The
INTERNATIONAL CRITICAL COMMENTARY
on the Holy Scriptures of the Old and New Testaments

GENERAL EDITORS

G. I. DAVIES, F.B.A.
Professor of Old Testament Studies in the University of Cambridge
Fellow of Fitzwilliam College

AND

C.M. TUCKETT
Professor of New Testament in the University of Oxford
Fellow of Pembroke College

CONSULTING EDITORS

J. A. EMERTON, F.B.A.
Emeritus Regius Professor of Hebrew in the University of Cambridge
Fellow of St John's College, Cambridge
Honorary Canon of St George's Cathedral, Jerusalem

AND

C. E. B. CRANFIELD, F.B.A.
Emeritus Professor of Theology in the University of Durham

FORMERLY UNDER THE EDITORSHIP OF

G.N. STANTON
General Editor of the New Series

S. R. DRIVER
A. PLUMMER
C. A. BRIGGS
Founding Editors

A CRITICAL AND EXEGETICAL COMMENTARY

ON

THE EPISTLE OF JAMES

BY

DALE C. ALLISON, JR.

*Errett M. Grable Professor of New Testament Exegesis and Early Christianity,
Pittsburgh Theological Seminary*

BLOOMSBURY
NEW YORK • LONDON • NEW DELHI • SYDNEY

Bloomsbury T&T Clark
An imprint of Bloomsbury Publishing Plc

50 Bedford Square
London
WC1B 3DP
UK

175 Fifth Avenue
New York
NY 10010
USA

www.bloomsbury.com

First published 2013
Paperback edition published 2025

© Dale C. Allison, Jr., 2013

All rights reserved. No part of this publication may be reproduced or transmitted in any form or by any means, electronic or mechanical, including photocopying, recording, or any information storage or retrieval system, without prior permission in writing from the publishers.

Dale C. Allison, Jr., has asserted his right under the Copyright, Designs and Patents Act, 1988, to be identified as Author of this work.

No responsibility for loss caused to any individual or organization acting on or refraining from action as a result of the material in this publication can be accepted by Bloomsbury Academic or the author.

British Library Cataloguing-in-Publication Data
A catalogue record for this book is available from the British Library.

ISBN: HB: 978-0-567-07740-0
PB: 978-0-567-71693-4

Library of Congress Cataloging-in-Publication Data
A catalog record for this book is available from the Library of Congress

Typeset by Forthcoming Publications

For Warren Farha
who carries many of my best memories

οὐθὲν κρεῖττον φιλίας ἐστίν· οὐδέποτε πίπτει

CONTENTS

General Editors' Preface   ix
Preface   xi

Literature   xiii

INTRODUCTION   1
    I. AUTHOR AND DATE   3
    II. *SITZ IM LEBEN*   32
    III. SOURCES   51
    IV. GENRE   71
    V. STRUCTURE   76
    VI. LITERARY CHARACTERISTICS   81
    VII. LEADING IDEAS   88
    VIII. LOCAL ORIGIN   94
    IX. TEXT   98
    X. THE RECEPTION OF JAMES   99

COMMENTARY   111
    I. SALUTATION AND ADDRESS (1.1)   113
    II. THE OUTCOME OF TRIAL (1.2-4)   135
    III. WISDOM, FAITH, DOUBT (1.5-8)   161
    IV. THE CONTRARY FUTURES OF POOR AND RICH (1.9-11)   192
    V. TEMPTATION AND GOD (1.12-15)   214
    VI. THE GOODNESS OF GOD (1.16-18)   255
    VII. QUICK TO HEAR, SLOW TO SPEAK, SLOW TO ANGER (1.19-21)   288
    VIII. HEARING AND DOING (1.22-25)   318
    IX. PURE RELIGION (1.26-27)   346

X.	PARTIALITY CONDEMNED (2.1-13)	367
XI.	FAITH WITHOUT WORKS (2.14-26)	425
XII.	THE SINS OF SPEECH (3.1-12)	509
XIII.	WISDOM, HUMILITY, PEACE (3.13-18)	561
XIV.	FRIENDSHIP WITH THE WORLD VERSUS FRIENDSHIP WITH GOD (4.1-12)	588
XV.	DENUNCIATIONS OF THE PROSPEROUS (4.13–5.6)	640
XVI.	THE NEAR END AND PATIENT ENDURANCE (5.7-11)	689
XVII.	PROHIBITION OF OATHS (5.12)	722
XVIII.	PRAYER, HEALING, RESTORATION (5.13-20)	740

GENERAL EDITORS' PREFACE

Much scholarly work has been done on the Bible since the publication of the first volumes of the International Critical Commentary in the 1890s. New linguistic, textual, historical and archaeological evidence has become available, and there have been changes and developments in methods of study. In the twenty-first century there will be as great a need as ever, and perhaps a greater need, for the kind of commentary that the International Critical Commentary seeks to supply. The series has long had a special place among works in English on the Bible, because it has sought to bring together all the relevant aids to exegesis, linguistic and textual no less than archaeological, historical, literary and theological, to help the reader to understand the meaning of the books of the Old and New Testaments. In the confidence that such a series meets a need, the publishers and the editors are commissioning new commentaries on all the books of the Bible. The work of preparing a commentary on such a scale cannot but be slow, and developments in the past half-century have made the commentator's task yet more difficult than before, but it is hoped that the remaining volumes will appear without too great intervals between them. No attempt has been made to secure a uniform theological or critical approach to the problems of the various books, and scholars have been selected for their scholarship and not for their adherence to any school of thought. It is hoped that the new volumes will attain the high standards set in the past, and that they will make a significant contribution to the understanding of the books of the Bible.

G.I.D
C.M.T

PREFACE

I began work on this commentary in 1997, having been invited by George W. Buchanan to contribute to a series he was then editing. I worked for only a few months, not getting very far. I set out much too soon after finishing another, very long commentary, and it proved impossible to go on. I needed a break from the sort of intensive reading and research required for a work such as this. So when invitations to work on other projects came in, I laid James aside.

Although, in subsequent years, I resolved several times to return to James full-time, the memory of the labor required proved too daunting, until a sabbatical in 2009–10 gave me the courage to take up the task again. By then the series for which I initially wrote was defunct, and in the meantime the late Graham Stanton, at the prompting of Charles Cranfield, had issued me a contract for the ICC. Putting most other work to the side, I was finally able to work on James until the end of 2011. The academic labor has been taxing. I have aspired to read as many relevant books and articles, of whatever date and provenance, as possible, including much outside the usual scope of standard academic study. I have inevitably been overwhelmed and deeply discouraged. The literature is far too large to read in its entirety, much less master. Thus I let this commentary go not only with a profound sense of its limitations, which are due to the many imperfections of its author, but also of the many paths not taken, which are due to the constraints of finite time and energy. I apologize in advance, moreover, for whatever contemporary contributions I have inadvertently overlooked: it is no longer possible to keep track of all the new publications that continue to appear each year.

I should like to thank my readers, Kristine Allison, Kathy Anderson, Chris Kettler, Joel Marcus, Nancy Klancher, and Tucker Ferda, for kindly commenting upon portions of an exceptionally difficult manuscript. I am also grateful to Pittsburgh Theological Seminary for its continued support of my scholarship as well as to the Pew Charitable Trust for a grant allowing me, in the 1997–98 academic year, to begin this project. Finally, my sincere thanks to the ICC editor, Chris Tuckett, for his encouragement, and to Duncan Burns, who patiently helped me prepare the manuscript for publication.

DCA

LITERATURE

Abbreviations are those of The SBL Handbook of Style, *ed. P.H. Alexander et al., Peabody, MA, 1999*

Achtemeier, *1 Peter*: P.J. Achtemeier, *1 Peter*, Minneapolis, 1996.
Adam: J. Adam, *An Exposition of the Epistle of James*, Edinburgh, 1867.
Adamson: J.B. Adamson, *The Epistle of James*, Grand Rapids, 1976.
Adamson, *Message*: J.B. Adamson, *James: The Man and the Message*, Grand Rapids, 1989.
Adderley: J. Adderley, *The Epistle of St James*, London, 1930.
Agourides, 'Origin': S.C. Agourides, 'The Origin of the Epistle of St. James', *GOTR* 9 (1963), 67-78.
Ahrens, *Arm*: M. Ahrens, *Der Realitäten Widerschein oder Arm und Reich im Jakobusbrief*, Berlin, 1995.
Alana, 'Rich': O.E. Alana, 'A Word with the Rich', *Verbum et ecclesia* 24 (2003), 1-14, 292-308.
Aland, 'Herrenbruder': K. Aland, 'Der Herrenbruder Jakobus und der Jakobusbrief', *TLZ* 69 (1944), 97-104.
Albl, 'Health': M.C. Albl, '"Are Amy among You Sick?" The Health Care System in the Letter of James', *JBL* 121 (2002), 123-43.
Alford: Henry Alford, *The Greek Testament*, vol. 4, Chicago, 1958.
Allison, 'Amnesia': D.C. Allison, Jr., 'Exegetical Amnesia in James', *ETL* 86 (2000), 162-66.
Allison, 'Audience': D.C. Allison, Jr., 'The Audience of James and the Sayings of Jesus', in *James, 1 and 2 Peter, and Early Jesus Traditions*, ed. A.J. Batten and J.S. Kloppenborg, London, 2013.
Allison, 'Blessing': D.C. Allison, Jr., 'Blessing God and Cursing People: Jas 3:9-10', *JBL* 130 (2011), 397-405.
Allison, 'Eldad': D.C. Allison, Jr., 'Eldad and Modad', *JSP* 21 (2011), 99-131.
Allison, *End*: D.C. Allison, Jr., *The End of the Ages has Come*, Philadelphia, 1985.
Allison, 'Ending': D.C. Allison, Jr., 'The Liturgical Tradition behind the Ending of James', *JSNT* 42 (2011), 3-18.
Allison, 'Fiction': D.C. Allison, Jr., 'The Fiction of James and Its *Sitz im Leben*', *RB* 108 (2001), 529-70.
Allison, *Jesus*: D.C. Allison, Jr., *Constructing Jesus*, Grand Rapids, MI, 2010.
Allison, *Tradition*: D.C. Allison, Jr., *The Jesus Tradition in Q*, Valley Forge, PA, 1997.
Allison, 'Polemic': D.C. Allison, Jr., 'Jas 2:14-26: Polemic against Paul, Apology for James', in *Ancient and New Perspectives on Paul*, ed. T. Nicklas, A. Merkt, and J. Verheyden, Göttingen, 2013, 123-49.
Alonso-Schökel, 'Culto': L. Alonso-Schökel, 'Culto y justicia en Sant 1,26-27', *Bib* 56 (1975), 537-44.
Alonso-Schökel, 'James 5,2': L. Alonso-Schökel, 'James 5,2 and 4,6', *Bib* 54 (1973), 73-76.
Althaus, 'Bekenne': P. Althaus, '"Bekenne einer dem andern seine Sünde": Zur Geschichte von Jak 5.16 seit Augustin', in *Festgabe für Theodor Zahn*, Leipzig, 1928, 165-94.
Ammassari, 'Law': A. Ammassari, 'Towards a Law of Liberty', *SIDIC* 10 (1977), 23-25.

Amphoux, 'Description': C.-B. Amphoux, 'Vers une description linguistique de l'épître de Jacques', *NTS* 25 (1978), 58-92.
Amphoux, 'Division': C.-B. Amphoux, 'Systèmes anciens de division de l'épître de Jacques et composition littéraire', *Bib* 62 (1981), 390-400.
Amphoux, 'Jacques 1, 17': C.-B. Amphoux, 'À propos de Jacques 1, 17', *RHPR* 50 (1970), 127-36.
Amphoux, 'Langue': C.-B. Amphoux, 'Langue de l'épître de Jacques', *RHPR* 53 (1973), 7-45.
Amphoux, 'Relecture': C.-B. Amphoux, 'Une relecture du chapitre 1 de l'épître Jacques', *Bib* 59 (1978), 554-61.
Amphoux, 'Témoins': C.-B. Amphoux, 'Quelques témoins grecs des formes textuelles les plus anciennes de l'épître de Jacques', *NTS* 28 (1982), 91-115.
Amphoux-Bouhot, *Lecture*: C.-B. Amphoux and J.-P. Bouhot, *La lecture liturgique des Épîtres catholiques dans l'Église ancienne*, Lausanne, 1996.
Ps.-Andrew of Crete, *Éloge*: Ps.-Andrew of Crete, *Un Éloge de Jacques, le frère du Seigneur*, ed. J. Noret, Toronto, 1978.
Andria: S. Andria, 'James', in *Africa Bible Commentary*, ed. T. Adeyemo, Nairobi, 2006, 1509-16.
Aretius: B. Aretius, *Commentarii in Omnes Epistolas*, vol. 3, Geneva, 1596.
Armerding, 'Afflicted': C. Armerding, 'Is Any Among You Afflicted? A Study of James 5:13-20', *BSacr* 95 (1938), 195-201.
Assaël, 'Oeuvre': J. Assaël, 'Mettre en oeuvre la foi, selon l'Épître de Jacques', *Bib* 90 (2009), 506-29.
Assaël-Cuvillier, 'Éléments': J. Assaël and É. Cuvillier, 'Quelques Éléments de christologie dans l'Épître de Jacques', *RHPR* 90 (2010), 321-41.
Assaël-Cuvillier, 'Interprétation': J. Assaël and É. Cuvillier, 'À propos de la traduction et de l'interprétation de Jacques 2.1', *NTS* 57 (2011), 145-51.
Assaël-Cuvillier, 'Traduction': J. Assaël and É. Cuvillier, 'À propos de la traduction de l'Épître de Jacques chapitre 1, verset 1', *Eruditio Antiqua* 2 (2010), 189-97.
Avemarie, 'Werke': F. Avemarie, 'Die Werke des Gesetzes im Spiegel des Jakobusbriefs', *ZTK* 98 (2001), 282-309.
Aymer, *Pure*: M.P. Aymer, *First Pure, then Peaceable: Frederick Douglass, Darkness, and the Epistle of James*, London, 2007.
Baasland: E. Baasland, *Jakobsbrevet*, Uppsala, 1992.
Baasland, 'Form': E. Baasland, 'Literarische Form, Thematik und geschichtliche Einordnung des Jakobusbriefes', *ANRW* 2/25.5 (1988), 3646-84.
Baasland, 'Weisheitsschrift': E. Baasland, 'Der Jakobusbrief als neutestamentliche Weisheitsschrift', *ST* 36 (1982), 119-39.
Backhaus, 'Condicio': K. Backhaus, 'Condicio Jacobaea: Jüdische Weisheitstradition und christlichen Alltagsethik nach Jak 4,13-17', in *Schrift und Tradition*, ed. K. Backhaus and F.G. Untergassmair, Paderborn, 1996, 137-57.
Bacon, 'Faith': B.W. Bacon, 'The Doctrine of Faith in Hebrews, James, and Clement of Rome', *JBL* 19 (1900), 12-21.
Baker: W.R. Baker, 'James' in W.R. Baker and P. Carrier, *James–Jude*, Cincinnati, 1990, 9-111.
Baker, 'Christology': W.R. Baker, 'Christology in the Epistle of James', *EvQ* 74 (2002), 47-57.
Baker, 'Contexts': W.R. Baker, '"Above All Else": Contexts of the Call for Verbal Integrity in James 5.12', *JSNT* 54 (1994), 57-71.
Baker, 'Daddy': W.R. Baker, 'Who's Your Daddy? Gendered Birth Images in the Soteriology of the Epistle of James (1:14-15, 18, 21)', *EvQ* 79 (2007), 195-207.

Baker, 'Holy Spirit': W.R. Baker, 'Searching for the Holy Spirit in the Epistle of James', *TynBul* 59 (2008), 293-315.
Baker, 'James': W.R. Baker, 'James', in *Theological Interpretation of the New Testament*, ed. K.J. Vanhoozer, London, MI, 2008, 200-208.
Baker, *Speech-Ethics*: W.R. Baker, *Personal Speech-Ethics in the Epistle of James*, Tübingen, 1995.
Baker-Ellsworth: W.R. Baker and T.D. Ellsworth, *Preaching James*, St. Louis, 2004.
Baljon: J.M.S. Baljon, *Commentaar op de Katholieke Brieven*, Utrecht, 1904.
Baltzer-Koester, 'Bezeichnung': K. Baltzer and H. Koester, 'Die Bezeichnung des Jakobus als ΩΒΛΙΑΣ', *ZNW* 46 (1955), 141-42.
Barclay: W. Barclay, *The Letters of James and Peter*, Philadelphia, 1958.
Bardenhewer: O. Bardenhewer, *Der Brief des heiligen Jakobus*, Freiburg im Breisgau, 1928.
Barlow, *Letters*: T. Barlow, *Two Letters...Concerning Justification by Faith Only*, London, 1701.
Barnes: A. Barnes, *Notes, Explanatory and Practical, on the General Epistles*, New York, 1859.
Barnett, 'Letter': A.E. Barnett, 'James, Letter of', *IDB* 2.794-99.
Barrett, *Acts 15–28*: C.K. Barrett, *Acts 15–28*, London, 1998.
Barrow, *Sermons*: I. Barrow, *Sermons, on Various Subjects*, vol. 1, London, 1823.
Bartlet, *Age*: J.V. Barlet, *The Apostolic Age*, New York, 1899.
Bartlett, 'Document': D.L. Bartlett, 'The Epistle of James as a Jewish-Christian Document', in *Society of Biblical Literature 1979 Seminar Papers*, vol. 2, ed. P.J. Achtemeier, Missoula, MT, 1979, 173-86.
Bartmann, *Paulus*: B. Bartmann, *St. Paulus und St. Jacobus über die Rechtfertigung*, Freiburg im Breisgau, 1897.
Basser: H. Basser, 'The Letter of James', in *The Jewish Annotated New Testament*, ed. A.-J. Levine and M.Z. Brettler, Oxford, 2011, 427-35.
Bassett: F.T. Bassett, *The Catholic Epistle of St. James*, London, 1876.
Batten, 'Asceticism': A. Batten, 'An Asceticism of Resistance in James', in *Asceticism and the New Testament*, ed. L.E. Vaage and V.L. Wimbush, New York, 1999, 355-70.
Batten, *Friendship*: A. Batten, *Friendship and Benefaction in James*, Dorchester, 2010.
Batten, 'Patron': A. Batten, 'God in the Letter of James: Patron or Benefactor?', *NTS* 50 (2004), 257-72.
Batten, 'Poor': A. Batten, 'The Degraded Poor and the Greedy Rich: Exploring the Language of Poverty and Wealth in James', in *The Social Sciences and Biblical Translation*, ed. D. Neufeld, Atlanta, 2008, 65-77.
Batten, *Saying*: A.J. Batten, *What Are They Saying About the Letter of James?*, New York, 2009.
Batten, 'Strategies': A.J. Batten, 'Ideological Strategies in the Letter of James', in Webb-Kloppenborg, *Reading*, 6-26.
Batten, 'Tradition': A.J. Batten, 'The Jesus Tradition and the Letter of James', *RevExp* 108 (2011), 381-90.
Bauckham, 'Spirit': R. Bauckham, 'The Spirit of God in Us Loathes Envy: James 4:5', in *The Holy Spirit and Christian Origins*, ed. G.N. Stanton, B.W. Longenecker, and S.C. Barton, Grand Rapids, MI, 2004, 270-81.
Bauckham, 'Tongue': R.J. Bauckham, 'The Tongue Set on Fire by Hell (James 3:6)', in *The Fate of the Dead*, Leiden, 1998, 119-31.
Bauckham, *Wisdom*: R.J. Bauckham, *James: Wisdom of James, Disciple of Jesus the Sage*, London, 1999.
Bauckham, 'Wisdom': R.J. Bauckham, 'The Wisdom of James and the Wisdom of Jesus', in Schlosser, *Epistles*, 75-92.

LITERATURE

Bauernfeind, 'Eid': O. Bauernfeind, 'Der Eid in der Sicht des Neuen Testaments', in *Eid, Gewissen, Treuepflicht*, ed. H. Gollwitzer, Frankfurt am Main, 1965, 79-112.
Bauernfeind, *Frieden*: O. Bauernfeind, *Eid und Frieden*, Stuttgart, 1956.
Baumgarten: S.J. Baumgarten, *Auslegung des Briefes Jacobi*, Halle, 1750.
Baur, *Paul*: F.C. Baur, *Paul the Apostle of Jesus Christ*, vol. 2, London, 1875.
BDAG: F.W. Danker and W. Bauer, *A Greek-English Lexicon of the New Testament and Early Christian Literature*, 3rd ed., Chicago, 2000.
BDF: F. Blass, A. Debrunner, and R.W. Funk, *A Greek Grammar of the New Testament*, Chicago, 1961.
Beasley-Murray: G.R. Beasley-Murray, *The General Epistles*, London, 1965.
D. Beck, 'Composition': D.L. Beck, 'The Composition of the Epistle of James', unpublished Ph.D. dissertation, Princeton Theological Seminary, 1973.
N. Beck, *Cryptograms*: N.A. Beck, *Anti-Roman Cryptograms in the New Testament*, New York, 1997.
Bede: Bede, *In Epistolas VII Catholicas*, in Bedae Venerabilis Opera Pars II Opera Exegetica 4, CCSL 121, ed. D. Hurst, Turnhout, 1983, 179-342.
Belser: J.E. Belser, *Die Epistel des heiligen Jakobus*, Freiburg im Breisgau, 1909.
Bendemann, 'Sünde': R. von Bendemann, 'Sunde: Zur Hamartiolgoie im Jakobusbrief', in *Fragmentarisches Wörterbuch*, ed. K. Schiffner *et al.*, Stuttgart, 2007, 367-77.
Bengel: J.A. Bengel, *Gnomon Novi Testamenti*, vol. 2, Tübingen, 1850.
Bennett: W.H. Bennett, *The General Epistles*, New York, 1901.
Benson: G. Benson, *A Paraphrase and Notes on the Seven (Commonly Called) Catholic Epistles*, London, 1756.
Béraudy, 'Sacrament': R. Béraudy, 'Le sacrament des malades', *NRT* 106 (1974), 600-34.
Bergauer, *Jakobusbrief*: P. Bergauer, *Der Jakobusbrief bei Augustinus*, Vienna, 1962.
Bernheim, *Brother*: P.-A. Bernheim, *James, Brother of Jesus*, London, 1997.
Bernheim, 'Mort': P.-A. Bernheim, 'Le mort de Jacques, l'Épître de Jacques et la dénonciation des riches', in Schlosser, *Epistles*, 249-61.
Betz, *Sermon*: H.D. Betz, *The Sermon on the Mount*, Minneapolis, 1995.
Beumer, 'Daemones': I. Beumer, 'Et daemones credunt (Iac. 2,19)', *Greg.* 22 (1941), 231-51.
Beyer, *Syntax*: K. Beyer, *Semitische Syntax im Neuen Testament*, vol. 1, Göttingen, 1962.
Beyschlag: W. Beyschlag, *Der Brief des Jacobus*, 6th ed., Göttingen, 1897.
Beyschlag, 'Geschichtsdenkmal': W. Beyschlag, 'Der Jakobusbrief als urchristliches Geschichtsdenkmal', *TSK* 48 (1874), 105-66.
Beza: T. Beza, *Annotationes maiores in Novum Testamentum*, Part II, Paris, 1594.
Bieder, 'Existenz': W. Bieder, 'Christliche Existenz nach dem Zeugnis des Jakobusbriefes', *TZ* 5 (1949), 93-113.
Bindemann, 'Weisheit': W. Bindemann, 'Weisheit versus Weisheit: Der Jakobusbrief als innerkirchlicher Diskurs', *ZNW* 86 (1995), 189-217.
Bischoff, 'Τὸ τέλος': A. Bischoff, 'Τὸ τέλος κυρίου', *ZNW* 7 (1906), 274-79.
Bishop, *Apostles*: E.F.F. Bishop, *Apostles of Palestine*, London, 1958.
Bishop, 'Three': E.F.F. Bishop, 'Three and a Half Years', *ExpTim* 61 (1950), 126-27.
Bisping: A. Bisping, *Erklärung der Sieben katholischen Briefen*, Munster, 1871.
Blackman: E.C. Blackman, *The Epistle of James*, London, 1957.
Bleek, *Introduction*: F. Bleek, *Introduction to the New Testament*, vol. 2, Edinburgh, 1874.
Blenker, 'Jakobs': A. Blenker, 'Jakobs brevs sammenhaeng', *DTT* 30 (1967), 193-202.
Blevins, 'Repent': W.L. Blevins, 'A Call to Repent, Love Others, and Remember God: James 4', *RevExp* 83 (1986), 419-26.
Blomberg-Kamell: C.L. Blomberg and M.J. Kamell, *James*, Grand Rapids, MI, 2008.
Blondel, 'Fondement': J.-L. Blondel, 'Le fondement théologique de la parénèse dans l'épître de Jacques', *RTP* 111 (1979), 141-52.
Bloomfield: S.T. Bloomfield, *ΉΚΑΙΝΗ ΔΙΑΘΗΚΗ*, vol. 2, Boston, 1837.

Böhmer, 'Glaube': J. Böhmer, 'Der "Glaube" im Jakobusbriefe', *NKZ* 9 (1898), 251-56.
Böttrich, 'Gold': C. Böttrich, 'Vom Gold, das rostet (Jak 5.3)', *NTS* 47 (2001), 519-38.
Boismard, 'Liturgie': M.-E. Boismard, 'Une liturgie baptismale dans la Prima Petri. II: Son influence sur l'épître de Jacques', *RB* 64 (1957), 161-83.
Bolich, 'Dating': G.G. Bolich, 'On Dating James', unpublished Ed.D. dissertation, Gonzaga University, 1983.
Bonsirven, 'Jacques': J. Bonsirven, 'Jacques', *DBSupp* 4, Paris, 1949, 783-95.
Bord, *Onction*: J.B. Bord, *L'Extrême Onction*, Brussels, 1923.
Borghi, 'Sagesse': E. Borghi, 'La sagesse de la vie selon l'épître de Jacques', *NTS* 52 (2006), 123-41.
Botha, 'Salvation': J.E. Botha, 'Simple Salvation, but not of Straw... Jacobean Soteriology', in *Salvation in the New Testament*, ed. J.G. van der Watt, Atlanta, 2005, 389-408.
Botha, 'Soteriology': J.E. Botha, 'Soteriology under Construction', *Acta Patristica et Bynzantina* 17 (2006), 100-18.
Bottini, 'Confessione': G.C. Bottini, 'Confessione e intercessione in Giacomo 5.16', *SBFLA* 33 (1983), 193-226.
Bottini, 'Correzione': G.C. Bottini, 'Correzione fraterna e salvezza in Giacomo 5.19-20', *SBFLA* 35 (1985), 131-62.
Bottini, *Introduzione*: G.C. Bottini, *Giacomo e la sua lettera: Una introduzione*, Jerusalem, 2000.
Bottini, 'Legislatore': G.C. Bottini, 'Uno solo è il legislatore e giudice (Gc 4.11-12)', *SBFLA* 37 (1987), 99-112.
Bottini, 'Minaccia': ' G.C. Bottini, 'Giacomo 1.9-11: Minaccia o parenesi', *SBFLA* 34 (1984), 191-206.
Bottini, *Preghiera*: G.C. Bottini, *La Preghiera di Elia in Giacomo 5,17-18*, Jerusalem, 1981.
Bottini, 'Sentenze': G.C. Bottini, 'Sentenze di Pseudo-Focilide alla luce della Lettera di Giacomo', *SBFLA* 38 (1986), 171-81.
Bouman: H. Bouman, *Commentarius Perpetuus in Jacobi Epistolam*, Utrecht, 1865.
Bouttier-Amphoux, 'Prédication': M. Bouttier and C.-B. Amphoux, 'Prédication de Jacques le Juste', *ETR* 54 (1979), 5-16.
Bowyer, *Conjectures*: W. Bowyer, *Conjectures on the New Testament*, London, 1772.
Boyle, 'Paradox': M.O'R. Boyle, 'The Stoic Paradox of James 2.10', *NTS* 31 (1985), 611-17.
Brandon, *Fall*: S.G.F. Brandon, *The Fall of Jerusalem and the Christian Church*, London, 1968.
Braumann, 'Hintergrund': G. Braumann, 'Der theologische Hintergrund des Jakobusbriefes', *TZ* 18 (1962), 401-10.
Braune: K. Braune, *Die Sieben Katholischen Briefe. Die Briefe des Jakobus und Judas*, Grimma, 1847.
Brightman-Hammond, *Liturgies*: F.E. Brightman and C.E. Hammond, *Liturgies, Eastern and Western*, vol. 1, Oxford, 1896.
Brinktrine, 'Jak 2.1': J. Brinktrine, 'Zu Jak 2.1', *Bib* 35 (1954), 40-42.
Brochmand: J.R. Brochmand, *In canonicam et catholicam Jacobi epistolam*, Copenhagen, 1641.
Broer, *Einleitung*: I. Broer, *Einleitung in das Neue Testament*, 3rd ed., Würzburg, 2010.
Brooks, 'Canon': J.A. Brooks, 'The Place of James in the New Testament Canon', *SWJT* 12 (1969), 41-56.
Brosend: W.F. Brosend II, *James and Jude*, Cambridge, UK, 2004.
Brown: C.C. Brown, *The General Epistle of James*, Philadelphia, 1907.
Brox, *Hirt*: N. Brox, *Der Hirt des Hermas*, Göttingen, 1991.
Brückner, 'Kritik': W. Brückner, 'Zur Kritik des Jakobusbriefs', *ZWT* 17 (1874), 530-41.
Brückner, *Reihenfolge*: W. Brückner, *Die chronologische Reihenfolge, in welcher die Briefe des Neuen Testaments verfasst*, Haarlem, 1890.

LITERATURE

Brunner, 'Rede': H. Brunner, '"Eure Rede sei ja ja, nein nein" im Ägyptischen', in *Das Hörende Herz*, ed. W. Röllig, Freiburg, CH, 1988, 396-401.
Bruston, 'Crux interpretum': C. Bruston, 'Une "crux interpretum"'. Jacques IV, 5', *RTQR* 4 (1907), 368-77.
Buchhold, 'Justification': J. Buchhold, 'La justification chez Jacques et chez Paul', *Hokhma* 98 (2010), 35-56.
Bultmann, *Theology*: R. Bultmann, *Theology of the New Testament*, 2 vols., New York, 1951, 1955.
C. Bultmann, 'Hiob': C. Bultmann, 'Hiob: Bild und Ton', in *Die Verheissung des Neuen Bundes*, ed. B. Kollmann, Göttingen, 2010, 226-45.
Bunyan: J. Bunyan, 'The General Epistle of James', in *The Works of John Bunyan*, vol. 2, ed. G. Offor, Glasgow, 1854, 410-13.
Burchard: C. Burchard, *Der Jakobusbrief*, Tübingen, 2000.
Burchard, 'Gemeinde': C. Burchard, 'Gemeinde in der strohernen Epistel', in *Kirche*, ed. D. Lührmann and G. Strecker, Tübingen, 1980, 315-28.
Burchard, 'Jakobus 2.14-26': C. Burchard, 'Zu Jakobus 2.14-26', *ZNW* 71 (1980), 27-45.
Burchard, 'Nächstenliebegebot': C. Burchard, 'Nächstenliebegebot, Dekalog und Gesetz in Jak 2,8-11', in *Die hebräische Bibel und ihre zweifache Nachgeschichte*, ed. E. Blum, C. Macholz, and E. Stegemann, Neukirchen–Vluyn, 1990, 517-33.
Burchard, 'Stellen': C. Burchard, 'Zu einigen christologischen Stellen des Jakobusbriefes', in *Anfänge der Christologie*, ed. C. Breytenbach and H. Paulsen, Göttingen, 1991, 353-68.
Burdick: D.W. Burdick. 'James', in vol. 12 of *The Expositor's Bible Commentary*, ed. F.E. Gaebelein, Grand Rapids, MI, 1981, 159-205.
Burge, 'Form': G.M. Burge, '"And threw them thus on paper": Recovering the Poetic Form of James 2:14-26', *Studia Biblica et Theologica* 7 (1977), 31-45.
Burger-Luthardt: K. Burger and G.C. Luthardt, *Die katholischen Briefe (Briefe des Jakobus, Petrus, Judas und Johannes)*, Nördlingen, 1888.
Burkitt: W. Burkitt, *Expository Notes*, New Haven, 1794.
F.C. Burkitt, *Beginnings*: F.C. Burkitt, *Christian Beginnings*, London, 1924.
Burtz, 'Meaning': H.W. Burtz, 'Meaning of "Religion" in James 1.27', *Homiletical Review* 31 (1896), 59-60.
G. Byron: G.L. Byron, 'James', in *True to Our Native Land: An African American New Testament Commentary*, ed. B.K. Blount, Minneapolis, 2007, 461-75.
J. Byron, 'Cain': J. Byron, 'Living in the Shadow of Cain: Echoes of a Developing Tradition in James 5:1-6', *NovT* 48 (2006), 261-74.
Cabaniss, 'Epistle': A. Cabaniss, 'The Epistle of Saint James', *JBR* 22 (1954), 26-28.
Cabaniss, 'Homily': A. Cabaniss, 'A Note on Jacob's Homily', *EvQ* 47 (1975), 219-22.
Cadoux, *Thought*: A.T. Cadoux, *The Thought of St. James*, London, 1944.
Cajetan: T. de Vio Cajetan, *Opera Omnia*, vol. 5, *In omnes Pauli et aliorum Apostolorum epistolas Commentarii*, Lyon, 1539.
Calduch-Benages, 'Trials': N. Calduch-Benages, 'Amid Trials: Ben Sira 2:1 and James 1:2', in *Intertextual Studies in Ben Sira and Tobit*, ed. J. Corley and V. Skemp, Washington, DC, 2005, 255-63.
Calloud-Genuyt, *Analyse*: J. Calloud and F. Genuyt, *L'Épître de Saint Jacques: analyse sémiotique*, Lyon, 1982.
Calmet: A. Calmet, *Commentarium literale in Biblia Epistolae S. Pauli, Epistolae canonicae et Apocalypsis*, 1735.
Calmet, 'Sagesses': A. Calmet, 'Vraie et fausse sagesses', *BVC* 58 (1964), 19-28.
Calvin: J. Calvin, 'The Epistle of James', in *A Harmony of the Gospels Matthew, Mark and Luke Volume III and The Epistles of James and Jude*, Edinburgh, 1972, 259-319.
Camp, 'View': A.L. Camp, 'Another View of the Structure of James', *RestQ* 36 (1994), 111-19.

Cantinat: J. Cantinat, *Les Épîtres de Saint Jacques et de Saint Jude*, Paris, 1973.
Cantinat, 'Foi': J. Cantinat, 'La foi vivante et salutative s'accompagne d'oeuvres (Jc 2)', *AsSeign* 55 (1974), 26-30.
Cantinat, 'Sagesse': J. Cantinat, 'Sagesse, Justice, Plaisirs. Jc 3.16–4,3', *AsSeign* 56 (1974), 36-40.
Cappel: J. Cappel, *Observationes in Novum Testamentum*, Amsterdam, 1657.
Cargal: T.B. Cargal, *Restoring the Diaspora: Discursive Structure and Purpose in the Epistle of James*, Atlanta, 1993.
Cargal, 'Prostitute': T.B. Cargal, 'When is a Prostitute not an Adulteress? The Language of Sexual Infidelity in the Rhetoric of the Letter of James', in *A Feminist Companion to the Catholic Epistles and Hebrews*, ed. A.-J. Levine, Cleveland, 2004, 114-26.
C. Carpenter, 'James 4.5': C.B. Carpenter, 'James 4.5 Reconsidered', *NTS* 46 (2000), 189-205.
W. Carpenter: W.B. Carpenter, *The Wisdom of James the Just*, New York, 1903.
Carr: A. Carr, *The General Epistles of St. James*, Cambridge, UK, 1905.
Carr, 'James iii. 6': A. Carr, 'The Meaning of ὁ κόσμος in James iii. 6', *Expositor* ser. 7.8 (1909), 318-25.
Carr, 'Patience': A. Carr, 'The Patience of Job', *Expositor* ser. 8.6 (1913), 511-17.
Carrington, *Catechism*: P. Carrington, *The Primitive Christian Catechism*, Cambridge, UK, 1940.
Carson, 'James': D.A. Carson, 'James', in *Commentary on the New Testament Use of the Old Testament*, ed. G.K. Beale and D.A. Carson, Grand Rapids, MI, 2007, 997-1013.
Cartwright, *Confutation*: T. Cartwright, *A Confutation of the Rhemists Translation*, Leiden, 1618.
Cassiodorus, *Ep. Jac.*: Cassiodorus, *Epistola S. Jacobi ad Dispersos*, in PL 70.1377-1380.
Catenae ed. Cramer: *Catenae Graecorum Patrum in Novum Testamentum. Tomus VIII*, ed. J.A. Cramer, Oxford, 1844.
Catharinus: A. Catharinus, *Commentaria in omnes divi Pauli et alias septem canonicas epistolas*, Venice, 1551.
Cedar: P.A. Cedar, *Mastering the New Testament: James; 1, 2 Peter; Jude*, Waco, TX, 1984.
Cellérier: J.E. Cellérier, *Étude et commentaire sur l'Épître de St. Jacques*, Geneva, 1850.
CEQ: J.M. Robinson, P. Hoffmann, J.S. Kloppenborg, *The Critical Edition of Q*, Hermeneia, Minneapolis, 2000.
Chaine: J. Chaine, *L'Épitre de Saint Jacques*, Paris, 1927.
Chaîne Arménienne: *Chaîne Arménienne sur les Épîtres Catholiques I. La chaîne sur l'Épître de Jacques*, Patrologia Orientalis 43.193, ed. C. Renoux, Brepols, 1985.
Chandler, 'Injustice': C.N. Chandler, 'Blind Injustice: Jesus' Prophetic Warning Against Unjust Judging (Matthew 7:1-5)', unpublished Ph.D. thesis, University of St. Andrews, 2009.
Chase, *Prayer*: F.H. Chase, *The Lord's Prayer in the Early Church*, Cambridge, UK, 1891.
Chester, 'Theology': A. Chester, 'The Theology of James', in A. Chester and R.P. Martin, *The Theology of the Letters of James, Peter, and Jude*, Cambridge, UK, 1994, 1-62.
Cheung, *Genre*: L.L. Cheung, *The Genre, Composition and Hermeneutics of James*, Carlisle, UK, 2003.
Childs, *Canon*: B.S. Childs, *The New Testament as Canon*, Philadelphia, 1984.
Chilton, 'Wisdom': B. Chilton, 'Wisdom and Grace', in Chilton-Evans, *Missions*, 307-22.
Chilton-Evans, *Missions*: B. Chilton and C.A. Evans, eds. *The Missions of James, Peter, and Paul*, Leiden, 2005.
Chilton-Evans, *Origins*: B. Chilton and C.A. Evans, *James the Just and Christian Origins*, Leiden, 1999.
Chilton-Neusner, *Brother*: B. Chilton and J. Neusner, eds., *The Brother of Jesus*, Louisville, 2001.

Chrysostom: John Chrysostom, *Fragmenta in Epistolas Catholicas in Epistolam S. Jacobi*, PG 64.1039-52.
Church: E. McKnight and C. Church, *Hebrews-James*, Macon, GA, 2004.
CII/P: *Corpus Inscriptionum Iudaeae/Palaestinae*, 2 vols., ed. H.M. Cotton *et al.*, Berlin, 2010-11.
CJZC: G. Lüderitz and J.M. Reynolds, *Corpus jüdischer Zeugnisse aus der Cyrenaika*, Wiesbaden, 1983.
Cladder, 'Anlage': H.J. Cladder, 'Die Anlage des Jakobusbriefes', *ZKT* 28 (1904), 37-57.
Cladder, 'Aufbau': H.J. Cladder, 'Der formale Aufbau des Jakobusbriefes', *ZKT* 28 (1904), 295-330.
Clarke: A. Clarke, *The New Testament of Our Lord and Saviour Jesus Christ*, vol. 2, New York, 1856.
Coker, 'Nativism': K.J. Coker, 'Nativism in James 2.14-26: A Post-Colonial Reading', in Webb-Kloppenborg, *Reading*, 27-48.
Collins, 'Anointing': C.J. Collins, 'James 5:14-16a: What is the Anointing For?', *Presbyterion* 23 (1997), 79-91.
Collins, 'Coherence': C.J. Collins, 'Coherence in James 1:19-27', *Journal of Translation and Textlinguistics* 10 (1998), 80-87.
Compton, 'Justification': R.B. Compton, 'James 2:21-24 and the Justification of Abraham', *DBSJ* 2 (1997), 19-45.
Condon, 'Healing': K. Condon, 'The Sacrament of Healing (Jas. 5:14-15)', *Scr* 11 (1959), 33-42.
Cone: O. Cone, *The Epistles*, New York, 1901.
D. Cooper, 'Analogy': D. Cooper, 'The Analogy of Faith in Puritan Exegesis: Scope and Salvation in James 2:14-26', *Stone-Campbell Journal* 12 (2009), 235-50.
D. Cooper, 'Recovery': D. Cooper, 'Saving the Strawy Epistle: The Recovery of James after Martin Luther', *Haddington House Journal* 11 (2009), 139-54.
R. Cooper, 'Prayer': R.M. Cooper, 'Prayer, A Study in Matthew and James', *Encounter* 29 (1968), 268-77.
Coppens, 'L'onction': J. Coppens, 'Jacq., V,13-15 et l'onction des malades', *ETL* 53 (1977), 200-207.
Coppieters, 'Signification': H. Coppieters, 'La signification et la provenance de la citation Jac. iv, 5', *RB* 12 (1915), 35-58.
Cothenet, 'Healing': E. Cothenet, 'Healing as a Sign of the Kingdom, and the Anointing of the Sick', in *Temple of the Holy Spirit*, New York, 1983, 33-51.
Countryman: L.W. Countryman, 'James', in *The Queer Bible Commentary*, ed. D. Guest *et al.*, London, 2006, 716-23.
Cox, 'Looking-Glass': S. Cox, 'The Divine Looking-Glass', *Expositor* ser. 4.4 (1891), 448-56.
Cox, 'Progress': S. Cox, 'The Sinner's Progress', *Expositor* ser. 4.4 (1891), 42-51.
Craddock, 'Connection': J.G. Craddock, 'A Possible Connection between the Letter of James and the Events of John 7 and 8', in *Studia Evangelica vol. VII*, ed. E.A. Livingstone, Berlin, 1982, 141-44.
Cranfield, 'Message': C.E.B. Cranfield, 'The Message of James', *SJT* 18 (1965), 182-93, 338-45.
Credner, *Einleitung*: K.A. Credner, *Einleitung in das Neue Testament*, Halle, 1836.
Crotty, 'Poor': R.B. Crotty, 'Identifying the Poor in the Letter of James', *Colloquium* 27 (1995), 11-21.
Crotty, 'Structure': R.B. Crotty, 'The Literary Structure of the Letter of James', *ABR* 40 (1992), 45-57.
Culpepper: R.A. Culpepper, 'James', in *Mercer Commentary on the New Testament*, ed. W.E. Mills *et al.*, Macon, GA, 2003, 1283-94.

LITERATURE

Culpepper, 'Words': R.A. Culpepper, 'The Power of Words and the Tests of Two Wisdoms: James 3', *RevExp* 83 (1986), 405-18.
Cuvillier, 'Paul': E. Cuvillier, '"Jacques" et "Paul" en débat', *NovT* 53 (2011), 273-91.
Dale: R.W. Dale, *The Epistle of James and Other Discussions*, London, 1900.
Dale, 'Temptation': R.W. Dale, 'St. James on Temptation. James i. 9, 10', *Expositor* ser. 2.5 (1883), 321-29, 426-34.
Darby, *Synopsis*: J.N. Darby, *Synopsis of the Books of the Bible*, vol. 5, New York, n.d.
Dassmann, *Stachel*: E. Dassmann, *Der Stachel im Fleisch*, Münster, 1979.
Daube, 'Reconstruction': D. Daube, 'Concerning the Reconstruction of the "Aramaic Gospels"', in *New Testament Judaism*, vol. 2, ed. C. Carmichael, Berkeley, 2000, 65-88.
Dautzenberg, 'Schwurverbot': G. Dautzenberg, 'Ist das Schwurverbot Mt 5,33-37; Jak 5,12 ein Beispiel für die Torakritik Jesu?', *BZ* 25 (1981), 47-66.
Davids: P.H. Davids, *The Epistle of James*, Grand Rapids, MI, 1982.
Davids, 'Discussion': P.H. Davids, 'The Epistle of James in Modern Discussion', *ANRW* 2.25.5 (1988), 3622-45.
Davids, 'Jesus': P.H. Davids, 'James and Jesus', in *Gospel Perspectives Volume 5*, ed. D. Wenham, Sheffield, 1985, 63-84.
Davids, 'Meaning': P.H. Davids, 'The Meaning of ἀπείραστος in James i.13', *NTS* 24 (1978), 386-92.
Davids, 'Message': P.H. Davids, 'James's Message', in Chilton-Neusner, *Brother*, 66-87.
Davids, 'Perspectives': P.H. Davids, 'Theological Perspectives on the Epistle of James', *JETS* 23 (1980), 97-103.
Davids, 'Peter': P.H. Davids, 'James and Peter: The Literary Evidence', in Chilton-Evans, *Missions*, 29-52.
Davids, 'Pseudepigrapha': P.H. Davids, 'The Pseudepigrapha in the Catholic Epistles', in *The Pseudepigrapha and Early Biblical Interpretation*, ed. J.H. Charlesworth and C.A. Evans, Sheffield, 1993, 228-45.
Davids, 'Suffer': P.H. Davids, 'Why Do We Suffer? Suffering in James and Paul', in Chilton-Evans, *Missions*, 435-66.
Davids, 'Test': P.H. Davids, 'The Test of Wealth', in Chilton-Evans, *Missions*, 355-84.
Davids, 'Tradition': P.H. Davids, 'Tradition and Citation in the Epistle of James', in *Scripture, Tradition, and Interpretation*, ed. W.W. Gasque and W.S. LaSor, Grand Rapids, MI, 1978, 113-26.
Davids, 'Traditions': P.H. Davids, 'Palestinian Traditions in the Epistle of James', in Chilton-Evans, *Origins*, 33-58.
Davidson, *Introduction*: S. Davidson, *An Introduction to the Study of the New Testament*, London, 1868.
Davies, *Paul*: W.D. Davies, *Paul and Rabbinic Judaism*, rev. ed., New York, 1967.
Davies, *Setting*: W.D. Davies, *The Setting of the Sermon on the Mount*, Cambridge, UK, 1966.
Davies-Allison, *Matthew*: W.D. Davies and Dale C. Allison, Jr., *A Critical and Exegetical Commentary on the Gospel according to Saint Matthew*, 3 vols., Edinburgh, 1988–97.
DDD: *Dictionary of Deities and Demons in the Bible*, ed. K. van der Toorn, B. Becking, and P.W. van der Horst, 2nd ed., Leiden, 1999.
Deems: C.F. Deems, *The Gospel of Common Sense*, New York, 1888.
Deines, 'Sources': R. Deines, 'Non-literary Sources for the Interpretation of the New Testament', in *Neues Testament und hellenistisch-jüdische Alltagskultur*, ed. R. Deines, J. Herzer, and K.-W. Niebuhr, Tübingen, 2009, 25-66.
Deiros: P.A. Deiros, *Santiago y Judas*, Miami, 1992.
Deissmann, *Studies*: G.A. Deissmann, *Bible Studies*, Edinburgh, 1901.
De Luca *et al.*, 'Transmissione': E. De Luca, M. Rescio, E. Stori, D. Tripaldi, and L. Walt, 'La transmissione delle parole di Gesù. Scandalo e prova, perseveranza e salvezza', *Annali di storia dell'esegesi* 25 (2008), 203-13.

LITERATURE

Denyer, 'Mirrors': N. Denyer, 'Mirrors in James 1:22-25 and Plato, *Alcibiades* 132C-133C', *TynBul* 50 (1999), 237-39.
Deppe, *Sayings*: D.B. Deppe, *The Sayings of Jesus in the Epistle of James*, Chelsea, MI, 1989.
de Wette: W.M.L. de Wette, *Kurze Erklärung der Briefe des Petrus, Judas, und Jakobus*, 3rd ed., ed. B. Brückner, Leipzig, 1865.
de Wette, 'Bemerkungen': W.M.L. de Wette, 'Exegetische Bemerkungen 1. Über Jakob. II., 14-16; 2. über Röm. XIV.; 3. über 5. Mos. 1-3', *TSK* 3 (1830), 348-57.
de Wette, *Introduction*: W.M.L. de Wette, *An Historico-Critical Introduction to the Canonical Books of the New Testament*, Boston, 1858.
Dibelius: M. Dibelius, *James*, ed. H. Greeven, Philadelphia, 1976.
Dickson: D. Dickson, *Expositio analytica omnium Apostolicarum Epistolarum*, Glasgow, 1645.
Didymus of Alexandria, *Ep. can.*: Didymus of Alexandria, *In epistolas canonicas brevis enarratio*, ed. F. Zoepfl, Münster, 1914, 1-8.
Dimont: C.T. Dimont, 'The Epistle of St. James', in *A New Commentary on Holy Scripture*, ed. C. Gore, H.L. Goudge, and A. Guillaume, New York, 1928, 627-39.
Diodati: G. Diodati, *Pious and Learned Annotations upon the Holy Bible*, London, 1664.
Dionysius bar Salībī: Dionysius bar Salībī, *In Apocalypsim, Actus et Epistulas Catholicas*, CSCO 53, 60 Scriptores Syri 101 ed. J. Sedlacek, Paris, 1910.
C.H. Dodd, *Bible*: C.H. Dodd, *The Bible and the Greeks*, London, 1935.
C.H. Dodd, *Scriptures*: C.H. Dodd, *According to the Scriptures*, London, 1965.
W. Dodd: W. Dodd, *A Commentary on the Books of the Old and New Testament*, vol. 3, London, 1770.
Doddridge: P. Doddridge, *The Family Expositor*, vol. 6, 13th ed., Charlestown, MA, 1839.
Döpp, 'Sozialtradition': H.-M. Döpp, 'Jakobus 2,1-13 im Horizont biblisch-rabbinischer Sozialtradition', in *Religionsgeschichte des Neuen Testaments*, ed. A. von Dobbeler, K. Erlemann, and R. Heiligenthal, Tübingen, 2000, 67-77.
Doering, 'Jeremia': L. Doering, 'Jeremia in Babylonien und Ägytpen', in *Frühjudentum und Neues Testament im Horizont Biblischer Theologie*, ed. W. Kraus and K.-W. Niebuhr, Tübingen, 2003, 51-79.
Donker, 'Verfasser': C.E. Donker, 'Der Verfasser des Jak und sein Gegner: Zum Problem des Einwändes im Jak 2.18-19', *ZNW* 74 (1981), 227-40.
Doriani: D.M. Doriani, *James*, Phillipsburg, N.J., 2007.
Dowd, 'Faith': S. Dowd, 'Faith that Works', *RevExp* 97 (2000), 195-205.
Draper, 'Apostles': J.A. Draper, 'Apostles, Teachers, and Evangelists', in van de Sandt-Zangenberg, *Matthew*, 139-76.
Dschulnigg, 'Enstehung': P. Dschulnigg, 'Wann sind die katholischen Briefe und die Offenbarung des Johannes entstanden?', *SUNT* A 31 (2006), 127-51.
Dschulnigg, *Gleichnisse*: P. Dschulnigg, *Rabbinische Gleichnisse und das Neue Testament*, Bern, 1988.
Duling, 'Oaths': D. Duling, 'Against Oaths', *Forum* 6 (1990), 99-138.
Dunn, *Beginning*: J.D.G. Dunn, *Beginning from Jerusalem*, Grand Rapids, MI, 2009.
Dunn, *Romans 1-8*: J.D.G. Dunn, *Romans 1-8*, Nashville, 1988.
Duplacy, 'Divisions': J. Duplacy, 'Les divisions du texte de l'Épître de Jacques dans B (03) du Nouveau Testament (Vatic. Gr. 1209)', in *Studies in New Testament Language and Text*, ed. J.K. Elliott, Leiden, 1976, 122-36.
Dyrness, 'Mercy': W. Dyrness, 'Mercy Triumphs over Justice', *Them* 6.3 (1981), 11-16.
Easton: B.S. Easton and G. Poteat, 'The Epistle of James', in vol. 12 of *The Interpreter's Bible*, ed. G.A. Buttrick, Abingdon, 1957, 3-74.
Eckart, 'Terminologie': K.-G. Eckart, 'Zur Terminologie des Jakobusbriefes', *TLZ* 89 (1964), 521-26.

Editio Critica Maior: *Novum Testamentum Graecum Editio Critica Maior IV: Catholic Letters, Part 1: Text. Installment 1: James*, ed. B. Aland et al., Stuttgart, 1997.
Edsman, 'Schöpferwille': C.-M. Edsman, 'Schöpferwille und Geburt Jac 1 18', *ZNW* 38 (1939), 11-44.
Edsman, 'Schöpfung': C.-M. Edsman, 'Schöpfung und Wiedergeburt: Nochmals Jac. 1:18', in *Spiritus et Veritas*, Eutin, 1953, 43-55.
J. Edwards: J. Edwards, *The 'Blank Bible'*, Part 2, Works of Jonathan Edwards 24.2, ed. S.J. Stein, New Haven, 2006, 1167-76.
Eichholz, *Glaube*: G. Eichholz, *Glaube und Werke bei Jakobus und Paulus*, Munich, 1961.
Eichholz, *Paulus*: G. Eichholz, *Jakobus und Paulus*, Munich, 1953.
Eichhorn, *Einleitung*: J.G. Eichhorn, *Einleitung in das Neue Testament*, Leipzig, 1812.
Eisenman, 'Rain': R. Eisenman, 'Eschatological "Rain" Imagery in the War Scroll from Qumran and in the Letter of James', *JNES* 49 (1990), 173-84.
Elliott, 'Perspective': J.H. Elliott, 'The Epistle of James in Rhetorical and Social Scientific Perspective', *BTB* 23 (1993), 71-81.
Elliott-Binns: L.E. Elliott-Binns, 'James', in *Peake's Commentary on the Bible*, ed. M. Black and H.H. Rowley, 1962, London, 1022-25.
Elliott-Binns, *Christianity*: L.E. Elliott-Binns, *Galilean Christianity*, London, 1956.
Elliott-Binns, 'Coincidence': L.E. Elliott-Binns, 'James i. 21 and Ezekiel xvi. 36: An Odd Coincidence', *ExpTim* 66 (1955), 273.
Elliott-Binns, 'Creation': L.E. Elliott-Binns, 'James I. 18: Creation or Redemption?', *NTS* 3 (1956), 148-61.
Elliott-Binns, 'Jas. iii. 5': L.E. Elliott-Binns, 'The Meaning of ὕλη in Jas. iii. 5', *NTS* 2 (1956), 48-50.
Elsner: J. Elsner, *Observationes sacrae in Novi Foederis libros*, vol. 2, Utrecht, 1728.
Engelhardt, 'Bemerkungen': E. Engelhardt, 'Bemerkungen zu Jac 4, V. 5 u. 6', *Zeitschrift für die gesammte lutherische Theologie und Kirche* 3 (1869), 232-43.
Enslin, *Beginnings*: M.S. Enslin, *Christian Beginnings*, New York, 1938.
Erasmus, *Annotationes*: D. Erasmus, *Desiderii Erasmi Roterodami in Novum Testamentum annotationes*, Basil, 1535; reprinted in *Erasmus' Annotations on the New Testament*, ed. A. Reeve, Leiden, 1993.
Erasmus, *Novum Testamentum*: D. Erasmus, *Novum Testamentum omne*, Basel, 1529.
Erasmus, *Paraphrase*: D. Erasmus, *Collected Works of Erasmus: New Testament Scholarship. Paraphrases on the Epistles to Timothy, Titus, and Philemon, the Epistles of Peter and Jude, the Epistle of James, the Epistles of John, the Epistle to the Hebrews*, ed. J.J. Bateman, Toronto, 1993.
Erdmann: D. Erdmann, *Der Brief des Jakobus*, Berlin, 1881.
Estius: G. Estius, *In omnes D. Pauli Epistolas*, vol. 1, Paris, 1891.
Evans, 'Law': M.J. Evans, 'The Law in James', *VE* 13 (1983), 29-40.
L. Evans, *Faith*: L.H. Evans, *Make Your Faith Work*, London, 1957.
Ewald: H. Ewald, *Das Sendschreiben an die Hebräer und Jakobos' Rundschreiben*, Göttingen, 1870.
Fabris: R. Fabris, *Lettera di Giacomo*, Bologna, 2004.
Fabris, *Legge*: R. Fabris, *Legge della libertà in Giacomo*, Brescia, 1977.
Fabris, 'Tradizione': R. Fabris, 'La Lettera di Giacomo nella tradizione sapienziale e apocalittica', in *'Il vostro frutto rimanga' (Gv 16,16)*, ed. A.P. Dell'Acqua, Bologna, 2005, 241-56.
Farley: L.R. Farley, *Universal Truth: The Catholic Epistles of James, Peter, Jude, and John*, Ben Lomond, CA, 2008.
Farrar, *Days*: F.W. Farrar, *The Early Days of Christianity*, New York, 1883.
Fausset: R. Jamieson, A.R. Fausset, and D. Brown, *A Commentary, Critical, Experimental, and Practical, on the Old and New Testaments*, vol. 6, Philadelphia, 1868.

Fay, 'Weisheit': S.C.A. Fay, 'Weisheit—Glaube—Praxis: Zur Diskussion um den Jakobusbrief', in *Theologie im Werden*, ed. J. Hainz, Paderborn, 1992, 397-415.
Feine, *Lehranschauungen*: P. Feine, *Der Jakobusbrief nach Lehranschauungen und Entstehungsverhältnissen*, Eisenach, 1893.
Feiner, 'Krankensalbung': J. Feiner, 'Die Krankheit und das Sakrament des Salbungsgebetes', in *Zwischenzeit und Vollendung der Heilsgeschichte*, vol. 5, Zurich, 1976, 494-550.
Felder: C.H. Felder, 'James', in *The International Bible Commentary*, ed. W.R. Farmer *et al.*, Collegeville, MN, 1998, 1786-1801.
Felder, 'Partiality': C.H. Felder, 'Partiality and God's Law: An Exegesis of James 2:1-13', *JRT* 39 (1982), 51-69.
Ferris, '1 Peter': T.E.S. Ferris, 'The Epistle of James in Relation to 1 Peter', *CQR* 128 (1939), 303-308.
Feuillet, 'Parousie': A. Feuillet, 'Le sens du mot Parousie dans l'Evangile de Matthieu. Comparison entre Matth. xxiv et Jac. v.1-11', in *The Background of the New Testament and Its Eschatology*, ed. W.D. Davies and D. Daube, Cambridge, UK, 1954, 261-80.
Findlay, 'James iv. 5,6': J.A. Findlay, 'James iv. 5,6', *ExpTim* 37 (1926), 381-82.
Findlay, *Way*: J.A. Findlay, *The Way, the Truth, and the Life*, London, 1940.
Fischer, 'Spruchvers': H. Fischer, 'Ein Spruchvers im Jacobusbrief', *Philologus* 50 (1891), 377-79.
Fletcher, 'Buddhism': R.J. Fletcher, 'Are There Any Links Between the Epistle of James and Buddhism? An Examination of James 3:6', *ExpTim* 117 (2006), 366-70.
Floor: L. Floor, *Jakobus: Brief van een broeder*, Kampen, 1992.
Forbes, 'Structure': P.B.R. Forbes, 'The Structure of the Epistle of James', *EvQ* 44 (1972), 147-53.
Forster, *Ethics*: G. Forster, *The Ethics of the Letter of James*, Cambridge, UK, 2002.
Fougeras, 'Sortie': D. Fougeras, 'L'Épître de Jacques, dernière Sortie avant la grande Église?', *FoiVie* 102 (2003), 9-17.
Francis, 'Form': F.O. Francis, 'The Form and Function of the Opening and Closing Paragraphs of James and 1 John', *ZNW* 61 (1970), 110-26.
Frankemölle: H. Frankemölle, *Der Brief des Jakobus*, 2 vols., Gütersloh, 1994.
Frankemölle, 'Gesetz': H. Frankemölle, 'Gesetz im Jakobusbrief', in *Das Gesetz im Neuen Testament*, ed. K. Kertelge, Freiburg im Breisgau, 1986, 175-221.
Frankemölle, 'Gespalten': H. Frankemölle, 'Gespalten oder ganz', in *Kommunikation und Solidarität*, ed. H.-U. v. Brachel and N. Mette, Freiburg, CH, 1985, 160-78.
Frankemölle, 'Netz': H. Frankemölle, 'Das semantische Netz des Jakobusbriefes', *BZ* 34 (1990), 161-97.
Frankemölle, 'Thema': H. Frankemölle, 'Zum Thema des Jakobusbriefes im Kontext der Rezeption von Sir 2,1-18 und 15,11-20', *BN* 48 (1989), 21-43.
Freeborn, 'Glory': J. Freeborn, 'Lord of Glory: A Study of James 2 and 1 Corinthians 2', *ExpTim* 111 (2000), 185-89.
Frick, 'Note': P. Frick, 'A Syntactical Note on the Dative τῷ κόσμῳ in James 2:5', *Filologia neotestamentaria* 17 (2004), 99-103.
Friesenhahn, 'Geschichte': H. Friesenhahn, 'Zur Geschichte der Überlieferung und Exegese des Textes bei Jak V,14f.', *BZ* 24 (1938), 185-90.
Fruchtenbaum: A.G. Fruchtenbaum, *Ariel's Bible Commentary: The Messianic Jewish Epistles*, San Antonio, TX, 2005.
Fry, 'Testing': E. Fry, 'The Testing of Faith: A Study of the Structure of the Book of James', *BT* 29 (1978), 427-35.
Fulford: H.W. Fulford, *The General Epistle of James*, London, 1901.
Fulford, 'James ii.1': H.W. Fulford, 'James ii.1', *ExpTim* 38 (1927), 469.
Fulke, *Confutation*: W. Fulke, *Confutation of the Rhemish Testament*, New York, 1834.

Fung, 'Justification': R.Y.K. Fung, '"Justification" in the Epistle of James', in *Right With God*, ed. D.A. Carson, Carlisle, UK, 1992, 146-62.
Furnish, *Love*: V.P. Furnish, *The Love Command in the New Testament*, Nashville, 1972.
Gabler, 'Iacobo': J.P. Gabler, 'Iacobo, epistolae eidem adscriptae auctore', in *Opuscula Academica*, ed. T.A. Gabler and J.G. Gabler, Ulm, 1831, 199-258.
Gaigny: J. Gaigny, *Brevissima & facillima in omnes diui Pauli epistolas scholia*, Paris, 1543.
Gans, *Gedankengang*: A.E. Gans, *Über Gedankengang, Gedankenentwicklung und Gedankenverbindung in Briefen des Jacobus*, Hannover, 1874.
Garland, 'Trials': J.E. Garland, 'Severe Trials, Good Gifts, and Pure Religion: James 1', *RevExp* 83 (1986), 383-94.
Garleff, *Identität*: G. Garleff, *Urchristliche Identität in Matthäusevangelium, Didache und Jakobusbrief*, Münster, 2004.
Gaugusch: L. Gaugusch, *Der Lehrgehalt der Jakobusepistel*, Freiburg im Breisgau, 1914.
Gebser: A.R. Gebser, *Der Brief des Jakobus*, Berlin, 1828.
Gemünden, 'Einsicht': P. von Gemünden, 'Einsicht Affekt und Verhalten: Überlegungen zur Anthropologie des Jakobusbriefes', in Gemünden-Konradt-Theissen, *Jakobusbrief*, 83-96.
Gemünden, *Vegetationsmetaphorik*: P. von Gemünden, *Vegetationsmetaphorik im Neuen Testament und seiner Umwelt*, Freiburg, CH, 1993.
Gemünden, 'Wertung': P. von Gemünden, 'Die Wertung des Zorns im Jakobusbrief auf dem Hintergrund des antiken Kontextes und seine Einordnung', in Gemünden-Konradt-Theissen, *Jakobusbrief*, 97-118.
Gemünden-Konradt-Theissen, *Jakobusbrief*: P. von Gemünden, M. Konradt, and G. Theissen, *Der Jakobusbrief*, Münster, 2003.
Gench: F.T. Gench, *Hebrews and James*, Louisville, 1996.
GenevaB.: *The Geneva Bible (The Annotated New Testament, 1602 Edition)*, ed. G.T. Sheppard, New York, 1989.
George, 'Perspectives': T. George, '"A Right Strawy Epistle": Reformation Perspectives on James', *RevExp* 83 (1986), 369-82.
Gertner, 'Midrashim': M. Gertner, 'Midrashim in the New Testament', *JSS* 7 (1962), 267-92.
Gertner, 'Terms': M. Gertner, 'Midrashic Terms and Techniques in the New Testament and The Epistle of James, a Midrash on a Psalm', in *Studia Evangelica 3*, ed. F.L. Cross, Berlin, 1964, 463.
Geyser, 'Condition': A.S. Geyser, 'The Letter of James and the Social Condition of his Addressees', *Neot* 9 (1975), 25-33.
Gibson: E.C.S. Gibson, *James*, in *The Pulpit Commentary*, ed. H.D.M. Spence and J.S. Exell, New York, 1910.
Giere, 'Midrash': S.D. Giere, 'The Midrash of James: A Study of the Connections between Leviticus 19 and the Epistle of James', unpublished M.Div. thesis, Wartburg Theological Seminary, 1997.
Gill: J. Gill, *An Exposition of the New Testament*, vol. 2, London, 1854.
Gilpin: W. Gilpin, *An Exposition of the New Testament*, London, 1790.
Giroud, 'Épître': M.C. Giroud, 'Épître de Saint Jacques: Chapitre III', *Sémiotique et bible* 22 (1981), 55-59.
Gloag, *Introduction*: P.J. Gloag, *Introduction to the Catholic Epistles*, Edinburgh, 1887.
Glossa Ordinaria: *Biblia Latin cum glossa ordinaria*, Strasburg, 1480/81; reprint ed., Brepols, 1992.
Goodspeed, *Introduction*: E.J. Goodspeed, *An Introduction to the New Testament*, Chicago, 1937.
Goodspeed, *Problems*: E.J. Goodspeed, *Problems of New Testament Translation*, Chicago, 1945.
Goguel, *Church*: M. Goguel, *The Primitive Church*, New York, 1964.

LITERATURE

Gollwitzer, 'Kantate': H. Gollwitzer, 'Kantate: Jakobus 1,17-21', *Pastoraltheologie, Wissenschaft und Praxis* 55 (1967), 225-33.

Gomar: F. Gomar, 'Explicatio Epistolae Apostoli Jacobi', in *Opera theologica Omnia*, vol. 2, Amsterdam, 1644, 381-402.

Gowan, 'Wisdom': D.E. Gowan, 'Wisdom and Endurance in James', *HBT* 15 (1993), 145-53.

Grafe, *Stellung*: E. Grafe, *Die Stellung und Bedeutung des Jakobusbriefes in der Entwicklung des Urchristentums*, Tübingen, 1904.

Gray, 'Job': P. Gray, 'Points and Lines: Thematic Parallelism in the Letter of James and the Testament of Job', *NTS* 50 (2004), 406-24.

Greeven, 'Gabe': H. Greeven, 'Jede Gabe ist gut, Jak. 1,17', *TZ* 14 (1958), 1-13.

Gregory-Tuckett, *Reception*: A. Gregory and C. Tuckett, eds., *The Reception of the New Testament in the Apostolic Fathers*, Oxford, 2005.

Grimm, 'Einleitung': W. Grimm, 'Zur Einleitung in den Brief des Jacobus', *ZWT* 13 (1870), 377-94.

Grimm, 'Stelle': W. Grimm, 'Über die Stelle Br. Jakobi IV. v. 5 und 6a', *TSK* 27 (1854), 934-56.

Grosheide: F.W. Grosheide, *De Brief van Jakobus*, 3rd ed., Kampen, 1961.

Grotius: H. Grotius, *Operum Theologicorum Tomi II. Volumen II*, Amsterdam, 1679.

Gruenwald, 'Death': I. Gruenwald, 'Ritualizing Death in James and Paul in Light of Jewish Apocalypticism', in Chilton-Evans, *Missions*, 467-86.

Grünzweig: F. Grünzweig, *Der Brief des Jakobus*, Wuppertal, 1973.

Gryglewicz, 'Matthieu': F. Gryglewicz, 'L'Épître de St. Jacques et l'Évangile de St. Matthieu', *Roczniki Teologiczno-Kanoniczne* 8 (1961), 33-55.

Gundry: R.H. Gundry, *Commentary on the New Testament*, Peabody, MA, 2010.

Gurney, 'Motive': T.A. Gurney, 'The Motive and Date of the Epistle of James', *ExpTim* 14 (1903), 320-22.

Guthrie, *Introduction*: D. Guthrie, *New Testament Introduction*, Downers Grove, Il., 1971.

Guyse: J. Guyse, *A Practical Exposition of the Epistle to the Galatians, and from thence Forward to the End of the Revelation*, London, 1761.

Haacker, 'Justification': K. Haacker, 'Justification, salut et foi', *ETR* 73 (1998), 177-88.

Haak: T. Haak, *The Dutch Annotations upon the Whole Bible*, London, 1657.

Haar: J. Haar, *Der Jakobusbrief*, Stuttgart, 1971.

Hadidian, 'Pictures': D.Y. Hadidian, 'Palestinian Pictures in the Epistle of James', *ExpTim* 63 (1952), 227-28.

Hagenbach, 'Aechtheit': K.R. Hagenbach, 'Ueber die Aechtheit des Abschnittes Jac. V. 12-20', *Kritisches Journal der theologischen Literatur* 7 (1828), 395-404.

Hagner, *Clement*: D.A. Hagner, *The Use of the Old and New Testaments in Clement of Rome*, Leiden, 1973.

Hahn, 'Genesis 15.6': F. Hahn, 'Genesis 15.6 im Neuen Testament', in *Probleme biblischer Theologie*, ed. H.W. Wolff, Munich, 1971, 91-107.

Hahn-Müller, 'Jakobusbrief': F. Hahn and P. Müller, 'Der Jakobusbrief', *ThR* 63 (1998), 1-73.

Hainthaler, *Ausdauer*: T. Hainthaler, *Von der Ausdauer Ijobs habt ihr gehört, Jak 5,11*, Frankfurt am Main, 1988.

Halévy, 'Lettre': J. Halévy, 'Lettre d'un rabbin de Palestine égarée dans l'évangile', *RevSém* 22 (1914), 197-201.

Halévy, 'Essénien': J. Halévy, 'Lettre d'un missionnaire Essénien égarée dans l'évangile', *RevSém* 22 (1914), 202-206.

Halson, 'Wisdom': B.R. Halson, 'The Epistle of James: Christian Wisdom?', in *Studia Evangelica* 4, ed. F.L. Cross, Berlin, 1968, 308-14.

Hamman, 'Prière': A. Hamman, 'Prière et cult dans la Lettre de Saint-Jacques', *ETL* 34 (1958), 35-47.

Hammond: H. Hammond, *A Paraphrase and Annotations upon all the Books of the New Testament*, London, 1702.
Hammond-Le Clerc: H. Hammond and J. Le Clerc, *Novum Testamentum Domini Nostri Jesu Christi*, vol. 2, Frankfurt, 1714.
Hanson, 'Report': A.T. Hanson, 'Seminar Report', *NTS* 25 (1979), 526-27.
Hardouin: J. Hardouin, *Commentarius in Novum Testamentum*, Amsterdam, 1741.
Harman, 'Faith': H.P. Harman, 'Faith and Works: Paul and James', *LTJ* 9 (1975), 33-41.
Harnack, *Geschichte*: A. Harnack, *Geschichte der altchristlichen Literature bis Eusebius, Teil II: Die Chronologie, Band I*, 2nd ed., Leipzig, 1958.
Harner: P.B. Harner, *What Are They Saying About the Catholic Epistles?*, New York, 2004.
G. and H. Hart, *Analysis*: G. Hart and H. Hart, *A Semantic and Structural Analysis of James*, Dallas, 2001.
Hartin: P.J. Hartin, *James*, Collegeville, MN, 2003.
Hartin, 'Context': P.J. Hartin, 'The Religious Context of the Letter of James', in *Jewish Christianity Reconsidered*, ed. M. Jackson-McCabe, Minneapolis, 2007, 203-31.
Hartin, 'Eschatology': P.J. Hartin, 'James and Eschatology', in *Eschatology of the New Testament and Some Related Documents*, ed. J.G. van der Watt, Tübingen, 2011, 451-71.
Hartin, 'Ethics': P.J. Hartin, 'Ethics in the Letters of James, the Gospel of Matthew, and the Didache', in van de Sandt-Zangenberg, *Matthew*, 289-314.
Hartin, *Jerusalem*: P.J. Hartin, *James of Jerusalem: Heir to Jesus of Nazareth*, Collegeville, MN, 2004.
Hartin, 'Perfect': P.J. Hartin, 'Call to Be Perfect through Suffering (James 1,2-4)', *Bib* 77 (1996), 477-92.
Hartin, *Perfection*: P.J. Hartin, *A Spirituality of Perfection*, Collegeville, MN, 1999.
Hartin, 'Poor': P.J. Hartin, 'The Poor in the Epistle of James and the Gospel of Thomas', *HvTSt* 53 (1997), 146-62.
Hartin, *Q*: P.J. Hartin, *James and the Q Sayings of Jesus*, Sheffield, 1991.
Hartin, 'Rich': P.J. Hartin, '"Come now, you rich, weep and wail..." (James 5:1-6)', *JTSA* 84 (1993), 57-63.
Hartin, 'Sermon': P.J. Hartin, 'James and the Q Sermon on the Mount/Plain', in *Society of Biblical Literature 1989 Seminar Papers*, ed. D.J. Lull, Atlanta, 1989, 440-57.
Hartin, 'Tradition': P.J. Hartin, 'James and the Jesus Tradition', in Niebuhr-Wall, *Tradition*, 55-70.
Hartin, 'Vision': P.J. Hartin, 'The Letter of James: Its Vision, Ethics, and Ethos', in *Identity, Ethics, and Ethos in the New Testament*, ed. J.G. van der Watt and F.S. Malan, Berlin, 2006, 445-71.
Hartin, 'Who is Wise?': P.J. Hartin, '"Who is wise and understanding among you?" (James 3:13)', in *Society of Biblical Literature 1996 Seminary Papers*, Atlanta, 1996, 483-503.
Hartmann, 'Aufbau': G. Hartmann, 'Der Aufbau des Jakobusbriefes', *ZKT* 66 (1942), 63-70.
Harvey: A.E. Harvey, *A Companion to the New Testament*, 2nd ed., Cambridge, UK, 2004.
Hasselhoff, 'Thought': G.K. Hasselhoff, 'James 2:2-7 in Early Christian Thought', in *Wealth and Poverty in Early Church and Society*, ed. S.R. Holman, Grand Rapids, MI, 2008, 48-55.
Hastings: J. Hastings, *The Speaker's Bible: James*, Aberdeen, 1926.
Hatch, *Essays*: E. Hatch, *Essays in Biblical Greek*, Oxford, 1889.
Hatch, 'Note': W.H.P. Hatch, 'Note on the Hexameter in James I 17', *JBL* 28 (1909), 149-51.
Hauck: F. Hauck, *Die Briefe des Jakobus, Petrus, Judas und Johannes*, 7th ed., Göttingen, 1954.
Hayden, 'Elders': D.R. Hayden, 'Calling the Elders to Pray', *BSac* 138 (1981), 258-66.
Heckel, *Segen*: U. Heckel, *Der Segen im Neuen Testament*, Tübingen, 2002.
Heide, 'Soteriology': G.Z. Heide, 'The Soteriology of James 2:14', *GTJ* 12 (1991), 69-98.
Heiligenthal, *Werke*: R. Heiligenthal, *Werke als Zeichen*, Tübingen, 1983.

Hemminge: N. Hemminge, *A Learned and Fruiteful Commentarie upon the Epistle of James*, London, 1577.
Hengel, 'Polemik': M. Hengel, 'Der Jakobusbrief als antipaulinische Polemik', in *Paulus und Jakobus: Kleine Schriften III*, Tübingen, 2002, 511-48.
Henry: M. Henry, *Commentary on the Whole Bible*, vol. 6, New York, n.d.
Henshaw, *Literature*: T. Henshaw, *New Testament Literature*, London, 1963.
Herder, 'Kanon': J.G. Herder, 'Briefe zwener Brüder Jesu in unserem Kanon', in *Herders Sämmtliche Werke*, vol. 7, ed. J.G. Müller, Vienna, 1819, 157-242.
Herzer, 'Hiob': J. Herzer, 'Jakobus, Paulus und Hiob', in *Das Buch Hiob und seine Interpretationen*, ed. T. Krüger *et al.*, Zurich, 2007, 329-50.
Hiebert, 'Theme': D.E. Hiebert, 'The Unifying Theme of the Epistle of James', *BSac* 135 (1978), 221-31.
Hilary of Arles: Hilary of Arles, *Exposito in Epistolas Catholicas*, PLSup 3.57-131.
Hilgenfeld, 'Brief': A. Hilgenfeld, 'Der Brief des Jakobus', *ZWT* 16 (1873), 1-33.
Hincks, 'Error': E.Y. Hincks, 'A Probable Error in the Text of James ii.18', *JBL* 18 (1899), 199-202.
Hobhouse, 'Law': R. Hobhouse, 'The Royal Law', *ExpTim* 29 (1918), 471-72.
Hodges: Z.C. Hodges, *The Epistle of James*, Irving, TX, 1994.
Hodges, 'Light': Z.C. Hodges, 'Light on James Two from Textual Criticism', *BSac* 120 (1963), 341-50.
L. Hogan, *Healing*: L.P. Hogan, *Healing in the Second Temple Period*, Göttingen, 1992.
M. Hogan, 'Law': M. Hogan, 'The Law in the Epistle of James', *SNTU* 22 (1997), 79-91.
Hollmann-Bousset: G. Hollman and W. Bousset, 'Der Jakobusbrief', in *Die Schriften des Neuen Testaments*, vol. 3, Göttingen, 1917, 219-47.
H. Holtzmann, 'Zeitlage': H.J. Holtzmann, 'Die Zeitlage des Jakobusbriefes', *ZWT* 25 (1882), 292-310.
O. Holtzmann: O. Holtzmann, *Das Neue Testament*, vol. 2, Giessen, 1926.
Hoppe: R. Hoppe, *Jakobusbrief*, 2nd ed., Stuttgart, 1999.
Hoppe, *Hintergrund*: R. Hoppe, *Der theologische Hintergrund des Jakobusbriefes*, Würzburg, 1977.
Hoppe, 'Zeugnis'; R. Hoppe, 'Der Jakobusbrief als briefliches Zeugnis hellenistisch und hellenistisch-jüdisch geprägter Religiosität', in *Der neue Mensch in Christus*, ed. J. Beutler, Freiburg im Breisgau, 2001, 164-89.
Horsley-Llewelyn, *Documents*: G.H.R. Horsley and S.R. Llewelyn, *New Documents Illustrating Early Christianity*, 10 vols., NSW Australia, 1981-2012.
Hort: F.J.A. Hort, *The Epistle of St. James*, London, 1909.
Howard, *Disease*: J.K. Howard, *Disease and Healing in the New Testament*, Lanham, MD, 2001.
Hug, *Introduction*: J.L. Hug, *Introduction to the Writings of the New Testament*, vol. 2, London, 1827.
Hugedé, *Métaphore*: N. Hugedé, *La Métaphore du Miroir dans les Epîtres de saint Paul aux Corinthiens*, Neuchatel, 1957.
Hus: J. Hus, 'In Epist. Apostolorum Canonicas Septem, Commentaii', in *Historia et monumeta Joannis Hus*, vol. 2, Nuremberg, 1715, 167-374.
Hutchinson Edgar, 'Love': D. Hutchinson Edgar, 'The Use of the Love-Command and the Shema' in the Epistle of James', *PIBA* 23 (2000), 9-22.
Hutchinson Edgar, *Poor*: D. Hutchinson Edgar, *Has God Not Chosen the Poor? The Social Setting of the Epistle of James*, Sheffield, 2001.
Huther: J.E. Huther, *Critical and Exegetical Handbook to the General Epistles of James, Peter, John, and Jude*, New York, 1887.
IJO: *Inscriptiones Judaicae Orientis*, 3 vols., ed. D. Noy *et al.*, Tübingen, 2004.
Immer, *Hermeneutics*: A. Immer, *Hermeneutics of the New Testament*, Andover, MA, 1877.

Ingelaere, 'Structure': J.-C. Ingelaere, 'La Structure littéraire de l'Épître de Jacques', *FoiVie* 4 (2003), 29-38.
Instone-Brewer, 'Sermon': D. Instone-Brewer, 'James as a Sermon on the Trials of Abraham', in *The New Testament in Its First Century Setting*, ed. P.J. Williams et al., Grand Rapids, MI, 2004, 250-68.
Iovino, 'Struttura': P. Iovino, 'La Lettera di Giacomo: Struttura letterario-tematica', *Ho Theológos* 10 (1992), 7-36.
Irwin, 'Lilies': M.E. Irwin, 'Consider the Lilies', *McMaster Journal of Theology* 2 (1991), 20-28.
Isaacs: M.E. Isaacs, *Reading Hebrews and James*, Macon, GA, 2002.
Isaacs, 'Suffering': M.E. Isaacs, 'Suffering in the Lives of Christians', *RevExp* 97 (2000), 183-93.
Isho'dad of Merv: Isho'dad of Merv, 'The Epistle of James', in *The Commentaries of Isho'dad of Merv*, vol. IV, ed. M.D. Gibson, Cambridge, UK, 1913, 36-37.
Ito, 'Question': A. Ito, 'The Question of the Authenticity of the Ban on Swearing (Matthew 5.33-37)', *JSNT* 43 (1991), 5-13.
Jackson-McCabe, 'Letter': M.A. Jackson-McCabe, 'A Letter to the Twelve Tribes in the Diaspora', in *Society of Biblical Literature 1996 Seminar Papers*, Atlanta, 1996, 504-17.
Jackson-McCabe, *Logos*: M.A. Jackson-McCabe, *Logos and Law in the Letter of James*, Leiden, 2001.
Jackson-McCabe, 'Messiah': M.A. Jackson-McCabe, 'The Messiah Jesus in the Mystic World of James', *JBL* 122 (2003), 701-30.
Jackson-McCabe, 'Politics': M.A. Jackson-McCabe, 'The Politics of Pseudepigraphy and the Letter of James', in *Pseudepigraphie und Verfasserfiktion in frühchristlichen Briefen*, ed. J. Frey et al., Tübingen, 2009, 599-623.
Jacobi: B. Jacobi, *Expository Lectures on the General Epistle of James*, London, 1838.
Jacobs, 'Background': I. Jacobs, 'The Midrashic Background for James ii. 21-3', *NTS* 22 (1976), 457-64.
Jebb, *Literature*: J. Jebb, *Sacred Literature*, London, 1820.
Jeremias, 'Jac 4 5': J. Jeremias, 'Jac 4 5: ἐπιποθεῖ', *ZNW* 50 (1959), 137-38.
Jeremias, 'Paul': J. Jeremias, 'Paul and James', *ExpTim* 66 (1955), 368-71.
JIGRE: W. Horbury and D. Noy, *Jewish Inscriptions of Graeco-Roman Egypt*, Cambridge, UK, 1992.
JIWE: D. Noy, *Jewish Inscriptions of Western Europe*, 2 vols., 1993, 1995.
Jobes, *Letters*: K.H. Jobes, *Letters to the Church: A Survey of Hebrews and the General Epistles*, Grand Rapids, MI, 2011.
Jobes, 'Minor Prophets': K.H. Jobes, 'The Minor Prophets in James, 1 & 2 Peter and Jude', in *The Minor Prophets and the New Testament*, ed. M.J.J. Menken and S. Moyise, London, 2009, 135-53.
Johanson, 'Definition': B.C. Johanson, 'The Definition of "Pure Religion" in James 1^{27} Reconsidered', *ExpTim* 84 (1973), 118-19.
John, 'Anointing': J. John, 'Anointing in the New Testament', in *The Oil of Gladness*, ed. M. Dudley and G. Rowell, London, 1993, 46-75.
Johnson: L.T. Johnson, *The Letter of James*, New York, 1995.
Johnson, *Brother*: L.T. Johnson, *Brother of Jesus and Friend of God: Studies in the Letter of James*, Grand Rapids, MI, 2004.
Johnson, 'Letter': L.T. Johnson, 'The Letter of James', in *The New Interpreter's Bible* 12, Nashville, 1998, 175-225.
B. Johnson: B.W. Johnson, *The People's New Testament*, vol. 2, Delight, AR, 1889.
S. Johnson, *Treasure*: S.R. Johnson, *Seeking the Imperishable Treasure*, Eugene, OR, 2008.
Johnston, 'Controversy': C. Johnston, 'The Controversy between Saint Paul and Saint James', *Constructive Quarterly* 3 (1915), 603-15.

Johnstone: R. Johnstone, *A Commentary on James*, rev. ed., Edinburgh, 1888.

Jülicher, *Einleitung*: A. Jülicher, *Einleitung in das Neue Testament*, Tübingen, 1931.

Kaiser, *Krankenheilung*: S. Kaiser, *Krankenheilung: Untersuchungen zu Form, Sprache, traditionsgeschichtlichem Hintergrund und Aussage von Jak 5,13-18*, Neukirchen–Vluyn, 2006.

Kamell, 'Economics': M.J. Kamell, 'The Economics of Humility: The Rich and the Humble in James', in *Engaging Economics*, ed. B.W. Longenecker and K.D. Liebengood, Grand Rapids, MI, 2009, 157-75.

Kamell, 'Faith': M.J. Kamell, 'Reexamining Faith: A Study of Hebrews 10:19–12:14 and James 1–2', in *The Epistle to the Hebrews and Christian Theology*, ed. R. Bauckham *et al.*, Grand Rapids, MI, 2009, 422-31.

Kamell, 'Grace': M.J. Kamell, 'The Implications of Grace for the Ethics of James', *Bib* 92 (2011), 264-87.

Kamell, 'Law': M.J. Kamell, 'Incarnating Jeremiah's Promised New Covenant in the "Law" of James', *EvQ* 83 (2011), 19-28.

Kamell, 'Soteriology': M.J. Kamell, 'The Soteriology of James in Light of Earlier Jewish Wisdom Literature and the Gospel of Matthew', unpublished Ph.D. thesis, University of St. Andrews, 2010.

Karrer, 'Christus': M. Karrer, 'Christus der Herr und die Welt als Stätte der Prüfung', *KD* 35 (1989), 166-88.

Karo, 'Versuch': G. Karo, 'Versuch über Jac. 2.18', *Protestantishce Monatshefte* 4 (1900), 159-60.

Karris, 'Angles': R.J. Karris, 'Some New Angles on James 5:13-20', *RevExp* 97 (2000), 207-19.

Kawerau, 'Schicksale': G. Kawerau, 'Die Schicksale des Jakobusbriefes im 16. Jahrhundert', *Zeitschrift für kirchliche Wissenschaft und kirchliches Leben* 10 (1889), 359-70.

Keenan: J.P. Keenan, *The Wisdom of James*, New York, 2005.

Keith, 'Citation': P. Keith, 'La citation de Lu 19,18b en Jc 2,1-13', in Schlosser, *Epistles*, 227-48.

Keith, 'Destinataires': P. Keith, 'Les Destinataires de l'Épître de Jacques', *FoiVie* 104 (2003), 19-27.

Keith, 'Foi'. P. Keith, 'Le foi, les oeuvres et l'exemple d'Abraham et Raab dans Jc 2,14-26', in *Bible et Terre Sainte*, ed. J.E.A. Chiu, K.J. O'Mahony, M. Roger, New York, 2008, 313-32.

Kennedy, 'Atmosphere': H.A.A. Kennedy, 'The Hellenistic Atmosphere of the Epistle of James', *Expositor* ser. 8.2 (1911), 37-52.

Kern: F.H. Kern, *Der Brief Jakobi*, Tübingen, 1838.

Kern, 'Charakter': F.H. Kern, 'Der Charakter und Ursprung des Briefes Jakoboi', *Tübinger Zeitschrift für Theologie* 8 (1835), 1-132.

Ketter: P. Ketter, *Hebräerbrief, Jakobusbrief, Petrusbriefe, Judasbrief*, Freiburg im Breisgau, 1950.

Kilmartin, 'Catena': E.J. Kilmartin, 'The Interpretation of James 5:14-15 in the Armenian Catena on the Catholic Epistles: Scholium 82', *OCP* 53 (1987), 335-64.

Kilpatrick, 'Übertreter': G.D. Kilpatrick, '"Übertreter des Gesetzes, Jak. 2,11', *TZ* 23 (1967), 433.

Kirk, 'Wisdom': J.A. Kirk, 'The Meaning of Wisdom in James', *NTS* 16 (1969), 24-38.

Kirn, 'Noch einmal': D. Kirn, 'Noch einmal Jakobus 4,5', *TSK* 77 (1904), 593-604.

Kirn, 'Vorschlag': D. Kirn, 'Ein Vorschlag zu Jakobus 4,5', *TSK* 77 (1904), 127-33.

Kistemaker: S. Kistemaker, *Exposition of the Epistle of James and the Epistles of John*, Grand Rapids, MI, 1986.

Kittel, 'Ort': G. Kittel, 'Der geschichtliche Ort des Jakobusbriefes', *ZNW* 41 (1942), 71-105.

Kittel, 'Stellung': G. Kittel, 'Die Stellung des Jakobus zu Judentum und Heidenchristentum', *ZNW* 30 (1931), 145-57.
Kittel, 'Τὸν τροχόν': G. Kittel, 'Τὸν τροχὸν τῆς γενέσεως', in *Die Probleme des palästinischen Spätjudentums und das Urchristentum*, Stuttgart, 1926, 141-68.
Kittel, 'Väter': G. Kittel, 'Der Jakobusbrief und die Apostolischen Väter', *ZNW* 43 (1950), 54-112.
Klein, *Werk*: M. Klein, *'Ein vollkommenes Werk': Vollkommenheit, Gesetz und Gericht als theologische Themen des Jakobusbriefes*, Stuttgart, 1995.
Klijn: A.F.J. Klijn, *De Brief van Jakobus*, Nijkerk, 1992.
Klöpper, 'Erörterung: A. Klöpper, 'Die Erörterung des Verhältnisses von Glauben und Werken im Jacobusbriefe', *ZWT* 28 (1885), 280-319.
Kloppenborg, 'Avoidance': J.S. Kloppenborg, 'Patronage Avoidance in James', *HvTSt* 55 (1999), 755-94.
Kloppenborg, 'Discourse': J.S. Kloppenborg, 'Diaspora Discourse: The Construction of *Ethos* in James', *NTS* 53 (2007), 242-70.
Kloppenborg, 'Emulation': J.S. Kloppenborg, 'The Emulation of the Jesus Tradition in the Letter of James', in Webb-Kloppenborg, *Reading*, 121-50.
Kloppenborg, *Gospel*: J.S. Kloppenborg, *Q, The Earliest Gospel*, Louisville, 2008.
Kloppenborg, 'Judaeans': J.S. Kloppenborg, 'Judaeans or Judaean Christians in James?', in *Identity and Interaction in the Ancient Mediterranean*, ed. Z.A. Crook and P.A. Harland, Sheffield, 2007, 113-35.
Kloppenborg, 'Poverty': J.S. Kloppenborg, 'Poverty and Piety in Matthew, James, and the Didache', in van de Sandt-Zangenberg, *Matthew*, 201-32.
Kloppenborg, 'Psychagogy': J.S. Kloppenborg, 'James 1:2-15 and Hellenistic Psychagogy', *NovT* 52 (2010), 37-71.
Kloppenborg, 'Reception': J.S. Kloppenborg, 'The Reception of the Jesus Traditions in James', in Schlosser, *Epistles*, 93-141.
Kloppenborg, 'Status': J.S. Kloppenborg, 'Status und Wohltägtigkeit bei Paulus und Jakobus', in *Von Jesus zum Christus*, ed. R. Hoppe and U. Busse, Berlin, 1998, 127-54.
Kloppenborg, 'Torah': J.S. Kloppenborg, '*Didache* 1.1–6.1, James, Matthew, and the Torah', in *Trajectories through the New Testament and the Apostolic Fathers*, ed. A.F. Gregory and C.M. Tuckett, Oxford, 2005, 193-221.
Klostermann, 'Texte': E. Klostermann, 'Zum Texte des Jakobusbriefes', in *Verbum Dei manet in aeternum*, ed. W. Foerster, Witten, 1953, 71-72.
Knoch: O. Knoch, *The Epistle of St. James*, New York, 1969.
Knoch, *Eigenart*: O. Knoch, *Eigenart und Bedeutung der Eschatologie im theologischen Aufriss des ersten Clemensbriefes*, Bonn, 1964.
Knowling: R.J. Knowling, *The Epistle of St James*, London, 1904.
Knox, 'Epistle': W.L. Knox, 'The Epistle of St. James', *JTS* 46 (1945), 10-17.
Könnecke, *Emendationen*: C. Könnecke, *Emendationen zu Stellen des Neuen Testaments*, Gütersloh, 1908.
Köster, 'Leser': F. Köster, 'Über die Leser, an welche der Brief des Jakobus ist und der erste Brief des Petrus gerichtet ist', *TSK* 4 (1831), 581-88.
Koester, *History*: H. Koester, *History and Literature of Early Christianity*, vol. 2, 2nd ed., New York, 2000.
Kollmann, *Jesus*: B. Kollmann, *Jesus und die Christen als Wundertäter*, Göttingen, 1996.
Kollmann, 'Schwurverbot': B. Kollmann, 'Das Schwurverbot Mt 5,33-37/Jak 5,12 im Spiegel antiker Eidkritik', *BZ* 40 (1976), 179-93.
Konradt, 'Brief': M. Konradt, 'Der Jakobusbrief als Brief des Jakobus', in Gemünden-Konradt-Theissen, *Jakobusbrief*, 16-53.
Konradt, 'Context': M. Konradt, 'The Historical Context of the Letter of James in Light of Its Traditio-Historical Relations with First Peter', in Niebuhr-Wall, *Tradition*, 43-54.

Konradt, *Existenz*: M. Konradt, *Christliche Existenz nach dem Jakobusbrief*, Göttingen, 1998.
Konradt, 'Gerechte': M. Konradt, '"Jakobus, der Gerechte": Erwägungen zur Verfasserfiktion des Jakobusbriefes', in *Pseudepigraphie und Verfasserfiktion in frühchristlichen Briefen*, ed. J. Frey *et al.*, Tübingen, 2009, 575-97.
Konradt, 'Kontext': M. Konradt, 'Der Jakobusbrief im frühchristlichen Kontext', in Schlosser, *Epistles*, 171-212.
Konradt, 'Love': M. Konradt, 'The Love Command in Matthew, James, and the Didache', in van de Sandt-Zangenberg, *Matthew*, 270-88.
Konradt, 'Theologie': M. Konradt, 'Theologie in der "strohernen Epistel"', *VF* 44 (1999), 54-78.
Konradt, 'Werke': M. Konradt, 'Werke als Handlungsdimension des Glaubens', in *Jenseits von Indikativ und Imperative*, vol. 1, ed. F.W. Horn and R. Zimmerman, Tübingen, 2009, 309-27.
Konradt, 'Wort': M. Konradt, '"Geboren durch das Wort der Wahrheit"—gerichtet durch das Gesetz der Freiheit"', in Gemünden-Konradt-Theissen, *Jakobusbrief*, 1-16.
Kot: T. Kot, *La Lettre de Jacques*, Paris, 2006.
Kotzé, *Brief*: P.P.A. Kotzé, *Die Brief van Jakobus*, Kaapstad, 1993.
Krüger, 'Definición': R. Krüger, 'Una definición muy peculiar de religión según Santiago 1:27', *Cuadernos de Teologia* 22 (2003), 79-91.
Krüger, *Kritik*: R. Krüger, *Der Jakobusbrief als prophetische Kritik der Reichen*, Münster, 2005.
Kühl, *Stellung*: E. Kühl, *Die Stellung des Jakobusbriefes zum alttestamentlichen Gesetz und zur Paulinischen Rechtfertigungslehre*, Königsberg, 1905.
Kümmel, *Introduction*: W.G. Kümmel, *Introduction to the New Testament*, rev. ed., Nashville, 1975.
Kugelman: R. Kugelman, *James and Jude*, Wilmington, DE, 1980.
Kuhn, 'Beiträge': G. Kuhn, 'Beiträge zur Erklärung des Jakobusbriefes', *NKZ* 41 (1930), 113-31.
Kutsch, 'Rede': E. Kutsch, '"Eure Rede aber sei ja ja, nein nein"', *EvT* 20 (1960), 206-17.
Kypke: G.D. Kypke, *Observationes sacrae in Novi Foederis libros*, vol. 2, Breslau, 1755.
Laato, 'Justification': T. Laato, 'Justification according to James: A Comparison with Paul', *TJ* 18 (1997), 43-84.
Lackmann, *Fide*: M. Lackmann, *Sola Fide: Eine exegetische Studie über Jakobus 2 zur reformatorischen Rechtfertigungslehre*, Gütersloh, 1949.
Lampe: G.W.H. Lampe, *A Patristic Greek Lexicon*, Oxford, 1961.
P. Lampe, *Paul*: P. Lampe, *From Paul to Valentinus*, Minneapolis, 2003.
Lange: J.P. Lange, *The Epistle General of James*, 5th ed., New York, 1867.
Lapide: C. à Lapide, *Commentaria in Epistolas Canonicas*, Antwerp, 1627.
Lardner, *Supplement*: N. Lardner, *A Supplement to the First Book of the Second Part of the Credibility of the Gospel History*, vol. 3, London, 1734.
Laurentius: J.S. Laurentius, *S. Apostoli Jacobi epistola catholica*, Amsterdam, 1662.
Lautenschlager, 'Gegenstand': M. Lautenschlager, 'Der Gegenstand des Glaubens im Jakobusbrief', *ZTK* 87 (1990), 163-84.
Lawrence, 'Note': E.A. Lawrence, 'Note on St. James i. 9, 10', *Expositor* ser. 2.6 (1883), 318-19.
Laws: S. Laws, *The Epistle of James*, San Francisco, 1980.
Laws, 'Basis': S. Laws, 'The Doctrinal Basis for the Ethics of James', *Studia Evangelica*, vol. 7, ed. E.A. Livingstone, Berlin, 1982, 299-305.
Laws, 'Scripture': S. Laws, 'Does Scripture Speak in Vain? A Reconsideration of James IV. 5', *NTS* 20 (1974), 210-15.
Leahy: T.W. Leahy, 'The Epistle of James', in *The New Jerome Biblical Commentary*, ed. R.E. Brown, J.A. Fitzmyer, and R.E. Murphy, Englewood Cliffs, N.J., 1990, 909-16.

Le Clerc: J. Le Clerc, *Novum Testamentum Domini Nostri Jesu Christi*, Frankfurt, 1714.
Leconte: R. Leconte, *Les Épîtres catholiques de Saint Jacques, Saint Jude, et Saint Pierre*, Paris, 1953.
Lee: E.T. Lee, *A Sheaf of Wheat... A Series of Brief Expository Studies on the Epistle of James*, Cincinnati, 1899.
Leigh: E. Leigh, *Annotations upon all the New Testament*, London, 1650.
Lenski: R.C.H. Lenski, *The Interpretation of the Epistle to the Hebrews and of the Epistle of James*, Columbus, OH, 1946.
Limberis, 'Provenance': V. Limberis, 'The Provenance of the Caliphate Church: James 2.17-26 and Galatians 3 Reconsidered', in *Early Christian Interpretation of the Scriptures of Israel*, ed. C.A. Evans and J.A. Sanders, Sheffield, 1997, 397-420.
Lindemann, *Paulus*: A. Lindemann, *Paulus im ältesten Christentum*, Tübingen, 1979.
Llewelyn, 'Prescript': S.R. Llewelyn, 'The Prescript of James', *NovT* 39 (1997), 385-93.
Lockett, 'God': D.R. Lockett, 'God and the World', in *Cosmology and New Testament Theology*, ed. J.T. Pennington and S.M. McDonough, London, 2008, 144-55.
Lockett, *Purity*: D.R. Lockett, *Purity and Worldview in the Epistle of James*, London, 2008.
Lockett, 'Spectrum': D.R. Lockett, 'The Spectrum of Wisdom and Eschatology in the Epistle of James and 4QInstruction', *TynBul* 56 (2005), 131-48.
Lockett, 'Strong': D.R. Lockett, 'Strong and Weak Lines: Permeable Boundaries between Church and Culture in the Letter of James', *RevExp* 108 (2011), 391-405.
Lockett, 'Structure': D.R. Lockett, 'Structure or Communicative Strategy? The "Two Ways" Motif in James' Theological Instruction', *Neot* 42 (2008), 269-87.
Lockett, 'World': D.R. Lockett, '"Unstained by the World": Purity and Pollution as an Indicator of Cultural Interaction in the Letter of James', in Webb-Kloppenborg, *Reading*, 49-78.
Lodge, 'Paul': J.G. Lodge, 'James and Paul at Cross-Purposes? James 2.22', *Bib* 62 (1981), 195-213.
Lohse, 'Glaube': E. Lohse, 'Glaube und Werke', in *Die Einheit des Neuen Testaments*, Göttingen, 1973, 285-306.
Longenecker, 'Faith': R.N. Longenecker, 'The "Faith of Abraham" Theme in Paul, James and Hebrews', *JETS* 20 (1977), 203-12.
Lorenzen, 'Faith': T. Lorenzen, 'Faith without Works does not count before God! James 2 14-26', *ExpTim* 89 (1978), 231-35.
Lowe, 'Debate': B.A. Lowe, 'James 2:1 in the Πίστις Χριστοῦ Debate', in *The Faith of Jesus Christ*, ed. M.F. Bird and P.M. Sprinkle, Milton Keynes, Bucks, 2009, 239-57.
Luck, 'Theologie': U. Luck, 'Die Theologie des Jakobusbriefes', *ZTK* 81 (1984), 1-30.
Luck, 'Theologie des Paulus': U. Luck, 'Der Jakobusbrief und die Theologie des Paulus', *TGl* 61 (1971), 161-79.
Luck, 'Weisheit': U. Luck, 'Weisheit und Leiden: Zum Problem Paulus und Jakobus', *TLZ* 92 (1967), 253-58.
Ludwig, *Wort*: M. Ludwig, *Wort als Gesetz*, Frankfurt am Main, 1994.
Lüdemann, *Opposition*: G. Lüdemann, *Opposition to Paul in Jewish Christianity*, Minneapolis, 1989.
Lührmann, *Glaube*: D. Lührmann, *Glaube im frühe Christentum*, Gütersloh, 1976.
S. Luther, 'Ethics': S. Luther, 'Protreptic Ethics in the Letter of James', in *Moral Language in the New Testament*, ed. R. Zimmermann and Jan G. van der Watt, Tübingen, 2010, 330-64.
Luz, *Matthew*: U. Luz, *Matthew*, 3 vols., Minneapolis, 2001–2007.
McCartney: D.G. McCartney, *James*, Grand Rapids, MI, 2009.
McDade, 'Jews': J. McDade, 'The Epistle of James for Jews and Christians', *Month* 254/second new series 26.1 (1993), 115-20.
MacDougall, *Conflict*: J. MacDougall, *The Modern Conflict*, London, n.d.

McGiffert, *History*: A.C. McGiffert, *A History of Christianity in the Apostolic Age*, New York, 1897.
MacGorman, 'Exposition': J.W. MacGorman, 'An Exposition of James 3', *SWJT* 29 (1986), 31-36.
MacGorman, 'Wisdom': J.W. MacGorman, 'A Comparison of the Book of James with the Jewish Wisdom Literature', unpublished D.Th. thesis, Southwestern Baptist Theological Seminary, 1956.
Macknight: J. Macknight, *A New Literal Translation from the Original Greek, of all the Apostolical Epistles*, Philadelphia, 1841.
McKnight: S. McKnight, *The Letter of James*, Grand Rapids, MI, 2010.
McKnight, 'Interlocutor': S. McKnight, 'James 2:18a: The Unidentifiable Interlocutor', *WTJ* 52 (1990), 355-64.
McKnight, 'Way': S. McKnight, 'A Parting within the Way: Jesus and James on Israel and Purity', in Chilton-Evans, *Origins*, 83-129.
Maclaren: A. Maclaren, *The Epistle to the Hebrews (Chapters VII. to XIII.). The General Epistle of James*, New York, 1910.
McNeile-Williams, *Introduction*: A.H. McNeile and C.S.C. Williams, *An Introduction to the Study of the New Testament*, 2nd ed., Oxford, 1953.
McNeile, *Teaching*: A.H. McNeile, *New Testament Teaching in the Light of St. Paul's*, Cambridge, UK, 1923.
März, 'Art': C.-P. März, 'Von der "evangelischen Art" der "strohernen Epistel"', in *Unterwegs zum einen Glauben*, ed. W. Beinert, K. Feifreis, and H.-J. Röhrig, Leipzig, 1997, 44-62.
Maier: G. Maier, *Der Brief des Jakobus*, Wuppertal, 2004.
Maier, 'Jakobusbrief': G. Maier, 'Inwiefern ist der Jakobusbrief missionarisch?', in *Martyria*, ed. J. Kniffka, Wuppertal, 1989, 88-94.
Maier, *Reich*: G. Maier, *Reich und Arm*, Giessen, 1980.
Manns, 'Jacques 2,24-26': F. Manns, 'Jacques 2,24-26 à la lumière du Judaïsme', *BeO* 26 (1984), 143-49.
Manns, 'Nazoréen': F. Manns, 'Le judéo-christianisme nazoréen', *EstBib* 63 (2005), 481-525.
Manns, 'Péchés': F. Manns, '"Confessez vos péchés les uns aux autres": Essai d'interprétation de Jacques 5,16', *RevSciRel* 58 (1984), 233-41.
Manns, 'Tradition': F. Manns, 'Une tradition liturgique juive sous-jacente à Jacques 1:21b', *RevSciRel* 62 (1988), 85-89.
Manton: T. Manton, *An Exposition of the Epistle of James*, Lafayette, IN, 2001 (reprint of 1693 edition).
Marchant: J. Marchant, *An Exposition of the Books of the New Testament*, London, 1743.
Marconi: G. Marconi, *La lettera di Giacomo*, Rome, 1990.
Marconi, 'Debolezza': G. Marconi, 'Le debolezza in fomra di attesa: Appunti per un'esegesi di Gc 5,7-12', *RivB* 37 (1989), 173-83.
Marconi, 'Malattia': G. Marconi, 'La malattia come "punto di vista": esegesi di Gc 5,13-20', *RivB* 38 (1990), 57-72.
Marconi, 'Nota': G. Marconi, 'Una nota sullo specchio di Gc 1.23', *Bib* 70 (1989), 396-402.
Marconi, 'Sapienza': G. Marconi, 'La "sapienza" nell'esegesi di Gc 3,13-18', *RevistB* 36 (1988), 239-54.
Marconi, 'Struttura': G. Marconi, 'La struttura di Giacomo 2', *Bib* 68 (1987), 250-57.
Marcus, 'Inclination': J. Marcus, 'The Evil Inclination in the Epistle of James', *CBQ* 44 (1982), 606-21.
Marshall, 'Δίψυχος': S.S. Marshall, 'Δίψυχος: A Local Term?', in *Studia Evangelica*, vol. 6, ed. E.A. Livingstone, Berlin, 1973, 348-51.
Martin: R.P. Martin, *James*, Waco, 1988.
Martin, 'Life-Setting': R.P. Martin, 'The Life-Setting of the Epistle of James', in *Biblical and Near Eastern Studies*, ed. G.A. Tuttle, Grand Rapids, MI, 1977, 97-103.

Martin of Legio: Martin of Legio, *Expositio in epistolam B. Jacobi*, in PL 209.183-216.
G.C. Martin, 'Storehouse': G.C. Martin, 'The Epistle of James as a Storehouse of the Sayings of Jesus', *Expositor* ser. 7.3 (1907), 174-84.
Marty: J. Marty, *L'Épître de Jacques*, Paris, 1935.
Marucci, 'Gesetz': C. Marucci, 'Das Gesetz der Freiheit im Jakobusbrief', *ZKT* 117 (1995), 317-31.
Marucci, 'Merkmale': C. Marucci, 'Sprachliche Merkmale des Jakobusbriefes', in Schlosser, *Epistles*, 265-71.
Marxsen, *Frühkatholizismus*: Marxsen, *Der 'Frühkatholizismus' im Neuen Testament*, Neukirchen–Vluyn, 1958.
Maser, 'Synagogue': P. Maser, 'Synagoge und Ekklesia', in *Begegnungen zwischen Christentum und Judentum in Antike und Mittelalter*, ed. D.-A. Koch and H. Lichtenberger, Göttingen, 1993, 271-92.
Massaux, *Influence*: É. Massaux, *The Influence of the Gospel of Saint Matthew on Christian Literature before Saint Irenaeus*, vol. 2, Macon, GA, 1992.
Massebieau, 'L'Épître': L. Massebieau, 'L'Épître de Jacques est-elle l'oevre d'un chrétien?', *RHR* 32 (1895), 249-83.
Matson, 'Dimensions': T.B. Matson, 'Ethical Dimensions of James', *SWJT* 12 (1969), 23-39.
Maurice, *Unity*: F.D. Maurice, *The Unity of the New Testament*, vol. 1, London, 1884.
B. Mayer, 'Bittgebet': B. Mayer, 'Jak 5,13-18—ein Plädoyer für das Bittgebet in der Kirche', in *Der Dienst für den Menschen in Theologie und Verkündigung*, ed. R.M. Hübner, B. Mayer, and E. Reiter, Regensburg, 1981, 167-78.
R. Mayer, 'Jakobusbrief': R. Mayer, 'Über den Jakobusbrief', in *Störenfriedels Zeddelkasten*, Berlin, 1991, 49-70.
Maynard-Reid, *Poverty*: P.U. Maynard-Reid, *Poverty and Wealth in James*, Maryknoll, 1987.
Mayor: J.B. Mayor, *The Epistle of St. James*, 3rd ed., London, 1913.
Mayordomo-Marin, 'Gericht': M. Mayordomo-Marin, 'Jak 5,2.3a: Zukünftiges Gericht oder gegenwärtiger Zustand?', *ZNW* 83 (1992), 132-37.
Mbwilo, 'Wisdom': E. Mbwilo, 'Heavenly Wisdom versus Earthly Wisdom', *Stylos Theological Journal* 16 (2008), 107-18.
Meecham, 'Epistle': H.G. Meecham, 'The Epistle of St. James', *ExpTim* 49 (1938), 181-83.
Mehlhorn, 'Erklärungsversuch': P. Mehlhorn, 'Noch ein Erklärungsversuch zu Jac 2,18', *Protestantische Monatshefte* 4 (1900), 192-94.
Meier, 'Oaths 1', 'Oaths 2': J.P. Meier, 'Did the Historical Jesus Prohibit All Oaths? Part 1', *JSHJ* 5 (2007), 175-204; 'Part 2', 6 (2008), 3-24.
Meinertz: M. Meinertz, 'Der Jakobusbrief', in M. Meinertz and W. Vrede, *Die Katholischen Briefe*, Bonn, 1932, 1-54.
Meinertz, 'Krankensalbung': M. Meinertz, 'Die Krankensalbung Jak 5,14f.', *BZ* 20 (1932), 23-36.
Meinertz, *Theologie*: M. Meinertz, *Theologie des Neuen Testaments*, Bonn, 1950.
Meinertz, *Verfasser*: M. Meinertz, *Der Jakobusbrief und sein Verfasser in Schrift und Überlieferung*, Freiburg im Breigau, 1905.
Ménégoz, *Étude*: E. Ménégoz, *Étude comparative de l'enseignment de saint Paul et de saint Jacques sur la justification par la foi*, Paris, 1901.
Metzger, *Canon*: B.M. Metzger, *The Canon of the New Testament*, Oxford, 1987.
Metzger, *Commentary*: B.M. Metzger, *A Textual Commentary on the Greek New Testament*, London, 1971.
Metzner, *Rezeption*: R. Metzner, *Die Rezeption des Matthäusevangeliums im 1. Petrusbrief*, Tübingen, 1995.
Meyer, *Rätsel*: A. Meyer, *Das Rätsel des Jacobusbriefes*, Giessen, 1930.
MHT: J.H. Moulton, F.W. Howard, and N. Turner, *A Grammar of New Testament Greek*, 4 vols., Edinburgh, 1906, 1929, 1963, 1976.

LITERATURE

J. Michaelis, *Introduction*: J.D. Michaelis, *Introduction to the New Testament*, vol. 4, Cambridge, UK, 1801.
W. Michaelis, *Einleitung*: W. Michaelis, *Einleitung in das Neue Testament*, 3rd ed., Bern, 1961.
Michl, *Briefe*: J. Michl, *Die Katholischen Briefe*, 2nd ed., Regensburg, 1968.
Michl, 'Spruch': J. Michl, 'Der Spruch Jakobusbrief IV, 5', in *Neutestamentliche Aufsätze*, ed. J. Blinzler, O. Kuss, and F. Mussner, Regensburg, 1963, 167-72.
J. Miller, *Romans*: J. Miller, *Commentary on Paul's Epistle to the Romans*, Princeton, NJ, 1887.
J.D. Miller, 'Birth': J.D. Miller, 'Can the "Father of Lights" Give Birth?', *Priscilla Papers* 19 (2005), 5-7.
Minear, 'Demand': P. Minear, 'Yes or No: The Demand for Honesty in the Early Church', *NovT* 13 (1971), 1-13.
Mitchell, 'Document': M.M. Mitchell, 'The Letter of James as a Document of Paulinism', in Webb-Kloppenborg, *Reading*, 75-98.
Mitton: C.L. Mitton, *The Epistle of James*, London, 1966.
Moffatt: J. Moffatt, *The General Epistles*, New York, 1928.
Moffatt, *Introduction*: J. Moffatt, *An Introduction to the Literature of the New Testament*, 3rd ed., Edinburgh, 1918.
Moo: D.J. Moo, *The Letter of James*, Grand Rapids, MI, 2000.
Morrell, *Conjectures*: W. Morrell, *Critical Conjectures and Observations on the New Testament*, London, 1812.
Motyer: A. Motyer, *The Message of James*, Downers Grove, IL, 1985.
Moule, *Birth*: C.F.D. Moule, *The Birth of the New Testament*, 3rd ed., San Francisco, 1982.
Moule, *Idiom*: C.F.D. Moule, *An Idiom-Book of New Testament Greek*, Cambridge, UK, 1960.
Moulton, 'Studies': J.H. Moulton, 'Synoptic Studies. II. The Epistle of James and the Sayings of Jesus', *Expositor* ser. 7.4 (1907), 45-55.
Moulton, 'Supplication': J.H. Moulton, '"Inspired" Supplication (James v.16)', *ExpTim* 26 (1915), 381-83.
Mozley, 'Faith': F.W. Mozley, 'Justification by Faith and Works in St. James and St. Paul', *Expositor* ser, 7,10 (1910), 481-503
Muraoka, *Lexicon*: T. Muraoka, *A Greek-English Lexicon of the Septuagint*, Louvain, 2009.
Mussner: F. Mussner, *Der Jakobusbrief*, 2nd ed., Freiburg im Breisgau, 1967.
Mussner, 'Christologie': F. Mussner, '"Direkte" und "indirekte" Christologie im Jakobusbrief', *Catholica* 24 (1970), 111-17.
Mussner, 'Motivation': F. Mussner, 'Die ethische Motivation im Jakobusbrief,' in *Neues Testament und Ethik*, ed. H. Merklein, Freiburg im Breisgau, 1989, 416-23.
Mussner, 'Rückbesinnung': F. Mussner, 'Rückbesinnung der Kirchen auf das Jüdische', *Catholica* 52 (1998), 67-78.
Mussner, 'Tauflehre': F. Mussner, 'Die Tauflehre des Jakobusbriefes', in *Zeichen des Glaubens*, ed. H. Auf der Mauer and B. Kleinheyer, Zurich, 1972, 61-67.
Myllykoski, 'History': M. Myllykoski, 'James the Just in History and Tradition', *CBR* 5 (2006), 73-122; 6 (2007), 11-98.
Nauck, 'Freude': W. Nauck, 'Freude im Leiden: Zum Problem einer urchristlichen Verfolgungstradition', *ZNW* 46 (1955), 68-80.
Navarre Bible: *The Navarre Bible: The Catholic Epistles*, ed. J.M. Casciaro *et al.*, Dublin, 1992.
NDL: P. Hermann and H. Malay, *New Documents from Lydia*, Vienna, 2007.
Neander: A. Neander, *The Epistle of James*, New York, 1852.
Neitzel, 'Crux interpretum': H. Neitzel, 'Eine alte *crux interpretum* im Jakobusbrief 2.18', *ZNW* 73 (1982), 286-93.

Neudorfer, 'Sachkritik': H.-W. Neudorfer, 'Ist Sachkritik nötig?', *KD* 43 (1997), 279-302.
Neuer Wettstein: *Neuer Wettstein*, vol. 2, ed. G. Strecker and U. Schnelle, Berlin, 1996.
Ng, 'Father': E.Y.L. Ng, 'Father-God Language and Old Testament Allusions in James', *TynBul* 54 (2003), 41-54.
Nicholas of Gorran: Nicholas of Gorran, *In Acta apostolorum, et singulas apostolorum, Iacobi, Petri, Iohannis & Iudæ canonicas epistolas, & Apocalypsin commentarij*, Antwerp, 1617.
Nicholas of Lyra: Nicholas of Lyra: *Postilla super totam Bibliam IV*, Strasburg, 1492.
Nicol, 'Faith': W. Nicol, 'Faith and Works in the Letter of James', *Neot* 9 (1975), 7-24.
Niebuhr, 'Diasporabriefe': K.-W. Niebuhr, 'Der Jakobusbrief im Licht frühjüdischer Diasporabriefe', *NTS* 44 (1998), 420-43.
Niebuhr, 'Ethik': K.-W. Niebuhr, 'Ethik und Anthropologie nach dem Jakobusbrief', in *Jenseits von Indikativ und Imperativ*, vol. 1, ed. F.W. Horn and R. Zimmermann, Tübingen, 2009, 329-46.
Niebuhr, 'Ethos': K.-W. Niebuhr, 'Jüdisches, jesuanisches und paganes Ethos im frühen Christentum', in *Neues Testament und hellenistisch-jüdische Alltagskultur*, ed. R. Deines, J. Herzer, and K.-W. Niebuhr, Tübingen, 2009, 251-73.
Niebuhr, *Gesetz*: K.-W. Niebuhr, *Gesetz und Paränese*, Tübingen, 1987.
Niebuhr, 'Minds': K.-W. Niebuhr, 'James in the Minds of the Recipients', in Niebuhr-Wall, *Tradition*, 43-54.
Niebuhr, 'Perspective': K.-W. Niebuhr, '"A New Perspective on James"? Neuere Forschungen zum Jakobusbrief', *TLZ* 129 (2004), 1019-1044.
Niebuhr, 'Seligpreisungen': K.-W. Niebuhr, 'Seligpreisungen in der Bergpredigt nach Matthäus und im Brief Jakobus', in *Neutestamentliche Exegese im Dialog*, ed. P. Lampe, M. Mayordomo, and M. Sato, Neukirchen–Vluyn, 2008, 275-96.
Niebuhr, 'Tora': K.-W. Niebuhr, 'Tora ohne Temple: Paulus und der Jakobusbrief im Zusammenhang frühjüdischer Torarezeption für die Diaspora', in *Gemeinde ohne Tempel*, ed. B. Ego, A. Lange, and P. Pilhofer, Tübingen, 1999, 427-60.
Niebuhr-Wall, *Tradition*: K.-W. Niebuhr and R. Wall, eds., *The Catholic Epistles and Apostolic Tradition*, Waco, TX, 2009.
Nielsen, *Heilung*: H.K. Nielsen, *Heilung und Verkündigung*, Leiden, 1987.
Nienhuis, *Paul*: D.R. Nienhuis, *Not By Paul Alone: The Formation of the Catholic Epistle Collection and the Christian Canon*, Waco, TX, 2007.
Nienhuis, 'Pseudepigraph': D.R. Nienhuis, 'The Letter of James as a Canon-Conscious Pseudepigraph', in Niebuhr-Wall, *Tradition*, 183-200.
Noack, 'Reichen': B. Noack, 'Jakobus wider die Reichen', *ST* 18 (1964), 10-25.
Nodet, 'Juste': É. Nodet, 'Jacques le juste et son épître', *RB* 116 (2009), 415-39, 572-97.
Nystrom: D.P. Nystrom, *James*, Grand Rapids, MI, 1997.
Obermüller, 'Contaminación': R. Obermüller, '¿Contaminación? En torno a una definición de la religión (Sant 1,27)', *RivB* 34 (1972), 13-19.
Obermüller, 'Themen': R. Obermüller, 'Hermeneutische Themen im Jakobusbrief', *Bib* 53 (1972), 234-44.
O'Callaghan, 'Papiros': J. O'Callaghan, '¿Papiros neotestamentarios en la cueva 7 de Qumrān?', *Bib* 53 (1972), 91-104.
Ps.-Oecumenius: Ps.-Oecumenius, *Epistolae Catholicae Jacobi*, in PG119.451-510.
Öhler, *Elia*: M. Öhler, *Elia im Neuen Testament*, Berlin, 1997.
Oeming, 'Glaube': M. Oeming, 'Der Glaube Abrahams', *ZNW* 110 (1998), 16-33.
Oesterley: W.E. Oesterley, 'The General Epistle of James', in vol. 4 of *The Expositor's Greek New Testament*, ed. W.R. Nicoll, New York, n.d., 385-476.
Ó Fearghail, 'Structure': F. Ó Fearghail, 'On the Literary Structure of the Letter of James', *PIBA* 19 (1996), 66-83.

Ogara, 'Verbo': F. Ogara, 'Voluntarie genuit nos verbo veritatis, ut simus initium aliquod creaturae eius', *VD* 15 (1935), 130-38.
Oliphant, 'Waiting': A. Oliphant, 'Waiting Patiently for the Coming of the Lord: James 5:7-11', *Ekklesiastikos Pharos* 77 (1995), 81-86.
Omanson, 'Judgment': R.L. Omanson, 'The Certainty of Judgment and the Power of Prayer: James 5', *RevExp* 83 (1986), 427-38.
Ong, *Strategy*: S.H. Ong, *A Strategy for a Metaphorical Reading of the Epistle of James*, Lanham, MD, 1996.
Orlando, *Lettera*: L. Orlando, *La Lettera di Giacomo. La Seconda Lettera di Pietro. La Lettera di Giuda*, Bari, 2008.
Orlando, 'Liturgia': L. Orlando, 'La lettera di Giacomo: Liturgia e medio Giudaismo', *Anton* 81 (2006), 431-61.
Osiander: L. Osiander, *Sacrorum Bibliorum*, vol. 3, Tübingen, 1592.
Painter, 'Catholic': J. Painter, 'James as the First Catholic Epistle', *Int* 60 (2006), 245-62.
Painter, *James*: J. Painter, *Just James*, Minneapolis, 1999.
Painter, 'Power': J. Painter, 'The Power of Words: Rhetoric in James and Paul', in Chilton-Evans, *Missions*, 235-73.
E. Palmer: E.F. Palmer, *The Book that James Wrote*, Grand Rapids, MI, 1997.
F. Palmer, 'Offering': F.H. Palmer, 'James i.18 and the Offering of First-Fruits', *TynBul* 3 (1957), 1-2.
Panackel, 'Poor': C. Panackel, 'The Option for the Poor in the Letter of St. James', *BiBh* 15 (1989), 141-53.
Paret, 'Wort': E. Paret, 'Noch ein Wort über Jac. 4, 5 nebst 1 Mos. 4, 7', *TSK* 36 (1863), 113-18.
Paret, 'Zitat': E. Paret, 'Nochmals das Zitat in Jak. 4,5', *TSK* 80 (1907), 234-46.
Paretsky, 'Two Ways': A. Paretsky, 'The Two Ways and *Dipsychia* in Early Christian Literature', *Ang* 74 (1997), 305-34.
Pareus: D. Pareus, 'S. Iacobi Apostoli', in *Operum theologicorum exegeticorum*, vol. 2, Frankfurt, 1647.
Parker, 'Text': D.C. Parker, 'The Development of the Critical Text of the Epistle of James', in *New Testament Textual Criticism and Exegesis*, ed. A. Denaux, Leuven, 2002, 317-30.
Parry, *Discussion*: R.S.J. Parry, *A Discussion of the General Epistle of St. James*, London, 1903.
Patry, *Prédication*: R. Patry, *L'Épître de Jacques dans ses rapports avec la Prédication de Jésus*, Paris, 1899.
Patterson, *Thomas*: S.J. Patterson, *The Gospel of Thomas and Jesus*, Sonoma, CA, 1993.
Paulsen, 'Jakobusbrief': H. Paulsen, 'Jakobusbrief', in *TRE* 16 (1987), 488-95.
B. Pearson, *Sense*: B.W.R. Pearson, *Corresponding Sense: Paul, Dialectic, and Gadamer*, Leiden, 2011.
J. Pearson, *Critici sacri*: J. Pearson, *Critici sacri*, vol. 7, London, Frankfurt am Main, 1660.Peck, 'James 5:1-6': G. Peck, 'James 5:1-6', *Int* 42 (1988), 291-96.
Pemble, *Vindiciae Fidei*: W. Pemble, *Vindiciae Fidei*, Oxford, 1629.
Penna, 'Giustificazione': R. Penna, 'La giustificazione in Paolo e in Giacomo', *RivB* 30 (1982), 337-62.
Penner, *Eschatology*: T.C. Penner, *The Epistle of James and Eschatology*, Sheffield, 1996.
Penner, 'Research': T.C. Penner, 'The Epistle of James in Current Research', *CurBS* 7 (1999), 257-308.
Perdue, 'Paraenesis': L. Perdue, 'Paraenesis and the Epistle of James', *ZNW* 72 (1981), 241-56.
Perkins: P. Perkins, *First and Second Peter, James, and Jude*, Louisville, 1995.
Perkins, 'James 3:16–4:3': P. Perkins, 'James 3:16–4:3', *Int* 36 (1982), 283-87.
Peters: H.-J. Peters, *Der Brief des Jakobus*, Wuppertal, 1997.

Pfeiffer, 'Zusammenhang': E. Pfeiffer, 'Der Zusammenhang des Jakobusbriefes', *TSK* 23 (1850), 163-80.
Pfleiderer, *Influence*: O. Pfleiderer, *The Influence of the Apostle Paul*, New York, 1885.
Pfleiderer, *Christianity*: O. Pfleiderer, *Primitive Christianity*, vol. 4, New York, 1911.
Pfligersdorffer, 'Demut': G. Pfligersdorffer, 'Demut und Gnade. Zu Jakobus 4,6 bei Augustus', in *Chartulae, Jahrbuch für Antike und Christentum*, Ergänzungsband 28, Münster in Westfalen, 1998, 243-52.
Philonenko, 'Écho': M. Philonenko, 'Un Écho de la Prédication d'Asoka dans L'Épître de Jacques', in *Ex Orbe Religionum*, ed. C.J. Bleeker *et al.*, Leiden, 1972, 254-65.
Pickar, 'Sick': C. Pickar, 'Is Anyone Sick among You?', *CBQ* 7 (1945), 165-74.
Piscator: J. Piscator, *Piscatoris commentarii in omnes libros Novi Testamenti*, Herborn, 1658.
Plummer: A. Plummer, 'The General Epistles of St. James and St. Jude', in vol. 6 of *The Expositor's Bible*, ed. W.R. Nicoll, Rahway, N.J., n.d., 555-643.
Plumptre: E.H. Plumptre, *The General Epistle of St James*, Cambridge, UK, 1886.
Poirier, 'Symbols': J.C. Poirier, 'Symbols of Wisdom in James 1:17', *JTS* 57 (2006), 57-75.
Pokorný-Heckel, *Einleitung*: P. Pokorný and U. Heckel, *Einleitung in das Neue Testament*, Tübingen, 2007.
Polhill, 'Prejudice': J.B. Polhill, 'Prejudice, Partiality, and Faith: James 2', *RevExp* 83 (1986), 395-404.
Polhill, 'Situation': J.B. Polhill, 'The Life-Situation of the Book of James', *RevExp* 66 (1969), 369-78.
Poole: M. Poole, *A Commentary on the Holy Bible*, vol. 3, London, 1846.
Popkes: W. Popkes, *Der Brief des Jakobus*, Leipzig, 2001.
Popkes, *Adressaten*: W. Popkes, *Adressaten, Situation und Form des Jakobusbriefes*, Stuttgart, 1986.
Popkes, 'Composition': W. Popkes, 'The Composition of James and Intertextuality', *ST* 51 (1997), 91-112.
Popkes, 'Justification': W. Popkes, 'Two Interpretations of "Justification" in the New Testament', *ST* 59 (2005), 129-46.
Popkes, 'Law': W. Popkes, 'The Law of Liberty (James 1:25; 2:12)', in *Festschrift Günter Wagner*, ed. Faculty of Baptist Theological Seminary, Bern, 1994, 131-42.
Popkes, 'Leadership': W. Popkes, 'Leadership: James, Paul, and their Contemporary Background', in Chilton-Evans, *Missions*, 323-54.
Popkes, 'Mission': W. Popkes, 'The Mission of James in his Time', in Chilton-Neusner, *Brother*, 88-99.
Popkes, 'Paraenesis': W. Popkes, 'James and Paraenesis, Reconsidered', in *Texts and Contexts*, ed. T. Fornberg and D. Hellholm, Oslo, 1995, 535-61.
Popkes, 'Scripture': W. Popkes, 'James and Scripture', *NTS* 45 (1999), 213-29.
Popkes, 'Traditionen und Traditionsbrüche im Jakobusbrief', in Schlosser, *Epistles*, 143-70.
Porter, '*Dipsuchos*': S.E. Porter, 'Is *dipsuchos* (James 1,8; 4,8) a "Christian" Word?', *Bib* 71 (1990), 469-98.
Porter, 'Temptation': S.E. Porter, 'Mt 6:13 and Lk 11:14: "Lead us not into temptation"', *ExpTim* 101 (1990), 359-62.
V. Porter, 'Sermon': V.V. Porter, 'The Sermon on the Mount in the Book of James', *BSac* 162 (2005), 344-60, 470-82.
Porubszky: G. Porubszky, *Jakobus, der Zeuge vom lebendigen Glauben*, Vienna, 1861.
Pott: D.J. Pott, *Epistolae Catholicae Graece*, Göttingen, 1816.
Powell, 'Faith': C.H. Powell, 'Faith in James and its Bearings on the Problem of the Date of the Epistle', *ExpTim* 62 (1951), 311-14.
Pratscher, *Herrenbruder*: W. Pratscher, *Der Herrenbruder Jakobus und die Jakobustradition*, Göttingen, 1987.

LITERATURE

Preisker, 'Eigenwert': H. Preisker. 'Der Eigenwert des Jakobusbriefes in der Geschichte des Urchristentums', *TBl* 13 (1934), 229-36.
Preisker, 'Verständnis': H. Preisker, 'Zum Verständnis Jakobus 2.18f.', *TBl* 4 (1925), 16-17.
Pretorius, 'Coherency': E.A.C. Pretorius, 'Coherency in James: A Soteriological Intent?,' *Neot* 28 (1994), 541-55.
Pretorius, 'Verklaringsopsies': E.A.C. Pretorius, 'Drie nuwe verklaringsopsies in die Jakobusbrief (Jak 2:1; 4:5; 5:6)', *HvTSt* 44 (1988), 650-64.
Preuschen, 'Jac 5,11': E. Preuschen, 'Jac 5,11', *ZNW* 17 (1916), 79.
Priestly: T. Priestly, *The Complete Family Bible*, London, n.d.
Prieto, 'Malédiction': C. Prieto, 'Malédiction des mauvais Riches de la communauté', *FoiVie* 102 (2003), 73-81.
Pritius, *Introductio*: J.G. Pritius, *Introductio in lectionem Novi Testamenti*, Leipzig, 1737.
Prockter, 'Noah': L.J. Prockter, 'James 4:4-6: A Midrash on Noah', *NTS* 35 (1989), 625-27.
Proctor, 'Faith': M. Proctor, 'Faith, Works, and the Christian Religion in James 2:14-26', *EvQ* 69 (1997), 307-32.
Puech, 'Qumrân': E. Puech, 'La Lettre de Jacques et Qumrân', *RivB* 59 (2011), 30-55.
Punchard: E.G. Punchard, 'The Epistle of St. James', in *A New Testament Commentary for English Readers*, vol. 3, ed. C.J. Ellicott, London, 1884, 351-81.
Pyle: T. Pyle, *A Paraphrase on the Acts of the Holy Apostles, upon all the Epistles of the New Testament, and upon the Revelations*, new ed., vol. 2, Oxford, 1817.
Quistorp: J. Quistorp, *Annotationes in omnes libros biblicos*, Frankfurt, 1648.
Rainbow, *Way*: P.A. Rainbow, *The Way of Salvation*, Bletchley, Milton Keynes, UK, 2005.
Rakestraw, 'Soteriology': R.V. Rakestraw, 'James 2:14-26: Does James Contradict the Pauline Soteriology?', *CTR* 1 (1986), 31-50.
Raphel: G. Raphel, *Annotationes in Sacram Scripturam*, vol. 2, n.p., 1747.
Rauch, 'Versuch': E.C. Rauch, 'Ueber den Brief Jakobi; ein exegetisch-kritischer Versuch', *Neues Kritisches Journal der theologischen Literatur* 6 (1827), 257-306.
Reese, 'Exegete': J.M. Reese, 'The Exegete as Sage', *BTB* 12 (1982), 82-85.
Reicke: B. Reicke, *The Epistles of James, Peter, and Jude*, Garden City, N.Y., 1964.
Reicke, *Diakonie*: B. Reicke, *Diakonie, Festfreude und Zelos*, Uppsala, 1951.
Reicke, 'L'onction': B. Reicke, 'L'onction des malades d'après Saint Jacques', *Le Maison-Dieu* 113 (1973), 50-56.
Rendall, *Christianity*: G.H. Rendall, *The Epistle of St James and Judaic Christianity*, Cambridge, UK, 1927.
Rendtorff: H. Rendtorff, *Hörer und Täter: Eine Einführung in den Jakobusbrief*, Hamburg, 1953.
Renouard, 'Foi': C. Renouard, 'La Maturité de la Foi selon Jc 2,14-26', *FoiVie* 52 (2003), 61-71.
Repschinski, 'Purity': B. Repschinski, 'Purity in Matthew, James, and the Didache', in van de Sandt-Zangenberg, *Matthew*, 379-95.
Resch, *Agrapha*: A. Resch, *Agrapha*, Leipzig, 1906.
Reumann, 'Christology': J. Reumann, 'Christology of James', in *Who Do You Say That I Am?*, ed. M.A. Powell and D.R. Bauer, Louisville, 1999, 128-39.
Reumann, *Righteousness*: J. Reumann, *'Righteousness' in the New Testament*, Philadelphia, 1982.
Reyes, 'Grito': G. Reyes, 'El Grito del Salario', *Recursos Teológicos* 5 (2004), 79-97.
Rheims: *The New Testament of our Lord and Saviour Jesus Christ*, New York, 1834.
Rhoads, 'Friend': D. Rhoads, 'The Letter of James: Friend of God', *CurTM* 25 (1998), 473-86.
Richardson: K.A. Richardson, *James*, Nashville, 1997.
Richardson, 'Job': K.A. Richardson, 'Job as Exemplar in the Epistle of James', in *Hearing the Old Testament in the New Testament*, ed. S.E. Porter, Grand Rapids, MI, 2006, 213-29.
Rico, 'Prière': C. Rico, 'Prière et paix en Jacques 5.13', *RB* 116 (2009), 440-44.

Riesenfeld, 'ΑΠΛΩΣ': H. Riesenfeld, 'ΑΠΛΩΣ. Zu Jak. 1,5', *ConNT* 9 (1944), 33-41.
Riesner: R. Riesner, 'James', in *The Oxford Bible Commentary*, ed. J. Barton and J. Muddiman, Oxford, 2001, 1255-63.
Ringe: S. Ringe, 'The Letter of James', in *A Postcolonial Commentary on the New Testament*, ed. F. Segoviah and R.S. Sugirtharajah, London, 2007, 369-79.
Robbins, 'Comparison': V.K. Robbins, 'A Comparison of Mishnah Gittin 1:1–2:2 and James 2:1-13', in J.N. Lightstone, *Mishnah and the Social Formation of the Early Rabbinic Guild*, Waterloo, ON, 2002, 201-16.
Robbins, 'Culture': V.K. Robbins, 'Making Christian Culture in the Epistle of James', *Scriptura* 59 (1996), 341-51.
D. Roberts, 'Definition': D.J. Roberts III, 'The Definition of "Pure Religion" in James 1^{27}', *ExpTim* 83 (1972), 215-16.
Roberts: J.W. Roberts, *The Letter of James*, Austin, TX, 1977.
Robertson: A.T. Robertson, *Studies in the Epistle of James*, New York, 1915.
A. Robertson, *Grammar*: A.T. Robertson, *A Grammar of the Greek New Testament in the Light of Historical Research*, 2nd ed., New York, 1914.
O. Robertson, 'Covenant': O.P. Robertson, 'Genesis 15:6: New Covenant Exposition of an Old Covenant Text', *WTJ* 42 (1980), 259-89.
Robinson, *Redating*: J.A.T. Robinson, *Redating the New Testament*, London, 1976.
Rolin, 'Foi': P. Rolin, 'Les Épreuves de la Foi', *FoiVie* 102 (2003), 51-59.
Rolland, 'Dialogue': P. Rolland, 'James and Paul in Dialogue', *Kephas* 1 (1997), 1-33.
Ropes: J.H. Ropes, *A Critical and Exegetical Commentary on the Epistle of St. James*, Edinburgh, 1916.
Ropes, 'Faith': J.H. Ropes, '"Thou Hast Faith and I Have Works" (James II. 18)', *Expositor* ser.7.5 (1908), 547-56.
Ropes, 'Text': J.H. Ropes, 'The Text of the Epistle of James', *JBL* 28 (1909), 103-29.
Rose, 'Chrétien': V. Rose, 'L'Épître de Jacques est-elle un écrit chrétien?', *RB* 5 (1896), 519-34.
Rosenmüller: J. Rosenmüller, *Scholia in Novum Testamentum*, vol. 5, Nuremberg, 1808.
Ross: A. Ross, *The Epistles of James and John*, London, 1954.
Rost, 'Bemerkungen': L. Rost, 'Archäologische Bemerkungen zu einer Stelle des Jakobusbriefes (Jak. 2,2f.)', *Palästinajahrbuch* 29 (1933), 53-66.
Roussel, 'Histoire': B. Roussel, 'Histoire de la Réception de l'Épître de Jacques', *FoiVie* 102 (2003), 39-49.
Rowston, 'Book': D.J. Rowston, 'The Most Neglected Book in the New Testament', *NTS* 21 (1975), 554-63.
Royster: D. Royster, *The Epistle of St. James*, Crestwood, NY, 2010.
Ruck-Schröder, *Name*: A. Ruck-Schröder, *Der Name Gottes und der Name Jesu*, Neukirchen–Vluyn, 1999.
Ruckstuhl: E. Ruckstuhl, *Jakobusbrief, 1.-3. Johannesbrief*, Würzburg, 1985.
Ruegg, 'Recherche': U. Ruegg, 'A la recherche du temps de Jacques', in *La mémoire et le temps*, ed. D. Marguerat and J. Zumstein, Geneva, 1991, 235-57.
Rusche: H. Rusche, *Der Brief des Apostels Jakobus*, Düsseldorf, 1965.
Rusche, 'Erbarmer': H. Rusche, 'Der Erbarmer hält Gericht: Einführung in die Grundgedanken des Jakobusbriefes (2:1-13a)', *BibLeb* 5 (1964), 236-47.
Rusche, 'Glaube': H. Rusche, 'Vom lebendigen Glauben und vom rechten Beten. Einführung in die Grundgedanken des Jakobusbriefes (2,14-26; 4.1-10)', *BibLeb* 6 (1965), 26-37.
Sadler: M.F. Sadler, *The General Epistles of Ss. James, Peter, John, and Jude*, London, 1891.
Sahlin, 'Obias': H. Sahlin, 'Noch Einmal Jacobus "Obias"', *Bib* 28 (1947), 152-53.
Salmon, *Introduction*: G. Salmon, *A Historical Introduction to the Study of the New Testament*, 7th ed., London, 1894.
Sanders, *Ethics*: J.T. Sanders, *Ethics in the New Testament*, Philadelphia, 1975.

LITERATURE

Sato, 'Brief': M. Sato, 'Wozu wurde der Jakobusbrief geschrieben?', *AJBL* 17 (1991), 55-76.
Sawicki, 'Person': M. Sawicki, 'Person or Practice? Judging in James and in Paul', in Chilton-Evans, *Missions*, 385-408.
Scaer: D.P. Scaer, *James: The Apostle of Faith*, St. Louis, 1983.
Scannerini, 'Giustificazione': S. Scannerini, 'Giustificazione per la fede, giustificazione per le opere. Linee di storia dell'esegesi di *Giacomo* 2,20-24 e 26', *Annali di storia dell'esegesi* 6 (1989), 165-87.
Schammberger, *Kampf*: H. Schammberger, *Die Einheitlichkeit des Jacobusbriefes im antignostischen Kampf*, Gotha, 1936.
Schanz, 'Jakobus': P. Schanz, 'Jakobus und Paulus', *TQ* 62 (1880), 1-22, 247-86.
Schegg: P. Schegg, *Jakobus der Bruder des Herrn*, Munich, 1883.
Schenk-Ziegler, *Correctio*: A. Schenk-Ziegler, *Correctio fraterna im Neuen Testament*, Würzburg, 1997.
Schille, 'Gespaltenheit': G. Schille, 'Wider die Gespaltenheit des Glaubens: Beobachtungen am Jakobusbrief', in *Theologische Versuche* 9, ed. J. Rogge and G. Schille, Berlin, 1977, 71-89.
Schlatter: A. Schlatter, *Der Brief des Jakobus*, 2nd ed., Stuttgart, 1956.
Schleiermacher, *Einleitung*: F. Schleiermacher, *Einleitung ins Neue Testament*, Berlin, 1845.
Schlosser, *Epistles*: J. Schlosser, ed., *The Catholic Epistles and the Tradition*, Leuven, 2004.
Schmidt, *Lehrgehalt*: W.G. Schmidt, *Der Lehrgehalt des Jacobus-Briefes*, Leipzig, 1869.
Schmitt, 'Adulteresses': J.J. Schmitt, 'You Adulteresses! The Image in James 4:4', *NovT* 28 (1986), 327-37.
Schnackenburg, *Teaching*: R. Schnackenburg, *The Moral Teaching of the New Testament*, New York, 1979.
Schneckenburger: M. Schneckenburger, *Annotatio ad Epistolam Jacobi*, Stuttgart, 1832.
Schneider: J. Schneider, *Die Briefe des Jakobus, Petrus, Judas, Johannes*, Göttingen, 1961.
Schnelle, *History*: U. Schnelle, *The History and Theology of the New Testament Writings*, Minneapolis, 1998.
Schnider: F. Schnider, *Der Jakobusbrief*, Regensburg, 1987.
Schoëkel, 'Culto': L.A. Schoëkel, 'Culto y justica en Sant. 1,26-27', *Bib* 56 (1975), 537 44.
Schökel, 'James 5,2': L.A. Schökel, 'James 5,2 and 4,6', *Bib* 54 (1973), 73-76.
Schoeps, 'Jacobus': H J. Schoeps, 'Jacobus ὁ δίκαιος καὶ 'Ωβλίας', *Bib* 24 (1943), 398-403.
Schoeps, *Theologie*: H.J. Schoeps, *Theologie und Geschichte des Judenchristentums*, Tübingen, 1949.
Schöttgen, *Horae Hebraicae*: C. Schöttgen, *Horae Hebraicae et Talmudicae in universum Novum Testamentum*, vol. 2, Dresden, 1742.
Schulthess: J. Schulthess, *Epistola Jacobi*, Zurich, 1824.
Schrage: W. Schrage, 'Der Jakobusbrief', in *Die 'Katholischen' Briefe des Jakobus, Petrus, Johannes und Judas*, 2nd ed., Göttingen, 1980, 1-39.
Schrage, *Ethics*: W. Schrage, *The Ethics of the New Testament*, Philadelphia, 1988.
Schulz, *Mitte*: S. Schulz, *Die Mitte der Schrift*, Berlin, 1976.
Schulze, *Charakter*: J.D. Schulze, *Der schriftstellerische Charakter und Werth des Petrus, Judas, und Jakobus*, Leipzig, 1802.
R. Scott: R. Scott, 'The General Epistle of James', in *The Holy Bible according to the Authorized Version (A.D. 1611)*, ed. F.C. Cook, New York, 1886, 104-53.
T. Scott: T. Scott, *The Holy Bible, Containing the Old and New Testaments*, vol. 6, Boston, 1844.
Seitz, 'Afterthoughts': O.J.F. Seitz, 'Afterthoughts on the Term "Dipsychos"', *NTS* 4 (1958), 327-34.
Seitz, 'Antecedents': O.J.F. Seitz, 'Antecedents and Significance of the Term ΔΙΨΥΧΟΣ', *JBL* 66 (1947), 211-19.

Seitz, 'Law': O.J.F. Seitz, 'James and the Law', in *Studia Evangelica*, vol. 2, ed. F.L. Cross, Berlin, 1964, 472-86.
Seitz, 'Hermas': O.J.F. Seitz, 'Relationship of the Shepherd of Hermas to the Epistle of James', *JBL* 63 (1944), 131-40.
C. Seitz, 'Job': C.R. Seitz, 'The Patience of Job in the Epistle of James', in *Konsequente Traditionsgeschichte*, ed. R. Bartelmus, T. Krüger, and H. Utzschneider, Freiburg, CH, 1993, 373-82.
Selwyn, *First Peter*: E.G. Selwyn, *The First Epistle of St. Peter*, 2nd ed., London, 1947.
Semmelink, 'Model': J.W. Semmelink, 'Daniel Patte's Semiotic Model applied to James', *Ekklesiastikos Pharos* 76 (1994), 31-47.
Sevenster, *Greek*: J.N. Sevenster, *Do You Know Greek?*, Leiden, 1968.
Shepherd, 'Matthew': M.H. Shepherd, Jr., 'The Epistle of James and the Gospel of Matthew', *JBL* 75 (1956), 40-51.
Shogren, 'Heal': G.S. Shogren, 'Will God Heal Us?—A Re-Examination of James 5:14-16a', *EvQ* 61 (1989), 99-108.
Sidebottom: E.M. Sidebottom, *James, Jude and 2 Peter*, Edinburgh, 1967.
Sigal, *Emergence*: P. Sigal, *The Emergence of Contemporary Judaism*, Pittsburgh, 1980.
Sigal, 'Halakhah': P. Sigal, 'The Halakhah of James', in *Intergerini Parietis Septum*, ed. D.Y. Hadidian, Pittsburgh, PA, 1981, 337-53.
Simeon: C. Simeon, *Horae Homileticae, vol. XX: James to Jude*, 8th ed., London, 1847.
Simon: L. Simon, *Une Ethique de la Sagesse*, Geneva, 1961.
Simon, 'Pourquoi': L. Simon, 'Pourquoi Aimer l'Épître de Jacques?', *FoiVie* 102 (2003), 83-90.
Simonis, *Paulus*: W. Simonis, *Der gefangene Paulus*, Frankfurt am Main, 1990.
Simpson: A.B. Simpson, *Practical Christianity*, Brooklyn, N.Y., n.d.
Sisti, 'Parole': A. Sisti, 'La parola e le opere (Giac. 1.22-27)', *BibOr* 6 (1964), 78-85.
Skarsaune-Hvalvik, *Believers*: O. Skarsaune and R. Hvalvik, *Jewish Believers in Jesus*, Peabody, MA, 2007.
Sleeper: C.F. Sleeper, *James*, Nashville, 1998.
D. Smit, 'Partiality': D.J. Smit, '"Show no partiality..." (James 2:1-13)', *JTSA* 71 (1990), 59-68.
P.-B. Smit, 'Background': P.-B. Smit, 'A Symposiastic Background to James?', *NTS* 58 (2012), 105-22.
Smith: H.M. Smith, *The Epistle of S. James*, Oxford, 1914.
J.R. Smith, 'Gospel': J.R. Smith, 'The Gospel in the Epistle of James', *JBL* 18 (1899), 144-55.
L.M. Smith, 'James ii.8': L.M. Smith, 'James ii.8', *ExpTim* 21 (1910), 329.
Soards, 'Abraham': M. Soards, 'The Early Christian Interpretation of Abraham and the Place of James within that Context', *IBS* 9 (1987), 18-26.
Songer: H.S. Songer, 'James', in *The Broadman Bible Commentary, vol. 12*, ed. C.J. Allen *et al.*, Nashville, 1972, 100-40.
Songer, 'Character': H.S. Songer, 'The Literary Character of the Book of James', *RevExp* 66 (1969), 379-89.
Songer, 'Introduction': H.S. Songer, 'Introduction to James', *RevExp* 83 (1986), 357-68.
Souček, 'Problemen': J.B. Souček, 'Zu den Problemen des Jakobusbriefes', *EvT* 18 (1958), 460-68.
Sparks, *Formation*: H.F.D. Sparks, *The Formation of the New Testament*, New York, 1953.
Spencer, 'Function': A.B. Spencer, 'The Function of the Miserific and Beatific Images in the Letter of James', *EvJ* 7 (1989), 3-14.
Spitaler, 'Dispute': P. Spitaler, 'James 1:5-8: A Dispute with God', *CBQ* 71 (2009), 560-79.
Spitaler, 'Shift': P. Spitaler, 'Διακρίνεσθαι in Mt. 21:21, Mk. 11:23, Acts 10:20, Rom. 4:20, 14:23, Jas. 1.6, and Jude 22—the "Semantic Shift" that went Unnoticed by Patristic Authors', *NovT* 49 (2007), 1-39.

Spitta: F. Spitta, *Zur Geschichte und Litteratur des Urchristentums, Zweiter Band: Der Brief des Jakobus; Studien zum Hirten des Hermas*, Göttingen, 1896.
Spurgeon: C.H. Spurgeon, *The Treasury of the Bible*, vol. 8, Grand Rapids, MI, 1981.
Stählin, 'Beteuerungsformeln': G. Stählin, 'Zum Gebrauch von Beteuerungsformeln im Neuen Testament', *NovT* 5 (1962), 115-43.
Stagg, 'Analysis': F. Stagg, 'An Analysis of the Book of James', *RevExp* 66 (1969), 365-68.
Stagg, 'Themes': F. Stagg, 'Exegetical Themes in James 1 and 2', *RevExp* 66 (1969), 391-402.
Stanley, *Sermons*: A.P. Stanley, *Sermons and Essays on the Apostolical Age*, 2nd ed., Oxford, 1852.
Stauffer, 'Gesetz': E. Stauffer, 'Das "Gesetz der Freiheit" in der Ordensregel von Jericho', *TLZ* 77 (1952), 527-81.
Stein, 'Faith': R.H. Stein, '"Saved by Faith [Alone]" in Paul Versus "Not Saved by Faith Alone" in James', *SBJT* 4 (2000), 4-19.
Stevartius: P. Stevartius, *Commentarius in canonicam d. Jacobi apostoli epistolam*, Ingolstadt, 1610.
Stewart, 'Synergism': A. Stewart, 'James, Soteriology, and Synergism', *TynBul* 61 (2010), 293-310.
Stewart-Sykes, 'Paraenesis': A. Stewart-Sykes, ' Ἀποκύησις λόγῳ ἀληθείας: Paraenesis and Baptism in Matthew, James, and the Didache', in van de Sandt-Zangenberg, *Matthew*, 341-59.
Stier: R. Stier, *The Words of the Risen Saviour; and, Commentary on the Epistle of James*, Edinburgh, 1859.
Stiglmayr, 'Jak 3,6': P.J. Stiglmayr, 'Zu Jak 3,6: rota nativitatis nostrae inflammata', *BZ* 1 (1913), 49-52.
Storr: G.C. Storr, 'Interpretatio Epistolae Jacobi', in *Opuscula Academia*, vol. 2, Tübingen, 1797, 1-74.
Strange, *World*: J.R. Strange, *The Moral World of James*, New York, 2010.
Streeter, *Church*: B.H. Streeter, *The Primitive Church*, New York, 1929.
Stringfellow, *Joy*: W. Stringfellow, *Count It All Joy*, Grand Rapids, 1967.
Strobel, *Untersuchungen*: A. Strobel, *Untersuchungen zum Eschatologischen Verzögerungsproblem*, Leiden, 1961.
Strotmann, *Vater*: A. Strotmann, *Mein Vater bist Du' (Sir 51.10)*, Frankfurt am Main, 1991.
Stuhlmacher, *Theologie*: P. Stuhlmacher, *Biblische Theologie des Neuen Testaments*, vol. 2, Göttingen, 1999.
Stulac: G.M. Stulac, *James*, Downers Grove, IL, 1993.
Stulac, 'Rich': G.M. Stulac, 'Who are "the Rich" in James?', *Presbyterion* 16 (1990), 89-102.
Surenhuys, *Sefer*: W. Surenhuys, *Sefer humash sive Biblios katallagēs in quo secundum veterum theologorum Hebraeorum formulas allegandi*, Amsterdam, 1713.
Symeon Metaphrastes: Symeon Metaphrastes, *Commentarius in sanctum Jacobum apostolum* 1 PG 115.200A-209A.
Syreeni, 'Legacy': K. Syreeni, 'James and the Pauline Legacy', in *Fair Play*, ed. I. Dunderberg, C. Tuckett, and K. Syreeni, Leiden, 2002, 397-437.
Taatz, *Briefe*: I. Taatz, *Frühjüdische Briefe*, Freiburg, CH, 1991.
Talbert, *Suffering*: C.H. Talbert, *Learning through Suffering*, Collegeville, MN, 1991.
Tamez, 'Bibel': E. Tamez, 'Elemente der Bibel, die den Weg der christlichen Gemeinde erhellen', *EvTh* 51 (1991), 92-100.
Tamez, 'Immigrants': E. Tamez, 'James: A Circular Letter for Immigrants', *RevExp* 108 (2011), 369-80.
Tamez, *Message*: E. Tamez, *The Scandalous Message of James*, New York, 1990.
Tasker: R.V.G. Tasker, *The General Epistle of James*, Grand Rapids, MI, 1956.
F. Taylor: F.J. Taylor, *The Apostle of Patience and Practice*, London, 1907.

M. Taylor, 'Scholarship': M.E. Taylor, 'Recent Scholarship on the Structure of James', *CBR* 4 (2004), 86-115.
M. Taylor, *Structure*: M.E. Taylor, *A Text-Linguistic Investigation into the Discourse Structure of James*, London, 2006.
Taylor-Guthrie, 'Structure': M.E. Taylor and G.H. Guthrie, 'The Structure of James', *CBQ* 68 (2006), 681-705.
TDNT: G. Kittel and G. Friedrich, eds., *Theological Dictionary of the New Testament*, 9 vols., Grand Rapids, MI, 1964–74.
Terry, 'Aspects': R.B. Terry, 'Some Aspects of the Discourse Structure of the Book of James', *JOTT* 5 (1992), 106-25.
Theile: C.G.G. Theile, *Commentarius in Epistolam Jacobi*, Leipzig, 1833.
Theissen, 'Ethos': G. Theissen, 'Ethos und Gemeinde im Jakobusbrief', in Gemünden-Konradt-Theissen, *Jakobusbrief*, 143-65.
Theissen, 'Intention': G. Theissen, 'Die pseudepigraphe Intention des Jakobusbriefes', in Gemünden-Konradt-Theissen, *Jakobusbrief*, 54-82.
Theissen, 'Nächstenliebe': G. Theissen, 'Nächstenliebe und Egalität: Jak 2,1-13 als Höhepunkt urchristlicher Ethik', in *Dielheimer Blätter zur Archäologie und Textüberlieferung der Antike und Spätantike*, ed. C. Nauerth and R. Grieshammer, Heidelberg, 1999, 179-92.
Theobald, 'Kanon': M. Theobald, 'Der Kanon von der Rechtfertigung', in *Worum geht es in der Rechtfertigungslehre?*, ed. T. Söding, Freiburg im Breisgau, 1999, 131-92.
Theophilus, 'Contra': P. Theophilus ab Orbiso, 'Contra acceptionem personarum (Iac 2,1-13)', *VD* 19 (1939), 22-32.
Theophilus, 'Iacobus': P. Theophilus ab Orbiso, '"Iacobus, Dei et...Christi servus"', *VD* 15 (1935), 139-43, 172-79.
Theophilus, 'Instans': P. Theophilus ab Orbiso, 'Instans et patientiam exhortation (Jac 5,7-11)', *VD* 28 (1950), 3-17.
Theophylact: Theophylact, *Expositio in Epistolam catholica S. Jacobi*, in PG 125.1131-90.
Thiele, 'Augustinus': W. Thiele, 'Augustinus zum lateinischen Text des Jakobusbriefes', *ZNW* 46 (1955), 255-58.
J. Thomas, 'Anfechtung': J. Thomas, 'Anfechtung und Vorfreude', *KD* 14 (1968), 183-206.
J.C. Thomas, *Devil*: J.C. Thomas, *The Devil, Disease and Deliverance*, Sheffield, 1998.
J.C. Thomas, 'Devil': J.C. Thomas, 'The Devil, Disease and Deliverance: James 5.14-16', *JPT* 2 (1993), 25-50.
Thomson, 'James iv. 5': P. Thomson, 'James iv. 5', *ExpTim* 29 (1918), 240.
Thurén, 'Rhetoric': L. Thurén, 'Risky Rhetoric in James?', *NovT* 37 (1995), 262-84.
Thurén, 'Writings': L. Thurén, 'The General New Testament Writings', in *Handbook of Classical Rhetoric in the Hellenistic Period 330 B.C.–A.D. 400*, ed. S.E. Porter, Leiden, 1997, 587-607.
Thurneysen: E. Thurneysen, *Der Brief des Jakobus*, Basel, 1941.
Tidball: D. Tidball, *Wisdom from Heaven*, Fearn, Scotland, 2003.
Tielemann, 'Verständnis': T. Tielemann, 'Zum Verständnis und zur Würdigung des Jakobusbriefes', *NKZ* 44 (1933), 256-70.
Tielemann, 'Versuch': T. Tielemann, 'Versuch einer neuen Auslegung und Anordnung des Jakobusbriefes', *NKZ* 5 (1894), 580-611.
Tiller, 'Rich': P.A. Tiller, 'The Rich and Poor in James', in *Conflicted Boundaries in Wisdom and Apocalypticism*, ed. B.G. Wright III and L.M. Wills, Atlanta, 2005, 169-79.
TLNT: C. Spicq, *Theological Lexicon of the New Testament*, 3 vols., Peabody, MA, 1994.
Tobac, 'Justification': É. Tobac, 'Le problème de la justification dans S. Paul et dans S. Jacques', *RHE* 22 (1926), 797-805.
Tollefson, 'Discourse': K.C. Tollefson, 'The Epistle of James as Dialectical Discourse', *BTB* 27 (1997), 62-69.
Torrey, 'Just': C.C. Torrey, 'James the Just, and his Name "Oblias"', *JBL* 63 (1944), 93-98.

Townsend: M.J. Townsend, *The Epistle of James*, London, 1994.
Townsend, 'Christ': M.J. Townsend, 'Christ, Community and Salvation in the Epistle of James', *EvQ* 53 (1981), 115-23.
Townsend, 'Epistle': M.J. Townsend, 'The Epistle of James', *ExpTim* 108 (1997), 134-37.
Townsend, 'Warning': M.J. Townsend, 'James 4:1-4: A Warning against Zealotry?', *ExpTim* 87 (1976), 211-13.
Trapp: J. Trapp, *A Commentary or Exposition upon all the Books of the New Testament*, 2nd ed., London, 1865.
Travis, 'Paul': A.E. Travis, 'James and Paul', *SWJT* 12 (1969), 57-70.
Trench, *Synonyms*: R.C. Trench, *Synonyms of the New Testament*, 11th ed., London, 1890.
Trenkle: F.S. Trenkle, *Der Brief des heiligen Jacobus*, Freiburg im Breisgau, 1894.
Trocmé, ' Églises': E. Trocmé, 'Le Églises pauliniennes vues du dehors: Jacques 2,1 à 3,13', in *Studia Evangelica*, vol. 2, ed. F.L. Cross, Berlin, 1964, 660-69.
Trollope: W. Trollope, *Analecta Theologica*, vol. 2, new ed., London, 1842.
Trudinger, 'Otherworldly': P. Trudinger, 'The Epistle of James: Down-to-Earth and Otherworldly?', *DRev* 12 (2004), 61-63.
Tsuji, *Glaube*: M. Tsuji, *Glaube zwischen Vollkommenheit und Verweltlichung: Eine Untersuchung zur literarischen Gestalt und zur inhaltlichen Kohärenz des Jakobusbriefes*, Tübingen, 1997.
Turnbull: R. Turnbull, *An Exposition upon the Canonicall Epistle of Saint James*, London, 1606.
Turner, *Insights*: N. Turner, *Grammatical Insights into the New Testament*, Edinburgh, 1966.
Urbach, *Sages*: E.E. Urbach, *The Sages*, 2 vols., Jerusalem, 1979.
Usteri, 'Glaube': L. Usteri, 'Glaube, Werke und Rechtfertigung im Jakobusbrief', *TSK* 62 (1889), 211-56.
Valpy: E. Valpy, *'Η ΚΑΙΝΗ ΔΙΑΘΗΚΗ*, vol. 3, 3rd ed., London, 1831.
van de Sandt, 'Law': H. van de Sandt, 'Law and Ethics in Matthew's Antitheses and James's Letter', in van de Sandt-Zangenberg, *Matthew*, 315-38.
van de Sandt, 'Way': H. van de Sandt, 'James 4,1-4 in the Light of the Jewish Two Ways Tradition 3,1-6', *Bib* 88 (2007), 38-63.
van de Sandt-Zangenberg, *Matthew*: H. van de Sandt and J.K. Zangenberg, eds., *Matthew, James, and Didache*, Atlanta, 2008.
van der Horst, *Sentences*: P.W. van der Horst, *The Sentences of Pseudo-Phocylides*, Leiden, 1978.
van der Westhuizen, 'Techniques': J.D.N. van der Westhuizen, 'Stylistic Techniques and their Functions in James 2:14-26', *Neot* 25 (1991), 89-107.
Van Zyl, 'Cosmic Dualism': S.M. Van Zyl, 'Cosmic Dualism in the Epistle of James', *Ekklesiastikos Pharos* 78 (1996), 35-49.
Vahrenhorst, *Matthäus*: M. Vahrenhorst, *'Ihr sollt überhaupt nicht schwören': Matthäus im halachischen Diskurs*, Neukirchen–Vluyn, 2002.
Vahrenhorst, 'Oath': M. Vahrenhorst, 'The Presence and Absence of a Prohibition of Oath in James, Matthew, and the Didache and Its Significance for Contextualization', in van de Sandt-Zangenberg, *Matthew*, 361-77.
Varner, *Perspective*: W. Varner, *The Book of James—A New Perspective*, Woodlands, TX, 2010.
Varner, 'Theme': W.C. Varner, 'The Main Theme and Structure of James', *MSJ* 22 (2011), 115-29.
Verheul, 'Sacrement': A. Verheul, 'Le caractère Pascal du sacrement des malades', in *La maladie et la mort du chrétien dans la liturgie*, Rome, 1975, 361-79.
Verheyden, 'State': J. Verheyden, 'Jewish Christianity, A State of Affairs', in van de Sandt-Zangenberg, *Matthew*, 123-35.

Verseput, 'Anger': D.J. Verseput, 'James 1:19-27: Anger in the Congregation', in *Interpreting the New Testament Text*, ed. D.L. Bock and B.M. Fanning, Wheaton, IL, 2006, 429-39.
Verseput, 'Genre': D.J. Verseput, 'Genre and Story: The Community Setting of the Epistle of James', *CBQ* 62 (2000), 96-110.
Verseput, 'Plutarch': D.J. Verseput, 'Plutarch of Chaeronea and the Epistle of James on Communal Behaviour', *NTS* 47 (2001), 502-18.
Verseput, 'Prayers': D.J. Verseput, 'James 1:17 and the Jewish Morning Prayers', *NovT* 39 (1997), 177-91.
Verseput, 'Puzzle': D.J. Verseput, 'Reworking the Puzzle of Faith and Deeds in James 2.14-26', *NTS* 43 (1997), 97-115.
Verseput, 'Wisdom': D.J. Verseput, 'Wisdom, 4Q185, and the Epistle of James', *JBL* 117 (1998), 691-707.
Via, 'Epistle': D.O. Via, 'The Right Strawy Epistle Reconsidered', *JR* 49 (1969), 253-67.
Vielhauer, *Geschichte*: P. Vielhauer, *Geschichte der urchristlichen Literatur*, Berlin, 1975.
Viviano, 'Loi': B.T. Viviano, 'La Loi parfaite de liberté. Jacques 1,25 et la Loi', in Schlosser, *Epistles*, 213-26.
Vollenweider, *Freiheit*: S. Vollenweider, *Freiheit als neue Schöpfung*, Göttingen, 1989.
von Soden: H. von Soden, *Hebräerbrief, Briefe des Petrus, Jakobus, Judas*, Freiburg im Breisgau, 1892.
Vorster, 'Diskriminasie': W. Vorster, 'Diskriminasie en die Vroeë Kerk: Gedagte oor Partydigheid in Jakobus 2:1-13', in *Eenheid en Konflik*, ed. C. Breytenbach and A. du Toit, Transvaal, 1987, 134-49.
Vouga: F. Vouga, *L'Épître de Saint Jacques*, Geneva, 1984.
Vouga, 'L'épître': F. Vouga, 'L'épître de Jacques', in *Introduction au Nouveau Testament*, ed. D. Marguerat, Paris, 2001, 407-18.
Vowinckel, *Grundgedanken*: E. Vowinckel, *Die Grundgedanken des Jakobusbriefes*, Gütersloh, 1898.
Vyhmeister, 'Rich': N.J. Vyhmeister, 'The Rich Man in James 2: Does Ancient Patronage Illumine the Text?', *AUSS* 33 (1995), 265-83.
Wachob, 'Intertexture': W.H. Wachob, 'The Apocalyptic Intertexture of the Epistle of James', in *The Intertexture of Apocalyptic Discourse in the New Testament*, ed. D.F. Watson, Atlanta, 2002, 165-85.
Wachob, 'Languages': W.H. Wachob, 'The Languages of "Household" and "Kingdom" in the Letter of James', in Webb-Kloppenborg, *Reading*, 151-68.
Wachob, 'Psalms': W.H. Wachob, 'The Epistle of James and the Book of Psalms', in *Fabrics of Discourse*, ed. D.B. Gowler, L.G. Bloomquist, and D.F. Watson, Harrisburg, PA, 2003, 264-80.
Wachob, *Voice*: W.H. Wachob: *The Voice of Jesus in the Social Rhetoric of James*, Cambridge, UK, 2000.
Wachob-Johnson, 'Sayings': W.H. Wachob and L.T. Johnson, 'The Sayings of Jesus in the Letter of James', in *Authenticating the Words of Jesus*, ed. B. Chilton and C.A. Evans, Leiden, 1999, 431-50.
R. Walker, 'Werken': R. Walker, 'Allein aus Werken. Zur Auslegung von Jakobus 2.14-26', *ZTK* 61 (1964), 155-92.
R.M. Walker, 'Moralizing James': R.M. Walker, 'The Mysterious and Moralizing James', *QR* 17 (1997), 169-87.
R. Wall: R.W. Wall, *Community of the Wise*, Valley Forge, PA, 1997.
R. Wall, 'Acts': R.W. Wall, 'Acts and James', in Niebuhr-Wall, *Tradition*, 127-52.
R. Wall, 'Context': R.W. Wall, 'James and Paul in Pre-Canonical Context', in R.W. Wall and E.E. Lemcio, *The New Testament as Canon*, Sheffield, 1992, 250-71.

R. Wall, 'Law': R.W. Wall, '"The Perfect Law of Liberty" (James 1:25)', in *The Quest for Context and Meaning*, ed. C.A. Evans and S. Talmon, Leiden, 1997, 475-98.
R. Wall, 'Letter': R.W. Wall, 'James, Letter of', in *Dictionary of the Later New Testament and Its Developments*, ed. R.P. Martin and P.H. Davids, Downers Grove, IL, 1997, 545-61.
R. Wall, 'Paraenesis': R.W. Wall, 'James as Apocalyptic Paraenesis', *ResQ* 32 (1990), 11-22.
R. Wall, 'Priority': R.W. Wall, 'The Priority of James', in Niebuhr-Wall, *Tradition*, 153-60.
R. Wall, 'Rahab': R.W. Wall, 'The Intertextuality of Scripture: The Example of Rahab (James 2:25)', in *The Bible at Qumran*, ed. P.W. Flint, Grand Rapids, MI, 2001, 217-36.
R. Wall, 'Theology': R.W. Wall, 'A Unifying Theology of the Catholic Epistles', in Niebuhr-Wall, *Tradition*, 13-40.
W. Wall: W. Wall, *Brief Critical Notes, Especially on the Various Readings of the New Testament Books*, London, 1730.
Wandel: G. Wandel, *Der Brief des Jakobus*, Leipzig, 1896.
Wandel, 'Auslegung': G. Wandel, 'Zur Auslegung der Stelle Jak. 3,1-8', *TSK* 66 (1893), 679-707.
Wanke, 'Lehrer': J. Wanke, 'Die urchristlichen Lehrer nach dem Zeugnis des Jakobusbriefes', in *Die Kirche des Anfanges*, ed. R. Schnackenburg and J. Wanke, Leipzig, 1978, 489-511.
Ward, 'Concern': R.B. Ward, Jr., 'The Communal Concern of the Epistle of James', unpublished Ph.D. dissertation, Harvard University, 1966.
Ward, 'Partiality': R.B. Ward, 'Partiality in the Assembly: James 2:2-4', *HTR* 62 (1969), 87-97.
Ward, 'Paul': R.B. Ward, 'James and Paul', *RQ* 7 (1963), 159-64.
Ward, 'Works': R.B. Ward, 'The Works of Abraham: James 2.14-26', *HTR* 61 (1968), 283-90.
Wardlaw: R. Wardlaw, *Lectures on the Epistle of James*, New York, 1862.
Warrington, 'Elijah': K. Warrington, 'The Significance of Elijah in James 5:13-18', *EvQ* 66 (1994), 217-27.
Warrington, 'Healing': K. Warrington, 'James 5:14-18: Healing Then and Now', *International Review of Missions* 93 (2004), 346-67.
Watson, 'Assessment': D.F. Watson, 'An Assessment of the Rhetoric and Rhetorical Analysis of the Letter of James', in Webb-Kloppenborg, *Reading*, 99-120.
Watson, 'Rhetoric': D.F. Watson, 'The Rhetoric of James 3:1-12 and a Classical Pattern of Argumentation', *NovT* 35 (1993), 48-64.
Watson, 'Schemes': D.F. Watson, 'James 2 in Light of Greco-Roman Schemes of Argumentation', *NTS* 39 (1993), 94-121.
Webb-Kloppenborg, *Reading*: R.L. Webb and J.S. Kloppenborg, eds., *Reading James with New Eyes*, London, 2007.
Webber, *Response*: R.C. Webber, *Reader Response Analysis of the Epistle of James*, San Francisco, 1996.
Weidner: F. Weidner, *Annotations on the General Epistles of James, Peter, John, and Jude*, New York, 1897.
Weiser, 'Edelmetall': W. Weiser, 'Durch Grünspan verdorbenes Edelmetall? Zur Deutung des Wortes "IOS" im Brief des Jakobus', *BZ* 43 (1999), 220-23.
B. Weiss: B. Weiss, *Die Katholischen Briefe*, Leipzig, 1892.
B. Weiss, *Manual*: B. Weiss, *A Manual of Introduction to the New Testament*, New York, 1889.
B. Weiss, *Kritik*: B. Weiss, *Der Jakobusbrief und die neuer Kritik*, Leipzig, 1904.
J. Weiss, *Christianity*: J. Weiss, *Earliest Christianity*, 2 vols., New York, 1959.
K. Weiss, 'Motiv': K. Weiss, 'Motiv und Ziel der Frömmigkeit des Jakobusbriefes', *Theologische Versuche* 7, ed. J. Rogge and G. Schille, Berlin, 1976, 107-14.

Welborn, 'Affirmation': L.L. Welborn, 'The Dangerous Double Affirmation: Character and Truth in 2Cor 1,17', *NovT* 86 (1995), 34-52.
Wells: E. Wells, *An Help for the More Easy and Clear Understanding of the Holy Scriptures, being the Epistles of St. James, St. Peter, St. John, and St. Jude*, Oxford, 1715.
L. Wells, *Healing*: L. Wells, *The Greek Language of Healing from Homer to New Testament Times*, Berlin, 1998.
Wenger, *Kyrios*: S. Wenger, *Der wesenhaft gute Kyrios: Eine Exegetische Studie über das Gottesbild im Jakobusbrief*, Zurich, 2011.
Weren, 'Community': W.J.C. Weren, 'The Ideal Community according to Matthew, James, and the Didache', in van de Sandt-Zangenberg, *Matthew*, 177-200.
Werner, 'Brief': K. Werner, 'Über den Brief Jacobi', *TQ* 54 (1872), 246-79.
Wesley: J. Wesley, *Explanatory Notes upon the New Testament*, London, 1950.
Wettlaufer, 'Variants': R.D. Wettlaufer, 'Unseen Variants: A Study of Conjectural Emendation in New Testament Textual Criticism with The Epistle of James as a Case Study', rev. ed., unpublished Ph.D. Dissertation, University of Toronto, 2011.
Wettstein: J.J. Wettstein, *Ἡ ΚΑΙΝΗ ΔΙΑΘΗΚΗ. Novum Testamentum Graecum*, vol. 2, Amsterdam, 1752.
Wheeler, *Wealth*: S.E. Wheeler, *Wealth as Peril and Obligation*, Grand Rapids, MI, 1995.
Whitby: D. Whitby, *A Paraphrase and Commentary on the New Testament*, 5th ed., vol. 2, London, 1727.
White, *Erstlingsgabe*: J. White, *Die Erstlingsgabe im Neuen Testament*, Tübingen, 2007.
Whitlark, 'Motif': J.A. Whitlark, '"Ἔμφυτος Λόγος: A New Covenant Motif in the Letter of James', in *Getting 'Saved'*, ed. C.H. Talbert and J.A. Whitlark, Grand Rapids, MI, 2011, 195-215.
Whitters, *Baruch*: M.F. Whitters, *The Epistle of Second Baruch*, London, 2003.
Wick, 'Murder': P. Wick, '"You shall not murder... You shall not commit adultery": Theological and Anthropological Radicalization in the Letter of James and in the Sermon on the Mount', in *The Decalogue in Jewish and Christian Tradition*, ed. H.G. Reventlow and Y. Hoffman, New York, 2011, 88-96.
Wieser, *Abrahamvorstellungen*: F.E. Wieser, *Die Abrahamvorstellungen im Neuen Testament*, Bern, 1987.
Wiesinger: J.T.A. Wiesinger, *Der Brief des Jakobus*, Königsberg, 1854.
Wifstrand, 'Problems': A. Wifstrand, 'Stylistic Problems in the Epistles of James and Peter', *ST* 1 (1947), 170-82.
Wikenhauser, *Introduction*: A. Wikenhauser, *New Testament Introduction*, New York, 1958.
Wilkinson, 'Healing': J. Wilkinson, 'Healing in the Epistle of James', *SJT* 24 (1971), 326-45.
Wilkinson, *Health*: J. Wilkinson, *Health and Healing*, Edinburgh, 1980.
H. Williams, 'Rags': H.H.D. Williams, 'Of Rags and Riches: The Benefits of Hearing Jeremiah 9:23-24 within James 1:9-11', *TynBul* 53 (2002), 274-82.
J. Williams, 'Law': J.G. Williams, 'The Law of Liberty (νόμος ἐλευθερίας)', *ExpTim* 16 (1905), 237-38.
R.L. Williams, 'Piety': R.L. Williams, 'Piety and Poverty in James', *WTJ* 22 (1987), 37-55.
R.R. Williams: R.R. Williams, *The Letters of John and James*, Cambridge, UK, 1965.
T. Williams: T. Williams and W. Patton, *The Cottage Bible and Family Expositor*, Hartford, 1841.
E. Wilson, 'Anointing': E.M. Wilson, 'The Anointing of the Sick in the Epistle of James, and Its Bearing on the Use of Means in Sickness', *PTR* 19 (1921), 64-95.
S. Wilson, *Strangers*: S.G. Wilson, *Related Strangers*, Minneapolis, MN, 1995.
W. Wilson, 'Sin': W.T. Wilson, 'Sin as Sex and Sex with Sin: The Anthropology of James 1:12-15', *HTR* 95 (2002), 147-68.

LITERATURE

W. Wilson, 'Turning': W.T. Wilson, 'Turning Words: James 4:7-10 and the Rhetoric of Repentance', in *Antiquity and Humanity*, ed. A.Y. Collins and M.M. Mitchell, Tübingen, 2011, 357-82.

Windisch-Preisker: H. Windisch and H. Preisker, *Die katholischen Briefe*, 3rd ed., Tübingen, 1951.

Winkler: E.T. Winkler, *Commentary on the Epistle of James*, Philadelphia, 1888.

Wischmeyer, 'Beobachtungen': O. Wischmeyer, 'Beobachtungen zu Kommunikation, Gliederung und Gattung des Jakobusbriefes', in *Das Gesetz im frühen Judentum und im Neuen Testament*, ed. D. Sänger and M. Konradt, Göttingen, 2006, 319-27.

Wischmeyer, 'Gebot': O. Wischmeyer, 'Das Gebot der Nächstenliebe bei Paulus', *BZ* 30 (1986), 161-87.

Wischmeyer, 'Milieu': O. Wischmeyer, 'Reconstructing the Social and Religious Milieu of James', in van de Sandt-Zangenberg, *Matthew*, 33-42.

Witherington: B. Witherington III, *Letters and Homilies for Jewish Christians*, Downers Grove, IL, 2007.

Wolf: J.C. Wolf, *Curae philologicae et criticae in SS. apostolorum Jacobi Petri Judae et Johannis Epistolas hujusque Apocal*, Hamburg, 1735.

Wolmarans, 'Male': J.L.P. Wolmarans, 'Male and Female Sexual Imagery: James 1:14-15, 18', *Acta Patristica et Byzantina* 5 (1994), 65-72.

Wolmarans, 'Misogyny': J.L.P. Wolmarans, 'Misogyny as a Meme: The Legacy of James 1:12-18', *Acta Patristica et Byzantina* 17 (2006), 349-61.

Wolmarans, 'Patterns': J.L.P. Wolmarans, 'Patterns of Thought in the Epistle of James', *Ekklesiastikos Pharos* 78 (1996), 50-57.

Wolmarans, 'Suffering': J.L.P. Wolmarans, 'Making Sense out of Suffering: James 1:2-4', *HvTSt* 47 (1991), 1109-21.

Wolmarans, 'θεός': J.L.P. Wolmarans, 'ὁ θεὸς ἀπείραστός ἐστιν κακῶν (James 1:13)', *Ekklesiastikos Pharos* 76 (1994), 106-108.

Wolmarans, 'Tongue': J.L.P. Wolmarans, 'The Tongue Guiding the Body: The Anthropological Presuppositions of James 3:1-12', *Neot* 26 (1992), 523-30.

Wolverton, 'Double-Minded Man': W.I. Wolverton, 'The Double-Minded Man in the Light of Essene Psychology', *ATR* 38 (1956), 166-75.

Wolzogen: J.L. Wolzogen, *Commentarium in Acts Apostolorum et reliqua ejus scripta didactica et polemica comprehendens*, Amsterdam, 1656.

Wordsworth: C. Wordsworth, *The New Testament of our Lord and Saviour Jesus Christ*, London, 1864.

J. Wordsworth, 'Corbey': J. Wordsworth, 'The Corbey St. James (ff), and Its Relation to Other Latin Versions, and to the Original Language of the Epistle', in *Studia Biblica*, Oxford, 1885, 113-50.

Wuellner, 'Rhetorik': W.H. Wuellner, 'Der Jakobusbrief im Licht der Rhetorik und Textpragmatik', *LingBib* 43 (1978), 5-66.

Wypadlo, *Gebet*: A. Wypadlo, *Viel vermag das inständige Gebet eines Gerechten (Jak 5,16)*, Würzburg, 2006.

Wypadlo, 'Gott': A. Wypadlo, 'Von Gott, dem Geber alles Guten, und vom rechten Beten', *TGl* 93 (2003), 74-92.

Young, 'Relation': F.W. Young, 'The Relation of 1 Clement to the Epistle of James', *JBL* 67 (1948), 339-45.

Zangenberg, 'Matthew': J. Zangenberg, 'Matthew and James', in *Matthew and his Christian Contemporaries*, ed. D.C. Sim and B. Repschinski, London, 2008, 104-22.

Zahn, 'Frage': T. Zahn, 'Die soziale Frage und die Innere Mission nach dem Brief des Jakobus', *ZWKL* 10 (1889), 295-307.

Zahn, *Geschichte*: T. Zahn, *Geschichte des neutestamentlichen Kanons*, 2 vols., Erlangen, 1888, 1890.

Zahn, *Introduction*: T. Zahn, *Introduction to the New Testament*, vol. 1, Edinburgh, 1909.
Zeller, 'Jak 1,12': E. Zeller, 'Über Jak 1,12', *ZWT* 6 (1863), 93-96.
Zimmer, 'Verhältnis': M. Zimmer, 'Das schriftstellerische Verhältnis des Jacobusbriefes zur paulinischen Literatur', *ZWT* 36 (1893), 481-503.
Zimmermann, *Lehrer*: A.F. Zimmermann, *Die urchristlichen Lehrer*, Tübingen, 1984.
Zmijewski, 'Vollkommenheit': J. Zmije, 'Christliche "Vollkommenheit": Erwägungen zur Theologie des Jakobusbriefes', *SUNT* A/5 (1980), 50-78.
Zodhiates, *Labor*: S. Zodhiates, *The Labor of Love*, Chattanooga, TN, 1981.
Zodhiates, *Patience*: S. Zodhiates, *The Patience of Hope*, Chattanooga, TN, 1981.
Zodhiates, *Work*: S. Zodhiates, *The Work of Faith*, Chattanooga, TN, 1981.
Zyro, 'Erklärung': F.F. Zyro, 'Zur Erklärung von Jakob. 4, 5.6', *TSK* 13 (1840), 432-50.
Zyro, 'Noch einmal': F.F. Zyro, 'Noch einmal Jakob. 4, 5.6', *TSK* 34 (1861), 765-74.
Zyro, 'Reinen': F.F. Zyro, 'Ist es mit Jakobus 4,5 nun im Reinen?', *TSK* 45 (1872), 716-29.

INTRODUCTION

The book of James has been dubbed 'the enigma of the New Testament',[1] and critical opinion regarding the letter is unusually diverse.[2] Some attribute James to a brother of Jesus and deem it to be the earliest extant Christian writing. Others assign it to an unknown individual who wrote in the first part of the second century or even later. Some espy in the letter a coherent global structure. Others regard the work as without overall plan. Some classify James as an example of paraenetical literature that does not require or reflect a particular *Sitz im Leben*. Others read between the lines any number of specific scenarios involving the author and his first readers. A few have doubted that the book was composed by a Christian. Most to the contrary read Christian doctrine and practice into almost every line.

Perhaps such disparity in judgment should cause despair. If the experts disagree so much over this 'oddity' within the canon,[3] are there really enough clues to solve the case? In this writer's judgment, however, some arguments are better than others, and we do indeed know enough to adjudicate plausibly between many of the conflicting proposals.[4] The following pages accordingly do not just catalogue opinions: they also as often as not take sides.

This commentary unapologetically continues the ICC tradition of pursuing historical-critical interests. It discusses at length issues of authorship and date. It catalogues textual variants and compiles parallels to James from Jewish and Graeco-Roman literature. And it seeks to uncover the interests of the author and to ask how an ancient audience might have received his words.

---

[1] So Deissmann, *Studies*, 52.

[2] Cf. Scott, *Literature*, 210, writing in the 1930s: 'There is no writing in the New Testament on which critical opinion has varied so widely as on this Epistle'. Time has not altered this assessment.

[3] 'Oddity' is from Laws, 1. One also recalls Herder, 'Kanon', 191: James is 'so easy to understand, and so difficult to grasp fully, to fathom'.

[4] Cf. Moffatt, *Introduction*, 475: 'the phenomenon of criticism upon the Jacobean homily are perplexing, but they are not to be taken as discrediting the science of NT research'.

At the same time, the present volume is much concerned with the history of interpretation and reception.⁵ Most critical commentaries tend instead to privilege recent work, their footnotes typically citing ancient sources and modern critics, with little in between.⁶ The habit is unfortunate. The history of interpretation and application of biblical texts invites our serious attention for multiple reasons. (i) Such history is intrinsically interesting in and of itself, as I hope readers of these pages concur. (ii) It instills humility by reminding exegetes of how much they owe to those who came before, and of the degree to which they are bearers of traditions. The line between present work and past work is much less distinct than many imagine. Most of our questions—as well as most of our answers—have been around for a long, long time. Further, much that we think of as new is really old.⁷ Reading through the sixteenth-century commentaries of Aretius and Diodati, for example, reveals that rhetorical criticism, which one might reckon to be a new method, has forerunners in much older works; and acquaintance with Grotius, Lapide, Wettstein, and Theile reveals the extent to which we remain indebted to our predecessors for uncovering so many relevant Graeco-Roman parallels. There is much less new under the sun than we vainly imagine.

(iii) Careful attention to older commentaries sometimes allows one to recover exegetical suggestions and profitable lines of inquiry that, from a historical-critical point of view, should never have dropped out of the commentary tradition.⁸ (iv) The history of the interpretation and reception of James reveals the plasticity of texts, and how easily and thoroughly they succumb to interpretive agendas. Readers make meaning, and awareness of this circumstance should move conscientious exegetes to ponder how their own interests and goals affect their work. Such awareness should equally make one mindful that all interpreters, including modern historical critics, belong to a centuries-long, unfinished history of effects. We do not somehow stand outside of that history; and we are no more its end than we are its beginning. We should not presume that our

---

⁵ There has been much discussion over the meanings of 'history of interpretation', *Wirkungsgeschichte*, and 'reception history'. This author regards the first as focused on formal theological and exegetical work. He equates the last two and understands them as broader and more inclusive: they take account of application and so extend to sermons, hymnody, general literature, and beyond, even to the readers outside ecclesiastical circles.

⁶ The custom has at least two major sources—the Reformers and their desire to read the Bible apart from Roman Catholic tradition, and later Protestant exegetes, who made themselves the informed purveyors of 'the original sense' as divined through historical study.

⁷ Including *Wirkungsgeschichte* itself; see N. Klancher, 'A Genealogy for Reception History', *BibInt* 21 (2013), 99-129.

⁸ On this subject see D.C. Allison, Jr., 'What I Have Learned from the History of Interpretation', *PRS* 35 (2008), 237-50.

own agendas and perspectives—which will soon enough give way to different agendas and perspectives—are superior to all that has come before us.

(v) Finally, reception history that looks beyond theologians and commentaries—as this volume sometimes does—reminds one that biblical texts are not the exclusive property of clerics and exegetes. They instead belong equally to popular piety and to literature in general, and likewise to artists, poets, and musicians. Those texts indeed belong to all who happen to ponder them. Moreover, the original meanings that historians regularly seek to uncover are far from being the only consequential meanings, just as historical-critical constructs are scarcely the only significant constructs. Critical historians are merely part of a much-larger story, or rather innumerable stories.

Recent decades have seen much discussion of what a commentary should be, and many have expressed discontent with traditional historical-critical approaches to texts. In this writer's judgment, there is no moral imperative here, no right or wrong. There remains rather room for manifold approaches. Commentators probably do best to write about what interests them, and as long as there are readers with similar interests—in the case of this commentary, readers who care about historical-critical questions and reception history—their books will continue to see the light of day.

I. AUTHOR AND DATE

The ms. tradition universally attributes our book to Ἰάκωβος. Early Christian sources know several men by that name: James the brother of Jesus;[9] James the father of Judas (not Iscariot);[10] James the son of Zebedee, one of the twelve;[11] James the son of Alphaeus, also one of the twelve;[12] and James the son of Mary, known variously as 'the Lesser', 'the Little', or 'the Younger', and sometimes identified with James the son of Alphaeus.[13] We know next to nothing about two of these, James the son of Mary and James the father of Judas, and our epistle has never been associated with them. Only a few have instead imagined the author

---

[9] Mt 13.55; Mk 6.3; Acts 12.17; 15.13; 21.18; 1 Cor 15.7; Gal 1.19; 2.9, 12; Jude 1.
[10] Lk 6.16; Acts 1.13.
[11] Mt 4.21; 10.2; 17.1; Mk 1.19, 29; 3.17; 5.37; 9.2; 10.35, 41; 13.3; 14.33; Lk 5.10; 6.14; 8.51; 9.28, 54; Acts 1.13; 12.2. This last verse reports that Herod Agrippa I had this James put to death, an event usually dated to CE 44.
[12] Mt 10.3; Mk 2.14; 3.18; Lk 6.15; Acts 1.13.
[13] Mk 15.40. W.K. Prentice, 'James the Brother of the Lord', in *Studies in Roman Economic and Social History*, ed. P.R. Coleman-Norton, Princeton, 1951, 144-51, identifies James the brother of the Lord not only with James of Alphaeus but also with James the Lesser. Criticism in Dibelius, 14 n. 32.

to be James of Zebedee[14] or urged that an unknown James produced our work.[15] Many more, especially in earlier times, have instead thought of James of Alphaeus—although usually they have taken him to be the same James as the brother or kinsman of Jesus.[16] The dominant opinion throughout exegetical history, beginning at least with Origen,[17] is that the James of 1.1 is the brother of Jesus, James of Jerusalem.

Two views dominate today: either James the brother of Jesus stands behind our text,[18] or it is a pseudepigraphon written in his name.[19] Both

---

[14] See 114 below n. 6.

[15] Cf. Pfleiderer, *Christianity*, 311; Moffatt, 2; V. Taylor, *The Atonement in New Testament Teaching*, 2nd ed., London, 1945, 43-44; W.K. Lowther Clarke, *Concise Bible Commentary*, London, 1952, 915; A.M. Hunter, *Introducing the New Testament*, Philadelphia, 1957, 165; Hauck, 3-4; Henshaw, *Literature*, 359-60; Kugelman, 12; Deppe, *Sayings*, 217; B. Ehrman, *The New Testament*, 4th ed., New York, 2008, 455-56.

[16] So most Roman Catholic tradition. Cf. Calvin, 260; Pareus, 539; Wolzogen, 179; Turnbull, 1-2; Burkitt, 1104; Gilpin, 589; Guyse, 561; Benson, 7; Jacobi, 1-2; Gabler, 'Iacobo'; Bouman, 14-24. The standard retort to this view is that, if one of Jesus' brothers had been a pre-Easter disciple or one of the twelve, Mk 3.21, 31-35 and Jn 7.5 are hard to explain. See further L.Á.M. Peral, 'A la búsqueda de identidades: Santiago el Zebedeo, Santiago el de Alfeo, Santiago de Nazaret', *EstBib* 67 (2009), 111-60.

[17] Origen, *Rom.* 4.8 FC 2.2 ed. Heither, 252: 'James, the brother of the Lord...says, "Whoever wants to be a friend of this world makes himself an enemy of God"'.

[18] So Zahn, *Introduction*, 101-51; Hort, xi-xxii; Beyschlag, 1-6; Mayor, i-lxxxiv; B. Weiss, *Kritik*, 43-49; Parry, *Discussion*; Knowling, xxiv-lxiv; Bardenhewer, 13-16; Rendall, *Christianity*, 38-40; Chaine, lxxviii-lxxxiv; Kittel, 'Ort'; idem, 'Väter'; Cadoux, *Thought*, 32-38; Tasker, 20-30; Mussner, 1-8; idem, 'Motivation'; Michl, 19-20; Mitton, 9; Geyser, 'Condition'; Guthrie, *Introduction*, 736-58; Robinson, *Redating*, 128-39; Grünzweig, 17; P. Stuhlmacher, *Vom Verstehen des Neuen Testaments*, Göttingen, 1979, 234; Adamson, 18-21; idem, *Message*, 3-52; Floor, 8-14; Maynard-Reid, *Poverty*, 5-11; Johnson, 108-21; Crotty, 'Poor', 12; Moo, 9-22; Riesner, 1256; Hartin, 16-24; Maier, 11; Brosend, 4-5; Dschulnigg, 'Enstehung', 130; Blomberg-Kamell, 27-35; Witherington, 395-401; McCartney, 8-32; Nodet, 'Juste'; Dunn, *Beginning*, 1123-29; McKnight, 13-38. According to M. Hengel, 'Early Christianity as a Jewish-Messianic, Universalistic Movement', in *Conflicts and Challenges in Early Christianity*, ed. D.A. Hagner, Harrisburg, PA, 1999, 4, James is 'perhaps' the real author.

[19] So Grimm, 'Einleitung'; Davidson, *Introduction*, 303; von Soden, 164-65; Bacon, 'Faith'; Grafe, *Stellung*, 46; Ropes, 47-52; Windisch-Preisker, 3-4; Dibelius, 11-21; Marty, 247-49; Jülicher, *Einleitung*, 210-13; Aland, 'Herrenbruder'; Jeremias, 'Paul'; Easton, 4-5; Souček, 'Problemen'; Blackman, 24-26; Trocmé, 'Églises'; Reicke, 3-5; Michl, 18-20; Rowston, 'Book', 559; Laws, 38-42; Cantinat, 44-52; Kümmel, *Introduction*, 413; Schnider, 16-19; Schrage, 11; Vouga, 18; Ruckstuhl, 8-9; Pratscher, *Herrenbruder*, 209-13; Hoppe, 12-13; Paulsen, 'Jakobusbrief', 492; Klijn, 24; Frankemölle, 45-54; Klein, *Werk*, 190-91; Tsuji, *Glaube*, 38-44; Hahn-Müller, 'Jakobusbrief', 64; Burchard, 1-6; Sleeper, 39-41; Bottini, *Introduzione*, 15-27; Fougeras, 'Sortie'; Burchard, 3-6; Theissen, 'Intention'; Fabris, 26; Popkes, 64-69; Jackson-McCabe, 'Politics'; Garleff, *Identität*, 231; Konradt, 'Gerechte'; Orlando, *Lettera*, 23; Broer, *Einleitung*, 601-606. Undecided is Michl, 20. Niebuhr, 'Diasporabriefe', 431, seems to leave the question open. One should not forget that, for many, theological issues remain inevitably involved in coming to a decision on this matter; see Jackson-McCabe,

views rightly assume that a lesser name requires qualification whereas a greater name does not. The Jesus of Col 4.11 is 'Jesus Justus'. An early Christian could never have simply called such a one 'Jesus': that name, if unqualified, would have signified Jesus of Nazareth. And so likewise, most suppose, is it with the simple Ἰάκωβος of Jas 1.1: the only James who could be introduced without further biographical specification, and who speaks with the authority that this writer does, must be the most famous James, which means the brother of Jesus. One may compare Jude 1, whose author identifies himself as 'the brother of James'. Here 'James' is not further specified, and most readers have naturally taken him to be James the Just. The same holds for Acts 12.17: 'Tell this to James and to the believers'. Although the narrative has earlier spoken of three men named 'James' (Acts 1.13; 12.2), this new James needs no introduction save his name,[20] and readers naturally identify him with James the brother of Jesus. Perhaps most important of all is 1 Cor 15.7: 'Then he appeared to James'. Here an unelaborated 'James' suffices to secure this individual's identity.

Paul's designation of this James as a 'pillar' as well as the several stories that found their way into Acts indicate that he was a foundational figure for early Palestinian Christianity.[21] The tradition in 1 Cor 15.7, which legend elaborated, names him as the recipient of a resurrection appearance.[22] We can surmise, from the portrait in Acts and from Paul's difficulties with delegates from James (Gal 2.2), that he observed Torah and worked primarily or exclusively among Jews. Later tradition, which nicknames him 'the Just', claims, with what warrant we know not, that he was an exceptionally pious Nazarite.[23] Josephus, who takes more note of James than Jesus, records the story of the former's execution: the high

---

'Politics'. Jobes, *Letters*, 6-12, deems canonicity and pseudonymity to be mutually exclusive: 'the embrace of pseudonymous New Testament writings insidiously turns the study of the New Testament into a study... not of what Jesus and his chosen eyewitnesses said and did, but merely of the religious ruminations of some anonymous people in the Roman period'.

[20] Cf. Barrett, *Acts 15–28*, 722: 'evidently a person of such consequence that he needs no introduction: Luke's readers are sure to know who is meant'.

[21] For overviews of what we know of James of Jerusalem see esp. Pratscher, *Herrenbruder*; R.B. Ward, 'James of Jerusalem in the First Two Centuries', *ANRW* 2.26.1 (1992), 779-812; Painter, *James*; Chilton-Evans, *Origins*; Hartin, *Jerusalem*; Y.Z. Eliav, 'The Tomb of James, Brother of Jesus, as Locus Memoriae', *HTS* 97 (2004), 33-59; Myllykoski, 'History'. On the controversial ossuary, which many suppose to have been forged, with the Hebrew inscription, 'James, son of Joseph, brother of Jesus', see R. Byrne and B. McNary-Zak, eds., *Resurrecting the Brother of Jesus*, Chapel Hill, NC, 2009.

[22] Cf. the fragment from the *Gospel of the Hebrews* in Jerome, *Vir. inl.* 2 TU 14.1a ed. Richardson 7-8.

[23] E.g. Hegesippus in Eusebius, *H.E.* 2.23.4-18.

priest Ananus had him stoned in the year 62.[24] Ecclesiastical history makes James the first bishop in Jerusalem.[25] His prestige and authority, which are underlined in apocryphal tales and writings,[26] no doubt were major factors in our epistle eventually receiving canonical status. What arguments favor identifying this figure not just with the purported author of our work but with its real author?[27] (i) The letter claims James as its author, and that it fails to make more of his status—it does not, for example, dub him an 'apostle', the brother of Jesus, or the head of the church in Jerusalem—bespeaks not pseudonymity but authenticity. 'A forger would not have been content with such simplicity and humility'.[28] (ii) The text is thoroughly Jewish in tone and at points seems to reflect acquaintance with Palestine or even Galilee.[29] (iii) Our epistle exhibits significant overlaps with the speech attributed to James in Acts 15.13-21 as well as with the letter of Acts 15.23-30, the latter issued by a group under James' leadership:[30]

χαρείν as an epistolary greeting	Acts 15.23	Jas 1.1
τὸ ὄνομα + passive ἐπικαλέω + ἐπί + pronoun	Acts 15.17	Jas 2.7

[24] Josephus, *Ant.* 20.200-203. The later account of Hegesippus *apud* Eusebius, *H.E.* 2.23, although legendary, conveys the impression many must have held of James, perhaps from early times.

[25] So already Clement of Alexandria *apud* Eusebius, *H.E.* 2.1.3; cf. the lists of bishops in Eusebius, *H.E.* 4.5; 5.12.

[26] Gos. Thom. 12 says that, when Jesus is gone, the apostles should go to James the righteous, 'for whose sake heaven and earth came into being'. Other books from Nag Hammadi present themselves as revelations given through James: the Apocryphon of James, the First Apocalypse of James, the Second Apocalypse of James. Ps.-Clem. Rec. 4.35 GCS 51 ed. Rehm, 164 tells readers to be wary of anyone not bringing from Jerusalem the testimony of James the Lord's brother.

[27] I make no attempt here to review all the arguments that have been forwarded one way or the other. The focus is rather on the most weighty considerations and on those claims that have been repeated again and again.

[28] So Knowling, xxiv. Cf. Gloag, *Introduction*, 27; Zahn, *Introduction*, 139; Mayor, clxxii; Wikenhauser, *Introduction*, 482; Sevenster, *Greek*, 14-15; Robinson, *Redating*, 129; R. Mayer, 'Jakobusbrief', 54. Oddly enough, Oesterley, 397-98, turns this argument around: 'one might reasonably have expected in an Epistle written by St. James that the fact of his having been the brother of the Lord would have been specially mentioned... The more authoritative the name of the person who addressed them, the more effective would be the influence of the Epistle upon them.'

[29] Cf. W. Dodd, preface to James; Hug, *Introduction*, 549-51; Alford, 101; Mayor, cxxiv-cxxv; Knowling, xxiv; Chaine, lxxxiii; Bishop, *Apostles*, 184-90; Wikenhauser, *Introduction*, 481-82; Johnson, 120-21; McCartney, 24-25; Jobes, *Letters*. The verses cited most often are 1.6, 11; 3.4, 11-12; 5.7, 17-18.

[30] Cf. Schulze, *Charakter*, 86-87; Zahn, *Introduction*, 119; Mayor, iii-iv; Oesterley, 392; Knowling, xxv-xxvi; Mitton, 230-31; Guthrie, *Introduction*, 742-43; Floor, 12; Moo, 10; McCartney, 25-26; McKnight, 24-25; Jobes, *Letters*, 153. Adamson, *Message*, 21-24, argues the point at length. Painter, *James*, 245-46, raises the possibility that the author of Acts had a hand in editing our epistle.

ἀκούσατε immediately before or after

ἀδελφοί	Acts 15.13	Jas 2.5
ἐπισκέπτομαι	Acts 15.14	Jas 1.27
ἐπιστρέφω	Acts 15.19	Jas 5.19-20
(δια)τηρέω	Acts 15.29	Jas 1.27; 2.10
ἀγαπητοί	Acts 15.25	Jas 1.16, 19; 2.5
ὄνομα	Acts 15.14, 17, 26	Jas 2.7; 5.10, 14

These parallels, it has been alleged, are 'remarkable', and 'of such a character that they cannot be explained by the common accidents of speech'.[31] (iv) Although James displays a knowledge of the Jesus tradition, the book shows no familiarity with Matthew, Mark, Luke, or John. This is consistent with an early date. In the eyes of some, furthermore, our epistle looks like the 'reminiscence of thoughts often uttered' by Jesus, thoughts that sank 'into the heart of the hearer' James, who reproduced them 'in his own manner'.[32] (v) Some have urged that knowledge of our text was early, well known, and authoritative, as attested by use of it in 1 Clement and Hermas, or even Paul and 1 Peter.[33] (vi) The social and religious circumstances reflected in James mirror the Christian situation in Palestine before 70; that is, the theology is undeveloped and the Christology understated;[34] rich and poor are at odds and wealth is a snare for some;[35] the Gentile issue and its controversies receive no mention, nor does the destruction of Jerusalem;[36] the recipients attend a synagogue (2.2), and

[31] So Guthrie, *Introduction*, 742. He thinks that the evidence from Acts 'while not conclusive, is yet corroborative of the traditional view of authorship'.

[32] So Mayor, lxii. Cf. Salmon, *Introduction*, 454-56; Patry, *Prédication*; G.C. Martin, 'Storehouse'; Kittel, 'Ort'; Tasker, 28; Guthrie, *Introduction*, 743; Adamson, 21-22; V. Porter, 'Sermon', 346. Contrast McNeile-Williams, *Introduction*, 204: James does not reflect the 'personal spell' of Jesus. Those who think that a brother of Jesus wrote our letter should acknowledge the theoretical possibility that Jesus borrowed ideas from a sibling; cf. Forster, *Ethics*, 7. Johnson, 119-20, infers an early Palestinian provenance from the resemblances to Q. So too Elliott-Binns, *Christianity*, 47.

[33] For discussion of the relationship between James and these sources see below, 17, 20-23, 62-70. According to L. Pullan, *The Books of the New Testament*, London, 1901, 231-32, both Peter and Paul knew our letter. So too Mayor, lxx-lxxix, who also finds a knowledge of James in the Didache, 1 Clement, 2 Clement, Barnabas, Ignatius, Polycarp, and Hermas.

[34] Cf. Salmon, *Introduction*, 464-65; G.V. Lechler, *The Apostolic and Post-Apostolic Times*, 3rd ed., Edinburgh, 1886, 291-92; Mayor, cxlvii-cxlix; Robinson, *Redating*, 123, the latter adding that there is no sense of the delay of the *parousia* or 'preoccupation with doctrinal orthodoxy', as in the Pastorals. According to Davids, 17, James 'may' preserve a 'primitive' Christology. For Botha, 'Soteriology', James represents an early stage of Christian theological development.

[35] According to Knowling, xxxiv, the year 70 saw an end to Jewish rank and wealth. Cf. Salmon, *Introduction*, 456-57; Guthrie, *Introduction*, 746; Robinson, *Redating*, 122; Adamson, *Message*, 25.

[36] Zahn, *Introduction*, 136-37; cf. Mayor, cxlv-cxlvi; Guthrie, *Introduction*, 761-62; Robinson, *Redating*, 120-23; V. Porter, 'Sermon', 344-45. The failure to mention the

the only offices mentioned are 'teacher' and 'elder', not 'bishop' and 'deacon'.[37] Some, moreover, believe that the references to wars and conflicts in 4.1 best fit the period leading up to 70.[38] What is the force of these claims and observations? (i) Pseudepigrapha, including pseudepigraphical epistles, do not always parade the credentials of their purported authors if those authors are sufficiently well known. Simple names, for example, suffice in the following instances (two of which name our James):

- 1 En. 1.1: 'The blessing of Enoch, with which he blessed...'
- Ep Jer 1.1: 'A copy of the letter that Jeremiah sent...'
- 3 Bar. Gk. 1.1: 'Narration and Apocalypse of Baruch concerning...'
- Apoc. Pet 1.1: 'The second coming of Christ and resurrection of the dead which Christ revealed through Peter to those who died for their sins...'
- Ap. Jas 1.1: 'James writes to...'
- PBod 5 Prot. Jas. title: 'Birth of Mary. Revelation of James'[39]
- Vis. Ezra 1.1: 'Ezra prayed to the Lord saying...'
- Correspondence of Paul and Seneca 1: 'Seneca to Paul. Greeting'
- Ep Peter to James 1.1: 'Peter to...'
- Apoc. Thom. Verona frag. 1: 'Hear, Thomas, the things which must come to pass...'
- Epistles of Socrates and the Socrates 15.1: 'Xenophon to the friends of Socrates'
- Epistles of Socrates and the Socrates 25.1: 'Phaedrus to Plato'

Furthermore, we have many instances of pseudepigrapha that fail to develop in obvious ways their fictional authorship: after naming their writer in the title or first sentence or two, they go on to other things.[40] So the argument that James is unlikely to be a pseudepigraphon because it fails to parade its author's credentials or status fails to persuade.

(ii) The broadly Jewish character of James is not in dispute. The fact, however, while consistent with ascription to James of Jerusalem, scarcely establishes it. Most early Christian leaders were Jewish, and Christian Judaism[41] flourished in several quarters into the second century and

Gentile controversy has been thought consonant with a date before the crisis related in Acts 15; cf. Eichhorn, *Einleitung*, 584-85; Salmon, *Introduction*, 458-59; J.V. Bartlet, *Age*, 233; Kittel, 'Ort'; Robinson, *Redating*, 138-40.

[37] Cf. Mayor, cxlvi-cxlvii; Robinson, *Redating*, 124-24; V. Porter, 'Sermon', 345.

[38] E.g. Gurney, 'Motive'; Martin, 'Life-Setting'.

[39] Origen, Mt 10.17 GCS 40 ed. Klostermann, 21, calls the Protevangelium simply βίβλος 'Ιακώβου.

[40] E.g. the Psalms of Solomon, the Epistle of Enoch A (1 En. 92.1-5; 93.11-14; 94.1-5; 104.9-105.2), Ps.-Phocylides, the Gospel of Thomas, the Gospel of Philip, the Sentences of Syriac Menander, the Apocalypse of Thomas, the Teachings of Silvanus, the Epistle of Titus.

[41] On the issues surrounding this term and the comparable 'Jewish Christianity' see M. Jackson-McCabe, 'What's in a Name? The Problem of "Jewish Christianity"', in *Jewish Christianity Reconsidered*, ed. M. Jackson-McCabe, Minneapolis, 2007, 7-38.

beyond. Thus, although the Jewish features of Revelation are patent, it is a post-70 document. The same is true of the Didache. Further, even if, as this writer believes, the author of James knew Hebrew, that scarcely directs us to a particular individual: it goes without saying that many in the early Christian movement did so. As for the alleged signs of a Palestinian or even Galilean author, the commentary addresses them at the appropriate junctures and finds cause for doubt in each case. Yet even were one to demur, the obvious remains: James of Jerusalem was not the only Christian to have lived in Palestine or Galilee. Even many diaspora Jews saw Israel first-hand when they visited for major festivals.

(iii) Regarding the correlations with Acts 15, several questions are in order. First, does Acts 15.13-21 report in near word-perfect detail a speech delivered in Greek by James of Jerusalem? Many doubt that, among them C.K. Barrett: 'It must be concluded, not with certainty but with high probability, that the quotation [of LXX Amos 9.12 in vv. 17-18], and probably therefore the whole speech, cannot be attributed to James'.[42] Certainly it is a commonplace of contemporary scholarship that the speeches in Acts are not likely to preserve slavishly recorded transcripts from eye-witnesses. Second, does the letter in Acts 15.23-30 really preserve Greek words dictated by James? Acts itself attributes the letter not to him alone but to 'the apostles and the elders' (15.22-23). Further, although the decree embedded in the letter is surely pre-Lukan, one wonders to what extent the setting is redactional. Harnack long ago called attention to the many Lukan features of Acts 15.23-29,[43] and Barrett is again skeptical: 'it is not unreasonable to suppose that he [Luke] created a fitting setting (including, it may well be, not only the letter but the whole account of the Council)'.[44]

This commentator uses 'Christian Judaism' in connection with James because of his conviction that the author of our epistle represents a group, of largely or exclusively Jewish descent, that considered itself to be within Judaism despite its beliefs about Jesus. It is even doubtful that his group should be labelled 'sectarian'; cf. E. Regev, 'Were the Early Christians Sectarians?', *JBL* 130 (2011), 785-86. One suspects that Rendall, *Christianity*, 26, was on target: 'Neither were they [the Jamesian Christians] Separatists', for 'the constitution of the synagogue allowed almost unlimited latitude in matters of religious opinion'. For an overview of the limits of tolerance in Diaspora Judaism see J. Barclay, 'Who was Considered an Apostate in the Jewish Diaspora?', in *Pauline Churches and Diaspora Jews*, Tübingen, 2011, 141-55.

[42] Barrett, *Acts 15–28*, 728. Although R. Bauckham, 'James and the Church of Jerusalem', in *The Book of Acts in Its Palestinian Setting*, ed. R. Bauckham, Grand Rapids, MI, 1995, 452, argues that Acts 15 accurately reflects the views and even arguments of James, he nonetheless deems it unlikely that Luke preserves a report of what James actually said. Contrast Mayor, iii, who, in his case for the authenticity of Jas 1.1, urges that, in Acts 15, 'the actual words of the speaker are recorded either in their original form or in a translation'.

[43] A. von Harnack, *Luke the Physician*, London, 1907, 219-23.

[44] Barrett, *Acts 15–28*, 741.

Third, are the verbal correlations truly remarkable?[45] Taken one by one, they do not impress. χαρείν was common in letter openings; see on 1.1. τὸ ὄνομα + passive ἐπικαλέω + ἐπί is a LXX formula; see on 2.7. ἀκούσατε immediately before or after ἀδελφοί is a well-attested idiom; see on 2.5. ἐπισκέπτομαι hardly qualifies as a rare word; see on Jas 1.27. ἐπιστρέφω is intransitive in Acts 15.19, transitive in Jas 5.19-20. διατηρέω appears in Acts 15.29 whereas Jas 1.27 and 2.10 employ τηρέω. And ἀγαπητοί (NT: 32×) occurs in roughly half of the NT letters, ὄνομα (NT: 230×) in most of them.

One might nonetheless maintain that the question is, so to speak, not one of quality but of quantity. In order to establish this, however, one would need to compare James not just with the relevant sections in Acts but with other ancient texts of about the same length. If it turns out that James finds more parallels in Acts 15 than anywhere else, a common tradition might suggest itself—although one could equally propose that James imitated Acts or one of the latter's sources. I am unaware that anyone has undertaken this task. As a trial run, this writer chose at random one pericope from the LXX where (as in Acts 15.17) τὸ ὄνομα + ἐπικαλέω in the passive occurs (Deut 28.1-14), and he quickly discovered these parallels with James:

θεός + δίδωμι	Deut 28.1	Jas 1.5
the importance of hearing, (εἰσ)ακούω	Deut 28.1, 2, 9, 13	Jas 1.19
the importance of doing, ποιέω	Deut 28.1, 13	Jas 2.12; 4.17
εὐλογία	Deut 28.2	Jas 3.10
πόλις	Deut 28.3	Jas 4.13
προσώπου + genitive pronoun	Deut 28.7	Jas 1.11
ἐπὶ τῆς γῆς	Deut 28.8	Jas 5.5, 17
κύριος + future ἀνίστημι/ἐγείρω	Deut 28.9	Jas 5.15
ὄμνυμι	Deut 28.9, 11	Jas 5.12
ἐν ταῖς ὁδοῖς αὐτοῦ	Deut 28.9	Jas 1.8
τὸ ὄνομα + ἐπικαλέω in the passive	Deut 28.10	Jas 2.7
God as source of good (ἀγαθά/όν/ἀγαθή)	Deut 28.11, 12	Jas 1.17
οὐρανός + δίδωμι + ὑετόν	Deut 28.12	Jas 5.17-18
ἔργον	Deut 28.12	Jas 1.4, 25, 14; etc.
divine λόγος/λόγοι	Deut 28.14	Jas 1.18, 21-23
πορεύομαι	Deut 28.9, 14	Jas 4.13

If one objects that these overlaps might be explained by James' knowledge of Deuteronomy—although no one to my knowledge has ever suggested that Deut 28.1-14 played a significant role in the composition of our text—here are the parallels between James and a very short letter in an extra-canonical pseudepigraphon:

---

[45] See further Deppe, *Sayings*, 198-202. Although Tasker, 26, believes that James wrote our epistle, he nonetheless observes, regarding Acts 15: 'Too much should not be made of these resemblances...for linguistic similarities can also be found between James' speech and other Epistles in the New Testament, where there is no question of similarity of authorship'. Cf. Robinson, *Redating*, 130-31.

addressees in the diaspora	4 Bar. 6.17	Jas 1.1
author + δοῦλος θεοῦ	4 Bar. 6.17	Jas 1.1
introductory χαίρειν/χαῖρε	4 Bar. 6.17	Jas 1.1
πόλις	4 Bar. 6.17	Jas 4.13
πατήρ + 'Αβραάμ	4 Bar. 6.18	Jas 2.21
ἄγγελος	4 Bar. 6.19	Jas 2.25
ὑψόω	4 Bar. 6.21	Jas 4.10
the importance of hearing, ἀκούω	4 Bar. 6.22, 23	Jas 1.19
ἀναφέρω	4 Bar. 6.22	Jas 2.21
testing (δοκιμάζω, δοκίμιον, δόκιμος)	4 Bar. 6.23	Jas 1.3, 12

One guesses that, if 4 Bar. 6.17-23 belonged not to a pseudepigraphon but to the canon, and if James were its purported author, some would parade these parallels as evidence of common authorship.

(iv) Does heavy dependence upon the Jesus tradition without formal citation suggest authorship by James? Several issues present themselves here. First, and as will be argued below, it is not entirely clear that James is independent of our canonical gospels. But, second, even if one thinks otherwise, some apostolic fathers cite sayings of Jesus without quoting Matthew, Mark, or Luke, so James cannot offer anything exceptional on that score. Third, this writer fails to detect signs that our author drew upon a first-hand knowledge of Jesus. Why does the recurrent but inexplicit borrowing from sayings attributed to Jesus point to an eye-witness rather than to someone steeped in early Christian traditions about Jesus?[46]

(v) As for the argument that second-century sources, including 1 Clement and Hermas, show a knowledge of James, the case for 1 Clement is doubtful. As for Hermas, it is very hard, as we shall see, to make up one's mind. But in any case the date of Hermas is not firmly established. Some expert opinion holds that the work, from a single hand, was produced in stages over the course of the first half of the second century.[47] So even if James was written as late as 120, it could still have influenced the final form of Hermas.

(vi) What about the social and religious circumstances reflected in James, that is, (a) the implications of the undeveloped Christology, (b) the polemic against rich, land-holding Jews, (c) the silence regarding Gentiles, (d) the failure to mention the destruction of Jerusalem, (e) the reference to a synagogue, and (f) the condemnation of violence, including murder? Against (a): one can scarcely plot a straightforward, one-way evolutionary history for early Christology. Thus, whereas John's Gospel displays a 'higher' Christology than the earlier Mark, the second-century Ebionites had a 'lower' Christology than the earlier Paul. Moreover, James' Christology appears to be less undeveloped than deliberately muted; see below, 36.

---

[46] Cf. Aland, 'Herrenbruder', 103-104.
[47] So Brox, *Hirt*, 22-33; C. Osiek, *Shepherd of Hermas*, Minneapolis, 1999, 18-20.

Against (b): the Jewish communities in Palestine that remained loyal to Rome, such as Sepphoris, retained their property after 70; and as for Palestine as a whole, 'probably in the course of time the land came to be regarded again as the private property of its tenants, and the rent as a tax on it. References in rabbinic literature give the impression that much Jewish land remained in or soon reverted to private ownership after 70 (for example, some of the rabbis were wealthy land-owners), and Jewish legislation about the purchase of land expropriated by the Roman authorities, apparently in force before as well as after Bar Cochba's revolt, however problematical and controversial in detail, implies the continuation of private ownership of land after 70.'[48] Even were the facts otherwise, James addresses itself to the diaspora, so it is unclear why the situation in Palestine should be the background for 4.13–5.6.

Against (c-d): the failure to discuss or allude to Gentiles or to the destruction of Jerusalem is readily explained in terms of the aims of the letter, for which they are not self-evidently to the point. The Didache, 2 Peter, and any number of post-70 Christian texts have no occasion to advert to the events of 70;[49] and why a Christian Jew addressing other Jews, Christian or not, should on every occasion speak of Gentiles is far from evident.[50] The extant fragments of the Gospel of the Nazoraeans, the Gospel of the Ebionites, and the Gospel of the Hebrews are mute on that subject.

Against (e): the use of 'synagogue' in Jas 2.2, on the assumption that the reference is to a Jewish community or building, does not require a date before 70, for we cannot say exactly when Christian Jews left the Jewish synagogues. The time and manner of the parting of the ways must have varied from place to place and from group to group;[51] and if we know of Christians attending synagogues in the fourth century[52] as well before 70, it seems far-fetched to insist that such never happened between those two periods.

Against (f): the censure of violent behavior, including murder, is without consequence for the issue of the authorship of James. Who would

---

[48] E. Mary Smallwood, *The Jews under Roman Rule*, Leiden, 1976, 341. Note that the Apocalypse of Peter, likely written by a Palestinian Christian around the time of the Bar Kokhba revolt, condemns the rich; see chap. 30.

[49] One could invert the argument. If James is a pseudepigraphon, it would be anachronistic for our fictional author, who died before the destruction of Jerusalem, to write of that destruction. He could, however, prophesy its destruction, which is how some have read 5.1-6.

[50] Some in fact turn this argument on its head: James of Jerusalem could not have written without discussing or alluding to the great controversy of his day, namely, the status of Gentiles; so e.g. Ruckstuhl, 8-9.

[51] P. Alexander, '"The Parting of the Ways" from the Perspective of Rabbinic Judaism', in *Jews and Christians*, ed. J.D.G. Dunn, Tübingen, 1989, 1-25; A.H. Becker, and A.Y. Reed, eds., *The Ways that Never Parted*, Tübingen, 2003.

[52] W.A. Meeks and R.L. Wilken, *Jews and Christians in Antioch in the First Four Centuries of the Common Era*, Missoula, MT, 1978.

contend that a Christian could have denounced such behavior only before 70? What makes the period before 70 a better candidate than, say, the years leading up to and including the revolt of 115–17?[53] In response to (a)–(f) as a group, one should not lose sight of a general consideration. Our knowledge of both early Christianity and early Judaism remains, despite new discoveries and the undeniable progress of scholarship, woefully incomplete. Compared to the large, concrete, complex historical realities of the first and second centuries, our extant sources are little more than ghosts. One can indeed slot James into pre-70 Palestine if so inclined. But one can equally read the epistle, as does this commentary, as a second-century pseudepigraphon composed in the diaspora. The vagaries of our letter and the gaping holes in our knowledge allow different scholars to place James in different times and different places.

If the usual arguments for authorship by James of Jerusalem do not compel, what of the case to the contrary? (i) We know that people wrote pseudepigrapha in his name.[54] The Protevangelium of James, the Apocryphon of James, the First Apocalypse of James, the Second Apocalypse of James, and the Epistle of James to Quadratus are examples.[55] And no one defends the authenticity of those writings. The only text attributed to James to receive such treatment belongs to the NT. Might there not be a canonical or theological bias at work here?

(ii) Our letter is not likely to have been written by a renowned authority, such as James of Jerusalem, because there is no clear knowledge of it in early times, or even before the time of Origen.[56] Here is an overview of the evidence:

- P20 (= POxy 1171), P23 (= POxy 1229), and P100 (= POxy 4449) are the earliest physical witnesses to James. All three are from the third century or, in the case of the latter, third or fourth century. The first preserves 2.19–3.9, the second 1.10-12, 15-18, the last 3.13–4.4; 4.9–5.1.

---

[53] For an overview of the troubles in these years see M.P. Ben Zeev, 'The Uprisings in the Jewish Diaspora, 116–117', in *The Cambridge History of Judaism*, vol. 4, ed. S.T. Katz, Cambridge, UK, 2006, 93-104.

[54] Cf. R.R. Williams, 95: 'it would be a most extraordinary thing if while Jesus left no written works behind him, two of his brothers...had written considerable tracts, in the Greek language, and that these had been preserved, had come into general use about two hundred years after they were written... When one knows the immense popularity in those times of attaching a new work to an old name...one cannot help hesitating long before accepting the traditional view.'

[55] On this last, little-known pseudepigraphon, which is extant only in Syriac and Armenian, see R. van den Broek, 'Der *Brief des Jakobus an Quadratus* und das Problem der judenchristlichen Bischöfe von Jerusalem', in *Text and Testimony*, ed. T. Baarda *et al.*, Kampen, 1988, 56-65. One also recalls, from a later time, The Liturgy of St. James.

[56] So Enslin, *Beginnings*, 332; Elliott-Binns, 1022; R.R. Williams, 95; Burchard, 4; Nienhuis, *Paul*, 101; *et al.*

- The Latin of the third-century Ps.-Clem. 1 Ep. virg. 11 ed. Funk, 19-20, cites Jas 3.1-2 as Scripture: 'Ne multi inter vos sint doctoresm, fratres... Qui in verbis suis non praevaricatur, hic homo perfectus est, potens domare et subigere totum corpus suum.'
- Origen (185–253) not only quoted or borrowed from James on multiple occasions, but for him the book was authoritative and written by James the brother of Jesus.[57]
- Origen's Latin contemporary, Cyprian (d. 258), Bishop of Carthage, however, shows no knowledge of James.[58]
- One wonders whether Nag Hammadi's Book of Thomas the Contender 140.10-30 offers a reinterpretation of Jas 3.6 and surrounding verses. It addresses 'the perfect' (ⲧⲉⲗⲉⲓⲟⲥ, cf. Jas 3.2), calls for 'wisdom' (ⲥⲟⲫⲓⲁ, cf. Jas 3.13-18), and speaks of a 'fire' that guides fools (cf. Jas 3.5-6), a fire that, 'like a bit in the mouth, leads them according to its own desires' (cf. Jas 3.3).[59] The relevant materials come from a layer of Thomas the Contender that has been dated ca. 200.[60]
- Ep. ad Diog. 10.2 has this: 'to them he sent his own and only Son, to them he promised the kingdom (βασιλείαν ἐπηγγείλατο) in heaven, and he will give it to those who loved him' (τοῖς ἀγαπήσασιν αὐτόν). This might draw upon Jas 2.5. Yet the date of the Epistle to Diognetus, which otherwise betrays no acquaintance with James, is unknown. Many place it at the end of the second century or in the first part of the third.
- The Teachings of Silvanus is a non-Gnostic Coptic wisdom text found at Nag Hammadi. It is usually dated to the late second or early third century. The book contains several phrases that recall James and could depend upon it.[61]
- Hippolytus (ca. 170–ca. 236?) may have known James, to judge by an imperfect citation of 1.1 which is misattributed to Jude.[62] But this reference survives only in a fragment belonging to an Arabic catena from the thirteenth century, so one can scarcely draw a secure conclusion.[63]
- The African Tertullian (b. 155), who manages to quote even Philemon, never cites James, nor does he anywhere indisputably allude to our book.[64] It is possible that he knew it and found it to be without utility or even unedifying;

[57] Note e.g. Origen, *Exod* 8.4 SC 321 ed. Borret, 254 ('the apostle James says'); *Josh* 10.2 SC 17 ed. Jaubert, 276 ('the apostle James declares'); Ps 30.6 PG 12.1300B ('according to James'); 65.4 PG 30.1500A ('as the apostle says'); 118.153 PG 30.1621B ('for James says'); *Prov* 18.51 PG 17.244C ('James says'); *Jn* frag. 126 GCS 10 ed. Preuschen, 570 ('the apostle James says'); *Rom* 4.8 FC 2.2 ed. Heither, 252 ('the apostle James says').

[58] Cf. Nienhuis, *Paul*, 45. Cyprian does use 1 Peter or 1 John.

[59] Note also that 143.17-18 employs the imagery of a wheel ('the wheel that turns in your minds').

[60] J.D. Turner, *The Book of Thomas the Contender*, Missoula, MT, 1975.

[61] See Johnson, 71-72. Note e.g. 101 (Jesus is 'the light of the Father', who 'gives light without being jealous'; cf. Jas 1.5, 17) and 115 ('God does not need to put any man to the test'; cf. Jas 1.13).

[62] Hippolytus, *Apoc.* 7.4-8 GCS 1.2 ed. Achelis, 231. The quotation of 2.13 in *Consumm.* 47 GCS 1.2 ed. Bonwetsch and Achelis, 308, is now recognized as Ps.-Hippolytus.

[63] See further Ropes, 101.

[64] So Nienhuis, *Paul*, 40-41; M.A. Frisius, *Tertullian's Use of the Pastoral Epistles, Hebrews, James, 1 and 2 Peter, and Jude*, New York, 2011, 10-13.

INTRODUCTION   15

but then he was quite capable of mentioning if only to criticize books that he disliked, such as Hermas.[65]
- James is missing from the list of scriptural books (including Jude) in the Muratorian canon, a list which likely comes from the latter half of the second century, although that is a disputed issue.[66]
- Clement of Alexandria (ca. 150–ca. 215) may have known James.[67] According to Eusebius, Clement in his *Hypotyposeis* 'gave concise explanations of all the canonical writings, not omitting even the disputed books, by which I mean the Epistle of Jude and the other catholic epistles, the Epistle of Barnabas, and Apocalypse known as Peter's'.[68] Photius, who still knew the *Hypotyposeis* first-hand, says the same thing.[69] It is true that the surviving Greek and Latin fragments of the *Hypotyposeis* include nothing from James,[70] but some of the resemblances between James and other extant writings of Clement seem suggestive.[71]
- The Greek Physiologus 13, 29 ed. Kaimakis, 42a-43a, 64a-65a, quotes Jas 1.8: 'Thus every double-minded man is unstable in all his ways. One should not walk two paths. Nor speak in two ways in prayer.' In its present forms, the Greek Physiologus is attributed to Epiphanius or other church fathers and must

---

[65] Tertullian, *Pud.* 10, 20 CSEL 20 ed. Reifferscheid and Wissowa, 240, 266. One can ask whether there are echoes of James in Tertullian's treatise on prayer. *Orat.* 8 CSEL 20 ed. Reifferscheid and Wissowa, 186, dismisses the idea that God tempts (cf. Jas 1.13), and in chap. 29, 199, *oratio iustitiae* ('prayer of righteousness') occurs near a mention of prayer stopping rain (cf. Jas 5.16-18). Yet note Ropes, 91: 'His omission to quote Jas. 1[13] in discussing the Lord's Prayer, *De orat.* 8, seems to show that he was not acquainted with it'.

[66] For the second-century dating see J. Verheyden, 'The Canon Muratori', in *The Biblical Canons*, ed. J.-M. Auwers and H.J. de Jonge, Leuven, 2003, 487-556. Some, however, have claimed that the fragment is defective and so may have mentioned James; so e.g. G.M. Hahneman, *The Muratorian Fragment and the Development of the Canon*, Oxford, 1992, 25-26.

[67] Cf. Ropes, 44: 'probably'. But later (92) he writes that 'the question must be left undecided'. Cf. H. von Lips, *Der neutestamentliche Kanon*, Zurich, 2004, 71: whether Clement knew James remains an open issue. Meyer, *Rätsel*, 42-48, argues the case against Clement knowing James.

[68] Eusebius, *H.E.* 6.14.1.

[69] Photius, *Bib.* 109 PG 103.384C: the work includes 'notes on Genesis, Exodus, the Psalms, the divine Paul's epistles, and the Catholic epistles and Ecclesiasticus'. But one might be excused for not putting too much stock in such generalizations. According to Cassiodorus, *Div. inst.* 1.8.4 FC 39 ed. Bürsgens, 160, Clement commented upon '1 Peter, 1 and 2 John, and James', yet in what survives of Cassiodorus' translation, Jude but not James is represented. Did Cassiodorus name the wrong book, or did a scribe introduce an error? See further Ropes, 91-92; Meyer, *Rätsel*, 42-48; Nienhuis, *Paul*, 48-50.

[70] See the collection of fragments in GCS 17 ed. Stählin, 195-215.

[71] Note esp. *Strom.* 7.7.44.2 GCS 17 ed. Stählin, 33 (οἱ μὲν γὰρ ἃ οὐκ ἔχουσιν εὔχονται κτήσασθαι, καὶ τὰ δοκοῦντα ἀγαθά, οὐ τὰ ὄντα, αἰτοῦνται; cf. Jas 4.3); 7.10.55, 40 (τελειοῦται ἡ πίστις; cf. Jas 2.22); 8.18.164.2, 516 (ἐὰν μή...σὺν τῷ μετὰ τῆς ἐν τούτοις τελειώσεως καὶ τῷ τὸν πλησίον ἀγαπᾶν...οὐκ ἔσεσθε βασιλικοί; cf. Jas 2.8); *Ecl.* 15.1 GCS 17 ed. Stählin, 141 (τῆς πίστεως τὴν εὐχὴν ἰσχυροτέραν; cf. Jas 5.16).

be late. But an early version was extant already in the second century.[72] Unfortunately, there is no way to determine at what stage or date the line from James entered the text.[73]
- Irenaeus (ca. 130–ca. 200), Bishop of Lyons, appears to borrow from Jas 2.23 in 4.16.2: '*Abraham*, without *circumcision* and without *Sabbath observance, believed God*, and it was reckoned to him as righteousness, and he was called the friend of *God*'.[74] Ropes, 223, however, thought this 'probably a mere coincidence', and otherwise there are few if any signs of our book.[75] The fact is puzzling given that Irenaeus cites even the Shepherd of Hermas as scripture.[76] If he knew James, he did not much use it. Indeed, he found it less helpful than the thirteen verses of 2 John, which he quotes more than once.
- The so-called Epistle of the Apostles was likely written not long after CE 150; and Ep. Apost. Coptic 31 (= Ethiopic 40) TU 43 ed. Schmidt, 19*—'I will hear the prayer of the righteous (ⲡϣⲗⲏⲗ ⲛⲛⲇⲓⲕⲁⲓⲟⲥ), that they make for them', that is, 'sinners'—might show the influence of James (see on 5.16); so too 47(39), 24: 'But if [someone] should fall [under the] load because of the sins he has [committed, then let] his neighbor admonish him... Now if his neighbor [has admonished] him and he returns he will be saved; (and) he who admonished him will receive a reward and life forever'; see on 5.20. But this evidence is slight.
- Hegesippus was a second-century heresiologist.[77] Although his works do not survive, excerpts from them appear in Eusebius. Those excerpts show much interest in James the brother of Jesus. So it is significant that, among those fragments, Hegesippus takes no notice of our epistle. Sometimes arguments from silence are weak. This one is not. Given Eusebius' keen interest in the development of the canon and in 'the disputed books' (τὰ ἀντιλεγόμενα), he would almost certainly have recorded any reference to the Epistle of James in Hegesippus.[78]
- The issue of the relationship between James and Hermas has been much discussed, and we shall consider the issue below in some detail. Many, however, have been content to attribute the similarities to a common paraenetical tradition, not Hermas' knowledge of James.

---

[72] See F. Sbordone, *Ricerche sulle fonti e sulla composizione del Physiologus greco*, Naples, 1936.

[73] Whatever the explanation, the quotation is absent in both places in mss. Vindobonesis theol.gr. 128 and Oxoniensis Barocc.gr. 95; see the edition of Kaimakis, 42b, 64b.

[74] 'Credidit Deo et reputatum est illi ad iustitiam et amicus Dei vocatus est'.

[75] Three possibilities—of uncertain weight—are *Haer*. 2.32.4 (ἄλλοι δὲ τοὺς κάμνοντας διὰ τῆς τῶν χειρῶν ἐπιθέσεως ἰῶνται καὶ ὑγιεῖς ἀποκαθιστᾶσιν; cf. Jas 5.14-15); 4.18.3 (this refers to those who 'had in themselves jealousy like that of Cain and so slew the just one [*occiderunt iustum*; cf. Jas 4.6], slighting the counsel of the Word, as did also Cain'); 5.1.1 (here Irenaeus depicts himself and his readers as 'the first fruits of creation' by means of the Word = Jesus Christ; cf. Jas 1.18, 22).

[76] Irenaeus, *Haer*. 4.20.2.

[77] On Hegesippus as a witness to second-century Christian Judaism see F.S. Jones, 'Hegesippus as a Source for the History of Jewish Christianity', in *Le Judéo-Christianisme dans tous ses états*, ed. S.C. Mimouni and F.S. Jones, Paris, 2001, 200-12.

[78] Burkitt, *Beginnings*, 70, offered that perhaps Hegesippus translated an Aramaic discourse into our Greek James—a conjecture for which there is not a shred of evidence.

- Polycarp's Epistle to the Philippians, likely composed shortly after the death of Ignatius (ca. 110), is densely intertextual. One recent author has concluded: 'In my estimation, he *certainly* employs Romans, 1 Corinthians, Galatians, Ephesians, Philippians, 1 Timothy, and 1 Peter; he *probably* uses Matthew, 1 Corinthians, 2 Timothy, and 1 John; and he *possibly* uses a variety of other works, including Luke, Acts, and 2 Thessalonians'.[79] Absent from this list is James.[80]
- There is no trace of James in the fragments of Papias, and Eusebius, who tells us that Papias knew 1 Peter and 1 John, fails to remark that he knew James.[81]
- The authentic writings of Ignatius—unlike the later, enlarged versions and the altogether spurious letters attributed to him—nowhere echo James.
- 2 Clement shows no sign of having known James.
- The same holds for Barnabas.
- The same holds for the Didache.
- The same holds for the Apocalypse of Peter.
- Although 1 Clement and James are linked in manifold and very interesting ways,[82] no literary dependence can be established.[83] The Oxford committee that produced *The New Testament in the Apostolic Fathers* did not even bother to discuss the issue, and the standard commentary on 1 Clement comes to a negative conclusion.[84] Even though Johnson, 72-75, argues to the contrary that Clement knew James, he concedes that the case is 'not conclusive'.
- A literary relationship between 1 Peter and James seems, as argued below, likely. Some would put our letter first, so that if 1 Peter appeared ca. 80–100 (see below), James would be pushed back into the first century. If, however, this commentator and others are right to argue that the truth is the other way around—James used 1 Peter—then dating 1 Peter to 80–100 requires a date long after James' martyrdom.
- A few have surmised that the Epistle of Jude—of uncertain date—presupposes James. The inference is drawn not from verbal parallels but from Jude 1: 'Jude, a servant of Jesus Christ and brother of James, to those who are called, who are beloved in God the Father and kept safe for Jesus Christ'. According to Dibelius, 'it seems to me very probable that the author of the Letter of Jude would not have chosen this obscure brother of the Lord as his patron unless the more well-known brother of the Lord already had a reputation as the author of

---

[79] P. Hartog, *Polycarp and the New Testament*, Tübingen, 2002, 195.
[80] The Martyrdom of Polycarp also nowhere draws upon James.
[81] Eusebius, *H.E.* 3.39.15.
[82] For the relevant data see Mayor, lxx-lxxi; Johnson, 72-75.
[83] So too Ropes, 87-88 ('the likeness is not sufficient to prove literary dependence, but only similar literary associations'); Moffatt, *Introduction*, 467; Dibelius, 32-33; Burchard, 27; Popkes, 9, 42. Contrast Hilgenfeld, 'Brief', 28-29; Grimm, 'Einleitung', 392; Spitta, 230-36; Mayor, *Rätsel*, 68-72; Mussner, 35-36; Johnson, *Brother*, 52-56. Hagner, *Clement*, 256, favors literary dependence but adds that the probability is 'not very considerable'. Young, 'Relation', raises the possibility that James used 1 Clement. One should perhaps note that the date of 1 Clement is far from certain; see K. Erlemann, 'Die Datierung des ersten Klemensbriefes', *NTS* 44 (1998), 591-607.
[84] H.E. Lona, *Der erste Clemensbrief*, Göttingen, 1998, 57—explaining the similarities in terms of 'Christian adoption of hellenistic-Jewish paraenetical tradition'. Cf. Knoch, *Eigenart*, 92-95.

a letter'.⁸⁵ The argument, however, is tenuous given that James had an impressive reputation apart from the circulation of our work.
- Few any longer hold that Paul knew James.⁸⁶

To sum up this overview: although there is room for legitimate debate over a number of issues, there are only uncertain hints that James was known before the last part of the second century. The data available to us confirm Eusebius' generalization: not many of 'the ancients' mention James.⁸⁷

(iii) James struggled to enter the canon. This is unexpected given its purported authorship.⁸⁸ The book is absent from Canon Mommsenianus (359).⁸⁹ The Cheltenham Canon (360) and the Muratorian canon (of uncertain date) likewise lack it, and it is not in the principal mss. of the Old Latin. In Codex Corbeiensis (ff), which may represent a fourth-century text, James appears together with patristic, not biblical texts. It was no part of the early Syrian canon.⁹⁰ There are no readings from it in the earliest extant Syriac lectionary,⁹¹ and Theodore of Mopsuestia did not accept it (although he received none of the Catholic Epistles).⁹² Latin authorities, as observed, take scant notice of it before the last half of the fourth century, and none quotes it as scripture.

(iv) There was a tradition that James was pseudonymous. Jerome wrote: 'James, who is called the Lord's brother…wrote only one epistle, which is one of the seven catholic epistles, which, it is asserted, was published under his name by another,⁹³ although little by little as time went on it obtained authority'.⁹⁴ These words recognize not only that, the

---

⁸⁵ Dibelius, 33; cf. Kümmel, *Introduction*, 428; Rowston, 'Book', 560-61; Burchard, 7, 47; Pokorný-Heckel, *Einleitung*, 726.

⁸⁶ But for those holding this opinion see 427 n. 10.

⁸⁷ Eusebius, *H.E.* 2.23.25: οὐ πολλοὶ γοῦν τῶν παλαιῶν αὐτῆς ἐμνημόνευσαν. Ropes, 51-52, conjectures that perhaps James was not widely known in the Greek churches until Origen ran across it in Palestine and took a copy back to Alexandria.

⁸⁸ Cf. Oesterley, 389; D.W. Riddle and H.H. Hutson, *New Testament Life and Literature*, Chicago, 1946, 199; Aland, 'Herrenbruder', 102-104; Paulsen, 'Jakobusbrief', 492; Schnider, 16-17; Deppe, *Sayings*, 207-209; Pratscher, *Herrenbruder*, 212; Schnelle, *History*, 387; Fabris, 25; *et al.*

⁸⁹ See Metzger, *Canon*, 231, for rejection of the conjecture that this source does after all implicitly refer to James.

⁹⁰ See further Ropes, 96-100.

⁹¹ F.C. Burkitt, *The Early Syriac Lectionary System*, London, 1923, 22.

⁹² Cf. Isho'dad of Merv pref. HSem 10 ed. Gibson, 49: Theodore 'does not even mention' it 'in a single place' nor 'bring an illustration' from it.

⁹³ 'Quae et ipsa ab alio quodam sub nomine eius edita adseritur'. The assertion of Jobes, *Letters*, 155, that there is 'no evidence' that the early church took James to be pseudonymous, is incorrect.

⁹⁴ Jerome, *Vir. inl.* 2 TU 14.1b ed. Gebhardt, 7. N. Lardner, 'A History of the Apostles and Evangelists', in *The Works of Nathaniel Lardner*, vol. 6, London, 1838, 197, urges that Jerome is here just reiterating the comments of Eusebius. Cf. Ropes, 44:

further back one goes, the less account one can find of James, but also that some regarded the epistle as pseudonymous. Eusebius also knew of such people: 'The first of the epistles named catholic is said to be by James the brother of the Lord, but some see it as forged'.[95] This opinion was further known to Origen, for that seems to be the best explanation for the odd phrase in *Jn* 19.23 GCS 10 ed. Preuschen, 325: ἐν τῇ φερομένῃ Ἰακώβου ἐπιστολῇ. This must mean something like 'the epistle current by the name of James'. Given what we otherwise know of Origen, this cannot reflect his own doubts. It must rather reflect awareness of the doubts of others.[96]

(v) Many have insisted that James, the brother of Jesus, a native speaker of Aramaic who grew up in Nazareth, is unlikely to have written an epistle in fairly accomplished Greek, an epistle that shows the influence of the LXX and contains Hellenistic literary *topoi*.[97] Although Alford thought that the brother of Jesus wrote James, he conceded: 'The Greek style of this Epistle must ever remain, considering the native place and position of its Writer, one of those difficulties, with which it is impossible for us now to deal satisfactorily' (108).

(vi) Our book, in the eyes of some, neglects issues with which James, as Acts 15 and 21 report, concerned himself. It says nothing about ritual observance, the status of Gentiles, circumcision, the Jerusalem decree, or the temple. Kümmel's verdict was this: 'It is scarcely conceivable that the Lord's brother, who remained faithful to the Law, could have spoken of "the perfect law of freedom" (1:25) or that he could have given concrete expression to the Law in ethical commands (2:11f.) without mentioning even implicitly any cultic-ritual requirements'.[98] Dibelius, 17-18, simi-

---

Jerome knew only what Eusebius wrote and that James did not belong to the Syrian and Latin canons.

[95] Eusebius, *H.E.* 2.23.25: ἰστέον δὲ ὡς νοθεύεται μέν. Eusebius himself accepted James as canonical; cf. Ps *ad* 100.5 PG 43.1244 line 36, where Jas 4.11 is the second part of a compound quotation introduced with τῆς Γραφῆς λεγούσης.

[96] Perhaps *Jn* 20.10 GCS 10 ed. Preuschen, 337, is also relevant, because it may imply that not all accept the validity of Jas 2.20 (οὐ συγχωρηθὲν ἂν ὑπὸ τῶν παραδεχομένων τὸ Πίστις χωρὶς ἔργων νεκρά ἐστιν). It remains odd on any account that, in his commentary on Matthew, where Origen speaks of James the brother of Jesus at length, he says nothing about our epistle. Cf. Nienhuis, *Paul*, 56.

[97] So de Wette, *Introduction*, 333; Davidson, *Introduction*, 300; Oesterley, 399-400; M. Jones, *The New Testament in the Twentieth Century*, London, 1914, 325-26; Ropes, 50; Jülicher, *Einleitung*, 205; Dibelius, 17; Windisch-Preisker, 36; Marty, 247-48; Easton, 6; Enslin, *Beginnings*, 332; Vielhauer, *Geschichte*, 579; Ruckstuhl, 8; Simonis, *Paulus*, 108; Pratscher, *Herrenbruder*, 210-11; Frankemölle, 52-53; Hoppe, 13; Tsuji, *Glaube*, 41-42; Hahn-Müller, 'Jakobusbrief', 62-63; Garleff, *Identität*, 231; Broer, *Einleitung*, 604; B. Ehrman, *Forged*, New York, 2011, 198.

[98] Kümmel, *Introduction*, 413. Cf. McGiffert, *History*, 581; Grimm, 'Einleitung', 386-87; Hollmann-Bousset, 220; Jülicher, *Einleitung*, 205-207; Marty, 248; Aland, 'Herrenbruder', 100-101; Blackman, 25-26; Vielhauer, *Geschichte*, 579; Deppe, *Sayings*, 207-208; Pratscher, *Herrenbruder*, 211-12; Hoppe, 13; Hahn-Müller, 'Jakobusbrief', 63;

larly judged that a 'strict legalist' or 'Christian ritualist', 'an advocate of hidebound Jewish-Christian piety', could not have spoken of 'the law of freedom'.

(vii) Some have reckoned James to be post-Pauline not just because it presupposes Paul's split between faith and works but because it fundamentally misunderstands the apostle, which is unlikely for someone who knew him.[99] Our letter must instead come from a time when Paul's rhetoric was no longer tied to the debate over circumcision and the status of Gentiles.[100]

How strong are these arguments? (i) The existence of late writings falsely attributed to James adds plausibility to the case for pseudonymity, but it does nothing more. If some wrote in Paul's name, that scarcely entails that he never did so. It is the same with James.

(ii) Is it true that there are no traces of James before 150? Having worked through James verse by verse and considered, at every relevant point, the parallels, this author has found no sure trace of James in literature from the first or first half of the second century. It is, however, very difficult to evaluate the parallels with the Shepherd of Hermas. Because the issue is so important, I here list the most frequently cited parallels:[101]

James	Hermas
1.1	*Sim.* 9.17.1 ('these twelve mountains are twelve tribes that inhabit the whole world')[102]
1.5	*Mand.* 2.4 (ὁ θεὸς δίδωσιν, δίδου ἁπλῶς, πᾶσιν δίδου, πᾶσαιν γὰρ ὁ θεὸς δίδοσθαι θέλει ἐκ τῶν ἰδίων δωρημάτων);[103] 9.4 (αἰτοῦ παρὰ τοῦ κυρίου καὶ ἀπολήψῃ πάντα); *Sim.* 5.4.3 (αἰτεῖται παρ' αὐτοῦ σύνεσιν καὶ λαμβάνει)[104]

Llewelyn, 'Prescript', 386 ('the author is not a nomist but a moralist'); Nienhuis, *Paul*, 111-12; Pokorný-Heckel, *Einleitung* 726; Broer, *Einleitung*, 605.

[99] Jülicher, *Einleitung*, 207; M. Goguel, *The Birth of Christianity*, New York, 1954, 374; Kümmel, *Introduction*, 413; Pratscher, *Herrenbruder*, 212-13; Tsuji, *Glaube*, 42-43.

[100] Cf. Ropes, 50-51; Ruckstuhl, 8-9. This argument appears to go back at least as far as Baur, *Paul*, 297-313. He took James to reflect reconciliation between Paul and strict Jewish Christianity.

[101] Literature: T. Zahn, *Der Hirt des Hermas*, Gotha, 1868, 396-409; C. Taylor, 'The Didache Compared with the Shepherd of Hermas', *Journal of Philology* 18 (1889), 297-325; Mayor, lxxiv-lxxviii; A Committee of the Oxford Society of Historical Theology, *The New Testament in the Apostolic Fathers*, Oxford, 1905, 108-13; Meyer, *Rätsel*, 60-68; Seitz, 'Afterthoughts'; 'Antecedents'; 'Hermas'; Massaux, *Influence*, 150-62; Johnson, 75-79.

[102] As Hermas (oddly) identifies the twelve tribes with the Gentile nations, his words are distant from Jas 1.1 if the latter refers to Jews, Christian or not.

[103] But in Hermas, δίδου ἁπλῶς refers to human, not divine giving. Moreover, the combination of those two words was traditional, as well the sentiment that God gives good gifts; see the commentary on 1.5 below.

[104] The 'ask' and 'receive' motif in these last two places appears often in early Christian texts; cf. Mt 7.8; 21.22; Mk 11.24; Lk 11.10; Jn 16.24; 1 Jn 3.22; 4 Ezra 2.13.

INTRODUCTION 21

1.6-8	*Mand.* 9.1-12 (αἰτήσασθαί τι παρὰ τοῦ θεοῦ, μὴ λήψῃ, τὸν διδόντα, οὐκ...μνησικακοῦντες ἀλλ' αὐτὸς ἀμνησίκακος, σπλαγχνίζεται ἐπὶ τὴν ποίησιν αὐτοῦ, ὁλοτελεῖς, ἐν τῇ πίστει, δίψυχος ἀνήρ, ἀδιστάκτως, πειρασμόν, ἐν παντὶ πράγματι, τελειοῖ)[105]
1.12	*Vis.* 2.2.7 (μακάριοι ὑμεῖς ὅσοι ὑπομένετε)[106]
1.17	*Mand.* 9.11 (πίστις ἄνωθέν ἐστι παρὰ τοῦ κυρίου); 11.5 (ἀπὸ θεοῦ δοθέν...ἄνωθέν ἐστιν ἀπὸ τῆς δυνάμεως τοῦ θεοῦ)[107]
1.21; 2.14	*Sim.* 6.1.1 (δυνάμεναι σῶσαι ψυχήν)[108]
1.27	*Mand.* 2.7 (καθαρὰ καί...ἀμίαντος)[109]
1.27	*Mand.* 8.10 (χήραις ὑπηρετεῖν, ὀρφανοὺς καὶ ὑστερουμένους ἐπισκέπτεσθαι); *Sim.* 1.8 (χήρας καὶ ὀρφανοὺς ἐπισκέπτεσθε)[110]
2.7	*Sim.* 8.6.4 (βλασφημήσαντες...τὸ ὄνομα τοῦ κυρίου τὸ ἐπικληθὲν ἐπ' αὐτούς)[111]
2.19	*Mand.* 1.1 (πίστευσον ὅτι εἷς ἐστὶν ὁ θεός)[112]
3.8	*Sim.* 9.26.7 ('just as snakes poison and kill a person with their venom [ἰῷ], so also the words of such people poison and kill a person');[113] *Mand.* 2.3 (πονηρὰ ἡ καταλαλιά· ἀκατάστατον δαιμόνιόν ἐστιν)[114]
3.15	*Mand.* 9.11 (πίστις ἄνωθεν ἐστι παρὰ τοῦ κυρίου); 11.5-6 (πνεῦμα ἀπὸ θεοῦ δοθέν...ἄνωθεν...ἐπίγειον)[115]
3.17	*Mand.* 11.8 ('the divine spirit from above is gentle and quiet and humble')[116]
3.18	*Sim.* 9.19.2 (καρπὸν δικαιοσύνης)[117]

[105] For the extensive parallels here see the discussion on 167-69. Note that James never uses ἀδιστάκτως, and Hermas does not have διακρίνω in this context.

[106] But Theod. Dan 12.12 (μακάριος ὁ ὑπομένων) is a closer parallel as both it and Hermas explicitly have to do with enduring the great tribulation of the latter days.

[107] One hesitates to make much of these parallels since the idea of divine gifts coming from above is well-attested beyond James and Hermas; see on 1.17; contrast Massaux, *Influence*, 152-53.

[108] σῴζω + ψυχή and δύναμαι + σῴζω were common; see on 1.21 and 2.4. It is their combination that is rare; but note Acts Thom. 139 ed. Bonnet, 246; Clement of Alexandria, *Ecl.* 26.2 GCS 17 ed. Stählin, 144; Ps.-Clem. Hom. 3.37.2 GCS 42 ed. Rehm, 70.

[109] These two adjectives often occur side by side; see on 1.27.

[110] But this language was traditional (cf. Pol. *Phil.* 6.1) and likely comes from the LXX (Jer 5.28).

[111] In James, the name—the good name—is blasphemed; in Hermas, sinners blaspheme the Lord and are ashamed of the name by which they are called. Also, 'the name called over you' is a Semitism often found in Jewish and Christian Greek texts; see on 2.7.

[112] Although εἷς ἐστὶν ὁ θεός was a standard confession, James and Hermas seem to supply the first instances of it being introduced with πιστεύω + ὅτι. For additional considerations see Massaux, *Influence*, 151.

[113] This is just a common *topos*; see on 3.8.

[114] Has LXX Prov 26.28—'A false tongue (γλῶσσα) hates truth, and an unguarded mouth works instability (ἀκαταστασίας)'—influenced both James and Hermas? Apart from ἀκαταστασία, there is no verbal overlap with James.

[115] Contrasts between ἐπίγειος and ἄνωθεν are rare; see on 3.15.

[116] Although James also has ἄνωθεν, his sentence is about 'wisdom', and none of his adjectives appear in Hermas.

4.3	*Mand.* 9.4 (αἰτοῦ παρὰ τοῦ κυρίου καὶ ἀπολήψῃ πάντα); *Sim.* 5.4.3 (αἰτεῖται παρ' αὐτοῦ σύνεσιν καὶ λαμβάνει)[118]
4.5	*Mand.* 3.1 (τὸ πνεῦμα, ὃ ὁ θεὸς κατῴκισεν ἐν); *Sim.* 5.6.5 (τὸ πνεῦμα τὸ ἅγιον...κατῴκισεν ὁ θεὸς εἰς σάρκα)[119]
4.7	*Mand.* 12.2.4 (ἀνθεστηκότα...φεύξεται); 12.5.2 (ὁ διάβολος... ἐὰν οὖν ἀντισταθῆτε αὐτῷ...φεύξεται ἀφ' ὑμῶν)[120]
4.11	*Mand.* 2.2 (μηδενὸς καταλάλει)[121]
4.12	*Mand.* 12.6.3 (δυνάμενον σῶσαι καὶ ἀπολέσαι); *Sim.* 9.23.4 (δυνάμενος ἀπολέσαι ἢ σῶσαι)[122]
5.4	*Vis.* 3.9.6 (ὁ στεναγμὸς αὐτῶν ἀναβήσεται πρὸς τὸν κύριον—a warning to the wealthy concerning the cries of the needy)[123]
5.11	*Mand.* 4.3.5 (πολυεύσπλαγχνος οὖν ὢν ὁ κύριος); *Sim.* 5.4.4 (ὁ δὲ κύριος πολυεύσπλαγχνός ἐστι); 5.7.4 (ὁ κύριος πάντως πολύσπλαγχνος ὢν)[124]

Informed opinion is dramatically divided over the meaning of these parallels. Mayor, lxxiv, thought it nearly obvious that Hermas used James. The Oxford committee that produced *The New Testament in the Apostolic Fathers* by contrast rated that option a 'C', which on their scale of probability ranked between B ('a high degree of probability') and D ('uncertain').[125] Ropes, 88-90, also doubted that James served Hermas as a source. Dibelius, 32, thought no firm decision on the matter could be reached and seemed content to posit a large, common store of paraenetical material. For Mayor, Hermas is instead evidence that James was popular in second-century Rome.[126] Seitz, in his articles on the issue, argued for the independence of Hermas and James by making the case that many of the parallels depend upon a lost Jewish apocryphon, Eldad and Modad. But according to Massaux, James 'inspired' Hermas,[127] and

---

[117] καρπὸς δικαιοσύνης was a traditional phrase that occurs in both Jewish and Christian sources. It is not sign of literary dependence; see on 3.15.

[118] Not much weight can be laid on this; see below, 604-605.

[119] See also *Mand.* 5.1.2, 5; 5.7.1. This is a very strong parallel as James and Hermas both offer the first Christian uses of κατοικίζω. But as argued in the commentary below, Jas 4.5 is cited from an apocryphal source also known to Hermas.

[120] One can find both the notion of resisting the devil and of the devil fleeing in Jewish and Christian sources; but James is the first extant source to combine them. See further Massaux, *Influence*, 153-54.

[121] This is not a substantial parallel for our purposes given the many similar texts; see on 4.11.

[122] The relationship between Hermas and James here is complicated by the parallel in Mt 10.28 diff. Lk 12.5; see on 4.12 and Massaux, *Influence*, 154-56.

[123] But surely Hermas depends here upon 1 En. 9.10.

[124] πολύσπλαγχνος is absent from pre-Christian sources. It occurs also in Clement of Alexandria, *Quis div.* 39.6 GCS 17 ed. Stählin, 186, and Acts Thom. 119 ed. Bonnet, 229 but remains rare.

[125] *The New Testament in the Apostolic Fathers* (as in n. 101), 108-13.

[126] Mayor, *Rätsel*, 60-68.

[127] Massaux, *Influence*, 161. Cf. Cantinat, 32 ('a utilization more or less direct of the letter of James').

for Johnson, 75-79, literary dependence is 'virtually certain'.[128] And yet two recent commentators on Hermas, N. Brox and C. Osiek, see no need to posit that Hermas was familiar with James.[129]

Given such regrettable disagreement and the nature of the data, which is indeterminate in part because of Hermas' habit of thoroughly rewriting his sources, assurance on the matter is inappropriate. This commentator has gone back and forth on the issue over the years and is still uncertain what to think. The pertinent footnotes show that most—but not all—of the parallels are poor evidence for literary dependence. Furthermore, this author, like Seitz, is persuaded that, were a copy of the defunct Eldad and Modad to come to light, we would learn that it significantly influenced both James and Hermas, and that it indeed accounts for many or most of the striking similarities between James and Mandate 12.[130] As an analogy, the large amount of material common to the summaries of Torah in Philo, *Hypoth.* 7.1-9; Josephus, *C. Ap.* 2.190-219; and Ps.-Phocylides is best explained as deriving either from a shared exegetical tradition or from a work that is no longer extant: those writers did not copy each other.[131]

Nonetheless, one is not wholly at ease attributing all the substantial parallels between James and Hermas to a lost source or sources. The unsatisfying conclusion, then, is that Hermas may be evidence for the circulation of James in Rome in the first third of the second century—although it is equally possible that common use of a defunct text and/or tradition explains the parallels.[132] One could also in theory imagine that James was familiar with an early stage of Hermas, which may have evolved over a period of three or four decades before appearing in the 140s.[133] The truth is very hard to make out.

We may, then, have one text from before 150 that used James. It, however, stands alone; and it remains conspicuous that, between Hermas and Origen, there are only passing traces of our text, traces so slight that many fail to see in them signs of literary contact. It is evident, then, that James was not, in the first two centuries, a well-known book, even though

---

[128] Cf. Johnson, *Brother*, 56-60, and the analysis of Laws, 22-23.

[129] Brox, *Hirt*, 46-47 (he is content to quote Dibelius); Osiek, *Shepherd* (as in n. 47), 26 ('both writings reflect the common world of Hellenistic Jewish moral instruction'). Cf. earlier O. von Gebhardt and A. Harnack, *Hermae pastor Graece*, Leipzig, 1877, lxxv.

[130] In addition to the commentary on 4.5 see Allison, 'Eldad', and cf. Harnack, *Geschichte*, 485 (Hermas may borrow from sources that James used).

[131] See Niebuhr, *Gesetz*, 5-72.

[132] Cf. Ropes, 88-89: that the 'resemblances are so numerous, while yet no one of them is conclusive, does not provide... cumulative evidence of literary dependence; on the contrary, it makes the opposite explanation all the more probable'. One might add that the silence of so many early western witnesses inclines one to wonder if Hermas alone can depend so extensively upon James.

[133] Nienhuis, *Paul*, 120, 237, raises the possibility that James knew Hermas. So too already Pfleiderer, *Christianity*, 296-97.

its content should have appealed to many.[134] It was far less popular than either 1 Clement or Hermas, two closely related writings. It appears to have circulated at the margins of the Christian circles we know about. Certainly it was not reckoned important enough to receive any discussion at all before Origen, and no one before him refers to it either as scripture or as written by James. Remarkably, one cannot even detect its influence in the second-century pseudepigrapha written in James' name.[135]

This does not prove our letter to be a pseudepigraphon. It is possible that James wrote something that remained unpublished until later, or that his letter was inadvertently laid aside for a few decades or had very limited circulation.[136] Aristotle's writings were not disseminated until long after his death. For decades they remained in the hands of descendants and admirers.[137] Yet, if we are trying to weigh probabilities, it seems unlikely, all else being equal, that a letter purporting to come from James of Jerusalem would have suffered the widespread neglect that our writing did.

Mayor, li, responds to this argument with the compound claim that 'the Epistle was probably written at Jerusalem and addressed to the Jews of the East Dispersion; it did not profess to be written by an apostle or to be addressed to Gentile churches and it seemed to contradict the teaching of the great apostle to the Gentiles'.[138] This retort does not suffice. (a) That James is addressed to 'the Jews of the East Dispersion' is without foundation. (b) Even if James does not claim to have been written by an apostle, 1.1 naturally implies authorship by James of Jerusalem, and he was an authority and hero for many. (c) The address to the twelve tribes is unlikely to explain the lack of attention. Hebrews was thought to be addressed to Jews—Clement of Alexandria already knows the title, Πρὸς Ἑβραίους—and yet it won a wide readership early on. Indeed, it is loosely quoted already in 1 Clem. 36.2-6. (d) Although one can imagine some disliked James because of its ostensibly anti-Pauline rhetoric, the

---

[134] Cf. Nienhuis, *Paul*, 103-104: 'A central feature of later second-century doctrinal debate was the concern to locate Paul in relationship with the Pillars of the Jerusalem church; yet though letters of Peter and John are utilized, no one mentions anything about a letter from James. One is left with the impression that the content of James as well as the mere existence of such a letter would in fact have been extremely useful for their purposes (as it clearly was for Origen) had they had access to it.'

[135] Cf. Nienhuis, *Paul*, 104: 'There was an explosion of hagiographical writings attached to James in the second century; yet in all of this there is no evidence of the letter we now attribute to him'.

[136] Brooks, 'Canon', 50, raises this possibility; cf. W. Michaelis, *Einleitung*, 287-88.

[137] See Strabo, *Geog.* 13.1.54; C.H. Roberts, *Buried Books in Antiquity*, London, 1963, 6-10.

[138] For related responses see Hug, *Introduction*, 574-75; Alford, 111; Gloag, *Epistles*, 24; Feine, *Lehrschauungen*, 150-53; Knowling, liii; Sparks, *Formation*, 129; Brooks, 'Canon', 51; Adamson, *Message*, 38-39, 47-51; Moo, 4; McKnight, 30-31. Contrast Nienhuis, *Paul*, 102-106. Hasselhoff, 'Thought', 55, ventures that perhaps James was not enthusiastically received because of its radical critique of wealth.

history of interpretation shows how simple it is to reconcile James and Paul, if one is so inclined. Harmonizing is easy, and it is the rule in pre-critical biblical interpretation. One recalls that although Matthew's take on the law (cf. 5.17-20) is discordant with Pauline theology, that Gospel received a warm welcome far and wide as soon as it appeared.[139]

What of arguments (iii) and (iv)? They too cannot be dismissed. The struggle of James to enter the canon is of a piece with its relative neglect until Origen; and that some thought of our letter as a pseudepigraphon can scarcely encourage those who defend its authenticity. What, other than a memory of the late and uncertain origin of the text that bears his name, explains the opinion that the brother of Jesus did not write it?

It is more difficult to evaluate (v), the argument from the nature of James' Greek. Given what we now know about first-century Judaism, it would be imprudent to insist that James of Jerusalem could not have composed a letter in Greek.[140] Greek was spoken—and not just in upper circles—in Jewish Palestine, Nazareth was close to Sepphoris and its Greek culture, and there were Greek-speaking Jews in Jerusalem from whom James, when he resided there, could have learned much were he so motivated. Perhaps it is worth noting that the legend in Hegesippus has him addressing diaspora Jews, presumably in Greek.[141]

Nevertheless, it is not simply a question of whether a first-century Galilean could have spoken or even written Greek, even good Greek. It is rather a question of how likely it is that *the brother of Jesus* could have written fairly accomplished Greek, possessed such a large Greek vocabulary,[142] employed the LXX, and adopted Hellenistic literary *topoi*.[143] Maybe Jesus spoke some Greek, but certainly the extent of his literacy in any language remains an unresolved problem;[144] and the traditions about his words, unlike the book of James, do not often recall Ecclesiasticus, Wisdom, or Philo.[145] Nor do they show many overlaps with Stoicism. We have no indication that Jesus could have produced anything like the

---

[139] On additional explanations for the apparent neglect of James see R. Wall, 'Theology', 53; he finds them wanting.

[140] See esp. Sevenster, *Greek*, passim; cf. Hengel, 'Polemik', 520-21; Johnson, 116-18; Nodet, 'Juste', 592-93. For an overview of the pertinent facts see P.W. van der Horst, 'Greek in Jewish Palestine in the Light of Jewish Epigraphy', in *Japheth in the Tents of Shem*, Leuven, 2002, 9-26. But for caution see M.A. Chancey, *Greco-Roman Culture and the Galilee of Jesus*, Cambridge, UK, 2005, 122-65. He concludes that 'enthusiastic claims about the high number of Galileans proficient in Greek are difficult to support' (161).

[141] Eusebius, *H.E.* 2.23.11. Prot. Jas 25.1 has James writing but does not tell us in what language.

[142] Our short letter has ca. 560 different words, 18 of which occur nowhere else in the Greek Bible, over 60 of which do not appear elsewhere in the NT.

[143] Cf. Jackson-McCabe, 'Politics', 620-22; Konradt, 'Gerechte', 579-81; also the remarks of R.R. Williams in n. 54.

[144] See esp. C. Keith, *Jesus' Literacy*, London, 2011.

[145] For the parallels between James and Philo see Kennedy, 'Atmosphere'.

Epistle of James, whose author 'uses with freedom rare [Greek] words and compounds, all of them correctly formed'.[146] How likely, then, that one of his siblings could have done so?

One might respond by offering that James had the advantage of a different course of study than his brother. Perhaps (as much Christian tradition has held) James was the son of Joseph by a former marriage and so had a dissimilar upbringing. Alternatively, maybe he received some sort of Hellenistic education in his later years.[147] But these are *ad hoc* hypotheses, supported only by a desire to deny that James is a pseudepigraphon. Would we not expect the brother of Jesus, a Galilean artisan purported to be uneducated (cf. Mk 6.3; Jn 7.15), to produce, if he could write at all, something more like Revelation, with its innumerable solecisms? Is it really credible that the son of Mary and Joseph of Nazareth wrote a letter which sometimes seems to avoid certain *koine* forms and even at points approximates Classical Greek, more so than Paul managed to do?[148] Or that he produced paragraphs which leave the impression that their author's native tongue was Greek? Moreover, was not the ability to write or dictate *literary* Greek, as opposed to the ability to speak everyday Greek, typically a privilege of the upper classes, to which James did not belong?[149] The Apocryphon of Jas 1.15 has James writing in Hebrew, not Greek, and the legends about him concern his piety, not his study. Once more, then, does not the evidence, fairly considered, incline—not prove but incline—one toward the view that James is a pseudepigraphon?[150]

What of the claim (vi) that our letter ill suits the law-observant James? Despite its long-running popularity, the proposition is insecure. First, if we leave aside the letter of James and later apocryphal material, we know very little about the brother of Jesus. Although Acts and Galatians depict him as law observant, do we really know enough to label him a 'strict legalist' or a 'Christian ritualist' (terms incidentally that are typically pejorative for Christian scholars)? Galatians 2 and Acts 15 do not portray him as unbending or narrow-minded but as willing at least to acknowledge the validity of a mission to Gentiles.[151]

---

[146] So Mayor, ccxlviii. See further below, 81-82.

[147] But can we name any first-century Christians who submitted to a Hellenistic education as adults?

[148] See further Chaine, ciii-civ.

[149] Cf. C. Hezser, *Jewish Literacy in Roman Palestine*, Tübingen, 2001, 90-94. Note L.H. Feldman, *Jew and Gentile in the Ancient World*, Princeton, 1993, 19: 'Josephus' admission (*Against Apion* 1.50) that he needed assistants in composing the version in Greek of the *Jewish War* illustrates that few attained the competence in the language necessary for reading and understanding Greek literature'.

[150] The Epistle of Jude complicates the question. Those who believe that Jude the brother of Jesus and James wrote it will find in this confirmation that the latter could likely write in Greek, too. But the authorship of Jude is another open question: many contemporary scholars judge it to be a pseudepigraphon.

[151] See further Chaine, lxxxiii-lxxxiv.

Second, as the commentary proper shows, our letter seemingly endorses the Torah and its practice. It certainly nowhere declares Moses to be over and done with.¹⁵² Indeed, one can plausibly construe 2.10 as forwarding a rigorous nomism.¹⁵³ Further, insisting that 1.25 ('the law of freedom', cf. 2.12) or 27 (pure religion is caring for orphans and widows) excludes strict Torah-observance is as unimaginative as the old argument that 'I desire mercy and not sacrifice' (Hos 6.6) entails opposition to the temple cult, or as unpersuasive as inferring from the minimal interest in ritual and cult in the gospels that the historical Jesus was antinomian.¹⁵⁴ We certainly know of non-Christian Jewish works that, despite their focus on moral teaching, keep in the background or altogether neglect ritual commandments.¹⁵⁵

As for the failure of our epistle to broach circumcision, Gentiles, or the temple, issues that presumably mattered much to James, this is a feeble argument from silence.¹⁵⁶ Our letter is not a systematic theology. It is not a systematic statement of anything. It is rather a cryptic text of less than obvious purpose, and its brevity alone insures that it neglects much its author thought important.¹⁵⁷ So just as one cannot insist, from our author's silence regarding the crucifixion and resurrection of Jesus, that he did not know of them or thought them insignificant,¹⁵⁸ so too one cannot infer, from their nonappearance, his indifference regarding the temple, Gentiles, or circumcision. One recalls that justification by faith, one of Paul's foundational beliefs, is not a theme in 1 and 2 Corinthians, both of which are much longer than James. Immediate purpose dictates the topic.

Also devoid of force is argument (vii), for although James does, it would appear, respond to Paul, it is not the case that polemic which misses its mark (if one judges James to miss) or devolves into caricature

---

¹⁵² Cf. B. Weiss, *Manual*, 112-13 ('It certainly does not follow from the fact that the so-called ceremonial law is nowhere expressly mentioned, that one who so emphatically asserts the solidarity of the whole law [ii. 10] regards it as no longer binding'); J. Marcus, review of Nienhuis, *Paul*, in *CBQ* 70 (2008), 385 ('if the letter was written by a Jewish Christian to other Jewish Christians, there would be no need to emphasize what all accepted: the unchallenged supremacy of the Torah, including all 613 commandments'). So too Dschulnigg, *Gleichnisse*, 262-64; idem, 'Enstehung', 128; Chester, 'Theology', 36-37; Bernheim, *Brother*, 235-38; Moo, 17-18; McKnight, 28-29.

¹⁵³ Cf. S. Wilson, *Strangers*, 154: the emphasis on keeping the whole law 'could be expressing an extremely rigorous stance rare even in Judaism'.

¹⁵⁴ S. Wilson, *Strangers*, 154: the distinction between ethical and ritual commands 'may have meant nothing to a Jewish Christian'.

¹⁵⁵ Cf. Philo, *Hypoth*. 7.1-9; Josephus, *C. Ap.* 2.190-219; Pseudo-Phocylides; m. 'Abot.

¹⁵⁶ Cf. Kittel, 'Väter', 56-58; Konradt, 'Gerechte', 577. Some urging authenticity have used similar observations to argue for a date before the conflict of Gal 2; see n. 36.

¹⁵⁷ Cf. Dunn, *Beginning*, 1127.

¹⁵⁸ Contrast however Freeborn, 'Glory', 186: James 'did not know about' the resurrection.

cannot come from an informed contemporary. A minimal awareness of modern political discourse should suffice to sink that idea.

To sum up the previous pages: although not all of the arguments marshaled to deny authorship by the brother of Jesus have merit, (ii)–(v), taken together, tip the scale. Hence this commentary adopts the thesis that James is a pseudepigraphon.

As for the date of James, opinion is here, as on so much else, remarkably diverse. Here is a sampling:

Harnack	120–50
Spitta	before 50
Zahn	44–66
Knowling	40–50
Ropes	75–125
Jülicher	120–50
Dibelius	80–130
Chaine	57–62
Marty	late first, early second century
Massebieau	before 50
Kittel	40–50
Enslin	70–125
Schoeps	100–150
Young	117–38
Hunter	60–100
Mussner	before the death of James the Just
Elliott-Binns	40–50
Kümmel	80–100
Cantinat	the last decades of the first century
Laws	post-60s
J.A.T. Robinson	47 or 48
Ruckstuhl	80–100
Frankemölle	the last quarter of the first century or beginning of the second century
Floor	40–50
Wolmarans	125–30
S. Wilson	the last quarter of the first century
Webber	late first or early second cent.
Penner	40–60
Hahn-Müller	not before the last third of the first cent.
Sleeper	75–85
P. Rolland	the year 56
Moo	the middle 40s
Riesner	before the middle 40s
Hartin	the late sixties, after James' death
Burchard	'the last decades of the 1st century'
Popkes	shortly before or after CE 100
Maier	before or around 50
Fabris	70–100
Dschulnigg	ca. 60
Nienhuis	the middle of the second century

Konradt	before 85
McKnight	the 50s
Varner	48 or earlier
Broer	70–100

The view of the present writer is that, since our letter, as we shall see, shows a likely knowledge of at least Romans and 1 Peter, it was likely not composed before 100. The inference is consistent with the lack of any firm first-century witnesses to our letter.[159] If, however, Hermas knew James—an uncertain issue—we cannot push the latter too far into the second century. A date of 100–120 would seem to fit the bill.

This inference gains support from, or is at least consistent with, four additional considerations:

(i) If 3.9-10, as argued below, adverts to some early version of the *birkat-ha-minim* that was promulgated after 70, James must be post-70.

(ii) 5.13-20, as the commentary shows, seems to depend upon a primitive church order; and we have no evidence for such a thing before Mt 6.1-18, from the late first-century, and the Didache, a text which likely took shape in the decades following 100.

(iii) As one works through James verse by verse, numerous parallels to 1 Clement and Hermas reveal themselves.[160] While some have taken these to suggest literary dependence, most of them must reflect a common Christian milieu. If so, placing James in the same general period as those post-apostolic writings makes sense.[161]

(iv) On formal grounds, the closest Jewish parallel to James is 2 Bar. 78–87.[162] This is intriguing because 2 Baruch is typically dated ca. 100. It is, then, credible that James, which is so much like it, comes from around the same time.

If all this is close to the truth, one needs to ask, Why James? Why write in the name of the brother of Jesus? Although we are here in the realm of conjecture, some suggestions are worth contemplating. (i) Attributing a book to a recognized leader such as James would, for those going along with the fiction, lend it an air of authority. (ii) It is likely that our author was a Christian Jew who took himself to represent the sort of faith that James was remembered, rightly or wrongly, as having embodied, a faith that traced its roots back to pre-70 Jerusalem. Our epistle, for example,

---

[159] Cf. already M. Luther, 'Preface to the Epistles of St. James and St. Jude', in *Luther's Works*, vol. 35, ed. Bachmann, Philadelphia, 1960, 397: James knew Paul and 1 Peter, 'so it seems that [this author] came long after St. Peter and St. Paul'.

[160] For a very telling chart see Popkes, 40-42.

[161] Bolich, *Dating*, instead argues, on the basis of statistics, that, linguistically and thematically, James belongs with earlier rather than later Christian documents. But his sampling is too meager to be representative (he studies only six texts besides James) and is badly skewed by an early dating for 1 Peter.

[162] See esp. Whitters, *Baruch*, 88-101.

counters Paul, and in certain circles James was thought to have done just that.[163]

(iii) Our letter presents itself as an address to Jews in the diaspora, and James was remembered as a Christian who had a good rapport with Jews at large. Eusebius claimed that 'the wise even of the Jews' attributed the siege of Jerusalem to the murder of James,[164] and according to Hegesippus, James addressed the 'whole people' at Passover, 'all the tribes' that had come together for the festival.[165] James also addresses 'all the people' (*omni populo*) of Jerusalem in the Pseudo-Clementines,[166] and Josephus, *Ant*. 20.201, reports: 'the most fair-minded and strict in the observance of the law' were offended at the execution of James.[167] Acts 21.18-25 also seems to belong here, for it has James and some elders encouraging Paul to take a vow so as to avoid conflict in Jerusalem. So if a Christian wished to address a letter to Jews, James was an obvious candidate for authorship.

(iv) The traditional image of James likely suited the author's agenda in additional ways. The brother of Jesus was remembered as living a life of poverty, as upholding the law, as being a man of prayer, and as having suffered greatly.[168] In short, he was 'James the Just'.[169] In line with this, our letter encourages those who suffer (1.2-4, 12; 5.7-11), offers instruction on prayer (1.5-8; 4.2-3; 5.13-18), upholds the law (see on 1.21, 25; 2.8), and pleads for the poor while criticizing the rich (1.9-11, 26-27; 2.1-7; 4.13–5.6).[170] All of this helps us to understand how the book might have been received by Christians familiar with the traditions about James, who was remembered as an individual of great integrity. Good character (ἦθος) strengthens argument.

Before passing to the next topic, brief notice should be taken of theories that link our book to James but do not assign its current form to

---

[163] See below, 444-57. It is also possible that our author thought of himself as a real channel of James, in the way that some of the apocalyptic visionaries thought that those in whose names they wrote spoke through them; cf. D.S. Russell, *The Method and Message of Jewish Apocalyptic*, London, 1964, 132-39.

[164] Eusebius, *H.E.* 2.23.19.

[165] Eusebius, *H.E.* 2.23.11.

[166] Ps.-Clem. Rec. 1.69.8 GCS 51 ed. Rehm, 47.

[167] For the argument that these people were not Pharisees—the conventional interpretation—but 'priests, wealthy laity, and Herodians' see J.S. McLaren, 'Ananus, James, and Earliest Christianity', *JTS* 52 (2001), 7-14.

[168] See esp. the traditions in Hegesippus *apud* Eusebius, *H.E.* 2.23.4-18.

[169] Cf. Gos. Thom. 12; Gos. Heb. 7 *apud* Jerome, *Vir. inl.* 2 TU 14.1 ed. Richardson, 8; 1 Apoc. Jas 5.32.2-3, 6-7; 2 Apoc. Jas 5.44.13-14; 59.21-22; Hegesippus in Eusebius, *H.E.* 2.23.7; etc.

[170] See further 121 below. Such correlations have often been observed, but typically by those urging authenticity; cf. Hug *Introduction*, 569-70. But note Konradt, 'Gerechte': our epistle was written under the name of James because of the tradition of James as ethical model and authority. Martin, xlv-xlvi, outlines connections between our epistle and the picture of James in the Pseudo-Clementine literature.

him. Some have supposed that our book is the product of two or more developmental stages, for the first of which alone James was responsible.[171] Others have surmised that James might have used a secretary or that Hellenistic-Jewish Christians aided him significantly in his work[172]— even Josephus needed 'assistants' when writing Greek (*C. Ap.* 1.50)—or that someone who once heard James subsequently wrote in his name,[173] or even that our document is a Greek edition or expansion of an Aramaic letter written by James.[174] Yet our book names neither secretary nor co-author. It rather presents itself as coming from James himself.[175] Also, the text is a unified whole that does not demand an involved compositional history,[176] and the various Greek wordplays and catchword links do not

---

[171] Proponents of some sort of redaction history include Oesterley, 390-91; Halson, 'Wisdom'; Davids, 12-13, 22; Martin, lxix-lxxvii; Popkes, *Adressaten*, 187-88; Felder, 1787. G.C. Martin, 'Storehouse', hypothesizes that James was originally a collection of sayings of Jesus made by his brother that, after the destruction of Jerusalem, was expanded by explanations and additional reflections. Knox, 'Epistle', proposes a complex tradition-history and thinks it 'possible that parts of chs. iv and v come from' James.

[172] Cf. Chaine, cviii; P. Feine, *Einleitung in das Neue Testament*, 3rd ed., Leipzig, 1922, 198-99; Meinertz, 18; Kittel, 'Ort', 79-80; Cadoux, *Thought*, 38; Bonsirven, 'Jacques', 793; Wikenhauser, *Introduction*, 484; Rendtorff, 1, 3; Beasley-Murray, 19; R. Mayer, 'Jakobusbrief', 54 ('perhaps'); Bauckham, *Wisdom*, 24; Witherington, 400; Farley, 15 ('possible'); McKnight, 33-34; Puech, 'Qumrân', 53 n. 52 ('peut être'). Cf. 2 Apoc. Jas 44.13-17: 'This is the discourse that James the Just spoke in Jerusalem, which Mareim, one of the priests, wrote'.

[173] Schleiermacher, *Einleitung*, 428-29. Cf. Barclay, 39 (somebody heard and wrote down a sermon of James which was later translated into Greek); S. Byrskog, *Story as History—History as Story*, Tübingen, 2000: 170-71 (students of James are responsible for our letter); Hartin, 25 ('a close associate of James' wrote up his teaching shortly after he died); Dunn, *Beginning*, 1128-29 (James contains oral traditions of its namesake put together after his death).

[174] So J. Wordsworth, 'Corbey'; M. Dods, *An Introduction to the New Testament*, 2nd ed., New York, n.d., 197-98; Burkitt, *Beginnings*, 69 (our Greek James is a second-century translation of an Aramaic discourse by James of Jerusalem); H.F.D. Sparks, *The Formation of the New Testament*, New York, 1953, 128; Agourides, 'Origin', 72 ('James made this address in Aramaic' and later 'put the speech in writing'; subsequently, 'some scribe of the first community translated the speech into the Greek language', adding 'the admonitory air, and with a preamble he gave it an epistolary character'); cf. Niebuhr, 'Diasporabriefe', 431: the translation hypothesis is 'thoroughly plausible'. R.A. Martin, *Syntax Criticism of Johannine Literature, the Catholic Epistles, and the Gospel Passion Accounts*, Lewiston, 1989, 99-108, posits an original Semitic letter to which 2.8–3.12 was later added. I have not had access to J.M. Faber, *Observationes in epistolam Jacobi ex Syro*, Coburgi, 1770, who appears to have been the first to defend the thesis of an Aramaic original. For criticism of Wordsworth see Chaine, cv.

[175] Contrast Rom 16.22; 1 Pet 5.12; 2 Apoc. Jas 44.13-17 (see n. 172). Sevenster, *Greek*, 10-14, argues against the secretary hypothesis.

[176] See further Konradt, 'Context', 118-19. Contrast Davids, 'Traditions', 41-42, who urges that the disjointedness and inconsistencies in James suggest a collection of 'originally independent sayings and sermons'.

comport with a translation hypothesis.[177] This exegete has failed to discover any solid evidence for the various theories of complex authorship or tradition-history. One suspects that they arise less from data within the text itself[178] than from a desire to retain some substance for the traditional ascription—which, such theories imply, is not, after all, exactly what we would expect from the brother of Jesus.[179]

II. *SITZ IM LEBEN*

Exegetes and scholars have proposed a large number of competing hypotheses as to our book's precise *Sitz im Leben*. A sampling:

- James is a response, by the brother of Jesus, to the deleterious effects that some of Paul's ideas—and perhaps even some of his letters—were having.[180]
- The people 'from James', whom Paul speaks of in Gal 2.12, were bearers of our epistle, whose aim was to calm the controversy that had arisen regarding Gentiles and to reject a perversion of Paul's doctrine of justification by faith.[181]
- In large measure James represents a reaction not to Paul but to later, post-70 Paulinism and the ethical lapses which it encouraged.[182]
- Certain rich individuals were oppressing poor members of the Christian community, which moved our author to intervene with his epistle.[183]
- James, sensing the revolutionary tendencies that eventuated in the Jewish war, sought an alternative in hope and patience that waits upon divine intervention.[184]
- Christians were being tempted to libertinism, which James abhorred.[185]
- James might be 'reacting against Jewish Christians with former ties to Essene, Therapeut, and Baptist circles'.[186]

---

[177] The only evidence that Burkitt offers for his theory of an Aramaic original is the unsatisfying conjecture that, in 3.6, James wrote נמבלא ('entrance'), which was misread as עלמא and so translated as κόσμος: *Beginnings*, 69.

[178] An exception is the article of Knox, 'Epistle', which argues from alleged tensions in the text.

[179] Cf. Frankemölle, 53; Broer, *Einleitung*, 604.

[180] Cf. Burkitt, 1104; Benson, 5-6; Hug, *Introduction*, 558-59, 576-77; Hengel, 'Polemik'; Pearson, *Sense*, 251-76; Limberis, 'Provenance'. There are many variants of this view. See further on 2.14-26 and note the comment of Rheims, 380: 'This Epistle... is directed specially, as S. Augustine saith, against the errour of only faith, which some held at that time also, by misconstruing Pauls words'.

[181] F.G. Chase, 'Peter (Simon)', in *A Dictionary of the Bible*, vol. 3, ed. J. Hastings, New York, 1900, 765. This view is idiosyncratic.

[182] So many modern authorities; see 428 n. 14.

[183] Agourides, 'Origin', 78; Camp, 'View'. Sato, 'Brief', considers this one of three important factors, the others being factionalism and problems stemming from Paulinism.

[184] Martin, lxvii-lxix; Townsend, xxxiv-xxxv. Cf. the much earlier, similar thesis of Whitby, 672-73, 689.

[185] Manton, 14; Pritius, *Introductio*, 75.

[186] So Riesner, 1257, citing 1 Cor 1.12; 3.4-6 and remarking on 'striking parallels with 1 Cor 1-4'.

- Our author wrote to oppose some type of Gnosticism.[187]
- During the reign of Domitian, Christians were tempted to join the larger social discontent and political rebellion, to which James responded with calls for humility, patience, and love.[188]
- James was composed in the middle of the second century in an attempt to counter Marcion and to interpret an incipient collection of Catholic Epistles.[189]
- 'James is an apology for Jewish Christianity against the distorted picture left behind by Paul's conflicts.'[190]

There is additionally the view that

- James 'was not written for a particular concrete occasion. There is not the slightest trace of any personal relationship between the author and the recipients.'[191]

Such a diversity of proposals should caution anyone who hazards to add another. It is this author's conviction, however, that several observations about the content of James direct us down a different path from those just introduced:

(i) The starting point is 1.1. As argued in the commentary proper, this is best taken literally: our book presents itself as a letter written to the tribes in the diaspora. There should be no objection to this from those who take James to be a pseudepigraphon: the audience is as fictional as the author. In any case, there is no sign of a Gentile audience whereas much lines up with a Jewish one. 2.21 calls Abraham 'our father' without any hint that the expression bears a transferred sense. The meeting place or gathering of the readers is called a 'synagogue' (2.2). In 2.19, their faith is embodied in the Shemaʻ: 'You believe that God is one'; cf. Deut 6.4. The writer, moreover, calls God 'the Lord σαβαώθ' without explanation (5.4), and all the moral exemplars are drawn from Jewish tradition—Abraham, Rahab, the prophets, Job, Elijah.[192] Gentiles are nowhere referred to nor are slaves, nor is there any mention of idolatry, drunkenness, or other sins that early Christian writers often imagined to be characteristic of Gentiles.[193] The Jewish ethos is ubiquitous.

---

[187] See esp. Schammberger, *Kampf*. Schoeps, *Theologie*, 344-45, finds Schammberger persuasive; cf. Reicke, *Diakonie*, 346-47. For earlier proponents of this thesis see Hammond, 687; Pfleiderer, *Christianity*, 301-305 (also positing that James attacks a 'secularised Christianity' that had gotten 'a foothold among the upper classes, the rich and the wise of this world', 299); H. Weinel, *Biblische Theologie des Neuen Testaments*, Tübingen, 1928, 510-11 (James fights 'gnostic Paulinists').

[188] Reicke, 5-7.

[189] So Nienhuis, *Paul*, passim.

[190] G. Theissen, *Fortress Introduction to the New Testament*, Minneapolis, MN, 2003, 140.

[191] Wikenhauser, *Introduction*, 475-76. Cf. Ropes, 2; Dibelius, *passim*; Enslin, *Beginnings*, 328.

[192] See further Schlatter, 95-96.

[193] Cf. Rom 1.24-27; 1 Cor 6.9-11; Gal 5.19-21.

(ii) James contains neither Christian salutation nor Christian benediction. Although unusual in an ancient Christian epistle,[194] the circumstance would be consistent with an attempt to pose as an address to non-Christian readers.

(iii) With the exception of 2.1, which is textually uncertain, the readers are nowhere explicitly characterized as followers of or believers in Jesus.

(iv) As a matter of exegetical history, many have found parts of James odd if taken to be addressed directly to Christians. Some have inferred that the rich of 1.9-10 cannot be believers, others that non-Christians are addressed in 1.20-21, in 4.1-10, in 4.13-17, and/or in 5.1-6. The documentation for all this appears in the relevant portions of the commentary.[195] Here I note only, by way of illustration, that those addressed in chaps. 4 and 5 are called to submit themselves to God, cleanse their hands, purify their minds, and mourn and weep. The reason is that they are 'adulterers' (4.4) and 'sinners' (4.8), that they are friends of the world and enemies of God (4.4). They are even guilty of murder (5.6). In calling them to account, James appeals to Scripture and Jewish tradition, not to the gift of the Holy Spirit or to specifically Christian convictions. Moreover, those denounced in 5.1-6 seem past repentance: they have fattened their hearts for slaughter; their flesh will be eaten like fire (5.1-5). Many have understandably doubted that these are believers in Jesus. Are there, in the first hundred years of Christianity, any other texts in which a Christian accuses Christians of murder? It is telling that most who think of James as addressed exclusively to Christians typically hold that, at least in 4.13-17 and/or 5.1-6, we have apostrophe: James is addressing those not present. This, however, is to concede that our writing does not consistently or in its entirety read well as a discourse to Christians.

(v) Commentators debate the identity of the rich in 2.1-7. That they are Christians ill fits the fact that they blaspheme 'the good name that was called over you'. There are also reasons, as the commentary shows, to doubt that they are unbelieving visitors, and the proposal that their identity is irrelevant seems an act of exegetical desperation. When, however, one thinks not of a Christian community but instead of a Jewish building or gathering—giving 'synagogue' one of its two usual senses—with Jewish as well as Christian participants, the problems dissipate.

(vi) Luther claimed that, although James 'names Christ', he 'teaches nothing about him, but only speaks of general faith in God'.[196] This is correct, and the fact explains why Jülicher could dub James 'the least Christian book in the New Testament'.[197] Jesus' crucifixion is neither

---

[194] Note, however, Acts 15:23.

[195] Schlatter, 92-93, thinks that the question of audience hangs over all of chaps. 3–5.

[196] M. Luther, 'Preface to the Epistles of St. James and St. Jude', in *Luther's Works*, vol. 35, ed. Bachmann, Philadelphia, 1960, 396. Cf. his remark in *Table Talk*, in Luther's Works, vol. 54, ed. T.G. Tappert, Philadelphia, 1967, 424 (no. 5443): 'Some Jew wrote it who probably learned about Christian people but never encountered any...'

[197] Jülicher, *Einleitung*, 209.

mentioned nor clearly alluded to. Nor is anything said about his resurrection or exaltation. His deeds merit no mention, and one searches in vain for any remark upon his character or status as a moral model—a striking omission given the appeals to other moral models. Harnack observed that James 'does not refer to Jesus Christ where one would expect'.[198] Further, our work says nothing explicit about baptism, about the Lord's Supper, or about the fulfillment of prophecy. Scholars have, to be sure, attempted to unfold James' Christology out of what they imagine is implicit, yet the truth remains that, as Gench, 79, puts it: 'James has more to say about Rahab the prostitute than about Jesus!'[199]

What explains these silences, which are so strange given James' canonical context? According to a few earlier scholars, James is a retouched Jewish writing.[200] No one defends this position today, for although it nicely explains some facts, it does not explain others, such as that our book borrows plentifully from Christian tradition, including the sayings of Jesus.

How else then might one account for what James fails to say? One could posit that the letter is so christologically quiescent because of its genre. Should we really expect much theology from a book of moral exhortation with wisdom affinities? Genre, however, does not clarify why James can mention the forgiveness of sins (5.15) and yet say nothing about Jesus' atoning death, or elucidate why, when James cites models of behavior, he refers to Abraham (2.21-23), Rahab (2.25), the prophets (5.10), Job (5.11), and Elijah (5.17-18), not Jesus. Nor does it help us understand why, even if one regards the 'Jesus Christ' of 2.1 as original, our book names 'Jesus' and 'Christ' less often than any other Christian writing of the NT period except the diminutive 3 John. Even the twenty-five verses of Philemon, the thirteen verses of 2 John, and the twenty-five verses of Jude beat the much longer James on this score.[201] Where else in

---

[198] Harnack, *Geschichte*, 490 n. 2. Cf. Bultmann, *Theology*, 2.143 ('That which is specifically Christian is surprisingly thin'); Sidebottom, 14 (one has 'the impression of an almost pre-crucifixion discipleship'); Kümmel, *Introduction*, 416 ('the lack of any distinctive Christian message in James'). The failure of James to name Jesus much, esp. at the beginning and end, or to refer to his life and work, have long drawn remark; see e.g. Osiander, 719; W. Wall, 344. Some have explained this by referring to Acts 5.40, where the apostles are commanded not to speak in the name of Jesus. According to Clarke, 1824, 'The style and manner [of James] are more that of a Jewish prophet than a Christian apostle. It scarcely touches on any subject purely Christian... It may be considered a sort of connecting link between Judaism and Christianity...'

[199] J.D.G. Dunn, *The Parting of the Ways*, London, 1991, 212, is correct: 'It is difficult to speak of James' christology. The references are too isolated, and the language too allusive for us to gain a real handle on the christology of the author.'

[200] Massebieau, 'L'Épître'; Spitta; Halévy, 'Lettre'; Meyer, *Rätsel*. For early criticism of this view see Rose, 'Chrétien'; Grafe, *Stellung*, 1-20. For criticism of Meyer see esp. the review of *Rätsel* by M. Meinertz, in *TRev* 39 (1931), 299-302.

[201] Ἰησοῦς: Philemon: 6×; 2 John: 2×; Jude: 7×. χριστός: Philemon: 8×; 2 John: 3×; Jude: 6×.

early Christianity do we have an epistle whose christological elements are so minimal that some have excised but a few words and then declared the result to be a non-Christian document? It is surely inadequate to say simply that James is *paraenesis*, for the paraenetical sections of other early Christian writings are full of christological affirmations. Even the laconic Q contains more Christology than James, so much so that according to one critic the teaching of Jesus in our epistle looks like it has been 'taken out of its dogmatic setting'.[202]

One also cannot elucidate James' conspicuous silences by urging that our book represents a type of Christianity akin to what some have glimpsed behind Q, or what Betz divines behind the Sermon on the Mount, namely, a faith that did not have at its center Jesus' death and resurrection or the sacraments of baptism and the Lord's Supper.[203] When one examines carefully the Christian parallels to James, time after time one discovers that he alone lacks christological elements. For instance, 1.2-4 has close parallels in Rom 5.1-5 and 1 Pet 1.6-9, and whereas the latter two name Jesus Christ and are in other ways explicitly Christian, James is not. The phenomenon recurs as one works through our text.

Again, then, what can be the explanation? Rendall offered that James must represent an early, undeveloped theology—'inchoate' or 'blanched'. He found the only alternative that he could think of—that James 'deliberately cancelled all references to the Christian hope and belief in which they lay embedded'—to be incredible.[204] But this is exactly what our author appears to have done.[205] Mayor, ii, wrote: in James, 'Christian ideas are still clothed in Jewish forms'. The formulation should rather be: 'Christian ideas are deliberately clothed in Jewish forms'.

(vii) A final observation about the content of James: the chief reason usually given for refusing to take 1.1 literally is the claim that, even apart

---

[202] Findlay, *Way*, 158. Cf. Pfleiderer, *Christianity*, 307: 'Undogmatic the Epistle of James certainly is, beyond any other document of Early Christianity'.

[203] See B. Mack, *The Lost Gospel*, San Francisco, 1993; Betz, *Sermon*. The secondary literature does contain the idea that the dearth of developed Christian theology in James is evidence for its primitive character. For a survey of older opinion see Moffatt, *Introduction*, 468-72. The claim appears more recently in Elliott-Binns, *Christianity*, 46-52; Sidebottom, 13-14; Robinson, *Redating*, 120-25, 137. According to Windisch-Preisker, 36, James represents a Jewish Christianity for which the person and history of Jesus did not yet have soteriological meaning. Nienhuis, *Paul*, 157-59, proposes that our author sought to assimilate his text to what he thought was the basically non-soteriological, ethical message of the real James.

[204] Rendall, *Christianity*, 108-109. Cf. Elliott-Binns, 1022: James comes 'from a very early period in the life of the Church, before theological ideas had been worked out'. It did not, however, take any time at all before Christians were at least referring to Jesus' death, resurrection, and exaltation as significant events. Helpful here is M. Hengel, 'Christologie und neutestamentliche Christologie', in *Neues Testament und Geschichte*, ed. H. Baltensweiler and B. Reicke, Zurich, 1972, 43-68.

[205] Ferris, '1 Peter', 303, speaks of 'a studied reserve about Christianity which indicates a purpose'.

INTRODUCTION

from the textually problematic 2.1, several verses presuppose a Christian readership. The four texts most often cited are 1.18 ('gave us birth by the word of truth'—interpreted as a reference to Christian regeneration), 25 ('the perfect law, the law of freedom'—interpreted as a reference to the gospel; cf. 2.12); 5.7-8 ('the coming of the Lord'—interpreted as a reference to Jesus' second coming); and 5.14 ('the elders of the ecclesia'—interpreted as a reference to officers of the church). The argument is not the clincher many suppose it to be.

Not one of the verses just cited names Jesus Christ, and we are still left with the question of why everything that we think of as being characteristically Christian remains at best tacit. Furthermore, in each case the history of interpretation shows us that the relevant texts can be and have been read in more than one way, and in ways that see Christian theology recede. The language of 1.18 has moved many—including Ps.-Oecumenius, Theophylact, Dionysius bar Salībī, Godfridus, Hort, Rendall, Meyer, Cadoux, Boismard, Frankemölle, Tsuji, Ludwig, Jackson-McCabe, and Kloppenborg—to think not of rebirth through the gospel but instead either of humanity's creation by God's word or the new creation of Israel through the giving of Torah on Sinai. As for the 'perfect law, the law of freedom', Jewish texts declare the Torah to be perfect and to be the source of freedom, which is why Spitta, R. Wall, Hartin, Jackson-McCabe, and Kloppenborg, among others, have thought not of the gospel but of Torah. As for 5.7-8, even though ἡ παρουσία τοῦ κυρίου is almost certainly a Christian formulation, it is striking that, in the verses that immediately precede and in those that immediately follow, ὁ κύριος is God, not Jesus (5.4, 11); so a few—Theile, Windisch-Preisker, Easton, Marxsen, Cantinat[206]—think that equation holds here too. Finally, regarding 5.14, James mentions neither 'deacons' nor 'bishops', and readers of the LXX would know about both Jewish ἐκκλησίαι and πρεσβύτεροι. In theory, a reader could take οἱ πρεσβύτεροι τῆς ἐκκλησίας to be the elders of a Jewish religious community.[207]

The very strange truth is that, aside from 1.1 and the textually dubious 2.1, James, although written by a believer in Jesus, offers nothing that requires Christian presuppositions on the part of readers.[208] The whole stays within a Jewish frame of reference. As P. Sigal observed: 'every sentence...could have been written by a proto-rabbi'.[209] Readers of James often miss this because, consciously or not, they are canonical readers,

---

[206] Hollmann-Bousset cannot make up their mind.
[207] See further below, on 5.15.
[208] The phenomenon has been noted before; cf. Maurice, *Unity*, 28-86; Schlatter, 138; McNeile-Williams, *Introduction*, 206-208. Most interpreters however ignore the fact and proceed on the 'supposition that the epistle presupposes what is taught in other parts of the New Testament'; so J.A. Alexander, 'The Christian's Duty in Times of Trial', in *The Gospel of Jesus Christ*, London, 1862, 555.
[209] Sigal, *Emergence*, 424. 1.1 and 2.1 are the only exceptions.

assuming that James must be saying what the NT says elsewhere. But he does not. He remains resolutely silent in remarkable ways.

Before proceeding to consider how all this bears on James' *Sitz im Leben*, it should be stressed that a pseudepigraphon typically has not only a fictional author but also a fictional audience. The real audience is, so to speak, addressed indirectly; it is expected to *overhear* what on the surface is addressed to others.[210] In the present case, James the brother of Jesus did not actually send a letter to all Jews of the diaspora, nor did someone do that in his name. Nor is there any more reason to think that the Jewish diaspora somehow got copies of our epistle than there is to imagine that Titus received a copy of the third Pastoral Epistle.

Although James presents itself as a letter from a Jerusalem authority to Jews in the diaspora, this is a literary fiction, and one can hardly promote some other interpretation by remarking upon this fiction's historical implausibility. This was the mistake of Ropes, 127, when he claimed, in his case against a literal reading of 1.1, that 'no time after the crucifixion is known to us when a Christian teacher could expect a respectful hearing for a didactic tract from both converted and unconverted Jews in the dispersion at large, or would have felt such responsibility for the general moral instruction of all diaspora Jews alike as this writer shows. The promptness of the separation of Christians and Jews in the diaspora is illustrated by all the mission narratives of Acts'. These words fail to distinguish between the literary claim and the historical reality. Like 2 Bar. 78–87, the purported readers of James may be the lost tribes in the diaspora, but that cannot have been the real audience. Similarly, although the Testaments of the Twelve Patriarchs are, on the literary level, addressed to the children of Reuben and his brothers, that tells us nothing about the historical addressees.[211] And so it is with James: if it is a pseudepigraphon, one can scarcely deny the plain meaning of 1.1 on the ground that it is historically implausible. That would be not much different than emending or reinterpreting 1 En. 1.1-2, which ascribes 1 Enoch to Enoch, on the ground that the book it heads looks Hellenistic rather than antediluvian.

Recognition of the pseudepigraphical character of James means that, even if we agree with Bede, Grotius, and so many others regarding the literal sense of Jas 1.1, we cannot simply resurrect their exegesis, for they took the claims of James at face value. The way ahead rather lies in showing how James makes sense as a pseudepigraphon.

For this task, two earlier interpreters prove helpful. In a nearly forgotten article, J.H. Moulton observed that, after the author of James

---

[210] Helpful here is R. Bauckham, 'Pseudo-Apostolic Letters', in *The Jewish World around the New Testament*, vol. 1, Tübingen, 2008, 123-49.

[211] Klein, *Werk*, 188, says that perhaps the historical James could have addressed all the Jewish people, but that this was not a possibility for anyone at a later date. Again this confuses the fiction of 1.1—the epistle is written for all diaspora Jews—with the actual historical circumstances of the letter, whatever they may have been.

INTRODUCTION

declares himself to be a servant of Jesus Christ, 'he drops all overt reference to Christian faith, and only names the Master in a verse [2.1] where the forced order of the words raises an extremely strong presumption of a gloss'.[212] The explanation for this, so Moulton argued, is that the letter is addressed to Jews: 'The "Twelve Tribes of the Dispersion", of course, most naturally suggests such a destination. The "synagogue" of ii. 2 will then be Jewish, and the rich men who are so sternly denounced will be more easily found than if we have to seek them in a Christian community of any date prior to the age of Constantine.'[213]

But why 'the absence of specifically Christian doctrine'?[214] Moulton suggested it was part of a missionary strategy. Most Jews 'would be deaf to all argument which even named the Crucified, and he who would reach them must try another way. Could there be a better way than to write as a Jew to Jews, threading the pearls of Christ's own teaching on a string of miscellaneous exhortation, all tending to shame them out of a blind unbelief rooted in party spirit (ἐριθεία)?[215] Jews who would read this Epistle could often without great difficulty be led on to read such a book as our First Gospel, in which they would learn with surprise that many of the sayings they had accepted as heavenly wisdom, when purporting to come from a pious and orthodox Jew, were really due to Him whom all orthodox Jews had agreed never to hear.'[216]

In making this proposal, Moulton cited a parallel from nineteenth-century India. A Christian missionary, he tells us, published a tract consisting of nothing but material from the *Mahābhārata*, material that the missionary found congruent with Christian belief. The purpose was to make Hindus more open to the appeal of the Christian message. 'The Epistle of James was a composition of this class, a Christian's appeal to non-Christians, which veils Christian terms and names in order to insinuate Christian truth into prejudiced minds.'[217]

It is unnecessary to go so far afield for examples of individuals who, for whatever reason, have found occasion to keep their religious convictions, or at least some of them, wholly in the background, or in the background for long stretches.[218] Both early Judaism and Christianity offer examples:

---

[212] Moulton, 'Studies', 45. For favorable remarks on Moulton's thesis see A.S. Peake, *A Critical Introduction to the New Testament*, New York, 1917, 89; Findlay, *Way*, 158.

[213] Moulton, 'Studies', 46.

[214] Moulton, 'Studies', 48.

[215] Moulton regarded the 'Jesus Christ' of 1.1, like that of 2.1, as an interpolation.

[216] Moulton, 'Studies', 47. A similar suggestion is already found in Herder, 'Kanon', 193: James did not name Jesus even when he had him in mind because he wanted to speak as a Jew to Jews, not as a sectarian.

[217] Moulton, 'Studies', 49-50.

[218] One should keep in mind that writers in all cultures regularly accommodate themselves in one way or another to projected audiences. For the sake of Gentile Greek

- Although Ps.-Phocylides is undeniably a Jewish text, 'it looks as if the author did his utmost to conceal the Jewish origin of many of his rules of conduct'.[219] One possible explanation for this is that, 'as a Jewish writer, he tried to provide a "pagan" text that could be used safely in Jewish schools to satisfy Jewish parents who wanted their children to be trained in the classical pagan authors'.[220] Another explanation is that he hoped for more than Jewish readers.[221]
- The Jewish Sibylline Oracles disguise their Jewish provenance. They attribute themselves to a pagan prophetess, the Sibyl, and clothe Jewish convictions and Jewish history in language designed to be comprehended by non-Jewish readers. All this reflects not only a desire to gain esteem for thinly disguised Jewish prophecies but represents an apologetical strategy that seeks common ground between Jew and pagan.
- Acts contains two speeches in which Christian elements are missing until the very end, and even then the language remains oblique. Stephen's speech in 7.2-53 lacks all Christology until the next to the last verse, when it speaks of the killing of 'the righteous one'. Paul's speech in Athens is similar. It seeks to explicate the religiosity of the Athenians and only at the end speaks of 'a man' whom God has appointed and raised from the dead. In both cases Luke thinks it appropriate to present two of his heroes as discoursing at length on religious subjects without being explicitly Christian.
- 5 Ezra claims to be the work of the famous scribe, Ezra. Although most likely Christian, its Christianity is inexplicit and conveyed in traditional Jewish language—so much so that, as with James, some have entertained the hypothesis that it is really Jewish.[222] The text does prophesy a shepherd (2.34) and, near its conclusion, it announces in a vision the future advent of 'the Son of God' (2.47); yet 'Jesus' is not named, and the author does his best to keep to the fiction that he is Ezra of old. He does not want to be thought of as a Christian but as a pre-Christian Jew looking into the future.
- Jerome observed that the Sentences of Sextus, although Christian, fail to mention 'the prophets, the patriarchs, the apostles, or Christ'.[223] The Christian writer evidently attempted to communicate by consciously setting aside overt Christian assertions. Why? According to Henry Chadwick, Sextus sought 'to bring the moral wisdom of the Greek sages under the wing of the church to whom all truth belongs. With adjustments here and there the language of Stoic or Pythagorean wisdom could pass in Christian circles. *Pythagoras saepe noster* might be his motto... The purpose was probably apologetic... Christianity brings to actuality what is potentially already there. *Anima naturaliter Christiana.*'[224]

readers, Josephus uses πρόνοια throughout *The Antiquities*. Modern textbooks are written on the level of anticipated students. Children's books eschew long words.

[219] P.W. van der Horst, 'Pseudo-Phocylides and the New Testament', *ZNW* 69 (1978), 189.

[220] P.W. van der Horst, 'Pseudo-Phocylides Revisited', *JSP* 3 (1988), 16.

[221] J. Thomas, *Der jüdische Phokylides*, Freiburg, CH, 1992, 352-61.

[222] Cf. T.A. Bergren, *Fifth Ezra*, Atlanta, 1990, 313-28.

[223] Jerome, *Ep.* 133.3 CSEL 56 ed. Hilberg, 247.

[224] H. Chadwick, ed., *The Sentences of Sextus*, Cambridge, UK, 1959, 160-61.

- Origen in one place tells us that, when in conversation with prejudiced pagans, he would hide his Christianity. That is, he would propound Christian teaching but not speak of 'Christ' or 'Christians' unless or until he had his listener's respect and attention: in that case he would then plainly declare his affiliation and the source of his wisdom.[225]
- Although Lactantius mentions God throughout the first three books of his *Divinae institutiones*, he nowhere names 'Jesus' or 'Christ'. In these long sections, Christian doctrine is off to the side as Lactantius attempts to argue with pagans on their own ground, offering criticisms of polytheism and secular philosophy. A similar silence marks *De opificio dei*, wherein Lactantius argues about the human body on the basis of reason, not Christian theology.
- The extant apologies of Athenagoras and Tatian fail to name Jesus or to speak of 'Christ'. The reason is that 'their projects were so focused on specific criticisms that they appear to support hardly more than monotheism, moral responsibility, and the expectation of resurrection and judgment and to be uninterested in Jesus as a human figure, in the corporate life of the Christian community, or in the deeper resources and expression of early Christian piety. The apologists were not disingenuous, but their task was of limited scope.'[226]
- The three extant books of *Ad Autolycum*, written by the second-century bishop Theophilus of Antioch, pass over the incarnation, fail to refer to the ministry of Jesus, and make no allusion to his passion. The canonical gospels are used only for their moral teachings. Moreover, Theophilus can define 'Christian' without naming Jesus Christ, and he can defend the idea of resurrection without referring to Jesus' resurrection.[227] *Ad Autolycum* promotes, evidently for apologetical purposes, 'a Christianity without Christ'.[228] One commentator has remarked that a sympathetic reader could have become a convert to Judaism as readily as to Christianity.[229]

One need not doubt, then, that a believer in Jesus might, in some circumstances, refuse to wear Christianity on his sleeve, or at least keep many of his important beliefs to himself.[230] Moulton's theory, however,

---

[225] Origen, *Jer* 20.5 SC 238 ed. Nautin, 274.

[226] H.Y. Gamble, 'Apologetics', in *Encyclopedia of Early Christianity*, 2nd ed., ed. E. Ferguson, New York, 1999, 86.

[227] Theophilus of Antioch, *Autol.* 1.12; PTS 44 ed. Marcovich, 31 (Christians are called such because they are anointed with the oil of God); 1.13; 2.27, 38 ed. Marcovich, 32-33, 77, 96 (the resurrection is proved by pagan examples, nature, and the prophets).

[228] So J. Bentivegna, 'A Christianity Without Christ by Theophilus of Antioch', in *Studia Patristica*, vol. 13, ed. E.A. Livingstone, Berlin, 1975, 106-30. See further R. Rogers, *Theophilus of Antioch*, Lanham, MD, 2000, 156-67.

[229] S. Laeuchli, *The Language of Faith*, New York, 1962, 165-66: if Theophilus 'pretends, in the interests of apologetics...that Christian faith is nomistic monotheism, why should the pagan not as well be converted to Diaspora Judaism?'; with his 'plea for monotheism and with the spiritualization of the law the Jew of the dispersion would have heartily agreed!'

[230] Kloppenborg, 'Discourse', 255, also cites a modern parallel: the Lubavichers publish 'tractates, essays, newspaper articles, and weblogs that often do not mention Chabad's messianic beliefs concerning Menachem Schneerson or other beliefs that set Chabad apart from other orthodox Jews. To the general readership, it is literature that encourages torah piety. A Lubavich reader would undoubtedly be able to recognize the

while rightly making that point, is not without difficulties. He argues that James originally styled himself a servant of God, not of Jesus Christ. Yet there is no solid reason to subtract 'Jesus Christ' from 1.1. Further, Moulton assumed that our letter was written by James of Jerusalem, who 'of all the Christians of the first century, who are known to us…is the only one who had in any sense the ear of the Jews'.[231] But there are, as we have seen, strong indications that our epistle is a pseudepigraphon from a later time. One also doubts that James was penned for non-Christian Jews alone. The title does nothing to exclude Christian Jews, and so much of James makes sense as practical advice for believers in Jesus that it seems unwise to imagine that the letter was intended only for outsiders.

A final problem with Moulton is his assumption that a Christian wishing or purporting to communicate with non-Christian Jews could have had only one goal in mind, namely, to proselytize them.[232] This is a narrow view. Do we really know that early followers of Jesus in all times and places sought the conversion of Jews to Christian doctrine? Perhaps the old idea that Judaism is concerned more with practice than with doctrine whereas Christianity is much more dogmatic in its orientation has unduly colored our perception of the early Jesus movement. However that may be, James does not drop a hint about missionizing, and we can without difficulty imagine situations in which stressing similarities rather than differences might have been the prudent course.[233] Indeed, is that not what one might expect of Christian Jews who wanted, despite opposition, to continue attending synagogue?

A.H. McNeile attempted to remedy the deficiencies in Moulton's thesis.[234] McNeile agreed that James' Christianity is intentionally quiescent and that our letter addresses itself to Jews.[235] But against Moulton he rightly held (i) that 'Jesus Christ' is an interpolation only in 2.1, not 1.1; (ii) that James is a pseudepigraphon; and (iii) that our epistle addresses

---

provenance of the literature from certain expressions and from the way in which standard Jewish authorities are cited and would understand how the general Torah exhortation fits in the larger theological schema of Chabad. But to a non-Lubavich Jew, the literature is simply exhortation to keep the Torah'.

[231] Moulton, 'Studies', 46.

[232] The presupposition appears again and again when scholars explain why 1.1 cannot envisage non-Christian Jews; cf. Rendtorff, 14; Bauckham, *Wisdom*, 16: 'James 1:1 does not specify that it is addressed to Christian members of the twelve tribes… Yet the letter presupposes its readers' allegiance to Jesus the Messiah. It is not Christian missionary literature which could be aimed at non-Christian Jews.' This assumes that a Christian would write to outsiders nothing save missionary literature.

[233] The attempt of Maier, 'Jakobusbrief', to argue that James, even though it is not a missionizing text, nonetheless contains hints of a missionizing theology, does not persuade.

[234] McNeile-Williams, *Introduction*, 201-208; McNeile, *Teaching*, 87-110. Moulton is mentioned in the former (206) but not the latter.

[235] McNeile, *Teaching*, 89: the people depicted in 1.9-11, 21; 2.1-3, 15; 3.13-16; and 5.6 do not sound like any other Christians we know of from the early decades.

both Jews and Christians.²³⁶ Why then the silences? 'There is little doubt that the writer is himself a Christian, but in his desire to reach the widest possible public he studiously selects language acceptable to Jew and Christian alike'.²³⁷ To that public he wanted 'to prove nothing doctrinal, and to "proselytize" no one, but to shew that the highest standard of ethics for Jew and for Christian could be one and the same'.²³⁸ In building his case McNeile correctly observed how often James is ambiguous, that is, how many times a Christian could take something one way, a non-Christian Jew another.²³⁹

Granted this, however, why might a Christian have wanted 'to prove nothing doctrinal, and to "proselytize" no one, but to shew that the highest standard of ethics for Jew and for Christian could be one and the same'? Can we find a plausible occasion for such an objective? This commentary, going beyond NcNeile, suggests that James represents Christian Jews who did not define themselves over against Judaism.²⁴⁰ That is, our book emerged from a Christ-oriented Judaism, from a group that still attended synagogue and wished to maintain irenic relations with those who did not share their belief that Jesus was the Messiah.²⁴¹

In such a context the Epistle of James makes good sense.²⁴² The emphasis upon convictions rooted in the common religiosity of the wisdom literature and the prophets, as well as the omission of potentially divisive Christian affirmations, would potentially make for good will among those in the synagogue.²⁴³ M. Hogan has written that 'James'

---

²³⁶ Like Moulton and McNeile, so also Cadoux, *Thought*, 85, and Beasley-Murray, 15, urge that James' doctrinal reserve can be explained in terms of his aims and audience.

²³⁷ McNeile, *Teaching*, 90. Cf. Elliott-Binns, *Christianity*, 50: 'If... the epistle was addressed to non-Christian Jews, as well as believers, it might have been considered advisable to preserve some reticence over specific Christian teaching'.

²³⁸ McNeile, *Teaching*, 95.

²³⁹ Cf. Ferris, '1 Peter', 303: 'there is an ambiguity perhaps designed'.

²⁴⁰ Note Farrar, *Days*, 340 (James draws 'no marked line of distinction between Jews and Christians in the communities which he is addressing'); also Robinson, *Redating*, 120: 'There is no sense of "we" and "they" such as we find, say, on the subject of sacrifice in Heb. 13.10 ("our altar is one from which the priests of the sacred tent have no right to eat") or fasting in Did. 8.1 (where "the hypocrites" keep the second and fifth days of the week, Christians the fourth and sixth)'. What Fletcher, 'Buddhism', 366, says about the readers of James—that they 'were unaware that being Christian meant anything different from being Jewish'—is more properly said of those on whose behalf James speaks.

²⁴¹ Cf. Felder, 1787: James seeks to 'alleviate tensions for Jewish Christians' who wanted to keep their allegiance to both church and synagogue.

²⁴² One should keep in mind that we know of other Christians who hoped for Jews as well as Christians to read what they wrote; see L. Lahey, 'Evidence for Jewish Believers in Christian-Jewish Dialogues through the Sixth Century (Excluding Justin)', in Skarsaune-Hvalvik, *Believers*, 588, 622-24.

²⁴³ Note Gruenwald, 'Death', 469: 'In contrast to the reports of the Gospel and the general spirit in the Letters of Paul, the Letter of James shows very little antagonism, if at all, to any of the Jewish groups of the time'.

grounding of his moral exhortations in theological rather than Christological principles provides a genuine bridge between Christians and Jews who share a belief in the One God, Creator, Lawgiver and Judge'.[244] Although this is a contemporary theological judgment, it harmonizes, I submit, with the original intention of our letter, which was to persuade sympathetic readers that the differences between James' version of Judaism and other forms was not so great. One recalls a line spoken by Peter in the Pseudo-Clementine Recognitions: 'only on this is there a difference between us, we who believe in Jesus, and those sons of our faith who do not believe'.[245]

James communicates, among other things, that Jesus' followers are not apostates from Judaism but rather faithful members of the synagogue who live according to the Jewish moral tradition, are faithful to Torah, and oppose those who want—as no doubt was rumored of other Christians—to divide faith from works. This is why 'his division does not fall between Judaism and Christianity, but rather between true and false religion'.[246]

4QMMT, Qumran's so-called Halakhic Letter, supplies a parallel to this view of James.[247] This Dead Sea Scroll differs from other scrolls in so far as it seemingly addresses outsiders: 'also we have written to you some of the precepts of the Torah which we think are good for you and for your people, for [we saw] in you intellect and knowledge of the Torah. Reflect on all these matters and seek from him so that he may support your counsel and keep far from you the evil scheming and the counsel of Belial, so that at the end of time, you may rejoice in finding that some of our words

---

[244] Hogan, 'Law', 91. Cf. Ferris, '1 Peter', 303 ('the author is writing to Christian Jews but he would also recommend his faith to Israel as a whole: he therefore concentrates on the ethic common to both but perfected in Christianity, and in certain passages there is an ambiguity perhaps designed'); Findlay, *Way*, 168 (James 'offers a meeting ground on which devout Jews and tolerant Christians can come together'); März, 'Art', 62; Musser, 'Rückbesinnung', 78 (James can be a 'genuine aid in Jewish-Christian dialogue'). It is noteworthy that James Parkes, who was so concerned to improve relations between Jews and Christians, believed that James is 'in many ways the most attractive of Apostolic writings' (*The Conflict of the Church and the Synagogue*, Cleveland, 1961, 58). Note also that A. Greenham, 'An Examination of the Role the Epistle of James Might Play in Introducing the New Testament to Muslims', *Faith and Mission* 19 (2002), 3-18, thinks that James serves as a good NT introduction to Muslims because of its affinity with Islamic beliefs and its lack of atonement theology.

[245] So the Syriac of Ps.-Clem. Rec. 1.43.2 TU 48.3 ed. Frankenberg, 48.

[246] So Childs, *Canon*, 443. It is helpful to keep in mind a comment of Broadhead, *Ways*, 389: 'It is probably no longer accurate to say that Christianity grew up alongside the synagogue or in the shadow of the synagogue or in dialogue and controversy with the synagogue. It appears more likely that in a number of important sites Jesus movements grew up within the synagogues.'

[247] I first proposed this parallel in Allison, 'Fiction'. Kloppenborg, 'Discourse', in essential agreement, has since developed it further. Peuch, 'Qumrân', 54, independently also suggests parallels between James and 4QMMT.

are true. And it shall be reckoned to you as justice when you do what is upright and good before him, for your good and that of Israel.'[248]

Although presumably the named addressees were real, not fictional—unfortunately we only have fragments—this diminishes only slightly the analogy with James. For 4QMMT was intended to be read outside the group of the author as well as within, and despite its concluding emphasis upon eschatology, 'it makes no attempt to argue from the experience of the sect that prophecy is being fulfilled, since the recipient of the letter could not be expected to accept such an argument. Instead, 4QMMT is framed in terms that might in principle be persuasive to any Jew, appealing primarily to the Law of Moses.'[249] In other words, the letter, which appears to have been written at a time when the community was still hopeful of reconciliation with an institutionalized opposition (probably some part of the Jerusalem establishment),[250] speaks in a language understandable to all learned Jews, even though its purpose is to describe sectarian laws. The analogy with James is manifest.

Despite the parallel, we must not overlook that James is often polemical. The attacks in chaps. 4 and 5 are in fact vicious. But they are not assaults upon the synagogue as such. From James' viewpoint, the synagogue has at least three sorts of members. There are Christian Jews, there are rich oppressors, and there are those belonging to neither group, whose sympathy James seeks to gain or preserve. He wants the latter to recognize in the opposition to his own kind the unjust oppression of the poor so fervently condemned by the Hebrew prophets. James rails, in the hope that others will see things as he does. He seeks not to proselytize but to promote tolerance for and understanding of his own group, to gain sympathy for Christians in a context where there is perhaps growing antipathy—the sort of antipathy that at some point led to the *birkat ha-minim*, a development James seems to know about; see on 3.9-10—but not yet formal expulsion.[251] This is why James' polemic is not against false teaching but against 'arrogance...anger, and the criticizing and insulting of others in the community, directly or otherwise'.[252] It is also why the epistle is so much concerned with 'the unity and proper

---

[248] 4Q398 14-17 2.2-8; cf. 4Q399 1 1-2.

[249] J.J. Collins, 'The Expectation of the End in the Dead Sea Scrolls', in *Eschatology, Messianism, and the Dead Sea Scrolls*, ed. C.A. Evans and P.W. Flint, Grand Rapids, MI, 1997, 81.

[250] According to E. Qimron and J. Strugnell, *Miqṣat Ma'aśe ha-Torah*, Oxford, 1994, 121, 4QMMT was written by the Qumran sectarians 'to an individual leader and his people Israel, with an exhortation to follow their own lead in certain points of Zadokite praxis'. They go on to speak of the relations between the sectarians and the other group as 'relatively eirenic'.

[251] The *birkat ha-minim* probably presupposes a situation in which Christian Jews want to remain in the synagogue.

[252] Chester, 'Theology', 29.

functioning of the [religious] community'.²⁵³ James wants to foster in the synagogue peace, gentleness, mercy, and impartiality (3.16-18), which should leave room for the Christian Jews for whom he speaks.²⁵⁴

To simplify, James has above all three groups in mind—those who are, in his view, mistreated and suffering, those who mistreat them, and those, belonging to neither of the first groups, whose sympathy he wishes to augment. The latter, he presumes, can effect change and make things better, and so he seeks their respect and support. Schematically:

A	Group defended (and addressed)	the suffering, the poor, those cursed
B	Group criticized	those who oppress and curse
C	Group addressed (potential sympathizers)	those who can effect or prevent change

The first group alone consists of followers of Jesus.

Again there is a formal parallel with 4QMMT, for it too envisages three groups—the 'we' group, the 'you' group, and the 'they' group. The 'we' group seeks to make common cause with the 'you' group against the 'they' group:²⁵⁵

A	Group defended (and addressed)	originators of the text
B	Group criticized	those currently in charge of temple ritual
C	Group addressed (potential sympathizers)	priestly circles not currently in charge

The first group alone consists of members of the Qumran movement.

The sort of Christianity herein envisaged for James is related to one of the groups scholarship has detected behind John's Gospel. J.L. Martyn has argued that John attests to the existence of Jews who attended synagogue and believed in Jesus but did not proselytize.²⁵⁶ His case has convinced many, including Raymond Brown, for whom the so-called Crypto-Christians had 'little taste for polemics against the synagogue'; they rather sought to 'work from within to bring...offended synagogue leaders back to a tolerance toward Christians that had previously existed'.²⁵⁷ One is tempted to extend the parallel even further. For if one

---

²⁵³ Keith, 'Destinataires', 24.

²⁵⁴ Just such a reading of James occurred to Moule, *Birth*, 219: 'Is it [James], then, perhaps, an attempt by a Jewish Christian to conciliate non-Christian Jews?'

²⁵⁵ See Qimron and J. Strugnell, *Miqṣat Ma'aśe ha-Torah*, 14-21; R. Deines, 'The Pharisees between "Judaisms" and "Common Judaism"', in *Justification and Variegated Nomism*, vol. 1, ed. D.A. Carson, P.T. O'Brien, and M.A. Seifrid, Tübingen, 2001, 443-504.

²⁵⁶ J.L. Martyn, *History and Theology in the Fourth Gospel*, rev. ed., Nashville, 1978.

²⁵⁷ See e.g. R.E. Brown, *The Community of the Beloved Disciple*, New York, 1979, 71-73.

is prepared to follow those who find in Nicodemus and Joseph of Arimathea[258] representatives of such people,[259] then they had among their number authorities in Jerusalem, and our epistle associates itself with James, who was head of the church in that place.[260]

However that may be, we certainly have evidence that, at least in later times, some Jews with Christian convictions, wishing to stay on friendly terms with those who did not share their convictions, did not always flaunt their beliefs about Jesus. Epiphanius reports that a certain Josephus of his acquaintance was encouraged, by 'an elderly scholar of the law', but only privately, to confess faith in Jesus Christ.[261] Epiphanius likewise purports to have known another Jew who was learned in the law, loved Christians, spent time in their company, and believed in the incarnation; and yet, 'from fear of the Jews', the man remained a non-Christian Jew.[262] Then there is the story in the Pseudo-Clementine Recognitions, regarding a certain Jewish authority, Gamaliel I, who was 'secretly' a believer in Jesus and used his prominent position to assist Christians.[263] Although this is a fiction, it expresses someone's belief that faith in Jesus did not necessarily entail evangelistic activity or abandoning Judaism.

One should also consider in this connection, because it is about James, the tale of his martyrdom in Hegesippus.[264] This has 'the Jews and the scribes and the Pharisees' asking James to restrain the people who have gone astray by belief in Jesus as the Messiah: 'Be good enough to make the facts about Jesus clear to all who come for Passover. We all accept what you say; we can vouch for it, and so can all the people, that you are a righteous man and do not show favoritism. So make it clear to the crowd that they must not go astray as regards Jesus.' In the event, James publicly confesses Jesus, whereupon the scribes and Pharisees realize their mistake. This is a remarkable legend, because it implies that, before James made his public statement, there were people in Jerusalem who knew of him and even admired him and yet were either unaware of his Christian affiliation or thought his beliefs about Jesus innocuous.[265] In other words, until shortly before he was executed, James according to this tale successfully passed himself off to many as a pious Jew.

---

[258] Note Jn 19.38: 'Joseph of Arimathea... was a disciple of Jesus, though a secret one because of his fear of the Jews'.

[259] See D. Rensberger, *Johannine Faith and Liberating Community*, Philadelphia, 1988, 37-61.

[260] For M. Goulder, 'Nicodemus', *SJT* 44 (1991), 153-68, Nicodemus represents 'the Jerusalem Christianity led by James and Peter'.

[261] Epiphanius, *Pan.* 30.9.2-3 GCS 25 ed. Hall, 344. In this a whole family holds their Christian convictions as a secret.

[262] Epiphanius, *Pan.* 30.9.4-6 GCS 25 ed. Hall, 344-36.

[263] Ps.-Clem. Rec. 1.65.2; 66.4 GCS 51 ed. Rehm, 45.

[264] Hegesippus *apud* Eusebius, *H.E.* 2.23.4-18.

[265] Cf. the analysis of Nienhuis, *Paul*, 134.

Recent work on ancient Judaism and Christianity has established that the two entities were not as clearly distinct as once taken for granted.[266] The Epistle of James, as read herein, accords with such work. Although writing in the name of James of Jerusalem and so openly speaking for Christians, our author does not clearly identify his readers as such. Hence the pseudepigraphical address: he evidently still hopes for an audience with non-Christian Jews. James is thus a sort of apology. It addresses Jews, which includes those who share the author's Christian convictions as well as those who do not. And it has a two-fold purpose—edification for the former and clarification for the latter.

On this view we understand why James is so Janus-faced, why it seems so Christian yet is so resolutely mute on peculiarly Christian themes, and why it contains so many passages that could be taken one way by a Christian and another by a non-Christian. James reflects a Christian group still battling for its place within the Jewish community, a group that wishes to remain faithful members of the synagogue, to be, as Jerome later said of the Nazoraeans, both Jew and Christian.[267]

It is no mystery that the book seems to be so Jewish, that it is largely a compilation of traditions,[268] and that it is often difficult to trace a logical connection between the larger units. James is not an argument but a presentation. From one point of view, that is, it is a sort of sampler, being someone's collection of what he wants Jews to know about Christians. It is designed to be Jewish; it is designed to look traditional.

Two final points regarding James' *Sitz im Leben*. First, if the hope to communicate solicitously with non-Christian Jews helps explain 1.1, we do not know who actually received copies of James or who paid it heed. Nor do we know whether, from the author's point of view, the text failed or succeeded, in his time and place, to achieve his goals.[269]

Second, perhaps we can link James' version of Christian Judaism with a group otherwise known. One candidate of course would be the Nazoraeans.[270] Yet we have little reliable information about them as our

---

[266] The evidence is surveyed in J.D.G. Dunn, 'Two Covenants or One? The Interdependence of Jewish and Christian Identity', in *Geschichte–Tradition–Reflexion*, vol. 3, ed. H. Canick, H. Lichtenberger, and P. Schäfer, Tübingen, 1996, 97-122. According to E.M. Myers, 'Response', in *American Bible Society Symposium Papers on the Bible in the Twenty-first Century*, ed. H.C. Kee, Philadelphia, 1993, 114, 'the inability of scholars to identify definitively any Christian burials prior to the fourth century in Syro-Palestine suggests strongly that Christian self-definition and beliefs were more closely aligned with Judaism than is normally believed'.

[267] Jerome, *Ep.* 112.13 CSEL 55 ed. Hilberg, 382.

[268] For a helpful overview of the various traditions in James see Popkes, 27-44.

[269] As a matter of later Christian history, apologetical works have tended to be read by insiders even when ostensibly addressed to outsiders.

[270] Cf. Moffatt, *Introduction*, 464; Manns, 'Nazoréen', 503-508 (James may be 'proto-Nazoraean'). For the sources and discussion see esp. R.A. Pritz, *Nazarene Jewish-Christianity*, Jerusalem, 1988. Given the links between James and Matthew, it might be

main sources—Epiphanius and Jerome—are late and second hand. Moreover, the Nazoraeans seem to have preferred Hebrew to Greek and to have accepted Paul's apostleship, which ill accords with what we find in James.

By contrast, the so-called Ebionites, if we can trust the sources, had no place for Paul. In this respect they stand closer to James.[271] They also employed an edited form of Matthew,[272] which matters given James' close relationship to special Matthean tradition. Even more suggestive for us are the links between James and the traditions behind the Pseudo-Clementine literature, especially Rec. 1.27-71. This last contains a source which has been called 'The Ascents of James'.[273] Perhaps composed in the mid-second century, it likely represents Ebionite circles.[274] The text bears witness to a Greek-speaking Christian Judaism that opposed Paul, upheld the law,[275] and regarded James as its hero. Moreover, it may not be coincidence that we find, in the Ascents, a number of themes and motifs that are prominent in James,[276] and further that both sources use Jesus

---

relevant that some have associated that gospel with the Nazoraeans; cf. Davies-Allison, *Matthew*, 3.721-27.

[271] A few have suggested or wondered about linking James and the Ebionites; cf. Herder, 'Kanon', 209-14; Schleiermacher, *Einleitung*, 426; Kern, 'Charakter'; A. Schwegler, *Das nachapostolische Zeitalter*, vol. 1, Tübingen, 1846, 418-443 ('a mild and attenuated form of Ebionitism'); Windisch-Preisker, 7, 36; Streeter, *Church*, 203 ('almost Ebionite outlook'); Moule, *Birth*, 218 ('the Epistle...might, for all the signs it shows of Christology, be near-Ebionite'). R. Wall, 'Context', while not classifying James as 'Ebionite', urges a similarity between the content of James and Ebionite critiques of Paul.

[272] So Irenaeus, *Haer*. 1.26.2 FC 8.1 ed. Brox, 316. For an overview of the evidence on the Ebionites see O. Skarsaune, 'The Ebionites', in Skarsaune-Hvalvik, *Believers*, 419-62; Broadhead, *Ways*, 188-212.

[273] See on this R.E. Van Voorst, *The Ascents of James*, Atlanta, 1989; F.S. Jones, *An Ancient Jewish Christian Source on the History of Christianity*, Atlanta, 1995. Is this the source that Epiphanius, *Pan*. 30.16.7, GCS 25 ed. Holl, 354-55, calls the Ἀναβαθμοὶ Ἰακώβου?

[274] See R. Bauckham, 'The Origin of the Ebionites', in *The Image of the Judaeo-Christians in the Ancient Jewish and Christian Literature*, ed. P.J. Tomson and D. Lambers-Petry, Tübingen, 2003, 167-80. Bauckham makes the case that the Ascents uses the Gospel of the Ebionites.

[275] And like our epistle, the Ascents upholds Mosaic praxis without mentioning the Sabbath, diet, or purity issues. Note, however, that Epiphanius, *Pan*. 30.16.5 GCS 25 ed. Holl, 354, preserves a fragment of the Gospel of the Ebionites that has Jesus do away with temple sacrifices, and that the source behind Ps.-Clem. Rec. 1.27-71 has the same teaching: 1.37.2-4; 39.2; 48.5-6; 54.1; 64.1-2 GCS 51 ed. Rehm, 30-31, 36, 39, 44. If our author thought this too, his silence on the matter could be interpreted as strategic.

[276] E.g. 'freedom' (Asc. Jas 1.37.5; 42.2; cf. Jas 1.25; 2.12), 'wisdom' (1.39.2; 40.3; cf. Jas 1.5; 3.13-18), 'perfection' (1.39.3; cf. Jas 1.4; 3.2), invocation of the divine name (1.39.2; cf. Jas 2.7), exile (1.39.3; cf. Jas 1.1), blasphemy (1.40.2; 60.5; cf. Jas 2.7), 'the crown of salvation' won by resisting and struggling against evil (1.42.2; cf. Jas 1.12), 'faith' = religious belief (1.43.1; cf. Jas 2.14-26), concern for the 'poor' (1.59.7; 61.2; cf. Jas 1.9-11; 2.1-6), *presbuteroi* (1.62.5; cf. Jas 5.14), divine giving (1.62.7; cf. Jas 1.5,

tradition unique to Matthew.²⁷⁷ Beyond all that, the Ascents has James address non-Christian Jews, knows of believers in Jesus who are in every outward respect Jewish,²⁷⁸ and—a fact relevant for those who deem 1 Peter to be a source for James—exalts Peter.²⁷⁹

So the Pseudo-Clementines preserve religious traditions that are in important respects akin to James.²⁸⁰ It is a reasonable hypothesis that our epistle and Rec. 1.27-71 witness to related, and perhaps closely related, forms of the Christian Judaism known as Ebionitism. The chief difference is that James represents a group that still holds out hope for irenic relations with the synagogue.²⁸¹ In the source behind the Recognitions, the separation from Judaism is a *fait accompli*.

If James is indeed to be related to Ebionite Christianity, it may not be coincidence that the book has so much to say about the poor, and that it indeed defends them at length in 2.1-13. Although some of the church fathers, following Tertullian, held that the Ebionites were named after a certain Ebion, modern scholars regard this as an error. The name rather derives from the Hebrew or Aramaic word for 'poor', either אביונים or אביוניא.²⁸² This was presumably a self-designation, inspired by scriptural texts that speak of the oppressed faithful as 'the poor'. One wonders whether our author intended 'the poor' to function as a sort of code word for his Christian group.²⁸³

---

17), non-Christian Jews as 'brothers' (1.67.3, 7; cf. Jas 1.2; etc.), eschatological *adventus* (1.69.4; cf. Jas 5.7-8), murder of the innocent (1.70.4-71.1; cf. Jas 4.1-2; 5.6); see GCS 51 ed. Rehm, 30-33, 42, 44, 46-48.

²⁷⁷ Ps.-Clem. Rec. 1.41.3 (opening of graves at the crucifixion); 42.4 (the rumor that Jesus' body was stolen); 55.4 ('kingdom of heaven') GCS 51 ed. Rehm, 32-33, 40; cf. Mt 4.17; 27.51-53, 64. Note also that Matthew is the first of the twelve apostles to speak in 1.55-61. The Ascents also plainly knows Acts, but it consistently disagrees with its account of events.

²⁷⁸ Ps.-Clem. Rec. 1.65.2; 66.4 GCS 51 ed. Rehm, 45. Bauckham, 'Origin', infers that the Ebionites defended themselves against the charge of apostasy from Judaism, a goal which accords with the nature of our Epistle. Incidentally, the Ascents clearly distinguishes between James the bishop of Jerusalem on the one hand and James the son of Zebedee and James the son of Alphaeus on the other.

²⁷⁹ Whereas James disputes Paul, he nowhere, in reworking 1 Peter, polemicizes against anything in that book.

²⁸⁰ So too S. Wilson, *Strangers*, 152-55, although Wilson does not regard the Ascents as Ebionite. Note, however, Epiphanius, *Pan.* 30.18.2 GCS 25 ed. Holl, 357: the Ebionites 'call their church a synagogue and not a church'. This fits perhaps with Jas 2.2 but not 5.14. Yet it would be incautious to consider Epiphanius' generalization the last word on an early second-century Christian group.

²⁸¹ One cannot use this fact to date James more precisely because there were Christians in synagogues for several centuries; see M. Simon, *Verus Israel*, Oxford, 1986, 306-38; J.G. Gager, 'A View of Early Christianity', in *Interwoven Destinies*, New York, 1993, 62-73.

²⁸² See O. Skarsaune, 'The Ebionites', in Skarsaune-Hvalvik. *Believers*, 424-27.

²⁸³ See further below, 376-78, 390.

INTRODUCTION

III. SOURCES

James appears to draw above all from five sources: the LXX, extra-canonical Jewish tradition, popular Hellenistic philosophy, the Jesus tradition, and other early Christian traditions and texts.

(i) Given its brevity, the extent to which our book manages to cite, refer to, allude to, or otherwise borrow from books that belong to our Bibles is striking:[284]

From the Pentateuch
- borrowing from LXX Gen 1.11 — see on 5.18
- borrowing from LXX Gen 1.26-27 — see on 3.7-9
- quotation of LXX Gen 15.6 — see on 2.23
- summary of LXX Gen 22.1-19 — see on 2.21-23
- citation of LXX Exod 20.13-14 = Deut 5.17-18 — see on 2.11
- allusion to Lev 19.13; Deut 24.14-15 — see on 5.4
- allusion to Lev 19.15 — see on 2.1, 9
- allusion to Lev 19.15-18 — see on 4.11-12
- citation of LXX Lev 19.18 — see on 2.8
- allusion to Deut 6.4 — see on 2.19

From the Former Prophets
- summary of episode in LXX Josh 2.1-22 — see on 2.25
- summary of episode in LXX 1 Kgs 17-18 — see on 5.17-18

From the Latter Prophets
- borrowing from LXX Isa 5.7-9 — see on 5.4
- borrowing from LXX Isa 32.15-20 — see on 3.18
- borrowing from LXX Isa 40.6-7 — see on 1.9-11
- borrowing from LXX Jer 5.24 — see on 5.7
- borrowing from LXX Jer 12.3 — see on 5.5
- borrowing from LXX Ezek 33-34 — see on 5.19-20
- borrowing from LXX Hos 14.10 — see on 3.13

From the Psalms[285] and Wisdom Literature
- citation of LXX Prov 3.34 — see on 4.6
- borrowing from Prov 10.12 (non-LXX form) — see on 5.20
- summary of Job — see on 5.11
- borrowing from LXX Wis 2 — see on 4.13–5.6
- borrowing from Ecclus 2 — see on 5.10
- borrowing from Ecclus 15.11-12 — see on 1.13

From an Unknown Scripture
- citation of lost Eldad and Modad (?) — see on 4.5

---

[284] This list represents the conclusions of this commentary. Many scholars would argue for additional borrowing, others for less. For example, Johnson, 'Leviticus', discerns greater use of Leviticus, and Frankemölle, passim; idem, 'Thema', sees extensive influence from Sirach.

[285] For an overview of all the possible echoes in James of the Psalms see Wachob, 'Psalms'.

A chart such as this only introduces part of the pertinent evidence. James is also full of scriptural and LXX idioms,[286] and every single paragraph carries forward themes at home in the Jewish Bible.[287] One's general impression, then, is that our author was well-versed in the scriptures.[288] He appears to have heard or read, at the very least, parts of the Pentateuch, parts of the Former Prophets, parts of the Latter Prophets, and parts of the poetic books, that is, Psalms and Wisdom writings. That he was familiar with most of what we think of as the LXX is a reasonable inference.[289]

He assumes such familiarity on the part of his audience. This is why he can summarize in the briefest manner stories about Abraham (2.22-23), Rahab (2.25), Job (5.11), and Elijah (5.17-18): in each case, a few words should suffice to call to mind a known episode. James says as much in 5.11: 'you have heard of the steadfastness of Job'. In like fashion, our author presumes readers know something about God's gift of the Torah to Moses on Sinai when he writes: 'For the one who said, "Do not commit adultery", also said, "Do not murder"' (2.11). Without such knowledge, the line, with its unspecified ὁ εἰπών, is an enigma.

This circumstance makes it likely that at least some of James' borrowing from the LXX is intended to be noticed; that is, certain lines are designed to function as allusions and so don divine authority. James 2.1, 9 (cf. Lev 19.15); 3.7-9 (cf. Gen 1.26-27); and 5.4 (cf. Lev 19.13; Deut 24.14-15) are strong candidates in this regard.

Our book nowhere pretends to dispense novelties, and its extensive intertextuality, which is often on the surface, at least for the biblically literate, prohibits the thought. James consistently interacts with a large network of authoritative texts. Biblical stories, wisdom, and prophecy are its chief memories and its dominant linguistic idiom. The upshot is an implicit claim faithfully to represent and reinscribe the divine revelation in the Jewish scriptures.

---

[286] See the list of Semitisms below, 86-87; also Chaine, xci-xcix.

[287] See further Mayor, cx-cxvi.

[288] Cf. Oesterley, 392-93: 'the mind of the writer was saturated with the spirit of the ancient Scriptures'.

[289] Popkes, 'Scripture', argues to the contrary that James' knowledge of the Bible, as reflected in both quotations and allusions, came to him 'second-hand'. One can, to be sure, theorize that James took some of his biblical materials from non-biblical sources. Perhaps, to illustrate, he knew Isa 40.6-7 and Prov 3.4 from 1 Pet 1.24 and 5.5, or the popular Lev 19.18 and Exod 20.13-14 = Deut 5.17-18 from Jewish or Christian *paraenesis*, or Gen 15.6 from Paul (cf. Rom 4.3; Gal 3.6). But this cannot be the whole story. The regular appearance of Septuagintalisms stands against positing nothing but a second-hand knowledge of scripture, as do the repeated and subtle use of Lev 19, the strong prophetic feel of 5.1-6, the use of Isa 5.7-9 in 5.4 (see *ad loc.*), and the fact that 5.17-18 seemingly reflects several lines in 1 Kgs 17-18; see on 5.17. For the same reason, Agourides, 'Origin', 67, fails to persuade when he claims that 'the author refers less to the Old Testament, than he does to Jewish paraphrases or commentaries on the holy texts'.

Such an understanding of James is bolstered by those words and phrases that, although they allude to no particular biblical text, nonetheless possess a biblical texture. An author whose phrases include 'the twelve tribes' (1.1), 'the word of truth' (1.18), 'the righteousness of God' (1.20), 'Go in peace' (2.16), 'purify your hearts' (4.8), 'the Lord Sabbaoth' (5.4), 'the day of slaughter' (5.5), 'establish your hearts' (5.8), 'the prophets who spoke in the name of the Lord' (5.10; cf. 5.15), and 'the Lord is merciful' (5.11) tacitly commends himself to those steeped in the Jewish scriptures.

As to how James came to his knowledge of the Bible, we can infer, on the basis of what we know of early Judaism and Christianity, that he heard texts in religious settings, and that he heard important texts again and again. As to whether he also had personal access to written copies of Greek scriptures, we cannot know. His intertextual finesse does not demand such. The ability to quote texts does not entail their physical presence. It requires only hearing them often enough so that they become memories. Surely James could readily have quoted Proverbs and alluded to Genesis without having had a copy of Genesis or of Proverbs to hand.[290]

One last point regarding James and scripture. It is natural to see a special relationship with the wisdom tradition.[291] James refers to σοφία (1.5; 3.13-18), quotes Proverbs twice, shows a likely knowledge of Wisdom and Ecclesiasticus,[292] and shares much vocabulary with LXX wisdom books.[293] He additionally recalls sapiential literature in that he

---

[290] One fails to see the need to postulate, as does Popkes, 'Scripture', that James copied quotations from texts he had run across and kept them in something like a 'file'.

[291] The most complete treatment of this subject known to the author is MacGorman, 'Wisdom'. This covers three large, general themes—the concept of wisdom, reward and retribution, the problem of sin—as well as several lesser themes—the tongue, the needy, the godless rich, trusting riches, humility, self-control, impartiality, envy, strife. He highlights differences (James is not 'just another work of Jewish Wisdom') as well as similarities (James 'resembles the Jewish Wisdom literature in its fundamental religious ideas and ethical precepts').

[292] Cf. J.V. Bartlet, *Age*, 233; Zahn, *Introduction*, 114, 121 (Sirach only); Dibelius, 27; Popkes, 28. Frankemölle's commentary consistently highlights parallels between James and Ecclesiasticus. Among the closest are these: Ecclus 2.9 and Jas 1.12; Ecclus 4.29; 5.8 and Jas 1.19; Ecclus 5.11 and Jas 1.19; Ecclus 7.10 and Jas 1.6; Ecclus 10.21 and Jas 1.9-10; Ecclus 15.11-12 and Jas 1.13; Ecclus 15.12 and Jas 1.13; Ecclus 18.15; 20.15 and Jas 1.5; Ecclus 19.16 and Jas 3.2; Ecclus 29.10-11 and Jas 5.2. For additional parallels see Mayor, cxvi-cxviii; Ropes, 19. The strongest agreements with Wisdom occur in Jas 4.11; 5.9 (cf. Wis 1.11); 5.1 (cf. Wis 5.8), 6 (cf. Wis 2.20). Additional parallels in Mayor, cxviii. This author has not had access to the 1860 Groningen dissertation of A. Boon, 'Dissertatio exegetico-theologica de Jacobi Epistolae cum Siracidae libro Sapientia dicto convenientia quam favente summo numine'.

[293] According to Halson, 'Wisdom', 308-309, James has 67 NT *hapax legomena*. Of these, 52 are Septuagintal. Of those, 34 appear in the wisdom literature as compared with 15 in the Pentateuch, 12 in the historical books, 9 in the Psalms, 18 in the Latter Prophets and Daniel, and 25 in non-wisdom apocryphal books. (Any one word can appear in more

uses the second person address,[294] likes aphoristic formulations (1.19; 2.13; 3.18), is fond of striking metaphors,[295] frets about anger (1.19-20), is interested in the dangers of speech (1.19; 3.1-12), focuses on practical guidance rather than speculative theology, is keen on imperatives, and sometimes juxtaposes sayings and paragraphs without evident rhyme or reason.

At the same time, one should not miss the significant ways in which James distinguishes itself from the wisdom tradition, both by what it says and by what it does not say. On the one hand, our letter lacks much that is characteristic of Proverbs and its cousins: there is no discussion of sex, no admonition about human friendship, no guidance for households, and no exhortation against laziness. On the other hand, James contains important theological ideas that set it apart from the dominant sapiential tradition, such as expectation of a near end (5.7-9), the prospect of Gehenna (3.6), and belief in demons and the devil (2.19; 4.17).[296]

(ii) James did not know biblical texts in isolation but received and understood them via Jewish tradition. There are, accordingly, Jewish parallels to the way he applies Isa 40.7 in 1.9-11 as well as to his notion that Job was patient; and 2.1-4 is his adaptation of a Jewish tradition associated with Lev 19.15, as the parallels in Sifra Lev 200; ARN A 10; Deut. Rab. 5.6 and elsewhere make evident. Our author, however, also knew Jewish traditions that were not immediately tied to biblical texts. This is why his text is full of ideas and expressions that appear exclusively in extra-biblical sources. The modern critical commentaries document this throughout. Two sources in particular, however, merit special mention in this Introduction—Philo and the Testaments of the Twelve Patriarchs.

According to several scholars, the correlations between Philo and James imply that the latter knew the former.[297] Among the abundant parallels are the following:[298]

---

than one category.) His conclusion: 'in his distinctive vocabulary... James has a marked predilection for words from the Septuagintal Wisdom literature'.

[294] For the second person address so common in wisdom literature see Prov 1.8-27; 2.1-10; 3.1-30; Wis 1.11; 6.2-25; Ecclus 1.26-30; 2.1-9; 3.10-23; etc.

[295] E.g. 1.6, 10-11; 4.14; 5.7. See further Schulze, *Charakter*, 68-73, and Frankemölle, 77, for full listings. According to S. Luther, 'Ethics', the metaphors in James 'aim at an intensification of the argumentation through vivid images which evoke the recipients' particular attention, irritation, reflexion or even fear' (338).

[296] See further Penner, 'Research', 275-80, on the combination of wisdom and eschatology in James. In this it is very much like the Synoptic tradition.

[297] So Plumptre, 80; Kennedy, 'Atmosphere'; Findlay, *Way*, 158. Contrast Dibelius, 27-28. C. Siegfried, *Philo von Alexandria als Ausleger des Alten Testament*, Jena, 1875, 310-14, argues that Philo influenced James, but only indirectly, through channels we know nothing about. Feine, *Lehranschauungen*, 142-46, doubts even that.

[298] C.F. Loesner, *Observationes ad Novum Testament e Philone Alexandrino*, Leipzig, 1777, 452-69, already compiled many parallels. Note also Mayor, cxxi-cxxiv; Johnson, 41-43.

- Jas 1.4: ἔργον τέλειον; cf. Philo, *Spec.* 2.59: ἔργον τέλειον
- Jas 1.14: ἐπιθυμίας ἐξελκόμενος καὶ δελεαζόμενος; cf. Philo, *Agr.* 103: πρὸς ἡδονῆς δελεασθὲν εἵλκυσται
- Jas 1.17: πᾶσα δόσις ἀγαθὴ καὶ πᾶν δώρημα τέλιον ἄνωθέν ἐστιν; cf. Philo, *Somn.* 1.162: ἄνωθεν δωρεὰς ἀγαθὸς καὶ τέλειος
- Jas 1.26: μὴ χαλιναγωγῶν γλῶσσαν; cf. Philo, *Somn.* 2.165: γλῶτταν ἀχαλίνωτον
- Jas 2.8: νόμον...βασιλικόν, followed by Lev 19.18; cf. Philo, *Post.* 101-102: 'the word of God' = the law is 'the royal road', βασιλικὴν ὁδόν, βασιλικῇ ὁδῷ, βασιλικῆς ὁδοῦ
- Jas 2.23: Ἀβραάμ...καὶ φίλος θεοῦ ἐκλήθη; cf. Philo, *Sobr.* 56: μὴ ἐπικαλύψω ἐγὼ ἀπὸ Ἀβραὰμ τοῦ φίλου μου;
- Jas 3.2: πταίομεν ἅπαντες; cf. Philo, *Deus* 75: 'No one...has run the course of life from birth to death without stumbling (ἄπταιστον)'
- Jas 4.4: φίλος εἶναι τοῦ κόσμου ἐχθρὸς τοῦ θεοῦ; cf. Philo frag. 2.649: 'It is impossible for love of the world to coexist with the love of God'

Although it would be easy to add to this list, the correlations do not establish that Philo influenced James, for the latter does not employ ideas or phrases that were demonstrably the exclusive property of the former. Instead, as this commentary confirms again and again, James and Philo have so much in common because they draw from the common river of Hellenistic-Jewish tradition.

The same may be said of the parallels between James and the Testaments of the Twelve Patriarchs, which include the following:[299]

- Jas 3.14: ψεύδεσθε κατὰ τῆς ἀληθείας; cf. T. Gad 5.1: τῷ ψεύδει λαλῶν κατὰ τῆς ἀληθείας
- Jas 4.7: ἀντίστητε δὲ τῷ διαβόλῳ καὶ φεύξεται ἀφ' ὑμῶν; cf. T. Iss. 7.7: πᾶν πνεῦμα τοῦ Βελιὰρ φεύξεται ἀφ' ὑμῶν; T. Dan 5.1: φύγῃ ἀφ' ὑμῶν ὁ Βελιάρ; T. Naph. 8.4: ὁ διάβολος φεύξεται ἀφ' ὑμῶν
- Jas 4.11: μὴ καταλαλεῖτε ἀλλήλων; cf. T. Iss. 3.4: οὐ κατελάλησά τινος; T. Gad 5.4: οὐ καταλαλεῖ ἀνδρός
- Jas 5.7: ἕως τῆς παρουσίας τοῦ κυρίου; cf. T. Jud. 22.2: ἕως παρουσίας τοῦ θεοῦ
- Jas 5.16: ἐξομολογεῖσθε...τὰς ἁμαρτίας; cf. T. Gad 2.1: ὁμολογῶ νῦν τὴν ἁμαρτίαν
- Jas 5.19-20: πλανηθῇ...ἐπιστρέψῃ...ἐπιστρέψας...πλάνης; cf. T. Zeb. 9.7-8: πλάνης...πλάνης...ἐπιστρέψει

Dibelius, 27, speaks for most students of James: 'a relationship of direct literary dependence cannot be deduced'. The lesson is the same as with Philo: the parallels are a measure of the common debt to Hellenistic Judaism.

(iii) James, it has been rightly said, 'is "multicultural". It unites early Christian traditions with popular Hellenistic philosophy and Greek rhetoric.'[300] In line with this, the present commentary is full not only of

---

[299] For longer lists see Mayor, xcviii-cxix; Johnson, 43-46.
[300] So Fay, 'Weisheit', 414.

parallels to Jewish and Christian sources but also to Graeco-Roman texts, above all Plutarch and Epictetus. It appears that James, like the author of Ps.-Phocylides, was open to Greek ideas so long as they could be assimilated to his Jewish-Christian tradition.

But how did he come by such ideas? The striking parallels that Graeco-Roman sources supply for 1.13 (the perfect goodness of God), 21 ('the implanted word'); 3.1-12 (the dangers of the tongue) and 6 (τὸν τροχὸν τῆς γενέσεως) have their close relatives in Philo and other Jewish writers, so we need not go beyond Judaism to account for a knowledge of them; and in view of his deep dependence upon the LXX, Jewish exegetical traditions, the sayings of Jesus, and early Christian tradition, one could insist that James' debt to secular currents of thought, including diatribe and Stoicism, were largely mediated through Jewish and/or Christian circles.

Perhaps that is the truth. But there are hints that our author had something more than a Jewish education, even though he can by no means be considered an ἀνὴρ λόγιος (Acts 18.24). His writing style, despite the relatively short sentences,[301] is not unaccomplished.[302] He seemingly attempts to construct a hexameter in 1.17, and he occasionally uses literary words (ἀποκυέω in 1.15, 18; ἔμφυτος in 1.21; κατήφεια in 4.9). Indeed, Classical forms appear in 1.6 and 23 (ἔοικεν), 3.10 (the impersonal imperfect χρή), and 5.12 (ὀμνύω + accusative for that by which one swears). Moreover, the twofold use of ἄγε νῦν in 4.13 and 5.1 is very suggestive. The idiom is not attested in Jewish sources or in Christian texts uninfluenced by James. It does, however, appear several times in Homer (e.g. *Il.* 19.108; *Od.* 12.298; 18.55)—the staple of all Greek education—and in other Classical sources as well; see on 4.13.

(iv) Few commentators fail to recognize James' recurrent dependence upon the Jesus tradition.[303] They disagree, however, on the extent of that dependence.[304] This commentator inclines to think that James probably knew at least the following synoptic logia:

Sayings found in Q
- Mt 5.3 = Lk 6.20   see on Jas 2.5
- Mt 5.11-12 = Lk 6.22-23   see on Jas 1.2; cf. 1.12
- Mt 7.1-5 = Lk 6.37, 41-42   see on Jas 4.11-12

---

[301] Note Mayor, 118: James 'never doubles the relative, never uses genitive absolutes, does not accumulate prepositions, or use the epexegetic infinitive—in a word, never allows his principle sentence to be lost in the rank luxuriance of the subordinate clauses'.

[302] See esp. Mayor, ccvi-ccxxxix (on 'the grammar of James'); Amphoux, 'Description'; idem, 'Langue'. Note e.g. James' proper use of participles (Mayor, ccxxxi-ccxxxii).

[303] The exceptions are those who argue that James is a lightly retouched Jewish text.

[304] The two most important surveys remain Deppe, *Sayings*, and Hartin, *Q*. The list of 65 parallel sayings in Mayor, lxxxvii-cv, represents the case for maximal dependence. Davids, 'Jesus', 66-67, also supplies a long list (47 entries). For a more modest catalogue see Hartin, *Q*, 141-42.

- Mt 7.24-27 = Lk 6.47-49   see on Jas 1.22-23
- Mt 7.7-11 = Lk 11.9-13   see on Jas 1.5, 17; 4.3
- Mt 6.19-21 = Lk 12.33-34   see on Jas 5.1-3

Saying found in Mark and Matthew
- Mk 11.23 = Mt 21.21   see on Jas 1.6

Saying found only in Matthew
- Mt 5.33-37   see on Jas 5.12

Sayings found only in Luke
- Lk 6.24   see on Jas 5.1-3
- Lk 6.25   see on Jas 4.9; 5.1

Readers are directed to the relevant sections for discussion. Here, several observations need to be appended. (a) A list such as this does not indicate the extent of our author's knowledge of the Jesus tradition. It necessarily includes only such sayings that seemingly entered our author's mind as he addressed a limited range of subjects. It would be foolish to imagine that James managed, in such a short letter, to draw upon all or even most of the logia that he knew. (b) The preceding list excludes the many places where James has often reminded readers of the gospels, yet the evidence falls short of establishing dependence.[305] In such cases, our inability to make a strong case does not exclude the possibility of influence.

(c) Just as James can rewrite the LXX in his own words (see e.g. on 3.7-9), so can he rewrite sayings of Jesus.[306] Indeed, with the exception of 5.12 = Mt 5.33-37, emulating logia without reproducing them is characteristic of him.[307] The circumstance is both encouraging and discouraging for attempts to discern the degree of James' debt to the Jesus tradition. It is encouraging because we know that there can be dependence upon tradition even when the verbal links are minimal. It follows that it would be unwise to object that a line in James draws upon a particular saying attributed to Jesus simply because few if any words are shared. At the same time, the presence of *aemulatio* is discouraging, for it can make intertextual judgments more difficult: if an author is deliberately not reproducing his sources but rather creatively rewriting them for his own ends, it may not be so easy to decide when to attribute parallels to design and when to give coincidence its due.

---

[305] See e.g. the commentary on 3.1, which has a close parallel in Mk 12.40, or on 3.12, where the possibility of the influence of Mt 7.18-18; 12.33-35 = Lk 6.43-45 is considered, or on 4.10, where the relationship to Mt 23.12 = Lk 14.11 is discussed.

[306] See esp. Bauckham, *Brother*, 74-111; Kloppenborg, 'Reception'; idem, 'Emulation'.

[307] One is reminded that the author of Revelation alludes to and reformulates scripture without ever formally quoting it.

(d) If we are investigating influence rather than attempting to detect allusions, we should not confine ourselves to asking whether a certain verse in James draws upon a certain saying attributed to Jesus. Our epistle exhibits a number of strong thematic parallels with the Jesus tradition.[308] Both for instance emphasize the goodness of God the Father, the peril of wealth, the importance of doing as opposed to hearing only, the exclusivity of divine allegiance, the piety of the poor, the priority of love, the danger of anger, the call to perseverance and joy in trial, the prospect of eschatological reversal, the priority of mercy over judgment, and the nearness of the end. It is reasonable to infer, given such correlations and what we otherwise know of James' knowledge of sayings attributed to Jesus, that the broader themes of the Jesus tradition influenced his thinking.

Beyond that, our epistle likely reflects the Jesus tradition even in some of its idioms and literary forms.[309] For example, the τίς σοφὸς καὶ ἐπιστήμων ἐν ὑμῶν of 3.13, the ὅπου γὰρ ζῆλος καὶ ἐριθεία, ἐκεῖ ἀκαταστασία καὶ πᾶν φαῦλον πρᾶγμα of 3.16, and the ἡ παρουσία τοῦ κυρίου ἤγγικεν of 5.8 employ language that mirrors the Jesus tradition.[310] James, moreover, like the Synoptic Jesus, employs aphoristic formulations, synonymous parallelism, and similitudes. In short, our text reflects not only individual sentences from the Jesus tradition but also some of its themes, literary forms, and modes of speech.

(e) It is unclear whether our author hoped or took for granted that all his readers would recognize the source of his materials and so appreciate his creative revisions. To borrow is one thing; to want to be seen borrowing is another. James never bothers to signal explicitly that this or that line draws upon this or that saying of Jesus. Why not write, in 5.12, 'Above all, my brothers, remember what our Lord Jesus commanded: Do not swear by heaven nor by earth nor with any other oath, but let your Yes be Yes and your No No, lest you fall under judgment'? Or why not write, in Jas 2.5, 'Listen, my beloved brothers: As our Lord Jesus taught, has not God chosen the poor in the world to be rich in faith and heirs of the kingdom which he promised to those who love him'? A twofold explanation suggests itself.

On the one hand, formal citations typically call attention to themselves for the purpose of adding authority.[311] Since *paraenesis*, by contrast, is

---

[308] For succinct lists see Chaine, lxiv, lxviii-lxix. For discussion see Hoppe, *Hintergrund*, 119-48; Hartin, *Q*, 140-217; Bauckham, *Brother*, 93-108; Penner, *Eschatology*, 241-53; Niebuhr, 'Ethik'.

[309] For idioms see Schlatter, 19-21; Allison, 'Audience'. For literary forms see Bauckham, *Brother*, 35-60.

[310] See the commentary on 3.13, 16; and 5.8.

[311] This explains why Philippians, Colossians, 1 Thessalonians, 2 Thessalonians, and Philemon contain no formal citations whereas the six chapters of Galatians contain ten such citations, and why Romans, with its 16 chapters, has 48. Paul strongly tends to quote Scripture explicitly in polemical situations in which his opponents also appeal to Scripture. Otherwise he can allude.

not argument but exhortation, sources are not usually cited.[312] Moreover, the implicit can serve positive rhetorical functions within the context of shared community discourse: individuals are encouraged to fill in the blanks and thus to appreciate an author's artistic reformulations of traditional materials.[313]

On the other hand, James poses as an address to the Jewish diaspora in its entirety, a group that, while it would include Jewish Christians, would also include others; so the failure to attribute material to Jesus is likely of a piece with the general failure, aside from the self-designation in 1.1, to be explicitly Christian about anything. That is, our text does not appeal to Jesus as an authority because Jesus was not an authority for all of the envisaged audience.

(f) The dominant opinion in current scholarship is that James did not know any of the extant written gospels. He was rather familiar with oral tradition, with written Q, or with a developing form of Q allied to Matthean tradition.[314] But the issue is far from closed. James shows overlap particularly with Matthew; and if the epistle was written in the first third of the second century, there might be as much as thirty years between James and Matthew, the latter being dated by one authority to 'not long after the year 80'.[315] Given what we know about the lines of communication among even distant churches of that period,[316] thirty years—a span greater than that between the composition of Matthew and Mark—is considerable time to pass without James becoming aware of Matthew. Further, other texts from the first part of the second century seem to betray a knowledge of the First Gospel. Luz at least detects Matthean influence in Ignatius and Polycarp as well as in the Didache and maybe 1 Peter.[317] To which one can add Papias as well as the Gospels

---

[312] Cf. S. Kim, 'Jesus, Sayings of', in G.F. Hawthorne, R.P. Martin, and D.G. Reid, eds., *Dictionary of Paul and His Letters*, Downers Grove, IL, 1993, 489.

[313] Cf. Kloppenborg, 'Reception', 141. Some have raised the possibility that James knew the sayings of Jesus as *paraenesis*, not as sayings of Jesus; cf. Klein, *Werk*, 196-97. In that case, obviously, one could not think of conscious allusions to the Jesus tradition.

[314] For the thesis of dependence upon oral tradition see Davids, 'Jesus'; H. Koester, *Ancient Christian Gospels*, London, 1990, 71-73; Johnson, 55-57; Wachob, *Voice*, 142; McCartney, 51-52. For the thesis that James reflects the influence of the written Q see Kloppenborg, *Gospel*, 111-20. His case depends largely upon James taking Q 11.9-10 to be about prayer, an interpretation which Kloppenborg assigns to Q redaction. Hartin, *Q*, emphasizes contact between James and the form of Q known to Matthew. Contrast Streeter, *Church*, 200: James 'read Q in the recension known to Luke'. For the thesis that the author himself drew upon first person memories of hearing Jesus see 7 n. 32.

[315] Luz, *Matthew 1–7*, 59.

[316] See M.B. Thompson, 'The Holy Internet', in *The Gospels for All Christians*, ed. R. Bauckham, Grand Rapids, MI, 1998, 49-70. Although Thompson concerns himself with the period, CE 30–70, there is no reason to imagine that circumstances were, in the relevant respects, much different during the following decades.

[317] Luz, *Matthew 1–7*, 58-59. His opinion is not idiosyncratic. According to P. Foster, 'The Epistles of Ignatius of Antioch and the Writings that Later Formed the New

of the Nazoraeans and of the Ebionites.[318] So one wonders whether James, who also wrote in the same general period as these witnesses to Matthew, can have been so isolated. Would not someone as indebted to the Jesus tradition as he have been interested in a large Gospel that was making the rounds and already having an impact?[319] That James did not live in a Christian backwater appears from his knowledge of Pauline theology and his likely dependence upon one or more of Paul's epistles.[320]

Another cause for querying the consensus emerges from the work of Hartin, who has discussed at length the significant number of parallels between Matthew and James. His carefully argued conclusion is this: 'Not only does James show an awareness of the Q tradition, but he is also conscious of the way it developed within the Matthean community. James shows that he has emerged from a world which holds as sacred traditions that are common to the Gospel of Matthew. This perspective…places James in an intermediary position between Q and the Gospel of Matthew. This does not mean that Matthew utilized the Epistle of James or *vice versa*. The knowledge that James has of the traditions and sources that go into the Gospel of Matthew is such that the epistle situates itself before the codification of these sources took place within the Gospel of Matthew.'[321]

From one point of view, this conclusion makes sense: in several respects James is indeed especially close to materials found only in the First Gospel—for example, the prohibition of oaths (Jas 5.12; Mt 5.33-37) and the emphasis upon 'perfection' (Jas 1.4; 3.2; Mt 5.48; 19.21). There is an issue, however, with Hartin's view of the originating circumstances of the epistle. In his judgment, the brother of Jesus wrote James

---

Testament', in Gregory-Tuckett, *Reception*, 185, 'It is most likely that Ignatius knew Matthew's gospel'. According to P. Hartog, *Polycarp and the New Testament*, Tübingen, 2002, 195, Polycarp 'probably' knew Matthew. According to C.M. Tuckett, 'The Didache and the Writings that Later Formed the New Testament', in Gregory-Tuckett, *Reception*, 126, 'in some instances the Didache appears to reflect elements of Matthew's redactional activity, and hence to presuppose Matthew's finished gospel rather than just Matthew's traditions'. Metzner, *Rezeption*, 283, contends that 1 Peter presupposes Matthew.

[318] For Papias see Eusebius, *H.E.* 3.39.16. One should also not forget that there appears to have been a harmony of the Synoptics or at least of Matthew and Luke before the middle of the second century; see A.J. Bellinzoni, *The Sayings of Jesus in the Writings of Justin Martyr*, Leiden, 1967.

[319] For the argument that James knew Matthew see Shepherd, 'Matthew' (Matthew was known to the church of James but he did not have a copy as he wrote); Gryglewicz, 'Matthieu'; Bottini, *Introduzione*, 116-24. For the argument to the contrary see Deppe, *Sayings*, 150-66. The resemblances between Matthew and James might inform the myth that Matthew and James were brothers, both being sons of Alphaeus; cf. Stanley, *Sermons*, 291.

[320] See below, 62-67.

[321] Hartin, *Q*, 242-43.

during the latter half of the 50s.³²² Given this, it is credible for him to propose that James is a witness to the Q tradition as it was developing before the publication of Matthew.

What happens, however, if one does not share Hartin's judgment about authorship, and especially if one dates James to the second century? How likely is it that a second-century source would be a witness to a pre-Matthean, mid-first-century state of affairs?³²³

Another consideration giving pause for thought arises out of Jas 2.5: ἀκούσατε, ἀδελφοί μου, ἀγαπητοί· οὐχ ὁ θεὸς ἐξελέξατο τοὺς πτωχοὺς τῷ κόσμῳ πλουσίους ἐν πίστει καὶ κληρονόμους τῆς βασιλείας ἧς ἐπηγγείλατο τοῖς ἀγαπῶσιν αὐτόν; These words likely borrow from a beatitude of Jesus, Mt 5.3 = Lk 6.20.³²⁴ πτωχός is nowhere associated with βασιλεία before Matthew and Luke, and that James uses βασιλεία only here is consistent with his line coming from tradition.

One could urge that James here shows a knowledge of Q or perhaps an independent oral tradition as opposed to Matthew, because James lacks two obviously redactional features of Matthew—τῷ πνεύματι and τῶν οὐρανῶν. The problem with this is that if one looks at the context of Mt 5.3, another parallel to James surfaces. Matthew 5.5—without parallel in Luke—has this: μακάριοι οἱ πραεῖς ὅτι αὐτοὶ κληρονομήσουσιν τὴν γῆν. This line, which reads like an explication of v. 3, may originally have immediately followed it.³²⁵ But whatever one makes of the text-critical issue, we find in Matthew, in a short space, πτωχός, βασιλεία, and the κληρονομ- root; and Jas 2.5 offers us the very same conjunction. Furthermore, the appearance of πτωχός, βασιλεία, and κληρονομ- within the space of four lines or fewer occurs nowhere in Jewish or secular Greek literature. Its first occurrence is in Matthew and then James. After that, all subsequent sources with this combination, beginning with Clement of Alexandria and Origen, are familiar with Matthew's Gospel. In other words, if James did not know Matthew, his use of πτωχός, βασιλεία, and κληρονομ- in close succession becomes the only instance of that concurrence in all of Greek literature not dependent upon the First Gospel. So once more one is moved to ponder the relationship of Matthew and James and to ask whether the latter betrays knowledge of the Gospel. If one believes that Matthew predates James by two or three decades, it is not so clear why we should decline to see a literary relationship.³²⁶

The hypothesis that James knew Matthew is a real possibility. It neatly accounts at a stroke for most of the Jesus tradition in our epistle. But it remains just that, a hypothesis. We have only hints, nothing approaching

---

³²² Hartin, *Q*, 240.

³²³ Another problem is Hartin's view that Q^Mt and Q^Lk differed considerably, but that is a large topic in itself which cannot be entered into here.

³²⁴ See the commentary on 2.5.

³²⁵ Some witnesses, including 05 33 S:C Or Eus, put v. 5 before v. 4.

³²⁶ On the issue of the relationship between Jas 5.12 and Mt 5.33-37 see, in addition to the commentary below, Allison, 'Audience'.

proof. Moreover, even if James did use Matthew, the latter may not have been his only source for the Jesus tradition. He may in addition have known oral materials related to Luke or perhaps even Luke itself, given that 5.17 agrees with Lk 4.25 (Elijah's prayer resulted in a three-and-a-half year drought) and that a couple of verses in James show correlations with the (redactional?) Lukan woes.[327]

(iv) James' dependence upon Christian tradition—beyond the Jesus tradition—is evident in many places, from 'the Lord Jesus Christ' in 1.1 to the final section, 5.13-20, which likely draws from a very early church order. Beyond that, however, many have supposed that our letter draws upon more than Christian oral tradition, that it indeed shows a knowledge of Christian texts known to us.

(a) Perhaps most have doubted that James knew any of the Pauline epistles, even scholars who have thought of him as responding to Pauline theology.[328] Others, however, have disagreed.[329] What are the relevant considerations?

If James belongs to the beginning of the second century, familiarity with some of Paul's correspondence would not be unlikely. Clement of Rome, presumably writing around the same time as James or before, already knew 1 Corinthians and in all probability Romans.[330] Not long thereafter, Ignatius made use of 1 Corinthians and seemingly Ephesians,

---

[327] See the commentary on Jas 4.9 (which resembles Lk 6.25) and on 5.1 (which resembles Lk 6.24). Cf. Aland, 'Herrenbruder', 99-100, 104; Bottini, *Introduzione*, 129-38. Contrast Shepherd, 'Matthew', 44; Deppe, *Sayings*, 150-66. If James did know Luke, then he may also have known Acts.

[328] Probably most see no literary relationship between James and Paul; so e.g. all of those who date James to the 40s or early 50s as well as Credner, *Einleitung*, 604-605; Gloag, *Introduction*, 85-87; Dibelius, 29-30; Polhill, 'Situation', 372-73; G. Strecker, *Theology of the New Testament*, Berlin, 2000, 674; Puech, 'Qumrân'.

[329] Scholars who believe that James knew one or more of the Pauline epistles include Wettstein, 659; de Wette, *Introduction*, 331 (probably Romans and Galatians); Hug, *Introduction*, 555-56 (Romans); Baur, *Paul*, 308-309; Pfleiderer, *Christianity*, 541 (the 'principal Pauline epistles'); Bleek, *Introduction*, 145; Brückner, 'Kritik'; idem, *Reihenfolge*, 287-95; Bartmann, *Paulus*, 151-59 (no doubt about Romans and Galatians); von Soden, 159 (Romans and probably 1 Corinthians); Hollmann-Bousset, 220 (Romans); J. Weiss, *Christianity*, 2.749 (Romans at least); Bonsirven, 'Jacques', 788 (Romans and Galatians); Cone, 268-69 (Romans, probably 1 Corinthians); Henshaw, *Literature*, 355; Bindemann, 'Weisheit'; Klein, *Werk*, 197-204 (Romans and 1 Corinthians); Sato, 'Brief', 67-68 (Romans and Galatians); Ludwig, *Wort*, 193 (Romans and Galatians); Bottini, *Introduzione*, 61-92 (Romans and Galatians, maybe 1 and 2 Corinthians, Philippians, 1 Thessalonians); Avemarie, 'Werke' (James used Romans); Nienhuis, *Paul*, 113-17, 163-31; Rolland, 'Dialogue' (James knew 1 Corinthians but Paul knew James when he wrote Romans). For Popkes, 39, James may have known a few Pauline 'Kerntexten', but only through oral tradition or mediated through other texts. Much less common is the view that Paul knew and used James; cf. Spitta, 202-24; Mayor, xci-cii.

[330] See A.F. Gregory, '1 Clement and the Writings that Later Formed the New Testament', in Gregory-Tuckett, *Reception*, 129-57.

1 Timothy, and 2 Timothy.³³¹ And Polycarp's sole surviving letter shows familiarity with 1 Corinthians, Ephesians, 1 Timothy, and 2 Timothy and maybe also Romans, Galatians, and Philippians.³³²

How does it stand with James? As observed in the commentary on 2.14-26, there are several very striking linguistic parallels between James and Paul: δικαιόω + ἐκ, ἐξ ἔργων, δικαιόω + ἐξ ἔργων, ἄνθρωπος/ν + a passive form of δικαιόω, ἐκ πίστεως, χωρὶς (τῶν) ἔργων. Yet all of these items appear in Rom 3.28 ('justified by faith apart from works of the law') and/or Gal 2.16 ('not justified by works of the law but through faith in Jesus Christ') and/or in the near vicinity of those verses. The agreement between Rom 3.28 and Gal 2.16 implies that we have here a standard Pauline formulation.³³³ So these phrases do not of themselves entail dependence upon either Romans or Galatians. One can just as readily think of an oral version of a well-known Pauline formulation, a formulation that was associated with Gen 15.6 as its proof text.³³⁴

But to reckon with that possibility scarcely closes the matter. There is more to consider. (1) Jas 2.14-26 and its immediate context share, beyond the parallels already noted, two 'minor agreements' with Romans. First, Jas 2.19 observes that James' opponent does well to believe that God is one (εἷς ἐστιν ὁ θεός), although the demons believe the same. This is of interest because the discussion of Abraham, faith, deeds, and justification in Rom 4 is preceded by reference to God's oneness or unity (3.30: εἷς ὁ θεός) while the discussion of those themes in Gal 3 is followed by the remark that 'God is one' (3.20: ὁ δὲ θεὸς εἷς ἐστιν ὁ θεός). One has to wonder whether James thought of Deut 6.4 because of an association in the Pauline material.³³⁵

Second, Jas 2.12 contains this phrase: ὡς διὰ νόμου ἐλευθερίας μέλλοντες κρίνεσθαι. Although Ecclus 46.14 (ἐν νόμῳ κυρίου ἔκρινεν); Jn 7.51 (ὁ νόμος...κρινεῖ); 18.31 (κατὰ τὸν νόμον...κρίνατε); Acts 23.13

---

³³¹ See P. Foster, 'The Epistles of Ignatius of Antioch and the Writings that Later Formed the New Testament', in Gregory-Tuckett, *Reception*, 159-86.

³³² See M.W. Holmes, 'Polycarp's *Letter to the Philippians* and the Writings that Later Formed the New Testament', in Gregory-Tuckett, *Reception*, 187-227. Some have also argued that Luke knew some of Paul's correspondence; see e.g. M.D. Goulder, *Luke*, vol. 1, Sheffield, 1989, 129-46; H. Leppä, 'Luke's Critical Use of Galatians', Academic Dissertation, University of Helsinki, 2002.

³³³ Cf. Dunn, *Romans 1–8*, 187: in Rom 3.28, 'as in 3:20, the train of thought comes so close to that of Paul's argument in Galatians that the phrasing of the earlier letter [see esp. Gal 2.16] is closely reproduced... Since it was also Gal 2:16 which was paralleled in 3:20, and since Paul was hardly writing Romans with a copy of Galatians to hand, the obvious conclusion is that the theological assertions formulated in Gal 2:16 were a fundamental part of Paul's understanding of the gospel, and fundamental in these terms.'

³³⁴ Cf. Rom 4.3; Gal 3.6. This incidentally reinforces the case that James responds to Paul: the striking overlap is with a generalizing statement that occurs in both Galatians and Romans, a statement near the heart of Paul's theology, one for which he was likely well-known.

³³⁵ Cf. Tsuji, *Glaube*, 192.

(κρίνων...κατὰ τὸν νόμον); and Demosthenes, *Arist.* 2 (κατὰ τοὺς νόμους κρῖναι) supply parallels, and although διὰ τοῦ νόμου appears in the LXX,[336] διὰ νόμου (without the article) occurs first in extant Greek literature in Paul. Moreover, given that he uses the expression six times and that, in Rom 2.12, he follows it with κριθήσονται, the parallel with Jas 2.12 is suggestive.

(2) James 2.18 is an expositor's nightmare. One cannot decide with any confidence whether the speaker is friend or foe or determine to whom the pronouns refer or divine how far the quoted material extends or answers any number of other issues crucial for interpretation. My own view is that nobody has yet successfully explained this verse, and I have reluctantly concluded that the text is corrupt, the original beyond recovery,[337] or that James expressed himself so poorly that we cannot offer any clear exposition of his thought.

One thing, however, is undeniable. The phrase, σὺ πίστον ἔχεις κἀγὼ ἔργα ἔχω, has reminded many of 1 Cor 12.8-9. In the latter, different individuals have different gifts. One of those gifts is faith, and another is a gift that features the ἐργ- root (ἑτέρῳ πίστις...ἄλλῳ δὲ ἐνεργήματα δυνάμεων). It is tempting to suppose that Ropes saw the truth here: James has heard of Paul's ideas about diversity in the church.[338] Might one go beyond that and entertain the possibility that James knew 1 Corinthians in particular?

(3) Mitchell has recently returned a positive answer to this question. She has compiled a long list of parallels between James and 1 Corinthians[339]—common phrases,[340] similar sentences,[341] shared terms for factionalism,[342] and identical *topoi*.[343]

---

[336] 2 Macc 2.18; Ecclus prol. 1; cf. Let. Aris. 122.

[337] If one judges James to oppose Paul, then it is possible that our text originally named the apostle and that later theological sensibility removed his name.

[338] Ropes, 'Faith', 553, 555.

[339] Mitchell, 'Document', 89-92.

[340] εἴ τις δοκεῖ + εἶναι (Jas 1.26; 1 Cor 3.18; 11.16; 14.37); τί τὸ ὄφελος (Jas 2.14, 16; 1 Cor 15.32); μὴ πλανᾶσθε (Jas 1.16; 1 Cor 6.9; 15.33).

[341] (i) 'Such a one has stood the test and will receive the crown (δόκιμος γενόμενος λήμψεται τὸν στέφανον) of life that the Lord has promised to those who love him (ἀγαπῶσιν αὐτόν)' (Jas 1.12); 'Athletes exercise self-control in all things; they do it to receive a perishable crown (στέφανον λάβωσιν), but we an imperishable one... But I punish my body and enslave it, so that after proclaiming to others I myself should not be disqualified (ἀδόκιμος γένωμαι)' (1 Cor 9.25-27); 'God has prepared for those who love him (ἀγαπῶσιν αὐτόν)' (1 Cor 2.9); (ii) 'Has not God chosen (ὁ θεὸς ἐξελέξατο) the poor in the world (τῷ κόσμῳ) to be rich in faith and to be heirs of the kingdom (κληρονόμους τῆς βασιλείας) that he has promised to those who love him (ἀγαπῶσιν αὐτόν)?' (Jas 2.5); 'But God chose what is foolish in the world (τοῦ κόσμου ἐξελέξατο ὁ θεός) to shame the wise; God chose what is weak in the world (τοῦ κόσμου ἐξελέξατο ὁ θεός) to shame the strong; God chose what is low and despised in the world (τοῦ κόσμου...ἐξελέξατο ὁ θεός), things that are not, to reduce to nothing things that are, so that no one might boast in the presence of God' (1 Cor 1.27-28); 'Do you not know that wrongdoers will not inherit the kingdom of God (βασιλείαν οὐ κληρονομήσουσιν)?' (1 Cor 6.9); 'God has

INTRODUCTION 65

Most of Mitchell's correlations are of uncertain or little value. τί τό ὄφελος, for example, occurs repeatedly in Epictetus and was characteristic of diatribe; and Philo and early Christian writers besides Paul also use the expression, which likewise has a precise Hebrew equivalent, מה־בצע.[344] Again, we may have enough evidence to infer that μὴ πλανᾶσθε was a conventional way of introducing a pointed assertion.[345] As for the similar sentences, common terms for factionalism, and shared *topoi*, the vast majority of them fail to intimate literary dependence, although perhaps their very number is suggestive.

Two of Mitchell's correlations, however, are not so easily dismissed. First, the construction, εἴ τις δοκεῖ + nominative adjective + εἶναι, appears nowhere in extant Greek writings until Paul and James. In subsequent literature, it occurs only in writers familiar with the NT, beginning with Origen. Second, the similarity between Jas 3.15-16 and 1 Cor 2.14-3.3 is indeed striking:[346]

Jas 3.15-16	ψυχική...	ὅπου γάρ	ζῆλος καὶ ἐριθεία
1 Cor 2.14–3.3	ψυχικός...	ὅπου γὰρ ἐν ὑμῖν	ζῆλος καὶ ἔρις

Mitchell also observes that the ἀκαταστασία of Jas 3.15-16 has its parallel in 1 Cor 14.33, to which one may add: in both places it stands in antithesis to εἰρήνη.

---

prepared for those who love him (ἀγαπῶσιν αὐτόν)' (1 Cor 2.9); (iii) 'Such wisdom does not come down from above, but is earthly, unspiritual (ψυχική), devilish. For where there is envy and selfish ambition (ὅπου γὰρ ζῆλος καὶ ἐριθεία), there will also be disorder (ἀκαταστασία) and wickedness of every kind' (Jas 3.15-16); 'The unspiritual (ψυχικός) man does not receive the gifts of God's Spirit, for they are foolishness to him, and he is unable to understand... For you are still of the flesh. For as long as there is jealousy and quarrelling among you (ὅπου γὰρ ἐν ὑμῖν ζῆλος καὶ ἔρις), are you not of the flesh, and behaving according to human inclinations?' (1 Cor 2.14–3.3); 'God is a God not of disorder (ἀκαταστασίας) but of peace' (1 Cor 14.33).

[342] ἀκαταστασία/ἀκατάστασος (1 Cor 14.33; Jas 1.8; 3.16); ζῆλος conjoined with ἔρις/ἐριθεία (1 Cor 3.3; Jas 3.14, 16); ζηλοῦσθαι (1 Cor 13.4; cf. 12.31; 14.1, 39; Jas 4.2); ψυχικός (1 Cor 2.14; 15.44, 46; Jas 3.15); μέλος (1 Cor 6.5; 12.12, 14, 18, 19, 20, 22, 25, 26, 27; Jas 3.5, 6; 4.1); (κατα)καυχᾶσθαι (1 Cor 1.29, 31; 3.21; 4.7; 13.3; Jas 1.9; 2.13; 3.14; 4.16); κενή (1 Cor 15.14, of πίστις; Jas 2.20 of a man with idle πίστις).

[343] The body and its members used for individuals and the corporate entity, one member or the other singled out for its relation to the health of the whole (1 Cor 6.15-20; 12.12-13; Jas 3.5-6; 4.1); factional strife related to the wisdom of 'this world', which is the antithesis of spiritual wisdom (1 Cor 1.18–4.21; Jas 3.13–4.12); criticism of bad boasts (1 Cor 5.6; Jas 4.16; etc.); importance of keeping eyes on eschatological reward (1 Cor 9.24-27; Jas 1.12; 3.1; 5.1-8); judging leads to strife; cognizance of the eschatological judgment will reduce strife (1 Cor 4.1-5; Jas 4.11-12).

[344] For all of this see below, on 2.14.

[345] See below, on 1.16.

[346] Which is why they have often been paired; cf. Gregory Palamas, *Heysch*. 1.1.9 ed. Meyendorff, 31, and the commentary tradition on James.

(4) Not only do the vocabulary and subject matter of Jas 2.14-24 have striking parallels in the vocabulary and subject matter of Rom 3-4, but the argument unfolds in the same way:[347]

- Issue posed in terms of faith and works   Rom 3.27-28   Jas 2.14-18
- Significance of claiming 'God is one'   Rom 3.29-30   Jas 2.19
- Appeal to 'father' Abraham as authorized test case   Rom 4.1-2   Jas 2.20-22
- Citation of proof text, Gen 15.6   Rom 4.3   Jas 2.20-22
- Conflicting interpretations of proof text   Rom 4.4-21   Jas 2.23
- Conclusion of argument   Rom 4.22   Jas 2.24

This common sequence cannot be due to chance, and an explanation is to hand if James knew Romans.

(5) There is an intriguing parallel between Rom 7.23 and Jas 4.2. The former has ἀντιστρατεύομαι + ἐν τοῖς μέλεσιν, which appears to be Paul's innovation as it is unattested before him. The latter has the very similar στρατεύω + ἐν τοῖς μέλεσιν, which has no precedent before James. Beyond that, James immediately goes on to write, ἐπιθυμεῖτε καὶ οὐκ ἔχετε, and the commandment not to covet looms large in Rom 7 (vv. 7-8).

(6) Jas 1.22-25 resembles in several respects Rom 2.13:[348]

- Rom 2.13   οὐ γὰρ οἱ ἀκροαταὶ νόμου δίκαιοι… ἀλλ' οἱ ποιηταὶ νόμου…
- Jas 1.22   γίνεσθε δὲ ποιηταὶ λόγου καὶ μὴ μόνον ἀκροαταί
- Jas 1.23   ἀκροατὴς λόγου ἐστὶν καὶ οὐ ποιητής
- Jas 1.25   οὐκ ἀκροατής… ἀλλὰ ποιητὴς ἔργου

These are the earliest Greek texts to contrast ποιηταί (in the sense of 'doers') with ἀκροαταί. Furthermore, Paul's 'hearers of the law' and 'doers of the law' are equivalent to James' 'hearers of the word' and 'doers of the word', for in James, 'word' = 'law'. In addition, both James and Paul negate ἀκροαταί/ής with οὐ(κ) or μή, and both draw their contrast with ἀλλά. Note especially the correlation between Rom 2.13 and Jas 1.25:

Rom 2.13   οὐ… ἀκροαταί…   ἀλλ'…   ποιηταί + genitive singular ending in -ου
Jas 1.25   οὐκ ἀκροατής…   ἀλλὰ   ποιητής + genitive singular ending in -ου

(7) The argument in Jas 2.14-26 employs the second person direct address ('you'), and rhetorical features characteristic of diatribe enliven the paragraph throughout. Verses 14 and 18 quote an unnamed opponent.

---

[347] Dunn, *Romans 1–8*, 197; idem, *Beginning*, 1142-43; Nienhuis, *Paul*, 115-16.

[348] The commentators regularly note the parallel, beginning with Bede *ad loc*. CCSL 127 ed. Hurst, 192; cf. also Ep. ad Adolescentem 3 PLSup 1.1377; Philoxenus, *Disc.* 1 ed. Budge, 4. For Klein, *Werk*, 124, Jas 1.22-25 reads 'almost as a commentary on Rom 2.13'. He adds that the opposition between νόμον τελεῖτε and παραβάται νόμου in Jas 2.8-11 is also reminiscent of the context in Romans; cf. 2.25, 27.

Verse 20 rebukes that opponent with a derogatory vocative (ὦ ἄνθρωπε κενέ). And rhetorical questions abound (vv. 14, 15-16, 20, 21, 25). All this interests not only because Rom 1–4 and Galatians, just like Jas 2.14-26, feature the second person direct address ('you') and employ condescending vocatives (ὦ ἄνθρωπε: Rom 2.1, 3; 9.20; ὦ ἀνόητοι Γαλάται: Gal 3.1) but also because Paul's arguments about justification and faith are presented, at least in Romans, amid obvious elements from diatribe.[349] Would it not be entirely appropriate for an author to respond to an opponent by mimicking his opponent's style? One recalls an observation of Soards: whereas James, in contrast to Paul, generally favors the article with nouns, his style changes in 2.14-16: here several anarthrous nouns appear.[350] So maybe James imitates the rhetorical pose of his opponent even as he turns his phrases and arguments upside down. Knowledge of Romans and/or Galatians would readily explain that.

Where does all this lead? The evidence is insufficient to establish with great assurance that James knew Romans, 1 Corinthians, or Galatians.[351] We nonetheless have here an attractive hypothesis, one to which this writer inclines: James was—or perhaps some of his sources were[352]—more likely than not familiar with Romans and perhaps also with 1 Corinthians and/or Galatians.

(b) Luther believed that James knew 1 Peter.[353] The parallels between the two works are extensive. The most obvious and impressive are these:

- Address to diaspora: Jas 1.1 (διασπορᾷ); 1 Pet 1.1 (διασπορᾶς)
- Rejoicing in suffering: Jas 1.2 (πειρασμοῖς... ποικίλοις); 1 Pet 1.6-9 (ἐν ποικίλοις πειρασμοῖς)
- Proving of faith and perfection: Jas 1.3-4 (δοκίμιον ὑμῶν τῆς πίστεως, τέλειον, τέλειοι); 1 Pet 1.7-9 (τὸ δοκίμον ὑμῶν τῆς πίστεως, δοκιμαζομένου, τέλος)
- Use of Isa 40.6-8: Jas 1.10-11 (allusion with ἄνθος χόρτου, ἐξήρανεν τὸν χόρτον, τὸ ἄνθος αὐτοῦ ἐξέπεσεν); 1 Pet 1.24 (quotation with ἄνθος χόρτου, ἐξηράνθη ὁ χόρτος, τὸ ἄνθος ἐξέπεσεν)
- Birth through the divine word: Jas 1.18 (λόγῳ); 1 Pet 1.23 (διὰ λόγου)

---

[349] S.K. Stowers, *The Diatribe and Paul's Letter to the Romans*, Chico, CA, 1981; T. Schmeller, *Paulus und die 'Diatribe'*, Münster, 1987.

[350] Soards, 'Abraham', 24. For criticism see Penner, *Eschatology*, 66-67.

[351] With Lüdemann, *Paul*, 140-41, Jas 1.2-4 does not evince a clear knowledge of Rom 5.3-5. Against Lüdemann, *Paul*, 141-43, Jas 2.10 ('For whoever keeps the whole law but fails in one point has become guilty of all of it') is not sufficiently close to Gal 5.3 ('every man who receives circumcision... is bound to keep the whole law') to suggest literary dependence. The Jewish parallels are in the way of this; see on 2.10.

[352] Given how much of James is revised tradition, it is possible that 2.14-26 is in large measure a traditional anti-Pauline fragment or argument.

[353] M. Luther, 'Preface to the Epistles of St. James and St. Jude', in *Luther's Works*, vol. 35, ed. Bachmann, Philadelphia, 1960, 396. Bengel, 503, also appears to think this a possibility.

- Call to rid self of evil: Jas 1.21 (ἀποθέμενοι πᾶσαν...κακίας); 1 Pet 2.1 (ἀποθέμενοι... πᾶσαν κακίαν)
- Call to good conduct: Jas 3.13 (καλῆς ἀναστροφῆς τὰ ἔργα); 1 Pet 2.12 (τὴν ἀναστροφήν...καλήν...καλῶν ἔργων)
- Warning about desires at war with the self: Jas 4.1-2 (στρατευομένων... ἐπιθυμεῖτε); 1 Pet 2.11 (ἐπιθυμιῶν αἵτινες στρατεύονται)
- Quotation of LXX Prov 3.34: Jas 4.6; 1 Pet 5.5
- Command to resist the devil: Jas 4.7 (ἀντίστητε δὲ τῷ διαβόλῳ); 1 Pet 5.8-9 (διάβολος...ᾧ ἀντίστητε)
- Promise that God will exalt those who humble themselves: Jas 4.10 (ταπεινώθητε...ὑψώσει ὑμᾶς); 1 Pet 5.6 (ταπεινώθητε...ὑμᾶς ὑψώσῃ)
- Quotation of portion of Prov 10.12: Jas 5.20 (καλύψει πλῆθος ἁμαρτιῶν); 1 Pet 4.8 (καλύπτει πλῆθος ἁμαρτιῶν)

Scholars have differed over the implications of these data. Some, appealing to the use of common Christian tradition, have seen no need to posit literary dependence.[354] Others have urged that 1 Peter borrows from James.[355] Still others turn this around: the author of James knew and used 1 Peter.[356]

In this writer's judgment, a literary relationship is likely. Not only are the similarities in theme and vocabulary extensive, but the agreement in the order of the parallels just listed is arresting. If the relevant verses from James are numbered 1-12, the order in 1 Peter is this:

1   2   3   5   4   6   7   8   9   11   10   12

[354] So e.g. Alford, 109; Ropes, 22; Carrington, *Catechism*, 27-29; Dibelius, 30-31; Baasland, 189; Johnson, 54-55; Achtemeier, *1 Peter*, 20; Konradt, 'Brief'; idem, 'Context' (positing that James and 1 Peter develop a specifically Antiochean tradition); McCartney, 52-53.

[355] So e.g. Wettstein, 659; Credner, *Einleitung*, 606; Wiesinger, 14; Hilgenfeld, 'Brief', 29; Gloag, *Introduction*, 89-92; Zahn, *Introduction*, 133-34; Spitta, 183-202; Mayor, ci-cvii; Vowinckel, *Grundgedanken*, 33-47; Meinertz, *Verfasser*, 57-59; Knowling, xlvi; Parry, *Discussion*, 69-72; Rendall, *Christianity*, 96-100; Mayor, *Rätsel*, 72-82; Cadoux, *Thought*, 39-43; Cantinat, 263, 279; Schlatter, 67-73; Hengel, 'Polemik', 519 n. 26; Bottini, *Introduzione*, 159-77.

[356] So e.g. Brückner, 'Kritik', 533-36; idem, *Reihenfolge*, 60-65; H. Holtzmann, 'Zeitlage', 295-96; Pfleiderer, *Christianity*, 296; C. Bigg, *A Critical and Exegetical Commentary on the Epistles of St. Peter and St. Jude*, New York, 1901, 23; Cone, 268-69; Grafe, *Stellung*, 24-27; O.D. Foster, 'The Literary Relations of "The First Epistle of Peter"', in *Transactions of the Connecticut Academy of Arts and Sciences* 17 (1913), 517-18 (conclusive 'is the naturalness with which' the common materials 'occur in their respective contexts... The contextual connection is much better in 1 Peter and not unfrequently does it appear that the thought of James has been introduced at the suggestion of another'); Ferris, '1 Peter'; Moffatt, *Introduction*, 466; J.C. Wand, *The General Epistles of St. Peter and St. Jude*, London, 1934, 24-25; McNeile, *Introduction*, 211 ('It is probable that the general expression "the twelve tribes that are in the Diaspora" (Jas. i.1) is borrowed from the more specific geographical description in I Pet. i.1'); Nienhuis, *Paul*, 169-231. Popkes, 'Composition', 101, entertains the option that James knew 'abstracts from a source' also known to 1 Peter or 'abstracts directly from 1 Peter'.

The odds of this being due to chance are remote.[357] One could contend, as did Carrington, that both James and 1 Peter reproduce 'the same system of oral teaching, which was so given that one formula tended to bring up the next one in the mind by association'.[358] Carrington had in mind a primitive catechism. Yet positing such a catechism scarcely explains the common address to the diaspora (Jas 1.1; 1 Pet 1.1). That address belongs to another genre, that of the letter. It would not have been at home at the beginning of a catechism or collection of moral imperatives. Furthermore, James and 1 Peter both deploy three OT texts (Isa 40.6-7; Prov 3.34; 10.12) that the NT nowhere else quotes or alludes to, so how likely is it that they were present in a catechetical tradition that had wide circulation?

One is strongly inclined instead to infer that James borrowed from 1 Peter. (i) If, as we have seen, there are no more than uncertain hints of a knowledge of James before Origen, the story is very different for 1 Peter. Tertullian, who never cites or refers to James, quotes 1 Peter by name.[359] The same is also true of Clement of Alexandria and Irenaeus.[360] Earlier still, Polycarp knew and used the book,[361] as did Papias, at least according to Eusebius.[362] The author of 2 Peter also evidently knew 1 Peter.[363] So whereas we have no clear evidence of second-century Christians reading and borrowing from James, it is otherwise with 1 Peter; and all else being equal, is it not more likely that a popular work, which we know was exerting its influence, was the source for a lesser known work, which was not wielding such influence?

(ii) The allusion to Isa 40.6-7 in Jas 1.10-11 cannot be the source or at least the sole source for the quotation in 1 Pet 1.24-25, because Peter includes whole lines from Isaiah that James lacks. Moreover, 1 Peter, unlike James, retains Isaiah's original application to the word of God (Isa 40.8; cf. 40.5). James thus seems secondary vis-à-vis 1 Peter.[364]

(iii) In like fashion, while the non-LXX rendering of Prov 10.12 in 1 Peter could be the source for Jas 5.20, it cannot work the other way

---

[357] In general, the odds of twelve items in one list occurring in the same order as twelve items in another, with only two adjacent transpositions, is less than 1.0×10^{-7}. One could, however, reject this calculation by adding less impressive parallels to the list.

[358] Carrington, *Calendar*, 28.

[359] Tertullian, *Scorp.* 12, 14; *Or.* 20 CSEL 20 ed. Reifferscheid and Wissowa, 172, 177, 192.

[360] Clement of Alexandria, *Paed* 1.6.44.1 ed. Marcovich, 28; *Strom.* 3.11.75.1 GCS 52 ed. Stählin and Früchtel, 229; etc.; Irenaeus, *Haer.* 4.9.2; 16.5.

[361] So M.W. Holmes, 'Polycarp's *Letter to the Philippians* and the Writings that Later Formed the New Testament', in Gregory-Tuckett, *Reception*, 220-23 ('virtually certain').

[362] So Eusebius, *H.E.* 3.39.5.

[363] Note 2 Pet 3.1 ('My dear friends, this is now my second letter to you') and see R. Bauckham, *Jude, 2 Peter*, Waco, TX, 1983, 146-47, 285-86.

[364] So too Brückner, 'Kritik', 534-35; idem, *Reihenfolge*, 64. Contrast Feine, *Lehranschauungen*, 129.

around: the fuller version in 1 Peter (with ἀγάπη as the subject) reflects MT Prov 10.12.[365]

(iv) We have seen above, and independently of the present question, that James was likely written between 100 and 120. This matters because the date of 1 Peter appears to be earlier. Three recent commentators on 1 Peter have offered these judgments: the book was written 80–100, 'most likely in the earlier years of that range' (Achtemeier);[366] it appeared in 'the early period of Domitian (between 81 and 100)' (Feldmeier);[367] it was composed between 73 and 92 (Elliott).[368] If these scholars are right—taken together they suggest a date for 1 Peter in the 80s—and if the arguments for a late dating of James persuade, then 1 Peter was in circulation before James, and the direction of literary borrowing, if any, is settled.[369]

The inference that James drew upon 1 Peter has important interpretive implications. 1 Peter is full of explicitly christological elements. Yet when James mines the book, he manages to reproduce none of them. He does not see fit to speak of 'the resurrection of Jesus Christ from the dead' (1.4; cf. 3.1) or of 'the Spirit of Christ' (1.11) or of 'the precious blood of Christ' (1.16). Nor does he so much as allude to Christ's suffering (2.21-23; 4.1; 5.1) or his redemptive death (2.24; 3.18). Such disparity likely tells us something about James' purposes. Whatever he had in mind, his intent was not to edify Christians by recalling for them the salvific work of Jesus Christ. On the contrary, he appears to have deliberately excised christological elements from one of his major sources.

(c) A few scholars—mostly of the nineteenth century—have supposed that James knew Hebrews.[370] Their case has typically rested upon parallels between Jas 2.22-25 and Heb 11.8-12, 30-31. Both sections discuss the faith of Abraham and Rahab, and they share some similar phrases.[371] The linguistic parallels do not really amount to much, however, and the common appeal to Rahab does not suffice to establish a literary relationship.

---

[365] See further Brückner, 'Kritik', 536.
[366] Achtemeier, *1 Peter*, 43-50.
[367] R. Feldmeier, *The First Letter of Peter*, Waco, TX, 2008, 40.
[368] J.H. Elliott, *1 Peter*, New York, 2000, 134-38.
[369] Cf. Moffatt, *Introduction*, 338: 'if 1 P. is on other grounds put early, the dependence of Jas. naturally follows'.
[370] E.g. de Wette, 'Bemerkungen', 349-50; idem, *Introduction*, 331 (probably); Hug, *Introduction*, 557-59; F. Bleek, *Der Hebräerbrief*, Elberfeld, 1868, 89-90; Grimm, 'Einleitung', 387-88; Hilgenfeld, 'Brief', 27; H. Holtzmann, 'Zeitlage', 292-93; Pfleiderer, *Christianity*, 295; Brückner, 'Kritik', 537; idem, *Reihenfolge*, 291; von Soden, 159; Zimmer, 'Verhältnis', 499-501; Bacon, 'Faith'; Cone, 268-70. Contrast Bartmann, *Paulus*, 157; Gloag, *Introduction*, 88-89; Feine, *Lehranschauungen*, 122-25. Mayor, xcviii-xcix, cviii-cix, thinks that Hebrews presupposes James.
[371] For the common expressions see Mayor, xviii-xix.

(d) Perhaps worth considering is the argument of Nienhuis, that James borrowed from 1 John.[372] His case highlights the parallels between the epistolary conclusions (Jas 5.13-20; 1 Jn 5.13-21) and between Jas 2.14-17 and 1 Jn 3.16-18. The similarities between the two endings, to which Francis, 'Form', first called attention, are especially interesting.[373] Whereas Francis saw them as evidence for a conventional way to end a letter, Nienhuis reckons them to be signs of literary borrowing. If he is right about that—the question is open—he is also right about the direction of such borrowing if one accepts, as does this writer, a second-century date for James.

(f) A few older scholars found traces of Revelation in James.[374] The parallels, however, amount to no more than a few common expressions that cannot bear the weight of such an inference.[375]

A final note about the sources of James. It is wildly unlikely that all of James' major sources have come down to us. Most books written in antiquity perished, and many oral traditions were never written down in the first place. So the literary remains known to us can be only a portion of a much larger corpus. Thus James must rely upon Jewish and Christian traditions and texts in ways that we can never learn. One suspects, for example, that our author was not the first to formulate the line of reasoning in 2.14-26 but that he rather preserves a standard argument common in anti-Pauline circles.

IV. GENRE

The vast majority of Greek mss. include the word ἐπιστολή in the *inscriptio* or *subscriptio*. Those that do not either lack an inscription and/or subscription or have the simple ΙΑΚΩΒΟΥ (03 2344). So according to the Greek textual tradition, James is an epistle.[376] One should not take such unanimity for granted. The Greek mss. of the Testament of Abraham variously call the book a 'testament', a 'narrative', an 'account', an 'apocalypse', or a 'bios'.

Despite the textual unanimity regarding our work, the last two centuries have seen many scholars break with the past.[377] de Wette was

---

[372] Nienhuis, *Paul*, 198-203, 212-15. For extensive discussion of the parallels between James and 1 John see Vowinckel, *Grundgedanken*, 48-66.

[373] This helps explain why Chrysostom, *Ps* 118.132.4 PG 55.704, can attribute 1 Jn 3.18 to James.

[374] E.g. Hilgenfeld, 'Brief', 27; Zeller, 'Über Jak 1,12'; Grimm, 'Einleitung', 388; Brückner, 'Kritik', 537; Pfleiderer, *Christianity*, 296. Contrast Bartmann, *Paulus*, 157-58; Feine, *Lehranschauungen*, 131-33.

[375] Cf. Jas 1.12 with Rev 2.10; Jas 2.5 with Rev 2.9; Jas 5.9 with Rev 3.20. For additional parallels see Mayor, cix.

[376] In this commentary, 'letter' and 'epistle' are used interchangeably.

[377] For an overview of developments since Dibelius see Penner, 'Research', 267-72.

perhaps the first to have second thoughts about how to categorize James.[378] Later, Deissmann argued that it is not a genuine letter, that is, a private communication to a definite audience, but rather 'literature' intended for a large public: 'Its pages are inspired by no special motive; there is nothing whatever to be read between the lines; its words are of such general interest that they might, for the most part, stand in the Book of Wisdom, or the Imitation of Christ'.[379] Dibelius, 1-11, furthered the argument, claiming that 1.1 is the only epistolary element: James lacks an epistolary ending, it conveys no personal messages, and it reflects no 'epistolary situation'. Rather, its 108 verses, which contain 54 imperatives, should be classified as *paraenesis*: the work 'strings together admonitions of a general ethical content'.[380] Comparable then are portions of Paul's epistles,[381] Heb 13,[382] the Didache, and Barnabas. The three little treatises in 2.1–3.12 are not, for Dibelius, evidence to the contrary, for they, like the Mandates in Hermas, are enlarged applications of paraenetical sayings. So as with Hebrews and Barnabas, the epistolary framework is 'veneer', an affectation, of no great significance. James contains eclectic, unrelated sayings and paragraphs of exhortation addressed to Christians at large.

Although Dibelius' judgment has been very influential,[383] his analysis of James' genre as *paraenesis* has not been the sole alternative to the traditional categorization of our work as a letter. Many have claimed that James is, like 2 Clement, a sermon.[384] Other proposed classifications include 'diatribe',[385] 'ethical scrapbook',[386] 'midrash',[387] 'prophetic

---

[378] de Wette, *Introduction*, 323: James lacks 'genuine epistolary character'.

[379] Deissmann, *Studies*, 51-52. For Deissmann, James is not a letter like Romans—a communication for a particular occasion with a particular end in view—but an 'epistle', a letter-like appeal to a broad audience with broad aims.

[380] Cf. already Aretius, 470, in the sixteenth century: 'Principale genus est exhortatorium'. Note also Baumgarten, 6.

[381] Rom 12–13; Gal 5.13–6.10; Col 3–4; 1 Thess 4.1-12; 5.1-22.

[382] Hebrews is the opposite of James in that it has an epistolary conclusion but no epistolary opening.

[383] Cf. Wikenhauser, *Introduction*, 476; Cantinat, 14-16; Vielhauer, *Geschichte*, 571-73; Schrage, 6; Songer, 'Introduction', 362-64; Cantinat, 14-16; Bottini, *Introduzione*, 231-43; Fabris, 11-13.

[384] So e.g. Feine, *Lehranschauungen*, 95-96; Jülicher, *Einleitung*, 203 (a sort of 'Busspredigt'); J. Weiss, *Christianity*, 2.744; Meyer, *Rätsel*, 300 (originally a Jewish synagogue sermon); Moffatt, 1-4; Findlay, *Way*, 159 (five sermon outlines); Leconte, 10; Cabaniss, 'Homily' (a homily addressed to different groups: 1.2-27 to bishops, 2.1-26 to deacons, 3.1-18 to teachers, 4.1-10 to widows, 4.11–5.12 to penitents, 5.13-20 to the faithful); H. Thyen, *Der Stil der Jüdisch-Hellenistischen Homilie*, Göttingen, 1955, 14-16 (he endorses Meyer's thesis); Elliott-Binns, 1022; Moo, 8; Instone-Brewer, 'Sermon' (a sermon on the trials of Abraham, with close ties to Jubilees); Witherington, 400-401. For criticism of this take on James see A. Stewart-Sykes, *From Prophecy to Preaching*, Leiden, 2001, 147-58.

[385] Ropes, 10-16. See further below, 88.

[386] A.M. Hunter, *Introducing the New Testament*, Philadelphia, 1946, 96.

pastoral',[388] 'collection of catechetical material',[389] 'wisdom poetry dressed as letter',[390] 'wisdom-prophecy genre',[391] and 'New Testament wisdom writing'.[392]

Since, however, the 1970 article of Francis, 'Form', the conviction that James should be understood, in accord with ecclesiastical tradition, as some sort of letter has been on the ascendancy.[393] This commentary joins that trend. Didactic letters were common in antiquity.[394] More importantly, James shares a number of features—family resemblances—with Jer 29; Bar 6 (= the Epistle of Jeremiah); 2 Macc 1.1-9; 1.10–2.18; 2 Bar. 78–87; 4 Bar. 6.16-25; t. Sanh. 2.6; and Tg. Jer 10.11, each of which is an example of what has been called the 'Diasporabrief':[395]

---

[387] So Gertner, 'Midrashim', 283-90; idem, 'Terms': James is a 'midrashic homily' on Ps 12 and Hos 10, although it has been 'de-midrashized', that is, the texts being commented on have been removed. For Giere, 'Midrash', James is a midrash on Lev 18. Giere supplies a review of all those who have thought of James or parts of James as midrash (76-85).

[388] So J.V. Bartlet, *Age*, 231.

[389] Halson, 'Wisdom', 312.

[390] W. Grundmann, *Die frühe Christenheit und Ihre Schriften*, Altenberg, 1973, 115. Cf. Schnelle, *History*, 392: 'a sapiential letter of admonition and instruction'.

[391] Tamez, 'Immigrants', 370.

[392] Baasland, 'Weisheitsschrift', 123-25. Cf. R. Mayer, 'Jakobusbrief', 54; Cheung, *Genre*, 5-52. Baasland emphasizes, however, that James distinguishes itself through its eschatological expectation and focus on faith and works. In 'Form', Baasland offers a slightly different take: James is a lecture in letter form, a protreptic wisdom discourse. According to Dunn, *Beginning*, 1131, 'there can be little dispute that the letter of James belongs to the genre of Wisdom literature'.

[393] Cf. Francis, 'Form' (emphasizing that letters often contain opening sections which introduce their main themes); Frankemölle, 66-70; Johnson, 23-24 ('a protreptic discourse in the form of a letter'); Wachob, *Voice*, 2-8; Ingelaere, 'Structure', 32-33. For criticism of Francis see Witherington, 421-23.

[394] E.g. 1 En. 92-105; Epistle of Jeremiah; 2 Bar. 78-87; Epistle of Peter to James; Epistle of the Apostles; Epistle of Titus; the Cynic Epistles; etc. See further the recognition of various types of epistles in Ps.-Demetrius, Τύποι Ἐπιστολικοί and Ps.-Libanius, Ἐπιστολιμαῖοι Χαρακτῆρες. The latter lists the paraenetic epistle as the first type (α΄ παραινετική).

[395] For this genre or subgenre see F. Schnider and W. Stenger, *Studium zum neutestamentlichen Briefformular*, Leiden, 1987, 34-41; Taatz, *Briefe*; L. Doering, 'Jeremiah and the "Diaspora Letters" in Ancient Judaism', in *Reading the Present in the Qumran Library*, ed. K. de Troyer and A. Lange, Atlanta, 2005, 45-72. Recent works that view James as such a letter include Niebuhr, 'Diasporabriefe'; Tsuji, *Glaube*, 5-50; Bauckham, *Wisdom*, 18-20; Verseput, 'Genre'; idem, 'Wisdom'; Whitters, *Baruch*, 86-101 (emphasizing esp. the parallels with 2 Bar. 78-87); Harvey, 721; Lockett, *Purity*, 70-76; Kloppenborg, 'Discourse', 268-70; Jobes, *Letters*, 165-67. For dissent see Hoppe, 'Zeugnis', 169-71; Blomberg-Kamell, 29; and the caution in Popkes, 61-64. Already Windisch-Preisker, 4, calls attention to Jer 29; 1 Pet 1.1; and 2 Bar. 78.1. Long before that, Hug, *Introduction*, 552-54, classified James with the relevant rabbinic letters. 4Q389 appears to be another example of the genre, but only fragments have survived; see Doering, 'Jeremia'. Perhaps note should also be taken of PMonac. III 49, a very

- Address to Jews in the diaspora (cf. Jas 1.1): note esp. 2 Bar. 78.1 ('to the nine and a half tribes'); t. Sanh. 2.6 ('to all the other exiles of Israel')[396]
- Authorship by recognized authority (cf. Jas 1.1): Jeremiah (Jer 29; Bar 6; 4 Bar. 6.16-25; Tg. Jer 10.11), 'the senate' (2 Mac 1.10–2.18), Baruch (2 Bar. 78–87), R. Gamaliel (t. Sanh. 2.6)
- Composition in Greek: the Epistle of Jeremiah; 2 Macc 1.1-9; 1.10–2.18; 4 Bar. 6.16-25
- Strong didactic/paraenetic elements: Jer 29.5-28; Ep Jer 6.2-73; 2 Bar. 83.1–86.1; 4 Bar. 6.20-25
- Strong prophetic features (cf. Jas 4.13-5.6): Jer 29.5-28; Ep Jer 6.2-73; 2 Bar. 78–87; 4 Bar. 6.16-25
- Consolation/encouragement in difficult circumstances (cf. Jas 1.2-4; 5.7-11): Jer 29.11-14; 1 Macc 1.2-6; 2 Bar. 78.2-7; 81.1–82.1; 85.3-9; 4 Bar. 6.20-21[397]
- Appeal to Torah/law (cf. Jas 1.25; 2.8-12): 2 Macc 1.4; 2.2-3; 2 Bar. 84.1-11; 4 Bar. 6.23-24
- Appeal to God's generous/merciful nature (cf. Jas 1.5, 13, 17-18): 2 Macc 1.2, 24-25; 2 Bar. 78.3; 81.4; 4 Bar. 6.21
- Hope for/promise of a divinely wrought salvation (cf. Jas 1.12; 2.5; 5.7-9): Jer 29.10-14; 2 Macc 1.27-29; 2.7-8, 18; 2 Bar. 78-85;[398] 4 Bar. 6.24[399]
- Judgment of the unrighteous (cf. Jas 2.13; 3.6; 5.1-6): Jer 29.21-23; 2 Bar. 82.1–83.23; 85.9-15; 4 Bar. 6.17

It is also pertinent, for those of us who regard James as a pseudepigraphon, that the Epistle of Jeremiah, 2 Macc 1.10-2.18,[400] 2 Bar. 78-87, and 4 Bar. 6.16-25 are likewise pseudepigraphical.

In any event, James combines the didactic letter with the diaspora letter; it is a 'paranetically oriented early-Jewish diaspora-letter'.[401]

fragmentary papyrus from Heracleopolis addressed 'to the elders of the Jews in Tebetnu'; see Horsley-Llewelyn, *Documents* 9.69-72. Might this be another diaspora letter?

[396] Regarding this point, it is important to remember that letters addressed to groups were not common in antiquity; see C. Forbes, 'Ancient Rhetoric and Ancient Letters', in *Paul and Rhetoric*, ed. J.P. Sampley and P. Lampe, New York, 2010, 143-60.

[397] See further Niebuhr, 'Diasporabrief', 433-34.

[398] In 2 Bar. 78-87, as in James, the motif of eschatological reversal is particularly prominent; cf. Jas 1.9; 2.5; 4.10; 5.1-5; 2 Bar. 83.3-23.

[399] On this and the following motif see further Niebuhr, 'Diasporabrief', 437-40.

[400] Against the authenticity of 2 Macc 1.10-2.18 see J.A. Goldstein, *II Maccabees*, Garden City, NY, 1983, 157-59.

[401] White, *Erstlingsgabe*, 242. Cf. Verseput, 'Genre', 99: 'a Jewish-Christian letter to the Diaspora regarding the regulation of the familiar areas of communal discord typical of ancient voluntary associations'. I exclude any reference to wisdom in categorizing James because, despite use of and some undeniable affinities with sapiential literature, those affinities do not suffice to define the genre of our writing. Cf. Ropes, 10-11; H. von Lips, *Weisheitliche Traditionen im Neuen Testament*, Neukirchen, 1990, 431-34; Davids, 23-24; Johnson, 33. Contrast Frankemölle, 68 (a 'wisdom writing in letter form'), 87; Hartin, 10-16. The latter recognizes that James is an example of a diaspora letter yet also says that it 'without doubt' belongs to 'the general category of Wisdom literature'. He further qualifies the work as 'protreptic discourse' in opposition to *paraenesis* because of its developed arguments, diatribe elements, and thematic focus; cf. J.G. Gammie, 'Paraenetic Literature', *Semeia* 50 (1990), 41-77.

Dibelius was far from being wholly wrong: James is indeed full of *paraenesis*, that is, moral exhortation.[402] He erred, however, in setting aside James' character as a letter, in denying that it could have a concrete situation in view,[403] and in failing to see that *paraenesis* can serve coherent argumentation.[404] Moreover, those who have thought of James as a sermon are likewise not wholly wrong, for our author clearly hoped that his work would be read to a group or to groups in a religious setting: the written was intended to become oral.[405] In certain important respects, then, the distance between letter and sermon is minimal.

What follows from the fact that James is 'paranetically oriented'? By its nature, *paraenesis* typically reminds rather than informs. So it should not be thought of as material for beginners, as though it were akin to catechetical material—an idea the history of interpretation does not strongly support: commentators do not read James as a book for novices. Typically, *paraenesis* reiterates the never-ending task of living out a philosophy or religion: it is a 'concise, benevolent injunction that reminds of moral practices to be pursued or avoided'.[406] In line with this, almost everything that James says has parallels elsewhere and can even be reckoned commonplace. This does not make the document trivial. Our author would have sympathized with Pascal—'All the good maxims are already current; what we need is to apply them' (*Pensees* 6.380)—and agreed with Seneca, *Ep.* 94.25-26: 'People say, "What good does it do to point out the obvious?" A great deal of good; for we sometimes know facts without paying attention to them. Advice is not teaching; it merely engages the attention and rouses us, and concentrates the memory, and keeps it from losing grip. We miss much that is set before our very eyes. Advice is, in fact, a sort of exhortation. The mind often tries not to notice even that which lies before our eyes; we must therefore force upon it the knowledge of things that are perfectly well known…'

Before turning to the next subject, one should add that determination of James' genre is not just a question about formal classification.[407] The decision about genre affects how one reads, for it cannot but prod one to

---

[402] On the problem of the various definitions that have been given to 'paraenesis' see Popkes, 'Paraensis'. He emphasizes that *paraenesis* is not a literary genre. See further Wachob, *Voice*, 41-52.

[403] See esp. Perdue, 'Paraenesis', who observes that authors necessarily make selections from their tradition, and that their choices cannot be independent of an immediate social setting.

[404] Important and influential here is the commentary of Davids.

[405] Cf. Col 4.16; 1 Thess 5.27; Rev 1.3; 22.8; 2 Bar. 86.1.

[406] So J. Starr, 'Was Paraenesis for Beginners?', in *Early Christian Paraenesis in Context*, ed. J. Starr and T. Engberg-Pedersen, Berlin, 2004, 79, adding: it 'expresses or implies a shared worldview, and does not anticipate disagreement'.

[407] For different ways of thinking about genre see C.A. Newsome, 'Pairing Research Questions and Theories of Genre', in *DSD* 17 (2010), 241-59.

construe a text in the light of others like it.[408] In the present case, reading James as a diaspora letter communicates much. It underlines the religious authority of the author. It encourages one to anticipate prophetic consolation and warning. It moves one to anticipate words for a broad audience as opposed to a small, well-defined community. And it positions the reader not as a dialogue partner but as a listener: one expects to hear exhortations that disallow discussion and instead call for obedience.

V. STRUCTURE

Echoing Luther's verdict that James 'throws things together chaotically',[409] de Wette wrote that the book is 'without plan or arrangement'.[410] Many have been of the same mind, including the influential Dibelius, who affirmed that 'the entire document lacks continuity in thought'.[411] For him, the frequent catchword connections[412] are purely formal, and the aphoristic formulations—especially in chap. 1—should be understood in isolation. Yet just as recent work on Proverbs has more and more tended to find coherence between nearby sayings and to offer contextual interpretations,[413] so too with James: Dibelius' practice of interpreting small units as though they were quarantined from their surroundings appears to

---

[408] Important here is 'prototype theory', which holds that human beings tend to classify not in terms of necessary features but prototypical examples; see B.G. Wright, 'Joining the Club', *DSD* 17 (2010), 260-85.

[409] M. Luther, 'Preface to the Epistles of St. James and St. Jude', in *Luther's Works*, vol. 35, ed. Bachmann, Philadelphia, 1960, 397. Cf. the comment in *Table Talk*, in Luther's Works, vol. 54, ed. T.G. Tappert, Philadelphia, 1967, 424 (no. 5443): 'there's no order or method'; the author 'is constantly shifting from one [topic] to the other'.

[410] de Wette, *Introduction*, 331.

[411] Dibelius, 2. Cf. Diodati, preface to James (the book is 'but a gathering together of diverse doctrines, exhortations, comforts, reproofs, instructions, and sentences'); W. Wall, 345 ('There are in this epistle many expressions in which it is hard to fit the signification of the words to the sense of the place'); Plumptre, 43 ('informal and unsystematic'); Harnack, *Geschichte*, 487; Marty, 236; Enslin, *Beginnings*, 328 ('destitute of structure'); McNeile-Williams, *Introduction*, 201 (no 'particular plan'); G.C. Martin, 'Storehouse', 181; Goodspeed, *Introduction*, 290 ('just a handful of pearls, dropped one by one into the hearer's mind'); E.F. Scott, *The Literature of the New Testament*, New York, 1957, 213; Reicke, 7 ('relative lack of plan'); Schrage, *Ethics*, 281 ('From beginning to end, injunctions and admonitions follow without apparent organization or logical development'); Hoppe, 10; Schnider, 13. E.A. Nida *et al.*, *Style and Discourse*, Cape Town, 1983, 116, even deem the structure of 1.2-8 to be based on 'stream of consciousness'.

[412] On these see below, 82.

[413] K.M. Heim, *Like Grapes of Gold Set in Silver*, Berlin, 2001, 7-66. Also relevant are the thematic clusters in and organization of other ancient sayings collections; see J.S. Kloppenborg, *The Formation of Q*, Philadelphia, 1987, 263-316.

belong to the past. Davids, 25, is typical of more recent work: James is 'a carefully constructed work'.[414]

Although rejection of Dibelius is the current consensus, there remains no agreement as to what to put in its place.[415] That is, those who agree that James displays thematic coherence disagree on how precisely the book is put together. This lack of concord has led Bauckham to suspect that 'something must be wrong with the goal that is being attempted', that is, with the attempt to uncover the overall literary structure of the work.[416] He rightly observes that coherence of thought does not require a carefully composed structure and that it further does not demand a sequential argument.[417] His own proposal finds in James three major parts:

[414] Cf. Luck, 'Theologie', 11: a 'Sprachkompetenz' without a 'Sachkompetenz' is unlikely. Mussner, 'Motivation', records a change of mind years after working on his commentary: he came to see more continuity between sections than he did earlier. For earlier attempts to find a unifying outline of James see Meyer, *Rätsel* (from 1.18 on, James creates an allegory that follows the birth order of at least eight of the twelve sons of Jacob); Hartmann, 'Aufbau' (James follows the names of the patriarchs in Gen 29.32–35.18, à la Meyer's thesis of a Jewish allegory); Cabaniss, 'Homily' (see n. 384); Blenker, 'Jakobs' (the order of James corresponds to the order of Job 1–2; 4–37; 42).

[415] Recent discussions, beyond the introductions to most commentaries, include Forbes, 'Structure' (positing division into sections for liturgical reading); D. Beck, 'Composition' (James mostly follows the order of 1QS and addresses 'Jewish Christian circles concerned with the problem of properly interpreting Essene traditions in terms of the Christian gospel'); Fry, 'Testing' (a thematic analysis that stresses 'testing'); Wuellner, 'Rhetorik' (introduction, 1.1-12; argument, 1.13-27; 2.1-13, 14-26; 3.1-18; 4.1-12; 4.13–5.6; 'call to action-impulse', 5.7-20); Baasland, 'Form' (1.2-18 is the *exordium*, 1.16-18 a *transitus*, 1.19-27 the *propositio*, 2.1–5.6 the *argumentatio* consisting of a *confirmatio* in 2.1–3.10 and a *confutatio* in 3.13–5.6, and 5.7-10 is the *peroratio*); Crotty, 'Structure'; Terry, 'Aspects'; Klein, *Werk*, 33-41 (1.2-18 + 19-27 is the double proposition; 2.1–5.6 is the argument, which has six parts: 2.1-13, 14-26; 3.1-12, 3.13-18; 4.1-12; 4.13–5.6; then 5.7-11 is the peroration, 5.12-20 the conclusion); Thurén, 'Rhetoric' (1.1-18, *exordium*; 1.19-27, *propsitio*; 2.1–5.6, *argumentatio*; 5.7-20, *peroratio*); Klein, *Werk*, 33-41 (prescript, 1.1; double *propositio*, 1.2-18, 19-27; *argumentatio*, 2.1–5.6, which includes six 'Mahnrede'; *peroratio*, 5.7-11; conclusion, 5.12-20); Frankemölle, 'Netz'; Elliott, 'Perspective' (a modification of Wuellner); Ó Fearghail, 'Structure' (1.2-11 is the introduction; three main parts follow: 1.12–2.26; 3.1–4.12; 4.13–5.20); Cheung, *Genre*, 53-85; M. Taylor, *Structure*; M. Taylor-Guthrie, 'Structure'. For surveys see M. Taylor, 'Scholarship'; idem, *Structure*, 8-34; McKnight, 47-55; Batten, *Saying*, 9-16; Orlando, *Lettera*, 33-42. Popkes, 47-49; idem, 'Composition', 93-95, briefly overviews the contribution of rhetorical critics and concludes that their work has, on the whole, not yielded many new insights into the problem of global structure. Cf. the doubts in J.T. Reed, 'Using Ancient Rhetorical Categories to Interpret Paul's Letters', in *Rhetoric and the New Testament*, ed. S.E. Porter and T.H. Olbricht, Sheffield, 1993, 292-324; also Thurén, 'Writings', 593: 'that James can be analyzed with ancient terminology proves only its general applicability'. Duplacy, 'Divisions', and Amphoux, 'Division', review the structural divisions evident in the mss. of James.

[416] Bauckham, *Wisdom*, 61. Cf. Ingelaere, 'Structure', 35.

[417] Bauckham, *Wisdom*, 67: 'It is the construction of each discrete section as a rhetorical unit that matters. The way in which these sections are placed in a sequence is of much less consequence.'

A   Prescript (1.1)
B   Introduction (1.2-27)
C   Exposition (2–5)[418]

This commentator largely agrees with Bauckham. 1.1 is the prescript, 1.2-27 serves as an introduction of sorts, and 2.1–5.20 is the main body, or at least the rest of the letter.

Regrettably it is hard to say much more, and one expects no forthcoming consensus on the issue. Some writers are more organized than others, and James was not one of the more organized; thus his work can be analyzed any number of ways. One recalls that it is much easier to identify major structural keys in Matthew than it is to divine the global organization of Mark. In this respect, James is more like the Second Gospel than the First. Exegetes have disputed and will forever dispute whether Jas 1.12 goes with 1.9-11 or with 13-15 or with 13-16 or with 13-18, or whether 4.11-12 belongs with 4.1-10 or constitutes an isolated section, or whether 4.13-17 and 5.1-6 are two halves of a whole or rather two independent pieces, or whether 5.12 is in any way tied to its immediate context. The debates regarding these and related issues—above all the coherence of the aphoristic units in chap. 1—will never conclude because James too often fails to demarcate its units in evident ways. Scholars may wish to draw straight lines, but James remains fuzzy.[419] One sympathizes with Popkes, 57, who makes no attempt to offer a comprehensive outline. A commentator, of course, must of necessity divide the text into discrete sections; but this writer freely confesses that his decisions have sometimes been dictated by convenience, not by a deep conviction that any other analysis would be inappropriate.

Despite the failure of our epistle to display a neat, clean structure, certain generalizations about its organization still hold. One is that James emphasizes through repetition, so that the more important topics are treated in more than one place: coping with trials and temptation (1.2-8, 12-18; 5.7-11),[420] the fate of rich and poor and the problem of partiality (1.9-11; 2.1-13; 4.13–5.6), the necessity for doing works (1.22-27; 2.14-26; 3.13-18), caution regarding speech (1.19, 26; 3.1-12; 4.11-12; 5.12), reflection upon and encouragement regarding prayer (1.5-8; 4.2-3; 5.13-18).

---

[418] Bauckham, *Wisdom*, 63-64, finds twelve sections within the exposition, an 'appropriate number...in a letter to the twelve tribes'. His analysis differs from that of the present commentary in that he regards 4.11-12 as independent, separates 4.13-17 and 5.1-6, and draws a line between 5.19-20 and 5.13-18.

[419] Perhaps part of the problem is that moderns think of a text as a writing and so naturally seek a visual outline. But our expectations may be foreign to a more oral environment; cf. M.E. Dean, 'The Grammar of Sound in Greek Texts', *ABR* 14 (1996), 53-70.

[420] For Hiebert, 'Theme', 1.3 announces the unifying theme: 'tests of a living faith'. Cf. Parry, *Discussion*, 11-12; Fry, 'Testing'; Semmelink, 'Model', 35; Tsuji, *Glaube*, 72 (the central theme is 'temptations of desire and obedience to God').

Another clear fact is that chap. 1 introduces all of these topics. Even though 1.2-27 is not exactly a table of contents, it does to significant degree portend what follows:[421]

1.2-4	
patient endurance	cf. 5.7-11
perfection	cf. 2.22; 3.2
1.5-8	
wisdom	cf. 3.13-18
divine giving	cf. 1.17-18
prayer of faith	cf. 4.2-3; 5.13-18
divided soul	cf. 4.8
1.9-11	
fate of poor	cf. 2.5
fate of rich	cf. 4.13–5.6
eschatological reversal	cf. 2.1-7; 4.10; 5.1-6
1.12-15	
enduring trial	cf. 5.7-11
human desire	cf. 4.2-3
1.16-18	
gift 'from above'	cf. 3.17
1.19-21	
slow to speak	cf. 3.1-12
1.22-25	
'the law of freedom'	cf. 2.12
doing the word/works	cf. 2.14-26
1.26-27	
bridle tongue	cf. 3.1-12
concern for the marginal	cf. 2.1-13, 14-17
'the world'	cf. 3.6; 4.4

---

[421] Exegetes have often observed that chap. 1 or some part of it effectively introduces the main themes of the epistle; cf. Bengel, 485-86; Wesley, 598; Leahy, 911; R. Wall, 34-37; Rauch, 'Versuch', 281-85; Pfeiffer, 'Zusammenhang' (see 293 below); R.N. Flew, *Jesus and His Way*, London, 1963, 117-33; Francis, 'Form' (contending for a double introduction, 1.2-11 and 12-27; effective criticism in Ó Fearghail, 'Structure', 69-71); Luck, 'Theologie', 11-12; Cantinat, 11; Wuellner, 'Rhetorik', 43; Klijn, 9-10 (1.2-3 introduces 1.12-26; 1.4 introduces 1.27–2.26; 1.5-8 introduces 3.1–5.10); Frankemölle, 165-74; idem, 'Netz' (1.3 is linked to 5.7-20; 1.4 is linked to 1.19-27 and 3.1-12; 1.5 is linked to 3.13-18; 1.6-8 is linked to 2.14-16; 1.9-11 is linked to 2.1-13 and 5.1-6; 1.13-15 is linked to 4.1-12); Johnson, 14-15; Davids, 26 (modifying Francis); Klein, *Werk*, 33-41; Tsuji, *Glaube*, 63-72; Bauckham, *Wisdom*, 71-73; Klein, *Werk*, 35-39; Cheung, *Genre*, 61-67; Ingelaere, 'Structure', 37-38; M. Taylor-Guthrie, 'Structure'. For Frankemölle, 153-65, 1.2-18 is the prologue or exordium. Burchard, 9-13, confines the introduction to 1.1-11, Ó Fearghail, 'Structure', to 1.2-11. Cladder, 'Anlage'; idem, 'Aufbau', makes 1.26-27 the structural key to a large chiasmus. For additional proposals regarding the extent of the prologue see Cheung, *Genre*, 61-62. Against the recent consensus, McKnight, 51, denies that chap. 1 is 'a consciously literary anticipation or whetting of the appetite for what is to come'. Note also the critical remarks of Popkes, 49-51.

Perhaps, then, 1.2-27 functions not unlike a πρόθεσις or *propositio*, an introductory statement of the chief matters to be discussed in what follows. As a parallel one can cite Ps.-Phoc. 3-8, which (following the title and prologue) introduces the themes of the letter.[422]

One might, in sorting through these correlations, wonder if they do not exhibit a chiastic pattern:[423]

1.2-8	prayer of faith
1.9-12	fate of rich + endurance
1.13-15	the evils of desire
1.16-18	divine gift from above
1.19-21	teaching about the tongue
1.22-24	deeds, not just words
1.25-27	law of freedom/concern for poor
2.1-13	law of freedom/concern for poor
2.14-26	deeds, not just words
3.1-12	teaching about the tongue
3.13-16	divine gift from above
4.1-12	the evils of desire
4.13–5.11	fate of rich + endurance
5.12-20	prayer of faith

The problems with such a tidy scheme, however, are manifold: (i) 1.2-4 is naturally viewed as its own paragraph, and it lines up most obviously with 5.7-11, not 5.12-20. (ii) The order of the topics in 1.9-12 and 4.13–5.11 is not reversed, so the chiasmus here fails. (iii) No ending corresponds to 1.1. One could offer additional criticism, but the point is made: the data do not establish that our author composed a large chiasmus. They rather reveal how easy it is to find correlations between Jas 1 and the rest of the book.

Although there is certainly much room for disagreement (especially regarding the place of 4.11-12), this commentator takes the main sections of the Exposition to be 2.1-13, 14-26; 3.1-12, 13-18; 4.1-12; 4.13–5.6; 5.12; and 5.13-20. These nine topical paragraphs are not only thematically coherent, but their introductions and conclusions share a few features:

- ἀδελφοί (μου) occurs in over half of the introductions: 2.1, 14; 3.1; 5.7, 12
- Three sections open with questions: 2.14; 3.13; 4.1
- All the others open with imperatives: 2.1; 3.1; 4.13; 5.1, 7, 12, 13
- ἐν ὑμῖν appears in 3.13; 4.1; 5.13
- 2.13, 26; 3.11-12, 18; and 5.20 offer concluding, proverb-like pronouncements

---

[422] W.T. Wilson, *The Sentences of Pseudo-Phocylides*, Berlin, 2005, 76-77.

[423] Chiastic analyses of James include Cladder, 'Anlage'; J.W. Welch, 'Chiasmus in the New Testament', in *Chiasmus in Antiquity*, ed. J.W. Welch, Provo, UT, 1981, 211-13; Reese, 'Exegete'; Davids, 25-26; Iovino, 'Struttura'; Crotty, 'Poor'; M. Taylor-Guthrie, 'Structure' (for 2.1–5.6); Krüger, *Kritik*, 105-109.

Some of these agreements surely reflect conscious design.

Lastly, some think that spotting instances of *inclusio* can help with the formal analysis of James. For instance, M. Taylor and Guthrie regard the parallels between 1.2-4 and 12 and between the latter and 1.25 as creating a double-paneled opening,[424] the parallels between 2.12-13 and 4.11-12 as marking the central portion of our letter, and the parallels between 4.6 and 5.6 as unifying another section. Perhaps they are right. Yet this commentator remains skeptical. The parallelism between 1.2-11 and 1.13-26 is far from perfect.[425] More importantly, James can repeat key phrases and ideas without thereby creating an *inclusio*, as in 1.25 = 2.12 ('the law of freedom'), 1.6-7 = 4.3 ('ask...not receive'), 1.9 = 4.10 (humility → exaltation), and 4.11-12 = 5.9 (μὴ κατα[λαλεῖτε] ἀλλήλων, ἀδελφοί, κριτής).[426] *Inclusio* does not seem to be the key to the structure of James.

Indeed, there does not seem to be any such key. James is too loosely structured, which is why meticulous outlines that attempt to account for every detail fail to convince. Like much Jewish wisdom literature, the author quickly moves from topic to topic without developing an overall argument. Dibelius underestimated the thematic links between the pieces. Nonetheless, the unity of the text is best sought not in a grand literary scheme but in the author's goals, as best we can judge them.[427]

VI. LITERARY CHARACTERISTICS

(i) *Style and tone.* James is, for the most part, written in idiomatic Greek. Leconte, 19, summarizes: 'its prose is graceful, its vocabulary varied; it uses rare and scholarly words, the precise use of the tenses is known and the conjunctions and adverbs are handled with ease'.[428] Paul and the author of Hebrews may be more rhetorically polished, but James composes good *koine*. He avoids anacolutha and can even on occasion use

---

[424] M. Taylor-Guthrie, 'Structure'; cf. Francis, 'Form'; Davids, 24-27; Tsuji, *Glaube*, 63-72.

[425] 1.2-4 is naturally set beside 1.12(13)-15 and 1.5-8 is naturally related to 1.16-18. But the links between 1.9-11 and 1.26-27 are less substantial, and 1.19-25 has few resonances with 1.2-11.

[426] One does wonder, however, whether there is a sort of large *inclusio* between chap. 1 and 5.7-20; the two sections do share a number of key words, and perhaps that is not coincidence. See below, 694-95; Crotty, 'Structure', 45-46 (on 5.19-20 and 1.15-18); M. Taylor-Guthrie, 'Structure', 700-701.

[427] See above, 32-50, on the *Sitz im Leben*. This is not to insist that only traditional historical scholarship as opposed to text-centered approaches can illumine James. For example, Cargal, 3-56, who prefers to read James through Greimasian structural semiotics, often proves illuminating.

[428] Cf. Dibelius, 34 ('relatively polished Greek'); Wifstrand, 'Problems', 176 ('a rather supple and idiomatic Greek in most parts').

literary words and Classical constructions.[429] His prose, however, features some very unGreek formulations[430] as well as a significant number of Semitisms.[431] Perhaps Wifstrand was justified to conclude: 'the author was a man who knew ordinary *koine* Greek as it was written by people of some education, but as soon as he felt a need to rise into a higher stylistic sphere, he had no Greek mode to follow, but had recourse to the higher style that he was really master of, the Semitic one'.[432] Wifstrand thought the language of James to be the language of the Hellenistic synagogue.

James is laconic. He often—as any commentator quickly learns— writes cryptically, without explanation.[433] He is also free of half-tones. He speaks with authority, and without a hint that anyone disagreeing could have anything credible to say. Both features must mirror a forceful, self-confident personality. At the same time, *paraenesis* is by nature commanding and free of nuance and qualifications. Furthermore, our letter assumes that author and reader share a tradition, that tradition being Jewish moral instruction rooted in Torah. So most of the imperatives, to the extent that they reverberate with the Tanak, require no justification, and James can formulate thoughts apodictically rather than expansively. The implied reader recognizes that what is being demanded has its warrant in a divine source.

(ii) Literary features. Several rhetorical devices recur often enough to qualify as being characteristic of our author:

(a) Catchword connections. Catchwords sometimes link sentences or even adjacent units, especially in chap. 1:[434]

1.1-2	χαίρειν...χαράν
1.4-5	λειπόμενοι...λείπεται
1.12-13	πειρασμόν...πειραζόμενος
1.21-22	λόγον...λόγου
1.26-27	θρῆσκός...θρησκεία. θρησκεία
2.12-13	κρίνεσθαι...κρίσις...κρίσεως
2.13	ἀνέλεος...ἔλεος...ἔλεος
3.13–4.2	ζῆλον...ζῆλος...ζηλοῦτε

[429] See above, 56.
[430] Note esp. the ἀκροατὴς ἐπιλησμονῆς of 1.25 and the ὁ κόσμος τοῦ ἀδικίας of 3.6.
[431] See below, 86-87.
[432] Wifstrand, 'Problems', 176. Cf. D.E. Aune, 'James', in *The Westminster Dictionary of New Testament and Early Christian Literature and Rhetoric*, Louisville, 2003, 239.
[433] Johnson, 10, observes that, when James is compared with Hellenistic moral treatises, his treatments of various *topoi* 'appear as precise miniatures'.
[434] Linking materials via catchwords was convention in James' world. For example, the device appears in both Proverbs (see S. Weeks, *Early Israelite Wisdom*, Oxford, 1994, 20-40) and the Jesus tradition; cf. Mk 9.43-50 and see A. Callahan, '"No Rhyme or Reason": The Hidden Logia of the Gospel of Thomas', *HTR* 90 (1997), 411-26. See further Dibelius, 7-11.

In like fashion, the same word, root, or phrase is regularly repeated in close proximity, sometimes even three or more times.[435]

(b) Wordplays. These appear throughout:

1.22	λόγου... παραλογιζόμενοι
2.4	διεκρίθητε... κριταί
2.20	ἔργων... ἀργή
2.22	συνήργει... ἔργοις
3.6	καὶ φλογίζουσα... τῆς γενέσεως // καὶ φλογιζομένη... τῆς γεέννης
3.17	ἀδιάκριτος... ἀνυπόκριτος
4.14	φαινομένη... ἀφανιζομένη

(c) Assonance, consonance, and alliteration. These three features are even more common. Among the more striking examples are these:[436]

1.2	π πειρ περι π π
1.6	ιζομενω ιζομενω
1.11	πε πρε προ π π πορ
1.11-12	μαρα μακαρ
1.14	ελ ομενος ελ ομενος
1.21	π πα αν πα αν π αν π
1.24	α πελ θε ε πελ θε
2.18	Χ Υ Υ Χ Χ Υ Υ
3.2	π πτα πα πτα
3.5	ηλικον ηλκην υλην
3.7	δαμαζ ται δαμασ ται
3.8	δ δ δ δ ακατα τατ κακ
3.17	επει ε επιε ης ε πει ης // α ων α ων // α κριτος α κριτος
4.1	πο εν πο εμ πο εν
4.13-14	πορ πο πο πορ πο προ
4.13-15	σομε σομε σομε σομε ομε ζομε σομε σομε

The reiteration of sounds has its parallels in Hebrew poetry,[437] and it is possible that James' penchant for repetition was partly inspired by scripture. It certainly gives his book a biblical feel.

(d) Parallelism. Even more reminiscent of the Bible is James' use of parallelism, that is, his repetition of similar constructions and phrases. Instances include:

---

[435] E.g. πειράζω / πειρασμός (1.12-14: 4×); λόγος (1.18-23: 4×); πτωχός (1.2-6: 4×); νόμος (2.9-12: 4×); πίστις (2.14-26: 10×); ἔργον (2.14-26: 12×); δικαιοσύνη / δικαιόω (2.21-25: 4×); ὅλον τὸ σῶμα (3.2-6: 3×); γλῶσσα (3.5-8: 3×); σοφία / σοφός (3.13-17: 4×); αἰτέω (4.2-3: 3×); καταλαλέω (4.11: 3×); ἀδελφός (4.11: 3×); νόμος (4.11: 4×); κριτής / κρίνω (4.11-12: 5×); ποιέω (4.13-17: 4×); μακροθυμέω (5.7-8: 3×); κύριος (5.10-11: 3×); προσεύχομαι / προσευχή (5.13-18: 6×). For a full list see Terry, 'Aspects', 114-16.

[436] Additional instances in Mayor, ccl-ccliv.

[437] Note e.g. Ps 122.6; Isa 1.18-20; 9.5; 53.4-7; Ezek 27.27; Amos 6.7; Nah 1.2.

1.9-10	καυχάσθω δὲ ὁ ἀδελφὸς ὁ ταπεινὸς ἐν τῷ ὕψει αὐτοῦ
	ὁ δὲ πλούσιος ἐν τῇ ταπεινώσει αὐτοῦ[438]
1.11	καὶ τὸ ἄνθος αὐτοῦ ἐξέπεσεν
	καὶ ἡ εὐπρέπεια τοῦ προσώπου αὐτοῦ ἀπώλετο
1.19	ταχὺς εἰς τὸ ἀκοῦσαι
	βραδὺς εἰς τὸ λαλῆσαι
	βραδὺς εἰς ὀργήν
2.2	ἐὰν γὰρ εἰσέλθῃ εἰς συναγωγὴν ὑμῶν ἀνὴρ χρυσοδακτύλιος
	ἐν ἐσθῆτι λαμπρᾷ
	εἰσέλθῃ δὲ καὶ πτωχὸς
	ἐν ῥυπαρᾷ ἐσθῆτι
2.3	εἴπητε· σὺ κάθου ὧδε καλῶς
	εἴπητε· σὺ στῆθι ἐκεῖ ἢ κάθου ὑπὸ τὸ ὑποπόδιόν μου
2.11	εἰπών· μὴ μοιχεύσῃς
	εἶπεν καί· μὴ φονεύσῃς
2.18	σὺ πίστιν ἔχεις
	κἀγὼ ἔργα ἔχω
2.21, 25	Ἀβραὰμ ὁ πατὴρ ἡμῶν
	οὐκ ἐξ ἔργων ἐδικαιώθη ἀνενέγκας Ἰσαάκ...;
	Ῥαὰβ ἡ πόρνη
	οὐκ ἐξ ἔργων ἐδικαιώθη ὑποδεξαμένη τοὺς ἀγγέλους...;
2.26	ὥσπερ γὰρ τὸ σῶμα χωρὶς πνεύματος νεκρόν ἐστιν
	οὕτως καὶ ἡ πίστις χωρὶς ἔργων νεκρά ἐστιν
3.9	ἐν αὐτῇ εὐλογοῦμεν τὸν κύριον καὶ πατέρα
	καὶ ἐν αὐτῇ καταρώμεθα τοὺς ἀνθρώπους
4.7	ὑποτάγητε οὖν τῷ θεῷ
	ἀντίστητε δὲ τῷ διαβόλῳ
4.8	ἐγγίσατε τῷ θεῷ
	καὶ ἐγγιεῖ ὑμῖν
4.8	καθαρίσατε χεῖρας, ἁμαρτωλοί
	καὶ ἁγνίσατε καρδίας, δίψυχοι
4.9	ὁ γέλος ὑμῶν εἰς πένθος μετατραπήτω
	καὶ ἡ χαρὰ εἰς κατήφειαν
4.13; 5.1	ἄγε νῦν οἱ λέγοντες
	ἄγε νῦν οἱ πλούσιοι
5.2-3	ὁ πλοῦτος ὑμῶν σέσηπεν
	καὶ τὰ ἱμάτια ὑμῶν σητόβρωτα γέγονεν
	ὁ χρυσὸς ὑμῶν καὶ ὁ ἄργυρος κατίωται
5.13-14	κακοπαθεῖ τις ἐν ὑμῖν, προσευχέσθω
	εὐθυμεῖ τις, ψαλλέτω
	ἀσθενεῖ τις ἐν ὑμῖν, προσκαλεσάσθω

The repetition of the same words and phrases, as in several of these examples, cannot be put down to a small vocabulary: the number of rare words is against that. We rather have a stylistic preference.[439]

---

[438] This is an instance of antithetical parallelism; for additional examples of antithetical formulations see Schulze, *Charakter*, 65-67.

[439] Cf. Chaine, xciii, who deems this a sign of Semitic influence. But James also likes to vary wording and use synonymous expressions; cf. Schulze, *Charakter*, 73-74.

(e) Aphoristic style. One feature that recalls both Jewish wisdom texts and the Jesus tradition is the prevalence of aphoristic formulations: 1.17, 19; 2.13b, 17, 26; 3.16; 4.4, 7, 8, 10, 17; 5.16b. Such occur in every chapter. Although one suspects that several aphorisms were to hand in the tradition, James is likely to be the author of at least a few.

(f) Antithetical formulations. Our letter gains much of its rhetorical force by regularly establishing antitheses.[440] For James there is a right way and a wrong way. He does not deal with shades of gray:

1.5-7	faith vs. doubt
1.9-11	poor vs. rich
1.13-15	temptation by God (impossible) vs. temptation by desire (ubiquitous)
1.19	quick to hear vs. slow to speak
1.20	anger of man vs. righteousness of God
1.21-25	doers of word vs. hearers only
1.26-27	worthless piety vs. undefiled piety
2.1-7	treatment of rich vs. treatment of poor
2.14-26	justification by works vs. justification by faith alone
3.9-10	blessing God vs. cursing human beings
3.13-18	wisdom from above vs. earthly wisdom
4.4	friendship with the world vs. friendship with God
4.6	divine opposition of the exalted vs. divine promotion of the humble
4.7-8	resisting the devil vs. drawing near to God
5.12	swearing vs. no no, yes yes

The preceding features run throughout. This establishes that James was not just a collector but also an author. His stamp is on the whole work.[441]

(iii) Vocabulary. James contains 67 NT *hapax legomena*. Of these words, the vast majority (49) are attested in the LXX.[442] Several, however, are unattested altogether before James, and their very number makes it likely that he coined at least a few of them, the strongest candidates being ἀνέλεος (2.13), ἀνεμιζόμενος (1.6), θρησκός (1.26), and χρυσοδακτύκος (2.2).[443] One is reminded of the author of 4 Maccabees, who enjoyed creating new words.

---

[440] See further Semmelink, 'Model'; Frankemölle, 'Netz', 184-87; Cargal, 229-32; Rhoads, 'Friend'; Tollefson, 'Discourse'. K. Weiss, 'Motiv', 108, sees the major antitheses as these: believing existence vs. secular existence; living from God vs. practical atheism; humble submission vs. hubris; love of neighbor in deed vs. unbounded egoism.

[441] Cf. Dibelius, 34: the language is 'relatively homogeneous'.

[442] See further Mayor, ccxlvi-ccxlvii. His statistics differ slightly from mine as my counts for the NT are based, aside from James, on Nestle-Aland[27].

[443] ἀπείραστος (1.13), ἀποσκίασμα (1.17), δαιμονιώδης (3.15), δίψυχος (1.8; 4.8), πολύσπλαγχνος (5.11), προσωπολημπτέω (2.9), or χαλιναγωγέω (1.26; 3.2) are additional rare words that are sometimes reckoned to be James' inventions. This commentator demurs. For the reasons see the verse-by-verse analysis.

(iv) Semitisms. James contains quite a few words, phrases, and constructions that, even when not contrary to Greek usage, likely reflect Semitic influence. This is unexpected given that the letter is written in fairly polished Greek. Note the following:

ἀκροατὴς ἐπιλησμονῆς*	see on 1.25
ἁμαρτία αὐτῷ ἐστιν	see on 4.17
ὁ ἄνθρωπος ἐκεῖνος	see on 1.7
ἀφεθήσεται αὐτῷ	see on 5.15
γέεννα	see on 3.6
δέησις δικαίου*	see on 5.16
δίδωμι + ὑετόν	see on 5.18
εἰς μαρτύριον	see on 5.3
ἐν τῇ διασπορᾷ	see on 1.1[444]
ἐν ἐσχάταις ἡμέραις	see on 5.3
ἐν πάσαις ταῖς ὁδοῖς αὐτοῦ	see on 1.8
ἐν ταῖς πορείαις αὐτοῦ	see on 1.11
ἐν τῇ ποιήσει αὐτοῦ	see on 1.25
ἐν τῷ ὀνόματι	see on 5.10, 14
ἐνώπιον κυρίου	see on 4.10
ἔστω πᾶς ἄνθρωπος	see on 1.19
τὸ καλὸν ὄνομα τὸ ἐπικληθὲν ἐφ' ὑμᾶς	see on 2.7
καρπὸν τῆς γῆς	see on 5.7
καρπὸς δικαιοσύνης	see on 3.18
ὁ κόσμος τῆς ἀδικίας	see on 3.6
κρίμα λημψόμεθα*	see on 3.1
κριταὶ διαλογισμῶν πονηρῶν*	see on 2.4
κύριος σαβαώθ	see on 5.4
λαλέω + ἐν τῷ ὀνόματι	see on 5.10
μακάριος ἀνὴρ ὅς	see on 1.12
μακροθυμέω + ἕως (?)	see on 5.7
μισθός + ἐργάτης	see on 5.4
ποιήσαντι ἔλεος	see on 2.13
ποιηταὶ λόγου	see on 1.22
ποιητὴς νόμου	see on 4.11
προσευχῇ προσηύξατο*	see on 5.17
προσηύξατο τοῦ μὴ βρέξαι	see on 5.17
προσωπολημψία/πτέω	see on 2.1, 9
πρόσωπον τῆς γενέσεως	see on 1.23
στηρίξατε τὰς καρδίας ὑμῶν	see on 5.8
συλλαβοῦσα τίκτει	see on 1.15
σῶσαι τὰς ψυχάς	see on 1.21
σώσει ψυχὴν αὐτοῦ ἐκ θανάτου	see on 5.20
ταπεινόω + ἐνώπιον	see on 4.10
ταχὺς εἰς τό*	see on 1.19
τίς...ἐν ὑμῶν	see on 3.13
τηρέω + ἑαυτοῦ + ἀπό*	see on 1.27
τὸ τέλος κυρίου (?)*	see on 5.11
ὑπάγετε ἐν εἰρήνῃ	see on 2.16

[444] For ἐν as a Semitism in James see Chaine, xcviii.

abstract genitive serving as adjective	1.25; 2.1, 4; 3.6; 5.15⁴⁴⁵
anarthrous participle for nominal subject	see on 4.17
conditional participle as subject	1.6, 25; 4.11; 5.20
genitive immediately after noun	1.12, 17, 18, 20; 2.2, 23; 3.7; 4.4; 5.4; *et al.*⁴⁴⁶
parallelism	1.9-11, 15, 19; 2.2-3, 18; 3.9; 4.8-9; 5.4, 13-14
pleonastic ἄνθρωπος or ἀνήρ	1.7, 8, 12, 19, 23; 3.2
possessive pronoun immediately after noun	1.2, 8-11, 16, 19, 21, 26; 2.2, 3, 5, 18, *et al.*⁴⁴⁷
rarity of μέν	see on 3.17
recurrent use of ποιεῖν = עשׂה	2.12, 13; 3.12, 18; 4.15, 17 (*bis*); 5.15
repeated asyndeton*	1.19, 27; 2.13b; 3.8-9, 15, 17; 4.2; 5.6; *et al.*⁴⁴⁸
repeated ἰδού	3.4, 5; 5.4, 7, 9, 11⁴⁴⁹
sentences joined by simple καί	1.11, 24; 2.22-23; 3.6; 4.7-8; 5.2-3, 14-18; *et al.*⁴⁵⁰
καί for logical hypotaxis	1.25; 2.2, 15; 4.17; 5.19
πᾶς immediately before anarthrous subject	1.2, 17 (*bis*), 19, 21; 3.7, 16; 4.16⁴⁵¹

Not all the items on this list are equally forceful, and surely many are due to the impact of the LXX. Nonetheless, it is not so easy to account for the entries marked by an asterisk (*), for these do not occur in the LXX.

Some have posited a Semitic original behind James,⁴⁵² but the Semitisms hardly suffice for that. Moreover, the Greek catchwords, wordplays, and paronomasia seem to prohibit a Hebrew or Aramaic original (although perhaps it is worth recalling that Josephus' *Jewish War* is written in excellent Greek even though it is a translation). One cannot object, however, to the possibility that our author was bilingual, perhaps a Greek-speaking Jew who, despite his knowledge of the LXX, also had some sort of education in the Hebrew Bible.⁴⁵³ That is the view to which this commentator is inclined.

---

⁴⁴⁵ See further Chaine, xcvii; BDF 165; Turner, *Grammar*, 118.

⁴⁴⁶ See further Chaine, xcvii; BDF 259. According to Mayor, ccxxxviii, leaving aside genitive pronouns, the genitive is placed immediately after the governing noun fifty times whereas it precedes it only three times. Cf. Schlatter, 77-78.

⁴⁴⁷ According to Davids, 'Traditions', 44, this occurs 57 times, as opposed to Colossians (28×) and 1 Peter (29×), which are of similar length.

⁴⁴⁸ Schlatter, 84, counts 79 instances. Turner, *Grammar*, 117, reckons this 'almost the exclusive Aramaism'. Cf. Chaine, xciv-xcv.

⁴⁴⁹ If this is a Semitism, it might be an Aramaism, because Hebrew strongly tends to preface הנה with ו whereas James never has καὶ ἰδού. Cf. Chaine, xcviii.

⁴⁵⁰ See further Chaine, xciv.

⁴⁵¹ Cf. Chaine, xcvi, and see further MHT 3.201-205.

⁴⁵² For arguments for a Semitic original see those cited in n. 174. For the case against earlier forms of this thesis see Mayor, cclx-cclxviii.

⁴⁵³ Cf. Rendtorff, 13: 'evidently the author is bilingual'.

(v) Elements from diatribe. Ropes, 10-18, emphasized James' debt to diatribe, and indeed classified James 'a diatribe'.[454] Dibelius, 6 n. 6, demurred, claiming that 'the absence of continuity, the scarcity of continuous trains of thought', prohibit that categorization. Dibelius did, nonetheless, concur that James does, at points, recall the dialogical style of the diatribe. The letter addresses the objections of a fictional interlocutor (2.14-26). It is full of rhetorical questions (2.2-7, 14-16, 21-22; 3.11-13; 4.1, 4, 12). It features dramatic characterizations (2.2-4, 16; 4.13-16; 5.1-6). It makes direct appeal to listeners ('my brothers'). And it treats subjects at home in the diatribe, including control of the tongue (3.1-12), the relationship of word to deed (1.22-27), and the problems brought by desire and the passions (1.14-15; 4.1-3).

Now as the commentary proper reveals, none of this is unique to the diatribe; indeed, all of it can be found in Jewish tradition.[455] Nonetheless, 'it is not the occurrence of isolated stylistic phenomena but the combination of multiple features in typical ways which identifies the style as diatribal'.[456] When one adds that Paul's epistles prove that an early Christian could borrow rhetorical features from diatribe, there is no cause to deny the same for James.

VII. LEADING IDEAS

Our letter is not a systematic or comprehensive statement of its author's personal theology or religious convictions.[457] The content is rather dictated and circumscribed by the particular goals its author had in mind; and as this commentary discerns an attempt to promote irenic relations between Christian Jews and non-Christian Jews, the dearth of unambiguously Christian beliefs is readily explained. So too the traditional character of most of the letter: it is full of conventional material because James wanted his group to be perceived as conventional. That is, he wanted Christian Jews to be perceived as Jews. So the letter is in large measure a statement of beliefs shared by Jews and Christians.

---

[454] For the nature of diatribe see esp. S.K. Stowers, *The Diatribe and Paul's Letters*, Chico, CA, 1981.

[455] Cf. the critical comments in Wifstrand, 'Problems', 177-78.

[456] S.K. Stowers, 'Diatribe', in *The Anchor Bible Dictionary*, vol. 2, ed. N. Freedman, New York, 1992, 193. Cf. Chaine, c-cii.

[457] It is not even clear to this writer that there is a unifying theme. Contrast Zmijewski, 'Vollkommenheit', 293-323, for whom 'perfection' serves as such (so too Wypadlo, 'Gott', 81), and Schille, 'Gespaltenheit', who summarizes James with this: because God is undivided (*haplos*), the faithful should not be divided (*dipsychos*).

Theology[458]

The God of James is the God of Abraham (2.21-23) and Rahab (2.25), the God of 'the prophets who spoke in the name of the Lord' (5.10), and of Job (5.11) and Elijah (5.17-18). In other words, he is the God of Israel; cf. 1.1.

Everything in the letter comports with this foundational fact. God is the creator (1.17) who fashioned humanity in the divine likeness (3.9). He is the one God of the Shema', who should be loved (1.12; 2.19). He is the giver of the law (4.12; cf. 2.11), whose will and word should be obeyed (1.22-25; 2.8-13; cf. 4.7, 15). He is 'the Lord of hosts' (5.4) who will judge the wicked and reward the righteous (1.12; 4.10). This is the God of the Jewish Bible.

To all these theological commonplaces one may add the following as attributes of the deity in James, many of them also routine for Judaism:

- God gives generously to all in response to prayers of faith, 1.5, 17; 4.3-4; 5.17-18
- God is not tempted to do evil and does not tempt others, 1.13
- God is unchanging, 1.17
- God is the father of all, 1.17, 18, 27; 3.9
- God is righteous, 1.20
- God favors the poor over the rich, 1.9-11; 2.5; 5.1-6
- God and 'the world' stand against each other, 4.4
- God gives grace to the humble, 4.6
- God heals the sick, 5.15
- God forgives sins, 5.15

None of this is distinctively Christian. On the contrary, and as the verse-by-verse commentary establishes, everything that James teaches about God has multiple parallels in the Bible and other Jewish texts.

Christology

James is theocentric, not christocentric.[459] In the standard critical editions, 'Jesus' is named twice, in 1.1 and 2.1; but the latter is likely corrupt. So attempts to reconstruct James' Christology have little with which to work.

---

[458] Dibelius, 21, famously asserted that James has 'no theology' (cf. 48). By this he meant that our author does not develop or elaborate 'religious ideas. At best, they are only touched upon, and in most instances they are merely presupposed. Yet we cannot determine with certainty either how much Jas presupposes or what is the precise nature of the religious property with which he credits his readers.' These words demand too much. If one forsakes 'certainty' and recognizes that reconstructions need not be wholly 'precise', it is possible to say much about James' religious ideas and even his theology in the proper sense of the word. Recent students of James have rightly passed beyond Dibelius in this respect. Indeed, we now have a hefty monograph—Wenger's *Kyrios*—dedicated to James' 'Gottesbild'.

[459] Cf. Frankemölle, 90 (James grounds his ethic primarily in theology, not Christology); Popkes, 22-23.

The truth is that, if we leave aside 1.1, James fails to ground a single proposition in the person and work of Jesus.[460] Christian readers and even most modern scholars have, to be sure, incessantly read christological elements into almost every single verse.[461] Some have even found in 1.1 an anticipation of fourth-century christological dogma.[462] But the text receives such eisegesis because it is part of the NT. Christian readers typically operate with an unconscious canonical synchronizing, assuming that, since James appears in the NT, it must say what other NT texts say. Although that may make sense for theological or sermonic ends, if one is trying to understand the original intent of James, the exegetical habit should be discarded: one should rather approach the book first on its own terms. When that is done, the christological elements must be deemed not largely quiescent but rather absent. Compared with other early Christian writings, James exhibits a 'christological deficit'.[463]

The upshot is that we know next to nothing about the Christology of our author. For failure to mention this or that is not proof of disbelief in this or that. James is short, and it is not an epitome. The attempt, moreover, to find common ground with non-Christian Jews would naturally result in downplaying or omitting divisive christological claims. At the same time, one cannot assume that James must have believed what Paul or the author of Acts believed. The diversity of early Christology and James' failure to say much about Jesus means that we simply do not know where to put our author on the christological map.

Batten has written: 'to determine the Christology of James is very difficult, other than to reiterate that clearly Jesus' teachings were a significant source of wisdom that inspired and shaped James' composition'.[464] It is hard to say more. Maybe James knew Matthew and believed in the virgin birth; and perhaps, if he had heard John, he would have found its high Christology congenial.[465] Yet it is no less possible, and indeed more likely if James was related to Ebionite circles, that he would rather have approved of Aphrahat's teaching—heretical by the standard of Nicaea— that scripture bestows exalted titles such as 'Lord' and 'Son of God' upon especially important and righteous human beings, and that Jesus is in this

---

[460] Cf. Schrage, *Ethics*, 281: 'Apart from James 2:1 there is no hint of a specifically Christian or christological foundation'.

[461] For an overview of the passages most often thought relevant see Reumann, 'Christology'. It is telling that Mussner, 'Christologie', has to speak of 'indirekte Christologie'.

[462] Riesner, 1255, suggests that James may see in Jesus 'the incarnation of God's pre-existent wisdom'.

[463] So Broer, *Einleitung*, 613.

[464] Batten, 'Tradition', 386.

[465] But against reading a Johannine—or a Pauline—Christology into James see Jackson-McCabe, 'Messiah', 711-12.

respect no different.⁴⁶⁶ The Ebionites, according to the church fathers, did not believe in Jesus' divinity.⁴⁶⁷ What did James believe? We do not know.⁴⁶⁸

Law
James offers no systematic statement about the law, so we must infer his views from passing remarks. These include 2.9 and 11, which assume that one should not transgress the law; 2.10, which posits the unity of the law; and 4.11, which pleads that one should do the law rather than speak against it or judge it (4.11). Given such verses and the fact that James nowhere criticizes Torah or hints that some parts of it no longer hold, it is plausible that he held the same opinion as the author of Mt 5.17-20: the whole law is still valid.

That James fails to refer to ritual commandments is no effective counter-argument. It is rather a frail argument from silence. Ritual is simply not relevant to any part of the argument—just as it is not to the point in certain Jewish moral texts where it also goes unmentioned.⁴⁶⁹ Moreover, the notion that 'the implanted word' cannot be Torah overlooks the not uncommon Jewish equation of the Mosaic law with natural law;⁴⁷⁰ and that no nomist could speak of the Torah as 'the perfect law, the law of freedom' (1.25; 2.12) is a purely Christian prejudice that reads Paul into James and overlooks Jewish texts in which obedience to the Torah is true freedom; see on 1.25.

Practical Teaching
James requires that Torah be not just heard but kept. Wholly in accord with that, he teaches that right religion is a means of bringing about concrete results in the world. Belief and piety are bankrupt if they tolerate hearing without doing (1.22-25; 2.14-26), if they do not lead to assistance of the disadvantaged (1.27; 2.14-17), if they do not issue in control of the tongue (1.19; 3.1-12), if they do not eliminate judging and cursing others (3.9-10; 4.11-12), or if they do not displace the desire to lay up riches (4.13–5.6). Faith is what it does, and religion is a way of being in the world for others, not a way of believing and living for oneself.

---

⁴⁶⁶ Aphraates, *Dem.* 17.2-8 SC 359 ed. Pierre, 730-40. See W.L. Peterson, 'The Christology of Aphrahat, the Persian Sage', *VC* 46 (1992), 241-56.

⁴⁶⁷ See Skarsaune, 'The Ebionites', in Skarsaune-Hvalvik, *Believers*, 429-35.

⁴⁶⁸ Even if this commentator is wrong and Ἰησοῦ Χριστοῦ belonged to the autograph of 2.1, the implications for James' Christology remain unclear, because the interpretation of the entire clause remains unclear; see the Excursus, 382-84.

⁴⁶⁹ See further above, 27.

⁴⁷⁰ 'The equation of Mosaic legislation and natural law took place on a routine or semi-routine basis in Second Temple Jewish circles'. So G.E. Sterling, 'Universalizing the Particular: Natural Law in Second Temple Jewish Ethics', *SPhilo* 15 (2003), 79. See further H. Najman, *Past Renewals*, Leiden, 2010, 87-118.

The imperatives in James—'he does not ask, he commands' (Meinertz, 16)—are relentless, and they are demanding. He calls readers to endure trials with patience (1.2-4, 12; 5.7-11), to seek wisdom (1.5-8; 3.13-18), to conquer anger (1.19), to control desire (1.14-16; 4.1-3), and to avoid relying upon wealth (1.9-11; 4.13–5.6). Batten indeed thinks that James' teaching is sufficiently stringent to merit the label, 'ascetical'.[471] Perhaps it would be better to speak of an incipient asceticism. Compared with later monastics or even the Gospel of Thomas, James remains undeveloped in the relevant respects. It is, moreover, not obvious that our book regards 'wealth in itself as an evil',[472] and it does not call for a sectarian existence.[473] Still, it does frown upon the pursuit of mammon, and it draws a heavy line between 'the world' and God and demands undivided loyalty to the latter (4.4-10).[474] It further presses hearers to overcome their passions (1.14-15; 4.1-3). In short, it rejects 'the world' and calls for renouncing customary goals and desires for the sake of a spiritual ideal.[475] Later ascetics, unsurprisingly, found the work congenial.[476]

One should not forget in this connection that the author chose to write under the name of James. The latter was remembered as having lived a life of self-denial, poverty, and suffering. Hegesippus, for example, says that he was 'holy from birth', that he 'drank no wine', that he was a vegetarian, that he did not shave his head, that he did not anoint himself with oil, that he took no baths, and that he prayed so much that his knees became calloused like those of a camel.[477] It does not surprise that a letter attributed to such a one is full of moral exhortations that display some ascetic-like tendencies.

Eschatology
Eschatological expectation is important for James, and it is present in every section.[478] It is nonetheless not a topic in and of itself, and it

---

[471] Batten, 'Asceticism'. For Wolmarans, 'Misogyny', 1.12-18 presupposes that sexual intercourse is sinful.

[472] So Scott, *Literature*, 214; cf. Preisker, 'Eigenwert', 235. Contrast Batten, 'Strategies', 25: although James is not aligned with the wealthy, he is not 'particularly focused upon attacking the rich. Rather James uses the dishonourable depictions of the rich and their future demise as a contrast to his audience's identity as the honourable poor, who must continue to support one another and withstand the trials of carving out an existence without patronal support'.

[473] See esp. Lockett, 'Strong'.

[474] On the corrupt cosmos in James see Jackson-McCabe, 'Messiah', 707-708.

[475] On the links between theology and ethics in James see esp. Konradt, 'Werke'.

[476] See 350, 589-90, 773; also Sahdona, *Perf.* 2.5.21-22 CSCO 214 Scriptores Syri 90 ed. Halleux, 57, and the references in Johnson, *Brother*, 72 n. 50. Johnson, 132, is correct: 'Monks found in James a clear and challenging support for flight from the world of sin and for combat with the devil and self-control'.

[477] Cf. Hegesippus *apud* Eusebius, *H.E.* 2.23.4-18.

[478] The most helpful treatment of eschatology in James is Penner, *Eschatology*. It is an effective antidote to the flawed view of Dibelius, 87, that James lacks eschatological

remains undeveloped. This is in large part due to the author's assumption that his audience will concur with him about much: 'the Lord' will return (5.7-9); there will be a final reckoning (2.12-13; 3.1; 4.12; 5.9);[479] that reckoning is near (5.7-9);[480] it will mean salvation and reward for the righteous in God's kingdom (1.12, 21; 2.5; 4.10; 5.20); it will mean the punishment of Gehenna for others (2.13; 3.6; 5.3).[481] Beyond these conventions, details are not necessary. Will judgment of the wicked mean extinction or everlasting punishment, or maybe temporal retribution? Will the punishment vary according to the crime? Will the kingdom be on earth or in heaven? Although our author may have pondered such subjects, for the purposes of his letter he is mute. All that matters is the consolation of hope and the threat of loss.[482]

Love of God and the *imitatio dei* may be, for our author, motives for fitting behavior (1.12; 2.5, 12-13), but he also invokes the threat of eschatological punishment and the promise of eschatological reward in order to incite people to change, or to keep them in the way that they should go.[483] He does not teach that people should do the good for its own sake. He nowhere says: *Virtus sibi ipsi praemium*. He rather takes human fear for granted and uses it to reinforce moral exhortations, confronting auditors with the possibility of a miserable final fate, just as he takes human hope as a given and promises its fulfillment in the kingdom of God. Josephus, *Bell*. 2.157, expresses what James assumes, that 'the good are made better in their lifetime by the hope of a reward after death, and the passions of the wicked are restrained by the fear that, even though they escape detection while alive, they will undergo never-ending punishment after their decease'.[484]

'passion'. Puech, 'Qumrân', 45, suggests that the eschatological statements in 1.2-12 and 4.6–5.12 form a sort of *inclusio* that helps unify the book. See further Fabris, 'Tradizione'. For Pretorius, 'Coherency', eschatological destiny is a consistent incentive in James. It is possible that James equated the difficulties of his present time (1.2-4, 12; 5.7-11) with the tribulations of the final days; see on 1.2.

[479] On the ubiquity of this belief see M. Reiser, *Jesus and Judgment*, Minneapolis, 1997. One should not forget that divine judgment is even a theme on epitaphs in the Jewish and Graeco-Roman worlds; cf. P.W. van der Horst, *Ancient Jewish Epitaphs*, Kampen, 1991, 56-58, and the collection of inscriptions in J. Strubbe, *Arai epitymbioi*, Bonn, 1997.

[480] This is also assumed in 5.1-6; cf. Klein, *Werk*, 175-76.

[481] Cf. Brosend, 147: 'The thoroughgoing nature of the eschatological expectations in the letter of James argues for similar expectations in the community for and to which he wrote'.

[482] Burchard, 203, is obviously right to caution that, given the brevity of James, one should not infer our author's ignorance or disbelief in eschatological expectations about which he says nothing (e.g. the resurrection of the dead).

[483] See further Mussner, 209-10; Spencer, 'Function'; Klein, *Werk*, 163-84.

[484] Cf. Origen *C. Cels*. 8.48 ed. Marcovich, 562-63 (the purpose of the subject of punishments is 'to induce those who have heard the truth to strive with all their might against those sins which are the causes of punishment'); Ephraem, *Ep. ad Publ*. 23 ed.

In James, eschatology is wholly in the service of ethics. That is why it makes no difference whether the author speaks about the near end (5.7-9) or reminds readers that life is brief so that death is nigh (1.10-11; 4.14). The two impending futures function the same way, because the chief purpose of each is to encourage right behavior and deter wrong conduct.

VIII. LOCAL ORIGIN

The proposals as to where James was written are various:

Rome	Brückner, Pfleiderer, Grafe, von Soden, Streeter, Henshaw, S. Marshall, Schulz, Laws, Deppe, Simonis, Orlando[485]
Egypt/Alexandria	Moffatt, Brandon, Cantinat, Schnider, Hoppe, Schnelle[486]
Syria	J. Weiss, Shepherd, Konradt, Pokorný-Heckel[487]
Antioch	Goodspeed, Zimmermann, Burchard[488]
Palestine	Knowling, Ropes, Marty, Mitton, Townsend, Davids, Johnson, Peuch[489]
Jerusalem	Mussner, Hartin, Dunn[490]
Galilee	Elliott-Binns[491]
Unknown	Popkes[492]

As there is no tradition that James the Brother of Jesus ever left Palestine, those who assign our letter to him have naturally thought of it as having been written in Jerusalem or Palestine. The inference is consistent with 1.1, which moves one to think of James of Jerusalem writing to the diaspora. It further harmonizes with the presence of Semitisms,[493] which are consistent with a bi-lingual author. Furthermore, several verses—above

---

Brock, 293 (rewards are explained 'so that people may yearn for them', and judgment is proclaimed so 'that they may restrain themselves').

[485] Brückner, *Reihenfolge*, 295; Pfleiderer, *Christianity*, 298; Grafe, *Stellung*, 45; von Soden, 164; Streeter, *Church* 196-206; Henshaw, *Literature*, 357; Schulz, *Mitte*, 283; Laws, 21-26; Schnider, 18; Deppe, *Sayings*, 211-15; Simonis, *Paulus*, 110-12; Orlando, *Lettera*, 25.

[486] Moffatt, 1; Brandon, *Fall*, 237-39; Cantinat, 53 (tentatively); Schnider, 18; Hoppe, 13-14; Schnelle, *History*, 388. Vouga, 18, suggests either Alexandria or Antioch.

[487] J. Weiss, *Christianity*, 2.751; Shepherd, 'Matthew', 49; Konradt, 'Context', 117; Pokorný-Heckel, *Einleitung*, 727. Preisker, 'Eigenwert', 236, suggests Syria or Asia Minor. For Garleff, *Identität*, 231, the choice is between Palestine or Syria.

[488] Goodspeed, *Introduction*, 291-92; Zimmermann, *Lehrer*, 194-96; Burchard, 7 (with hesitation).

[489] Knowling, xxiv; Ropes, 41-42; Marty, 280; Mitton, 233-34; Townsend, xxxi-xxxiii; Johnson, 120; Puech, 'Qumrân'; Davids, 'Tradition' (the most extensive defense of a Palestinian provenance).

[490] Mussner, 23; Hartin, 27; Dunn, *Beginning*, 1128.

[491] Elliott-Binns, *Christianity*, 43-52.

[492] Popkes, 69.

[493] On these see above, 86-87.

all 1.6, 11; 3.4, 11-12; 5.7, 17-18—have often been thought to imply a Palestinian or even Galilean author.[494]

This commentary, however, argues that our letter is a pseudepigraphon, so 1.1 cannot be taken at face value. Nor can 1.6, 11; 3.4, 11-12; 5.7, and 17-18 support the weight often laid upon them. Most of those verses contain biblical *topoi* or otherwise rhetorical common places, as the verse-by-verse commentary shows. It is instructive to keep in mind how easily they can be turned into an argument for some other location. To illustrate: Brandon bolstered his case for an Alexandrian origin of James with these words: 'The use of the simile of the tossing of waves as an illustration in 1.6 would indicate a familiarity with the sea, which might be expected of a writer in a seaport city, and further, the great interest in ships, and especially the note about their size, would well fit in with an Alexandrian authorship, for Alexandria was famous for its great corn ships; again the reference to trading in 4.13 would be natural to an inhabitant of a great commercial centre such as Alexandria'.[495]

Some would insist, against the commentary below on 5.7, that at least James' mention of the early and late rains is evidence for the author's first-hand knowledge of Palestine. According to Davids, the phrase 'could indicate either the author's origin or his location at the time of writing'.[496] Yet πρόϊμος + ὄψιμος with reference to rain occurs five times in the LXX and so would be known to the biblically literate. One recalls the modern Pentecostals who reckon themselves part of 'the latter-rain movement'. They borrowed the expression from the Bible. They did not learn it from their travels abroad.[497]

The appeal to Semitisms is also not decisive. Our unknown author, in addition to knowing the LXX, could have studied Hebrew scriptures in a diaspora context. Or maybe our text represents a diaspora Christianity with strong roots in pre-70 Jerusalem, some of whose members continued to speak Aramaic for a time. We simply do not know. But one can scarcely urge that all post-70 Jews or Christians living in the diaspora were unacquainted with a Semitic language. Hebrew is well attested in diaspora inscriptions.[498]

If the case for a Palestinian origin is inconclusive, there are perhaps hints favoring another verdict. This author, while conceding that the evidence is circumstantial and fragile, believes that the best bet is Rome.

---

[494] See above, 6.

[495] Brandon, *Fall*, 238. It is true enough that the writings of Philo, who lived in Alexandria, are full of nautical metaphors; cf. Deines, 'Sources', 43-44.

[496] Davids, 'Tradition', 48.

[497] For additional examples from Christian history see 702 n. 80; 703 n. 82.

[498] JIWE 1.48, 61, 75, 80, 82, 84, 111 = CIJ 1.594, 599, 609, 569, 570, 593; etc. Recall that the Monteverde catacomb in Rome preserves Semitic epitaphs: JIWE 33, 47, 53, 58, 92 = CIJ 1.291, 294, 292, 290, 293. There are even a few inscriptions from Egypt in Hebrew or Aramaic, such as JIGRE 3, 4, 5 = CIJ 2.1424, 1425, 1426.

(i) James shares many linguistic and thematic parallels with 1 Clement and Hermas, both written in Rome. Some deem those parallels sufficient to establish that Hermas and Clement knew James. If they are correct, then the two earliest witnesses to James would be Roman texts. If, on the other hand, 1 Clement and Hermas are independent of James, the numerous striking agreements necessarily reflect common traditions that we know circulated in Rome.

(ii) There are extensive, numerous parallels between James and 1 Peter, another book composed in Rome.[499] The explanation of the agreements is, as we have seen, disputed. Some contend that the two books draw upon a common text or tradition. In that case the common text or tradition was known in Rome. Others urge that 1 Peter used James. In that case 1 Peter would be another early Roman witness to James. Still others, including this commentator, have concluded that James knew 1 Peter. In this case James was familiar with a writing that appeared in Rome at the end of the first century. Whatever solution one adopts, the links between James and 1 Peter are links to a Roman text or tradition.

(iii) This commentary argues elsewhere that James not only knew something of Pauline theology but that he plausibly knew Romans and perhaps 1 Corinthians.[500] This is relevant not only because Romans must have been read in the Christian communities in Rome but also because the author of 1 Clement, writing in Rome at the end of the first century, appears, like our author, to have read or heard both 1 Corinthians and Romans.[501]

(iv) The commentary on 4.5 makes the case that the unnamed γραφή there cited is the defunct Eldad and Modad. This matters because that book was known to Roman Christians in the period when James wrote. It is cited by name in Herm. *Vis.* 2.3.4, and it is highly likely that the quoted material common to 1 Clem. 23.3-4 and 2 Clem. 11.2-4 comes from the same source[502]—and Hermas and 1 Clement came out of Rome.[503]

(v) At points James seems to reflect an urban setting. The text assumes that readers are familiar with a court (2.7), with wealthy individuals (2.2; 5.1-6), and with merchants who travel from city to city (4.13-16, with πόλις).[504] An urban origin would also account for the author's Greek

---

[499] Cf. the greeting in 1 Pet 5.13: 'Babylon' = Rome; see Achtemeier, *1 Peter*, 353-55. For the links between 1 Peter and James see above, 67-70.

[500] See above, 62-67; below, 444-57.

[501] See A.F. Gregory, '1 Clement and the Writings that later formed the New Testament', in Gregory-Tuckett, *Reception*, 129-57—'very likely' for Romans, 'certain' for 1 Corinthians.

[502] For the details see Allison, 'Eldad'.

[503] Where 2 Clement was written is not known. Suggestions include Rome, Corinth, and Alexandria.

[504] Cf. Simonis, *Paulus*, 109; Batten, *Friendship*, 183.

education[505] as well as for the contacts between our book and popular Graeco-Roman philosophy, including Stoicism.

(vi) James, as argued above, represents a form of Christian Judaism, and we know that Rome was home to Christian Jews in both the first and early second centuries.[506] The famous line in Suetonius, *Claud.* 25.4, about Claudius expelling from Rome Jews 'who were making disturbances at the instigation of Chrestus', likely adverts to a dispute between Jews and Jewish Christians.[507] Romans 16.3-5 speaks of a house church led by the Jews Aquila and Prisca (cf. Acts 18.2), while 16.7 dubs two additional Jewish Christians, Andronicus and Junia, 'prominent among the apostles'; and Paul's letter to the Romans elsewhere assumes that Christian Jews as well as Gentile Christians will hear it.[508] The presence of such Christians in Rome is further indicated by Philippians, if that letter was written there and if 1.15-18 refers to Judaizers.[509] Just as important, because of the later date of James, is 1 Clement, a Roman writing full of lightly Christianized Jewish traditions. 1 Clement is a witness either to on-going contact between church and synagogue or to the influence upon Clement of Christians who had attended synagogue at one time.[510]

One possible protest against a Roman provenance is that James seems to have suffered widespread neglect until the third century, at least if one doubts that it influenced 1 Clement or Hermas. Would not a book circulating in Rome or sponsored by churches there have won a wider hearing?[511] The problem with this objection is that the Roman church was not a monolithic entity, and there is no reason to imagine that the product of one of its Jewish Christian groups would have been welcomed by all of its Gentile groups. Moreover, the case of Marcion shows that what

---

[505] For signs of such an education see above, 56.

[506] See esp. R. Hvalvik, 'Jewish Believers and Jewish Influence in the Roman Church until the Early Second Century', in Skarsaune-Hvalvik, *Believers*, 179-216.

[507] Incidentally, the common assumption that the event Claudius refers to permanently separated all Christians from all Jews is scarcely warranted. Cf. P. Lampe, *Paul*, 79: 'individual Christians continued to have contacts with Jews' and 'for the second century, too, one must still reckon with a direct influx of individuals carrying tradition from the synagogue'.

[508] See Dunn, *Romans 1-8*, xliv-liv; R.K. Jewett, *Romans: A Commentary*, Minneapolis, 2007, 70-72.

[509] See M. Bockmuehl, *The Epistle to the Philippians*, London, 1998, 25-32, 76-80.

[510] Note P. Lampe, *Paul*, 76: 'Christians from the sphere of influence of the synagogues, Jewish Christian as well as Gentile Christian, exercised an astonishing influence on the formation of theology in urban Roman Christianity in the first century. These Christians from the sphere of influence of the synagogues presumably formed the majority. Most Christians of the first generation, at least before their conversion, would have had contacts with a synagogue. As *sebomenoi* or as members of Judaism, they would in varied intensity have taken in its wealth of ideas.'

[511] For use of James in third and fourth century Rome see Johnson, 136-37.

mattered ultimately was content, not provenance. His writings, although composed in Rome, were not read and copied by the dominant Christian movement that opposed him. Similarly, if James emerged from an Ebionite-like community, the book's failure to become an immediate best seller scarcely surprises.

IX. TEXT

Although this commentary prints for the most part the Greek text in the *Editio Critica Maior* of 1997, it does not regard that critical edition as the last word.[512] Our earliest Greek witnesses are P20, P23, and P100.[513] The first two are from the third century while P100 is from the third or fourth century. All three are woefully incomplete.[514] The earliest patristic source is Origen, from the first half of the third century. His quotations cover only a small part of James and have their own uncertain textual history. Thus, even if our letter appeared as late as 120, a century or more lies between the original and the earliest fragmentary witnesses, and we have no cause to believe that our letter was miraculously immune to the sorts of scribal errors and corrections that attended the transmission of all other early Christian writings.[515]

This commentary prefers one reading that the *Editio Critica Maior* relegates to its apparatus (see 5.19) and in two instances opts for conjectural emendations, that is, texts without external support (see on 2.1 and 4.2).[516] The justification is the great distance between the autograph and our extant witnesses, along with the conviction that James could not have passed through the second century without suffering alteration.[517]

This commentary makes no attempt to supply a large apparatus. Variants are cited (i) when this commentator is unusually uncertain of the original (see e.g. on 2.3; 4.13). Also noted are readings that (ii) have a

---

[512] For a helpful survey of where the *Editio Critica Maior* differs from early critical Greek editions see Parker, 'Text'.

[513] The imperfect Greek leaves of Jas 1–2 published in C. Simonides, *Facsimiles of Certain Portions of the Gospel of St. Matthew and of the Epistles of St. James & Jude*, London, 1861, and purported to be from the first century, were forged.

[514] P20 contains 2.19–3.9. P23 contains 1.10-12, 15-18. P100 contains 3.13–4.4; 4.9–5.1.

[515] In general see the overview of M.W. Holmes, 'Text and Transmission in the Second Century', in *The Reliability of the New Testament*, ed. R.B. Stewart, Minneapolis, 2011, 61-79. With regard to James in particular, note the old article of Ropes, 'Text', which demonstrates concretely that 'no Ms. or version gives an untouched, "neutral", text free from emendations'. Papyri published since then do not alter the picture.

[516] This commentator would also happily endorse conjectural emendations in 2.18 and 3.6 if he could find any sufficiently convincing.

[517] See further Wettlaufer, 'Variants', who argues for conjectural emendations in 3.1; 4.2, 4.

decent chance of being original even if not favored by modern critical editions; (iii) have aroused scholarly interest and discussion; (iv) affect notably the sense of the text; or (v) illustrate a significant tendency in the textual tradition, such as assimilation to the LXX, other NT texts, or other parts of James itself. The abbreviations and symbols in the apparatus are those of the *Editio Critica Maior*.

X. THE RECEPTION OF JAMES

The commentary proper offers a history of interpretation and influence section by section, and sometimes verse by verse. Here, then, we need only make some large, introductory generalizations about the *Wirkungsgeschichte* or reception history of James.

We have already seen that evidence for the circulation of James before Origen is slight. Some would regard Hermas as the exception; but if they are correct, Hermas may stand alone. Other writers before the third century betray at best, in this or that phrase, a passing acquaintance with the book.[518] No one discusses it, and no one quotes it by name.

Given this large silence, it is no surprise that James continued to have a checkered history for some time. Important patristic authorities, including Tertullian, Cyprian, and Novatian, appear to have paid it no heed, and in the west in general it garnered little attention before the middle of the fourth century,[519] although by that time it must have been translated into Latin.[520] Eusebius, while he regarded the book as canonical, observed that its status was contested,[521] and it is absent from several early lists—the Muratorian Canon (of disputed date), the Canon Mommsenianus (359), and the Cheltenham Canon (360)—as well as from the principal mss. of the Old Latin. Theodore of Mopsuestia did not use it,[522] and James was furthermore no part of the earliest Syrian canon[523]—which is all the more remarkable given the prominence of its alleged author among eastern Christians. The book gained widespread acceptance among Syrian Christians only with its inclusion in the Peshitta and the

---

[518] E.g. Irenaeus and Clement of Alexandria; see above, 15-16.

[519] Cf. Meyer, *Rätsel*, 8-18. Ambrose makes some use of James; cf. e.g. *Lk* 8.13 SC 52 ed. Tissot, 106; *Off*. 2.7 ed. Davidson, 272. Hilary quotes 1.17 in *Trin*. 4.8 CCSL 62 ed. Smulders, 108. Ambrosiaster cites 5.20 in *Gal ad* 5.10 CSEL 81.3 ed. Vogels, 57. For the argument that Athanasius had a hand in the western acceptance of James see J.P. Yates, 'The Reception of the Epistle of James in the Latin West', in Schlosser, *Epistles*, 273-88.

[520] See Ropes, 'Text', 120-21.

[521] Eusebius, *H.E.* 2.23.25; 3.25.3. According to Ropes, 94, Eusebius was here thinking of 'the Syrians'.

[522] Both Leontius Byzantinus, *Nest. et Eut.* 3.13 PG 86.1365C, and Isho'dad of Merv *ad loc.* HSem 10 ed. Gibson, 50, remark upon Theodoret's failure to recognize James.

[523] See Meyer, *Rätsel*, 18-22.

Philoxenian version.[524] This is why it plays no role in Aphraates, Ephraem, or the Doctrine of Addai.[525] Even after the Peshitta appeared, the Nestorians tended to regard the book as possessing a lesser authority.[526]

By the end of the fourth century, however, it had won for itself canonical standing in most Christian quarters, east and west. It appears in Sinaiticus and Vaticanus, in the canon lists of Codex Claromontanus (D), Athanasius,[527] Cyril of Jerusalem, Gregory of Nazianzus,[528] Amphilochius, Philaster of Brescia, Epiphanius, Rufinus, and Innocent I, as well as in the lists of the Councils of Laodicea (364), Hippo (393), and Carthage (397).[529] Chrysostom quoted occasionally from James,[530] and the book eventually was taken up into the Greek lectionary cycle.[531] Jerome included James in the Vulgate, and Augustine esteemed it authoritative scripture.[532]

There were few commentaries before the Reformation, never large.[533] Didymus the Blind may have been the first to write on James. In any event, only fragments survive.[534] Augustine wrote a now lost and presumably unsubstantial work on James.[535] The *Catenae* of Andreas published by Cramer, with its many quotations from Chrysostom and Cyril of Alexandria, could descend from a sixth-century catena.[536] Bede wrote his

---

[524] B. Aland, *Das Neue Testament in syrischer Überlieferung I*, Berlin, 1986, 94-104, finds no evidence for an earlier translation of James into Syriac.

[525] That is, authentic Ephraem. The Greek corpus of Ps.-Ephraem often uses James.

[526] See Metzger, *Canon*, 219-20. For a survey of James in the Syrian church see Ropes, 96-100.

[527] The *Synopsis sacrae scripturae*, with its very short summary of James in PG 28.405D-408A, is wrongly attributed to Athanasius.

[528] But in general the Cappadocians make sparse use of James; see Johnson, 131.

[529] Athanasius, *Ep. fest.* 39 PG 26.1437B; Cyril of Jerusalem, *Cat.* 4.36 PG 33.499B; Gregory of Nazianzus, *Poem* 1.1.12 PG 37.474; Amphilochius, *Seleuc.* PG 37.1597; Filaster of Brescia, *Haer.* 88.4 CCSL 9 ed. Bulhart, 255; Epiphanius, *Haer.* 3.1.76; Rufinus of Aquileia, *Exp. symb.* 35 CCSL 20 ed. Simonetti, 171; Innocent 1, *Ep.* 6.7 PL 20.502A.

[530] See R.A. Krupp, *Saint John Chrysostom: A Scripture Index*, Lanham, MD, 1984, 251-52.

[531] See C.-B. Amphoux, 'Les lectionnaires grecs', in Amphoux-Bouhot, *Lecture*, 19-47. For surveys of James in later Eastern and Byzantine sources see Meinertz, *Verfasser*, 193-203; Johnson, *Brother*, 61-83.

[532] But against the usual story, it is not clear that Jerome and Augustine are chiefly responsible for the acceptance of James in the West; see J. Yates, 'The Canonical Significance of the Citations of James in Pelagius', *ETL* 78 (2002), 482-89; also Yates, 'Reception', as in n. 519.

[533] See further the brief, helpful review of earlier commentaries in Ropes, 110-13.

[534] K. Staab, 'Die Griechischen Katenenkommentare zu den Katholischen briefen', *Bib* 5 (1924), 296-353, makes it likely that the relevant fragments represent not a later catena but a commentary of Didymus.

[535] Augustine, *Retr.* 2.32 ed. Perl, 196.

[536] See Ropes, 110-11; Staab, 'Katenenkommentare' (as in n. 534). Ps.-Oecumenius often depends upon this, and the commentary attributed to Theophylact is partly derivative of it.

influential, verse-by-verse commentary in the eighth century.[537] The work of Isho'dad of Merv comes from the next century.[538] The Glossa Ordinaria, traditionally but wrongly assigned to Walafrid Strabo,[539] may not have appeared before the early twelfth century.[540] After that, it became the standard commentary in the West.[541] Nicholas of Gorran, Nicholas of Lyra, and Jan Hus also penned pre-Reformation commentaries.

From Origen on, James was read in terms of Paul, and Paul was read in terms of James. The ruling assumption was that there could be no conflict. This is why Origen's commentary on Romans makes significant use of James without raising the issue of possible contradiction. Sometimes—beginning with Pelagius and Augustine—the undeniable tensions were duly contemplated,[542] but the issue was never in doubt: it was impossible for two apostles to contradict one another. The same harmonizing hermeneutic governed the recurrent attempts to bring the content of 1.2 and 13 into line with the Lord's Prayer and its petition to be delivered from evil.

This is why Luther marks such a radical break with Jamesian exegetical tradition. His understanding of Paul entailed a rejection of James,[543] and 'in this way attention was drawn for the first time to the fact that within the New Testament there are material differences between the books of instruction—differences that cannot be reconciled—and as a consequence it became possible to observe the multiplicity of the ways of thinking'.[544] Although Luther often quoted James to positive effect[545] and

---

[537] Subsequent Latin work on James is full of quotations—acknowledged and unacknowledged—from Bede. Indeed, Rabanus Maurus, *Hom.* 34, 40, and 42 PL 110.207D-209C, 219D-220D, 223A-224B, simply reproduce Bede.

[538] For later Syriac commentaries see Dionysius bar Salībī, *In Apocalypim, Actus et Epistulas Catholicas*, CSCO 53, 60 Scriptores Syri 101 ed. Sedlacek; Gregory Bar-Hebraeus, in M. Klamroth, *Gregorii Abulfaragii Bar Ebhraya in Actus Apostolorum et Epistolas catholicas adnotationes*, Göttingen, 1878.

[539] K. Froehlich, *Biblical Interpretation from the Church Fathers to the Reformation*, Farnham, Surrey, 2010, 192-96.

[540] M.T. Gibson, 'The Twelfth Century Glossed Bible', in *Studia Patristica*, vol. 23, ed. E.A. Livingstone, Leuven, 1989, 232-44.

[541] See chaps. 2–8 of Froehlich, *Interpretation* (as in n. 539). For a survey of James in the Latin Middle Ages see Meinertz, *Verfasser*, 206-15.

[542] See e.g. Pelagius, *Rom ad* 3.28 TU 9.2 ed. Robinson, 34; Augustine, *En. Ps* 31.2.2-3 CCSL 38 ed. Dekkers and Fraipont, 225-27; *Fide et op.* 14.21-23 CSEL 41 ed. Zycha, 61-64; also the overview of Augustine in Bergauer, *Jakobusbrief*, 45-81.

[543] Perhaps the earliest statement along these lines came in his famous 1519 debate with John Eck; cf. 'Resolutiones Lutherianae super propositionibus suis Lipsiae disputatis', in *D. Martin Luthers Werke*, vol. 2, Weimar, 1884, 425.

[544] W.G. Kümmel, *The New Testament: The History of the Investigation of Its Problems*, Nashville, 1972, 26.

[545] See F. Graf-Stuhlhofer, 'Martin Luthers Bibelgebrauch in quantitativer Betrachtung', *Theologisches Gespräch* 24 (2000), 111-20. Even in the 'Preface to the Epistles of St. James and St. Jude', in *Luther's Works*, vol. 35, ed. E.T. Bachmann, Philadelphia, 1960, 395-97, where he criticized James, Luther also wrote: 'I praise it and

even preached on the book,[546] he yet denied the letter's apostolic authority.[547] His reason was that it teaches 'works-righteousness' and fails to mention the sufferings of Christ. He famously spoke of James as 'a right strawy epistle'—perhaps alluding to 1 Cor 3.12?[548]—without 'evangelical character'.[549] He also asserted that the unknown author,[550] who may not even have been a Christian, 'throws things together chaotically'.[551] Indeed, he even, when discussing once what James has to say about justification, could assert that the author 'raves'.[552] Luther placed James along with Hebrews, Jude, and Revelation at the back of his Bible and failed to enumerate those Catholic Epistles in the table of contents.[553]

Luther's views have had a far-flung effect.[554] They are reflected in Osiander's great commentary, which argues that James was not an apostle and that he contradicts Romans.[555] The Wüttenberg Confession of 1552, drawn up by Johann Brenz, excluded James from the canonical books. The Swiss German Bible sponsored by Zwingli (1527–1529) followed Luther in relegating Hebrews, James, Jude, and Revelation to a

---

consider it a good book'; 'I cannot include him among the chief books, though I would not...prevent anyone from including or extolling him as he pleases, for there are otherwise many good sayings in him'. Luther was not even unremittingly negative about 2.14-26; cf. H. Heinz, 'Jakobus 2, 14-26 in der Sicht Martin Luthers', *AUSS* 19 (1981), 141-46.

[546] See 'Sermon for the Fourth Sunday after Easter', on Jas 1.16-21, in *The Sermons of Martin Luther*, vol. 7, Grand Rapids, MI, 1989, 289-300. The sermon was first printed in Wittenberg in 1536.

[547] Yet in the sermon cited in the previous note, he repeatedly calls James an 'apostle'.

[548] If so, the implication is that one should not build with straw, that is, construct theology with this book.

[549] 'Preface to the New Testament', in *Luther's Works* (as in n. 159), 362 ('eyn rechte strohern Epistel'). These words have often been echoed; note e.g. Blackman, 33: James offers 'simple things for the ordinary member who is not interested in theology, has no deep religious experience, and yet feels called to be faithful in that which is least: who asks for no spiritual banquet, but is content with a diet of straw!' Luther himself withdrew the remark from later editions of the NT.

[550] Erasmus anticipated Luther in doubting that James the apostle wrote James. See below, 114 n. 8.

[551] Luther, 'Preface to the Epistles of St. James and St. Jude', in *Luther's Works* (as in n. 159), 397.

[552] Luther, *In Genesin Enarrationum*, vol. 2.3, in *Exegetica Opera Latina*, Erlangen, 1830, 1830, 227 (*delirat*).

[553] Before Luther, James was ordinarily placed at the front of the Catholic Epistles. That is its place in the Vulgate and the Byzantine ms. tradition.

[554] On James in the sixteenth century, Kawerau, 'Schicksale', remains instructive. For later responses to Luther see M. Meinertz, 'Luthers Kritik am Jakobusbriefe nach dem Urteile seiner Anhänger', BZ 3 (1905), 273-86.

[555] See e.g. his brief introduction to James: Osiander, 719. M. Flacius Illyricus, *Ecclesiastic historia*, vol. 2, *Secunda Centuria*, Basel, CH, 1559, 71-72, also adopts Luther's critical conclusions as well as his reasons for them.

INTRODUCTION

separate section as the end of the NT and left them unnumbered.[556] Similarly, the NTs of Tyndale (1525) and Coverdale (1535) placed Hebrews, James, Jude, and Revelation at the end, as books of uncertain or secondary status.[557] Jacob Lucius published a Bible (1596) in which James was classified among the NT 'Apocrypha', and David Wolder's Bible (also 1596) listed James as non-canonical.[558]

Eventually, and after the permanent split of Catholicism and Protestantism, James made a recovery among Lutherans.[559] The view of Melanchthon, which harmonized Paul and James and upheld the authority of the latter, came to dominate popular German piety and theology.[560] Thus the Formula of Concord (1577) treated James as an authoritative member of the canon.[561] In Anglican circles, the publication of the Bishops' Bible (1568), in which the NT is printed in the traditional order, signaled a rejection of Luther's skepticism.

Nevertheless, in critical theological circles, unease with or uncertainty about James never wholly vanished and indeed made a come-back of sorts in the nineteenth century, with the critical contributions of Kern and de Wette.[562] This is the larger historical context for Bultmann's negative

---

[556] Yet Zwingli himself did not question the authority of James; see F. Schmidt-Clausing, 'Die unterschiedliche Stellung Luthers und Zwinglis zum Jakobusbrief', *Reformatio* 18 (1969), 568-85; T. George, '"A Right Strawy Epistle": Reformation Perspectives on James', *RevExp* 83 (1986), 373-75.

[557] H.H. Howorth, 'The Origin and Authority of the Biblical Canon in the Anglican Church', *JTS* 8 (1907), 1-40.

[558] Cf. Metzger, *Canon*, 245. See further A. Wikgren, 'Luther and "New Testament Apocrypha"', in *A Tribute to Arthur Vööbus*, ed. R.H. Fischer, Chicago, 1977, 379-90.

[559] Although Luther had Protestant opponents from the beginning. Karlstadt, *De Canonicis Scripturis libellus* (1520; reprinted in K.A. Credner, *Zur Geschichte des Kanons*, Halle, 1847, 402-406), already rejected Luther's arguments against James, contending that, even if the author is unknown, the book is canonical and authoritative.

[560] The commentaries of Neander, Weidner, and Scaer are all energetic attempts to claim James without embarrassment for Lutheran theology. Note that the latter closes his commentary with a chapter entitled, 'Luther, the Lutherans, and James: An Attempt at a Defense' (138-41).

[561] Kawerau, 'Schicksale', 369, suggests that the Formula of Concord marked the turning point regarding the status of James among Lutherans. By contrast, H.H. Howorth, 'The Canon of the Bible among the Later Reformers', *JTS* 10 (1909), 193-95, documents continued and significant support for Luther in the seventeenth century and suggests that it was only eighteenth-century pietism that resolved the issue. That century, however, witnessed the advent of deism and the Enlightenment, so the canonical question was never fully closed; see H. von Lips, *Der neutestamentliche Kanon*, Zurich, 2004, 164-74.

[562] Note e.g. K.F.A. Kahnis, *Die Lutherische Dogmatik*, vol. 1, Leipzig, 1861, 533-36. But one should observe that criticism of James has not been confined to theologians and academics. E.g. the famous Chinese preacher, Witness Lee, in his *Life-Study of James, First Peter, Second Peter*, Anaheim, CA, 1985, remarks that 'James may not have had a clear view concerning the distinction between grace and law' (20), that 'he did not have a clear vision concerning God's New Testament economy'. These critical views are embedded in his NT study notes as found in the so-called Recovery Bible, and they are

take on James: 'Every shred of understanding for the Christian's situation...is lacking here. The moralism of the synagogue-tradition has made its entry, and it is possible that James not merely stands in the general context of this tradition but that its author took over a Jewish document and only lightly retouched it.'[563]

The Reformed tradition has, by contrast, typically given a more positive reception to James. This is in large part because Calvin wrote a favorable commentary on the book. The preface contains these words: 'I am fully content to accept this epistle, when I find it contains nothing unworthy of an apostle of Christ. Indeed, it is a rich source of varied instruction, of abundant benefit in all aspects of Christian life. We may find striking passages on endurance, on calling upon God, on the practice of religion, on restraining our speech, on peace-making, on holding back greedy instincts, on disregard for this present life' (259). The detailed commentary then argues—against 'the false reasoning that has trapped the sophists'—that Jas 2.14-26, understood aright, does not contradict Paul. Zwingli, Beza, and John Knox were of the same mind, and they were followed by Pareus and subsequent Reformed exegetes.

Nonetheless, Luther's discomfort with James does find occasional echoes in the Reformed tradition. Barth wrote to Eduard Thurneysen in 1923: James 'speaks one-sidedly as a preacher of repentance and always *ad hominem*, to the individual as such. There are indeed quite striking things in it that give some light if one examines them carefully. But I am glad...that in the summer I shall be taking up Paul (I Cor. 15) again'.[564]

---

promulgated among his followers. Cf. R. Kangas, 'The Pattern of Paul and the Religion of James', *Affirmation & Critique* 1 (1996), 32-43, which includes these remarks: 'the "godliness" of the religion of James is something apart from God's New Testament economy; that is, it is something that is not the product of the Triune God' (41); 'the religion of James might have been "pure and undefiled" in his eyes, but in the eyes of God it was an intolerable mixture' (42). Even among Christian groups that do not officially criticize James, the book has often been treated as a second-class citizen; cf. P.R. Jones, 'Approaches to the Study of the Book of James', *RevExp* 16 (1969), 425: speaking for American Baptists of fifty years ago Jones observed: 'Its bare contents are not familiar to the average layman beyond a faint memory of the refrain, "Be ye doers of the word and not hearers only"'.

[563] Bultmann, *Theology*, 2.162-63. Cf. 143: 'that which is specifically Christian is surprisingly thin'. It is not so unexpected that Bultmann's student, H. Conzelmann, in his *Outline of the Theology of the New Testament*, New York, 1969, does not, to judge by the index, contain a single reference to the Epistle of James. Cf. E.F. Scott, *The Gospel and Its Tributaries*, Edinburgh, 1928, 97 (the book represents a 'decline', 'profound ideas' have become 'formal' and 'commonplace'; the book marks a 'growing externalism' in Christian circles); Elliott, 'Perspective', 71 (James is 'customarily ranked among the "junk mail" of the Second Testament').

[564] *Revolutionary Theology in the Making: Barth-Thurneysen Correspondence, 1914–1925*, Richmond, VA, 1964, 127. Thurneysen, in his collection of sermons, *Der Brief des Jakobus*, 3rd ed., Basel, n.d., 6, refers to an unpublished lecture of Barth on Jas 1–2. To my knowledge it remains unpublished.

Post-Trent Roman Catholicism, by contrast, regularly blasted Luther's view of James[565]—to Catholics it appeared to be obvious special pleading: he dismissed what disagreed with him—and found in the book a scriptural ally with which to counter Protestant ideas about faith and works.[566] Again and again, in Catholic commentaries and polemical works of theology, James has been leveraged against *solo fide* and perceived attempts to separate faith from behavior. Justification must be real, not just imputed.[567] One nineteenth-century theologian wrote: 'The doctrine taught in the Epistle of St. James is avowedly in harmony with that of the Catholic Church, which teaches that "by works a man is justified and not by faith only" (ii. 24); these words do not exclude the part played by faith, but are totally opposed to the Lutheran view. Attempts have been made to exclude the Epistle of St. James from the Protestant canon, solely on account of its doctrine', but it is in harmony with 'the doctrine set forth at Trent'.[568]

James has been a battlefield not only for the one-time heated conflicts between Protestants and Catholics regarding justification by faith. Augustine and the Pelagians also disputed the meaning of 2.14-26; the early Anabaptists used the passage to counter what they perceived as an incipient antinomianism among Lutherans; and modern evangelical proponents of 'Lordship salvation' have appealed to the same passage in their debates with the so-called free grace movement.[569] In addition, certain Mennonites and Quakers have wielded 5.12 very effectively in their opposition to the common Christian habit of swearing.[570] Roman Catholics have routinely explained that 5.14-16 validates extreme unction as a sacrament and supports the practice of confessing one's sins to a priest. Protestants, to the contrary, have adamantly argued at length that James offers no support for Catholic tradition in these matters.[571] Again, charismatics and faith-healers have habitually urged that those same verses constitute proof that the faithful should engage in ministries of miraculous healing. But others, such as B.B. Warfield, have earnestly disagreed.[572] Although most contemporary commentaries, produced in an ecumenical age, have become irenic, it was not always so.

---

[565] For samples see H.H. Howorth, 'The Canon of the Bible among the Later Reformers', *JTS* 10 (1909), 189-91. Lapide, 3, accuses Luther of blasphemy and puts him on the side of the devil because of what he wrote about James. Note, however, that the English divine Manton likewise reproaches Luther and his followers for 'blasphemies'.

[566] For a very early, point-by-point response to Luther's main points about James see *Annotationes Hiëronymi Emsers Saligen über Luthers Neu Testament*, n.p., 1528, clii-clvi.

[567] See further below, 434.
[568] S.J. Hunter, *Outlines of Dogmatic Theology*, New York, 1896, 125.
[569] On all this see below, 436.
[570] See further below, 724.
[571] See further below, 740-43.
[572] See further below, 744-45.

The marginalizing of many of the earlier ecclesiastical debates in the commentary tradition has gone hand in hand with the rise of modern critical exegesis. Modern commentaries and monographs have tended to move historical and literary issues to center stage. Thus they typically compile vast amounts of comparative Jewish and Graeco-Romans materials. They regularly discuss the structure of the book. Some now seek understanding from the categories of classical rhetoric.[573] They deliberate over literary relations and sources. And more often than not they take multiple pages to address questions of authorship and date. In addition, most of the implicit theology in recent commentaries is generic; that is, it seems aimed at Christians in general, not Christians of this stripe or that denomination. One can hardly tell the difference any more between a commentary by a Methodist and a Baptist, or a Catholic and an Anglican, or a Presbyterian and a Lutheran.[574] We are far removed from Lapide, for whom James was largely an opportunity to quote the church fathers and medieval Catholic theologians and saints, or John Trapp, whose seventeenth-century commentary is a cache of polemical aphorisms directed against everybody but faithful Anglicans.

The historic quarrels about James and the modern turn to historical and literary questions should not lead one to lose sight of the fact that James has, more than anything else, been a source for Christian exhortation. Over and over again, in homilies and popular commentaries, its sentences—usually without concern for their context—have been employed to stress that bare belief is insufficient faith, that baptism is not the end of the line, that being a modestly 'good' Christian is not enough, and that one must sincerely care for others, which means more than wishing them well from afar. The implicit assumption has been that the ethical issues in James are timeless concerns,[575] and the emphasis has been upon the practical, and indeed the necessity for the practical. The Puritan, Thomas Manton, prefaced his mammoth commentary with these words: 'In Christ there are no dead and sapless branches; faith is not an idle grace; whatever it is, it fructifieth in good works. To evince all this to you, I have chosen to explain this epistle. The apostle wrote it upon the same reason, to wit, to prevent or check their misprisions who cried up naked apprehensions for faith, and a barren profession for true religion. Such unrelenting lumps of sin and lust were there even in the primitive times, gilded with the specious name of Christians' (9). It does not surprise that Kierkegaard found James congenial when assailing and mocking a lax, state-subsidized 'official Christianity', a religion that he

---

[573] See D.F. Watson, 'Rhetorical Criticism of Hebrews and the Catholic Epistles since 1978', *CurBS* 5 (1997), 187-90; idem, 'Assessment'; Batten, *Saying*, 16-26.

[574] As always, there are exceptions. E.g. the work of Royce is clearly that of an Eastern Orthodox Christian.

[575] Cf. Maston, 'Dimensions', 36-37, affirming that 'human nature has never basically changed'.

deemed nearly antithetical to 'the Christianity of the New Testament'. A book that upholds law, emphasizes works over *sola fide*, and disparages wealth was just what he needed.[576] And in less profound but not dissimilar fashion, myriads of preachers have called upon James to rebuke seemingly complacent congregants and prod them to 'good works'.

What have recent times contributed to the interpretation and reception of James? Several things stand out.[577] One is appreciation of the degree to which James is indebted to Jewish tradition. Before the Reformation, the only Jewish sources in the commentaries are, in addition to the OT, the biblical apocrypha. After the Reformation, a few rabbinic quotations began to appear in the literature. Few earlier exegetes, to be sure, knew anything firsthand about the rabbis, but many, including such influential writers as Poole, Henry, and Gill, came to see their importance for interpreting James.

The next major step was taken near the turn of the twentieth century, with the rediscovery of the Pseudepigrapha, and especially with the publications of Jewish pseudepigrapha in the collections of Kautzsch (in German, 1900) and Charles (in English, 1913). Ever since, citations from intertestamental, non-canonical sources have worked their way into all academically serious commentaries. The discovery of the Dead Sea Scrolls added yet more comparative materials, the importance of which was on display for the first time in Mussner's commentary. Yet even before the Qumran findings, the developing apprehension of just how Jewish James really is led a few to argue that the book was originally not Christian at all; that is, it is a lightly-retouched Jewish work.[578]

Perhaps perception of the Jewish character of James is not unrelated to another significant development in the commentary tradition. As this work documents, the Christian literature on James gives copious expression to anti-Jewish sentiments. Negative stereotypes abound, and it always occurs to multiple commentators that, whatever vice this verse or that

---

[576] W. Lowrie, in his Introduction to *Kierkegaard's Attack Upon 'Christendom' 1854–1855*, Princeton, 1944, xvii, speaks of Kierkegaard's 'marked preference for the Epistle of St. James'. On Kierkegaard and James see Bauckham, 158-74; K.A. Roberts, 'James: Putting Faith into Action', in *Kierkegaard and the Bible Tome II: The New Testament*, ed. L.C. Barrett and J. Stewart, Surrey, 2010, 209-17 (with bibliography).

[577] For surveys of recent scholarship on James see Davids, 'Discussion'; Popkes, *Adressaten*, 9-52; Hahn-Müller, 'Jakobusbrief'; Penner, 'Research'; Konradt, 'Theologie'; Wachob, *Voice*, 25-58; P.B. Harner, *What are they Saying about the Catholic Epistles?*, New York, 2004, 5-28; Orlando, 'Liturgia'; Batten, *Saying*. For reviews of earlier scholarship see Huther, 23-30; Meinertz, *Verfasser*, 237-312; Knowling, lxviii-lxxii; Moffatt, *Introduction*, 465-75; Johnson, 143-52.

[578] Massebieau, 'L'Épître'; Spitta; Halévy, 'Lettre'; Meyer, *Rätsel*. The modern commentaries also recurrently cite Graeco-Roman sources for comparison, but here there is more continuity with the past. The habit of citing numerous Greek and Latin texts is already on display in Grotius (seventeenth century), Wettstein (eighteenth century), Theile (nineteenth century), *et al*.

paragraph combats, it must be because that vice characterized Jews.[579] This is much less the case these days. The Shoah has had an impact here, as have improved Jewish-Christian relations. Today far fewer Christian exegetes employ James to attack or belittle Judaism.

Related to this change is the circumstance that James is becoming part of inter-religious dialogue, and not just between Christians and Jews. Keenan, an Episcopal priest, has written a provocative commentary with the subtitle: *Parallels with Mahāyāna Buddhism*. This combines more traditional, section-by-section exegesis with comparison of James and Buddhist perspectives. The Dalai Lama has also written on James, arguing that 'this beautiful letter' exhibits striking similarities with his Buddhist faith. Claiming that 'many of our fundamental spiritual values' are 'universal' and 'perennial', he finds that James lines up with his own tradition in that it attacks double-mindedness, calls one to be slow to wrath, slow to speak, and quick to listen to others, demands that faith be translated into action, warns that life is transient, opposes discrimination, and teaches respect for the poor.[580]

Another development is still in its infancy, but it may be mentioned because it has the potential to alter perception of James. I refer to interpreting James within the context of the canon. Nienhuis has argued that our book is a canon-conscious pseudepigraphon, written in order to lend a theological and aesthetic unity to a primitive collection of Christian letters.[581] Whatever one makes of the details of his thesis, James exhibits very strong parallels with Paul, 1 Peter, and 1 John, and these cry out for explanation. They cannot all be put down either to coincidence or to common Christian 'oral tradition'.[582] So if, like this commentator, one dates James after Paul, 1 Peter, and 1 John, deliberate interaction with sources that are now in the canon seems to follow.

There is another way of thinking about James within its canonical context. Some Hebrew Bible scholars now contend that the Minor Prophets constitute a coherent collection. Hosea, Amos, and the rest may have had separate origins and tradition histories, but someone brought them together, put them in a particular order, and redacted them so that they function as a unit.[583] Might there be a rough parallel here with the Catholic Epistles? Was the common—although not exclusive—order, James, 1 Peter, 2 Peter, 1 John, 2 John, 3 John, Jude, due to design? Was James perhaps placed at the front for theological reasons?[584] Was the

---

[579] See below, 291, 513, 592, 642-43.

[580] The Dali Lama, 'The General Epistle of James', in *Revelations*, Edinburgh, 2007, 359-64. For a Hindu interpretation of Jas 4.4 see 590 below.

[581] Nienhuis, *Paul*; idem, 'Pseudepigraph'.

[582] See above, 62-71.

[583] See *Reading and Hearing the Book of the Twelve*, ed. J.D. Nogalski and M.A. Sweeney, Atlanta, 2000.

[584] James is first in the list of Eusebius, but that was not always so in the west; see Ropes, 103-104.

collection as a whole intended to balance the Pauline collection and interpret it aright?[585] The questions are worth exploring.

The academic study of James is prospering at the moment. The last two decades have witnessed not only significant new commentaries—Martin, Frankemölle, Johnson, Moo, Hartin, Burchard, Popkes, Maier, Fabris, McKnight—but a torrent of articles and a number of very significant monographs. If, however, one stands back and looks at the larger world, the most important and far-reaching business with James has taken place elsewhere, outside of both church and academy.

Alcoholics Anonymous is one of the most remarkable movements of modern times. Countless individuals throughout the world have benefitted from the Twelve Steps Program and its many offshoots—Narcotics Anonymous, Overeaters Anonymous, etc. And without for the most part knowing it, beneficiaries owe a large debt of gratitude to James. For this NT letter was of key importance to the founders of A.A., who stressed again and again that 'faith without works is dead'.[586] Indeed, the book of James was so popular among early members of A.A. that some wanted their fellowship to be called 'The James Club'.[587] Furthermore, Jas 5.16—'confess your sins to one another'—directly inspired the famous and effective strategy of requiring members, when meeting together in small groups, to share honestly their failings with one another.[588]

---

[585] See esp. R. Wall, 'Acts'; idem, 'Priority'; idem, 'Theology'.
[586] *'Pass It On': The Story of Bill Wilson and How the A.A. Message Reached the World* (New York, 1984), 147, 195.
[587] *Dr. Bob and the Good Old Timers*, New York, 1980, 71, 96.
[588] *'Pass It On'* (as in n. 586), 128.

COMMENTARY

I

SALUTATION AND ADDRESS (1.1)[1]

James, a servant of God and of the Lord Jesus Christ, to the twelve tribes that are in the diaspora: Greetings.

History of Interpretation and Reception

The author of our letter has more often than not been identified with James the brother of Jesus,[2] although those who have believed in Mary's perpetual virginity have considered him either Jesus' cousin or a son of Joseph by a former marriage.[3] Jerome moreover identified this individual—he took him to be Jesus' cousin—with 'James the son of Alphaeus'.[4] This then became, in Roman tradition, the dominant view as to who

---

[1] Recent literature: Assaël-Cuvillier, 'Traduction'; Baltzer-Koester, 'Bezeichnung'; Bauckham, *Wisdom*, 14-25; Garleff, *Identität*, 232-47; Jackson-McCabe, 'Letter'; Karrer, 'Christus'; Klein, *Werk*, 185-90; Köster, 'Leser'; Konradt, *Existenz*, 64-66; Llewelyn, 'Prescript'; Lockett, *Purity*, 66-76; Penner, *Eschatology*, 181-83; Rendall, *Christianity*, 11-15; Sahlin, 'Noch Einmal'; Schmidt, *Lehrgehalt*, 44-49; Schoeps, 'Jacobus'; Tsuji, *Glaube*, 22-25, 44-49; Theophilus ab Orbiso, 'Iacobus'; Torrey, 'Just'; Zahn, *Introduction*, 73-83.

The most common forms of the inscription are these: Ἰακώβου ἐπιστολή – ἐπιστολή Ἰακώβου – Ἰακώβου ἐπιστολή καθολική – Ἰακώβου καθολική ἐπιστολή – ἐπιστολή Ἰακώβου καθολική – ἐπιστολή καθολική Ἰακώβου – καθολική ἐπιστολή Ἰακώβου. Most mss. include the designation 'catholic', and some early Protestants, unhappy with the connotations of that word, either dropped it or substituted another adjective, such as 'general'. Catholics accused them of not following the Greek mss. Cf. the Rheims edition of James, 380, asserting that Protestants 'fear and abhor' the word 'catholic'. Protestants responded by insisting that the title was secondary and so no proper part of the word of God, and further that 'catholic' here means 'universal' and so has nothing to do with Catholicism; cf. Fulke, *Confutation*, 354.

[2] For modern proponents of this view see 4 n. 18; and for recent critical literary on James of Jerusalem see 5 n. 21.

[3] The author is 'the brother of God' in the title of mss. 104C 945 1739 1875. Many of the older commentaries, and not just those of Roman Catholics, discuss the issue—brother, half-brother, or cousin?—at length. It receives a full fifty pages in Mayor (v-lv), which is more space than he gives to any other introductory issue. Even the more recent, popular commentary of Barclay devotes nine pages to the subject (16-24).

[4] Known from Mt 10.3; Mk 2.14; 3.18; Lk 6.15; Acts 1.13.

wrote our letter, and many Protestants have gone along.[5] Only occasionally has the writer been identified with James the son of Zebedee.[6]

Those in the ancient church who rejected our letter's authority or canonical status[7] presumably rejected its authorship by the brother of Jesus. Maybe some attributed it to another, unknown James, as did Erasmus, Thomas de Vio (Cardinal Cajetan), and Luther later on.[8] A few exegetes still think this.[9] It was not until the nineteenth century that the theory of pseudepigraphy, adopted in this commentary, came into its own.[10] Now, at the beginning of the twenty-first century, it is a common opinion.

A few have thought the issue of authorship relatively unimportant. Calvin, 259-60, was not sure which James wrote our epistle;[11] and according to J.A. Alexander, a decision about authorship 'cannot materially affect our view of the design and meaning of the book itself'.[12] Throughout exegetical history, however, the conviction that our letter was written by James of Jerusalem, the brother of Jesus, has been thought to add to the book's authority[13] and to elucidate much, such as the book's seemingly

---

[5] Cf. Jerome, *Perp. virg. adv. Helv.* PL 23.183-206; Pareus, 541; Wolzogen, 179; Henry, *ad loc.*; Gill, 778; Wells, 2-3; Wesley, 506; Schneckenburger, 1; *et al.*

[6] So Ps.-Epiphanius, in T. Schermann, ed., *Prophetarum vitae fabulosae*, Leipzig, 1907, 109; also the subscription of the Latin Codex Corbeiensis (ff), Spanish tradition, and Dante, *Paradisio* 25; cf. the confusion in Irenaeus, *Haer*. 3.12.15 and see further Lardner, *Supplement*, 66-75; Ropes, 45. For the modern period note above all Bassett, i-xxxvii. He fancifully links our letter with the transfiguration as well as with Lk 9.51-56, where Jesus rebukes the sons of Zebedee for wanting to call down fire from heaven: the latter episode taught our author the folly of anger (cf. Jas 1.19-20) while the transfiguration called his attention to the importance of Elijah (cf. Jas 5.17).

[7] For references to these see Eusebius, *H.E.* 2.23.25, 3.25.3; Jerome, *Vir. inl.* 2 TU 14.1a ed. Richardson, 7; Isho'dad of Merv *ad loc.* HSem 10 ed. Gibson, 49.

[8] Erasmus, *Annotationes*, 744 ('It just does not add up to that apostolic majesty and gravity. Nor should we expect so many Hebraisms from the Apostle James who was bishop of Jerusalem'); Cajetan, 362; M. Luther, *Table Talk*, in Luther's Works 54, ed. T.G. Tappert, Philadelphia, 1967, 424 (no. 5443): 'Some Jew wrote it who probably learned about Christian people but never encountered any'. Luther, it should be remembered, accepted the doctrine of Mary's perpetual virginity and so denied that Jesus had a uterine brother.

[9] For representatives of this opinion see above, 4 n. 15.

[10] For proponents see 4 above n. 19, and the survey of criticism in Johnson, 146-52. de Wette (1826) appears to be the first proponent of pseudepigraphy; cf. his *Introduction*, 332-33.

[11] Cf. Isho'dad of Merv *ad* 1.1 HSem 10 ed. M.D. Gibson, 49 ('perhaps James is the author of it, whatever his name may be'); also the hesitation of Lapide, 4-8. Calvin, incidentally, took the pillar of Gal 2.9 to be James the son of Alphaeus.

[12] J.A. Alexander, 'The Christian's Duty in Times of Trial', in *The Gospel of Jesus Christ*, London, 1862, 555. So too Mitton, 9; Songer, 'Introduction', 360-61.

[13] Note E. Palmer, viii: 'When I became convinced that this very James was the author of the Book of James, I then read its earnest discipleship advice with new eyes and new anticipation'.

SALUTATION AND ADDRESS (1.1)

modest theology,[14] its thoroughly Jewish character,[15] its alleged Galilean color,[16] and its knowledge of sayings of Jesus.[17] Belief in James' authorship has also been an interpretive guide, as when readers have doubted, in view of Acts 15 and Gal 1.18-24, that James could truly disagree with Paul about anything important.[18] Our book, in turn, has been thought to illuminate what we otherwise know of James. Lardner, for instance, believed that James was executed because of offense taken at our epistle.[19]

Most commentators over the centuries have identified 'the twelve tribes in the diaspora' with scattered Christian Jews living outside of Palestine.[20] The equation has been reckoned consistent with James' commission as a minister of the circumcision (Gal 2.9). Quite a few, moreover, have linked the word διασπορά with the 'scattering'

---

[14] Cf. Moo, 11; McCartney, 15. The argument is airtight: if James wrote our book, and if he was martyred in the early 60s, our book must date from before then and so it represents an early phase of Christian theology. Adamson, *Message*, 12, explains the scarcity of christological statements by appeal to Acts 5.40: 'they ordered them not to speak in the name of Jesus'. But B. Weiss, *Manual*, 113-14, attributes our author's failure to cite the example of Jesus to his not having been a disciple before the resurrection.

[15] Cf. Scaer, 25-26; Deiros, 24; Hartin, 21-24; McKnight, 23-24; *et al.*

[16] Cf. Bishop, *Apostles*, 184-91; Hadidian, 'Pictures'; McCartney, 25; *et al.*

[17] Cf. Wordsworth, 13; Kittel, 'Ort'; idem, 'Väter'; Cadoux, *Thought*, 33-34; Tasker, 28; Adamson, *Message*, 186-92; *et al.*

[18] Cf. Herder, 'Kanon', 194-97; Bartmann, *Paulus*, 154; Oesterley, 391 (Paul's positive references to James in 1 Corinthians and Galatians make contradictions between the two men unlikely); Davids, 20.

[19] Lardner, 'A History of the Apostles and Evangelists', in *The Works of Nathaniel Lardner*, vol. 6, London, 1838, 199-200.

[20] So e.g. the title of ms. 94 (πρὸς τοὺς ἐν τῇ διασπορᾷ πιστεύσαντας 'Ιουδαίους); Hippolytus, *Apoc. ad* 7.4-8 GCS 1.2 ed. Achelis, 231; Ps.-Euthalius the Deacon, *Cath. ep. ad loc.* PG 85.676B; Dionysius bar Salībī *ad loc.* CSCO 60 Scriptores Syri 101 ed. Sedlacek, 89; *Catenae ad loc.* ed. Cramer, 1; *Chaîne Arménienne* 1 ed. Renoux, 68; Nicholas of Gorran, 66; Nicholas of Lyra *ad loc.*; Hus, 179; Calvin, 261; Beza, 547; GenevaB. *ad loc.* ('to all the believing Jewes, of what tribe soever they be, and are dispersed thorow the whole world'); Aretius, 472; Hemminge, 2; Wolzogen, 180, 193; Aretius, 471-72; Gomar, 385 (synecdoche: the whole—the twelve tribes—stands for the part—the Jewish Christians); Pareus, 541; Dickson, 680; Calmet, 666; Gill, 778-79; Burkitt, 1105; Hammond, 688; Pritius, *Introductio*, 73; Benson, 13, 27; Guyse, 563; Wesley, 596; Storr, 6; Eichhorn, *Einleitung*, 582-83; Jacobi, 3; Schulthess, 2; Kern, 79-80; Gebser, 5; Rosenmüller, 322; Pott, 322; Wiesinger, 30, 49-50; Cellérier, xiv; Huther, 10-13; Alford, 99, 274; Eerdman, 54-62; Adam, 5-6; Valpy, 235; Gloag, *Introduction*, 46-53; Bleek, *Introduction*, 144; B. Weiss, 93; Bisping, 11-12; Schegg, 3-4; Davidson, *Introduction*, 286-87; Trenkle, 14-21; Wandel, 26-27; Weidner, 14, 24; Hort, xxiii, 2-3; Belser, 30-31; Plummer, 562-66 (arguing for a 'literal construction' that yet does not really have non-Christian Jews in mind); Bardenhewer, 11-13, 24; Gaugusch, 1; Chaine, lxxxiv-lxxxv; Meinertz, 11, 19; H.E. Dana, *Jewish Christianity*, New Orleans, 1937, 106-107; Schneider, 5; Mussner, 11; Scaer, 28; Davids, 63-64; Martin, 8-10; Townsend, 4-5; P.J. Tomson, *'If this be from Heaven...': Jesus and the New Testament Authors in their Relationship to Judaism*, Sheffield, 2001, 341; Bauckham, *Wisdom*, 16; Moo, 23-24, 50; Hartin, 25-27; Keith, 'Destinataires'; Doriani, 12; Church, 335; Farley, 17; Gundry, 919.

(διεσπάρησαν, διασπαρέντες) of the Jerusalem church in Acts 8.1; 11.19.[21]

Perhaps the most prevalent reading today—although it was rare before the last two centuries—gives 'the twelve tribes in the diaspora' figurative sense and identifies those tribes with Christians, Jew and Gentile, abroad in the world; that is, the church universal is here the new Israel.[22] A literal reading, which identifies the twelve tribes in the diaspora with Jews, whether Christian or not, has had fewer modern proponents. But it appears in Bede and Isho'dad of Merv, and it was quite popular in the seventeenth and eighteenth centuries. It is the view of this commentary.[23]

---

[21] So already Bede *ad loc.* CCSL 121 ed. Hurst, 183; cf. Dionysius bar Salībī *ad loc.* CSCO 60 Scriptores Syri 101 ed. Sedlaeck 89; George Syncellus, *Ecl. chron.* 623 ed. Mosshammer, 400; Stevartius, 10-11; Gomar, 385; Manton, 16; Le Clerc, 499; Gebser, 5; Winkler, 14; Salmon, *Introduction*, 454; Geyser, 'Condition'; Robinson, *Redating*, 136; Tidball, 10-11; Kistemaker, 7; Scaer, 28; Baker, 18; Hodges, 17; R. Wall, 'Paraenesis', 15; Moo, 50; Fruchtenbaum, 213; Carson, 'James', 998; G. and H. Hart, *Analysis*, 6; Gundry, 919; Jobes, *Letters*, 157.

[22] E.g. de Wette, *Introduction*, 329; Hilgenfeld, 'Brief', 4-6; Schmidt, *Lehrgehalt*, 45-46; McGiffert, *History*, 584; Baljon, 3-4; von Soden, 162; Hollmann-Bousset, 222; Ropes, 118-27; O. Holtzmann, 823; Dibelius, 67; Jülicher, *Einleitung*, 204; Dimont, 628; Moffatt, 6; Easton, 20; Hauck, 6; Schnider, 25; Burger-Luthardt, 210; Grünzweig, 19-22; Simon, 13; Barnett, 'Letter', 795; Schulz, *Mitte*, 281; Knoch, 141; Vielhauer, *Geschichte*, 570; Wuellner, 'Rhetorik, 22-23; Vouga, 37; Garland, 'Trials', 383-84; Ruckstuhl, 11; Schrage, 14; Leahy, 910; Kugelman, 12-13; D. Sänger, 'διασπείρω', *EDNT* 1.312; Frankemölle, 54-57, 125-27; Johnson, 171; Llewelyn, 'Prescript'; Cargal, 48; Klein, *Werk*, 185-90; Tsuji, *Glaube*, 22-25, 47-49; Konradt, *Existenz*, 64-66; Isaacs, 178; Burchard, 50; Fabris, 53; Popkes, 71-72; Harvey, 721; Konradt, 'Brief', 50-51; Royster, 32. According to Hahn-Müller, 'Jakobusbrief', 65, this is the consensus of recent exegetes. Many of those who hold this position construe 'in the diaspora' not geographically but theologically: 'the diaspora' = 'the world'; so e.g. Dibelius; Isaacs. Cf. Dimont, 628 ('exiles from their true home in heaven'); E. Palmer, 18-19 (to be scattered is to be 'homeless', and 'home is first of all the relationship with the Lord of every place'). But the Protestant Turnbull, 8, emphasized the literal geographical element in order to attack Catholicism for being headquartered in a single city.

[23] See Bede *ad loc.* CCSL 121 ed. Hurst, 183; Isho'dad of Merv *ad* 1.1 HSem 10 ed. M.D. Gibson, 49; cf. Ps.-Andrew of Crete, *Éloge* 4 ed. Noret, 44; Grotius, 1073 (to all Jews, but with parts pertinent above all to those who believe in Jesus); Trapp, 693; Manton, 13, 398-99 (he compares the Sermon on the Mount, where Jesus addresses the disciples but the crowd overhears); C. Ness, *History and Mystery of the New Testament*, London, 1696, 501; Whitby, 2.672; Wells, 1 (James seeks to establish orthodox Jewish Christians in their faith and to stop unbelieving Jews and Judaizing Christians from persecuting believers); Wolf, 8-9; Lardner, *Supplement*, 94-99; Baumgarten, 17-18; Doddridge, 135-36; Guyse, 560; Wells, 3; Macknight, 584, 596; Pyle, 308; J. Priestley, *Notes on all the Books of Scripture*, vol. 4, Northumberland, 1803, 502; Herder, 'Kanon', 192 (for James 'Jews and Christians are not yet separated'); T. Scott, 564, 586 (James wrote 'principally' but not exclusively to Christians); Pyle, 308; Clarke, 798; Hug, *Introduction*, 552-54; Credner, *Einleitung*, 593-94; Macknight, 584; Theile, 48-51; Bouman, 33-40; Fulford, 17-20; Maurice, *Unity*, 285; Wordsworth, 4, 13 ('St. James was writing an Epistle, not only for the use of Christians, but of Jews; and of Jews who at that

A text attributed to Hippolytus used Jas 1.1 (wrongly attributed to Jude) to prove how many Christian converts there were in the diaspora.[24] Later on, Gill, 779, with a perfect faith in the scriptures, took the verse to imply that the Jewish diaspora had early on converted to Christianity.[25]

Some have understood the first part of our verse to mean: 'James, a servant of Jesus Christ, God and Lord', or they have otherwise found in the verse evidence of Jesus' divinity.[26] Such a reading, however, appears to have played little or no role in the Arian controversy.[27] Common nonetheless has been the conviction that, even though God and Jesus Christ may here be distinguished,[28] James' statement that he is the slave

---

time were exasperated against Christianity'; he compares the speech of Stephen in Acts 7, which does not name Jesus until the very end); Winkler, 7; Bassett, xxxvii-xlv; Plumptre, 35-38; W. Carpenter, 71-72. H. Heisen, *Novae hypotheses interpretandae felicius epistulae Iacobi apostoli*, Bremen, 1739, reportedly belongs on this list, but I have been unable to see a copy of this book. Many of these commentators felt an apologetical need to argue that the twelve tribes still existed in Jesus' time; see e.g. the five-page discussion in Benson, 14-18; also Whitby, 676-77; Clarke, 798. More recent proponents of Jewish addressees include: J.V. Bartlet, *Age*, 231-32; Mayor, cxliii, 31 (but on cxcvii he says that James is 'to believers by a believer', and this is the position generally presupposed in his exegesis); Knowling, 4; Moulton, 'Studies'; M. Jones, *The New Testament in the Twentieth Century*, London, 1914, 321 ('The non-Christian tone of the Epistle' may be due 'partly to the fact that the Epistle was meant to influence unconverted as well as converted Jews'); McNeile, *Teaching*, 87-110; McNeile-Williams, *Introduction*, 201-208 (they assert that the people depicted in 1.9-11, 21; 2.1-3, 15; 3.13-16; and 5.7 do not sound like any other Christians we know of from the early decades); Meyer, *Rätsel*, 108 (although for him this is part of his thesis that the letter was originally Jewish, not Christian); Schlatter, 91-97; Rendall, *Christianity*, 29-30, 89; Cadoux, *Thought*, 10-18, 85; Beasley-Murray, 12-18 (Beasley-Murray cites Schlatter and Cadoux as among 'the few' who have observed that several passages in James are for individuals 'who acknowledge God but who are yet strangers' to Christianity; he then cites 5.1-6; 4; 1.19-20, 26-27; 2.10-12; and 3.13-18 as places where James possibly 'addresses himself to non-Christians as well as Christian Jews'); Adamson, 50-51; idem, *Man and Message*, 11-18, 50-51; Maynard-Reid, *Poverty*, 10-11, 65; McDade, 'Jews'; R. Murray, 'Jews, Hebrews and Christians', *NovT* 24 (1993), 204 (James is 'addressed, as it says, to diaspora Jews, its Christian content being somewhat concealed; those who were attracted would be "followed up" locally'); R.L. Williams, 'Piety', 39-41; R.R. Williams, 97; Keenan, 14; Kloppenborg, 'Discourse'; idem, 'Judaeans'. For Windisch-Preisker, 5, this is a possibility. Such a view is also implicit in Ps.-Epiphanius (as in n. 6), for here we read: James ταῖς δώδεκα φυλαῖς τῆς διασπορᾶς ἐκήρυξε τὸ εὐαγγέλιον τοῦ Χριστοῦ. This depends upon Jas 1.1 and identifies the twelve tribes of the diaspora with Jews to be evangelized.

[24] Hippolytus, *Apoc.* 7.4-8 GCS 1.2 ed. Achelis, 231.

[25] For an updated, critical variant of this view see Bardenhewer, 12.

[26] Cf. Ps.-Andrew of Crete, *Éloge* 4 ed. Noret, 44; Hus 179; Hardouin, 681; Burkitt, 1104; Guyse, 563; Hort, 1 ('at least some Divineness of nature'); Oesterley, 419; Vouga, 31, 36; Baker, 18; Motyer, 27; the Navarre Bible, 35; Assaël-Cuvillier, 'Traduction'. Contrast Baumgarten, 14.

[27] Burkitt, 1104, to the contrary.

[28] See the textual variants in n. 52: these introduce 'Father'.

of both shows their equal honor and nature.²⁹ Moffatt, 6, offered that 'the collocation here and the phrase in ii.1 imply a divine authority for Christ'.³⁰

James' description of himself as a 'slave' has often been the starting point for homiletical reflections on or exhortations to humility. Manton, 17, cited Ps 84.10: 'I would rather be a doorkeeper in the house of my God than dwell in the tents of wickedness'.³¹ Only occasionally have exegetes or preachers stopped to ponder the tension with Jn 15.15, 'No longer do I call you slaves'.³² More common has been the claim that James' manner of introduction, which eschews claiming to be the brother of Jesus, establishes that spiritual affinity matters more than physical kinship.³³

1.1 has been appealed to in the debate over British Israelism. Proponents have alleged that the verse is proof that the so-called lost tribes were still in existence in the first-century: 'James would not have written to the Twelve Tribes if he had known they were not within reach of this epistle'.³⁴ Detractors, to the contrary, have insisted that, 'in New Testament days the "Jews", though the term was originally confined to Judahites only, are regarded as the living representatives not of Judah, Benjamin, and Levi alone, but of all the tribes. When S. James writes to "the twelve tribes of the Dispersion", he writes, unless he refers to the Church of Christ, to the whole body of the Israelite people'; that is, the twelve tribes are not some 'lost' group but 'the Jews of Palestine and the Dispersion who are still known to be practising their religion'.³⁵

---

²⁹ Cf. Theophylact *ad loc.* PG 125.1133D-1136A, and the closely related exposition in Ps.-Oecumenius *ad loc.* PG 119.456A. From our own time one may note R.L. Reymond, *Jesus, Divine Messiah*, Phillipsburgh, N.J., 1990, 282. Reymond finds, in James, Jesus' 'equality' with God the Father. Popkes, 71, labels Jas 1.1 'binitarian'. Cf. Sadler, 4 ('co-equal'); Gundry, 919.

³⁰ See further Karrer, 'Christus', 168-70.

³¹ Cf. Didymus the Blind, *Ps* 858 PTS 16 ed. Mühlenberg, 155; Ps.-Andrew of Crete, *Éloge* 4.5-10 ed. Noret, 44; Nicholas of Lyra *ad loc.*; Stevartius, 8; Henry, *ad loc.*; Benson, 26; Deems, 30-32; Adderley, 1; Cedar, 18-19; *et al.*

³² Noticed by the author of the Greek scholia to Revelation printed in C. Diobouniotis and A. von Harnack, *Der Scholienkommentar des Origenes zur Apokalypse Johannis*, TU 38/3, Leipzig, 1911, 21 (I [post 1,1]). Laws, 45, cites Jn 15.15 in commenting on Jas 1.1.

³³ See esp. W. Carpenter, e.g. 77-83; R. Bauckham, *Jude and the Relatives of Jesus in the Early Church*, Edinburgh, 1990, 125-30. Cf. Manton, 16-17; Johnstone, 25; Grünzweig, 23-24.

³⁴ E. Odlum, *God's Covenant Man: British-Israel*, London, 1927, 283.

³⁵ H.L. Goudge, *The British Israel Theory*, London, 1933, 6-7. Cf. Dimont, 630; Fruchtenbaum, 212.

SALUTATION AND ADDRESS (1.1) 119

Exegesis

James opens not with a liturgical formula but with a common epistolary formula found in Jewish,[36] Christian,[37] and secular Greek[38] letters:[39]

    Name (and identification) of sender +
        Name (and identification) of recipient(s) +
            Salutation ('Greetings')[40]

[36] E.g. Add Esth 16.1 ('The Great King, Artaxerxes, to the rulers of the provinces from India to Ethiopia, one hundred and twenty-seven satrapies, and to those who are loyal to our government: Greetings'); 1 Macc 10.25 ('King Demetrius to the nation of the Jews, Greetings'); 12.6 ('Jonathan the high priest, the senate of the nation, the priests, and the rest of the people to their brethren the Spartans: Greetings'); 2 Macc 1.10 ('Those in Jerusalem and those in Judea and the senate and Judas, to Aristobulus, who is of the family of the anointed priests, teacher of Ptolemy the king, and to the Jews in Egypt: Greeting and good health'; cf. 2.1); Eupolemus in Eusebius, *Praep. ev.* 9.31.1 GCS 43 ed. Mras 539 ('King Solomon to Vaphres, king of Egypt, friend of my father: Greetings'; cf. 9.32.1 [540]; 33.1 [540]; 34.1 [541]); 3 Macc 7.1 ('King Ptolemy Philopator to the generals in Egypt and all who have charge of our affairs: Greetings and good health'); Josephus, *Vita* 217 ('Jonathan and his fellow deputies from Jerusalem to Josephus: Greetings'); *4 Bar.* 6.19 ('Baruch, the servant of God, writes to Jeremia in the captivity of Babylon: Greetings, and rejoice that…').

[37] E.g. Acts 15.23 (A to B + χαίρειν); *Ep. Pet. Phil.* 8.132.12-15 (A to B + xe[ιpe]); POxy. 1162 (A to B + χαρᾷ χαίρειν). The openings of the Pauline letters regularly expand the greeting (e.g. Rom 1.1-7; 1 Cor 1.1-3; 2 Cor 1.1-2; Phil 1.1-2), as do later Christian letters, probably under Pauline influence (e.g. 1 Clement; Ign. *Ephesians*; *Magnesians*; Pol. *Philippians*).

[38] E.g. PHib 1.41 ('Polemon to Harimouthes: Greetings'); PYale 42 ('Nechthosiris to Leon his brother: Greetings'); SelPap 1.99 ('Serapion to his brothers, Ptolemy and Apollonios: Greetings'); SelPap 1.104 ('Athenagoras, the chief physician, to the priests of the stolistai at the Labyrinth and to the stolistai. Greetings'); PRyl 2.229 ('Ammonios to his dearest Aphrodisios: Greetings'); Ps.-Plato, *Ep.* 3.315A ('Plato to Dionysius: Greetings'). For a large sampling and commentary see F.X.J. Exler, *A Study in Greek Epistolography*, Washington, D.C., 1923, 23-68.

[39] For the debate regarding the genre of James and whether it should be classified as a letter see the Introduction, 71-76.

[40] According to J.L. White, 'New Testament Epistolary Literature in the Framework of Ancient Epistolography', *ANRW* II.25.2 (1984), 1734, 'about two-thirds of the Greek papyrus letters have as their opening formula, "A (= the sender) to B (= the recipient) greeting"', and 'familiar letters almost always take "A- to B- greeting (χαίρειν)"'. See further his article, 'Epistolary Formulas and Clichés in Greek Papyrus Letters', in *Society of Biblical Literature 1978 Seminar Papers*, ed. P.J. Achtemeier, Missoula, MT, 1978, 289-319. One should not, however, overlook the closely related openings in Semitic letters. D. Pardee *et al.*, *Handbook of Ancient Hebrew Letters*, Chico, CA, 1982, contains the following parallels: Arad 16 ('Your brother Hananyahu sends greetings to [you] Elyashib', 48); Arad 21 ('Your son Yehukal [hereby] sends greetings to [you] Gedalyahu [son of] Elyair and to your household', 57); Arad 40 ('Your son Gemar[yahu] as well as Nehemyahu [hereby] sen[d greetings to (you)] Malkiyahu', 63-64); papMur 42 ('From the village managers of Beth-Mashko, from Yeshua and Elazar, to Yeshua son of Galgula, camp commander: Greetings', 123-24); papMur 43 ('From Shimon ben Kosiba

'Ιάκωβος. A popular name at the turn of the era.⁴¹ For the argument that our text is a pseudepigraphon, see the Introduction, 3-32. The use of 'James'⁴²—the text assumes knowledge of his identity; he is sufficiently well known to require no further introduction⁴³—lends authority to the book. It also implicitly communicates a connection with biblical history. For 'Ιάκωβος represents the Hebrew יעקב, 'Jacob'. So just as once, long ago, the patriarch gave instructions to his twelve sons (Gen 49), so now another Jacob offers wisdom to their descendants, the twelve tribes of Israel.⁴⁴ In line with this is the ancient habit of designating Jacob/Israel as God's 'servant' or 'slave',⁴⁵ for this is the title our author immediately gives to himself.⁴⁶

to Yeshua ben Ga[l]gula and to the men of your company: Greetings', 129-30); papMur 44 ('From Shimon to Yeshua son of Galgula: Greetings', 132); 5/6Hev 12 ('From Shimon bar Kosiba to the men of Ein-Gedi, to Masbala [and] to Yeho[n]atan [s]on of Beyan: Greetings', 143). Pardee observes that 'letters written in Hebrew in the military and administrative circles of the time of Bar Kokhba...had the following set structure: a) "From PN (+ title) to PN (+ title)" b) "Greetings"' (157). Cf. also Midr. Tannaim on Deut 26.13 ed. Hoffmann, 175-76: 'From Simeon b. Gamaliel and from Yohannan ben Zakkai to our brothers in the Upper and Lower South, to Shahlil and to the seven southern toparchies: Greetings'. All these letters remind us that we should not overlook the many elements common to Greek and Semitic letter-writing; see further P.E. Dion, 'The Aramaic "Family Letters" and Related Epistolary Forms in Other Oriental Languages and in Hellenistic Greek', *Semeia* 22 (1981), 59-76. For the closely related opening formulas in Aramaic letters from various times and places see idem, 'A Tentative Classification of Aramaic Letter Types', in *Society of Biblical Literature 1977 Seminar Papers*, ed. P.J. Achtemeier, Missoula, MT, 415-41.

⁴¹ The NT knows several Jacobs; see the Introduction, 3-4. Josephus, in addition to referring to James the brother of Jesus, speaks also of James son of Judas the Galilean (*Ant.* 20.102), of James the bodyguard of Josephus (*Vita* 96, 240), and of James the son of Sosas, an Idumaean leader (*Bell.* 4.235, 521-28). 'Ιάκωβ is common in Jewish inscriptions: CIJ 1.340, 594, 623, 715; 2.796, 801, 820, 861, 879; IJO 1.Mac15; 2.Syr51n.96; Syr92; CII/P 1.588, 995; 2.1481; etc.

⁴² The English 'James' comes from the French 'Gemmes', which in turn derived from the Latin 'Iacomus', this last being a late form of 'Iacobus', the Latin transliteration of 'Ιάκωβος.

⁴³ Contrast Jude 1, where the author claims to be 'brother of James'.

⁴⁴ Cf. Lapide, 11; Knoch, 141-42; Frankemölle, 123-24; Konradt, 'Gerechte', 582 (the latter thinking this an argument for pseudonymity). Against Meyer, *Rätsel*, we cannot go further and see in James developed allegories based on the traditions about Jacob. Johnson, 167, rightly observes that the readers are nowhere placed in a filial relationship with James, but that one would expect this if the author were setting forth a detailed correlation between the author and his readers on the one hand and Israel and his twelve children on the other.

⁴⁵ Gen 32.10; Isa 41.8; 48.20; Jer 30.10; 46.27; 4Q176 1-2 1.9; 4Q379 19; Ezek 28.25; Sifre 27 on Deut 3.24; etc.

⁴⁶ Such typological sense would be even stronger if our author viewed the patriarch Jacob as did Philo, namely, as a doer (*Sacr.* 5; *Fug.* 39) who was wise (*Sacr.* 18; *Virt.* 223) and perfect (*Fug.* 39-40; *Migr.* 199-201)—all virtues that our epistle emphasizes.

Although our pseudepigraphon does not elaborate the identity of its author, its contents are consistent with traditions and legends about Jesus' brother:[47]

- James was a writer (cf. 1.1): Prot. Jas 25.1; the Apocryphon of James; the First Apocalypse of James; the Second Apocalypse of James
- James was an authoritative figure who had the ear of the Jewish people (cf. 1.1): Hegesippus *apud* Eusebius, *H.E.* 2.23.10-12; Ps.-Clem. Rec. 1.66-69 CGS 51 ed. Rehm, 45-47
- James was a 'servant' (cf. 1.1): 1 Apoc. Jas 31-32; 2 Apoc. Jas. 59
- James lived in Jerusalem (implicit in 1.1): Acts 15; Gal 1.18-19; Prot. Jas 25; 2 Apoc. Jas. 44; Eusebius, *H.E.* 2.23.1; Ps.-Clem. Rec. 1.66.1; 1.71.2 CGS 51 ed. Rehm, 45, 48
- James did not show favoritism (cf. 2.1: μὴ ἐν προσωποληµψίαις): Hegesippus *apud* Eusebius, *H.E.* 2.23.10 (πρόσωπον οὐ λαµβάνεις)
- James was concerned for the poor and chose a life of deprivation (cf. 1.9-11; 2.1-7, 15-17; 4.1-4): Gal 2.10; Hegesippus *apud* Eusebius, *H.E.* 2.23.4-7
- James was a priest and so presumably concerned about 'purity' (cf. 1.27; 3.17; 4.8): Hegesippus *apud* Eusebius, *H.E.* 2.23.6; Epiphanius, *Pan.* 29.4.1-4 GCS 25 ed. Holl, 324[48]
- James was extraordinarily pious, even ascetical (cf. 1.13-15; 4.2-10): Hegesippus *apud* Eusebius, *H.E.* 2.23.5; Jerome, *Vir. ill.* 2 TU 14.1a ed. Richardson, 7-8; Epiphanius, *Pan.* 29.4.2 GCS 25 ed. Holl., 324
- James opposed Paul (cf. 2.14-26): Gal 2.12; Ps.-Clem. Rec. 1.70 CGS 51 ed. Rehm, 47-48
- James was a man of prayer (cf. 1.5-8; 4.1-2; 5.13-18): 1 Apoc. Jas 30-32; 2 Apoc. Jas. 48, 62; Hegesippus *apud* Eusebius, *H.E.* 2.23.6
- James practiced Torah (cf. 1.25; 2.8-12): Acts 21.17-26; Josephus, *Ant.* 20.200-203;[49] Hegesippus *apud* Eusebius, *H.E.* 2.23.4-18
- James was murdered as 'the just one' (cf. 5.6): 1 Apoc. Jas. 32-33, 43; 2 Apoc. Jas. 61; Hegesippus *apud* Eusebius, *H.E.* 2.23.12, 15-16[50]

Such congruency, for those who accept the fiction of 1.1, makes the author a person of integrity, one who lived as he spoke and spoke as he lived.[51]

---

[47] In addition to the following see Konradt, 'Context', 119-25.

[48] On this tradition see J.J. Scott, 'James the Relative of Jesus and the Expectation of an Eschatological Priest', *JETS* 25 (1982), 323-31.

[49] Although his words can be taken in more than one way, it seems likely that Josephus remembers James as law-observant; see Painter, *James*, 138-41.

[50] These are only the most striking correlations between our epistle and the traditions about James; others include God as the giver of wisdom (Prot. Jas. 25.1; cf. Jas 1.2-4), knowledge/wisdom coming from above (2 Apoc. Jas. 47; cf. Jas 3.13-18), rejection of judging others (2 Apoc. Jas. 59; cf. Jas 4.11-12; Hegesippus *apud* Eusebius, *H.E.* 2.23.16), and James' association with 'all the tribes' (Hegesippus *apud* Eusebius, *H.E.* 2.23.22; cf. Jas 1.1). Perhaps it is worth observing that contradictions between our letter and traditions about James are harder to find, although the Gospel of the Hebrews *apud* Jerome, *Vir. inl.* 2 TU 14.1 ed. Richardson 7-8, has him taking an oath, in contrast to Jas 5.12.

θεοῦ καὶ κυρίου Ἰησοῦ Χριστοῦ δοῦλος.[52] The expression is unparalleled in early Christian sources.[53] It looks like a conflation of the traditional Jewish δοῦλος θεοῦ[54] with the Pauline δοῦλος Χριστοῦ Ἰησοῦ, the latter of which occurs at the beginning of Romans and Philippians. Those who find in James a knowledge of Paul might find such here.[55]

θεοῦ refers not to Jesus[56] but rather to God 'the Father'; cf. 1.17, 27; 3.9. Everywhere else in James θεός = God (the Father),[57] and straightforward statements of Jesus' divinity in early Christian sources are rare. κυρίου to the contrary goes with Ἰησοῦ Χριστου. There is debate as to whether κύριος[58]—which clearly refers to God in 1.7; 3.9; 4.10; and 5.10—anywhere else in James designates Jesus. Many think it does in at least 5.7-8, 14.[59] This commentary argues to the contrary.[60]

The author does not dub himself 'apostle', in contrast to Paul's regular although not invariable habit.[61] Nor, in summarizing 'the defining

---

[51] Cf. M. Hole, *Practical Discourses on the Liturgy of the Church of England*, ed. J.A. Giles, London, 1837, 431: the imperatives in James are equally taught 'by the example of the saint...who underwent many sharp and difficult trials for the cause of Christ'.

[52] 206 429 522 *et al.* insert πατρός in third place, before καί (378 inserts it in fourth place, after καί). Given the weak attestation, one infers assimilation to convention, for 'Father' often appears with 'God' in the introductions to early Christian epistles: Rom 1.7; 1 Cor 1.3; 2 Cor 1.2; Gal 1.1; Eph 1.2; Phil 1.2; Col 1.2; 1 Thess 1.1; 2 Thess 1.1; 1 Tim 1.2; 2 Tim 1.2; Tit 1.4; 1 Pet 1.2; Jude 1; Ign. *Eph* salutation; etc.

[53] Tit 1.1 ('Paul, a slave of God and an apostle of Jesus Christ') is perhaps the closest parallel before Origen.

[54] As in LXX 2 Esd 20.30; Theod. Dan 6.21; 9.31; 4 Bar. 6.17; Apoc. Sedr. 16.8; cf. Rev 15.3. δοῦλος appears only here in James.

[55] Contrast O. Holtzmann, 823, for whom James' use of χαίρειν tells against dependence upon Paul

[56] Although epexegetical καί is linguistically possible; for proponents see n. 26. Yet even M.J. Harris, *Jesus as God*, Grand Rapids, MI, 1992, who believes that the NT otherwise equates Jesus with God, leaves Jas 1.1 out of account. The proposal of Cabaniss, 'Homily', 219, that 'God and Lord' evoke the title of the emperor Domitian, seems to have been ignored.

[57] 1.5, 13, 20, 27; 2.5, 19, 23; 3.9; 4.4, 6, 7, 8.

[58] Jas: 13×: 1.1, 7; 2.1; 3.9, 4.10, 15; 5.4, 7, 8, 10, 11, 14, 15.

[59] The use of 'lord' for both Jesus and God led Schlatter, 88, to assert that the one who serves God serves Jesus Christ and *vice versa*

[60] For the argument that Ἰησοῦ Χριστοῦ in 2.1 is secondary, so that both Ἰησοῦς and Χριστός occur only here in James, see the Excursus, 382-84.

[61] According to Frankemölle, 129, the 'James tradition' knew that its hero was not an apostle, which accounts for Jas 1.1. Acts 1.13-14 distinguishes the apostles from Jesus' brothers, and Paul nowhere clearly calls James an apostle (although the import of Gal 1.19 and 1 Cor 15.7 has been debated). On the uncertain issue of whether James the brother of Jesus was actually known in early Christianity as an 'apostle' see R. Bauckham, *Jude, 2 Peter*, WBC, Waco, TX, 1983, 23-24. Later tradition had no doubt: it happily bestowed the title upon him; it appears in the title for many mss. of James (020 025 049 0142 1 43 69 88 93 254 *et al.*); cf. Cyril of Alexandria, *Hom. Pasch.* PG 77.944A; Ps.-Ephraem, *De pan. ad mon.* ed. Phrantzoles, 10; Bede *ad loc.* CCSL 121 ed.

relationships of his life' (Brosend, 29), does James give himself any institutional or geographical affiliation. To this there are many parallels. Some pseudepigrapha fail to state anything save an author's personal name when that name in and of itself establishes an authoritative identity.[62]

On the thesis that James addresses itself to Jews of the diaspora, the absence of ἡμῶν does not puzzle. On the thesis that James addresses Christians exclusively, it is unexpected.[63] Some textual witnesses naturally add it.[64]

James designates himself as God's 'servant' or 'slave', in accord with the habit of subordinates using the term for themselves in an epistolary prescript.[65] The claim can be understood as setting the author beside the readers: both are about the task of serving God. In line with this, in Jewish sources—most notably the Psalms[66]—Israel is sometimes called God's עבד or δοῦλος,[67] and in early Christian literature believers in general can be called 'servants' or 'slaves'.[68] Yet the number of examples of the latter usage is more than balanced by those places where, in continuity with many Jewish texts,[69] עבד and δοῦλος are reserved for

---

Hurst, 183; Anastasius of Sinai, *Hodegos* 8.2.25-26 CCSG ed. Uthemann, 118; Rufinus of Aquileia, *Exp. symb.* 3.35 CCSL 20 ed. Simonetti, 171; Godfridus, *Hom. dom.* 55 PL 174.174C; Zahn, *Introduction*, 107; P. Theophilus ab Orbiso, '"Iacobus, Dei et... Christi servus"', 176-78; and the entire commentary tradition until Erasmus and Luther. For later doubts see Wiesinger, 4-12. Jerome's identification of James the Lord's brother with James the son of Alphaeus gave the author of our letter undoubted apostolic status for those who accepted that identification; cf. Mt 10.3.

[62] See further the Introduction, 8. Thus the argument, that the simple 'James' speaks against pseudonymity, fails to persuade.

[63] Contrast 1 Cor 1.2; 2 Cor 1.3; Gal 1.3; Eph 1.3; 1 Pet 1.3; Jude 17; 1 Clem. salutation; Mart. Pol. salutation; etc.

[64] L:V K:B A^ms Ä.

[65] Note e.g. the judicial plea in the Yavneh-Yam Ostracon from Mesad Hashavyahu (Hebrew: 'Let my lord, the governor, listen to the word of his servant'); Lachish 3 (Hebrew); 4 Bar. 6.19 (Greek). For examples from Aramaic letters see J.A. Fitzmyer, 'Notes on Aramaic Epistolography', *JBL* 93 (1974), 211, 213. δοῦλος is also prominent in the prefaces of NT letters: Rom 1.1; Phil 1.1; Tit 1.1; 2 Pet 1.1; Jude 1.

[66] E.g. Ps 86.2; 102.14 119.38, 76; 134.1; 135.1; 143.10. In each case the LXX has δοῦλος, the MT עבד.

[67] E.g. Pss 134.1; Isa 49.3; Ezek 28.25; Josephus, *Ant.* 11.101; b. Qidd. 22b.

[68] 1 Cor 7.22; Eph 6.6; 1 Pet 2.16; 2 Clem. 20.1; Herm. *Mand.* 5.2.1; *et al.* Discussion in I.A.H. Combes, *The Metaphor of Slavery in the Writings of the Early Church*, Sheffield, 1998.

[69] E.g. Exod 14.31 (Moses); 24.13 (Joshua); Num 12.7 (Moses—cited by Dionysius bar Salībī *ad loc.* CSCO SS 101 ed. Sedlacek, 89); Judg 2.8 (Joshua); 2 Kgs 17.13 (the prophets); Ezra 9.11 (the prophets); Ps 36 title (David); Ps 105.42 (Abraham); Isa 20.3 (Isaiah); Ezek 34.23-24 (David); Dan 9.6 (the prophets); Amos 3.7 (the prophets); Zech 1.6 (the prophets); Mal 4.4 (Moses); 1QS 1.3 (the prophets); 4Q292 2 (the prophets); 4Q504 6 12 (Moses); LAB 20.2 (Moses); 4 Bar. 1.4 (Jeremiah); 6.17 (Baruch); m. 'Abot 1.3 (a generality about those who serve God). See further Fabris, 50 n. 17. For

leaders or particularly righteous individuals;[70] and the Graeco-Roman world in general was familiar with the enslaved leader as a rhetorical *topos*.[71] Moreover, Paul's uses of δοῦλος in the epistolary introductions to Romans and Philippians seem to be implicit claims to authority and leadership,[72] and the reappearance of 'slave of God/Jesus Christ' in the openings to other pseudepigrapha (see n. 53) imply that the title could be one of honor.[73] We do not, then, have here self-abnegation[74] but high station: the author is like those fortunate slaves in the Graeco-Roman world who had powerful masters and, accordingly, status. He speaks with authority.[75]

It is possible that James was known not only as 'the Just'[76] but also as '(the) slave of God'. Hegesippus refers to James as 'Oblias' ('Ωβλίας), a word otherwise unattested.[77] One explanation for the odd title is that it is a corruption of 'Obadiah' = עבדיה = עבד יהוה = עבד יה = δοῦλος θεοῦ. On this view, 'ΩΒΔΙΑΣ ('Obadiah') became 'ΩΒΛΙΑΣ ('Oblias') when, through a simple scribal error, Δ became Λ.[78] This solution is all the more attractive as Hegesippus goes on to say that James was a 'rampart (περιοχή) of the people', an apparent allusion to LXX Obad 1 (περιοχὴν εἰς τὰ ἔθνη). Yet

---

Jacob/Israel see above n. 45. For a rabbinic discussion of those honored with the title, 'servant of God', see Sifre Deut 27.

[70] E.g. Lk 1.38 (Mary the mother of Jesus); Acts 4.29 (the apostles); 16.17 (Paul and his fellow missionaries); Jas 2.23 v.l. (Abraham); Rev 10.7 (the prophets); 15.3 (Moses).

[71] D.B. Martin, *Slavery as Salvation*, New Haven, 1990.

[72] Contrast Ropes, 118, who asserts that 'Paul uses this form of description in the address of Romans and Philippians only, two epistles in which he is consciously striving to avoid the assumption of personal authority and to emphasize the give and take of an equal comradeship in faith'. Schnider, 24, is rather correct to say that 'slave' connotes authority, if not as much as 'apostle'.

[73] Cf. Didymus of Alexandria, *Ep. can. ad loc.* ed. Zoepfl, 1; Nerses of Lambron in the *Chaîne Arménienne* 1 ed. Renoux, 70; Hort, 2; Schrage, 14; Bauckham, *Wisdom*, 17; Koester, *History*, 161 ('weighty honorary title'); Tsuji, *Glaube*, 24-25; Moo, 48-49; Burchard, 48; Gundry, 919; *et al.* The parallels are one reason to doubt whether Cargal, 212-13, is right when he asserts that James is a 'slave' precisely because he restores those who have wandered from the truth (5.19): this likely reads too much into the text.

[74] An idea found in quite a few older commentaries; cf. Hole, *Discourses* (as in n. 51), 426: '"James a servant of God"... shews the lowliness and humility of his mind'. So still G. and H. Hart, *Analysis*, 14.

[75] According to Tsuji, *Glaube*, 25, James implicitly claims prophetic status. Those who attribute our epistle to the historical James sometimes combine the two possible senses of 'slave': it is both a special office and a sign of humility; so e.g. Mussner, 60.

[76] Cf. Gos. Thom. 12 (ιακωβος πδικαιος); Gos. Heb. 7 *apud* Jerome, *Vir. inl.* 2 TU 14.1a ed. Richardson, 8; 1 Apoc. Jas 5.32.2-3 (this may associate James' status as 'the Just' with his being a servant, but the text is fragmentary), 6-7; 2 Apoc. Jas 5.44.13-14; 59.21-22; Hegesippus in Eusebius, *H.E.* 2.23.7.

[77] Hegesippus *apud* Eusebius, *H.E.* 2.23.7.

[78] Cf. the textual variants for Lk 3.32 ('Ιωβήλ, 'Ιωβήδ). Discussion in Torrey, 'Just'; Schoeps, 'Jacobus'; Sahlin, 'Obias'; Baltzer-Koester, 'Bezeichnung'; Bauckham, 'Jerusalem Church'.

even if this is the correct explanation—many doubt that it is—we cannot know whether the appellation was bestowed upon James before or after our book was written, or how widely the tag became known, so one should not assume knowledge of it for exegesis.

Another possibility, consistent with but not dependent upon the previous suggestion, is that James' status as 'slave' involves an intertextual allusion. Deutero-Isaiah more than once identifies the suffering servant with 'Ἰάκωβος.[79] Moreover, several of the key words in LXX Isa 49.5-6 reappear in Jas 1.1:

LXX Isa 49.5-6	Jas 1.1
Thus says the Lord (κύριος), who formed me from the womb a servant (δοῦλον) to himself to gather Jacob ('Ἰάκωβ) and Israel to him... and he said to me: 'It is a great thing for you that you are called my servant to establish the tribes (φυλάς) of Jacob ('Ἰάκωβ) and to bring back the diaspora (διασποράν) of Israel'.	James ('Ἰάκωβος), a slave (δοῦλος) of God and of the Lord (κυρίου) Jesus Christ, to the twelve tribes (φυλαῖς) that are in the diaspora (διασπορᾷ): Greetings.

Although one can hardly be confident that ancient readers linked the two texts, early Christian literature otherwise quotes or alludes to Isa 49.5-6, and it belongs to a portion of Scripture—Isa 49–51—often mined for proof texts.[80] Further, other intertextual links with Isaiah appear throughout James,[81] and a few modern expositors have indeed thought of Isaiah's servant when reading Jas 1.1.[82]

If, in Judaism, the faithful are servants of God,[83] and if in the Graeco-Roman world the pious can be thought of (albeit rarely) as the slaves of a particular deity,[84] in the early church Christians are 'slaves' of 'Jesus Christ' (a name at home in liturgical contexts).[85] This is already implicit in the parables in which the faithful serve and wait for their returning master,[86] and Jesus' status as 'Lord' in the early Palestinian community is confirmed by the pre-Pauline and Aramaic μαράνα θά = מרנא תא ('Lord,

---

[79] 44.1-2, 21; 45.4; 48.20; 49.5-6.

[80] Quotations: Acts 13.47 (applying Isa 49.6 to the ministry of Paul and Barnabas); Barn. 14.8; Justin, Dial. 121.4. Allusions: Lk 2.32; Acts 1.8; Sib. Or. 14.214. See C.H. Dodd, *Scriptures*, 91-92.

[81] See above, 51, and for some additional possibilities note Mayor, *James*, cxiv.

[82] E.g. Keenan, 31-32; Cargal, 212-13; R. Wall, 41 (citing Isa 49.5-6).

[83] See n. 69 and J. Byron, *Slavery Metaphors in Early Judaism and Pauline Christianity*, Tübingen, 2003; also Philo, *Cher.* 107. Mt 6.24 = Lk 16.13 presupposes the idea.

[84] E.g. Plato, *Phaedo* 85B; Sophocles, *Oed. tyr.* 140; Euripides, *Ion* 309; MAMA 4.279.

[85] W. Kramer, *Christ, Lord, Son of God*, London, 1966, 215-22.

[86] E.g. Mt 24.43-51 = Lk 12.39-46.

come!').[87] That 'Jesus is Lord' is the basis for James being a 'slave'. According to most exegetes, κύριος is again a title for Jesus in 5.7-8 (this commentator demurs) whereas in 1.7; 3.9; 4.10; and 5.10 it refers to God.

The double name, 'Jesus Christ', probably goes back to the Aramaic confession, משיחא ישוע, 'Jesus [is] the Messiah', which became, in Greek, the compound designation, ᾽Ιησοῦς + Χριστός.[88] Most modern commentators assume that, in James, 'Jesus Christ' functions as a proper name, as it does so often in early Christian literature. That is, 'Christ', although it derives from the Hebrew משיח, has lost its titular status.[89] But caution is in order. One doubts that, in a Jewish Christian setting, Χριστός was ever wholly devoid of traditional messianic associations. In line with this, although Matthew, John, and Paul use ᾽Ιησοῦς Χριστός as though it were a name,[90] they also exploit the messianic meaning of Χριστός.[91] For them, 'Jesus Christ' is a name with titular significance.[92] It may be the same with James.

In accord with his unlikely thesis that James is a lightly Christianized Jewish text, Massebieau argued that an editor added ᾽Ιησοῦ Χριστοῦ. Spitta and Meyer, offering a similar hypothesis, urged that καὶ κυρίου ᾽Ιησοῦ Χριστοῦ is an interpolation.[93] These conjectures depend wholly upon the strength of their compositional theories, which this commentary rejects, and neither supposition finds support in the Greek mss. or the translations. External evidence is also lacking for the more plausible conjecture that an originally Christian document of *paraenesis*, without prescript, was turned into a letter in order to assimilate it to other works in the canon.[94] It is best to regard 1.1 as the original opening and to observe the following: (i) the content of our epistle corresponds with

---

[87] Known from 1 Cor 16.22; Did. 10.6; Apost. Const. 7.26.5 ed. Funk, 414; cf Rev 22.20. See J.A Fitzmyer, 'The Semitic Background of the New Testament *Kyrios* Title', in *A Wandering Aramean*, Missoula, MT, 1979, 115-42; M. Hengel, 'Abba, Maranatha, Hosanna und die Anfänge der Christologie', in *Studien zur Christologie: Kleine Schriften IV*, ed. C.-J. Thornton, Tübingen, 2006, 496-534.

[88] See J. Frey, 'Der historische Jesus und der Christus der Evangelien', in *Der historische Jesus*, ed. J. Schröter and R. Brucker, Berlin, 2002, 302-303.

[89] Cf. Davids, 63, who thinks the nontitular use of 'Christ' would 'be unusual for a Jew who spent most of his time in Jerusalem where the titular use would have been meaningful, but it is very similar to the normal Pauline (i.e. Hellenistic) usage. Thus it is an indication that this verse stems from a Hellenistic Christian.'

[90] Mt 1.1, 18; Jn 1.17; 17.3; Rom 1.1; etc.

[91] E.g. Mt 2.4; 16.13-20; 24.5, 23, 24; 26.63, 68; Jn 1.41; Rom 9.5

[92] Helpful here is D.R. Hare, 'When Did "Messiah" Become a Proper Name?', *ExpTim* 121 (2009), 70-73.

[93] Massebieau, 'L'Épître'; Spitta, 7-8, 14; Meyer, *Rätsel*, 118-23. So too Easton, 21.

[94] McGiffert, 585; Cone, 273; and R. Wall, 39-40, raise this possibility. Llewelyn, 'Prescript', argues for it at length. Cf. Harnack, *Geschichte*, 485-91; J. Weiss, *Christianity*, 743 n. 4; Streeter, *Church*, 197-98; Findlay, *Way*, 158; Elliott-Binns, 1022. As James may not have circulated widely before the latter half of the second century, by which time Christian letters existed as parts of collections, one can imagine it then gaining an epistolary opening if it lacked one before.

Christian tradition about James; (ii) the catchword connection between vv. 1 and 2 harmonizes with the writer's procedure throughout chap. 1; (iii) vv. 2-4 closely resemble 1 Pet 1.6-7 (see 140-41), just as v. 1 closely resembles 1 Pet 1.1. The similarities suggest that, if 1 Peter lies behind James, all of Jas 1.1-4 comes from the same compositional stage.[95] If, on the other hand, 1 Peter rewrote James, it already knew it in its present form.

ταῖς δώδεκα φυλαῖς ταῖς ἐν τῇ διασπορᾷ. The phrase is all-inclusive: every region and every Jewish group in the diaspora is in view. δώδεκα, φυλή, and διασπορά are all Jamesian *hapax*. Particularly instructive for comparison are the openings of other letters written to Jewish exiles:[96] Jer 29.1 ('These are the words of the letter which Jeremiah sent from Jerusalem to the elders of the exiles...and all the people, whom Nebuchadnezzar had taken into exile...'); Ep Jer 6.1 ('A copy of the letter which Jeremiah sent to those who were to be taken to Babylon as captives by the king of the Babylonians');[97] 2 Macc 1.1 ('The Jewish brothers in Jerusalem and those in the land of Judea, to their Jewish brothers in Egypt: Greetings and good peace'); 2 Macc 1.10 ('Those in Jerusalem and those in Judea and the senate and Judas, to Aristobulus, who is of the family of the anointed priests, teacher of Ptolemy the king, and to the Jews in Egypt...'); 1 Pet 1.1 ('Peter, an apostle of Jesus Christ, to the exiles of the dispersion [διασπορᾶς] in Pontus, Galatia, Cappadocia, Asia, and Bithynia...'); 2 Bar. 78.1 ('These are the words of the letter which Baruch, the son of Neriah, sent to the nine and a half tribes which were across the river in which were written the following things'); 4 Bar. 6.17 ('Baruch, the servant of God, writes to Jeremiah in the captivity of Babylon...');[98] t. Sanh. 2.6 (Rabban Gamaliel writes a letter to the exiles in Babylon and in Media and 'to all the other exiles of Israel').[99] Clearly there was a tradition of authorities in Judea writing to those outside of Palestine.[100] Perhaps indeed the first line of our letter puts James on a par with the rabbinic authorities who sought to legislate matters in the diaspora. However that may be, 1.1 implies that James is a Jew writing from Palestine, probably Jerusalem,[101] which is consistent with the

---

[95] See further the Introduction, 67-70.

[96] On the diaspora letter as a literary type of which James is a member see 71-75.

[97] Here the exiles have not yet left the land of Israel. 4QApocryphon of Jeremiah Cᵃ (4Q389) was probably another Jeremiah letter to exiles—so D. Dimant in DJD 30.233—but all we have are fragments; see Doering, 'Jeremia'.

[98] Note 6.16 v.l.: ἀποστείλας δὲ εἰς τὴν διασπορὰ τῶν ἐθνῶν.

[99] לאחנא בני גלותא דבבבל ובני גלותא דימדי ושאר כל גלוותא דישראל. Cf. y. Maʻaś. Š. 31c (5.4); y. Sanh. 18d (1.2); b. Sanh. 11a.

[100] See further Taatz, *Briefe*. She differentiates between institutional letters dealing with cultisc, calendric, and related matters on the one hand and prophetic letters of instruction on the other. She does not discuss James at any point.

[101] Almost all the older commentaries assume this. Cf. also Brückner, 'Kritik', 540; Tsuji, *Glaube*, 25; Niebuhr, 'Minds', 46; and the title of ms. 330: γραφεῖσα ἀπὸ Ἰηρουσαλήμ.

traditions about our purported author in Acts and Galatians as well as later legends that have him live out his life in the capital; cf. Prot. Jas 25.1: 'I, James, wrote this history in Jerusalem'.

αἱ δώδεκα φυλαί = שנים עשר שבטי was a common way of referring to all Israel.[102] Its qualification by the phrase, ἐν τῇ διασπορᾷ, appears, however, to be without parallel.[103] διασπορά—a rare word outside biblical Greek and patristic texts[104]—can mean, depending upon the context, the state of dispersal or the area in which people are scattered.[105] As the ἐν indicates, the local meaning holds for Jas 1.1;[106] and as τῇ διασπορᾷ is unqualified, one should think of the universal diaspora, east and west.[107] Often διασπορά bears a negative sense: the scattering of God's people is punishment for their sins.[108] This does not, however, tell us much about the self-conception of those who lived in the diaspora nor anything about James. For more than one word was used for the experience of exile, and in any case evaluations must have varied from place to place and time to time and group to group.[109] Seemingly more relevant is the observation that many thought of the diaspora as a place of suffering.[110] This makes it appropriate that the theme of suffering receives attention immediately in v. 2.[111]

---

[102] Gen 49.28; Exod 24.4; 28.21; 39.14; LXX Josh 4.5; Ezek 47.13; Ecclus 44.23; 1QM 3.14; 5.1, 2; 4Q379 1.5; 4Q158 4.3; 11QTemple 5.7; Ecclus 44.23; Philo, *Fug.* 185; Sib. Or. 3.249; LAB 45.4; T. Mos. 2.4; T. Benj. 9.2; T. Abr. RecLng. 13.6; Mt 19.28; Lk 22.30; Acts 26.7; Rev 21.12; 2 Bar. 77.2; 78.4; 1 Clem. 55.6 v.l.; Prot. Jas. 1.1, 3; etc.

[103] The most common qualification of 'the twelve tribes' is 'of Israel', but there are others; see Ropes, 119.

[104] The few instances include Manetho frag. 5c; Plutarch, *Mor.* 1105A, 1109F; *Sol.* 32; Epicurus, *Deperd. libr. reliq.* frag. 21.2. NT: 3×: Jn 7.35; Jas 1.1; 1 Pet 1.1. LXX: 10-12×, for several Hebrew equivalents but never גלוה or גלות. Gk. Pseudepigrapha (Denis): 3×: T. Ash. 7.2; Pss. Sol. 8.28; 9.2. Philo: 2×: *Conf.* 197; *Praem.* 115. Josephus: 0×. The corresponding verb, διασπείρω ('to scatter'), is, by contrast, common enough.

[105] For the former see LXX Deut 28.25; Jer 41.17; Neh 1.9; Pss. Sol. 8.28; 9.2. For the latter see Jdt 5.19; T. Ash. 7.2; 1 Pet 1.1; Justin Martyr, *Dial.* 117.2 PTS 47 ed. Marcovich, 271; Hippolytus, *Antichr.* 53-54 CGS 1.2 ed. Achelis, 36.

[106] Cf. the ב in בגולה, בגלותא, בגלות.

[107] Earlier commentators, assuming James to be authentic, debated whether the eastern or western diaspora is in view, and whether one can determine more precisely the locale of the envisaged audience.

[108] J. Becker, *Untersuchungen zur Entstehungsgeschichte der Testamente der zwölf Patriarchen*, Leiden, 1970, 172-77; W.C. van Unnik, *Das Selbstverständnis der jüdischen Diaspora in der hellenistisch-römischen Zeit*, ed. P.W. van der Horst, Leiden, 1993. Contrast K.L. Schmidt, 'διασπορά', *TWNT* 2 (1964), 100.

[109] J.M.G. Barclay, *Jews in the Mediterranean Diaspora*, Edinburgh, 1996; J.M. Scott, 'Exile and the Self-Understanding of Diaspora Jews in the Greco-Roman Period', in *Exile*, ed. J.M. Scott, Leiden, 1997, 173-218.

[110] See esp. van Unnik, *Selbstverständnis* (as in n. 108).

[111] Cf. Niebuhr, 'Diasporabriefe', 432; Tsuji, *Glaube*, 25-26; Verseput, 'Wisdom'.

James' use of ἐν τῇ διασπορᾷ is unexpected. It is likely a Semitism. The expression appears nowhere in the Greek Pseudepigrapha, Philo, Josephus, or in any other Christian source before Justin.[112] The obvious Hebrew equivalent is the well-attested בגולה,[113] for which however the LXX has ἐν ἀποικίᾳ (Jer 48.7; 49.3), ἐν ἀποικισμόν (Jer 48.11), ἐν μετοικεσίᾳ (Ezek 12.11), or ἐν αἰχμαλωσίᾳ (Ezek 25.3; Amos 1.15; Zech 14.2). But ἐν διασπορᾷ (without the article) is attested in LXX Deut 28.25; Jer 15.7; T. Ash 7.2-3; and some LXX witnesses have, as the title for Ps 138, τῷ Δαυὶδ ψαλμὸς Ζαχαρίου ἐν τῇ διασπορᾷ.[114] Although this is from a psalm, not a letter, it is the opening line and so seems to be a significant parallel.

Those who find in 1.1 a metaphorical way of addressing Christians conceptualized as the new Israel or of addressing Christian Jews outside Palestine have made the following claims and observations against a strictly literal interpretation. (i) The twelve tribes did not exist when our book was written. (ii) By then those tribes were a symbol of the elect, or the people of God, and some Christians applied that symbol to themselves.[115] Further, διασπορά could be used metaphorically.[116] (iii) James is clearly written to followers of Jesus, not non-Christian Jews. (iv) 1 Peter opens with an address to Christians, most of whom appear to have been Gentiles, under the guise of the exiled.[117] (v) 'Literally the twelve tribes was a synonym for Israel as a whole, which could by no means be described as in the Dispersion.'[118] In other words, one cannot address the

[112] Justin, *Dial.* 117.2, 4 (both referring to the Jewish dispersion).

[113] As in Jer 29.16; 48.7, 11; 49.3; Ezek 12.11; 25.3; Amos 1.15; Zech 14.2; 4Q169 3-4 4.1; 4Q385a 17a-eii7. Cf. Aramaic בגלותא, as in Tg. Ps.-J. Lev 26.41; Deut 4.27; 29.27.

[114] The line remains enigmatic, although one may note that some LXX mss. attribute Pss 145-48 to 'Haggai and Zechariah', and further that Ps 139 evokes the thought of distance (cf. vv. 2, 9) and so perhaps exile.

[115] Jn 11.51-52 ('he prophesied that Jesus was about to die for the nation, and not for the nation only, but to gather into one the dispersed children of God'); 1 Pet 1.1 ('Peter, an apostle of Jesus Christ, to the exiles of the dispersion in Pontus, Galatia, Cappadocia, Asia, and Bithynia'), 17 ('live in reverent fear during the time of your exile'); 2.11 ('I urge you as aliens and exiles to abstain from the desires of the flesh that wage war against your soul'). Also pertinent are (i) the use of πάροικος, παροικία, and παροικέω in still other texts (e.g. 1 Clem. inscription; 2 Clem. 5.1, 5; Pol. *Phil.* inscription; Mart. of Pol. inscription; Diogenes, *Ep.* 5.5; on this see R. Feldmeier, *Die Christen als Fremde*, Tübingen, 1992); (ii) 5 Ezra's apparent reinterpretation of the expectation of the eschatological gathering of diaspora Jews as fulfilled in the church; see T.A. Bergren, 'The "People Coming from the East"', *JBL* 108 (1989), 675-83; and (iii) the identification of the 144,000 out of every tribe of the people of Israel Rev 7 with the church, if one supposes that to be the correct interpretation.

[116] Note Philo, *Praem.* 115 (διασπορᾶς ψυχικῆς; cf. *Cherub.* 120); Justin, *Dial.* 113.3 (Jesus restored τὴν διασπορὰν τοῦ λαοῦ); Clement of Alexandria, *Prot.* 8.8 ed. Marcovich, 131; Eusebius, *Ecl.* 41 PG 22.1172A (τῆς διασπορᾶς τοῦ πνευματικοῦ).

[117] Achtemeier, *1 Peter*, 82.

[118] So Moffatt, 7. See further Zahn, *Introduction*, 73-83.

twelve tribes in the diaspora because not all Jews lived outside Palestine. (vi) If our author envisioned non-Christian Jews, his letter would be more evangelistic.[119]

All this is unpersuasive. (i) The belief that all the tribes of Israel still existed, albeit most of them might be hidden in exile, was widespread, and many hoped for their literal return to the land.[120] E.P. Sanders reckons this hope to have been 'common'.[121] (ii) The occasional application of diaspora language to the church universal does not annul the fact that many Christians still believed in the continued existence of the lost tribes and in their eschatological return.[122] In other words, there were Christians for whom the twelve Jewish tribes remained a literal reality. Furthermore, early Christians did not typically employ διασπορά in the metaphorical

---

[119] Cf. Erdmann, 40; Huther, 10; Beyschlag, 10.

[120] Pertinent texts include Deut 30.1-5; 1 Chr 16.35; Neh 1.8-9; Pss 106.47; 147.2; Isa 11.11-13; 27.12-13; 43.5-6, 14-21; 49.6; 56.8; 60.3-7; 66.18-24; Jer 23.8; 29.10-14; 31.1, 8, 10; 32.37-41; Ezek 11.17-20; 20.33-44; 28.25; 34.11-16; 36.24; 37.11-28; 39.26-17; 47–48; Hos 11.11; Zech 2.6; 3.20; 8.7; 10.6-12; 2 Macc 1.27; 2.7, 18; Tob 13.5, 13; 14.5; Ecclus 36.11; 48.10; Bar 4.37; 5.5; Jub. 1.15; Pss. Sol. 8.28; 11.2-3; 17.4, 21, 26-28, 44; 90.33; 1QM 2.1-3; 11QTemple 57.5-6; 4QpsEzek^b 1 col. 2; 4Q509 3; 4Q243 24; 4Q504 1-2 6.12-14; 1 En. 57.1; Philo, *Praem*. 164-65, 168; 4 Ezra 13.32-50; 2 Bar. 78.1-7; Sib. Or. 2.170-73; T. Iss. 6.2-4; T. Dan 5.8-9; T. Naph. 4.2-5; T. Ash. 7.3; T. Benj. 9.2; 10.11; T. Jos. 19.3-8 (Arm.); Mek. on Exod 14.31; m. Sanh. 10.3; t. Sanh. 13.12; y. Sanh. 29c (10.6); b. Sanh. 110b; Tg. Neof. 1 Num 24.7; Tg. Isa 6.13; 53.8; Tg. Hos 2.2; Tg. Mic 5.3; Commodian, *Inst*. 2.1 CSEL 15 ed. Combart, 58-61. The Epistle of Aristeas recounts that the LXX was translated in the post-exilic period by 72 men, six from each tribe of Israel (47-51); and the content of the tenth benediction of the Amidah—'Sound the great horn for our freedom, and lift up a banner to gather in our exiles. You are praised, O Lord, who gathers in the outcasts of his people Israel'—goes back to pre-70 liturgical texts; see E.G. Chazon, '"Gathering the dispersed of Judah"', in *Heavenly Tablets*, ed. L. LiDonnici and A. Lieber, Leiden, 159-75. The inscribing of the names of the twelve tribes on the gates of the new Jerusalem in 4Q554 and Rev 21.12 also belongs here; and Luke's Paul, in Acts 26.6-7, may implicitly endorse the expectation. At the very least, he speaks as though 'the twelve tribes' (δωδεκάφυλος, cf. Sib. Or. 3.248) still exist. The tradition that all twelve tribes did not become extinct lived on in medieval times; see A. Neubauer, 'Where are the Ten Tribes?', *JQR* 1 (1988–89), 14-28, 95-114, 185-201, 408-23. It even survived into some nineteenth-century Christian circles in the form of 'British Israelism'. See Z. Ben-Dor Benite, *The Ten Lost Tribes*, Oxford, 2009.

[121] E.P. Sanders, *Judaism*, London, 1992, 290-91. He writes: 'The general hope for the restoration of the people of Israel is the most ubiquitous hope of all. The twelve tribes are sometimes explicitly mentioned and often indirectly referred to (e.g. by the name "Jacob"), but sometimes the hope is stated more vaguely: the children of Israel will be gathered from throughout the world. In such instances we cannot be sure that the lost ten tribes were explicitly in mind, though it seems likely enough; in any case the reassembly of the people of Israel was generally expected' (294).

[122] See Allison, *Tradition*, 177-92; A.S. Geyser, 'Some Salient New Testament Passages on the Restoration of the Twelve Tribes of Israel', in *L'Apocalypse johannique et l'Apocalyptique dans le Nouveau Testament*, ed. J. Lambrecht, Gembloux, 1980, 305-10; and n. 120 above.

way it employed πάροικος and παρεπίδημος;[123] and with the doubtful exception of Rev 7 and the idiosyncratic Herm. *Sim.* 9.17,[124] 'the twelve tribes' always, in early Christian literature, designates the Jewish people in its totality.[125] (iii) This commentary argues throughout that James envisages a mixed audience, one that includes Christian and non-Christian Jews.[126] Beyond that, there would be nothing odd about a letter that addresses believers in Jesus under the guise of a pseudepigraphon written to Jews. The Greek Apocalypse of Ezra, the Vision of Ezra, and 4 Ezra 1–2, 15–16 are Christian pseudepigrapha with pretended Jewish authors and audiences. One also thinks of the Testaments of the Twelve Patriarchs and 4 Baruch in their present Christian forms. (iv) If 1 Peter supplies an example of a letter addressed to Christians as exiles,[127] it is the only example; that is, no other Christian writing from the first two centuries refers to the church with the term, διασπορά. Moreover, and as observed above, other ancient letters are ostensibly addressed to literal Jewish exiles. Beyond that, James, unlike 1 Peter, does not otherwise use exile terminology for its readers.[128] (v) Schlatter, 93, arguing that our text can address non-Christian Jews in the diaspora who belong to the twelve tribes, cites as a linguistic parallel t. Sanh. 2.6, where Gamaliel writes to 'our brothers, sons of the Babylonian diaspora and sons of the Media diaspora and sons of all the other Israelite diasporas'. Here the universal, 'our brothers', is immediately qualified by particulars, 'sons of the Babylonian diaspora, etc.'. Aside from this parallel, in Greek a second term can narrow or limit a preceding one, as in 1 Cor 1.2, where Paul writes to τῇ ἐκκλησίᾳ τοῦ θεοῦ τῇ οὔσῃ ἐν Κορίνθῳ. In addition, Jews could speak of 'Israel' (without qualification) as scattered among the nations.[129] 2 Baruch 78.4 probably reflects a general sentiment: 'Are we

[123] See Kloppenborg, 'Judaeans', 116-17.

[124] Here 'the twelve tribes' are usually said to be the nations of the world.

[125] Mt 19.28; Lk 22.30; Acts 26.7; Rev 21.12; 1 Clem. 31.4; 43.2; 55.6; Justin, *Dial.* 68.6; Ep. Apost. 30; Prot. Jas. 1.1, 3. One should keep in mind that the earliest undisputed evidence for the church reckoning itself the new Israel does not occur until Justin; see P. Richardson, *Israel in the Apostolic Church*, Cambridge, UK, 1969.

[126] See esp. the Introduction, 32-50.

[127] But for a different view see W.C. Van Unnik, *Sparsa Collecta, Part Three*, Leiden, 1983, 95-105. He observes that not even the allegorist Origen applied the word 'diaspora' to the church, not even when alluding to 1 Pet 1.1: *Gen* frag. PG 12.92A. For Origen, as for Eusebius, *H.E.* 3.4.2, 1 Peter was written to Jews in the diaspora. Perhaps modern scholarship has often not considered this a serious option because (as with James) it has confused the fictional readers of the address with the likely real readers.

[128] And even 1 Peter retains a literal dimension through the mention of geographical areas (1.1).

[129] E.g. b. Pesaḥ. 87b; cf. Jub. 1.12-18; 4Q504 5.7-21; 2 Macc 2.7; Ecclus 36.10; Tob 13.2. Note also Josephus, *Ant.* 11.133, where two of the tribes live in Asia and Europe while the other ten live beyond the Euphrates. For the theme of post-exilic Israel as still in exile see M.A. Knibb, 'The Exile in the Literature of the Intertestamental Period', *HeyJ* 17 (1976), 253-72; C.A. Evans, 'Jesus and the Continuing Exile of Israel',' in *Jesus and the Restoration of Israel*, ed. C.C. Newman, Downers Grove, IL, 1999, 76-100.

not all, the twelve tribes, bound by one captivity?' Not all Judeans returned from the Babylonian exile, and others lived in Egypt and elsewhere. Which is to say: all twelve tribes were thought to be represented in the dispersion. This would no doubt have seemed all the more true after the destruction of Jerusalem in CE 70, when James was written, for by then most Judeans had been removed from their homeland. Against Ropes, 128, then, we can construe 1.1 as though it read: ταῖς ἀπὸ τῶν δέδεκα φυλῶν διασπαρεῖσιν,[130] that is, 'to those persons from the twelve tribes who reside in the dispersion'. (vi) The objection that James would be more evangelistic if its author hoped for non-Christian Jewish readers[131] blatantly assumes that early Christians communicated with others only in order to convert them, and that there is only one way to persuade, namely, by parading one's beliefs. Both assumptions are demonstrably false.[132]

If the arguments for a metaphorical reading of ταῖς δώδεκα κτλ. fail, the case for the literal reading recommends itself. (i) 1.1, unlike 1 Pet 1.1-2, contains no hint that it is to be given figurative sense or applied to the churches. Nor does the rest of the book in any way intimate how the church might be thought of as in the diaspora. (ii) In the words of Adamson, 49, if James 'has a new spiritual meaning for the twelve tribes he must not at once add of the Dispersion, for this at once anchors it again in the old historical application'. (iii) The quiescence of *explicit* Christian themes in James is, as explained in the Introduction, consistent with a desire to address non-Christian recipients. (iv) As the commentary tradition shows, exegetes have regularly had trouble thinking of all of James as addressed to churches. The damning rebuke of 5.1-6, for example, is often for this reason regarded as an apostrophe. If, however, James poses as an address to the whole Jewish diaspora, those rebuked by 5.1-6 can be part of the declared audience.[133] The puzzling fact that the implied readers seemingly belong to different groups makes sense if James poses as an address to the twelve tribes. (v) Hegesippus records the legend that a contingent of Jewish authorities asked James to address the people: 'Stand then upon the pinnacle of the temple, so that from on high you will be clearly seen and so that all the people may readily hear your words. For because of Passover all the tribes (πᾶσαι αἱ φυλαί) with the Gentiles have come together.'[134] We do not know the provenance of this legend wherein James speaks to 'all the tribes'. But it appears to be independent of our letter,[135] and it in any event reflects somebody's assumption that the brother of Jesus could address all Israel.

---

[130] So the *prothesis* of the *Catenae* ed. Cramer, 1.

[131] Cf. Huther, 10; Gloag, *Introduction*, 46; Vielhauer, *Geschichte*, 570; *et al.*

[132] See further the Introduction, 39-44.

[133] See further 33, 38-50 of the Introduction.

[134] Hegesippus in Eusebius, *H.E.* 2.23.10-11. James also addresses a large Jewish crowd in Ps.-Clem. Rec. 1.66-69 CGS 51 ed. Rehm, 45-47.

[135] Cf. the Introduction, 16.

Taking everything into account, Cadoux was probably right: although Christians in our day and age may believe that 'the Church has inherited the privileges of Israel...if they found a circular letter beginning, "My dear fellow Jews", they would unhesitatingly conclude that it was written by a Jew to Jews; nor is there less reason for taking the address of this Epistle to mean what it says.'[136] This, to be sure, still leaves open the question of the actual audience; for if, as argued in the Introduction, James is a pseudepigraphon, its audience is likely as fictional as the author. That issue can only be settled by the verse-by-verse commentary.

Should James be read in the light of the hoped-for ingathering of the twelve tribes at the consummation?[137] Since our letter addresses scattered Israel with moral exhortations, and since it expresses the conviction that the end is near (5.9), and since Israel's repentance before the end was a stock item of Jewish eschatology,[138] it may be that James presents itself as the same sort of writing as 2 Bar. 78–87, namely, an attempt to encourage and stir up the dispersed tribes to repent in preparation for the approaching day of judgment. Such a reading coheres with the possible allusion to LXX Isa 49.5-6 (see above), for that passage envisages the eschatological restoration of the entire Jewish people.

χαίρειν. The use of this lone infinitive in an epistolary greeting appears also in the LXX[139] and in Acts 15.23 (in a letter associated with James); 23.26.[140] It was quite common in Hellenistic letters.[141] Our verse reveals no influence from the liturgical variant in the Pauline prescripts, 'grace to you and peace'. The simple verb links up with 1.2 (χαράν) and so inaugurates the string of catch-word connections that follows. See further on v. 2.

---

[136] Cadoux, *Thought*, 11. Cf. Bassett, xxxvii-xlv: 'The whole question, To whom is this Epistle written? is settled for us without any inquiry being necessary, in the fewest words, "To the twelve tribes". It is really painful, as being utterly obstructive to the discovery of truth, after reading this address with which the letter is inscribed, to find critics, like postmen who are ill-skilled in deciphering hand-writing, conveying the letter to every house except that of the person whose name is specified on the envelope.'

[137] See n. 120 and cf. Penner, *Eschatology*, 181-83; Jackson-McCabe, 'Letter', 515; idem, 'Messiah', 724. Maybe it is relevant that Jas 1.1 refers to Jesus as 'the Christ', and in 4 Ezra 13.12-13, 39-50, the Messiah returns the scattered tribes to their land; cf. Pss. Sol. 17.28-30; 4Q521 2.13 (?); b. Meg. 12a; Gen. Rab. 98.9; Frag. Tg. on Num 24.7; and Tg. on Cant 1.1. The idea probably stems from Isa 11.10-12: 'On that day the root of Jesse shall stand as a signal to the peoples... On that day the Lord will extend his hand yet a second time to recover the remnant that is left of his people.'

[138] See Allison, *Tradition*, 192-204.

[139] 1 Esd 6.8; 8.9; 1 Macc 10.18, 25; 11.30, 32; 12.6, 20; 13.36; 14.20; 15.2, 16; 2 Macc 11.16, 22, 27, 34. Cf. Let. Aris. 41.

[140] Commentators regularly instruct us that χαίρειν assumes λέγει or some such.

[141] See nn. 37, 38 and note also XHev/Se 67.3. One is also reminded of the simple Aramaic שלם ('wellbeing, greetings') in Ezra 4.17 and b. Sanh. 95a and the simple Hebrew שלום ('shalom') in the Bar Kokhba correspondence (e.g. papMur 43, 44, 46; 5/6 Hev 10, 12; cf. Midr. Tannaim on Deut 26.13, as cited in n. 40).

A few have found the common use of the plain greeting, χαίρειν, in Acts 15.23 and Jas 1.1 to be a sign that James produced both.[142] Yet the isolated infinitive as a greeting is otherwise common enough. One could, moreover, just as easily take the coincidence as evidence that the author of our epistle imitated the opening of a well-known letter associated with James the Just.

---

[142] E.g. Gill, 779; Fausset, 582 ('an undersigned coincidence and mark of genuineness'); Mayor, 32; Cadoux, *Thought*, 33; Moo, 58. See further the Introduction, 6-7.

II

THE OUTCOME OF TRIAL (1.2-4)[1]

(2) Consider it utmost joy, my brothers, when you fall into various tribulations, (3) knowing that this means of testing your faith works patient endurance; (4) and let patient endurance have in you its perfected work, so that you may be perfect and complete, lacking in nothing.

History of Interpretation and Reception

Ecclesiastical commentators have usually been anxious, when commenting on 1.2, to distinguish between two types of trial. Ps.-Euthalius the Deacon even makes this one of the major themes of the epistle.[2] Gill, 770, is typical when he says that the faithful should not rejoice over the temptations brought by Satan or stirred up by sin, which can only be matters of grief, but only over 'afflictions and persecutions for the sake of the Gospel…because they are trials of the faith of God's people…'[3] This distinction has allowed Christians to eliminate the seeming contradiction between Jas 1.2, which enjoins rejoicing in trials, and the Lord's Prayer, which instructs praying for deliverance from them.[4] Ps.-Oecumenius and Theophylact, for instance, asserted that saints should rejoice in the trials that God sends but, when temptation to sin arises from within, they should ask for deliverance.[5] In line with this point of view, Abraham and Job, whose trials originated from without rather than from within, are

---

[1] Recent literature: Boismard, 'Liturgie'; Calduch-Benages, 'Trials'; Cheung, *Genre*, 162-94; Davids, 'Suffer'; Deissmann, *Studies*, 259-62; Garland, 'Trials'; Gowan, 'Wisdom'; Hartin, 'Perfect'; idem, *Q*, 81-89, 198-207; Hoppe, *Hintergrund*, 18-43; Isaacs, 'Suffering'; Kirk, 'Wisdom'; Klein, *Werk*, 44-81; Kloppenborg, 'Psychagogy'; Luck, 'Weisheit'; Nauck, 'Freude'; Nienhuis, *Paul*, 174-80; Penner, *Eschatology*, 183-201; Rolin, 'Foi'; Selwyn, *First Peter*, 439-59; Stagg, 'Themes'; Talbert, *Suffering*, 24-41; Tamez, *Message*, 34-43; Theophilus, 'Iacobi'; J. Thomas, 'Anfechtung'; Tsuji, *Glaube*, 123-24; Wenger, *Kyrios*, 122-34; Wolmarans, 'Suffering'.

[2] Ps.-Euthalius, *Cath. ep. ad loc.* PG 85.676B. Cf. the *Catenae ad loc.* ed. Cramer, 2.

[3] Cf. John Scottus Eriugena, *Jn.* 6.1 SC 180 ed. Jeauneau, 328; Manton, 5-6. Pelagius, *Rom ad* 5.3-4 ed. Souter, 42, cites Jas 1.2 in connection with suffering 'for the Lord's name'.

[4] And also the oft-perceived tension with Jas 1.13-15; see below, 214-15.

[5] Ps.-Oecumenius *ad loc.* PG 119.456C-457A; Theophylact *ad loc.* PG 125.1136B. Cf. the *Catenae ad loc.* ed. Cramer, 3; Theodore the Studite, *Ep.* 33 ed. Fatouros, 250; Whitby, 676.

most frequently mentioned as illustrations of what our verse has in mind.[6] This is appropriate given their mention in 2.21-23 and 5.11.

Ps.-Cyril of Jerusalem, however, found another way of establishing harmony between the Lord's Prayer and Jas 1.2: Jesus' words have to do with being overwhelmed by temptation, James' words with besting it: 'But perhaps the entering into temptation means being overwhelmed by temptation? For temptation is, as it were, like a winter torrent difficult to cross. So those who are not overwhelmed in temptations pass through, showing themselves excellent swimmers, while those who are not such enter into them and are overwhelmed.' He went on to cite Judas as an example of one who was overcome by temptation, Peter as an illustration of one who overcame it.[7]

Many commentaries and sermons have addressed themselves to people in relatively comfortable situations. So in the attempt to render vv. 2-4 relevant, some have made it about getting through day-to-day life with equanimity,[8] or even dealing with the drudgery of an unfulfilling job.[9] Others have sought to employ James to awaken people from supposed complacency; thus preachers and exegetes have again and again stressed that suffering should be a part of authentic Christian existence,[10] or even of all human existence.[11] To establish this, proof texts on the inevitability of suffering for the faithful—for example Ecclus 2.1[12] and

[6] Cajetan, 364; Hemminge, 3; and Piscator, 728 e.g. refer to Abraham. Gregory Palamas, *Hom. xxi–xlii* 32.1-2 ed. Chrestou and Zeses, 306-308; Dionysius bar Salībī *ad loc.* CSCO 60, Scriptores Syri 101 ed. Sedlacek, 89; Henry, *ad loc.* (citing Job 5.17); Schöttgen, *Horae Hebraicae*, 1010; and Plummer, 571, refer to Job. Ps.-Oecumenius *ad loc.* PG 119.457A; Gill, 779; Manton, 34; Hort, 4; R. Wall, 48; and Hartin, 58, refer to both.

[7] *Myst. cat.* 5.17 SC 126 bis ed. Piédagnel, 164-66. For yet additional discussions of the Lord's Prayer and Jas 1.2 see Chrysostom, *Job* 2.6 SC 346 ed. Sorlin and Neyrand, 166-68; Maximus the Confessor, *Quaest. ad Thal.* 8.34ff. CCSG 22 ed. Laga and Steel, 29; Nerses of Lambron in the *Chaîne Arménienne* 5 ed. Hus, 72; Stevartius, 14-15; R. Hooker, 'Ecclesiastical Polity', in *The Ecclesiastical Polity and Other Works*, vol. 2, London, 1830, 165-66; Makarios of Corinth, *Η ΚΥΡΙΑΚΗ ΠΡΟΣΕΥΧΗ* ed. Dragas, 94-104.

[8] Cf. Origen, *Hom. Gen* 8.10 SC 7bis ed. de Lubac, 232; Macarius/Symeon, *Logos MS¹* 1.5 GCS ed. Berthold, 85; Radulphus Andrens, *Hom. de sanct.* 9 PL 155.1522A-B; Martin of Legio *ad loc.* PL 209.185B; R. Collyer, *That Life that Now Is*, Boston, 1871, 264-83; W.H. Hutton, *A Disciple's Religion*, Edinburgh, 1911, 12-24.

[9] A.W. Momerie, 'Patience', in *Inspiration and Other Sermons*, Edinburgh, 1889, 245-54.

[10] Cf. Peter Damian, *Ep.* 76.5 ed. Reindel, 379-80. To this end Bede *ad loc.* CCSL 121 ed. Hurst, 184, cites 1 Pet 2.19; Rom 8.18; Acts 5.41.

[11] Cf. Deems, 36: 'The fish was made to swim, as the bird was made to fly, and man was "born to trouble"'.

[12] Cf. Chrysostom, *Frag. in Jac. ad loc.* PG 64.1040A; Ps.-Oecumenius *ad loc.* PG 119.455B; Theophylact *ad loc.* PG 125.1136A. Modern commentators also often cite this verse; see e.g. Knowling, 6; Dibelius, 71; Blackman, 44; Garland, 'Trials', 385; Frankemölle, 189-97. The latter contends that Ecclus 2 in its entirety has significantly influenced James.

Jn 16.33[13]—have regularly been drawn upon. Commentators have also found it helpful to buttress the import of Jas 1.2 by recalling sayings of Jesus himself.[14] Yet 1.2-4 has also become the opportunity not to exhort but to console, to address the religious perplexities that can assail people facing the slings and arrows of outrageous fortune.[15]

Although modern commentators tend to be unruffled by the problem, exegetes in the past often sensed tension with Rom 5.3-4, where Paul says that θλῖψις produces ὑπομονή, which in turn fosters δοκιμή. In James, by contrast, πειρασμός produces δοκίμιον, which fosters ὑπομονή and finally an ἔργον τέλειον. Bede assured readers that Paul and James 'ought not to be considered contradictory' and found harmony by asserting that patient endurance produces character (so Paul) because the one whose patient endurance cannot be overcome is shown to be perfect (so James).[16] Calvin, 262, took this route: 'James says that to be proved results in patience, for if God did not test us, but left us undisturbed, we would not have patience... Paul's sense is that our actual experience of overcoming evil leads us to grasp the value of God's help in the crisis.' Poole, 880, observing that Romans uses δοκιμή whereas James has δοκίμιον, urged that James refers to the testing that works steadfastness, Paul to the outcome of steadfastness.[17] Beginning in the nineteenth century, historical-critical commentators began to cite Rom 5.3-4 (along with 1 Pet 1.7) to raise source-critical issues.

1.3-4 has played a role in debates over the nature of Christian perfection. Wesley identified the 'perfect work' of v. 4 with full sanctification. He fretted much over whether it is typically the outcome of a protracted process or—as he eventually came to believe—is more often than not rather an instantaneous work of God.[18] Some of his followers have occasionally cited the passage to prove that God requires perfection, which must include sinlessness. To this others have responded that 3.2 indicts everyone, including the author, as a sinner, and that 1.2 has to do with the perfection of steadfastness, not a second work of the soul leading to sinlessness.[19]

---

[13] Cf. Athanasius, *Ep.* 14.6 PG 26.1417C-D; Chrysostom, *Frag. in Jac. ad loc.* PG 64.1040A; Ps.-Oecumenius *ad loc.* PG 119.455B; Theophylact *ad loc.* PG 125.1136A; et al.

[14] Esp. Mt 5.10-12 and its Lukan parallel; so Calmet, 666; Stevartius, 12; Lapide, 12; Brochmand, 31; Pareus, 541, 543; Manton, 24; Gill, 779; MacDougall, *Conflict*, 19-20; McKnight, 77; *et al.* See further n. 44.

[15] E.g. F.D. Huntington, 'Trials of Faith', in *Sermons for the People*, Boston, 1862, 225-37.

[16] Bede *ad loc.* CCSL 121 ed. Hurst, 184. Cf. Nicholas of Gorran, 66; Calmet, 667; Lapide, 20; Wolzogen, 183.

[17] Cf. Didymus of Alexandria, *Ep. can.* ad loc. ed. Zoepfl, 2; Radulphus Ardens, *Hom. de sanct.* 9 PL 155.1523A-B; Manton, 27-28; Mayor, 37-38.

[18] See esp. his sermon, 'On Patience', in *Sermons on Several Occasions*, vol. 2, New York, 1839, 219-24.

[19] Cf. S. Franklin, *A Critical Review of Wesleyan Perfection*, Philadelphia, 1875, 490-91.

The exegetical and homiletical traditions have been mostly blind to the ethical problem of exhorting those in difficult situations to rejoice. Joseph Alexander was an exception, candidly observing that 'the moral sense...shrinks from what is here commanded, to rejoice in temptation'. His response was to contend that the joy is retrospective: James does not call people to rejoice while they are suffering but only after they have suffered, when they are far enough away to be able to see the good that has come out of their hardship or evil.[20] More recently, Tamez, writing from a South American liberationist standpoint, remarked: 'We must recognize that [for] those of us who want to read the text from the perspective of the poor, it will be difficult for us to accept passages like James 1:2... We may very well decide to read a different biblical text with a more obvious meaning for liberation.'[21] Most commentators and homileticians, however, show no sign of wondering whether Jas 1.2-4 might foster a fatalism that discourages people in oppressive circumstances from working for justice, or whether it can be cruel to advise victims of suffering to rejoice because oppression will ultimately strengthen their character.[22]

Exegesis

Unlike the Pauline epistles, and against general Greek custom, James does not open with an introductory paragraph of good wishes or congratulations. Rather, like Hebrews, 1 John, and Jude, our letter commences with instruction. Specifically, it begins with an unexpected imperative— rejoice in trials (v. 2)—followed by a complex justification:

First imperative	'Consider it utmost joy', v. 2a
Circumstance	'when you fall into various tribulations', v. 2b
Justification	'this means of testing your faith works patient endurance', v. 3
Second imperative	'let patient endurance have in you its perfected work', v. 4a
Result	'so that you may be perfect and complete, lacking in nothing', v. 4b[23]

The pericope and the following two verses offer the first of two instances of the rhetorical device known as 'gradatio' or 'climax'. The

---

[20] J.A. Alexander, 'The Christian's Duty in Times of Trial', in *The Gospel of Jesus Christ*, London, 1862, 555-67.

[21] Tamez, *Message*, 7.

[22] An occasional commentator does, however, condemn masochism; cf. Gench, 91; McCartney, 84.

[23] Some regard vv. 2-8 as the first unit; so e.g. Gaugusch, 1; Floor, 50; Kotzé, 69-79; Johnson, 176; Fabris, 43; McCartney, 83-84. Others see vv. 1-12 as the first unit; cf. Simon, 34-38; Kot, 48-60.

THE OUTCOME OF TRIAL (1.2-4)   139

second occurs in 1.14-15. 'Gradatio' also appears in Paul,[24] 2 Pet 1.5-7,[25] and elsewhere in ancient Christian sources.[26] Jewish[27] and Graeco-Roman writings[28] likewise employ it. Indeed, it belongs to worldwide literature and folklore.[29] In Jas 2.2-4, the device is part of lengthy series of catchwords:[30]

1   χαίρειν
2   χαράν
3   κατεργάζεται ὑπομονήν
4a ὑπομονὴ ἔργον τέλειον
4b   τέλειοι λειπόμενοι
5   λείπεται αἰτείτω
6a   αἰτείτω διακρινόμενος
6b   διακρινόμενος

[24] Rom 5.3-5 (see below); 10.14 (calling upon the name of the Lord requires belief, belief requires hearing, hearing requires a preacher, and a preacher must be sent).

[25] Faith needs virtue, virtue needs knowledge, knowledge needs self-control, self-control needs steadfastness, steadfastness needs godliness, godliness needs brotherly affection, brotherly affection needs love.

[26] E.g. Gos. Thom. 2 ('Jesus said: Let him who seeks not cease seeking until he finds, and when he finds, he will be troubled, and when he has been troubled, he will marvel and he will rule over all'; cf. Clement of Alexandria, *Strom.* 5.14.96 GCS 15 ed. Stählin, 389; POxy. 654); Herm. *Mand.* 5.2.4 ('Ill temper is first foolish, frivolous, and silly; then from silliness comes bitterness, from bitterness wrath, from wrath rage, and from rage fury; then fury, being compounded of such great evils, becomes great and inexpiable sin').

[27] Wis 6.17-20 explains how the desire for wisdom leads to the kingdom, to wit: the beginning of wisdom is the desire for instruction, such desire is love of wisdom, such love means keeping the Torah, keeping the Torah is assurance of immortality, and immortality brings one near to God. Additional examples: LXX Hos 2.23; m. 'Abot 1.1; 4:12; m. Yoma 7:1; m. Soṭah 9.15 (cf. Cant Rab. 1.1.9); y. Sanh. 28b (10.2); and the Dayenu hymn of the Passover liturgy.

[28] Dibelius, 96-98, cites these: Homer, *Il.* 2.102ff.; Demosthenes, *Or.* 18.179; Epicharmus frag. 148; Aelius Aristides, *Or.* 28.116; 50.52; Cicero, *Mil.* 61; idem, *Pro Roscio Amerino* 75; Corp. Herm. Kore Kosmou frag. 23.5 ed. Nock and Festugière, 4.2; Porphyry, *Ad. Marc.* 24.

[29] Dibelius, 94-99, gives a good many samples. To those one may add Bhagavad-Gita 2.62-62 ('From attachment springs desire, and from desire comes anger, and from anger arises bewilderment, and from bewilderment loss of memory, and from loss of memory the destruction of intelligence'); Theodore the Studie, *Parva cat.* 105 (conflict does not come 'from teaching and admonition; but where there is teaching and admonition, there is peace and soundness; and where there is peace and soundness, there the Holy Spirit rests'); and the old English fairy tale, 'A Woman and her Pig', which ends with this: 'As soon as the cat had lapped up the milk, the cat began to kill the rat; the rat began to gnaw the rope; the rope began to hang the butcher; the butcher began to kill the ox; the ox began to drink the water; the water began to quench the fire; the fire began to burn the stick; the stick began to beat the dog; the dog began to bite the pig; the little pig in a fright jumped over the stile; and so the old woman got home that night'.

[30] For catchword links in James see the Introduction, 82-83.

The progression in vv. 2-4—trials → patient endurance → perfection—has a close parallel in Rom 5.3-5, which opens with Paul boasting about suffering that leads to steadfastness that leads to character that leads to hope.[31] The parallel is all the closer in view of the shared vocabulary:

Romans   εἰδότες ὅτι
          ὑπομονὴν κατεργάζεται. ἡ δὲ ὑπομονὴ δοκιμήν... δοκιμή
James   γινώσκοντες ὅτι
          δοκίμιον... κατεργάζεται ὑπομονήν. ἡ δὲ ὑπομονή

If James does not know Romans or *vice versa*, use of a common source or tradition must be postulated.[32] If, however, one suspects, as does the present commentator, that James is familiar with Romans, and especially if one sees polemic against Paul in 2.14-26, it is possible to see intentional deviation here. Paul's sequence ends in hope. Does James go one better by demanding perfection?

James is even closer to 1 Pet 1.6-7: 'In this you rejoice (ἀγαλλιᾶσθε), though now for a little while you may have to suffer various trials (ἐν ποικίλοις πειρασμοῖς), so that the genuineness of your faith (τὸ δοκίμιον ὑμῶν τῆς πίστεως), more precious than gold, which though perishable is tested (δοκιμαζομένου) by fire, may redound to praise and glory and honor at the revelation of Jesus Christ'.[33] This follows 1 Pet 1.1, which resembles Jas 1.1, and it precedes verses that, just like Jas 1.2-4, feature both χαρά and the τελ- root: 'you believe in him and rejoice with an indescribable and glorious joy (χαρᾷ), for you are receiving the outcome (τέλος) of your faith, the salvation of your souls' (1.8-9).[34] This writer believes

---

[31] Didymus of Alexandria, *Job* 94 ed. Henrichs, 264, conflates Paul and James, and the two texts are often quoted together outside of the commentary tradition; note e.g. Martyrius, *Perf.* 4.2.39 CSCO 200 Scriptores Syri 86 ed. Halleux, 98; Carlstadt, 'Whether We should go slowly and avoid offending the Weak in Matters pertaining to God's Will', in *The Essential Carlstadt*, ed. E.J. Furcha, Waterloo, ON, 1995, 256; *et al.*

[32] A.E. Barnett, *Paul becomes a Literary Influence*, Chicago, 1941, 187, contends that James here depends upon Romans. So too Barnes, 22; Brückner, *Reihenfolge*, 289; Nienhuis, *Paul*, 174-80. The latter believes that James draws upon both Romans and 1 Peter, and further that, 'while James 1:2-4 is terminologically and structurally closer to 1 Peter 1:6-9, it is thematically closer to Romans 5:3-4. Though in context both Romans and 1 Peter are celebrating *hope*, James and Paul ultimately agree in their praise of the virtuous, enduring *character* that results from suffering'. Smith, 47, suggests Paul rewrote James. Bouman, 48, supposes Paul and Peter imitate James. Lüdemann, *Opposition*, 140-41, argues for literary independence; so too Frankemölle, 187; Burchard, 52-53; Maier, 58; Fabris, 58; Wenger, *Kyrios*, 125.

[33] Christians have regularly linked these two texts; note e.g. Didymus of Alexandria, *Zech* 5.12 SC 85 ed. Doutreleau, 972; Wolzogen, 181; and the commentary tradition on 1 Peter.

[34] James agrees with Paul against 1 Peter in three particulars: εἰδότες ὅτι // γινώσκοντες ὅτι; ὑπομονήν // ὑπομονήν; κατεργάζεται // κατεργάζεται. James agrees with 1 Peter against Paul in three particulars: χαράν // ἀγαλλιᾶσθε; πειρασμοῖς ποικίλοις // ποικίλοις πειρασμοῖς; τὸ δοκίμιον ὑμῶν τῆς πίστεως // τὸ δοκίμιον ὑμῶν τῆς πίστεως.

that James was familiar with 1 Peter (which in its turn may borrow from Romans).[35] Those who reject this hypothesis and also doubt that 1 Peter depends upon James will infer that the two works independently take up a tradition that may also have influenced Romans. They could adopt the view of W. Nauck, that the material common to Romans, James, and 1 Peter grew out of a Jewish tradition that originated during the Maccabean revolt.[36] Or they could accept the theory of Carrington, that our texts reflect a primitive Christian catechism,[37] or of Selwyn, that the three writers adopt an 'oral or written' Christian 'admonition compiled in view of persecution'.[38] Whatever the source-critical solution, James, by composing a closing imperative and referring to maturity (v. 4), has redacted his source(s) to stress his ideal of moral integrity.[39] Note also that, unlike Paul and 1 Peter, he does not link the material to christological themes.[40] Exegetes, by contrast, repeatedly refer to the cross, the afflictions of Jesus, suffering for Christ, faith in Christ, and so on.[41] This disparity between text and interpretation is striking.

1.2-4, although fictively envisaging the difficult circumstances of Jewish exiles (1.1), does not elaborate. Although commentators are full of suggestions,[42] some deny that a precise situation of oppression is in

[35] See the Introduction, 67-70. Brückner, 'Kritik', 533-34, contends that 1 Pet 1.6-7 is organically linked to the rest of 1 Peter whereas Jas 1.2-4 is not so linked to the rest of James. Contrast Wesley, 'Patience' (as in n. 18), 220: Peter had 'an eye to this very passage of St. James'.

[36] Nauck, 'Freude'. For discussion see L. Ruppert, *Der leidende Gerechte*, Würzburg, 176-79, and the response to Ruppert in Hoppe, *Hintergrund*, 19 n. 3. Dibelius, 74-77, similarly argues for literary independence and the influence of Jewish *paraenesis*. D. Daube, *The New Testament and Rabbinic Judaism*, London, 1956, 113-19, raises the possibility of a pre-Christian catechetical tradition.

[37] P. Carrington, *The Primitive Christian Catechism*, Cambridge, UK, 1940. For a related theory see Boismard, 'Liturgie'.

[38] Selwyn, *First Peter*, 439-59. Criticism in Blackman, 46-47. Johnson, 182, speaks of an 'early Christian *topos* on suffering'.

[39] See further Klein, *Werk*, 50-54.

[40] Rom 5.3-5 follows an affirmation about peace with God through Jesus Christ and introduces a statement about Christ's death. 1 Pet 1.6-7 refers to the appearance of Jesus Christ, 1.8 to the readers' love of him.

[41] Cf. Hus, 180-81; Stevartius, 12; Gaigny, 155; Wells, 5; Wesley, 'Patience', 219; Stier, 229; T. Scott, 565; Smith, 47; Blackman, 45; Grünzweig, 26-27; McKnight, 73-74; *et al.*

[42] Erasmus, *Paraphrase*, 136: the pains of exile; cf. 1.1. Grotius, 1073, refers to the edict of Claudius, which expelled Jews from Rome in CE 49. Piscator, 717: persecution on account of the gospel; cf. Aretius, 473; Benson, 29; T. Scott, 565; Farley, 19; *et al.* Calmet, 666: social ostracization. Barnes, 21: 'sickness, poverty, bereavement, persecution'; cf. Moo, 54. Deems, 34: 'a doubly-hard life; hard because they were Jews, and hard because they were Christians'; cf. Bassett, 4. Fausset, 582: illness; cf. 5.15. Weidner, 25: 'afflictions of all kinds'. Mitton, 19: 'inevitable disappointments, griefs, sorrows and annoyances which no human life can avoid'. Reicke, 13: 'persecution, sickness, and poverty'. Frankemölle, 188: difficulties stemming from being a 'social minority' in a non-Christian environment. Konradt, *Existenz*, 109-23: the temptation to

mind.⁴³ Such is the view of this commentary. The text refers to 'various' (ποικίλοις) trials, and it links itself formally to both 1.12 and 5.7-11, where again we meet with broad generalizations, not a well-defined situation. So attempts to be more precise, even when based on other parts of James, likely read too much into the text. It accords with this judgment that the blessedness or joy of those suffering appears in the Jesus tradition⁴⁴ and elsewhere in early Christianity,⁴⁵ so we have here familiar and thus general advice which does not in itself evoke a specific *Sitz im Leben*.⁴⁶ This is all the more so as good parallels appear also in Jewish and Graeco-Roman texts. Indeed, we have here a far-flung *topos*.⁴⁷

assimilate to a worldly system of norms; cf. 4.4 and Burchard, 55. Davids, 'Message', 69-71: economic persecution (cf. 5.1-6) and slander (cf. 4.1-2, 11-12). Hartin, 57: every 'situation of adversity that could befall the believer', and not just the individual but also the community. Felder, 1788: 'stresses incidental to daily living under difficult socio-economic circumstances'. Fabris, 55: not persecution but social and religious conflict. Gundry, 919: 'displacement from homeland, social ostracism, economic boycott, and the loss of loved ones and friends through martyrdom'. McKnight, 75-76: religious persecution including economic oppression. Ringe, 376-77: 'the greed and competition for wealth, status and honour that undergird the structures and values of the Roman imperial project'. Wenger, *Kyrios*, 129-30: social hostility in the diaspora.

⁴³ Cf. Ropes, 1134; Blackman, 44-45; Laws, 52. If James depends upon 1 Peter here, it is worth noting that the latter clearly speaks of persecution and the former does not.

⁴⁴ Mt 5.10-12 = Lk 6.22-23; Gos. Thom. 68. Against Plummer, 571; Smith, 45; Bardenhewer, 25; Adamson, 53; and Maier, 59, the beatitude is unlikely to lie behind Jas 1.2. See Deppe, *Sayings*, 61-65; Tsuji, *Glaube*, 123-24.

⁴⁵ Acts 5.41; Rom 5.3-5; 2 Cor 7.4; Phil 4.10-13; 1 Thess 1.6; Heb 10.34; 1 Pet 1.6; 3.14; 4.12-14; Pol. *Phil*. 2.3.

⁴⁶ Konradt, *Existenz*, 109-23, urges that James, unlike 1 Peter, does not really contain a 'Leidenstheologie' but rather puts ethical interests front and center.

⁴⁷ Cf. Jdt 8.25 ('In spite of everything let us give thanks to the Lord our God, who is putting us to the test as he did our forefathers'); 2 Macc 6.30 ('I am enduring terrible sufferings in my body under this beating, but in my soul I am glad to suffer these things because I fear him [God]'); Pr Azar 1-3, 28-68 (praise from Azariah and his companions in the fiery furnace); 1 En. 108.10 ('While they were being trampled by evil men and heard from them reviling and reproach and were abused, they still blessed me'); 1QS 10.17 ('When affliction starts I will laud him [God]'); 4Q525 2 ('Blessed are those who rejoice' in Wisdom; 'blessed is the man who...is constrained by her discipline and always takes pleasure in her punishments'); 2 Bar. 52.6 ('Rejoice in the suffering that you suffer now'); Josephus, *Bell*. 1.653 ('"And why [are you] so exultant when you will shortly be put to death?" "Because after our death we will enjoy greater felicity"'); b. Šabb. 88b ('Rejoice in suffering'); b. Ta'an. 8a ('The one who joyfully bears the chastisement that befalls him brings salvation to the world'); Exod. Rab. 31.3 ('Happy is the man who can withstand the test, for there is none whom God does not prove'); Seneca, *M.L.* 71.7 ('Socrates said: "Follow these rules if you wish to be happy, and let some think you even a fool. Allow anyone who desires to insult you and work you wrong. But if only virtue dwells with you, you will suffer nothing. If you wish to be happy, if you would wish in good faith to be a good person, let one person or another despise you"'); *Prov*. 4.4 ('Great men rejoice oft-times in adversity'); Epictetus, *Diatr*. 2.19.24 ('Show me one who though sick is happy, though in danger is happy, though dying is happy, though condemned to exile is happy, though in disrepute is happy. Show

Our paragraph, with its close parallel in 1.12,[48] fails to answer how one is to endure trial, but this appears in the following unit, beginning with v. 5: 'If any of you lacks in wisdom...' Wisdom does not, in James, deliver from trial—contrast Ps 1.3, which has the wise prospering in all that they do—but is rather that which allows enduring and/or understanding and/or profiting from such. The idea is at home in the wisdom literature.[49] Throughout 4 Maccabees wisdom enables faithful martyrs to endure torment, even with joy (6.30), and according to Wis 10.5, σοφία preserved Abraham before God. In these texts, as in James, wisdom is less the upshot of trials[50] than what enables enduring them to a good end.

Verse 2. The imperative to rejoice in the midst of trials, which can be construed as consolation,[51] is paradoxical. For not only do people often view trials as punishment or calamity, but everyone avoids trials precisely because they bring misery, not joy. So James calls for a counter-intuitive or unnatural interpretation of events, which then become educational.[52]

πᾶσαν χαρὰν ἡγήσασθε. Cf. Euripides, *Med.* 454 (πᾶν κέρδος ἡγοῦ); 4 Bar. 6.17 (Baruch writes to Jeremiah 'in the captivity of Babylon': χαῖρε καὶ ἀγαλλιῶ). Wordplays on χαίρειν in letter openings appear to have been conventional; cf. Chionis, *Ep.* 3.1 (χαίρειν. πολλὴν χάριν οἶδα); PPetr 1.29 (χαίρειν. χάρις τοῖς θεοῖς πολλή); BGU 531 (χαίρειν... ἐχάρην); PGiss 1.21 (χαίρειν. λίαν ἐχάρην); PNeph. 9.3-5 (χαίρειν. χάριν ὁμολογεῶ τῇ θείᾳ προνοίᾳ); IKPrusaOlymp 54 (" Απφηι Πανταύχου, χαῖρε· μῆτερ Τιμοῖ, τὸ χαίρειν λέγετε τειμωρούμενοι. χαρὰ γὰρ ὑμεῖν ἔμενεν εἰ ἔζων ἐγώ).[53] Also similar is the wordplay in IG 9.2.988 (= CIJ

---

him! By the gods, I would fain see a Stoic!'). See further Schnider, 28-30; H. Millauer, *Leiden als Gnade*, Bern, 1976, 135-88. (One is unsure of the consistent utility of Millauer's distinction between joy *nach*, *trotz*, and *über* suffering: these sometimes cannot be distinguished.) Unpersuasive is the attempt of B. Estrada, 'The Last Beatitude: Joy in Suffering', *Bib* 91 (2010), 187-209, to argue that Christian texts offer something new vis-à-vis Jewish tradition in this connection. Only the christological element seems novel.

[48] 1.2-4 and 12 are often linked even outside the commentaries on James; cf. Didymus of Alexandria, *Zech.* 2.72-73 SC 84 ed. Doutreleau, 462; Antiochus the Monk, *Hom.* 78 PG 89.1668C; *et al.*

[49] For this and what follows see Gowan, 'Wisdom and Endurance'.

[50] A common idea: Ps 119.67; Job 36.5-12; etc.

[51] Verseput, 'Genre', 99, speaks of 'consolation' in tribulation. Cf. Nicholas of Gorran, 66; Osiander, 719. The *Chaîne Arménienne* 1 ed. Renoux, 69, calls James a 'letter of consolation'. So too Stanley, 'The Epistle of St. James', in *Sermons*, 294.

[52] Popkes, 'Composition', 96, dubs 1.2 'the very core statement of James'.

[53] This is a grave inscription from the second or third century CE. Note also 2 Tim 1.2-3 (χάρις...χάριν); Euripides, *Hec.* 426-27 (Polyxena: χαῖρ', ὦ τεκοῦσα, χαῖρε Κασσάνδρα τέ μοι. Hecuba: χαίρουσιν ἄλλοι). Theodore the Studite, *Ep.* 392 ed. Fatouros, 543 (χαίρειν. πᾶσαν χαρὰ ἡγητέον) draws upon James. Johnson, 176, compares Ps.-Plato, *Ep.* 8 352A-B: Πλάτων τοῖς Δίωνος οἰκείοις τε καὶ ἑταίροις εὖ πράττειν. ἃ δ' ἂν διανοηθέντες μάλιστα εὖ πράττοιτε ὄντως...

1.701 = IJO 1.Ach1c), a Jewish epitaph (first–fourth centuries CE) from Larissa in Thessaly: Μαρία 'Ιούδα Λεοντίσκου δὲ γυνὴ τῷ λαῷ χαίρειν. [χαί]ροις ἀνθρώπων πεπ[νυμέν]ε ὅστις ὑπάρχει.

James, like Wisdom, Pseudo-Phocylides, and the Sentences of Syriac Menander, commences with an imperative. Only here in biblical Greek is χαρά[54] the object of ἡγέομαι (Jas: 1×). There are also no secular parallels, and the expression is odd: it is as though James is commanding one to think an emotion.[55] The verb means 'regards as, consider', as often in the LXX and the NT.[56] Cargal, 61-63, suggests it is indicative: 'You considered it supreme joy…' This makes it possible to find a harsh tone in 1.4: 'Do you think that your steadfastness is a sign that you have come to maturity and completeness and lack nothing?' Few understand the text this way, and imperatives run throughout James. Further, such blunt confrontation at the beginning of a general letter is unexpected (although Galatians admittedly supplies an example).

πᾶσαν χαράν, which adds to the assonance in our verse (α αν α αν), probably means 'utmost' or 'supreme joy', πᾶσαν having the sense of 'complete' or 'utter'.[57] Some, however, take the sense to be 'pure joy', as in Luther's translation,[58] or 'every kind of joy'.[59] Do we have here a Semitism? Although secular Greek nowhere qualifies χαρά with πᾶς, כל־שמחה, as in Isa 24.11 and Eccl 2.10, supplies an exact equivalent. Maybe that Hebrew expression also lies behind Tob 13.16 S (πᾶσαν τὴν χαράν); Rom 15.13 (πάσης χαρᾶς); Phil 2.29 (πάσης χαρᾶς).

It may have mattered to an early Christian audience that the purported author of James was remembered as having exhibited an exceptional and painful piety, even enduring a martyr's death.[60] They could have thought of his life as matching his words.[61]

ἀδελφοί μου. The phrase, which appears throughout James,[62] most often in transitions of subject matter, puts the author beside the readers.

---

[54] Jas: 2×; cf. 4.9. The latter is the antithesis of the imperative in 1.2.

[55] BAGD, s.v., ἡγέομαι 2, cites for comparison POxy. 528.8: πένθος ἡγούμην.

[56] E.g. LXX Job 13.24 (for חשב); 41.23; 42.6; Wis 15.9; 2 Macc 4.15; 9.21; Acts 26.2; Phil 3.7-8; Heb 10.29; 2 Pet 1.13; 2.13. Cf. Let. Aris. 124, 292; Jos. Asen. 3.3; Diogenes, *Ep.* 2.10.

[57] See the full discussions in Theile, 6-9; Ropes, 130-32; Adamson, 88-89. Cf. Phil 1.20; 2.29; 1 Tim 2.2; Jude 3. According to Hort, 3, it is not 'quantitative' but expresses 'the full abandonment of mind to this one thought'.

[58] 'Eitel Freude' = 'nothing but joy'; so also Moffatt, 7; BDF 275.3; the NIV.

[59] So Theile, 6; Alford, 275; cf. Clement of Alexandria, *Strom.* 2.21.130.9 GCS 52 ed. Stählin and Früchtel, 185: 'every joy (πᾶσαν χαράν) of the soul arises from previous sensations of the flesh'.

[60] See esp. Josephus, *Ant.* 20.197-203; Hegesippus in Eusebius, *H.E.* 2.23.4-18. For a full collection of the relevant traditions see Pratscher, *Herrenbruder*.

[61] Gundry, 919, mentions James' martyrdom when commenting on 1.2-4.

[62] 1.2, 16, 19; 2.1, 5, 14; 3.1, 10, 12; 5.12, 19; with ἀγαπητοί in 1.16, 19; 2.5. For unqualified ἀδελφοί see 4.11; 5.7, 9, 10. 'Brothers' is also characteristic of Paul's epistles.

This makes for a contrast with the common, potentially condescending address, '(my) son', typical of much wisdom literature.[63] The latter might be awkward here given the demand for maturity: the author does not want the readers to see themselves as children.[64]

Those who think of the audience as exclusively Christian or Jewish Christian naturally compare NT passages that use familial language for community relations.[65] But ἀδελφός and אח were common terms for Jewish co-religionists,[66] and this is the sense demanded if the twelve tribes of 1.1 are Jews of the diaspora.[67] This meaning of 'brother(s)' is attested in early Christian literature,[68] and '(my) brothers' also appears in Jewish letters written to diaspora Jews; indeed, in 2 Bar. 78–87, which is addressed to the nine and a half tribes, it is a refrain.[69] Note also the use of 'brothers' for those in the diaspora in Isa 66.20; Mic 5.3; and Tob 14.4.[70] On this second reading, our Christian writer repeatedly addresses non-Christian Jews as 'brothers'.

One cannot confidently argue, on the basis of 2.15 ('brother or sister') and the appeal to Rahab (2.25), that 'my brothers' must be gender inclusive. We cannot exclude the possibility that our author, unacquainted with modern notions of equality, had in mind a predominantly or pre-

---

[63] With either υἱός or τέκτον: Prov 1.8; 2.1; 3.1; Eccl 12.12; Ecclus 2.1; 4.1; etc., and frequently in the Testaments of the Twelve Patriarchs.

[64] Observed by the *Catenae ad loc.* ed. Cramer, 2; cf. Didymus of Alexandria, *Ep. can. ad loc.* ed. Zoepfl, 2; Knowling, 5 ('brothers' may be 'an exhortation to manliness and courage; St. James calls them not children, but brethren'). Contrast Paul in 1 Cor 4.14-17; Gal 4.19; 1 Thess 2.11. The failure of James to characterize himself as a father coheres with Mt 23.9: 'call no one your father on earth'.

[65] Mt 18.15; 23.8; Mk 3.35; Jn 21.23; Rom 1.13; 7.4; 1 Cor 6.5-6; Gal 1.2; Col 1.2; Heb 10.19; 13.22; 2 Pet 1.10; 1 Jn 2.9-11; Rev 1.9; 6.11; 12.10; 2 Clem. 1.1; etc. See K. Schäfer, *Gemeinde als 'Bruderschaft'*, Frankfurt am Main, 1989.

[66] Exod 2.11; 4.18; Lev 19.17; 25.25, 46; Num 20.3; Deut 3.18; 15.3; 17.15; 18.15; 24.7, 14; Judg 14.3; 20.13; Neh 5.1, 8; Isa 66.20; Jdt 7.30; 1 Macc 12.10, 17; 2 Macc 1.1; 4 Macc 13.23, 26; 14.1; Ecclus 10.20; 25.1; 1QS 6.10, 22; 1QSa 1.18; CD 6.20; 7.1; 20.18; 1QM 13.1; 11Q5 19.17; 11Q19 56.14-15; Acts 13.26; Josephus, *Bell.* 2.122; Sifre Deut 112; m. Ta'an. 2.1; y. Sanh. 30a (11.2); etc.

[67] Ropes, 132, observing how often '(my) brothers' appears in speeches (e.g. Acts 1.16; 2.29; 3.17; 7.2; 13.15; 15.7; 22.1; 23.1; 28.17), suggests that 'it belonged to the homiletical style of the synagogue and was brought thence into Christian hortatory language'. Cf. Chaine, 5.

[68] Mt 5.22-24; Acts 2.29; 3.17; 7.2, 23; 13.26, 38; 22.1; 23.1, 5, 6; Rom 9.3; Heb 7.5; Ps.-Clem. Rec. 1.67.3, 7 GCS 51 ed. Rehm, 46; Didascalia 5.14.23 ed. Funk, 280.

[69] 2 Bar. 78.2, 3; 79.1; 80.1; 82.1; cf. the letters in t. Sanh. 2.6 ('to our brothers'); y. Sanh. 18d (1.2) ('to our brothers'); and b. Sanh. 11a-b ('to our brothers'); also Cowley 2.1, 11 ('to my brothers').

[70] Despite the oft-expressed doubt to the contrary, 'brothers' was at least occasionally used in Greek guilds and associations; see P.A. Harland, 'Familial Dimensions of Group Identity', *JBL* 124 (2005), 491-513; idem, *Dynamics of Identity in the World of the Early Christians*, New York, 2009, 63-81.

eminently male audience. The use of ἀνήρ in 1.8, 12, 23; 2.2; 3.2 seemingly suggests this.[71]

ὅταν πειρασμοῖς περιπέσητε ποικίλοις. Note the strong alliteration and assonance: πειρ-περι // π-π-π-π // οις-οις. James employs ὅταν (Jas: 1×), not ἐάν. The assumption seems to be that suffering is inevitable.[72] πειρασμός[73] recurs in v. 12. It is exceedingly rare in secular Greek[74] and should be considered a Greek biblicism. Here the term refers, as in the Lord's Prayer, to a test of religious faithfulness,[75] presumably occasioned by circumstances that have fallen upon the recipients through no fault of their own. It remains unspecified and so allows readers to think of their own difficulties.

James employs περιπίπτω[76] and ποικίλος[77] only here. The two words do not appear together before 1 Pet 1.6. By contrast, περιπίπτω +

---

[71] According to Burchard, 'Hiob', 13, James has men first of all in view, without excluding women. According to Wolmarans, 'Male and Female', James promotes a patriarchal agenda. Johnson, *Brother*, 221-34, takes the other side, making these observations: (i) 'although James's language and focus are androcentric, his value system is one in which traits stereotypically associated with male patterns of aggressiveness and domination are evil, while traits associated with stereotypical female patterns of passivity, patience, and self-donation are good, even when expressed by males' (226); (ii) 'his language about God giving birth [1.18] and his association of *sophia* with God suggest that his sense of gender is both fair and flexible' (230); (iii) apart from 2.11, James pays no attention to sexual behavior; he does not speak of women as a problem for males; and 'the topics that have to do with the establishing of civic and domestic social order are absent...and since in antiquity this social order invariably subordinated women, such studied silence is not insignificant'. But see further below, on 1.12, and recall that James labels Rahab a 'prostitute' (2.25) and that women are objects of charity in 1.27 and 2.15-16.

[72] Cf. Jn 16.33; Acts 14.22. Commentators regularly recall the latter in connection with Jas 1.2-4; cf. Hilary of Arles *ad loc*. PLSupp 3.63; Gomar, 386; Gill, 779; *et al*. James might well have approved of the saying preserved in Apophthegmata Patrum Evagrius 5 PG 65.176A: 'Take away temptations, and no one will be saved'.

[73] NT: 21×. LXX: 19×, mostly for מסה and ענה. Gk. Pseudepigrapha (Denis): 2×. Philo: 0×. Josephus: 0×. For discussion see especially J.H. Korn, *ΠΕΙΡΑΣΜΟΣ*, Stuttgart, 1937.

[74] Note Ps.-Ptolemy the Grammarian, *Diff. vocab*. 146 (νόσων καὶ πειρασμῶν); Pedanius Dioscorides, *Mat. med. praef*. 5.12 (τοὺς ἐπὶ τῶν παθῶν πειρασμούς); Aelius Heroedianus, *Part*. ed. Boissonade, 110; Cyranides 1.21 (πειρασμῶν ἔν τε γῇ καὶ θαλάσσῃ).

[75] Cf. Gk. Jub. 10.8; T. Jos. 2.7; 1 Cor 10.13; 1 Pet 1.6; 2 Clem. 18.2; Herm. *Mand*. 9.7; Pol. *Phil*. 7.2; Acts Jn 21 ed. Bonnet, 162; etc. For discussion of the sense see J.B. Gibson, *The Temptations of Jesus in Early Christianity*, Sheffield, 1995, 245 n. 33. The older English translations had 'temptations', which seems awkward here (as opposed to vv. 13-14) if one takes 'temptation' to imply being lured to wrong-doing ('temptation to sin').

[76] NT: 3×; cf. Lk 10.30; Acts 27.41. It is often used of falling into unpleasant circumstances; cf. LXX Prov 11.5; Dan 2.9; 2 Macc 6.13; 9.7, 21; 10.4; 4 Macc 1.24; T. Dan 4.5; T. Jos. 10.3; Gk. LAE 5.2; Josephus, *Ant*. 10.25; T. Abr. RecLng. 19.12; so

πειρασμός seems to have no precise precedent at all, although 2 Macc 10.4 (περιπεσεῖν τοιούτοις κακοῖς) and 1 Tim. 6.9 (ἐμπίπτουσιν εἰς πειρασμόν) are similar.

Typically in early Christianity, God 'tries' or 'tests' (πειράζω or δοκιμάζω), with hope of a good outcome.[78] The devil, on the other hand, 'tempts' (πειράζω), with nothing save an evil end in view.[79] One might urge that the two things cannot always be clearly distinguished, as in Job, where Satan works with God's approval, or in the Testament of Job, where the hero attributes directly to God things done by Satan,[80] or in Mt 4 and Lk 4, where the Spirit leads Jesus into the wilderness so the devil can tempt him, or in rabbinic literature, where God implants the יצר הרע, the evil impulse. Yet all this does not obliterate the distinction, probably implicit in James, between a demonic trial and a divine test, for even when both God and Satan are involved, the intention of the one party cannot be that of the other.[81]

Given the many biblical texts in which God 'tries' the saints,[82] it is unclear whether, for James, God does nothing more than 'allow' the situation of 1.2.[83] As the history of interpretation shows, some readers find in 1.2 the concept of a divine 'trial'.[84] On their view, 1.2-4 is not about temptation by sin or the devil, which is a different topic, treated in 1.12-16.[85] Yet one must acknowledge that 1.2 fails to address the

---

too in secular Greek. Johnstone, 30, taking περιπίπτω to imply a situation not sought, rejects 'asceticism, or a perverse ambition for martyrdom in any form'. Cf. Scaer, 40.

[77] NT: 10×. LXX: 26×, for several Hebrew words. Gk. Pseudepigrapha (Denis): 11×. Philo: 62×. Josephus: 46×. The chief sense is variety: the notion of quantity ('many') is present only insofar as diversity entails it. Cf. 3 Macc 2.6: 'You tested the proud Pharaoh...with various and numerous punishments' (ποικίλαις καὶ πολλαῖς δοκιμάσας τιμωρίαις). Wesley, 'Patience' (as in n. 18), 219, colorfully comments: 'temptations innumerable as the stars of heaven; and those varied and complicated a thousand ways'. Kloppenborg, 'Psychagogy', 55-56, suggests that James may here recall the beguiling and seducing Aphrodite, whose famous girdle was of 'various' colors.

[78] Note 1 Thess 2.4; 1 Tim 3.10; Heb 11.17; cf. Wis 3.5; 11.9-10.

[79] E.g. Mt 4.1; Mk 1.13; Lk 4.2; 1 Cor 7.5; Rev 2.10.

[80] 37.3-4: 'And again he (Baldad) said to me (Job), "Who destroyed your goods or inflicted you with these plagues?" And I said, "God".'

[81] See further below, 214-15 on 1.12-15.

[82] Gen 22.1; Exod 15.25; 16.4; Deut 8.2; 13.3; 2 Chr 32.21; Pss 26.2; 95.8; 139.23; Jer 9.7; 17.10; Zech 13.9; Jdt 8.25-27; Wis 3.5-6; etc. One might think it relevant that the notion of the dispersion being a punishment for sin was a *topos*; see 128 n. 108.

[83] According to Mussner, 65, trials are 'permitted by God'. Cf. Guyse, 563; Wells, 5; Wordsworth, 13.

[84] So Methodius of Olympus, *Cibis* 2.3 GCS 27 Bonwetsch, 428 (who erroneously attributes words from Jas 1 to Paul), and many commentators; see above, 135-36; also Ropes, 13; Laws, 51. Poole, 880, thinks of trials occasioned by divine providence. Burkitt, 1105, speaks of 'correcting trials for sin', of 'castigatory, probatory trials', and of 'afflictions sanctioned by God'. According to Kistemaker, 33, nothing happens by chance, and 'God stands behind every trial and test'.

[85] Note also that sickness is associated with sin in 5.13-20.

proximate or ultimate cause of 'various tribulations': the situation is just a given, without explanation. Furthermore, 1.13-15 does not encourage the thought that God is the subject behind the temptations of 1.2.[86]

In Rev 3.10 and probably the Lord's Prayer (Mt 6.13 = Lk 11.4), πειρασμός is an eschatological term signifying the great tribulation that precedes the return of Jesus.[87] Given, then, the interpretation of present experience in terms of eschatological tribulation in the Jesus tradition and 1 Peter, two of James' sources as well as in other early Christian texts,[88] plus the nearness of the *parousia* in Jas 5.8, our author and his first Christian readers might have thought of the messianic woes.[89] When Schnider, 27, asserts, to the contrary, that Jas 1.2 has to do not with eschatological affliction but rather with the continual opposition met by the faithful, he makes a distinction foreign to those early Christians who construed their present existence in eschatological categories.[90]

περιπέσητε implies that one has not gone seeking for trouble, for the main sense of περιπίπτω is 'to come on something accidentally'.[91] The situation is akin to that of the poor who are oppressed unjustly in 2.1-7, 15; and 5.4-6. Gregory Palamas, in commenting on Jas 1, appropriately asserts that whereas virtue is in one's power, falling into trials is not.[92]

ποικίλοις, which seems strictly superfluous[93] but balances πᾶσαν and adds to the assonance (see above), appears with πειρασμοῖς in 1 Pet 1.6, in a context with other links to Jas 1; see above. Either one book draws upon the other or both depend upon a lost source or common tradition. Whether one should think of falling into diverse difficulties at once or over time or of both is unclear: a decision one way or the other asks too much of the text.

---

[86] See esp. Wenger, *Kyrios*, 122-34.

[87] R.E. Brown, *New Testament Essays*, Garden City, NY, 1968, 314-19.

[88] Allison, *End*; M. Dubis, *Messianic Woes in First Peter*, New York, 2002; S. McKnight, *Jesus and His Death*, Waco, TX, 2005; C.M. Pate and D.W. Kennard, *Deliverance Now and Not Yet*, New York, 2003 (335-49 on James); B. Pitre, *Jesus, the Tribulation, and the End of the Exile*, Tübingen, 2005.

[89] See Dan 7.21-22; 12.2; Jub. 23.1-31; T. Mos. 9.1-7; Mk 13.8; Liv. Proph. Jer. 12; b. Sanh. 98b; etc. Cf. Mussner, 207-208; Kugelman, 14; Pate and Kennard, *Deliverance* (as in n. 88), 335-49.

[90] Cf. Hoppe, *Hintergrund*, 11.

[91] Cf. LXX Ruth 2.3; 2 Macc 10.4 (περιπεσεῖν τοιούτοις κακοῖς); Lk 10.30 ('fell into the hands of robbers'); Acts 27.41; Ps.-Origen, *Comm. Ps ad* Ps 2.2 PG 12.1088C (πειρασμοῖς περιπίπτομεν); CIG 4 9668 ('I know in myself that I have never done anything evil, but falling into an evil fate [εἱμαρμένῃ δὲ περιπεσὼν κακῇ] and bitter malevolence, I suffered'). Josephus uses the word of falling into sickness: *C. Ap.* 1.305, 313; *Ant.* 10.25; 15.244. See further W. Michaelis, 'περιπίπτω', *TDNT* 6.173.

[92] Gregory Palamas, *Hom. xxi–xlii* 32.3 ed. Chrestou and Zeses, 310. Nothing in James commends the attitude of Clement of Alexandria, who admired the wise who could pray, 'O Lord, put me to the test' (*Strom.* 4.7 GCS 15 ed. Stählin, 273).

[93] As also in 2 Tim 3.6 and Heb 13.9. Adamson, 53, however, thinks it emphatic.

Verse 3. Trials are, in accord with Jewish, Christian, and Graeco-Roman teaching on educative discipline,[94] arduous means to a good end. Here the proximate end is patience, regarding which J.A. Alexander remarked: 'A temptation to which patience is the proper antidote, must be specifically a temptation to impatience'.[95]

γινώσκοντες ὅτι τὸ δοκίμιον ὑμῶν τῆς πίστεως κατεργάζεται ὑπομονήν.[96] τὸ δοκίμιον ὑμῶν τῆς πίστεως also occurs in 1 Pet 1.7 and otherwise only in patristic sources, beginning with Origen. Both the thought and the language are conventional.[97] γινώσκοντες ὅτι[98] presumably reflects the author's awareness that he is expressing a common sentiment; cf. 3.1: εἰδότες. One might wonder whether the participle here, as so often in rabbinic materials,[99] functions as in imperative: 'Know

---

[94] Note e.g. Deut 8.5; Job 5.17; Ps 94.12; Prov 3.11-12; Jer 5.3; 2 Macc 6.12-17; Jdt 8.27; Philo, *Det.* 146 ('if he punishes us, he will of his gracious goodness gently and kindly correct our faults'); Heb 12.6; Rev 3.19; Sifre Deut 32; Aeschylus, *Ag.* 176-78 (Zeus 'established as a fixed ordinance that learning is by suffering'); Herodotus 1.207 ('disaster has been my teacher'); Seneca, *Prov.* 1.5-6 (God 'does not make a spoiled pet of a good man; he tests him, hardens him, and fits him for his own service'); 2.5-6 (God says to good men: 'Let them be harassed by toil, by suffering, by losses, in order that they may gather true strength'); 4.5, 12; Epictetus, *Diatr.* 1.24.1-3 ('It is difficulties that show what men are'); Musonius Rufus, *Diss.* 6. For full discussion of suffering as education see Talbert, *Suffering*.

[95] Alexander, 'Duty' (as in n. 20), 557.

[96] ὑμῶν τῆς πίστεως (01 02 03* 04 025 044 5 33 69 81 *et al.* **Byz** MaxConf PsMaxConf PsOec) becomes τῆς πίστεως ὑμῶν in 629 Did **G**:G-D **Sl**:D (this clarifies that ὑμῶν goes with πίστεως), τῆς πίστεως in 206 429 522 614 630 *et al.* S:P., ὑμῶν in 03C2 Did **L**:F. It is conceivable that the whole phrase is an addition, borrowed from 1 Pet 1.7. Bowyer, *Conjectures*, 313, supposes an original nominative ὑπομονή: 'knowing that patience draweth after it the trial of your faith'. This is in fact the reading of 522.

[97] See the texts cited in n. 147; also Ecclus 2.1, 5 ('If you come forward to serve the Lord, prepare yourself for temptation [πειρασμόν]...and in times of humiliation be patient. For gold is tested [δοκιμάζεται] in fire, and acceptable people in the furnace of humiliation'; for Frankemölle, 189-97, Eccl 2 has much influenced James); 4 Macc 9.7-8 ('Put us to the test [πείραζε], tyrant, and if you take our lives for the sake of our religion, do not think you can harm us with your torments. By our suffering and steadfastness [ὑπομονῆς] we will obtain the prize of virtue and will be with God'); Jub. 19.8 ('This is the tenth trial with which Abraham was tried, and he was found faithful'); Pss. Sol. 16.14-15 ('When a person is tried by the hand of his mortality, your [God's] testing [δοκιμασία] is in his flesh, and in the difficulty of poverty. If the righteous endures [ὑπομεῖναι] all these things, he will receive mercy from the Lord'); T. Jos. 2.7 ('In ten testings [πειρασμοῖς] he [God] showed that I [Joseph] was approved [δόκιμον], and in all of them I persevered, because perseverance is a powerful medicine and steadfastness [ὑπομονή] provides many good things'); Did. 16.5 ('Then will the creation of human beings come to the fiery trial [δοκιμασίας] and many will fall away and be lost, but those who endure [ὑπομείναντες] in their faith [πίστει] will be saved').

[98] Cf. Gk. 1 En. 98.10; 4 Macc 18.2; Rom 6.6; Eph 5.5; 2 Pet 3.3; Josephus, *Ant.* 4.186. γινώσκω: Jas: 3×; cf. 2.20; 5.20 (γινωσκέτω ὅτι).

[99] See David Daube, 'Participle and Imperative in 1 Peter', in Selwyn, *First Peter*, 467-88.

then...'[100] Against this is the parallel in the closely related Rom 5.3: 'knowing (εἰδότες) that suffering produces steadfastness'.

That falling into trial is a means of putting to proof one's faith is a generality. In 5.10-11, however, ὑπομονή is exhibited when undergoing unmerited suffering (like Job), and the dominant history of interpretation reads our present verse accordingly. That is, 'when you are beset by various trials' likely refers to undeserved or seemingly unfair difficulties, perhaps above all those effected by religious commitment, not to problems created by personal passion (1.14-15) or temptations from the devil (4.7). Mayor, 34, speaks of 'outward trial'.[101]

δοκίμιον[102] is difficult. (i) One might print the more common word found in some witnesses: δόκιμον.[103] The latter means, according to the dictionaries, 'genuine', 'tried and true', 'esteemed'.[104] (ii) According to Deissmann, δόκιμος (used in Jas 1.12) and δοκίμιον are synonymous, and the latter carries the meaning of the former in our passage.[105] The upshot is the same as (i): Jas 1.3 concerns the genuineness of one's faith being proved.[106] In the closely related 1 Pet 1.7, δοκίμιον means 'genuine' or 'proved character' (although there, too, we find textual variants). And yet in this case, would we not expect δοκίμιον to be the culmination of James' series, not a step in the middle? (iii) δοκίμιον is often said to mean 'testing' or 'trial'.[107] The NRSV translates: 'the testing of your faith'. (iv) But James' sentence makes most sense if δοκίμιον is rendered 'means of

---

[100] So Luther's translation; Mussner, 64; McCartney, 85-86.

[101] Cf. the use of ὑπομονή for endurance in the midst of trial inflicted by others in 4 Macc 1.11; 9.7-8; Lk 21.19 (often cited in the commentaries; cf. also Antiochus the Monk, *Hom.* 78 PG 89.1668C); 2 Cor 1.6; 1 Thess 1.3-6; Rev 1.9; T. Jos. 2.7; etc. Peter Damian, *Ep.* 76.5 ed. Reindel, 379-80, uses Jas 1.2 to illustrate 'calamities caused by others'.

[102] NT: 2×; cf. 1 Pet 1.7. LXX: 4×: 1 Chr 29.4; Ps 11.6; Prov 27.21; Zech 11.13. Gk. Pseudepigrapha (Denis): 0×. Philo: *Somn.* 1.226. Josephus: 0×. Readers almost always attach ὑμῶν to what follows, namely, πίστεω. But it is possible to take it with δοκίμιον, as does Schlatter, 104-105. For him, the Greek means: τὸ δοκίμιον ὑμῶν τὸ τῆς πίστεως.

[103] It appears in 431 1241 Did instead of δοκίμιον; cf. the variants for LXX Zech 11.13; 1 Pet 1.7. This results in the phrase, 'knowing that the genuineness (or: approved character) of your faith works steadfastness'. This is not likely to be original, even though δόκιμος appears again in 1.12. The weak attestation inclines one to postulate either a scribal slip or alteration to bring the meaning into line with 1 Pet 1.7. One would, moreover, expect the more common word to replace the less common in the textual tradition. 2818 omits the word altogether.

[104] E.g. BAGD, s.v. Cf. LXX 1 Chr 29.4 (ἀργυρίου δοκίμου = 'tried/refined silver'); Ps 11.7 (ἀργύριον πεπυρωμένον δοκίμιον = 'silver refined by fire'); Zech 11.13.

[105] Deissmann, *Studies*, 259-62. Cf. Knowling, 7.

[106] Cf. Ps.-Oecumenius *ad loc.* PG 119:457B; Calvin, 262; Piscator, 728; Huther, 36; Baumgarten, 23; Bisping, 13; Beyschlag, 45; Hodges, 19.

[107] E.g. Ropes, 134; Bardenhewer, 26; Laws, 52.

testing',[108] which is a sense the word plainly has elsewhere, including once in the LXX.[109]

πίστις occurs in our book sixteen times.[110] According to Bultmann, for James the word is 'merely the theoretical conviction of the existence of the one God'.[111] This may be largely true for 2.14-26, where 'faith' can plausibly be understood not as 'trust' or 'obedience' but 'credence', that is, 'belief', the antithesis of 'doubt'. Such 'faith' has as its object either God or religious teaching. Yet elsewhere in our letter it is hard to rid the word of all connotations of loyalty and steadfastness, connotations present in the Hebrew אמונה, which the LXX often translates with πίστις. In 1.6 and 5.15, 'faith' is associated with prayer, and in 2.5 it obviously involves trust: the poor are rich in faith because they trust in and depend upon God. In 1.3, furthermore, it is precisely one's faith, or rather constancy in that faith, that is tested by trial,[112] so here the word appears to be something like a comprehensive term for right religion, as is typical of Paul.[113]

ὑπομονή—also associated with χαρά in Col 1.11—appears again in 5.11, where we read, in a passage featuring μακροθυμέω and μακροθυμία

---

[108] So Grotius, 1073; Gebser, 13; Pott, 137; Schneckenburger, 6; de Wette, 209; Theile, 9-11; Immer, *Hermeneutics*, 152; Wandel, 29; Mayor, 34-35; Belser, 39; Baljon, 6; Dibelius, 72-73; Burchard, 56.

[109] LXX Prov 27.21: δοκίμιον ἀργύρῳ καὶ χρυσῷ πύρωσις, ἀνὴρ δὲ δοκιμάζεται διὰ στόματος ἐγκωμιαζόντων αὐτόν ('Fire is the means of testing gold and silver, but a person is tested through the mouth of those who praise him'). Cf. Plutarch, *Mor.* 230B (Ναμέρτης... ἠρώτησεν εἰ δοκίμιον ἔχει τίνι τρόπῳ πειράζεται ὁ πολύφιλος: 'Namertes... asked if he had any sure means of testing the man of many friends'); Iamblichus, *Vit.* 30.185 (ταύτην δέ μοι θεῶν τις ἐνῆκε, δοκίμιον ἐσομένην τῆς σῆς περὶ συνθήκας εὐσταθείας: 'one of the gods implanted this forgetfulness in me as a means of testing your steadfastness about an agreement'); Origen, *Mart.* 6 GCS 2 ed. Koetschau, 8 (δοκίμιον οὖν καὶ ἐξεταστήριον τῆς πρὸς τὸ θεῖον ἀγάπης νομιστέον ἡμῖν γεγονέναι τὸν ἑστηκότα πειρασμόν: 'we must believe then that the present trial is a means of testing and a scrutiny of our love for God'). Further examples in Mayor, 34-35.

[110] 1.3, 6; 2.1, 5, 14 (*bis*), 17, 18 (*ter*), 20, 22 (*bis*), 24, 26; 5.15. Literature: W.H.P. Hatch, *The Idea of Faith in Christian Literature from the Death of Paul to the Close of the Second Century*, Strasbourg, 1925 (64-68 on James); Meyer, *Rätsel*, 123-41; Bultmann, 'πιστεύω κτλ.', *TDNT* 6.174-228; Mussner, 133-36; Lührmann, *Glaube* (78-84 on James); G. Barth, 'Glaube', *RAC* 11 (1981), 47-122; C. Spicq, 'πίστις', *TLNT* 3.110-16; J.E. Botha, 'The Meanings of πιστεύω in the Greek New Testament', *Neot* 21 (1987), 225-40; E. Brandenburger, 'Pistis und Soteria', *ZTK* 85 (1988), 165-98; W. Rebell, *Alles ist möglich dem, der glaubt*, Munich, 1989; G. Barth, 'πίστις', *EDNT* 3.91-97. On 'faith' in James specifically see A. Schlatter, *Glaube im Neuen Testament*, Stuttgart, 1896, 265-326; Hoppe, *Hintergrund*, 72-118; Frankemölle, 222-31.

[111] Bultmann, *Theology*, 2.163.

[112] Not the truth of one's faith or whether God is faithful.

[113] Cf. Powell, 'Faith'. James says nothing about faith in Jesus—unlike his interpreters, who incessantly define faith with reference to Jesus: Benson, 29; Beyschlag, 45; Mitton, 22; *et al.*

(vv. 7, 8, 10), of Job's 'steadfastness'.[114] The word, elsewhere allied with ἐλπίς[115] and set over against ὀργή,[116] suggests not passivity but being bravely patient with suffering until it dissipates; cf. Theod. Dan 12.12 ('Blessed is the one ὑπομένων'); Mk 13.13 ('the one ὑπομείνας to the end will be saved').[117] It is the opposite of despondency and resignation. In the words of Dibelius, 73: 'There is more heroism in this word than the translation "patience" [so KJV] would suggest'.[118] The noun, which the NEB renders 'fortitude', appears throughout 4 Maccabees (11×), where it applies to the religious constancy of martyrs;[119] and the Testament of Job—which declares that μακροθυμία, a near synonym of ὑπομονή,[120] is 'better than anything' (27.7)[121]—has its main character declare at the beginning: 'I am your father Job, fully engaged in ὑπομονῇ' (1.5). The virtue was probably much discussed in the Judaism known to James,[122] and it is not surprising that it appears frequently in early Christian literature, most often with reference to constancy in suffering.[123]

---

[114] Literature: C. Spicq, ''Ὑπομονή, Patientia', *RSPT* 19 (1930), 95-106; idem, 'ὑπομένω, ὑπομονή', *TLNT* 3.414-20; A.M. Festugière, ''Ὑπομονή dans la tradition grecque', *RSR* 30 (1931), 477-86; F. Hauck, 'ὑπομονή', *TWNT* 4.581-88; M. Spanneut, 'Geduld', *RAC* 9.243-94; W. Radl, 'ὑπομονή', *EDNT* 3.405-406. Adamson, 90-92, contends that we should read ὑπομονῇ instead of the accusative at the end of v. 3. But the text can be understood as it is and there is no external evidence for the proposal, which wrecks the climactic nature of v. 4. Cf. Klein, *Werk*, 47 n. 21.

[115] LXX Ps 70.5; 4 Macc 17.4; Rom 5.4; 8.25; cf. Rom 12.12. In the LXX, over half the time ὑπομονή translates מקוה or תקוה, both of which mean 'expectation', 'hope'.

[116] E.g. Acts Jn 4 ed. Bonnet, 153; Ps.-Macarius, *Serm.* 64 B 3 GCS ed. Berthold, 217. Tertullian, *Pat.* 15 CSEL 47 ed. Kroymann, 22-23, argues that *patientia* assuages anger, bridles the tongue, guards peace, breaks wrongful desire, checks the power of the rich, soothes the poor, fosters humility and gentleness, and enables one to resist temptation—all of which are concerns of James. Cf. Aquinas, *Summa* 2/2 q. 136 a. 2, expounding Jas 1.4: 'Patience is said to have a perfect work in bearing hardships: for these give rise first to sorrow, which is moderated by patience; secondly, to anger, which is moderated by meekness; thirdly, to hatred, which charity removes; fourthly, to unjust injury, which justice forbids'.

[117] Note also Plutarch, *Mor.* 208C, where the word is ethically neutral: 'When a malefactor endured tortures without flinching, Agesilaus said, "What an out-and-out villain the man is, devoting his endurance (ὑπομονή) and fortitude to such base and shameful purposes"'.

[118] Cf. Philo, *Mut.* 153: the 'brave man' has learned what it is necessary ὑπομένειν. According to F. Hauck, 'ὑπομονή', *TDNT* 5, 582, ὑπομονή is, in the system of Greek virtues, 'a sub-division of ἀνδρεία'.

[119] 1.11; 7.9; 9.8, 30; 15.30; 17.4, 12, 17, 23.

[120] James himself brings ὑπομονή into close association with μακροθυμία; see 5.7-11.

[121] Cf. Philo, *Cherub.* 78: ὑπομονή is among 'the mightiest of virtues'.

[122] Note further Pss. Sol. 2.36 ('the Lord is good to those who call out to him in ὑπομονῇ'); 1 En. 47.2 (the righteous pray that 'endurance might not be theirs forever'); T. Jos. 2.7 (ὑπομονή 'bestows many gifts'); 10.1 (ὑπομονή works 'great things'), 2 ('ὑπομονῇ and in humility of heart').

[123] Lk 8.15; 21.19; Rom 15.4-5; 2 Cor 1.6; 2 Thess 1.4; Heb 12.1; 2 Pet 1.6; Rev 1.9; 2.2, 3, 19; 1 Clem. 5.5; etc. The two earliest Christian treatises on patience, those of Tertullian (*De patientia*) and Cyprian (*De bono patientiae*), make no use of James.

If ὑπομονή occurs here in close connection with πειρασμός (v. 2) and δοκίμιον (v. 3), v. 12 blesses the one who ὑπομένει πειρασμόν and has been tested, δόκιμος. The repetition lends thematic unity to James' opening; cf. also the repetition of πειράζω in vv. 13-14.

κατεργάζομαι,[124] a Pauline favorite, occurs in Rom 5.3 in connection with ὑπομονή: ἡ θλῖψις ὑπομονὴν κατεργάζεται. Although κατεργάζομαι with ὑπομονήν as its object eventually became a common Christian idiom, its first attestation is in Paul,[125] and the verb does not appear in the parallel in 1 Pet 1.6-7.

Verse 4. 1.3 ends with the virtue ὑπομονή, so 1.4 now explains the value of that virtue.[126] From the worst (1.2) comes the best (1.4). Note the rhythm, assonance, and consonance of the closing words:

ἵνα ἦτε τέλειοι	λε οι
καὶ ὁλόκληροι	λ λη οι
ἐν μηδενὶ λειπόμενοι	λε οι

ἡ δὲ ὑπομονὴ ἔργον τέλειον ἐχέτω. Cf. 2.22: ἐκ τῶν ἔργων ἡ πίστις ἡ ἐτελειώθη. For ἔχω + ἔργα/ον see on 2.14.[127] The singular, ἔργον, corresponds to James' concern for integrity, for unified commitment; cf. 1.6-8; 4.4. τέλειος (see below) is a favorite of James.[128] ἡ δὲ ὑπομονή... ἐχέτω serves as a transition: ὑπομονή picks up the previous clause, and ἔργον τέλειον leads to the following statement about those who are τέλειοι. James is envisaging the outcome of a process. One may compare T. Jos. 2.7 ('perseverance is a powerful medicine, and ὑπομονή provides many good things'); 10.1 ('how great are the things that patience [ὑπομονή] and prayer with fasting accomplish' [κατεργάζεται]). The imperative, ἐχέτω, entails that suffering does not in and of itself produce virtue: what counts is the response to that suffering.

Mayor, 36, takes ἔργον τέλειον[129] to mean 'full effect'; so too the NRSV.[130] But, as Dibelius, 73-74, observes, 'the expression sounds

---

[124] Jas: 1×. LXX: 11×, for various Hebrew words. NT: 22× (all but three in authentic Pauline epistles). Gk. Pseudepigrapha (Denis): 7×. Philo: 14×. Josephus: 12×.

[125] Although ὑπομονή as the subject of κατεργάζομαι occurs in T. Jos. 10.1.

[126] Was Hort, 6, justified to observe, 'Here the Stoic constancy is at once justified, and implicitly pronounced inadequate, because it endeavours to be self-sufficing and leads the way to no diviner virtue'?

[127] According to Maier, 60, the Hebrew מעשה lies behind James' ἔργον. But there appears to be no tradition of associating that word with תמים or שלם, which one naturally thinks of as the Hebrew equivalents of τέλειος and ὁλόκληρος.

[128] 1.4 (bis), 17, 25; 3.2; cf. τελειόω in 2.22.

[129] Of God's creation in Philo, Spec. 2.59; so too Celsus in Origen, Cels. 4.99 ed. Marcovich, 316. Elsewhere however Philo uses the superlative, τελειότατον ἔργον: Opif. 9; Conf. 97; Her. 199; Abr. 74 (τελεώτατον ἔργον); Mos. 2.267. In Spec. 1.71, τελειότατον ἔργον designates the temple.

[130] For Calvin, 263, ἔργον τέλειον ἐχέτω is a call for patient endurance until it becomes perfect patient endurance.

strangely specific for this rather bland idea'. Dibelius also rejects reference to an unspecified manifestation of endurance.[131] He instead maintains that ἔργον τέλειον corresponds to the term '"produce" (κατεργάζεσθαι) in the preceding member of the catena; the thought, "Let endurance effect a perfect work", finds its completion in the final clause: "*You* are that perfect work"'. Dibelius translates: 'Let this endurance effect a perfect product, so that, etc.' More persuasive is Klein, who shows that elsewhere in early Christian literature, ἔργον and ἔργον τέλειον refer to a person's lifework as judged by God.[132] So Klein understands ἔργον τέλειον to be the climactic member of James' 'gradatio': trial → patient endurance → perfected work, this last then being clarified by the words that follow.[133]

ἵνα ἦτε τέλειοι. Cf. 2.22: πίστις ἐτελειώθη. James uses ἵνα only twice, the other time in 4.3. Oddly enough, ἵνα ἦτε is first attested in Paul, in 1 Cor 5.7 and Phil 1.10, and in the latter it closely follows δοκιμάζειν (cf. James' δοκίμιον) and immediately precedes a pair of plural nominatives that characterize the eschatological goal of faith (εἰλικρινεῖς καὶ ἀπρόσκοποι). τέλειος[134] seems to mean 'perfect' in 1.17 ('perfect gift') and 25 ('perfect law'). Elsewhere in early Christian literature it may signal maturity or adulthood (1 Cor 14.20; Eph 4.13), perfection of kind (1 Clem. 55.6; Ign. *Pol*. 1.3), or some sort of moral perfection (Mt 5.48; 19.21; Did. 1.4; 6.2). The following points are relevant to the understanding of Jas 1.4:

---

[131] Ropes, 137, refers to 'those further fruits which make up completeness of character'. Cf. Kypke, 419, who glosses ἔργον with 'fruit'

[132] Klein, *Werk*, 54-56. For ἔργον alone see 1 Cor 3.13-15; Heb 6.10; 1 Pet 1.17; Rev 22.12; 1 Clem. 14.3; cf. T. Abr. RecLng. 13.12-13. For ἔργον τέλειον see Ign. *Smyr*. 11.2 ('In order then that your work may be perfect [τέλειον ὑμῶν γένηται τὸ ἔργον] both on earth and in heaven'); Ps.-Ign. *Smyr*. 11.2 ed. Zahn, 250 ('τὸ ἔργον τέλειον on earth and in heaven'); Acts Jn 107 ed. Bonnet, 205; Clement of Alexandria, *Strom*. 4.4.14.3 GCS 52 ed. Stählin and Früchtel, 255. Cf. Jn 17.4: 'I glorified you on earth by finishing the work (τὸ ἔργον τελειώσας) that you gave me to do'.

[133] For Lange, 37, the end is acknowledgment of Gentile Christians by Jewish Christians and the latter forsaking 'judaistic faith-pride and fanaticism'. This idiosyncratic reading is bound up with Lange's anti-Semitism, as becomes obvious on the next page: 'the Jewish people itself became most emphatically the λειπόμενοι of the world's history. James with a prophet's eye foresaw all the growing decay.'

[134] LXX: 24×. NT: 19×. Gk. Pseudepigrapha (Denis): 13×. Josephus: 36×. The word was one of Philo's favorites, occurring over 300× in his extant writings. Literature: R.N. Flew, *The Idea of Perfection in Christian Theology*, Oxford, 1934; P.J. Du Plessis, *ΤΕΛΕΙΟΣ*, Kampen, 1959 (233-40 on James); K. Prümm, 'Das neutestamentliche Sprach- und Begriffsproblem der Vollkommenheit', *Bib* 44 (1963), 76-92; Davies, *Setting*, 209-15; G. Delling, 'τέλειος', *TDNT* 8.67-78; Hoppe, *Hintergrund*, 27-32; Zmijewski, 'Vollkommenheit'; Peterson, *Hebrews and Perfection*, Cambridge, UK, 1982; H. Hübner, 'τέλειος', *EDNT* 3.342-44; Martin, lxxix-lxxxii; W. Popkes, 'New Testament Principles of Wholeness', *EvQ* 64 (1992), 319-32; Klein, *Werk*, 56-65; Konradt, *Existenz*, 267-85; Hartin, 'Perfect'; idem, *Perfection*; D. Cheung, *Genre*, 162-96.

(i) In the LXX, τέλειος usually translates שלם or תמ(ים) and means 'unblemished', 'undivided' or 'whole', as in 'unblemished offering'[135] or 'undivided heart'.[136] In Gen 6.9; Deut 18.13; 2 Βασ 22.26; and Ecclus 44.17, undivided loyalty to God is the meaning. This is surely part of what Jas 1.4 connotes. The 'perfect' are, unlike those who are double-minded and divided within themselves (1.7-8; 4.8), characterized by whole-hearted, undivided allegiance. One may compare Tg. Neof. 1 on Gen 22, where Abraham has both a 'perfect heart' (6, 8: לבה שלמה) and an 'undivided heart' (14: לבי פלגו).

(ii) Deuteronomy 18.13 demands: 'You must be perfect (תמים; LXX: τέλειος) before the Lord your God'; and 1 Kgs 11.4; 15.3, and 14 criticize several kings for not being 'perfect' of heart. So the imperative to be 'perfect' is already embedded in the law and the prophets. It is nothing new to James or the early church.

(iii) The notion of sinlessness is unlikely to play a role here. Although the idea was not foreign to Judaism,[137] Jas 3.2 confesses that *all* make many mistakes.[138] Moreover, the following words ('lacking in nothing') show that 'wholeness' or 'completeness' is the chief content; cf. Philo, *Spec.* 1.252: 'even the τέλειος...never escapes from sinning'.[139] So the formulation of Burchard, 58, seems justified: James demands perfection, but he is no perfectionist.

(iv) The Dead Sea Scrolls speak of 'men of perfection', a 'house of perfection', and a 'perfection of way',[140] and they regularly associate such language with the faithful keeping Torah. A link to the law is also required in James, where the Torah is the perfect revelation (1.25) which one must perform (1.22-25).

(v) Some have thought that Mt 19.16-22 distinguishes between two sorts of believers, the 'perfect'—those who give up all they have to follow Jesus—and those of lesser commitment. Whether or not that rightly construes Matthew, the Didache seems to make just this distinction

---

[135] Exod 12.5. A few earlier commentators thought of pentateuchal laws of sacrifice; cf. Clarke, 799; Pott, 138.

[136] 3 Βασ 8.61; 11.4, 10; 15.3, 14; 1 Chr 28.9; cf. T. Jud. 23.5.

[137] See Tob 3.14; Pry. Man. 8; Wis 10.5; Ecclus 44.7; Jub. 23.10; 27.17; Pss. Sol. 17.41; T. Iss. 7.1-7; T. Mos. 9.4; 2 Cor 5.21; Heb 4.15; 7.26; T. Abr. RecLng. 10.13-14; 2 Bar. 9.1; 4 Bar. 6.6; 9.1; Hist. Rech. 11.2; t. Sanh. 13.3; b. Qidd. 40b; Deut. Rab. 10.10.

[138] Cf. Mt 7.11 = Lk 11.13; Rom 3.9-18; 1 Jn 1.8; etc.

[139] Until recently, the major English translations, following the Vulgate (*perfecti*), have preferred to translate τέλειοι with 'perfect'. Contemporary translations have often departed from this long-standing tradition—e.g. NEB ('complete'), NIV ('mature'), NRSV ('mature'). One guesses that these newer versions are trying to avoid the idea of 'sinlessness'. One might additionally consider 'perfection' problematic because it wrongly 'suggests a 100% result reached at a certain stage and maintained unchanged' (Popkes, 'Wholeness', 321). But 'mature' and 'complete' are also less than ideal equivalents.

[140] 1QS 1.8; 2.2; 4.22; 5.24; 8.10, 26; 9.2; 1QM 14.7; 4Q418 172 4; 4Q510 1 9; 4Q525 5; 11Q5 27.3; etc.

(6.2; cf. 1.2), which became popular in later Christianity.[141] James, however, shows no trace of this sort of thinking.[142]

(vi) Given the mention of wisdom in 1.5 and its importance throughout our epistle, it matters that a link between 'wisdom' and 'perfection' was probably traditional.[143] 1QS 4.22 speaks of God giving the Spirit so that 'upright ones may have insight into the knowledge of the Most High and the wisdom (חכמת) of the sons of heaven, and the perfect in the way (תמימי דרך) may receive understanding'. In 1QH 9(1).34-36, the wise (חכמים) are the 'perfect of way' (תמימי דרך). In 4Q525 5.11, those who walk in 'perfection' (תמים) do not reject Wisdom's admonishments. In 1 Cor 2.6, Paul writes that he speaks a 'wisdom' (σοφίαν) among the 'perfect' (τελείοις). Colossians 1.28 depicts the teaching of 'wisdom' (σοφία) as the prerequisite for presenting everyone 'mature' (τέλειον) in Christ. Matters are similar in Jas 1.4, where wisdom enables one to endure patiently, which in turn leads to a 'perfected work'.[144]

(vii) Patient endurance and its 'perfected work' depend upon wisdom, as the next verse makes plain; and because wisdom is the gift of God (1.5, 17), it seemingly follows that the one who is steadfast and perfect has been made such by divine favor.[145]

(viii) James' use of τέλειος probably does not have an exclusively Jewish background but also owes something to popular Hellenistic philosophy.[146] Philo uses τέλιος with reference to moral perfection;[147] so too the Stoics[148] and yet others.[149] The Stoic maxim preserved in Stobaeus, *Ecl.* 2.7.11G, supplies a good parallel to James: πάντα δὲ τὸν καλὸν καὶ ἀγαθὸν ἄνδρα τέλειον εἶναι λέγουσι διὰ τὸ μηδεμιᾶς ἀπολείπεσθαι ἀρετῆς.[150] Further, the combination of ὁλόκληρος and τέλειος is seemingly unattested in Palestinian sources but common elsewhere (see below),

---

[141] See e.g. Cyprian, *Hab. virg.* 23 CSEL 3 ed. G. Hartel, 203-204; Eusebius, *Dem. ev.* 1.8 GCS 23 ed. Heikel, 39.

[142] Hemminge, 3-6, argues from James against 'the Papists' and the old distinction between 'the perfect' (= the religious) and lay Christians.

[143] See further Hoppe, *Hintergrund* 32-33.

[144] See further Ecclus 34.8; 1Q28a 1.28; Philo, *Leg.* 3.207; and cf. Ps.-Dionysius, *Ep.* 9.4 PTS 36 ed. Heil and Ritter, 204: σοφία... τελεσιουργός.

[145] So also Hoppe, *Hintergrund*, 32-33.

[146] See esp. Klein, *Werk*, 56-65.

[147] G. Delling, 'τέλειος', *TDNT* 8.70-72, conveniently gathers the relevant texts.

[148] In Stoicism, one is τέλειος when one has all the virtues. Cf. Plutarch, *Mor.* 1046F: 'Neither [according to the Stoics] is one perfect (τέλειον) if he have not all the virtues...'

[149] Note the hyperbolic description on a first-century BCE marble stele from Lydia: ἀνὴρ τετελησμένος εἰς ἀρετήν (NDL 58). The term, τέλειος φιλόσοφος, may have had some currency; cf. Diogenes of Sinope, *Ep.* 25.1; Simplicius, *Epict.* 130; David, *Proleg. phil.* 17.1, 10. For Epicurean use see Philodemus, *On Frank Criticism* 6b.13; 8a.3-5; 10a.11.

[150] 'They say that every good and noble person is perfect, since he lacks no virtue'. Cf. Philo, *Abr.* 34: that Noah became 'perfect' (τέλειον) means that 'he acquired not one virtue but all', that is, he lacked no virtue.

and ὑπομονή is linked with moral perfection in Diogenes of Sinope, *Ep.* 27.[151]

(ix) Philo perceived the human goal as perfection, which he thought could be obtained.[152] For him, perfection included ridding oneself of anger, being peaceable, and uniting word and deed: 'we have found the perfect man cutting out the seat of anger entirely from the wrangling soul, and so rendering it gentle and submissive and peaceable, and cheerfully ready to face every demand both in act and word' (*Leg.* 3.140). All this has its parallel in James, which condemns anger (1.19-20), promotes peace (1.17), and insists on deed as well as word (1.22-25; 2.14-17).

(x) James 1.2-4 envisages a series and so a process. With this in mind, one recalls Phil 3.12-16, where Paul calls himself 'perfect' (v. 15) and yet declares that he has not yet obtained 'perfection' (v. 12), for that consists precisely in moving ever forward (v. 14).[153] James may similarly have imaged 'perfection' as an on-going endeavor, as the struggle to produce a 'perfected work' acceptable to God at death or the *parousia*;[154] cf. Heb 6.1 ('Let us go on to τελειότητα') and recall the importance of the *prokopton*—the individual making moral progress—for Panaetius of Rhodes and other Stoics.

(xi) As 1.4 belongs to the first paragraph of James, one should let the rest of the book offer illumination; that is, what follows should clarify 'perfection' by bringing to the fore the virtues the author promotes most. To judge from 3.17-18, for instance, the 'perfect' will be peaceable, meek, willing to yield, full of mercy and good works, and bereft of partiality and hypocrisy.

(xii) Although James, unlike Matthew (5.43-48), does not explicitly root the imperative to be 'perfect' in the divine perfection, the text may take such for granted. Not only was the imitation of God at home in James' world—being prominent in Plato, Philo, and the Jesus tradition[155]—but it appears in Jas 2.5-6, where God's favoring of 'the poor'

---

[151] 'Pitiable indeed are those people who do not understand that the things they seem to be practicing are in fact brought to perfection (κατορθοῦσθαι) by me alone... Who would boast of patience (ὑπομονήν) under frightful circumstances with Diogenes present?'

[152] See *Agr.* 159; Delling as in n. 147; M.L. Satlow, 'Philo on Human Perfection', *JTS* 59 (2008), 500-19; H. Najman, *Past Renewals*, Leiden, 2010, 291-34.

[153] Cf. perhaps Philo, *Mos.* 1.159: 'Happy are those who imprint' the model (παράδειγμα) of Moses—'the most perfect (τελειοτάτου) man' in 1.1—'or strive to imprint, that image in their souls. For it were best that the mind should carry the form of virtue in perfection (τέλειον) but, failing this, let it at least have the unflinching desire to possess that form.'

[154] Ezek 28.15 apparently rewrites a version of the Eden story in which the first person was originally 'perfect' (תמים). It follows that a return to 'perfection' would be a return to the beginning.

[155] Plato, *Theaet.* 176A-B; Philo, *Fug.* 63; Mt 5.44-48; Lk 6.35-36; cf. Exod 20.10-11; Lev 11.45-46; 19.2; 20.26; Deut 10.18-19; Let. Aris. 188, 254, 281; Eph 5.1; Sextus, *Sent.* 144-45, 148; Mek. on Exod 15:2; Sifra 121 on Lev 11:44; Sifre 49 on Deut 11.22;

rebukes human beings who do not favor 'the poor'.[156] Moreover, James presumably believed that God is 'perfect',[157] and Matthew's Gospel, which otherwise shares so much with James, correlates human perfection with divine perfection: 'Be perfect, therefore, as your heavenly Father is perfect' (5.48).[158]

καὶ ὁλόκληροι. According to the dictionaries, ὁλόκληρος (cf. ὁλοκληρία), which appears only one other time in the NT,[159] means first 'whole' or 'complete',[160] then 'without defect' or 'blameless',[161] although often one can scarcely distinguish the two senses.[162] The word, otherwise applied to this or that virtue,[163] is a near synonym of τέλειος.[164] The LXX four times uses ὁλόκληρος to translate שלם or מתים, words also translated by τέλειος, and Philo, *Abr.* 47, says that 'the perfect one (τέλειος) is complete (ὁλόκληρος) from the beginning'.[165] So the appearance of ὁλόκληρος and τέλειος together is expected, and it is otherwise well-attested.[166]

y. Ber. 9c (5.3); y. Pe'ah 15b (1.1); y. Meg. 75c (4.10); b. Šabb. 133b; b. Soṭah 14a; Tg. Ps.-J. on Lev 22:28; Dio Chrysostom 1.37-41. Discussion in H. Crouzel, 'L'imitation et la "suite" de Dieu et du Christ dans les premières siècles chrétiens, ainsi que leurs sources gréco-romaines et hebraïques', *JAC* 21 (1978), 7-41.

[156] On imitating God in James see further Laws, 'Basis'.

[157] See Judg 9.5 (the proper name יותם probably means 'Yahweh is perfect'); 2 Kgs 15.32; Ps 38.17 ('This God—his way is perfect'); Job 37.16 (God's 'knowledge is perfect'); Mt 5.48.

[158] Cf. Lev. Rab. 2.10, which correlates God being perfect with the patriarchs being perfect. For an attempt to correlate James' idea of 'perfection' with that of Matthew see Hartin, *Q*, 199-207. Against Plummer, 572, and a few others, James does not seem to be recalling Mt 5.48; see Deppe, *Sayings*, 65-67.

[159] 1 Thess 5.23 ('may your spirit... be preserved complete'). The context is eschatological. Cf. Herm. *Mand.* 5.2.3: τὴν πίστιν ἐχόντων ὁλόκληρον. LXX: 9-10×. Gk. Pseudepigrapha (Denis): 1×. Philo: 70×. Josephus: 11×.

[160] Cf. LXX Lev 23.15; Deut 16.9; 27.6; Jos. Asen. 16.16b.

[161] Cf. LXX Zech 11.16; Philo, *Spec.* 1.283; Josephus, *Ant.* 3.228.

[162] As in 1 Thess 5.23; Herm. *Mand.* 5.2.3.

[163] Cf. Wis 15.3 ('perfect righteousness'); 4 Macc 15.17 ('perfect piety'); Philo, *Deus* 4 ('the perfect virtues'); Ps.-Lucian, *Amor.* 51 ('perfect virtue').

[164] Trench, *Synonyms*, 77, divines this distinction: 'The ὁλόκληρος is one who has preserved, or who, having once lost, has now regained, his *completeness*: the τέλειος is one who has attained his moral *end*, that for which he was intended'; cf. Hort, 6; Mussner, 66. For Popkes, 85, τέλειος is qualitative, ὁλόκληρος quantitative; cf. W. Foerster, 'ὁλόκληρος', *TDNT* 3.766-67.

[165] Cf. Philo, *Sacr.* 111: offerings are to be made 'perfect (ὁλόκληρα) and complete' (τέλεια).

[166] Cf. Ps.-Aelius Aristides, *Ars. rhet.* 1.Arg.1.1 (ὁλόκληρος καὶ τελείως ἔχων); Dio Chrysostom 12.34 (τὴν ὁλόκληρον καὶ τῷ ὄντι τελείαν τελετήν); Philo, *Prov.* frag. 1 (οὐκ ἂν ἐγένετο τέλειος οὐδ'... ὁλόκληρος); Plutarch, *Mor.* 1069F (τέλειον... καὶ ὁλόκληρον... βίον); *Mor.* 636F ('the complete [τὸ τέλειον = the world] is earlier than the incomplete just as the perfect [ὁλόκληρον] pre-exists the defective'); Alexander of Aphrodisias, *Analyt. prior.* 48.24; Origen, *Cels.* 4.99 ed. Marcovich, 316; Iamblichus, *Myst.* 5.21. The peculiar view of Lapide, 22, that the terminology comes from the Grecian games, where the winner of any contest was supposedly τέλειος, the winner of the pentathlon ὁλόκληρος, is without foundation.

Originally ὁλόκληρος seems to have had a physical application, and in Philo, *Sacr*. 33, and Josephus, *Ant*. 3.228, it refers to sacrificial offerings. But Greek literature, including the LXX,[167] shows a transfer to moral excellence.[168]

ἐν μηδενὶ λειπόμενοι. So far from adding clarity, this elliptical phrase leaves one asking, Not lacking in what? Perfection? Virtue? Character? Faith? Patience? Love? All that would make for authentic faith? Presumably ἐν κτλ. is tacked on partly for formal reasons: it creates a catchword connection with the next verse—εἰ δέ τις ὑμῶν λείπεται. Further, James likes to qualify positives with negatives; cf. 1.5 (ἁπλῶς καὶ μὴ ὀνειδίζοντος), 6 (ἐν πίστει μηδὲν διακρινόμενος), 22 (ποιηταὶ λόγου καὶ μὴ μόνον ἀκροαταί). The verb, λείπω,[169] recurs in 2.15, μηδείς again only in chap. 1 (vv. 6, 13). Their combination with the sense, 'lack for nothing', is attested, although not in Jewish sources.[170]

1.4 does not indicate when patient endurance will produce its perfected work. For Laws, 52, 'there is no eschatological term to James' series...the process of probation leads to an achieving of personal integrity, apparently an end in itself'. Against this, (i) πειρασμός (v. 2) and ὑπομονή (vv. 3-4) often carry eschatological meaning in early Christian texts;[171] (ii) Jewish sources offer more of the same;[172] (iii) the close parallel in 1 Pet 1.7 culminates in a reference to the return of Jesus

---

[167] Wis 15.3: ὁλόκληρος δικαιοσύνη; 4 Macc 15.17: τὴν εὐσέβειαν ὁλόκληρον.

[168] Cf. Plato, *Phaed*. 250C (celebration of mysteries in a state of 'perfection', ὁλόκληροι); Suetonius, *Claud*. 4 ('if he be sound and so to speak "complete"', *holocleros*).

[169] LXX: 8×, exclusively in the wisdom literature and 2-3 Maccabees, and never with the meaning the word has in James. NT: 6×. Gk. Pseudepigrapha (Denis): 22×. Philo: 22×. Josephus: 70×. For the sense 'lack' see Jas 2.5; T. Abr. RecLng. 14.3; Ign. *Pol*. 2.2 (μηδενὸς λείπῃ); and next note.

[170] Cf. Corpus Hermeticum frag. 23.52 ed. Nock and Festugière, 4.17 (μηδενί... λείπεσθαι); Porphyry, *Herm. Ptolem*. ed. Düring, 163 (τὸ λεῖπον ἐν μηδενί); Proclus, *Plat. Alc*. 1.249 (μηδενὶ λείπουσαν). The closest Semitic equivalent seems to be לֹא אחסר, as in Ps 23.1 (although Royster, 17, is reminded of the last verse, the commentary tradition otherwise appears to overlook it); Eccl 9.8; m. Suk. 3.6; or לֹא חסר, as in Tg. Onq. Exod 16.18. Without explanation, McCartney, 88, suggests that ἐν κτλ. may carry 'forward the priestly notion of proper investiture and preparation, but may be more closely associated with military imagery, being fully outfitted for battle'.

[171] For πειρασμός see 148 and K.G. Kuhn, 'New Light on Temptation, Sin, and Flesh in the New Testament', in *The Scrolls and the New Testament*, ed. K. Stendahl, New York, 1957, 94-113. For ὑπομονή/ένω see Mt 10.22; Mk 13.13; Lk 21.19; Rom 8.25; 2 Thess 1.4-7; Rev 1.9; 2.2 (with ἔργον), 19 (with ἔργα); 14.12-13 (with ἔργα); Did. 16.5. Note esp. Rev 3.10: 'Because you have kept my word of patient endurance (ὑπομονῆς), I will keep you from the hour of trial (πειρασμοῦ) which is coming on the whole world, to try (πειράσαι) those who dwell upon the earth'.

[172] E.g. Dan 12.12 Theod. ('Blessed is the one who continues ὑπομένων'); LXX Zech 6.14 ('The crown will be to those who continue ὑπομένουσιν'); 4Q177 2.9-10 ('the purification of the heart of the men of [the community]...in the last days [...] to test them and to refine them'); 4Q174 1-3 2 ('the time of trial which co[mes]...the just [...shall be whi]tened and refined').

while the parallel in Rom 5.3-4 has to do with eschatological hope; and (iv) Jas 1.12 associates the overcoming of temptations with receiving 'eternal life'. One concurs then with Mussner, 67: Jas 1.2-4 should be set against the background of eschatological reward. The perfection for which one strives in the present will be realized at the end.[173] Cf. 4 Macc 9.8, where suffering works both virtue in the present and eschatological reward in the future: 'through this severe suffering and endurance, we will have the prize of virtue and will be with God'.

---

[173] Cf. Theodore the Studite, *Parva cat.* 68 ed. Auvray, 238; Peter Damian, *Ep.* 94.2 Reindel, 32; Ancrene Wisse 4.5-7 ed. Millett, 69; Aquinas, *Summa* 2/1 38 a. 5; Erasmus, *Paraphrase*, 137-38; Gill, 779; Guyse, 564; A.G. Fuller, 'The Work of Patience', in *The Complete Works of the Rev. Andrew Fuller*, vol. 1, Philadelphia, 1845, 374-79; Cone, 274; J. Thomas, 'Anfechtung', 190; Martin, 17; Betz, *Sermon*, 323; R. Wall, 49-50; Penner, *Eschatology*, 183-201; Wenger, *Kryios*, 131 (stressing that if eschatological perfection is the goal, it must be pursued even now).

III

WISDOM, FAITH, DOUBT (1.5-8)[1]

(5) If anyone of you lacks wisdom, let him ask of God, who gives to all unreservedly and without reproach, and it will be given to him. (6) But let him ask in faith, without doubting; because the doubter is like a surging wave of the sea, driven and tossed about by the wind. (7-8) For that person, being double-minded and unstable in all his ways, should not suppose that he will receive anything from the Lord.

History of Interpretation and Reception

Most commentators have, until recent times, perceived a direct thematic connection between 1.5-8 and 1.2-4. Bede wrote: James 'seems to be talking about that wisdom which is necessary for us to use in trials. If anyone of you, he says, cannot understand the utility of trials that beset the faithful in order to test them, let him pray to God that he...be able to recognize with what great kindness the father punishes the sons whom he carefully makes worthy of an eternal inheritance'.[2] Calvin, 263, commented: 'Our reason, and indeed all our senses, find it strange that we should think ourselves blessed in time of woe, and so we are told to ask the Lord to bring us this wisdom... So we see that our Lord does not make demands on us beyond our powers, but is in fact all ready to send resources, once we ask for them. As soon as He tells us our task, we should ask from Him the means to fulfil it.'[3]

---

[1] Recent literature: Baker, *Speech-Ethics*, 241-43; Bartlett, 'Document'; Cheung, *Genre*, 196-216; R. Cooper, 'Prayer'; Frankemölle, 'Netz'; Garland, 'Trials'; Gowan, 'Wisdom'; Hadidian, 'Pictures'; Hartin, *Q*, 174-76; Hoppe, *Hintergrund*, 32-40; Isaacs, 'Suffering'; Kirk, 'Wisdom'; Klein, *Werk*, 92-97; Kloppenborg, 'Psychagogy', 43-53; idem, 'Reception'; Konradt, *Existenz*, 267-74; Marshall, 'Δίψυχος'; Porter, '*Dipsuchos*'; Riesenfeld, 'ΑΠΛΩΣ'; Seitz, 'Afterthoughts'; idem, 'Antecedents'; Spitaler, 'Dispute'; idem, 'Shift'; J. Thomas, 'Anfechtung'; Tsuji, *Glaube*, 64-65, 119-21; Wenger, *Kyrios*, 156-71; Wolverton, 'Double-Minded Man'; Wypadlo, *Gebet*, 37-183; idem, 'Gott'.

[2] Bede *ad loc*. CCSL 121 ed. Hurst, 185.

[3] For similar sentiments see Martin of Legio *ad loc*. PL 209.186A; Hemminge, 5-6 (insisting that wisdom will reveal that 'we are tempted and oppressed with diverse afflictions because of our sinnes'); Diodati, *ad loc*. ('wisdom to judge rightly of afflictions, of their causes, and properties, of their aim, fruit, and issue, and of the duty we must perform to moderate the passions of the soul, and by means of an inward tranquility, and lively apprehension of eternal benefits, overcome all affaults, and escape all dangers that

Implicit in Calvin's remark is a strong doctrine of grace, and 1.5 has often been employed to underline the helplessness of human beings left on their own and, as a result, the importance of divine favor and supernatural aid.[4] Bede found the verse anti-Pelagian,[5] and for Dante, 1.5-8 spoke of 'the abundant gifts of our heavenly court'.[6]

Whereas most expositors have linked 1.5-8 to 1.2-4 via the idea that σοφία is necessary for understanding and enduring trials, a lesser number have joined the two passages with the thought that σοφία is the cause of maturity or perfection (v. 4). As Theophylact put it, the spiritual wisdom from above empowers believers to achieve the perfected work of 1.4.[7]

Despite the frequent focus upon wisdom as needed to endure trials, exegetes, encouraged no doubt by the indefinite τι of v. 7, have often, by the time they reach v. 8, passed from talking about prayer for wisdom in particular to prayer in general. Gill, 779, in commenting on v. 7, says that the doubter will not receive 'wisdom or anything else he is seeking after'. Manton, 45, ends up stressing that, when praying, one must ask for what is 'good' and to 'a holy purpose', thereby betraying that he is no longer thinking about wisdom.[8]

Given that many have understood vv. 5-8 to be a general statement about prayer,[9] the verses have become problematic given the habitual

---

may be met with therein'); Dickson, 681; Wolzogen, 182; Brochmand, 37; Manton, 37; Trapp, 693; Hammond, 688; Bengel, 487; Gill, 779; Lange, 38; Macknight, 586-87; Barnes, 22; Trollope, 603; Johnstone, 37; B. Weiss, 93; Mayor, 38; Easton, 23; Reicke, 14; Luck, 'Weisheit'; Roberts, 36; Thomas, 'Anfechtung und Vorfreude', 90-93; Hoppe, *Hintergrund*, 43; R. Wall, 51; Deiros, 67; Richardson, 64; Fruchtenbaum, 219. Ps.-Andrew of Crete, *Éloge* 4.18-22 ed. Noret, 46, even quotes 1.2-5 as a unit.

[4] E.g. Augustine, *De dono pers.* 17(43) PL 45.1019-20; Leo the Great, *Tract.* 49.4 CCSL 138A ed. Chavasse, 288; Whitby, 677; Belser, 43; Stringfellow, *Joy*, 47-51; Frankemölle, 215 ('Sola gratia'); Kamell, 'Grace', 276-77.

[5] Bede *ad loc.* CCSL 121 ed. Hurst, 184. Cf. Prosper of Aquitaine, *Contra collatorem* 16.1 PL 51.259B-C (defending Augustine against Semi-Pelagians); Wordsworth, 14.

[6] Dante, *Paradisio* 25.29-30, where Beatrice asks James—an 'illustrious living soul'—to examine Dante regarding the virtue of hope. Although James fails to explain the motive for divine grace, ecclesiastical tradition typically holds that God gives because God loves; cf. Lapide, 30; Johnstone, 39; *et al.*

[7] Theophylact *ad loc.* PG 125.1137B. Cf. the *Catenae ad loc.* ed. Cramer, 3; de Wette, 210 (emphasizing that σοφία is 'moral wisdom'); Kern, 114; Bisping, 14; S. Cox, *Expositions*, 4th series, New York, 1888, 76-78; C. Gore, 'Faith as an Active Force', *Christian World Pulpit* 104 (1923), 97; Ropes, 138; Spitta, 20; Ruckstuhl, 12; Schrage, 16; *et al.* Many relate vv. 5-8 both to trial and to perfection; cf. Ps.-Oecumenius *ad loc.* PG 119.458C; Schegg, 32; Wandel, 32-33; Davids, 71-72; Frankemölle, 212-14; Moo, 57; Hartin, 67; Fabris, 62; McKnight, 84; Wenger, *Kyrios*, 158-59; *et al.*

[8] Cf. *Catena Havniensis in Ecclesiasten* 8.17 CCSO 24 ed. Labate, 140-41.

[9] Most exegetes appear to reason as does Moo, 60: 'James does not return to the topic of wisdom in vv. 6-8, and his teaching here finds parallels in other NT texts about prayer in general. So we are probably justified in taking his teaching in these verses to apply to any prayer.' Contrast Fruchtenbaum, 219-21, who interprets the whole passage as pertaining to wisdom.

reality of unanswered petitions. So although the pericope plays no role in the earliest discussion of that subject, namely, Origen's *De oratione*, later musings on that topic have regularly included it. To illustrate: the seventeenth-century Puritan Thomas White preached a sermon on Jas 1.6 in which he labored to explain how 'it will be given to him' fits Christian experience. He insisted that prayers for 'temporal things' should be 'moderate as to their measure, and conditional as to their effect upon us; that is, if it be for our good'; and 'since our desires are to be conditional, and God's promises of temporals are conditional, we must not absolutely believe we shall receive what we ask: a conditional promise cannot be a foundation for an absolute faith'. In other words, people can ask for something in faith and still not receive it. At the same time, 'though we cannot nor ought not certainly to believe the obtaining the thing we ask, if it be temporal…yet, by virtue of an immediate assurance God may give us of receiving the very thing we ask, we may, and indeed cannot choose but, expect it'.[10] Lapide, 34, quoted Augustine, to the effect that the individual 'who supplicates God in faith for the necessary things of life is both mercifully heard and also unmercifully unheard. For the doctor knows better than the patient what is useful', which is why God did not remove Paul's thorn in the flesh.[11]

1.5 belongs to the foundational myth of Mormonism. Joseph Smith reported that, on a spring day in 1820, while he was 'laboring under extreme difficulties', he was reading that verse, and 'never did any passage of scripture come with more power to the heart of man that [sic] this did at this time to mine… I reflected on it again and again.' Determining then to ask God for wisdom, Smith retreated into the woods, where he had a vision of Jesus Christ, who informed him that 'all the sects' were mistaken, and that he should join 'none of them'. So Smith 'found the testimony of James to be true', and three years later the angel Moroni appeared to him, which led to the discovery of the golden tablets and the founding of Mormonism.[12]

Some exegetes, in response to those who have invoked 1.6 to promise people that, if only they overcome all doubt, their prayers will certainly

---

[10] T. White, 'What Faith is that which except we have in Prayer, we must not think to obtain any thing of God?', in *Puritan Sermons 1659–1689, being the Morning Exercises at Cripplegate, St. Giles in the Fields, and in Southwark by Seventy-Five Ministers of the Gospel in or Near London*, vol. 1, Wheaton, IL, 1981, 292-305. For related comments see Blomberg-Kamell, 52. According to Wordsworth, 14, God will always answer prayers for 'necessary graces' but not always answer prayers for 'common graces'. Sadler, 8, suggests rather that so few prayers are answered because so few pray with real faith. Adderley, 4, is sure that God answers all 'right prayers', it is just that they may be answered in unexpected ways or in ways not understood or after a great passing of time.

[11] See further Jacobi, 19-24, who argues that Christians should not want all their prayers answered, because they do not know what is truly good for them.

[12] For Smith's own testimony see D. Vogel, *Early Mormon Documents*, vol. 1, Salt Lake City, 1996, 59-67.

be answered, have opposed such magical thinking as misinterpretation.[13] More interesting is the problem of how to reconcile v. 6—does it lies behind our expression, 'waves of doubt'?—with the fact that even pious Christians have religious doubts.[14] How can a text counter something that plagues all thoughtful people? The verse moves Kistemaker, 40, to ask, 'Is doubt always sinful?'[15] John of Kronstadt would appear to think that it is, because he glosses v. 6 with this: 'Doubt is blasphemy against God, an insolent lie of the heart or of the lying spirit that nestles in the heart, against the spirit of truth'.[16] The Protestant pastor, E.M. Bounds, thought the same: 'Doubting is always put under the ban, because it stands as a foe to faith and hinders effectual praying... All questioning must be watched against and eschewed.'[17] Yet in the modern world, where doubt is often thought the key to knowledge (Descartes), where the Zen saying, 'No doubt, no awakening', rings true to many, and where knowledge of the physical world and human psychology have advanced precisely because people have doubted the wisdom of convention and traditions of the past, including religious traditions, it is common to find sympathy for doubt. Some make room for doubt by distinguishing the intellectual sort from the moral sort, allowing the former but not the latter.[18] Tholuck took another approach, writing that the one 'who sincerely desires to believe is already a believer', and that there is nothing wrong with praying, 'Lord, I believe, help my unbelief'.[19] Similarly, Sylvester Horne, citing the same synoptic prayer, distinguished between doubters who mock religion and those who want Christianity to be true but feel unsure that it is.[20] Moo, 60-61, reminds his readers that Abraham had doubts (Gen 17.15-18), so James, it follows, cannot claim 'that some prayers will never be answered where any degree of doubt exists—for some degree of doubt on at least

---

[13] Benson, 31: 'I see no reason, from this text, to conclude that we shall be heard, in any particular request, if we be strongly persuaded in our own minds, that we shall be heard. But it is very right to ask wisdom of God, even now-a-days, though the age of miracles is over.' Cf. Moo, 60: James does not support 'false prophets who claim that God has promised "health and wealth" to every Christian—if only his or her faith is strong enough'.

[14] As Hemminge, 7, wrote: faith and doubt co-exist, for although 'fayth is a firme consent nothing wavering' in the 'spirite in the regenerate', nonetheless 'doubts do oftentimes arise, which are the work of ye flesh, against which the works of the spirit do strive'.

[15] He argues that it is not because authentic perplexity is different from unbelief.

[16] John of Kronstadt, *My Life in Christ*, Jordanville, N.Y., 2008, 8.

[17] E.M. Bounds, 'Prayer and Faith', in *The Complete Works of E. M. Bounds on Prayer*, Grand Rapids, MI, 2000, 23, commenting on Jas 1.5-8. Cf. Cedar, 29.

[18] E.g. Punchard, 356. Cf. Ropes, 140: the doubter of 1.5-8 is one 'whose allegiance wavers, not one tormented by speculative intellectual questions, which do not fall within James's horizon'. Already Chrysostom *Exp. Ps.* 12.3 PG 55.154, contrasts the doubt of Jas 1.6-8 not with certainty but with hope (he cites the example of David in the Psalms).

[19] A. Tholuck, *Hours of Christian Devotion*, New York, 1875, 171-72.

[20] C.S. Horne, 'Doubt', *Christian World Pulpit* 66 (1904), 33-35.

some occasions is probably inevitable in our present state of weakness. Rather, he wants us to understand that God responds to us only when our lives reflect a basic consistency of purpose and intent: a spiritual integrity'. Stringfellow, *Joy*, 72-77, when contemplating faith and doubt in James, even holds up the agnostic Albert Camus as an example of 'an exceptionally mature human being' with a 'wondrous sort of faith'.

In the nineteenth century, the long poem of the Oxford Victorian Arthur Hugh Clough, *Dipsychus* (1850), made the δίψυχος of Jas 1.8 a well-known word in the English-speaking world. The poem itself, however, is no exposition of James but rather a statement of the struggle between idealism and worldliness, in which one of the refrains is, 'Dong, there is no God; dong!'

The last few decades have perhaps brought a new slant on 1.5-8. Traditional exegetes, some of whom have been unmarried monastics or single clergy, have typically envisaged an individual praying in isolation.[21] But Tamez, the liberation theologian, has instead underlined the communal orientation of the text: it 'refers to those who pray with vacillation, with hesitancy. James says that they are like the waves of the sea moved this way and that by the wind. Such people are a problem for the community principally because no one can trust them, because they are both with the community and not with it'.[22] A related exegesis appears in Johnson, 184: 'When James suggests that "they [double-minded persons] should not think that they will receive anything from the Lord", he suggests something about the dynamics of community life: those who share the group's ethos with only half a mind are already half out of the community'.

Exegesis

The verbal link with the previous paragraph continues the catchword linkage of vv. 1-4, as do the connections between vv. 5 and 6a and between vv. 6a and 6b:

v. 4:	λειπόμενοι		
v. 5:	λείπεται...	αἰτείτω	
v. 6a:		αἰτείτω...	διακρινόμενος
v. 6b:			διακρινόμενος

For Dibelius, 77, the association of 1.2-4 and 1.5-8 is purely formal, due to catchword only: there is no thematic tie.[23] As just observed, however, many commentators have, more plausibly, supposed that it is precisely

---

[21] Note e.g. Evagrius, *Log.* 26 SC 438 ed. P. Géhin, C. Guillaumont, and A. Guillaumont, 246; John Cassian, *Inst.* 15.2 SC 109 ed. Guy, 312.

[22] Tamez, *Message*, 59. Cf. Hartin, 68.

[23] Cf. Grafe, *Stellung*, 11; Oesterley, 422; Grosheide, 17; Cantinat, 68-69.

wisdom that enables the faithful to endure and learn from the trials of vv. 2-4, while others have highlighted a link between wisdom (the subject of 1.5) and perfection (the climax of 1.4).[24] To this one should add that, if vv. 2-4 culminate in talk of 'perfection' (ἔργον τέλειον, τέλειοι), vv. 5-8 culminate in talk of being 'double-minded' (δίψυχος), and that the latter is, in James, the opposite of the former. To be 'perfect' is to be 'complete', 'whole', 'undivided'; cf. v. 4: ὁλόκληροι. To be 'double-minded' is, to the contrary, to suffer divided loyalty, divided faith. In short, 1.2-4 and 5-8 are contrasting panels: the one sets up the ethical and eschatological goal; the other warns of what stands in the way of reaching that goal.

The structure and logic of 1.5-8 are straightforward:[25]

i. Hypothetical condition/deficiency ('If anyone of you lacks wisdom'), v. 5a
ii. Right response to condition/deficiency ('ask God'), v. 5b
iii. Encouragement ('who gives to all unreservedly and without reproach'), v. 5c
iv. Qualification ('But let him ask in faith, without doubting'), v. 6a
v. Twofold clarification of qualification
   a. A similitude ('because the doubter'), v. 6b
   b. A concluding generalization ('For that person should not suppose'), vv. 7-8[26]

Characteristic for James are paired phrases, which either elaborate or supply synonyms:

v. 5   ἁπλῶς καὶ μὴ ὀνειδίζοντος
v. 6   ἐν πίστει μηδὲν διακρινόμενος
v. 6   ἀνεμιζομένῳ καὶ ῥιπιζομένῳ
v. 8   δίψυχος, ἀκατάστατος

Implicit in the section is a set of opposites that Cargal, 69, sets forth thus:

Positive	Negative
1. Having 'faith'	1. Having 'doubt'
2. Asking for 'wisdom' from God	2. Not asking for 'wisdom' from God
3. Receiving 'wisdom' from God	3. Receiving nothing from God

---

[24] This was perhaps a traditional association; cf. Wis 9.6 ('even one who is perfect among human beings will be regarded as nothing without the wisdom that comes from you'; Spitta, 20, thinks this verse influenced James; cf. Wypadlo, *Gebet*, 61-63; contrast Konradt, *Existenz*, 250 n. 9); Ecclus 34.8 ('wisdom is perfect in the mouth of the faithful'); Philo, *Leg.* 3.207 ('the wise and the perfect'); 1 Cor 2.6; Col 1.28. See further on 1.4 and McKnight, 86-87.

[25] Frankemölle, 211, divides 1.6b-8 from 1.5-6a; but with Theissen, 'Intention', 65 n. 31, v. 6 does not introduce a new theme.

[26] Contrast Dickson, 680: vv. 6b, 7, and 8 are three 'reasons' for 6a. Wypadlo, *Gebet*, 51, offers this outline: introduction of case (v. 5a), summons to prayer (vv. 5b-d), renewed, clarified summons with supporting analogy (v. 6), utilization of analogy with warning (vv. 7-8).

Did a precise setting in life call forth 1.5-8? Hilary of Arles thought of Simon Magus, who wanted to buy the Holy Spirit when he should instead have asked God.[27] For Hammond, 689, James was opposing Gnostics who sought to avoid persecution. Macknight attributed to 'some' the view that James refers to 'those Jews who were not resolved whether they would adhere to the law or to the gospel'.[28] According to Neander, James addresses churches which featured 'a proneness to a vain show of wisdom, to the over-estimation of mere knowledge, the conceit of knowledge and wisdom'.[29] Martin, 17, by contrast, supposes that 'the readers are facing real problems arising from persecution'.[30] But McKnight, 84, surmises that the readers were likely suffering 'economic destitution and exploitation'. All of this is guesswork. We just do not know.

The commentators have long observed the many parallels between 1.5-8 and Herm. *Mand.* 9:

	Jas 1.5-8	Herm. *Mand.* 9
Topic: asking God for something	αἰτείτω παρὰ τοῦ... θεοῦ; αἰτείτω	αἰτήσασθαί τι παρὰ τοῦ θεοῦ; αἰτήσασθαι παρὰ τοῦ κυρίου; αἰτοῦ παρὰ τοῦ κυρίου; αἰτήσῃς παρὰ τοῦ κυρίου; αἰτησάμενός ποτε παρὰ τοῦ κυρίου
Outcome: one receives or does not receive	λήμψεται τι παρὰ τοῦ κυρίου	λαβεῖν; οὐ μὴ λήψῃ; λαμβάνουσιν; λήψῃ; λαμβάνῃς; ἔλαβες; λαμβάνεις; λήψῃ
Character of God: God gives	διδόντος θεοῦ	τὸν διδόντα
Character of God: God's goodness is universal	διδόντος... πᾶσιν	σπλαγχνίζεται ἐπὶ τὴν ποίησιν αὐτοῦ
Character of God: God holds no grudges, does not rebuke, is without malice	μὴ ὀνειδίζοντος	οὐκ... μνησικακοῦντες ἀλλ' αὐτὸς ἀμνησίκακός ἐστι
Requirement: faith	ἐν πίστει	ἐν τῇ πίστει; πίστιν; πίστευε; πίστεως; πιστούς; πίστιν; πίστις; πίστις; τῇ πίστει

[27] Hilary of Arles *ad loc.* PLSupp 3.64.
[28] Macknight, 587. So too Clarke, 799.
[29] Neander, 48. He gratuitously labels this 'a fruit of the Jewish spirit'.
[30] Scaer, 43, is of the same mind: the Jewish Christian audience was, under the pain of persecution, being 'lured back into the full communal life of the Jewish culture'. R.L. Williams, 'Piety', largely follows Martin.

Problem: being double-minded	ἀνὴρ δίψυχος	διψυχίαν; διψυχήσης; δίψυχοι; διψυχοῦντες; δίψυχος ἀνήρ; διψυχίας; διψχήσης; διψυχήσης; διψυχίαν; διψυχία; διψυχίας; διψυχία; διψυχίας
Problem: doubt	διακρινόμενος	ἀδιστάκτως, ἀδιστάκτως, διστάσης, διστάζοντες, ἀδιστάκτως
Scope of issue: comprehensive	ἐν πάσαις ταῖς ὁδοῖς	ἐν παντὶ πράγματι
Related theme: perfection	τέλειοι καὶ ὁλόκληροι, v. 4	ὁλοτελεῖς, τελειοῖ
Related theme: temptation/trial	πειρασμοῖς, vv. 2-4	πειρασμόν

One understands why many have thought these correlations sufficient to establish literary dependence.[31] Perhaps Hermas knew James. Two considerations, however, leave this writer uncertain.[32] First, the precise date of Hermas remains unknown. Parts of the book may go back to the end of the first century, or maybe, as the current consensus holds, it belongs in its entirety to the first half of the second century. In either case, James is, in the view of this writer, from the same period. Given this, the chronological order of the two documents is unclear. That James knew Hermas or some early or developing form of the document is possible.

Beyond that, one suspects dependence upon a common source, at least in part. The lost document behind 1 Clem. 23.3-4 = 2 Clem. 11.2-4, which James and Hermas probably knew,[33] condemned the double-minded (δίψυχοι), those who doubt (διστάζοντες). Moreover, 1 Clement introduces its quotation from that source with references to God's goodness (σπλάγχνα), universal benevolence (ὁ οἰκτίρμων κατὰ πάντα), and divine gift-giving (χάριτας…ἀποδιδοῖ, δωρεαῖς αὐτοῦ) whereas 2 Clement includes, in its version of the common citation, references to instability (ἀκαταστασίας) and receiving (ἀπολήψεται) from God, which it follows with an exhortation to patient endurance (ὑπομείνωμεν)—all of which is paralleled in Jas 1.4-8 and/or Herm. *Mand.* 9. To complicate matters even more, Hermas agrees with 1 and 2 Clement against James in clarifying δίψυχος with διστάζω and with 2 Clement against James in having more precisely διστάσης/οἱ διστάζοντες τῇ καρδίᾳ. James alone,

---

[31] For a helpful overview of estimations of Hermas' dependence or lack thereof upon the NT, including James, see J. Verheyden, 'The Shepherd of Hermas and the Writings that later formed the New Testament,' in Gregory-Tuckett, *Reception*, 292-329.

[32] See further the Introduction, 20-33.

[33] For this inference see Seitz, 'Hermas'; Knoch, *Eigenart*, 111-25; Allison, 'Eldad'.

then, cannot be the explanation for all the parallels. Instead they likely derive in large measure from a book, now lost, known to James, Hermas, and 1 and 2 Clement.[34]

Although Jas 1.5-8 says nothing about prayer that a non-Christian Jew could not equally say,[35] the verses are clearly Christian as they reflect, as we shall see, the influence of the Q saying in Mt 7.7 = Lk 11.9, and perhaps also the logion in Mk 11.23 = Mt 21.21. Some have further suspected—this could be true at the same time—a debt to 2 Chr 1.7-13 or Ecclus 20.15.

Verse 5. This elaborates the end of v. 4: those who are not ἐν μηδενὶ λειπόμενοι need to petition God for wisdom. 'It is a direction on how to behave, and not a reproof' (Benson, 30).

εἰ δέ τις ὑμῶν λείπεται σοφίας. εἴ τις recurs in 1.23, 26; 3.2. λείπεται + σοφία does not appear to have been a traditional Greek idiom, although Philostratus supplies a couple of parallels,[36] and rough equivalents appear in Ecclus 19.23 (ἐλαττούμενος σοφίᾳ); 37.21 (σοφίας ἐστερήθη). λείπω, which creates a verbal link with 1.4, recurs again in 2.15, with the same meaning. τις ὑμῶν[37] appears only here in James, but εἴ τις occurs in 1.23, 26; 3.2, τις ἐξ ὑμῶν in 2.16, τις ἐν ὑμῖν in 5.13, 14, 19 (ἐάν τις ἐν ὑμῖν). The conditional implies that readers—a few? many? most?[38]—have not yet reached the goal of 1.4.

σοφία, one of the prerequisites for the 'perfection' of v. 4,[39] is not wisdom gathered from experience (as in Job 12.12) or gained from education.[40] Further, it is not personified[41] nor is there speculation about its role in creation or any association with Christology.[42] And here (in

[34] See further Seitz, 'Afterthoughts'; idem, 'Antecedents'. For Seitz, that book must be Eldad and Modad. This writer concurs; see Allison, 'Eldad'. Contrast Ropes, 88 (James and Hermas 'are independently using a mass of religious and moral commonplaces, probably characteristic of the Jewish hortatory preaching with which both were plainly familiar'); Dibelius, 31-32; Brox, *Hirt*, 237; Popkes, 41-42.

[35] So rightly Wypadlo, 'Gott', 91.

[36] Philostratus, *Apoll.* 6.6.1 (σοφία...λείπεσθαι); 8.7.9 (σοφίας...λείπονται). Note also Aelian, *Hist.* 1.23 (τῇ δὲ σοφίᾳ τοσοῦτον ἐλείποντο).

[37] LXX: 0. NT: 1 Cor 6.1; Jas 1.5; 1 Pet 4.15. Philo: 0×. Josephus: 3×.

[38] Some expositors wish to clarify that all lack wisdom to some degree; cf. Pareus, 542-43; Guyse, 564; Cox, *Expositions* (as in n. 7), 78.

[39] On wisdom and 'perfection' see above, 156.

[40] As in Wis 6.17; m. 'Abot 2.7. On wisdom in James see Luck, 'Weisheit'; Hoppe, *Hintergrund*, 18-71; Hartin, *Q*, 81-115; Frankemölle, 561-91; Konradt, *Existenz*, 249-65; Hartin, 75-81; Cheung, *Genre*, 134-61; Burchard, 155-58; McCartney, 280-92.

[41] Contrast Prov 8; Mt 11.19; 7.35; 11.49; etc.

[42] Contrast Aymer, *Pure*, 73: in James, wisdom is not a 'what' but a 'who'. Cf. Hartin, *Q*, 134-37: for James, wisdom = Jesus. But that our book anywhere personifies wisdom is not evident; see further Konradt, *Existenz*, 258-60. Also, and against Bieder, 'Existenz', 111; Kirk, 'Wisdom'; and Hartin, *Q*, 102-104, our epistle does not imply an equation of Wisdom with the Holy Spirit. See further Baker, 'Holy Spirit'; Cargal, 71-72. James develops no pneumatology; cf. Isaacs, 183. This is not to say that its author

contrast to 3.13-18) it has nothing directly to do with the tongue. Wisdom is instead a 'divine χάρισμα' (Huther, 39), the 'revelation addressing and directing' those who seek it.[43] It is a gift, enabling one, notwithstanding circumstances, to know and, above all, do God's will.[44] The background is in the Jewish tradition, where God gives wisdom to the deserving faithful.[45] It thus comes down from above (3.15).

Notwithstanding James' obvious and extensive debt to the wisdom tradition, and despite the usual thematic importance of a topic treated near a text's beginning, σοφία will occur again only in 3.13-18. In James, it is an important but not controlling idea. Here, in vv. 5-8, our author fails to elaborate upon σοφία, immediately turning rather to the subject of prayer.

αἰτείτω παρὰ τοῦ διδόντος θεοῦ πᾶσιν ἁπλῶς καὶ μὴ ὀνειδίζοντος. Cf. Wis 7.7 ('Therefore I prayed, and understanding was given me; I called upon God, and the spirit of wisdom came to me');[46] Pss. Sol. 5.13-15 ('Human kindness is grudging and tomorrow, and if it comes a second time without complaint, this is remarkable. But your gift is abundantly good and rich, and the one whose hope is in you will not be lacking gifts. Lord, your mercy is upon the whole world in goodness'); Philo, *Leg.* 1.34 ('God loves to give and so bestows good things on all, even those who are not perfect'); Plutarch, *Mor.* 63F ('I imagine the gods confer benefits...since it is their nature to take pleasure in the mere act of being gracious and doing good'). αἰτέω[47] + παρά (= שאל + מן)[48] + θεοῦ/θεῶν or an equivalent was a common idiom.[49]

---

[43] Barth, *CD* III/1 41.1 ed. Bromiley and Torrance (1958), 52-53, citing Jas 1.5-6.

[44] But Evagrius, *Log.* 26 SC 438 ed. Géhin, Guillaumont, and Guillaumont, 244-46, applies Jas 1.5 to 'knowledge (γνῶσιν) of discernment'.

[45] See 1 Kgs 3.9-12; 2 Chr 1.7-13; Prov 2.6; Wis 7.7; 8.21; 9.4, 9-10, 17; Ecclus 1.1-4; 24.1-22; 51.17; 1 En. 101.8; b. Nidd. 70b; b. Ber. 33a, 55a, 58b; ARN B 43; etc.; cf. Eph 1.17; Col 1.9; Ign. *Pol.* 1.3; Pry. Jacob 17 ('Fill me with wisdom').

[46] Many have associated the text from Wisdom with James; e.g. Bonaventure, *Lk* 8.18 Opera Omnia 10 ed. Peltier, 426; Oesterley, 422; Frankemölle, 214; Burchard, 59; Popkes, 96; *et al.*

[47] αἰτέω of prayer: 1.6; 4.2-3. προσεύχομαι of prayer: 5.13-14, 17-18. εὔχομαι of prayer: 5.16. εὐχή of prayer: 5.15. προσευχή of prayer: 5.17.

[48] As in Deut 10.12; Judg 8.24; 2 Sam 3.13; m. Ned. 4.6; etc.

[49] 1 Βασ 1.17 (ὁ θεός...δῴη σοι πᾶν αἴτημά σου, ὃ ᾐτήσω παρ᾽ αὐτοῦ; cf. v. 27); 3 Βασ 3.11 (ᾐτήσω παρ᾽ ἐμοῦ, sc. τοῦ κυρίου); LXX Ps 2.8 (αἴτησαι παρ᾽ ἐμοῦ [τοῦ κυρίου] καὶ δώσω σοι); Prov 30.7 (αἰτοῦμαι παρὰ σοῦ, sc. τοῦ θεοῦ); Philo frag. 27 (αἰτεῖν παρὰ θεοῦ); T. Abr. RecLng. 8.7 (ὁ θεός says: δώσω σοι ὅσα ἂν αἰτήσῃς παρ᾽ ἐμοῦ); 9.4 (ὃ ᾐτησάμην παρὰ σοῦ, sc. τοῦ ὑψίστου), 5 (αἰτοῦμαι παρὰ σοῦ, sc. τοῦ κυρίου); Herm. *Vis.* 3.10.6 (ὃ αἰτεῖς παρὰ τοῦ κυρίου); Apoc. Sed. 2.1 (αἰτῆσαι παρ᾽ αὐτοῦ, sc. τοῦ θεοῦ); Ps.-Plato, *Eryx.* 398E (προσευχόμενος αἰτεῖς παρὰ τῶν θεῶν δοῦναί σοι ἀγαθά); Xenophon, *Cyr.* 1.6.5 (αἰτεῖσθαι τἀγαθὰ παρὰ τῶν θεῶν); Artemidorus, *Onir.* 4.2 (αἰτεῖν τι παρὰ θεοῦ); Libanius, *Ep.* 1249.3 (αἰτεῖν παρὰ τῶν θεῶν); etc.

---

necessarily had none, only that, if he did, his silence entails that we know nothing about it. Perhaps he preferred 'wisdom' over 'spirit' because he believed it would more easily establish common ground with non-Christian Jews.

Although God grants wisdom—does James imply that human beings cannot gain wisdom apart from the deity?[50]—it is not given indiscriminately. It rather comes to those who seek it, or rather ask for it.[51] The divine gift does not annul human responsibility.

James will return to the subject of prayer in 5.13-18, where those suffering are exhorted to pray. This makes for a nice thematic link with 1.5 and so creates a sort of *inclusio* that spans the epistle, for it is precisely those suffering the trials of 1.2-4 who pray in 1.5-8.

The theme of God's exceptional giving—a popular Jewish sentiment[52]—is here expressed by διδόντος[53] + ἁπλῶς,[54] another traditional idiom.[55] ἁπλῶς, as well as the related noun, ἁπλότης (= 'simplicity', 'liberality', or 'integrity'),[56] and the adjective ἁπλοῦς (= 'single' or 'sincere'),[57] often describe virtuous human beings.[58] In James, the subject instead is God.[59] Yet in this particular, the deity may be an implicit model for human beings, as many exegetes infer.[60]

---

[50] Cf. 3.15; Augustine, *Nat. et. grat.* 16(17) CSEL 60 ed. Urba and Zycha, 243-44; *Ep.* 214 CSEL 57 ed. Goldbacher, 387.

[51] Cf. Didymus of Alexandria, *Zech.* 3.1 SC 84 ed. Doutreleau, 614. At the same time, Spurgeon, 283 observes: 'No form of asking is prescribed, no words laid down, no method dictated... But there it stands in gracious simplicity, "let him ask".' Cf. Bonaventure, *Lk* 12.11 Opera Omnia 10 ed. Peltier, 555.

[52] Note e.g. Ps 145.15-19 (with 'all' repeated); T. Gad 7.2 (God 'provides good and beneficial things for all humanity'); Philo, *Leg.* 1.34 ('God loves to give, and so bestows good things upon all'); *Cher.* 123 ('God is...a free giver of all things, pouring forth eternal fountains of free bounties, and seeking no return'); Mek. on Exod 18.12 ('The Holy One...gives to all their wants and to everybody according to their needs').

[53] δίδωμι: 1.5; 2.16; 4.6 (with 'God' as subject); 5.18 (with 'heaven' as subject).

[54] NT: 1. LXX: Prov 10.9; Wis 16.27; 2 Macc 6.6. Gk. Pseudepigrapha (Denis): 4×. Philo: 22×. Josephus: 1×. For relevant background see J. Amstutz, *ΑΠΛΟΤΗΣ*, Bonn, 1968; Wypadlo, *Gebet*, 67-94. It is worth noting, given the use of τέλειος and ὁλόκληρος in 1.4, that the LXX can render תם with ἁπλότης (2 Βασ 15.11), תמם (Hiphil) with ἁπλοῦν (Job 22.3).

[55] See n. 58; also Aristotle, *Soph.* 181B (τῷ ἁπλῶς δόντι); Plutarch, *Demetr.* 19.6 (διδοὺς ἁπλῶς); Aelius Aristides, *Or.* 3.497 (ἁπλῶς δόντες); Demosthenes, *Cor.* 179 (ἔδωκ'...ἁπλῶς); etc.

[56] Cf. Wis 1.1; T. Job 26.6; 2 Cor 11.3; Eph 6.5; Col 3.22; Herm. *Vis.* 1.2.4.

[57] Cf. Prov 11.25; Ps.-Phoc. 50; Mt 6.22 = Lk 11.34.

[58] Cf. T. Reub. 4.1; T. Sim. 4.5; T. Levi 13.1; T. Iss. 3.2, 4, 6-8; 4.1-2, 6; 5.1, 8; 6.1; 7.7; T. Benj. 6.7; Rom 12.8 (ὁ μεταδιδοὺς ἐν ἁπλότητι); Herm. *Mand.* 2.4 (δίδου ἁπλῶς). In the Testaments of the Twelve Patriarchs, such simplicity and sincerity are set over against διπλόος (T. Benj. 6.6, 7) and διπρόσωπος (T. Ash. 2.1–3.2; 4.1-3; 6.2). Cf. Jas 1.5-8 (with δίψυχος) and see Amstutz, *ΑΠΛΟΤΗΣ*, 64-85.

[59] Cf. Philo, *Leg.* 2.2 (ὁ θεός...φύσις ἁπλῆ); T. Iss. 3.7 ('Jacob knew that God collaborated τῇ ἁπλότητί μου'). Divine simplicity became a Hellenistic *topos*: Plato, *Resp.* 382E (ὁ θεὸς ἁπλοῦν); Philo, *Her.* 183; *Abr.* 122; etc. See Amstutz, *ΑΠΛΟΤΗΣ*, 53-54.

[60] Cf. Bonaventure, *Lk* 19.8 Opera Omnia 11 ed. Peltier, 103; Aquinas, *Summa* 2/2 q. 117 a. 6; Wordsworth, 14; Paretsky, 'Two Ways', 317 n. 27; Hartin, 68; *et al.* Cf. Sifra Shemini 1 (43d): 'Just as he (God) is singular in the world, so let your service be singular before him'.

Prayer in James is directed to God (the Father), not Jesus Christ. That is to be expected and is in accord with Christian liturgy up to and including most of the fourth century. Less expected in a Christian work is no mention of prayer being 'through Jesus Christ' (Rom 1.8; Col 3.17) or 'in his name' (Eph 5.20).[61] In this particular James remains in the Jewish tradition.

For a few commentators, ἁπλῶς means not 'unreservedly'[62] but 'generously',[63] so that one thinks of individuals who do not fully deserve what they get. Matthew 20.1-16, where those who have worked less than some are not paid the less for it, would then supply a parallel. Most, however, hold that the Greek suggests less God's excess liberality and more God's undivided intent or unreservedness.[64] In this case, one might translate, 'without second thought'.[65] Such a rendering is preferable.[66] (i) Hermas, which supplies so many parallels to the vocabulary and thought of Jas 1.5-8, uses ἁπλῶς in connection with giving to mean 'unreservedly'.[67] (ii) James has a habit of putting two near synonyms side by side,[68] and ἁπλῶς stands beside μὴ ὀνειδίζοντος. (iii) 'Unreservedly' stands as an appropriate contrast to the divided individual of v. 8; cf. the contrasts in 1 Clem. 23.1-2 (ἁπλῇ διανοίᾳ is set over against μὴ διψυχῶμεν); T. Benj. 6.7 ('Every work of Beliar is διπλοῦν and has no ἁπλότητα'). (iv) James knew Ecclesiasticus, and in LXX 20.14, the gift of a fool profits nothing, for the fool has 'many eyes instead of one'—that is, gives with multiple motives.

---

[61] The phrase in Jas 5.14, ἐν τῷ ὀνόματι τοῦ κυρίου, is naturally interpreted in the light of 5.10—'the prophets who spoke ἐν τῷ ὀνόματι κυρίου'—and the latter cannot refer to Jesus.

[62] Cf. LXX Prov 10.9; Epictetus, *Diatr*. 2.2.13.

[63] See esp. Hort, 7-9. Cf. Grotius, 1074; Bloomfield, 483; Ropes, 139-40; Johnson, 179. This is the translation of the AV and NRSV. The Vulgate has *affluenter*; cf. Rheims and 2 Cor 8.2; 9:11, 13; Josephus, *Ant*. 7.332 ('the king admired him for his ἁπλότητος'); Plutarch, *Mor*. 63F (unlike the gods, who enjoy being gracious and doing good, the flatterer lacks ἁπλοῦν); as well as the use of ἁπλοῦς in Mt 6.22 = Lk 11.34. On this last see H.J. Cadbury, 'The Single Eye', *HTR* 47 (1954), 69-74. The meaning of ἁπλότης in T. Iss. 3.8 ('In the ἁπλότητι of my heart I supplied everything from the good things of the earth to all the poor and the oppressed') is unclear.

[64] E.g. Bouman, 53; Bassett, 6; Mayor, 39, and 25-26 of 'Further Studies', printed at the end of the volume; Belser, 44; Knowling, 10; Dibelius, 77-79 (with full discussion of the relevant texts); Marty, 16; Spicq, 'ἁπλότης', *TLNT* 1.172-73; Davids, 72-73; Martin, 18; Moo, 59; Hartin, 59; Popkes, 88-89; Maier, 62; McKnight, 86-87; Wenger, *Kyrios*, 160-62; Wypadlo, *Gebet*, 93-94. Cf. Tyndale and Cranmer: 'indifferentyle'.

[65] Cf. Polybius 27.13.2.3, of Ptolemy: ἐδίδου δ' ἁπλῶς οὐδὲν οὐδενί.

[66] But according to Laws, 55, the author probably intended both meanings. Cf. Isaacs, 184.

[67] Herm. *Mand*. 2.4: 'Give unreservedly [δίδου ἁπλῶς] to all who need'; cf. *Sim*. 2.7. Also relevant is *Sim*. 9.24.2-3, where God sees the ἁπλότητα of those who give from 'the fruit of their labors without upbraiding (ἀνονειδίστως) or doubting'.

[68] From the immediate context note e.g. 1.4 ('perfect' and 'complete'), 6 ('driven' and 'tossed'), and 11 ('its flower falls' and 'its beauty perishes').

πᾶσιν[69] is not universal, although the thought that God, through the natural processes, is good to all[70] would presumably have been congenial to James.[71] Given that vv. 6-8 know of those who do not receive, one must understand 'all' to be hyperbole, to mean 'all who ask in faith without doubting'.[72] This includes, in the light of 1.1, faithful Jews as well as Christians.[73] Similarly, 'without reproach' must apply to 'all (Jews and Christians) who ask in faith without doubting'.

What, if anything, does μὴ ὀνειδίζοντος[74] add?[75] Ecclesiasticus 20.15 speaks of the one who gives (δώσει) little and reproaches (ὀνειδίσει) much,[76] and 41.22 counsels one not to upbraid (μὴ ὀνείδιζε) after making a gift (τὸ δοῦναι; cf. 18.15-18). Whether or not those lines are echoed here,[77] the point is that ungracious gift-giving, which presumably involves

---

[69] Riesenfeld, "ΑΠΛΩΣ. Zu Jak 1,5', shows that ἁπλῶς, especially in connection with πᾶς, often means 'without exception'. But in James ἁπλῶς qualifies διδόντος; see BDF 474.5a.

[70] Let. Aris. 207 ('God guides all in kindness'); Mt 5.44-47 = Lk 6.32-35; Seneca, *Benef.* 7.26.1 ('If you are imitating the gods, you say, "Then bestow benefits also upon the ungrateful; for the sun rises also upon the wicked, and the sea lies open to pirates"'); b. Ta'an. 7a (God rains upon the wicked as well as the righteous); b. Šabb. 88b; b. Giṭ. 36b; etc.

[71] Spurgeon, 284, uses Jas 1.5 to go on at length about the goodness of God through the natural order—only then to admit that the passage probably has nothing to do with that subject. Here homiletics consciously triumphs over exegesis.

[72] Cf. Augustine, *Nat. et. grat.* 17(19) CSEL 60 ed. Urba and Zycha, 245: God gives wisdom to all 'who ask in such a manner, and to such an extent, as so great a matter requires in earnestness of petition'.

[73] Cf. Bassett, 7; Schlatter, 112. Note the parallel in t. Ber. 3.7 = y. Ber. 8b (4.4): 'Let it be your will...to give (שתתן) to each (כל) and every creature its lack (צרביה) and to each (כל) and every person his lack' (מחסורה). The gratuitous remark of Dimont, 631, that James stands 'in contrast to the Jewish representation' of God 'as a great and exacting creditor', is uninformed although sadly not idiosyncratic.

[74] ὀνειδίζω: Jas 1×; NT: 10×. LXX: most frequently for חרף. The NT uses it often of the persecution of Christians (Mt 5.11; Lk 6.22; 1 Tim 4.10 v.l.; 1 Pet 4.14) or the treatment of Jesus (Mt 27.44; Mk 15.32, 34; Rom 15.3). The verb is associated with ἁπλᾶς in Philodemus, *Περὶ εὐσεβαίας* frag. 6, but the context is fragmentary.

[75] Stylistically it accords with James' habit of following a positive assertion with a corresponding denial; cf. Schulze, *Charakter*, 64-65, and note esp. 1.6, 17, 22, 23; 5.12.

[76] Cf. y. Ber. 7d (4.2): 'do not let our welfare depend upon the gifts that come through the hands of flesh and blood...because their giving is little and their reproach great'.

[77] So Frankemölle, 219-20. Also comparable are Sib. Or. 2.272-73 (many of the wicked 'ὀνειδίζουσιν when they give from the fruit of their own labors'); Pss. Sol. 15.13 ('Human kindness is sparing, and tomorrow, if it [kindness] comes a second time without grumbling, this is marvelous'); 1 Pet 4.9; Did. 4.7 ('You shall not hesitate to give, nor will you grumble when you give'); Barn. 19.11 ('You shall not hesitate to give, and when you give you shall not grumble'); Sent. Sextus 339 ('Whoever combines gift-giving with ὀνείδους acts insultingly'); Seneca, *Benef.* 2.10.4 ('it is a first and indispensable requirement, never to reproach a man with a benefit'; cf. 7.25.1-2). Further references in Mayor, 39-40; *Neuer Wettstein*, 1249-54. Burchard, 59, speaks in this connection of a 'widespread maxim'. 'Common sentiment' would be a more appropriate term.

taking offense when one's gift is not sufficiently appreciated, is foreign to God, who is gracious both before and after the giving.[78] Huther, 40, wonders whether there is not a 'side glance' at the rich (cf. 1.10-11) who give yet reproach. More common is associating μὴ ὀνειδίζοντος with the behavior of the father in the parable of the prodigal son.[79]

Calvin, 264, supposes that 'without reproach' is 'added in case a man should fear that he is approaching God too often. Among men, the most open-handed remember their previous donations, even if a man approaches them for aid repeatedly, and make excuse for another time; so that we grow ashamed to bother our fellow man, however generous, with too much asking. But with God, says James, there is no comparison. He is prepared to heap new benefits on top of the old, with neither limit nor calculation.'[80] For Wesley, 597, however, μὴ ὀνειδίζοντος encourages those who fret over much about past or present sins. Mayor, 40, takes this line of interpretation a step further: the words are 'intended to encourage those who were tempted to regard their trials [see 1.2-4] as a sign of God's displeasure for their sin'. Cargal, 64-65, even contends that the implicit readers hold that God rebukes the saints, that is, gives them wisdom through various trials (vv. 2-4). But these various interpretations read too much into the text, which remains silent on why individuals might worry about God's 'reproach'. Indeed, even to ask the question is to pass beyond what appears to be little more than a rhetorical way of saying that one may have utter confidence in the God who unreservedly gives gifts.[81]

καὶ δοθήσεται αὐτῷ. This precise phrase (with καί) occurs before James only in the LXX, in Ps 71.15 and Dan 5.7.[82] δοθήσεται (divine

---

[78] J. Schneider, 'ὄνειδος κτλ.', *TDNT* 5.240: people 'often accompany their gifts with discontented utterances which degrade and wound the recipient. But God gives and does not upbraid'. Cf. Plautus, *Amph.* prol. 41-47: Jupiter does not have 'the habit of casting in good people's teeth what good turns he's doing them'. In the Hebrew Bible, God sometimes takes away 'reproach' (LXX: ὄνειδος or ὀνειδισμός); see Gen 30.23; Josh 5.9; Ps 119.39; Isa 4.1; 25.8; Ezek 34.29; etc. But God can also do the opposite: Ezek 22.4; Joel 2.17-19.

[79] Lk 15.11-32; cf. Stevartius, 27; Johnstone, 41; Maier, 63; Wegner, *Kyrios*, 163-64; et al.

[80] Cf. Cassiodorus, *Ps* on 26(27).13-14 CCSL 97 ed. Adriaen, 241: 'God does not submit an account when He bestows. As the apostle James says, "Who gives to all..."'

[81] A few earlier exegetes worried that whereas James says that God gives without reproach, Jesus reproaches (ὀνειδίζειν) cities of Galilee in Mt 11.20. For this problem see Manton, 38-39. Moreover, some copies of Mk 15.34 have God reproaching (ὠνείδισας) Jesus, and one could argue that, were this reading original, Jas 1.5 would have encouraged its emendation.

[82] Cf. also Ecclus 15.17 (ינתן לו); LXX: δοθήσεται αὐτῷ); 4Q381 46 2 (ותנתן לי); t. B. Bat. 9.13 (תנתן לו); b. B. Qam. 129a (ותנתן לו). Even without the καί, secular Greek offers no instances of δοθήσεται αὐτῷ. By contrast, the expression appears 5× in the LXX (Lev 24.20; Ps 71.15; Prov 12.14; Ecclus 15.17; Dan 5.7; cf. Theod. Dan 4.16, for the Aramaic יתיהב לה), 5× in the NT (Mt 13.12; Mk 4.25; Lk 8.18; Acts 24.26; Jas 1.5).

passive) picks up διδόντος, αὐτῷ answers to τις ὑμῶν. This promise, which reflects not only the wisdom tradition but also, and like 5.13-18, the optimistic enthusiasm of primitive Christianity,[83] recalls especially the saying attributed to Jesus in Mt 7.7 = Lk 11.9, and some find a deliberate allusion to or use of that particular saying:[84]

Mt 7.7 = Lk 11.9   αἰτεῖτε καὶ δοθήσεται ὑμῖν
Jas 1.5   αἰτείτω... καὶ δοθήσεται αὐτῷ

One might object that the case falls short because the link between human petition and divine giving was at home in the Jewish tradition.[85] But the argument to the contrary persuades. In both lines (i) the subject is prayer, (ii) there is an imperatival form of αἰτέω, (iii) δοθήσεται is a divine passive, and (iv) the verb is followed by a personal pronoun in the dative. Moreover, (v) λαμβάνω appears in both Mt 7.8 = Lk 11.10[86] and Jas 1.7; (vi) James' remark on God's generosity has its thematic parallel in Mt 7.9-11 = Lk 11.11-13, which argues that God gives good gifts to God's children; (vii) whereas the synoptic unit concludes by speaking of ὁ πατήρ and δόματα ἀγαθά, Jas 1.17 says that every δόσις ἀγαθή comes from τοῦ πατρός; (viii) if the subject in Jas 1.5 is σοφία, the formulation

---

[83] Yet one should recall the common characterization of God or the gods as 'hearing', that is, as answering prayer, in the Graeco-Roman world: Plato, *Leg.* 931c ('it is natural for God to hearken especially to their prayers'); *Menex.* 247D; NDL 33 (θεῷ ἐπηκόῳ = 'to the god who hears'), 76 (Ἑρμῷ ἐπηκόῳ = 'to Hermos who hears'), 99 (Διὶ Διγινδηνῷ μεγάλῳ καὶ ἐπηκόῳ = 'for the great and listening Zeus Digindenos'); Dionysius of Halicarnassus, *Dem.* 30; etc.

[84] So e.g. Kern, 115; Alford, 277 ('The whole verse seems to be written in remembrance of Matt. vii.7-12'); Johnstone, 38; Knowling, 10; Belser, 45 ('certainly'); Easton, 24; Mussner, 69; Knoch, 150; Hoppe, *Hintergrund*, 40; Laws, 56; Deppe, *Sayings*, 67-70; Deiros, 68; Porter, 'Dipsuchos', 480-81; Hartin, *Q*, 174-76; Townsend, 10; Johnson, 180-81; Klein, *Werk*, 93; Tsuji, *Glaube*, 119-20; Bauckham, *James*, 85-86 ('the way in which James in these two verses re-expresses the teaching of Jesus on prayer is very similar to the way in which Ben Sira frequently re-expresses the wisdom of Proverbs'); Wachob-Johnson, 'Sayings', 439-42; Moo, 58; Maier, 62; Popkes, 87; Felder, 1789; Kloppenborg, 'Reception'; Blomberg-Kamell, 51. Cf. Augustine, *De spiritu et lit. ad Marc.* 32(56) CSEL 60 ed. C.F. Urba and J. Zycha, 214; *Catena Havniensis in Ecclesiasten* 8.17 CCSO 24 ed. Labate, 140-41; Bonaventure, *Lk* 11.9 Opera Omnia 10 ed. Peltier, 523; Calvin, 264; Poole, 881; Gill, 780; Karl Barth, *CD* III/4 ed. Bromiley and Torrance, Edinburgh, 1961, 106-107. Contrast Dibelius, 79; Burchard, 58-59. Oddly, given that v. 5 follows a paragraph in which the subject is trial and affliction (vv. 2-4), few—Benson, 30-31, being an exception—have called attention to the parallel in Mt 10.19-20; Mk 13.11; Lk 21.14-15, where those brought before authorities will be given what they are to say.

[85] See e.g. LXX 1 Chr 1.7; Ps 105.15 (ἔδωκεν αὐτοῖς τὸ αἴτημα αὐτῶν).

[86] According to Luz, *Matthew*, 1.357-58, Mt 7.8-11 = Lk 11.11-13 belonged with Mt 7.7 = Lk 11.10 from the beginning. Contrast Kloppenborg, *Gospel*, 112-14: the link to prayer should be attributed to Q's editorial work, so James shows direct or indirect knowledge of Q.

of Mt 7.7-11 = Lk 11.9-13 has regularly turned biblically literate minds to sayings about 'wisdom';[87] (ix) Jas 4.2 likely reflects knowledge of Mt 7.7 = Lk 11.9;[88] and (x) the synoptic logion was popular among early Christians.[89]

One also wonders whether there is a relationship between our text and 2 Chr 1.7-13:[90]

LXX 2 Chr 1.7-13	Jas 1.5
That night God appeared to Solomon in a dream and said, Ask (αἴτησαι) what I should give (δῶ) to you. Solomon said to God... Grant (δός) me now wisdom (σοφίαν)...	If any of you lack wisdom (σοφίαν), ask (αἰτείτω) God, who gives (διδόντος)... and it will be given (δοθήσεται)...

Three key words run throughout 2 Chr 1.7-13—σοφία (vv. 10, 11, 12), αἰτέω (vv. 7, 11 [three times]), and δίδωμι (vv. 7, 10, 12)—and these are precisely the key words of Jas 1.5.[91] It is no wonder that some commentators on James are reminded of Chronicles and that some commentators on Chronicles are reminded of James.[92] As Kloppenborg shows, moreover, there are additional possible parallels between the different versions of Solomon's prayer (see n. 90) and the initial verses of James.[93] For Kloppenborg, these suffice to establish that our author 'has constructed the ethos of the speaker by invoking the figure of Solomon, who stands behind "James" and whose virtues James evinces: he, like Solomon, knows *how* to obtain wisdom—by prayer to a god who rewards ungrudgingly; he, like Solomon, shows an abiding concern for the poor and he understands that justice involves defending the poor against rich aggressors; and he, besting the Deuteronomist's Solomon, is insistent that wisdom must always be practiced in the context of Torah observance.'[94]

---

[87] Cf. Prov 1.28 ('they will seek me [wisdom] diligently but not find me'); 8.17 ('those who seek me diligently find me'); Wis 6.12 (wisdom is 'found by those who seek her').

[88] See further the commentary on 4.2.

[89] Variants include Mt 21.22; Jn 11.22; 14.13-14; 15.7, 16; 16.23-24; Gk. Apoc. Ezra 7.13

[90] Cf. the other versions of the same materials in 1 Kgs 3.3-9; Ps 72; Wis 9.1-18; Josephus, *Ant.* 8.23-25. Bonaventure, *Lk* 18.1 Opera Omnia 11 ed. Peltier, 74, already associates James and the passage from the OT; cf. Lapide, 28; Schneckenburger, 11; Wordsworth, 14; Bassett, 7 ('an unmistakable reference'); Johnstone, 40; Weidner, 26; Spitta, 20; Townsend, 9; Knoch, 149; Hartin, 59, 66; Fabris, 63; *et al.*

[91] Note also the occurrence of πιστωθήτω (cf. Jas 1.6) in LXX 2 Chr 1.9.

[92] E.g. Radulph Ardentis, *Hom. de Sanctis* 9 PL 155:1524A; Alford, 276; Mayor, 38; Knowling, 9; Chaine, 9; Schneider, 6; Mitton, 29; Laws, 54; R.B. Dillard, *2 Chronicles*, WBC, Waco, 1987, 15 ('James may...be reflecting on this supreme example of the gift of wisdom'); McKnight, 87.

[93] Kloppenborg, 'Discourse', 259-67.

[94] Kloppenborg, 'Discourse', 265.

WISDOM, FAITH, DOUBT (1.5-8)

James nowhere informs readers how, that is, by what means, God gives wisdom to those who ask for it in faith.[95] Does wisdom come via sacred texts, an inner voice, providential circumstances, or some other channel? Whatever the answer, James presumably believed, as did Philo, that somehow God can directly instruct the faithful.[96] The theme of God as teacher appears in the Hebrew Bible,[97] where it develops into an eschatological expectation,[98] which some early Christians then made their own.[99]

Verse 6. This verse and the next two, which were presumably formulated in the knowledge that prayers often go unanswered,[100] do four things: they (i) move attention from God to human beings (note the adversative δέ); (ii) offer teaching that applies not just to prayer for wisdom but to prayer of any sort;[101] (iii) explicitly specify a condition that must be met if prayer is to be answered; (iv) implicitly explain why some prayers appear to have no effect: human beings, not God, are to blame.[102] All this prepares for the argument in 4.3, where unanswered prayer is explicitly mentioned.

αἰτείτω δὲ ἐν πίστει μηδὲν διακρινόμενος.[103] Cf. Herm. *Mand.* 9.6: 'Those who are perfect in faith (ὁλοτελεῖς...ἐν τῇ πίστει) make all their requests (αἰτοῦνται) trusting in the Lord, and they receive (λαμβάνουσιν) them, because they ask (αἰτοῦνται) unhesitatingly, without any doublemindedness' (διψυχοῦντες). The vocabulary borrows from previous verses. For αἰτέω see on 1.5. On πίστις, which seems to mean something like persistent trust full of expectation,[104] see on 1.3. It is more moral than

---

[95] Homileticians have been more expansive; cf. F.B. Meyer, *The Present Tenses of the Blessed Life*, New York, 1892, 135-36: 'It shall be given in the strong impression on the heart; in the clear conviction of duty; in the concurrence of circumstances; in the indication of slight symptoms which could only be discerned by the eye fixed steadfastly on the eye of God'. Barnes, 24, makes similar remarks. For T. Williams, 1360, this verse belongs to 'natural religion'.

[96] Philo, *Cher.* 127-28; cf. Cyril of Alexandria, *Trin.* 1.387 SC 231 ed. Durand, 136.

[97] E.g. Exod 4.12; Pss 25.5; 27.11.

[98] E.g. Isa 2.2-4; 30.20-21; Jer 31.31-34.

[99] Jn 6.45; 1 Thess 4.9. Further texts and discussion in S.E. Witmer, *Divine Instruction in Early Christianity*, Tübingen, 2008. Witmer does not discuss James.

[100] Cf. 4.3 and note Dibelius, 81: James is probably 'familiar with disappointments which such confidence [in prayer] has encountered, and therefore in 1:5 he urges his readers to pray for wisdom, in 4:3, to pray correctly, and in 5:16, to confess sins before prayer'.

[101] Cf. Klein, *Werk*, 92. He notes the unqualified τι of v. 7.

[102] Cf. 1.13 and the reasoning of Herm. *Mand.* 9.8: 'But if you grow weary, and are double-minded in your request, blame yourself and not him who gives to you'.

[103] 429T 630 2200 replace διακρινόμενος with ἀπίστων ὅτι λήψεται. This anticipates v. 7, makes the warning more ominous, and recalls 2 Clem. 19.2: 'the double-mindedness (διψυχίαν) and unbelief (ἀπιστίαν) that is in our breasts'.

[104] Others, however, equate 'faith' here with 'the faith' (= traditions and orthodoxy) of the church; so e.g. John of Damascus, *Imag.* 3.41 PTS 17 ed. Kotter, 143; Stevartius, 23-24 (there are three sorts of wisdom: i. wisdom given by the Holy Spirit; ii. doctrinal

intellectual, and it presumably characterizes not a moment but a life:[105] if the one whose prayers go unanswered is 'unstable in all his ways', surely the one whose prayers are answered is faithful 'in all his ways'. Against Burchard, 60, 1.6 does not entail that efficacious petitions must be Christian. The purported audience is Israel of the diaspora, not the Christian churches (1.1), and the object of faith in James is not Jesus but God.

ἐν πίστει, which recurs in 2.5, typically connotes, in secular literature (where it is uncommon), being trustworthy.[106] James rather reflects Christian usage, which took up Septuagintal usage (usually for the Hebrew בֶּאֱמוּנָ[ה])[107] and regularly made God or Jesus Christ the objects.[108] The contrast between doubt and faith likewise comes from Christian discourse; cf. Mt 21.21; Mk 11.23 (see below); Rom 4.20 (οὐ διεκρίθη τῇ ἀπιστίᾳ ἀλλ' ἐνεδυναμώθη τῇ πίστει); 14.23 (ὁ διακρινόμενος…οὐκ ἐκ πίστεως).[109] For μηδείς see on 1.4 and cf. Acts 10.20: μηδὲν διακρινόμενος.

James does not tell us exactly what he means by διακρινόμενος.[110] In the LXX, διακρίνω has three meanings: 'pass judgment', 'subject to thorough examination', 'argue'.[111] What of the middle in Jas 1.6? The possibilities are several—a psychological state of uncertainty,[112] a lack of

---

wisdom; iii. moral wisdom); Hammond, 689. Still others take ἐν πίστει to signal prayer 'in the name of Jesus Christ'; cf. Nicholas of Gorran, 67; Hus, 182.

[105] Cf. Bede *ad loc.* CCSL 121 ed. Hurst, 185: 'Let him, by living well, show himself to be worthy of being heard when he begs'. Bede equates faith with right conduct throughout one's life—a commonplace in Christian *paraenesis*; cf. Clement of Alexandria, *Strom.* 5.14 GCS 15 ed. Stählin, 335; *Apophthegmata Patrum* Poemen 69 PG 65.337D. Many, however, think of a single prayer or occasion. So e.g. Burkitt, 1016: 'The petitioner must be a believer; the thing asked for must be an object of faith, by being the subject-matter of some promise… Again, The manner of asking must be faithful, with a pure intention.' Cf. Sadler, 8; O. Holtzmann, 825; Haar, 42-43 (excluding prayer that belongs 'to daily ritual').

[106] E.g. Aristotle, *Rhet.* 1418A; *Mag. mor.* 2.11.5; Plutarch, *Pub.* 19.2; *Cic.* 41.4; etc. See further Spicq, 'πίτστις', *TLNT* 3.110-16.

[107] 4 Βασ 12.16; 22.7; 1 Chr 9.26; 2 Chr 31.12, 15, 18; 34.12; 3 Macc 6.25; Ps 32.4; Ecclus 41.16; 45.4; 46.15; 49.10; Hos 2.22; Jer 35.9; 39.41. Cf. Ps Sol. 17.40; T. Levi 16.5; T. Ash. 7.7.

[108] Cf. Gal. 2.20; 1 Tim 1.2, 4; 2.7, 15; 3.13; 4.12; 2 Tim 1.13; Tit 3.15; Heb 11.28; 1 Clem. 42.5; 60.4; Ign. *Magn.* 1.1; 6.1; *Trall.* 8.1; *Smyr.* 1.1; Pol. *Phil.* 9.2; Barn. 11.8; Acts Thom. 143; Acts Phil. 44, 91; etc. With one exception, these are all post-Pauline.

[109] Note however the comparable contrast in Philo, *Somn.* 1.12: τὰ ἐνδοιαζόμενα τῶν πραγμάτων ὅρκῳ διακρίνεται…καὶ τὰ ἄπιστα λαμβάνει πίστιν.

[110] διακρίνω: LXX: 30× (most often for a form of שפט). Gk. Pseudepigrapha (Denis): 9×. Philo: 89×. Josephus: 24×. NT: 19×; James: 3× (cf. 2.4, where the meaning is 'to distinguish'). Dibelius, 80, assumes that 'in faith' and 'without doubting' are synonymous, but the latter may be intended to add clarification to the former.

[111] Muraoka, *Lexicon*, s.v.

[112] So Calvin, 265: the saints should be so convinced of God's once-and-for-all promise that they will have no doubt about prayers being heeded. Cf. Dibelius, 80-81; Laws, 57; and the use of the verb in Prot. Jas. 11.2 ('When she [Mary] heard this she

faith caused by divided loyalties,[113] unsteadiness under oppressive circumstances,[114] a bad conscience.[115] Although commentators regularly argue for this or that choice, the text itself offers us nothing by which to decide. If, however, there is indeed a link with the Jesus tradition (see below), we should probably find in James what we find in Mark, in which case the meaning is 'doubt' or 'uncertainty'—a meaning BAGD, s.v., says is first attested in the NT. James is then saying that 'the chief and principal thing required in prayer, is that without all doubting we steadfastly believe that God our Father will grant what we do ask; so that it be neither unprofitable for us to receive, nor unfit for him to give'.[116] James does not combat unbelief but vacillating faith.[117] One recalls the function of ὀλιγόπιστος in Matthew and Luke.[118]

Spitaler has vigorously challenged this conventional interpretation.[119] Among his observations and claims are these: (i) In Classical Greek sources, the middle διακρίνομαι means, without exception, 'take issue, dispute'. (ii) Despite standard reference works, this meaning holds for all pertinent NT texts, including James. (iii) Patristic remarks on those texts do not give a new meaning to διακρίνομαι. (iv) The clear equation of διακρίνομαι with 'doubt' is late.

This writer is not persuaded. Spitaler has shown that a number of texts thought to establish a new Christian meaning do not do so (e.g. Jude 9, 22-23), or are at best ambiguous.[120] Nonetheless, the traditional position remains plausible. (i) As Spitaler concedes, Photius offers this definition of διακρίνομαι: ἀμφιβάλλει, ἀπιστεῖ, διαχωρί-

debated/doubted in herself'); also perhaps the use of διψυχέω in Did. 4.4 ('You shall not be of two minds [διψυχήσεις] whether it will be or not'; cf. Barn. 19.5).

[113] Ropes, 140-41: the doubter is one whose 'allegiance wavers', as 'is indicated by v. 7, which shows...that the kind of waverer whom James has in mind fully *expects* to receive some benefit from God.' Cf. Davids, 73. Criticism in Dibelius, 80. Perhaps Ign. *Magn.* 15.1, is comparable: 'Farewell in godly concord and may you possess a spirit that knows no ἀδιάκριτον'. But the meaning here is not transparent.

[114] So N. Baumert, 'Das paulinische Wortspiel mit κριν-', *Filologia Neotestamentaria* 15 (2002), 31.

[115] So Bede *ad loc.* CCSL 121 ed. Hurst, 185; Ps.-Oecumenius *ad loc.* PG 119.460A. One can compare Herm. *Mand.* 9.1, where the command not to be double-minded is clarified by the imperative not to say, 'How can I ask anything from the Lord and receive it after having sinned so greatly against him?'

[116] John Ponet, *Short Catechism* LCC 26 ed. T.H.L. Parker, 180. Cf. Cyril of Alexandria *ad loc.* PG 74.1008A; Theophylact *ad loc.* PG 125.1137B.

[117] Cf. Huther, 41: διακρινόμενος is neither Yes nor No but the conjunction of Yes and No.

[118] Mt 6.30; 8.26; 14.31 (ὀλιγόπιστε, εἰς τί ἐδίστασας;); 16.8; Lk 12.28.

[119] Spitaler, 'Dispute'; idem, 'Shift'; idem, 'Doubt or Dispute (Jude 9 and 22-23)', *Bib* 87 (2006), 201-22. For related arguments see Baumert, 'Wortspiel' (as in n. 114), 31; D. De Graaf, 'Some Doubts about Doubt', *JETS* 48 (2005), 733-55. De Graaf, 742, reads Jas 1.6 this way: 'Let him ask in faith, free from divided motives and divisive attitudes, for such a person is like an ocean wave'.

[120] The reason one cannot always establish one meaning rather than the other is obvious. If something is disputed, it is in doubt. The upshot is that, in a number of texts, both 'contest' and 'doubt' work equally well.

ζεται. At some point, then, διακρίνομαι indisputably came to be thought of in some Christian circles as religious doubt.[121] (ii) It remains credible that διακρίνομαι is antithetical to 'belief' in sentences such as Mt 21.21 (ἐὰν ἔχητε πίστιν καὶ μὴ διακριθῆτε) and Mk 11.23 (μὴ διακριθῇ ἐν τῇ καρδίᾳ αὐτοῦ ἀλλὰ πιστεύῃ). This is all the more so as the Synoptics do not, on the whole, prod one to think about disputing God whereas they do concern themselves often with religious doubt, including doubt in prayer.[122] Further, it seems natural to relate Mt 21.21 directly to 14.31, where Jesus addresses Peter with: ὀλιγόπιστε, εἰς τί ἐδίστασας; That is, if in 14.31 Jesus rebukes a 'little faith' that doubts (ἐδίστασας), in 21.21 he commends a faith that does not doubt (μὴ διακριθῆτε). (iii) διακρίνομαι and διστάζω appear to be synonymous in a passage in Cyril of Scythopolis, where Jas 1.6 is quoted: 'He who attempts to hear or say anything without faith labors in vain, unable to procure himself any benefit; but he who has attained a faith powerful in everything is able to do whatever he wishes, especially if he keeps this faith unwavering (ἀδίστακτον) and does not yield to unbelief (ἀπιστίαι) but is always vigorous and strengthened in his faith (πίστει), not hesitating or doubting (διστάζων ἢ διακρινόμενος). "He who doubts is like a billow of the sea, driven by the wind and tossed", and so on. I for my part place unwavering faith (τὴν ἀδίστακτον τίθημι πίστιν) as the origin, root, and foundation of the account of holy Euthymius.'[123]

(iv) διακρίνομαι is also most plausibly understood as 'doubt' in Chrysostom, *Rom. ad* 4.20 PG 60.461[124] as well as in Ps.-Oecumenius *ad* Jas 1.6 PG 119.457D[125] and Theophylact, *ad* Jas 1.6 PG 125.1137C.[126] (v) The interpretation of διακρινόμενος in terms of belief rather than debate is also reflected in a variant reading for Jas 1.6: 429T 630 2200 replace that word with ἀπίστων.

(vi) Herm. *Mand*. 9 is very closely related to Jas 1.5-8.[127] However one solves the source-critical issue, James and Hermas work with the same materials; and where James

[121] Cf. Suda, *Lex*. Δ 606: διακρίνεται· ἀμφιβάλλει, ἀπιστεῖ, διαχωρίζεται.

[122] Cf. Mt 6.30; 8.26; 14.31; 16.8; 17.20; 28.17; Mk 4.40; 9.24; Lk 1.20; 8.12, 25; 12.28; 20.5; 22.67. De Graaf, 'Doubts', contends that διακριθῇ ἐν τῇ καρδίᾳ in Mk 11.22-24 means 'divided in heart'. This requires translating ἀλλά in ἀλλὰ πιστεύῃ ὅτι as 'but also'.

[123] Cyril of Scythopolis, *V. Euthym*. 1 TU 49 ed. Schwartz, 5. This is the translation of R.M. Price, *Lives of the Monks of Palestine by Cyril of Scythopolis*, Kalamazoo, 1991, 1. Spitaler discusses this text in 'Shift', 20, but I cannot see that he effectively rebuts Price's interpretation: the context is all about faith or belief, not disputation.

[124] οὐ διεκρίθη· τουτέστιν, οὐδὲ ἐνεδοίασεν, οὐδὲ ἀμφέβαλε. Spitaler, 'Shifts', 23-24, argues that Chrysostom is in effect saying that Abraham did not object to God's promise. Is this not over subtle? Moreover, the parallel in *Scand*. 10.7 SC 79 ed. Malingrey, 154, so far from supporting Spitaler, refers explicitly to 'doubt' (ἀμφιβάλλειν). I am equally unpersuaded by Spitaler's reading of Theophylact, *Mk ad* 11.23 PG 123.617: ἐὰν μὴ διακριθῶμεν, τουτέστι, διστάσωμεν.

[125] ὁ γὰρ διακρινόμενος ἀμφίβολος ὢν περὶ τὰς ἑαυτοῦ αἰτήσεις.

[126] διακρινόμενος ἔστω, ὁ διαστέλλων ἑαυτὸν ἀπὸ βεβαίου πράγματος καὶ ἐνδοιάζων. Theophylact continues: οὗτος γὰρ οὐδὲ λήψεται, ἀμφίβολος περὶ τὸ ἐλπισθὲν γινόμενος.

[127] See above, 167-68. Cf. Ps.-Athanasius, *Doctr. Ant*. 1.9 PG 28.568B ('You then purify your reasoning and soul from all unclean evil and ask from the Lord [αἴτησαι παρὰ τοῦ κυρίου], and you will receive if you ask for something [λήψῃ εἴ τι αἰτήσῃ], because he does not abandon those who hope in him. For those who doubt [διστάζοντες] in God are the double-souled [δίψυχοι], and they will receive [λαμβάνουσιν] nothing at all of their requests. But those perfected in faith [ἐν πίστει] will receive all which they ask for with their whole soul. For every double-souled man [δίψυχος ἀνήρ]...');

has διακρίνομαι, Hermas has διστάζω.[128] (vii) The Latin tradition renders διακρίνομαι with *haesito* (e.g. Vulgate Jas 1.6). Spitaler regards this as 'interpretation', not accurate translation. Translations, however, typically reflect interpretive traditions; and how likely is it that *haesito*, in the relevant NT texts, represents a novel (mis)interpretation instead of an exegetical tradition? (viii) *Pace* Spitaler, it is hard to see that the classical sense works well in Jas 1.6.[129] Thinking in terms of disputing God and/or disputing others has nothing to do with the letter of James to this point. The issue of 'doubt', however, is already implicit within ἐν πίστει. Moreover, Spitaler's interpretation, if I understand it correctly, requires that someone who is disputing with God is at the very same time beseeching God for assistance. Does that make good sense? (ix) ὁ διακρινόμενος in James is δίψυχος. The latter word is rare in early Christianity. It occurs in James, 1 Clement, 2 Clement, and Hermas. All three of the extra-canonical sources associate δίψυχος with 'doubt': 1 Clem. 11.2 (διστάζοντες); 23.3 (διστάζοντες); 2 Clem. 11.2 (διστάζοντες); Herm. *Mand.* 9.5 (διστάσῃς, διστάζοντες). Should we not speak here of a tradition,[130] and are not the implications for Jas 1.6 patent?[131]

μηδὲν διακρινόμενος following ἐν πίστει in connection with prayer recalls Mk 11.22-24 = Mt 21.21-22:

Mk 11.22-24
Have faith (πίστιν) in God. Truly I tell you, if you say to this mountain,
Be taken up and thrown into the sea,
and if you do not doubt (μὴ διακριθῇ) in your heart,
but believe (πιστεύῃ) that what you say will come to pass, it will be done for you.
Therefore I say to you,

Jas 1.6-7
But ask (αἰτείτω) in faith (πίστει)

without doubting (μηδὲν διακρινόμενος)

Antiochus the Monk, *Hom.* 85 PG 89.1693A ('You then cleanse your heart from doubt [τοῦ διστάζειν], and ask from him [αἰτοῦ παρ' αὐτοῦ], and you will receive [λήψῃ] your request. But if ever you doubt [διστάζεις], you will not receive [οὐ λήψῃ]. For those who doubt [διστάζοντες] God, they are the double-souled [οἱ δίψυχοι], and they will gain nothing of their requests. But the perfect, who ask [αἰτοῦνται] for all in faith [ἐν πίστει], they prevail with the Lord, and they receive whatever they, undoubting [ἀδιστάκτως], ask for [αἰτοῦνται]').

[128] Spitaler, 'Dispute', 577-79, anticipates this objection. But the case against him does not require that Hermas knew James, nor is it clear why observing differences between James and Hermas carries much weight.

[129] According to Spitaler, 'Dispute', 572, who sees communal strife throughout James, 1.6 introduces '"the disputer" as an example of a person who fails to achieve the inner–outer life consistency that he exhorts the recipients of his letter to develop'.

[130] Cf. also Ps.-Ign. *Her.* 7 ed. Zahn, 270 ('Do not be δίψυχος in your prayer, for blessed is the one who does not doubt [μὴ διστάσας]'); Origen, *Frag. 1 Cor* 90 ed. Jenkins, 51 (ὁ δίψυχος οὐχ ἕστηκεν ἐν τῇ πίστει ἢ ὁ ἀμφιβάλλων περὶ τῶν κατὰ τὴν πίστιν πραγμάτων); Apost. Const. 7.11 ed. Funk, 398 ('Do not be δίψυχος in your prayer, whether it will come to pass or not. For the Lord said to me, Peter, on the sea: "O you of little faith; why did you doubt?"').

[131] As to why διακρίνομαι took on the meaning 'doubt', the question is open. Did someone use the word to translate the Aramaic פלג, which can mean both 'divide' and (in the passive) 'divided in opinion', that is, 'doubtful'?

Whatever you ask (αἰτεῖσθε) in prayer,
believe (πιστεύετε) that you will receive
(ἐλάβετε) it and you will   will receive (λήμψεται) anything[132]

Does James depend upon dominical tradition here?[133] In favor of this are not only the common appearance of four words in passages dealing with the same subject, prayer, but also James' use of the Jesus tradition elsewhere as well as the apparent popularity of the logion behind Mk 11.23-24.[134] The sentiment in James is in any case congruent with the Synoptic Jesus, who finds that he can do no mighty works when human faith is deficient (Mk 6.5).

ὁ γὰρ διακρινόμενος ἔοικεν κλύδωνι θαλάσσης ἀνεμιζομένῳ καὶ ῥιπιζομένῳ. ἔοικα,[135] which appears only twice in the NT, both times in James (cf. 1.23), here means 'be like'.[136] κλύδων[137] + θάλασσα (Jas: 1×) was a traditional expression.[138] Whether the image is of a full-blown storm[139] is unclear. Ps.-Oecumenius *ad loc*. PG 119.460, envisages waves

---

[132] Although the parallel in Mt 17.20 = Lk 17.6 does not mention doubt, this variant has also been cited to illustrate our text; see e.g. Radulph Ardentis, *Hom. de Sanctis* 9 PL 155.1524C.

[133] For Easton, 24, 'the source of these three verses [6-8] may unhesitatingly be pronounced to be the teaching of Jesus'. Cf. Theile, 21; Sadler, 7; Leahy, 910; Floor, 56; Hartin, *Q*, 196; Tsuji, *Glaube*, 120-21; Doriani, 25; Royster, 19. Note the association of the two texts in Zwingli, *Von Klarheit und Gewißheit des Wortes Gottes* 47 Corpus Reformatorum, Zwingli 1.379. For doubt that James here alludes to a particular logion see Deppe, *Sayings*, 74-77. An affirmative answer regarding dependence would be consistent with speaking either of an allusion designed to be perceived or of influence without such intention.

[134] Cf. Lk 17.6 (Q); 1 Cor 13.2; Gos. Thom. 48, 106.

[135] LXX: 0. Gk. Pseudepigrapha (Denis): 3×. It is common in Philo and Josephus.

[136] BAGD, s.v., cites for comparison Hesiod frag. 263: ποταμῷ ῥέοντι ἐοικώς Elsewhere the word means 'seem'—LXX Job 6.3, 25; Josephus, *Ant.* 3.183; Plutarch, *Per.* 30.2. Early Christian writers tend rather to use ὅμοιός ἐστιν.

[137] Jas: 1×. Cf. Lk 8.24; Gk. 1 En. 101.4; 102.1. LXX: 9×, most often for רעש. Sadler, 8, observes 'the similarity in sound' between κλύδωνι and διακρινόμενος (δ, κ, ν are common).

[138] Philo, *Gig.* 51 (κλύδωνι κυμαινούσης θαλάττης); *Mos.* 1.41 (κλύδωνα θαλάττης); T. Abr. RecLng. 19.12 (θαλάσσῃ κλυδωνίῳ); Ps.-Hippocrates, *Herm.* 19 (κλύδωνος θαλάσσης); cf. משברי־ים in Ps 93.4; גלי הים in Isa 48.18; סער ים in Tanḥ. Buber Noah 7; also LXX Isa 48.18 (ὡς κῦμα θαλάσσης); Lk 8.24 (τῷ κλύδωνι τοῦ ὕδατος; Moffatt, 12: 'It is perhaps an undesigned coincidence that the rebuke of Jesus to the disciples, "Where is your faith?" (in Luke viii. 24, 25) comes after the only other use of the Greek word for surge in the N.T.'). According to Hort, 10, κλύδων appears never 'to mean a "wave", but always "rough water"...or "roughness of water"'. BAGD, s.v., defines the word as 'a succession of waves, rough water'.

[139] As in 1 En. 101.4; Philo, *Gig.* 51; T. Abr. RecLng 19.12. Cf. the colorful elaboration in T.G. Selby, *The Unheeding God*, New York, n.d., 59: 'like the wave of the sea, which may be bent, deflected from its first course, moulded to the contour of any coast on to which it is driven at the will of the storm, sucked back into the sea out of which it came, or shattered into useless spray upon the rocks'. For the argument that James does not suggest a storm see Hort, 10-11.

WISDOM, FAITH, DOUBT (1.5-8) 183

drifting to and fro. As ἀνεμίζω (in the passive = 'driven by the wind') occurs nowhere else in the Greek Bible, as our author has a fondness for verbs ending in -ιζω, as the word is unattested before James, and as every occurrence of it thereafter, with one possible exception, appears to be Christian,[140] he may have coined it. ῥιπίζω[141] is a NT *hapax legomenon*. In the passive the word means 'blown by the wind'.[142] Sadler, 9, remarks, perhaps aptly: a wave 'has no will of its own' but is 'drawn by what is exterior to it'.[143]

This illustration from the natural world,[144] with its repetition in Greek (-ιζομένῳ... -ιζομένῳ), has reminded some readers of the NT of Peter's failure to walk on the sea.[145] Already Apost. Const. 7.11 ed. Funk, 398, connects the imperative, 'Be not of divided mind (δίψυχος) in your prayer', with this: 'For the Lord said to me, Peter, upon the sea, "O you of little faith..."' More to the point are the ancient texts that illustrate human instability by referring to the billowing or tossing waves of the sea, among which are Isa 57.20 ('the wicked are like the tossing sea that cannot keep still; its waters toss up mire and mud');[146] Ecclus 29.18

---

[140] The earliest occurrences are, to my knowledge, in Basil the Great, *Ep.* 42 LCL ed. Defarrari, 258 (not seemingly alluding to James); Chrysostom, *Exp. in Ps* 12.3 PG 55.154 (quoting James); Cyril of Alexandria, *Lk* PG 72.848 (also quoting James). The only use of the word that is not obviously Christian is in Scholia in Homerum on *Od.* 12.336: ἔνθα ἦν σκέπη πρὸς τὸ μὴ ἀνεμίζεσθαι. For related words see Hort, 10. Oddly enough, Hesychius, *Lex.* A 4689, defines ἀναψῦξαι as ἀνεμίσαι.

[141] LXX: Dan 2:35: ἐρρίπισεν αὐτὰ ὁ ἄνεμος. Gk. Pseudepigrapha (Denis): 1×. Philo: 2×. Josephus: 0×.

[142] Cf. Let. Aris. 70 ('the arrangement of the leaves seemed actually to receive a movement of breath in the air fanning [ῥιπίζοντος] them'); Philo, *Aet. mund.* 125 ('if water is not ῥιπίζοιτο by the wind'). It was not traditionally associated with θάλασσα. See further Hort, 10-11. He asserts that the verb was formed from ῥιπίς, fire-fan, not ῥιπή. But proper etymology may be no guide to James, who could have had in mind something thrown with force; cf. Bassett, 7.

[143] Contrast Hartin, 60: 'the person who doubts is not compared to the wave itself, but to the tempestuous sea that is blown about by the wind'. Dimont, 631, is not alone in claiming that ancient Jews were uncomfortable with the sea; cf. Maier, 63. Many commentators romantically think of James the brother of Jesus growing up near and observing the Sea of Galilee; so e.g. Bishop, *Apostles*, 184. Adamson, 59, even imagines that 1.6 'corroborates the ascription of this Epistle to the Lord's brother, James of Galilee'. But a literary commonplace proves no such thing.

[144] Cf. the similes in 1.10-11; 3.4, 6, 11-12. For other maritime analogies in wisdom literature see Prov 23.34 and Wis 14.5 (with κλύδων).

[145] Mt 14.28-33. See e.g. Stevartius, 29; Wordsworth, 15; Robertson, 67; Oesterley, 423; Cooper, 'Prayer', 274; Scaer, 43-44 ('James is holding up Peter...an example to all Christians to show that no one is exempt from the temptations of doubting and denial'). As noted, κλύδων appears only twice in the NT, in Jas 1.6 and in Lk 8.24, and the latter is Luke's version of Jesus walking on the sea. Bonaventure, *Lk* 1.9 Opera Omnia 10 ed. Peltier, 453, instead links Jas 1.6 with Herod's indecision over what to do with John the Baptist.

[146] LXX: 'But the wicked will be tossed like waves (κλυδωνισθήσονται) and will be unable to rest'. Schlatter, 115, thinks they may lie behind James.

('surety has destroyed many who were prosperous and tossed them about like a wave of the sea'); 33.2 ('A wise person will not hate the law but the one who is hypocritical about it is like a boat in a storm'); Philo, *Gig.* 51 (in each individual is 'the fierce mysterious storm in the soul, whipped into fury [ἀναρριπίζεται] by the wild blast of life and its cares'; one can 'wonder that another should find fair weather in the storm, or calm amid the surges [κλύδωνι] of the tempestuous sea'); 4 Macc 15.31 ('overwhelmed on every side in the flood of passions and by the mighty gales of your sons' torments'); Eph 4.14; Jude 14.[147]

Some exegetes try to divine a distinction between 'driven' and 'tossed'. Wesley, 597, following Bengel, 487-88, comments: 'driven from the wind—From without; and tossed—From within, by his own unstableness'. For Theile, 22, ἀνεμιζομένῳ is the cause, ῥιπιζομένῳ the result. Fruchtenbaum, 221, offers: 'The word *driven* means "to be driven laterally by the wind", and *tossed* means "to rise and fall by the wind". Therefore, this is two-dimensional instability, lateral and vertical.' All this is overdone. The two words, 'driven' and 'tossed', are near synonyms; the addition of the one to the other adds rhetorical force, not extra meaning; cf. REB: 'tossed hither and thither by the wind'.

Verse 7. The tone changes. The unhappy consequences of a lack of whole-hearted faith, of a lack of unanimity of heart and mind, now appear.

μὴ γὰρ οἰέσθω ὁ ἄνθρωπος ἐκεῖνος ὅτι λήμψεταί τι παρὰ τοῦ κυρίου.[148] Cf. 4.3: 'you ask and do not receive'. Perhaps Dibelius, 82, is

---

[147] Additional parallels: LAB 29.4 ('Do not let your heart be like the waves of the sea. But just as a wave of the sea understands nothing except what is in the sea, so let your heart ponder nothing else except what belongs to the Law'); Philo, *Sacr.* 90 (God brought you to Canaan not for you 'to be carried hither and thither, ever passive amid the swell and eddy and surges [κλύδωνα], but that quit of the wild sea you should spend your days under clear sky and in calm water, and reaching virtue as an anchorage or roadstead, or haven of most sure shelter, might there find a stable place of rest'); *Migr.* 148 ('Some are irresolute, facers both ways, lurching to either side like a boat tossed by winds from opposite quarters'); Ps.-Clement, *Ep. Clem. Jas.* 14.4 GCS 42 ed. Rehm, 17 ('the meeting of two seas' is like 'unreasonable people and those who doubt the promises of truth'); Demosthenes, *Or.* 19.136 ('a democracy is the most unstable and capricious thing in the world, ὥσπερ ἐν θαλάττῃ πνεύματι κῦμα ἀκατάστατον...κινούμενον'); Dio Chrysostom 32.23 (quoting Homer, *Il.* 2.144-46: 'Then stirred was the assembly, as the sea sends forth long billows on the Icarian deep, billows the southeast wind raises, with force rushing from out the clouds of Father Zeus...ἄστατον and evil is the populace, and θαλάσσῃ πάνθ᾽ ὅμοιον ὑπ᾽ ἀνέμου ῥιπίζεται'); Virgil, *Aen.* 12.486 ('Vainly he [Aeneas] tosses on a shifting tide, and conflicting cares call his mind this way and that'); Seneca, *Ep.* 23.7-8 ('wavering and unstable persons' are like objects swept along by a river or carried out to sea); 95.57 ('the rest of humanity continually ebb and flow in their decisions, floating in a condition where they alternatively reject things and seek them').

[148] 01 04*V **L**:G lack τι. So too 018 522 1241 *et al.* with λήψεται. The omission could be accidental, an eye having skipped from the ι in λήμψεται to the ι in τι.

right to cite BDF 452.2 and claim that here γάρ means 'to be sure' rather than 'for'. However that may be, the warning addresses the doubter of v. 6, not the one who prays in faith; and the focus is upon the human side of things: answered prayer requires faith.

Regarding οἴομαι,[149] it frequently means 'suppose' or 'imagine'.[150] Mayor, 42, notes that it 'is often used in Philo in a bad sense = δόξα, as opposed to ἐπιστήμη'. That seems so here, as also in LXX Job 11.2 and Phil 1.17: the person of doubt supposes *wrongly*.[151] The move from the second person of v. 5 to the more formal third person of vv. 6-8 distances the writer from those warned.[152]

ὁ ἄνθρωπος[153] ἐκεῖνος is, as in Mk 14.21, a likely Semitism. The LXX uses it to translate אִישׁ הַהוּא on several occasions.[154] Also as in Mk 14.21, 'that man' is derogatory, as a number of times in the Hebrew Bible.[155]

λαμβάνω[156] + object + παρά (cf. 1.5) τοῦ κυρίου was a conventional way of speaking.[157] 'The Lord' (for κύριος see on 1.1) is God the Father, not Jesus Christ, despite a few exegetes,[158] for surely the one who gives in v. 7 is the one who also gives in v. 5, namely, God; cf. v. 17. No Christology is implicit.

On τι, Bassett, 6, remarks: 'Much less the high and precious gift of wisdom'.

---

[149] LXX: 22×. Muraoka, s.v., gives the LXX meaning as: 'to assume as probable though not absolutely certain'. NT: 3×: Jn 21.25; Phil 1.17; Jas 1.7. BAGD, s.v., defines the word as 'to consider someth. to be true but with a component of tentativeness, think, suppose, expect'.

[150] Cf. the expressions in Mt 3.9 (μὴ δόξητε λέγειν ἐν ἑαυτοῖς); 5.17 (μὴ νομίσητε ὅτι); 4 Ezra 8.28 (*neque cogites*).

[151] Cf. further 1 Macc 5.61 ('the people suffered a great rout because, supposing [οἰόμενοι] to do a brave deed, they did not listen to Judas and his brothers'); 2 Macc 5.21 (of Antiochus—'supposing [οἰόμενος] in his arrogance that he could stand on the land and walk on the sea'); Josephus, *Ant.* 19.16 ('those who suppose [οἰομένοις] that good fortune is eternal').

[152] Burkitt, 1016, anxiously remarks that although 'doubtful and unbelieving persons' can 'expect nothing' when they pray, they nonetheless 'receive something'—because God yet gives to the undeserving. Cf. Hus, *ad loc.*, recalling Mt 5.45.

[153] Contrast ἀνήρ in v. 8.

[154] LXX Lev 17.9; Num 9.13; Deut 17.12; Job 1.1, 3; Jer 20.16. Cf. 11Q19 65.14; y. Ber. 6c (3.4); 14c (9.5); b. Pesaḥ. 91b; etc.

[155] E.g. Lev 17.4, 9; 20.3, 4, 5; cf. LXX Jer 45.4; 11QTemple 55.21; 56.10; 65.14; Mt 12.45; Mk 14.21. Cf. Huther, 42: 'in the whole mode of expression, there is something disparaging'.

[156] Cf. 1.12; 3.1; 4.3 (also of prayer); 5.7, 10.

[157] Cf. LXX Ps 23.5 (λήμψεται εὐλογίαν παρὰ κυρίου); Wis 5.16; Let. Aris. 225 (δῶρον εἰληφέναι παρὰ θεοῦ); Acts 20.24; 1 Cor 11.23; 4 Ezra 2.33, 39; Herm. *Mand.* 9.1.

[158] E.g. Grotius, 1074; Wolzogen, 183; Manton, 52; Knowling, 11; Schlatter, 115; Scaer, 46.

Verse 8. According to Calvin, 265, 1.8—clearly quoted by the Philiologus[159]—'can be read as a separate sentence, expressing a general comment on hypocrisy, but I think it is more like a conclusion to the foregoing teaching'. Calvin is likely right: v. 8, which addresses the same individual as the one warned in v. 7,[160] is a conclusion. It offers not a new exhortation but an explanation of v. 7: the two subjects are in apposition;[161] cf. the NRSV: 'for the doubter, being double-minded and unstable in every way, must not expect to receive anything from the Lord'.

ἀνὴρ δίψυχος.[162] Although ἀνήρ[163] occurs only twice in Wisdom, the other canonical wisdom writers favor it.[164] It is unclear to what degree the word in and of itself reflects a patriarchal outlook.[165] δίψυχος (cf. 4.8) may be unattested before James, yet he did not coin the term.[166] The word occurs twice in quotations from a lost Jewish apocryphon,[167] and it and its cognates, διψυχία and διψυχέω, occur often in early patristic literature.[168]

---

[159] Gk. Physiologus 23.6-7 ed. Muradyan, 127: 'Thus every double-minded man is unstable in all his ways. One should not walk two paths. Nor speak in two ways in prayer.' On the problem of dating this see the Introduction, 15-16.

[160] A few, however, have wanted to translate this way: 'For let not that person suppose that the double-minded...will receive anything from the Lord'.

[161] Cf. Ropes, 142, calling attention to similar constructions in 3.2, 8; and 4.12 and observing that this view 'underlies the punctuation of Cod. B and the rendering of the Peshitto'. So too Dibelius, 82. Contrast Burchard, 61.

[162] 61 88 326 378 *et al*. Chrys Cyr S:H^A A K:S^mss insert γάρ in second place. This increases the parallelism with vv. 6 and 7 and entails that v. 8 is not an independent statement.

[163] Jas: 6×. Contrast ἄνθρωπος in v. 7

[164] Proverbs: 144×; Ecclesiastes: 12×; Ecclesiasticus: 85×.

[165] See 146 n. 71. For Easton, 24, however, ἀνήρ 'shows that men alone are in mind: Jewish and early Christian ethical exhortations presupposed a male audience unless women are expressly named'.

[166] Burchard, 62, compares a number of other δι-words: δίγνωμος, διγνώμων, δίθυμος, διχόνους, δίφροντις, δίγλωσσος, δικάρδιος, δίκρανος, δίλογος, διπρόσωπος, δίστομος, δισώματος. Greek literature, moreover, displays a keen interest in the divided self; see C. Gill, *Personality in Greek Epic, Tragedy, and Philosophy*, Clarendon, 1996.

[167] 1 Clem. 23.3-4; 2 Clem. 11.2-4. The argument of Porter, '*Dipsuchos*', that James coined the word (so too Frankemölle, 238), fails to establish that the saying common to 1 Clem. 23.3-4 and 2 Clem. 11.2-4, which 1 and 2 Clement attribute not to James but to ἡ γραφή and ὁ προφητικὸς λόγος respectively, goes back directly or indirectly to James. J.B. Lightfoot, *The Apostolic Fathers: Clement, Ignatius, and Polycarp, Part One. Clement*, vol. 2, London, 1890, 81, argues that 1 Clement and 2 Clement both drew upon the lost Eldad and Modad for their use of δίψυχος; so too Allison, 'Eldad'. Aside from that, nothing excludes an origin in Judaism (see Lichtenberg, *Menschenbild*, 190-200), even if there are no indisputable uses of δίψυχος in extant non-Christian literature, Jewish or not.

[168] δίψυχος: 1 Clem. 11.2; 23.3; 2 Clem. 11.2; and often in Hermas. Literature: Wolverton, 'Double-Minded Man'; Marshall, 'Δίψυχος'; Knoch, *Eigenart*, 111-25; Porter, '*Dipsuchos*'; Paretsky, 'Two Ways'. διψυχία: 2 Clem. 19.2 and often in Hermas. διψυχέω: 1 Clem. 23.2; 2 Clem. 11.5; Did. 4.4; Barn. 19.5; and often in Hermas. Adamson, 60, appears implausibly to see the influence of James behind all these texts.

δίψυχος—an attribute inconsistent with wisdom—presumably represents the Hebrew idiom, לב ולב ('double heart') or שתי לבבות ('two hearts'), which is the antithesis of לב אחד = 'single heart'[169] or כל־לב = 'whole heart.'[170] Even though the LXX does not translate the one with the other,[171] this is the view of many commentators, and it is consistent with the other Semitisms in vv. 7-8 (ὁ ἄνθρωπος ἐκεῖνος, pleonastic ἀνήρ, ἐν πάσαις ταῖς ὁδοῖς αὐτοῦ). One should note that, in LXX Deut 6.5, ἐξ ὅλης τῆς καρδίας and ἐξ ὅλης τῆς ψυχῆς are parallel,[172] and if a 'whole heart' and 'whole soul' are synonymous or nearly so, it would seem to follow that a double heart (שתי לבבות/לב ולב) would entail a double soul (δίψυχος).

The various meanings of לב ולב—the copula expresses more than one kind (GCK 123-24)—and שתי לבבות appear from the following: 1 Chr 12.34 ('to serve David without double purpose', לב ולב); Ps 12.3 ('with flattering lips and a double heart', לב ולב; LXX: ἐν καρδίᾳ καὶ ἐν καρδίᾳ);[173] 1QH 12(4).14 ('They [hypocrites] look for you [God] with a double heart', לב ולב);[174] 4Q542 1 1.9 ('holding on to the truth and walking in uprightness and not with a double heart [לבב ולבב, Aramaic], but with a pure heart and with a truthful and good spirit'); 1 En. 91.4 ('Do not draw near uprightness with a double heart [kāle' leb], and do not associate with hypocrites'); Mek. on Exod 14.3 (Pharaoh's heart was divided—לבו חלוק—whether to pursue the Israelites); b. B. Bat. 12b ('Before eating and drinking a person has two hearts' [שתי לבבות], but after eating and drinking there is only one heart'); Tanḥ. Buber Ki-Tavo 3

On the later Christian disinclination to use δίψυχος much see Paretsky, 'Two Ways'. He contends that the word did not fit the idea either of humans as triadic or of the soul as struggling against the flesh and spirit; cf. Gal 5.17. By contrast, the antonym, ὁλόψυχος/ ὕχως, became quite popular.

[169] See 2 Chr 30.12; Jer 32.39; Ezek 11.19; 4Q183 1 2.4; 4Q215a 1 2.8; b. Ber. 57a; etc. Note also the prayer Ps 86.11: יחד לבבי = 'unify my heart'.

[170] See Deut 6.5; 2 Kgs 23.3; Ps 119.2, 34, 145; Zeph 3.14; Ecclus 7.27; CD 15.9, 12; 1QS 5.8-9; 1QH 6.26; T. Levi 13.1; etc.

[171] See further Seitz, 'Afterthoughts'; 'Antecedents'. One should not however overlook the parallels outside the biblical tradition, such as Homer, Il. 16.435 (διχθὰ δέ μοι κραδίη); 20.32 (δίχα θυμόν); Theognis 1.91 (δίχ'...νόον); Herodotus 6.109 (δίχα αἱ γνῶμαι); Plato, Resp. 554D (the rascal will be at war with himself and so οὐδὲ εἷς ἀλλὰ διπλοῦς); Xenophon, Cyr. 6.1.41 (δύο...ψυχάς).

[172] The point is the stronger as the LXX uses ψυχή to render (ב)לב on over two dozen occasions.

[173] The connection of this verse with Jas 1.8 has long been a staple; see already Cassiodorus, Ps on 11(12).2(3) CCSL 97 ed. Adriaen, 118; cf. Lapide, 37—attributing the quotation from James to Solomon. But against Hanson, 'Report', 526, signs that part of Jas 1 is 'a midrash on Psalm 12' are lacking.

[174] Is this an allusion to Ps 12.3? Note also Ecclus 2.12 v.l.: 'Woe to double hearts [613 755: καρδίαις δισσαῖς; 421: καρδίαις δυσαῖς; Vetus Latina: duplici corde] and to slack hands and to a sinner treading a double path'. Both Bede ad loc. CCSL 121 ed. Hurst, 185, and Martin of Legio ad loc. PL 209:187A, cite this last. One might also take note of the divided heart of Hos 10.2: חלק לבם.

('When you pray to the Holy One, you will not have two hearts [שתי לבבות], one before God and the other directed toward some other object'). One Hebrew expression or the other presumably lies behind the lost Semitic original of Ecclus 1.28: 'Be not faithless to the fear of the Lord, nor approach him with duplicity of heart' (ἐν καρδίᾳ δισσῇ).[175]

The use of שתי לבב/לב ולב or δίψυχος in connection with prayer, found in James, Tanḥuma, and probably Ecclesiasticus, as well as in Herm. *Mand.* 9; Apost. Const. 7.11 (see 130 above); and Apoc. Elijah 1.26,[176] must have been traditional; and one recalls the importance of an undivided heart for prayer in rabbinic literature.[177] An association with doubt was also likely traditional, for this appears not only in James but also in 1 Clem. 11.2 ('Those who are double-minded [δίψυχοι] and have doubts concerning the power of prayer incur judgment'); 23.3 ('Wretched are the double-minded [δίψυχοι] who doubt in their soul'—attributed to 'Scripture'); 2 Clem. 11.2 ('Wretched are the double-minded [δίψυχοι] that doubt in their heart'—attributed to 'the prophetic word'); and Herm. *Mand.* 9.5 ('For those who have doubts towards God, these are the double-minded [δίψυχοι], and they will not by any means obtain any of their petitions').[178] Moreover, given that Eldad and Modad is likely to have been the source behind not only 1 Clem. 23.2 = 2 Clem. 11.2 but also Jas 4.5,[179] one suspects the influence of that lost apocryphon in Jas 1.

The double heart involves divided loyalty or attention in 1 Chr 12.33; b. B. Bat. 12b; and Tanḥ. Buber Ki-Tavo 3 (cf. Ecclus 1.28-29), hypocrisy in Ps 12.3; 1QH12(4).14; and 1 En. 91.4.[180] James 1.8 belongs with the former texts: the individual who is double-minded exists in two worlds, in the world of faith and in the world of doubt.[181] Such a one is 'religiously schizoid',[182] or like those who 'limp with two different

---

[175] This line, which seems to be about prayer, has sometimes been cited in ecclesiastical commentaries as illustrating Jas 1.8; see e.g. Dionysius bar Salībī *ad loc.* CSCO 60 Scriptores Syri 101 ed. Sedlacek, 89.

[176] 'The one who is double-minded in his prayer is darkness to himself'. This may belong to the Jewish stratum of the Apocalypse, which was perhaps written before James.

[177] m. Ber. 5.1; t. Ber. 2.7; 3.6, 18; b. Ber. 30b; b. B. Bab. 164b; etc.

[178] Note also the tendency of Indo-European languages to associate doubt with the root for two—'duwo', as in the Latin 'duobus', the German 'Zweifel', the English 'doubt', the French 'doute', etc.

[179] See n. 167 above and the commentary below, 617-22.

[180] With the latter cf. Midr. Ps 12.1: 'with a double heart do they speak' means: 'there is one word in their mouths, and a different one in their hearts'.

[181] Cf. Herm. *Vis.* 3.4.3 ('the double-minded... question in their heart whether these things are so or not'); *Mand.* 9.5; *Sim.* 8.7.1-2 (the double-minded 'are neither alive nor dead' and 'are never at peace among themselves'). But in *Sim.* 9.21.1, the double-minded are like hypocrites, for they 'have the Lord on their lips but do not have him in their hearts'.

[182] Garland, 'Trials', 389. The Physiologus 16.5-11 ed. Muradyan, 113-14, likens the double-minded of Jas 1.8 to the onocentaurs that are half-man, half-ass.

opinions', as 1 Kgs 18.21 puts it.[183] Just as Jesus declares that one must decide between God and mammon (Mt 6.24 = Lk 16.13), and just as the risen Lord of Revelation rebukes the lukewarm for not being cold or hot (Rev 3.15-16), so James demands undivided faith.[184] Prayer is to be whole-hearted, not half-minded. One may compare the criticism elsewhere in James of those who lack integrity or wholeness (cf. 1.4), who listen and do not do (1.23), who have faith but not works (2.14-26), and who bless while they curse (3.9-10).

God, in biblical texts, seeks the 'whole/entire heart'[185] or 'singleness of heart' (Col 3.22) or 'purity of heart'.[186] This is indeed the fundamental demand of the Shema': 'You shall love the Lord your God with all your heart, and with all your soul, and with all your might'.[187] For James, this imperative is realized in 'the person who has consented to become the close friend of faith and of prayer' and 'lives in single-mindedness'.[188]

In rabbinic literature, the heart is closely related to the יצר הטוב (the good inclination) and to the יצר הרע (the evil inclination),[189] and in T. Ash. 3.2, being double-faced (διπρόσωποι) is linked with 'desires' (ἐπιθυμίαις) and (in some manuscripts) 'the inclination' (διαβούλιον).[190] This interests because James' use of ἐπιθυμία should be linked with the

---

[183] Midr. Ps 119.113 associates 1 Kgs 18.21 with the סעפים or 'double-minded' of Ps 119.113.

[184] Theodoret of Cyrus, *Ps* 62.5 PG 80.1333A, draws the connection with the saying of Jesus. So too Lapide, 37; Guyse, 565; Weidner, 28; Belser, 46; Hartin, 67; *et al.* The contrast between δίψυχος and 'faith' also appears in Herm. *Mand.* 11.1-2; cf. Theodoret of Cyrus, *Ps* 62.5 PG 80.1333A

[185] Cf. Deut 30.10; 2 Kgs 20.3; Ps 119.2; Jer 24.7; Joel 2.12; Wis 1.1; 1QS 5.8-9; Wis 1.1; T. Levi 13.1; Acts 8.37; Herm. *Sim.* 8.11.3; *Mand.* 6.1.5; 9.1-2.

[186] Ps 24.3; Mt 5.8; T. Naph 3.1; T. Jos. 4.6.

[187] See further 2 Chr 22.9 (Jehoshaphat 'sought the Lord with all his heart'); T. Benj. 6.5-7 ('The good set of mind does not talk from both sides of its mouth: praises and curses, abuse and honor, calm and strife, hypocrisy and truth, poverty and wealth, but it has one disposition, uncontaminated and pure, toward all men. There is no duplicity in its perception or its hearing... The works of Beliar are twofold, and have in them no integrity'); Sifre Deut 32 ('"With all your heart" (Deut 6.5): With all the heart that is within you; your heart should not be divided in regard to God').

[188] Ephraem, *Hymns Preserved in Armenian, no. 1* 3 CS 101, trans. Brock, 36.

[189] E.g. m. Ber. 9.5 (God is to be loved with 'all your heart' and with 'both of your inclinations, your good inclination and your bad inclination'); Sifre Deut 32 (see n. 187); Midr. Prov 12.20 ('Does man have two hearts [Ps 7.10]? Hence you must conclude that "hearts" refers to the inclination to good and the inclination to do evil'). See further F.C. Porter, 'The Yeçer Hara', in *Biblical and Semitic Studies*, New York, 1902, 110-11 (observing that the rabbis associated the two impulses with the two בs in the longer form of לב, that is, לבב; see e.g. Tanḥ. Buber Bereshit 7). The verb יצר is already associated with the heart in Gen 6.5, a text crucial for the rabbinic understanding of the two impulses; cf. also 1 Chr 28.9, with לבבות and יצר. Midr. Ps. 14.1 explains the plural לבבות this way: 'He meant the two hearts of the two inclinations, the heart that is evil because of the evil inclination and the heart that is good because of the good inclination'.

[190] On the numerous links between T. Asher and James see Cheung, *Genre*, 201.

יֵצֶר הָרַע.[191] So in its original setting James might have been taken to imply that those who doubt are double-minded because they do not successfully resist the evil inclination. This would help explain why 1.6b-8 comes down so hard on the doubter. There is, moreover, a close parallel in Hermas, for if *Mand.* 12.2.2 identifies ἡ ἐπιθυμία ἡ πονηρά = יֵצֶר הָרַע with 'the daughter of the devil', *Mand.* 9.9 equates διψυχία with that daughter.[192]

ἀκατάστατος ἐν πάσαις ταῖς ὁδοῖς αὐτοῦ. This clause, with its string of six sigmas, may indicate the consequence of being δίψυχος,[193] or it may rather just supply a rough synonym for δίψυχος. ἀκατάστατος,[194] which the LXX has only once—Isa 54.11: 'afflicted and unsettled (ἀκατάστατος) you have not been comforted'[195]—means 'restless' or 'unstable'.[196] It resonates with or carries forward the imagery of v. 6, where the doubter is like the billows of the sea.[197] A 'double-minded' individual who is 'unstable in all his ways' = 'the doubter' who 'is like a surging wave of the sea, driven and tossed about by the wind'. So, as Bloomfield, 484, has it: 'what was before expressed figuratively is now expressed in plainer terms'. The correlation makes plain that doubt (see vv. 6-7) goes with instability, that is, vacillation in conduct. We have here the antithesis of the blameless; cf. Ps 15.5: 'Those who do these things will never be moved'.[198]

---

[191] See below on 1.14; but contrast Burchard, 62.

[192] αὕτη ἡ διψυχία θυγάτηρ ἐστὶ τοῦ διαβόλου.

[193] Cf. Hort, 13. For Spitaler, 'Dispute', 570-71, ἀκατάστατος is the external manifestation of the internal δίψυχος; thus ὁ διακρινόμενος is described inside and out. Athanasius, *Decr.* 4.2 PG 25.421B-C, applies the line to Arians who in his view are guilty of changing their minds on dogmatic issues; cf. C. Nic.(787) 2 act. 6; Nicephorus I, *Ref. def. syn. an. 815* 77 CCSG 33 ed. Featherstone, 131. John Cassian, *Inst.* 7.15.1 SC 109 ed. Guy, 312, refers it to failed monastics who need to return to secular life.

[194] NT: Jas 1.8; 3.8. Gk. Pseudepigrapha (Denis): 2×. Philo: 0×. Josephus: 0×.

[195] Martin, 20-21: 'If there is an allusion taken from Isa 54:11, the maritime analogy from v. 6 is continued, since LXX has ἀκατάστατος as a rendering of סֹעֲרָה, *sō ʿărāh*, "storm-tossed"'. Note also MT Gen 49.4: Reuben is 'unstable/wanton as water' (פַּחַז כַּמַּיִם).

[196] Cf. Sib. Or. 1.164; T. Job 36.3-4 ('the earth and those who dwell in it are unstable'); Herm. *Mand.* 2.3 (slander is a ἀκατάστατον δαιμόνιον); Plutarch, *Mor.* 286C (birds in the mating season are 'unstable'); 437D (ἐμπαθῆ καὶ ἀκατάστατον); and note the ἀκαταστασία of Jas 3.16.

[197] Cf. Demosthenes, *Or.* 19.136, cited above, n. 147; also Dio Chrysostom 39.19 (one needs prayer in order to get rid of the vices that excite and disturb and to avoid being in a constant state of instability or thrown into confusion, 'just as happens at sea when contrary winds prevail'). Apart from the use of ἀκατάστατος in Symmachus Gen 4.12, the word is not associated with Cain, and against Hanson, 'Report', 526, one need not wonder about an allusion to that figure.

[198] Cf. T. Dan 4.7 ('when the soul is continually perturbed, the Lord withdraws from it and Beliar rules'); Orsiius in Apophthegmata Patrum PG 65.315B ('those who are firm in faith remain unmoved'). See further the long discussion in Wypadlo, *Gebet*, 159-68.

1.17 will affirm that God does not change but is always the same. Human instability is the antithesis of divine constancy.

ἐν πάσαις ταῖς ὁδοῖς αὐτοῦ is another Semitism—בכל דרכיו—known from both the Hebrew Bible and the Dead Sea Scrolls.[199] It means something like 'in all of one's conduct'; cf. v. 11: ἐν ταῖς πορείαις. Its comprehensive character, which πάσαις underlines, shows how far-ranging, for James, are the effects of doubt and double-mindedness.

In the texts cited in n. 199, בכל דרכיו and ἐν πάσαις ταῖς ὁδοῖς αὐτοῦ are positive: the ways are the ways of God or the just or (several times in the scrolls) of 'the perfect'. In James, however, the idiom describes not the way of faith but the way of doubt. 1QS 4.11 supplies precedent for this ironic use of a traditional idiom: 'walk in all the ways of darkness'.[200]

---

[199] Deut 10.12; 11.22; LXX 19.9; 30.16; Josh 22.5; 1 Βασ 18.14; 1 Kgs 8.58; Pss 91.11; 145.17; Prov 3:6; 1QS 2.2; 3.9-10; 5.4; CD 2.15-16; 2Q22 2.5; 4Q381 31 3; 11QPsᵃ 27.3. Cf. 1 En. 8.2; Jub. 36.23; b. Roš. Haš. 17b; y. Sanh. 23d (6.7); etc. ὁδός: Jas: 4×: 1.8 (figurative); 2.25 (literal); 5.19, (figurative), 20 (figurative).

[200] Cf. Prov 2.13. Also comparable are Herm. Mand. 5.2.7 (ἀκαταστατεῖ ἐν πάσῃ πράξει αὐτοῦ); Midr. Ps 119.46 ('I hate those who are of two minds' [Ps 119.113] refers to one 'who hates the way of life walks in the way of evil', to one who 'forks off from the ways of the Holy One').

IV

THE CONTRARY FUTURES OF POOR AND RICH (1.9-11)[1]

(9) But let the brother who is lowly glory in his exaltation, (10) and the rich by contrast glory in his humiliation, because like a flower of the field he will pass away. (11) For the sun rises and, together with the scorching wind, withers the grass, and its flower falls, and the beauty of its appearance perishes. So also the rich in the midst of his pursuits will fade away.

History of Interpretation and Reception

1.9-11 has, to judge by the relatively low number of relevant sermons and academic articles, garnered less attention than any other part of James. Its interpretation nonetheless has hardly been free of controversy. Contemporary critical exegetes have been most exercised over the identity of the rich. Were they within the community or without?[2] Opinion has been close to evenly divided. Earlier ecclesiastical commentaries tended to think of members of the ecclesia.

Those more or less comfortable with the economic circumstances around them, and especially those keenly aware of their church's dependence upon well-to-do benefactors, have been anxious to emphasize that the condemnation of the rich in 1.10-11 does not damn all with wealth. As Bede put it, James 'is speaking not about every rich person but only about the one who trusts in the uncertainty of riches. For in contrasting a rich man with a humble brother, he has shown that he was speaking about that sort of rich man who is not humble.'[3] Even stronger was T. Scott, 566: our text must not be taken to 'imply, that no rich man, however humble, poor in spirit, liberal, and condescending to his poor brethren, could have any ground of rejoicing, or glorying in Christ, in the hope of

---

[1] Recent literature: Ahrens, *Arm*; Bottini, 'Minaccia'; Dale, 'Temptation'; Garland, 'Trials'; Garleff, *Identität*, 248-51; Hainthaler, *Ausdauer*, 306-11; Hutchinson Edgar, *Poor*, 146-49; Irwin, 'Lilies'; Isaacs, 'Suffering'; Klein, *Werk*, 97-101; Konradt, *Existenz*, 145-48; Krüger, *Kritik*, 111-34; Lawrence, 'Note'; Maynard-Reid, *Poverty*, 38-47; Penner, *Eschatology*, 204-10; Stulac, 'Rich'; Tiller, 'Rich'; H. Williams, 'Rags'; R.L. Williams, 'Piety'; Wypadlo, *Gebet*, 168-82; Zahn, 'Frage'.

[2] See below, on v. 10.

[3] Bede *ad loc*. CCSL 121 ed. Hurst, 186, then cites Abraham as an example of a rich saint. Cf. Henry *ad loc*. ('Good Christians may be rich in the world'); Manton, 67 ('Riches are not altogether inconsistent with Christianity').

glory; unless he voluntarily relinquished, or were forcibly deprived of, his estate and possessions, and so reduced to entire poverty!' Scott turns v. 10 into a call for humility.[4]

In striking contrast, those uncomfortable with or antagonistic toward the wealthy—a distinct minority among commentators—have rather called upon 1.9-11 to criticize them. For example, Maynard-Read insists that the rich cannot have been members of James' community. Our letter rather condemns them, a circumstance Maynard-Reid finds supportive of his critical stance against contemporary economic structures.[5]

Still others have found not economic but religious polemic in our text. The Protestant Winkler, 20, attacked the Vatican for seeking 'temporal sovereignty and secular possessions'. T. Scott, 566, also turned vv. 9-11 against the Roman church. He denounced, however, not the proverbial wealth of the Vatican but, to the contrary, the Franciscans, who commend poverty: their 'doctrine [is] well suited to some order of papist, but not at all to genuine Christianity'.

Perhaps most exegetes have thought that the exaltation of the poor in v. 9 and the withering of the rich are events that will take place either at death or at the *parousia*.[6] According to Tamez, the boast of the lowly in 1.9 anticipates eschatological joy, and vv. 10-11 have to do with 'the future reversal of the present unjust order'.[7] Laurentius, *ad loc.*, even equated the rising of the sun with the second coming of Christ. Others, however, have wished to stress that the lowly are exalted even now. For Hort, 15, the lowly Christian exults 'not [in] any future elevation in this or the other world, but [in] the present spiritual height conferred by his outward lowliness, the blessing pronounced on the poor, the possession of the Kingdom of God'.[8] Perhaps most have found in 1.19 both present and future blessing. Gill, expansive as ever, is representative: the 'height of honor and grandeur, of which he may boast and glory, amidst his outward poverty, lies in his high birth and descent, being born from above, and of God and belonging to his family; in being an adopted son of God; and so an heir of God, and a joint-heir with Christ, and of the

---

[4] Cf. Ps.-Andrew of Crete, *Éloge* 4.29-34 ed. Noret, 46; Poole, 881; Gill, 780-81; Clarke, 800.

[5] Maynard-Read, *Poverty*. For Fruchtenbaum, 222, James stands against the so-called prosperity gospel, against 'name it and claim it' theology.

[6] Cf. Godfrey of Bouillon, *Hom—II. De sanctis* 9 PL 155.1525C (referring to 'eternal damnation' in connection with our verse); Hemminge, 7; Wells, 7; Weidner, 28; Dibelius, 84 (the imminent *parousia*); Mussner, 74; Vouga, 48; R.L. Williams, 'Piety', 43 (death); Scaer, 49; Isaacs, 185-86; Burchard, 64; Witherington, 432; Gundry, 920; *et al.* Contrast Pfleiderer, *Christianity*, 300: 'the Christian rich... are told in i. 10 that they ought to seek their glory in a (spontaneous) self-humiliation, in humbly taking the same level as their (in the worldly sense) inferior brother, who glories in his (spiritual) exaltation'.

[7] Tamez, *Message*, 42. Cf. Dibelius, 84 ('In vv 9-11, Jas voices the expectation of an imminent reversal of circumstances'); Blackman, 51; Blomberg-Kamell, 55; *et al.*

[8] For focus on the present rather than the future cf. Diodati *ad loc.*; Brosend, 43.

heavenly inheritance and kingdom; in the present riches of grace he is possessed of, as justifying, pardoning, and sanctifying grace.'[9]

Recent critical work has sought to avoid reading modern assumptions about wealth and poverty into a first-century text. It is, for instance, crucial to Batten, 'Poor', that people tended, in James' Graeco-Roman world, to think in terms of limited goods: goods are finite, so one person's gain is necessarily another's loss.[10] She thinks it equally important to understand, when interpreting James, that many in his world regarded wealth as in itself morally problematic and inevitably the result of greed.

By contrast, Christians in modern capitalistic societies often deny that goods are limited, in part because of their experience that technology can usually produce more of something; and they likewise may be convinced, with Adam Smith, of the economic virtue of self-interest. The complex hermeneutical questions all this might raise should be evident. Nonetheless, most ecclesiastical use of James continues to move from past text to contemporary situation with relative ease, as though wealth and poverty and their causes are cross-cultural absolutes.

Exegesis

1.9-11 is the third introductory subsection. The topic becomes God's exaltation of the poor and—this is where the stress lies[11]—the coming abasement of the rich.[12] What then is the link with the previous paragraph? Does it suffice to observe that here, as in 1.2-4 and 5-8, the text introduces a subject to which the letter will return, that is, that 1.2-11 is a bit analogous to a table of contents?

Bede finds two links with the immediate context: (i) it is wealth that makes people double-minded (v. 8); (ii) the lowly who boast about their high estate are the very same who reckon it joy when they encounter various trials (vv. 2-4).[13] Fewer interpreters exploit the first possible connection[14] than the second, which ties 1.9-11 to 1.2-4, so that poverty

---

[9] Gill, 780. Cf. Hus, 184; Simeon, 17-23; Easton, 24; Schrage, 18; Konradt, *Existenz*, 146. McKnight, 97, thinks v. 9 has in view the 'perfection' of vv. 2-4 but adds that being raised up now is a 'proleptic realization' of the eschaton.

[10] Here she relies upon G.M. Foster, 'Peasant Society and the Image of Limited Good', *American Anthropologist* 67 (1965), 293-315; idem, 'A Second Look at Limited Good', *Anthropological Quarterly* 45 (1972), 57-64; J.H. Neyrey and R.L. Rohrbaugh, 'He Must Increase, I Must Decrease', *CBQ* 63 (2001), 468-76.

[11] So already Hilary of Arles *ad loc*. PLSupp 3.65, observing that vv. 10-11 are longer than v. 9.

[12] Exegetes often compare Lk 1.46-56, the Magnificat, where God sends the rich away empty and lifts up the lowly; cf. Lapide, 39; Punchard, 357; Moo, 65; Isaacs, 185; Fabris, 71; Brosend, 43; Blomberg-Kamell, 63; McKnight, 96; Royster, 21; *et al.*

[13] Bede *ad loc*. CCSL 121, ed. Hurst, 185-86.

[14] Others who connect the double-minded with the problems of wealth and/or poverty include Ps.-Oecumenius *ad loc*. PG 119.460C-D; Theophylact *ad loc*. PG 125.1140B;

is an instance of the sort of trial referred to in 1.2-4[15] or so that the boasting of v. 9 is related to the rejoicing of v. 2.[16] Still other proposals have been forwarded—that the boast of the lowly is the remedy for double mindedness,[17] or that wealth (rather than poverty) can be one of the trials of true faith,[18] or that the link between 1.9-11 and 1.5-8 is purely formal: both present antitheses, the one believer versus doubter, the other poor versus rich.[19] Then there are those who deny any real connection between 1.9-11 and its immediate context[20] or who fail to address the issue.[21]

In this writer's judgment, 1.5-8 and 9-11 have been formulated so as partly to mirror one another. Both (i) open with a third person singular present imperative that ends in -ω; (ii) feature an antithetical contrast—in vv. 5-8 faith receives what it asks for and doubt receives nothing whereas in vv. 9-11 the humble are exalted and the rich pass away; (iii) link the two contrasts by means of a catchword connection (αἰτείτω/αἰτείτω in vv. 5-6, ταπεινός/ταπεινώσει in vv. 9-10); (iv) commence with a positive example but focus upon and conclude with a negative example; (v) cite an illustration from the natural world (v. 6, vv. 10-11); (vi) use γάρ to introduce that illustration; (vii) end with similar phrases (ἐν πάσαις ταῖς ὁδοῖς αὐτοῦ/ ἐν ταῖς πορείαις αὐτοῦ); and (viii) contain almost the same number of words (vv. 5-8: 55; vv. 9-11: 54).

In view of all this, and because the units immediately before and after 1.9-11 clearly relate themselves to vv. 2-4 and the theme of trial, it is natural to connect also vv. 9-11 with that theme. So vv. 2-4 introduce the

---

Lapide, 38; Wandel, 41; Hort, 14 ('poverty, riches, and the change from the one to the other may be among the "ways" in all of which the waverer is found unstable'); Spitta, 25; Lawrence, 'Note'; Tasker, 42; Mitton, 99; Haar, 43 (linking doubt to wealth); McKnight, 94. Ewald, 187, rather finds in vv. 9-10 instances of what poor and rich Christians should pray for.

[15] Cf. Martin of Legio *ad loc.* PL 209.187D-188A; Lapide, 38; Manton, 21 (calling 1.5-8 a 'digression'; so too Burkitt, 1016; Bisping, 18); Wells, 5; Theile, 26; Kern, 118; Huther, 44-46; Bouman, 59; Smith, 52; Fulford, 41 (calling attention to the Litany from the Book of Common Prayer: 'In all time of our tribulation; in all time of our wealth... Good Lord deliver us'); Plummer, 575; Ropes, 144; O. Holtzmann, 825; Hodges, 22 (remarking that vv. 5-8 are parenthetical); Kotzé, 80-83; Isaacs, 185.

[16] Cf. Beyschlag, 55; Mitton, 33.

[17] So Bengel, 488; Wesley, 597. Cf. Martin, 24: the readers who remain faithful in poverty will avoid becoming double-minded.

[18] So Martin, 22-23 (although he also suggests that 'poverty provides an arena for the testing of one's faith in God', 24). For Barnes, 25-26, reversal of circumstances—from poor to rich or rich to poor—is a sort of trial.

[19] So Schnider, 8; Windisch-Preisker, 7.

[20] Most famously Dibelius, 83-84 ('the hopelessness of establishing any connection in thought, and the dubiousness of finding any external length'; cf. 70). Cf. Belser, 50; Oesterley, 424; Schrage, 17; Cantinat, 76 (1.9-11 is 'un ensemble indépendant'); Laws, 62.

[21] E.g. Poole, 881; Henry *ad loc.*; Trapp, 694.

subject; vv. 5-8 discuss the wisdom that is required for enduring trials; vv. 9-11 put difficulties in eschatological perspective by foretelling the fate of both poor (= oppressed; cf. 2.6; 5.4-6) and rich (= oppressor; cf. 2.6-7; 5.4-6);[22] and vv. 12-18 serve to clarify that, although trials may come, God is not the author of bad things. Such a reading is supported by the similar sequence in 4.13–5.11, where the rebuke of the rich who oppress the poor (4.13–5.6) is immediately followed by a paragraph on the *parousia* of the eschatological judge and the saints' 'endurance' (cf. 1.2-4) to the end (5.7-11).

1.9-11, which prepares for 2.1-7, 14-16; and 4.13–5.6, is artfully constructed. Two formally parallel but antithetical imperatives are followed by an elaboration of the second:

first imperative	καυχάσθω δὲ ὁ ἀδελφὸς ὁ ταπεινὸς ἐν τῷ ὕψει αὐτοῦ
second imperative	ὁ δὲ πλούσιος ἐν τῇ ταπεινώσει αὐτοῦ
Elaboration (with future tense)	ὅτι ὡς ἄνθος χόρτου παρελεύσεται
Elaboration of elaboration (aorist series)	ἀνέτειλεν ὁ ἥλιος
	καὶ ἐξήρανεν τὸν χόρτον
	καὶ τὸ ἄνθος αὐτοῦ ἐξέπεσεν
	καὶ ἡ εὐπρέπεια…ἀπώλετο
Résumé (with future tense)	οὕτως καὶ ὁ πλούσιος…μαρανθήσεται

If, as the history of interpretation suggests, 1.9-10 is indeed oriented to the last judgment, then it is pertinent to observe that, in Jewish and Christian documents, that judgment generally functions in one of three ways—to console, to exhort, and/or to rebuke. How is it with James? Is the author consoling the lowly or exhorting the rich or condemning the rich? The question arises also in chaps. 4–5, where James again addresses the rich and again condemns them. Many deem the direct address to be rhetorical posturing, a way of speaking indirectly to one group while pretending to speak to another: the real targets are not the rich but the 'poor folk who are impressed by the power and status which wealth provides'.[23] This commentary, however, takes the envisaged audience of 1.1 to be the Jewish diaspora, which would include rich as well as poor and all in between. So whoever as a matter of history heard James read, the implied readers belong to all classes. Our letter operates with the assumption that James of Jerusalem had the authority to encourage both poor Jews and to rebuke rich Jews.

---

[22] But for Brosend, 40, the passage is 'not about possessions as such as much as about status'.

[23] Cf. L.E. Keck, 'The Poor among the Saints in the New Testament', *ZNW* 56 (1965), 117. He writes: 'Their weakness is not a wistful recollection of previous wealth which they gave up when they became "the Poor" but their tendency to honor the rich man more than is really warranted or proper (2 1-7). A church…which consists of members who impoverished themselves to enter it, does not face this problem.' Contrast Klein, *Werk*, 99-100: the implicit audience is neither rich nor poor but people between them.

Although commentators typically observe that James recalls Isa 40.6-7, Davids, 77, leaves the impression that we may have here little more than an ornamental borrowing of traditional scriptural language: although there is 'perhaps some rough allusion' to Isaiah, 'one cannot press this, for the verbal parallels are equally close' to LXX Ps 102.15-16, and 'the saying had certainly been or become a common proverb'.[24] It is not evident, however, that any part of Jas 1.9-11 preserves a proverb,[25] and Davids seemingly overestimates the parallels with the psalm[26] while overlooking the degree to which Jas 1.9-11 reflects the language of Isa 40.2-9:

(Isa 40.2) Speak, priests, to the heart of Jerusalem. Comfort her, for her humiliation (ταπείνωσις) is fulfilled, her sin is put away. For she has received double from the Lord's hand for her sins. (3) A voice of one crying in the wilderness, Prepare the way of the Lord, make straight the paths of our God. (4) Every valley will be filled, and every mountain and hill will be brought low (ταπεινωθήσεται)... (6) A voice of one saying, Cry; and I said, What will I cry? All flesh is grass (χόρτος), and all the glory of humanity is as the flower of grass (ὡς ἄνθος χόρτου). (7) The grass withers (ἐξηράνθη ὁ χόρτος) and the flower falls (καὶ τὸ ἄνθος ἐξέπεσεν), (8) but the word of our God abides forever. (9) Go up on a high (ὑψηλόν) mountain, O proclaimer of good tidings to Zion; lift up (ὕψωσον) your voice with strength...lift it up (ὑψώσατε)...

(Jas 1.9) Let the brother who is lowly (ταπεινός) glory in his exaltation (ὕψει), (10) and the rich by contrast in his humiliation (ταπεινώσει), because like a flower in the field (ὡς ἄνθος χόρτου) he will pass away. (11) For the sun rises and, together with the scorching wind, withers the grass (ἐξήρανεν τὸν χόρτον), and its flower falls (καὶ τὸ ἄνθος αὐτοῦ ἐξέπεσεν), and the beauty of its appearance perishes. So also the rich in the midst of his pursuits will fade away.

---

[24] Cf. Estius, 382-83; Beyschlag, 58; Spitta, 26-27. Contrast Wolzogen, 184; Barnes, 27 ('it is probable that James had his eye on the passage'); Gibson, 3 ('a clear reference'); Belser, 52; Weidner, 28 ('quotation'); Bennett, 148; Oesterley, 425; Dibelius, 86; Grosheide, 18-19; Scaer, 50-51; Vouga, 47; Hanson, 'Report', 526 ('a midrash on Isa. 40.6-7'); Deppe, *Sayings*, 43-45; Frankemölle, 246-47; Penner, *Eschatology*, 204-10; Fabris, 74; Hartin, 62-63 ('certainly alludes'); Burchard, 65; Nienhuis, *Paul*, 181-85; Blomberg-Kamell, 63 ('clearly alluding'); Batten, 'Poor', 72; McKnight, 102.

[25] Davids cites two texts to buttress his claim, namely, T. Job 33 and Pliny the Elder, *N.H.* 21.1. The former says that 'the whole world will pass away and its splendor shall fade', and that 'kings will pass away, and rulers come and go; but their splendor and boast shall be as in a mirror'. For the latter see below, on v. 11.

[26] Which are confined to two words:
LXX Ps 102.15-16   χόρτος...   ἄνθος τοῦ ἀγροῦ
Jas 1.10-11   ἄνθος χόρτου... τὸν χόρτον καὶ τὸ ἄνθος

The shared vocabulary is considerable:

Isa 40.2-4	ταπείνωσις...	ταπεινωθήσεται	
Jas 1.9-10	ταπεινός...	ταπεινώσει	
Isa 40.6	χόρτος...	ὡς ἄνθος χόρτου	
Jas 1.10		ὡς ἄνθος χόρτου	
Isa 40.7	ἐξηράνθη ὁ	χόρτος καὶ τὸ ἄνθος	ἐξέπεσεν
Jas 1.11	ἐξήρανεν τὸν	χόρτον καὶ τὸ ἄνθος αὐτοῦ	ἐξέπεσεν
Isa 40.9	ὑψηλόν...	ὕψωσον...ὑψώσατε	
Jas 1.9		ὕψει	

When one adds that the first part of Isa 40 was popular among Christians[27] and that it appears to have been important for various groups within Judaism,[28] we may infer that it was a well-known portion of the Bible and that the observed parallels constitute an allusion: the informed reader of James is supposed to think of Isa 40.

James' use of Isa 40.6-7 to characterize the wealthy wicked lines up with the interpretation of the targum. For whereas the MT and LXX apply the imagery to human beings in general,[29] the targum thinks of the wicked in particular: '(6) All the wicked are as the grass, and all their strength like the chaff of the field. (7) The grass withers, its flower fades, for the spirit from the Lord blows upon it; surely the wicked among the people are reckoned as the grass. (8) The wicked dies, his conceptions perish; but the word of our God abides forever.' Beyond the concordance of James with the targum, the antiquity of this application is further established by 2 Bar. 82.7: 'And we think about the beauty of their gracefulness while they go down in impurities; but like grass which is withering, they will fade away'. This clear allusion to Isa 40.6-7 also has to do with the wicked; see 82.1-6. Similar is the eschatological application in Midr. Ps 1.20: 'There will come a time when the wicked will be blown like grass from the face of the earth, as it is said, "The grass withers, etc." In this world the righteous are smitten, but in the world-to-come they will have firm footing and great strength.'

---

[27] Quotations: Mt 3.3 (Isa 40.3); Mk 1.3 (Isa 40.3); Lk 3.4-6 (Isa 40.3); Jn 1.23 (Isa 40.3); 1 Pet 1.24-25 (Isa 40.6-9); Barn. 9.3 (Isa 40.3); Justin, Dial. 50.3 (Isa 40.1-17). Allusions: Mt 24.35 (Isa 40.8); Lk 2.25 (Isa 40.1), 30 (Isa 40.5); 21.33 (Isa 40.8); Jn 12.15 (Isa 40.9); Acts 28.28 (Isa 40.5); Rev 1.5 (Isa 40.2); 18.6 (Isa 40.2); Sib. Or. 1.336-38 (allusion to Isa 40.3); 8.234 (Isa 40.4). Note also that Job 14.2 appears to depend upon Isaiah.

[28] See e.g. 1 En. 1.6 (allusion to Isa 40.4); 4QTanḥumin 1-2 1 (quoting Isa 40.1-5); 1QS 4.2 (allusion to Isa 40.3); 8.13-14 (quotation of Isa 40.3); 9.19-20 (allusion to Isa 40.3); Pss. Sol. 8.17 (allusion to Isa 40.3); 11.4 (allusion to Isa 40.4); T. Mos. 10.4 (allusion to Isa 40.4); LAE 10.2 (allusion to Isa 40.6); 2 Bar. 82.7 (see above).

[29] This happens again in later, incidental uses of Jas 1.11; e.g. Braulio of Saragossa, Ep. 19 PL 80.666C.

One final remark concerning Jas 1.9-11 and Isa 40. The theme of the latter is preparing the 'way' (ὁδός) of the Lord, and there is a second use of 'way' (ὁδός) in Isa 40.4. So one wonders whether the use of 'way' (ὁδός) at the end of Jas 1.8 played its part in the process that led our author to Isa 40.[30]

Given the attribution of our book to James (1.1), one should note that 1.9-11, which exalts the poor and debases the rich, harmonizes with Christian memories of that figure. Galatians 2.10 has it that he, along with Cephas and John, asked Paul to remember the poor, and Hegesippus reported that James was an ascetic Nazarite who wore linen instead of wool.[31]

Verse 9. As with the introductory v. 5 in the previous paragraph, so too here: the passage opens with an imperative.

The chiastic structure of 1.9-10 is this:

Shame	Let the brother who is lowly
Honor	glory in his exaltation
Honor	but the rich
Shame	in his humiliation

This has the same structure as the aphoristic saying in Mt 20.16 and Lk 13.30 (cf. *Teach. Silv.* 104.21-24):

Shame	The last
Honor	will be first
Honor	and the first
Shame	will be last

James 1.9-10 also resembles the paradoxical, anti-proverb of eschatological reversal in Lk 14.11:

Honor	The one who exalts himself
Shame	will be humbled,
Shame	and the one who humbles himself
Honor	will be exalted[32]

Beyond the structural parallels is a similarity in thought. James, like the complexes in the Jesus tradition, offers not common sense akin to Prov 29.23 ('A person's pride will bring humiliation, but one who is

---

[30] Cf. Penner, *Eschatology*, 207.
[31] Hegesippus *apud* Eusebius, *H.E.* 2.23.4-5.
[32] See also Mt 10.39 = Lk 17.33; Mt 23.12; Mk 8.35; 10.31; Lk 18.14; Gos. Thom. 4. There is also a close rabbinic parallel. In b. Pesaḥ. 50a, Rabbi Joseph ben Joshua catches a glimpse of the next world, which is 'topsy-turvy', for 'those who are on top here are at the bottom there, and those who are at the bottom here are on the top there'.

lowly in spirit will obtain honor') but rather eschatological forecast. It is true that the divinity does, in some texts, exalt the humble and humble the exalted even now.[33] Proverbial wisdom, however, knows that the rich get richer and the poor get poorer. In contrast to this, Jas 1.9-11 looks beyond the present, as the future tenses (παρελεύσεται, μαρανθήσεται) and the tenor of the whole book intimate. James has in mind the eschatological turning of the tables, in anticipation of which the lowly may even now rejoice; cf. Mt 5.3-12; Lk 6.20-23. This conclusion is confirmed by the circumstance that James draws upon Isa 40, which received an eschatological reading from other Jews.[34]

καυχάσθω δὲ ὁ ἀδελφὸς ὁ ταπεινὸς ἐν τῷ ὕψει αὐτοῦ. This, like the call to rejoice in 1.2,[35] goes against the norm. The lowly typically mourn while the rich exult in their privileged status; cf. Ps 49.6. James, however, rejects the present arrangement as final. Despite appearances, God has chosen the poor; cf. 2.5. καυχάομαι[36]—here in emphatic position—recurs in 4.16, where traveling merchants arrogantly boast.[37] δέ is often regarded as transitional, a mild adversative that need not be translated.[38] It appears also in 1.5 and 22 to mark the turn from one subject to another. One can, however, also translate the particle with 'but' and draw a contrast with the double-minded of v. 8.[39] On ἀδελφός see on 1.2. Although Christian readers would identify themselves with the lowly brother, this commentary—against most others[40]—takes 1.1 to imply that 'brother' need not be an exclusively Christian term.

---

[33] E.g. Hesiod, *Op.* 6-7 (Zeus 'easily humbles the proud and raises the obscure'); Diogenes Laertius 1.69 (Zeus 'is humbling the proud and exalting the humble'); 1 Sam 2.4-5; Job 22.29; Ps 18.27; Prov 3.34; Ezek 21.26; Lk 1.52-53; Tanḥ. Buber Wayyetse' 10 ('as soon as He sees someone whose power is down, he gives him a hand and raises him up'); Ahiqar 60 ed. Lindenberger ('If [y]ou wis[h] to be [exalted], my son, [humble yourself before Šamaš], who humbles the [exalted] and [exalts the humble]'). Hilary of Arles *ad loc.* PLSupp 3.65, thinks of the exaltation of the Hebrew slaves and the humiliation of the Egyptians.

[34] See above; also K.R. Snodgrass, 'Streams of Tradition Emerging from Isaiah 40:1-5 and their Adaptation in the New Testament', *JSNT* 8 (1980), 24-25; Penner, *Eschatology*, 204-205; R. Davidson, 'The Imagery of Isaiah 40:6-8 in Tradition and Interpretation', in *The Quest for Context and Meaning*, ed. C.A. Evans and S. Talmon, Leiden, 1997, 37-55.

[35] Burchard, 63-64, observes that καυχάομαι connotes joy and so belongs with v. 2.

[36] NT: 37×, all in Paul and James (2×). LXX: 41×, most often for the Hitpael of הלל. Philo: 1×. Josephus: 1×. With the exception of Pss. Sol. 17.1, the verb, in the Gk. Pseudepigrapha, carries negative sense: T. Reub. 3.5; T. Jud. 13.2, 3; T. Iss. 1.9; T. Job 15.6; 41.3; T. Abr. RecLng. 19.4; 4 Bar. 1.6; 4.8. καυχάομαι is much more popular in Christian texts than in secular sources.

[37] Cf. κατακαυχάομαι in 2.13 (positive); 3.14 (negative).

[38] Cf. Benson, 31: here δέ = μέν.

[39] Cf. Winkler, 19; Maynard-Reid, *Poverty*, 39.

[40] Lapide, 38, is typical: 'Frater] id est, Christianus'.

ταπεινός[41] occasionally means 'humble' as a virtue,[42] and it became a common self-designation of Christians.[43] It usually, however, means 'miserable' or 'of low position'.[44] Many modern commentators, against the moralizing tendency of their exegetical predecessors, choose the second and more usual sense because of the opposition thereby created with 'rich' in v. 10. But in Jas 1.9 it may be unwise to set the two meanings against each other. For ταπεινός has an ethical sense in 4.6;[45] and just as both the Hebrew עני and Greek πτωχός can denote individuals who are economically poor and therefore spiritually dependent upon God,[46] so too is it sometimes impossible to distinguish the two senses of ταπεινός because both seem applicable.[47] It may be the same with our verse: the lowly are poor in fact and humble in spirit.[48] This was presumably the case with the alleged author, James of Jerusalem, for the traditions about him depict an ascetic of great spirituality and humility.[49]

The theme of the humble being exalted and the exalted being humbled appears, as already seen, in a number of ancient texts, Jewish, Christian, and pagan. But it is particularly prominent in the Jesus tradition, so

---

[41] NT: 8×; Jas: 2×; cf. 4.6; Isa 40.2. LXX: most often for עני and שפל.

[42] LXX Ps 33.19 (God will save 'the lowly [ταπεινούς] in spirit'); Let. Aris. 263 (God 'exalts the gentle and lowly [ταπεινούς]'); T. Gad 5.3 ('For the righteous and lowly [ταπεινός] is ashamed to do injustice'); Mt 11.29 (a virtue of Jesus); 1 Pet 5.5 (quotation of Prov 3.34); 1 Clem. 30.2 (quotation of Prov 3.34); cf. ταπεινοφροσύνη, as in Herm. Vis. 3.10.6 ('Every request needs humility', ταπεινοφροσύνης); Sim. 5.3.7 ('you shall thus be humble-minded that through your humility [ταπεινοφροσύνης] he who receives it may fill his soul and pray to the Lord for you'); etc. On the rarity of this usage see R. Leivestad, 'Ταπεινός – ταπεινόφρων', NovT 8 (1966), 36-47.

[43] Lampe, s.v., ταπεινός 7. One of the baptismal graffiti at Dura-Europos ends with: ΣΙΣΕΟΝ ΤΟΝ ΤΑΠΙΝΟΝ; cf. C.B. Welles, ed., The Excavations at Dura-Europos, vol. 8.2, New Haven, 1967, 95.

[44] E.g. 1 Βασ 18.23 (David's poverty: κἀγὼ ἀνὴρ ταπεινὸς καὶ οὐχὶ ἔνδοξος); LXX Ps 9.39 (the 'lowly' [ταπεινῷ] is coupled with the orphan); 81.3 ('Judge the orphan and poor; do justice to the low [ταπεινόν] and needy'); Josephus, Bell. 4.365 (a reference to 'humble' [ταπεινός] birth); Lk 1.52; Barn. 3.3 (do not despise 'the poor', ταπεινόν); Crates, Ep. 19 (Odysseus begged even from 'the poor', ταπεινούς).

[45] Quoting Prov 3.34; cf. also 4.10: ταπεινώθητε.

[46] Documentation in Davies-Allison, Matthew, 1.442-44. For the overlap of meaning between πτωχός and ταπεινός see Hatch, Essays, 73-77.

[47] Cf. LXX Ps 17.28 (God will save 'the lowly', ταπεινόν); Prov 3.34 (quoted in Jas 4.6); Isa 49.13 (God 'has comforted the lowly ones [ταπεινούς] of his people'); 2 Cor 7.6 (quotation of Isa 49.13); 1 Clem. 59.3 (God raises up 'the lowly', ταπεινούς); Did. 3.9 ('walk with righteous and lowly people', ταπεινῶν).

[48] Cf. Huther, 46 (the Christian is 'despised and persecuted by the world... is inwardly distressed... and walks in humility before God'); Blackman, 51; Maynard-Reid, Poverty, 40-41; Konradt, Existenz, 147-48 (emphasizing that, in 4.6-10, humility is set over against δίψυχος, and that 1.9 immediately follows a line with δίψυχος); Burchard, 64 (insisting that it is not a question of either/or but of emphasis). Unsurprisingly, Dionysius bar Salībī ad loc. CSCO 60, Scriptores Syri 101, ed. Sedlacek, 89, speaks of the 'poor in spirit'; cf. Mt 5.3.

[49] See especially the account of Hippolytus preserved in Eusebius, H.E. 2.23.4-18.

although 1.9-11 does not allude to any particular saying of Jesus[50]—the language of exaltation and lowliness is rather from Isaiah and has numerous parallels[51]—there is continuity in theme.[52]

The structure of v. 9—καυχάσθω + subject + ἐν τ. + noun [the object of glorying] + αὐτοῦ—seemingly has no classical parallel but does appear several times in the LXX:[53]

1 Βασ 2.10	μὴ καυχάσθω	ὁ φρόνιμος	ἐν τῇ φρονήσει	αὐτοῦ
ibid.	μὴ καυχάσθω	ὁ δυνατὸς	ἐν τῇ δυνάμει	αὐτοῦ
ibid.	μὴ καυχάσθω	ὁ πλούσιος	ἐν τῷ πλούτῳ	αὐτοῦ
Jer 9.22:	μὴ καυχάσθω	ὁ σοφὸς	ἐν τῇ σοφίᾳ	αὐτοῦ
ibid.	μὴ καυχάσθω	ὁ ἰσχυρὸς	ἐν τῇ ἰσχύι	αὐτοῦ
ibid.	μὴ καυχάσθω	ὁ πλούσιος	ἐν τῷ πλούτῳ	αὐτοῦ
Jas 1.9	καυχάσθω δὲ	ὁ ἀδελφὸς ὁ ταπεινὸς	ἐν τῷ ὕψει	αὐτοῦ

Dibelius, 84, rightly observes that in all these instances we do not find 'an actual demand'[54] but rather 'a form of speech' used 'when reality is being distinguished from appearance'.

The biblical or Semitic influence upon James' Greek is further evident from ἐν τῷ ὕψει αὐτοῦ = 'in his exaltation'. For although ἐν τῷ ὕψει is exceeding rare in secular Greek,[55] it occurs four times in the LXX.[56]

As noted, 4.16 declares that 'boasting' is evil; cf. 3.14. Just as Paul, however, condemns boasting[57] and yet boasts (typically about things that would seem to the uninitiated to be shameful or undesirable),[58] so is it

---

[50] But Johnson, 187, finds here an 'echo' of Mt 23.12 = Lk 14.11; 18.14. Cf. Mitton, 36: 'the words of Jesus...may well have been in James's mind'.

[51] For contrasts between ταπεινός/ω and ὑψόω/ὕψος/ὑψηλός see on 4.10; also LXX 1 Βασ 2.7; Esth 1.1k (with ὁ ἥλιος ἀνέτειλεν; Klein, *Werk*, 99, suggests an allusion to this); Pss 74.5-8; 93.1-5; Prov 3.34-35; Job 5.11; Eccl 10.6; Isa 2.11; 5.15-16; 10.33; 25.11-12; 26.5-6; Ezek 17.24; Ecclus 11.1; Philo, *Mos*. 1.31; *Spec*. 4.88; Mt 23.12; Lk 1.51; 14.11; 18.14; 2 Cor 11.7; 1 Pet 5.5 (quoting Prov 3.34); Josephus, *Bell*. 4.189; 5.12; 1 Clem. 30.2 (quoting Prov 3.34); 59.3; Did. 3.9; Barn. 19.3, 6; T. Abr. RecShrt 7.9; Aesop, *Sent*. 9; Plutarch, *Consol. ad Ap*. 103D; Epictetus, *Diatr*. 2.6.25; Diodorus Siculus 19.23.1; Dio Chrysostom 4.118.

[52] Yet note Preisker, 'Eigenwert', 235: he argues that James is more hostile to the rich than is the Jesus tradition.

[53] The underlying Hebrew is: אל + יתהלל + subject + ב + noun ending in possessive ו.

[54] Contrast the interpretation of Punchard, 357: James is encouraging those who may not feel pleasure 'at a prospect of a rise in the world...finer spirits who fain would shrink from anything like exaltation...to these the kindly Apostle writes that they may take heart, and not fear the greater dangers which of necessity accompany a higher call'. This assumes that the subject is change of status in this life; so too Barnes, 26-27.

[55] I have found only two examples: Apollodorus of Damascus, *Polior*. ed. Wescher 175; Cleomedes, *Mot. circ.* ed. Ziegler, 106.

[56] Isa 38.10; Ezek 31.2 (MT: בגדלך, of exalted status), 7 (MT: בגדלו), 14.

[57] Boasting is a bad thing in Rom 2.17, 23; 3.27; 4.2; 1 Cor 1.29; 4.7; 5.6; 2 Cor 11.18; and Gal 6.13; cf. Eph 2.9.

[58] E.g. Rom 5.3 (boasting in afflictions); 2 Cor 11.30 (boasting in weakness); 12.9 (boasting in weakness).

in James.⁵⁹ This double usage, and the fact that the verb James uses (καυχάσθω) appears often in the Pauline corpus but not elsewhere in the NT might lead one to detect Paul's influence in James' use of καυχάσθω.⁶⁰ But both positive and negative uses of 'boasting' or 'glorying'—in James one naturally thinks of an attitude rather than speech—appear in the Hebrew Bible and elsewhere.⁶¹

Verse 10. We now pass from the lowly to the rich, who, against Jer 9.23-24 ('Do not let the wealthy boast in their wealth'),⁶² typically pride themselves in their possessions; cf. Herm. *Vis.* 1.1.8: 'those who pride themselves on wealth bring death'. Verse 10, taken with v. 9, implies that 'everyone will, at some point or another, be ταπεινός. The question merely is whether this humility is self-chosen (and temporary) or enforced by God (and permanent)'.⁶³

ὁ δὲ πλούσιος ἐν τῇ ταπεινώσει αὐτοῦ. The words stand in parallel with the preceding line:

δὲ ὁ ἀδελφὸς ὁ ταπεινὸς ἐν τῷ ὕψει   αὐτοῦ
ὁ δὲ πλούσιος   ἐν τῇ ταπεινώσει αὐτοῦ

πλούσιος⁶⁴ recurs in 1.11; 2.5-6; 5.1.⁶⁵ James, like 2 Sam 12.1-7 (the parable of Nathan) and Lk 16.19-31 (the parable of the rich man and Lazarus), stereotypes 'rich' and 'poor': one is good, the other bad. He says nothing like Plato, *Resp.* 421B: poverty is just as evil as wealth, for 'the one is the parent of luxury and indolence, and the other of meanness and viciousness, and both of discontent'. He rather, foreshadowing the desert monastics, who found in poverty a divine blessing,⁶⁶ presumes that God is especially with the poor (2.5).

---

⁵⁹ See further Painter, 'Power', 242-48.

⁶⁰ For Brückner, *Reihenfolge*, 289, James shows a knowledge of Rom 5.3. McKnight, 97, suggests rather use of 'a similar tradition about inaugurated eschatology'.

⁶¹ Positive use: 1 Chr 16.35; Ps 5.11; 31.11; 149.5; Ecclus 39.8; etc. Negative use: Prov 11.7; 20.9; 25.14; 9.23; Ecclus 10.26-27; 11.4; 32.12; T. Jud. 13.2; T. Reub. 3.5; T. Job 15.5-7; 1 Clem. 13.2; Ign. *Pol.* 5.2; Sent. Sext. 432; etc.

⁶² H. Williams, 'Rags', argues at length that James shows dependence upon this passage; so too Spitta, 25; Dibelius, 84 ('possibly'); R. Wall, 55; McKnight, 97. Contrast Belser, 50-51. Other texts that quote or allude to Jer 9.23-24 include Ecclus 10.22; 11.1-6; LAB 50.2; Ps.-Phoc. 53; 1 Cor 1.31; 2 Cor 10.17; 1 Clem. 13.1

⁶³ Kamell, 'Economics', 169.

⁶⁴ LXX: most often for עשיר.

⁶⁵ On the rich in James see C. Osiek, *Rich and Poor in the Shepherd of Hermas*, Washington, D.C., 1983, 32-37; Maynard-Reid, *Poverty*; Maier, *Reich*; Frankemölle, 251-59; Tamez, *Message*; Ahrens, *Arm*; Hutchinson Edgar, *Poor*; Tsuji, *Glaube*, 135-48; Tiller, 'Rich'; Theissen, 'Ethos'; Kamell, 'Economics'.

⁶⁶ A. Solignac, 'Pauvreté chrétienne, Pères de l'Église et moines des origines', in *Dictionnaire de Spiritualité*, vol. 12/1, ed. M. Viller *et al.*, Paris, 1984, 634-47.

Most ecclesiastical readers, despite the plain sense of James, stress that wealth does not in itself amount to condemnation. This is understandable given that they interpret James in its canonical context. For the Bible praises the fabulously wealthy Solomon and makes Joseph of Arimathea a rich disciple (Mt 27.57). Indeed, James himself regards Abraham and Job, two rich men, as heroes.[67] Yet James fails to remind readers of the social status of those two men, and he otherwise does not qualify his rebukes of the rich. It appears that he shared with the author of the Epistle of Enoch an uncompromisingly negative view of the rich in his time and place.[68] One guesses that he would have seen nothing amiss in how Revelation blasts merchants, or in Aristotle's generalization, in *Rhet.* 1390b-91A, that the wealthy are 'insolent and arrogant, being mentally affected by the acquisition of wealth, for they seem to think that they possess all good things; for wealth is a kind of standard of value of everything else, so that everything seems purchasable by it... In a word, the type of character produced by wealth is that of a fool favored by fortune.' In this particular, James is seemingly close to Luther: 'The matter, form, effect, and goal of riches are worthless. That's why our Lord God generally gives riches to crude asses to whom he doesn't give anything else.'[69]

The identity of the rich in vv. 10-11 has generated much discussion. Most commentators insist that the rich belong to the Jamesian community because v. 10 depends upon v. 9 for its verb (καυχάσθω),[70] so ὁ πλούσιος naturally also draws to itself the ὁ ἀδελφός of v. 9. Visually:

9	Let the brother who is lowly	glory	in his exaltation
10	but (let the brother) who is rich	(glory)	in his humiliation

On this interpretation, the paradoxical imperative is real, and well-to-do Christians are being exhorted to heroic humility. They are to rejoice that their wealth will disappear or has in some cases (perhaps because of their Christian confession) disappeared already; or they are to appreciate whatever might humble them in this life.[71] 1 Timothy 6.17 is then a close

---

[67] 2.21-24; 5.11. Exegetes occasionally note this; so e.g. Wordsworth, 15; Robbins, 'Culture', 347.

[68] Cf. 1 En. 94.8-9; 96.4-8; 97.8-10; 103.5-8.

[69] M. Luther, *Table Talk*, in Luther's Works, vol. 54, ed. T.G. Tappert, Philadelphia, 1967, 452 (no. 5559).

[70] Sometimes exegetes supply another missing verb. Ps.-Oecumenius *ad loc.* PG 119.461A inserts αἰσχυνέσθω: 'Let the rich one be ashamed...' Cf. Estius, 382. Grotius, 1074, inserts ταπεινούσθω. Barrett, 10, suggesting 'grieve', appeals to instances of brachylogy that require supplying a word different from or even opposite to another just used: 1 Cor 3.2; 10.24. Alford, 278, rather proposes: 'Let the ταπεινός glory in his exaltation, whereas the rich man glories [καυχᾶται, indicative] in his debasement', that is, wrongly takes pride in what he should not.

[71] So Erasmus, *Paraphrase*, 139; Hemminge, 7-8; Manton, 24; Pyle, 308-309; Guyse, 566; Bloomfield, 484 (comparing 1 Cor 7.22, which he finds 'remarkably similar... in its

parallel: 'As for those who are rich in the present age, exhort them not to be haughty or to set their hopes on the uncertainty of riches'. Interpreters of this persuasion sometimes remark that the early church had well-to-do adherents such as Nicodemus and Joseph of Arimathea.[72]

But there are problems, and many suppose the rich to be outside the community.[73] (i) In 2.6-7 and 5.1, where οἱ πλούσιοι turn up again,[74] they oppress the faithful and blaspheme and are headed for misery. Can they then be Christians? (ii) The omission of 'brother' from v. 10 can be deliberate. (iii) In v. 11, the rich have no hope. That it is only wealth that withers and not the rich themselves goes against the plain sense of the words.[75] (iv) The ταπείνωσις of the rich seems to be equivalent not to the virtue of humility[76] but to the passing away of the flowers. (v) Our text depends upon Isa 40, which 2 Baruch and the targum take to depict the fate of the wicked; see above. (vi) In the words of Dibelius, 85, the Jewish 'literature of the poor' speaks of 'the fate of the rich man...without any sentimentality'. The same is true of the Jesus tradition.[77]

On the understanding of James offered throughout this commentary, according to which the fictional audience of James is broader than the church, justice can be done to the conflicting indicators. For if the entity

---

nature and scope'); Valpy, 237; Wordsworth, 15; Macknight, 587; Neander, 54-55; de Wette, 213; Bisping, 18; Dale, 'Temptation', 432-33; Mayor, 44-46 (citing as a parallel Ecclus 10.22—'The rich, and the eminent, and the poor—their glory is the fear of the Lord'—and the many texts in which Christians are exhorted to humble themselves); Stier, 242-43; von Soden, 166; Knowling, 12-14; Ropes, 145-46; Dimont, 631; Chaine, 14; Mussner, 74; Simon, 49; Mitton, 36-37; Adamson, 61; Schnider, 35-36; Cantinat, 78; Grünzweig, 39; Bottini, 'Minaccia'; Davids, 77; Scaer, 49 ('rich and poor pastors'); Frankemölle, 241-43; Moo, 68; G. and H. Hart, *Analysis*, 30; Popkes, 95; H. Williams, 'Rags'; Theissen, 'Ethos', 154-55; Fabris, 72; Maier, 67-68; Doriani, 27; Witherington, 430; Blomberg-Kamell, 57-58; *et al.* Tsuji, *Glaube*, 135-36, thinks of Christian and non-Christian rich.

[72] E.g. Weidner, 28; Smith, 52. Wordsworth, 15, noting that Abraham was rich, contends that 'fade away' refers to this life only, not to heavenly reward.

[73] Dionysius bar Salībī *ad loc.* CSCO 60, Scriptores Syri 101, ed. Sedlacek, 89-90; Pott, 146; Huther, 44-46; Alford, 278; Gibson, 3; Bassett, 9-10; Plummer, 576; Beyschlag, 56; Windisch-Preisker, 7; Dibelius, 87-88; Bardenhewer, 37; Easton, 25; Schneider, 8; Laws, 62-64; Kistemaker, 43; Martin, 25-26; Maynard-Reid, *Poverty*, 41-44; Stulac, 'Rich'; R. Wall, 56; Klein, *Werk*, 97-98; Konradt, *Existenz*, 145; Hutchinson Edgar, *Poor*, 148; Verseput, 'Wisdom', 703-704; Isaacs, 186; Brosend, 42; Krüger, *Kritik*, 118-21; McKnight, 99 (wondering if the rich might be the Jerusalem priesthood); Gundry, 920. Johnson, 185-86, raises the possibility that while the rich thought themselves in, James thought them out. Burchard, 64, speaks of the 'half-Christian'. Dibelius, 87, cannot decide.

[74] In the latter they are again addressed directly.

[75] Contrast Diodati *ad loc.*: James condemns riches, not the rich.

[76] Although ταπεινός can be a virtue in early Christian texts: Mt 11.29; Jas 4.6; 1 Pet 5.5; 1 Clem. 30.2; 55.6; etc.

[77] See e.g. Mt 6.19-21, 24; Mk 10.17-27; 12.41; Lk 6.20-23; 12.16-21; 14.12-14; 16.1-15, 19-31.

to which poor and rich belong is not the church but the Jewish diaspora (cf. 1.1), the parallelism between vv. 9 and 10 can stand—both groups belong to the same Jewish community—and yet the rich need not be Christian.[78]

This interpretation requires that the implicit command to boast is, as Bede already observes,[79] ironic, for, as v. 11 makes plain, the rich are headed for eschatological destruction. In line with this, James is ironic and sardonic elsewhere (2.19; 5.5), and one may compare the sarcasm of Mt 6.2, 5, and 16, where of wrongdoers it is said, 'They have their reward'.

ὅτι ὡς ἄνθος χόρτου παρελεύσεται. ἄνθος (NT: 3×), χόρτος (NT: 15×), and παρέρχομαι occur in James only here and (in the case of the two nouns) the next verse. Although the use of plants to represent a short-lived existence was common enough,[80] ἄνθος χόρτου—not a traditional Greek expression but a Semitism, the equivalent of ציץ השדה—comes from Isa 40.6.[81] The verb, which means 'he [the rich man] will pass away', not 'it [the rich man's wealth] will pass away',[82] is the first of five verbs that together tell the preordained story:

'pass away', παρελεύσεται[83]
  'withers', ἐξήρανεν
    'falls', ἐξέπεσεν
      'perishes', ἀπώλετο
        'fade away', μαρανθήσεται[84]

---

[78] This is also the view of Maynard-Reid, *Poverty*, 44; R.L. Williams, 'Piety'.

[79] Cf. Bede *ad loc*. CCSL 121 ed. D. Hurst, 185: 'Quod per inrisionem quae Graece hironia uocatur dictum esse constat'. This comment has been influential; cf. Glossa Ordinaria *ad loc*.; Godfrey of Bouillon, *Hom—II. De sanc.* 9 PL 155.1525B; Martin of Legio *ad loc.* PL 209.187B; Nicholas of Gorran, 67; Nicholas of Lyra *ad loc.*; Hardouin, 682; Schegg, 41; Belser, 51-52; Bardenhewer, 37; Beyschlag, 57; Plummer, 376; Dibelius, 85; Blackman, 51; Konradt, *Existenz*, 146 ('bittere Ironie'); Hutchinson Edgar, *Poor*, 148; Isaacs, 186; *et al.*

[80] Cf. Homer, Il. 6.144 ('As is the generation of leaves, so is that of humanity. The wind scatters'); Job 14.2; Pss 90.5-6; 103.15-16; Ecclus 14.18; Isa 5.24; Mt 6.25-33; Lk 12.22-31; b. 'Erub. 554a ('The children of men are like the grasses of the field, some blossom and some fade'); etc.

[81] See above. Although ὡς ἄνθος χόρτου literally means 'as flower of the grass', we may translate as though the Greek were, ἄνθος τοῦ ἀγροῦ; cf. LXX Ps 102.15, which uses the latter phrase to translate ציץ השדה. That is, we have here *synecdoche*. Not only is this the meaning of the MT behind the LXX, but in early Christian literature, χόρτος almost always has to do with the grass of a field or meadow: BAGD, s.v.

[82] Cf. v. 11; also T. Job 33.8 (kings will 'pass away'); Mk 13.30 ('this generation will not pass away'); 1 Cor 5.17; 1 Clem. 50.3 (previous generations have 'passed away'). James' intertext, Isa 40, says 'all *flesh* is grass'.

[83] Irwin, 'Lilies', denies that the verb here connotes passing away or disappearing: 'I translate James 1:10 "the rich will grow up like a flower of the field" taking it to indicate, not the ultimate fate of the rich...as most translators take it, but the flowering which is followed by fading in the sun's heat' (28).

[84] Wordsworth, 15, compares the famous declaration of Caesar: *veni, vidi, vici.*

These verbs, transferred from plants to human beings, remind readers of the obvious and inevitable, that human beings are no different than other forms of life in so far as death and decay are their future. Doom is universal. And wealth makes no difference.[85] Goods are transient, uncertain, and ineffective against death—a truth, it goes without saying, as proverbial in James' day as in ours,[86] and no doubt also then as in our day pushed to the back of many minds and so fitting content for exhortations.

Verse 11. This verse clarifies the end of the previous verse; that is, it is amplification, colorfully explaining why the flower in the field will pass away. Wesley, 857, remarks: there is 'beauty and elegance, both in the comparison itself, and in the very manner of expressing it, intimating both the certainty and the suddenness of the event'. Gill, 781, dramatically expounds: 'Riches are uncertain things now, they often make themselves wings and flee away; they are things that are not, that are not solid and substantial; they are a vain show; they sometimes fade away in a man's life-time, before he dies; and he fades away, and comes to decay, amidst all the ways and means, designs and schemes, he forms and pursues, and all the actions and business he does; and if not, when he fades away, and dies amidst all his riches, his glory does not descend after him, but falls off from him, as the flower of the field before the heat of the sun.'

ἀνέτειλεν γὰρ ὁ ἥλιος σὺν τῷ καύσωνι καὶ ἐξήρανεν τὸν χόρτον. ἀνέτειλεν, like the other aorists that follow, may be, as often claimed, gnomic.[87] But note the ungnomic sequence in LXX Nah 3.17 (ἀνέτειλεν...

---

[85] Blomberg-Kamell, 55, cite the saying: 'the person with the most toys still dies'.

[86] Cf. Job 15.29 ('their wealth will not endure'); 24.24 (the mighty 'are exalted a little while and then they are gone'); Ps 49.16-20 (mortals cannot take wealth to the grave); Ecclus 11.18-19 (the rich individual with many goods 'does not know how long it will be until he leaves them to others and dies'); 1 En. 97.10 ('your wealth shall not endure but shall take off from you quickly'); 100.6 ('their wealth shall not be able to save them'); Philo, *Jos.* 140-41 ('the events of life... are ever swept away'); *Spec.* 1.311 (riches, reputation, dominion, comeliness, and strength quickly come to 'the hour of their passing, how they wither away [μαραινόμενα]'; cf. Jas 1.11); Mt 6.19-21 = Lk 12.33-34 (treasure on earth is subject to corruption); Lk 12.13-21 (the rich fool); Gos. Thom. 76 ('Seek also for the treasure that fails not, that endures, where no moth comes near to devour and no worm to destroy'); Ps.-Phoc. 27 ('wealth is unstable'), 109-10 ('When you are rich, do not be sparing; remember that you are mortal. It is impossible to take riches and money into Hades'); Pindar, *Nem.* 11.13-16 ('If a man having riches surpasses others in beauty of form... let him remember that mortal are the limbs he clothes and that the earth will be the last garment of all he will wear'); Sent. Syr. Menander 110-12 ('For neither riches are everlasting... for subject to change are all things'); and the epitaph from Emircik/Eumeneia (4.12) printed in G.J. Johnson, *Early-Christian Epitaphs from Anatolia*, Atlanta, 1995, 134-36: 'No one deluded by wealth should dare to exult, for there is one Hades and an equal end [awaiting us] all. Is someone great in possessions? He receives for a tomb no more than this same measure of earth.'

[87] Cf. LXX Isa 40.7 and see BDF 333.

ἀφήλατο...ἔγνω). Perhaps instead James' aorists represent the Hebrew perfect tense and so emphasize suddenness and completeness.[88] ἀνατέλλω (Jas: 1×) + ἥλιος (Jas: 1×) was a common Greek idiom which occurs in the LXX for זרח + שמש.[89] Although ἐξήρανεν τὸν χόρτον[90] is from LXX Isa 40.7,[91] Isaiah does not refer to the sun. This is James' addition. Most have assumed that the direct connection with the sun implies that σὺν (Jas: 1×) τῷ καύσωνι[92] is an effect of the sun; so they translate 'with (its scorching) heat' or some such, a well-attested meaning.[93] Others, however, urge that σὺν τῷ καύσωνι here means 'with scorching wind'.[94] They may be correct: (i) In the LXX, καύσων often—maybe as much as eleven out of fourteen times—refers to 'hot wind', that is, the desert wind (קדים).[95] (ii) This appears to be the case in particular in LXX Isa 49.10, the only LXX passage to couple καύσων and ἥλιος: 'neither shall the heat [καύσων] nor the sun [ἥλιος] smite them'. (iii) The wind causes the flowers of the field to perish in Ps 103.15-16[96] and 4Q185 1.10-11,[97]

---

[88] So Moule, *Idiom*, 12 (the aorist represents the Hebrew perfect so as 'to emphasize the suddenness and completeness of the withering: the grass has withered and flower has faded before you can look round, as it were'), followed by Maynard-Reid, *Poverty*, 46 ('thus the judgment upon the rich will be abrupt and final'); cf. Bassett, 11.

[89] LXX Gen 32.31; Exod 22.2; Judg 9.33; 2 Βασ 23.4; 4 Βασ 3.22; Esth 1.1k; Ps 103.22; Jon 4.8; Nah 3.17; Wis 5.6; Ecclus 26.16; cf. Philo, *Leg.* 3.35; *Somn.* 1.84; Mt 5.45; 13.6; Mk 4.6; 16.2; Herodotus 7.233; Plato, *Leg.* 887E; Diodorus Siculus 14.70; Lucian, *Gall.* 1.20; Galen, *In Hipp. lib. vi epid. comm. vi* ed. Kühn, 155; PGM 4.33, 37; etc.

[90] While χόρτος can mean 'hay' (as in 1 Cor 3.12) or '(early) stalks of grain' (as in Mk 4.28), the dominant meaning is '(green) grass', as clearly here; cf. Mk 6.30; Rev 8.7.

[91] ἐξηράνθη ὁ χόρτος. For metaphorical application of ξηραίνω to people see LXX Pss 36.2; 101.12; Isa 37.27.

[92] This precise phrase does not appear to occur anywhere in Greek literature before James, and then only rarely after that, in Christian sources quoting James. καύσων: NT: 3×; cf. Mt 20.12; Lk 12.55. LXX: 14-15×. Gk. Pseudepigrapha (Denis): 0×. Philo: 0×. Josephus: 0×.

[93] So Beyschlag, 59; Dibelius, 86; Bardenhewer, 38; Davids, 77-78; Hartin, 63. Cf. καίω and T. Gad 1.4 ('faint from the heat'); Mt 20.12 ('the burden of the day and the scorching heat').

[94] So Bengel, 488; Benson, 33; Rosenmüller, 329; Bassett, 12; Mayor, 47; Chaine, 15; Schlatter, 122; Ross, 31; Martin, 27; Moo, 67 ('viable'). Cf. Lk 12.55 ('And when you see the south wind blowing, you say, "There will be scorching heat"'); also the Hebrew שרב, which originally meant 'heat of the sun' but came to designate the intense desert wind that blows in May–June and September–October.

[95] Job 27.21; Isa 49.11; Jer 18.17; Ezek 17.10; 19.12; 51.1; Hos 12.1; 13.15; Jon 4.8; Ecclus 18.16; 31.16. In Gen 31.40; Jdt 8.3; and Ecclus 43.22 the reference may be to the sun's heat.

[96] Windisch-Preisker, 7: the καύσων 'ist das πνεῦμα von Ps 102 16'.

[97] 'For see, (man) sprouts like grass and his loveliness blooms like a flower. His grace makes the wind blow over him and his root shrivels, and his leaves: the wind scatters them until hardly anything is left in his place'. This alludes to Isa 40.7-8. On the

texts reminiscent of Isa 40.7-8. The same is also true of the ears of grain in Gen 41.5, of the vine in Ezek 17.10, and of the reed in Hos 13.15. (iv) Although the τῷ in σὺν τῷ καύσωνι might stand for the possessive,[98] one can no less plausibly urge that the definite article introduces an independent item: 'along with the scorching wind'. (v) James 1.9-11 is a deliberate adaptation of Isa 40, and MT 40.7-8 has this: 'Grass withers, the flower fades when the Spirit of Yahweh blows against them. Surely the people are but grass. Grass withers, flowers fade...' Although the reference to the wind withering the grass and flower is absent from the original of 1QIsa[a] and the LXX (cf. 1 Pet 1.24), the omission is likely due to haplography,[99] and if James knew the longer text—which appears in the Lucianic recension, some Hexaplaric texts, the Syraic, the Vulgate, and the targum—this could explain his addition of v. 11a, understood as referring to wind. (vi) The objection, that a hot wind has nothing to do with the sun, fails because (a) it is equally true that heat is typically associated not with the rising of the sun (ἀνέτειλεν γὰρ ὁ ἥλιος) but with its mid-day height, so that on any account James' Greek is not perfectly felicitous and (b) Jon 4.8 joins the rising of the sun with the east wind[100] just as Philo associates the dry south wind of Egypt with the scorching sun,[101] and the same link lies behind the Arabic 'sherkiyeh', that is, 'sirocco', whose etymological meaning is, according to the dictionaries, 'the rising of the sun, the east'.[102]

The closest parallel to our line appears to be in the Jesus tradition, in Mk 4.6 (cf. Mt 13.6):

---

interesting links between 4Q185 and James see Verseput, 'Wisdom'. Note also Gen 41.6, 23, 27; Job 37.17; Ezek 17.10; 19.12 (LXX: ἄνεμος ὁ καύσων ἐξήρανεν); 1 En. 76.7 ('winds of heat').

[98] See A. Robertson, *Grammar*, 684.

[99] On the original text see H.G.M. Williamson, *The Book Called Isaiah*, Oxford, 1994, 255-56.

[100] LXX: καὶ ἐγένετο ἅμα τῷ ἀνατεῖλαι τὸν ἥλιον καὶ προσέταξεν ὁ θεὸς πνεύματι καύσωνος. Bassett, 12, conjectures the influence of this passage upon our text: James, 'having mentioned the waves of sea tossed by the wind is reminded of Jonah's storm; then the man of two purposes reflects the wavering prophet; then the sun arising with the vehement east wind...which withers the gourd...is all but reproduced *verbatim*'.

[101] Philo, *Mos.* 1.120: 'when the wind sets it in motion the scorching of the sun is pushed forward with it and burns up everything'.

[102] The conclusion that James refers to the desert winds does not entail that the author lived in Palestine, much less Galilee: 'such a reference could come through the literary medium of the LXX' (Laws, 65) or from a one-time visit to the Middle East, and other parts of the Mediterranean can experience winds from the Sahara and Arabian deserts or drying winds from other causes. (Drying siroccos can reach southern Greece.) Many, however, see our verse as more than consistent with a Palestinian origin for James, or for authorship by someone who knew the Palestinian sirocco; cf. Smith, 54 ('he is thinking of Galilee'); Bishop, *Apostles*, 184; Hadidian, 'Pictures', 228; *et al.*

Mark	ἀνέτειλεν	ὁ ἥλιος	ἐκαυματίσθη... ἐξηράνθη
James	ἀνέτειλεν γὰρ	ὁ ἥλιος σὺν τῷ καύσωνι καὶ	ἐξήρανεν

One might raise here the possibility of an allusion,[103] especially as James elsewhere borrows from words of Jesus and as Isa 40, James' intertext, does not refer to the sun. Furthermore, the parable of the sower, like Jas 1.10-11, warns about wealth. On the other hand, (i) ἐξήρανεν is from Isaiah; (ii) LXX Jon 4.7-8 contains a similar sequence: ἀπεξηράνθη... ἀνατεῖλαι τὸν ἥλιον...καύσωνος, so the words common to James and Mark are likely a natural and/or traditional concatenation;[104] (iii) whereas, as just argued, σὺν τῷ καύσωνι (James) likely has to do with the wind, ἐκαυματίσθη (Mark) has to do with the sun's heat; and (iv) the line in James characterizes the rich, but in the parable of the sower the rich are associated not with the seed withered by the sun but with the seed sown among thorns: Mk 4.18-19.

καὶ τὸ ἄνθος αὐτοῦ ἐξέπεσεν.[105] James, with reference to χόρτου in the previous verse, has inserted αὐτοῦ into LXX Isa 40.7 (καὶ τὸ ἄνθος ἐξέπεσεν).[106] According to Ropes, 149, ἐξέπεσεν 'is used in the sense not only of "fall off", but also of "fail", "come to naught". The specific meaning "fade" is contained in the Hebrew נבל, and so in translation became attached to ἐκπίπτειν.'[107] The flowers are the ornamentation of the grass, the multicolored decoration of the green field, both of which are here today, gone tomorrow. In Cant 2.12 the appearance of flowers (LXX: τὰ ἄνθη) is the sign of springtime. Perhaps that is so here too, and we should think of the short-lived Mediterranean spring.

καὶ ἡ εὐπρέπεια τοῦ προσώπου αὐτοῦ ἀπώλετο.[108] Cf. 4Q185 1.10-11 (see n. 97) and 2 Bar. 82.7,[109] both of which also mention 'beauty' in contexts alluding to Isa 40.6-7. εὐπρέπεια occurs only here in the NT.[110] In the LXX it appears sixteen times, but only once in close connection with προσώπον.[111] ἡ εὐπρέπεια τοῦ προσώπου, which anticipates 2.2-3, where the rich have gold rings and fine clothes, is not a traditional Greek

---

[103] So Martin, 23: James 'seems to draw from the parable in Mark 4:6'.

[104] Cf. 4 Ezra 15.50: 'sicut flos siccabitur, qum exsurget ardor qui emissus est super te'.

[105] 206 254 429 522 et al. S:H **A**^mss **G**:AA1 omit αὐτοῦ. Is this assimilation to LXX Isa 40.7?

[106] Cf. also LXX Job 14.2; 15.30, 33; Isa 28.1, 4 (all with ἄνθος).

[107] Cf. Oesterley, 426: 'נבל contains the idea of dying'.

[108] 03 1827 1893 omit αὐτοῦ.

[109] 'And we think about the beauty of their gracefulness while they go down in impurities; but like grass which is withering, they will fade away'.

[110] Gk. Pseudepigrapha (Denis): 7×. Philo: 2×. Josephus: 14×.

[111] Jer 23.9: ἀπὸ προσώπου εὐπρεπαίας δόξης αὐτοῦ = 'because of the appearance of the beauty of his glory'. Ecclus 24.14 uses the closely related εὐπρεπής of nature: 'like a lovely olive tree in a plain'. Cf. Herm. Vis. 1.3.4.

expression but rather a Semitism, τοῦ προσώπου being pleonastic.[112] ἀπόλλυμι often has eschatological connotations in early Christian literature, including Jas 4.12.[113] Here the aorist emphasizes 'the outcome of an irreversible process' (Fabris, 75).

The fleeting nature of beauty was proverbial in antiquity as it has been in all times and places. From Scripture it suffices to recall Isa 28.1 ('Woe to the proud crown of the drunkards of Ephraim, and to the fading flower of its glorious beauty', cf. v. 4); Nah 1.4 ('the bloom of Lebanon fades'); Mt 6.25-33 = Lk 12.22-31 (the lilies of the field that surpass Solomon in beauty are 'alive today and tomorrow thrown into the oven');[114] cf. from outside the Bible Pliny the Elder, *N.H.* 21.1 (nature has given to flowers 'birth but for a day—a mighty lesson to man, we see, to teach him that which in its career is the most beauteous and the most attractive to the eye is the very first to fade and die'); Apoc. Sed. 7.8 ('What is the use of beautiful things if they wither away to dust?').

οὕτως καὶ ὁ πλούσιος ἐν ταῖς πορείαις αὐτοῦ μαρανθήσεται.[115] οὕτως also concludes units in 2.17 and 26. Most assume that καί belongs to the comparison: just as the grass withers, so also does the rich person.[116] The repetition of ὁ πλούσιος from v. 10a makes for an *inclusio* and so further signals closure. In the LXX, πορεία[117] most often represents a form of הלך, with several senses: 'walking' (Isa 3.16), 'journey' (Num 33.2), 'conduct' (Isa 8.11), 'route, course' (Nah 1.8). μαραίνω is a NT *hapax*, which the LXX uses for the piel of יבש in Job 15.20 (τὸν βλαστὸν αὐτοῦ μαράναι ἄνεμος).[118] Its future tense corresponds to the future that ends v. 10, παρελεύσεται. When Sadler, 10, offers that, if the rich choose 'the reproach of Christ rather than the treasures of Egypt', they will not pass away but abide forever, he undoes the rhetorical posture of the text.

---

[112] Cf. LXX 1 Βασ 16.7 ('a human being looks εἰς πρόσωπον' = 'a human being looks at outward appearances'); Jer 23.9 (see n. 112); Mt 16.3 = Lk 12.56 ('the face of heaven' = 'the appearance of the sky'); 2 Cor 5.12 ('those who boast in face' = 'those who boast in outward appearance'). These locutions go back to the use of the Hebrew פנים to mean 'appearance', as in 2 Sam 14.20 ('In order to change פני הדבר' = 'In order to change the appearance of the thing'; LXX: τὸ πρόσωπον τοῦ ῥήματος); m. Yoma 3.1 (האיר פני כל־המזרח = 'the whole east is lit up').

[113] Cf. Mt 10.28, 39; 16.25; Jn 3.16; Rom 14.15; 2 Pet 3.9; Did. 16.5; Barn. 20.1; etc. The same is true in Jewish literature: Bar 3.3; 1 En. 1.7, 9; T. Levi 4.6; T. Abr. RecLng. 11.11; etc.

[114] Brosend, 40-41, wonders whether James depends upon this passage.

[115] Erasmus proposes an original πορίαις, which he takes to be the equivalent of εὐπορίαις, 'in prosperity'; cf. Tyndale's translation: 'with his aboundance'. For this and other conjectures see Bowyer, *Conjectures*, 313-14.

[116] But for Frankemölle, 245-46, 249, καί reaches back to v. 9: the rich like the poor also pass away.

[117] LXX: 29×. NT: 2×; cf. Lk 13.2. Gk. Pseudepigrapha (Denis): 10×. Philo: 9×. Josephus: 36×.

[118] LXX: 4×. Gk. Pseudepigrapha (Denis): 3×. Philo: 9×. Josephus: 7×.

Occasionally ἐν ταῖς πορείαις αὐτοῦ is taken to mean 'in their travelling'.[119] This is a possibility, for the first meaning of πορεία in BAGD, s.v., is 'journey, trip',[120] and in Jas 4.13 merchants travel to acquire profit. For several reasons, however, πορεία is more likely to mean 'activities', 'way of life', 'pursuits'[121] and so to be the equivalent of the common Hebrew expression, בכל־דרכיו.[122] (i) This second meaning is well attested.[123] (ii) There is much parallelism between 1.5-8 and 9-11, and this argues for giving the closing clauses similar import: 'in all their ways' (v. 8) corresponds to 'in the midst of his pursuits' (v. 11); this then explains the plural in the latter phrase.[124] (iii) The rich will perish whether or not they gain their wealth locally or journey to gain it, so it is hard to see what would be added here by a reference to travel. (iv) James may use ἐν ταῖς πορείαις αὐτοῦ because this avoids wooden repetition of ἐν ταῖς ὁδοῖς (v. 8) and adds consonance with π: ἐξέπεσεν...εὐπρέπεια... προσώπου...ἀπόλετο...πλούσιος...πορείαις.

μαραίνω, which climactically ends the unit, is used both of human circumstances[125] and of plants withering.[126] This makes it especially

---

[119] This is the view of Piscator, 728; Hort, 18; Mayor, 47; Weidner, 29; Chaine, 16; Moffatt, 15; Tasker, 43; Mussner, 75; Maynard-Reid, *Poverty*, 46-47; Batten, 'Poor', 73. So too Punchard, 358, with anti-Jewish stereotyping: 'to no people could the rebuke apply more sharply than to the Jews, the lenders unto "many nations" (Deut. xv. 6), the merchants and bankers of the world'.

[120] Cf. Let. Aris. 283; Lk 13.22; Josephus, *Bell.* 1.328, 345; *Ant.* 4.358; 3 Bar. 2.2; 3.2; 4.2. Note the use of ἐν ταῖς πορείαις in Ps.-Plato, *Ep.* 11 (358E: 'in travelling'); Xenophon, *An.* 7.3.37 ('in marches'); Aristotle, *Prob.* 870B (= 'in walking'); Polybius 5.78.1 ('in the march'). LXX Nah 2.6 translates בהלכותם (= 'in their journey') by ἐν τῇ πορείᾳ αὐτῶν (A: ἐν ταῖς π. α.).

[121] So Ps.-Oecumenius *ad loc.* PG 119.461A; Theophylact *ad loc.* PG 125.1140D; Dionysius bar Salībī *ad loc.* CSCO 60, Scriptores Syri 101, ed. Sedlacek, 90; Rosenmüller, 329; Ropes, 149; Dibelius, 87; Davids, 78; *et al.* Cf. LXX Isa 8.11; T. Job 38.5; 1 Clem. 48.4; Herm. *Sim.* 5.6.6; Ps.-Socrates, *Ep.* 27.5.

[122] See on v. 8. Krüger, *Kritik*, 116-17, leaves the issue undecided. The older translations tend to have 'in his ways' (e.g. Wycliffe, Geneva, Rheims, AV).

[123] E.g. LXX Ps 67.25 ('Your doings [πορεῖαι], O God, have been seen, the doings [πορεῖαι] of my God, the king, in the sanctuary'); Prov 2.7 (God protects the πορείαν of the upright); Prov 4.27b ('God will guide your steps [πορείας] in peace'); Isa 8.11 ('the course [πορείᾳ] of the way of this people'); Ecclus 1.5 v.l. ('the ways [πορεῖαι] are its eternal commandments'); Ps.-Socrates, *Ep.* 27.5 ('guide him on a course of life [πορείαν]'; 1 Clem. 48.4 ('make straight their way [τὴν πορείαν] in holiness and righteousness'); Herm. *Sim.* 5.6.6 ('the conduct [ἡ πορεία] of this flesh pleased him').

[124] But for Bengel, 488, the plural represents the burdensome extent of the rich man's undertakings.

[125] E.g. Josephus, *Bell.* 6.274 (of starvation); T. Sim. 3.3 ('the envious one languishes', μαραίνεται).

[126] E.g. LXX Job 15.30 (with ἄνθος and ἄνεμος, and with metaphorical application to the wicked rich); Wis 2.7-8 (with ἄνθος); Herm. *Sim.* 9.1.7; 9.23.1; 4 Bar. 6.8 (of figs); Apoc. Sed. 7.8.

appropriate in the present context.[127] One might think only that the rich are headed for the grave. But the mention of heat prepares for 5.1-6, where they suffer in eschatological fire. Further, it is only the eschatological future that makes real the difference between rich and poor. So 1.9-11 seems to miss its mark without an implicit appeal to the last judgment.[128]

---

[127] Note also Philo, *Spec.* 1.311: riches wither away (μαραινόμενα) quickly.

[128] See further Krüger, *Kritik*, 127-30. After surveying multiple exegetical options, his conclusion is that 1.11 envisages the death and eternal damnation of the rich, and that finding anything more—e.g. their conversion or loss of riches in this life—is eisegesis.

V

TEMPTATION AND GOD (1.12-15)[1]

(12) Blessed is the one who endures trial, because having stood the test he will receive the crown of life that he [God] promised to those who love him. (13) Let no one, when tempted, say, 'I am tempted by God'. For God cannot be tempted to do evil, and he himself tempts no one. (14) But each one is tempted by his own desire, being lured and enticed by it. (15) Then, when desire has conceived, it gives birth to sin, and sin, when it comes to completion, gives birth to death.

History of Interpretation and Reception

Most exegetes have concurred in associating the πειρασμόν of v. 12 with the πειρασμοῖς of v. 2 and in arguing that vv. 13-15, which use the verb πειράζω, envisage a closely related but different topic. Bede drew these contrasts:[2]

1.2 + 12		1.13-15
outer trial	vs.	inner temptation
the Lord's assent	vs.	the devil's instigation
testing	vs.	deceiving

Calvin, 267, had a similar take: 'All outward trials, of which we have been speaking so far, come to us by God's will. In this sense God tempted Abraham (Gen. 22), and daily tempts us: that is, he tests us to see what we are like, by putting something in our path which will reveal our inner self. But it is quite one thing to draw the secrets of the heart into the open, and another to harass the inner man with foul desires. Now he [James] is dealing [in 1.13-15] with inward temptations, which are, simply, excessive lusts driving us to sin. Quite rightly, he states that God

---

[1] Recent literature: Baker, 'Daddy'; Cox, 'Progress'; Davids, 'Meaning'; idem, 'Message'; Garland, 'Trials'; Hoppe, *Hintergrund*, 40-43; Isaacs, 'Suffering'; Jackson-McCabe, *Law*, 196-213; Klein, *Werk*, 65-66, 82-91; Kloppenborg, 'Reception'; idem, 'Psychagogy'; Konradt, *Existenz*, 115-25; Ludwig, *Wort*, 144-50; Marcus, 'Inclination'; Niebuhr, 'Seligpreisungen'; Penner, *Eschatology*, 158-213; Porter, 'Temptation'; Tsuji, *Glaube*, 104-105; Turner, *Insights*, 161-63; Van Zyl, 'Dualism'; W. Wilson, 'Sin'; Wolmarans, 'Male'; idem, 'Misogyny'; idem, 'θεός'; Zeller, 'Jak 1,12'.

[2] Bede *ad loc.* CCSL 121 ed. Hurst, 187.

is not the source of these, for they flow from the evil of our flesh.'[3] Most commentators have felt that, unless one distinguishes between tests and temptations or between two sorts of temptations, James becomes not only incoherent but also at odds with the many biblical passages in which God tries individuals.[4]

James 1.13, read with some such distinction, has again and again been called upon to explicate the difficult line from the Lord's Prayer, 'Lead us not into temptation'. In the words of Cassian, Jesus' petition holds 'a problem that is not a minor one. If we pray that we be not permitted to be tempted, where will that constancy come from for which we are to be tested? There is the scriptural statement that everyone who has not been tempted has not been approved of. There is "Blessed is the man who endures temptation". So this cannot be the sense of "Lead us not into temptation". It is not "Do not allow us ever to be tempted" but rather "Do not allow us to be overcome when we are tempted".'[5] Dionysius of Alexandria argued to like effect: God tempts but does not actually lead people into sin, that is, actually make them succumb to it: the blame for that lies with the devil and human beings.[6] Lancelot Andrewes made a related distinction when he wrote: 'God's temptation maketh us happy, "Blessed is he that endureth temptations"; but the devil's temptation bring us to misery, and this latter is that against which we pray...'[7]

---

[3] Cf. Origen, *Exod ad* 15.25 PG 12.288D-89A; Augustine, *Serm.* 57.9 PL 38.399-400; *Con. ev.* 2.(30)71 CSEL 43 ed. Weihrich, 175; the *Catenae ad loc.* ed. Cramer, 5; Dionysius bar Salībī *ad loc.* CSCO 60, Scriptores Syri 101, ed. Sedlacek, 90; Aelred of Rievaulx, *Serm.* 54.1-6 CCCM 2B ed. Raciti, 66-68; Glossa Ordinaria *ad loc.* PG 114.672A-B; Martin of Legio *ad loc.* PL 209.188A-D; Martin Bucer, *Enarr. perpet. in ev.* fol. 67r.30; Peter Martyr Vermigli, *An Deus sit author pecatti* 26 ed. McLelland, 245-46; Stevartius, 47-50; S. Clark, *A Survey of the Bible*, London, 1693, 307-308; J. Tillotson, 'Sermon LXI', 'Sermon LXII', in *Works*, vol. 2, London, 1752, 377-94; Gill, 781; Benson, 36 (39-41 are devoted to discussion of James' seeming contradiction of the Lord's Prayer and other biblical texts); E.J. Chapman, *Critical and Expository Notes on Many Passages in the New Testament*, Canadaigua, 1819, 140 (citing Gen 22.1); Mayor, 50; Ropes, 153; Robertson, 72-74; Marty, 30; Schnider, 39; Popkes, 103-104; *et al.* Although not citing James, Tertullian, *Orat.* 8 CSEL 20 ed. Reifferscheid and Wissowa, 186, already contrasts demonic temptation (*temptandae*) with divine testing (*probandae*; the older commentaries often cite this). This notion of two sorts of temptation was not just an exegetical contrivance: one also finds it as a report of and reflection upon first-hand experience; see e.g. Francisco de Osuna, *The Third Spiritual Alphabet*, trans. M.E. Giles, New York, 1981, 515-46.

[4] For Laws, 70, James 'could hardly ignore OT references to God's testing of, for instance, Abraham, to whom he refers in ii.21, even though in later parts of the OT this teaching is increasingly attributed to the Satan'. But see below n. 151.

[5] John Cassian, *Conf.* 9.23 SC 54 ed. Pichery, 60-61.

[6] Dionysius of Alexandria, *Frag. on Lk* 22.42ff. ed. Feltoe, 247-48.

[7] Lancelot Andrewes, 'But Deliver Us from Evil', in *Ninety-Six Sermons*, vol. 5, Oxford, 1843, 455. Cf. Chrysostom, *Job* 2.6 SC 346 ed. Sorlin and Neyrand, 166; Cyril of Jerusalem, *Myst. cat.* 5.17 PG 33.1121A-B; Augustine, *Serm.* 57.9 PL 38.399-400; Chromatius of Aquileia, *Serm.* 40.2 SC 164 ed. Lemarié, 228; Ps.-Oecumenius *ad loc.*

Our verse has also been wielded to interpret additional biblical texts that could be taken to imply that God can lead or has led people into sin. The Sermon of Abba Amphilochius on the sacrifice of Isaac tones down Gen 22.1-2 by interpreting it in the light of James' assertion: 'The One who is not tempted, did not tempt Abraham to evil'.[8] And Peter Martyr Vermigli, in commenting on 2 Sam 16.5-14 (the cursing of Shimei) and 20-23 ('I [God] will raise up evil against you...and I will take your wives before your eyes and give them to your neighbor, and he shall lie with your wives in the sight of this sun'), cites James to the contrary: 'James asserted that God tempts no one. Through temptations men are provoked to sin: if God were the cause of sin, we could not say that he tempts no one. It is *concupiscentia* that tempts us, and that is not from God, but from the world.'[9]

How does one go about overcoming temptation? One might gain guidance from surrounding verses. Perhaps one should ask for wisdom (1.5) or be quick to hear, slow to speak, slow to anger (1.19) or be a doer of the word rather than a hearer only (1.22). In vv. 12-15, however, James offers no concrete counsel. He does not commend the imperatives just

---

PG 119.461B-D = Theophylact *ad loc.* PG 125.11140D-41A; Albertus Magnus, *Super Mt cap. I-XIV ad* Mt 6.13 Opera Omnia 21/1 ed. Schmidt, 214; Calvin, *Inst.* 3.20.46 ('To some it seems rude and harsh to ask God not to lead us into temptation, since, as James declares, it is contrary to his nature to do so. This difficulty has already been partly solved by the fact that our concupiscence is the cause, and therefore properly bears the blame of all the temptations by which we are overcome. All that James means is, that it is vain and unjust to ascribe to God vices which our own consciousness compels us to impute to ourselves'); Knoch, 159-60; Michl, 31; *et al.* Luther, in his *Small Catechism*, in the commentary on the sixth petition in the Lord's Prayer, says: 'God indeed tempts no one; but we pray in this petition that God would guard and keep us, so that the devil, the world, and our flesh may not deceive us, nor seduce us into misbelief, despair, and other great shame and vice'. Porter, 'Temptation', prefers a contextual solution: James addresses people who are 'persecuted and deprived', and although 'it is easy to blame God for the deprivations...in this context God tempts no one'—implying in other contexts God might tempt.

[8] *Orat. de Abr. pat.* 22-23 CCSG 3 ed. Datema, 275. The same contradiction was handled in like fashion centuries later by J. Dick, *Systematic Theology*, Cincinnati, 1856, 56: 'The apostle James seems to be at variance with Moses, because the one says, "Let no man say when he is tempted, I am tempted by God", and the other tells us that the Lord "did tempt Abraham": but the difficulty is removed by the simple observation, that James means by tempting, soliciting to sin, while Moses means, making trial of faith and obedience.' Already the *Catenae ad loc.* ed. Cramer, 5, asserts that God tempted Abraham for good. Many readers of Jas 1.12-15 have wondered esp. how to relate it to Gen 22 (cf. Jas 2.21); cf. Jerome, *Adv. Jov.* 2.3 PL 23.286C (James prevents readers from supposing that God will tempt them the way God tempted Abraham; that sort of event seemingly belongs to the past); Bede *ad loc.* CCSL 121 ed. D. Hurst, 187; Ps.-Oecumenius *ad loc.* PG 119.461D; John of Damascus, *Parall.* Π 35 PG 96.324C; Hus, 187; Osiander, 720; Calmet, 669; Pareus, 545; Brochmand, 55; Ewald, 188; Mussner, 86-87; *et al.*

[9] Peter Martyr Vermigli, *An Deus sit author pecatti* 1 ed. McLelland, 217.

cited; nor does he extol apatheia[10] or reason or contentment with one's lot. He says simply: if you overcome, you are blessed. Readers have been more expansive, insisting that one should repeat the commandments and pray,[11] or focus on the joy of holiness instead of on prohibition,[12] or cultivate sincerity and truthfulness,[13] or avoid bad company and contemplate the example of the tempted Christ,[14] or seek 'a refined moral sense which can discriminate between the true and the false, and which can discern the enemy even when he comes as "an angel of light"'.[15] Hemminge, 9-12, distinguished various sorts of temptations and offered various remedies for each—reading, meditating, pondering Providence, contemplating the brevity of life, considering the example of Jesus, reflecting upon 'tragicall and lamentable examples', etc. More succinctly, Wesley, 597, interpreting our verse via 1 Cor 13.7, affirmed: 'it is love only that endureth all things'.[16]

One of the chief applications of 1.12 has been to encourage people in difficult straits;[17] that is, rather than bemoaning one's lot, one should take heart and appreciate that successfully enduring trials issues in great reward, both in this world—confronting obstacles builds character[18]—and the world to come ('the crown of life').[19] It is no surprise then that our passage is often linked to 1 Cor 10.13—'No testing has overtaken you

[10] Note Kloppenborg, 'Psychagogy', 48: 'It is unclear whether' James 'would side with the Stoic view that the passions are to be extirpated or the Peripatetic view that they are only to be moderated'.
[11] So W. Wynn, 'Temptation and How to Overcome It', *Christian World Pulpit* 54 (1898), 102-104.
[12] H. Macmillan, *The Daisies of Nazareth*, London, 1897, 191-203.
[13] W.H.M.H. Aitken, *Temptation and Toil*, New York, 1895, 203.
[14] Sadler, 11; R.J. Campbell, 'The Two Sides of Temptation', in *Sermons to Young Men*, London, 1904, 153-69. Campbell is chiefly concerned with sexual sins.
[15] J.H. Jowett, *My Daily Meditation*, Nashville, 1914, 49.
[16] Cf. Nicholas of Lyra *ad loc.*; Lapide, 43; Bengel, 488 ('amor parit patientiam').
[17] In James, the difficulties are not specified. Readers have thought, among other things, of sexual sins (see n. 220; cf. Cyril of Alexandria, *Lk* 77 CSCO 140 Scriptores Syri 70 ed. Tonneau, 314), sickness (Ancrene Wisse 4.7 ed. Millett, 69), economic injustice (cf. Tamez, *Message*, 43; W. Wilson, 'Sin', 161), and persecution (see n. 54).
[18] So Dale, 'Temptation', 323 ('the stumbling block becomes a stepping-stone'); R.J. Drummond, *Faith's Perplexities*, New York, n.d., 161-62.
[19] So e.g. Didymus of Alexandria *ad loc.* ed. Zoepfl, 2-3; Epistola Magnum cumulatur PLSup 1.1698; W.L. Watkinson, *The Supreme Conquest*, New York, 1907, 136-50. Lapide, 41, offers examples, including Athanasius' battles with Arius and Simeon Stylites' battles with temptation. K. Barth, *CD* 2.1 § 27.2 ed. Bromiley and Torrance, 248, characteristically thinks rather in terms of faith: 'By temptation faith is completely destroyed, and in that way completely established. In temptation faith is taken from man that it may be restored by its object. In temptation faith is killed that it may be quickened again by Him in whom it believes. This is the blessedness of temptation'. Also idiosyncratic is Barsanuphius and John, *Ep.* 386 SC 450 ed. Neyt and Angelis-Noah, 435, which asks what James means for those who do not suffer, the answer being humility, for God does not bring affliction upon those too weak to endure it.

that is not common to everyone. God is faithful, and he will not let you be tested beyond your strength, etc.'[20] At the same time, vv. 14-15 hold readers responsible for their failures, so homileticians have appealed to our text to warn congregants that they have no excuses before God.[21]

Verses 14-15 have produced polemical exchanges regarding concupiscence, for the verses might be taken to entail that the first stirrings of wrongful desire are not sinful. But Poole, 882, objected to this that 'the least motions of it [lust] are forbidden', and appealed to Mt 5.28. Calvin, 269, was equally adamant: 'Papists show their ignorance in seizing on this text, in a wish to prove from it that vicious, filthy, criminal, and unspeakable desires are not sins, so long as one does not fall in with them'. He went on to reject the 'foolish notion of taking from these words the sense that there is no mortal sin, until it breaks out into (what they call) an external act. This is not James' point...he is concentrating on the fact that the root of our destruction lies within ourselves'.[22] The object of this attack is the view, taught by Aquinas, upheld by Trent (Session 5), and enshrined in the Rheims annotation on our verse,[23] that concupiscence[24]—the inordinate internal tendency that precedes active desire—is, while a consequence of the fall, not itself sin.[25]

Occasionally v. 13 has been directly related to the second person of the Trinity. If God cannot be tested, then in what sense did the devil tempt Jesus, as the Synoptics report?[26] One answer distinguishes between

---

[20] Cf. Grotius, 1075; Wolzogen, 185; Tillotson, 'Sermon LXI', 381; Adderley, 12; Hartin, 91; Maier, 77. Brückner, *Reihenfolge*, 289, even imagines that this text has influenced James.

[21] E.g. Cyril of Jerusalem, *Hom.* 17 PG 33.1152A-B; Manton, 82-86; Tillotson, 'Sermon LXII', 392 ('We have many powerful enemies; but we are much more in danger of treachery from within, than of assaults from without. All the power of our enemies could not destroy us if we were but true to ourselves'); F. Temple, 'Temptation from Within', in *Sermons Preached in Rugby School Chapel*, London, 1871, 226-33; A. Shepherd, 'Temptation and Moral Responsibility', *Christian World Pulpit* 68 (1905), 101-104; cf. Brosend, 47.

[22] Calvin, *Inst.* 3.3.13. Cf. Pareus, 545-46; C. Jansen, *Augustinus*, vol. 2, Louvain, 1640, 188; Manton, 99; Fulke, *Confutation*, 355 ('we see there is distinction of concupiscence from actual sin, as of the mother from her daughter, but yet as one serpent conceiveth and bringeth forth another serpent, so both the mother and daughter are sin, and Paul plainly testifieth that concupiscence is sin. Rom. 7.7').

[23] Rheims 381: 'concupiscence, we see here, of itself is not sin as Heretics falsely teach; but when by any consent of the mind we do obey or yield to it, then is sin engendered and formed in us'.

[24] 'Concupiscence' was, following the Vulgate's *concupiscentia*, the old standard English translation for ἐπιθυμία in our verse; so Tyndale, Cranmer, Geneva, Rheims, AV.

[25] See further *Concilii Tridentini Actorum Pars Altera: Acta post Sessionem Tertiam usque ad Concilium Bononiam Translatum*, ed. Stephanus Ehses, Freiburg, 1911, 185 (citing James and Augustine); Stevartius, 52-53. Lapide, 44, finds in 1.13 occasion to blast Calvin for making God the agent of evil.

[26] Cf. R.O. Yeager, *The Renaissance New Testament*, vol. 16, Gretna, 1985, 507.

different modes of temptation while another insists that Jesus was tempted by legitimate desire rather than by corrupt desire.[27]

Although our passage does not name the devil, readers have incessantly read him in: they have found it all but impossible to speak or write about temptation without speaking of the devil.[28] Some modern Christians, however, have appealed to Jas 1.14-15 to downplay the importance of or even to deny the existence of the devil. For E.W. Lewis, 'If James, the Apostle, was able to explain temptation by the known facts of human nature, he was compelled to say, not "Every man is tempted when the devil comes to him and allures him with his wiles"; but "Every man is tempted when he is drawn away of his own lust and enticed". And if I can explain the origin of moral evil on the ground of human freedom, I am compelled by the law of parsimony to be content with that explanation, without postulating the unnecessary...existence of an evil spirit outside of me.'[29]

Another issue for modern readers of a book that assumes human moral responsibility has been how to respond to the sort of materialism Laplace expounded, for it eliminates free acts and so seemingly destroys ethical accountability. Such accountability has also taken a beating from modern psychology, sociology, and medicine, all of which reveal how much people are products of circumstances beyond their control. Plummer, 578, responded to 'the Positivist' and 'the Determinist' by appealing to self-reproach and remorse, which he could not discount as convenient fictions, and by claiming that 'there is probably no language, certainly no civilised language, which has no word to express the idea of sin. If sin is an illusion, how came the whole human race to believe in it, and to frame a word to express it?'[30] Reinhold Niebuhr, by contrast, cited Jas 1.13-15 in his defense of an Augustinian doctrine of 'responsibility despite inevitability'.[31]

---

[27] Cf. Gregory Palamas, *Hom. i-xx* 32.12 ed. Chrestou and Zeses, 324; Albertus Magnus, *Super Mt cap. I-XIV ad* Mt 4.1 Opera Omnia 21/1 ed. Schmidt, 85; J.E. McKinley, *Tempted for Us*, Milton Keynes, UK, 2009 (282-85 discuss James).

[28] Cf. Athanasius, *Vit. Ant.* 21 SC 400 ed. Bartelinnk, 192-94; John of Damascus, *Parall.* A 9 PG 95.1113C; Nicholas of Gorran, 69; Cajetan, 364; Aretius, 475; Calvin, 26; Stevartius, 55; Osiander, 720; Calmet, 669; Tillotson, 'Sermon LXII' (as in n. 3), 389-92; T. Scott, 567; W. Bates, *The Whole Works of the Rev. W. Bates*, vol. 2, London, 1815, 224; Robertson, 74; Ross, 34; *et al.*

[29] E.W. Lewis, *Some Views of Modern Theology*, London, 1905, 141. Cf. Schleiermacher, *Christliche Glaube* 45.1 (Jas 1.12 is among those passages where the devil is not mentioned even though 'sin is being discussed, and we should most expect it'); G. Dawson, 'Endurance of Temptation', in *Sermons on Life and Duty*, London, 1883, 165-83 ('you have no enemy but yourself'). Contrast Moo, 75: 'Nor should we make anything of James's omission of Satan as a source of temptation'.

[30] Cf. Adderley, 13: 'No man is obliged to sin. His will is always really free, however much he may be beset by evil forces which seem omnipotent.'

[31] R. Niebuhr, *The Nature and Destiny of Man*, vol. 1, New York, 1964, 253-54.

Our passage's vivid depiction of sin has left its mark in English literature, in a gruesome passage in Milton's *Paradise Lost*. In 2.745-814, Sin, addressing Satan, recalls how she mated with him, and how their incestuous union begat Death:

> At last this odious offspring whom thou seest
> Thine own begotten, breaking violent way
> Tore through my entrails, that with fear and pain
> Distorted, all my nether shape thus grew
> Transform'd: but he my inbred enemie
> Forth issu'd, brandishing his fatal Dart
> Made to destroy: I fled, and cry'd out *Death*.

The influence of James upon this passage is obvious.

Exegesis

Following the introductory makarism, which blesses those who endure trial (v. 12), the text makes a theological denial (v. 13) and then an anthropological affirmation (vv. 14-15). Verse 13 draws an inference from the divine nature: because God is ἀπείραστος κακῶν, God cannot tempt human beings.[32] As this asseveration, within a monotheistic framework, leaves temptation unexplained, vv. 14-15 make up the lack by faulting human nature. They do this via a climactic sequence, a résumé of 'the fool's biography':[33]

> First: being lured and enticed, one is tempted by ἐπιθυμία
> Second: ἐπιθυμία conceives (sin)
> Third: ἐπιθυμία gives birth to sin
> Fourth: sin grows up
> Fifth: sin brings death[34]

---

[32] Contrast Teach. Sylv. 115.36–116.5: God does not tempt because God knows everything beforehand.

[33] The phrase is from R. Wall, 61.

[34] Blomberg-Kamell, 72, refer to the 'life cycle of sin'. Death, however, begets nothing. J. Owen, *The Nature, Power, Deceit, and Prevalency of the Remainders of Indwelling Sin in Believers*, Glasgow, 1825, 137, in accord with much earlier ecclesiastical exegesis, interprets the sequence this way: 'The first of these relates to mind; that is drawn off or drawn away by the deceit of sin. The second unto the affections; they are enticed or entangled. The third to the will, where sin is conceived; the consent of the will being the formal conception of actual sin. The fourth to the conversation wherein sin is brought forth; it exerts itself in the lives and courses of men. The fifth respects an obdurate course in sinning, that finisheth, consummates, and shuts up the whole work of sin, whereon ensues death or eternal ruin.'

Verses 12-15 function then as a practical—not philosophical—theodicy, an explanation of sin and spiritual death.[35]

This paragraph, which contains nothing specifically Christian,[36] takes readers back to previous verses. Verse 12 recalls the vocabulary of vv. 2-4 and restates their basic content:

| v. 12 | ὑπομένει πειρασμόν... δόκιμος |
| vv. 2-4 | πειρασμοῖς... δοκίμιον... ὑπομονήν... ὑπομονή[37] |

Verse 12 also links itself also to vv. 9-11, for both sections have to do with eschatology: the crown of life for the one enduring temptation in the former is the functional equivalent of the eschatological exaltation of the lowly in the latter.[38] It is further natural to contrast the fate of the rich with the fate of those who endure.[39] Moreover, the triadic catena in 1.2-4 has its antithesis in the triadic sequence of 1.12-15:

	1.2-4	1.14-15
situation	trial	temptation by desire
response	faithful endurance	sin
result	maturity (τέλειον)	death (ἀποτελεσθεῖσα)[40]

One might even discern a link between vv. 12-15 and vv. 5-8: the focus on 'desire' in the present paragraph could be related, via the Jewish doctrine of the יצר הרה, to the 'double-minded' individual mentioned earlier. However that may be, vv. 12-15 help unite the opening segments of James.

Although this commentary views vv. 12-15 as a unit,[41] there is no consensus on the matter. Indeed, the diversity of opinion is stunning,

---

[35] The word 'theodicy' is borrowed from Mussner, 86.

[36] Cf. Easton, 28: 'While the teaching of this section would undoubtedly represent common-sense Christianity, it would also represent common-sense Judaism; there is no reason to think of it as a Christian creation'.

[37] Kotzé, 87, displays the parallels this way:

1.2	πᾶσαν χαράν	1.12	μακάριος
	πειρασμοῖς		πειρασμόν
	δοκίμιον		δόκιμος
	ὑπομονήν		ὑπομένει

He further sees receiving the crown of life (1.12) as balancing perfection (v. 4)

[38] Pace Spitta, 28-29, who makes the rich person the object of the blessing. McKnight, 106, regards v. 12 as a recapitulation of the themes in vv. 2-11. See Taylor, *Structure*, 48-49, for ways in which v. 12 isolates itself from what comes before and what comes after.

[39] Cf. Bengel, 488: 'blessed' and 'the crown of life' are opposed to 'shall fade away'.

[40] Cf. Baasland, 23. Calloud-Genuyt, *Analyse*, 7, relate vv. 2-4 to vv. 12-15 this way:
trial → faith → endurance → works → crown of life
trial → seduction → yielding to impulse → sin → death

[41] So too Neander, 55; Plumptre, 53; R. Wall, 59.

perhaps even an indictment of the endeavor to fathom a distinct organization. For Dibelius, 88-90, v. 12 is isolated, vv. 13-18 a unit.[42] For Schnider, 37-39, v. 12 stands alone while vv. 13-15 constitute the next paragraph.[43] Cantinat, 80-88, also thinks v. 12 independent but then reckons vv. 13-16 to be the subsequent section. Mussner, 84-85, views vv. 12-18 as a single piece.[44] Burchard, 12, 67-68, rather takes 12-25 to be a unified whole.[45] Johnson, 184-92, joins v. 12 to vv. 9-11 and sees vv. 13-21 as a cohesive paragraph.[46] Pritius reckons vv. 12-16 to be a coherent subsection between vv. 9-11 and 17-27.[47] For Martin, 28, the unit extends from 1.12 to 19a. Tsuji deems vv. 2-12 to be the introduction, vv. 13-27 the second section.[48] For Hauck, 6-10, vv. 2-12 are the initial unit, vv. 13-18 the following unit.[49] Bengel, 485, by contrast, construes vv. 2-12 and 13-15 as the first two subsections of the opening *adhortatio*. According to Pareus, 1.2-13 concerns external temptation, 1.14-18 internal temptation, 1.19-25 hearing, receiving, and doing the word of God, 1.26-27 false and true religion. Popkes, makes vv. 2-15 the opening segment, vv. 16-27 the second segment.[50] Bisping, 11, judges the opening portion to be vv. 1-18.[51] For Gaugusch, 10, 1.9-27 is the second section, following the introductory 1.1-8.[52] Fortunately, few fundamental exegetical decisions hang upon the proper division—if there can be such a thing—of these verses.

If one chooses to view vv. 12-15 as a unit, it would appear to be largely triadic:[53]

---

[42] So too Lange, 46-48; Michl, 29-30; Stagg, 'Analysis', 367; Schrage, 18-19; Frankemölle, 259-60, 276-78; Moo, 69-71.

[43] So too Weidner, 29-31; Easton, 26-27.

[44] So too W. Carpenter, 119; Plummer, 577; Bardenhewer, 39; Laws, 66; Kotzé, 86 97; Hartin, 88; Felder, 1787; Brosend, 44; Blomberg-Kamell, 65-66; Orlando, *Lettera*, 48-50; McKnight, 104-105.

[45] Cf. Garleff, *Identität*, 271-84: 1.13-25 is a unit.

[46] Cf. Klein, *Werk*, 43-45.

[47] Pritius, *Introductio*, 76.

[48] Tsuji, *Glaube*, 64-72. So too Kern, 106, 123. Cf. Manton, 74: v. 12 'concludeth all the former discourse with a general sentence'. Amphoux, 'Relecture', considers 13-27 to be of a piece, vv. 13-20 being its first subdivision. Calloud-Genyut, *Analyse*, 11, treat vv. 1-13 as the first unit, vv. 14-26 as the second.

[49] So too Pareus, 541, 544; Piscator, 717; G. and H. Hart, *Analysis*, 18-43; Maier, 56, 73.

[50] Popkes, 74, 110. So too Iovino, 'Struttura', 9-11, with this analysis: first section: 1.2-4 (A) + 5-11 (B) + 12-15 (A'); second section: 1.16-21 (A) + 22-25 (B) + 26-27 (A'). Varner, *Perspective*, 37, likewise sees 1.2-15 as a unity but then judges 1.16-18 and 19-27 to be the next two sections.

[51] So too Gans, *Gedankengang*, 2, who then views 1.19–2.26 as the next major section. For Fabris, 14-15, 1.1-18 is the exordium. Meinertz, 8, sees 1.2-18 as the first section, 1.19-27 as the second.

[52] For additional analyses of chap. 1 see Popkes, 49-50.

[53] For a related analysis that discerns triads see already Hus, 185-87.

12	Blessing	Blessed is the one who endures trial
	Justification	having stood the test he will receive the crown of life
	Explanation	that he promised to those who love him.
13	Prohibited thought	Let no one, when tempted, say 'I am tempted by God'
	Justification (premise)	For God cannot be tempted to do evil
	Justification (inference)	God tempts no one
14-15	Alternative justification	Each is tempted by desire, being lured and enticed
	First Consequence	when desire conceives, it gives birth to sin
	Second Consequence	when sin comes to completion, it gives birth to death

Catchwords hold the whole together:

12	πειρασμόν	
13	πειραζόμενος... πειράζομαι... πειράζει	
14	πειράζεται...	ἐπιθυμίας
15a		ἐπιθυμιά... ἁμαρτίαν
15b		ἁμαρτία

Note also that vv. 13-14 are the antithesis of v. 12:

12	trial	13-14	temptation
	enduring the test		succumbing to desire
	the crown of life		sin and death

The antithetical presentation lines up with the rest of the chapter. Verses 2-8 contrast the perfect individual with the doubter. Verses 9-11 contrast rich and poor. Verses 22-25 contrast those who do the word with those who simply hear. Verses 26-27 contrast false religion with true religion.

Exegetes have speculated about the *Sitz im Leben* of 1.12-15. Perhaps the recipients were suffering persecution.[54] Or perhaps some were 'being tempted to use violence against their oppressors in order to establish justice'.[55] Or perhaps they interpreted all evils as divinely imposed discipline, to be embraced nobly[56] or experienced for the sake of knowledge.[57] Or perhaps they less nobly blamed God for their afflictions, excusing their own failings.[58] Or perhaps some attributed their misfortunes to the

---

[54] Cf. Tillotson, 'Sermon LXI' (as in n. 3), 380; Benson, 35-36 (imagining that recent Jewish converts to Christianity were unused to persecution); Neander, 55; Scaer, 53; Brosend, 47; *et al.*

[55] So McKnight, 117. Martin, 31, holds a related idea: Christians are tempted to go along with 'Zealot policy'.

[56] Blackman, 54, raises this possibility.

[57] For Wordsworth, 16, 'St. James may perhaps refer to the false tenet of some of the heretics of the early Church, who said that it was the duty of men to have experimental knowledge of all evil, in order to the attainment of perfection [*sic*]'. Cf. Pfleiderer, *Christianity*, 301-305: James is polemicizing against Gnostics.

[58] Blomberg-Kamell, 70, suggest this. Cf. Floor, 63; Maier, 'Jakobusbrief', 90.

fates or to an astrological determinism.[59] Or maybe James here attacks Paul, who might be thought to have taught that God tempts people;[60] or maybe James rather defends Paul, correcting perceived misinterpretation of him.[61] The evidence for all such suggestions is thin. James does not plausibly envisage definite scenarios until chap. 2, where the units become longer. Here, at the beginning, the shorter units offer instead advice of more general relevance.[62]

Although 1.12-15 shows no obvious indebtedness to the Jesus tradition, v. 12 is reminiscent of Mt 5.11-12 = Lk 6.22-23,[63] and the subject of God and temptation also famously belongs to the Lord's Prayer, Mt 6.13 = Lk 11.4.[64] As for scriptural intertextuality, James could borrow from Ecclus 15.11-20 (see on v. 13) and Ps 7.14 (see on v. 15). But the chief background for our passage is Hellenistic Judaism.[65] Philo depicts ἐπιθυμία (as well as ἡδονή) as a licentious woman who seduces and begets, and he otherwise uses the image of reproduction for how the soul, overtaken by vices and passions, begets undesirable offspring.[66] He further speaks of the 'baits' and 'lures' that desire and pleasure use to draw the soul away from its proper goal.[67] 4 Maccabees exalts ὑπομονή and ties the virtue to mastering ἐπιθυμία, promising that those who are tested (πείραζε, ἐπειρᾶτο, πειρασθεῖσα) and approved (δοκιμάζουσα) will gain life (ζωήν,

---

[59] Cf. Hanson, 'Report', 526: 'James may be resisting Greek notions of determinism'. Bardenhewer, 41, cites Agamemnon's speech in Homer, *Il.* 19.85-90: 'It is not I who am at fault, but Zeus and Fate and Erinys... since in the place of assembly they cast on my mind fierce blindness on that day when on my own authority I took from Achilles his prize. But what else could I do? It is a god that brings all things to their end'. See 262 for those who find such fatalism behind v. 17. Bisping, 21, thinks the Pharisees might be in mind since Josephus, *Bell.* 2.162, asserts that they 'attribute everything to Fate and God'. Cf. Schneckenburger, 21; Winkler, 22. Lapide, 44, imagines that James opposes Simon Magus, to whom he attributes the view that God authors temptation and sin.

[60] E.g. Rom 9.17-18; 11.8.

[61] Hengel, 'Polemik', 528, divines possible anti-Pauline polemic. So too Henshaw, *Literature*, 356. For Benson, 36-37, and Bisping, 21, James may be responding to 'misinterpretation' of Paul. Cf. Estius, 384-85.

[62] Ps.-Andrew of Crete, *Éloge* 5 ed. Noret, 48, takes the idiosyncratic view that v. 13 is prophetic: it corrects an evil that will come to pass at a later date.

[63] James: 'Blessed' – enduring temptation – eschatological crown
Matthew/Luke: 'Blessed' – persecution – reward in heaven

[64] For other suggestions as to links between our text and the Jesus tradition see n. 91.

[65] See esp. W. Wilson, 'Sin'; Kloppenborg, 'Psychagogy'.

[66] E.g. Philo, *Cher.* 71; *Deus* 14-15 (the soul separated from God brings forth a multitude of children, mostly abortions, including desire); *Jos.* 64 ('Like a licentious woman the desire of the multitudes makes love to the statesman'); *Leg.* 1.75-76 ('Travailing' is the name of folly, which produces 'wretched abortions and miscarriages... an evil tantamount to the death of the soul'); 3.148; *Spec.* 4.79-80 (ἐπιθυμία—the most troublesome of passions—'breeds fierce and endless yearnings'); *Praem.* 117 (ἡδονή and ἐπιθυμία are 'mistresses').

[67] Philo, *Agr.* 103; *Sob.* 23-24; *Migr.* 67; etc. See further W. Wilson, 'Sin', 153.

TEMPTATION AND GOD (1.12-15) 225

ζωῆ) and be crowned (στεφανοῦσα).[68] In the Testament of Joseph, the hero exhibits ὑπομονή by proving (δοκιμάσαι, δόκιμον) himself when tempted (πειρασμοῖς), when Potiphar's wife, full of ἐπιθυμία, seeks to lure (ἐφελκύσθησαν, ἐφελκύσατο, ἐφελκομήνη) him into sin.[69]

Verse 12. The importance of the themes in this verse appears not only from the connections with vv. 2-4 but also from 5.11 (μακαρίζομεν τοὺς ὑπομείναντας), which echoes our verse and so reinforces its teaching.[70]

Dibelius, 90, separates v. 12 from what follows. Surely, however, as with the catchword connections between the previous paragraphs, the link is more than formal. The question answered by vv. 13-15—'Does God do evil things?'—arises out of v. 12, where evil results in good. It is true that πειράζω in vv. 13-15 conjures up a different set of ideas than πειρασμός in vv. 2-4 and 12. These last have to do with 'trials' that fall upon the faithful for ultimate good[71] whereas vv. 13-15 deny that God directly 'tempts' to evil. Yet the sequence is altogether natural. After first extolling suffering, the author next addresses the problem of evil.[72]

μακάριος ἀνὴρ ὃς ὑπομένει πειρασμόν.[73] Cf. the πᾶσαν χαρὰν ἡγήσασθε of v. 2 and the καυχάσθω of v. 9: at this point in the letter, encouragement abounds. For ἀνήρ see on 1.8. The word need not be gender specific here.[74] Yet given that the feminine ἐπιθυμία tempts readers in vv. 14-15 and begets a child (sin), 'man' is contextually appropriate. It is also relevant that, for Philo as for other ancients, '"male" and "manly" refer generally to what is rational, complete, superior, and

---

[68] 4 Macc 1.10-11; 9.5-8; 12.2; 15.3, 16; 17.11-16.

[69] T. Jos. 2.6-7; 3.8-10; 4.7; 5.3; 7.6-8; 8.2; 10.1-2. W. Wilson, 'Sin', 165, also notes parallels with the Testament of Job, but these are less extensive.

[70] According to Lange, 47, v. 12 'contains the proper theme of the whole Epistle and indicates the dominant fundamental idea of the same'.

[71] As Ropes, 150, says regarding the πειρασμόν of v. 12, 'Inner enticement to evil would have to be *resisted*, not *endured*'. In other words, 'trial', not 'temptation', is the right translation.

[72] Cf. Johnson, 203: 'If God is an active agent in the process by which humans are proven worthy of the crown of life, is it not fair to place responsibility for every sort of testing and temptation on God?'

[73] 02 044 1448 Cyr Dam have ἄνθρωπος in second place. Is this a pre-modern attempt at gender inclusion? The future ὑπομενεῖ appears in 018 020 025 049 1 6 93 104 et al. L156 L427 L590 A^mss Sl:ChMS. Bengel, 489, and Bowyer, *Conjectures*, 314, support this reading by appealing to 1.3-4 and 1 Pet 2.20.

[74] Blomberg-Kamell, 69, argue that it is generic, given that ἀνήρ and ἄνθρωπος are interchanged in vv. 7-8. Cf. Manton, 75; Belser, 54; Hartin, 89; Gundry, 920. Some earlier commentators thought otherwise (see Huther, 48), and Wolmerans, 'Male', 139, contends that James 'envisages his audience as male' and reinforces patriarchal values. For the contemporary translation debate note D.A. Carson, *The Inclusive Language Debate*, Grand Rapids, MI, 1998, 161-62. Scaer, 51-53, exploits the singular to suggest a christological reference: Jesus is the man who endured temptation. So too Felder, 1790.

active, while "female" and "effeminate" designate their opposites'.[75] ὑπομένω[76] recurs in the closely related 5.11. Here the verb means 'patiently and constantly beareth' (Manton, 75). For πειρασμός see on v. 2, and on the relationship between that verse and this one see above, 214-15.

μακάριος[77] is first found in Pindar (fifth century BCE).[78] The basic meaning, like that of ὄλβιος, is 'free from daily cares or worries' or 'prosperous'. It originally describes the blessed state of the gods, who neither toil nor suffer.[79] But human beings can also be considered 'blessed' because of their good children, virtue, piety, wisdom, or fame. The formula, μακάριος ὅσ(τις), was common,[80] although the beatitude took many forms on Greek soil.[81]

In Jewish texts, אשרי and ברך are the key words. The difference between them is that the former, which is never applied to God, is less sacred and solemn and usually has to do with a condition of happiness.[82] The latter is the liturgical word used for blessing God. The LXX uses μακάριος (64×) only for אשרי, never for ברוך (= εὐλογητός).

μακάριος occurs fifty times in the NT, almost exclusively for religious joy.[83] μακάριος ἀνήρ ὅς (or οὗ) + verb is not found in secular Greek

---

[75] So W. Wilson, 'Sin', 151, citing Philo, *Spec.* 1.200-201; *QG* 4.15. Cf. his comment on 164: 'The inability to counteract one's desire not only marks one with attributes ascribed by Graeco-Roman sensibilities to femininity (powerlessness, passivity, instability), it is tantamount to a man subordinating himself to a woman, yielding to female sexual initiative'. Recall the masculine nature of virtue in Hermas, e.g. *Vis.* 1.4.3 (ἀνδρίζου, Ἑρμᾶ).

[76] Jas: 2×. LXX: most often for קוה.

[77] Jas: 2×; cf. 1.25. Note the repetition with the concluding word of v. 11: μαρα-// μακαρ-.

[78] Literature: G. Bertram and F. Hauck, 'μακάριος κτλ.', *TDNT* 4.362-70; W. Janzen, '"Ašrê" in the Old Testament', *HTR* 58 (1965), 215-26; E. Lipiński, 'Macarismes et psaumes de congratulation', *RB* 75 (1968), 321-67; W. Käser, 'Beobachtungen zum alttestamentlichen Makarismus', *ZAW* 82 (1970), 225-50; H. Cazelles, *TDOT* 1.445-8; M. Hengel, 'Zum matthäischen Bergpredigt und ihrem jüdischen Hintergrund', *TRu* 52 (1987), 332-41; Betz, *Sermon*, 97-105; Heckel, *Segen*.

[79] Cf. Homer, *Od.* 5.7 ('O Father Zeus and other gods blessed [μάκαρες] forever'); Epicurus, *Ep. ad Men.* 123 (God is immortal and μακάριον); Ps.-Socrates, *Ep.* 6.4 ('God is happy and μακάριος').

[80] Cf. Pindar, *Pyth.* 5.46; Menander frag. 114; Euripides frag. 256; etc. For Jewish and Christian texts see below.

[81] ὄλβιος ὅσ(τις) was also common (e.g. Hesiod, *Theog.* 95, 954-5; Theocritus 12.34; Pindar, *Olymp.* 7.11; Euripides frag. 910; Sib. Or. 14.307), as were expressions employing τρισμακάριος (e.g. Aristophanes, *Ach.* 400; Philo, *Praem.* 30).

[82] Cf. the Aramaic synonym, טובא, as in 4Q196 18.3; Tg. 1 Kgs 10.8 (for אשרי): the basic meaning of this word is 'good' or 'goodness'.

[83] Mt: 13×; Lk: 15×; Jn: 2×; Acts: 2×; Pauline epistles: 7× (three beatitudes); Jas: 2×; 1 Pet: 2×; Rev: 7×. The related noun, μακαρισμός, appears three times (Rom 4.6, 9; Gal 4.15), the verb, μακαρίζω, twice (Lk 1.48; Jas 5.11). The NT does not use ὄλβιος or εὐδαίμων.

sources. It is a formula taken over by early Christians[84] from the Psalms and the wisdom literature of the LXX:

- LXX Ps 1.1   μακάριος ἀνὴρ ὃς οὐκ ἐπορεύθη
- LXX Ps 33.9   μακάριος ἀνὴρ ὃς ἐλπίζει
- LXX Prov 8.34   μακάριος ἀνὴρ ὃς εἰσακούσεται
- LXX Prov 28.14   μακάριος ἀνὴρ ὃς καταπτήσσει
- LXX Ecclus 14.1   μακάριος ἀνὴρ ὃς οὐκ ὠλίσθησεν
- LXX Ecclus 14.20   μακάριος ἀνὴς ὅς... μελετήσει[85]

There are several corresponding Hebrew formulas: אשרי האיש אשר + verb (Ps 1.1), (אשר הגבר) אשרי (Ps 34.9; 4Q173 3.1), (שהוא) אשרי אדם + verb (Ps 84.13; Prov 8.34; 28.14; 4Q185 1-2 2.8, 13; 4Q525 2ii + 3.3), אשרי אנוש (Ecclus 14.1, 20), אשרי איש ש (traditional Morning Prayer).[86] Exodus Rabbah 31.3 supplies a parallel of both form and content: אשרי אדם שהוא עומד בנסיונו שאין בריה שאין הקב״ה מנסה אותה.[87] The late rabbinic line goes on to speak about the rich and the poor and their rewards in the world to come; cf. Jas 1.9-11.[88]

In each of the texts from the LXX, as in James, the blessed individual is a moral or religious model. But explanatory ὅτι after μακάριος does not occur. Its appearance rather reminds one of the beatitudes in the Jesus tradition, which so often have μακάριοι/ος...ὅτι.[89] James further recalls the Jesus tradition in that his beatitude has eschatological content.[90] But

---

[84] Cf. Rom 4.8 (citing LXX Ps 31.2); *Gos. Thom.* 58 (ⲟⲨⲘⲀⲔⲀⲢⲒⲞⲤ ⲠⲈ ⲠⲢⲰⲘⲈ ⲚⲦⲀϨϨⲒⲤⲈ); 103 (ⲟⲨⲘⲀⲔⲀⲢⲒⲞⲤ ⲠⲈ ⲠⲢⲰⲘⲈ ⲠⲀⲈⲒ ⲈⲦⲤⲞⲞⲨ); Barn. 10.10 (quoting Ps 1.1); Justin, *1 Apol.* 40.8 (quoting Ps 1.1); *Dial.* 61.5 (citing Prov 8.34).

[85] For μακάριος ἀνὴρ οὗ see LXX Ps 31.2; 39.5; 83.6; Ps Sol. 6.1; 10.1; Sextus, *Sent.* 40. For μακάριος ἀνὴρ ὁ see LXX Ps 111.1; Isa 56.2; also LAE 29.15 v.l.: 'Felix est omnis homo qui...'; on this see J.H. Mozley, 'The Vitae Adae', *JTS* 30 (1929), 121-49

[86] *Daily Prayer Book: Ha-Siddur Ha-Shalem*, ed. P. Birnbaum, New York, 1977, 79. Cf. also the rabbinic אשרי + מי, as in t. Suk. 4.2; y. Ta'an. 69b (4.5); b. Ber. 17a.

[87] 'Blessed is the man who stands in his temptations, for there is none whom God does not prove'.

[88] 'If the rich man withstands his test and practises charity, then he will enjoy his wealth in this world while the capital will be preserved for him in the life to come, and the Holy One, blessed be he, will redeem him from the punishment of Gehenna... If the poor man withstands his test without rebelling he takes a double portion in the world to come.'

[89] Mt 5.3, 4, 5, 6, 7, 8, 9, 10; 13.16; 16.17; Lk 1.45, 48; 6.20, 21; 12.38; 14:14. Other beatitudes with ὅτι or an equivalent include Ps.-Plato, *Hipp. maj.* 304B; Gen 30.13; 1 Sam 23.21; 1 En. 58.2-3 ('Blessed are you, righteous and elect ones, for glorious is your portion. The righteous one shall be in the light of the sun'); Tob 13.16 S (μακάριοι πάντες οἱ ἄνθρωποι, οἵ...ὅτι—with eschatological content); Bar 4.4; 1 Pet 4.14; Acts Paul 5, 6 ed. Lipsius, 238-39; Acts Thom. 94 ed. Bonnet, 207-208; Apost. Const. 5.2.3 ed. Funk, 241.

[90] For beatitudes with an eschatological promise see Dan 12.12; Tob 13.14; 1 En. 58.2-3 (see n. 89); 81.4 ('Blessed is the one who dies righteous and upright, against whom no record of oppression has been written, and who received no judgment on that day'); Pss. Sol. 17.44 ('Blessed are those born in those days to see the good fortune of Israel'); 18.6 ('Blessed are those born in those days'); 2 En. 42.6-14; 52.1-14.

if there is an allusion in Jas 1.12 it is less likely to a word of Jesus[91] than to Dan 12.12, which in Theodotion reads: μακάριος ὁ ὑπομένων.[92] The possibility of an allusion is perhaps strengthened by the appearance of πειράζω in LXX Dan 12.10 ('Many will be tried'). There are, however, also good parallels in Isa 30.18 (LXX: μακάριοι οἱ ἐμμένοντες ἐν αὐτῷ); LXX Zech 6.14 (ὁ δὲ στέφανος ἔσται τοῖς ὑπομένουσι);[93] 2 Bar. 52.5-7 ('Rejoice in the suffering which you now suffer… Prepare your souls for the reward which is held for you'); Herm. *Vis.* 2.2.7 (μακάριοι ὑμεῖς ὅσοι ὑπομένετε τὴν θλῖψιν τὴν ἐρχομένην τὴν μεγάλην). So James may not allude to any particular text but rather express a theological commonplace.

ὑπομένει πειρασμόν takes the reader back to 1.2-4, where various trials (πειρασμοῖς) test faith and lead to ὑπομονή.[94] ὑπομένω + πειρασμόν is not classical and is foreign to the LXX. Its earliest appearance besides James appears to be in Origen.[95] Before that, the closest parallel is T. Jos. 2.7— 'In ten πειρασμοῖς he (God) showed that I (Joseph) was δόκιμον, and in all of them I persevered, because perseverance is a powerful medicine and ὑπομονή provides many good things'—and Paul has the comparable ὑποφέρω + πειρασμόν in 1 Cor 10.13.

---

[91] Some—e.g. Gill, 781; Kloppenborg, 'Reception', 122-29—suspect dependence upon Mt 5.11-12 = Lk 6.22-23 or Mt 10.22. Deppe, *Sayings*, 245-46, argues to the contrary. For Knoch, 157, 1.12 is an application of Mt 5.11. Hoppe, *Hintergrund*, 41, asks whether the near association of temptation with beatitudes in Q (in modern reconstructions, Q 6.20-23 immediately follows Q 4.1-13) has anything to do with our verse. Hort, 20, wonders whether James refers to Mt 19.29 or Lk 18.29-30; cf. Grotius, 1075. G.C. Martin, 'Storehouse', 177-78, urges that we have here a word of Jesus, for the sayings about crowns in Rev 2.10; Acts Phil 135 ed. Bonnet, 67 ('Blessed is he who has his garment white, for he it is who receives the crown of joy'); and Liber Graduum 3.3 ed. Kmosko, 52 ('Our Lord said: "If after…receiving blows, you have won and come up from the contest, received the wreath and with it departed from this world, then your faults will not be remembered. As you are found in victory, so you will be taken, wearing your wreath"') are attributed to Jesus; note also 2 Tim 4.7-8. Cf. Belser, 55; Mayor, lxiii; Resch, *Agrapha*, 34-35; Weidner, 30 (an oral tradition like Acts 20.35); Plummer, 577; MacDougall, 23; W. Grundmann, 'στέφανος, στεφανόω', *TDNT* 7, 630; Adamson, 68; Scaer, 55 (maybe a word of the risen Jesus); Fruchtenbaum, 224; De Luca *et al.*, 'Transmissione'.

[92] LXX: ἐμμένων; MT: הַמְחַכֶּה.

[93] On this parallel see Bouman, 70-71. For Easton, 26, this verse is 'possibly' in mind.

[94] See the remarks there. Dibelius, 88, surmises that there 'is only one difference [between vv. 2-4 and 12]: the trials which are presupposed in the earlier verses are troubles involving the community addressed collectively as "brothers"; here, where it is the individual person who is being discussed, we may imagine the misfortune of the individual'. Whether the two things should be distinguished is unclear.

[95] Origen, *Hom. Lk* 26 GCS 35 ed. Rauer, 155 (ὅταν δὲ πειρασμοῦ γενομένου ὑπομείνῃς τὸν πειρασμόν); *Frag. Lk* 93 GCS 35, ed. Rauer, 264 (κἂν πειρασμόν τις ὑπομείνῃ).

ὅτι δόκιμος γενόμενος λήμψεται τὸν στέφανον τῆς ζωῆς. δόκιμος[96] and στέφανος[97] are Jamesian *hapax legomena*. ζωή recurs in 4.14, with different sense. Elsewhere James uses λαμβάνω (6×)—common with στέφανος as object[98]—of receiving from God: in 1.7 (answers to prayer); 3.1 (eschatological judgment); 4.3 (answers to prayer).

In Judaism and Christianity, the eschatological beatitude is typically addressed to those in dire straits: it promises future consolation and thereby brings comfort. So in contrast to the wisdom beatitude, where moral exhortation is, despite the declarative form, generally the object, assurance and hope are the goal: eyes become focused on the future, which will reverse everyday values and the present situation. Our beatitude combines elements from both types. As in Dan 12.12 and the nine beatitudes in Mt 5.3-12, those suffering trial are being both comforted and called to further faithfulness.

δόκιμος here means 'tried and true' or 'approved (by test)',[99] so δόκιμος γενόμενος[100] makes plain the outcome of enduring trials. Readers are reminded of the related δοκίμιον (= 'means of testing') in 1.3, which follows a verse having to do with 'trials' (πειρασμοῖς). The combination of δόκιμος and πειρασμός also makes for resemblance with T. Jos. 2.7 (see above); 1 Pet 1.6-7 ('you have to suffer various πειρασμοῖς so that the δοκίμιον of your faith...');[101] and the agraphon, 'A man ἀδόκιμος is a man ἀπείραστος by God'; see n. 171. ὅτι δόκιμος κτλ. also recalls Christian texts that associate salvation with suffering: Acts 14.22 ('It is through many persecutions that we must enter the kingdom of God'); Barn. 7.11 ('Jesus says, "Those who will see me, and attain to my kingdom must lay hold of me through pain and suffering"'); Gos. Thom. 58 ('Blessed is the man who has suffered, he has found life'); Tertullian, *De bapt.* 20 CSEL 20 ed. Reifferscheid and Wissowa, 217 ('No one can enter the kingdom of heaven without having been tested').

James 1.12 does not, however, appear to be a true variant of any of these but rather an independent formulation with similar content. It also has striking parallels in 2 Tim 4.8 ('From now on there is laid up for me a

---

[96] NT: 6×, all but once in the Pauline corpus. LXX: 6×, always of metals or coins; cf. Let. Aris. 57. Gk. Pseudepigrapha (Denis): 3×. Philo: 74×. Josephus: 14×. Cf. δοκίμιον in Jas 1.3 and δοκιμάζω in T. Ash. 5.4; T. Jud. 2.6.

[97] Most often for עטרה in the LXX.

[98] Cf. Aristophanes, *Nub.* 256; Demosthenes, *Or.* 51.17; LXX Ecclus 32.2; Josephus, *Ant.* 7.161; Acts Thom. 158 ed. Bonnet, 268; etc.

[99] Cf. Rom 16.10; 2 Cor 13:7; 2 Tim 2.15. Even though, in the LXX, the word is consistently used in connection with refined metals, it seems unlikely that readers of James should have in mind a concrete image. But Beyschlag, 61, like many, envisions the purification of metals. Others, such as Pott, 152, think rather of athletic competition. See further Huther, 48.

[100] Cf. Philo, *Mos.* 2.187: γέγονε δοκιμώτατος, of Moses.

[101] On the possible literary relationship between James and this as well as with Rom 5.3-5 (where ὑπομονή and δοκιμή appear) see above, 140-41.

crown of righteousness, which the Lord, the righteous judge, will give me on that day, and not only to me but also to all who have loved his appearing'); Rev 2.10 ('Be faithful unto death and I will give you the crown of life');[102] Acts Phil. 135 ed. Bonnet, 67 ('Blessed is he who has his garment white, for he it is who receives the crown of joy'). Once again it is best not to seek a genealogical relationship: we simply have to do with commonly associated motifs.

τὸν στέφανον τῆς ζωῆς[103] is referred to also in Rev 2.10, just quoted.[104] Whether ancient readers would have envisaged a crown of vegetation, of the sort given to winners of athletic contests[105] or for honoring

---

[102] For Pfleiderer, *Christianity*, 296, James here depends upon Rev 2.10. So too Zeller, 'Über Jak 1,12'; Grimm, 'Einleitung', 388.

[103] This expression does not appear in secular Greek literature, nor does the obvious Semitic equivalent, עטרת החיים, appear until the Middle Ages. The nearest ancient parallel (not counting Rev 2.10) seems to be the epitaph printed in *IG* 14 (1890), 441: λιφθεὶς τὸν βιότου στέφανον, 'I was defeated [?] for the crown of life'. See *Hellenica* 11-12 (1960), 330-42. Also reminiscent of our phrase are Aelius Aristides, *Or.* 27.36 ('these are adorned τῷ τῶν ἀθανάτων στεφάνῳ') Odes Sol. 1.1-4 ('The Lord is like a wreath on my head...you are alive on my head'); 17.1 ('God is my living crown'); 20.7 (a wreath from 'the tree [of life]'); and the scholion to Aristophanes, *Lys.* 601 ed. Rutherford, 2.198: the crown is given to the dead 'as to those who have won the contest of life'.

[104] Literature: L. Deubner, 'Die Bedeutung des Kranzes im klassischen Altertum', *Archiv für Religionswissenschaft* 30 (1933), 70-104; K. Baus, *Der Kranz in Antike und Christentum*, Bonn, 1940; E.R. Goodenough, 'The Crown of Victory in Judaism', *Art Bulletin* 28 (1946), 139-59; idem, *Jewish Symbols in the Greco Roman Period*, vol. 7, New York, 1958, 135-71; vol. 12 (1965), 138-41; H. Kosmala, *Hebräer-Essener-Christen*, Leiden, 1959, 246-50; W. Grundmann, 'στέφανος, στεφανόω', *TDNT* 7.615-36; M. Blech, *Studien zum Kranz bei den Griechen*, Berlin, 1982; F.W. Danker, *Benefactor*, St. Louis, 1982, 467-71; Z. Stewart, 'Greek Crowns and Christian Martyrs', in *Mémorial André-Jean Festugière*, ed. E. Lucchesi and H.D. Saffrey, Geneva, 1984, 119-24; M. Mach, *Entwicklungsstadien des jüdischen Engelglaubens in vorrabinischer Zeit*, Tübingen, 1992, 185-208; G.M. Stevenson, 'The Conceptual Background to Golden Crown Imagery in the Apocalypse of John (4:4, 10; 14:14)', *JBL* 114 (1995), 257-72.

[105] Such is the interpretation of Methodius Olympus, *Cibis* 4.4 GCS 27 ed. Bonwetsch, 431; Didymus of Alexandria *ad loc.* ed. Zoepfl, 3; Chrysostom *ad loc.* PG 64.1040B-C; Clarke, 800 ('There may be an allusion here to the contests in the Grecian games'); Pott, 152; cf. Hort, 20, who nevertheless adds that James' phrase 'probably came from Jewish usage not now recorded'. Contrast Theile, 37-38; Ropes, 152. See Herodotus 8.26 ('the wreath of olive leaves' awarded at the Olympic festival); Aeschines, *Ctes.* 179 ('games that confer a crown'); Philo, *Prob.* 26 ('he will finally quit the arena without a crown'); T. Job 4.10 (see n. 114); Ps.-Diogenes, *Ep.* 31 (the crowning of Cicermus with the Olympic wreath and his coming to learn of things that matter more); Tab. Cebes 22.1 ('one crowns those who have been victorious in the mightiest contests'); and the many references in Blech, *Kranz*, 109-81, and Oscar Broneer, 'The Isthmian Victory Crown', *AJA* 66 (1962), 259-63. For early Christian texts note 1 Cor 9.25; 1 Pet 5.4; 2 Clem. 7.3 ('Let us run the straight course, the immortal contest, and let many of us sail to it, and contend, that we may also receive the crown, and if we cannot all receive the crown, let us at least come near to it').

TEMPTATION AND GOD (1.12-15)   231

benefactors,[106] or rather crowns such as those sometimes worn by royalty[107]—this would harmonize with 2.5—or other honored public figures,[108] including victorious soldiers,[109] is unclear.[110] Dibelius, 88, doubts that the expression alludes to any concrete metaphor,[111] and a few exegetes seemingly deem it unworthy of explanation.[112] In any case the promise of a (metaphorical) crown bestowed by wisdom[113] became, in

---

[106] See e.g. IGRR 1.1077; CJZC 70, 71; CPJ 1530A; IJO 2.36 = CIJ 2.738.

[107] Although we must distinguish the 'diadem' (διάδημα) from the 'crown' (στέφανος), and while 'throughout the Hellenistic and Roman periods it was the diadem (διάδημα), rather than the wreath (στέφανος), that functioned primarily as a symbol of royalty' (so Stevenson, 'Crown Imagery', 259), one cannot isolate the στέφανος altogether from royal associations. The two terms were not always distinct (*pace* Trench, *Synonyms*, 78-81; so rightly Mayor, 48-49), and the latter could be used with reference to the headgear of royalty (sometimes a wreath was placed over or wound about a diadem); see e.g. Josephus, *Bell.* 1.671; 7.105; *Ant.* 17.197; Plutarch, *Caes.* 61.5; *Mor.* (*Fort. Rom.*) 325E (στεφάνους βασιλέων); Cassius Dio 51.6.5 (Cleopatra sent to Mark Antony a golden scepter, a golden crown [στέφανον] together with the royal throne). The generalization holds for the LXX: 2 Βασ 12.30; Esth 8.15 (a king with both crown and diadem); Ps 21.3; Jer 13.18; Ezek 21.26; Ecclus 40.3-4 (always translating עטרה); cf. the כתר מלכות ('kingly crown') and כתרי מלכות ('kingly crowns') of 3 En. 12.4 and 17.8 respectively and the *regni coronam* in Virgil, *Aen.* 8.505. One recalls that the 'crown (στέφανος) of thorns' in the canonical gospels is part of a mock coronation. In connection with the possibility that the crown in Jas 1.12 is a royal motif, Mayor, 49, cites texts in which the saints reign in the coming world (e.g. Dan 7.27; Mt 19.28).

[108] Note CIJ 2.738 = IJO 2.36, where the patron of a synagogue is honored with 'a gold crown and a seat of honor'; IMylasa I 119 (in Horsley-Llewelyn, *Documents*, 9.1), where a gold crown and bronze statue are given to an accomplished dignitary; AthMitt 33.147.4.9, where a 'gold crown in Christ' awaits a dead Christian. For the controversy over the crowning of Demosthenes see Demosthenes, *Or.* 18.54-55, 84. According to Tertullian, *Cor.* 13 CSEL 70 ed. Kroymann, 181, 'the various orders of citizens are crowned with laurel crowns, but the magistrates with golden ones, as at Athens and Rome'.

[109] See e.g. Demosthenes, *Or.* 18.116 (a golden crown for bravery in battle); Josephus, *Bell.* 7.14 (Titus presenting crowns of gold to officers who served well during the Jewish war); Arrian, *Anab.* 7.5.4-6 (gold crowns for 'conspicuous bravery'). Full discussion in V.A. Maxfield, *The Military Decorations of the Roman Army*, Berkeley, 1981, 67-81. But the military also awarded wreaths; see Tertullian, *Cor.* 12 CSEL 70 ed. Kroymann, 178.

[110] In any case, the homiletical remark of Wynn, 'Temptation', 103, seems fitting: 'It is a suggestive figure. The man who conquers in his struggle with sin of self is the uncrowned king among men.'

[111] He speaks of 'the use of the concept as a mere byword, a use in which the concrete prospect no longer stood in the background' (89). Cf. Ropes, 151-52: 'It may even be that στέφανος, like στεφανόω, had already gained the simple meaning "reward"'. Cf. Ps 103.4 ('crowns you with steadfast love and mercy'); the use of עטרה in 11Q5 19.7-8 ('crowns his devout with kindness and compassion'); m. 'Abot 4.13 ('the crown of a good name'). See also n. 113.

[112] Bede *ad loc.* CCSL 121 ed. D. Hurst, 187, passes it over in silence.

[113] Prov 4.19; 14.24; Ecclus 1.18; 6.31; 15.6; cf. CPJ 3.1530a ('crowned in his wisdom'). For additional metaphorical uses of 'crown' in the wisdom tradition see

apocalyptic and related literature, surpassed by hope for a crown in the afterlife or the new age.[114] This may have happened because of the application of athletic imagery to Jewish martyrs.[115] It may also have had something to do with the secular practice of awarding crowns posthumously[116] or with the fact that graves were sometimes decorated or

---

Prov 12.4; 16.31; 17.6; Ecclus 1.11; 25.6. Frankemölle, 262-63, stresses also in this connection the importance of 'life' for the wisdom tradition. Note further Ps 103.4; Isa 62.3; LXX Ezek 28.12; Let. Aris. 280; 1Q28b 4.3; m. 'Abot 4.13; and from the Christian tradition Phil 4.1; 1 Thess 2.19; Pol. *Phil.* 1.1; Odes Sol. 5.12; 9.8; 17.1; 20:7. עטרה means both 'protection' and 'crown' in rabbinic sources: Jastrow, s.v. Graeco-Roman literature also attests to metaphorical usage: Euripides *Iph. Aul.* 194 ('Salamis's crown' = 'Salamis's pride'); Aristophanes, *Nu.* 959 ('to crown' = 'to adorn'); Ps.-Heraclitus, *Ep.* 4 (Heraclitus crowned himself through his virtuous behavior); Tab. Cebes 22.1 ('Happiness crowns him with her power', cf. 23.3; 24.2); etc.

[114] E.g. Wis 5.15-16 ('But the righteous live forever, and their reward is with the Lord; the Most High takes care of them. Therefore they will receive a glorious crown and a beautiful diadem from the hand of the Lord'); 1QH 17(9).25 ('a crown of glory for me'); 1QS 4.7-8 ('a crown of glory together with a resplendent attire in eternal light'); 1 Cor 9.25; 2 Tim 4.8; 1 Pet 5.4; Rev 3.11; T. Benj. 4.1 ('crowns of glory'); T. Job 4.9-10 ('And you shall be raised in the resurrection. For you will be like a sparring athlete, both enduring pains and winning the στέφανον'); 40.3; 2 Bar. 15.8 ('a crown of great glory'); 4 Ezra 2.46 (the reception of palms and crowns upon entrance into immortality); Herm. *Sim.* 8.2.1; 8.3.6 ('those who are crowned are the ones who have wrestled with the devil and conquered him'); Apoc. Elijah 1.8 (crowns prepared in heaven); Asc. Isa. 7.22 (heavenly robes and a crown laid up for Isaiah; cf. 8.26; 9.10-18); Mart. Pol. 17.1 ('crowned with the crown of immortality'); Gk. Apoc. Ezra 6.17 ('the crown is ready for you'); b. Ber. 17a ('In the future world... the righteous sit with crowns on their heads'); b. Šabb. 104a ('a crown on you in the world to come'); h. Sanh. 111b ('a crown on the head of every righteous one'). These parallels and James' future tense (λήμψεται) explain why Hodges, 25-26, is almost alone in equating the crown with 'enrichment of our *temporal* experience of life (spiritually always, materially sometimes)'—although for Knowling, 18, the 'crown' indicates 'a life which is at all events commenced for the Christian, cf. Rom. v. 17, and of which he is already in possession at least in germ'. But the eschatological sense is patent; so already Origen, *Hom. in Gen.* 15.6 SC 7, ed. Doutreleau, 368. For the possibility of an Egyptian background to the eschatological crown see J.G. Griffiths, *The Divine Verdict*, Leiden, 1991, 238-39.

[115] See 4 Macc 6.10; 11.20; 15.29; 17.11-16 (v. 15: 'Piety won the victory and crowned her own contestants'). Cf. Sib. Or. 2.38-39 (perhaps Christian): 'For then he will show from heaven a crown to men who strive in contest'. Following Jewish precedent, crown symbolism became associated particularly with Christian martyrs; note e.g. Rev 2.10; Mart. Pol. 17 (Polycarp 'was crowned with the crown of immortality'), 19 (Polycarp 'received the crown of immortality'). See further V. Saxer, 'The Influence of the Bible in Early Christian Martyrology', in *The Bible in Greek Christian Antiquity*, ed. P.M. Blowers, Notre Dame, IN, 1997, 361-63.

[116] Note OGIS 339.6; IGRom 3.739 cols. 4, 5, 11; MAMA 8 (1962) 408.13-14 (one deceased is crowned with 'the crown of excellence'). See further Horsley-Llewelyn, *Documents*, 2.50. One might also note Heb 2.9, where Jesus is crowned with glory and honor after his suffering and death.

inscribed with wreaths, so that they became a sign of immortality.[117] Sometimes the language surrounding the eschatological crown is metaphorical,[118] and if that is so here we may have an epexegetical genitive: the wreath that is life.[119] Just as often, however, the extant sources seem to anticipate a literal crown.[120] If this is the case here—so Burchard, 70—then James' genitive is either a genitive of definition—the promised crown is that which belongs to the future world, when the saints will be adorned as are the angels and God[121]—or a genitive of quality—the crown

[117] Cf. e.g. NDL 48 ('Doddous... crowned her husband Athenodikos with the wreath above' refers to an inscribed wreath on the grave marker), 96. See further Blech, *Kranz* (as in n. 104), 81-108, and Goodenough, 'Crown of Victory' (as in n. 104), offering Jewish examples. In Plato, *Resp.* 363C-D, the righteous in the house of Hades recline on couches and are crowned in wreaths. Dibelius, 88, citing Apuleius, *Met.* 11.24 ('a beautiful garland was wound around my head, with bright palm leaves shooting out like rays of light; thus adorned to resemble the sun'), assumes that James' expression ultimately derives from the mystery cults. This is supposition only, although it is true that 'initiates were "crowned". The Orphics crowned themselves with flowers. The Graeco-Roman vase of Monaco shows, amid some eschatological scenes, an initiate with a crown on his head. The *pinax* of Ninnion and the relief of Lacratides represent the Eleusian candidate crowned with myrtle, the nuptial plant sacred to Aphrodite'; so S. Angus, *The Mystery-Religions*, New York, 1975, 91. See further Goodenough, *Jewish Symbols* (as in n. 104), 7.158-61.

[118] E.g. 1Q28b 4.3; 4Q257 5.5; 1 Cor 9.25; 2 Bar. 15.8; Odes Sol. 17.1.

[119] Cf. Erasmus, *Paraphrase*, 140; Trapp, 694 ('Eternal life is called "a crown": 1. For the perpetuity of it; for a crown hath neither beginning nor ending. 2. For the plenty; because as the crown compasseth on every side, so there is nothing wanting in this life. 3. The dignity; eternal life is coronation-day'; Manton, 75-76, says much the same thing); T. Scott, 567; Hort, 20; Mayor, 49; Meinertz, 23; Mussner, 86; Johnson, 188; Gundry, 920; and most.

[120] E.g. 1QS 4.7-8; 4 Ezra 2.43-46 (Lapide, 42, imagines that James alludes to this text); Asc. Isa. 7.22; 8.26; 9.10-18; Apoc. Paul 12 v.l.; b. Ber. 17a; b. Šabb. 104a. In Rev 4.4 and 10 and throughout 3 Enoch, the crowns must be literal crowns. One might think either of metallic crowns (as in Revelation) or of a nimbus (as in the morning Amidah: 'You placed a crown of glory on his [Moses'] head') or of both together (as seemingly in 3 Enoch). In T. Abr. RecShrt 13.19-20, the metaphorical appears to be mixed with the literal: 'If anyone is righteous, they [the angels] take all his righteousness and it becomes a crown on my [Death's] head, and I go to him in persuasiveness and in his own righteousness. But if anyone is a sinner, I go to him in great putrefaction, but also they [the angels] make all his sins into a crown on my head, and in great fear I disturb him greatly.'

[121] For the crowns of angels see Jos. Asen. 14.9 (of Michael the archangel); Rev 14.14 (of one like the Son of man; the figure is Jesus but he is presented as an angel; see P.R. Carrell, *Jesus and the Angels*, Cambridge, UK, 1997, 175-95); 2 En. 14.2 A (the crown of the sun); 3 Bar. 6.2 (the crown of the sun); Apoc. Zeph. frag. *apud* Clement of Alexandria, *Strom*. 5.11.17 GCS 15 ed. Stählin, 377 (diadems upon the lords of heaven); 3 En. 12.4 (the crown of Metatron: 'a crown in which 49 refulgent stones were placed, each like the sun's orb'); 16.2 ('all the princes of kingdoms crowned with crowns'); 17.8 ('crowned with kingly crowns'); 18.23, 25; 21.4; Hekalot Rabbati 11.1; and A. Green, *Keter*, Princeton, 1997, 58-67. For God's crown see 3 En. 15B.2; 29.1; 48B.1; b. Ḥag.

of life, unlike those that wither,[122] is eternal.[123] Beyond that, ancient Jewish or Christian readers might have associated the crown with their own priestly[124] or royal[125] status. Almost certainly they would have associated it with joy.[126]

ὃν ἐπηγγείλατο τοῖς ἀγαπῶσιν αὐτόν.[127] Cf. LXX Ps 5.12-13 ('those who love [ἀγαπῶντες] your name will boast in you, because you will bless [εὐλογήσες] the righteous...you crowned [ἐστεφάνωσας] us');

13b; and Green, *Keter*, passim. Divinities in the Graeco-Roman world regularly appear with crowns: Ep Jer 8 ('People take gold and make crowns for the heads of their gods'); Philo, *Legat.* 103 ('Apollo wears a crown adorned with rays'); Epictetus, *Diatr.* 4.8.30 (the diadem of Zeus); Tertullian, *Cor.* 7 CSEL 70 ed. Kroymann, 164-68 (a list of examples); etc.

[122] Cf. Isa 28.1 ('the fading flower of its glorious beauty, which is on the head of those bloated with rich food, of those overcome with wine'; cf. vv. 3-4). Some exegetes draw a contrast with the short-lived rich in vv. 10-11.

[123] Cf. 1 Pet 5.4 ('you will win the crown of glory that never fades away'); Odes Sol. 17.1; Ps.-Chrysostom, *Paen. 1* PG 60.685 (τὸν ἀμαράντινον στέφανον τῆς ζωῆς). For Gill, 781, the crown of life 'differs from the corruptible crown given to the victors in the...games, which were made of fading herbs, and leaves of trees'.

[124] Cf. Exod 19.6; 1 Pet 2.9. For crowns of priests see Exod 28.36-38; 29.5-9; Zech 6.11; 1 Macc 10.20; Ecclus 45.12; Philo, *Mos.* 2.114; Josephus, *Ant.* 3.157; T. Levi 8.9-10; m. 'Abot 4.13; etc. Cf. Plato, *Resp.* 328C ('He had a garland on, for he had just sacrificed in the courtyard'); Xenophon, *An.* 7.1.40 ('a garland on his head all ready for the sacrifice'); Virgil, *Aen.* 7.135 (Aeneas binds his head with a leafy branch before praying).

[125] Cf. Dan 7.27; Sib. Or. 2.288-90; 4Q521; T. Levi 13.9; 2 Tim 2.12; Rev 3.21; 20.4; 22.5; Pol. *Phil.* 5.2; and the targumim on Exod 19.6. Note also the Acts of the Scillitan Martyrs 17 v.l. ed. Musurillo, 88 n., where the martyrs at the end have crowns and reign. Here the notion of collective messianism becomes relevant; see H. Roose, *Eschatologische Mitherrschaft*, Göttingen, 2004. For Knowling, 17-18, the parallel in Jas 2.5 favors finding a motif of sovereignty in 1.12.

[126] Dionysius bar Salībī *ad loc.* CSCO 60, Scriptores Syri 101, ed. Sedlacek, 89, speaks of a crown of 'eternal joy'. So too Gill, 781. Cf. Jub. 16.30 (a crown for the feast of booths); Jdt 15.13 (garlands with dancing and singing and celebration at the death of Holofernes); Ecclus 15.6 ('a crown of rejoicing'); Phil 4'1 ('my joy and crown'); Odes Sol. 20.7-8 ('make for yourself a wreath...and set it on your head and rejoice'); b. Roš. Haš. 8b ('they ate and drank and made merry, wearing garlands on their heads'); Tg. on Isa 28.5 ('for a crown of joy and for a diadem of glory'); also Sophocles, *Trach.* 178 ('a messenger, bay-wreathed—he brings good news'); Aelian 3.3 (removing a garland for mourning and putting it back on at good news); Tab. Cebes 27.1 ('Some of them are wearing crowns and present an appearance of exultation, while others are without crowns and give the appearance of grief and confusion'). See further Deubner, 'Bedeutung' (as in n. 104), 103-104. The common wearing of crowns at weddings—which lives on in Eastern Orthodoxy—is here relevant; cf. Cant. 3.11; Euripides, *Iph. Aul.* 905-906; Chariton 3.2.16; Jos. Asen. 21.5; Acts Thom. 5 ed. Bonnet, 107; b. Soṭah 49b; etc.; see Baus, *Kranz* (as in n. 104), 93-112; Blech, *Kranz* (as in n. 104), 75-81; Green, *Keter* (as in n. 121), 78-87.

[127] The unstated subject of ἐπηγγείλατο is (ὁ) κύριος in 04 025 0246 5 61 69 88 180T *et al.* **Byz** L593 AnastS PsOec A^mss, ὁ θεός (cf. 2.5) in 322 323 945 *et al.* Ath Cyr^T Dam Did **L**:V **S**:P **G**:ABG-D **SI**:DM. 1751 2374 2805 assimilate to Tit 1.2: ὁ ἀψευδὴς θεός.

Pss. Sol. 14.1 ('The Lord is faithful to those who love him [τοῖς ἀγαπῶσιν αὐτόν] in truth, to those who endure [ὑπομένουσι] his discipline'). Manton, 76-77, asks, 'Why them that love, rather than them that serve or obey him, or some other description?' He answers, among other things: 'Because patience is the fruit of love'.

Both ἐπαγγέλλομαι[128] and ἀγαπάω (Jas: 3×) recur in 2.5, in the same phrase.[129] The subject of the line is unspecified, and the secondary insertions of (ὁ) κύριος and ὁ θεός in the textual tradition are expected. Most modern commentators assume that the textual variants offer correct interpretation.[130] The recurrence of the same phrase in 2.5, where ὁ θεός is the subject, seems decisive.[131] We have here 'the style of rabbinical writings, where the word "God" is sometimes to be supplied mentally'.[132] Christian readers have nonetheless sometimes thought rather of Jesus, and they have for support appealed to 2 Tim 4.8 and Rev 2.10, where Jesus Christ gives the saints their crowns.[133]

ἐπηγγείλατο τοῖς ἀγαπῶσιν αὐτόν reflects a thoroughly Jewish notion: one should love God. The imperative is enshrined in the Shema' (Deut 6.6), which the Jewish James presumably recited (cf. 2.19), and it is all over early Christian writings.[134] Indeed, τοῖς ἀγαπῶσιν + τὸν θεόν or αὐτόν (derived from לאהביו)[135] was a formula for both Jews and Christians.[136]

---

[128] Jas: 2×; NT: 15×. LXX: 10×. Gk. Pseudepigrapha (Denis): 8×. Philo: 15×. The word is a favorite of Josephus (62×).

[129] In 2.8 James speaks of loving one's neighbor. But he never uses the substantive, ἀγάπη, which appears so often in Paul. Mussner, 86 n. 5, wonders whether this is a sign of a Jewish-Christian milieu.

[130] Schlatter, 125: 'The naming of God is not necessary. Everyone thinks of him.' Cf. Didymus of Alexandria *ad loc.* ed. Zoepfl, 3-4; Chrysostom *ad loc.* PG 64.1040C. According to Windisch-Preisker, 7, the subject is Scripture, maybe Dan 12.12 or LXX Zech 6.14 (see above). Others have thought of a word of Jesus; see n. 91.

[131] Cf. also LXX Ps 5.13 ('you [God] have crowned us'); LXX Isa 22.21 ('I [God] will put your crown on his head'); Philo, *Leg.* 1.80 ('crowned by God and awarded a recompense'); b. Šabb. 104a ('The Holy One' will 'bind a crown on you in the world to come').

[132] Metzger, *Commentary*, 679. See the texts cited in Billerbeck 3.751.

[133] Cf. Gill, 781; Baumgarten, 45; Schneckenburger, 19; Plumptre, 54; *et al.*

[134] Mt 22.37; Mk 12.30; Lk 10.27; 1 Cor 8.3; 2 Thess 3.5; 2 Tim 3.4; 1 Jn 2.5; 5.2; Did. 1.2; 1 Clem. 29.1; etc.

[135] As in Deut 7.9; Neh 1.5; Dan 9.4; CD 20.21; Tanḥ. Buber Wayyishelah 8; etc.

[136] From the LXX: Deut 7.9 (αὐτόν); Neh 1.5 (αὐτόν); Ecclus 1.10 (αὐτόν); cf. Pss. Sol. 6.9 (αὐτόν); 14.1 (αὐτόν); T. Abr. RecLng 3.3 (αὐτόν). Christian texts: Rom 8.28 (τὸν θεόν); 1 Cor 2:9 (αὐτόν); Diog. 12.1 (αὐτόν); Ps.-Clement, *1 Ep. virg.* 9.4 ed. Diekamp, 16 (αὐτόν); Acts Thom. 22 v.l., 36 (αὐτόν *bis*) ed. Bonnet, 135, 154. Cf. the τοῖς ἀγαπῶσι + object in LXX Exod 20.6 (μέ); Deut 5.10 (μέ); Ps 121.6 (σέ); Dan 9.4 (σέ); the τοὺς ἀγαπῶντας + object in LXX Ps 144.20 (αὐτόν); Ecclus 31.19 (αὐτόν); Bel 38 (σέ); the ἀγαπώντων αὐτόν of 1 Macc 4.33; and the nominative οἱ ἀγαπῶντες + object in Judg 5.31 (αὐτόν); Tob 13.14 (αὐτόν); 14.7 (κύριον τὸν θεόν); Ps 96.10 (τὸν

ἐπηγγείλατο comes without explanation, and no one biblical text can be in mind.[137] Perhaps then we have a generalization about Scripture or about multiple promises;[138] cf. 2 Bar. 14.13: 'They leave this world without fear and are truly with joy that they will receive the world which you have promised them'. It is just possible, however, that James alludes to or borrows from a lost writing attributed to Elijah. For 1 Cor 2.9-10 ('As it is written, "What no eye has seen, nor ear heard, nor the human heart conceived, what God has prepared for those who love him"') appears to be, as Origen claimed, from an Apocalypse or Apocryphon of Elijah,[139] and 'to/for those who love him' is cited along with 'What no eye has seen, nor ear heard' in texts besides 1 Cor 2.9-10.[140] Moreover, a reference to 'enduring' or 'waiting' (cf. James' ὑπομένει) also appears in several variants of the saying, not all of which can depend upon James.[141]

κύριον); Ecclus 2.15-16 (αὐτόν). Note also Pss. Sol. 4.29 (τοὺς ἀγαπῶντάς σε); 6.9 (τοῖς ἀγαπῶσιν αὐτόν; so too 14.1); 10.4 (τοὺς ἀγαπῶντας αὐτόν); T. Sim. 3.6 (τῶν ἀγαπώντων αὐτόν); 4 Bar. 6.6 (τοῖς ἀγαπῶσί σε); Odes Sol. 41.16; Theophilus, *Autol.* 1.3.3 PTS 44 ed. Marcovich, 18 (τοὺς ἀγαπῶντας... αὐτόν). See further J.B. Bauer, '"...τοῖς ἀγαπῶσιν τὸν θεόν" Rm 8 28 (I Cor 2 9, I Cor 8 3)', *ZNW* 50 (1959), 106-12; Ludwig, *Wort*, 146-48.

[137] For Hort, 21, 'probably the promise comes from Deut. xxx. 15, 16, 19, 20'. Zeller, 'Jak 1,12', thinks Rev 2.10 is being cited. Cf. Pfleiderer, *Christianity*, 296; Brückner, *Reihenfolge*, 289.

[138] Cf. Hus, 185; Piscator, 717; Wolzogen, 184; Mitton, 45-46. Many commentaries neglect the issue.

[139] See M.E. Stone and J. Strugnell, *The Books of Elijah Parts 1–2*, Missoula, 1979, 42-73. But Brückner, *Reihenfolge*, 289, suggests James' dependence upon Paul.

[140] Asc. Isa. 11.34 ('what neither eye has seen nor ear heard, nor has it come up into a man's heart, how much God has prepared for all who love him'); Acts Thom. 36 ed. Bonnet, 154 ('concerning which eye has not seen nor ear heard nor has entered into the heart of sinful people, what God has prepared for those who love him'); Apost. Const. 7.32.5 ed. Funk, 422 ('inheriting those things which eye did not see and ear did not hear, nor went up into a man's heart, which God prepared for those who love him'); 4 Ezra 5.40 arm ('the good things from him which he has promised to his loved ones, which eye has not seen and ear has not heard').

[141] 1 Clem. 34.8 ('Eye did not see, and ear did not hear, nor did it come up into a man's heart, how much he prepared for those who wait [ὑπομένουσιν] upon him'); 2 Clem. 11.5-7 ('let us not be double-minded but patiently endure [ὑπομείνωμεν] in hope...and receive the promises that ear has not heard nor eye seen nor the heart of man imagined'); Mart. Pol. 2.3 ('those good things which are kept for those that wait [ὑπομείνασιν], which ear did not hear, and eye did not see, and which did not come up into a man's heart'); Theophilus of Antioch, *Autol.* 1.14 PTS 44 ed. Marcovich, 35 ('To those who, with ὑπομονήν, through good works seek the incorruptible, he will give eternal life, joy, peace, rest, and an abundance of good things which neither eye has seen nor ear heard nor entered into the heart of the human being'); Sifre Num 27.12 ('For of old no one has heard or perceived by the ear, no eye has seen a God besides you, who works for him who waits for you'); Ps.-Callisthenes, *Hist. Alex. Magn.* Eth. ed. Budge, 539 ('Hitherto eye has not seen and hitherto ear has not heard, neither can it be described or conceived by the mind the things that God has prepared for those who have endured patiently'). LXX Isa 64.3 ('From of old we have not heard, neither have our eyes seen a

The language of promise is, in early Christianity, prominently associated with God's pledge to give the land to Abraham and his descendants; but ἐπαγγέλλω and ἐπαγγελία are also characteristically linked with the promise of the Holy Spirit and, as here in James and already in Judaism,[142] with eschatological hope in general.[143] So much is the latter the case that 'the promise of God' comes to mean 'salvation', 'resurrection', 'immortality'.[144]

Verse 13. Verses 13-15—which can seem paradoxical following v. 12— are occasioned not by news of the audience's situation, nor are they designed as 'practical ammunition against the excuse of those who had fallen under temptation'.[145] They rather refute a potential misunderstanding generated by the text itself. If temptation is a blessing (v. 12), then God, it would seem, must do evil that good may come. The inference, spoken by a 'pseudo-Job',[146] might appear to be in accord with biblical texts:

- Gen 22.1: 'After these things God tested (LXX: ἐπείραζεν) Abraham'
- Exod 16.4: 'I [God] will test (LXX: πειράσω) them [Israel]'
- Exod 20.20: 'God has come only to test (LXX: πειράσαι) you and to put the fear of him upon you'
- Deut 13.4: 'The Lord your God is testing (LXX: πειράζει) you'
- Job 42.11: 'they showed him sympathy and comforted him for all the evil that the Lord had brought upon him'[147]
- Ps 26.2: 'Prove me, O Lord, and try (LXX: πείρασον) me'
- Jdt 8.25: 'The Lord is putting us to the test (πειράζει) as he did our ancestors'
- Wis 3.5: 'God tested (ἐπείρασεν) them'[148]

God beside you, and your works that you will perform to those who wait [ὑπομένουσιν] for mercy') appears to lie in the background, and for Lapide, 43, James 'alludes' to this text.

[142] See 4 Ezra 7.49 ('an eternal age has been promised to us'), 50 ('an everlasting hope has been promised us'); 2 Bar. 57.2 ('the promise of the life that will come later'); 59.2 ('the promise of their reward'); Gk. LAE 41.3 ('Now I promise to you the resurrection').

[143] As in 2 Tim 1.1; Tit 1.2; Heb 10.23; 2 Pet 3.4, 9; 1 Jn 2.25.

[144] See Acts 26.6 and the epitaphs printed in G.J. Johnson, *Early-Christian Epitaphs from Anatolia*, Atlanta, 1995, 140-43.

[145] Dibelius, 91. Cf. Ropes, 153, and 1 Cor 10.13. Tillotson, 'Sermon LXI' (as in n. 3), 378, remarks: 'When he says, Let no man say so, he intimates, that men are apt to say so, and it is very probable some did say so'.

[146] The phrase is from Burchard, 71.

[147] Cf. also Job 2.10; 5.17-18; 9.17-18; 10.8; 12.14-25; 13.26.

[148] Cf. 4Q378 6 2 ('For God tests...and he will test'); 4Q299 3 2.14 (God 'tested our heart'). Note also Exod 7.3 (God hardens Pharaoh's heart); Deut 2.30 (God hardens the spirit of Sihon king of Heshbon and makes his heart obstinate); 1 Kgs 22.19-23 (God puts a lying spirit into prophets); 2 Chr 34.24 (God says: 'I will bring disaster'); Job 2.10 (Job receives 'bad' as well as 'good' from God; cf. 5.18; 9.17; 10.8; 12.14-16); Ps 69.27

For James, the inference is faulty. His view is instead that of 1 Jn 2.16 ('For all that is in the world—the desire of the flesh, the desire of the eyes, the pride in riches—comes not from the Father but from the world') and Ps.-Clem. Hom. 3.55.2 GCS 42 ed. Rehm, 77 ('To those who imagine that God tempts [πειράζει], as the scriptures say, he said, "The Tempter is the wicked one"'). These two texts grew out of a post-exilic tendency—one which had two very different outcomes in Marcion and Augustine—to dissociate God altogether from all evil.[149] The idea that the Almighty makes woe as well as weal (Isa 45.7) became a stumbling block to many. Thus 1 Chr 21.1 transfers to Satan an act thought unworthy of the deity even though 2 Sam 24.1 attributes that same act to God. Jubilees 17.16 makes the sacrifice of Isaac Mastema's idea.[150] Deut 13.4 is revised in Ps.-Clem. Hom. 16.13.3 GCS 42, ed. Rehm, 224, so that instead of God testing (πειράζει) in order to learn it is ὁ πειράζων tempting in order to learn. The targum rewrites Lam 3.38 ('Is it not from the mouth of the Most High that good and evil come?') by adding that evil 'does not go forth without a Bat Qol intimating [that it is] because of the robberies with which the earth is filled'. Regarding the reading of Isa 45.7 ('I make weal and create woe'), b. Ber. 11b instructs that one should substitute the euphemism 'all things' for 'woe'. James shares the unease manifest in such texts.[151] For him, not only is every good and perfect gift from God (1.17), but God gives only such gifts.

μηδεὶς πειραζόμενος λεγέτω ὅτι ἀπὸ θεοῦ πειράζομαι.[152] Note the artistic, chiastic parallelism created by the next clause:

(a prayer for God to add guilt to the guilt of the psalmist's enemies); Isa 63.17 (God leads people astray); Lam 3.38 (bad as well as good comes from God's mouth), Ezek 14.9 (God can deceive prophets).

[149] Already the Tanak by and large associates God with only some misfortune, not all; see F. Lindström, *God and the Origin of Evil*, Lund, 1983.

[150] Cf. LAB 32.1-2 (the offering is prompted by the envy of the heavenly hosts); Ps.-Clem. Hom. 3.43.2 GCS 42 ed., Rehm, 73 (it is false that 'the Lord tempted Abraham in order that he might learn if he would endure'); b. Sanh. 89b (God, knowing the outcome in advance, commanded Abraham to kill Isaac in response to a challenge from the devil, and in order to prove Satan wrong). On the relationship of Jubilees to James see Davids, 'Pseudepigrapha', 228-30.

[151] According to McKnight, 115, 'it is not possible to deny that God "tests" in scriptural Judaism: Abraham and Isaac in Genesis 22 and the wilderness wanderings of Exodus–Deuteronomy are driven by such a theme, and Job is filled with it'. One must be careful here, as the passages just cited show. Our straightforward reading of texts can be no guide as to how all ancients read them, especially when those texts could be taken to contradict others; see D.C. Allison, Jr, 'Rejecting Violent Judgment', *JBL* 121 (2002), 459-78. Davids, 'Message', 72-73, suggests that James knew the tradition that an honor contest led to the offering of Isaac.

[152] A few witnesses supply the article before θεοῦ. The preposition becomes ὑπό (cf. v. 14) in 01 81 206 *et al.*, probably without any distinction of meaning; see BDF 210.2.

μηδεὶς
   πειραζόμενος
      θεοῦ πειράζομαι
      θεὸς ἀπείραστος
   πειράζει
οὐδένα

For μηδείς see on v. 4. πειράζω[153] picks up on the πειρασμός of the previous verse. Here the verb can mean either 'being tested' or 'being tempted'. Most commentators, assuming the same sense for πειραζόμενος and πειράζομαι, opt for 'being tempted'. McKnight, 115, prefers 'when tested' for πειραζόμενος—'No one, when tested, should say, "I am being tempted by God"'. This works equally well and makes for a smooth transition with v. 12.[154] The choice matters little because the stress is not on the situation (πειραζόμενος) but on the problematic explanation (ἀπὸ θεοῦ πειράζομαι).

λέγω (Jas: 7×) introduces authoritative citations in 2.23; 4.5, 6, but here, as in 2.14 and 4.13, it prefaces faulty opinions. Although μηδεὶς λεγέτω is a Greek idiom otherwise absent from Jewish sources,[155] the Hebrew equivalent, אל יאמר אדם, is attested,[156] and James' μηδεὶς λεγέτω is the rough equivalent of μὴ εἴπῃς (= אל האמר), which commonly prefaces defective remarks in the LXX wisdom literature, including Ecclus 15.11-12, which likely lies behind our text.[157]

ἀπό (Jas: 6×) can indicate 'distance from a point, away from',[158] so perhaps the idea is not that God directly tempts but that a particular situation can ultimately be traced back to God.[159] One thinks of canonical Job, where God permits Satan to torment Job. It is not clear whether the parallel in 1.17 (ἀπὸ τοῦ πατρός) supports this interpretation; but the possible contrast with ὑπό in the next verse seemingly does.

The impulse to blame another for one's problems is human nature if anything is, and the temptation to blame God does not require a specific historical setting or background in the history-of-religion. Recall the complaints of Adam and Eve (Gen 3) as well as Prov 19.3: 'One's own heart rages to ruin, yet the heart rages against the Lord'.

---

[153] NT: 37×; Jas: 4×, all in 1.13-14. LXX: 51×, often for the piel of נסה. Gk. Pseudepigrapha (Denis): 4×. Philo: 9×. Josephus: 29×.

[154] Cf. NJB; Moo, 72.

[155] Cf. Xenophon, *An.* 1.3.15; Dionysius Halicarnassus, *Ant.* 7.17.5; Heraclitus, *Quaest. Hom.* 24.1; Clement of Alexandria, *Strom.* 3.13.91.1 GCS 52 ed. Stählin and Früchtel, 238; etc. Note also μὴ λεγέτω in LXX Isa 56.3; 2 Clem. 9.1

[156] Tanḥ. Buber Wayyiqra' 14; b. 'Abod. Zar. 71a; b. Ta'an. 10b, 11a. Cf. also אל־יאמר as in 1 Kgs 22.8; Isa 56.3; etc.

[157] See below and cf. Prov 3.28; 20.9; 24.29; Eccl 5.5; 7.10; Ecclus 5.1, 3, 4, 6; 7.9; 11.23, 24; 15.11, 12; 16.17; 31.12. Cf. 4Q418 9.13.

[158] BAGD, s.v. 4.

[159] Cf. Huther, 50; Alford, 280; Mayor, 50; Weidner, 31; Schlatter, 128. Contrast Wordsworth, 15: 'ἀπό marks the immediate cause of the temptation'. The NT, as Bisping, 21, rightly notes, usually shows no sharp division between ἀπό and ὑπό.

The closest parallel to James' admonition is Ecclus 15.11-12: 'Do not say, "It was the Lord's doing that I fell away"; for he does not do what he hates. Do not say, "It was he who led me astray"; for he has no need of a sinful man'; cf. v. 20: 'He has not commanded anyone to be impious, nor has he given anyone leave to sin'. Some commentators suspect, probably rightly, that this passage lies behind James.[160] Not only is the content similar, but so is the form: both teach that God does no evil, and they do so through a command not to say such (Sirach: μὴ εἴπῃς ὅτι; James: μηδεὶς...λεγέτω ὅτι). Yet whether one should speak of an allusion to be picked up by informed readers or rather of borrowing not necessarily intended to be noticed can hardly be decided.

James quotes an imaginary interlocutor, as he does again in 2.3, 16, 18; and 4.13. The citation of direct speech and use of the first person singular not only intensify the rhetoric but prepare for the following emphasis upon *individual* responsibility.[161] Many have been reminded of Paul's style in Rom 1-11; 1 Cor 15; and Gal 3, a style presumably taken over from Hellenistic diatribe, which in turn presumably adopted the oral habits of wandering Cynic and Stoic philosophers.[162] James, however, does not relate a dialogue but quotes only a single, short phrase, so it is equally relevant that Jewish wisdom literature quotes statements in order to refute them.[163]

J. Jeremias supposed that Jas 1.13 alludes to the Lord's Prayer: 'And let us not fall into temptation' could 'be taken to imply that God himself tempts us. The Letter of James had already rigorously rejected this misunderstanding when—probably with direct reference to our petition—it said, "Let no one say when he is tempted, 'I am tempted by God'; for God cannot be tempted with evil and he himself tempts no one"'.[164] The conjecture cannot be sustained, for whether or not James knew the Lord's Prayer—the odds of that are good given his knowledge of the Jesus tradition—the problem of 1.13-15 arises naturally from its context: one need not call upon the Lord's Prayer to explain it.

ὁ γὰρ θεὸς ἀπείραστός ἐστιν κακῶν, πειράζει δὲ αὐτὸς οὐδένα. ὁ γάρ + nominative subject occurs also in 1.6. For θεός see on v. 5. ἀπείραστος[165]

---

[160] Cf. Mussner, 89 ('perhaps'); Frankemölle, 190-98, 278-80, 286; Witherington, 433. Contrast Konradt, *Existenz*, 116 n. 104.

[161] So also Schnider, 39.

[162] D.E. Aune, *The New Testament in Its Literary Environment*, Philadelphia, 1987, 200-202. For both Floor, 63, and W. Wilson, 'Sin', 160, 1.13 belongs to 'diatribe-style'.

[163] Cf. Prov 3.27-28; 20.22; 24.29; Ecclus 5.3-6; 11.23-26; etc.

[164] J. Jeremias, *The Prayers of Jesus*, London, 1967, 104. Hartin, *Q*, 178-79, is more guarded: 'James could have had this prayer in mind'. Cf. Windisch-Preisker, 8. F.G. Peabody, *Mornings in the College Chapel*, Boston, 1897, 217, calls Jas 1.12-17 'a commentary on the last petition of the Lord's Prayer'.

[165] LXX: 0×. NT: 1×. Gk. Pseudepigrapha (Denis): 0×. Philo: 0×. It occurs in Josephus, *Bell*. 5.364 v.l.; 7.262 v.l; Acts Jn 57 (of God), 90 (of Jesus) ed. Bonnet, 179, 196; Ps.-Ign. *Phil*. 11 ed. Zahn, 224 (of Jesus); Leontius of Cyprus, *Vit. Jn.* 8 ed. Festugière and Rydén, 352 (of God); in the agraphon, ἀπείραστος ἀνὴρ ἀδόκιμος (see

is a passive verbal adjective: 'cannot be tempted'.[166] If, as the next verse asserts, temptation arises from ἐπιθυμία, then a God free of the latter will be free of the former.[167] κακός[168] recurs in 3.8, as does οὐδείς. Does the genitive plural[169] mean evil in general, or is there 'an allusion to the supernatural forces of evil'?[170] πειράζω (see n. 153) is active and so the pattern is: affirmation about God in the passive, affirmation about God in the active.

Several patristic texts preserve the agraphon, ἀπείραστος ἀνὴρ ἀδόκιμος.[171] One guesses that this derives from James: it is a succinct, aphoristic version of v. 12 that borrows ἀπείραστός from v. 13. Twice the correspondence of Barsanuphius and John closely links the byword with Jas 1.12.[172]

'For he himself tempts no one' is in effect a restatement of 'Let no one, when tempted, say, "I am tempted by God"' (v. 13a); but ὁ γὰρ θεὸς ἀπείραστός ἐστιν κακῶν is new. It functions to justify both what precedes (μηδείς... πειράζομαι) and what follows (πειράζει κτλ.). The proposition comes as though self-evident. There is clear precedent in Greek thought (see n. 182), and the idea of God's goodness was near the center of much Jewish theology[173] and became a commonplace of Christian reflection.[174]

---

n. 171); as well as in Chrysippus (1×); Demetrius Lacon (1×); Onasander (1×); Galen (5×); and various scholia on pagan works.

[166] Cf. BDF 117.1. See esp. the long note in Mayor, 51-53; also Burchard, 71.

[167] One guesses that James, like Philo and Ignatius (*Eph.* 7.2; *Pol.* 3.2), would be familiar with Hellenistic notions of divine apatheia. On the topic generally see H. Frohnhofen, *Apatheia tou Theou*, Frankfurt am Main, 1987.

[168] Jas: 2×; most often in the LXX for (ה)רע.

[169] With the genitive construction cf. Sophocles, *Ant.* 583 (κακῶν ἄγευστος); Chrysippus, *Frag. mor.* 609 (ἄγευστον... παθῶν ἢ κακιῶν); Philo, *Sacr.* 111 (quoting Chrysippus); Origen, *C. Cels.* 4.40 ed. Marcovich, 257 (ἄγευστον κακίας).

[170] So W. Wilson, 'Sin', 160.

[171] Eusebius, *Ps ad* 65.10-13, 76.2 PG 23.661A, 889A; Chrysostom, *Res. mort.* 4 PG 50.424; Apost. Const. 2.8.2 ed. Funk, 45; Didascalia 2.8.2 ed. Funk, 44 ('Vir, qui non est temptatus, non est probatus a Deo'); etc. See further Resch, *Agrapha*, 130-32.

[172] Barsanuphius and John, *Ep.* 386, 499 SC 450, 451, ed. Neyt and Angelis-Noah, 434, 622.

[173] See Gen 1 (God creates a 'good' world); 1 Chr 16.34 ('he is good'); Ezra 3.11 ('he is good'); Neh 2.8 ('the good hand of my God'); Ps 25.8 ('Good... is the Lord'); 34.8 ('the Lord is good'); 73.1 ('God is good'); 145.9 ('The Lord is good to all'); Ecclus 39.33 ('the works of the Lord are all good'); Philo, *Fug.* 79 ('the treasuries of evils... are in ourselves; with God there are only good things'); *Mut.* 7 (God 'alone is good'); *Somn.* 1.149 (God is 'the good one'); *Dec.* 176 ('He was God, and it follows at once that as Lord he was good, the cause of good only and of nothing ill'); m. Ber. 9.2 ('Blessed be he [God] who is good and does good'); etc. When Mark's Jesus says, 'No one is good but God alone' (10.18; cf. Lk 18.19), the proposition is assumed to be manifest to all.

[174] Cf. Rom 8.28; 12.2; 4 Ezra 2.14 ('I left out evil and created good'); *Teach. Silv.* 115.26-28 ('But this divine is not pleased with anything evil. For it is this that teaches all people what is good'; the same text a few lines later affirms that God need not test people because God already knows everything); Ps.-Clem. Hom. 8.10 GCS 42 ed. Rehm, 125; etc.

Whatever the precise background, the application here appears to be that if God is all good, God can hardly tempt human beings to do what is not good; cf. Ecclus 15.11: God 'does not do what he hates'.[175]

Hort, 22-23, takes ἀπείραστος κακῶν to mean that God has no contact or experience with evil; cf. ἀπείρα[η]τος = 'inexperienced'.[176] But one wants to relate ἀπείραστος as closely as possible to the πειράζομαι that immediately precedes it and to the πειράζει that immediately follows, so the idea of 'temptation' is unlikely to be absent. Davids' suggestion, that we have here an imperative—God ought not to be tempted by evil people—is also less than likely, even if it harmonizes with the wilderness traditions.[177] It (i) has scant support from the commentary tradition[178] and (ii) sets aside the usual interpretation of the close parallel in Ecclus 15.11-20 (see above). Further (iii) the suggestion that ἀπείραστος means something other than 'unable to be tempted' in *Acts Jn.* 57 and Ps.-Ign. *Phil.* 11 (see n. 165) is very far from obvious. Even less plausible, however, is the active interpretation of the Vulgate: 'a tempter to evil'.[179] This makes the two halves of v. 13b tautologous to no end: 'except the word be taken passively, the Apostle saith one thing twice immediately together, without any cause of such vain repetition'.[180]

The Jewish character of Jas 1.12-15 is manifest: μακάριος ἀνὴρ ὅς = אשרי האיש אשר; τοῖς ἀγαπῶσιν αὐτόν = לאהביו; ἐπιθυμία likely reflects the Jewish idea of the יצר הרע (see below); συλλαβοῦσα τίκτει = הרה + ילד; and the specific associations of πειράζω and ἁμαρτία come from biblical tradition. But the alpha-privative (ἀ – πείραστος) to characterize God and the removal of God from all evil (κακῶν, genitive of separation) probably reflect ideas from the Hellenistic world. As Dibelius, 93 n. 127,

---

[175] Aitken, *Temptation*, 197, and a few others find implicit the imitation of God: one should strive to be above temptation, as is God. Sadler, 12, draws a contrast between God and the myth of Satan: 'Why is the devil the tempter? Because he was first to be tempted, and to fall under the temptation. Because he fell under the temptation he unceasingly desires that others share his condemnation'.

[176] So too Alford, 280; Bassett, 14-15; Martin, 35; NEB (but not REB).

[177] Davids, 'Meaning'. See e.g. Exod 17.2 ('Why do you test [LXX: πειράζετε] the Lord?'); Deut 6.16 ('Do not put the Lord to the test [LXX: ἐκπειράσεις]', cf. Mt 4.7 = Lk 4.8). Marty, 31-32, observes that the texts which speak of tempting God uniformly speak against such.

[178] Yet note Spitta, 33-34. Wolmarans, 'θεός', offers a related reading: 'God cannot be tested [for the giving] of evil things'. Didymus of Alexandria, *Trin.* 2.10 PG 39.641A; Gill, 782; Benson, 37; Spitta, 34; and Chaine, 19, otherwise recall the wilderness narrative.

[179] *Deus enim intentator malorum est.* The same sense appears in Luther's translation ('Gott ist nicht ein Versucher zum Bösen'). Cf. Lapide, 44: James argues not from the passive to the active but from the general to the particular.

[180] So Fulke, *Confutation*, 355, for whom this is a divide between Protestants and Catholics. At one time, the latter tended to defend the active in the Vulgate and to accuse Protestants of diminishing the force of the text; cf. the note *ad loc.* in Rheims, 381, and the polemic in Hardouin, 682. Manton, 82, attributes to the Jesuit Alfonso Salmeron this interpretation: 'God is not the tempter of evil persons, but only of the good'.

affirms, James' ἀπείραστος κακῶν is 'materially rooted in that Hellenistic theology which describes God's essence by means of circumlocutions with negatives'.[181] Many texts (anticipating later apophatic theology) give the deity negative attributes[182] or isolate the deity from evil and/or blame humans for evil.[183]

---

[181] Klein, *Werk*, 86-88, contends that the Hellenistic James is here trying to correct his more traditional Jewish readers who took texts such as Gen 22.1 and Isa 45.7 at face value.
[182] Cf. Epicurus *apud* Diogenes Laertius 10.139 (God is ἄφθαρτος, has no trouble, brings no trouble upon others, is exempt from anger and partiality); Lactantius, *De ira dei* 4 CSEL 27 ed. Brandt and Laubmann, 71-73 (summarizing Epicurus); Albinus, *Did.* 10.3 (God is ἄρρητος, αὐτοτελής, ἀπροσδεής); Philo, *Cherub.* 51 (God is ἀγένητος, ἄφθαρτος, ἄτρεπτος), 86 (God is ἄλυπος, ἄφοβος, ἀκοινώνητος κακῶν); *Abr.* 202 (God is ἄλυπος, ἄφοβος, παντὸς πάθους ἀμέτοχος); Plutarch, *Comp. Arist. Cat.* 4.2 (God is wholly ἀπροσδεής; so too 1 Clem. 52.1); Alexander Rhetor in *Rhetores Graeci* ed. Spengel, 3.4 (God is ἀγέννητος, ἀνώλεθρος); Corpus Herm. frag. 30 ed. Nock and Festugière, 4.135 (the logos is ἀναυξής, ἀμείωτος, ἀμετάβλητος, ἄφθαρτος); Apoc. Abr. 17.8 (the Slavonic list presumably translates a list of alpha-privatives: 'incorruptible, unsullied, unborn, immaculate, immortal...without mother, without father, without birth'); 4 Bar. 9.6 (God is ἀγένηητος, ἀπερινόητος); Apost. Const. 7.35.9 ed. Funk, 432 (God is ἀόρατος, ἀνενδεής, ἀκάματος, ἀπερίγραφος, ἀπρόσιτος, ἀμετανάστευτος; his knowledge is ἄναρχος; his truth ἀναλλοίωτος; his work ἀμεσίτευτον; his dominion ἀνεπιβούλευτον; his monarchy ἀδιάδοχος; his kingdom ἀτελεύτητος; his strength ἀνανταγώνιστος; perhaps this borrows from a Jewish prayer text); Ap. John 3 (God is without lack, illimitable, unsearchable, immeasurable, invisible, ineffable, immaculate, imperishable); Zostrianos passim; Eugnostos the Blessed 3.71-72 (God is ineffable, unbegotten, immortal, nameless, infinite, incomprehensible, imperishable, faultless, unknowable, immeasurable; in the retroversion into Greek of D. Trakatellis, *The Transcendent God of Eugnostos*, Brookline, MA, 1991, 161-63, the relevant Coptic words are translated as follows: ἄρρητος, ἀθάνατος, ἀγέννητος, ἀνωνόμαστος, ἀπέραντος, ἀκατάληπτος, ἄφθαρτος, ἀναλλοιώτος, ἄμωμος, ἀνεννόητος, ἀμέτρητος, ἀνίχνευτος; on the possibility that the text is Jewish see R. van den Broek, 'Eugnostos and Aristides on the Ineffable God', in *Knowledge of God in the Graeco-Roman World*, ed. R. van den Broek, T. Baarda, and J. Mansfeld, Leiden, 1988, 202-18); Theophilus, *Autol.* 1.3.1 PTS 44 ed. Marcovich, 18 (God is ἄρρητος, ἀνέκφραστος; his glory is ἀχώρητος; his greatness ἀκατάληπτος; his height ἀπερινόητος; his strength ἀσύγκριτος; his goodness ἀμίμητος; his kindness ἀνεκδιήγητος); Acts Jn. 107 ed. Bonnet, 205 (God is ἀμίαντος, ἄυλος, ἀμετάβολος, ἄδολος, ἀόργητος). Note also these NT examples: ἀόρατος (Rom 1.20; Col 1.15; 1 Tim 1.17; Heb 11.27; cf. Jn 1.18); ἄφθαρτος (Rom 1.23; 1 Tim 1.17); ψευδής (Tit 1.2). For discussion of early apophatism see A.-J. Festugière, *La révélation d'Hermès Trismégiste IV*, Paris, 1954; C.L. Hancock, 'Negative Theology in Gnosticism and Neoplatonism', in *Neoplatonism and Gnosticism*, ed. R.T. Wallis and J. Bregman, Albany, 1992, 167-84.
[183] Homer, *Od.* 1.32-34 (Zeus: 'My word, how mortals take the gods to task! All their afflictions come from us, we hear. And what of their own failings? Greed and folly double the suffering in the lot of men'; but Homer otherwise blames the gods: *Il.* 15.109; *Od.* 20.199-203; etc.); Euripides, *Tr.* 914-1032 (Helen's attempt to blame the gods for everything is followed by Hecabe's extended rebuttal); Plato, *Resp.* 379C ('Of the good things God and no other must be described as the cause, but of the evil things we must look for many different causes, only not God'); ibid. 380B ('To call God a cause of evil to anyone, being good himself, is a falsehood to be fought tooth and nail'); ibid. 617E

Verse 14. Having insisted that God is not the author of temptation, James is obliged to explain its true genesis: ἐπιθυμία. Again comparable is Ecclus 15.11-20: God has handed human beings over to the power of their own free choice.

Cladder observes that v. 14—which recounts, in the words of Mic 1.13, 'the beginning of sin'—and the verses on either side seem to have an effective poetic rhythm:

13 μηδεὶς πειραζόμενος λεγέτω,
 ὅτι ἀπὸ θεοῦ πειράζομαι
 ὁ γὰρ θεὸς ἀπείραστός ἐστιν κακῶν
 πειράζει δὲ αὐτὸς οὐδένα
14 ἕκαστος δὲ πειράζεται
 ὑπὸ τῆς ἰδίας ἐπιθυμίας
 ἐξελκόμενος καὶ δελεαζόμενος
15 εἶτα ἡ ἐπιθυμία συλλαβοῦσα
 τίκτει ἁμαρτίαν
 ἡ δὲ ἁμαρτία ἀποτελεσθεῖσα
 ἀποκυεῖ θάνατον.[184]

ἕκαστος δὲ πειράζεται ὑπὸ τῆς ἰδίας ἐπιθυμίας. ἕκαστος—antithetical to the μηδείς in v. 13—and ἴδιος are Jamesian *hapax*.[185] In contrast to v. 14 (ἀπὸ θεοῦ denied), ὑπό (Jas: 5×) is used for the source of temptation, perhaps stressing proximity. For the verb see n. 153. ἐπιθυμία[186] recurs in the next verse, and the related ἐπιθυμέω in 4.2.

('No destiny shall cast lots for you, but you shall all choose your own destiny... The blame is for the chooser; God is blameless'); *Tim.* 29E-30A (God lacks all envy and desires nothing evil); Epicurus *apud* Diogenes Laertius 10.139 (see n. 182; Ps.-Oecumenius *ad loc.* PG 119.464A quotes this); Philo, *Opif.* 75 (God cannot 'be the cause of an evil thing to his offspring'), *Det.* 122 (see n. 188); *Fug.* 79-81 (see n. 188); *Leg.* 2.53 (God 'is exempt from all evil, filled with perfect forms of good, or rather, if the real truth be told, is himself the good'); Marcus Aurelius, *Med.* 6.1.1 (the reason that governs the universe 'has no malice, nor does it do evil to anything, nor is anything harmed by it'); Sextus, *Sent.* 113-14 ('Consider God the cause of all you do well. God is not the cause of evil'); ibid. 440 ('Consider nothing that is evil as belonging to God'); Hierocles *apud* Stobaeus 2.9.7 ('a god is never the cause of any evil, that is entirely from wickedness alone'); Porphyry, *Ad Marc.* 12 ('let us consider God responsible for all the good that we do, but as for the evils, we who have chosen them are responsible; God is not responsible'); Ps.-Libanius, *Ep. char.* 78 ('Do not think that God caused the terrible things that have befallen you. For God is completely free of evil. For he who orders others to flee evil would never cause evil to someone'); Asclepius 27 ed. Nock and Festugière, 2.331 ('it is the very being of God to purpose good'). See further I. Ramelli, 'La "colpa antecedente" come ermeneutica del male in sede storico-religiosa e nei testi biblici', *RStB* 19 (2007), 11-64.

[184] Cladder, 'Aufbau', 316.
[185] ἕκαστος δέ: LXX: 0×. NT: 4× (1 Cor 3.8, 10; 15.23; Jas 1.14). Gk. Pseudepigrapha (Denis): 0×. Philo: 0×. Josephus: 4×.
[186] LXX: 71× (often for the root חמד). NT: 38× (19× in the Pauline corpus). Gk. Pseudepigrapha (Denis): 26× (19× in the Testaments of the Twelve Patriarchs). Philo: 218×. Josephus: 95×.

How does the biblical monotheist come to terms with human sin and ruin? The old texts adopt several strategies.[187] Some proclaim human freedom and/or accountability and thereby reduce or eliminate divine responsibility for the world's evils.[188] Others offer that the sin of Adam and Eve has contaminated the world,[189] or that the story of the watchers in Gen 6 largely explains the sorry condition of things.[190] It was also common to pin the blame for evil on Satan.[191] Still others did not shrink

---

[187] In addition to what follows see A.L. Thompson, *Responsibility for Evil in the Theodicy of IV Ezra*, Missoula, MT, 1977, 20-66.

[188] E.g. Ecclus 15.11-20; Pss. Sol. 9.4 ('Our works [are] in the choosing and power of our souls, to do right and wrong in the works of our hand'); 1 En. 98.4 ('Neither has sin been sent into the world. It is the people who have themselves invented it'); Gk. 1 En. 98.5 ('Neither was sin given from above but because of transgression'); Philo, *Deus* 47 ('For it is mind alone that the Father who begat it judged worthy of freedom, and loosening the fetters of necessity, suffered it to range as it listed... Man, possessed of a spontaneous and self-determined will, whose activities for the most part rest on deliberate choice, is with reason blamed for what he does wrong with intent, praised when he acts rightly of his own will'); *Leg.* 2.78 ('It is when the mind has sinned and ceased to cleave to virtue that it blames God's ways, fastening its own defection on God'); *Det.* 122 ('For Moses does not, as some impious people do, say that God is the author of ills. No, he says that "our own hands" cause them'); *Conf.* 161 ('There are many who, wishing to shirk all charges to which they are liable and claiming to escape the penalties of their misdeeds, ascribe the guilty responsibility, which really belongs to themselves, to God, who is the cause of nothing evil, but of all that is good'); *Fug.* 79-80 ('It is not right to say that any secret wrongs committed with secret hostility... are done as God ordains; they are done as we ordain. For... the treasuries of evil things are in ourselves; with God are those of good things only'); *Dec.* 142 (while passions 'seem to be involuntary, an extraneous visitation, an assault from outside, desire alone originates with ourselves and is voluntary'); *Spec.* 4.79-135; 2 Bar. 54.19 ('Adam is, therefore, not the cause, except only for himself, but each of us has become our own Adam'); T. Jud. 20.1-2 ('two spirits await an opportunity with humanity: the spirit of truth and the spirit of error. In between is the conscience of the mind which inclines as it will'); 2 En. J 30.15 ('And I [God] gave him [Adam] his free will; and I pointed out to him the two ways—light and darkness... so that I might come to know whether he has love toward me or abhorrence, and so that it might become plain who among his race loves me'); Apoc. Sed. 8.1 ('I left him [man] to his own desires because I loved him'). Rom 7, whatever its precise interpretation, is relevant here.

[189] E.g. Rom 5 and the *Vita Adae et Evae*; cf. 4 Ezra 7.48: 'O Adam, what have you done? For though it was you who sinned, the fall was not yours alone, but ours also who are your descendants'. See F. R. Tennant, *The Sources of the Doctrine of the Fall and Original Sin*, New York, 1968.

[190] See 1 En. 1-36; Jub. 5.1-2; CD 2.15-21; the Book of Giants.

[191] E.g. Jubilees (in many places; in 17.16 e.g. the sacrifice of Isaac is the Mastema's idea); 1 En. 69.4-15; Wis 2.24; the Testaments of the Twelve Patriarchs (in many places); cf. 1 Chr 21.1; Job 1-2; Zech 3.1-2 (although these biblical texts must be distinguished from later speculations about 'Satan'). The cosmic dualism of the Dead Sea Scrolls belongs here, as does the condemnation of Azazel in Apoc. Abr. 13.9: 'Through you (are) wrath and trials on the generations of men who live impiously'. Also related is the speculation of Philo, *Opif.* 75, in his comment on the 'Let us make' of Genesis: 'When man orders his course aright, when his thoughts and deeds are blameless, God the

from assigning much of the responsibility for sin and/or misfortune to God,[192] who created the evil impulse (יצר) and planted it in human hearts.[193]

These several explanations were not mutually exclusive, and they sometimes appear together, as in James. In our epistle, the idea of the evil impulse is probably present (see below), and 4.7 assumes the interference of the devil in human affairs.[194] We also find the insistence that human beings make their own decisions and that God does not tempt. One is still left with the philosophical question of whether James falls back upon a distinction without a difference. Maybe God does not directly tempt, but if the deity created human beings (3.9), how is God exonerated?[195] The causes of sin and the origin of evil are not so easily disentangled. James (unlike the author of 4 Ezra) does not, however, address the puzzle.

ὑπὸ τῆς ἰδίας—ἰδίας is emphatic—ἐπιθυμίας goes with the main verb, πειράζεται, and supplies the subject for the two subsequent participles. It likely reflects the then-evolving doctrine of the human יצר,

universal ruler may be owned as their source; while others from the number of his subordinates are held responsible for thoughts and deeds of a contrary sort, for it could not be that the Father should be the cause of an evil thing to his offspring.'

[192] Note Exod 11.10 ('but the Lord hardened Pharaoh's heart'); 2 Sam 24.1 (God 'incited David against them' [Israel]—corrected in 1 Chr 21.1); Isa 45.7 ('I make weal and create woe'); Jer 6.21 ('I am laying against this people stumbling blocks'); Lam 3.38 ('Is it not from the mouth of the Most High that good and evil come?'); Ezek 3.20 ('I lay a stumbling block before them'); 20.25-26 ('I gave them statutes that were not good and ordinances by which they could not live. I defiled them through their very gifts... in order that I might horrify them'); Amos 3.6 ('Does evil befall a city, unless the Lord has done it?'); T. Job 26.4; 37.3-4 (Baldad: 'Who destroyed your goods or inflicted you with these plagues?' Job: 'God'). One presumes that James, like many other post-exilic Jews, would have found all these texts problematic. Here one part of the canon is at odds with other parts.

[193] Literature: F.C. Porter, 'The Yeçer Hara', in *Biblical and Semitic Studies*, New York, 1902, 93-156; G.H. Cohen Stuart, *The Struggle in Man between Good and Evil*, Kampen, 1984; J. Cook, 'The Origin of the Tradition of the יצר הטוב and יצר הרע', *JSJ* 38 (2007), 80-91; E. Tigchelaar, 'The Evil Inclination in the Dead Sea Scrolls, with a Re-Edition of 4Q468I (4QSectarian Text?)', in *Empsychoi Logoi—Religious Innovations in Antiquity*, ed. A. Houtman, A. de Jong, and M.M-v. de Weg, Leiden, 2008, 347-57. Cook and Tigchelaar show that likely evidence for something approximating rabbinic doctrine appears already in the second century BCE, in Ben Sira (Heb. 15.14), LXX Proverbs (2.11-12), and the Dead Sea Scrolls (1Q18 1-2 3-4; 4Q370 1.3; 4Q417 2 2.12; 4Q435 1 1.10; 4Q468i (?); 11Q5 19.15-16). Surely, moreover, Col 3.5 (ἐπιθυμίαν κακήν) presupposes it. At the same time, the idea of two impulses, a good יצר matching a bad יצר, seemingly remained undeveloped until much later; cf. I. Rosen-Zvi, 'Two Rabbinic Inclinations?', *JSJ* 39 (2008), 513-39.

[194] Cf. 11Q5 19.15-16, which refers Satan, evil spirits, and an evil yetzer. Later texts can identify the יצר הרע with Satan—e.g. b. B. Bat. 16a. The equation was no doubt encouraged by the nearness of διαβούλιον (one of the Greek equivalents of יצר) to διάβολος.

[195] One might, however, on the basis of our text, distinguish good human nature from its wrongful desires; cf. Ps.-Andrew of Crete, *Éloge* 5 ed. Noret, 4.

'impulse'.¹⁹⁶ It is true that the LXX never uses ἐπιθυμία to translate יצר, but (i) Ecclus 15.11-20, which James may reflect here (see above), refers in the Hebrew to the יצר.¹⁹⁷ (ii) Paul and the Ps.-Clementine Homilies reflect that doctrine in passages employing ἐπιθυμία.¹⁹⁸ (iii) In Hermas, which has so many parallels with James, ἐπιθυμία πονηρά = יצר הרע.¹⁹⁹ (iv) The יצר is sometimes personified in rabbinic sources,²⁰⁰ just as ἐπιθυμία is in James. (v) Some blamed the evil יצר for death, which is the upshot of ἐπιθυμία in Jas 1.15.²⁰¹ (vi) The יצר was associated with topics of great interest to James, including being perfect,²⁰² being deceived,²⁰³ and being 'double-faced'.²⁰⁴

---

¹⁹⁶ For this and what follows see Marcus, 'Inclination'. Others who find the idea of the יצר reflected in James include Grotius, 1075; Schöttgen, *Horae Hebraicae*, 1011; Clarke, 800; Hort, 25; Oesterley, 408-11; Mussner, 88; Cantinat, 86-87; Schnider, 41; Davids, 83; R. Wall, 61; Hartin, 91; Fruchtenbaum, 226; Cheung, *Genre*, 206-22; McKnight, 118-19. Contrast Ropes, 156; Johnson, 194; Isaacs, 188; Popkes, 106; Fabris, 84. Easton, 27, raises the possibility that James is polemicizing against the teaching of the two impulses. G.F. Moore, *Judaism in the First Centuries of the Christian Era*, vol. 1, Cambridge, MA, 1927, 481, summarizes rabbinic teaching by saying that 'the opportunity or the invitation to sin may come from without, but it is the response of the evil impulse in man to it that converts it into a temptation. It pictures in imagination the pleasures of sin, conceives the plan, seduces the will, incites to the act.' This could almost serve as a paraphrase of what James says. Note that, in the Hellenistic philosophical schools, 'desire' became the chief source of human problems, and Klein, *Werk*, 91, wonders whether the doctrine of the יצר הרע developed under Hellenistic reflections about 'desire'. This seems likely.

¹⁹⁷ Verse 14: God put into the hand of man יצרו (= LXX διαβουλίου αὐτοῦ).

¹⁹⁸ For Rom 7.7-8 see Davies, *Paul*, 19-35, and for Gal 5.16 J.L. Martyn, *Galatians*, New York, 1977, 292, 492-493. For the general point see J. Marcus, 'The Evil Inclination in the Letters of Paul', *IBS* 8 (1986), 8-21. For the Ps.-Clementine literature note e.g. Hom. 19.21 GCS 42 ed. Rehm, 264, where God implants ἐπιθυμία, which is required for the perpetuation of the species.

¹⁹⁹ Herm. *Vis.* 1.1.8; 1.2.4; 3.7.3; 3.8.4; *Mand.* 12.1.1-3; cf. Brox, *Hirt*, 78.

²⁰⁰ E.g. b. Šabb. 105b (the impulse speaks); b. Ḥag. 16a (it speaks); b. Suk. 52a (the impulse is likened to a weak woman and a strong man); b. Qidd. 81a (it is cast out like an evil spirit).

²⁰¹ See esp. Herm. *Mand.* 12.1; 12.2.2; *Sim.* 6.2.1-2; and cf. b. B. Bat. 16a: the evil impulse = the angel of death.

²⁰² See 1QH 9(1).35-36 ('Be of staunch inclination [יצר]... And all of you, of perfect way'); CD 2.15-16 ('that you may walk in perfection in all his ways and that you may not be drawn by the thoughts of the guilty inclination', יצר); Herm. *Sim.* 5.3.6; cf. Jas 1.4; 2.22; 3.2.

²⁰³ Note 1QH 21.9-10, where the יצר is linked with רמיה; also Herm. *Sim.* 6.2.1; cf. Jas 1.16, 26; 3.17.

²⁰⁴ T. Ash. 3.2 says that those who serve their own desires (ἐπιθυμίαις) are double-faced; cf. Jas 1.8; 4.8. The association of the double-faced or double-souled or double-hearted with the doctrine of the יצר was almost inevitable: the person with two inclinations is divided. Perhaps it is also worth noting that, if James explicates ἐπιθυμία with an analogical depiction of its development, b. Sanh. 99b speaks of the evil impulse as being initially like a spider's thread but later like a cart rope.

Nothing suggests that ἐπιθυμία in James means all desires. Rather, as often in the LXX and NT, and like the rabbinic יֵצֶר הָרָע, it refers to evil desires in particular.[205] If so, James—like Philo[206] and Herm. *Mand*. 12— opens itself to the later distinction between natural appetites and postlapsarian passions; cf. the exegesis of Bonhoeffer: 'Desire in itself does not make me sinful... Desire conceives by the union of my "I" with it... As long as desire remains untouched by my self, it is an "It". But sin occurs only through the "I". Thus the source of temptation lies in the ἐπιθυμία, the source of sin is in my self, and in my self alone.'[207]

ἐξελκόμενος καὶ δελεαζόμενος.[208] This is a picturesque way of speaking about deceit (ἀπάτη, ἀπατάω), which is otherwise associated with ἐπιθυμία and ἁμαρτία.[209] Note the concluding rhyme, reminiscent of the concluding rhyme in v. 6. There is no reason for taking ἐξελκόμενος to mean 'lured from the good' and δελεαζόμενος to mean 'enticed to evil'.[210]

ἐξέλω is a NT *hapax legomenon*; δελεάζω[211] recurs in 2 Pet 2.14, 18. The former appears several times in the LXX, where it consistently has its literal meaning, 'drag away'.[212] But the figurative use of the simplex, ἕλκω,[213] is attested, as is its association with ἐπιθυμία and the closely related ἡδονή.[214] δελεάζω, like the noun, δέλεαρ (= 'bait'), was also

---

[205] See BAGD, s.v., ἐπιθυμία 3. Recall that the decalogue prohibits the desire of a neighbor's wife (LXX Exod 20.17; Deut 5.21: οὐκ ἐπιθυμήσεις); cf. 4 Macc 2.5-6: 'since the law has told us not to covet, I could prove to you all the more that reason is able to control desires (ἐπιθυμιῶν)'.

[206] Note e.g. Philo, *Leg*. 3.140-41, 147. Here Philo follows Plato.

[207] D. Bonhoeffer, *Temptation*, London, 1955, 27. Cf. Augustine, *Civ. dei*. 1.25. Like Origen, *Princ*. 3.4.1-5 GCS 22 ed. Koetschau, 263-70, James presumably implies two wills, not two souls.

[208] Adamson, 72, conjectures an original ὀφελκόμενος without external support.

[209] E.g. Plutarch, *Mor*. 990C; Sus 56; Pss. Sol. 16.8; Rom 7.11 (ἁμαρτία... ἐξηπάτησεν... ἀπέκτεινεν); Eph 4.22 (τὰς ἐπιθυμίας τῆς ἀπάτης); Heb 3.13 (ἀπάτῃ τῆς ἁμαρτίας); Acts Phil. 142 ed. Bonnet, 81 (ἡ ἐπιθυμία... ἀπατήσασα).

[210] But see Nicholas of Lyra *ad loc.*; Grotius, 1075; Baumgarten, 50; Theile, 44-45.

[211] LXX: 0×. But Philo was fond of the word (31×); cf. also Gk. LAE 19.1; 26.3; Jos. Asen. 21.21; Josephus, *Bell*. 3.22, 100; 5.170; *Ant*. 8.225; 13.220; Acts Jn. 69 ed. Bonnet, 185.

[212] LXX Gen 37.28; Judg 20.31; Job 20.15; 36.20; Prov 24.68; 3 Macc 2.23; cf. Philo, *Migr*. 196, 197; *Prob*. 130; Josephus, *Bell*. 2.448; *Ant*. 8.47.

[213] Cf. 2.6, with literal sense.

[214] Plato, *Phaedr*. 238A (ἐπιθυμίας... ἑλκούσης ἐπὶ ἡδονάς); *Resp*. 538D (ἐπιτηδεύματα ἡδονὰς ἔχοντα, ἅ... ἕλκει); Xenophon, *Cyr*. 8.1.32 (ὑπὸ τῶν... ἡδονῶν ἑλκόμενον); Aelian, *Hist. an*. 6.31 (ὑπὸ τῆς ἡδονῆς ἑλκόμενοι); Soranus, *Gyn*. 1.33.4 (ἕλκουσι τὰς ἐπιθυμίας); Philo, *Mos*. 2.139 (ἐπιθυμίας... ἑλκούσης); Josephus, *Ant*. 15.27 (πρὸς τὰς ἡδονὰς ἑλκύσαι); Dio Chrysostom 4.111 (ἐπιθυμιῶν... ἑλκουσῶν); Athenagoras, *Res*. 22.3 ed. Marcovich, 47 (ἑλκούσης... ἐπιθυμίας... ἡδονάς); Libanius, *Progymn*. 8.6.9 (πρὸς τὰς ἀτόπους ἡδονὰς ἑλκύσῃ); etc. Note also 2 Clem. 17.3 (ἀντιπαρελκώμεθα ἀπὸ τῶν κοσμικῶν ἐπιθυμιῶν) and Lk 8.14, which has 'ἡδονῶν of life' where Mk 4.19 has 'ἐπιθυμία for other things'. ἡδονή and ἐπιθυμία are often parallel: Plato, *Phaed*. 83B; *Leg*. 788B; Philo, *Det*. 110; *Agr*. 17; *Ebr*. 215; *Conf*. 90; *Migr*. 219; Tit 3.3; etc.

commonly used with ἐπιθυμία and ἡδονή.²¹⁵ It is further relevant that δέλεαρ and its cognates are often linked with ἕλκω and its cognates.²¹⁶ Note especially Philo, *Agr.* 103: 'For there is no single thing that does not yield to the enticement of pleasure and get caught and dragged along' (πρὸς ἡδονῆς δελεασθὲν εἵλκυσται).

As the dictionaries make clear, ἐξέλω and δελεάζω—are the words practical synonyms, or do they mark a sequence?²¹⁷—had to do originally and principally with fishing and hunting. One wonders, however, whether they have sexual connotations in James.²¹⁸ Certainly ἐπιθυμία often does in Christian literature,²¹⁹ and readers of this verse and the next—who can speak of desire as a 'harlot' or 'mistress'—sometimes think so.²²⁰ One

---

²¹⁵ Plato, *Tim.* 69D (ἡδονή is a δέλεαρ to evil); Xenophon, *Mem.* 2.1.4 (ἐπιθυμία... δέλεαρ); Dionysius Halicarnassus, *Ant.* 11.40.6 (δελεαζόμενος...ἡδοναῖς); Diodorus Siculus 12.12.3 (ἡδοναῖς δελεασθέντες); Philo, *Ebr.* 165 (δέλεαρ...ἡδονῆς); *Migr.* 29 (δελεαζούσαις ἡδοναῖς); *Mos.* 1.295 (ἡδονὴν δέλεαρ); *Prob.* 31, 159 (ἐπιθυμίας...ἡδονῆς δελεάζεται); 2 Pet 2.18 (δελεάζουσιν ἐν ἐπιθυμίαις); Marcus Aurelius, *Med.* 2.12.1 (ἡδονῇ δελεάζοντα; the context has to do with the transitory nature of things; cf. Jas 1.10-12); 2 Pet 2.18; Julian, *Apaid. kun.* 185A (δελεασθέντες ἡδονῆς).

²¹⁶ Herodotus 2.70 (on catching crocodiles: 'They baited [δελεάσῃ] a hook...[and] hauled [it] out [ἐξελκυσθῇ] of the water'); Plutarch, *Mor.* 1093D (the pleasures of geometry and harmonics have a δέλεαρ that gives them 'the potency of a love charm' as they 'draw' [ἕλκουσαι] people); Oppian, *Hal.* 3.437 ('fishers easily take them [ἕλκουσιν] with smelly δελέασσιν'); Aelian, *NA* 5.3 ('When the δέλεαρ is secured on the hook...the men ἀνέλκουσι').

²¹⁷ So Cox, 'Progress', 47. Cf. Hemminge, 12: 'the Apostle compareth concupiscence to a bayt, wherewith the fisher coverth his hooke, that he may deceive and catch the fishes'. Mayor, 54, cites texts in which ἕλκω and its cognates depict 'the first drawing of the fish out from its original retreat' and then suggests that 'the first effect of ἐπιθυμία is to draw the man out of his original repose, the second to allure him to a definite bait'. The sermon, 'Drawn and Dragged', by W. Arnot in his *The Lesser Parables of Our Lord*, London, 1885, 212-16, starts from this analysis and explicates Jas 1.14 entirely through fishing analogies. Bishop, *Apostles*, 184-85, includes Jas 1.15 in his list of 'echoes of Palestine in Saint James'. Cf. Moo, 75, who wonders whether James, who grew up near the Sea of Galilee, was thinking of fishing. Moo goes on, however, to compare our own 'I took the bait' and to suggest that the metaphor was dead by James' day. O. Holtzmann, 826, asserts that the order of the verbs is wrong if fishing is in view. For other options see Manton, 95.

²¹⁸ Note also T. Jos. 3.8 (εἰς πορνείαν με ἐφελκύσατο); 8.2 (ἐφελκομένη με εἰς συνουσίαν); 2 Pet 2.14, 18.

²¹⁹ Cf. BAGD, s.v. 2; Lampe, s.v. C. Add to their references Ep. Clem. ad Jas 7 GCS 42, ed. Rehm, 10-11.

²²⁰ So e.g. Bede *ad loc.* CCSL 121 ed. D. Hurst, 188; Bengel, 489 ('concupiscentia est pellex'); Owen, *Indwelling Sin* (as in n. 34), 136 ('there is a secret allusion to an adulterous deviation from conjugal duties, and conceiving or bringing forth children of whoredom and fornication'); Alford, 281; Macknight, 588; Winkler, 23; Mussner, 88; Wolmarans, 'Misogyny' (for James, sexual intercourse is sinful). Clarke, 800, speaks of 'illicit connexions' with 'impure women'. Oesterley, 428, thinks that throughout vv. 13-15 James has in view specifically 'temptation to lust'. For Plummer, 578, 'James represents the evil desire as playing the part of Potiphar's wife'. Many mention the loose woman in Prov 5–9: Wordsworth, 16; Bassett, 15; Plumptre, 55; R. Wall, 62; Moo, 76;

might compare Prov 7.22-23 (the fool follows the loose woman and 'bounds like a stag toward the trap... He is like a bird rushing into a snare'); Ecclus 7.26 ('I found more bitter than death the woman who is a trap, whose heart is snares and nets, whose hands are fetters; one who pleases God escapes her, but the sinner is taken by her'); 4Q184 2 ('her heart weaves traps, her kidneys [nets]', cf. 16-17).[221] The next verse, which speaks of conception and pregnancy, is consistent with thinking along these lines. At the same time, even if sexual connotations are present, ἐπιθυμία can hardly be simply equated with or reduced to sexual desire; see further below.

Verse 15. The lineage of death continues. Unlawful desire, having enticed and lured its victim, first conceives, then gives birth to sin, which in turn engenders death.[222] What at first delights, in the long run destroys. Verse 18 introduces a very different genealogy.

Verses 15a and b stand in parallel. Not only are they structurally identical—ἡ + subject + participle + main verb + object—but the final letters of the corresponding words are all the same (η ια σα ει ν):

εἶτα ἡ ἐπιθυμία συλλαβοῦσα τίκτει ἁμαρτίαν
ἡ δὲ ἁμαρτία ἀποτελεσθεῖσα ἀποκύει θάνατον

εἶτα ἡ ἐπιθυμία συλλαβοῦσα τίκτει ἁμαρτίαν. This contains three Jamesian *hapax*: εἶτα, συλλαμβάνω, τίκτω. By contrast, ἁμαρτία[223] is, as with the Paul of Romans and the author of Hebrews, one of our author's favorites (7×). In the LXX, the combination of the two verbs, uncommon in secular Greek,[224] again and again renders תהר ותלד.[225] So συλλαβοῦσα τίκτει should be judged a Semitism or a Septuagintalism.[226] Here the idiom seems to stand for mental consent to temptation.[227]

Isaacs, 189; Fruchtenbaum, 226; Witherington, 435; *et al.* Poole, 882, cannot decide whether the analogy is with fishing or with sexual seduction in v. 14; but he supposes that v. 15 envisages harlotry. Clarke, 800-801, and Knoch, 161, see both connotations at the same time.

[221] For other metaphorical uses of hunting language see Ecclus 9.12; Ezek 12.13; 17.20; 1QH 11(3).26; 13.5(8); 4Q185 2.5.

[222] Against the suggestion that 'desire', 'sin', and 'death' are spirits from a myth see Dibelius, 93-94. On the catena as a literary form see on 1.2-4.

[223] LXX: most often for חטאת.

[224] But note Hippocrates, *Mort. pop.* 2.2.17: συλλαμβάνουσα ἔτεκεν ἄρσεν.

[225] Gen 4.17, 25; 21.2; 29.32-35; 30.17, 19; Ps 7.15; Hos 1.3, 6, 8; etc.; cf. 4Q215 1-3 4.

[226] As in T. Levi 11.2; T. Iss. 1.14; T. Benj. 1.5; Philo, *Cher.* 46; *Quaest. Gen* 3.18; Jos. Asen. 21.9; Lk 1.31. For metaphorical use of the verbs see Burchard, 74, and below n. 230.

[227] Recall the patristic use of the Stoic συγκατάθεσις for assent to temptation (Lampe, s.v. 5) and cf. Evagrius, *Cap. pract.* A 75 SC 171 ed. Guillaumont, 663.

εἶτα does not entail an inevitable sequence.[228] That would go against common experience, which is that much temptation is successfully resisted. It would also, moreover, go against Jas 5.19-20, which holds out hope for a sinner turning back from death. So James narrates what must have happened when sin has led to death, not what must happen when sin is conceived.[229]

That συλλαβοῦσα alludes to the sex act is clear from the following τίκτει. The metaphor[230] interests because the Jewish idea of the יצר, which likely lies behind our passage, could be associated with the sexual impulse.[231] Perhaps that association encouraged James in his choice of metaphors. A few readers, as already observed, have thought of sexual sin in particular.[232] Yet it would be unwise to reduce the scope of the sin that leads to death, and there are texts that, so far from identifying the οὐκ ἐπιθυμήσεις of Exod 20.17 = 5.21 with sexual sin, enlarge it to cover all unlawful desires, making it indeed the sin behind all other sins. Philo, *Spec.* 4.84, labels ἐπιθυμία 'the fountain of all evils', a sentiment he repeats elsewhere,[233] and one which probably had some currency in

---

[228] Yet because the sequence is narrated as though it is strictly cause and effect, sermons on the text rarely focus upon forgiveness and God's ability to break the chain. P. Brooks, *Christ the Light and Life*, London, 1905, 63-68, is an exception.

[229] Maier, 79, affirms: 'The legitimate continuation of the Letter of James...is not (Luther's) Bondage of the Will but Irenaeus' chapter on free will in Adv. haer. IV,37'. See further the exposition in Jerome, *Adv. Jov.* 2.3 PL 23.286C-D, which takes James to imply that God created human beings with free will, so that they are not compelled to either virtue or vice. One guesses that James shared something like Philo's idea of free will, on which see D. Winston, 'Freedom and Determinism in Philo of Alexandria', *SPhilo* 3 (1974), 47-70.

[230] Cf. Justin Martyr, *Dial.* 100.5 PTS 47 ed. Marcovich, 242, of Eve: 'Conceiving (συλλαβοῦσα) the word from the serpent, she gave birth (ἔτεκε) to disobedience and death'. The parallel is interesting but hardly proves dependence upon James. For other metaphorical uses of συλλαμβάνω see LXX Ps 7.14; T. Benj. 7.2 ('The sword is the mother of the seven evils; it receives them [συλλαμβάνει] through Beliar'). τίκτω was also used metaphorically: LSJ, s.v., IV, lists examples, to which may be added LXX Prov 10.23 ('Wisdom τίκτει prudence for a man'); Ecclus 8.18 ('you do not know what tomorrow will τέξεται'; cf. Prov 3.28; 27.1); Sib. Or. 3.235 ('love of money...τίκτει innumerable evils').

[231] See Sifre Num 88; b. Qidd. 81a, 81b; b. Suk. 52a; b. 'Abod. Zar. 17a; Urbach, *Sages*, 1.471-83. For earlier sources see CD 2.16 ('a guilty יצר and lascivious eyes'); Rom 7 (on which see D. Boyarin, *A Radical Jew*, Berkeley, 1994, 158-79); T. Jud. 11.1-2 ('youthful διαβούλιον [the usual word in the Testaments for יצר; see R.H. Charles, *The Testaments of the Twelve Patriarchs*, London, 1908, 162] blinded my reason... and I had intercourse with her'). Yet one should be cautious here; the sexual connotations of the יצר הרע are less common in earlier than in later rabbinic literature; see I. Rosen-Zvi, 'Sexualising the Evil Inclination', *JJS* 60 (2009), 264-81

[232] See above n. 218. Note also perhaps the use of 'she' in some of the older English translations of v. 15: Tyndale, Cranmer, Geneva.

[233] Cf. Philo, *Decal.* 142, 173 (from ἐπιθυμία 'flows the most iniquitous actions, public and private, small and great, dealing with things sacred or things profane, affecting bodies and souls and what are called external things. For nothing escapes desire,

Jewish circles given its reappearance in Gk. LAE 19.3 ('ἐπιθυμία is the κεφαλή of every sin')[234] and Apoc. Abr. 24.9 (in the hand of 'desire'[235] is 'the head of every kind of lawlessness').[236] The same idea appears outside Jewish circles.[237]

Conceptually the closest passage in the Tanak to our line is Ps 7.14: 'See how they conceive evil and are pregnant with mischief and bring forth lies'.[238] Here the reproductive process is turned into a three-stage metaphor for the transition from evil thought to evil deed. A surprisingly large number of commentators seem to miss the parallel;[239] but given the similar imagery, the verbal overlap (Jas: συλλαβοῦσα τίκτει; Ps: συνέλαβεν...ἔτεκεν), the reference to death in both texts (cf. Ps 7.13) as well as the shared stress on human responsibility (Ps 7.16: 'Their mischief returns on their own heads') and the common focus on human error (Jas: ἁμαρτία; Ps 7.14: ἀδικίαν...ἀνομίαν),[240] one wonders whether the psalm has informed James.

ἡ δὲ ἁμαρτία ἀποτελεσθεῖσα ἀποκύει θάνατον. 'Sin is born pregnant with death'.[241] Note the assonance:

```
ἁ           μαρτία
ἁ π οτελεσθ εἶ σ     α
ἁ π ο κύ    ει
```

ἀποτελέω[242] occurs only here in James. Although it means 'perform' in Lk 13.32 and elsewhere, here it must mean 'come to completion'.[243] The word was not typically associated with coming to term and giving birth but presumably occurs here because it supplies the antithesis of the positive τέλειος called for in 1.4, 17. 25.[244] ἀποκυέω recurs in v. 18, with

---

and...like a flame in the forest, it spreads abroad and consumes and destroys everything'); *QG* 1.47 ('desire becomes the evil origin of sins').

[234] If a Hebrew text lies behind this, κεφαλή probably renders ראש = 'first', 'chief'.

[235] 'Slav[onic] *želanie*, a neuter, but the following possessives are feminine, surely reflecting mechanical translation of pronouns referring to Gk. *epithymia*'. So R. Rubinkiewicz, 'Apocalypse of Abraham', in *The Old Testament Pseudepigrapha*, vol. 1, ed. J.H. Charlesworth, Garden City, NY, 1983, 701.

[236] See further below, on 4.2.

[237] Cf. Maximus of Tyre, *Dial.* 24.4A ('ἐπιθυμία is the greatest evil for man'); Ps.-Diogenes, *Ep.* 50 ('ἐπιθυμία for money is the cause of all evil').

[238] LXX: ἰδοὺ ὠδίνησεν ἀδικίαν, συνέλαβεν πόνον καὶ ἔτεκεν ἀνομίαν. Related are MT Job 15.35; Isa 59.4.

[239] Baumgarten, 51; Lange, 50; Oesterley, 428; and Leahy, 911 ('the verse partially echoes Ps 7:15') are exceptions.

[240] Note also that ἁμαρτωλόν appears in v. 10.

[241] So Wesley, 598. Equally memorable is Hesychius *ad loc.* PG 93.1389A: 'the desires of sinners are the birth-pangs of death'.

[242] LXX: 2×. NT: 2×. Gk. Pseudepigrapha (Denis): 7×. Philo: 104×. Josephus: 3×.

[243] Cf. BAGD, s.v., and the texts cited in Mayor, 55-56.

[244] Is it also worth noting that the verb is otherwise associated with ἐπιθυμία, as in Plato, *Gorg.* 503D; *Resp.* 580D; Galen, *Placit. Hippocr. et Platon.* 4.4.21?

God as the subject; see the discussion there. It literally means 'give birth' but can have figurative sense, as in its one LXX occurrence.[245] θάνατος is appropriately last in the sentence because death is the end of life. The word also appears in 5.20, in James' concluding line, and again in close connection with ἁμαρτία. In this way the beginning ties itself to the end, unifying the book. Only here, however, is sin—which must be unnatural, out of accord with the divine intent—personified.[246] Is the reader supposed to envision the gruesome event of a stillborn child?[247]

Jews and Christians sometimes linked sin and death with Adam and Eve.[248] Our text, however, does not clearly allude to the primeval myth of the fall[249] or offer an aetiology of physical death. It rather diagnoses the cause of any individual's spiritual death, which means alienation from God in this world and the world to come;[250] cf. 5.20, where being saved

---

[245] 4 Macc 15.17: 'Ὁ woman who alone among women brought to birth (ἀποκυήσασα) perfect piety'. NT: 2×. Gk. Pseudepigrapha (Denis): 0×. Philo: 24×. Josephus: 0×. There seems to be no justification for the remark of Plumptre, 55, that the verb was 'used for extraordinary or monstrous births (such e.g. as a woman's bearing four or five children), and so is appropriate here'.

[246] The personification of Death is attested in the Tanak (Ps 49.15; Isa 25.8; 28.15, 18; Jer 9.21; Hos 13.14; Hab 2.15), in the Pseudepigrapha (Pss. Sol. 7.4; Asc. Isa. 9.16 [this is Christian]; T. Abr. RecLng. 16-20), in the NT in Revelation (1.18; 6.8; 20.13-14; 21.4) and perhaps Paul (Rom 5.14, 17; 6.9; 1 Cor 15.26, 54-55), and in later Christian writings (e.g. Orig. World 106.23-29; Melch. 2.5; Ps.-Bartholomew, *Book of the Resurrection of Jesus Christ*; Timothy of Alexandria, *Discourse on Abbaton*; History of Joseph the Carpenter; the Coptic Assumption of the Virgin); etc. In Graeco-Roman mythology, death is personified as Thanatos, the brother of Sleep: Hesiod, *Theog.* 211-12, 756-57; Homer, *Il.* 14.231; 16.667-75, 682; Aeschylus frag. 141 (255); Sophocles, *Oed. col.* 1223, 1574-77; *Aj.* 854-55; *Phil.* 797; Euripides, *Alcestis*; Horace, *Carm.* 1.4.13-14; Virgil, *Aen.* 11.197; etc. Pausanias, *Descr.* 3.18.1, says that there were statues of Death and Sleep in Sparta. See further G. Röhser, *Metaphorik und Personifikation der Sünde*, Tübingen, 1987.

[247] Contrast Popkes, 109: James narrates not a stillbirth but the birth of death.

[248] See Ecclus 25.24 ('From a woman sin had its beginning, and because of her we all die'); Wis 2.24; Rom 5.12 ('Sin came into the world through one man, and death came through sin'); 6.23 (Brückner, *Reihenfolge*, 289, thinks James influenced by these two verses in Romans); 4 Ezra 3.7 ('you laid upon him [Adam] one commandment of yours; but he transgressed it, and immediately you appointed death for him and for his descendants'). All these texts derive ultimately from Gen 2.17; 3.3-4.

[249] Contrast Martin, 36: 'echoes of the temptation in Gen 3 are to be detected at a subsurface level in this verse'; cf. Stevartius, 55; Grotius, 1075; Quistorp, 395; Sadler, 13-14; Weidner, 32; Mussner, 89; Reicke, 17 (in 'the background is Jewish speculation about Adam and the fall'); Popkes, 108 ('possible'); McKnight, 122. Note Ecclus 15.14 and 4Q422, where Adam's sin is associated with the evil impulse; see T. Elgvin and E. Tov, in *Qumran Cave 4, VIII: Parabiblical Texts, Part I*, Oxford, 1994, 422-23.

[250] Cf. Gregory Palamas, *Hom. xxi–xlii* 32.13 ed. Chrestou and Zeses, 324 (the death of Jas 1.15 is 'eternal' because it is 'the separation of the soul from God through sin'); Hemminge, 12 ('death and damnation'); Calmet, 670 ('damnationem, aeternamque infelicitatem'); Manton, 100 (death 'is but a modest word for damnation'); Bassett, 15 ('lust and hell are grandparent and grandchild'); Bardenhewer, 44; Michl, 31 ('Ver-

from death means sins being covered.[251] In other words, people die to God because they allow wrongful desire to lead them astray; for when sin, like a foetus come to term, is fully formed, it alienates the individual from God, with death the result. The thought is similar to Philo, *Leg.* 2.77 ('pleasures...bring death, not the death which severs soul from body, but the death which ruins the soul by vice'); Rom 6.21-23 ('the wages of sin is death');[252] 7.5 ('our sinful passions...were at work in our members to bear fruit for death');[253] Herm. *Mand.* 4.1.1 ('This desire is a great sin for the servant of God. And if any one commit this wicked deed he works death for himself'); b. Ber. 33a (החטא ממית: 'sin kills').[254] Bede observes that the mention of death makes for an antithesis with 'the crown of life' (v. 12): 'Just as someone who, when tempted, wins the rewards of life, so surely someone who, when lured by his own concupiscence, is overcome by temptation rightly incurs the ruin of death'.[255] In brief and in a picture:

v. 12: testing → endurance → life
v. 15: desire → sin → death[256]

dammnis'); R. Wall, 62; Burchard, 74 ('life without salvation and meaning, that eventuates in physical and eternal death'); etc. The commentary tradition often refers in this connection to the 'second death' of Revelation; cf. Origen, *Apoc. 1–27* Scholion 11 TU 38.2 ed. Diobouniotis and Harnack, 25; Fulgentius, *Ad Mon.* 1.5.1 CCSL 91 ed. Fraipont, 6; Guyse, 567; Chaine, 22; Gundry, 921; *et al.* Contrast Knowling, 22 ('spiritual death', not 'eternal death'); Schnider, 42 ('every area of life that is destroyed through sin').

[251] Note also 2 Bar. 78.6: 'If you reckon that you have now suffered these things for your good, that you may not be condemned at the end and be tormented, then you will receive eternal hope'.

[252] Barnes, 31, opines: 'There is a strong similarity between this declaration and that of the apostle Paul...and it is probable that James had that passage in his eye'.

[253] On the parallels between Rom 7 and our text see Klein, *Werk*, 88-90.

[254] Cf. also b. Šabb. 55a ('There is no death without sin') and recall the fact that death is the consequence of birth (cf. Heraclitus frag. 120), which in turn can be traced to the sexual impulse; cf. the Gospel of the Egyptians *apud* Clement of Alexandria, *Strom.* 3.9.63.1-2 GCS 52 ed. Stählin and Früchtel, 225.

[255] Bede *ad loc.* CCSL 121 ed. Hurst, 189. Cf. Wandel, 57; Klein, *Werk*, 84; Popkes, 108.

[256] Oesterley, 429, raises the possibility that the author and his Christian readers, who hoped the *parousia* to be near (5.7), imagined they might not die: they would neither die physically nor suffer what Revelation calls 'the second death' (2.11; 20.6).

VI

THE GOODNESS OF GOD (1.16-18)[1]

(16) Do not be deceived, my beloved brothers. (17) Every good gift and every perfect present is from above, coming down from the Father of lights, with whom there is neither variation nor shadow due to change. (18) Of his own will he brought us forth by the word of truth so that we might become a kind of first fruits among his creatures.

History of Interpretation and Reception

1.17-18 has given rise to three very different interpretations. (i) The majority of readers, glossing the passage with concepts found elsewhere in the NT, have identified the 'word of truth' with the gospel, the event of birth with regeneration, and 'the first fruits' with either the early (predominantly Jewish-Christian) church or all Christians. In other words, the passage has to do with salvation through Christian rebirth, which is thus the great illustration of God's goodness.[2] (ii) Others, however, have

---

[1] Recent literature: Amphoux, 'Jacques 1, 17'; Baker, 'Daddy'; Boismard, 'Liturgie'; Cadoux, *Thought*, 19-24; Edsman, 'Schöpferwille'; idem, 'Schöpfung'; Elliott-Binns, 'Creation'; Fischer, 'Spruchvers'; Gollwitzer, 'Kantate'; Greeven, 'Gabe'; Hartin, *Q*, 174-76; Hatch, 'Note'; Isaacs, 'Suffering'; Klein, *Werk*, 66-68, 129-34; Konradt, *Existenz*, 41-66; idem, 'Wort'; Ludwig, *Wort*, 151-59; J.D. Miller, 'Birth'; Mussner, 'Tauflehre'; Ng, 'Father'; Ogara, 'Verbo'; F. Palmer, 'Offering'; Parry, *Discussion*, 18-24; Poirier, 'Symbols'; Tsuji, *Glaube*, 67-70; Verseput, 'Prayers'; Walker, 'Werken'; Wenger, *Kyrios*, 104-22, 134-42; White, *Erstlingsgabe*, 238-60; Wolmarans, 'Male'; idem, 'Misogyny'.

[2] Bede *ad loc*. CCSL 121 ed. D. Hurst, 189-90; Martin of Legio *ad loc*. PL 209.190A; Nicholas of Gorran, 69; Nicholas of Lyra *ad loc*.; Erasmus, *Paraphrase*, 143; Luther (see J. Haar, *Initium creaturae Dei*, Gütersloh, 1939); Calvin, 270; Wolzogen, 186; Bengel, 489-90; Gill, 783; Storr, 15; de Wette, 218-19; Rosenmüller, 334-35; Mayor, 62-64; Dibelius, 104-107; Chaine, 25-27; Tielemann, 'Verständnis'; Ogara, 'Verbo', 131; Meinertz, *Theologie*, 239 (the word of truth = 'the gospel' that 'perfects, deepens, and intensifies the OT law'); Knoch, 162-64; Michl, 32; Cantinat, 97-98; Cargal, 85-86; Moo, 79-80 (with hesitation); Konradt, *Existenz*, 42-44; Popkes, 123-27; Fabris, 89-90; Blomberg-Kamell, 75 (the word = 'the story of Christ's incarnation, death and resurrection'); Orlando, *Lettera*, 50-55; *et al*. Some who adopt this interpretation refer specifically to baptism; cf. Aretius, 476; Weidner, 34; Belser, 68; Bardenhewer, 46-47; Mussner, 'Tauflehre'; Ruckstuhl, 14; Stewart-Sykes, 'Paraenesis'; Farley, 23. See further n. 172. C.F. Aked, 'First Fruits: The Inspiring Gospel of Eternal Hope', *Christian World Pulpit* 104 (1923), 121-24, counters a perceived 'slump in idealism' by construing

read our passage not against the background of the NT but rather of the Hebrew Bible. They have identified the 'word of truth' with God's creative word, the event of birth with the creation of Adam, and the 'first fruits' with humanity.³ (iii) Yet a third interpretation has appealed to a small minority of exegetes, all modern: the 'word of truth' is the Torah, the event of birth is God's creation of Israel, and the 'first fruits' are the Jewish people.⁴

'Every good gift and every perfect present' is nowadays usually thought of as a general, comprehensive expression: 'good gift' and 'perfect present' are rough synonyms, together denoting God's numerous benefits. In the past, however, many drew a distinction between 'good gift' (δόσις ἀγαθή) and 'perfect present' (δώρημα τέλειον). Dionysius bar Salībī raised the possibility that the former is something given by grace to the undeserving whereas the latter refers to bishops, presbyters, and deacons.⁵ John Scottus Eriugena urged that the divine *datum* is existence, the divine *donum* heavenly grace.⁶ Much more common has been the proposition that 'good gifts' have to do with things for this life, 'perfect presents' with things for the life to come. As Lancelot Andrewes put it, 'By "giving" he understandeth...every transitory thing whereof we stand

---

the idea of Christians as the 'first fruits' as reason for optimism about the world's redemption. For application to Jewish-Christians in particular see Calmet, 670; Clarke, 802; T. Scott, 568 ('an earnest of a vastly larger increase from the Gentile world'); T. Williams, 1360; Pyle, 310; Beyschlag, 75; Gaugusch, 17; Mussner, 96; White, *Erstlingsgabe*, 257 (stressing the nearness to Rom 11.6).

³ So Dionysius bar Salībī *ad loc.* CSCO 60, Scriptores Syri 101, ed. Sedlacek, 91; Ps.-Oecumenius *ad loc.* PG 119.464D; Theophylact *ad loc.* PG 125.144B-C; Godfridus, *Hom. dom.* 52 PL 174.349D; Spitta, 45-47; Hort, 31-32; Fulford, 44-45; Parry, *Discussion*, 11; Cadoux, *Thought*, 18-24; Rendall, *Christianity*, 64-65; Edsman, 'Schöpferwille' (positing an androgynous demiurge in the pre-James tradition); Sidebottom, 33; Elliott-Binns, 'Creation'; Laws, 75-78 (arguing that the language of creation and redemption intermingle but that 'creation remains...the primary and dominant idea'); Frankemölle, 298-304; Tsuji, *Glaube*, 68-69; Jackson-McCabe, *Logos*, 233-38. This interpretation lies behind B. Wilberforce, 'Our Mother which art in Heaven', in *New (?) Theology*, London, 1907, 150-59, a sermon which divines in James not only the notion of God as mother (ἀπεκύησεν) but also 'the reality and the universality of sonship and human brotherhood' as well as 'Divine Immanence in man'. Baker, 'Daddy', combines interpretations (i) and (ii): 'birth in a new life is an extension of God's original purpose for creating humanity in the first place'. Cf. Leahy, 911.

⁴ Maurice, *Unity*, 287-90; Bassett, 19; Windisch-Preisker, 10; Meyer, *Rätsel*, 157-59; Boismard, 'Liturgie', 171-72; Lautenschlager, 'Gegenstand', 168; Ludwig, *Wort*, 157-59; Giere, 'Midrash', 93-94; Kloppenborg, 'Discourse', 246-48. According to Schlatter, 138, a non-Christian Jewish reader of James would identify the 'word of truth' with Torah and the 'first fruits' with Israel.

⁵ Dionysius bar Salībī *ad loc.* CSCO 60, Scriptores Syri 101, ed. Sedlacek, 90.

⁶ John Scottus Eriugena, *Exp. Ier. cael.* 1.1 PL 122.127-31. This is not far from W. Bates, 'Spiritual Perfection', in *Whole Works*, vol. 2, London, 1815, 488: the good gifts are 'blessings in the order of nature', the perfect gifts the sanctifying graces and comforts of the Holy Spirit. So too Stevartius, 57; Bisping, 24.

in need, while we are yet in our journey towards our heavenly country...
By "gift" he meaneth the felicity that is reserved for us after this life.'[7]
Closer to our time, Mayor, 58, urged that one could illustrate δόσις by
referring to God's granting of wisdom in v. 5 and illuminate δώρημα by
referring to the 'crown of life' in v. 12.

Whatever the precise meaning given to 'every good gift and every
perfect present', the phrase has often been taken to teach that human
beings should not boast: good things come from God alone,[8] or only as
an answer to prayer.[9] In other words, Jas 1.17—the opening line in
Pseudo-Dionysius' *Celestial Hierarchy*[10]—has been used paraenetically,
as an exhortation to humility. Luther went further in this direction, even
employing the verse to counter belief in free will, which he reckoned
vanity.[11] On the other hand, John of the Cross insisted that gifts must be
accepted: what God gives is useless unless people hold out their hands
and receive.[12]

The assertion that *all* good gifts are from God has led Christians to
contemplate good things outside of the Bible or their own tradition.
Sopford Brooke preached an eloquent sermon on 1.17, the purpose of

[7] L. Andrewes, 'A Preparation to Prayer', in *Ninety-Six Sermons*, vol. 5, Oxford, 1843, 314. Cf. Martin of Legio *ad loc.* PL 209.189C; Nicholas of Gorran, 69; Trapp, 695; Wordsworth, 16. Baumgarten, 55, rejects this interpretation, which modern commentators no longer mention. Bucer included free will among the good gifts of 1.17, which is eisegesis, yet it accords with the spirit of James; see the sermon printed in *Die letzten Strassburger Jahre 1546–1549*, ed. R. Stupperich, Gütersloh, 1981, 500.

[8] Augustine, *Ep.* 186.10 CSEL 57 ed. Goldbacher, 53-54; Cassian, *Conf.* 3.16 SC 42 ed. Pichery, 161; 13.3 SC 54 ed. Pichery, 151; Fulgentius, *Ad Mon. I* 14.1 CCSL 91 ed. Fraipont, 15; *Ep. III ad Proba* CCSL 91 ed. Fraipont, 214; Fulgentius of Ruspa, *Ep.* 3.5; 4.6 SC 487 ed. Bachelet, 156-58, 212; Leo the Great, *Tract.* 5.1 CCSL 138 ed. Chavasse, 22; Caesarius of Arles, *Serm.* 226.6 CCSL 104 ed. Morin, 896; John of the Cross, *Llama de Amor* 3.47 ed. S.P. de Santa Teresa, 782 (the saints can do nothing about certain things they desire: they can only wait upon God); Stier, 259-62. Augustine, *Spir. et lit.* 7.11; 13.22; 35.63 CSEL 60 ed. Urba and Zycha, 163, 175, 223, turns the verse against the Pelagians. It is no surprise that Jas 1.17 has often been cited along with Jn 3.27 ('No one can receive anything except what has been given from heaven') and/or 1 Cor 4.7 ('What do you have that you did not receive? And if you received it, why do you boast as if it were not a gift?'), and not just in the commentary tradition; note e.g. Augustine, *Serm.* 185.2 PL 38.998; 'The Doctrinal Chapters of the Synod of Orange' (conclusion), in *Creeds and Confessions of Faith in the Christian Tradition*, vol. 1, ed. J. Pelikan and V. Hotchkiss, New Haven, 2003, 697; Maximus the Confessor, *Quaest. ad Thal. I* 100ff. CCSG 7 ed. Laga and Steel, 385; Andrewes, 'Preparation to Prayer' (as in n. 7), 315; Barth, *CD* 3.3.51.2 (435).

[9] Cf. John of Damascus, *F.O.* 88 PTS 12 ed. Kotter, 204; Andrewes, 'Preparation to Prayer' (as in n. 7), 312, 320; Wordsworth, 17.

[10] SC 58 ed. Roques, 70. It is also the opening line of an obscure poem by Alan of Lille; see N.M. Häring, 'Two Theological Poems probably composed by Alan of Lille', *Analecta Cisterciensia* 32 (1976), 249.

[11] M. Luther, *De Servo Arbitrio*, in *Luthers Werke in Auswahl*, 6th ed., vol. 3, ed. Clemen, 253.

[12] John of the Cross, *Spiritual Cant.* 30.6 ed. P.S. de Santa Teresa, 655.

which was to commend the reading of Shakespeare, whose inspiration was 'of God'.[13] Robert Flint, in preaching the same text, crafted a paean to beauty, arguing that art is from God and admonishing artists to take their divine task seriously.[14] In a more academic context, E. Reeves Palmer found in 1.17 justification of the fact that biblical religion borrowed important elements from the Zoroastrians and the Greeks.[15]

Calvin, 270, and most exegetes since the Reformation have understood 'the father of lights'—a phrase that entered the liturgies[16]—to relate God to the heavenly orbs. In the past, however, several other proposals were common. Origen equated the lights with the spiritual light of Jn 1.9 that 'enlightens everyone'.[17] Bede took the lights to be spiritual gifts.[18] Isho'dad of Merv thought they were the apostles and other religious teachers.[19] For the *Catenae* ed. Cramer, 6, they might be those enlightened by the Holy Spirit.[20] Pseudo-Dionysius seemingly equated the lights with the Son and the Holy Spirit,[21] as did certainly Nicholas of Methone later on.[22] Many have thought the sense to be manifold, so that it includes both physical and spiritual lights of every beneficial kind.[23]

James' comment that God does not change has been an important proof text for the doctrine of divine immutability. For 'with whom there is neither variation nor shadow due to change' has typically been taken to be a metaphysical statement.[24] Athanasius argued from Jas 1.17 not only

---

[13] S.A. Brooke, 'Shakespeare and Human Life', in *The Spirit of the Christian Life*, London, 1881, 333-46. The sermon was preached at Stratford, at the inauguration of the theatre in 1879.

[14] R. Flint, 'The Good and Perfect Gift of Art', in *Sermons and Addresses*, New York, 1899, 28-38. This sermon was preached in Edinburgh in 1889 before the National Association for the Advancement of Art.

[15] E.R. Palmer, *The Development of Revelation*, London, 1892, 207-18.

[16] Note e.g. Basil the Great, *Liturg.* PG 31.1656A; the Liturgy of John Chrysostom (in Brightman-Hammond, *Liturgies*, 398); Testamentum Domini 1.23, 26 ed. Rahmani, 38, 52 (אבא דנוהרא); the Byzantine Armenian Rite (in Brightman-Hammond, *Liturgies*, 456).

[17] Origen, *Jn ad* 1.8 GCS 10, ed. Preuschen, 488. Cf. Theophylact *ad loc.* PG 125.1137B; Godfridus, *Hom. dom.* 52 PL 174.348B-C; Poole, 882.

[18] Bede *ad loc.* CCSL 121 ed. D. Hurst, 189.

[19] Isho'dad of Merv *ad loc.* HSem 10 ed. Gibson, 49. Cf. Dionysius bar Salībī *ad loc.* CSCO 60, Scriptores Syri 101, ed. Sedlacek, 90, referring to Mt 5.14 ('You are the light of the world'). Mt 5.14 is also referred to by Fulgentius, *Ep. XIV ad Ferrandus* 7 CCSL 91 ed. Fraipont, 393, but he identifies the lights more generally with the saints.

[20] Cf. Kuhn, 'Beiträge', 120: the lights are in the first instance Christians themselves.

[21] Ps.-Dionysius, *Div. nom.* 2.7 PTS 33 ed. Suchla, 132. Cf. Albert Magnus, *Summae theologiae pars prima* Q 32.1 ed. Borgnet, 339. For additional texts that apply 1.17 to the Son and the Holy Spirit see Johnson, *Brother*, 80-81.

[22] Nicholas of Methone, *Ref. Procl.* 54 ed. Angelou, 66.

[23] E.g. Gill, 782; Wesley, 598; Knowling, 24. Cf. Wordsworth, 16; Johnstone, 79; Hort, 30.

[24] Cf. Hilary, *Trin.* 4.8 CCSL 62 ed. Smulders, 108 (the Arians use this against there being any change in God); Severus of Antioch, *Hom. cath.* 42 PO 167 ed. Brière and

THE GOODNESS OF GOD (1.16-18)

that God is incapable of change (ἀπαράλλακτος)[25] but also that the divinity must thus be a 'simple essence'.[26] For Augustine, James' assertion that God does not change meant that within God there can be no past, present, or future.[27] Cyril of Alexandria used 1.17 to contend that the blending of the Son of God with human flesh did not change the divine nature of the Word.[28] John of Damascus found in the text support for a platonic conception of the divine mind: all images and models have always existed in God.[29] The unknown author of the *Libellus de tribus epistolis* cited the verse to urge that God 'knows how to create things without any novelty of will. He knows how to be at work although resting and how to be at rest although working'.[30] The Westminster Confession of Faith lists Jas 1.17, along with Mal 3.6 ('For I am the Lord, I change not'), as the confirmation that God is 'immutable'.[31] Some recent theologians, however, instead insist that James has in view not metaphysical change but only moral change.[32] This reading is perhaps reflected in the twentieth-century hymn, 'Great is Thy Faithfulness': 'Great is Thy

---

Graffin, 50; and note the comment of Servetus, *Errors of the Trinity* 5.9 trans. Wilbur, 157: 'nor do I understand light as meaning here the assertion of a quality. But inasmuch as the rays of being, and shining angels, flow from God, the breath of being comes out of his storehouse, from the Father's breast, as sons from a father's bosom; manifold rays of divinity proceed, which are all Essences of God, and he is in them'.

[25] Athanasius, *Ep. I ad Serap.* 26 PG 26.592A. The word was subsequently the object of some debate; see the references in Lampe, s.v., IIB.

[26] Athanasius, *Afros* 8 PG 26.1044B. Cf. Gregory of Nyssa, *Ep.* 24.12 ed. Pasquali, 78 (there is no 'variation'—παραλλαγήν—among the members of the Trinity); Alexander Nequam, *Spec. spec.* 3.9.6 ed. Thomson, 266.

[27] Augustine, *Civ. dei.* 11.21.

[28] Cyril of Alexandria, *Symbol. Eph.* ed. Pusey, 50; *Adv. Nest. blasph.* 5.4 PG 76.229C. See conveniently J.A. McGuckin, *St. Cyril of Alexandria*, Leiden, 1994, 281, 284, 318, 339-40. Cf. Severus of Antioch, *Philal.* 20 CSCO 113 Scriptores Syri 68 ed. Hespel, 19; Gregory Palamas, *Hom. xliii-lxiii* 53.33 ed. Chrestou and Zeses, 302. For Augustine, *Serm.* 23.15 PL 38.161, Jas 1.17 applies not just to the Father and the Son but also the Holy Spirit; cf. Athanasius, *Ep. IV ad Serap. ep. Thum.* 1.26 PG 26.591A.

[29] John of Damascus, *Imag.* 1.10 PTS 17 ed. Kotter, 84.

[30] *Lib. de trib. ep.* 7 PL 121.992C.

[31] Cf. the *Catenae ad loc.* ed. Cramer, 6; Novatian, *Trin.* 4 PL 3.919C; Ps.-Andrew of Crete, *Éloge* 4.18-22 ed. Noret, 48 (God is ἄτρεπτόν τε καὶ ἀναλλοίωτον). The same two texts are combined as early as Hilary, *Trin.* 4.8 PL 10.101B, and Didymus of Alexandria, *Zech.* 2.195; 5.35 SC 84, 85, ed. Doutreleau, 516, 986, and thereafter often; see e.g. Ps.-Oecumenius *ad loc.* PG 119.464D; Theophylact *ad loc.* PG 125.1144B; Aquinas, *Comm. Sent.* 1.8.3.1; Peter Martyr Vermigli, *Provid.* 12 ed. McLelland, 191; E. Roberts, *The Works of the Right Reverend Father in God, Ezekiel Roberts*, ed. Josiah Pratt, vol. 1, London, 1809, 196-97; C. Hodge, *Systematic Theology*, vol. 1, New York, 1872, 390.

[32] So e.g. I.A. Dorner, 'Über die richtige Fassung des dogmatischen Begriffs der Unveränderlichkeit Gottes', in *Gesammelte Schriften*, Berlin, 1883, 247 ('God's inner ethical essence'); A.G. Padgett, *God, Eternity, and the Nature of Time*, New York, 1992, 33. Kierkegaard, *Edifying Discourses*, ed. P. Holmer, New York, 1958, 253-54, takes the meaning to be that the father of lights 'has no other ambition, nor any other thought, than invariably to send good and perfect gifts'.

faithfulness, O God my Father! There is no shadow of turning with Thee; Thou changest not, Thy compassions, they fail not: As Thou hast been Thou forever wilt be.'

Modern Christians, concerned for gender equality, have sometimes found support for their cause in the ἀπεκύησεν of v. 18, because the verb means 'give birth to' and so associates God with a feminine function.[33] Already Bengel, 489, remarked: God 'stands in the place of father and mother'. Wordsworth, 17, was like-minded: 'With reverence be it said, in the work of our Regeneration, He is both our Father and Mother... He is a Father, the Father of lights, and He is like a Mother also, and gives birth to us...' Most translations, however, have avoided such an idea.[34] Unease with depicting God as giving birth may also explain the textual variant, ἐποίησεν.[35]

Despite the relative dearth of christological elements throughout James, a canonical reading has often espied them. In the present case, and despite the theocentric language, the 'word of truth' has been equated with the light of John's prologue and so identified with Jesus. This interpretation appears in Athanasius, Theophylact, Nicholas of Lyra, and George Bull.[36] Anselm read 1.17 as depicting not just the relationship between God and human beings in general but also the relationship between God the Father and God the Son: Jesus Christ 'could only have the will by which he was willing to die, to achieve such a great good, only from the Father of lights, from whom comes every best and perfect gift'.[37] Scaer argues that this is in fact that true sense of v. 17: 'the one perfect and good gift for salvation [the incarnate Christ] has already come down from heaven'.[38] Related is the view of Hus: one can think of the

---

[33] See e.g. B. Wilberforce, 'Our Mother which art in Heaven' (as in n. 3); R.M. Groothuis, *Good News for Women*, Grand Rapids, MI, 1997, 93. Contrast Wolmarans, 'Male', who argues that, in context, the God of 1.18 is masculine whereas, in 1.14-15, sin and desire are feminine; the upshot is that James 'strengthens male patriarchal values'.

[34] E.g. RSV, NASB, and NewKJV have 'brought us forth'. Contrast KJV ('begat'); NIV ('give us birth'); NRSV ('gave us birth').

[35] See n. 162 and cf. J.D. Miller, 'Birth'. Maier, 85, is quick to caution: God should not be compared with birth-giving goddesses because 'the biblical God, in contrast to gods and goddesses, is not sexualized'.

[36] Athanasius, *Orat. III contra Arianos* 61 PG 26.452B; Theophylact *ad loc.* PG 125.1144C; Nicholas of Lyra *ad loc.*; G. Bull, *Defensio fidei Nicaenae* 1.1.17-19; *Harm. apost. doct.* 2.15. Cf. Ps.-Oecumenius *ad loc.* PG 119.465A; Godfridus, *Hom. dom.* 52 PL 174.349C; Lapide, 61; Wordsworth, 17-18 (urging that although James may not have intended such, the Holy Spirit did); Cedar, 41; Scaer, 61 (James may anticipate John, and 'the influence of James on the Fourth Gospel should not be discounted'). Note that Irenaeus, *Haer.* 5.1.1, depicts himself and his readers as 'the first fruits of creation' by means of the Word = Jesus Christ, and further that, in this connection, he uses *optimo et bono* of God, which is comparable to James' 'good and perfect'.

[37] Anselm, *Cur deus homo* 1.10 ed. Schmitt, 34.

[38] Scaer, 57-59. Burchard, 79, recognizes how puzzling it is, if v. 18 is about redemption, that James is silent about Jesus Christ.

Son as the good gift (cf. Isa 9.6; Jn 3.16) and of the Holy Spirit as the perfect gift (cf. Lk 11.13).[39]

Meister Eckhart preached a memorable sermon on 1.17 which argues that if one abandons one's will to God, then all that happens will be the best of all, even when it seems otherwise. Even suffering and pain can be, for Eckhart, good and perfect gifts from above.[40]

In the nineteenth century, Walter Chalmers Smith (1824–1908) took an old Welsh melody and composed for it 'Immortal, Invisible', which has become, in English-speaking countries, a staple of mainline Protestant hymnals. The hymn is in part a creative rewriting of 1.17, and the theme is largely God as light: God dwells 'in light inaccessible hid from our eyes',[41] is 'silent as light', and ''Tis only the splendor of light hideth Thee'. God is indeed addressed, in line 1 of the fourth stanza, as 'Great Father of glory, pure Father of light'. The dependence upon James is here unmistakable. The theme of God's immutability is likewise central to the hymn. God is 'unhasting', 'silent', and without 'wanting', and the third stanza ends with: 'We blossom and flourish as leaves on the tree, And wither and perish but naught changeth Thee'. These words take up 1.11.[42] Given all this, it may well be that the opening line of the third stanza, 'To all life Thou givest—to both great and small', depends upon James' words about God being the giver of every good and perfect gift.

Exegesis

Verses 16-18—which are, for Burchard, 74, 'the foundational theological passage of the letter'[43]—serve as 'warrant for the readers to accept the conviction expressed in Jas 1:13-14 by relating it to beliefs the readers already hold about God'.[44] 1.13 denies that God can be the source of temptation on the ground that the divinity has nothing to do with evil.

---

[39] Hus, 188. Christological doctrine has also led to theologians insisting on the difference between the begetting of Christ and all others; cf. Augustine, *Cons.* 2.3.6 CSEL 43 ed. Weihrich, 87; Bede, *ad loc.* CCSL 121 ed. D. Hurst, 189-90; Aquinas, *Summa* 3 q. 23 a. 2; Wesley, 858.

[40] *Serm.* 4 in *Meister Eckharts Predigten* ed. Quint, 60-74. In *Serm.* 9 ed. Quint, 149, he argues that God = the good gifts from above, that is, God gives God.

[41] This is from 1 Tim 6.16.

[42] KJV: the sun '*withereth* the grass, and the flower thereof falleth, and the grace of the fashion of it *perisheth*'.

[43] Cf. Schmidt, *Lehrgehalt*, 59: v. 18 expresses the author's fundamental idea about Christianity.

[44] So Cargal, 82. Linking vv. 16-18 to v. 13 is ubiquitous in the commentary tradition. Cf. the *Catena ad loc.* ed. Cramer, 6; Neander, 59; and note the exposition of the former in terms of the latter in Calvin, *De Occulta Dei Providentia* Corpus Reformatorum 37 Ioannis Calvini 9, 280. For Bisping, 23, vv. 16-17 are 'closely joined' to v. 13. Tsuji, *Glaube*, 68, labels vv. 16-18 a 'pendant' to vv. 14-15. Kot, 61, discerns a concentric structure in 1.13-18: vv. 17-18 balance vv. 13-15; v. 16 is the center.

That point is reinforced here: God, as readers should know, gives good gifts and is of constant character, so of course God does not tempt people to do evil. In Lancelot Andrewes' words, 'As before the Apostle shewed that God is not the cause of any evil, so in this verse [17] he teacheth that there is no good thing but God is the author of it; if He be the fountain of every good thing, then He cannot be the cause of evil, for "no one fountain" doth out of the same hole "yield sweet and bitter water"'.[45]

The structure of the unit is straightforward:

I. Warning ('Do not be deceived') and address ('my beloved brothers'), 16
II. Characterization of the deity, 17-18
    a. Good gifts are from God, 17a
    b. God is the father of lights, 17b
    c. God is without change or shadow, 17c
    d. God gave birth to 'us', the 'first fruits', by 'the word of truth', 17d

The paragraph contains a series of words that offers a stark contrast with the language of the previous unit:

1.13-15: 'tempted'—'evil'—'desire'—'lured'—'enticed'—'sin'—'death'
1.16-18: 'good'—'perfect'—'gift'—'lights'—'truth'—'first fruits'

James is moving from the undesirable to the desirable. Note that the contrast between vv. 16-18 and 13-15 is highlighted by the common verb, ἀποκυέω:

15 sin gives birth to (ἀποκύει) death
18 God gives birth to (ἀπεκύησεν) the first fruits

Commentators sometimes try to divine a concrete *Sitz im Leben*. McKnight, 123, supposes that some in 'the messianic community', which is suffering economic hardship and is 'tempted to react with violence and verbal abuse', question God's goodness and constancy. Maier, 81, urging that James 'does not theorize in a vacuum', infers that some in James' church believed God could work evil.[46] Vouga, followed by Martin, argues that 1.17-18 is polemic against the fatalism of astral religion.[47] Some of James' readers thought themselves at the mercy of fate because they believed that the stars dictated their destiny.[48] Although this last

---

[45] Lancelot Andrewes, 'Preparation to Prayer' (as in n. 7), 312.
[46] Cf. Lapide, 54-55, who ascribes this error to Simon Magus.
[47] Vouga, 57-58; Martin, 31-42. Cf. Doddridge, 839: 'it has been the opinion of some persons that this is intended to oppose some heretical notion of the influence of the stars'. Henry *ad loc.* speculates that James here opposes 'the loose opinions of Simon, and the Nicolaitans (from whom the Gnostics, a most sensual corrupt set of people, arose afterwards)'. Hammond, 688, also refers to Gnostics.
[48] Cf. already Hilary of Arles *ad loc.* PLSupp 3.66: James counters heretics who believe in divine fatalism. Appealing to passages in Josephus, G. Bull, *Harmonia*

hypothesis explains the astrological language of our passage, it does not persuade. The proposed polemic remains indirect, the topic is not taken up elsewhere in the letter, and vv. 17-18 can be adequately explained as commentary arising out of the exhortations in vv. 13-16: they do not require positing a particular community problem.

Verse 16. As in previous sections (1.2, 5, 9), James opens with an imperative. Perhaps 'what follows...[is] an inference from what went before' (Benson, 41). But one can also view vv. 16-18 as the theological justification for vv. 13-14.

μὴ πλανᾶσθε. This appears to have been a customary way of introducing a pointed assertion.[49] It is often said that the imperative is from Stoic diatribe.[50] The evidence for this conclusion appears to be texts from Epictetus (see n. 49) as well as the general presumption that Paul, who has the phrase three times, otherwise borrows elements from the Stoic–Cynic diatribe. One should observe, however, that there are parallels in the LXX[51] and 1 En. 104.9 (μὴ πλανᾶσθε τῇ καρδίᾳ), that a Semitic original underlies LAB 62.2 (*quid seduceris*) and perhaps Bel 7 (LXX: μηδείς σε παραλογιζέσθω; Theod.: μὴ πλανῶ), and that the exact Hebrew equivalent, אל תטעו, occurs in Tanḥ. Yel. Wayyestse 4.[52]

πλανάω[53] here connotes more than just a misunderstanding. One should think of serious moral failing that threatens salvation—a circumstance clarified by the rest of the letter, especially chaps. 4-5. The verb has just such drastic sense elsewhere,[54] and in some contexts it gains eschatological resonance: one must take care not to be 'deceived' in the latter days.[55]

---

apostolica, Oxford, 1842, 179-81; Benson, 43; and Wells, 8, attribute such fatalism to the Pharisees.

[49] Cf. 1 Cor 6.9 (μὴ πλανᾶσθε); 15.33 (μὴ πλανᾶσθε); Gal 6.7 (μὴ πλανᾶσθε); 1 Jn 3.7 (μηδεὶς πλανάτω ὑμᾶς); Ign. *Eph.* 5.2 (μηδεὶς πλανάσθω); 16.1 (μὴ πλανᾶσθε, ἀδελφοί μου); *Magn.* 8.1; (μὴ πλανᾶσθε); *Phil.* 3.3 (μὴ πλανᾶσθε, ἀδελφοί μου); *Smyr.* 6.1 (μηδεὶς πλανάσθω); Acts Thom. 96 ed. Bonnet, 209 (μὴ πλανῶ). There are three parallels in Epictetus: *Diatr.* 2.20.7 (μὴ ἐξαπατᾶσθε, ἄνθρωποι); 2.22.15 (μὴ ἐξαπατᾶσθε); 4.6.23 (μὴ πλανᾶσθε, ἄνδρες).

[50] Cf. Dibelius, 99 ('probably'); Marty, 37; H. Braun, 'πλανάω κτλ.', *TDNT* 6.244; Laws, 72 ('an idiom of Hellenistic rhetoric'). Burchard, 75, disagrees.

[51] Deut 4.19 (μὴ... πλανθείς); Isa 41.10 (μὴ πλανῶ); 44.8 B L C (μηδὲ πλανᾶσθε); 2 Macc 7.18 (μὴ πλανῶ).

[52] Cf. also אל + פתח in 4Q417 2 2.12-13 (*bis*).

[53] Jas: 2×; cf. 5.19. LXX: most often for a form of תעה.

[54] See e.g. Mt 18.12-13; 22.29; Mk 12.24, 27; 2 Tim 3.13; Rev 2.20; and the texts in the following note.

[55] E.g. Mt 24.4, 5, 11, 24; Mk 13.5, 6; Lk 21.8 (βλέπετε μὴ πλανηθῆτε); 2 Pet 2.15; Rev 12.9; 13.14; 19.20; 20.3, 8, 10; Apoc. Elijah 1.14. James does not specify the deceiving agent. Blomberg-Kamell, 73, suggest a middle sense: 'do not deceive yourselves'. Cf. Popkes, 119, appealing to 1.22.

ἀδελφοί μου ἀγαπητοί. This expression, which brings together 'my beloved' and 'my brothers',[56] appears elsewhere in the NT outside of James in 1 Cor 15.58 and Phil 4.1.[57] It recalls 1.2 and reappears in 1.19 and 2.5, where it again adds emphasis.[58] It has its parallels in the vocatives in several of the injunctions cited in n. 49: Epictetus, *Diatr.* 2.20.7 (ἄνθρωποι); 4.6.23 (ἄνθρωποι); Ign. *Eph.* 16.1 (ἀδελφοί μου); *Phil.* 3.3 (ἀδελφοί μου). The nearness of these last two lines to Jas 1.16— μὴ πλανᾶσθε ἀδελφοί μου is common to James and Ignatius—moves one to suspect that our letter reproduces specifically Christian language, for evidence that either writer knew the other is lacking.[59]

That James addresses his readers as 'beloved' is particularly apt given their characterization in 1.1: they are the tribes scattered abroad. Jewish tradition reckoned Israel to be God's 'beloved'.[60]

Although sometimes 1.16 or 16a has been thought the conclusion to 1.12(13)-15,[61] most have rather understood it to be an introduction. This accords with at least three observations. (i) 'Do not be deceived' is commonly a formula of introduction.[62] (ii) The vocative 'brothers' more often than not, in James, opens a new section or marks a shift of some sort,[63] and 'my beloved brothers' belongs to a new beginning in 1.19. (iii) Throughout James imperatives are a bit more characteristic of openings than of conclusions.[64] One should not, however, deny the obvious link with 1.12-15. Perhaps then it is best to speak of a formula of transition.[65]

---

[56] ἀγαπητοί μου (LXX: 0×): 1 Cor 10.14; Phil 2.12; Ign. *Magn.* 11.1; Mart. Pet. 9 ed. Lipsius, 96; etc. ἀδελφοί μου (LXX: not used as an address): Rom 7.4; 15.14; 1 Cor 1.11; 11.33; 14.39; Phil 3.1; Jas 2.1; 3.1, 10, 12; 5.12, 19; Ign. *Phil.* 5.1; Barn. 4.14; 5.5; 6.15; 2 Clem. 7.1; 10.1; 11.1; etc.

[57] Cf. also Tob 10.13 BA (ἄδελφε ἀγαπητέ); Col 4.7 (ὁ ἀγαπητὸς ἀδελφός), 9 (ἀγαπητῷ ἀδελφῷ); Phlm 16 (ἀδελφὸν ἀγαπητόν); 2 Pet 3.15 (ὁ ἀγαπητὸς ἡμῶν ἀδελφός); T. Abr. RecLng. 20.15 (ἀδελφοί μου ἀγαπητοί, a Christian addition); P. Köln. 2.109.1, 25. ἀγαπητοί occurs often by itself: 1 En. 10.12; 1 Pet 2.11; 4.12; 2 Pet 3.1, 8, 14, 17; 1 Jn 2.7; 3.2, 21; 4.1, 7, 11; Jude 3, 17, 20; Ign. *Smyr.* 4.1; etc.

[58] Scaer, 57, sees this is an address to teachers in particular: James does not want them teaching falsehood.

[59] Burchard, 75, thinks that James knew μὴ πλανᾶσθε as 'church language'.

[60] Recall the traditional identification of 'the beloved' in Canticles with Israel, as in the targum, and cf. Hos 11.1; Sifre Num 1.10; Sifre Deut 97; b. Ber. 6a; etc.

[61] E.g. Bede *ad loc.* CCSL 121 ed. D. Hurst, 189; Poole, 882; Gill, 782; Doddridge, 838-39; Bassett, 15-16; Spitta, 39; Grünzweig, 46; Haar, 59; Cantinat, 89; Cargal, 81; Martin, 37.

[62] See many of the texts cited in n. 49. Contrast the use of μηδ᾽ ὑμεῖς ἐξαπατᾶσθε as a conclusion in Ps.-Lysias, *And.* 41.

[63] 1.2, 19; 2.1, 5, 14; 3.1; 4.11; 5.7, 12. Contrast 3.10, 12; 5.9, 10.

[64] Imperatives in openings: 1.2, 5, 9, 19, 22; 3.1; 5.1, 7, 13. Imperatives in closings: 1.4, 21. Some would add 4.10.

[65] For Schlatter, 132, 'Do not be deceived' goes both with what precedes and with what follows. So too Knowling, 22-23.

One might paraphrase: 'Do not go astray by supposing that God is the author of temptation but know rather this...'[66]

Given, as we shall see, that so many other terms in 1.16-18 have to do with the heavens, one wonders whether James chose μὴ πλανᾶσθε because the verb, πλανάω, and its cognates were so often used with reference to the movements of the heavenly bodies (cf. our English word, 'planet').[67] Jackson-McCabe thinks so and unfolds the logic of vv. 13-17 this way: 'Though God is the "father" of the "lights", any wandering on their part reflects not his nature but represents, on the contrary, a deviation from the path which God had marked out for them. So too, though God is our "father", the human experience of πειρασμός does not reflect God's nature—for he is ἀπείραστος—but rather stems from each individual's own desire.'[68]

Verse 17. As in Ps 136.7-9, where creation of the heavenly lights is a sign that God's 'steadfast love endures forever',[69] so likewise in Jas 1.17—a favorite of Kierkegaard, which he called 'beautiful'[70]—the heavens are evidence of God's goodness to human beings.

πᾶσα δόσις ἀγαθὴ καὶ πᾶν δώρημα τέλιον ἄνωθέν ἐστιν. Cf. 1.5; 3.15 (ἔστιν...ἄνωθεν); also Philo, *Somn.* 1.103 (δώρημα κάλλιστον ἐδόθη παρὰ θεοῦ), 162 (ἄνωθεν δωρεὰς ἀγαθὸς καὶ τέλειος); *Abr.* 54 (δώρημα τέλειον καὶ κάλλιστον); Dionysius of Halicarnassus, *Ant.* 2.62.5 (παντὸς ἀγαθοῦ θεοὶ δοτῆρές εἰσι). If it is from God it is good;[71] if it is good it is from God.[72] Implicit is: if it is not good, it is not from God; cf. v. 13. Equally

---

[66] Cf. the *Catenae ad loc.* ed. Cramer, 6.

[67] Note Democritus, *Test.* 40.13; Plato, *Tim.* 39D; Ocellus, *Univ. nat.* 3.2; Diodorus Siculus 2.30.3; Dionysius Halicarnassus, *Ant.* 2.5.2; Jude 13; etc. The possibility is mentioned in a few of the older commentaries, e.g. Theile, 49. Note more recently Scaer, 59, who calls attention to the wordplay in Jude 13.

[68] Jackson-McCabe, *Logos*, 210-13.

[69] Ng, 'Father', 46-48, urges that 'James had Psalm 136 in mind as he wrote 1:17-18'.

[70] S. Kierkegaard, *Eighteen Upbuilding Discourses*, ed. Howard V. Hong and Edna H. Hong, Princeton, 1990, 41. Three of the discourses in this book are on Jas 1.17-22 (32-48, 125-39, 141-58).

[71] Cf. Philo, *Post.* 80 ('God's gifts are all good'); *Plant.* 88-92; *Migr.* 73 ('God bestows on those who obey him no imperfect boon. All his gifts are full and complete [τέλεια]'); *Spec.* 1.224 ('God...gives...good unmixed with evil'); Dio Chrysostom 32.15 ('the gods themselves control all blessings everywhere...evils come from quite a different source'). See further on 1.13. Immer, *Hermeneutics*, 160, suggests that πᾶσα here effectively means 'only'.

[72] Carr, 19, observes: 'the position of ἀγαθήν and τέλιον gives the force of an adverbial clause; if it be good or perfect it is a divine gift'. Cf. Plato, *Resp.* 379C ('for the good we must assume no other cause than God'); Philo, *Sacr.* 63 ('there is no good thing which is not divine and is not of God'); Dio Chrysostom 32.14-15 ('all things which happen to people for their good are without exception of divine origin...there is no good fortune, no benefit, that does not reach us in accord with the will and the power of the gods; on the contrary').

implicit is: if it is not from above, it is not good.[73] Piscator, 729, glosses τέλιον with: *ad hominis perfectionem pertinens*.

Printing the text with a comma after ἐστιν separates ἄνωθεν ἐστιν from the following καταβαῖον κτλ., so that the latter is an independent participial clause.[74] Yet one could, with many, insert a comma after καταβαῖον—'is coming down from above, from the Father of lights'.[75] Greeven suggests instead putting a full stop after τέλιον, so that ἄνωθέν begins a new sentence.[76]

As in v. 19, the parallelism, rhythm, and consonance are obviously deliberate:

        πᾶσα   δόσις   ἀγαθὴ
    καὶ πᾶν   δώρημα   τέλειον

Because of James' habit of using near synonyms in parallel[77] and because πᾶσα δόσις[78] and πᾶν δώρημα[79] are unexplained and undeveloped, we should, against much of the commentary tradition, probably resist pressing for any significant distinction between the twin expressions. It is true that one might compare the δόματα καὶ δωρεάς = מתנן ונבזבה ('gifts and rewards') of Theod. Dan 2.6 (cf. 5.17; 2 Chr 32.23), where two near synonyms do indeed convey different meanings. It is also true that δόσις strictly means '(act of) giving' (cf. Phil 4.15), δώρημα 'thing given, gift'.[80] Moreover, Philo, *Cherub*. 84, draws this distinction: 'Among existing things there are some which rank lower as benefits, and this benefit is called "giving" (δόσις). In others the benefit is

---

[73] Cf. Popkes, 121, who compares 3.15-16 and remarks that the division between God and the world (4.4) is already clear. See further below, 365-66.

[74] Cf. 1.14 and see Mayor, 58.

[75] But that we should translate, 'All giving is good, but every perfect gift comes down from God' (so Tasker, 47), seems implausible. In this case we should expect ἀλλά instead of καί; and 'all giving is good' is scarcely a truism: people often give hoping to get in return.

[76] Greeven, 'Gabe', 8. Leahy, 911, concurs. Contrast Popkes, 120-21, and the vast majority of exegetes.

[77] Cf., from chap. 1, vv. 4, 6, 21, 27.

[78] δόσις: NT: 2×; cf. Phil 4.15; Herm. *Mand*. 5.2.2 (δόσεως ἢ λήψεως = 'giving or receiving'). The word appears 2× in LXX Proverbs, 18× in Sirach, 6× in Aristeas, 11× in Philo, 21× in Josephus. It is used of divine gifts in Plato, *Philb*. 16C; Euripides, *Alc*. 1071 (with ironic sense); Sophocles, *Oed. Tyr*. 1518; Iamblichus, *Myst*. 1.13; Ecclus 11.17; 26.14; 32.13; Let. Aris. 229.

[79] Besides Jas 1.17, δώρημα is used in the NT only in Rom 5.16; cf. Herm. *Mand*. 2.4; *Sim*. 2.7. LXX: Ecclus 34.18. Gk. Pseudepigrapha (Denis): 3×. Philo: 5×. Josephus: 1×. For the noun used of God's gifts see Ezekiel the Tragedian *apud* Eusebius, *Praep. ev*. 9.28.3; 9.29.8 ed. Holladay, 354, 370; Let. Aris. 276 (θεοῦ δώρημα καλόν); Philo, *Deus* 5; *Somn*. 1.103 (δώρημα κάλλιστον ἐδόθη παρὰ θεοῦ); *Abr*. 54 (δώρημα τέλειον καὶ κάλλιστον); Josephus, *Ant*. 4.318 (δώρημα κάλλιστον); IG IV² 1.128 (a μέγα δώρημα from Apollo and Asklepios).

[80] See further Carr, 19.

of a higher kind and this has the special name of "bounty" (δωρεά)'. BAGD, s.v., however, shows that, in NT times, δόσις and δώρημα could be equivalents. With this in mind it seems more in keeping with James' style to remark, as does Johnson, 195, on 'the rhetorical force of repetition with variation'. It is not, however, rhetoric for rhetoric's sake, but a way of being emphatic.[81]

One also hesitates to specify exactly what James has in mind by 'good gift'[82] and 'perfect gift'.[83] Some commentators have thought of the Spirit or of wisdom (cf. 1.5), or of what is necessary to gain victory over temptation[84] or of the birth brought by the 'word of truth' (v. 18).[85] Still others have insisted or assumed that the good things are given in response to prayer.[86] But the text offers no specificity.[87] Indeed, are not πᾶσα and πᾶν[88] comprehensive,[89] so that although they obviously include wisdom,[90]

---

[81] So too Popkes, 121; Wenger, *Kyrios*, 109.

[82] ἀγαθός: Jas: 2×: 1.17; 3.17. Cf. T. Zeb. 1.3 (δόσις ἀγαθή); Ps.-Justin, *Qu. chr.* 1.2 ed. Otto, 242 (ἀγαθὴν δόσιν). McKnight, 125, suggests that ἀγαθή here means 'beneficial' or 'generous'; cf. the exposition of 1.17 in Ps.-Dionysius, *C.H.* 1.1 PTS 36 ed. Heil and Ritter, 7: this uses ἀγαθοδότως. McKnight also proposes, on the assumption that James of Jerusalem was our author, that there might be a reference to Paul's gifts for the poor in Jerusalem (Acts 11.27-30; Gal 2.10; Phil 4.15).

[83] For the notion that God gives gifts see, in addition to the texts cited in nn. 71, 78, 79, Deut 33.13; Eccl 3.13; 5.19; Ecclus 38.2; 2 Macc 15.16; Let. Aris. 231; Jn 4.10; Acts 8.20; Rom 5.15-17; 6.23; 11.29; 1 Cor 2.12, 14; 7.7; 2 Cor 9.15; Eph 2.8; 3.7; 2 Tim 1.6; y. Qidd. 65b (4.1); Tanḥ. Buber Mattot 7; b. Ber. 52a; cf. Plutarch, *Mor.* 780E. Most of these use δωρεά or δῶρον. The idea was not foreign to the pagan world; note Aelius Aristides, *Or.* 43.29: Zeus is δοτὴρ ἀπάντων. For the pairing of ἀγαθός (Jas: 2×; cf. 3.17) and τέλειος (see on 1.4), which is unattested in the LXX, see Philo, *Somn.* 1.162; Rom 12.2 (the will of God is ἀγαθόν and τέλειον); Isocrates, *Ant.* 200; Plutarch, *Mor.* 84D, 75C, 789F; *Mar.* 23.5; Galen, *Crisibus libri iii* 9.725; *Diebus decretoriis libri iii* 9.856; Hippolytus, *Ref.* 5.23.3 PTS 25 ed. Marcovich, 199 (τελείου καὶ ἀγαθοῦ—of God).

[84] Cf. Lapide, 55 (victory over concupiscence); Davids, 85 (God's 'gift of wisdom or the spirit which will help one in the test'). Cargal, 83; Perkins, 102; *et al.* think of wisdom above all, an interpretation that appears to be as old as Origen, *Num* 27.6.1 SC 461 ed. Doutreleau, 296. Poirier, 'Symbols', who also sees wisdom as the chief referent, further detects an allusion to the Urim and Thummim, observing that LXX Ezra 2.63 renders אורים ותמים by τοῖς φωτίζουσιν καὶ τοῖς τελείοις. Although he fails to note the fact, older commentaries are sometimes aware of the possible connection with the Urim and Thummim; see e.g. Bassett, 17.

[85] So Wenger, *Kyrios*, 140, equating the word with the gospel.

[86] See John of Damascus, *F.O.* 88 PTS 12 ed. Kotter, 204. For additional proposals see 257 above and the list of options in Lapide, 55-56.

[87] Cf. the generalizations in Tanḥ. Buber Wayyera 18 ('The Holy One does not send down anything bad from above, only rain'); Gen. Rab. 51.3 ('Nothing evil descends from above').

[88] Against πᾶσα here meaning 'only' see Ropes, 158.

[89] Cf. the application in the Liturgy of St. John Chrysostom: 'Give peace to the world, to thy churches, to thy Priest, to our kings, their armies, and to all thy people; for every

they yet embrace more than wisdom? All true blessings are from God,[91] or as Philo has it, 'There is no good thing which...is not of God'.[92] The thought, conventional by James' day,[93] appears already in Plato, *Resp.* 379C: 'Of the good things God and no other must be described as the cause, but of the evil things we must look for many different causes, only not God'.

There are at least two productive intratextual links between 1.17a and the rest of James. First, according to 3.17, the wisdom ἄνωθεν is full of 'good (ἀγαθῶν) fruits'. So twice James associates 'from above' with 'good'. In 3.15-17, moreover, 'earthly' is linked with 'unspiritual' and 'devilish', so we have in James a spatial dualism: up is good, down is bad.[94] Second, 'perfect gift' resonates with 1.4 ('perfect work') and is echoed in 1.25 ('perfect law'). Now because τέλειος is, in 1.4, a goal for human beings, and because, in 1.17 and 25, it characterizes the deity, tacit is the notion that the divine quality of 'perfection' is a standard: the divine perfection beckons human perfection.[95]

'Good gift' was a traditional Jewish expression (מתנה טובה), often used of divine gifts.[96] But it also appears in Mt 7.7-11 = Lk 11.9-13, which argues that if human parents give to their children δόματα ἀγαθά, how much will the Father 'in the heavens' (so Matthew) or 'of heaven' (so Luke) give good gifts to his children. Does James draw upon this saying of Jesus?[97] This is plausible since Jas 1.5 alludes to the same

good gift and every perfect blessing, etc.' (*Divine Prayers and Services of the Catholic Orthodox Church of Christ*, compiled by S. Nassar, Brooklyn, 1961, 134).

[90] Note the connections back to 1.4-5 (τέλειον, τέλειοι, διδόντος, δοθήσεται) and forward to 3.13-18 (ἄνωθεν, ἀγαθῶν), passages which explicitly refer to wisdom. Cf. Philo, *Deus* 5: τῆς τοῦ θεοῦ δώρημα σοφίας.

[91] This is the interpretation of Cassiodorus, *Ps* 92.4 CCSL 98, ed. Adriaen, 845.

[92] Philo, *Sacr.* 63. See further the texts in n. 71.

[93] Cf. Tob 4.19 (God δίδωσιν πάντα τὰ ἀγαθά); POxy 15 1786.5 (a late third cent. Christian hymn: δ[ωτ]ῆ[ρι] μόνῳ πάντων ἀγαθῶν = 'to the one [God] who alone gives all good things'); b. Sanh. 59b ('No unclean thing descends from heaven').

[94] Some commentators find in 1.17 an implicit denigration of human goodness, as though good things come only from God, never human beings; so Ps.-Andrew of Crete, *Éloge* 4.18-22 ed. Noret, 48: our verse teaches that people should not assign what virtue they may have to themselves. See further above, 257.

[95] Cf. Klein, *Werk*, 68: the divine indicative is the human imperative.

[96] Note Prov 4.2 (δῶρον ἀγαθόν); Tob 4.11 (δῶρον ἀγαθόν); Ecclus 18.17 (δόμα ἀγαθόν); 26.3 (quoted in b. Sanh. 100b; b. Yeb. 63b); Let. Aris. 225 (καλὸν δῶρον); 276 (δώρημα καλόν); T. Zeb. 1.3 (δόσις ἀγαθή); PGM 35.23; Mek. on Exod 20.20 ('The three good gifts given to them [Israel] which the nations of the world covet were all given only at the price of chastisements'; the same line or variations appear in Sifre Deut 32; t. Soṭah 11.18; y. Qidd. 23d (6.7); 65b (4.1); Tanḥ. Buber Mattot 7; b. Ber. 5a.); Tanḥ. Buber Ki Tissa 15; Tanḥ. Buber Wayyetse' 22; ARN A 13; b. Šabb. 10b; b. Beṣah 16a; b. Ta'an. 5a. The traditional connotations of the expression exclude the interpretation of Grünzweig, 46-47, who appeals to Isa 45.7; Amos 3.6; and Ecclus 11.14 and includes suffering and trials within 'good gifts'; see further on v. 13.

[97] So Hartin, *Q*, 174-76. For the case to the contrary see Deppe, *Sayings*, 239.

THE GOODNESS OF GOD (1.16-18)

synoptic unit. Already Origen conflates the two texts, and many after him have linked them.[98]

ἄνωθεν,[99] which is another of way of saying 'from heaven',[100] should be taken literally given that the following words refer to the lights in the sky and that Jews and Christians believed God and the angels to dwell above their heads.[101] In any event James' use of ἄνωθεν in connection with divine giving has close parallels which establish the conventional nature of the language.[102]

Many exegetes have suspected that 'every good gift and every perfect present' is a quotation.[103] Davids, 592, calls it a 'pagan proverb' whose original meaning was something like, 'Every gift is good and every gift is perfect', that is, 'Don't look a gift horse in the mouth'. The argument is that James then recasts the saying.[104] In favor of this proposal are at least

---

[98] Origen, *Frag. Jn* ad 3.12 GCS, ed. Preuschen, 514; cf. Didymus of Alexandria, *Zech.* 3.242 SC 83 ed. Doutreleau, 730; Augustine, *Serm.* 159.9 PL 38.872; D. Philips, *Van die Ghemeynte Godts* Ib, ed. Pijper, 393; Grotius, 1076; Andrewes, *Ninety-Six Sermons* (as in n. 7), 309-31 (a series in which a sermon on Jas 1.16-18 prefaces one on Mt 7.7); Manton, 112; Johnstone, 77; Kierkegaard, *Discourses* (as in n. 70), 129; Knowling, 23; Marty, 38; Floor, 65; Haar, 69; Simon, 84; Kistemaker, 52; Michl, 32; Davids, 66; Maier, 82; *et al.*

[99] The word (cf. Hebrew מעל and the Aramaic ל(י)עלד, as in Frag. Tg. Gen P V 40.23: 'grace from above') recurs in 3.15 and 17, both times of wisdom from above. With James' construction cf. Sib. Or. 3.307 (ἄνωθεν αὐτὰρ ἀπ' οὐρανόθεν καταβήσεται); Philo, *Her.* 274 (ἄνωθεν ἀπ' οὐρανοῦ καταβάς); Herm. *Mand.* 11.5 (ἄνωθεν ἐστιν ἀπὸ τῆς δυνάμεως τοῦ θείου πνεύματος).

[100] Cf. Gen 27.28 (LXX: τοῦ οὐρανοῦ ἄνωθεν), 39 (השמים מעל, τοῦ οὐρανοῦ ἄνωθεν); Josh 2.11 (בשמים ממעל, LXX: ἐν οὐρανῷ ἄνω); Philo, *Her.* 274 (ἄνωθεν ἀπ' οὐρανοῦ καταβάς); *Mos.* 2.69 (ἄνωθεν ἀπ' οὐρανοῦ); etc.

[101] Cf. LXX Ps 113.11: ὁ δὲ θεὸς ἡμῶν ἐν τῷ οὐρανῷ ἄνω.

[102] Gk. 1 En. 98.5 (slavery ἄνωθεν οὐκ ἐδόθη, nor was lawlessness ἄνωθεν ἐδόθη); Philo, *Somn.* 1.162 ('δωρεάς showered upon him ἄνωθεν'; interestingly enough this goes on to use the pair, ἀγαθός and τέλειος: 'As the result of the gifts showered upon him from above he [Abraham] showed himself good and perfect from the outset'); Jn 19.11 (δεδομένον... ἄνωθεν); Herm. *Mand.* 9.11 ('Faith ἄνωθέν ἐστι παρά the Lord'); 11.5 (a spirit from God 'ἄνωθέν ἐστι ἀπό the power of the divine spirit'); Gen. Rab. 51.3 ('Nothing evil יורד מלמעלה'; this assertion is rebutted in its immediate context, which reminds us that there were rabbis who did not share James' conviction; see C.G. Montefiore and H. Loewe, *A Rabbinic Anthology*, New York, 1974, 541-55); Tanḥ. Buber Wayyera 18 ('The Holy One does not send down anything bad from above', מוריד מלמעלה); Tanḥ. Buber Emor 21 ('The breath of man is given from above', שניתנה מלמעלה). Cf. the notion of divine gifts 'from heaven': Deut 33.13; Tanḥ. Buber Mattot 7; etc.

[103] E.g. Benson, 41 (see n. 105); Fischer, 'Spruchvers'; Wandel, 59; Mayor, 57 ('a quotation from some Hellenistic poem'; he calls attention to the verse quotations in Acts 17.28; 1 Cor 15.33; Tit 1.12); Hauck, 11; Greeven, 'Gabe'; Schneider, 10 ('presumably a citation from a Jewish-hellenistic writing'); Moo, 78 ('may').

[104] Greeven, 'Gabe', however, believes that James retains the proverb's original meaning. He paraphrases: 'Do not be deceived, beloved brothers. You know the proverb, "Every gift is good, and every present is perfect". And why? Because it is from above,

four considerations. (i) 'Do not be deceived' can in fact introduce a quotation; see above. (ii) The Greek is a hexameter:[105]

πᾶσα δόσις ἀγαθὴ καὶ πᾶν δώρημα τέλειον
- ∪ ∪ | - ∪ ∪ | - - | - - | - ∪ ∪ | - ∪

(iii) δόσις and δώρημα occur only here in James, so they are not characteristic of our author; indeed, they are uncommon in early Christian literature in general.[106] (iv) The logic of vv. 13-18 is incomplete. That God is without change and is the source of all good things does not entail that God does not also give bad things. To insure that inference, James would need to say: only good and perfect gifts come from God.[107] Maybe the explanation of his failure is reproduction of a traditional line.[108]

On the other hand, (i) against the last point, one could urge, with Ropes, 159, that 'the omission of the writer to make the implied complementary statement, that bad gifts do *not* come from God, adds to the rhetorical effect'. Readers, informed by the emphatic denial in 1.13, do regularly make the all-important inference.[109] (ii) There is no independent attestation of such a saying. (iii) 'Do not be deceived' does not invariably

coming down from the father of lights...' Amphoux, 'Jacques 1, 17', urges that the quotation extends through 'father of lights'. For criticism of these theories see Klein, *Werk*, 66-67.

[105] Cf. Benson, 42 ('This seems to have been an hexameter verse, quoted, by the Apostle James, from some of the Greek poets. But from what particular author does not now appear. St. James was indeed a native of Palestine; and had lived mostly, if not altogether, in that country. But, as he wrote in greek; he might, possibly, have read some of the greek poets'); Ewald, 190; Adderley, 15; Greeven, 'Gabe'. See further the discussion in Hatch, 'Note'. More than one scholar reports that Benson first made this observation (in 1756), but it appears at the same time in Baumgarten, 54 (who rejects it). It is relevant that we do have examples of Jews attempting to write in Homeric meters; cf. the Sentences of Ps-Phocylides, the fragments of Philo the epic poet and Theodotus preserved in Eusebius, and two inscriptions from Beth She'arim, one of them being, like the line in James, imperfect; see M. Schwabe and B. Lifshitz, *Beth She'arim*. Vol. 2, *The Greek Inscriptions*, New Brunswick, NJ, 1974, nos. 127, 183.

[106] They are paired only in James and later Christian literature, unless there is an exception in Ps.-Callisthenes, *Hist. Alex. Mag*. recs. E F 16.1: ἀμὴ ὅπου θέλει ὁ θεὸς νὰ δώση δώρημα, ἀπὸ τῆς ἄνωθεν προνοίας φωτίζεται; cf. rec. V ed. Mitsakis, 29. Given the complex history of the Alexander Romance, this line—which concerns God's will, refers to divine illumination, and includes δόσις, δώρημα, ἀπό, and ἄνωθεν—may be Christian. If, however, it is not, the question of its relationship to James is open.

[107] See the argument in Jackson-McCabe, *Logos*, 199, who notes that Hort, 27, and Mayor, 56, also sense the difficulty here.

[108] Cf. Dibelius, 99.

[109] Cf. Lapide, 55 (evil things are from the devil or concupiscence); Cargal, 83. But some commentators, aware that the Bible can assign evil acts to God (e.g. Isa 28.5; 45.7; Mic 1.12), are quick to add that God's judgment may bring bad things upon people; so e.g. Didymus of Alexandria *ad loc*. ed. Zoepfl, 4. Roberts, 53, clarifies this way: although some things that seem bad might be from God, things that are positively evil cannot be from God.

introduce a quotation.[110] (iv) The language of our line may reflect the Jesus tradition; see above. (v) The hexameter is defective.[111] (vi) τέλειον, which does not make obvious good sense in the proposed proverb,[112] is likely from James,[113] while the parallelism and use of synonyms are characteristic of him. (vii) Our author otherwise likes to use uncommon words and expressions.[114] (viii) The character of our line as a hexameter may be coincidence[115] or (ix) one might follow Frankemölle, 291-94, and hold that James himself was capable of composing a hexameter. (x) The closest parallels to James' language appear in Jewish, not pagan sources, so postulating a non-Jewish origin, as does Davids, is puzzling. (x) Not only is James fond of parallelism and double-membered clauses, but the structure of v. 17 has a close match in the redactional v. 21:

1.17   πᾶσα δόσις ἀγαθὴ   καὶ πᾶν δώρημα τέλειον
1.21   πᾶσαν ῥυπαρίαν   καὶ περισσείαν κακίας

In both case two near synonyms are joined by καί and universalized through words that create alliteration and consonance. Note the common πᾶσα(ν) + καί + π(-)αν.

In this commentator's judgment, James likely constructed the aphorism. He expressed a conventional sentiment, that God gives good gifts, using traditional language as well as his own τέλειον.[116] The mechanical parallelism is not, in this case, evidence for a Greek proverb but a Semitism of the sort one finds throughout Matthew's Gospel, where such parallelism is abundant,[117] and the failed hexameter is either coincidence or, more likely, James' conscious but imperfect work.

---

[110] Cf. Epictetus, *Diatr.* 4.6.23.

[111] Hatch, 'Note'. The second foot has a tribrach. Hatch, appealing to instances of faulty meter in inscriptions, wonders whether James offers an 'example of popular or non-literary verse-making'.

[112] In a world that knew the stories of the Trojan horse and Pandora's box, would the goodness and indeed perfection of every gift have found proverbial expression?

[113] It also appears in 1.4, 25; and 3.2.

[114] E.g. θρησκός in 1.26, δαιμονιώδης in 3.15. See further the Introduction, 85.

[115] So Kern, 135 ('inadvertent'); Beyschlag, 71 n. ('coincidence'); Robertson, 82 ('Just accidental rhythm common enough in good prose'). B.F. Westcott, *The Epistle to the Hebrews*, 3rd ed., London, 1914, 1973, 405, observes that the v.l. ποιήσατε in Heb 12.13 'gives an accidental hexameter'. See further Bassett, 17, citing other examples of accidental rhythm. Rendtorff, 62, finds a hexameter in Jas 4.5.

[116] Although δώρημα τέλιον appears before James only once—in Philo, *Abr.* 54—the expression was natural given the use of τέλειος for sacrificial animals (Exod 12.5; Judg 20.26; Josephus, *Ant.* 3.230; cf. תמים) and of δῶρον for offerings (LXX Gen 4.4; Lev 1.2; 17.4; Num 28.2; Mt 5.23-24.

[117] See e.g. Mt 5.39-40 diff. Lk 6.29; Mt 6.19-21 diff. Lk 12.33-34; Mt 6.22-23 diff. Lk 11.34-36; Mt 7.24-27 diff. Lk 6.47-49; Mt 10.24-25 diff. Lk 6.40; and Mt 18.8-9 diff. Mk 9.43-47.

καταβαῖνον ἀπὸ τοῦ πατρὸς τῶν φώτων.[118] καταβαίνω and φῶς are both Jamesian *hapax*; πατήρ recurs in 1.27 (of God), 2.21 (of Abraham), 3.9 (of God). The image of good gifts 'coming down from'[119] heaven is at least as old as the story of manna 'from heaven'.[120] The 'lights' are the sun and the moon and the stars,[121] which God, for the benefit of humanity,[122] set in the firmament according to Gen 1 (cf. Isa 45.6-7); that is, 'father' = 'begetter', 'maker'.[123] The title is akin to the rabbinic יוֹצֵר הַמְּאוֹרוֹת, 'the one forming the luminaries',[124] and recalls Ps 136.7: God 'made the great lights' (LXX: φῶτα). The thought is conventional, even if the expression, 'Father of lights', seemingly has, if we leave aside quotations of James, true parallels only in variant readings in Gk. LAE

---

[118] 322 323 424Z 945 1241 1739 G:G-D have κατερχόμενον (assimilation to 3.15?; cf. also Lk 9.37; Acts 11.27; 12.19; 15.1; 18.5; 21.10; Acts Thom. 41, 91, ed. Bonnet, 158, 205 [κατελθόντα ἀπ' οὐρανοῦ]). The following preposition is παρά in 018 056 0142 5 104 312 *et al*. AndrCr Cyr Dam Did Eustr MarcEr Or (assimilation to 1.5, 7?; cf. also LXX Mic 1.12; Isa 63.14; Josephus, *Bell*. 5.405; Herodotus 8.134).

[119] Although καταβαίνω + ἀπό was a common Greek idiom (cf. Xenophon, *An*. 7.3.45; Plutarch, *Mor*. 406E; Philo, *Legat*. 145; etc.), it is particularly prevalent in the LXX, for יָרַד + מִן: Gen 38.1; Exod 32.15; Ezek 47.1; etc. Cf. also the idiom, καταβαίνω + ἀπὸ τοῦ / ἀπ' οὐρανοῦ, as in Theod. Dan 4.13, 23; Sib. Or. 3.308; Philo, *Abr*. 205; Lk 9.54; 10.30; Jn 6.38; 1 Thess 4.16; Rev 3.12; 21.2; Liv. Proph. Elijah 10; etc.

[120] Exod 16; Num 11. One of the 'good gifts' given to Israel in t. Soṭah 11.10 is manna.

[121] Cf. LXX Gen 1.14-16 ('φωστῆρες in the firmament of heaven', 'two great φωστῆρας'); Ps 135.7 ('the great φῶτα'); Jer 4.23 (τὰ φῶτα of heaven); Gk. 1 En. 2.1 ('the φωστῆρας in heaven'). Outside of biblical tradition, the sun, moon, and stars are less commonly called φῶτα = 'lights (in the sky)'; but see Dio Chrysostom 40.38, where the sun is the φωτός. Amphoux, 'Jacques 1, 17', refers to the poetic use of φώς to mean 'human being' (cf. LSJ, s.v.; Sib. Or. 3.391, 665) and implausibly suggests this may be so in our verse.

[122] Schlatter, 133, observes that 'father of stars' would not so obviously direct readers to their service to those on earth.

[123] This is the consensus of recent commentators. Cf. Plato, *Tim*. 28C ('maker and father of this universe'); Philo, *Leg*. 1.18 (πατήρ ὢν τῶν γινομένων); *Decal*. 134 ('father of the world'); *Spec*. 1.96 ('father of the world'); *Ebr*. 81 (τὸν πατέρα τῶν ὅλων; this title appears often in Philo); *Contempl*. 90 ('father and maker of all'); 1 Cor 8.6; Heb 12.9 ('father of Spirits'—Bowyer, *Conjectures*, 314, wonders whether this might be the original reading in James); Josephus, *Ant*. 7.380 ('father and source of the universe'). Many earlier exegetes thought not of the lights in the sky but found metaphorical sense, or did both at the same time; cf. Bede, *ad loc*. CCSL 121 ed. D. Hurst, 189; Estius, 389-90 (he contrasts 'the Father of lights' with 'the father of lies'); Osiander, 721; Gomar, 390; Pareus, 546; Grotius, 1076; Calmet, 670; Lapide, 56-58. Hemminge, 13: 'all good things'. Benson, 43: 'all joy and happinesse'. Macknight, 588: 'all virtue and happiness'. Wordsworth, 16, like several of those just cited, sees here all lights—the lights in the sky, the light of reason, the light of the law, *et al*. So too Plumptre, 56. See further the list of interpretive options in Bassett, 17.

[124] Tanḥ. Buber Berakhah 7; b. Ber. 12a; y. Ber. 3c (1.4).

36.3 (τοῦ φωτὸς ὅλων, τοῦ πατρὸς τῶν φώτων);[125] 38.1 v.l. (τὸν πατέρα τῶν φώτων); T. Abr. RecShrt. 7.6 (πατὴρ τοῦ φωτός)—these all may be Christian interpolations—and P. Heidelberg 1686.[126] There are, however, comparable expressions.[127] One suspects that either אל(והי) אורים or יוצר המאורות lies behind James' Greek, and that he altered the traditional title in anticipation of God's 'procreative' activity in v. 18, where God is implicitly contrasted with unlawful desire and its offspring (vv. 14-15). The idea was in any case congenial given the belief that God is light.[128]

For James' readers, the lights in the sky were not inanimate objects but living beings, to be identified with angels[129] and/or departed saints.[130]

---

[125] See Strotmann, *Vater*, 294-96, for the case that the reading here is original. It is not present in all mss.; see J.R. Levison, *Texts in Transition: The Greek Life of Adam and Eve*, Atlanta, 2000, 101.

[126] This last belongs to a Christian Coptic text of uncertain date, 'The Praise of Michael the Archangel'; see M. Meyer and R. Smith, eds., *Ancient Christian Magic*, San Francisco, 1994, 323-41. For the Coptic text (line 29: ⲡⲓⲱⲧ ⲙⲡⲟⲩⲁⲓⲛ) see A.Kropp, *Der Lobpreis des Erzengels Michael*, Brussels, 1966, 15. C. Keener, in a private communication, has observed that 'Father of the luminaries/stars' may have appeared in the Ugaritic text UT 76 I:4; see plates xv-xvi in A. Hernder, *Corpus des tablettes en cunéiformes alphabétiques découvertes à Ras Shamra-Ugarit de 1929 à 1939*, Paris, and the transcription in fig. 33. The text, however, is fragmentary.

[127] E.g. Job 38.28 (where God is 'father of rain', LXX: ὑετοῦ πατήρ); 1QS 3.20 and CD 5.18 (the 'prince of lights' [שר האורים] is an angel; cf. 4Q405 46 2: אלוהי אורים, 'angels of lights'); 4Q403 1 2.35 (אלי אור, 'gods of light'); 4Q503 13-16 1 (אלוהי אורים, 'God of lights'); 29-32 9 (אל אורים, 'God of lights'); 215 7 (אלוהי אורים, 'God of lights'); *Poimandres* 1.21 ed. Nock and Festugière, 1.14 (ἐκ φωτός...ὁ πατήρ τῶν ὅλων). Is there any connection with the Indo-European name for the chief deity, *dyeupoder* (cf. 'Zeus Pater' and 'Jupiter')? 'Poder' means 'father' and 'dyeu' means 'to shine'. Note Macrobius, *Sat.* 1.15.14: Jupiter is *luci auctorem*. Against Isaacs, 289, there is no allusion to Gen 1.14-16, and against O. Holtzmann, 826, there is no need to regard the expression as reminiscent of Zoroastrianism.

[128] Cf. Ps 35.9; Isa 60.19; Wis 7.26; 1QH 15(7).25 ('you are my everlasting luminary', מאור); Philo, *Somn.* 1.75; *Heres.* 264; *Abr.* 70; LAB 12.3; 1 Jn 1.5; Rev 21.23; 22.5; etc. The notion of God's 'glory' lies in the background; cf. Piscator, 729. Bassett, 17, thinks τῶν φωτῶν may equal τῆς δόξης.

[129] Cf. the *Catena ad loc.* ed. Cramer, 6 (τὰς λογικὰς δυνάμεις, 'the rational [heavenly] powers'); Theophylact *ad loc.* PG 125.1144A; Schulthess, 36; Kern, 136; Spitta, 42; Baljon, 27; Smith, 62-63; G. Schrenk, 'πατήρ κτλ.', *TDNT* 5.1013-14; Grünzweig, 48-49; McKnight, 126-27. Contrast Frankemölle, 295; Isaacs, 189. Relevant are Judg 5.20; Neh 9.6; Job 25.4-6; 38.7; Ps 148.1-4; Isa 24.21-23; Jer 19.13; Dan 8.10; 1 En. 18.11-14; 43.1-2; 86.1-6; 90.20-27; Ezekiel the Tragedian *apud* Eusebius *Praep. ev.* 9.29.5 ed. Holladay, 364; 1QH 9(1).9-12; Bar 3.34; Philo, *Opif.* 73; *Gig.* 8; *Somn.* 1.135; *Plant.* 12; LAB 32.15; Jos. Asen. 14.1-7; Rev 1.20; 9.1-2; 12.3-4; Lat. LAE 19.3; 2 Bar. 51.10; Apoc. Abr. 19.9; Ps.-Phoc. 71-75; 2 En. 29.3A; T. Sol. 6.7; 20.14-17; 2 En. 29; 3 En. 46; Origen, *Prin.* 1.7; *C. Cels.* 5.11; Jerome, *Ep.* 124.4 CSEL 56 ed. Hilberg, 99-101; b. 'Abod. Zar. 43a-b; Exod. Rab. 15.6. For discussion see A. Scott, *Origen and the Life of the Stars*, Oxford, 1991. Note that the traditional Jewish eulogy to God as the creator of the luminaries (in the morning service) equates them with the angelic host: 'He

(In Job 38.7 the 'morning stars' are even called 'the sons of God', which is interesting in view of James' expression, 'father of lights'.) The image is of an animate sky that serves human beings: the former share their glorious light with the latter.[131] One must also remember that, before Newtonian science, people did not assume that God created the heavens and then left them to run by themselves forever. If the passage about the birds and the lilies in Mt 6.25-34 = Lk 12.22-32 and the supernatural darkness and earthquake in Matthew's passion narrative presuppose God's continual working through nature, so too in James: the lights in the sky are not just signs of a great past act but ongoing evidence of the creator's care for the creation.[132] Beyond this, James' readers probably shared Philo's understanding of the stars as not just animate but good: some existences 'have partnership with virtue only, and have no part or lot in vice. Such are the heavenly bodies; for these are said to be not only living creatures but living creatures endowed with mind...excellent through and through and unsusceptible of any evil.'[133]

In 1.17, that which is 'above', a region associated with 'light', comes 'down'; cf. 3.15, 17. This reminds one of John's dualism. In Jn 8.23 Jesus is 'from above' and 'not of this world' whereas those he is speaking to are 'from below' and 'of this world'; elsewhere John features a dualism of light and darkness. James moreover is familiar with the pejorative use of 'the world' (cf. 1.27) and of 'earthly' (cf. 3.15).

παρ' ᾧ οὐκ ἔνι παραλλαγὴ ἢ τροπῆς ἀποσκίασμα.[134] A poetic statement of divine faithfulness.[135] παραλλαγή,[136] ἀποσκίασμα,[137] and

placed luminaries around his majesty. His chief hosts are holy beings that extol the Almighty. They constantly recount God's glory and holiness. Blessed are you, Lord our God, for your excellent handiwork and for the luminaries that you have made.'

[130] See Dan 12.2-3; 1 En. 104.2-7; 4 Macc 17.5; 2 Bar. 51.10; LAB 33.5; As. Mos. 10.9; CIJ 2.788 = IJO 2.236. Astral immortality was the dominant conception of the afterlife in the post-classical world. It was held by, among others, Pythagoreans, Platonists, and Stoics. See F. Cumont, *After Life in Roman Paganism*, New Haven, 91-109; idem, *Lux Perpetua*, Paris, 1949, 142-88.

[131] See further Spitta, 41-43.

[132] Cf. Job 38.12-41; Ps 104.19-23; Isa 40.26; Ecclus 43.5 (at God's 'command it [the sun] hastens on its course'); Pss. Sol. 18.10 (God 'arranges the stars into orbits'); Pry. Jacob 16 (God's creating power makes the stars and planets run); Philo, *Spec.* 1.279 (God is 'the sun of the sun...and from invisible fountains he supplies the visible beams to the sun which our eyes behold').

[133] Philo, *Opif.* 72. He goes on (73): 'It was most proper to God the universal father to make those excellent things by himself alone, because of their kinship to him'.

[134] ἐστί(ν) takes the place of the rarer ἔνι in 01 025 197 206 *et al.* L590 L593 L1440 AndrCr Dam Did. Most witnesses have παραλλαγὴ ἢ τροπῆς ἀποσκίασμα: 01C2 02 04 025 5 69 81 88 206 *et al.* **Byz** Ath CyrH Dam Did IohPhil[v] Phot PsOec **S**:H. Less well attested are παραλλαγὴ οὐδὲ τροπῆς ἀποσκίασμα (044 1509 AndrCr **L**:V S:P); παραλλαγὴ ἢ τροπῆς ἀποσκιάσματος (01* 03); παραλλαγὴ ἢ τροπὴ ἀποσκιάσματος (614 1505 2412 2495); παραλλαγῆς ἢ τροπῆς ἀποσκιάσματος (P23 **Sl**:ChMS); and there are additional variations. This is the only place where Westcott and Hort, in their critical edition, decided not to follow the agreement of Sinaiticus and Vaticanus. Ropes, 162,

THE GOODNESS OF GOD (1.16-18)   275

τροπή[138] are all NT *hapax legomena*. παρά to indicate possession—here a sort of reverential circumlocution?—is not unusual in biblical Greek.[139] James is fond of ἥ.[140] ἔνι = ἔνεστι, 'there is'.[141]

The gist of the line seems clear. First, there is no variation in God, a fact perhaps attested by the regularity of the heavenly orbs,[142] a regularity which witnesses to the constancy of their creator: 'the father of lights' must be the same yesterday, today, and forever. Second, although the heavenly bodies are not always the same—the sun goes dark, the seasons change, eclipses occur[143]—their creator is by contrast constant light, without change, without shadow, without darkness.[144] Cf. Sextus, *Sent.*

suggests ἥ instead of ᾗ: 'with whom is none of the variation that belongs to ("consists in", "is observed in") the turning of the shadow'. Some earlier scholars conjectured an original παραλλαγὴ ἢ ῥοπῆς ἀποσκίασμα on the basis of L:F's *modicum* and Augustine's *momenti*; but according to Ropes, 163, 'the Latin versions merely show that Jerome and Augustine had the reading of ℵᶜ A C, while ff [= L:F] represents a different text, identical with that of 614 1108 boh'. See further W. Thiele, 'Augustinus', 256. To all this one may add the conjectures of Könnecke, *Emendationen*, 13 (παραλλαγὴ τροπῆς ἢ ἀποσκίασμα; he supposes use of Wis 7.18); Dibelius, 101-102 (παραλλαγὴ τροπῆς ἢ ἀποσκιάσματος), and Adamson, 96-97 (παραλλαγὴ τροπῆς ἢ ἀποσκιάσματος αὐτός). We can construct several plausible genealogies, but most modern editions and commentators have thought it wisest to print the reading best attested. See further Metzger, *Commentary*, 679-80. At the end of v. 17, οὐδὲ μέχρι ὑπονοίας τινὸς ὑποβολὴ ἀποσκιάσματος ('not even the least suspicion of a shadow') appears in 876 1765 1832 1890 2138 2494*C. This is presumably an early gloss. Ropes, 164, traces it to the influence of Ps.-Oecumenius *ad loc*. PG 119.464D: τὸ δέ, Τροπῆς ἀποσκίασμα, ἀντὶ τοῦ, οὐδὲ μέχρις ὑπονοίας τινὸς ὑποβολή.

[135] Gundry, 921, speaks of God's 'stability'.
[136] LXX: 4 Βασ 9.20, where it translates שׁובב and means 'disorderly' or 'furiously'. Note also Let. Aris. 75; Josephus, *Ant.* 15.245; and the use of ἀπαραλλάκτῳ in T. Job 33.5: the 'unchangeable' world is heaven. Philo: 0×.
[137] LXX: 0×. Gk. Pseudepigrapha (Denis): 0×. Philo: 0×. Josephus: 0×. Some older commentaries state that the word appears first in Christian sources, but it does occur in Democritus (fifth–fourth centuries BCE) and Theopompus (fourth century BCE?).
[138] LXX: 11×. The word seems to mean 'solstice' in Deut 33.4 and Wis 7.18. Job 38.33 refers to 'the changes [τροπάς] of heaven'. In Ecclus 45.23 the word just means 'turning' ('and standing firm when the people turned away', ἐν τροπῇ λαοῦ). Gk. Pseudepigrapha (Denis): 3×. Philo: 111×. Josephus: 21×.
[139] E.g. LXX Gen 24.25; Ps 35.10; Job 12.13; Ecclus 5.6; Rom 2.11; 9.14; Eph 6.9.
[140] 1.17; 2.3, 15; 3.12; 4.5, 11, 13, 15.
[141] BDF 98: '"Ενι, which properly stands for ἔνεστιν (ἔνι = ἐν) as πάρα stands for πάρεστιν, and which in M[odern] Gr[eek] (in the spelling εἶναι, pronounced *ēně*) has driven out ἐστίν and εἰσίν, appears in the NT with the meaning "there is" (always with negative)'.
[142] The regularity of the heavenly orbs was proverbial; cf. Jer 31.35-36; Ep Jer 60; 1 En. 2.1; 41.5; 69.20; T. Naph. 3.2; Sifre Deut 306 ('Have the heavens ever changed their nature?').
[143] Cf. Ecclus 27.11: 'the fool changes like the moon'.
[144] Cf. Philo, *Post.* 19 ('whereas the heavenly bodies...are themselves in motion, God...is motionless'); 1 Jn 1.5 ('God is light and in him there is no darkness at all'); Apoc. Abr. 7.7 ('I would not account it [the sun] God, for by night a cloud obscures its

30: 'God is the wise light that has no room for its opposite'. As Meister Eckhart says somewhere: the Father of lights is the light of lights.

Given the reference to heavenly bodies in the first part of our verse, it intrigues that, according to LSJ, s.v., παραλλαγή can refer either to the change of the sun's position[145] or to a heavenly body 'passing beyond the degree occupied by another'.[146] Moreover, according to the same source, τροπή is sometimes used of a 'point on the horizon, prob. the West or place where the sun sets',[147] and it at other times refers to the winter or summer solstice.[148] James 1.17, then, uses sometime- or quasi-astronomical terms.[149] But that they here have technical or fixed sense is not obvious, even if Wis 7.17-18 shows that some Greek-speaking Jews knew astronomical terms.[150] παραλλαγή might refer to the motion of the sun or the movement of the constellations, and τροπῆς ἀποσκίασμα[151] could be a reference to the sun going down or to eclipses or to the changes of the seasons. Yet the terms are also, as LSJ makes clear, often used with more general sense, as in most translations of James.[152] So we can no more determine exactly what, if any, particular heavenly phenomena the text

course. Nor, again, would I call the moon and stars God, for they too in their season are darkened in their light at night'); 17.19 (in God's dwelling place is 'an inexhaustible light of invincible dawning'). Poirier, 'Symbols', 59 n. 6, cites A. Chourfrine, *Gnosis, Theophany, Theosis*, New York, 2002, 155: for Philo, 'the true Light has as its opposite not darkness, but the very interchange of light and darkness characteristic of the sublunary realm'. Commentators often cite Rev 22.5, where God replaces lamp and sun, to illustrate the idea; cf. Gregory Palamas, *Hom. xxi-xlii* 34.15 ed. Chrestou and Zeses, 376. Although Irenaeus, *Haer*. 2.4.3, rebuts the notion that the Pleroma has shadow as well as light, James' point arises out of his own argument, not the perceived error of others.

[145] Cf. Strabo, *Geog*. 17.3.10: τὸ τάχος τῆς παραλλαγῆς = 'the speed of the sun's transit'.

[146] LSJ cites Antiochus Atheniensis, *Cat. Cod. Astr.* 8(3).113.

[147] Cf. Homer, *Od.* 15.404.

[148] E.g. Hesiod, *Op.* 479; Gk. Jub. 3.9. Cf. the usage in LXX Deut 33.14 ('the sun's changes'); Job 38.33 ('heaven's changes'). But Plato, *Tim.* 39D, uses the word of the turning of the stars: τῶν ἄστρων ὅσα δι' οὐρανοῦ πορευόμενα ἔσχε τροπάς.

[149] Hence the RV: 'shadow that is cast by turning'. Note Geminus, *El. astr.* 8.23: παραλλαγὴν πρὸς τὰς χειμερινὰς τροπάς. Ropes, 162, observes further the resemblance of παραλλαγή to παράλλαξις. Clarke, 806-808, offers a detailed explanation of James that involves using logarithms to answer the question, 'When the moon's horizontal parallax is a degree, what is her distance from the earth's centre in semidiamteres of the earth'!

[150] Recall also all the astronomical lore in 1 En. 72–82 (originally composed in Aramaic) and the calendrical texts among the Dead Sea Scrolls (e.g. 4Q317-330).

[151] The suggestion that 'shadow' = 'trace', so that James is denying that there is any trace of change in the divinity seems unlikely. Contrast Ps.-Oecumenius *ad loc.* PG 119.464D; the Old Latin (*modicum obumbrationis*); and KJV ('shadow of turning', implying the least trace of change).

[152] For the history of the various English translations of 1.17 see Goodspeed, *Problems*, 189-90.

was designed to evoke than we can specify precisely the content of LXX Job 38.33 (τροπὰς οὐρανοῦ) or of Ps.-Eupolemus in Eusebius, *P.E.* 9.17.4 ed. Holladay, 173 (τροπὰς ἡλίου καὶ σελήνης). Sunsets, eclipses—which were widely reckoned evil omens[153]—the phases of the moon, the alternation of night and day, and the movements of the constellations are all things that might occur to a reader. One might even think of all of them together, that is, of the entirety of celestial changes.[154] The general point, however, remains the same: unlike the lights in the sky,[155] God varies not.[156] The contrast resembles that in Philo, *Leg.* 2.33: 'Every created thing must necessarily undergo change, for that is its property, even as unchangeableness is the property of God'.

The commentary tradition neglects the fact that, in the Jewish Bible, shadows are regularly spoken of as fleeting.[157] When James refers to a 'shadow' (ἀποσκίασμα), he refers to the proverbially ephemeral.

That God cannot change was an idea at home among Graeco-Roman thinkers.[158] The same was true of Hellenistic Jews,[159] who no doubt took the Tanak to teach as much.[160]

---

[153] Note Philo *apud* Eusebius, *Praep. ev.* 8.14; Prov. 2.50; Josephus, *Ant.* 14.309; 17.167; Ovid, *Met.* 15.779-86; Valerius Maximus, *Mem.* 8.11 ext. 1; etc.

[154] The words of Bassett, 18, are worth pondering: 'A comprehensive figure capable of embracing many allusions is likely to awake in a poetical mind, such as St. James evidently possessed, many side-thoughts, and the fundamental idea first conceived would be likely to attract to itself various after thoughts, suggested by the terms employed'.

[155] For the observation that the heavens change see 1 En. 41.8 ('the many changes of the sun'); 72.2-37 (detailed observations on the courses of the sun and its effects); Wis 7.29-30 (light is succeeded by night); Ecclus 17.31 ('What is brighter than the sun? Yet it can be eclipsed'); 27.11 ('the fool changes like the moon'); cf. Epictetus, *Diatr.* 1.4.4: 'Whence are there seen, on the waxing and waning of the moon, and the approach and departure of the sun, so great changes and transformations in earthly things?'

[156] Mayor, 61, suggests that 'God is alike incapable of change in his own nature (παραλλαγή) and incapable of being changed by the action of others' (ἀποσκίασμα). This distinction, however, reads Plato, *Resp.* 380, into James.

[157] 1 Chr 29.15 ('our days on the earth are like a shadow, and there is no abiding'); Job 8.9 ('our days on earth are a shadow'); 14.2 ('he flees like a shadow and continues not'); Ps 102.11 ('my days are like an evening shadow; I wither away like grass'); 109.23 ('I am gone, like a shadow at evening'); 144.4 ('Man is like a breath, his days are like a passing shadow'); Eccl 6.12 ('he passes like a shadow'); Cant 2.17 ('the shadows flee'); 4.6 ('the shadows flee'); Wis 2.5 ('our allotted time is the passing of a shadow'); 5.9 ('vanished like a shadow'); cf. 1 En. 49.2 ('iniquity will pass like a shadow').

[158] Recall Aristotle's 'unmoved mover' (cf. *Cael.* 279A: 'the highest divinity must be entirely immutable') and note Xenophanes, frags. 26 + 25 (God 'always remains in the same place, moving not at all'); Plato, *Resp.* 381C ('It is impossible even for a god to wish to alter himself'); ibid. 371E ('the gods themselves do not change'); Maximus of Tyre, *Or.* 5 ('Changing one's mind or repenting is not only unfitting for a god but even to a good person'; this goes on to associate change with evil and then to affirm, 'but the divine and evil are far apart'); Aelius Aristides, *Or.* 43.22 ('it is not fitting for him to change'); Hermes to Tat 5 ed. Nock and Festugière, 1.62 (God is ἀκίνητον). See further W. Maas, *Unveränderlichkeit Gottes*, Munich, 1974 (28-30 on James).

Verseput, 'Prayers', departing from patristic exegesis and most modern commentators, has urged that Jas 1.17 'does not suggest an ontological immutability, but refers quite plainly to the unwavering character of God's faithfulness. That is, God remains unchanged relative to his activity of providing good and perfect gifts, confirming what is asserted in vv. 13-15, namely, that he does not tempt his creatures in a manner leading to their death. Thus, it is God's lovingkindness rather than his self-identity which elicits James' most conspicuous comment regarding divine invariability' (178). This could be correct interpretation. Yet maybe the antithesis is false. For while James' focus is on God's invariable goodness, such goodness is easily rooted in the more metaphysical notion of God's immutability, a notion neither foreign to James' larger world, as the comparative materials prove, nor at odds with his thought in particular.

Verseput supports his claim with the suggestion that Jas 1.17 alludes to the Jewish morning prayer. This is an attractive possibility, especially given the appearance of 'God of lights' and a reference to the creation in the morning prayers of 4Q503. Also suggestive are the parallels with Jewish prayers in the Apostolic Constitutions; see n. 159. Unfortunately, our fragmentary knowledge of the evolution of Jewish liturgy means that we cannot know what forms of morning prayer were known to James.

Verse 18. This verse—which Luther, despite his problems with James, loved[161]—evidently offers an illustration of what has just been defended, that is, God's goodness. The contrasts with vv. 14-15 are forceful: the

---

[159] Philo wrote an entire tract on the subject: *Quod Deus immutabilis sit*. See further Philo, *Post*, 23 ('That which is unwaveringly stable is God, and that which is subject to movement is creation'); *Mut.* 28 (God is ἄτρεπτον); *Leg.* 2.33 ('Every created thing must necessarily undergo change, for this is its property even as unchangeableness [ἄτρεπτον] is the property of God'); ibid. 2.89 ('All other things change but he [God] is unchangeable'); idem, *Deus* 22 ('What greater impiety can there be than to suppose that the unchangeable changes [ἄτρεπτον τρέπεσθαι]?'; for a comparison of God in Philo and in James see Wenger, *Kyrios*, 109-16); T. Job. 33.5 v.l. (Job's throne is in 'the world of the changeless one'); 2 En. 33.4 (God says, 'My thought is without change'); Apost. Const. 7.35.9 ed. Funk, 432 (ἄτρεπτος καὶ ἀνελλιπὴς ἡ διαμονή); 8.12.6 ed. Funk, 496 (τὸν πάντοτε κατὰ τὰ αὐτὰ καὶ ὡσαύτως ἔχοντα); 8.15.7 ed. Funk, 520 (ὁ τροπῆς ἀνεπίδεκτος, ὁ φύσει ἀναλλοίωτος). The selections from the Apostolic Constitutions have often been thought to derive from Jewish sources, and E. R. Goodenough, *By Light, Light*, New Haven, 1935, 338, took the parallel between 8.15.7 (which immediately precedes ὁ φῶς οἰκῶν ἀπρόσιτον, cf. 1 Tim 6.16) and James to indicate the latter's dependence upon a Hellenistic synagogue liturgy. For discussion of Philo see Maas, *Unveränderlichkeit Gottes* (as in n. 158), 87-124.

[160] Cf. Num 23.19; 1 Sam 15.29; Pss 90.2; 102.25-27 (the foundations of the earth will perish 'but you [God] are the same, and your years have no end'); Isa 46.10; Mal 3.6 ('I am the Lord; I change not'; LXX: οὐκ ἠλλοίωμαι). Also relevant is the 'I am he' of Isa 41.4; 43.10, 13; and 48.12; see H. Ringgren, 'הוא', *TDOT* 3.344.

[161] J. Haar, *Initium creaturae Dei*, Gütersloh, 1939, 28-29.

divine good will is the opposite of illicit human desire (v. 14), and the divine begetting produces the first fruits of creation whereas sin gives birth to death (v. 15).

βουληθεὶς ἀπεκύησεν ἡμᾶς λόγῳ ἀληθείας εἰς τὸ εἶναι ἡμᾶς ἀπαρχήν τινα τῶν αὐτοῦ κτισμάτων.[162] Cf. Poimandres 9 ed. Nock and Festugière, 1.9: God 'gave birth by a word (ἀπεκύησε λόγῳ) to another mind, the demiurge'. βούλομαι recurs in 3.4 and 4.4; only here is the subject God.[163] For ἀποκυέω see on 1.15. As the verb means 'give birth to', the subject is usually female; but this is not the case here or in Poimandres 9 (quoted above) or 12 ed. Nock and Festugière, 1.10: ὁ δὲ πάντων πατὴρ ὁ Νοῦς...ἀπεκύησεν " Ἄνθρωπον.[164] See further below. ἡμᾶς[165] does not help with interpretation: it could mean 'us Christians', 'us human beings', or 'us Jews'. λόγος (Jas: 5×) becomes a catchword holding this part of James together (1.18, 21, 22, 23). ἀλήθεια (Jas: 3×) is absolute in 3.14 and 5.19 ('the truth). 'Word(s) of truth' was more or less a fixed expression without fixed meaning.[166] εἰς τό + infinitive (Jas: 4×) makes for a formal tie to the next verse, where the construction occurs twice. ἀπαρχή and κτίσμα are Jamesian *hapax legomena*.[167] The former has figurative sense elsewhere in ancient literature, especially in Christian sources.[168]

---

[162] 1367 1853 1893 2298 L427 Cyr L:V^mss Ä insert γάρ in second place, and ἐποίησεν becomes the main verb in 206 378T 429 522 *et al.* S:H. αὐτοῦ becomes ἑαυτοῦ in 01C2 02 04 025 044 88 *et al.* Cyr Dam. MacSym.

[163] For examples of this verb used of the will of the gods or God—common in Homer—see BDAG, s.v., 2b.

[164] But Knox, 'Epistle', 14, observes that the deity in Poimandres is bisexual.

[165] Cf. 2.1, 21; 3.3, 6; 4.5; 5.17.

[166] Cf. Pss 45.5 (דבר־אמת); 119.43 (of the Torah: דבר־אמת; LXX: λόγον ἀληθείας; cf. vv. 142, 151); Prov 22.21 (of true statements: אמרים אמת; LXX: λόγους ἀληθείας); Eccl 12.10 (of true proverbs: דברי־אמת; LXX: λόγους ἀληθείας); Jer 23.28 (אמת; LXX: τὸν λόγον μου ἐπ' ἀληθείας); 1 En. 104.9 (of divine revelation: 'Do not alter the words of truth'; Gk: τοὺς λόγους τῆς ἀληθείας; cf. v. 10); Pss. Sol. 16.10 (of true words: ἐν λόγοις ἀληθείας); Philo, *Somn.* 1.23 (λόγῳ τῆς ἀληθείας); *Her.* 143 (λόγῳ τῆς ἀληθείας = 'the standard of truth'); T. Gad 3.1 v.l. (of divine revelation: λόγον ἀληθείας); 2 Cor 6.7 (ἐν λόγῳ ἀληθείας = 'truthful speech'); Eph 1.13 (of the gospel: τὸν λόγον τῆς ἀληθείας); Col 1.5 (of the gospel: ἐν τῷ λόγῳ τῆς ἀληθείας); 2 Tim 2.15 (of the gospel or scripture: τὸν λόγον τῆς ἀληθείας); Josephus, *Ant.* 16.108 (λόγον τῆς ἀληθείας = 'frankness of speech'); Odes Sol. 8.8 (פתגמא דשררא); Treat. Res. 43.34 (of Christ (?): 'stood within the word of truth'; cf. 45.3-4); Clement of Alexandria, *Strom.* 1.13.57.2 GCS 52 ed. Stählin and Früchtel, 36 (τοῦ τῆς ἀληθείας λόγου seems to be akin to the Stoic logos); Pistis Sophia 2.98 (of revelation: ⲉⲡϣⲁϫⲉ ⲛ̄ⲧⲁⲗⲏⲑⲓⲁ); Ψαλμοὶ Σαρακωτῶν ed. Allberry, 158 (Christ is ⲡⲥⲉϫⲉ ⲛ̄ⲧⲙⲏⲉ); Sifre Deut 41 (דברי אמת = 'true words'). For discussion of these and additional texts see Ludwig, *Wort*, 153-56; he finds nomistic associations to be predominant.

[167] ἀπαρχή: NT: 9× (7× in Paul). The word is common in the LXX, most often for תרומה. κτίσμα: LXX: 6× (confined to Wisdom, Sirach, 3 Maccabees). NT: 4×: 1 Tim 4.4; Jas 1.18; Rev 5.13; 8.9. Gk. Pseudepigrapha (Denis): 12×. Philo: 0×. Josephus: 3×.

[168] Cf. Pss. Sol. 15.3; Rom 8.23; 11.16; 16.5; 1 Cor 15.20, 23; 16.15; 2 Thess 2.13; Rev 14.4; 1 Clem. 42.4; Dio Chrysostom 71.2 and see G. Delling, 'ἀπαρχή', *TDNT* 1.484-86. For the topic of 'first fruits' in general see White, *Erstlingsgabe*.

κτίσμα, characteristic of the LXX wisdom tradition,[169] means in the LXX, as here, 'that which has been created by God'.[170]

The history of interpretation, as we have seen, offers three rather different choices for understanding this line. A few think of the birth of Israel, more of humanity's creation. But the dominant tradition is that our text is about the supernatural begetting of Christians.[171] The reasons are these: (i) Christians sometimes referred to themselves as 'first fruits'.[172] (ii) 'The word of truth' is the Christian proclamation in some early Christian writings.[173] (iii) The language of birth was used of Christian conversion.[174] (iv) Our passage has some parallels in NT texts often presumed to be baptismal.[175] (v) God is, in v. 16, the Father of lights, and Christians associated baptism with light or being enlightened, as is evidenced by the use of φώτισμα for that ritual.[176]

---

[169] Wis 9.2; 13.5; 14.11 (κτίσματι θεοῦ); Ecclus 36.14 (κτίσμασίν σου); 38.34; 3 Macc 5.1. Cf. Gk. Jub. 2.2 (κτισμάτων αὐτοῦ); 11.16, 17; Jos. Asen. 9.5 (κτίσματα αὐτοῦ); 12.2; T. Job 47.12 (τὰ τοῦ θεοῦ κτίσματα); 1 Tim 4.4 (κτίσμα θεοῦ); Rev 5.13; 8.9; Herm. Mand. 12.4.3 (κτισμάτων τοῦ θεοῦ).

[170] Muraoka, Lexicon, s.v. Cf. the expansion in Didymus of Alexandria, Ps frag. 1061 ed. Mühlenburg, 267: ἀπαρχήν τινα τῶν αὐτοῦ κτισμάτων καὶ ποιημάτων. Note, however, that κτίσμα seems to mean 'humankind' in Ps.-Mk 16.15.

[171] Or of the church; cf. Hardouin, 682.

[172] E.g. Rom 16.5 (Epaenetus was the 'first fruits' of Asia for Christ; cf. 1 Cor 16.15); 2 Thess 2.13 ('God chose you as the first fruits for salvation'); Rev 14.4 (the 144,000 are 'redeemed from humankind as first fruits for God and the Lamb'—yet maybe this refers to Israel). In Rom 8.23, Christians have the 'first fruits of the Spirit'.

[173] E.g. Eph 1.13; Col 1.5; 2 Tim 2.15; and often in the Ps.-Clementine literature. But in each of these instances the article appears before both Greek words; cf. Odes Sol. 8.8 (פתגמא דשררא) Moreover, in both Eph 1.13 and Col 1.5, defining clauses are required ('the word of truth, the gospel of your salvation' and 'the word of truth, the gospel that has come to you' respectively). Both the articles and a defining clause are missing from 2 Cor 6.7, but there the meaning of the expression is debated. One should further keep in mind that the texts cited are from Paul or Pauline circles; they do not necessarily reflect the usage of other Christian circles. Pace Mayor, 63, λόγος ἀληθείας was not clearly a 'vox technica of early Christianity'. Smith, 65, supposes James was likely thinking of the parable of the sower. Mussner, 'Tauflehre', 63, raises the possibility that the word of truth is the baptismal formula.

[174] E.g. Jn 1.13 ('born...of God'); 3.1-10 (Nicodemus must be born again/from above'); Tit 3.5 ('through the water of rebirth'); 1 Pet 1.23 ('You have been born anew...through the living and abiding word of God'); 1 Jn 2.29 ('everyone who does right is born of him' [God]). See further Konradt, Existenz, 44-59.

[175] This is the argument of Mussner, 95-96. He refers to Col 1.10; Eph 2.15; 4.21-24; 5.26; 1 Pet 1.23 and suggests that the 'word' might be catechetical instruction. For a similar argument see Boismard, 'Liturgie'. Bede ad loc. CCSL 121, ed. D. Hurst, 189, already finds here a reference to baptism (per aquam regenerationis). But our text says nothing about baptism, and 'first fruits' does not appear in connection with that ritual in our sources. One may also doubt whether all the parallel texts are in fact baptismal; on 1 Pet 1.23 e.g. see Achtemeier, 1 Peter, 139 ('allusion to baptism is...unlikely here').

[176] Lampe, s.v., φώτισμα B2.

THE GOODNESS OF GOD (1.16-18)

These observations are not decisive. Cadoux writes: 'If Jas. I. 18 speaks of regeneration, it says nothing of what man is regenerated from, nothing of what he is born again to, nothing of the means of rebirth; all of which would be not only very unusual, but very misleading'.[177] Laws, 77, observes: 'when the language of birth is used of Christian conversion, it is usually expressly defined as new birth, as being born again: thus Jniii. 3ff.; Tit. iii. 5; 1 Pet. i. 3, 23 (though not 1 Jn iii. 9); and in Paul's comparable idea of the new creation (2 Cor. v. 17) or of the new man (Col. iii. 10)'. James speaks of being born, not of being reborn or born again;[178] and the notion of a spiritual rebirth is not in any case very common in first-century Christian sources.[179] Beyond this, nothing in the epistle to this point prepares the reader to see a reference to regeneration, and the idea does not appear later. In sum, the interpretation in terms of redemption and/or baptism depends upon reading into James ideas found in other early Christian texts, and they may or may not reflect the sort of Christianity James represents.[180]

What then of the possibility that the reader should think of creation rather than redemption? In favor of this reading, which despite the current consensus is no less plausible than that just introduced, are these facts: (i) It has pre-modern support; see n. 3. (ii) It harmonizes well with the context, for the previous verse clearly refers to God's creative work. (iii) Elsewhere God creates the world by the divine word,[181] so one can construe James' λόγῳ ἀληθείας to refer to the speech by which God created the world, including human beings. Allusions to God's creative word often use a dative construction, as does James; see n. 181. (iv) Philo uses ἀποκυέω ('give birth to') in connection with the creation of the

---

[177] Cadoux, *Thought*, 23.
[178] Cf. Kloppenborg, 'Discourse', 247: 'nothing else in the letter suggests that James viewed salvation as a matter of *re*birth'.
[179] Outside of John and 1 John see Tit 3.5; 1 Pet 1.3, 23; Justin, *1 Apol*. 61.1-10; 66.1.
[180] See further Walker, 'Werken', 159-61, and cf. the complaint of Baker, 'Daddy', 197-98: 'despite the fact that James never refers to the Holy Spirit, the cross, the death of Christ, redemption, or many other key ideas, the spiritual anthropological model that depends on these developed concepts is still used to read James'.
[181] Ps 33.6 ('By the word [LXX: λόγῳ] of the Lord the heavens were made'); Wis 9.1 (all was made ἐν λόγῳ σου); Jub. 12.4 (God 'created everything by his word', *baqalu*); Sib. Or. 3.20 ('created everything λόγῳ'); Jn 1.1-4; Heb 11.3 ('the worlds were prepared by the ῥήματι θεοῦ'); 2 Pet 3.5 ('τῷ τοῦ θεοῦ λόγῳ heavens existed long ago and an earth was formed'); 4 Ezra 6.38 ('your word accomplished the work'), 43 ('your word went forth, and at once the work was done'); 2 Bar. 14.17 ('you devised and spoke by means of your word [במלתא] and immediately the works of your creation stood before you'); 21.4 ('fixed the firmament by the word [במלתה]'); 48.8 ('with the word [במלתא] you bring to life that which does not exist'); Herm. *Vis*. 1.3.4 (God 'by his mighty ῥήματι fixed the heavens and founded the earth'); Corp. Herm. frag. 33 ed. Nock and Festugière, 4.140 (God 'spoke with his own holy and creative λόγῳ and said, "Let the sun be"'); m. 'Abot 5.1 ('By means [ב] of ten words the world was created'). The original text of Tg. Neof. 1 on Gen 1.1 probably declared that the Lord's מימר = 'word' created the world.

world,[182] and God was sometimes spoken of as the begetter of humanity.[183] (v) When 1.18 is taken to refer to human beings as the first fruits of creation, one can view all of 1.13-18 as a developed allusion to Gen 1–3. The temptation that leads to sin and death (vv. 13-15) mirrors the tragic decision of Adam and Eve, which, according to an interpretation known in James' day, brought death into the world (Gen 3). That God's gifts are good reflects the refrain in Gen 1, 'and God saw that it was good'.[184] God's status as the creator of the heavenly lights (v. 17) recalls Gen 1.14-19: 'And God said, "Let there be lights in the dome of the sky"'. And God's will to make 'us', through the word of truth, the first fruits of the creation (v. 18) alludes to Gen 1.26ff.—to which James also alludes in 3.7-9—where God says, 'Let us make mankind in our image', and then gives human beings dominion over the world;[185] cf. Wis 9.2 ('by your wisdom you have formed humankind to have dominion over the creatures [κτισμάτων] you have made'); Herm. *Mand.* 12.4.3 ('Man is the lord of all the creatures [κτισμάτων] of God').

As attractive as is the second option, it fails to explain why James speaks specifically of the 'word of truth'. There does not appear to have been any traditional link between 'truth' and the creation of the world. Furthermore, the use of λόγος in the verses immediately following has nothing to do with the divine word of creation (1.21, 22, 23).

We come, then, to the third possibility, which most scholars have tended to dismiss too quickly or even ignore altogether. It has much to be said for it. (i) James ostensibly addresses itself to the twelve tribes in the diaspora (1.1) and to those who meet in synagogues (2.2); and if we take the epistolary fiction seriously, it is altogether natural to identify ἡμᾶς with the Jewish people. (ii) God gives birth to Israel in Deut 32.18: 'You were unmindful of the rock that begat you;[186] you forgot the God who gave you birth'.[187] One may also recall the late rabbinic texts which teach that those who sin can be born anew by keeping Torah.[188] (iii) Israel is

---

[182] Philo, *Ebr.* 30: God had union with Wisdom, which 'bore' (ἀπεκύησε) the only beloved son, the world. Cf. Poimandres 1.16 ed. Nock and Festugière, 1.12: nature 'gave birth to' [ἀπεκύησεν] the original human beings); Ps.-Clem. Hom. 2.52.2 GCS 42 ed. Rehm, 55 (Adam was 'fashioned'—κυοφορηθείς—by God's hands).

[183] E.g. Mal 2.10 ('Have we not all one father? Has not one God created us?'); Sib. Or. 3.278 (God is 'the immortal begetter [γενετῆρα] of…all people'). Cf. Aelius Aristides, *Or.* 43.21 ('our γένεσις is originally from God'); Acts 17.28 (quoting Aratus: 'we too are his offspring'); Asclepius 20 ed. Nock and Festugière, 2.322 (God 'unceasingly brings into being all that he was willed to generate [*uoluerit procreare*]'), 26, 2.331; and the Gnostic creation myths.

[184] Cf. Spitta, 40. Note, however, that the LXX uses καλόν.

[185] Cf. Rendall, *Christianity*, 64: 'the act of will referred to…is the divine resolve, "Let us make man in our image, after our likeness" (Gen. i. 26), the charter of man's being, as he issued from the womb of creation'.

[186] MT: ילדך; LXX: γεννήσαντα.

[187] מחללך; the LXX changes the sense completely.

[188] Exod. Rab. 15.6; Lev. Rab. 35.7; Midr. Ps. 102.18.

called 'first fruits' in Jer 2.3;[189] Philo, *Spec.* 4.180;[190] and 1 Clem. 29.3;[191] and Israel is God's 'first born'—a closely related concept—in several sources.[192] (iv) 'The word of truth' is the Torah or divine revelation in several texts,[193] above all in Ps 119, which exhibits many parallels to this part of James;[194] and the 'Torah' or 'law' is otherwise associated with 'truth'.[195] (v) The λόγος of 1.22 is the same as 'the law of freedom' in 1.25, and the latter, as this commentary argues, is the Torah, not the divine word of creation or the law of love or the proclamation of the gospel. But then the λόγος of 1.22 is naturally identified with the immediately preceding λόγος of 1.21 ('the implanted word'), which is itself readily associated with the λόγος of our verse.[196] It is of course possible that James is using the same word with multiple senses in brief space, but if a proposed single meaning—Torah—unites them, should it not be preferred? One might even then propose, in an attempt to unify vv. 16-26, that 'every good gift and every perfect present' includes or envisages above all the law, because it was (a) thought of as 'given' and sometimes called a 'gift',[197] (b) said to be 'from heaven',[198] (c) associated with light,[199] and (d) reckoned to be 'good' and 'perfect'.[200]

[189] 'Israel was holy to the Lord, the first fruits (MT: ראשית; LXX: ἀρχή) of his harvest'. Cf. Mek. on Exod 14.15; Lev. Rab. 36.4. According to W. Dodd, *ad loc.*, James alludes to Jer 2.3.

[190] 'Moses tells us that the orphan-like, desolate state of his people is always an object of pity and compassion to the ruler of the universe whose portion it is, because it has been set apart out of the whole human race as a kind of first fruits (ἀπαρχή) to the maker and father'. Ludwig, *Wort*, 158-59, also finds a reference to Israel as the firstborn in T. Mos. 1.13; but against this see J. Tromp, *The Assumption of Moses*, Leiden, 1933, 141-42.

[191] 'Behold, the Lord takes for himself a nation out of the midst of the nations, as a man takes the first fruits of his threshing floor; and the Holy of Holies will come forth from that nation'. The source of this quotation is unknown, although perhaps it is an artificial composite; cf. Num 18.27; Deut 4.34; 14.2; Jer 2.3; Ezek 48.12.

[192] Exod 4.22 ('Israel is my firstborn [בכרי; πρωτότοκος] son'; Bassett, 19, supposes this 'the key to the passage before us'); Jub. 2.20 ('And I [God] have chosen the seed of Jacob from among all that I have seen [cf. James' τῶν αὐτοῦ κτισμάτων]. And I have recorded him as my first born [bak^wr] son'); Pss. Sol. 18.4 (Israel is 'an only, firstborn [בוכרא; πρωτότοκον] son'); Ecclus 36.11 ('Israel, whom you have likened to a firstborn son', πρωτογόνῳ); 4Q369 1 2.6 ('you made him a firstborn [בכור] son'); LAB 32.16 ('God killed the firstborn of the Egyptians on account of his own firstborn'); 4 Ezra 6.58 ('But we your people, whom you have called your *primogenitum*, only begotten'). For later rabbinic parallels see Billerbeck 3.257-58. Burchard, 79-80, although he interprets v. 18 in terms of Christian rebirth, nonetheless wonders whether James, in using ἀπαρχή, appropriates 'an Israel-predication'.

[193] See n. 166; cf. also 2 Sam 7.28 ('You are God, and your words are true'); Ps 119.142 ('your law is the truth'), 151 ('all your commandments are true').

[194] See below, 339-41, and cf. Frankemölle, 301.

[195] Cf. Neh 9.13; Ps 118.142; Mal 2.6; T. Gad 3.1; Philo, *Aet.* 1; Rom 2.20; etc.

[196] See further Jackson-McCabe, *Logos*, 214-15.

[197] Note e.g. Exod 24.12 (LXX: δώσω—of the stone tablets); Neh 9.13 (LXX 2 Esd 19.13: ἔδωκας αὐτοῖς κρίματα εὐθέα καὶ νόμους ἀληθείας, προστάγματα καὶ ἐντολὰς

(vi) Verse 17 calls God 'the father of lights', that is, the creator of the heavenly orbs, and in Judaism there was a tradition that the twelve signs of the zodiac represent the twelve tribes of Israel.[201] In this way then one could discern continuity between vv. 17 and 18: the creator of the constellations (v. 17) is the very same as the creator of the twelve tribes of Israel (v. 18). (vii) If Verseput if right to connect Jas 1.17 with the Jewish morning prayer, it is pertinent that the blessing of the creator of the luminaries was immediately followed by benedictions thanking God for his love for Israel and his election of them when he redeemed them from Egypt.[202] Our sources for this are, to be sure, Amoraic;[203] but the antiquity of the sequence is strongly suggested by 4Q503, a fragmentary collection of morning prayers. This repeatedly thanks God for the light of morning, and frags. 21-25 have this: '[And when the sun ascends to illuminate] the earth, they will bless. [Starting to speak, they will say: Blessed be] the God of Israel who has chosen us from among all the nations.'

Perhaps the chief objection to this third reading is that the immediate context seems to have more to do with creation than the Jewish people and the giving of the law. This, however, is not the difficulty it may seem,

ἀγαθάς); 1 Esd 8.3 (τῷ Μωυσέως νόμῳ τῷ ἐκδεδομένῳ ὑπὸ τοῦ θεοῦ τοῦ Ἰσραήλ); 9.39 (τὸν νόμον Μωυσέως τὸν παραδοθέντα ὑπὸ τοῦ κυρίου); Wis 18.4 (τὸ ἄφθαρτον νόμου φῶς τῷ αἰῶνι δίδοσθαι); Jn 1.17; 4 Ezra 3.19 (*dares semini Iacob legem*; cf. 5.27; 7.94); Tg. Ps 68.19 (the commandments are מתנן, 'gifts'); Midr. Ps 68.11 (the Torah 'was bestowed upon Israel as a gift, at no cost').

[198] Note Philo, *Cher*. 106 (νόμους ἀπ' οὐρανοῦ) and recall the rabbinic term, תורה מן השמים, as in Sifre Deut 102; m. Sanh. 10.1; y. Sanh. 27c (10.1; ניחוה תורה מן השמים); b. Sanh. 90a, 99a; b. 'Abod. Zar. 18a; etc.

[199] Note. Ps 119.105 ('Your word is a lamp to my feet and a light to my path'), 130 ('The unfolding of thy words gives light'); Wis 18.4 ('the imperishable light of the law'); T. Levi 14.4 ('the light of the law'); b. Ketub. 111b ('the light of the law').

[200] For the latter see on 1.25. For the Torah as 'good' note Neh 9.13 (LXX: ἀγαθάς); Ps 119.72 (LXX: ἀγαθόν); 4Q369 1 2.5 (הטובים); T. Ash. 6.1-3 (καλόν); Rom 7.12 (ἀγαθή); etc.

[201] See the commentaries on Gen 37.9 and Rev 12.1; also Exod. Rab. 15.6; Tanḥ. Buber Wayehi 16. Whereas according to Exod 28.21 the twelve stones on the breastplate of the high priest correspond to the twelve tribes, in Philo, *Mos*. 3.14, and Josephus, *Ant*. 3.186, they correspond to the circle of the zodiac. Undoubtedly the zodiacs in synagogue mosaic floors (as at Beth Alpha) were commonly associated with the twelve tribes; see E. R. Goodenough, *Jewish Symbols in the Greco Roman Period*, vol. 8, New York, 1958, 167-218.

[202] 'You are praised, O Lord, creator of the luminaries' is followed immediately by 'with a great love you have loved us' (Israel), by prayers to do Torah, and by the line, 'You have chosen us from all peoples and nations, and have forever brought us near to your truly great name... Blessed are you, O Lord, who has graciously chosen your people Israel.'

[203] Although not for morning prayer itself; that practice is attested early on; cf. Ps 88.13; Wis 16.28; 4Q503; T. Jos. 3.6; Josephus, *Ant*. 4.212-13.

for Jews could construe the exodus as a new creation.²⁰⁴ Wisdom 19.6 affirms that 'the whole creation in its nature was fashioned anew' when God preserved the Israelites as they fled from Egypt. LAB 15.5-6 compares the parting of the Red Sea to the creative act of Gen 1.9 ('Let the waters under the heavens be gathered together into one place'; cf. Exod. Rab. 21.6). Ecclesiasticus 36.14 asks God, with reference to Israel, to 'bear witness to those whom you created in the beginning' (ἐν ἀρχῇ κτίσμασίν σου).²⁰⁵ Already the Hebrew Bible moves Rahab, the female monster of chaos, from creation (Job 9.13; 38.8-11) to the exodus (Ps 89.11; Isa 51.9-10), and additional texts seemingly present Moses himself as a new creation and a new Noah.²⁰⁶ Christians, too, could merge language about the creation of the world with language about the birth of God's people. Matthew and John open their accounts of the Christian dispensation by recalling creation themes from Genesis,²⁰⁷ and Paul not only describes the Christian as 'a new creation' (2 Cor 5.17) but associates Abraham's becoming 'the father of many nations' with the God 'who calls into existence the things that do not exist' (Rom 4.17-18). So the presence of creation motifs in Jas 1 scarcely counts against taking v. 18 to be about Israel's birth at Sinai.

All three interpretations have something to be said for them and something to be said against them. In a case such as this, the commentator will prefer the reading that best fits his or her understanding of James as a whole. This exegete, who does not give ecclesiastical sense to the 'twelve tribes' of 1.1, accordingly inclines to the second and third options. He adds, however, that the author may at points have wished for some ambiguity in his text, in accord with the mixed audience envisioned.²⁰⁸

βουληθείς stresses God's deliberate and sovereign choice,²⁰⁹ the upshot of a set purpose.²¹⁰ So here βούλομαι = θέλω.²¹¹ The former is used of

---

²⁰⁴ There is much useful material in I.R. Chernus, 'Redemption and Chaos', unpublished Ph.D. diss., Temple University, 1975, 111-276.

²⁰⁵ Frankemölle, 303, stresses the importance of this verse as immediate background for James.

²⁰⁶ J.S. Ackerman, 'The Literary Context of the Moses Birth Story (Exodus 1-2)', in *Literary Interpretations of Biblical Narratives*, ed. K.R.R. Gros Louis, Nashville, 1974, 74-119; I.M. Kikawada and A. Quinn, *Before Abraham Was*, Nashville, 1985, 107-26.

²⁰⁷ See Davies-Allison, *Matthew*, 1.149-54, and the commentaries on Jn 1.1, which takes up the ἐν ἀρχῇ of Gen 1.1; also P. Borgen, *Philo, John and Paul*, Atlanta, 1987, 75-101.

²⁰⁸ See further the Introduction, 36-44. According to Maurice, *Unity*, 285-86, our passage is designed to be read one way by baptized Christians, another way by Jews.

²⁰⁹ Cf. Job 23.13 ('What he desires, that he does'); Ps 115.3 ('Our God is in the heavens; he does whatever he pleases').

²¹⁰ Commentators sometimes read in the thought that God's decision was independent of human merit; so e.g. Bede *ad loc.* CCSL 121 ed. Hurst, 189. Calvin, 270, can even find implicit in our phrase a doctrine of election. Burkitt, 1018, and Scaer, 276, espy in βουληθείς confirmation of their belief that God alone is the source of salvation.

²¹¹ Cf. BDF 101 and see further G. Schrenk, 'βούλομαι κτλ.', *TDNT* 1.629-32.

human volition in 3.4 and 4.4, the latter of human volition in 2.20 and of divine volition in 4.15. No difference in meaning is discernible. In any case, God's good 'will' (βουληθείς) stands in stark contrast to the human ἐπιθυμία that wreaks so much havoc (vv. 14-15).

Unlike sin, which begets (ἀποκύει) death (1.15), God produces—depending upon which interpretation one favors—the church, humanity, or Israel (ἀπεκύησεν ἡμᾶς). That the verb properly applies to the female was once the basis for speculation that a gnostic myth of a male–female divinity lies behind James.[212] But the biblical tradition contains other texts which give God feminine attributes or functions, including giving birth;[213] and the metaphorical use of (ἀπο)κυέω is attested.[214] The choice of the verb, it seems, should be explained by a rhetorical desire to set what God does over against what sin does in 1.15.[215]

ἀπαρχήν τινα[216]—which might have eschatological connotations[217]—takes up an expression well known from the Hebrew Bible. There the first fruits (ראשית) are that part of the annual crop set aside for sacrifice to God.[218] It might be objected (against interpretation 3) that since Israel was not created first, it cannot be the first fruits of creation. But one should not insist on the chronological element in a metaphorical application. When we read in Jer 2.3 that Israel was the first fruits, the point has to do with the nation's sanctified status, not chronological priority. Matters are similar in Tanḥ. Buber Noah 1, where Adam, created only on the sixth day of creation, is said to be 'first'. It is relevant that ἀπαρχή translates חלב ('fat' = 'best') in Num 18.12, 30, 32, and further that

---

[212] Edsman, 'Schöpferwille'; Schammberger, *Kampf*, 58. Edsman's article remains a helpful survey of the use of the verb that highlights James' rare usage. Baker, 'Daddy', argues that the dominant image in the wider context is paternal (e.g. 'Father of lights'), so interpretation should not make much of the maternal verb here.

[213] E.g. Num 11.12; Deut 32.18; Pss 2.7; 90.2; Prov 8.24-25; Isa 42.14; 66.13; 1QH 17(9).36 (God is like a wet-nurse); Philo, *Ebr.* 30 (see n. 182); Tanḥ. Buber Shemot 18 (God says to Moses: 'I am making you into a new creature, as in the case of a woman, who conceives and gives birth'). In Odes Sol. 16.14 Christ says, 'I prepared my own breasts for them, that they might drink my holy milk and live by it' (cf. 14.2; 19.2). Cf. also the use of γεννάω with divine subject in Philo, *Leg.* 2.47; 3.219; *Conf.* 63; *Migr.* 1.142; Jn 1.13; 1 Pet 1.3; etc.

[214] E.g. Irenaeus, *Haer.* 1.15.1; Clement of Alexandria, *Paed.* 1.42.2 GCS, ed. Stählin, 115; Acts Thom. 45 ed. Bonnet, 162 (ὡς ἐξ αὐτοῦ [God] ἀποκυηθείς). See also Poimandres 9, 12 ed. Nock and Festugière, 1.9, 10, quoted above, 279.

[215] Some commentators recall Gal 4.19, where Paul uses feminine terminology of himself; cf. Wordsworth, 17.

[216] For τις softening a metaphorical expression see BDF 301.1. Cf. esp. Philo, *Spec.* 4.180 (Israel has been set apart as 'a kind of first fruits [τις ἀπαρχή] to the Maker and Father'); Alexander of Aphrodisias, *Fato* ed. Bruns, 164 (τινὰ ἀπαρχὴν ὑμῖν τῶν ἡμετέρων καρπῶν: 'a sort of first fruit of our fruits').

[217] Cf. Schlatter, 137: in view is 'the final goal of God', which embraces all humanity and all the creation.

[218] Exod 23.19; 34.22; Lev 23.10, 15-22; Num 15.20-21; 28.26; Deut 16.9-12; 26.1-11; etc.

ראשית itself clearly means 'the best' in 1 Sam 2.29 and 15.21.[219] BAGD quotes the scholion on Euripides, *Or*. 96: 'first fruits' refers not just to 'the first in order but also to the first in honor'.[220] Throughout patristic literature, ἀπαρχή often means 'what is best' or 'what is representative'.[221] One presumes a similar sense here, although as is his wont James refrains from defining his terms.[222]

Is εἰς τὸ εἶναι ἡμᾶς descriptive or hortatory? Given the nature of James as a whole, the latter seems more likely; cf. Hemminge, 14: 'When as he called the saintes the first fruites, he alludeth unto the outcome of the lawe, whereby the first fruites were consecrated unto God, whereupon we are admonished continually to meditate on true holines'.

---

[219] Cf. also Pss. Sol. 15.5, where a 'new psalm' is 'the first fruits (Gk: ἀπαρχήν) of the lips from a devout and righteous heart'.

[220] BAGD, s.v., 2. Cf. the *Catenae ad loc*. ed. Cramer, 7, and Theophylact *ad loc*. PG 125.1144C—the first fruits are 'first and most honorable'.

[221] So Lampe, s.v., B.

[222] Ps.-Macarius, *Hom. 1–50* 49.4 PTS 4 ed. Dörries, Klostermann, Kroeger, 319, clarifies: the first fruits are God's 'wisdom and communion, his own habitation, his own honorable and pure bride'. For Macknight, 588, the term shows 'how acceptable such are to God, and how excellent in themselves through the renovation of their nature'. J.A.T. Robinson, 'Kingdom, Church and Ministry', in *The Historic Episcopate*, ed. K.M. Carey, London, 1954, 16, asserts that 'first-fruits' stands for and anticipates the destiny of whole, implying the salvation of all. Cf. Gollwitzer, 'Kantate', 230: implicit in James is apocatastasis. Stier, 262, and F. Palmer, 'Offering', argue to the contrary.

VII

QUICK TO HEAR, SLOW TO SPEAK, SLOW TO ANGER (1.19-21)[1]

(19) You must understand this, my beloved brothers. Let everyone be quick to listen, slow to speak, slow to anger. (20) For human anger does not effect God's righteousness. (21) Wherefore, ridding yourselves of all sordidness and profusion of evil, in humility receive the implanted word that is able to save you.

History of Interpretation and Reception

Two issues stand out from discussions and applications of this passage. First, does James disqualify all anger or only anger for the wrong reasons? Second, what exactly is 'the implanted word'?

Bede represents the majority of ecclesiastical readers in urging that James does not prohibit anger altogether. If, for instance, one cannot otherwise correct a person for whom one is responsible, then, according to Bede, anger may have a just cause, and it may be necessary to be harsh in speech or to issue a severe judgment—provided one takes as much care as possible to remain calm.[2] Similarly, Dionysius bar Salībī—contrasting anger against Satan with Paul's anger against the Corinthians and Galatians—made our text opportunity to expound upon the differences between legitimate and illegitimate anger while Martin of Legio affirmed that James is writing about anger that is without cause or reason.[3] Manton, 140-41, went into the topic at length. He made room both for 'propassions', that is, 'sudden and irresistible alterations, which are the infelicities of nature, not the sins; tolerable in themselves, if

---

[1] Recent literature: Amphoux, 'Relecture'; Baker, 'Daddy'; idem, *Speech-Ethics*, 23-104; Boismard, 'Liturgie'; A. Calmet, 'Sagesses'; Cheung, *Genre*, 86-92; Cladder, 'Anlage'; Collins, 'Coherence'; Elliott-Binns, 'Coincidence'; Fabris, *Legge*; Jackson-McCabe, *Logos*; Kamell, 'Law'; Klein, *Werk*, 119-20, 135-37; Konradt, 'Wort'; Lockett, *Purity*, 108-12; Ludwig, *Wort*; Manns, 'Tradition'; Ogara, 'Verbo'; Tsuji, *Glaube*, 68-70, 108-109; von Gemünden, 'Wertung'.

[2] Bede *ad loc*. CCSL 121 ed. Hurst, 191.

[3] Dionysius bar Salībī *ad loc*. CSCO 60 Scriptores Syri 101 ed. Sedlacek, 92; Martin of Legio *ad loc*. PL 209.190B. Cf. Glossa Ordinaria *ad loc*.; Aquinas, *Summa* 3a q. 15 a. 9 (Jas 1.19 is consistent with Jesus' apparent display of anger because he was always controlled by reason); Nicholas of Gorran, 70.

rightly limited', as well as 'holy anger, which is the whetstone of fortitude and zeal'.[4] Richardson, 89-90, by contrast, doubts that James allows for righteous anger. Citing Rom 12.19-21, he associates anger with temptation and rejects it utterly: 'Whether in relationship with God (2.23) or in relationship with others (3.18), anger must be ruled out'.[5] This interpretation harmonizes 1.19-20 with one plausible reading of Mt 5.21-26.[6]

Most commentators have understood the 'implanted word' to be the gospel accepted at baptism or conversion.[7] A minority, however, have understood it to be something innate, such as reason, or the human ability to tell right from wrong (conscience), akin to Paul's notion of a law written on the heart.[8] Still others have given a christological sense to λόγος—the word is Christ[9]—while a few modern scholars propose that James is instead referring to the Jewish Torah: it is the implanted word

---

[4] Cf. Stevartius, 77-81; Burkitt, 1018 ('anger, justly moderated, is a duty'); Trapp, 695 (appealing to the anger of Moses and Jesus); Moo, 84 (one should not read wisdom sayings as absolute assertions).

[5] Maier, 91, is of like mind; cf. also von Gemünden, 'Wertung', 110-11. Hort, 36, takes our verse to speak against 'holy anger': it is 'nothing better than spite'.

[6] See Jerome, *Mt ad* 5.22 SC 242 ed. Bonnard, 112; John Cassian, *Inst.* 8.21 SC 109 ed. Guy, 364; Luz, *Matthew*, 1.234-41. Basil the Great, in his homily on anger (PG 31.353-72), fails to appeal to James.

[7] E.g. Bede *ad loc.* CCSL 121, ed. Hurst, 191; Aretius, 476; Piscator, 729; Cappel, 129; Whitby, 680; Poole, 883; Wesley, 859; Rosenmüller, 339; Valpy, 239; Bisping, 28; Beyschlag, 83; Bouman, 91; Bardenhewer, 51; Hauck, 12; Mussner, 102; Michl, 33; Kugelman, 20; Martin, 48-49; Johnson, 202; Whitlark, 'Motif'; *et al.*

[8] Rom 1.15. Cf. Ps.-Oecumenius *ad loc.* PG 119.468A-B; Theophylact *ad loc.* PG 125.1145D; Dionysius bar Salībī *ad loc.* CSCO 60 Scriptores Syri 101 ed. Sedlacek, 120; Gregory Palamas, *Hom. i–xx* 3.7 ed. Chrestou and Zeses, 82; Hort, 37-38 (he thinks of 'the original capacity involved in the Creation in God's image which makes it possible for man to apprehend a revelation at all'); Parry, *Discussion*, 21-23; Meyer, *Rätsel*, 156-57; Cadoux, *Thought*, 20; Boismard, 'Liturgie', 171-72; Jackson-McCabe, *Logos*. Ropes, 173 (who supplies a useful overview of what various translations have made of the expression) combines two interpretations: 'It seems to mean the sum of present knowledge of God's will. It is inwrought into a man's nature and speaks from within, but this does not exclude that it should also exist for man's use in written or traditional form, whether in the law of Moses or in the precepts of Jesus.' Cf. Laws, 83: 'The reference is primarily to the word of the gospel, yet because of this interaction of ideas, and because the creation word of v. 18 is still in mind, the word of the gospel is described in terms of the word of creation, part of the nature of man from his birth'. Baker, *Speech-Ethics*, 91, follows Laws.

[9] So e.g. Godfridus, *Hom. dom.* 52 PL 174.351D; Wordsworth, 19; T. Zahn, *Bread and Salt from the Word of God*, Edinburgh, 1905, 180; cf. Carr, 24 ('the implanted Word is scarcely distinguishable from the indwelling Christ'); Scaer, 66 ('it is tempting to see James' concept of the Word...as resembling John's incarnate Word'); Assaël-Cuvillier, 'Éléments'. Note also the occasional application of the language of v. 19 to Christ, as in Theodore the Studite, *Ep.* 127 ed. Fatouros, 244 (the Lord is ὁ βραδὺς εἰς ὀργὴν καὶ ταχὺς εἰς οἰκτιρμούς); Adderley, 19; also the juxtaposition of Jas 1.19-20 with Jesus' example in Bonaventure, *Lk* 9.56 Opera Omnia 10 ed. Peltier, 484.

that can save souls.¹⁰ Modern treatments regularly discuss the possible debt to Stoicism.¹¹

Christians who have identified the word with an innate element of human nature have sometimes ended up sounding like Justin Martyr when he spoke of the *spermatikos logos*. In 1896, Basil Wilberforce preached a sermon in Westminster Abbey in which he insisted that 'a ray of the Father's own life, capable of boundless expansion, and destined ultimately to work out...a perfect sonship', exists in each individual from birth. This ray is the 'inborn Word or Reason of God, ceaselessly acting on the conscience, formulating unwritten laws, impelling the desires of man to centre on God alone'; it is the germ of the divine in each human, the inborn 'Christ-nature', which became 'pre-eminently incarnate in Jesus', so 'that men might know what their own capacity, possibility, and destiny is'. On Wilberforce's reading, James counters Calvinistic election because he presumes that all share in the universal divine nature.¹²

James' imperatives are laconic in that they offer no hint as to how to achieve them.¹³ Readers have remedied this defect. Manton, 137, for example, recalled the counsel to repeat the alphabet when overcome by sudden rage, and Thomas Senior went on at length about how to 'receive the implanted word', which word he identified with Scripture and its public interpretation: listen attentively, do not let your thoughts wander, do not give in to drowsiness.¹⁴ Charles Gore recommended the silence of solitude as the best way to overcome anger and to receive the implanted word, which he identified not only with 'the message of Christ' but also with 'the human soul in the conscience'.¹⁵

---

¹⁰ E.g. Spitta, 50; Meyer, *Rätsel*, 149-57; Boismard, 'Liturgie', 171-73; Klein, *Werk*, 135-37; Tsuji, *Glaube*, 108-10; Jackson-MacCabe, *Logos*. Those who hold this position can combine it with the idea of an inborn or innate law; see the commentary on v. 21.

¹¹ See esp. Jackson-MacCabe, *Logos*, for a review of the discussion and the case that James does reflect Stoic ideas.

¹² B. Wilberforce, 'The Inborn Word', *Christian World Pulpit* 49 (1896), 296-98. Wilberforce was a universalist, which circumstance clearly informs his interpretation.

¹³ He also does not explain why his demands are prudent. Contrast Lapide, 63-66, who offers multiple reasons, including the need for discipline, angelic example, and secular wisdom. Surprisingly, J. de Valdés, *Diálogo de doctrina cristiana*, Alcalá de Henares, 1529, 46r-v, who permits righteous anger, says that James offers 'remedies' for wicked anger. He seems to have in mind being quick to listen and slow to hear, although he adds that this is not enough: one must also learn to control emotions.

¹⁴ T. Senior, 'Sermon VII', in *The Morning Exercises at Cripplegate, St. Giles in the Fields, and in Southwark by Seventy-Five Ministers of the Gospels*, vol. 2, 5th ed., ed. J. Nichols, London, 1844, 52-53.

¹⁵ C. Gore, 'The Implanted Word', *Christian World Pulpit* 56 (1899), 22-24. For a long list of what to do in order to control speech see N. Lardner, 'The Difficulty of Governing the Tongue', in *The Works of Nathaniel Lardner*, vol. 9, London, 1838, 279-80. This includes fearing God, loving neighbor, reflecting on the consequences of past slips of the tongue, contemplating moral exemplars, and mortifying pride, envy, and 'inordinate self-love'.

One of the more memorable applications of Jas 1.21 came in a sermon, entitled 'Toleration', that the Scottish minister Robert Lee preached in 1852. He turned the verse into an indictment of those who hunt Christian heretics. Persecution, Lee proclaimed, 'can compel only an outward compliance, not an inward change of opinion', an idea that he believes accords with James: 'The righteousness of God here is the righteousness which God requires, which is faith in the first instance; and the wrath of man is another name for all those penalties by which man expresses his wrath. These penalties have no tendency to produce in others that faith in God which we would diffuse... Translated, the text reads thus: "Thou shalt not persecute, because by persecution thou canst not convince. Thy wrath, O man, is not the appropriate means of making the fellow-man righteous before God".'[16]

Although failing to listen and being angry are scarcely the privileged sins of any one human group, some commentators condescendingly assert that the sins of vv. 19-20 typified ancient Jews. T. Williams, 1360, opined: the Jews were 'a very irritable people'. Benson, 45, explained: at that time Jews 'were exceedingly impatient in hearing others'. Baumgarten, 63, was even worse: it was 'the evil habit of Jews of that time to dispute about everything, to speak against all things which they did not understand, and even to dispose of a teacher of unknown things'. Such gratuitous stereotyping is, alas, not hard to find.[17]

Exegesis

Heretofore James has been concerned above all with trials and temptations (1.2-18). But with v. 19 those subjects recede. They are succeeded by lines and paragraphs[18] related in one way or another to the imperative in 1.22: 'Be doers of the word and not hearers only'.[19] Believers are no longer told how to behave in situations not of their own making but rather how to avoid or repair situations that are wrong.

---

[16] R. Lee, 'Sermon X. Toleration', in *Sermons*, Edinburgh, 1874, 137. Cf. the applications in Benson, 45-46 ('religion is a matter of pure choice'); Clarke, 802 ('The zeal that made the Papists persecute and burn the Protestants, was kindled in hell'); Adderley, 19.

[17] See further Bisping, 27; Bassett, 21. According to Scaer, 64, Judaism 'in Jesus' day had deteriorated into a Law preaching which taught the possibility of actually living up to its own demands', so some Jewish Christians, raised in that religion, 'might have been preaching God's displeasure over the failure of some to fulfill... ceremonial obligations', and James' admonition about anger could have in view their proclamation of 'soul-scorching damnation'.

[18] These extend all the way to 2.26.

[19] Collins, 'Coherence', urges that vv. 19-27 are also united in that they have to do with 'the manner, the frame of soul, in which James wanted his audience to listen to their leader/teacher when he spoke in their worship service' (84).

The section may be analyzed this way:

I. Address: 'You must understand this, my beloved brothers' (19a)
II. Three specific imperatives (19b)
    a. Positive: Be quick to hear
    b. Negative: Be slow to speak
    c. Negative: Be slow to anger
III. Justification of IIc: 'For human anger, etc.' (20)
IV. Two general imperatives (21)
    a. Be rid of all sordidness and excesses of evil
    b. In humility receive the implanted word that can save[20]

Alliteration, assonance, and consonance run throughout:

```
v. 19:
       ἀ   δελφ           οί
       ἀ        γαπητ     οί
                          πᾶ              ς
                          ἄνθρωπ ο ς
                          τ α χ ὺς    εἰς  τὸ       ἀκοῦ    σαι
                          βρ αδ ὺς    εἰς  τὸ   λαλῆ        σαι
                          βρ αδ ὺς    εἰς       ὀργήν
v. 20:                                          ὀργή
v. 21: ἀ   π οθέμενοι
            πᾶ        σ        αν
       ῥυ π α  ρ ί              αν
         π ε ρ ι    σσεί        αν
          π     ρ       αὐτητι
                                  τὸν
                            ἔμφυ τον
                            λόγ    ον
                                   ιόν
                            δυνάμενον
                                         σῶσαι
                                    τ    άς
                                    ψυχ  άς
```

1.19-21 can be connected with preceding verses in various ways. Amphoux, 'Relecture', suggests that 'slow to speak' takes one back to v. 13: one should be slow to charge God with temptation. For Johnson, 199, ἴστε is an indicative that takes up 'the principle just enunciated in 1:17-18, thus providing the warrant for the command that follows concerning hearing and speaking. The *adelphoi agapētoi* is, therefore, not

---

[20] Contrast Moo, 81, who separates vv. 19-20 from 21-27. McKnight, 135, suggests a chiasm:
    1. three commands about speech (1.19b-d)
        2. the reason for the commands (1.20)
        2'. inference that sums up the three commands (1.21a)
    1'. command that re-expresses the three commands (1.21b)

to be taken simply as a transition but, above all, as an *inclusio* with 1:16 for the sake of emphasis'. Some such thought presumably lies behind the v.l., ὥστε, in v. 19 (see n. 41), a variant that, enshrined in the KJV and other translations, led many to posit that 'swift to hear' harks back to 'the word of truth' in v. 18.[21] Boismard, 'Liturgie', 170, to the contrary, offers a source-critical conjecture: v. 21 once directly followed upon v. 18. James, that is, interpolated vv. 19-20 into a traditional sequence he took over from his liturgy.[22]

Despite the parallelism and catchword links between 1.16-18 and 19-21—both open with ἀδελφοί μου ἀγαπητοί, use εἰς τό + infinitive (vv. 18, 19 [*bis*]),[23] and close with a sentence featuring 'word' (v. 18: λόγῳ; v. 21: λόγον)[24]—and even if 'the shift from God's word to human words is easy',[25] most exegetes, ancient and modern, regard v. 19 as a new beginning, a point of topical shift[26] and so prefer to relate v. 19 to what follows.[27] According to Wesley, 598, swiftness of hearing is treated from 1.21–2.26, slowness of speaking throughout the third chapter, and slowness to anger throughout chaps. 3, 4, and 5. Many have said similar things.[28] For example, Pfeiffer (without acknowledging predecessors) associates 'quick to hear' with 1.21ff., 'slow to speak' with 3.1ff., and

---

[21] Cf. Manton, 128: James 'had spoken of the word of truth as being the instrument of conversion, and upon that ground persuades them to diligent hearing and reverent speaking of it; for so these sentences must be constrained, and then the coherence is more fluent and easy'. Huther, 59, lists Estius, Gataker, Gomar, Piscator, Homejus, Baumgarten, Rosenmüller, Pott, Hottinger, Gebser, de Wette, and Wiesmiger as supplying 'the word of truth' as the object of 'quick to hear'. According to Calvin, 271, v. 19 is 'placed straight onto the last sentence about the Word of truth, without breaking the sense...' Cf. Trapp, 695; T. Scott, 568.

[22] For another compositional theory see Knox, 'Epistle': James redacted a source that contained, among other things, 1.2-4, 9-12, 19-20, 26-27.

[23] Elsewhere in James only in 3.3.

[24] One might also observe the antithesis between πᾶσαν ῥυπαρίαν καὶ περισσείαν κακίας (1.21) and πᾶσα δόσις ἀγαθὴ καὶ πᾶν δώρημα τέλειον (1.17).

[25] So Davids, 91, adding: 'especially since chap. 3 shows how closely God's gift of wisdom is tied to how people speak'.

[26] According to Ps.-Andrew of Crete, *Éloge* 4.18-22 ed. Noret, 48, with v. 19 James moves from theology (θεολογικόν) and piety (τὴν πρὸς θεὸν εὐσέβειαν) to ethics (ἠθικοῦ). Cf. Frankemölle, 322: 1.19 is the beginning of the 'Briefkorpus' and we turn here from the indicative in the prologue (vv. 2-18) to the imperative.

[27] But Maier, 88, regards it as an independent section not closely aligned with vv. 22-27.

[28] E.g. Bengel, 490; Leahy, 911; R. Wall, 34-37. Particularly common is the attempt to connect not being angry with chap. 3: Mitton, 60; Adamson, 78; Davids, 91-92; *et al.* This link lies behind attempts to refer v. 19 to teachers (cf. 3.1); see e.g. Augustine, *Ep.* 266.2 CSEL 57 ed. Goldbacher, 648-49; Bede *ad loc.* CCSL 121 ed. Hurst, 190; Hort, 35 (the reference must be to speaking in God's name or on God's behalf); Ross, 38. It may also explain the v.1. in v. 21, πραΰτητι σοφίας; see n. 146. For a connection between hearing and chap. 2 see Adamson, 78, and for one between the prohibition of anger and chap. 4 Davids, 92.

'slow to anger' with 3.13ff.[29] Dibelius, 108, however, links 1.19-21 primarily with the remainder of chap. 1: '1:20 seems to be an appendix to the last part of the saying in 1:19b, just as 1:26 is evidently connected with the second part of this "triplet". What comes in between, 1:21-25, is an elaboration about hearing and doing, and therefore is a supplement to the first part of 1:19b: "be quick to hear"...; this thought seems to be the primary interest of the author here. This is confirmed also by 1:27, which externally represents a supplement attached to 1:26 by means of a catch-word...but which in its content signifies a return to the author's chief interest...'[30]

Dibelius seems to be correct. Although vv. 20-6 are not exactly exegesis of v. 19, they do elaborate its elements. At the same time, and along the lines of Wesley's proposal, vv. 19-21 are fitting preface to 1.22–2.26 because they (i) use λόγος, a key word in the next paragraph (vv. 22, 23); (ii) instruct people to listen, a theme developed in 1.22-25; 2.12; (iii) commend being slow to speak, which anticipates 1.26; and (iv) refer, as we shall see, to the Torah, which is the key concept throughout the following paragraphs: one should do Torah. Beyond that, 1.19-21 equally anticipates 3.1-12 and 4.11-12, where sins of the tongue are discussed at length, and 3.13-18, which demands communal peace (cf. the words about anger and meekness in 1.19-20). So 1.19-21, even if not a table of contents, is a crossroads where many of the themes in James meet.[31] This implies that one should read the verses less as general proverbs and more as maxims applicable to the situations reflected in subsequent sections.

The parallels between this part of James and 1 Pet 1.23–2.2 are remarkable:

1 Pet 1.23:   'You have been born anew', cf. Jas 1.18
1 Pet 1.23:   reference to 'the word', ὁ λόγος, cf. Jas 1.18, 21-23
1 Pet 1.24:   citation of Isa 40.7-8, cf. Jas 1.11
1 Pet 2.1:   ἀποθέμενοι οὖν πᾶσαν κακίαν καὶ πάντα δόλον, cf. Jas 1.21
1 Pet 2.2:   resulting salvation, εἰς σωτηρίαν, cf. Jas 1.21

What accounts for these similarities? Moo, 85, speaks for many in postulating 'a familiar teaching from the early church in which a reminder of the spiritual birth God had graciously given his people through his word was followed by exhortation to shun the kind of behavior associated with the old life and to begin living by the standard of the word that had saved

---

[29] Pfeiffer, 'Zusammenhang'; he thus speaks of the unity of 1.19–4.13. But the remainder of James remains, on his analysis, not so neatly arranged.

[30] Cf. Moffatt, 23. For additional opinions see below, 322-23.

[31] Hodges, 37, sees in v. 19 an 'outline' of the 'kephalaia' of James. For Gaugusch, 18, v. 19 is the 'Grundthema' of the letter. For Werner, 'Brief', 266, vv. 19-20 are the 'Grundthema'.

them'. Also tenable is the hypothesis that James revised not a Christian scheme of teaching but rather borrowed from a traditional Jewish sequence that other Christians also adopted.[32] This commentary, however, instead supposes James' familiarity with 1 Peter.[33]

Verse 19. Transparently good advice, presumably not news to the readers.

The three aphoristic imperatives are succinct, unencumbered by discussion of how one might learn to listen better, hold one's tongue, or forsake anger. This stands in contrast to Graeco-Roman reflections on anger (see n. 55), which regularly offer advice on achieving such ends. But it is reminiscent of the Jesus tradition, where 'how to' advice is sparse, obedience often demanded without elaboration.

ἴστε, ἀδελφοί μου ἀγαπητοί.[34] For 'my beloved brothers' see on 1.16. The chief issue is the first word, ἴστε. It is usually translated as an imperative: 'You must understand this'.[35] But it could also be reckoned an indicative: 'You understand this' (cf. the Vulgate: *scitis*) or (as the NEB has it) 'Of that you may be certain'.[36] In favor of this last are these considerations: (i) Besides 1.19, ἴστε appears twice in the NT, in Eph 5.5 and Heb 12.17, and some interpreters find indicatives in those verses. (ii) The following δέ—which some have found strange enough to consider part of a traditional sentence[37]—can be given adversative sense if ἴστε is indicative: 'You know this, my beloved brothers. But let...' (iii) An imperative makes for a rougher transition from v. 18.

Other observations outweigh these: (i) James, in the manner of the diatribe, likes to open new sections with imperatives, including in chap. 1.[38] (ii) James typically uses the vocative ἀδελφοί with imperatives.[39]

---

[32] So Boismard, 'Liturgie', 172.

[33] See the Introduction, 67-70. On the lack of a christological element see above, 34-36, 70.

[34] P74V 02 629*V 2464 **K**:S^mss B^mss insert δέ in second place whereas a few late mss. (1751 1838 2147) and over a dozen lectionaries altogether omit the verb, whose significance interpreters debate. 025 044 5 69 93* 206 312 *et al.* **Byz** L1442 PsOec S:H^T read ὥστε instead. This ties v. 19 to v. 18. Adamson, 78, finds this cause to accept the reading; cf. Bouman, 84-87. Davids, 91, offers decisive criticism.

[35] So NRSV. Cf. Hort, 35; Ropes, 168; MHT 2.222; Dibelius, 109; Mussner, 99; Davids, 91; Martin, 44; Hartin, 95; Burchard, 80-81; Fabris, 99; *et al.*

[36] Cf. Bede *ad loc.* CCSL 121, ed. Hurst, 190; Bassett, 20; Wandel, 63-64; Bisping, 27 (urging that the reference is not to v. 18 but to what follows); Mayor, 65; Gaugusch, 18; Bardenhewer, 48; Chaine, 27; Schlatter, 139; Reicke, 19-20; Johnson, 199; Popkes, 128; McKnight, 135 n. 8. Note 3 Macc 3.14: ἧς ἴστε καὶ αὐτοί = 'of which you yourselves are aware'.

[37] E.g. Jülicher, *Einleitung*, 202; Dibelius, 109; Davids, 91.

[38] 1.2, 5, 9, 16, 22; 2.12; 3.1; 4.11; 5.1, 7, 12.

[39] 1.2, 16; 2.5; 3.1; 4.11; 5.7, 9, 10, 12, 19. In 2.1, 14; and 3.12 the vocative appears in questions. Only in 3.10 does it belong to a declarative sentence.

(iii) The indicative in 4.4 is οἴδατε, not ἴστε. (iv) δέ—assuming it is original; see n. 41—need not be adversative. Often in James it has continuative or transitional sense,[40] and in 2.23 the καί of LXX Gen 15.6 becomes δέ with no alteration in meaning. (v) A thematic transition from v. 18 to v. 19 is likely, and there are rough transitions throughout James. It is best, then, to hold that 1.19a introduces a new section with a series of fresh imperatives.

ἔστω δὲ πᾶς ἄνθρωπος ταχὺς εἰς τὸ ἀκοῦσαι, βραδὺς εἰς τὸ λαλῆσαι, βραδὺς εἰς ὀργήν.[41] The readers should be all ears. ἔστω appears only here in James, but 1.13 supplies another example of a third person imperative (λεγέτω). The function of δέ, as just noted, is unclear; it is often not translated.[42] For ἄνθρωπος (only here in James with πᾶς) see on v. 7. ταχύς is a Jamesian *hapax* occurring over 50× in the LXX; ταχὺς εἰς τό, however, is a non-LXX Semitism.[43] ἀκούω recurs in 2.5 and 5.11, but in neither case does it have the general scope it does here. Adderley, 18, paraphrases: 'be teachable'.[44] Ps.-Oecumenius *ad loc.* PG 119.465B, however, thinks rather of a listening that leads to action. βραδύς[45] shows up elsewhere as a contrast for ταχύς in balanced, proverbial-like statements.[46] λαλῆσαι[47] is as unqualified as ἀκοῦσαι.[48] On the issue of whether ὀργή[49] is comprehensive or covers only unjustified anger see below, 299-300.

---

[40] 1.5, 9, 15; 2.2, 3, 16, 23, 25; 3.18. For this use of δέ see A. Robertson, *Grammar*, 1181-83.

[41] Presumably in order to eliminate a perceived contrast between vv. 19a and b, δέ is dropped in 025C 044 0246 5 69 88 206 *et al.* **Byz** Antioch Carp Dam GregAgr PsOec S:H **A G**:G-D. And 02(*Vf) 33 81 **L**:PS-AM fi have καὶ ἔστω, which might be construed as proper interpretation: the δέ is not adversative but continuative.

[42] Burchard, 81, suggests it either marks opposition to the negation in v. 16 or the change from second to third person; cf. LSJ, s.v., II.4.

[43] See below. James supplies the earliest instance of ταχὺς εἰς τό + infinitive. Ps.-Lucian, *Epig.* 11.431 appears to be the earliest non-Christian example, of which there are next to none.

[44] Cf. Diodati *ad loc.*

[45] NT: 3×: Lk 24.25; Jas: 1.19 *bis*. LXX: 1×. Gk. Pseudepigrapha (Denis): 1×. Philo: 25×. Josephus: 14×.

[46] Cf. Aristophanes, *Ran.* 1428 (πάτραν βραδὺς πέφανται, μεγάλα δὲ βλάπτειν ταχύς); Philo, *Conf.* 48 (βραδὺς ὠφελῆσαι, ταχὺς βλάψαι); Plutarch, *Mor.* 1006A (ὀξὺς μὲν γὰρ ὁ ταχὺς γίγνεται βαρὺς δὲ ὁ βραδύς); Libanius, *Ep.* 957.2 (ὁ βραδὺς μὲν εἰς δίκην, ταχὺς δὲ εἰς χάριν); *Progymn.* 8.8.12 (ταχὺς ὁ ἵππος, ἀλλ' οὐδὲ ὁ βοῦς βραδύς).

[47] λαλέω: cf. 2.12; 5.10.

[48] But James would not have objected to Gill, 783: 'to hear' is not an exhortation about 'any thing; not idle and unprofitable talk, or filthy and corrupt communication'. Cf. Godfridus, *Hom. dom.* 52 PL 174.350B; Wolzogen, 187. Some have similarly explained that 'slow to speak' has nothing to do with either the language of adoration or evangelical witness; see e.g. E. de Pressensé, *The Mystery of Suffering and Other Discourses*, New York, 1869, 174-80.

[49] Jas: 2×: 1.19-20.

Although James' advice is thoroughly conventional,[50] Samuel Johnson says somewhere that we 'are more often required to be reminded than informed'. One presumes James would agree as he could not have been under the mistaken impression that he was promoting novelties.

Of the first two imperatives Trapp remarks: 'We read oft, "He that hath an ear to hear, let him hear"; but never, he that hath a tongue to speak, let him speak; for this we can do fast enough, without bidding'.[51] On the third imperative, Bede comments: James 'does not forbid the swiftness of anger in such a way that he approves of its slowness but rather advises that even at a time of upset and quarreling we avoid letting anger creep in...'[52]

Texts that recommend listening,[53] that counsel measured speech,[54] that warn against anger,[55] and that combine directions about speech or listening

---

[50] Ecclesiastical commentators have recognized this. Bede *ad loc.* CCSL 121 ed. Hurst, 190, for instance, illustrates our verse by referring to the Pythagoreans; cf. Lapide, 63; Gill, 783 (who also cites Jewish proverbs). Pareus, 548, *et al.* refer to the Stoics.

[51] Trapp, 695. He tacks on a bit of natural theology: 'hath not Nature taught us the same that the apostle here doth, by giving us two ears, and those open; and but one tongue, and that hedged in with teeth and lips?' Cf. Plutarch in n. 53.

[52] Bede *ad loc.* CCSL 121, ed. Hurst, 190.

[53] Cf. Prov 19.20; Ecclus 5.11 (with ταχὺς ἐν ἀκροάσει); 6.33; 4Q412 1 5 ('Place a binding on your lips and for your tongue doors of protection'); 4Q420 1 2.1 ('one should not answer before one has listened'); Philo, *Abr.* 29 (the 'unbridled mouth' always 'gives utterance where silence is due'); *Her.* 10-11 (some should 'be silent with the tongue and listen with the ears'); b. Šabb. 88a (this rebukes those who 'gave precedence to your mouth over your ears'); Plutarch, *Mor.* 39B ('It is a common saying that nature has given us two ears and one tongue because we ought to do less talking than listening'; Diogenes Laertius 7.23 attributes this proverb to Zeno); ibid. (people should 'hear much but not speak much'); Dio Chrysostom 32.2 ('I...should prefer to praise you as being slow to speak', βραδύ...φθεγγομένους); Lucian, *Dem.* 51 ('Speak little, hear much').

[54] Cf. Plato, *Leg.* 701C ('I must, every time, rein in my discourse like a horse, and not let it run away with me as though it had no bridle in its mouth'); Diogenes Laertius 1.88 (ταχὺ λάλει), 94 ('be listeners rather than talkers'); 104 ('Bridle speech'—a maxim of Anacharsis); Plutarch, *De garrulitate passim* (see on this W.A. Beardslee, 'De Garrulitate (Moralia 502B-515A)', in H.D. Betz, ed., *Plutarch's Ethical Writings and Early Christian Literature*, Leiden, 264-88); Pss 39.1; 141.3; Prov 10.19; 13.3; 15.1; 17.27, 28; 21.23; 29.20 (with ταχὺν ἐν λόγοις); Eccl 3.7; 4.29 (with ταχύς); 5.2; Ecclus 5.11-6.1; 14.1; 19.16; 20.1-8; 21.26; 22.27; 25.8; 28.13-26; 4Q525 14 2.24-25 ('First hear his words and afterwards answer with [...and with] patience bring them out'); Mt 12.36; Ps.-Phoc. 20 ('Take heed of your tongue, keep your word hidden in [your] heart'); Barn. 19.8 ('do not be quick to speak, for the mouth is a deadly snare'); m. 'Abot 1.15 ('Say little, do much'), 17 ('Too much talk causes sin'); b. Meṣi'a 87a ('The righteous speak little and do much; the wicked speak much and do little'); Sextus, *Sent.* 152-57 ('It is better to toss a stone without purpose than a word. Think carefully before speaking lest you say things that you should not. Words without thought deserve reproach. Excessive talking cannot avoid sin. Wisdom accompanies brevity of speech. Speaking at length is a sign of ignorance'); Sent. Syr. Menander 30.1 ('Hateful is loquacity'); Ahikar Papyrus Insinger 3.6 ('Do not let yourself be known as "the prattler" because your tongue is

with admonitions about anger[56] are beyond abundant.[57] Moreover, James' complex admonition is as conventional in form as in content. Not only was it common to issue imperatives about hearing, speaking, and being angry in short, self-contained, pithy imperatives or generalizations, but Prov 14.29 and 16.32 speak of being 'slow to anger',[58] Eccl 7.9 of being 'quick to anger',[59] and Ecclus 5.11 of being 'quick to hear'.[60] Also inviting special comparison is m. 'Abot 5.11, where we read of four different temperaments—easy to anger and easy to be appeased,[61] hard to anger and hard to be appeased,[62] hard to anger and easy to be appeased,[63] and easy to anger and hard to be appeased[64]—and 5.12, which refers to

everywhere'); al-Ghazzali, *Revival of Religious Sciences* 3.80.6 ('Jesus was asked guidance about entering paradise. He said: "Do not ever speak". His disciples said: "We cannot do that". He said: "Then never speak anything but good"').

[55] Cf. Ps 37.8; Prov 14.29; LXX 15.1; 16.32; 29.11; Eccl 7.9; Ecclus 1.21-22 (Frankemölle, 328, suggests that James draws on this); 27.30; 30.24; Let. Aris. 253-54 ('God governs the whole universe with kindliness and without any anger, and you, O King, must follow him'); 1QH 9.36-37 (האריכו אפים: 'be slow to anger'); 1QS 5.25; Mt 5.22; Josephus, *Bell.* 2.135 (the Essenes are praised because they hold 'righteous anger in reserve' and are 'masters of their temper'); T. Dan 2.2 ('there is blindness in anger'); 3.1 ('anger is evil'); 4.3 ('When anyone speaks to you, do not be moved to anger'); Ps.-Phoc. 57 ('Bridle your wild anger', cf. 63-64); Did. 3.2; Herm. *Mand.* 5.1-2; m. 'Abot 2.10 ('Do not be easily angered'); Sifre Num. 157 (the few times Moses fell into error it was because he gave way to anger); b. Pesaḥ. 66b ('As to every man who becomes angry, if he is a sage, his wisdom departs from him. If he is a prophet, his prophecy departs from him'); b. Ned. 22b (angry students forget what they learn and become more and more stupid, and the sins of angry people outweigh their merits). Some dedicated entire treatises to this subject; recall Seneca's *De ira*. For an introduction to the subject see W.V. Harris, *Restraining Rage*, Cambridge, MA, 2001; see 127-28 for a list of fragments of and references to additional treatises.

[56] Cf. Prov 17.27; Pss. Sol. 16.10 ('Protect my tongue and my lips with words of truth; put anger and thoughtless rage far from me'); Mt 5.21-26; Col 3.8; Lucian, *Demon.* 5.1 ('Do not lose your temper... Do little talking and much listening'); Ahiqar saying 15 ed. Lindenberger, 75 ('Above all else, guard your mouth; and as for what you have h[eard], be discreet! For a word is a bird, and he who releases it is a fool'); Pap. Insinger 21.14-17 ('He who guards his heart and his tongue sleeps without an enemy. He who reveals a secret matter, his house will burn. He who repeats it out of impatience is one who defiles his tongue. He who turns away from his anger is one who is far from the anger of the god'); ARN A 1 ('One should be patient in his speech and not lose temper in his speech'). Cicero, *Ep. (Q. Fr. I.1)* 30.13, writes: 'when the mind is most under its [anger's] influence is just the time when you should be most careful to bridle your tongue'. He adds that the ability to do so is 'a mark of no slight natural ability'.

[57] See further Baker, *Speech-Ethics*, 23-83.
[58] ארך אפים, *bis*; LXX: μακρόθυμος, *bis*; cf. 1QH 9.36-37.
[59] תבהל...לבעוס; LXX: σπεύσῃς... τοῦ θυμοῦσθαι.
[60] היה ממהר להאזין; ταχὺς ἐν ἀκροάσει. On this see below, 299.
[61] נוח לבעוס ונוח לרצות.
[62] קשה לבעוס וקשה לרצות.
[63] קשה לבעוס ונוח לרצות.
[64] נוח לבעוס וקשה לרצות.

students 'quick to learn and quick to forget'[65] or 'slow to learn and slow to forget'[66] or 'quick to learn and slow to forget'[67] or 'slow to learn and quick to forget'.[68] It was common to combine the advice to speak slowly or little on the one hand with the advice to listen on the other just as it was also common to link the theme of controlling speech with that of controlling anger.[69] Perhaps implicit in James then is the idea that those who are quick to hear will be slow to speak, and that those thus acting will find it easier to avoid anger.[70]

James does not appear to cite or allude to any text in particular, although some have thought Ecclus 5.11 ('Be quick to hear and deliberate in answering')[71] such a candidate.[72] Others have suspected that James here reproduces a proverb.[73] There is no proof of this.[74] It is more likely, given the links to the broader context, that he composed the triadic injunction.[75] The many related texts establish only dependence upon tradition, not the mechanical reproduction of a fixed sentence. One guesses that James, who was adept at aphoristic formulations, reworked traditional materials the same way others in turn later reworked our sentence; cf. Theodore the Studite, *Catech. magn.* 17 ed. Papadopoulos-Kerameus, 119 (ἔστω βραδὺς εἰς ὀργήν, ταχὺς εἰς ὑπακοήν, ταχύτερος εἰς τὸ λέγειν συγχώρησον); *Ep.* 127 ed. Fatouros, 244 (ὁ βραδὺς εἰς ὀργὴν καὶ ταχὺς εἰς οἰκτιρμούς).

The Hebrew Bible, like Aristotle, allows for justified anger.[76] The same is true of many early Christian writings. Eph 4.26 counsels, for example, 'Be angry, but do not sin; do not let the sun go down on your anger'. In Mt 5.21-26, on the other hand, Matthew's Jesus (at least

---

[65] מהר לשמוע ומהר לאבד.
[66] קשה לשמוע וקשה לאבד.
[67] מהר לשמוע וקשה לאבד.
[68] קשה לשמוע ומהר לאבד.
[69] Note also Pss. Sol. 16.10: 'Establish my tongue and my lips in words of truth; remove from me anger and wrath which is unreasoning'.
[70] So Baker, *Speech Ethics*, 87. According to G. Stählin, 'ὀργή κτλ.', *TDNT* 5.446, by anger James has in mind mainly sins of the tongue.
[71] היה ממהר להאזין ובארך רוח השב פתגם; γίνου ταχὺς ἐν ἀκροάσει σου καὶ ἐν μακροθυμίᾳ φθέγγου ἀπόκρισιν.
[72] Cf. Bisping, 27; Frankemölle, 327; Farley, 24.
[73] See esp. Dibelius, 108-11. Cf. Davids, 91; Cheung, *Genre*, 66; Witherington, 438-39; Blomberg-Kamell, 85.
[74] There appears to be no pre-Jamesian example of a succinct, threefold imperative dealing with listening, speaking, and being angry.
[75] So too Frankemölle, 327; Popkes, 128.
[76] E.g. Ps 4.4 ('When you are angry, do not sin'); Ecclus 1.22 ('unrighteous anger cannot be justified'—a sentiment which implies that a righteous anger can be justified). There are also scriptural examples of heroes becoming angry for a righteous cause—Moses (Exod 32.19) and Jeremiah (Jer 6.11), for instance. God, furthermore, is often said to be angry or full of wrath: Exod 4.14; Deut 1.37; Josh 22.18; etc. From the Greek tradition one may note, in addition to Aristotle's discussion in *Nichomachean Ethics*, Plutarch, *Mor.* 448D: there is an irrational anger and a justified anger.

according to the modern critical texts)[77] does not say that people should not be angry for the wrong reason nor imply that there might be some good reason for being angry with another. He seemingly, like the Stoics and some later monastics,[78] prohibits the emotion altogether.[79] One could suppose that James' phrase, 'slow to anger' (1.19), belongs with Eph 4.26, that is, with those texts that warn against anger yet imply its inevitability and perhaps even occasional usefulness; see above, 288. 1.20, however, appears to be a general prohibition: human anger does not achieve God's righteousness. Perhaps the tension is illusory and 'slow to anger' does not imply any sort of justified anger; or, on the contrary, maybe v. 20 assumes there is another sort of anger—justified anger—that is beyond its scope.[80] Then again maybe the tension is real, in which case one may compare Matthew, in which Jesus condemns anger and yet, to the consternation of interpreters, angrily makes protest in the temple and angrily rebukes the scribes and Pharisees.

Although πᾶς ἄνθρωπος is not uncommon in Greek texts, it is characteristic of the LXX, and ἔστω πᾶς ἄνθρωπος, with or without δέ, is not a Greek expression. It occurs only in James and later quotations of James. πᾶς ἄνθρωπος is likely Semitic, reflecting the common Hebrew כל־איש or כל־אדם,[81] or maybe the Aramaic כל (בר) אנש.[82] The rest of the line also looks Semitic. James' ἔστω δὲ πᾶς ἄνθρωπος is the precise equivalent of the common rabbinic יהא כל אחד.[83] Moreover, the expected μέν...δέ contrast is missing from James;[84] ταχὺς εἰς τό[85] + infinitive followed by

[77] Most modern scholars and exegetes reckon the εἰκῆ in v. 22 secondary.

[78] See esp. John, *Inst.* 8 SC 109 ed. Guy, 336-66. Cassian cites Jas 1.19 near the beginning of his discussion, in 8.1.2. Jerome, *Mt ad* 5.22 SC 242 ed. Bonnard, 112, rejects *sina causa* as secondary and cites James when construing Mt 5.22 as an absolute prohibition of anger.

[79] Maier, 92, thinks it possible that James has Jesus' teaching in that passage in mind. So too Witherington, 439. Others cite it to illustrate James: Nicholas of Gorran, 70; Hus, 191; *et al.* For von Gemünden, 'Wertung', James, Mt 5.21-26 and Did 3.2 ('Do not become angry, for anger leads to murder') attest a radical rejection of anger on the part of Jewish Christians in Syria near the beginning of the second century. Popkes, 129, rather suggests a customary instruction for Christian neophytes.

[80] In this case, one could even regard the command to be slow to anger as part of the *imitatio dei*, because the prophets more than once speak of God as being slow to anger: Joel 2.13; Jon 4.2; Nah 1.3 (in each case the Hebrew is ארך אפים, the Greek μακρόθυμος). Note also Neh 9.17; Pss 103.8; 145.8.

[81] πᾶς ἄνθρωπος translates כל־איש in LXX Lev 21.18; 22.3; Deut 4.3; and Esth 4.11, כל־אדם in LXX Gen 7.21; Lev 16.17; Deut 27.26; Job 21.33; 36.25; 37.7; Jer 10.14. For πᾶς ἄνθρωπος in the NT see 1.9; 2.10; Gal 5.3; Col 1.28; cf. Jos. Asen. 28.7; T. Abr. RecLng. 13.3, 5, 7.

[82] πᾶς ἄνθρωπος and כל בר אנש appear in the Greek and Syriac versions of Pss. Sol. 2.11, and the former translates כל־אנש in Ezra 6.11; Dan 3.10; 6.13.

[83] Cf. m. Suk. 4.4; t. Raš. Haš. 1.18; t. Ḥag. 3.19; y. Ber. 6b (3.3). ἔστω translates יהי in LXX Gen 1.6; 30.34; 33.9; Deut 33.6; etc.

[84] Contrast Dio Chrysostom 32.2 (βραδὺ μὲν φθεγγομένους, ἐγκρατῶς δὲ σιγῶντας, ὀρθῶς δὲ διανοουμένους); also the quotations from Isocrates and Aristotle in n. 86.

βραδὺς εἰς (τό) + infinitive (*bis*) seemingly has its closest parallel in m. 'Abot 5.11-12, where ל + קשה alternates with ל + נוח or ל + מהר;[86] and James' memorable triadic arrangement—

ταχὺς εἰς τὸ ἀκοῦσαι
βραδὺς εἰς τὸ λαλῆσαι[87]
βραδὺς εἰς ὀργήν—

reminds one of how often 'Abot passes on proverbial-like utterances with three clauses in close parallel[88]—sometimes with the last irregular member receiving the emphasis.[89]

Even if, as in this commentary, one identifies the 'word' of vv. 18 and 21 with Torah, it seems unlikely that v. 19 has special application to the law in particular—or to the gospel, if one equates James' λόγος with that.

[85] εἰς τό here means 'with respect to'; cf. 1 Thess 4.19. In 1.18 it denotes purpose.

[86] These are the closest Greek parallels: Theognis, *Eleg.* 1.329 (βραδὺς εὔβουλος εἷλεν ταχὺν ἄνδρα διώκων); Isocrates, *Ad Dem.* 34 (βουλεύου μὲν βραδέως, ἐπιτέλει δὲ ταχέως τὰ δόξαντα); Aristotle, *Eth. nic.* 1142B (πράττειν μὲν δεῖν ταχὺ τὰ βουλευθέντα, βουλεύσται δὲ βραδέως); Philo, *Conf.* 48 (βραδὺς ὠφελῆσαι, ταχὺς βλάψαι); Dio Chrysostom 32.2 (see n. 84). Pace Klein, *Werk*, 119 n. 2, James' wordplay with ταχύς and βραδύς is not, despite these parallels, typically Greek rather than typically Jewish, nor is Dibelius, 111, correct to assert that Jas 1.19b 'has its real charm only in Greek'. Why would

מהר לשמוע
קשה לדבר
וקשה לכעוס

lack 'real charm'?

[87] Note that the first two clauses rhyme and have the same number of syllables.

[88] E.g. 1.1, 2, 4, 5a, 7, 15, 16, 17, 18; 2.10, 12, 13. Cf. Sent. Syr. Men. 99-101 ('Do not laugh at the words of the aged, nor curl your lips at the aged, and do not despise the poor'), 173-74 ('Do not leave the way, and do not go astray, and do not walk wickedly'), 213-16 ('Do not despise your friends, and do not dishonor those who honor you; and he with whom you had a meal, do not walk with him in a treacherous way'); Ahiqar saying 5 ed. Lindenberger, 53 ('A blow for a serving-boy, a rebuke for a slave-girl, and for all your servants, discipline').

[89] 1.6: 'Get yourself a teacher
and get yourself a fellow-disciple
and when you judge any man incline the balance in his favor'

1.10: 'Love labor
and hate mastery
and do not make yourself known to the ruling power'

3.1: 'Know whence you come
and (know) whither you go
and (know) before whom you are to give a strict account'

3.13: 'Be submissive to the ruler
and patient under oppression
and receive every person with cheerfulness'

For additional examples of the concluding member of a series being irregular for emphasis or for closure see Allison, *Tradition*, 97-104.

The meaning is rather comprehensive: one should always be swift to hear and slow to speak.[90] One could surmise that one should be quick to hear Scripture or the gospel and/or slow to teach others.[91] But 'slow to anger' then seems out of place;[92] and neither 'to hear' nor 'to speak' is given an object (such as 'word' or 'law'). It seems better, then, to interpret v. 19 as the sort of general advice applicable to all sorts of situations.[93] Thus those who link 1.19 with various parts of James are in harmony with the spirit of the text even if, in the manner of proverbial wisdom, the verse intentionally leaves itself open to wide application. Cf. Cassian: 'In every respect be quick to hear and slow to speak'.[94]

Verse 20. It seems likely that, in v. 19, the irregularity of βραδὺς εἰς ὀργήν over against the preceding clauses—it lacks τό + infinitive—as well as its position in last place make it emphatic. Thus it is natural that James, in the very next verse, elaborates not on listening and speaking but on anger. At the same time, and as already noted, perhaps being slow to speak and quick to hear are aspects of controlling anger, in which case v. 20 grounds not just the last part of v. 19 but the verse in its entirety. In either case there is again no need to posit opponents or misinformed Christians who take the position James refutes: the sins of vv. 19-21 scarcely characterizes any particular group.

One can oppose anger for prudential reasons, such as that anger begets more anger. James, however, justifies his imperative on theological grounds: anger does not accord with God's will.

ὀργὴ γὰρ ἀνδρὸς δικαιοσύνην θεοῦ οὐκ ἐργάζεται.[95] For ἀνήρ see on v. 8. Bisping, 27, remarks: the wrath of man does not work the

[90] So most interpreters. This is the common paraenetical application; cf. John Cassian, *Conf.* 14,9,5 SC 54 ed. Pichery, 194. As usual, Gill, 783, spreads his interpretive net as wide as possible: 'to hear' refers to 'wholesome advice, good instructions, and the gracious experiences of the saints, and, above all, the word of God'.

[91] Cf. Dionysius bar Salībī *ad loc.* CSCO 60 Scriptores Syri 101 ed. Sedlacek, 119; Pareus, 548; Poole, 883; Manton, 128; Burkitt, 1018; Trapp, 695 ('life doth now enter into the soul at the ear, as at first death did, Gen. iii'); Guyse, 569; Baumgarten, 62; Gibson, 16; Bardenhewer, 49; Cranfield, 'Message', 186; Simon, 96-98; Grünzweig, 54-56; Cantinat, 100; Collins, 'Coherence'.

[92] Cf. Schrage, 22. Contrast Collins, 'Coherence': James opposes anger occasioned by the moral exhortation of teachers in church; cf. Manton, 136-37; Senior, 'Sermon VII', 53-54; Grünzweig, 56; Roberts, 56. Also dubious are the proposals that James opposes anger against God in particular (Bengel, 490) or anger linked to agitation against Rome (Reicke, 21; Martin, 48) or anger occasioned by Judaizing Christians (Hammond, 679).

[93] So too Moo, 82, who observes that the many parallels in the Jewish wisdom tradition support a more general application. The common application of 1.19 to teachers in particular overlooks the global address—'my beloved brothers…everyone'.

[94] John Cassian, *Inst.* 14.9.5 SC 54 ed. Pichery, 194.

[95] 04* 025 0246 88 206 *et al.* **Byz** Antioch Ath PsOec Sl:ChDMSiS have οὐ κατεργάζεται (cf. 1.3). This accords with a scribal tendency to strengthen verbs; cf. Hort, 36: 'A natural correction: this word more distinctly expresses result'.

righteousness of God but its opposite, the wrath of God. γάρ[96] makes v. 20 the basis for the preceding assertion. ὀργὴ ἀνδρός—the genitive, instead of being generic, 'of man', might be a particular individual: 'of a man'[97]—is not a traditional term but appears to be James' *ad hoc* formulation on the analogy of the conventional δικαιοσύνη θεοῦ.[98] ἐργάζομαι recurs in 2.9: ἁμαρτίαν ἐργάζεσθε.

ἐργάζομαι + δικαιοσύνη appears only once in the LXX, in Ps 14.2.[99] One might wonder whether our text alludes to that one.[100] It is indeed striking that both passages use the combination in a context having to do with speech ethics. Still, we have inadequate cause to see an allusion, and the history of interpretation offers negligible support. It probably suffices to see here simply a traditional expression: ἐργάζομαι + δικαιοσύνη, which derives from עשׂה + צדק(ה),[101] occurs in other texts.[102]

Some exegetes seek to clarify ὀργή by distinguishing it from θυμός. Mitton, 61, suggests that the latter 'means a passionate outburst of anger', the former 'not so much a passing display of temper, but rather that which expresses persistent dislike of another person and hostility to him'.[103] This allows one to argue that James is not condemning the inevitable momentary outburst but only cultivated hatred. Perhaps this reading is not just wishful thinking. For although ὀργή and θυμός are usually indistinguishable in the biblical tradition, Hellenistic thinkers and the church fathers did tend to define them differently. In the words of Diogenes Laertius 7.114, θυμός is the beginning of ὀργή; that is, the former is the transient passion which can harden into the fixed hostility that is the latter.[104]

---

[96] Jas: 15×, only here separating nominative subject and genitive.

[97] So Rosenmüller, 338. Even if it contradicts contemporary sensitivities, Mayor, 65, may be right: 'The choice of ἀνήρ here, instead of ἄνθρωπος, was probably determined by the facts of the case; the speakers would be men, and they might perhaps imagine that there was something manly in violence as opposed to the feminine quality of πραΰτης...' Bengel, 490, has the same thought. Burchard, 81, leaves this possibility open.

[98] Cf. Deut 33.21 (צדקת יהוה); Bar 5.2 (τῆς παρὰ τοῦ θεοῦ δικαιοσύνης); 1QS 1.21 (צדקות אל); 10.23 (צדקות אל), 25 (צדקת אל); 11.12 (צדקת אל); 1QM 4.6 (צדק אל); T. Dan 6.10 v.l. (τῇ δικαιοσύνῃ τοῦ θεοῦ); T. Abr. RecLng. 13.10; Mt 6.33; Rom 1.17; 3.5, 21, 22, 25-26; 10.3; 2 Cor 5.21; Phil 3.9; 2 Pet 1.1; 1 Clem. 18.15; Pol. *Phil.* 5.2.

[99] 'O Lord, who will sojourn in your tabernacle? and who will encamp in your holy mountain? The one walking blamelessly and doing righteousness (ἐργαζόμενος δικαιοσύνην; MT: פעל צדק), speaking truth in his heart.'

[100] There is no real connection with Ecclus 1.22 (οὐ δυνήσεται θυμὸς ἄδικος δικαιωθῆναι), which is often cited for comparison.

[101] As in Gen 18.19; Ps 106.3; Prov 21.3; Isa 56.1; 64.5; 4Q421 1 2.13; 11Q5 19.7; t. Sanh. 1.4, 5; etc.

[102] Cf. Philo, *Congr.* 31; Acts 10.35; Heb 11.33; Herm. *Vis.* 2.2.7; 2.3.3; *Mand.* 5.1.1; 12.3.1.

[103] Cf. Bassett, 21: ὀργή is the feeling of anger, θυμός its outward eruption.

[104] But contrast Jerome, *Gal ad* 5.19-21 CCSL 77A ed. Raspanti, 188, where the 'anger' of Jas 1.20 is occasional, 'wrath' by contrast constant. See further the texts cited in Trench, *Synonyms*, 130-33; van der Horst, *Sentences*, 156-57.

What does δικαιοσύνη θεοῦ mean?[105] One hesitates, despite Pauline usage, to equate it with the gift of righteous status divinely bestowed on human beings.[106] Nor is it likely to mean 'justice', if that means God, through God's people, making things right in this world or the world to come.[107] Most believe that, as so often with צדק in the Dead Sea Scrolls and Tannaitic literature,[108] and as with δικαιοσύνη in Matthew, Luke–Acts, and Hebrews, the word here refers to conduct in accord with the divine will—'the righteousness that God desires of us'.[109] ἐργάζομαι + δικαιοσύνην is thus the antithesis of ἐργάζομαι + ἁμαρτίαν (2.9). One may compare δικαιοσύνη in LXX Ps 14.1-2 (see n. 99) and Herm. *Mand.* 12.3.1 (ἔργασαι δικαιοσύνην)[110] as well as Tgs. Ps.-J. and Onq. on Deut 33.21, which turn 'he executed the righteousness of God' into 'he did righteous deeds before the Lord'. In Jas 2.23 and 3.18, δικαιοσύνη also appears to refer to proper human behavior.[111]

21. Although usually joined to vv. 19-20, several commentators have thought of v. 21 as the introduction to vv. 22-25.[112] But (i) the only other occurrence of 'wherefore' (διό) does not introduce a new section; see 4.6. (ii) Linking v. 21 with vv. 19-20 leaves intact the structural parallel

---

[105] One cannot regard 'the righteousness of God'—see the texts in n. 98—as a technical term with a fixed meaning; see M.A. Seifrid, *Justification by Faith*, Leiden, 1992, 99-108.

[106] Pace Mayor, 66; Frankemölle, 328; McKnight, 139, the latter construing 'righteousness' as not only obedience to the moral code but also God's gift. Royster, 31-32, takes James to refer to God's faithfulness to redeem humanity. It remains possible that James here stands under Pauline influence; but the phrase could come from Paul and yet bear unPauline meaning; cf. Dibelius, 111. Much less likely is influence from the Jesus tradition, although Cantinat, 102, citing Mt 5.6, 20; 6.33, thinks otherwise.

[107] But some have compared Rom 12.19, where vengeance is to be left to God; and others have supposed James to be combatting people with a theocratic agenda during the Jewish war; so e.g. Martin, 47-48, citing in agreement Reicke and Townsend.

[108] See B. Przybylski, *Righteousness in Matthew and His World of Thought*, Cambridge, UK, 1980. One should note that the LXX translators 'understood that the meaning of "righteousness" could not be reduced to the idea of "salvation", and in at least some instances entirely shift the meaning to a forensic or ethical field'; so M.A. Seifrid, 'Paul's Use of Righteousness Language against Its Hellenistic Background', in *Justification and Variegated Nomism*, vol. 2, ed. D.A. Carson, P.T. O'Brien, and M.A. Seifrid, Tübingen, 2004, 52.

[109] So Valpy, 239; cf. Grotius, 1076 (citing Mt 5.20); Wolzogen, 188; Poole, 883; Wesley, 858; Schneckenburger, 37; Gaugusch, 19; Ropes, 168-69; Bardenhewer, 49; R. Wall, 71; Moo, 83-84; Isaacs, 192; Fabris, 102-103; Blomberg-Kamell, 86; Gundry, 922; *et al.*

[110] Note also Herm. *Mand.* 5.2.1, where 'ill temper' leads God's servants away from δικαιοσύνη.

[111] Godfridus, *Hom. dom.* 52 PL 174.350D-351B, bases his interesting exposition of our passage upon the proposal that the 'justia' of God is returning good for evil, the 'justia' of human beings is returning good for good and evil for evil, and the 'justia' of the devil is returning evil for good.

[112] E.g. Oesterley, 431; Dibelius, 112; Moo, 85.

between vv. 16-18 and 18-21; see above, 293. (iii) Verse 21 does not directly bear on the theme of hearing and doing, which is the chief concern of vv. 22-25. (iv) Verse 21 directly relates itself to vv. 19-20 in two ways. ἐν πραΰτητι implicitly continues the condemnation of anger, and anger must be included within 'all sordidness and profusion of evil'.

διὸ ἀποθέμενοι πᾶσαν ῥυπαρίαν καὶ περισσείαν κακίας. διό—some suggest this refers back not to vv. 19-20 but to v. 18a—recurs in 4.6; ἀποτίθημι, ῥυπαρία, περισσεία, and κακία appear only here in James. This commentary takes πᾶσαν ῥυπαρίαν and περισσείαν κακίας to be two separate albeit closely related items.[113] One could, however, link πᾶσαν ῥυπαρίαν as well as περισσείαν to the genitive κακίας: 'all sordidness (of evil) and all excesses of evil'.[114] Structurally, πᾶσαν ῥυπαρίαν καὶ περισσείαν κακίας recalls v. 16: πᾶσα δόσις ἀγαθὴ καὶ πᾶν δώρημα τέλειον. In both cases two synonyms or near synonyms are joined by καί and are universalized through words that create alliteration and consonance. Our line also resembles 1.13-15, where human beings are held responsible for their own sins; for the present verse assumes, in the words of Richardson, 91, that 'however much evil practices are rooted in the memory and structure of desire within the human soul, they are effectively dealt with as activities distinct from believers themselves'. In other words, sordidness and evil are seemingly neither necessary nor permanent elements of human nature: one can be rid of them.

ἀποθέμενοι takes up traditional paraenetical language which, many have guessed, had its setting in baptismal ritual, perhaps in the shedding of garments.[115] One may compare the following:

- Rom 13.12: 'Let us then lay aside (ἀποθώμεθα οὖν) the works of darkness...'
- Eph 4.21-22: 'You were taught to put away (ἀποθέσθαι) your former life, your old self, corrupted and deluded by its lusts'
- Eph 4.25: 'Wherefore putting away (διὸ ἀποθέμενοι) falsehood...'
- Col 3.8: 'But now you must get rid (ἀπόθεσθε) of all (πάντα) such things—anger (ὀργήν), wrath, malice (κακίαν), slander, and abusive language from your mouth'
- Heb 12.1: 'Therefore (τοιγαροῦν)...let us lay aside (ἀποθέμενοι) every (πάντα) weight and the sin that clings so closely...'

---

[113] Hilary of Arles *ad loc.* PLSup 3.67, traces them both to the sin of anger. Maier, 93, thinks anger is their 'representative'; cf. von Gemünden, 'Wertung', 111: πᾶσαν ῥυπαρίαν κτλ. takes up the ὀργή of v. 20.

[114] Windisch-Preisker, 10, translates: 'die ganze Schmutzmasse der Schlechtigkeit', that is, 'the great filthy mass of wickedness'. One can also think of πᾶσαν as qualifying both ῥυπαρίαν and καὶ περισσείαν.

[115] Cf. Knoch, 167 ('we can be sure St. James is thinking here of baptism'); Schrage, 22; Popkes, *Adressaten*, 146-56; Scaer, 65; Fabris, *Legge*, 191-94; *et al.* Contrast Frankemölle, 330-32. For the verb used of taking off clothes see 2 Macc 8.35; Jos. Asen. 10.10; 13.3; 14.12; Acts 7.58; Mart. Pol. 13.2; etc.

- 1 Pet 2.1: 'Rid yourselves therefore (ἀποθέμενοι οὖν) of all malic (πᾶσαν κακίαν), and all (πάντα) guile, insincerity, envy, and all (πάσας) slander'[116]
- 1 Clem. 13.1: 'Let us, therefore (οὖν), be humble-minded, brothers, putting aside (ἀποθέμενοι) all (πᾶσαν) arrogance and conceit and foolishness and wrath (ὀργάς)...'
- Herm. Sim. 9.23.5: 'Whoever holds this view must put it aside (ἀπόθεσθε) and repent...'
- Mart. Mt 6 ed. Bonnet, 223: τὸ ἀμέτρητον μέγεθος τῆς κακίας ἀποθέμενοι.

Clearly James falls in line with a Christian convention in using an inferential conjunction with ἀποθέμενοι[117] and in associating that verb with 'all'[118] as well as with κακία[119] and injunctions about speech and anger.[120] It is further noteworthy that 1 Pet 2.1 follows ἀποθέμενοι with πᾶσαν κακίαν whereas James uses πᾶσαν ῥυπαρίαν καὶ περισσείαν κακίας, and further that 1 Clem. 13.1 links ἀποθέμενοι with a call for humility, ταπεινοφρονήσωμεν.[121] Finally, one should observe the striking correlation between Jas 1.21 and 1 Pet 3.21: σαρκὸς ἀπόθεσις ῥύπου. Either 1 Peter and James 'are drawing on a common pattern of instruction, most probably for new converts'[122] and/or there is a literary relationship between James and 1 Peter.[123]

Whatever the correct solution to the source-critical issue, it is undeniable that James stands out by its lack of Christology. Romans 12.13 leads to this: 'put on the Lord Jesus Christ' (v. 14). Ephesians 4.22 is preceded by 'that is not the way you learned Christ' (v. 20). Hebrews 12.1 is followed by a call to 'look to Jesus the pioneer and perfector of our faith' (v. 2). 1 Clement 13.1 includes the demand to 'remember the words of the Lord Jesus'. As elsewhere, however, James makes no statement about Jesus. This commentary takes the view that this reflects a deliberate strategy: our author does not write as a Christian to Christians, or not only to such.

ῥυπαρία[124] appears only here in the Greek Bible.[125] The word, often used in medical writers, literally means 'filth' or 'dirt'.[126] It and its

---

[116] Cyril of Jerusalem, Catech. 19–23 5 inscription SC 126bis ed. Piédagnel, 146, understandably conflates this with Jas 1.19, borrowing διό from the latter.

[117] Rom 13.12; Eph 4.25; Heb 12.1; 1 Pet 2.1; 1 Clem. 13.1.

[118] Col 3.8; Heb 12.1; 1 Pet 2.1; 1 Clem. 13.1.

[119] Col 3.8; 1 Pet 2.1; Mart. Mt 6 ed. Bonnet, 223.

[120] Col 3.8; 1 Pet 2.1. Note also the use of ὀργίζω and παροργίζω in Eph 4.26.

[121] Davids, 94, uses the parallel with 1 Pet 2.1 to construe κακίας as 'malice' and then draws a connection with chap. 3. Cf. Hort, 36.

[122] So Laws, 84-85; E. Kamlah, Die Form der Katalogischen Paränese im Neuen Testament, Tübingen, 1967, 34-38, 183-89; Popkes, 133. Origen, Lk 14 GCS 49 ed. Rauer, 88, speaks of the one who 'lays aside' (ἀποτίθεται), through baptism, 'filth' (ῥύπου).

[123] For this question see the Introduction, 67-70; also above, 294.

[124] Gk. Pseudepigrapha (Denis): 0×. Philo: 0×. Josephus: 0×.

cognates were naturally transferred to the moral sphere.[127] But the related adjective, ῥυπαρός, is used in 2.2 with nonmetaphorical sense: 'a poor person in ῥυπαρᾷ clothes'.[128] So perhaps ἀποθέμενοι—here the participle might be an imperative[129]—suggests the removal of clothing, that is, maybe the metaphor is not altogether dead.[130] Martin, 48, however, proposes that the metaphor has to do with cleaning the ears: ῥύπος = 'earwax'.[131] This is a well-attested meaning.[132] Perhaps then ἀποθέμενοι πᾶσαν ῥυπαρίαν is a metaphorical way of emphasizing 'be quick to hear': clean out your ears.

---

[125] But note the use of the related ῥυπαρός in 2.2 and Rev 22.11. James appears to be the first extant text to make ῥυπαρία the direct subject of ἀποτίθημι.

[126] Cf. the verb, ῥυπαίνω, as in Rev 22.11. There are yet other suggestions regarding the image in v. 21. Poole, 883, thinks of excrement. For Gill, 783, the image is of 'a boiling pot, which casts up scum and filth, which must be taken off'.

[127] Cf. Philo, *Deus* 7 ('the things that make filthy [καταρρυπαίνοντα] our lives in word and thought and deed'); *Mut.* 49 ('the things making filthy [καταρρυπαίνοντα] the soul'), 124 (the soul 'washed away its defilements', καταρρυπαίνοντα); T. Jud. 14.3 ('filthy [ῥυπαροῖς] thoughts'); Epictetus, *Diatr.* 2.9.4 ('in a filthy [ῥυπαρῶς] fashion'); 2.18.25 ('throw out this filthy one' [sc. impression; ῥυπαράν]); 4.11.7 (erroneous decisions can make a soul 'dirty', ῥυπαράν); Rev 22.11 ('Let the evildoer still do evil, and the filthy [ὁ ῥυπαρός] still be filthy [ῥυπανθήτω], and the righteous still do right'); Ign. *Eph.* 16.2 ('such a one shall go in his foulness [ῥυπαρός] to the unquenchable fire'); Justin Martyr, *Dial.* 116.3 PTS 47 ed. Marcovich, 270 ('filthy [ῥυπαρά] garments' are 'sins'). Oesterley, 432, supposes that sexual sin may be particularly in view in James: 'the Syriac has טנפולא which is the same word used in Ezek. xliv. 6 for the Hebrew תועבה "abomination", meaning that which is abhorrent to God...it occurs a number of times in the later literature in reference to unchastity, this more especially in Proverbs... [In James] the word...probably means "filthiness" in the sense of lustful impurity.' Cf. Henry *ad loc.*

[128] Clothing is also involved in Zech 3.3-4 LXX ('clothed in filthy garments', ἐνδεδυμένος ἱμάτια ῥυπαρά; 'take away the filthy garments from him', ἀφέλετε τὰ ἱμάτια τὰ ῥυπαρὰ ἀπ' αὐτοῦ; MT: הסירו הבגדים הצאים). These verses are often cited in illustration of Jas 1.21, and sometimes an allusion to them is proposed; cf. Spitta, 49.

[129] See on this D. Daube, 'Participle and Imperative in I Peter', in Selwyn, *First Peter*, 467-88. One commentator or another has found imperatival force in the participles in 1.3, 6; 3.1; and 5.14; see Mussner, 32.

[130] Cf. Wesley, 859; Gundry, 922; *et al.* Contrast Robertson, 93: 'probably James means to carry the figure of the garden through the verse': one clears all the foul rank growth and the weeds of filthiness and then receives the implanted word. So too Johnstone, 106. Trapp, 695, unaccountably finds an allusion 'to the garbage of the sacrifices cast into the brook Kedron, that is, into the town-ditch', and he further records the odd notion that 'the word rendered filthiness, properly signifies "the filth under the nails and armholes"'.

[131] So too Keenan, 147; Witherington, 441. Royster, 32, leaves the question open. Mayor, 64, records this possibility and attributes it to Heisen.

[132] Cf. Ps.-Aristotle, *Prob.* 960B (ἐν τοῖς ὠσὶ ῥύπος πικρός ἐστιν); Hippocrates, *Epid.* 6.5.1 (ὠτὸς ῥύπος); Clement of Alexandria, *Paed.* 2.10.87.1 ed. Marcovich, 122 (ῥύπος εἰς ὦτα); Artemidorus, *Onir.* 1.24 (ὦτα καθαίρειν μεστὰ ῥύπου); PGM 36.332 (ῥύπον ἀπὸ ὠτίου μούλας).

What of περισσείαν κακίας?[133] Gill, 783-84, thinks of circumcision: 'There seems to be an allusion to the removing of the superfluous foreskin of the flesh, in circumcision, typical of the foreskin of the heart, spoken of in Jer. iv. 4, which the Targum in that place, calls רשע לבבון, *the wickedness*, or *naughtiness of your hearts* to be removed...' Although this suggestion does not appear in modern commentaries on James, it was once well known.[134] Recently, moreover, and independently, W.J. Dalton has proposed it in a book on 1 Peter.[135] It merits consideration. (i) It would allow one to give περισσείαν a natural sense. (ii) A case can be made for seeing in 1 Pet 3.21 ('not as a putting off [ἀπόθεσις] of the filth [ῥύπου] of the flesh') a reference to circumcision,[136] and Peter's vocabulary approaches that of James. (iii) Philo, *Leg.* 1.5, argues that one purpose of circumcision was to promote cleanliness of the body; so the use of ῥυπαρία of the foreskin, which tradition regarded as 'unclean',[137] would be understandable. (iv) Philo also, in the same place, refers to the foreskin with the word περιττῆς, and his rare pejorative use of this word is very close to James' rare pejorative use of περισσείαν. (v) Both Jewish and Christian texts offer metaphorical applications of circumcision.[138]

Although the first meaning for περισσεία[139] in LSJ is 'surplus', supposing that to be the meaning here runs into the objection—if one does not think of circumcision—that κακία 'in the smallest measure is already excess'.[140] The Vulgate translates with *abundantiam*, and the word means 'abundance' in Rom 5.17 and 2 Cor 8.2; cf. περισσεύω. BAGD, s.v., suggests that the sense of περισσείαν κακίας—did James coin the expression?—is 'all the evil prevailing (around you)'. Other possibilities

---

[133] κακία (NT: 11×; in the LXX most often for רעה) occurs only here in James

[134] Cf. Grotius, 1076 (James alludes to the ערלה, the prepuce, which stands for all that is useless); Hammond, 689; Hammond-Le Clerc, 504; Benson, 47-48; Macknight, 589; Clarke, 802 ('perhaps'). Theile, 67, still lists this as an exegetical option.

[135] W.J. Dalton, *Christ's Proclamation to the Spirits*, 2nd ed., Rome, 1989, 205.

[136] P.J. Achtemeier, *1 Peter*, Minneapolis, 1996, 269.

[137] Isa 51.1 ('the uncircumcised and the unclean'); Jer 4.1-4 ('remove your abominations' is followed by 'circumcise yourselves to the Lord'); b. Pesah. 92a; etc. LXX Lev 19.23 translates ערלה = 'foreskin' by ἀκαθαρσία = 'uncleanness'.

[138] Exod 6.12, 30 (uncircumcised lips); Deut 10.16 (circumcision of the heart); 30.6 (circumcision of the heart); Jer 9.25-26 (circumcision of the heart); 6.10 (uncircumcised ears); Rom 2.29 (real circumcision is a matter of the heart); Col 2.11 (circumcision 'made without hands'); Sifra Shemini 1 (43d) ('remove the evil yetzer from your hearts', followed by a quotation of Deut 10.16).

[139] NT: 4×: Rom 5.17; 2 Cor 8.2; 10.15; Jas 1.21. LXX: 12×-14×, all in Ecclesiastes, most often for יתרון, and with the meaning, 'advantage'; see 1.3; 2.11, 13; 3.9, 19; 5.8, 15; 6.8; 7.12, 11; 10.10, 11. Gk. Pseudepigrapha (Denis): 0×. Philo: 0×. Josephus: 0×. The word is exceedingly rare in secular Greek; cf. Aelius Herodian, *Pros. cath.* ed. Lentz, 291.9; *Περὶ ὀρθ.* ed. Lentz, 453. In James, the word may or may not be qualified by the preceding πᾶσαν.

[140] So Oesterley, 432. Cf. Poole, 883: 'all sin is superfluous in the soul, as being that which should not be in it'.

include: 'overflowing (ebullition) of malice',[141] 'remainder of evil',[142] and 'rank growth'.[143] Whatever the precise sense, we have passed beyond the subjects of speech and anger to sin in general, to all manner of sin.

Even aside from the suggestions just introduced, exegetes have drawn several distinctions between πᾶσαν ῥυπαρίαν and περισσείαν κακίας.[144] But it is also possible to hold that the latter does not communicate anything concrete beyond the former, that the addition of περισσείαν κακίας rather (i) reflects James' fondness for repeating sounds, (ii) illustrates his habit of offering near synonyms in parallel, and (iii) enhances the impression of comprehensiveness: every evil is in view.[145]

ἐν πραΰτητι δέξασθε τὸν ἔμφυτον λόγον.[146] With vices laid aside, the way is cleared for reception of 'the implanted word', which implicitly appears to be a divine gift; cf. vv. 5, 17. It has appropriately been called an 'enablement motif': whatever its precise definition, it enables James' audience to do what is asked of them.[147] ἐν πραΰτητι[148]—which some link with ἀποθέμενοι[149] instead of δέξασθε[150]—refers to a virtue important for

---

[141] Mayor, 66-67; cf. Lk 6.45.

[142] So Cantinat, 103-104 ('reste de vice'), calling attention to περισσόν = 'remainder' in LXX Exod 10.5 and περισσεύματα = 'what remains' in Mk 8.8; cf. Tasker, 51; Mitton, 63; Davids, 94; and the v.l. περίσσευμα in 02 33 436 442 1409 2344 2541 L596.

[143] Alford, 286; NRSV. These and other possibilities are outlined and assigned to various authorities in Theile, 67; Mayor, 67-68.

[144] Bede *ad loc.* CCSL 12 1, ed. Hurst, 191, links 'sordidness' with bodily sins, 'evil' with inward sins. Charles Taylor, in a note appended to Mayor, 68, asks whether 'sordidness' denotes 'the passively mean and base', in opposition to 'evil', an 'active form of vice'. Some take κακίας, because of the context, to mean 'malice'; so e.g. Mayor, 68; Laws, 81. The former refers to Trench, *Synonyms*, 37-38. Cf. Rom 1.29; Eph 4.31; Col 3.8; Tit 3.3; 1 Pet 2.1; Did. 5.1; Barn. 20.

[145] Cf. Burchard, 82. But for McKnight, 141-42, πᾶσαν ῥυπαρίαν καὶ περισσείαν κακίας designates 'verbal sins and anger' in particular.

[146] 025 and 1852 insert σοφίας: 'humility of wisdom'. This is drawn forward from 3.13. Given how often interpreters connect our verses with chap. 3, the insertion stands in an exegetical tradition.

[147] See Whitlark, 'Motif'. Contrast Scott, *Literature*, 216: James thinks in terms of 'law', not in terms of 'a power which creates a new life'.

[148] For the expression see the texts from Sirach cited in n. 153; also 2 Tim 2.25; 1 Clem. 61.2; Ign. *Pol.* 2.1 (ἐν πραΰτητι); 6.2 (ἐν πραΰτητι); Diognetus, *Ep.* 7.4 (ἐν ἐπιεικείᾳ καὶ πραΰτητι); and for the construction Jas 2.1. The Hebrew equivalent, בענוה, is well attested: 1 Sam 1.11; 1QS 3.8; 4Q259 2.11; m. 'Abot 6.6; etc. In the LXX, πραΰτης and πραότης translate ענו(ה). Literature: A. Harnack, 'Sanftmut, Huld und Demut in der alten Kirche', in *Festgabe für Julius Kaftan zu seinem 70. Geburtstag*, Tübingen, 1920, 113-19; F. Hauck and S. Schulz, 'πραΰς, πραΰτης', *TDNT* 6.645-51; J. Dupont, *Lés Beatitudes*, vol. 3, rev. ed., Paris, 1973, 457-69; H. de Romilly, *La douceur dans la pensée grecque*, Paris, 1979; H. Frankemölle, 'πραΰτης κτλ.', *EDNT* 3.146-47; Spicq, 'πραϋπάθεια κτλ.', *TLNT* 3.160-71; D.J. Good, *Jesus the Meek King*, Harrisburg, PA, 1999.

[149] Laws, 44, notes this possibility. Nestle-Aland[26] puts a comma between πραΰτητι and δέξασθε. Lockett, *Purity*, 110, links ἐν πραΰτητι to both verbs. So too Baker, *Speech-Ethics*, 89.

Matthean[151] and Pauline circles.[152] It was also, more generally, a virtue in both the Jewish and certain Greek circles.[153] πραΰτης, like πραΰς, is often contrasted with wrath or anger, as implicitly here in James.[154] Its nature as both kindness and humility appears from its pairing with ἐπιεικής/ίκεια,[155] ἡσύχιος/ία,[156] ὑπομονή,[157] μακρόθυμος/ία,[158] ἐλεήμων/ἔλεος,[159] as well as with ταπεινός (cf. Jas 1.9) and ταπεινόφρων/οσύνη.[160] Dibelius, 112, believes that 'in humility' is here comprehensive: it refers to one's life in general, not to reception of the word in particular. He translates: 'Therefore, put away...and be meek, when you receive the implanted word...'

[150] This is the interpretation of the vast majority of commentators and translations; cf. Lk 8.13 (μετὰ χαρᾶς δέχονται τὸν λόγον); Acts 17.11 (ἐδέξαντο τὸν λόγον μετὰ πάσης προθυμίας); 1 Thess 1.6 (δεξάμενοι τὸν λόγον ἐν θλίψει πολλῇ μετὰ χαρᾶς).

[151] See 5.5; 11.29; 21.5.

[152] 1 Cor 4.2 1; 2 Cor 10.1; Gal 5.23; 6.1; Eph 4.2; Col 3.12; 2 Tim 2.25; Tit 3.2.

[153] For the Jewish tradition see LXX Ps 24.9; 33.2; 36.11; 75.9; 146.6; 149.4; 1QS 2.24 (ענות טוב); 4.3 (רוח ענוה); Ecclus 1.26; 3.17-18 (ἐν πραΰτητι); 4.8 (ἐν πραΰτητι); 10.28 (ἐν πραΰτητι); 36.28; 45.4 (ἐν... πραΰτητι); Philo, Det. 146 (God acts πράως); Legat. 335 (of all people the Jews are πραοπαθέστατοι); m. 'Abot 4.4 ('Be very, very humble'), 12 ('Be humble of spirit'); 5.22 ('humility' in a list of virtues); b. Abod. Zar. 20b (ענוה is 'the greatest of virtues'). Moses was the exemplar of this trait; see on 3.13. For the Greek tradition see Plato, Crito, 120E (the Atlantians, so long as they retained 'the inherited nature of God', showed πραότητι 'joined with wisdom'); Phaedo 116C (Socrates was 'the noblest and gentlest', πραότατον); Aristotle, Eth. nic. 1125B (see next note); Epictetus, Diatr. 3.20.9 (the reviler serves the good purpose of exercising others' patience, dispassionateness, and 'gentleness', πρᾷον); 4.7.12; Ench. 42; Plutarch, Mor. 395A (of a student: what most merits admiration is his winning πραότης); Tab. Cebes 20.3 (πραότης in a list of virtues).

[154] So Hemminge, 14; Poole, 883; Senior, 'Sermon VII' (as in n. 14), 49, 53-54; Bengel, 491; Burchard, 83, Fabris, 104, 106; et al. Didymus of Alexandria, Ps frag. 358 ad 36.8a ed. Mühlenberg, 299, follows a quotation of Jas 1.20 with a call to become tame and meek (πραΰτητος). Cf. Aristotle, Eth. nic. 1125B (πραότης 'is the observance of the mean in relation to ὀργάς'); Rh. 1380A; Isocrates, Adv. Nic. 23; 1QS 5.24-25 ('They shall admonish one another in truth and humility [ענוה] and merciful love to another. He must not speak to his fellow with anger or with a snarl'); Josephus, Ant. 19.334; Ign. Eph. 10.2 ('towards their ὀργάς be πραεῖς'); Plutarch, Mor. 453B; Herm. Mand. 5.2.3; Didymus of Alexandria, Ps ad 36.8a ed. Mühlenberg, 299. In Philo, Spec. 1.145, sacrificial fat from the breast is a symbol of πραότητος applied to the 'spirited element', that is, θυμός = 'passion/anger'.

[155] E.g. Philo, Opif. 103; Jos. Asen. 15.8; Tit 3.2; 2 Cor 10.1; 1 Clem. 21.7; 30.8; Diognetus, Ep. 7.4; Plutarch, Per. 39; Caes. 15.4.

[156] E.g. 2 Cor 10.1; 1 Pet 3.4; 1 Clem. 13.4; Barn. 19.4; Herm. Mand. 5.2.6; 5.11.8; T. Abr. RecLng. 1.1; Plutarch, Fab. 1.4.

[157] E.g. Did. 5.2; Barn. 20.2; Justin, 1 Apol. 16.3. Cf. 2 En. 50.2: 'live in patience and meekness'.

[158] E.g. Gal 5.23; Col 3.12; Did. 3.7-8; T. Dan 6.9; Ign. Pol. 6.2. Cf. 1QS 4.3 ('a spirit of humility and patience').

[159] E.g. Ecclus 36.23; Jos. Asen. 8.8; Did. 3.7-8.

[160] E.g. T. Dan 6.9; Mt 11.29; 2 Cor 10.1; Eph 4.2; Col 3.12; 1 Clem. 30.8; Ps.-Demosthenes, Erot. 14.

But the linguistic parallels favor linking ἐν πραΰτητι with δέξασθε; see n. 150.

What does τὸν ἔμφυτον λόγον mean? Most commentators, arguing that one cannot receive something that is inborn or innate—the first meaning of ἔμφυτος[161]—think of the gospel or baptismal instruction,[162] and δέχομαι + λόγον[163] does elsewhere refer to reception of the Christian gospel.[164] On this view, 'implanted'[165] refers not to that which is innate but rather to that which has become implanted through acceptance of the Christian message,[166] and James' point is that conversion is not the end of accepting the word: it must constantly be received, that is, heeded and lived.[167] Jeremiah 31.33, a text certainly well known to early Christians,[168] could then be in the background: 'This is the covenant that I will make with the house of Israel after those days, says the Lord: I will put my law within them, and I will write it on their hearts; and I will be their God, and they shall be my people'.[169] One might also compare Jesus' parable of the

---

[161] NT: 1×; cf. Barn. 1.2; 9.9. LXX: Wis 12.10, of 'inborn wickedness'. Gk. Pseudepigrapha (Denis): Ps.-Phoc. 128. Philo: 6×. Josephus: 4×. LSJ, s.v., gives the first meaning of the word as 'inborn, natural', the second as 'planted', the third as 'implanted'. The first is illustrated by fifteen texts, the third only by Jas 1.21. Lampe, s.v., lists the meanings for patristic texts as (i) 'inborn, natural', (ii) 'implanted, engrafted', (iii) 'deeply rooted'.

[162] See those cited in n. 7. Senior, 'Sermon VII', 49 (see n. 14), thinks of the word of God read and expounded, Knoch, 168 of 'the teaching of the faith as a formulated doctrine'. McKnight, 143-44, wonders whether the Holy Spirit is thus indicated. R. Wall, 90, suggests that the implanted word is wisdom.

[163] Cf. the rabbinic idiom, קבל + דבר: m. Roš. Haš. 2.9; b. Šeb. 36a; b. ʿAbod. Zar. 39a; y. Maʿaś. Š. 55b (4.4); etc.

[164] Lk 8.13; Acts 8.14; 11.1; 17.11; 1 Thess 1.6; 2.13—although this is hardly decisive given that the expression appears in other connections, too; see LXX Prov 1.3; 2.1; 4.10; Jer 9.20. Often the idiom means 'hear' or 'hear agreeably'; cf. Plato, Lach. 187D; Plutarch, Mor. 150B; Josephus, Ant. 18.369. Ludwig, Wort, 36-37, calling attention to LXX Deut 33.3—the people 'accepted from his words a law (ἐδέξατο ἀπὸ τῶν λόγων αὐτοῦ νόμον), which Moses commanded us'—urges that the idiom here belongs to a nomistic tradition; cf. Zech 1.6; Acts 7.38; 4 Ezra 9.33, 36; 14.30; 2 Bar. 15.5; 48.24; Tg. Isa 9.5.

[165] Or, as Oesterley, 432, has it: 'rooted'. The KJV's 'engrafted word' (cf. Tyndale, Cranmer, Rheims) implies its foreign nature. Cf. Irenaeus, Haer. 5.10.1, where we read about those who use diligence and receive the word of God as a 'graft' (insertionem).

[166] Note the v.l. in K:B (νεόφυτον) and 1 Cor 3.6: Paul 'planted (ἐφύτευσα), Apollos watered, but God gave the growth'.

[167] Cf. Cheung, Genre, 92: 'the emphasis is not on receiving the gospel of truth in conversion, but rather on learning and understanding the word of truth'.

[168] C.H. Dodd, Scriptures, 44-46, 85-86.

[169] Cf. Gregory Palamas, Hom. xliii–lxiii 45.2 ed. Chrestou and Zeses, 70-72; Poole, 883; Cappel, 129; B. Weiss, 96; Cantinat, 105; Cargal, 89; Bauckham, Brother, 141, 146; Moo, 32 ('almost certainly' an allusion), 87; Blomberg-Kamell, 88; Kamell, 'Soteriology', 140-44; idem, 'Law'. Contrast Jackson-McCabe, Logos, 192: dependence upon Jer 31-35 is 'most doubtful'.

sower, which the Synoptics interpret as being about 'the word',[170] as well as Barn. 1.2 ('Exceedingly and abundantly do I rejoice over your blessed and glorious spirit for the greatness and richness of God's ordinances towards you; so implanted [ἔμφυτον] a grace of the gift of the spirit have you received') and 9.9 ('He knows this who implanted [ἔμφυτον] the gift of his teaching in our hearts').[171]

James, however, immediately goes on to enjoin readers to 'do' the word, and the gospel is typically not performed but rather believed. Moreover, when δέχομαι + λόγον has to do with receiving the Christian message, it is otherwise about conversion, not post-baptismal appropriation of that message. For these reasons, and because ἔμφυτον typically means 'inborn', and means this the only other time it appears in the Greek Bible,[172] some exegetes hold that τὸν ἔμφυτον λόγον is 'the innate word'. Our verse then refers to the inborn capacity of humanity, created in the image of God, to receive divine revelation. In Cadoux's words: 'The context favors "inborn" [rather than implanted], which is to be reached by discarding accretions—"all filthiness and superfluity of wickedness", and in 1.23 the man who hears this word but does not act on it is likened to a man who for a moment sees himself in a mirror and then goes away and forgets what manner of man he was. He is said to see the face "of his genesis", an addition needless if not emphatic, and the reference seems to be to his creation, as "made after the likeness of God", and, where James later quotes this Genesis story, "made" is the verb corresponding to "genesis".'[173] Although Cadoux's take on v. 23 is far from obvious, Hellenistic philosophy had made familiar the idea of a universal 'law' (νόμος) or 'word' (λόγος)[174] 'planted' in human nature,[175] and it is hard not to read ἔμφυτος λόγος without recalling Stoic ideas.[176]

---

[170] Mt 13.19-23; Mk 4.14-20; Lk 8.11-15. See below, 341 n. 180. Many readers of James here recall Jesus' parable: Hus 191; Erasmus, *Paraphrase*, 144; Senior, 'Sermon VII' (as in n. 14), 49, 55-56; Schneckenburger, 40; Kern, 142; Rosenmüller, 338; Gibson, 17; Knowling, 30; J.C. Gibbons, *Discourses and Sermons*, Baltimore, n.d., 253-54; Gaugusch, 20; Mayor, 64; Spitta, 52; Hauck, 12; Mussner, 102; Cranfield, 'Message', 187; Grünzweig, 54; Ruckstuhl, 14-15; Cantinat, 105; Royster, 32-33; *et al*. Alford, 286; Bassett, 22-23; Davids, 'Jesus', 71; Maier, 94, find an allusion to or use of Jesus' parable. Deppe, *Sayings*, 246, makes the case to the contrary.

[171] Ps.-Ign. *Eph*. 17 ed. Zahn, 286, also uses ἔμφυτος with the meaning 'implanted': 'having received as implanted (ἔμφυτον) from Christ the faculty of judgment concerning God'.

[172] Wis 12.10 refers to 'inborn' wickedness.

[173] Cadoux, *Thought*, 20. For related expositions see those cited in n. 8. Note also Frankemölle, 329-30.

[174] See e.g. Zeno *apud* Diogenes Laertius 7.88 (the universal νόμος runs through everything); Marcus Aurelius 5.32 (the λόγος 'that informs all substance and governs the whole').

[175] Cicero, *Leg*. 1.18(6) ('Law is the highest reason, implanted [*insita*] in nature'); *Rep*. 3.33(22) (true law is 'right reason' [*recta ratio*] congruent with nature; whoever disobeys this law is 'fleeing from himself and denying his human nature'); Epictetus, *Diatr*. 2.11.3 (the concept of what is good and evil is 'innate', ἔμφυτον). Stoics also

This commentary interprets ἔμφυτος λόγος as an innate reality. It is necessary to add, however, that reference to the 'implanted word' is flanked by texts that refer to the Torah as λόγος,[177] and further that, by James' day, some within Judaism had begun to interpret Wisdom and Torah in terms of the Stoic idea of the cosmic νόμος,[178] the 'common' λόγος that is in all and steers all things, and upon which human law and moral behavior should be based.[179] This helps explain why the Torah is internal and taught by or in accord with nature in Philo,[180] in Rom 1.32; 2.14-15,[181] and in the Hellenistic Jewish synagogal prayers preserved in the *Apostolic Constitutions*. These last speak of the law that God 'planted

---

spoke of the 'seminal (σπερματικός) word' and of 'implanted (ἔμφυτοι) ideas'. For review of the relevant materials see Jackson-McCabe, *Logos*, 29-86.

[176] See esp. Jackson-McCabe, *Logos*, passim.

[177] See the commentary on vv. 18 and 22.

[178] M. Hengel, *Judaism and Hellenism*, vol. 1, Philadelphia, 1974, 153-75. For wisdom as Torah more generally see E.J. Schnabel, *Law and Wisdom from Ben Sira to Paul*, Tübingen, 1985.

[179] Marcus Aurelius 4.4 ('If the faculty of understanding is common to us all, the reason [λόγος] also, through which we are rational beings, is common. If this is so, common also is that reason [λόγος] which tells us what to do, and what not to do'); 7.53 ('every act must be performed in accord with the reason [λόγον] which is common to gods and men'); Diogenes Laertius 7.88 ('The universal law [ὁ νόμος] is the right reason [λόγος] that pervades all things'); Proclus, *In Plat. rem. pub.* ed. Kroll, 2.307 (νόμος is 'unchangeably aligned according to a single word [λόγος]; among human beings it rules according to the appointed seasons; among animals it fulfills the way of life that is natural for each. So then this law [νόμον] must be regarded as divine, the link between the necessary laws which the demiurge of the Timaeus wrote into souls, and the laws that extend into every polity of the universe'); Stobaeus 2.7.11i ('The Stoics say that law [νόμου] is... the reason [λόγος] stipulating what is to be done and forbidding what is not to be done').

[180] *Abr.* 275-76: Abraham followed the commandments 'not taught by written words, but unwritten nature gave him the zeal to follow where wholesome and untainted impulse led him. And when they have God's promises before them what should men do but trust in them most firmly? Such was the life of the first, the founder of the nation, one who obeyed the law, some will say, but rather, as our discourse has shown, himself a law and an unwritten statute'. Cf. *Mos.* 1.162 (Moses was a 'living impersonation of law', νόμος ἔμψυχος); 2.12-14 (Moses' law bears 'the seals of nature herself'), 52 (the commandments of Moses are 'in agreement with the word [λόγῳ] of eternal nature'); *Opif.* 3 ('the world... is in harmony with the law, and the law with the world, and... the man who observes the law is constituted thereby a loyal citizen of the world, regulating his doings by the purpose and will of nature, in accordance with which the entire world itself also is administered). In *Virt.* 127, Philo refers to the Torah with the Stoic term, 'right reason', ὀρθῷ λόγῳ. See further P. Borgen, *Bread from Heaven*, Leiden, 1965, 136-41; R.A. Horsley, 'The Law of Nature in Philo and Cicero', *HTR* 71 (1978), 35-59; H. Najman, 'The Law of Nature and the Authority of Mosaic Law', *SPhilo Annual* 22 (1999), 55-73. One recalls the rabbinic belief that the world was created by Torah: e.g. m. 'Abot 3.15; Gen. Rab. 1.1.

[181] On this see esp. G. Bornkamm, *Studien zu Antike und Urchristentum, Gesammelte Aufsätze*, vol. 2, Munich, 1970, 93-118.

deeply' in human souls[182] and of 'implanted knowledge and inborn judgment'.[183] The adoption of the Stoic doctrine was natural given that Jewish tradition could call Torah λόγος and think of it as both 'internal', that is, as something within the heart,[184] and as something that could be 'implanted'.[185] Also relevant is the tradition, grounded in Gen 26.5, that the patriarchs kept the law even before Moses delivered it.[186] One can then find in Jas 1.21 a reference to the Torah, but by way of a traditional expression that conveyed the belief that the νόμος is the λόγος that is everywhere present to everyone, yet above all present in and manifested through the Mosaic Torah.[187] A similar idea appears in Justin Martyr, writing not long after James: for him even pagans have a share in the 'seminal word', which is yet only fully revealed in the Christian proclamation.[188] To what extent James' expression, 'the implanted word',

---

[182] 7.26.3 ed. Funk, 412: νόμον κατεφύτευσας; cf. 6.20.10 ed. Funk, 353 (τὸν νόμον τὸν ὑπ' ἐμοῦ τῇ φύσει καταβληθέντα πᾶσαιν ἀνθρώποις); 8.9.8 ed. Funk, 486 (God gave νόμον...ἔμφυτον καὶ γραπτόν); 8.12.18 ed. Funk, 500-502 (God has given to humanity a νόμον...ἔμφυτον). For discussion see Jackson-McCabe, *Logos*, 105-22.

[183] 7.33.3 ed. Funk, 424: τῆς ἐμφήτου γνώσεως καὶ φυσικῆς κρίσεως. This likely belongs to a Jewish layer of the document.

[184] Deut 30.14 ('the word is...in your heart for you to observe'); Ps 37.31 ('the law of God is in their hearts'); 40.8 ('your law is in my heart'); Isa 51.7 ('in whose heart is my law'); Jer 31.33 ('I will put my law within them'—this, however, is prophecy); 1QH 12.10 ('your law, which you engraved in my heart'). Cf. 1 Clem. 2.8 ('The commandments and ordinances of the Lord were written on the tables of your hearts'); Herm. *Sim.* 8.3.3 (Michael 'puts the law into the hearts of those who believe'). According to Philo, *Mos.* 2.11, the laws in the books of Moses are 'copies of the patterns enshrined in the soul'.

[185] 4Q504 1-2 2.13: 'Remember your marvels which you performed in view of the peoples, for we have been called by your name...with all (our) heart and with all (our) soul and to implant (לטשמ) your law in our heart, [so that we do not stray] either to the right or to the left'. Cf. also Ecclus 24.12 (where Wisdom = Torah says, 'And I took root among a honored people'); Philo, *Prob.* 68 (virtue's 'roots have been set by their maker even so near to us, as the wise legislator of the Jews also says, "in your mouth, in your heart, and in your hand"'); *Legat.* 210 (the Jews 'carry the likeness of the commandments enshrined in their souls'); 4 Ezra 9.31 ('I [God] sow my law in you'); 2 Bar. 32.1 ('if you [Israel] prepare your minds to sow into them the fruits of the law'; cf. 51.3, where being righteous on account of the law is parallel to planting 'the root of wisdom'); b. Ḥag. 3b (the Torah is 'well planted', נמועים). According to Ludwig, *Wort*, 163, Judaism commonly spoke of the internalization of the law through an agricultural picture: the law or words of wisdom were sown or planted.

[186] Cf. Ecclus 44.20; Jub. 6.17-19 (here however the pre-Mosaic Torah is not innate but a primitive revelation); Philo, *Abr.* 275-76; m. Qidd. 4.14; ARN 33; Gen. Rab. 64.4; 61.1 (God arranged for Abraham's 'two kidneys to be as two rabbis to him'). Apost. Const. 6.20.4 ed. Funk, 351, continues this tradition: the patriarchs were moved φυσικῷ νόμῳ.

[187] Cf. Ecclus 24; Meyer, *Rätsel*, 155-57; Boismard, 'Liturgie', 171-72. Klein, *Werk*, 136-37, who sees Deut 30.11-14 as the key to Jas 1.21, makes a similar argument but goes on to speak of 'the law of Christ'.

[188] Justin, *2 Apol.* 7(8).1-3 (although the σπέρμα τοῦ λόγου is 'implanted' [ἔμφυτον] in all, the Stoics live 'according to a part only of the seminal word [σπερματικοῦ λόγου]'

retained Stoic connotations for him and his first readers we do not know. Boismard, who observes the philosophical tone of v. 17, may be correct to conjecture that James took the phrase from Jewish propaganda, which had borrowed a Stoic idea to underline the rapport between Moses and human reason: there is only one law, but it has two successive forms, first the natural law, the 'implanted word', and then the Mosaic law, the written word.[189]

How then does one 'receive' or 'welcome' the 'implanted word'? In Heraclitus, the λόγος is accessible to all—he calls it 'common', ξυνός—and yet most people fail to heed it.[190] Similarly, Cicero, *Leg.* 1.33(12), can say that although Nature gives right reason and law to all, the sparks of such law and reason can be extinguished by the corruption of bad habits—just as they can equally be sensed and heeded. There is a parallel here with Torah in Judaism. Deuteronomy 30.14 says that the word is near, in the heart—and there 'for you to observe'. Nonetheless, one might choose not to observe it.[191] An analogous idea is also implicit in Rom 2.12-16. Paul's assertion, 'When the Gentiles who have not the law do by nature what the law requires, they are a law to themselves', does not assume, as Rom 1 makes plain, that all Gentiles do the law: the nations are free to sin and ignore the law written upon their hearts. Comparable too is 4 Ezra 9.33: the faithless descendants of Jacob 'did not keep what had been sown in them'. James presupposes that the word can be implanted yet not received, not welcomed.[192] One recalls the relationship between indicative and imperative in Paul: the one who has already died to sin (Rom 6.2) is nonetheless exhorted not to sin any more (6.12-14).[193]

Perhaps one should note that the Syriac translations use קבל for James' δέξασθε, and that the former, in Aramaic, means 'receive', yet

---

whereas Christians live 'by the knowledge and contemplation of the whole word, which is Christ'); 13.2-5. Cf. Athenagoras, *Res.* 24.4 ed. Marcovich, 49 (human beings are regulated by τὸν ἔμφυτον νόμον καὶ λόγον); Methodius, *Res.* 2.6-7 GCS 27 ed. Bonwetsch, 339-42 (τὸν κατὰ τὸ ἔμφυτον ἐν ἡμῖν ἀγαθόν, ὃν καὶ νόμον σαφῶς νοὸς ἐκάλεσεν); idem *apud* Epiphanius, *Pan.* 64.60.4-6 ed. Holl, 495-96 (the commandment has been given as an ἔμφυτον...καὶ φυσικὸν νόμον); Procopius of Gaza, *Gen ad* 4.2 PG 87/1.236A (ὁ δὲ νόμος ὁ ἐν ἡμῖν τῆς ἐμφύτου θεογνωσίας).

[189] Boismard, 'Liturgie', 171-73.

[190] Frags. 1 (Sextus, *Adv. math.* 7.132), 2 (ibid. 7.133), 50 (Hippolytus, *Haer.* 9.9.1 PTS 25 ed. Marcovich, 344).

[191] Basser, 429, wonders if James does not here refer to Deut 30.14.

[192] Cf. Jackson-McCabe, *Logos*, 188-89: James is calling for 'repentance', not 'conversion'; δέχομαι can mean 'give ear to' or 'accept without complaint'; and 'the "receiving" of the logos in 1:21 must...be understood more on the analogy of the "hearing" of 1:22-25 than the "implanting" of 1:21'. Ludwig, *Wort*, 163, observes that James is no odder than 2 Bar. 32.1: 'prepare your minds to sow into them the fruits of the law'. Seeds are sown, not fruit.

[193] See further Whitlark, 'Motif', remarking on how Paul can say that Christians have put on Christ and at the same time demand that they put Christ on; cf. Rom 13.14; Gal 3.27.

often with the connotations of 'listen' and 'obey'.[194] Could James' Greek, which otherwise contains Semitisms, retain such connotations?[195]

A few commentators sense that 1.19 would read well if addressed to non-Christians Jews.[196] The fact accords with this commentary's take on 1.1 as well as with other parts of James that seem aimed at non-Christian Jews.[197] Furthermore, James here distances himself from his readers by forsaking the first person plural of v. 18 (ἡμᾶς) and reverting to the second person plural (ὑμῶν),[198] and he does not say that the word has in fact saved the recipients but only that it is *able* (δυνάμενον) to do so.[199] So their salvation is not a present reality but rather a future possibility.[200]

τὸν δυνάμενον σῶσαι τὰς ψυχὰς ὑμῶν.[201] This adds strong warrant for putting off evil and receiving the 'implanted word', Torah.[202] For δύναμαι + σῴζω, a traditional combination, see on 2.14. σῴζω + ψυχήν (which recurs in 5.20) was also conventional.[203] Did James first combine the two idioms,[204] so that Herm. *Sim.* 6.1.1 (δυνάμεναι σῶσαι ψυχήν) shows a knowledge of our book, or does the agreement rather reflect a common tradition or milieu?[205] Whatever the answer, the subject in Hermas is 'the

---

[194] Cf. Jastrow, s.v., and the translation of שמע = 'hear, obey' by קבל in the targums, as in Tg. Judg 3.4; 9.7; 1 Kgs 15.20; etc. Note also Ludwig, *Wort*, 161. δέχομαι translates קבל in LXX 2 Chr 29.16, 22; 2 Esd 8.30; Job 2.10.

[195] Cf. Boismard, 'Liturgie', 172; Cantinat, 104.

[196] E.g. Clarke, 802; Oesterley, 432.

[197] See the Introduction, 32-50.

[198] The v.l. ἡμῶν (see n. 201) undoes this distance.

[199] Cf. 4.12, in a rebuke: 'There is one lawgiver and judge who is able to save (ὁ δυνάμενος σῶσαι) and to destroy'.

[200] Cf. Knowling, 30: 'It is remarkable that this language is addressed to those who had been already described as begotten by the word of truth, so that salvation is regarded by the writer as in a sense still in the future...'

[201] 020 049 056 0142 1 6 38 43 88 180 *et al.* K:S^ms and several lectionaries change ὑμῶν, which distances author from reader, to ἡμῶν. This eliminates the possibility that 1.21 be read as addressed to non-Christians.

[202] For the Torah as the means of salvation see 1 En. 99.10; T. Gad 4.7 ('the spirit of love works by the law of God through forbearance for the salvation of humanity'); Mek. on Exod 12.6; Tg. Ps.-J. Deut 30.15; etc. Jn 5.24 and 8.51 associate salvation with hearing and doing 'the word', although here it is the word of Jesus; cf. Barn 19.10: εἰς τὸ σῶσαι ψυχὴν τῷ λόγῳ (of the gospel).

[203] See LXX Gen 19.17; 1 Βασ 19.11; Jer 31.6; Amos 2.14 (all four times for מלט in Niphal or Piel + נפש); Mt 16.25 = Mk 8.35 = Lk 9.24; Josephus, *Ant.* 9.240; 11.255; T. Abr. RecLng. 11.10, 12; Barn. 19.10. Cf. 1Q27 1.4 ('and they will not save [מלטו] their souls [נפשמה] from the future mystery'); 1 Pet 1.9 (σωτηρίαν ψυχῶν). Although the phrase also occurs outside the biblical tradition—e.g. Diodorus Siculus 37.19.5: 'to save the lives [σῶσαι ψυχάς] of young children')—surely in James it has a Semitic pedigree.

[204] Which together have their antithesis in Mt 10.28: τὸν δυνάμενον καὶ ψυχὴν... ἀπολέσαι.

[205] See the Introduction, 20-24. The idiom also occurs in Acts Thom. 139 ed. Bonnet, 246; Clement of Alexandria, *Ecl.* 26.2 GCS 17 ed. Stählin, 144; Ps.-Clem. Hom. 3.37.2 GCS 42 ed. Rehm, 70.

commandments' (ἐντολῶν), which falls in line with a nomistic reading of James.

ψυχάς means 'selves' or 'lives'[206]—one guesses that James believed in the resurrection of the body as well as the salvation of the soul[207]—and although there is no necessary antithesis, the focus is not upon being saved from evil in this life but upon finding salvation in the next.[208] That is, as with the other instances of σῴζω in James,[209] the last judgment is in view:[210] those who receive the 'implanted word' and live accordingly will enter the world to come.[211]

---

[206] So Poole, 883; Gill, 784; Gundry, 921; *et al.* Cf. Mt 10.39 = Lk 17.33 and see G. Dautzenberg, *Sein Leben bewahren*, Munich, 1966, 13-48.

[207] A few, however, equate ψυχάς with 'soul' in the immaterial sense; so e.g. Alford, 286; Spitta, 52; cf. Punchard, 361. Pareus, 548, speaks of synecdoche: the part (soul) stands for the whole (body and soul).

[208] Protestant exegetes sometimes feel bound to insist that 'the word' is not the cause of salvation, only a divine instrument; cf. Poole, 883; Gill, 784; Burkitt, 1018. The Catholic Lapide, 71, by contrast, finds it prudent to add that the word saves only those who obey.

[209] 2.14; 4.12; 5.20.

[210] So most commentators; cf. Lapide, 71; Wolzogen, 188; Burkitt, 1018; Simon, 98; Moo, 88; Burchard, 83; Cheung, *Genre*, 93; *et al.* Cf. 1.11, 12, 15; 2.13; 4.10, 12; 5.1-11, 20. Adderley, 20-21, however, insists on a present application simultaneously: Christians are being 'restored to spiritual health' even now. Cf. Konradt, *Existenz*, 175-76.

[211] Manns, 'Tradition', cites as a parallel the late *Siddur of Rab Sa'adia Ga'on*: 'Blessed art you O Lord our God, king of the universe, who has given to us the law of truth and who has planted in us eternal life. Blessed are you, giver of Torah.'

VIII

HEARING AND DOING (1.22-25)[1]

(22) But show yourselves to be doers of the word, and not hearers only, deceiving yourselves; (23) for if someone is a hearer of the word and not a doer, that one is like a man who contemplates his face in a mirror; (24) for he looks at himself and then, having gone away, instantly forgets what he was like. (25) But the one who looks into the perfect law, the law of freedom, and perseveres, showing himself to be not a hearer who forgets but a doer who works, that one will be blessed in his doing.

History of Interpretation and Reception

Homiletical and devotional treatments of this passage have tended to move in four directions, depending upon whether the focus has been the necessity of doing, the character of 'the word', the nature of liberty, or the importance of self-awareness. (i) The most common application of 1.22-25 has been to demand that Christians do more than just listen to homilies, or that catechumens practice what they have learned.[2] Lancelot

---

[1] Recent literature: Ammassari, 'Law'; Assaël, 'Oeuvre'; Assaël-Cuvillier, 'Éléments'; Baker, *Speech-Ethics*, 92-96; A. Calmet, 'Sagesses'; Cheung, *Genre*, 92-96, 129-32; Collins, 'Coherence'; Cox, 'Looking-Glass'; Denyer, 'Mirrors'; Deppe, *Sayings*, 83-87; Eckart, 'Terminologie'; Evans, 'Law'; Fabris, *Legge*; Frankemölle, 'Gesetz'; Hugedé, *Métaphore*, 71-74; Jackson-McCabe, *Logos*; Johnson, *Brother*, 168-81; S. Johnson, *Treasure*, 91-93; Klein, *Werk*, 121-25, 137-44; Konradt, *Existenz*, 171-76; Ludwig, *Wort*; S. Luther, 'Ethics', 344-46; Marconi, 'Nota'; Marucci, 'Gesetz'; Nauck, 'Lex'; Parry, *Discussion*, 25-31; Popkes, 'Law'; Seitz, 'Law'; Sigal, 'Halakhah'; Sisti, 'Parola'; Stauffer, 'Gesetz'; Tsuji, *Glaube*, 67-71, 124-25; Viviano, 'Loi'; Vollenweider, *Freiheit*, 184-88; R. Wall, 'Law'; Walker, 'Werken'; Ward, 'Concern', 108-27; J. Williams, 'Law'.

[2] Cf. Augustine, *Serm.* 179 1 PL 38.966; Ps.-Oecumenius *ad loc.* PG 119.468C-D; Erasmus, *Paraphrase*, 144; W. Beveridge, 'Sermon CXI', in *The Works of the Right Reverend Father in God William Beveridge*, vol. 5, Oxford, 1818, 207-24 ('as if they served God only by hearing how to serve him, or did any good only by hearing how to do it. And yet this is the case of too many among us, who never think they can hear too much, or do too little'); Barnes, 36; A. Maclaren, 'The Perfect Law and Its Doers', *Homiletical Review* 21 (1891), 40-45 (observing that some people complain when pastors quit 'preaching the Gospel' and insist upon fitting conduct); Dale, 44-47; Cox, 'Looking-Glass', 456 (warning about 'Bibleworms', people who know all about the Bible but do not live it); Adamson, 84. According to G.H. Williams, *The Radical Reformation*, Philadelphia, 1962, 804, 1.22 was a favorite admonition among the early Anabaptists.

Andrewes, in a sermon on our passage, complained of 'the common error', that 'sermon-hearing is the *consummatum est* of all Christianity', and warned those who imagine that, if they hear 'sermons duly, all is safe'.[3] This sort of application found its way into the Liturgy of Saint James, in one of the priestly prayers: 'God...enlighten our sinful souls to comprehend what has been written beforehand, so that we may not only...be hearers (μὴ μόνον ἀκροατάς) of spiritual songs but also doers (ποιητάς) of good deeds'.[4] Sometimes the exhortations have turned into musings on why words are often ineffective;[5] other times they have become polemical. As illustration of the latter, the Catholic bishop J.C. Hedley, in a sermon on Jas 1.22, complained about the 'partial Christianities' of Protestantism, which do not sincerely demand doing, because they teach that one need only believe.[6]

(ii) Although this commentary identifies 'the word' of vv. 22-23 with the Jewish Torah, commentators have almost always thought otherwise, identifying the term with the words of Jesus,[7] 'the gospel',[8] 'the Faith and Revelation of Jesus Christ',[9] or the Bible/word of God.[10] They have also

---

John of Salisbury, *Ep.* 185 ed. Millor and Brooke, 224, included preachers among the hearers. Moo, 90, includes 'even seminary professors': they too can deceive themselves. Theognostus, *Thes.* 16.29 CCSG 5 ed. Munitiz, 153, turned the exhortation upside down: one should not do what one hears if the speaker is the devil.

[3] L. Andrewes, 'Of the Doing of the Word', in *Ninety-Six Sermons*, vol. 5, new ed., London, 1843, 186-202. Cf. Smith, 83: one 'may have an audience without having disciples'. Robertson, 96; Ross, 39; and Townsend, 27, use the Scottish expression, 'sermon taster'. R. Sanderson, 'Sermon IV', in *The Works of Robert Sanderson*, vol. 3, Oxford, 1854, 360-63, attacked those who make predestination an excuse not to practice piety. He wound down with this: 'Who are the enemies of God's word? not the infidels and unbelieving Pagans, but the unfruitful Christians, such as daily hear the word and never practise it: these are the enemies.'

[4] Brightman-Hammond, *Liturgies*, 38-39.

[5] This is the chief topic of A. Raleigh, *Quiet Resting Places*, Edinburgh, 1885, 106-22, and it has sometimes been in mind when Jas 1.22-25 is linked to the parable of the sower; see n. 180. H.S. Holland, 'Hearing and Doing', *Christian World Pulpit* 63 (1903), 337-40, stressed the overwhelming power of sin as well as the ease with which humans regularly forget important things.

[6] J.C. Hedley, *The Christian Inheritance*, London, n.d., 171-90. Cf. Stevartius, 90-91, 83, 98. S.T. Coleridge, *Aids to Reflection*, London, 1913, 13 n. turned v. 25, with its mention of a 'perfect law', into criticism of the Familists and 'similar enthusiasts', who fail to understand the nature of 'law'. On the problem that a blessing for good works has raised for Lutheranism see A. Ritschl, *The Christian Doctrine of Justification and Reconciliation*, New York, 1900, 509-13.

[7] Cf. Davids, 96: 'primarily the ethical teaching of Jesus'.

[8] So e.g. Paulinus of Nola, *Ep.* 5.6 CSEL 29 ed. de Hartel, 28; Erasmus, *Paraphrase*, 144; Gill, 784; Doddridge, 840; Huther, 65; Beyschlag, 85; Adamson, 82 ('the gospel as taught by Jesus'); Baker, *Speech-Ethics*, 93; Maier, 95; Gundry, 922. Cf. Cantinat, 107: 'the Christian proclamation'.

[9] Hedley, *Christian Inheritance* (as in n. 6), 171.

[10] Theognostus, *Thes.* 16.29 CCSG 5 ed. Munitiz, 153; Beveridge, 'Sermon CXI' (as in n. 2), 208-209; Carr, 24; *et al.*

often equated the mirror of v. 23 with scripture, an idea read back from v. 25,[11] where one looks into the law of freedom, which has often been equated with the Bible.[12] So our passage has inevitably been the occasion for reflections on how either the gospel or the Bible reveals the true nature of human beings, above all—even though there is no hint of this in James[13]—their sins and failings.[14]

(iii) 'The law of freedom' in 1.25—chosen by the Digger Winstanley as the title for one of his books[15] and perhaps echoed in 'America the Beautiful' ('thy liberty in law')[16]—has encouraged much reflection on the nature of true freedom. Common has been the conviction that 'the Christian gospel is a law of liberty because it creates in the hearts of those who perfectly receive it the disposition and the power to obey it'.[17] Implicit here is the notion of an internalized law, in accord with v. 21.[18]

---

[11] And also encouraged by 2 Cor 3.12-18, where hearing scripture is the topic, freedom is mentioned, and a mirror analogy is employed; cf. Didymus of Alexandria, *Ps ad* 25.6 ed. Gronewald, 168-70; Lapide, 72, 76; F. Taylor, 32; Royster, 35-36; *et al.* See further below n. 110.

[12] Cf. Didymus of Alexandria, *Ps ad* 25.6 ed. Gronewald, 168; Gregory the Great, *Mor.* 2.1.1; Symeon the New Theologian, *Cat.* 31 SC 113 ed. Krivochéine and Paramelle, 226; Hilary of Arles *ad loc.* PLSup 3.68 (the OT is a small mirror, the NT a large mirror); Martin of Legio *ad loc.* PL 209.191A; Manton, 159; Poole, 883 ('the glass of the word'); Trapp, 695; Wesley, 859; de Wette, 221; J. Keble, *The Christian Year*, Philadelphia, 1845 ('our mirror is a blessed book'); Bisping, 29-30; Stier, 229; Bassett, 25; *et al.* This idea is the foundation for Kierkegaard's reflections in the first part of *For Self-Examination*, Princeton, 1990. According to Stulac, 73, Christians can apply James' teaching to the entire Bible because he is writing about the OT and the teaching of Jesus, and the latter forms 'the heart of the New Testament'. Idiosyncratic but affecting is G. Matheson, *Leaves for Quiet Hours*, New York, n.d., 25-27, who identifies the mirror with yesterday: recollection of one's past, with its many failures, leads to human sympathy.

[13] Although Martin, 50, has a point in observing that people typically look into a mirror in order to improve their appearance, that is, to remedy a defect.

[14] Cf. Nicholas of Lyra *ad loc.*; GenevaB., 115; Beveridge, 'Sermon CXI' (as in n. 2), 216; Burkitt, 1019; Doddridge, 839; Barnes, 37; T. Scott, 569; Plumptre, 60; A. Maclaren, 'Perfect Law' (as in n. 2), 40-45; Cox, 'Looking-Glass' (as in n. 2), 454; H.S. Holland, 'The Mirror of the Word of God', *Christian World Pulpit* 54 (1898), 49-51; Easton, 32; Roberts, 60; Sleeper, 64; Doriani, 52-53; McKnight, 153. One may compare in this connection Odes Sol. 3.1-3, where 'our mirror is the Lord' is apparently followed—the text is corrupt—by a reference to wiping one's face and being unblemished.

[15] G. Winstanley, 'The Law of Freedom', in *The Works of G. Winstanley*, ed. G.H. Sabine, Ithaca, NY, 1941, 501-600. His book, however, fails to interact at any point with James.

[16] The author of the lyrics, Katharine Lee Bates, was the daughter of a Congregationalist minister so presumably had some biblical literacy.

[17] So Dale, 48-50; cf. Aquinas, *Summa* 2/1 q. 108 a. 1; Sadler, 21; Maclaren, 'Perfect Law' (as in n. 2), 42 ('liberty is not exemption from commandment, but the harmony of will and commandment').

[18] Calvin, 273-74, and J. Williams, 'Law', 238, are here representative. Many commentators cite Jer 31.31-33 ('I will put my law within them, and I will write it upon

1.25 has also sometimes led to criticism of popular or secular ideas of freedom[19] or to the observation that so much of what human beings think of as freedom leads to bondage.[20]

(iv) Much attention has also been paid to the subject of self-awareness, to the importance of introspection in order to gain a true view of oneself.[21]

Apart from closely associating Jesus Christ with the perfect law of freedom, christological readings of Jas 1.23-25 are surprisingly rare. Only a few have observed that Jesus was a doer of the word or that he exhibited freedom.[22]

The anti-Judaism of the older commentary tradition is on full display in remarks on our passage. Exegetes have regularly asserted that Jews were or are hearers only, not doers.[23] Commentators have also defined the 'freedom' of v. 25 over against the imagined lack of such in Judaism, against the onerous Torah apart from Jesus Christ; and Paul's negative assertions about the Mosaic law and Mosaic dispensation have been read into James. Benson wrote: 'The law was so burdensome a service, and treated men with such rigor, it produced a spirit of bondage. Whereas; the easie service and mild treatment of the gospel provides a spirit of live and filial freedom. And this is a subject, which St. Paul has often touched upon.'[24]

---

their hearts'); cf. Calvin, 273; Baljon, 23; Belser, 82; Mitton, 71-72; Ruckstuhl, 15; Ammassari, 'Law'; Fabris, *Legge*, 158-59; Martin, 51; Moo, 94; *et al.*

[19] E.g. Hedley, *Christian Inheritance* (as in n. 6), 332-47.

[20] E.g. F.D. Maurice, *Sermons Preached in Country Churches*, London, 1873, 284-90; H.H. Henson, 'A Law of Liberty', in *Westminster Sermons*, London, 1910, 289-301.

[21] Cf. F. Paget, *Faculties and Difficulties for Belief and Disbelief*, London, 1887, 21-34 (observing that forgetting oneself is good if that means unselfishness but bad if that means unconscious assimilation to appetites, fashions, and irrational customs); H.S. Holland, 'The Mirror of the Word of God', *Christian World Pulpit* 54 (1898), 49-51; W.L. Watkinson, *Studies in Christian Character, Work, and Experience*, London, 1901, 55-60. A novel twist on this approach to our text appears in Anonymous, 'Mirror', *ExpTim* 31 (1887), 225-26: the mirror of the soul reflects the company with which one associates, and one's behavior affects the mirrors of others.

[22] But note D.J. Burrell, *The Unaccountable Man*, New York, 1900, 66-76; MacDougall, *Conflict*, 38-39; Roberts, 61; Scaer, 67-68; Royster, 37. For W.R. Inge, *Faith and Knowledge*, Edinburgh, 1905, 151, self-knowledge comes from assimilation to the image of Christ.

[23] E.g. Ps.-Oecumenius *ad* 2.23-25 PG 119.469A-B; the *Catenae ad loc.* ed. Cramer, 8 (indicting the scribes and Pharisees); Erasmus, *Paraphrase*, 144 (Jews 'memorize their law but do not express it in their way of life'); Manton, 152-53; Whitby, 680; Wordsworth, 19; Pyle, 311; Sanderson, 'Sermon IV' (as in n. 3), 361; Plummer, 580. One finds this accusation—which could likely be lodged against any group of human beings with a serious moral tradition—as recently as Chaine, 31.

[24] Benson, 48-49. Cf. Pareus, 549; Calmet, 672; Wolzogen, 190; Wells, 11; Guyse, 571; Simon, 103 (although 'the law is an empty tomb', it is no longer a 'prison that surrounds us and condemns us, but is rather a sign of victory won by Jesus Christ. Jesus is no longer in the tomb as we are no longer under the law. By him and with him we have passed from nothingness to freedom').

Exegesis

The structure of this passage—which for Brosend, 51, constitutes 'the thesis statement' of the whole letter—is straightforward. An opening imperative (v. 22) is unfolded by a simile or miniature parable illustrating failure (vv. 23-24) and by a commendation of that which leads to blessedness (v. 25):[25]

I. Complex imperative (v. 22)
   a. Be doers of the word (positive)
   b. Do not be hearers only (negative)
   c. (Do not) deceive yourselves
II. Case 1, illustrating I.b-c: Those who hear and do not (vv. 23-24)
   a. They are like one who look into a mirror
   b. and goes away
   c. and forgets
III. Case 2, illustrating I.a: Those who hear and do (v. 25a-b)
   a. They contemplate the perfect law of freedom
   b. and remain steadfast
   c. and become doers
IV. Blessing of those who do the word (v. 25c)

The whole is held together not only by theme but verbal repetition:

22	γίνεσθε	ποιηταὶ λόγου	ἀκροαταί			
23		ποιητής λόγου	ἀκροατής	κατανοοῦντι		οὗτος
24				κατενόησεν	ἐπελάθετο	
25	γενόμενος ποιητής		ἀκροατής		ἐπιλησμονῆς	οὗτος

The section, which implicitly moves auditors to decide which of two antithetical types best represents them, enlarges the exhortations to be quick to hear (v. 19) and to receive 'the implanted word' (v. 21). The verses also effectively preface the rest of the letter which, among other things, commands observance of the law (2.8-12; 4.11-12), emphasizes the importance of deeds (1.26-27; 2.14-26; 3.13-18), and declares that it is sin to know the good and yet not do it (4.17).

As with the rest of the sections in chap. 1, there is no agreement as to how 1.22-25 relates to surrounding verses. Some approach it as an independent unit.[26] Others see it and vv. 26-27[27] or 1.21-27[28] or 1.19-25[29] or 1.19-2.6[30] or 1.16-27[31] or 1.13-27[32] or 1.12-25[33] or 1.9-27[34] as a distinct

---

[25] See further Cheung, *Genre*, 129; Klein, *Werk*, 122; Marconi, 'Nota'.
[26] E.g. Weidner, 37; Cantinat, 11, 106-107; Mitton, 66.
[27] E.g. Kern, 143; Forbes, 'Structure', 151; Johnson, 205-206; R. Wall, 76.
[28] So Moo, 84-85.
[29] E.g. Pareus, 547; Piscator, 727; Simon, 95; Schnider, 45; McCartney, 114.
[30] So Bisping, 26.
[31] So Popkes, 110-11.

subsection. Perhaps most think of 1.19-27 as a large unit.[35] This is the view of Hartin, 106, who deems v. 19 the key: 'quick to hear' introduces vv. 22-25, 'slow to anger' introduces vv. 20-21, 'slow to speak' introduces vv. 26-27.[36]

Whatever the solution to that issue, the central point of the passage is clear. Our author is adamant that knowledge without corresponding action is worthless. In his own way, he anticipates Kierkegaard, who wrote: 'Truth is for the particular individual only as he himself produces it in action. If the truth is for the individual in any other way, or if he prevents the truth from being for him in that way, we have a phenomenon of the demonic. Truth has always had its loud proclaimers, but the question is whether a person will in the deepest sense acknowledge the truth, will allow it to permeate his whole being, will accept all its consequences, and not have an emergency hiding place for himself...'[37]

1.22-25 neither quotes nor obviously alludes to any particular text in the Tanak, although there are, as we shall see, several instructive parallels with Ps 119. There are also parallels with sayings in the Jesus tradition, sayings which insist on acting upon what one hears. Some have indeed thought that James rewrites Mt 7.24-27 = Lk 6.47-49 in particular; see on v. 23.

Because 2.14-26 more than suggests that our author understood the Pauline gospel to exalt faith at the expense of deeds, it is plausible that 1.22-25—which may well betray a knowledge of Romans (see on v. 22)— also consciously distances itself from Paul.[38] The apostle emphasized the importance of hearing (cf. Rom 10.14-17), and indeed spoke of the ἀκοὴ τῆς πίστεως (Gal 3.2, 5). James instead puts doing ahead of hearing, relativizing the latter as of no consequence in and of itself. In line with this, 1.22-25 clearly anticipates 2.14-26, where Paul is implicitly rejected: hearing without doing amounts to the same thing as having faith without works. Moreover, as Paul associated the law with slavery and stressed freedom from the law (cf. Galatians), one wonders whether 1.25, which links the law to freedom, is likewise intended to distance James from Paul.[39] It is notable that many have sensed tension here between James

---

[32] So Beyschlag, 62; Tsuji, *Glaube*, 67; M.F. Taylor, *Structure*, 122.

[33] So Burchard, 13, 67-68.

[34] So Gaugusch, 10-11.

[35] E.g. Lange, 60-61; Bardenhewer, 48; Chaine, 27; Moffatt, 23; Hauck, 12; Marty, 47; Grosheide, 24-25; Mussner, 98; Schneider, 11; Laws, 79; Kotzé, *Brief*, 98-109; Frankemölle, 320; Fabris, 93-94; Brosend, 48; McKnight, 55.

[36] Cf. Punchard, 362; Kotzé, *Brief*, 100-101; Frankemölle, 323; Blomberg-Kamell, 82-84. See further above, 293-94.

[37] S. Kierkegaard, *The Concept of Anxiety*, Princeton, 1980, 138.

[38] Cf. Limberis, 'Provenance', 411-12; Nienhuis, *Paul*, 189-90. Contrast Hoppe, 48.

[39] Jackson-McCabe, *Logos*, 178-79, and Kloppenborg, 'Torah', 217, also raise this possibility. Kern, 146, considers James' formulation to be modeled upon Pauline ideas, but he does not set James against Paul. Cf. Popkes, 'Law': James corrects certain heirs of Paul. Mayor, 73, turns all this around: Rom 8.2 'may serve as a comment on St. James'.

and Paul.[40] Luther wrote: James 'calls the law a "law of liberty", though Paul calls it a law of slavery, of wrath, of death, and of sin.'[41] One in any case surmises that James would have found Galatians problematic, just as he would have found Mt 5.17-20 congenial.

Verse 22. This, the thesis statement for vv. 22-25,[42] seems to be partial clarification of v. 21: receiving the word means not merely hearing it but also doing it.[43]

γίνεσθε δὲ ποιηταὶ λόγου καὶ μὴ ἀκροαταὶ μόνον.[44] Cf. Theophrastus frag. 96 (οὐκ ἀκροατὴς μόνον ἀλλὰ καὶ μάρτυς σου); Josephus, *Ant.* 20.44 ('you ought not merely to read the law but also, and even more, to do what is commanded in it'); m. 'Abot 1.17 ('doing [המעשה] is the essential thing').[45] On the striking parallel in Rom 2.13 see the Introduction, 66. Although works should 'follow knowledge as the shadow the body',[46] James knows it is otherwise.

James is fond of γίνομαι (10×), and γίνεσθε recurs in 3.1 (following μή).[47] Surprisingly, secular Greek rarely employ the imperative form, γίνεσθε.[48] By contrast, the imperative appears 4× in Philo,[49] 2× in

---

[40] E.g. Pareus, 549; Calmet, 671; I. Watts, 'The Form of the Gospel', in *The Works of Isaac Watts*, vol. 2, Leeds, 1810, 428; Neander, 65-67; Maclaren, 387; idem, 'Perfect Law', 40; Mussner, 107-108; Roberts, 62; Hodges, 44; R. Wall, 98; Stulac, 80; Hoppe, 48; McCartney, 123-24; Royster, 36-37. Most attempt to dispel that tension.

[41] M. Luther, 'Preface to the Epistles of St. James and St. Jude', in *Luther's Works*, vol. 35, ed. Bachmann, Philadelphia, 1960, 397. Note also Schrage, 23: James nowhere shows Paul's awareness that even the aspiration to deeds can be corrupted; James knows only the problem of 'Nicht-Tun'. Cf. R. Wall, 82, 87.

[42] According to Moo, 89, 1.22 is 'the best-known verse in the letter'. One is unsure how to judge such an assertion, but this author's impression is instead that, beginning with the patristic period, 1.17; 4.6, and 8 have been quoted most often.

[43] Cf. Mussner, 104; Reicke, 21-22; Klein, *Werk*, 121 (1.22-25 is not a 'continuation' of v. 21 but a 'clarification'); Moo, 88 ('Essentially, James argues in vv. 22-25, to "accept" the word is to "do" it'); Witherington, 442 ('When I say receive the word I mean do it, not just listen to it'). Manton, 152, puts it this way: v. 22 'catcheth hold of the heel of the former' verse.

[44] (τοῦ) νόμου appears in 04C2 88 254 378 398 *et al.* L623 L938 L1440 L2087 Dam. This is assimilation to 4.11 and/or Rom 2.13. The same change appears in v. 23; see n. 76. Whether μόνον originally followed (03 206 254 *et al.* **L**:FV **S**:PH **G**:B—so the *Editio Critica Maior*) or preceded ἀκροαταί (P74 01 02[*f] 04 025 044 5 69 81 88 218 *et al.* **Byz** Dam PsOec—so NA[27]) is uncertain.

[45] For Graeco-Roman texts that stress the importance of turning theory into practice see Johnson, 206-207.

[46] So Clement of Alexandria, *Strom.* 7.82.7 GCS 17 ed. Stählin, 59.

[47] According to Tasker, 52, the imperative 'has the implication "Make sure that you are"'.

[48] The few instances include Herodotus 1.126; 8.22; Dionysius of Halicarnassus, *Ant.* 3.30.3; Epictetus, *Diatr.* 2.6.2; (Ps.?-)Plutarch, *Mor.* 221A.

[49] Philo, *Jos.* 266; *Mos.* 1.223; *Decal.* 114; *Leg.* 4.213.

Josephus,⁵⁰ 4× in the Testaments of the Twelve Patriarchs,⁵¹ 24× in the NT (half of them in Paul),⁵² 9× in the apostolic fathers,⁵³ and otherwise not infrequently in early Christian literature.⁵⁴ Presumably the chief explanation for the wide attestation in Jewish and Christian texts is the LXX's translation of היו by γίνεσθε.⁵⁵

ποιητής⁵⁶ + λόγος⁵⁷ also has a likely Semitic background, for although דבר + עשה most often means 'do a thing',⁵⁸ it can also mean 'perform a word'.⁵⁹ Moreover, the usual Greek sense of ποιητής is 'maker'.⁶⁰ In James, by contrast, ποιητής means 'doer'.⁶¹ Additionally, ποιηταὶ λόγου is analogous to 4.11's ποιητὴς νόμου,⁶² for 'the word' of v. 22 takes up 'the word' of v. 21, which is the Torah.⁶³ So in the background are those Jewish texts in which one 'does' Torah.⁶⁴ For James, to do the 'word' is to do Torah, that is, to obey the commands of God.

---

⁵⁰ Josephus, *Ant.* 6.21; *Bell.* 6.51.

⁵¹ T. Zeb. 8.5; T. Naph. 8.10; T. Ash. 3.1; 7.1.

⁵² E.g. Mt 10.16; 24.44; Lk 6.36; Rom 12.16; 1 Cor 4.16; 11.1; 15.58; Gal 4.12; Eph 4.32; 5.1; Phil 3.17; Col 3.15.

⁵³ Did. 16.1; Ign. *Eph* 4.2; *Rom.* 7.1; *Phil.* 6.2; 7.2; Barn. 21.4, 6; Herm. *Vis.* 3.6.7; 3.9.7.

⁵⁴ E.g. Justin, *Dial.* 96.3; Acts Thom. 85, 86 ed. Bonnet, 200, 202; Acts Jn 31, 107 v.l. ed. Bonnet, 167, 204.

⁵⁵ As in Exod 19.15; Num 16.16; 1 Sam 4.9; 2 Sam 2.7; 13.28. Cf. the LXX's rendering of אל־תחיו with μὴ γίνεσθε; see on 3.1.

⁵⁶ 4×; cf. 1.23, 25; 4.11; NT: 6×; cf. Acts 17.28; Rom 2.13. LXX: only 1 Macc 2.67, πάντας τοὺς ποιητὰς τοῦ νόμου. Gk. Pseudepigrapha (Denis): 5×. Philo: 114×. Josephus: 10×.

⁵⁷ Jas: 4×; cf. 1.18, 23; 3.2.

⁵⁸ Gen 18.25; 21.6; Judg 6.29; etc.

⁵⁹ Cf. Ps 103.20 (MT: עשי דברו; LXX: ποιοῦντες τὸν λόγον αὐτοῦ); 148.8 (MT: עשה דברו; LXX: τὰ ποιοῦντα τὸν λόγον αὐτοῦ); Jer 22.4 (LXX: ποιήσητε τὸν λόγον). Note also Deut 1.18; Exod 33.17; Esth 5.5; Joel 2.11.

⁶⁰ Cf. Thucydides 1.11.2 (τοὺς ποιητὰς λόγου = 'creators of the word, poets'); Acts 17.28; Plotinus, *Enn.* 5.8.3 (ποιητὴς τοῦ πρώτου λόγου = 'maker of the first principle'). Assaël, 'Oeuvre', exploits Hellenistic usage to urge an aesthetic dimension to our text.

⁶¹ Cf. 1 Macc 2.67; Ecclus 19.20; Rom 2.13; Josephus, *Ant.* 18.63; Apost. Const. 7.18.2 ed. Funk, 402.

⁶² Cf. the textual variant, (τοῦ) νόμου for λόγου, in some witnesses (n. 44) and the revision in Apophthegmata Patrum sys. 10.188 SC 474 ed. Guy, 132: χρὴ τὸν μοναχὸν μὴ ἀκροατὴν εἶναι μόνον ἀλλὰ καὶ ἐργάτην τῶν ἐντολῶν.

⁶³ See the discussion on 1.21. Those who believe that the 'word' of v. 22 = Torah include Spitta, 52; Oesterley, 432 (arguing also that Jesus is 'the word' in a 'higher' sense); Ludwig, *Wort*, 169; Giere, 'Midrash', 95-96; Hartin, 98, 111-12 (adding that 'not too sharp a distinction should be made between the word of the gospel, the message of Jesus, and the biblical Torah'); Jackson-McCabe, *Logos*, 136-37; Keenan, 57-58; McKnight, 147. For the equation of 'the word' with the Christian gospel see above n. 8.

⁶⁴ E.g. Exod 18.20; Deut 17.19; 27.26; 28.58; 29.29; 31.12; 32.46; Josh 1.7; 22.5; 23.6; 2 Kgs 17.34, 37; 2 Chr 14.4; Ezra 7.10; Neh 10.29; Ps 40.8; Jer 32.23; 1QpHab 7.11; 8.1; 12.4-5; 1QS 8.15; 4Q171 2.15, 23; 4Q174 1 2.2; CD 4.8; 6.14; 16.8; 4Q528 2.1, 3-4; 4Q261 1 3; 4Q470 1 4; 11QTemple 56.3; m. 'Abot 6.7; Sifra Lev 209.11. For

ἀκροατής[65] in this context means 'hearer'.[66] Its association with λόγος is well attested.[67] The qualifier, μόνον (cf. 2.24), excludes the connotation that שמע and ἀκούω often have, of a hearing that becomes doing.[68] This explains the choice of ἀκροατής, which rarely if ever has that connotation. James in any case writes of a listening that is nothing more than listening, in contradiction to the old formula, 'hear and do'.[69]

παραλογιζόμενοι ἑαυτούς. Cf. v. 26 (ἀπατῶν καρδίαν αὐτοῦ) and note the wordplay with λόγου (vv. 22-23). Although the verb appears only twice in the NT (cf. Col 2.4), it occurs eleven times in the LXX.[70] To imagine that there is some virtue to being ἀκροαταὶ μόνον is to be deluded.[71] Interpreters often think in terms of a deception that leads to losing salvation.[72] The point seems rather to be that some people are deluded about the nature of authentic religion: they believe—or through their inactions appear to believe—that listening to religious instruction is in itself meritorious.[73]

According to Davids, 97, Origen attributed Jas 1.22 to Jesus.[74] The text he refers to does not bear this out.[75] But Ps.-Cyprian, *Mont. sina et sion*

Grunewald, 'Death', 466, Jas 1.22 'clearly echoes' Exod 24.3, 7, and McKnight, 147, writes: 'Torah and "do" (*'asah*) are brought together so often in the Hebrew Bible that instinct ought to lead us to see here a form of Torah observance'.

[65] NT: 4×: Rom 2.13 (οἱ ἀκροαταὶ νόμου); Jas 1.22, 23, 25. LXX: 2×: Ecclus 3.29; Isa 3.3. Gk. Pseudepigrapha (Denis): Let. Aris. 266. Philo: 13×. Josephus: 11×.

[66] Cf. Philo, *Sacr.* 78; Josephus, *Ant.* 1.161; 4.43; Epictetus, *Diatr.* 3.23.10; Herm. *Vis.* 1.3.3; Diognetus, *Ep.* 2.1; Acts Jn 56 ed. Bonnet, 178; etc. The classical sense, 'pupil' (cf. Plato, *Soph.* 237C; Plutarch, *Mor.* 80F), is foreign to James.

[67] E.g. Aristotle, *Rhet.* 1358a; Philo, *Congr.* 70 (οὐκ ἀκροατὴν λόγων); Josephus, *Ant.* 4.40; Papias frag. 2.2 ed. Bihlmeyer, 134; Clement of Alexandria, *Paed.* 3.12.99.1 ed. Marcovich, 203. Cf. Thucydides 3.38.4: θεαταὶ μὲν τῶν λυγῶν...ἀκροαταὶ δὲ τῶν ἔργων.

[68] Contrast Deut 18.15, 19; Mt 17.6; 4 Bar. 6.25.

[69] As in Deut 5.27; 30.12, 13; T. Job 4.2; Herm. *Vis.* 3.8.11; etc.

[70] Mostly for רמה. Gk. Pseudepigrapha (Denis): 2×. Philo: 0×. Josephus: 2×. For the verb with the reflexive pronoun see Aristotle, *Top.* 156a; Galen, *Simp. med. temp.* ed. Kühn, 12.219.

[71] Not all commentators agree that the verb is consequential; some deem it attributive instead, descriptive of those who only hear. The distinction matters little. Johnson, 207, translates παραλογιζόμενοι ἑαυτούς as an independent sentence—'that would be to deceive yourselves'—and comments: 'those who learn but don't do are both "deceiving themselves" (into thinking that passive profession is enough) and "defrauding themselves" (by missing out on the path to perfection through the doing of the word)'.

[72] Cf. the *Catenae ad loc.* ed. Cramer, 8 (the Pharisees and scribes, who hear but fail to do, will be handed over to destruction); Gill, 784 (citing Lk 13.25-26); Dibelius, 114; Reicke, 21-22; Davids, 97; Stulac, 74-75; Maier, 96; Witherington, 442 ('probably').

[73] E.g. Ropes, 175; Mussner, 97; Martin, 49. McKnight, 149, finds both interpretations true at the same time.

[74] He adds: 'While not impossible when one considers Jas. 5:12, this theory is not provable'.

[75] Is Davids' remark a misinterpretation of Cantinat, 108: 'Certain authors have even thought that the verse reproduces an agraphon of Jesus (cf. Origen, *Hom. in. Gn*, 2, 16)'?

13 CSEL 3 ed. Hartel, 117, does credit an agraphon related to v. 23 to Jesus: 'you see me in yourselves, as one of you sees himself in water or as in a mirror'.

Verse 23. One's imagination naturally envisages a religious setting in which Torah is read, after which it is up to the listeners to decide how to act. Some auditors will respond rightly. Others will go their own way.

ὅτι εἴ τις ἀκροατὴς λόγου ἐστὶν καὶ οὐ ποιητής.[76] Cf. 3.2 (εἴ τις...οὐ); Lk 14.26 (εἴ τις...καὶ οὐ); 2 Thess 3.10 (ὅτι εἴ τις οὐ).[77] Taking up the vocabulary of the previous verse—the repetition makes for emphasis—James poses the hypothetical situation of one who ignores the imperative in that verse: he hears without resolving to obey or resolves to no later effect. The arrangement is partly chiastic:

```
a   (22)          ποιηταί
b   (22)                    ἀκροαταί
b'  (23)                    ἀκροατής
a'  (23)          ποιητής
```

But a and b' and b and a' also reflect each other:

```
a   (22)   λόγου
b   (22)           negation with καὶ μή
b'  (23)   λόγου
a'  (23)           negation with καὶ οὐ
```

οὗτος ἔοικεν ἀνδρὶ κατανοοῦντι τὸ πρόσωπον τῆς γενέσεως αὐτοῦ ἐν ἐσόπτρῳ. We have here a brief parable or, in Calvin's words, 'an elegant simile' (273). Some modern—but not ancient or medieval—commentators find it odd that James moves from hearing (vv. 22-23a) to seeing (vv. 23b-25a) and back to hearing (v. 25b). They further puzzle over whether v. 25 continues the parable or comments upon it. In response it suffices to refer to Dibelius, 116, who acknowledges that the incongruous rhetoric is 'contrary to Western logic' but at home in James' world. Note that LXX Deut 4.9 even seems to speak of seeing words: πάντας τοὺς λόγους οὓς ἑωράκασιν οἱ ὀφθαλμοί σου.[78]

οὗτος recurs in 1.25. ἔοικεν ἀνδρί appears to be James' own formulation, not a traditional Greek expression.[79] It, like the parallels in the

---

Origen, in the place cited (*Hom. Gen* 2.6 SC 7Bis ed. Doutreleau, 112), rewrites Jas 1.23 without attributing it to anybody.

[76] νόμου replaces λόγου (correct interpretation) in 18 35 88 104 326Z 378 *et al.* L623 L921 L938 L1440 L2087 Dam L:Car **Sl**:S. The same variant occurs in v. 22; see n. 44.

[77] On οὐ after εἰ see Mayor, 70.

[78] Clarke, 803, finds in James 'a reference to Deut. iv. 9'.

[79] Nor did it become one, being otherwise confined to the Apophthegmata Patrum and John of Damascus.

gospels,[80] presumably reflects הוא[81] דומה לאדם or some closely related expression. For ἔοικα see on 1.6. ἀνδρί followed by αὐτοῦ moves one to think of a man, but the earlier τις is generic, and mirrors were associated with females no less than with males, so a gender inclusive translation might be in order.[82] Yet some earlier commentators thought the masculine ἀνδρί crucial for interpretation, alleging that men forget their faces more easily than women, so our text must be about the former.[83]

κατανοέω, which recurs in the next verse, was not common with πρόσωπον, although Jdt 10.14 supplies a parallel: κατενόησαν τὸ πρόσωπον αὐτῆς. Given that κατανοέω—which here means 'look at'[84]—translates ראה half a dozen times in the LXX, perhaps the familiar Hebrew ראה + פנה[85] suggested the construction. On the oft-alleged contrast with παρακύψας in v. 25 see the commentary there.

τὸ πρόσωπον[86] τῆς γενέσεως is yet another unusual Greek expression, probably a Semitism—the noun + genitive reflecting the Hebrew construct state—although no precise parallel is known. The peculiar phrase, which has never been satisfactorily explained, is most often thought to mean something like 'the way he has turned out to be, the way he really looks'.[87] Comparable then are Jdt 12.18 and Wis 7.5, where γένεσις (cf. 3.6) means 'physical existence'.[88] But what τῆς γενέσεως then adds is unclear.[89] The line would make perfect sense without it, or with a simple ἑαυτοῦ;[90] cf. the ἑαυτόν of v. 24. For Potts, 173, the meaning instead is: 'the native form of the face', that is, the face he was born with.[91] Gundry,

---

[80] Mt 7.24, 26 (ὁμοιωθήσεται ἀνδρί); 13.24 (ὡμοιώθη...ἀνθρώπῳ), 45 (ὁμοία...ἀνθρώπῳ), 52 (ὅμοιος...ἀνθρώπῳ); 20.1 (ὁμοία...ἀνθρώπῳ); Lk 6.48-49 (ὅμοιος...ἀνθρώπῳ).

[81] As in Tanḥ. Buber Balaq 16; b Taʿan. 16a, 19b; Moʿed Qat. 21b; etc.

[82] Cf. Gundry, 922. the masculine noun has figurative sense.

[83] So e.g. Guyse, 570; Clarke, 803. For criticism of this reading see Manton, 159; Hammond, 690.

[84] Cf. LXX Gen 3.6; Exod 2.11; Mt 7.5; Acts 27.39; Josephus, Ant. 5.5; Gk. LAE 16.2; 4 Bar. 5.12.

[85] As in Gen 33.10; 43.3, 5; 46.30; 48.11; Exod 10.28; 33.20; 2 Sam 2.13; Ezek 10.22; b. Ber. 19b; etc.

[86] For πρόσωπον see on v. 11. It can mean either 'face' (e.g. Mt 17.2) or 'appearance' (e.g. Jas 1.11). Carr, 25, et al., think of one's character as reflected in one's appearance.

[87] So BAGD, s.v., γένεσις, 2a. Contrast BDAG, s.v. πρόσωπον, 1a: 'the face he was born with'.

[88] Cf. Muraoka, Lexicon, s.v. 2. Note the translations of Tyndale ('bodyly face'); Cranmer ('bodely face').

[89] It is also unclear whether αὐτοῦ modifies πρόσωπον or γενέσεως.

[90] Cf. the NRSV: 'they are like those who look at themselves in a mirror'. But Baker, Speech-Ethics, 93, thinks that τῆς γενέσεως and κατανοοῦντι add to the absurdity: 'How could anyone after close study of his very own face in a mirror so easily and quickly forget it?'

[91] So too Grotius, 1077; Storr, 17; et al.; cf. the REB: 'the face nature gave him'. Potts cites for comparison Plato, Tim. 42C (τὴν ὁμοιότητα τῆς τοῦ τρόπου γενέσεως) and—like Wettstein, 664—a twelfth-century text, Eustathius, Comm. ad Hom. Od. ed.

HEARING AND DOING (1.22-25)

922, offers that τῆς γενέσεως refers to the rebirth of the Christian.[92] For Hort and Frankemölle, James has the creation story in mind; cf. 3.9. In Hort's words: 'The face which a man beholds when he received the Divine word is the representation of what God made him to be, though now defaced by his own wrong doings'.[93] The truth remains opaque.[94]

ἔσοπτρον[95] appears twice in the LXX.[96] Like the synonymous κάτοπτρον (cf. LXX Exod 38.26) and ἔνοπτρον (cf. Let. Aris. 76),[97] the word means 'mirror'. In the Roman world, mirrors were made of polished metal,[98] above all of bronze (Exod 38.8), copper, and (of most value and so more rare) silver.[99] Glass mirrors akin to ours, consisting of plate glass over a thin leaf of silver—probably invented ca. 400 BCE in Phoenicia— were known but rare.[100] Although highly polished cups and basins served as mirrors,[101] more popular were looking glasses, which were typically more or less round with a handle made of wood, ivory, bronze, or bone.[102]

Stallbaum, 173: τὴν εἰκόνα τοῦ ἐκ γενέσεως προσώπου. Cf. also LXX Gen 31.13: 'the land of your birth (γενέσεως)'. The Vulgate has: *vultum nativitatis*; cf. Rheims, 381: 'the countenance of his nativity'. According to Bassett, 24, who adopts this interpretation, 'the word seems to point to the idiosyncrasy of each man's physiognomy, which ought to make it more easy of remembrance'.

[92] Cf. the *Catenae ad loc*. ed. Cramer, 8; Reicke, 23; Hodges, 43. Johnstone, 113, seems related: 'we are...to think of the spiritual countenance, the face of the soul'. Bardenhewer, 54, argues just the opposite: one sees one's inherited nature, not the state of grace.

[93] Hort, 38; Frankemölle, 340-41. Cf. the *Catenae ad loc*. ed. Cramer, 8; Dionysius bar Salībī *ad loc*. CSCO 60 Scriptores Syri 101 ed. Sedlacek, 120; Carr, 24; MacDougall, *Conflict*, 39; Rendall, *Christianity*, 65 ('a clear and unmistakable reference to the book of the Genesis of men'); Simon, 102; Sidebottom, 35; Martin, 50; Jackson-McCabe, *Logos*, 142 n. 26; Marconi, 'Nota', 399-400. Contrast Mitton, 69; Moo, 90-91; and see further the discussion in Konradt, *Existenz*, 174-75.

[94] Assaël-Cuvillier, 'Éléments', 334-35, offer a christological reading: the face is the image of Jesus Christ. For additional proposals see Alford, 287.

[95] NT: 2×; cf. 1 Cor 13.12. Gk. Pseudepigrapha (Denis): T. Job 33.8. Philo: 1×. Josephus: 1×.

[96] Wis 7.26; Ecclus 12.11.

[97] According to Horsley-Llewelyn, *Documents*, 4.150, James chose ἔσοπτρον as opposed to several synonyms common in the papyri because it was 'appropriate for a more literary level of language'.

[98] Cf. Job 27.18; Ecclus 12.11; 1QM 5.4-5.

[99] See Pliny, *N.H.* 34.48.

[100] Pliny, *H.N.* 36.26.

[101] Cf. Pliny, *N.H.* 33.45; 34.48; Jos. Asen. 18.9.

[102] Literature: G. Bénédite, *Catalogue général des antiquités Égyptiennes du Musée du Caire N°s 44001–44102: Miroirs*, Cairo, 1907; F. Endell, *Antike Spiegel*, Munich, 1952 (a collection of the pictures on the backs of hand mirrors); G. Lloyd-Morgan, 'The Antecedents and Development of the Roman Hand Mirror', in *Papers in Italian Archaeology I: The Lancaster Seminar, Part I*, ed. H. McK. Blake, T.W. Potter, and D.B. Whitehouse, Oxford, 1978, 227-38; G. Zimmer, *Spiegel im Antikenmuseum*, Berlin, 1987; idem, *Frühgriechische Spiegel*, Berlin, 1991; Horsley-Llewelyn, *Documents*,

James likely has this last in mind, or perhaps the compact mirror which the Greeks invented. The latter consisted of two metal discs fastened by a hinge.

Looking into a mirror was commonly associated, for obvious reason, with self-knowledge.[103] Johnson has discussed the relevant texts, urging that James' simile assumes use of the mirror in popular Graeco-Roman philosophy.[104] He could be correct. For although James' parable does not require such a background, the tradition of likening a human being who embodies virtue to a mirror would help explain James' choice of illustration.[105] Is Church, 345, right to suggest that James' appeal to a mirror 'may be subtle jab' at the rich who enjoy 'consumptive lifestyles'.[106]

James does not imply that the person sees in his mirror things that need to be changed, or that his face is dirty or blemished, or that he beholds good things only to forget them, or that he sees bad things only to forget them.[107] Although such suggestions appear again and again in the

---

4.149-50; Spicq, 'ἔσοπτρον', *TLNT* 2.73-76; A. Schwarzmaier, *Griechische Klappspiegel*, Berlin, 1997.

[103] Cf. Seneca, *N.Q.* 1.17.4 ('mirrors were invented so that man might know himself'); *Ira* 2.36.1 ('it has been good for some to see themselves in a mirror when they are angry; the great change in themselves alarmed them, brought, as it were, face to face with the reality they did not recognize themselves'); Philo, *Migr.* 98; *Mos.* 2.139; *Contempl.* 78 (the soul that looks into the law contemplates 'what belongs to itself' as through a mirror); 1 Cor 13.12 (although often cited in the commentaries, it is hard to see that Paul's famous reference to seeing in a mirror has much to with James; cf. Schlatter, 149); Plutarch, *Mor.* 42B; Theophilus of Antioch, *Autol.* 1.2.4-5 PTS 43 ed. Marcovich, 17; POxy. 31.2603. See further Hugedé, *Métaphore*, 101-14. Note also the tradition that the mind or soul is like a mirror, as in Ps.-Plato, *Alc.* 133C; Sent. Sext. 450 ('the mind of the wise man is the mirror of God'). This motif lived on especially in Ephraem; see E. Beck, 'Das Bild vom Spiegel bei Ephräm', *OCP* 19 (1953), 5-24. For Knox, 'Epistle', 15, v. 23 is 'completely unintelligible' because it presupposes 'that it is ridiculous to look at your face in a glass but not your own soul'. This is far from obvious. Also, the later christological applications of the mirror *topos*, as in 1 Clem. 36.2 (through Jesus Christ 'we see as in a mirror his faultless and transcendent face; through him the eyes of our hearts have been opened'); Odes Sol. 13.1-3; Teach. Silv. 113.2-7; Acts Jn 95 ed. Bonnet, 198, seem irrelevant here.

[104] Johnson, *Brother*, 168-81. Cf. Klein, *Werk*, 122-23. Johnson cites, in addition to several of the texts in the previous note, Seneca, *Clem.* 1.1-15; Epictetus, *Diatr.* 2.14.17-23; Plutarch, *Mor.* 14A; 42A; 85A-B; 139F, 141D, 967D.

[105] Note further Johnson, *Brother*, 176: 'A reader schooled in' the relevant 'conventions would readily supply what is lacking in James' elliptical use of the metaphor of the mirror' and surmise that the law functions as a moral teacher. Cf. Tsuji, *Glaube*, 70: the mirror is a 'metaphor' for the law.

[106] Cf. R. Wall, 80, who wonders whether James wants to 'create an impression of personal vanity'.

[107] Contrast Erasmus, *Paraphrase*, 144 ('He cannot change the face he was born with and he steps back from the mirror no different from what he was when he stepped up to it. No, since he stepped up to it only to see what he looked like, the thought of changing the defects in his appearance does not even occur to him'); Martin, 50; *et al.* Christian ideas of sin have influenced this reading; cf. above, n. 5.

HEARING AND DOING (1.22-25)

commentaries, they go beyond the parable, which stresses only seeing and forgetting. The point is the lack of a permanent effect; cf. T. Job 33.8 ('rulers pass away, and their glory and boast will be ὡς ἐν ἐσόπτρῳ'); Dio Chrysostom 21.2 ('fades away like reflections in a mirror').[108]

Readers sometimes identify the mirror with the gospel[109] or scripture.[110] This may read too much into the text, even if there are analogies in Wis 7.26, where wisdom is 'a spotless mirror',[111] and Philo, *Contemp.* 78, which compares studying the law to looking through a mirror (ὥσπερ διὰ κατόπτρου). James may be (as in 1.11) just drawing a negative analogy: looking into a mirror and then forgetting is unlike looking into Torah in order to live it.[112]

1.22-23 has moved many to recall Mt 7.24-27 = Lk 6.47-49, the parable of the two builders, where doing the word of Jesus is like building on rock while not doing what he says is like building on sand.[113] Indeed, for some, James here borrows from the Jesus tradition or even intends readers to recall it.[114] The thematic parallel—one must not just hear but do—is obvious, and both passages offer parabolic illustration. There is an overlap in vocabulary as well:

---

[108] Note also Ps.-Plato, *Alc. maj.* 128A-29B; POxy. 31.2603. On the latter see Horsley-Llewelyn, *Documents*, 4.150. On the former see Denyer, 'Mirrors', who thinks it supplies the closest ancient parallel to James.

[109] Cf. Ephraem, *Ad Publius* 1 ed. Brock, 272 ('the mirror of the gospel'); Lapide, 72.

[110] See those cited in n. 11. This allows Stier, 229, *et al.* to think of looking into the Bible to see one's inner person or character.

[111] For a similar text, presumably independent of James but not Wisdom, see Ephraem, *Fide* 67.8 CSCO 154 Scriptores Syri 73 ed. Brock, 207.

[112] Cf. Dibelius, 115: v. 25 moves many to equate the 'mirror' with the 'law' or 'word', and 'from that one then moves to the further question of what is the object which is reflected in this mirror; finally one makes observations about the manner of the seeing, and thus the subtilizations go on forever. Over against all that...the simile itself...is completely contained within vv 23, 24'. So too Popkes, 130-31.

[113] Cf. Philoxenus, *Disc.* 1 ed. Budge, 4; John of Damascus, *Parall.* E 2 PG 95.1424B; Wolzogen, 189; Andrewes, 'Of the Doing of the Word' (as in n. 3), 201; Rosenmüller, 338; Schneckenburger, 41; Kern, 144; Neander, 66; Beveridge, 'Sermon CXI', 220-21; Plumptre, 59; Cox, 'Looking-Glass', 449-50; Smith, 82; Windisch-Preisker, 11; Schlatter, 148; Hauck, 12; Grosheide, 27; Mitton, 74; Scaer, 66-67; Martin, 50; Hoppe, 45; Klein, *Werk*, 124; Sisti, 'Parola', 84; Blomberg-Kamell, 89; Royster, 33; *et al.* Commentators on Mt 7.24-27 have also often called Jas 1.22-25 to mind; note e.g. Cyril of Alexandria, *Comm. Mt* frag. 89 TU 61 ed. Reuss, 180; Albertus Magnus, *Super Mt cap. I–XIV ad* Mt 7.24, 26 Opera Omnia 21/1 ed. Schmidt, 269, 271. Almost as many exegetes of James cite the preceding Mt 7.21(-23): Hus, 193; Aretius, 476; Wolzogen, 189; Pareus, 549; Stevartius, 94; Benson, 47; Poole, 883; Potts, 171-72; Lange, 64; Smith, 82; Ropes, 175; Knowling, 31; Marty, 54; Grünzweig, 59-60; Hoppe, 49; McKnight, 149; *et al.* For Wordsworth, 20, 'there seems to be a reference to our Lord's own speech, Matt. xii. 46-48'.

[114] E.g. Winkler, 28; Sadler, 19 ('no doubt'); Valpy, 239 ('seems'); Hort, 38; Knowling, 31 ('may well be'); Tsuji, *Glaube*, 124-25 ('possible'); Johnson, *Treasure*, 91-93 ('possibility'); Batten, 'Tradition', 387 ('surely'). Kugelman, 21, uses the term 'echo'.

Jas 1.22-23		Mt 7.24-27 = Lk 6.47-49
ποιηταὶ λόγου καὶ μὴ μόνον ἀκροαταί	Mt:	ἀκούει...λόγους...ποιεῖ
	Lk:	ἀκούων...λόγων...ποιῶν
ἀκροατὴς λόγου...οὐ ποιητής	Mt:	ἀκούων...λόγους...μὴ ποιῶν
	Lk:	ἀκούσας καὶ μὴ ποιήσας
ἔοικεν ἀνδρί	Mt:	ὁμοιωθήσεται ἀνδρί
	Lk:	ὅμοιός ἐστιν ἀνθρώπῳ

Deppe objects to discerning dependence here.[115] (i) The verbal similarities are not substantial.[116] (ii) James' γίνεσθε and παραλογιζόμενοι ἑαυτούς are without Synoptic parallel. (iii) The imagery of gazing into a mirror has nothing to do with building. (iv) The contrast between doing as opposed to just hearing was a common Jewish *topos*[117] and it also appears in Lk 8.21; Rom 2.13; 1 Jn 3.17-18.[118]

Is Deppe right? (ii) is weak while the impact of (i) is diminished by James' habit of freely rewriting the Jesus tradition. (iii) and (iv), by contrast, carry weight. At the same time, many of the texts Deppe cites fail explicitly to contrast hearing with doing,[119] and James otherwise creatively rewrote the Jesus tradition. Further, Jas 1.23 and Mt 7.24 are the only early Christian instances of ἀνδρί following ὅμοιος or a synonym, and the concentration of words featuring ποιη- (see on v. 25) has its parallel in the heavy use of ποιέω in Mt 7.12-26. Finally, gazing and forgetting are not unlike building something that falls apart whereas looking and persevering are analogous to building a house that endures storms. So perhaps the issue is not closed. We can at least safely infer, given the history of interpretation, that readers of James familiar with Matthew or Luke or the parable of the two builders might have been put in mind of words attributed to Jesus.

---

[115] Deppe, *Sayings*, 83-87. Laws, 85, also rejects an allusion to the Jesus tradition.

[116] James has ποιηταί and ποιητής, not a form of ποιέω, the singular λόγου rather than a plural form of the noun, ἀκροαταί and ἀκροάτης instead of a form of ἀκούω, and ἔοικεν rather than ὁμοιωθήσεται or ὅμοιος.

[117] He cites Deut 30.8-10; Ezek 33.31-32; Prov 6.3; Ecclus 3.1; 4 Macc 7.9; 1QS 2.25-3.12; 1QpHab 7.11; 8.1; 12.4-5; 4QpPs37 2.15, 23; Philo, *Praem.* 79; Josephus, *Ant.* 20.44; m. 'Abot 1.17; 2.10; 5.14; b. Šabb. 88a ('when the Israelites gave precedence to "we will do" over "we will hearken", six hundred thousand ministering angels came and set two crowns upon each man of Israel, one as a reward for "we will do" and the other as a reward for "we will hearken"'). To these one may add Deut 4.1, 5-6, 13-14; 6.6; 15.5; 30.11-14; 1 Macc 2.67; 13.48; Jub. 24.11; Philo, *Congr.* 70; Sifra Lev. 193.8 ('it is not the repetition of traditions that is the important thing but doing them is the important thing'); 209.11; 260.1; m. 'Abot 3.18; ARN A 24.

[118] The commentary tradition consistently associates Jas 1.22-23 with Rom 2.13-15.

[119] Note however Ezek 33.31-32 ('they hear your words but will not obey them...they hear what you say but will not do it'; many commentators on James cite this); Philo, *Praem.* 79 ('not merely to hear them [the commandments] but to carry them out by your life and conduct'). Cf. also Philo, *Congr.* 70 ('the practiser must be the imitator of a life, not the hearer of words'). Josephus, *Ant.* 20.44, contrasts doing with just reading.

In 1972, J. O'Callaghan, 'Papiros', made the sensational claim that several Dead Sea Scroll fragments are of NT books, and he identified 7Q8 with Jas 1.23-24. The Greek text has four lines, the first with initial σ, the second with initial εσ and perhaps ο, the third with initial λη, the fourth with perhaps initial ν (although O'Callaghan assigned this to another hand and another text). So he reconstructed this reading:

σ[ωπον τῆς γενέσεως αὐτοῦ ἐν]
ἐσό[πτρῳ· κατενόησεν καὶ ἀπε-]
λή[λυθεν καὶ εὐθέως ἐπελάθε-]

Very few have concurred. Not only (despite O'Callaghan) is there no other convincing evidence for Christian texts in Qumran caves, but the amount of text to work with is minimal. The reconstruction, moreover, requires omitting γὰρ ἑαυτόν, and while some witnesses omit γάρ,[120] all witnesses have the pronoun.[121]

Verse 24. We have here a parable, the moral of which is this: momentary perception is useless unless acted upon; hearing is not an end in itself.

Verse 24, taken with the second half of v. 23, sounds proverbial. Davids, 97, reckons it such. There is, however, no independent evidence that James preserves a traditional saying.

κατενόησεν γὰρ ἑαυτὸν καὶ ἀπελήλυθεν καὶ εὐθέως ἐπελάθετο ὁποῖος ἦν. Out of sight, out of mind. Human beings are slow to learn, quick to forget. κατανοέω comes from v. 23. The reflexive ἑαυτοῦ (Jas: 4×) makes for a link with v. 22. ἀπέρχομαι, εὐθέως (which here seems hyperbolic), ἐπιλανθάνομαι, and ὁποῖος[122] occur only here in James. On the transience of looking into a mirror see on v. 23. The perfect, ἀπελήλυθεν, likely emphasizing an on-going result,[123] stands out over against what are often said to be gnomic aorists, κατενόησεν and ἐπελάθετο.[124] Wesley, 859, following Bengel, glosses ἀπελήλυθεν with: 'to other business'. Cheung

---

[120] 206 429 522 630 1799 1890T 2200 L:FV^{ms},Hl K:S^{mss}.

[121] See further C.H. Roberts, 'On Some Presumed Papyrus Fragments of the New Testament from Qumran', *JTS* 23 (1972), 446-47; K. Aland, 'Neue Neutestamentliche Papyri III', *NTS* 20 (1974), 357-81; Puech, 'Qumrân', 29-31. In his later book, *Los primeros testimonios del Nuevo Testamento*, Cordoba, 1995, O'Callaghan defends his claims that some Qumran fragments are of the NT, but he no longer discusses the proposal regarding James.

[122] NT: 5×. LXX: 1-2×. Gk. Pseudepigrapha (Denis): 7×. Philo: 26×. Josephus: 25×.

[123] Cf. Lk 4.18; Heb 2.14. But according to Wifstrand, 'Problems', the perfect here stands for the aorist and so is a vulgarism. For Ropes, 177, the aorists themselves are 'a form of popular expression'.

[124] Bauckham, *Brother*, 52, dissents: 'It is better to read the verbs as telling a particular story...the comparison narrates a single imagined story'. So too Bardenhewer, 54. According to Moule, *Idiom*, 12, the aorists 'represent the Hebrew Perfect' and emphasize suddenness: 'No sooner has he looked...than he has gone away and...forgotten'. Cf. Mayor, 72: 'just a glance and he is off'.

appropriately observes, given the content of the next verse, how often the LXX uses ἐπιλανθάνομαι of forgetting God and God's law.[125] Maier, 99, recalls m. 'Abot 2.8: 'Eliezer b. Hyranus is a plastered cistern which loses not a drop'.

25. The imagery shifts from contemplating oneself to contemplating the Torah. The verse reverts to and expands v. 22a ('be doers of the word') and supplies a foil to vv. 23b-24:[126]

- 'looks into the perfect law' stands over against

    'who contemplates his face in a mirror'

- 'and perseveres' stands over against

    'having gone away'

- 'not a hearer who forgets but a doer who acts' stands over against

    'instantly forgets what he was like'

ὁ δὲ παρακύψας εἰς νόμον τέλειον τὸν τῆς ἐλευθερίας καὶ παραμείνας. δέ marks a contrast with vv. 22b-24. παρακύπτω[127] is a Jamesian *hapax*, here meaning 'look'.[128] Poole, 883, remarks: the word 'seems to be opposed to looking into a glass [v. 24], which is more slight, and without such prying and inquisitiveness'. Although this notion recurs incessantly in the commentaries, it is problematic: κατανοέω, the verb used in v. 24, need not mean 'glance' as opposed to 'observe carefully'.[129] It is more likely that we have here only a stylistic variation.

[125] Cheung, *Genre*, 132, citing Deut 4.23; 6.12; 26.13; Ps 119.16, 61, 93, 141; Hos 4.6; 1 Macc 1.49; 2 Macc 2.2. See further n. 178. O Holtzmann, 827, drawing an implicit contrast with his own world, offers that James 'knew nothing of vain people, young and old, who accurately keep their mirror-image in mind'.

[126] A fact often observed; cf. Kotzé, *Brief*, 106; *et al.*

[127] NT: 5×. LXX: 8×. Note especially Ecclus 14.20-23: 'Blessed (μακάριος) is the man who meditates on wisdom…who peers through (παρακύπτων) her windows'. Gk. Pseudepigrapha (Denis): 4×. Philo: 1×. Josephus: 0×.

[128] Cf. Ecclus 21.23 (with εἰς); Gk. 1 En. 9.1; Gk. LAE 17.2; Jn 20.11 (with εἰς); 1 Pet 1.12 (with εἰς); Lucian, *Pisc.* 30 (with εἰς). The verb can mean 'bend over for the purpose of looking' (BAGD, s.v.), as in Lk 24.12; cf. Mayor, 72. For Alford, 288, the verb is used because one must bend over to look into a mirror placed on a table. Oesterley, 434, envisions someone 'pouring over a roll of the Torah' (which seemingly assumes a literacy foreign to most in James' audience); cf. Schlatter, 150; Grosheide, 28. Benson, 47, is reminded of the cherubim over the ark, 'their heads bowing down; as if they wanted to pry into the ark, and see what it contained'.

[129] See further Field, *Otium Norvicense*, 59, 147; Hort, 40-41; Davids, 99; Baker, *Speech-Ethics*, 94-95; Moo, 92-93; Cheung, *Genre*, 129-30. Contrast Calvin, 273; Bengel, 491; Wesley, 859; Huther, 67; J. Williams, 'Law', 238; Hartin, 108; Witherington, 443. Simpson, 5, turns this around: 'Is it that, though the man took a good look at himself in the glass (κατανοεῖν, consider, *is* a very strong word; cf. Rom. iv. 19), yet he forgot what he was like, while the man who only peeps into the law of liberty is led on to abide…and so to act?' Cf. Baker-Ellsworth, 35-36.

Commentators often take νόμος (Jas: 8×) to mean 'the gospel'[130]— even though that expression occurs nowhere in our letter—or (less often) the teaching of Jesus,[131] the revealed will of God,[132] the law of love,[133] or some other specifically Christian idea.[134] All this is eisegesis due to harmonizing James with the rest of the Christian canon.[135] When the book is instead interpreted on its own terms, none of this is plausible. If 1.1 declares the ostensible audience to be Jews, if the rest of the letter is not marked by explicitly Christian themes, if the 'lawgiver' of 4.12 is God, and if the apparent sense of νόμος in 2.8-12 (which quotes three different Pentateuchal texts and alludes to another) is Torah, there is no good reason to discern any other meaning here: 'the law'—which is the same as 'the word' in vv. 21 and 22[136]— is the biblical Torah, or as 2.10 has

[130] Cf. Irenaeus, *Haer.* 4.34.4; Bede *ad loc.* CCSL 127 ed. Hurst, 192; Nicholas of Lyra *ad loc.*; Osiander, 725; Stevartius, 97; Grotius, 1077; Calmet, 672; Whitby, 677; Poole, 883; Henry, *ad loc.*; Gilpin, 592; Schneckenburger, 43; Macknight, 589; T. Williams, 1360; Weidner, 38; Baljon, 23; Gaugusch, 24; Moffatt, 28; J. Williams, 'Law', 238; Michl, 34; Schnider, 50-51; Kotzé, *Brief*, 106; Blomberg-Kamell, 91 ('particularly in its role as fulfilling the OT prophecies about a new or renewed covenant'); S. Luther, 'Ethics', 345; *et al.*

[131] Cf. Plumptre, 61 ('the spiritual code of ethics, which had been proclaimed by Christ, and of which the Sermon on the Mount remains as the great pattern and example'); Parry, *Discussion*, 27; W. Carpenter, 147-48. For Davids, 99-100, James has in mind the teaching of Jesus, understood as a new law. Cf. Davies, *Setting*, 402-405. For Baker, *Speech-Ethics*, 96, the text adverts to 'Jesus' reformulation of Jewish moral law'. According to Mayor, 73, James' recollection of Mt 5.17 and Jn 8.32 were probably the source of νόμον τέλειον τὸν τῆς ἐλευθερίας.

[132] So e.g. T. Scott, 569; Gench, 98. Cf. Ropes, 178-79 (the OT plus 'the precepts and truths of the Gospel'); Songer, 113; Maier, 98; Witherington, 444 (the OT, Jesus' teaching, Christian ethics).

[133] Cf. Wesley, 859; Knowling, 33; Mussner, 107; Hoppe, 47; Martin, 216. For Eckart, 'Terminologie', 524, and Laws, 14, the 'law' is Lev 19.18 plus the decalogue.

[134] Trapp, 695, thinks of moral law as opposed to ceremonial law; cf. Windisch-Preisker, 12; Seitz, 'Law', 484; Vollenweider, *Freiheit*, 185-86. Pott, 174-75, writes of the Christian religion, Carrington, *Catechism*, 78, of baptismal Torah, Lohse, 'Glaube', of the moral instruction of James itself. For Alford, 288, the referent is not the gospel but 'the rule of life as revealed in the gospel'. Beyschlag, 89, thinks of the new covenant, which involves the law being written on the heart. Lange, 66, speaks of the gospel in its role as completing and transforming the law. Roberts, 61, thinks of the preaching of the apostles that became the NT. According to McKnight, 158, 'James has a Christian hermeneutic of the Torah in mind here'; cf. Moo, 94: 'the law of Moses as interpreted and supplemented by Christ'. Many interpreters borrow from Paul and speak of 'the law of Christ': Ps.-Oecumenius *ad loc.* PG 119.469C; Theophylact *ad loc.* PG 1148D; Wolzogen, 190; Schneckenburger, 43; Carr, 26; Mayor, 73; Bouman, 96; Schlatter, 151; Easton, 32; Hauck, 13; Schneider, 13; Blackman, 68; Ruckstuhl, 15; Cantinat, 111; Isaacs, 193; Witherington, 445; *et al.* For histories of interpretation see Fabris, *Legge*, 13-32; Evans, 'Law'.

[135] The reception history of Mt 5.17-20 shows precisely the same phenomenon.

[136] The equation of 'word' and 'law' is natural in the light of the refrain in Deuteronomy, 'all the words of this law': 17.19; 27.3, 8, 26; 28.58; 29.29; 31.12, 24; 32.46; cf. Josh 8.34; 24.26; 2 Kgs 22.11; 23.24; 2 Chr 34.19; Neh 8.9, 13; 1Q22 1.4, 12; 1QS

it, ὅλον τὸν νόμον.[137] As in Mt 5.17-20, so in James: the Mosaic commandments are still in full force.

There is insufficient reason to claim that our text adverts not to all of Torah but only to portions of it, such as its ethical components.[138] To argue otherwise is to argue from silence,[139] and parallels make this hazardous. Ps.-Phocylides avoids all reference to cultic rules or indeed to any laws that might be thought distinctively Jewish—not because the author deems those rules or laws passé but because his goals lie elsewhere.[140] Similarly, the Testaments of the Twelve Patriarchs, which enjoin observing 'the whole law of the Lord',[141] contain few if any references to ritual Torah, yet one hardly comes away with the idea that the ritual law must be defunct.[142] Again, what should we infer from the fact that Sirach does not discuss the individual laws of Moses (even when naming Moses himself)? Beyond all this, Jewish diaspora texts in general often fail to pay much attention to sabbath or circumcision or—for obvious reasons—the temple cult or other laws associated with the land (such as tithing and purity regulations). Omission of those topics reflects primarily the situation of the addressees and the occasional nature and brevity of the relevant discourses. The same likely holds for James.[143]

That the Torah is 'perfect'[144] accords with Jewish tradition; cf. MT Ps 19.8 (MT: תורת יהוה תמימה; LXX: ὁ νόμος τοῦ κυρίου ἄμωμος; Aquila has τέλειος);[145] Let. Aris. 31 (ἀκέραιον); Rom 7.12 ('the law is holy and

---

8.22; 11Q19 59.10. Note also that 'word' and 'law' are synonyms in Ps 119; Isa 5.24; Jer 6.19; Mic 4.2; Philo, *Opif.* 143; *Jos.* 29; *Prob.* 46; *et al.* For discussion of this phenomenon see Ludwig, *Wort, passim.*

[137] Cf. Spitta, 54-55; Ammassari, 'Law'; R. Wall, 83, 86-87; Hartin, 100; Jackson-McCabe, *Logos*, 176-85; Hartin, 'Vision'; Kloppenborg, 'Torah', 217-18; Viviano, 'Loi'; Weren, 'Community', 194-95. Contrast Goguel, *Church*, 492 ('James wished to make it clear by his definition that he was not referring to the Mosaic law'); Via, 'Epistle', 260 (James insists 'that he does not mean the law of Moses'). For Ludwig, *Wort*, James has in mind the Torah, but chiefly its ethical content.

[138] Contrast Pfleiderer, *Christianity*, 308: the law of freedom consists of 'the moral duties of the decalogue'.

[139] Here Dibelius, 119-20, is typical: James pays no attention to ritual commandments, so he must have thought in terms of moral law alone. Cf. Schmidt, *Lehrgehalt*, 62-63; *et al.*

[140] van der Horst, *Sentences*, 70-76.

[141] T. Jud. 26.1; cf. Jud. 23.5; T. Gad 3.1.

[142] J. Marcus, 'The Testaments of the Twelve Patriarchs and the Didascalia: A Common Jewish Christian Milieu?', *JTS* 61 (2010), 596-626; D. Slingerland, 'The Nature of *Nomos* (Law) within the Testaments of the Twelve Patriarchs', *JBL* 105 (1986), 39-48.

[143] See further above, 27; also Dschulnigg, *Gleichnisse*, 262-64; Niebuhr, 'Torah'.

[144] τέλειος: see on 1.4.

[145] The line is quoted in Sifre Deut 48; Mek. on Exod 15.1; Tanḥ. Buber Yitro 5.12; y. Ber. 9c (5.3); b. Qidd. 2b; Exod. Rab. 29.4; etc., and it is discussed in Midr. Ps. 19.14. Some think James echoes or depends directly upon Ps 19.8; so A.T. Hanson, *The Living Utterances of God*, London, 1983, 147; Sigal, *Emergence*, 424; idem, 'Halakhah',

the commandment holy and just and good'); Philo, *Mos.* 2.12-16;[146] 3 En. 11.1 ('the perfect Torah'); Alphabet of Akiba BHM 3.14 ('the perfect Torah').[147] Note also 2 Sam 22.31 and Ps 18.30: God's 'way' is 'perfect'. The perfection of the Torah is implicit in the widespread conviction of its immutability and eternal nature.[148]

But what exactly νόμον τέλειον is supposed to connote in James is unclear. Perhaps it correlates with the application of τέλειος to human beings (1.4; 3.2): the obedient become perfect by living the perfect law.[149] Commentators offer additional suggestions: it is perfectly true,[150] it sets forth 'the true ideal of character and conduct',[151] it derives from the perfect deity,[152] or it replaces and/or completes once and for all the transitory Mosaic Torah.[153] Some exegetes opt for several of these at the same time.[154] The text, however, offers no definitive guidance, and that the author himself had some single, clear-cut idea in mind is far from obvious.[155]

That Torah brings—paradoxically[156]—freedom[157] is attested elsewhere;[158] cf. m. 'Abot 6.2 ('no one is free except he who labors in the

---

344-45. Sigal argues, against C.H. Dodd, *Bible*, 39-40, that James rewrites Ps 19.8: his τέλειον renders the MT's תמימה better than the LXX's ἄμωμος, and ἐλευθερίας interprets משיבת נפש according to 'midrashic exegesis': James 'has in mind *meshibat* in the sense of restoring, refreshing or allowing the *nefesh* to take a new breath, metaphorically to find new freedom or renewal of life'.

[146] Note also that Philo, *Fug.* 12, can speak of the τέλειος λόγος, and that he can further identify law and logos; see n. 136.

[147] On the perfection of the law in Jewish sources see further Fabris, *Legge*, 121-25.

[148] Cf. Bar 4.1; Mt 5.17-20; 4 Ezra 9.37; 2 Bar. 59.2; 77.15; etc.

[149] One of several suggestions in Rusche, 38. Cf. Spitta, 54 (adding that it is also perfect because 'anything better is unthinkable'); Reicke, 23.

[150] So Gill, 784 (but, as is typical of Gill, it is perfect in many additional ways as well); Kern, 146.

[151] So Cox, 'Looking-Glass', 454.

[152] So Darby, *Synopsis*, 356; Schnider, 51; Kamell, 'Soteriology', 148 (adding that it 'perfectly represents his will'). Cf. Doriani, 53: it 'reflects God's perfect character'.

[153] Carr, 26; Mayor, 74; Knowling, 33; Roberts, 62. Cf. Henry, *ad loc.*: it is perfect because nothing can be added to it. Commentators often cite Mt 5.17 here. For Popkes, 'Law', 133, the perfection of the law is 'eschatological', and 'the law is unsurpassable by its very relation to freedom'.

[154] Manton, 163-64, accepts six diverse explanations. Cf. Gill, 784.

[155] Sometimes exegetes observe that, as James' phrase 'is not precisely defined it must have been familiar to his readers'; so Goguel, *Church*, 493. But this is not obvious: an author may deem an open-ended term appropriate.

[156] Cf. the Latin *cui servire, regnare est*, and the later English liturgies with their phrase, 'in whose service is perfect freedom'. Schlatter, 152, appropriately recalls here 1.1: the author is a slave.

[157] ἐλευθερία: NT: 11×; Jas 2×; cf. 2.12. LXX: 7×. Gk. Pseudepigrapha (Denis): 0×. Philo: 97×. Josephus: 107×.

[158] Contrast R. Wall, 92, who writes that 'while the Torah's perfection is known from Jewish literature...the Torah's "liberty" is not'.

Torah'); Tanḥ. Buber Ki Tissa 12 (that the law was inscribed on tablets means 'freedom from the empires' or 'freedom from the angel of death' or 'freedom from tribulation'; cf. Num. Rab. 16.24); b. B. Meṣi'a 85b ('the one who, for the sake of the words of Torah, makes himself a slave in this world, will be a free person in the world to come'); Gen. Rab. 53.7 ('when the law came into the world, freedom came into the world'). There indeed developed a homiletical tradition of reading, in Exod 32.16, not חָרוּת ('engraved') but חֵרוּת ('freedom'), resulting in this: 'the writing was the writing of God, freedom upon the tables'.[159]

'The perfect law of freedom', like 'the implanted word' in v. 21, likely has also a Stoic background.[160] The Stoics, who spoke of the natural law as 'the word', regarded that law as bestowing freedom.[161] Moreover, Philo and the author of 4 Maccabees conflated Stoic ideas about the law with the Mosaic law and further linked that law with freedom.[162] So James may have become acquainted with Stoic terminology through Jewish sources. To what extent that terminology carried for him distinctively Stoic ideas, such as the universality of the implanted logos or the autonomy of the wise man, we do not know.[163] But James' central point, that one must do and not just hear, is characteristically Jewish.

Perhaps because νόμον...τὸν τῆς ἐλευθερίας (cf. 2.12: νόμου ἐλευθερίας) forwards a conventional conviction, it remains unelaborated. That is, James does not explain how the law brings freedom. Given the Stoic derivation, perhaps he thought of the law as offering freedom from ἐπιθυμία.[164] Christians, identifying the 'law' with the gospel or some related idea, and influenced by what the NT otherwise has to say about freedom,[165] have offered any number of suggestions,[166] most of them

---

[159] E.g. Exod. Rab. 32.1; 41.7. For discussion of rabbinic evidence see further Fabris, *Legge*, 84-91. Does Rom 8.2 assume traditional rhetoric about the law bringing freedom? Sigal, 'Halakhah', 344-45, believes that James knew the exegetical tradition regarding Exod 32.16. Stauffer, 'Gesetz', finds the phrase, 'law of freedom' (חוק חרות), in 1QS 10.6, 8, 11, but his proposal has not held up; see Nauck, 'Lex'; Fabris, *Legge*, 109-13.

[160] So too Dibelius, 116-17; Jackson-McCabe, *Logos*.

[161] Cf. Chrysippus frag. 360 ('as many as live with law are free'); Cicero, *Parad.* 34 (the free individual follows and respects the laws); Seneca, *Vit. beat.* 15.7 ('to obey God is freedom'); Epictetus, *Diatr.* 4.1.158 (Diogenes needed nothing but 'the law', and this 'allowed him to be a free man'). On freedom in Stoicism see Vollenweider, *Freiheit*, 23-104.

[162] Cf. Philo, *Opif.* 3; *Conf.* 93-94; *Mos.* 2.48; *Quod Omnis probus liber sit passim*; 4 Macc 1.13-35; 2.1-3.5; 14.2. See further Dibelius, 117-18; Fabris, *Legge*, 37-42; Jackson-McCabe, *Logos*, 87-105.

[163] Irenaeus, *Haer.* 4.39.3, can think in terms of free agents with power over themselves. Jackson-McCabe, *Logos*, stresses the Stoic background more than other interpreters.

[164] Cf. 1.14-15 and note Rosenmüller, 338; B. Weiss, 97; Moffatt, 28; Gench, 98.

[165] Note e.g. Mt 17.26 ('the sons are free'); Jn 8.32 ('the truth will make you free'); Acts 13.39 ('freed from everything from which you could not be freed by the law of Moses'); Rom 6.7 ('freed from sin'; cf. vv. 18, 22); 8.2 ('free from the law of sin and death'); 1 Cor 10 (freedom of conscience); 2 Cor 3.17 ('where the Spirit of the Lord is,

summed up by Poole, 883: 'freedom from sin,[167] the bondage of the ceremonial law,[168] the rigour of the moral, and from the wrath of God'. While this is eisegesis, Poole's remark may accord with our text insofar as it, lacking specificity, allows readers to supply the content.[169] James in any case fails to indicate whether the law leads to freedom—and if so to what sort of freedom—or is rather related to freedom in some other way.[170] The only certainty is that freedom is positive and associated with the law; cf. the various expositions of 'freedom upon the tables' (of the law, Exod 32.16) in Tanḥ. Buber Ki Tissa 12, quoted above.

Verse 25 and its context resemble in certain respects Ps 119, the famous lengthy paean to the Torah:

	Jas 1.22-25	Ps 119
Blessing of those who keep the law	v. 25: 'that one will be blessed in his doing'	vv. 1-2: 'Blessed are those whose way is blameless, who walk in the law of the Lord. Blessed are those who keep his decrees'

there is freedom'—commentators on James cite this again and again); Galatians (freedom from the law); Rev 1.5 ('freed us from our sins'). Cf. Barn. 2.6 ('the new law of our Lord Jesus Christ, which is free from the yoke of compulsion'); Irenaeus, *Haer.* 4.13.2; 4.34.4 (*libertatis lex*); 4.37.1. See further K. Niederwimmer, *Der Begriff der Freiheit im Neuen Testament*, Berlin, 1966 (he does not discuss James). Eckart, 'Terminologie', explains James in terms of Christian ideas about freedom. Klein, *Werk*, 143, argues for dependence upon Paul.

[166] See Theile, 79. R. Wall, 93-95, thinks of the levitical jubilee and its liberty for the oppressed. Cf. Ward, 'Concern', 112-27 (with hesitation). Marucci, 'Gesetz', contends that James is the first Christian to write of the relative freedom of the individual to make religious and ethical decisions. Cf. the discussion of freedom, obedience, and forgetting in Mek. on Exod 15.26; also b. 'Erub. 54a. W. Carpenter, 149, seems to be alone in thinking of freedom from self-deception (v. 22).

[167] This is the most common proposal in the commentary tradition. Cf. Gaugusch, 24: the new birth (1.18) means that Christians are no longer slaves to sin.

[168] Cf. Pyle, 311, who sets Christian liberty over against 'the slavish observance of Jewish ceremonies'. So too Estius, 395; Benson, 48; and many earlier commentators. See further above n. 24.

[169] Construing freedom in terms of multiple oppressions has been a common homiletical and theological strategy; cf. Dickson, 685; Manton, 164-66; Gill, 784; J. Keble, 'The Law of Liberty', in *Sermons for the Christian Year*, Grand Rapids, MI, 2004, 172-78; Macknight, 589; Schlatter, 154; Hauck, 13; H.U. von Balthasar, *The Glory of the Lord*, vol. 7, San Francisco, 1989, 500; 'Catechism of the Catholic Church' § 1972. That John of Damascus can apply 'the law of freedom' differently depending upon the rhetorical goal—note e.g. *F.O.* 96 (4.23) PTS 12 ed. Kotter, 226; *Volunt.* 44 PTS 32 ed. Kotter, 230—is typical of the tradition: there has been no rigid definition. Cf. Cheung, *Genre*, 95: freedom from the evil inclination, freedom to love God, freedom to be perfect.

[170] According to Ammassari, 'Law', the law is a law of liberty because Jesus instructed his followers to observe it in a spirit of freedom. He cites Mt 17.24-27.

Forgetting and not forgetting	vv. 24-25: 'for he looks at himself and then, having gone away, instantly forgets (ἐπελάθετο) what he was like...not a hearer who forgets' (ἐπιλησμονῆς)	v. 16: 'I will not forget your word'; LXX v. 30: 'your statutes I did not forget'; v. 61: ' I do not forget your law'; v. 83: 'I have not forgotten your statutes'; v. 93: 'I will never forget your precepts'; v. 109: 'I do not forget your law'; v. 139: 'my foes forget your words'; v. 141: 'I do not forget your precepts'; v. 153: 'I do not forget your law'; v. 176: 'I do not forget your commandments'—all with ἐπιλανθάνομαι in the LXX
Freedom	v. 25: 'the law...of freedom'	v. 45: 'I will walk in liberty'[171]
Perseverance	v. 25: 'perseveres'	v. 33: 'I will keep it to the end'; v. 44: 'I will keep your law continually, forever and ever'; v. 112: 'to perform your statutes forever, to the end'
'Word' = 'law'	vv. 21-22, 23, 25: 'the word' = 'the law'; note also 'the word of truth' in v. 18, with its parallel in Ps 118.43[172]	vv. 1, 9, 11, 16, 17, 18, 25, 28, 29, 34, 43-44, 49, 51, 53, 55, etc.: 'word' and 'law' (λόγος and νόμος in the LXX) alternate as synonyms
Doing/keeping the law	v. 22: 'doers (ποιηταί) of the word'; v. 23: 'not a doer (ποιητής)'; v. 25: 'a doer (ποιητής) who acts...in his doing (ποιήσει)'	v. 4: 'to be kept diligently'; v. 5: 'keeping your statutes'; v. 44: 'keep your law'; v. 55: 'keep your law'; v. 60: 'keep your commandments'; v. 112: 'to do (LXX: ποιῆσαι) your statutes forever'; v. 115: 'keep the commandments'; v. 121: 'I did (ἐποίησα) what is right and just'; v. 129: 'my soul keeps them'; v. 145: 'I will keep your statutes'; v. 158: 'they do not keep your commands'; v. 166: 'I fulfill your commandments'; v. 167: 'my soul keeps your decrees'; v. 168: 'I keep your precepts and decrees'; etc.

---

[171] On this see J.F.A. Sawyer, 'Spaciousness', *ASTI* 6 (1968), 29.
[172] See further Frankemölle, 301-302.

HEARING AND DOING (1.22-25)   341

Given the lack of strong verbal overlap,[173] the evidence is insufficient for claiming a conscious allusion.[174] The parallels do, however, establish that a Jewish audience would naturally have associated all that James says with the Torah.

παραμένω[175]—perhaps selected to match παρακύπτω—means 'continue', 'stay', 'endure'.[176] One may compare James' use of ὑπομένω (1.12; 5.11) and μακροθυμέω (5.7, 8): the theme of endurance is important to him. Here continued hearing and doing are likely envisaged,[177] and one may compare the many Jewish texts that warn about forgetting the commandments.[178] Readers sometimes recall Jn 8.31 ('if you remain in my word'),[179] or the interpretation of the parable of the sower, where certain hearers of the word receive it but do not endure.[180] Hort, 41, cites Ps 1.2: 'on his law he meditates day and night'.[181]

According to Dibelius, 120, James could have coined or spoken of 'the law of freedom' 'only where there was certainty that it would not be

---

[173] The common use of κατανοέω (Jas 1.24; LXX Ps 118.15) is presumably coincidence.

[174] Kamell, 'Law', however, offers that James 'may echo' Ps 119 'in his celebration of the law', and commentators do often refer to this psalm; note e.g. Stevartius, 91; Lapide, 73; Manton, 167 (referring to the delight in the law in Ps 119 and observing that 'affection... is a great friend to memory; men remember what they care for'); Grosheide, 28; Johnson, 209; R. Wall, 80; *et al.* Augustine, in his commentary on Ps 119, makes use of Jas 1.23-25: *Ps* 118 4.3 CCSL 40 ed. Dekkers and Fraipont, 1675.

[175] Jas: 1×. NT: 4×. LXX: 9×. Gk. Pseudepigrapha (Denis): 2×. Philo: 13×. Josephus: 47×.

[176] Cf. Gk. 1 En. 97.10; T. Job 20.10; Heb 7.23; Herm. *Mand.* 5.2.3 (patience 'remains' gentle and quiet); *Sim.* 7.6 (of serving God in humility). Marty, 61, observes that, in many inscriptions and papyri, the word conveys staying in order to serve.

[177] One can associate the verb either with continued looking (e.g. Winkler, 30; Mussner, 109) or with continued doing of the law (e.g. Burchard, 90); but one suspects that the text may well move many readers to think of both at the same time.

[178] See above n. 125; also Prov 3.1; Jub. 1.9 (= 4Q216 2.16: 'they will forget all my laws'), 14; 6.34; 23.19; 1Q22 2.4 ('Beware of... forgetting what I command you today'); 4Q436 1 1.5 ('not to forget your laws'); 4Q525 2 2.3-7 (on not forgetting wisdom); 2 Bar. 44.7; m. 'Abot 3.9; 5.12 (on forgetting what one studies); ARN A 23; b. Menaḥ. 99b.

[179] Poole, 883; Rosenmüller, 338; Schegg, 71-72; Carr, 26; Bardenhewer, 55; *et al.*

[180] Cf. 'The Egyptian Liturgy of Saint Mark', in Brightman-Hammond, *Liturgies*, 117; W. Wall, 345; Beveridge, 'Sermon CXI' (as in n. 2), 207-24; Bassett, 23; Johnstone, 116; Knowling, 31; Robertson, 96; Plummer, 580; Ross, 39; Scaer, 68-69; Richardson, 94; Maier, 96-97; Kamell, 'Soteriology', 147; *et al.* Although likely coincidence, the parallels between Jas 1.21-23 and the parable of the sower are perhaps worth noting:
sowing/planting of 'the word'   Jas 1.21 (ἔμφυτον); Mk 4.3 (σπεῖραι)
hearing of 'the word'   Jas 1.22 (ἀκροαταί); Mk 4.15 (ἀκούσωσιν, cf. 20)
reception of 'the word'   Jas 1.21 (δέξασθε); Mk 4.20 (παραδέχονται)

[181] According to Gill, 785, 'there seems to be an allusion to the blessed man in Psal. i. 1,3'. Cf. Manton, 162; McCartney, 125.

misinterpreted by Judaizers; this certainly may have existed either because Judaizing influences were not active at all in the communities in question or because Judaizers no longer constituted a danger'. This commentary rather takes the view that James speaks of 'the law of freedom' because he represents Christian Jews who, like other Jews, thought of the Mosaic Torah as a liberating gift.

οὐκ ἀκροατὴς ἐπιλησμονῆς γενόμενος ἀλλὰ ποιητὴς ἔργου.[182] Cf. the OT idiom, 'remember (to do) the/his commandments'[183] and the refrain in Ps 119 about not forgetting God's law/word. James passes by the possibility that one might remember and yet still not do.[184] The qualifying genitives are formally parallel, even though only the first is adjectival. ἀκροατής takes up the language of vv. 22-23, ἐπιλησμονή[185] harks back to v. 24's ἐπελάθετο, γενόμενος recalls the imperative in v. 22 (γίνεσθε), and the singular ποιητὴς ἔργου amounts to the same thing as the plural ποιηταὶ λόγου of v. 22. The line recapitulates, adding emphasis.

ἀκροατὴς ἐπιλησμονῆς, with its adjectival genitive,[186] is 'Hebraistic'.[187] One suspects, further, that ποιητὴς ἔργου, like ποιηταὶ λόγου, has a Semitic background, given that ποιητής must mean not 'maker' but 'doer', and that עשה (= ποιέω) + מעשה (for which the LXX has ἔργον well over a hundred times) was a very common Hebrew idiom.[188] Note the parallel in the Christian interpolation in Josephus, *Ant.* 18.63: Jesus was παραδόξων ἔργων ποιητής. Cox observes: one 'who is habitually occupied in doing the word must find it impossible to forget the word he is doing'.[189]

The concluding ἔργον (see on 1.4), which is strictly unnecessary—Robertson, 99, calls ποιητὴς ἔργου 'tautological'—ties chaps. 1 and 2 together. The latter contains a section that repeats ἔργον again and again (12×), and the former opens with an exhortation to aspire to a 'perfect work' (v. 4).[190]

---

[182] οὗτος in first place may be original; it occurs in 025 044 5 69 88 206 *et al.* **Byz** PsOec **S**:H **G**:G-D **Sl**:ChMSiS. Omit: 01 02 03 04 0173 33 81 436 *et al.* L596 **L**:FV **S**:P.

[183] Num 15.39, 40; Ps 103.18; cf. Josh 1.13; Mal 4.4. Gregory Palamas, *Hesych.* 2.2.20 ed. Meyendorff, 365, links LXX Ps 102.18 with Jas 1.25.

[184] See the discussion of this possibility in Sifre Deut. 48.

[185] NT: 1×. LXX: Ecclus 11.27. The word is rare, occurring before Sirach in literary texts only in a fragment assigned to the Comic Cratinus or the Comic Alexis. Is its occurrence in James then a sign of his knowledge of Sirach? So Plummer, 582. Gk. Pseudepigrapha (Denis): 0×. Philo: 0×. Josephus: 0×.

[186] Cf. 3.6: ὁ κόσμος τῆς ἀδικίας.

[187] So Hort, 42; this is a refrain in the commentaries. See further on 3.6 and Moule, *Idiom*, 175. Wifstrand, 'Problems', 176, speaks of 'a rather astonishing mode of expression to a Greek'.

[188] Cf. Gen 2.2; Exod 23.12; Isa 28.21; 59.6; 4Q271 3.11; m. Ber. 2.5; m. Sanh. 7.11; etc.

[189] Cox, 'Looking-Glass', 451. Unlike b. Menaḥ. 99b, James fails to observe that forgetting can be due to any number of causes, not all of them blameworthy.

[190] See R. Wall, 81, for additional connections with vv. 2-4.

Given the νόμον in v. 25, it is natural to suppose that ποιητὴς ἔργου denotes one who does the work that Torah demands. This makes it equivalent to the ποιητὴς νόμου of 4.11, and one may compare 'work(s) of the law' in Paul,[191] מעשי התורה (= 'works of the Torah') in 4Q398 14-17 2.3, and עבדא דפוקדנא (= 'work of the commandments') in 2 Bar. 57.2.

οὗτος μακάριος ἐν τῇ ποιήσει αὐτοῦ ἔσται. Blessed in doing, not in hearing; cf. Calvin, 274: 'the blessing lies in the action itself, not in the empty sound'. The closest formal parallel is a makarism attributed to Menander: οὗτος μακάριος ἐν ἀγορᾷ νομίζεται.[192] With the content one may compare Ps 106.3 ('Blessed are they who observe justice, who do righteousness at all times'); Isa 56.2 (LXX: μακάριος ἀνὴρ ὁ ποιῶν ταῦτα); Gk. 1 En. 99.10 ('blessed are all who heed the words of wisdom and understand them, to do the commandments of the Most High');[193] 4Q185 1-2 2.13 ('Blessed is the man who performs her', that is, wisdom); 4Q525 2 2+3 3-4 ('Blessed is the man who attains wisdom and walks in the law of the Most High'); Lk 11.28 ('Blessed are those who hear the word of God and keep it');[194] 4 Ezra 7.45 ('Blessed are those who are alive and keep your commandments'); Jn 13.17 ('If you know these things, blessed are you if you do them');[195] Rev 1.3 ('blessed are those who hear, and who keep what is written therein'); Jos. Asen. 16.14 ('Blessed are those who attach themselves to the Lord God in repentance'); the agraphon in Ps.-Clem. Hom. 12.29.1 GCS 42 ed. Rehm, 189 ('It is necessary that good things come, but blessed, he says, is the one through whom they come'); Seneca, *Ep.* 75.7 ('Non est beatus, qui scit illa, sed qui facit'). That the emphatic οὗτος (cf. 1.23; 3.2) is in first place in James may be due to conscious parallelism with v. 23 (οὗτος ἔοικεν ἀνδρί).

On μακάριος and beatitudes see on 1.12.[196] In accordance with probable Egyptian influence,[197] OT אשרי/μακάριος formulas appear first in wisdom literature or in literature influenced by wisdom, in sentences praising the wise man and holding him up for emulation.[198] Later,

---

[191] Rom 2.15; 3.20, 28; Gal 2.16; 3.2, 5, 10.

[192] 'This man is considered blessed in the public throng'. Cf. Plutarch, *Mor.* 100E, 471B; Themistius, *Metr. phil.* 4.18 ed. Hardin, 357; Orion, *Anth.* 8.9.

[193] Gk.: μακάριοι... οἱ ἀκούσαντες... λόγους... ποιῆσαι.

[194] The commentators very often recall this: Hus, 193; Calvin, 273; Piscator, 729; Stevartius, 94; Lapide, 71; Manton, 153, 169; Baumgarten, 70; Johnson, 210; Moo, 89; *et al.*

[195] This verse is often associated with James; cf. Theodore the Studite, *Catech. magn.* 34 ed. Papadopulos-Kerameus, 95; Andrewes, 'Of the Doing of the Word' (as in n. 3), 198-99; Theile, 76; Bisping, 29; Tasker, 53; Maier, 100; *et al.*

[196] M.F. Taylor, *Structure*, 61-62, finds several parallels between 1.12 and 25 and urges that this helps give a 'balanced structure to the opening chapter of James'.

[197] J. Dupont, '"Béatitudes" égyptiennes', *Bib* 47 (1966), 185-222.

[198] E.g. Gen 30.13; Job 5.17; Pss 1.1-2; 2.12; 32.1-2; 34.8; 41.1; 84.12; 119.1; 127.5; Prov 3.13; Wis 3.13-14; Ecclus 14.1-2, 20; 25.8; 26.1; 28.19; 31.8; 34.15; 48.11; 50.28; Tob 13.14.

beatitudes begin to appear with eschatological content (cf. Jas 1.12), particularly in apocalyptic writings.[199] But 1.25 may have nothing to do with this phenomenon.[200] Maybe those who listen and then act upon what they have heard are blessed even now, as they go about their work: ἐν τῇ ποιήσει αὐτοῦ.[201] Comparable then would be texts in which divine blessing in this life is a response to human obedience.[202] Barnes, 38, extrapolates: doing the word will 'produce peace of conscience; it will impart happiness of a high order of mind; it will exert a good influence over his whole soul'. This may not be so far from James' intention; cf. Deut 5.29 ('to keep all my commandments, that it might go well with them and with their children for ever'); Ps 19.11 ('in keeping them [God's commandments] is great reward'); Ecclus 1.26 (keeping the commandments brings wisdom); 1 Macc 2.64 (to grow strong in Torah is to gain honor); Josephus, *Ant.* 3.87-88 (keeping the law makes for happiness); m. 'Abot 6.4 (working in Torah leads to happiness); Midr. Ps 119.4 (if one obeys Torah one will live to see grandchildren).

ποίησις is a NT *hapax legomenon*.[203] Here it means 'doing' or 'working'.[204] For its use with νόμου (implicit here) see LXX Ecclus 19.20 and 51.19 (ἐν ποιήσει νόμου). It adds to the string of words featuring ποιη-: ποιηταί (v. 22), ποιητής (v. 23), ποιητής (v. 25), ποιήσει (v. 25).

---

[199] E.g. Ps 72.17; LXX Isa 30.18; 31.9; Dan 12.12; Tob 13.14; Ecclus 48.11; 1 En. 58.2-3; 81.4; 82.4; Pss. Sol. 18.6; Rev 19.9; 20.6; 22.7, 14; 2 Bar. 10.6-7; 2 En. 42.6-14; 52.1-14. The beatitudes of Jesus in the sermon on the mount and the sermon on the plain also belong here.

[200] Although commentators sometimes see eschatological blessedness here; so e.g. Poole, 884; Spitta, 55-56; Windisch-Preisker, 12; Bardenhewer, 56; Mussner, 110; Schrage, 23; Davids, 100; Klein, *Werk*, 124 ('little doubt'); Maier, 100; McCartney, 124; Gundry, 922. Contrast Popkes, 146 (the future is 'logical', not eschatological), Blomberg-Kamell, 93. Some others posit blessing both now and in the future: Johnstone, 124; Simeon, 44; Laws, 87-88; Hartin, 108; McKnight, 161. According to Huther, 68, although the blessing does not directly refer to the world to come, James presumably thought the blessedness 'permanent'. So too Baumgarten, 78; Beyschlag, 91. Schrage, 24, fails to judge between a present or future blessing: both it seems are equally possible for him.

[201] One could, however, construe ἐν as instrumental—'by means of'. Note that Protestant commentators are often anxious to insist that doers will be blessed *in* their doing, not *because* of it; cf. Burkitt, 1019; Kern, 144-45; Evans, 'Law', 38; Scaer. 69; Maier, 99. Manton, 162, protests: 'Here the Papists come upon us, and say—Lo! here is a clear place that we are blessed for our deeds'.

[202] E.g. Gen 22.17-18 (Abraham); 26.3-5 (Abraham); Deut 11.27 (Israel); 28.2-3 (Israel).

[203] LXX: 11×, most often for מעשה. Gk. Pseudepigrapha (Denis): 3× (all in Aristeas). Philo: 3×. Josephus: 15×.

[204] Cf. LXX Exod 28.8; Ps 18.1; Ecclus 16.26; Let. Aris. 31, 60, 258; Josephus, *Ant.* 17.94; 1 Clem. 27.7. W. Carpenter, 149, remarks: 'Not observe, in his deed, but in his doing. The point is not the success of the action but the blessing which comes to the honest doer, whether the special act is successful to human eyes or not'.

ἐν τῇ ποιήσει αὐτοῦ is a Semitism, the equivalent of ב + מעשה + pronominal suffix.[205] The Greek phrase is unattested in pre-Christian sources, and when it occurs in Dio Chrysostom, *Or.* 53.9, it means 'in his poetry'.

---

[205] Cf. 2Q21 1.6 (במעשיך); 4Q398 11-13 6 (במעשיהמה); 4Q418 158 4 (במעשיבה); t. Sanh. 8.7 (במעשו); Gen. Rab. 4.8 (במעשיך).

IX

PURE RELIGION (1.26-27)[1]

(26) If any one imagines himself to be religiously observant and yet does not keep a tight rein on his tongue but rather deceives his heart, that person's religion is empty. (27) Religion that is pure and undefiled before God the Father is this, to visit orphans and widows in their affliction, and to guard oneself against the world, unstained.

History of Interpretation and Reception

Burdick, 176, is candid enough to note that James fails to indicate what sin of the tongue v. 26 has in view. Readers have filled in the blank. Abba Isaiah thought of hypocrisy,[2] Gregory the Great of idle talk,[3] Henry of censuring others,[4] Weidner, 39, of 'zeal in talking about religion', Clarke, 803, of not teaching 'according to the oracles of God'. John of the Cross surmised that the imperative 'is to be understood no less of inward speech than of outward'.[5] Bede found comprehensive sense: James urges restraint from slanders, lies, blasphemies, foolishness, verbosity, and all speech leading to sin.[6] This reading, which allows the largest possible application, has been common.[7] Butler, however, in his well-known sermon on

---

[1] Recent literature: Alonso-Schökel, 'Culto', Baker, *Speech-Ethics*, 96-99; Burtz, 'Meaning'; A. Calmet, 'Sagesses'; Cheung, *Genre*, 124-28; Collins, 'Coherence'; Elliott, 'Reflections'; Johanson, 'Definition'; Krüger, 'Definición'; idem, *Kritik*, 135-43; Lockett, *Purity*; idem, 'World'; McKnight, 'Way'; Ng, 'Father'; Obermüller, 'Contaminacion'; D. Roberts, 'Definition'; Schoëkel, 'Culto'; Trudinger, 'Otherworldly'; Verseput, 'Puzzle'.

[2] Apophthegmata Patrum sys. 10.30 SC 474 ed. Guy, 32: 'whoever says one thing but holds another in his heart in malice, the liturgy of that man is empty' (ἡ λειτουργία τοῦ τοιούτου ματαία ἐστίν).

[3] Gregory the Great, *Mor.* 7.58 CCSL 143 ed. Adriaen, 378.

[4] Henry, *ad loc.* So too Calvin, 274, followed by Tasker, 54. Pyle, 311, refers to uncharitable slanders, revilings, and reproaches. Johnstone, 132, and Moffatt, 29, think of religious censoring.

[5] John of the Cross, *Cautelas* 9 ed. P.S. de Santa Teresa, 818.

[6] Bede *ad loc.* CCSL 127 ed. Hurst, 192.

[7] Cf. Martin of Legio *ad loc.* PL 209.191D; Lapide, 78-79; Poole, 884 ('the common vices of the tongue'); Gill, 785; Ropes, 182; Cantinat, 115. Manton, 172, first stresses the sin of speaking against others but then goes on to consider lying, cursing, swearing, railing, and ribaldry. Oesterley, 435, asserts that 'the reference is to the threefold misuse of the tongue, slander, swearing and impure speaking; see Eph. v. 3-6'.

the subject, isolated the sin of 'talkativeness', defined as a disposition to be talking, 'abstracted from consideration of what is to be said; with very little or no regard to, or thought of doing, either good or harm'; this is 'talking for its own sake'.[8] Butler, one suspects, was influenced by 'Talkative' in Bunyan's *Pilgrim's Progress*, for that character, who constantly and cheerfully converses on all subjects because what he loves above all is conversation, is associated with an explicit quotation of Jas 1.26-27.[9] T. Scott, 570, observing that bridles keep horses in the right way and that, in some situations, keeping silence is wrong, emphasized instead the importance of learning to say exactly the right thing. Cargal, 110-11, linking v. 26 to v. 27, infers that bridling involves speaking only what one truly enacts.[10]

James is also mute regarding how one gains the ability to bridle the tongue. Burkitt, 1019, offered that this comes through grace and God's word. A similar issue arises in v. 27—what moves people to minister to unfortunates or to keep oneself from the world? According to F.W. Robertson, one should cultivate sympathy, for that leads to helping others;[11] and as for guarding oneself against the world, one achieves that by avoiding excess social stimulation and exhilaration, focusing instead on 'the simplicities' of life.[12] P. Brooks, however, contended that one stays unstained precisely by carrying out ministry to the poor.[13] This makes the state envisaged in the last half of v. 27 a consequence of the state envisaged in the first half. So too Hodges, 47, who takes the Greek to mean: 'to visit orphans and widows in their trouble in order to keep oneself unspotted from the world'.[14] Others have been content to invoke divine power or the Holy Spirit.[15]

---

[8] J. Butler, *Sermons*, 1836, 75-88. Cf. Schlatter, 157: 'without regulation or goal the words thoughtlessly flow from the person'.

[9] J. Bunyan, *The Pilgrim's Progress*, New York, n.d., 165. Ross, 42, also recalls Bunyan's figure.

[10] Cf. Martin, 52: the reference is to uttering 'merely formal religious platitudes that have no substance evidenced by practical deeds'.

[11] Cf. Cyril of Alexandria, *Fest. Ep.* 5.8 SC 372 ed. Burns, 328.

[12] F.W. Robertson, *'The Human Race'*, New York, 1881, 163-64, 167-68.

[13] P.S. Brooks, 'Unspotted from the World', in *Sermons*, New York, 1879, 189: 'Go close up to this world, and help it...sacrifice yourself for it; so shall you be safest from its infection; so shall you be surest not to sacrifice yourself to it'.

[14] Schneider, 14, has it the other way around: holiness leads to serving one's neighbor.

[15] E.g. Anthony, *Ep.* 1.53-56 CSCO 148 SI 5 ed. Garitte, 4-5; T. Scott, 570; H. Macmillan, *The Daisies of Nazareth*, London, 1897, 226-30; J.S. Holden, *Redeeming Vision*, New York, 1908, 96 (James 'expresses the necessary moral attitude which conditions all spiritual experience. God's keeping power can only be known in any life in answer to the fulfilment of easily recognised conditions, and if by His grace you determine to keep yourself "unspotted from the world", His response will be power sufficient to make the unspotted life not merely a possibility but a reality'); Maier, 101.

Commentators have universally interpreted 1.26-27 'according to its spirit, and not its letter'.[16] Thus for Diodati, *ad loc.*, visitation of widows and orphans stands for 'all the duties of Christian charity', and in the words of Baumgarten, 81, we have here a 'synecdochen speciei pro genere'.[17] Calvin, 275, wrote: 'by synecdoche, he refers to the widows and the orphans. There can be no doubt that by this single instance he is commending the general range of charity'. Remarks similar to this are all over the literature.[18] Moo brings the application up-to-date by referring to 'immigrants...impoverished third-world dwellers, the handicapped, or the homeless'.[19] Church, 349, mentions HIV positive patients, abused children, undocumented aliens, minimum-wage workers living in privation, the impoverished elderly.

Control of the tongue in v. 26 has also, if only rarely, been generalized. The *Ancrene Wisse* 2.19 ed. Millett, 30, observes: 'A bridle is not only in a horse's mouth, but sits above the eyes, and goes around the ears, for there is great need that all three be bridled'. According to Richardson, 100: 'Control of the tongue stands for control of the whole self against temptation to indulge evil desire and to become deceptive about one's own double-mindedness. Control of the tongue also stands for persevering under trial, praying God for wisdom, and using the tongue, indeed the entire body, for the obedience of faith.'

Some have found James' equation of religion with social action and personal piety justification for relativizing the importance of liturgy, church buildings, and/or Christian rituals.[20] The deists naturally found

---

[16] Robertson, *Human Race* (as in n. 12), 163. A.C. Dixon, *Milk and Meat*, London, 1893, 199-200, observes that one cannot be literal here simply because some widows and orphans are well to do and do not need help.

[17] Cf. Dickson, 686; Grotius, 1077 (*ex specie genus intelligitur*); Wolzogen, 192; Pott, 178; Rosenmüller, 340; Theile, 86.

[18] In addition to those named in the previous notes, cf. Ps.-Clement, *1 Ep. virg.* 12.1 ed. Diekamp, 22; Acts Thom. 19 ed. Bonnet, 130; Cyril of Alexandria, *Fest. Ep.* 6.12 SC 372 ed. Burns, 398; Bede *ad loc.* CCSL 127 ed. Hurst, 192; Aquinas, *Summa* 2/2 q. 187 a. 2; Erasmus, *Paraphrase*, 146-47; Poole, 884 ('He doth not exclude others from being the objects of our charity and compassion, but instanceth in fatherless and widows, as being usually most miserable, because destitute of those relations which might be most helpful to them'); Henry, *ad loc.*; Plumptre, 62 ('proverbial types of extremest affliction'); Knowling, 36 ('a kind of proverbial expression for those most in need of help and sympathy'); Maclaren, 398; Mussner, 113; Gench, 99; Doriani, 59.

[19] Moo, 97. Tamez, 'Immigrants', with an eye on modern global conditions, sees the entire letter as advice to immigrants on 'how to survive in a hostile Greco-Roman society'.

[20] Note e.g. Gibson, 18-19; John Greenleaf Whittier's poem, 'O Brother Man' (on which see Church, 351-52); Maclaren, 403 ('we are accustomed as Nonconformists to think that texts of this sort hit the adherents of a more elaborate, sensuous, and ceremonial form of worship than finds favour in our eyes'). Wordsworth, 20, encourages pastors to limit the number of services they conduct so as to leave enough time to visit the sick and needy.

the passage congenial.[21] This explains the claim of Coleridge, that it has 'been perverted into a support of a very dangerous error' and become 'the favourite text and most boasted authority of those divines who represent the Redeemer of the world as little more than a moral reformer, and the Christian faith as a code of ethics'.[22] Later liberal Christians also sometimes appealed to James to esteem doing over orthodox doctrine, which is why, in response, more conservative Christians have stressed that what one believes is as important as what one does.[23] All sides, however, have appealed to 1.27 to promote philanthropy or fund-raising projects[24] as well as to counter class consciousness[25] and, more generally, to demand immersion 'in the social, economic, and political realities of the larger world', something that 'inevitably leads to being doers, and not just hearers, of the word' (G. Byron, 464). Blomberg-Kamell, 95, 100, represent many contemporary Protestants when they insist that James requires both social justice and personal piety, both orthopraxy and orthodoxy.[26]

Like so much of the rest of James, our verses have occasioned hostile generalizations about Jews. Erasmus wrote: 'Those who savour Judaism establish the glory of their religion in cloaks and phylacteries, in discrimination among foods, in ritual washing, in long prayers, and other ceremonies... Among the Jews the godly and pure person is someone who has not touched a dead body or someone who has washed in a running stream. In God's view the one who helps orphans and widows in their afflictions or raises up an oppressed brother or aids the needy with money is godly and pure. To a Jew whoever eats pork is impure. To God anyone is impure whose soul has been tainted and sullied by the passions of this world.'[27] These words are sadly representative.[28]

---

[21] Cf. M. Tindal, *Christianity as Old as Creation*, London, 1731, 293-94.

[22] S.T. Coleridge, *Aids to Reflection*, London, 1913, 13. Cf. Smith, 95 ('Men have used this text to prove that true religion and mere morality are convertible terms, that faith is of no importance, and that philanthropy is everything'); also the polemic of Manton, 174; Johnstone, 128.

[23] Cf. Maclaren, 399-400 (too many are so full of 'Christian work' that they have no 'intelligent grasp of the principles of the gospel'; the '"Christian worker" has all but blotted out the conception of "Christian thinker" and "Christian scholar"'), 405-406; Dale, 52-53.

[24] E.g. H.S. Holland, 'Works of Charity', *Christian World Pulpit* 49 (1886), 408-11; W. Ogg, 'Charity and Purity', *Christian World Pulpit* 58 (1900), 408-10; J. Rogan, 'Pure Religion', *Christian World Pulpit* 99 (1921), 286-87; Church, 350.

[25] A.W. Patten, 'Religion in Action', *Christian World Pulpit* 79 (1906), 152-56; Rogan, 'Pure Religion'.

[26] Cf. T. Zahn, 'Die soziale Frage und die Innere Mission nach dem Brief des Jakobus', *Zeitschrift für kirchliche Wissenschaft und kirchliches Leben* 10 (1889), 295-307; J.C. Nicholas, *Pure Religion*, Boston, 1922, 13-22; Songer, 113. W. Paley, 'Sermon XXXVI', in *The Works of William Paley*, vol. 5, London, 1830, 332-34, castigates those who engage in public benevolence but in private act immorally.

[27] Erasmus, *Paraphrase*, 146.

[28] Cf. Poole, 884 ('the hypocritical Jews, whose religion consisted so much in external observances, and keeping themselves from ceremonial defilements, when yet

Although nothing about 1.26-27 is explicitly Christian, commentators have consistently read Christian ideas and themes into the text. They have done this by, among other things, citing NT texts to illustrate every word and phrase, by equating θρησκεία with 'Christianity' (so Hus, 194), by appealing to the imitation of Christ,[29] by stressing the Christian content of 'Father',[30] by asserting that visitation of the needy is of little or no value unless rooted in 'Christian love',[31] by equating 'the world' with the non-Christian world,[32] and even by opining that the widows and orphans of v. 27 belong to the Christian community.[33]

Cyril of Alexandria associated the end of 1.27 with fasting, and Lapide thought purity related to mortification of the appetites and senses.[34] During the Middle Ages, moreover, 1.27 was thought to endorse anchoritism. Thus the *Ancrene Wisse* pref. 7 ed. Millett, 4, found two sorts of 'religious' in the verse—those who live 'in the world' and so can minister to the needy, and those who guard themselves from the world and so become recluses.[35] In contrast to this, Protestant commentators, lacking much sympathy for asceticism and anchoritism, have again and again confidently remarked that James promotes neither. Gibson, 18, and Martin, 53 are typical in asserting, as altogether obvious, that 1.27 does not require becoming an ascetic or a hermit.[36] Protestants have also been quick to insist that 1.26-27 does not teach salvation by works.[37]

---

they were sullied with so many moral ones'); Benson, 49 ('The jews were, many of them, very much addicted to cursing and swearing, and to passionate and reproachful language. And the charging such as different from them, with dangerous errors and designs, and censuring their practices'); Macknight, 589; Smith, 90-91. Knowling, 38, after citing a Zoroastrian parallel to v. 27, adds that Zoroastrianism 'was burdened with superstitions and fettered by ceremonial purity and externalism'. Lange, 66, takes a swipe at 'Mohammedans' and 'Jesuits'. Lapide, 79, dismisses Jews, pagans, Gnostics, Carpocrations, Orphites, Luther, Calvin, and Muslims as unclean.

[29] E.g. A. Fuller, 'The Characteristics of Pure Religion', in *The Complete Works*, Philadelphia, 1845, vol. 1, 398-404; Brooks, 'Unspotted' (as in n. 13), 182-86; Holden, *Redeeming Vision* (as in n. 15), 100; Robertson, *Human Race* (as in n. 12), 164; Macmillan, *Daisies* (as in n. 15), 224-26.

[30] Lange, 67; Maier, 101 (James' formula is an 'actualization' of the Lord's Prayer); *et al.*

[31] Cf. Johnstone, 136: 'Many visits—many visits to "the fatherless and widows" even—may have nothing of religion connected with them'.

[32] Cf. Maier, 103: the world is 'the human world outside the effective action of Christ'.

[33] Cf. Guyse, 572; Reicke, 25 ('works of love within the church'). Contrast Grünzweig, 63: v. 27 envisions more than members of the Christian community.

[34] Cyril of Alexandria, *Fest. Ep.* 1.3 SC 372 ed. Burns, 158; Lapide, 82.

[35] Bonaventure, *Lk* 1.80 Opera Omnia 10 ed. Peltier, 254, seems to associate bridling the tongue with religious retreat. Cf. Clarke, 803.

[36] One does, however, occasionally find a Protestant longing to leave the present life. Burkitt, 1020, wrote: 'we should more and more grow weary of the world, and long for heaven where there is nothing that defileth... Lord! When shall we ascend on high, to live with thee in purity.' In a different way, Charles Wesley's 'Love Divine, All Loves

Although 1.26-27 has occasioned little speculation about the *Sitz im Leben* of James, Hammond, 691, appealing to the supposed licentiousness of Gnostics as reported by Irenaeus, took the verses to be aimed at such. Whitby, 680, disputed this conjecture and instead proposed that James' target may have been the Zealots.[38] Both proposals are idiosyncratic. Most commentators offer little more than that there must have been religious strife in James' community.[39] Scaer, however, relates our passage to Acts 6.1, to the complaint of the Hellenists against the Hebrews, that their widows were being ignored.[40]

Exegesis

1.26-27 is a succinct, threefold characterization of authentic religion. Such religion involves measured speech, requires social action, and entails separation from 'the world'. It is the antithesis of a sham religion that fails to control the tongue, shuns unfortunates, and assimilates itself to 'the world'.

The verses are firmly linked to sections before and after.[41] They look back to 1.22-25, which emphasizes the importance of doing, and further back to 1.19-21, which uses purity language and demands measured speech.[42] They appropriately precede 2.1-13 insofar as care for widows and orphans correlates with not showing favoritism to the rich and with not dishonoring the poor.[43] They also link up with 2.14-26, which

---

Excelling', also gives 1.27 an eschatological reading: 'Finish, then, thy new creation; pure and spotless let us be. Let us see thy great salvation perfectly restored in thee.'

[37] Note e.g. Cartwright, *Confutation*, 655 (this responds to the gloss of Rheims, 381: 'True religion standeth not only in talking of the Scriptures, or only faith, or Christ's justice: but in purity of life, and good works... This is the Apostolical doctrine, and far from the heretical vanity of this time'); C.S. Robinson, *Studies in the New Testament*, New York, 1880, 158.

[38] Schlatter, 161-62, contrasts James' advice with the retreat of the Zealots to the desert.

[39] So e.g. Mussner, 111-12; Davis, 101. Reicke, 25, unaccountably thinks of Christians who complain about state authorities.

[40] Scaer, 69. Cf. Wordsworth, 20, who cites Acts 2.44; 6.1 and remarks that James' words were 'rendered specially appropriate by the circumstances of the Jewish Christian at this time'.

[41] Some commentators see them as belonging to a larger section—1.12-27 (Hartin, 88-89) or 1.16-27 (Popkes, 110) or, most commonly, 1.19-27; cf. Mussner, 98; Grosheide, 24-25; Martin, civ; Frankemölle, 321; Hoppe, 43 (yet calling 1.26-27 an 'excursus'); Fabris, 14. Many, however, including Pareus, 549; Plumptre, 61; Mitton, 74; Cantinat, 113; Burchard, 12; and the present commentator, treat the lines separately. A decision on the matter is not crucial for exegesis.

[42] For Verseput, 'Anger', 437, vv. 26-27 are the 'culmination' of vv. 19ff.

[43] Thus Penner, *Eschatology*, 144, can urge that 1.26-27 is 'both a recapitulation of the opening sections, and a bridge to the first section of the main body (2.1ff.)'.

dismisses those who fail to help people in need (2.14-17), and they are closely related to the discourse on the tongue in 3.1-12, which also employs χαλιναγωγέω and the imagery of bridling (3.2-3).⁴⁴ They further anticipate both 3.13-18 and 4.1-12 in that the latter passages speak of the 'heart' (3.14; 4.8) and use the language of purity (3.17; 4.8; cf. also 3.6). Finally, 1.27 foreshadows 4.4, which warns about friendship with 'the world'.⁴⁵

The passage as a whole has a nice rhythm and reads almost like a poem with two four-line stanzas:

εἴ τις δοκεῖ θρησκὸς εἶναι
μὴ χαλιναγωγῶν γλῶσσαν αὐτοῦ
ἀλλὰ ἀπατῶν καρδίαν αὐτοῦ
τούτου μάταιος ἡ θρησκεία

θρησκεία καθαρὰ καὶ ἀμίαντος
παρὰ τῷ θεῷ καὶ πατρί αὕτη ἐστίν
ἐπισκέπτεσθαι ὀρφανοὺς καὶ χήρας ἐν τῇ θλίψει αὐτῶν
ἄσπιλον ἑαυτὸν τηρεῖν ἀπὸ τοῦ κόσμου

Structurally, 1.26-27 is in large measure a collocation of dyads:

26   θρησκός... θρησκεία
     μὴ χαλιναγωγῶν   γλῶσσαν   αὐτοῦ
     ἀλλὰ   ἀπατῶν   καρδίαν   αὐτοῦ
27   καθαρὰ καὶ ἀμίαντος
     θεῷ καὶ πατρί
        ἐπισκέπτεσθαι... τηρεῖν
        ὀρφανοὺς καὶ χήρας

Note also the characteristic antitheses:

δοκεῖ θρησκὸς εἶναι   vs.   τούτου μάταιος ἡ θρησκεία
μάταιος ἡ θρησκεία   vs.   θρησκεία καθαρὰ καὶ ἀμίαντος
τῷ θεῷ καὶ πατρί   vs.   τοῦ κόσμου

In ancient texts, θρησκεία, καθαρός, ἀμίαντος, and ἄσπιλος refer to both cultic and moral purity. The immediate context and the history of interpretation suggest that the latter is exclusively to the fore here.⁴⁶ But Lockett, *Purity*, has argued that the traditional antithesis, literal purity vs. metaphorical purity, is reductionistic. He documents five different uses of (im)purity language in ancient Jewish sources: (i) natural purity and impurity (cf. 'pure' and 'impure' gold, which have nothing to do with a

---

⁴⁴ Oesterley, 434: 1.26-27 'would stand at least equally well before iii.1ff.'

⁴⁵ Blomberg-Kamell, 83, dub v. 27 'the thesis statement of the letter'.

⁴⁶ Lockett, *Purity*, 6-20, offers a helpful overview of what commentators have had to say about purity in these verses and in the rest of James.

ritual, moral, or social condition); (ii) ritual purity and impurity (of which there are different degrees); (iii) moral purity and impurity (which, unlike most ritual purity and impurity, involves willful action); (iv) figurative or spiritualized purity and impurity (attested in Graeco-Roman as well as Jewish and Christian texts);[47] and (v) ritual impurity as the occasion for intentional moral impurity; cf. Lev 7.20-21. In James, according to Lockett, purity, in the figurative sense, is closely related to perfection, to whole-hearted devotion. The two are not identical, but the former is a necessary although insufficient condition for the latter; and without purity, one is not just metaphorically or figuratively impure but truly separated from God. The argument, in its main points, persuades, as does Lockett's conclusion that purity language in James constructs a firm value boundary between sympathetic readers and the larger culture. At the same time, the social boundaries are not so fixed as to imply that our letter represents what we might call a sectarian community. In this James is different from the Qumran sectarians and the group behind John's Gospel. He does not represent an introversionist sect. He rather seeks common cause with diaspora Judaism (1.1).

That James uses cultic language without reference to cultic practices says nothing about his religious observance or his understanding of Torah. Christian commentators, reading themselves into our text, sometimes affirm that our author could not have been an observant Jew.[48] Dibelius, 121-22, for instance, contends that 'it is impossible to assign our passage to a Jewish-Christian who strictly' observed Jewish rituals: such a Christian would have been 'more specific' about ritual concerns, and he would have had to address the Gentile issue. This is a tenuous argument from silence.[49] Law-abiding Jews could use purity language in a figurative and moral fashion, and the status of Gentiles might not be

---

[47] Lockett, *Purity*, 58, cites Plato, *Leg.* 716D-E ('the bad man is impure in soul... and neither a good man nor a god may rightly receive gifts from the polluted'); Epictetus, *Diatr.* 2.8.12 (students should not defile the indwelling god 'with unclean thoughts and filthy actions'). To these one may add Isocrates, *Nic.* 20 (quoted below, 360); Diodorus of Sicily 12.20.2. Relevant Jewish texts include Pss 24.4; 51.2, 7; Prov 12.27; 20.9; Isa 1.15-16; 64.5-6; Jer 3.2; 13.27; Lam 1.17; Ezek 7.19-20; 36.17, 25-26; Dan 11.35; Mal 3.2-3; Wis 4.2; 8.20; Jub. 2.22; Pss. Sol. 17.36; T. Jos. 4.6; T. Benj. 8.2; 2 En. J 45.3. For early Christianity note Mk 7.15, 20 = 15.11, 23; Lk 11.41; 2 Cor 7.1; Eph 5.27; 1 Thess 4.7; 1 Tim 5.22; 2 Tim 2.22; Heb 7.26; 13.4; Jas 4.8; 1 Pet 1.4, 22; 2 Pet 2.13; Jude 23-24; Rev 14.4-5; Herm. *Sim.* 5.7.1. See further M. Newton, *The Concept of Purity at Qumran and in the Letters of Paul*, Cambridge, UK, 1985; J. Klawans, *Impurity and Sin in Ancient Judaism*, Oxford, 2000; also n. 96 below.

[48] Cf. Schrage, *Ethics*, 288: 'James's total lack of interest in ritual matters is shown above all by 1:27... It would be hard for the author to express more clearly his reservations about everything cultic'. See further above, 336.

[49] McKnight, 167, calls it a *non sequitur*. According to Laws, 92, 'the absence of specific contrast with ritual prescriptions... tells against polemical intention [against the ritual law] on the part of James'. Cf. Frankemölle, 360; Burchard, 93.

relevant in an epistle ostensibly addressed wholly to Jews (1.1). There is, moreover, no antithesis here between external ritual and internal purity, nothing to indicate that maintenance of the latter requires jettison of the former.[50] One thinks of Matthew, which quotes Hos 6.6 ('I desire mercy and not sacrifice') not once but twice (9.13; 12.7), declares that it is not what goes in but what comes out of a person that defiles (15.11), and yet affirms the continuing validity of every letter and stroke in the Torah (5.17-20; cf. 23.23). One should also not forget that our author chose to write in the name of James, who was remembered as having been Torah-observant.[51]

Verse 27 gives us the author's definition of right religious practice. It is, then, seemingly deficient from a Christian point of view, lacking as it does any specifically Christian elements. Hemminge, 16, imagining this to be a point favored by those who would denigrate James, responded: 'It was not the purpose of James perfectly to define religion, but onely to set downe certayne properties thereof disagreeing with the vanitie of hipocrites. Wherefore they are not to be heard, which here sharply reprove and find fault with James as a man ignorant of true religion. For it is one thing to define a thing and an other to signifie or shew it by certayne signes and tokens. Which, it is an unseemely thing and a shame, for the sharpe reprovers and taunters of James not to know.' This a fair retort.[52] But Hemminge himself goes on to define 'religion' with reference to Jesus Christ, and it remains striking that James can discuss central aspects of 'religion' without saying anything distinctively Christian. This commentary finds the explanation in 1.1, which does not confine the audience to believers in Jesus. James hopes to win the sympathy of some who do not share his Christian faith.

Verse 26. James advances his argument by highlighting inconsistency;[53] being religious and not controlling the tongue are incompatible. 2.14-17, which declares faith to be of no account if one neglects those in need, and 3.9-10, which makes blessing God incompatible with cursing human beings, adopt the same rhetorical strategy.

The structure seems to be chiastic—

---

[50] Cf. Painter, 'Rhetoric', 251: 'separation of the moral and ritual elements in the law is nowhere suggested by the letter of James'. McKnight, 'Way', urges that purity for James must involve observance of Torah.

[51] See further above, 121.

[52] Cf. Hort, 43: 'It is not ἡ καθ. καὶ ἀμ. θρ. He does not say or mean that what follows includes all that can be called pure and undefiled religion.' Commentators often state that James is not here really defining true religion, or that he assumes Christian ritual and doctrine; cf. Poole, 884; Gill, 785; Lange, 68; Barnes, 39; Knowling, 37; Ropes, 182; Robertson, 103; Easton, 34; Davis, 102; *et al.* Paley, 'Sermon XXXVI' (as in n. 26), dedicates several pages to the issue, contending that James sets forth the chief 'effects' of true religion, not its 'motives and principles'.

[53] Frankemölle, 358, uses 'schizophrenic' to describe the hypothetical addressee.

PURE RELIGION (1.26-27)

a θρησκός
  b -ων + -αν + αὐτοῦ
  b¹ -ων + -αν + αὐτοῦ
a¹ θρησκεία.

εἴ τις δοκεῖ θρησκὸς εἶναι.[54] The construction, εἴ (δέ) τις δοκεῖ + nominative adjective + εἶναι, appears nowhere in extant Greek writings until Paul and James:

1 Cor 3.18	εἴ	τις δοκεῖ σοφὸς	εἶναι
1 Cor 11.16	εἰ δέ	τις δοκεῖ φιλόνεικος	εἶναι
1 Cor 14.37	εἴ	τις δοκεῖ προφήτης	εἶναι
Jas 1.26	εἴ	τις δοκεῖ θρησκὸς	εἶναι

After Paul and James, it appears only in writers quoting the NT.[55]

θρησκός is a *hapax* in the Greek Bible, although the related θρησκεία (see below) occurs in both the LXX and the NT, and the LXX uses θρησκεύω.[56] Indeed, the exceedingly rare word occurs first in James and might be his coinage.[57] It must, given the sense of the related and well-attested θρησκεύω and θρησκεία, mean 'religious', in the sense of cultic devotion or public, ceremonial worship.[58] That is, it is the visible side of religious faith, the external manifestation of εὐσεβής; cf. Josephus, *Ant.* 13.244: Antiochus was called Εὐσεβῆ because of his exaggerated devoutness (θρησκείας).[59]

---

[54] 04 025 0173V 33 69 88 252 *et al.* L596 Antioch **L**:FV **S**:P^ms add δέ. This may be due either to assimilation to 1 Cor 11.16 or to a desire to strengthen the connection with v. 25. Some witnesses add ἐν ὑμῖν either before or after εἶναι. The most common of these readings, εἶναι ἐν ὑμῖν (5 69 88C 206 *et al.* **Byz** Cyr PsOec **G**:G-D **Sl**:ChMSi), may mark influence from 1 Cor 3.18.
[55] Cf. also Gal 6.3: εἰ γὰρ δοκεῖ τις εἶναι. On whether James knew 1 Corinthians see the Introduction, 62-67.
[56] LXX: 2×: Wis 11.15; 14.16; cf. T. Job 2.2.
[57] The earliest secular attestation of θρησκός is (Ps.-?)Aelius Herodianus, *Part.* ed. Boissonade 59.3: θρησκεύω· θρησκεία· θρῆσκος, ὁ περί τι πιστός. Hort, 42, has an interesting discussion of θρησκός, but it is marred by a denigration of Judaism.
[58] Cf. 4 Macc 5.7 and the Latin *religiosus*. Burtz, 'Meaning', prefers to translate James with 'worship'. For a wealth of relevant materials see Spicq, 'θρησκεία, θρησκός', *TLNT* 2.200-204; also Hatch, *Essays*, 55-57; Mayor, 75-76. Plutarch, *Alex.* 2, associates θρησκεύω with 'the celebration of extravagant and superstitious ceremonies'. Spicq observes that θρησκεία 'is normally an expression of an internal piety or a truly religious sentiment' and that 'James sided with the contemporary religious movement in the direction of the spiritualization of worship'. He cites Josephus, *Ap.* 2.192: 'It is God...all must serve by practicing virtue, for that is the holiest manner of serving God'.
[59] Cf. *Ant.* 6.90 (τὴν θρησκείαν καὶ τὴν εὐσέβειαν); Dittenberger, *Syl.* 783.42-43 (τοὺς μὲν θεοὺς ἐθρήσκευσεν εὐσεβῶς); Porphyry, *Abst.* 4.17 (θρησκεύουσί τε τὸ θεῖον καὶ εὐσεβοῦσαι περὶ αὐτὸ καθορῶνται).

δοκέω[60] can mean 'seem' or 'appear' as well as 'suppose' or 'imagine'. Either meaning would work here. But the theme of deception (ἀπατῶν) argues for the latter; so too the Pauline parallels noted above.

The situation in Jas 1.26-27 is, as already noted, analogous to that in 2.14-17, where someone professes 'faith' yet nonetheless lack works. In both cases, moreover, there is a sin of speech. Here it is not bridling the tongue; there it is speaking without doing.

What precisely θρησκὸς εἶναι connotes—one could think of communal worship, private prayer, and fasting, among other practices—is unclear. As so often, James is not concrete. Yet he clearly would have agreed with Philo, *Det.* 21: people go astray from the road of piety (θρησκείαν) when they practice ritual but not holiness, and when they lavish expense upon 'externals'. All that is 'mere display'.

μὴ χαλιναγωγῶν γλῶσσαν αὐτοῦ. The law of freedom (1.25) does not mean liberty of the tongue.[61] Although the Greek moral tradition likens control of the passions to a charioteer in control of steeds, James may have been the first to link χαλιναγωγέω[62] = 'bridle' with γλῶσσα.[63] At least he is the first extant author to do so, although there are other examples of χαλιναγωγέω (or the related χαλινόω) being used figuratively,[64] and Greek tradition could associate bridling with the human γλῶσσα or στόμα.[65] Philo especially was fond of the association.[66] One should not, however, overlook the possibility that the image of a human being with an animal's bit in his mouth owes something to Jewish tradition. Relevant texts include MT Ps 32.9 ('Do not be like a horse or a mule, without understanding, whose temper must be curbed with bit and bridle'); Ps 39.2 ('I will guard my ways, that I may not sin with my

---

[60] Jas: 2×; cf. 4.5.

[61] Albertus Magnus, *Par. an.* 28 Opera Omnia 37 ed. Borgnet, 490, speaks of *libertas linguae* in connection with Jas 1.26.

[62] NT: 2×; Jas 1.26; 3.2. LXX: 0. Gk. Pseudepigrapha (Denis): 0×. Josephus: 0×. Against Davids, 101, the verb does not appear here for the first time in Greek. This overlooks Philo, *Opif.* 86. Second-century pagan authors also know the word: Vettius Valens, *Anth. lib.* 9 6.3; 8.5; Lucian, *Tyr.* 4; *Salt.* 70.

[63] Jas: 5×: 1.26; 3.5, 6 (bis), 8. On bridles see on 3.3.

[64] Herm. *Mand.* 12.1.1; Pol. *Phil.* 5.3. Cf. Lucian, *Tyr.* 4; *Salt.* 70.

[65] Cf. Plato, *Leg.* 701C ('I must, every time, rein in my discourse like a horse, and not let it run away with me as though it had no bridle [ἀχάλινον] in its mouth [τὸ στόμα]'); Euripides, *Bacch.* 386 (ἀχαλίνων στομάτων); Philostratus, *Apoll.* 4.26 (χαλινὸς οὐκ ἦν ἐπὶ τῇ γλώττῃ); Libanius, *Ep.* 315 (ἐπέστω τῷ στόματι χαλινός). Note also Plutarch, *Mor.* 967B: geese, fearing eagles, can put large stones in their beaks and so bridle their gaggling loquacity (χαλινοῦντες τὸ φιλόφωνον καὶ λάλον) and so pass in silence. Does Gregory Thaumaturgus, *Pan. Or.* 97 ed. Koetschau, 20 (ὡς ὑπὸ χαλινῷ τῷ ἐκ στόματος ἡμῶν λόγῳ) depend upon James or show rather the conventional nature of the thought?

[66] Cf. *Det.* 44 (ἀχαλίνῳ κεχρημένους γλώττῃ), 174 (ἀχαλίνου γλώττης); *Somn.* 2.132 (ἀχαλίνου στόματος καὶ κακηγόρου γλώττης), 165 (γλῶτταν ἀχαλίνωτον); *Her.* 110 (ἀχαλίνῳ στόματι); *Abr.* 29 (ἀχαλίνῳ στόματι); *Jos.* 246 (ἀχαλίνοις στόμασιν); *Mos.* 2.198 (ἀχάλινον στόμα); *Leg.* 1.53 (ἀχαλίνῳ γλώσσῃ); *Legat.* 163 (στόμασι καὶ ἀχαλίνοις). For the general idea see *Sacr.* 49 and the overview in Deines, 'Sources', 42.

tongue; I will put a muzzle [מחסום] in my mouth');[67] Isa 30.28 ('to place on the jaws of the peoples a bridle [רסן] that leads astray'); 37.29 = 2 Kgs 19.28 ('Because...your arrogance has come up to my ears, I will put my hook in your nose and my bit [MT: מתגי; LXX: χαλινόν] in your mouth').

What restraining the tongue means, beyond not saying everything that enters one's head (cf. 1.19), is not indicated. This explains the variety of suggestions in the history of interpretation.[68] We might think of 1.13: one should hold the tongue when inclined to attribute temptation to God. More plausible and closer to hand is a connection with 1.19-21: one should be slow to speak, above all when one is angry.[69] The imperative, however, remains vague at this point. Is this because its content will be unfolded in 3.1-12, which implores one to beware of teaching, to avoid boasting, and to refrain from cursing others? Whatever the answer, the envisaged offense involves a disjunction—conscious or not—between outward appearance and inward reality,[70] and James would surely have agreed with m. 'Abot 1.17: those who multiply words occasion sin. Many commentators cite for comparison Mt 12.32-37.[71]

Why exactly James characterizes irreligion above all as failure to bridle the tongue is unclear.[72] Any number of other sins would have worked just as well. Perhaps it is because he is looking back to 1.19—be slow to speak[73]—and/or ahead to 3.1-12. Or maybe it is because he believes the heart speaks through the mouth (Lk 6.45), so that words accurately manifest one's identity. Or maybe the explanation is, at least in part, that he thinks of words as deeds, which do as much harm or good as actions. Barnes, 38-39, appears in any case to be correct: 'a single unsubdued sinful propensity...shows that there is no true piety'.

ἀλλὰ ἀπατῶν καρδίαν αὐτοῦ. Cf. Acts Phil. 142 ed. Bonnet, 81: ἡ ἀπατήσασα τὴν καρδίαν Εὕας. ἀπατάω[74] + καρδία (see on 3.14) is not a

---

[67] For Gill, 785, 'there seems to be an allusion to Psal. xxxix. 1'.

[68] See above, 346-47. For relevant materials from the Graeco-Roman world see Johnson, *Brother*, 155-67, documenting praise of brevity, self-controlled speech, and silence.

[69] Cf. Bouman, 98; Moffatt, 29; McKnight, 164. Most commentators on v. 26 refer to v. 19.

[70] Cf. Simeon, 49. Many speak of 'hypocrisy' when writing on 1.26-27; so e.g. Calvin, 275; Aretius, 477; Dickson, 686; Piscator, 730; Guyse, 572; Doriani, 57; Chaine, 37; Songer, 113; Royster, 39.

[71] E.g. Dionysius bar Salībī *ad loc.* CSCO 60 Scriptores Syri 101, ed. Sedlacek, 92; Lapide, 77; Punchard, 362; Blomberg-Kamell, 94. Also sometimes cited is Jesus' tirade against the scribes and Pharisees in Mt 23; cf. Hus, 195; Chaine, 37; Royster, 39. The latter wonders whether James 'had in mind the Lord's denunciation'.

[72] Townsend, 31, deems it 'slightly odd'.

[73] Cf. Tg. Ps 39.4: 'Is there such a thing as a bridle for a person's mouth? The verse means, however, "I will be silent and not occupy myself with idle words, only with words of Torah".'

[74] NT: 3×: Eph 5.6; 1 Tim 2.14; Jas 1.26. Gk. Pseudepigrapha (Denis): 12×. The word is common in both Philo and Josephus.

Greek idiom but represents the Hebrew פתה[75] + נפש/לב.[76] 'Heart' here means 'self'/'soul'; cf. T. Naph. 3.1, where the subject is also speech: 'Do not deceive your souls with empty phrases', ἐν λόγοις κενοῖς ἀπατᾶν τὰς ψυχὰς ὑμῶν.

James' sentence is inelegant. Does ἀπατῶν κτλ. modify μὴ χαλιναγωγῶν κτλ., so that somebody thinks he bridles his tongue when he does not, or does it modify all that comes before, so that somebody thinks he is religious when he is not? One expects καί instead of ἀλλά,[77] or ἀλλὰ ἀπατῶν κτλ. to precede μὴ χαλιναγωγῶν κτλ. If, however, James could write the enigmatic 2.18,[78] we need not be surprised at the present awkwardness. At least here the main point is more or less clear.[79] The envisaged individual supposes himself to be appropriately religious, and at the same time he does not control his tongue. James believes such a lack of control is in conflict with authentic piety.[80]

Johnson, 210-11, prefers to translate ἀπατάω as 'indulge'—'while indulging his heart'. This is an intriguing possibility.[81] Although LSJ, s.v., does not list that meaning for the verb, BDAG, s.v., claims it for Herm. Sim. 6.4.1; 6.5.3-4. No less importantly, Muraoka, Lexicon, s.v., finds this sense in Ecclus 14.16; 30.23. Certainly the related ἀπάτη can mean 'pleasure'.[82] So perhaps Johnson is correct to relate v. 26 not to the theme of self-deception in 1.6-7, 14, 16 but rather to link it to the condemnation of 'pleasures' and 'desires' in 4.1-3; cf. 5.5.[83]

---

[75] The LXX uses ἀπατάω for פתה 14×; cf. Exod 22.16; Judg 14.15; 16.5; etc.

[76] Grotius, 1077: *locutio Hebraea*. Cf. Lapide, 77; Pott, 177. See Job 31.9 (MT: נפתה לבי), 27 (MT: יפת בסתר לבי; LXX: ἠπατήθη λάθρᾳ ἡ καρδία μου); Ecclus 30.23 (פת נפשך ופייג לבך; LXX: ἀπάτα τὴν ψυχήν σου καὶ παρακάλει τὴν καρδίαν σου); Mek. on Exod 14.2 (משרים לבן של משרים). Cf. also the Aramaic טעא + לב, as in Tg. Ps.-J. 1 Kgs 11.2, 4.

[77] Schoëkel, 'Culto', argues that ἀλλά does not here mean 'but'. Cheung, *Genre*, 125, deems it 'emphatic'—'in fact', 'indeed'.

[78] Which like our clause shows symmetry—
μὴ χαλιναγωγῶν γλῶσσαν αὐτοῦ
ἀλλὰ ἀπατῶν καρδίαν αὐτοῦ
Both of these lines consist of a negation or disjunction + a participle ending in -ων + noun ending in -αν + αὐτοῦ.

[79] According to Dibelius, 121, 'the construction here is inexact' because James wants to 'introduce a double antithesis'—'religious' vs. 'without bridling'; 'thinks' vs. 'deceives'. According to Baker, *Speech-Ethics*, 97, the disjunction 'is placed before the second participle because the author's main point has to do with self-deception of which uncontrolled speech is only one instance'.

[80] Some interpreters, however, think the deception might be blindness brought on by a self-conceit that censures and speaks evil of others; so e.g. Poole, 884.

[81] McKnight, 165, is open to Johnson's proposal. Contrast Cheung, *Genre*, 125.

[82] See Spicq, 'ἀπάτη', *TLNT* 1.153-55. Cf. perhaps Mk 4.19.

[83] For Knowling, 35, the verb does not just refer to an intellectual error but 'emphasises the moral nature of the error'.

τούτου μάταιος ἡ θρησκεία. θρησκεία (cf. עבודה) was a particular favorite of Josephus (91×).[84] It can bear either negative[85] or positive sense.[86] Here, where it connotes both inward and outward piety, it recalls θρησκός and so unifies the sentence. It also creates a link with the following verse (θρησκεία καθαρά). Its appearance with μάταιος[87] makes for yet one more combination unattested before James,[88] although Jewish sources supply conceptual parallels.[89] The unusual combination of the two words prepares for 2.20, where a foolish (κενέ) individual has a 'useless' (ἀργή) faith.

As the verses in n. 89 indicate, μάταιος was regularly associated with false worship. Most notably, the LXX links the word to idol worship.[90] So it makes for strong contrast with καθαρός, ἀμίαντος, and ἄσπιλος in the rest of the passage. To be impure and undefiled before God and stained by the world is to be an idolater.[91]

James does not elaborate on the implications of 'vain'. Perhaps it is best to leave it at that. One could think either in terms of losing eternal salvation[92] or—perhaps at the same time?—of the consequences for those, such as widows and orphans, who need support from those who profess religious faith.[93] Most commentators do not address the issue clearly.

Verse 27. This verse, attached by catchword to the previous line, is nicely balanced. It contains three word pairs (καθαρὰ καὶ ἀμίαντος, θεῷ καὶ πατρί, ὀρφανοὺς καὶ χήρας), two prepositions introducing dative cases (παρὰ τῷ θεῷ, ἐν τῇ θλίψει), and two parallel infinitives (ἐπισκέπτεσθαι, τηρεῖν). The ἄσπιλον in the third line, moreover, compliments the first line's καθαρά.

---

[84] LXX: 5×. NT: 4×: Acts 26.5; Col 2.18; Jas 1.26-27. Gk. Pseudepigrapha (Denis): 0×. Philo: 5×.

[85] Cf. Philo, Det. 21 (θρησκείαν ἀντὶ ὁσιότητος); Col 2.18.

[86] Cf. v. 27; 1 Clem. 45.7.

[87] NT: 6×; Jas: 1×. LXX often for הבל, ר(י)ק, and שוא. Gk. Pseudepigrapha (Denis): 12×. Philo: 20×. Josephus: 8×.

[88] Ps.-Clement, 1 Ep. virg. 3.4 ed. Diekamp, 4 (θρησκεία ἐστὶν μάταιος) depends upon James.

[89] Cf. LXX Isa 29.13 (quoted in Mt 7.7 = Mt 15.9: 'in vain [ματήν] do they worship me'); Mal 3.14 ('You have said, "It is vain [LXX: μάταιος] to serve God"'); Let. Aris. 134 ('the gods whom they vainly [ματαίως] worship'); Sib. Or. 3.547-48 ('you give vain [μάταια] gifts to the dead and sacrifice to idols'); 5.83 ('they have made them [gods] of bronze and gold and silver, vain [ματαίους]').

[90] E.g. Lev 17.7; 2 Chr 11.15; Jer 2.5; 8.19; 10.3, 15; Ezek 8.10; Hos 5.11; Amos 2.4; Zech 11.17. Cf. Acts 14.15.

[91] More recent commentators often see this; cf. Knowling, 35 ('perhaps'); Blackman, 69-70; Johnson, 211; Hartin, 101; Moo, 96; McCartney, 129; et al.

[92] So e.g. Davids, 102; Burchard, 92; Gundry, 922.

[93] So McKnight, 166: 'mataios... pertains to jeopardizing the social conditions created (or not created) by those who choose (choose not) to control the tongue and refrain from violence and anger'.

Because 'negatives in religion are not enough' (Manton, 173), v. 27 supplies the antithesis to v. 26. While the one sentence characterizes vain religion, the other characterizes 'pure and undefiled' religion. James would probably have assented to the analysis of Lactantius: 'It is impossible that those who are not deceived in all the (other) actions of their lives should err in what is essential, namely, in religion, the foundation of all. For if one adopts an impious attitude toward what is essential, that carries into everything else. Equally it is impossible that those who are deceived in all the actions of their lives should be undeceived in religion, because piety, if it rules over what is essential in life, maintains the same rule in all of its life. So the general character of each of the two sides may be known from the quality of their actions.'[94]

θρησκεία καθαρὰ καὶ ἀμίαντος. Cf. Isocrates, *Nic*. 20 (ἡγοῦ δὲ θῦμα τοῦτο κάλλιστον εἶναι καὶ θεραπείαν μεγίστην, ἂν ὡς βέλτιστον καὶ δικαιότατον σαυτὸν παρέχῃς); T. Jos. 4.6 (οὐκ ἐν ἀκαθαρσίᾳ θέλει κύριος τοὺς σεβομένους αὐτόν); Hermes to Tat 12.23 ed. Nock and Festugière, 1.183 (θρησκεία δὲ τοῦ θεοῦ μία ἐστί, μὴ εἶναι κακόν); Marcus Aurelius 2.13.1 (service to the divinity within means keeping that divinity 'unsullied by passion', καθαρὸν πάθους διατηρεῖν). Ps.-Clement, *1 Ep. virg*. 4.1 ed. Diekamp, 6 (ἐν θρησκείᾳ καθαρᾷ καὶ ἀμιάντῳ) depends upon our line, which recalls other texts that qualify θρησκεία by an adjective in order to characterize what religion or act of piety one has in mind.[95] For θρησκεία see on v. 26. We have here the spiritualization of cultic language, so common in early Christianity.[96]

καθαρός[97] was not a traditional modifier of θρησκεία, but the association is natural against the backdrop of Jewish tradition, which spoke of both the worship of the heart and the purity of the heart.[98] In the LXX, καθαρός describes cultic purity[99] as well as moral purity.[100] The adjective was traditionally paired, through καί, with the nearly synonymous

---

[94] Lactantius, *Inst*. 5.9.23-24 SC 204 ed. Monat, 176. Cf. E. Hawarden, *The True Church of Christ*, vol. 3, London, 1715, 263: visitation of widows and orphans is θρησκεία 'because Religion is the Spring or Source from whence it proceeds'.

[95] E.g. Philo, *Fug*. 41; Josephus, *Ant*. 5.101; Cassius Dio 45.30.4; etc.

[96] Cantinat, 114-15, cites Acts 10.4; Rom 12.1; 15.16; Phil 2.17; 4.18; Heb 13.15; 1 Pet 2.5, 9; Rev 8.3. For Jewish precedent and parallels see n. 47; also Pss 50.14, 23; 51.16-17; 141.2; Tob 4.10; Ecclus 35.1-5; 1QS 8.5-6; 9.3-5; Philo, *Mos*. 2.107; *Leg*. 1.271; 2 En. 45.3; ARN A 4. Literature: H. Wenschkewitz, *Die Spiritualisierung der Kultusbegriffe*, Leipzig, 1932; G. Klinzing, *Die Umdeutung des Kultus in der Qumrangemeinde und im Neuen Testament*, Göttingen, 1971; E. Ferguson, 'Spiritual Sacrifice', *ANRW* II.23.2 (1980), 1152-89.

[97] Jas: 1×. LXX: most often for טהור.

[98] For the former see Deut 11.13; 2 Macc 1.3; b. Ta'an. 2a. For the latter see Ps 24.3-4; T. Naph. 3.1; T. Jos. 4.6.

[99] E.g. Gen 7.2; Mal 1.11; and often in Leviticus; cf. Heb 10.22.

[100] E.g. Gen 20.5; Ps 51.10; Job 33.9; Hab 1.13; cf. Josephus, *Bell*. 6.48. Clarke, 804, unaccountably relates the two adjectives to diamonds, whose perfection lies in them being free of flaws and not cloudy.

ἀμίαντος.[101] The latter means 'undefiled' or 'pure'[102] and describes the temple in 2 Macc 14.36; 15.34.

παρὰ τῷ θεῷ καὶ πατρί αὕτη ἐστίν.[103] One might imagine 'God and Father' to be a distinctively Christian formulation.[104] But the divinity is often enough called 'Father' in Jewish texts,[105] which in addition can combine 'God' with 'Father'.[106] A Jewish audience would hear nothing unusual. For θεός see on 1.1. For πατήρ see on 1.17.

The precise connotation of 'Father' is unclear. Does James use 'Father' in order to imply that human beings are siblings, something forgotten by those who fail to visit the undeservedly helpless, a category represented by orphans and widows?[107] Or is there an echo of Ps 68.5, where God is 'father of orphans and protector of widows'?[108] Or does it suffice to observe that, in early Jewish literature, 'father' often designates 'God as the refuge of the afflicted and persecuted'?[109]

παρά (Jas: 4×) also governs a dative in 1.17: παρ᾽ ᾧ, 'in whom'. Here, however, the preposition marks a viewpoint: 'in the sight/judgment of

---

[101] Cf. Dionysius of Halicarnassus, *Ant.* 8.33.4; 8.52.3; Plutarch, *Mor.* 267C, 290A, 382F (Osiris is ἀμίαντος καὶ καθαρός from all matter that is subject of destruction and death), 388F (Apollo is known as Phoebus because of his καθαρῷ καὶ ἀμιάντῳ), 395E, 612B; *Numa* 9.6; *Per.* 39.2; Philo, *Cherub.* 50; *Det.* 169 (ἐν σοφοῦ ψυχῇ ἀμίαντα καὶ καθαρά); *Leg.* 1.50, 250; *Fug.* 114; Jos. Asen. 15.14; Herm. *Mand.* 2.7 (καθαρά καὶ ἄκακος καὶ ἀμίαντος); *Sim.* 5.7.1. Note also Acts Jn 107 ed. Bonnet, 205: God is ὁ καθαρός, ὁ ἀμίαντος. ἀμίαντος: NT: 4×: Heb 7.26; 13.4; Jas 1.27; 1 Pet 1.4. LXX: 5× (all in Wisdom and 2 Maccabees). Gk. Pseudepigrapha (Denis): 2×. Philo: 15×. Josephus: 1×.

[102] Cf. Wis 4.2; Josephus, *Bell.* 6.99.

[103] On the textual variations surrounding τῷ θεῷ καὶ πατρί see Ropes, 183-84.

[104] Cf. Rom 15.6; 1 Cor 15.24 (τῷ θεῷ καὶ πατρί); Gal 1.4; Eph 4.6; 5.20 (τῷ θεῷ καὶ πατρί); Phil 4.20 (τῷ δὲ θεῷ καὶ πατρί); 1 Thess 3.11, 13; Rev 1.6 (τῷ θεῷ καὶ πατρί); Justin, *Dial.* 74.2 (τῷ θεῷ καὶ πατρί); 133.6, 301; Mart. Isa 2.37; Mart. Pol. 19.2; Odes Sol. 9.5; etc. The expression is Christian in T. Abr. RecLng. 20.13-14 and probably 6.6 v.l.

[105] Deut 32.6; 2 Sam 7.14; Ps 68.6; Jub. 1.24, 28; 19.29; Tob 13.4; Wis 2.16; 11.10; 14.3; Ecclus 51.10; 1QH 9.35; 4Q372 1.16; 4Q460 5.5; 3 Macc 2.21; 5.7; 6.3; 7.6; T. Job 33.3, 9; 52.12 v.l.; Jos. Asen. 12.8, 14-15; T. Jud. 24.2; T. Levi 18.6; Josephus, *Ant.* 2.137; Apoc. Ezek frag. 2; m. Ber. 5.1; b. Taʿan. 23b; etc. See further Strotmann, *Vater*.

[106] Cf. LXX 1 Chr 29.10 (κύριε ὁ θεὸς 'Ισραήλ, ὁ πατὴρ ἡμῶν); Wis 2.16; Ecclus 23.4 (κύριε πάτερ καὶ θεὲ ζωῆς μου); Tob 13.4 BA (αὐτὸς κύριος ἡμῶν καὶ θεός, αὐτὸς πατὴρ ἡμῶν); 3 Macc 5.7 (ἐλεήμονα θεὸν αὐτῶν καὶ πατέρα); 4Q372 1.16 (אבי ואלחי); Philo, *Leg.* 2.67 (θεοῦ τοῦ πατρός); *Abr.* 75 (θεοῦ καὶ τοῦ συμπάντων πατρός); *Decal.* 51 (θεὸν καὶ πατέρα). 'God and Father' is also common in the Corpus Hermeticum—Hermes Trismegistus, *Poim.* 1.21; 31.1 ed. Nock and Festugière, 1.14, 17; etc.

[107] Cf. Hort, 44; Mitton, 78; Baker, *Speech-Ethics*, 98.

[108] Cf. Ewald, 193; Bassett, 27; Leahy, 912; Fabris, 127; *et al.*

[109] M.R. D'Angelo, 'Abba and "Father"', *JBL* 3 (1992), 621, citing 3 Macc 6.3-4, 8; 7.6; 4Q372 1.16-18; Ecclus 23.1; 51.10; Wis 2.16-20; 11.10; 1QH 9.35; Jos. Asen. 12.8-15.

God and the Father'.[110] The implicit contrast is with παρὰ ἀνθρώποις. Maybe, as Chrysostom thought, the words assume the *imitatio dei*: divine care for widows and orphans demands human care of the same.[111]

ἐπισκέπτεσθαι ὀρφανοὺς καὶ χήρας ἐν τῇ θλίψει αὐτῶν. Cf. Herm. *Sim.* 1.8: ψυχὰς θλιβομένας...χήρας καὶ ὀρφανοὺς ἐπισκέπτεσθε. The LXX often uses ἐπισκέπτομαι (NT: 11×) to translate the Hebrew פקד. Both words can mean 'visit'[112] as well as 'care for'/'watch over'.[113] The two senses—both of which imply more than almsgiving[114]—cannot be distinguished here,[115] and Henry, *ad loc.*, is likely correct: 'Visiting is here put for all manner of relief which we are capable of giving to others'. That is, the verb carries the idea of ministry in general. The parallels from Hermas and Polycarp show the traditional nature of James' language,[116] which might derive from LXX Jer 5.28-29: 'they did not judge the cause of the orphan, and the cause of the widow they would not judge. μὴ ἐπὶ τούτοις οὐκ ἐπισκέψομαι;'[117]

---

[110] So BAGD, s.v., B2; cf. T. Ash. 4.1 (παρὰ τῷ θεῷ); also לפני and (as in Lk 16.15) ἐνώπιον.

[111] Chrysostom *apud Catena* ed. Cramer, 9. Cf. Lev 19.2; Ecclus 4.10; and see further n. 29. Note also Cyril of Alexandria, *Fest. Ep.* 12.6 SC 434 ed. Burns, 78; Barnes, 39; Gaugusch, 27; Sidebottom, 36; Moo, 97; Hartin, 109; Doriani, 59. Knowling, 36, makes the idiosyncratic proposal that we should associate 'Father' with visitation of the down and out, 'God' with keeping oneself unspotted by the world.

[112] Cf. LXX Gen 21.1; 1 En. 25.3; T. Sim. 1.2; T. Ash. 7.3.

[113] LXX Ecclus 7.22, 35; Ezek 34.11; Heb 2.6; 4 Bar. 7.35; etc.

[114] Fuller, 'Pure Religion', 400-401; Johnstone, 136-37; and Dale, 52, insist that Christians need to do more than write checks or fill a collection box. Cf. Didymus of Alexandria, *Zech* 144-45 SC 83 ed. Doutreleau, 488: support entails not only almsgiving but 'other' (ἄλλης) types of assistance.

[115] Cf. Pss. Sol. 3.14, T. Jud. 23.5, Mt 25.36, 43, Herm. *Mand.* 8.10 (χήραις ὑπηρετεῖν, ὀρφανοὺς καὶ ὑστερουμένους ἐπισκέπτεσθαι); *Sim.* 1.8 (see above); Pol. *Phil.* 6.1 (ἐπισκεπτόμενοι πάντας ἀσθενεῖς, μὴ ἀμελοῦντες χήρας ἢ ὀρφανοῦ). Many commentators recall the Matthean verses here; so e.g. Cyril of Alexandria, *Fest. Ep.* 13.4 SC 434 ed. Burns, 118; Bede *ad loc.* CCSL 121 ed. Hurst, 193; Martin of Legio *ad loc.* PL 209.192A; Lapide, 81; Grotius, 1077; Manton, 176; Pott, 179; B. Weiss, 98 ('perhaps' reminiscence); Mitton, 78-79; Townsend, 31; Kugelman, 23; Scaer, 70; Maier, 102; Royster, 40; *et al.* Cf. how Cyril of Alexandria, *Os.-Mal. ad* Amos 2.7 ed. Pusey, 403, moves from Mt 25.31-46 to Jas 1.27. Yet the Matthean text says nothing about widows or orphans.

[116] Which later readers might have associated with the ἐπίσκοπος, given that bishops came to be responsible for the care of widows and orphans; cf. Ign. *Pol.* 4.1; Apost. Const. 2.4.2; 2.25.2 ed. Funk, 37, 93; De viduitate servanda PL 67.1094-98; etc. Some texts, however, give this office to 'elders'—so e.g. Pol. *Phil.* 6.1—others to widows; see n. 00. The reason is obvious and clearly stated by Ambrose, *Off.* 1.20.87 ed. Davidson, 168: younger male clergy visiting widows may be tempted to sin, or such visitation may give rise to scandalous rumors. More recently, one can find commentators insisting that visitation is not just a duty for pastors: elders and the general membership of the church should also undertake this task; cf. MacDougal, *Conflict*, 42.

[117] The commentary tradition, however, offers no support for this suggestion.

ὀρφανός[118]—which sometimes meant not parentless but fatherless or motherless[119]—and χήρα[120] occur only here in James. Widows and orphans presumably stand for those most needing of help in James' world.[121] Their nearly constant combination in Jewish and Christian sources goes back to Exod 22.21: 'You will not afflict any widow or orphan'.[122] This text could, given James' choice of θλῖψις, inform our verse, for in Exod 22.20-21, οὐ κακώσετε is parallel to μὴ θλίψητε. But James also reminds one of Exod 4.31. This last employs θλῖψις of the affliction of the Israelites in Egypt, and there we find ἐπισκέπτομαι: 'And the people believed and were glad because God had taken regard for (ἐπεσκέψατο) the sons of Israel and because he had seen their tribulation (αὐτῶν τὴν θλῖψιν)'.

Whether or not James echoes a particular scriptural text, Exodus' prohibition not to harm widows and orphans[123] became, in Jewish and Christian tradition, a positive admonition to do good to them, one often rooted in the imitation of God, guardian of widows and orphans.[124] A reader of James might think of the command to love neighbor; cf. 2.8.

---

[118] Cf. Mk 12.40 v.l.; Jn 14.18. LXX: repeatedly for יתום.
[119] See Horsley-Llewelyn, *Documents*, 4.162-64, with examples from the papyri.
[120] NT: 26×. LXX: most often for אלמנה. On widows in early Christianity see G. Stählin, 'χήρα', *TDNT* 9.448-65. For relevant Graeco-Roman texts see W. Den Boer, *Private Morality in Greece and Rome*, Leiden, 1979, 34-50. On 56-61, the latter discusses orphans in Judaism.
[121] Cf. Wesley, 859. Poole, 884, comments: 'lest any should think it sufficient to visit them that were rich, or in a prosperous condition'.
[122] MT: כל־אלמנה ויתום לא תענון; LXX: πᾶσαν χήραν καὶ ὀρφανὸν οὐ κακώσετε.
[123] Cf. Deut 27.19; Job 6.27; 22.9; 24.9; Ps 94.6; Prov 23.10; Isa 10.2; Jer 5.28; 7.6; 22.3; Ezek 22.7; Zech 7.10; Mal 3.5; CD 6.16-17; Sib. Or. 2.270-71; Mt 23.14; Mk 12.40; Apoc. Paul 35 (a bishop is in hell because he neglected widows and orphans).
[124] Cf. Deut 10.18; 14.29; 24.17-21; 26.12-13; Job 31.18; Pss 10.14, 18; 68.5 (God is 'father of orphans and protector of widows'; Ng, 'Father', 48-49, thinks James alludes to LXX Ps 67.6; cf. Witherington, 447-48); 82.3; 146.9; Isa 1.17 (quoted in 1 Clem. 8.4; according to Verseput, 'Puzzle', 104, James may have Isa 1.16-17 in mind), 23; Ep Jer 38 ('they cannot take pity on a widow or do good to an orphan'); Tob 1.8; 2 Macc 8.28 ('they gave some of the spoils to...the widows and orphans'; cf. v. 30); Ecclus 4.10; 35.17 (for Frankemölle, 362-64, these and other verses in Sirach have influenced James); Philo, *Spec.* 1.310 (God provides for widows and orphans because they have lost their protectors); 2.108; 4.176; T. Job 9.3; 10.2; 13.14; 14.2; 16.3; 53.3; Sib. Or. 2.76; 3.242; Acts 6.1-6; 1 Tim 5.3-16; Josephus, *Ant.* 4.240; Ign. *Smyr.* 6.2; Herm. *Vis.* 2.4.3; *Sim.* 5.3.7; Barn. 20.2; 4 Ezra 2.20 ('Guard the rights of the widow...defend the orphan'); Sextus, *Sent.* 340; Apoc. Zeph. 7.4-5; Acts Thom. 19 ed. Bonnet, 130; m. Ketub. 4.12; 11.1-6; Exod. Rab. 30.8; Midr. Esth 2.5; etc. 'Orphan' often bore figurative sense (cf. Jn 14.18; Epictetus, *Diatr.* 3.24.14), and 'widows' came to be a class of Christian ministers; cf. Tertullian, *Virg. vel.* 9 CSEL 76 ed. Bulhart, 92. There is no trace of either of these special senses in James. Note, however, Article 9 of the Mennonite Confession adopted at Dordrecht in 1632: ordained widows are to visit widows and orphans.

James has θλῖψις[125] only here. The word can, in both Jewish and Christian texts, advert to the woes of the latter days.[126] Hartin, 102, takes such to be the case here.[127] That is quite possible given the nearness of the end in James (5.8) and the fact that some Jewish and Christian groups did conceptualize their own time as belonging to the eschatological tribulation.[128] But the unspecified[129] plight of widows and orphans could equally belong to ordinary time.[130] θλῖψις need not have eschatological connotations,[131] and the same is true of ἐν + θλῖψις and the comparable Hebrew (ה)בצר.[132]

There is nothing new in the notion that, without love of neighbor, one can have a false religious consciousness. This is a staple of the biblical tradition.[133] Indeed, the attack on empty ritualism in Isa 1.10-17 includes the imperatives: 'defend the orphan, plead for the widow'; cf. Jer 7.1-15.

ἄσπιλον ἑαυτὸν τηρεῖν ἀπὸ τοῦ κόσμου.[134] ἄσπιλος[135] means, in a cultic context, 'without blemish',[136] but early Christian writings (and

[125] Most often for צר(ה) in the LXX. NT: 45×.
[126] LXX Dan 12.1; Zeph 1.15; Hab 3.16; Mt 24.9; Mk 13.9; Acts 14.22; Col 1.24; Rev 7.14; Herm. Vis. 2.2.7; etc.
[127] Cf. Laws, 89-90; Martin, 53 ('may'); R. Wall, 101 ('may'). Contrast Ng, 'Father', 49; Fabris, 127; McKnight, 171.
[128] See the discussion above, 148, on 1.2.
[129] Despite occasional attempts to be concrete—maybe e.g. James has in mind poverty (Laws, 89) or the grief process (cf. Ropes, 184)—the lack of specification is effective: it leaves open multiple possibilities.
[130] Cf. Hilary of Arles *ad loc*. PLSup. 3.68-69: the robbing of widows (cf. Mk 12.40) was common. One recalls the lengthy descriptions of the plight of widows in Gregory of Nyssa's *De virginitate*.
[131] Cf. Jos. Asen. 11.13 (ὁ πατὴρ τῶν ὀρφαῶν...τῶν τεθλιμμένων βοηθός); Ign. *Smyr*. 6.2 (οὐ περὶ χήρας, οὐ περὶ ὀρφανοῦ, οὐ περὶ θλιβομένου); Herm. *Sim*. 1.8 (ψυχὰς θλιβομένας...χήρας καὶ ὀρφανούς); Acts Thom. 19 ed. Bonnet, 130 (ὁ τροφεὺς τῶν ὀρφανῶν καὶ οἰκονόμος τῶν χηρῶν, καὶ πᾶσι τοῖς τεθλιμμένοις αὐτὸς γίνεται ἄνεσις καὶ ἀνάπαυσις); Apost. Const. 2.25.2 ed. Funk, 93 (ὀρφανοῖς καὶ χήραις καὶ θλιβομένοις); 3.3.2, 187 (χήραις καὶ ὀρφανοῖς...καὶ τοῖς ἐν θλίψει).
[132] Cf. Deut 4.30; 28.53, 55; Ps 46.2; Hos 6.1; 1QH 13.17; 4Q460 7.7; etc.
[133] Note Isa 29.13; 58.1-14; Jer 6.19-20; Hos 6.6 (quoted in Mt 9.13; 12.7); Amos 5.21-23; Mic 6.6-8; Zech 7.1-7; Ecclus 34.21-27; ARN A 38; etc. See further Ahrens, *Arm*, 89-91.
[134] There are seven different variants for ἄσπιλον ἑαυτὸν τηρεῖν, all poorly attested. The most interesting of them, and the only one not an obvious variation of ἄσπιλον ἑαυτὸν τηρεῖν, is that of P74: ὑπερασπίζειν αὐτούς. This results in: 'to visit orphans and to protect widows in their afflictions from the world'. Although M. Black, 'Critical and Exegetical Notes on Three New Testament Texts', in *Apophoreta*, Berlin, 1964, 45, thinks this 'no doubt...a corruption,' he yet observes that it 'makes singularly good sense in the context—even (it is arguable) giving a more suitable meaning than the usual Greek Text'. D. Roberts, 'Definition', defends P74 as original; so too R.B. Ward, 'James', in *IDBSup*, 470. Although Roberts' arguments—which include the unlikelihood that James would have encouraged separation from the world; cf. Trudinger, 'Otherworldly'—fail, one should note the parallels in T. Job 53.1-3 (Job was ὁ πατὴρ τῶν ὀρφανῶν and τῶν

Job 15.15 Sym.) give it an ethical sense, 'morally pure', that is, undivided.[137] Its appearance after καθαρός and ἀμίαντος is natural.[138] There is no sacrificial metaphor here. Although τηρέω[139] + ἑαυτοῦ is otherwise attested,[140] τηρέω + ἑαυτοῦ + ἀπό is rare.[141] Like the comparable διατηρήσατε οὖν ἑαυτούς...ἀπὸ παντὸς ἔργου πονηροῦ of T. Dan 6.8, the τηρήσῃς αὐτοὺς ἐκ of Jn 17.15, and the σε τηρήσω ἐκ of Rev 3.10, it presumably reflects the Hebrew idiom, שמר + pronominal suffix + מן.[142] 'Guard against' might be as accurate a translation as the conventional 'keep from'—'to guard yourself against the world, unspotted'.[143] For κόσμος see on 3.6.

Presumably 'world' does not include all activities and relationships outside the religious community. More likely, it is the practical antithesis of 'God and Father' and the functional equivalent of 'sin' or 'evil'.[144] That is, 'the world' means, in effect, 'all the evils and sins in the world'.[145] James is censuring all ethical compromise, so that ἄσπιλον κτλ. is moral distancing, not physical separation. The choice of 'world' instead of 'sin' or 'evil' simply emphasizes that the things to be avoided are practically ubiquitous.[146] Unrighteousness is everywhere (3.6), even within the

χηρῶν ὁ ὑπερασπίστης); Jos. Asen. 11.13 (ὄψεται τὴν ὀρφανίαν μου καὶ ὑπερασπιεῖ μου).

[135] Jas: 1×; NT: 4×. LXX: 0×. Gk. Pseudepigrapha (Denis): 0×. Philo: 0×. Josephus: 0×.

[136] Cf. ἄμωμος and 1 Pet 1.19; Cyranides 1.10, 18; (Ps.-?)Aelius Herodianus, Part. ed. Boissonade 203; Prot. Jas 8; PGM 2.25; 3.694; 12.213, 260; 13.370.

[137] Cf. 1 Tim 6.14 (τηρῆσαί σε τὴν ἐντολὴν ἄσπιλον); 2 Pet 3.14; Jude 25 v.l.; Herm. Vis. 4.3.5; Sim. 59.6.7; 2 Clem. 8.6; Justin, Dial. 110.6; Apost. Const. 6.18.10 ed. Funk, 345; etc.

[138] Cf. Herm. Vis. 4.3.5 (ἄσπιλοι καὶ καθαροί); Sim. 5.6.7 (ἀμίαντος καὶ ἄσπιλος); Hippolytus, Dan. 1.13 GCS N.F. 7 ed. Bonewitsch and Richard, 30 (καθαρὸν καὶ ἄσπιλον); Apost. Const. 7.45.3 ed. Funk, 452 (σῶμα ἄσπιλον, καρδίαν καθαράν).

[139] Jas: 2×; cf. 2.10.

[140] E.g. Cor 11.9; Jude 21.

[141] It seemingly appears only in James and later ecclesiastical sources.

[142] As in Pss 121.7; 141.9; 1QS 2.3; cf. y. Pe'ah 16b (1.1); y. Sanh 27c (10.1: שומר אדם את עצמו מן).

[143] Cf. LXX Prov 7.5 (ἵνα σε τηρήσῃ ἀπὸ γυναικὸς ἀλλοτρίας καὶ πονηρᾶς); Hippolytus, Dan 4.59 GCS N.F. 7 ed. Bonwetsch and Richard, 334 (φυλάξαι, τηρῆσαι ἀπὸ παντὸς πειρασμοῦ).

[144] Cf. Gundry, 923: 'the world' = 'the sinful ways of unbelievers'. Barnes, 39, is specific: 'religion will keep us from the maxims, vices and corruptions which prevail in the world'.

[145] Cf. Gibson, 18 ('its pursuits, ambitions, counsels, and grosser pleasures'); Lockett, 'God', 150 ('the entire cultural value system or world-order which is hostile toward what James frames as the divine value system').

[146] Cf. 1 En. 48.7 (the righteous have 'hated and despised this world of oppression'); T. Iss. 4.6 (ἀπὸ τῆς πλάνης τοῦ κόσμου); T. Abr. RecLng. 1.7 (τοῦ ματαίου κόσμου τούτου); Rom 12.2 ('do not be conformed to this world'); 1 Cor 2.12 (τὸ πνεῦμα τοῦ κόσμου); 2 Pet 2.20 (τὰ μιάσματα τοῦ κόσμου); 1 Jn 2.17 ('the whole world is in the

faithful (1.14). Not only that, but the dominant social order—as 2.1-13 implies—is estranged from God[147] and so hostile. Jewish readers, especially in view of the language of cult and purity, might think in the first instance of the Gentile world.[148]

A cosmic dualism (cf. 3.15; 4.4) informs this conviction, and one recalls the similar use of κόσμος in John's Gospel and 1 John. James might have approved the formulation in Jn 17.11-14—'in the world' yet 'not of the world'.[149] In any case, human beings can mirror the division in the cosmos, for they too can be split, δίψυχος (1.8; 4.8).

power of the evil one'); Gos. Thom. 27 ('fast from the world'), 56 (the κόσμος is a πτῶμα; for a comparison of what Thomas and James have to say about 'the world' see Hartin, 'Poor'); 2 Bar. 40.3 ('the world of corruption'); Corpus Hermeticum 6.4 ed. Nock and Festugiére, 1.74 ('the κόσμος is the fullness of evil').

[147] Cf. Lk 16.15 (that which 'is exalted among people is an abomination in the sight of God'); Theophylact *ad loc.* PG 125.1152A (the world = the many who are corrupted by their desires and errors).

[148] Cf. Bardenhewer, 58.

[149] Commentators often cite or allude to this last text; cf. Schneckenburger, 49; Cantinat, 118; *et al.* Hort, 45, suggests the Hebrew תבל, which has negative sense especially in the first few chapters of Isaiah, lies in the background. Blackman, 72-73, argues against this.

X

PARTIALITY CONDEMNED (2.1-13)[1]

(1) My brothers, do not hold faith in the Lord of glory with favoritism. (2) For if a man with gold rings and in fine clothes enters a synagogue of yours, and if a poor person with filthy clothes also enters, (3) and if you look favorably upon the one wearing the fine clothes and say, 'You sit here, in a good place', but to the one who is poor you say, 'Stand there or sit at my feet', (4) have you not made distinctions among yourselves and become judges with evil thoughts? (5) Listen my beloved brothers. Has not God chosen the poor in the world to be rich in faith and to be heirs of the kingdom that he promised to those who love him? (6) But you have dishonored the poor. Do not the rich oppress you and drag you into court? (7) Do they not blaspheme the good name that was invoked over you? (8) Now if you really fulfill the royal law according to the scripture, 'You will love your neighbor as yourself', you do well. (9) If, however, you show partiality, you commit sin, being convicted by the law as transgressors. (10) For whoever keeps the law in its entirety yet fails in one point has become guilty of all of it. (11) For the one who said, 'Do not commit adultery', also said, 'Do not murder'. If you do not commit adultery but nonetheless commit murder, you have become a transgressor of the law. (12) Thus speak and thus act, as those about to be judged by the law of freedom. (13) For the judgment will be merciless to the one not showing mercy. Mercy triumphs over judgment.

---

[1] Recent literature: Ahrens, *Arm*; Assaël-Cuvillier, 'Éléments'; idem, 'Interprétation'; Batten, *Friendship*, 123-34; Boyle, 'Paradox'; Brinktrine, 'Jak 2.1'; Burchard, 'Nächstenliebegebot'; idem, 'Stellen'; Carson, 'James', 998-1003; Chandler, 'Injustice', 224-53; Cheung, *Genre*, 93-24; Deppe, *Sayings*, 87-99, 246-47; Döpp, 'Sozialtradition'; Dschulnigg, *Gleichnisse*, 262-64; Dyrness, 'Mercy'; Felder, 'Partiality'; Frankemölle, 'Gesetz'; Frick, 'Note'; Furnish, *Love*, 175-82; Garleff, *Identität*, 251-57, 284-89; Hartin, *Q*, 89-97; Hasselhoff, 'Thought'; Hobhouse, 'Law'; Hoppe, *Hintergrund*, 72-99, 120-21; Hutchinson Edgar, 'Love'; idem, *Poor*, 111-36; Jackson-McCabe, *Logos*, 135-92; Keith, 'Citation'; Kilpatrick, 'Übertreter'; Klein, *Werk*, 145-54, 165-75, 177-80; Kloppenborg, 'Avoidance'; idem, 'Didache'; Konradt, *Existenz*, 97-99, 135-45, 184-87; idem, 'Love'; Krüger, *Kritik*, 145-85; Kühl, *Stellung*, 4-26; Lowe, 'Debate'; Ludwig, *Wort*; Maier, *Reich*, 11-24; Marconi, 'Struttura'; Maser, 'Synagoge'; Maynard-Reid, *Poverty*, 48-67; Meyer, *Rätsel*, 118-23, 146-49, 248-52; Nienhuis, *Paul*, 187-97; Patry, *Prédication*, 20-46, 83-100; Polhill, 'Prejudice'; Popkes, *Adressaten*, 53-55; idem, 'Law'; Pretorius, 'Verklaringsopsies'; Robbins, 'Comparison'; Rost, 'Bemerkungen'; Rusche, 'Erbarmer'; Seitz, 'Law'; D. Smit, 'Partiality'; P.-B. Smit, 'Background'; L.M. Smith, 'James ii.8'; Theissen, 'Nächstenliebe'; Theophilus, 'Contra'; Tiller, 'Rich'; Trocmé, 'Églises'; Tsuji, *Glaube*, 73-77, 125-27, 135-71; Vorster, 'Diskriminasie'; Vyhmeister, 'Rich'; Wachob, *Voice*; Walker, 'Werken', 161-63; Ward, 'Concern'; idem, 'Partiality'; Watson, 'Schemes'; Wettlaufer, 'Variants', 202-35; P. Wick, 'Murder'; J. Williams, 'Law'; R.L. Williams, 'Piety'; Wischmeyer, 'Gebot'.

History of Interpretation and Reception

Discussions of congregational seating arrangements have often attended to 2.1-4. During the Church of Scotland's nineteenth-century controversy concerning the renting of church seats, for instance, our text was effectively quoted. Thus James Begg, in his pamphlet on the subject, appealed to vv. 1-5 to counter 'contempt for the poor which the apostle condemned': James 'desired the poorest man to meet with the richest on a level in the House of God,—and that as a matter of right, not favour. As they shall all meet in the grave, and at the judgment, it is the aim of Scripture that they should equally meet under the sound of the Gospel.'[2] The renting and reserving of church pews explains the prominent display of Jas 2.2-3 on a marble tablet in the ante-chapel of a nineteenth-century church in Holmbury.[3]

Yet ecclesiastical readers have also blunted James' rebuff of acts of favoritism. Hildegard of Bingen wrote that 'rich and poor must not be regarded as equals because such a judgment would be lacking in discretion'.[4] For Calvin, 276, James' admonition appears 'difficult and inconsistent', because it is a duty 'to pay respect to those who are of high rank in the world'. James then cannot be 'making a one-sided condemnation of the respect they [the readers] pay to the rich, but of the fact that they do this to bring insult to the poor'. On this reading, it is not wrong to bestow honors upon the rich; sin is bestowing honor *only* upon the rich.[5] A related defense of the *status quo* appears in Wordsworth, 21: 'Differences are fitly made between man and man in regard to *social* order and degree, but not in spiritual respects, such as the administration of the Lord's Supper...and in Christian assemblies for public worship, to which St. James refers'.[6] The guilty pragmatism of T. Scott, 572, reveals part of the motive behind such commentary: 'As places of worship cannot be built and maintained, without much expense; it may be proper that they,

---

[2] J. Begg, *Seat Rents brought to the Test of Scripture, Law, Reason, and Experience; or, the Spiritual Rights of the People of Scotland vindicated against Modern Usurpations, both within and without the Establishment*, Edinburgh, 1838, 23.

[3] See Hastings, 100-101, and further below, 370-72.

[4] Hildegard of Bingen, *Ep.* 378 CCCM 91B ed. Acker and Klaes-Hachmöller, 135. Cf. Rheims, *ad loc.*: 'The Apostle meaneth not, as the Anabaptists and other seditious persons sometime gather hereof, that there should be no difference in common weales or assemblies, betwixt the Magistrate and the subject, the free man and the bond, the rich and the poore, betwixt one degree and another, for God and nature, and the necessity of man, have made such distinctions'. The same words are in W. Fulke, *The Text of the New Testament of Iesus Christ*, London, 1601, 787.

[5] Similar comments appears in many commentators; cf. Dionysius bar Salībī, *ad loc.* CSCO 60 Scriptores Syri 101, ed. Sedlacek, 93; Theile, 105; Robertson, 116; Kugelman, 25-26; *et al.* Calvin further argued that James does not encourage thoughts of revenge against the moneyed classes, for that would contradict the command to love enemies.

[6] So too Burkitt, 1020; Johnstone, 146.

who contribute towards defraying it, should be accommodated accordingly: but were all professed Christians more spiritually minded, less disparity would be made, and the poor would be treated with far more attention and regard, than they commonly are in worshipping congregations'.

Christians have not only often justified preferential treatment of the rich but also relativized the affirmation that God has chosen the poor. According to Gill, 786, 2.5 holds true only 'generally speaking', for some poor people are 'not chosen, and are miserable here and hereafter; and there are some rich men that are chosen'.[7] L. Evans cautioned against 'maintaining our prejudices against those who are financially prosperous. We adopt a "soak the rich" attitude, which is unchristian... Some men strike the ground with industry, and it smiles back at them with produce.'[8] We read in Bengel, 493, that 'all the poor are not here meant, nor the poor only, for poverty and riches by themselves make no one good or evil'. Bede gained the same end by affirming that the poor are identical with the humble who disregard visible things.[9] Another redefinition, one that wholly abandons economics, appears in a popular series of children's books from the late twentieth century, *The Incredible Worlds of Wally McDoogle*. The inscription to volume 2 is Jas 2.1, and the story offers a reinterpretation of Jas 2.1-7 in terms of friendship and fame: the poor are poor in friendship while the rich have many friends, and it is wrong to pay attention to the latter and ignore the former.[10]

Much closer to the spirit of James are the English Puritan Manton, who clearly insisted that being rich is no sign of God's favor,[11] and G. Byron, who discusses, in a North American context, the 'serious challenges' that 'the black elite' raise 'for leaders of the black church'.[12] All this is, however, still a long way from the view of the liberation theologian Tamez: the rich in James 'do not belong to the Christian community, or at least the author does not think they should belong to it'.[13]

---

[7] So already Isho'dad of Merv *ad loc*. HSem 10 ed. Gibson, 49. Cf. Erasmus, *Paraphrase*, 148 ('Not everyone who is wealthy is impious of course'); Cranfield, 'Message', 191.

[8] L. Evans, *Faith*, 50-51.

[9] Bede *ad loc*. CCSL 127 ed. Hurst, 94.

[10] B. Myers, *My Life as Alien Monster Bait*, Dallas, 1993. See esp. 65-68 (a child's exegesis of his pastor's sermon).

[11] Manton, 193-95. Cf. Andria, 1512, who counters 'discrimination in favour of the rich' among 'Christian communities in Africa'. Note also the occasional use of Jas 2 in the cause of women's equality in the church: to exclude women from the pulpit is to commit the sin of partiality; cf. K.C. Bushnell, *God's Word to Women*, North Collins, NY, n.d., # 734.

[12] Byron, 465. Cf. C.H. Felder, *Troubling Biblical Waters*, Maryknoll, 1990, 118-34, who uses Jas 2.1-7 to counter social stratification in African-American churches.

[13] Tamez, *Message*, 31.

It has been natural to expand the theme of impartiality to areas of life other than wealth. Cranfield makes James an opponent of racial discrimination.[14] The Navarre Bible finds in our chapter opposition 'to every form of discrimination' (44). Countryman takes James' rejection of preferential treatment to speak to modern Christians who discriminate against 'sexual minorities'.[15]

The received—but probably not original—text of 2.1 contains one of the few explicit christological texts in James, and interpreters have made the most of it. Some have even taken it to mean that Jesus is the Shekinah, the divine glory.[16] B.B. Warfield found in Jas 2.1 evidence that Jesus is 'Jehovah come to be with His people... God manifest to men'.[17] More recently, Spicq has judged that the 'Lord' (κύριος) of 2.1 'is a title of supremacy and even of deity'.[18] Commentators have also, however, sought christological meaning in other verses of this section. Erasmus, 147, thought that the equality James calls for is founded upon Christ's dying for all. Manton, 194, believed that Jesus himself stands for the poor who are despised.[19]

First in his 1966 Harvard dissertation ('Concern') and then in a 1969 article based upon that dissertation ('Partiality'), Ward argued that our passages depict a Christian court scene. The thesis has appealed to many and is now defended in several commentaries.[20] Recent literature leaves the impression, however, that Ward's proposal is his discovery. According to Stulac, 90, while 'the traditional understanding has been that the meeting is a gathering for worship', Ward's position is a 'more recently advocated possibility'.[21] Watson, 'James 2', 99 n. 18, says it was 'first proposed by Ward'.

The history of interpretation shows otherwise. In the eighteenth century, Matthew Henry, *ad loc.*, wrote that, in Jas 2.2, 'synagogue' means 'those meetings which were appointed for deciding matters of difference among the members of the church, or for determining when censures should be passed upon any, and what those censures should be; therefore the Greek word here used, συναγωγή, signifies such an

---

[14] Cranfield, 'Message', 190. So too L. Evans, *Faith*, 58-62.

[15] Countryman, 719-20. So too Crotty, 'Poor', 19: 'the "poor" of today would be those marginalised by sexist practices, racism, ethnocentrism as well as unjust economic strategies'.

[16] See 383 and cf. Cyril of Alexandria, *Trin.* 6.603A SC 246 ed. Druand, 58. But J.D.G. Dunn, *The Parting of the Ways*, London, 1991, 212, thinks that 'the Lord of glory' means that Jesus has regained the glory Adam lost.

[17] B.B. Warfield, *The Lord of Glory*, New York, 1907, 265.

[18] Spicq, 'δόξα κτλ.', *TLNT* 1.370 n. 49.

[19] Cf. Letter 22 of J. Newton in *The Works of John Newton*, vol. 1, London, 1820, 291: the poor who are rich in faith 'are honoured with the nearest external conformity to Jesus their Saviour'.

[20] E.g. Davids, 109; Martin, 57-59; Johnson, 223-24; R. Wall, 103-105; Hartin, 118. Cf. Patterson, *Thomas*, 181-82; Ahrens, *Arm*, 114-16; Chandler, 'Injustice', 231-39.

[21] Stulac deems this interpretation possible but uncertain.

PARTIALITY CONDEMNED (2.1-13) 371

assembly as that in the Jewish synagogues, when they met to do justice'. Before Henry, Manton, 185-87, read our text the same way: 'the synagogue here spoken of is not the church assembly, but the ecclesiastical court, or convention, for the decision of strifes, wherein they were not to favour the cause of the rich against the poor'. Manton did not claim originality but attributed his position to 'others', and indeed this interpretation recurs in English-language commentaries of the seventeenth, eighteenth, and early nineteenth centuries.[22] The allegedly new interpretation was once exceedingly common.

The popularity of the reading was encouraged because application to a Jewish or Christian judicatory allowed commentators to live with the circumstance that many churches had preferred seating. Referring Jas 2.1-7 to the worship service would have posed embarrassing questions about that practice. As Henry, *ad loc.*, wrote: 'we must be careful not to apply what is here said to the common assemblies for worship; for in these certainly there may be appointed different places for persons according to their rank and circumstances, without sin'.

When one examines the older commentaries, one finds that their reasons for identifying our scene with ecclesiastical and civil judicatures are clearly summed up by Whitby, 588:[23] (i) προσωπολημψία (v. 1) and its relatives appear in judicial contexts.[24] (ii) If James speaks of the poor being under a footstool (v. 3), judges on tribunals had footstools.[25] (iii) Verse 4 uses the language of the courts when it refers to 'judges' (κριταί) and asks, 'Have you not judged (διεκρίθητε) among yourselves'.[26] (iv) Verse 9—'if you show partiality, you commit sin and are convicted by the law as transgressors'—refers to the biblical legislation banning partiality in court.[27] (v) Jewish tradition has it that when the rich and poor have a seat together in the courtroom, either both must sit or both must stand in order to avoid all marks of partiality.[28]

---

[22] Cf. Marchant, 797; Hammond, 691; Poole, 884; Whitby, 681; W. Wall, 345; Burkitt, 1020; Le Clerc, 505-506; Wells, 13; Pyle, 299; Guyse, 573-74; Wolf, 29; Gill, 786; Benson, 54; Macknight, 590-92; Gilpin, 591; Doddridge, 146-47; Clarke, 809; Valpy, 241; Trollope, 607; R. Scott, 123. Although all of these writers note the proposed interpretation, not all endorse it. This exegetical tradition is also known to the German Schöttgen, *Horae Hebraicae*, 1015-16.

[23] Whitby's list of reasons or something like it appears again and again; see e.g. Hammond, 692-93; Le Clerc, 506; Guyse, 573.

[24] Lev 19.15 ('You shall not render an unjust judgment; you shall not be partial to the poor or defer to the great: with justice you shall judge your neighbor') is most frequently cited. Note also Ecclus 35.14-16; Pss. Sol. 2.18; Rom 2.11; 1 Pet 1.17; Did. 4.3; Barn. 4.12.

[25] This assertion is made repeatedly, although without documentation.

[26] Indeed, the forensic language continues through v. 13.

[27] In this connection Guyse, 573-75, cites Lev 19.15 and Deut 1.17.

[28] Whitby documents this last assertion with a reference to 'R. Levi Barcinon *l.* 142. Juris Hebraici'. Cf. Marchant, 797; Hammond, 692-30 ('For by a canon of the Jews it is

Excepting (ii), these arguments, which enlarge the case made by Ward, are of considerable weight, and there does not appear to be any detailed or convincing refutation of them. One can only wonder why, in the latter half of the nineteenth century and the first half of the twentieth, this very interesting understanding of 2.1-7 unaccountably fell by the wayside and then had to wait a century before being resurrected.

Verses 8-13, which deal with the law, have given Christian exegetes opportunity to make any number of uninformed, disparaging, gratuitous comments about Jews. Trapp, 607, claimed that 'Jews at this day senselessly argue, "Cursed is he that abides not in all things", therefore he is not cursed that abides in some things only'. Similarly, Wordsworth, 22, asserted that the Pharisees 'imagined that if a man took pains to observe some portions, especially the ceremonial portion of the Law, he might safely indulge himself in the neglect of others, and in the commission of acts contrary to the spirit and letter of the Law'.[29] Lange, 78, managed to attack not only Jews but also Catholics and modern political philosophers: 'mercy boasteth over judgment' is 'the triumphant assurance with which the evangelizing mercy of believers...excelled the judging spirit of Judaism, the cheerful Gospel excelled the gloomy Talmud, the Church of the world the synagogue of the Jewish quarter and the evangelical confession the inquisition of the Middle Ages, to say nothing of the triumph of Christian philanthropy over modern particularism'.[30]

Christians have often appealed to v. 10—'one of the hardest verses in the Bible to a great many people'[31]—to promote moral rigorism,[32] and to scare people into obedience by stressing that no offenses against God are minor. Isaac Watts was typical: even just 'one willful sin...abuses

provided, that when a rich man and a poor have a fight together between their consistories, either both must sit or both stand in the same rank, and avoid all marks of partiality'); Trollope, 607 (the Jews 'had a canon, very analogous to the terms here employed, that when the rich and poor had a suit together, either both must sit or both must stand, to avoid all appearances of partiality'). The assertion of Ward, 'Partiality', 91 n. 17, that 'the rabbinic passages which speak of sitting and standing have gone altogether unnoticed' needs to be qualified.

[29] Adamson, 117, misconstruing moral exhortation as halakah, perpetuates this sort of misreading of certain rabbinic texts. Cf. Winkler, 37: James wrote what he did because 'the Jews...were possessed by an insatiable spirit of casuistry... Some regarded the law as to fringes and phylacteries as of first importance.'

[30] M. Skaballanovitch, *Tolkovii Tipikon*, 2nd ed., Moscow, 2008, 28, contrasts the admonitions in Jas 2.2-4 with the rules of the ancient synagogue. In this way Judaism represents concern for social status, Christianity a lack of concern for the same.

[31] So P. Brooks, 'The Law of Liberty', in *The Candle of the Lord*, New York, 1881, 193.

[32] Note e.g. C.G. Finney, *Sermons on the Way to Salvation*, Goodrich, 1891, 165-86. According to B.R. Rees, *The Letters of Pelagius and His Followers*, Woodbridge, Suffolk, 1991, 202 n. 34, the Pelagians often used Jas 2.10 to support their moral demands.

that governor and affronts that authority by which all the commands are enjoined. Nor is any willful sin small in the sight of divine justice, for it is the fruit of a presumptuous heart, and is therefore highly criminal.'[33] Others, however, remarking that it is impossible even after baptism to keep invariably all the commandments,[34] have emphasized divine grace. Augustine asked, in response to v. 10, 'Who could quit this life with any hope of obtaining eternal salvation with that sentence impending?' He answered by appealing to v. 12: mercy triumphs over judgment.[35]

Augustine also discussed at length how it could be that 'whoever keeps the law in its entirety yet fails in one point has become guilty of all of it'.[36] He showed some sympathy for the idea that to have one virtue is to have all and that to lack one is to lack all, although he eventually qualified that view. His chief worry was the Stoic doctrine of the equality of sins, which he found highly objectionable. To avoid finding this idea in 2.10, he appealed to 3.2, which implies that all, including the author of James, must fail in numerous ways; and yet no one would contend that all Christians are altogether without virtue or that their sins are on the same level as those of everybody else. Once again, then, Augustine interpreted one verse in James *via* another verse in James.

While Augustine's discussion of the relationship of vv. 8-13 to Stoicism still finds parallels in the critical literature, wholly foreign to the modern commentaries is the use Meister Eckhart made of v. 10. He found in it a proof text for his notion that multiplicity is both an illusion and a sin because it is a fall or departure from the One.[37]

During the medieval period, some theologians appealed to the threatening principle that 'the judgment will be merciless to the one not showing mercy' to confirm their view that the torments of the damned will last forever and be without interruption.[38] But during and after Reformation

---

[33] I. Watts, 'Orthodoxy and Charity United', in *The Works of the Rev. Isaac Watts*, vol. 3, London, 1812, 145.

[34] This is a regular theme in the commentaries, which often insist that 'Whoever keeps, etc.', must be purely hypothetical; cf. e.g. Gill, 787.

[35] Augustine, *Pecc. merit.* 2.3 CSEL 60 ed. Urba and Zycha, 73. Cf. Milton, *Paradise Lost* 3.132-34:
 In mercy and justice both,
 Through heaven and earth, so shall my glory excel;
 But mercy, first and last shall brightest shine.

[36] Augustine, *Ep.* 167 CSEL 44 ed. Goldbacher, 586-609. Note also the discussion of W. Covel, *A Just and Temperate Defence of the Five Books 'Of Ecclesiastical Polity' written by Mr. Richard Hooker* (1603), reprinted in *The Ecclesiastical Polity and Other Works of Richard Hooker*, ed. R. Hanbury, vol. 2, London, 1830, 498-99.

[37] He cites the text several times in his writings; note e.g. *Exp. Sap.* 110 ed. Fischer, Koch, and Weiss, 446

[38] Peter Lombard, *Sent.* 4.265 (Dist. 46.2) ed. Brady, 529. Cf. the application in Rheims *ad loc.* and the counter to this in Cartwright, *Confutation*, 656.

times, the comforting v. 13b, which exalts mercy over judgment,[39] was sometimes employed to counter the cruelty inherent in religious persecution.[40]

Exegesis

2.1-7, which harks back to 1.9-11 and enlarges upon the sentiment of 1.26-27, consists of three parts:

I. General admonition (1)
    A. Address (1a)
    B. Imperative (1b)
II. Concrete illustration of general admonition (2-4, a long question)
    A. Hypothetical situation (2)
        i. Entry of rich individual (2a)
        ii. Entry of poor individual (2b)
    B. Hypothetical response (3)
        i. Favoritism towards the rich (3a)
        ii. Mistreatment of poor (3b)
    C. Evaluation of hypothetical situation (4, rhetorical question)
        i. Wrongful discrimination (4a)
        ii. Judges with evil thoughts (4b)
III. Grounding of admonition (5-7)
    A. Defense of the poor (5-6a)
        i. Address (5a)
        ii. Divine exaltation of the poor (5b, rhetorical question)
        iii. The readers' failure (6a)
    B. Criticism of the rich (6b-7)
        i. Their oppression of the readers (6b, rhetorical question)
        ii. Their blasphemy of the name (7, rhetorical question)

Watson applies the terminology of Graeco-Roman rhetoric: I is the *propositio*, II is the *ratio*, and III is the *confirmatio*.[41]

Verses 8-13—which abandon the interrogatory mode of vv. 2-7—supply additional confirmation by appealing to scripture and then concluding with two aphorisms that warn and exhort:

---

[39] The half-verse has occasionally been cited as evidence that James does not teach 'strict work-righteousness'; so e.g. Kamell, 'Faith'.

[40] G. Kleinberg, 'On How Persecution Hurts the World', in the sixteenth-century collection of S. Castellio, *Concerning Heretics, Whether They are to be persecuted and How They are to be Treated*, ed. Bainton, 216.

[41] Watson, 'James 2', 102-105. Cf. Kloppenborg, 'Avoidance', 759-68; also the analysis of Hartin, 125-28, who regards vv. 8-11 as embellishment (*exornatio*) and vv. 12-13 as the conclusion (*complexio*). Robbins, 'Comparison', outlines the passage this way: Introduction, v. 1; Case/Rationale, vv. 2-4; Argument (*Probatio*), vv. 5-11; Case Argument from the Opposite (v. 6a); Case/Social Example (vv. 6b-7); Argument from Judgment in Four Parts (vv. 8-11); Conclusion (vv. 12-13).

IV. Grounding in scripture (8-12)
   A. Quotation of Lev 19.18 (8)
   B. Application of Lev 19.18 to situation (9)
   C. Unity of the Torah (10-11)
      i. Principle (10)
      ii. Illustration (11)
   D. Judgment by the law (12)
V. Eschatological conclusion (13)
   A. Warning: there will be no mercy for those without mercy (13a)
   B. General principle: mercy is greater than judgment (13b)

The entire section features parallelism and strong contrasts:

1	ἀδελφοί μου
5	ἀδελφοί μου ἀγαπητοί
2a	εἰσέλθῃ...ἐν ἐσθῆτι λαμπρᾷ
2b	εἰσέλθῃ...ἐν ῥυπαρᾷ ἐσθῆτι
3a	εἴπητε· σὺ κάθου ὧδε
3b	εἴπητε· σὺ στῆθι ἐκεῖ ἢ κάθου ὑπὸ τὸ ὑποπόδιόν μου
5b	ὁ θεὸς ἐξελέξατο τοὺς πτωχούς
6a	ὑμεῖς δὲ ἠτιμάσατε τὸν πτωχόν
6b	οὐχ οἱ πλούσιοι καταδυναστεύουσιν
7a	οὐκ αὐτοὶ βλασφημοῦσιν
6b	αὐτοὶ ἕλκουσιν ὑμᾶς
7b	αὐτοὶ βλασφημοῦσιν... ὑμᾶς
8	εἰ μέντοι... τελεῖτε ... ποιεῖτε
9	εἰ δὲ προσωπολημπτεῖτε ... ἐργάζεσθε
10a	ὅλον τὸν νόμον τηρήσῃ
10b	πταίσῃ δὲ ἐν ἑνί
10c	γέγονεν πάντων ἔνοχος
11c	γέγονας παραβάτης νόμου
11a	εἰπών μὴ μοιχεύσῃς
11a	εἶπεν... μὴ φονεύσῃς
11b	εἰ δὲ οὐ μοιχεύσεις
11b	φονεύσεις δέ
12a	οὕτως λαλεῖτε
12b	οὕτως ποιεῖτε
13a	ἡ γὰρ κρίσις ἀνέλεος τῷ μὴ ποιήσαντι ἔλεος
13b	κατακαυχᾶται ἔλεος κρίσεως

Our text is crucial for interpreting James. Three groups are involved—the poor (vv. 2-3, 5-6), the rich (vv. 2-3, 6-7), and the recipients of James, who honor the latter and dishonor the former (vv. 2-4, 6). The first two classes are spoken of in the third person; the other class is addressed directly with the second person plural. But all three are found together in the synagogue (v. 2). When read in the light of 1.1, according to which James addresses Jews in the diaspora, 2.1-7 is ostensibly aimed at synagogue members who tend to disparage co-religionists less fortunate than themselves while honoring the wealthy, even when the latter take them to court (v. 6) and bring disrepute to their religion (v. 7). Given that the writer is a professed Christian (1.1), one suspects that some Christians are among the poor, and that he is seeking here, as elsewhere, to maintain or make room for them in the community.

This reading is supported by the long-standing debate over the identity of the rich in our passage. Four solutions have been offered: (i) They are Christians.[42] This makes sense of the fact that they are in a religious assembly with the readers, and it is consistent with the ἐν ἑαυτοῖς ('among yourselves') of v. 4. This view, however, is hard to harmonize with what James elsewhere has to say about the rich (e.g. 1.10-11; 5.1-6). Moreover, one must, on this view, distinguish the rich of vv. 2-4 from the blaspheming and oppressing rich of vv. 6-7, which hardly commends itself.[43] As vv. 2-4 introduce the poor, who are then considered in vv. 5-6, it is unnatural to dissociate vv. 6-7 from vv. 2-4. Further, the impact of vv. 6-7 is reduced if the rich described there are not those honored in vv. 2-3. Above all, v. 6a is left without antecedent if it does not explicate vv. 2-4.[44] BDF 139, 263 even uses the τόν before πτωχόν (v. 6) to illustrate anaphoric sense: 'that beggar' refers to v. 2.

(ii) The rich do not belong to the community but are visitors, perhaps attending out of curiosity.[45] This is why they do not know where to sit.[46]

---

[42] Hilgenfeld, 'Brief', 9; P.H. Furley, 'ΠΛΟΥΣΙΟΣ and Cognates in the New Testament', *CBQ* 5 (1943), 251; Ward, 'Concern', 97-98; idem, 'Partiality', 96-97; Schnider, 58, 62; Cargal, 106. Burchard, 103, thinks this possible.

[43] Dibelius, 136, separates vv. 5-7 from vv. 2-4 by contending that the former 'do not warn against partiality in the distribution of seats, but rather against partiality of any sort'. Cf. Ward, 'Partiality', 96-97 (making much of πλούσιος being present in v. 6 but not v. 2); Tsuji, *Glaube*, 137.

[44] Contrast the unconvincing argument of Dibelius, 138.

[45] E.g. W. Dodd *ad* 2.2; Jacobi, 81; Feine, *Lehranschauungen*, 85; Ropes, 191; Dale, 55; Cantinat, 130-31; Easton, 36; L.W. Countryman, *The Rich Christian in the Church of the Early Empire*, New York, 1980, 82-83 (identifying the rich with Sadducees); Laws, 99-100; Burchard, 'Gemeinde', 323. Hutchinson Edgar, *Poor*, 117-20, thinks the rich are prospective patrons. Theissen, 'Nächstenliebe', 189-91, sees the rich as well as the poor as 'potential members' and so argues that, in James, love of neighbor is not confined to insiders but is truly universal in scope.

[46] But the poor individual is likewise shown seating yet seemingly belongs to the group God has elected (v. 6). Further, the brief speeches in 2.18 and 4.13 express

One can cite in this connection 1 Cor 14.23-25, where unbelievers attend a Christian meeting.[47] Yet, against this, how likely is it that individuals behaving with the hostility indicated by vv. 6-7 would be receiving seats of honor? Beyond that, the rich and poor are co-religionists in the close parallel in *Didascalia Apostolorum* 12; see below. (iii) Precise identification of the parties involved is a matter of exegetical indifference.[48] This solution seems to have arisen largely because of the failure to make sense of the text on the presupposition that 'synagogue' refers to a Christian assembly.

(iv) The difficulties vanish, however, when we think not of a Christian church but instead of a Jewish synagogue with Christians in attendance. Those who dishonor the poor, drag people into court, and blaspheme are members of the assembly—but they are not Christians, not even visiting Christians. They are rather, as Mayor, 88, and a few others have seen, well-to-do Jewish members of the synagogue.[49] Nothing hints that the rich do not worship the same God as the poor or those being addressed. On this reading, James' auditors attend religious services that are not exclusively Christian. This is consistent with the use of 'synagogue' in v. 5; see below.

Dibelius, 125, argues that 2.2-4 offers us 'an example, and not a special case which has motivated the introductory admonition; and this example is narrated without any concern for its reality, and hence, without any consideration of the question of the community in which, or the circumstances under which, this or even something similar could have taken place'.[50] One doubts, however, that our text is only hypothetical.[51] If an example is foreign to the readers' experience, its force is diminished,[52] and the very fact that, with 2.1, James moves from loosely connected

---

attitudes more than anything else, and one may likewise understand the speeches of v. 3 as stylized ways of saying that the congregation has seats of greater and lesser honor, not necessarily that the people do not know where to sit.

[47] Cf. the Iranian inscriptions on the walls at Dura-Europos: these record the visits of outsiders; see C.H. Kraeling, *The Synagogue*, New Haven, 1956, 283-317.

[48] See esp. Dibelius, 131-32. Cf. Popkes, 161-62.

[49] Mayor, 88: these people 'profess to know God, but by their works deny him... On the whole I think the general sense of the passage suits better with the idea that the blasphemers are unbelieving Jews...' Cf. Clarke, 837; Credner, *Einleitung*, 596; J. Weiss, *Christianity*, 2.668, 745-46; Mussner, 81-82; Maynard-Reid, *Poverty*, 53-55.

[50] Dibelius uses the words 'stylized' and 'unrealistic' and asserts, 'we are not able to say how much he [James] is relating and criticizing actual events in the life of the church' (129). Cf. Mussner, 116-17.

[51] The vast majority of commentators have not thought so; cf. Marty, 71; Martin, 60-61; Schnider, 57; Kloppenborg, 'Avoidance', 764-65; Ahrens, *Arm*, 63-69, 112-13; *et al.* The observation of Dibelius, 129-30, that Epictetus sometimes uses fictional examples, proves little. Graeco-Roman rhetoricians (including Epictetus) used both real and assumed situations; cf. Watson, 'James 2', 120-21: rhetoric cannot answer whether vv. 2-4 depict an actual situation.

[52] Cf. Maser, 'Synagoge', 277-76; Popkes, 160-61.

sayings to a discourse proper poses the question of a concrete situation, as does the amount of space dedicated to the issue. Verses 2-4 are, moreover, not unrealistic, and vv. 6-7 seem on their face to rebuke a real offense. All this is not to deny that the speeches in v. 3 are stylized for a dramatic end, only that they probably reflect a real circumstance, namely, the seating of people from different classes in different places—something for which, as we shall see, we otherwise have evidence.

Our text is very close to a passage in the Didascalia: 'But if, when you are seated, some other man or woman should come who has worldly honor, whether from the same district or from another congregation, you O bishop, if you are speaking or listening or reading, should not leave off your ministry of the word in order to show them a place but should remain as you are and not interrupt the world. Let the brothers receive them... But if a poor man or woman should come, whether from the same district or another congregation, and especially if they are exceedingly old in years, and they have no place, you O bishop, should act from your heart and find a place for them, even if you have to sit upon the ground. There should be no respect of persons with you.'[53] Similar directions appear in Apost. Const. 2.58 ed. Funk, 167, 169, 171. These texts either stand under the influence of James or—more likely—go back to a common tradition.[54]

This is all the more credible because Jas 2.1-7 and the Didascalia 12.4-6 closely resemble a rabbinic tradition. Sifra Lev 200, applying Lev 19.15 ('You will not render an unjust judgment; you will not be partial to the poor or defer to the great') to a judge, takes it to mean, among other things, that a judge should not seat a rich person in court while letting a poor person stand: 'R. Judah said: "I have heard a tradition that if they wanted to let both of them sit down, they let them sit down. What is prohibited is only that one of them should sit while the other is standing".' ARN A 10 and b. Šeb. 30a-b preserve a generalizing form of this ruling that does not apply it to rich and poor specifically. But the variant in Deut. Rab. 5.6 maintains the application to rich and poor. It further, recalling James, discusses the matter of dress:[55] the rich individual must either dress as the poor individual dresses or give the latter better clothes. Given the early date of Sifra, its attribution of this teaching to tradition (מקובלני), and the fact that the rabbinic teaching cannot be derived from James but is rather exegetically based upon Lev 19.15, one must infer that Jas 2.1-4 (which alludes to Lev 19.15) is Jewish tradition lightly revised.[56] Verses 5-13 then become application of and commentary on that tradition.

---

[53] Didascalia apostolorum 12.4-6 ed. Vööbus CSCO 407 Scriptores Syri 179, 147-48.
[54] Both Ropes, 191, and Ward, 'Concern', deny literary dependence upon James.
[55] So too the variants in t. Sanh. 6.2; b. Šeb. 31a.
[56] According to Hanson, 'Report', 527, 'James 2.1-13 seems to be based on Lev. 9.11-18: the themes of blaspheming the Name, showing partiality to the rich and powerful, and loving one's neighbor as oneself are all in common'.

In addition to taking up the exegetical tradition behind vv. 1-4, James cites Lev 19.18 (v. 8) and two commands from the decalogue (v. 10). He further draws upon the saying behind Mt 5.3 = Lk 6.20 in v. 5 and may, in addition, betray knowledge of Mt 5.5; see below. It also seems likely that our author knew the traditional combination of the imperative to love God (Deut 6.5) with the imperative to love neighbor (Lev 19.18), which Christian tradition attributed to Jesus.[57] But whether he knew that combination from the Jewish tradition or the Jesus tradition or both cannot be ascertained.

Verse 1. This general admonition, which introduces all of 2.1-13,[58] exposes some of the readers as hypocrites: their behavior toward rich and poor is out of line with a religion that prohibits partiality.

ἀδελφοί μου. See on 1.2. Here—unlike in v. 5—the address marks a transition to a new subject. It is also, as some commentators have observed, particularly appropriate given James' call to eliminate hierarchical attitudes: ἀδελφός is a term of equality.[59]

μὴ ἐν προσωπολημψίαις ἔχετε τὴν πίστιν τοῦ κυρίου τῆς δόξης.[60] The precise prepositional phrase, ἐν προσωπολημψίαις,[61] appears only here in Greek literature, although προσωπολη(μ)ψία occurs in Rom 2.11; Eph 6.9; Col 3.25. Vouga, 70, is not alone in inferring that Paul coined the noun, yet it occurs also in T. Job 43.10 (where it is linked with κρίμα and κρίνω);[62] and Dibelius, 126, remarks that, in Eph 6.9 and Col 3.5 as well as Pol. *Phil.* 6.1, the word occurs in *Haustafeln* and so likely derives from paraenetical tradition. James uses the related verb, προσωπολημπτέω, in v. 9.[63] Note that the noun also occurs in Apost. Const. 2.58 ed. Funk, 171, in the section parallel to Jas 2.1-7: ἵνα μὴ πρὸς ἄνθρωπον αὐτοῦ γένηται ἡ προσωπόληψις.

In the background is the LXX's translation of נשא + פנים with πρόσωπον λαμβάνειν, and perhaps our line would have been 'unintelligible to non-Jews or Christians of Gentile background'.[64] The Hebrew may even

---

[57] Mt 22.34-40; Mk 12.28-31; Lk 10.25-28; see on v. 8.

[58] Cf. the general admonition in 3.1, which introduces another discourse.

[59] So Wesley, 599: 'The equality of Christians, intimated by this name ["brothers"], is the ground of the admonition'. Cf. Gill, 785; Chaine, 39.

[60] See the Excursus below, 382-84.

[61] Cf. the ἐν πραΰτητι of 1.21.

[62] 'Righteous is the Lord, trustworthy are his judgments; with him there is no favoritism (προσωποληψία) for he will judge us with consistency'. When Adamson, 104, says that the word is 'definitely' Christian, this requires that its appearance in the Testament of Job is not Jewish, which is far from certain. See Gray, 'Job', 410-11.

[63] The related προσωπολήμπτης (= 'one who shows partiality') is found in Acts 10.34, the related ἀπροσωπολήμπτως (= 'impartialy') in 1 Pet 1.17; 1 Clem. 1.3; and Barn. 4.12; and the related ἀπροσωπόλημπτος ('without respect of persons') in T. Job 4.7; Clement of Alexandria, *Strom.* 6.8.64 GCS 52 ed. Stählin and Früchtel, 463.

[64] So Vyhmeister, 'Rich', 274. Cf. Easton, 35: 'pure "translation Greek"'.

account for James' plural.[65] נשא + פנים—the antithesis of פנים + הפיל = 'to make the countenance fall'—can mean 'to receive kindly' as well as (less often) 'show partiality towards' or 'be unduly influenced by'.[66] But when πρόσωπον λαμβάνειν becomes 'an independent Greek phrase...the bad sense [exclusively] attaches to it, owing to the secondary meaning of πρόσωπον as "a mask", so that πρόσωπον λαμβάνειν signifies "to regard the external circumstances of a man", his rank, wealth, etc., as opposed to his real intrinsic behavior. Thus in the NT it has always a bad sense.'[67]

Favoritism is the antithesis of divine impartiality, the latter being a fundamental theme of Jewish theology[68] that Christians adopted.[69] So to be impartial is to be like God.[70] James links impartiality with mistreatment of the poor in particular, as do Job 34.19 ('who shows no partiality to nobles, nor regards the rich more than the poor') and Ps.-Phoc. 10 ('Do not cast the poor down unjustly, judge not partially', μὴ κρίνε πρόσωπον).[71]

---

[65] Yet according to Mayor, 78, the plural 'refers to the many ways in which partiality may show itself'.

[66] For the latter see Lev 19.15 ('you will not be partial to the poor' [לא־תשא פני־דל; LXX: οὐ λήμψη πρόσωπον πτωχοῦ]; Johnson, 221, rightly asserts that 'the connection with the citation of Lev 19:18 is critical to James' argument'); Deut 10.17-18 ('For the Lord your God is God of gods and Lord of lords, the great God, mighty and awesome, who is not partial [לא־ישא פנים; LXX: ὅστις οὐ θαυμάζει πρόσωπον) and takes no bribe, who executes justice for the orphan and the widow, and who loves the strangers, providing them food and clothing'); Ps 82.2 ('How long will you...show partiality to the wicked?' [ופני רשעים תשאו]; LXX: πρόσωπα ἁμαρτωλῶν λαμβάνετε]; cf. 11QMelch 2.11); Ecclus 4.22 ('Do not show partiality' [אל תשא פניך]; LXX: μὴ λάβῃς πρόσωπον]); 1QH 6(14).19 ('I do not show partiality to evil' [לא אשא פני רע]); m. 'Abot 4.22 (with God there is no respect of persons—לא משוא פנים); Sifre Deut 304 ('Blessed is the judge of truth, the lord of all deeds, before whom there is neither injustice nor favoritism' [שאין...משוא פנים לפניו]).

[67] J.B. Lightfoot, *The Epistle of St. Paul to the Galatians*, 6th ed., London, 1980, 108. See further J.M. Bassler, *Divine Impartiality*, Chico, CA, 1982, 189-91.

[68] See Deut 10.17-19; 2 Chr 19.7; Job 34.19; Jub. 5.16; 21.3-5; 33.18; Pss. Sol. 2.18-19; Wis 6.7; Ecclus 35.12-15 (according to Frankemölle, 'Gesetz', 207, this text has influenced James); 1 En. 63.8; T. Job 4.7; 43.10; LAB 20.4; 2 Bar. 13.8; 44.4-5; m. 'Abot 4.22; etc. Full discussion of these texts and others can be found in Bassler, *Divine Impartiality* (as in n. 67). See also the very helpful review of partiality in Jewish and Christian texts in Ward, 'Concern', 41-77.

[69] See e.g. Acts 10.34; Rom 2.11; Gal 2.6; Eph 6.9; Col 3.25; 1 Pet 1.17; Did. 4.10; Barn. 4.12; 19.7. For rejection of human partiality see Deut 1.17; 16.19; Ps 82.1-4; Mal 2.9; 1 Esd 4.39; Prov 18.5; 24.23; Ecclus 4.22, 27; 7.6; 35.13; Philo, *Jos*. 72; Mt 22.16; Mk 12.14; Lk 20.21; 1 Clem. 1.3; Did. 4.3; Barn. 19.4; Pol. *Phil*. 6.1; Ep. Apost. 42, 46 (condemnation of partiality toward the rich); Ps-Heraclitus, *Ep*. 7.1.

[70] So also Eph 6.9. The idea is implicit in Deut 10.17, where the statement of God's impartiality is followed by the command to love the stranger.

[71] See also Ps 82.1-2 (rejection of partiality to the wicked followed by a plea for justice for the weak and the orphan).

PARTIALITY CONDEMNED (2.1-13)   381

The latter text takes up Lev 19.15: 'You will not render an unjust judgment; you will not be partial to the poor or defer to the great'.[72] The same scripture lies behind James. This follows from several considerations.[73] (i) Jas 2.1-7 and LXX Lev 19.15 are of the same intent insofar as they prohibit discrimination against the poor. (ii) The two passages show verbal overlaps:

LXX Leviticus	James
οὐ λήμψῃ πρόσωπον, v. 15	μὴ ἐν προσωπολημψίαις, v. 1
πτωχοῦ, v. 15	πτωχός, πτωχούς, vv. 2, 5
κρίσει, κρινεῖς, v. 15	διεκρίθητε, κριταί, v. 4

(iii) The closely related rabbinic tradition to which we have called attention was associated with Lev 19.15: t. Sanh. 6.2 cites it, and Sifra Lev 200 is commentary on it. (iv) Our passage leads directly to an exposition of Lev 19.18; see Jas 2.8-13. (v) Exegetes regularly refer to Lev 19.15 when commenting on Jas 2.1.[74] (vi) The same is true with regard to 2.10; see below. (vii) 4.11-12 also seems to allude to Lev 19.15.

2.1 might be interrogatory. But that would make the γάρ in v. 2 unexpected.[75] For πίστις see on 1.6. Here the word can mean either 'trust' (cf. v. 5) or 'belief'. The point in either case is that the religious faith of the readers, their trust or belief 'in'[76] God, is incompatible with acts of favoritism, a proposition at home in the Jewish tradition. For ἔχω + πίστιν see on 2.14.[77]

'Lord of glory'[78] is a title in both Jewish and Christian texts. It is especially prominent in 1 Enoch.[79] What precisely it adds here is unclear.

---

[72] See Niebuhr, *Gesetz*, 21.
[73] In addition to what follows see Chandler, 'Injustice', 228-31.
[74] E.g. Poole, 884; Theile, 91; Dale, 60; Beyschlag, 95; Mayor, 78; Ropes, 186; Meyer, *Rätsel*, 140 n. 5; Chaine, 39-40; Marty, 69; Mussner, 115; Schneider, 15; Laws, 93; Frankemölle, 373; Johnson, 221; Giere, 'Midrash', 87-88; Döpp, 'Sozialtradition', 71; Hartin, 117; Burchard, 97; Fabris, 138; Garleff, *Identität*, 252-53; McKnight, 176.
[75] See further Mayor, 79; Ropes, 186.
[76] Cf. Mk 11.22, where πίστιν θεοῦ = 'faith in God', and Acts 3.16, where τῇ πίστει τοῦ ὀνόματος αὐτοῦ = 'faith in his name'. Those who do not amend the text but read πίστιν τοῦ κυρίου ἡμῶν Ἰησοῦ Χριστοῦ can find here a subjective genitive: 'the faith of our Lord Jesus Christ'. Cf. R. Wall, 109-10; Johnson, 220; Lowe, 'Debate'.
[77] Wifstrand, 'Problems', 176, finds μὴ ἔχετε τὴν πίστιν after μὴ προσωπολημψίαις 'extremely strange and un-Greek'. Mayor, 79, by contrast, remarks that μὴ ἔχετε 'is a more personal way of putting μὴ ἔστω ἡ πίστις, implying free-will and responsibility...' He cites for comparison Mk 9.50; Rom 10.2; Jas 2.18.
[78] δόξα: Jas: 1×. Cf. 'God of glory' (Ps 19.3; Acts 7.2), 'king of glory' (Ps 24.7-10; Hippolytus, *Dan*. 2.36 GCS N.F. 7 ed. Bonewitsch and Richard, 126), 'father of glory' (Eph 1.17).
[79] Cf. Gk. 1 En. 22:14 (τὸν κύριον τῆς δόξης; cf. 4Q205 1 1.2: רבותא [מרא]); 25.3 (but the Greek is ὁ ἅγιος τῆς δόξης); 27.3 (τὸν κύριον τῆς δόξης), 5 (τὸν κύριον τῆς

Is it simply a stylistic variant of θεός, which was used in the previous verse? Is the implicit thought akin to Jn 5.44: 'How can you believe when you accept glory from one another and do not seek the glory that comes from the one who alone is God'?[80] Is the stress on divine transcendence, which is above all human division? Is God's glory supposed to turn to naught the splendor of the rich (v. 2)? Or does 'glory' refer to the divine throne and so emphasize God's role as judge?[81] Whatever the answer, perhaps 'Lord of glory' was known from James' liturgy, for, 'with one exception', it appears in 1 Enoch 'in doxologies or references to blessing and prayer'.[82]

Excursus

Most mss. have τὴν πίστιν τοῦ κυρίου ἡμῶν ᾽Ιησοῦ Χριστοῦ τῆς δόξης at the end of v. 1. But 33 631 Antioch omit the last two words because they are so awkward. Those words are also omitted in the readings of 2344 (τὴν πίστιν τοῦ Χριστοῦ) and K:S^ms (τὴν πίστιν ᾽Ιησοῦ Χριστοῦ). 206 429 436 522 614 630 *et al*. K:S^mssB S:PH attempt improvement by putting τῆς δόξης before τοῦ κυρίου ἡμῶν ᾽Ιησοῦ Χριστοῦ. The inability of modern exegetes to make much sense of the passage as it stands reveals how clumsy it is. Mayor, cxciii, concedes that, despite the weight of the textual tradition, a 'strong case' can be made 'for an interpolation in chap. ii. 1'. He is correct, and it is no surprise that others have come to the same conclusion. Cf. Massebieau, 'L'Épître'; Spitta, 4-7; Halévy, 'Lettre', 199, 201; Meyer, *Rätsel*, 119-21; Windisch-Preisker, 13-14 (either 'our Jesus Christ' or 'of glory' is an interpolation); McNeile-Williams, *Introduction*, 206; Meecham, 'Epistle', 183; Findlay, *Way*, 158; Boismard, 'Liturgie', 176; Fulford, 'James ii.1'; Kloppenborg, 'Judaeans'. This commentator concurs. (i) 'The whole phrase is syntactically extremely awkward, being a string of genitives of which the last…reads like an appendage without any clear connection with what precedes it' (Laws, 94). Should we expect this from a writer who, apart from a number of spontaneous Semitisms, writes 'rather supple and idiomatic Greek in most parts' (Wifstrand, 'Problems', 176)? (ii) Although τῆς δόξης 'has been variously interpreted as having an objective, a subjective, or a qualitative force, and been connected in turn by different commentators with every substantive in the sentence' (Mayor, 79), none of the proposed interpretations is persuasive: (a) δόξης goes with προσωπολημψίαις: 'partiality arising from opinion'. Erasmus translates: 'ne cum respectu personarum habeatis fidem Domini nostri Jesu Christi ex opinione' (although he offers a different exegesis in his paraphrase of James). Calvin, 277, follows Erasmus. But the words are too far apart, and δόξα never means 'opinion' in early Christian literature. No contemporary commentator opts for this reading. (b) δόξης goes with πίστιν: 'faith in the glory of our Lord Jesus Christ' (so the v.l. noted above and Zahn, *Introduction*, 151; Burchard, 'Stellen', 357) or 'Christ-given faith in the glory (we shall receive)' or 'glorious faith in Christ'; cf. Reicke, 26.

δόξης); 36.4; 40.3; 63.2; 83.8 (all of God); 1 Cor 2.8 (of Jesus); Barn. 21.9 (of God); Apoc. Elijah Akh 1.3 (of God); Asc. Isa. 9.32 v.l. (of God); Apost. Const. 3.27 ed. Funk, 213 (of Jesus).

[80] Cf. Knowling, 41; Mussner, 116.

[81] For the argument that, in 1 Cor 2.8, 'Lord of glory' has its background in Jewish apocalyptic throne visions see C.C. Newman, *Paul's Glory-Christology*, Leiden, 1992, 236-39.

[82] G.W.E. Nickelsburg, *1 Enoch 1*, Minneapolis, 2001, 316. The phrase is common in the Byzantine collection of hymns known as the Analecta Hymnica Graeca.

According to Ropes, 'The last two of these are forced, and the first involves too strange an order of words to be acceptable...' Dibelius, 127, is more expansive: 'There is no intention in v 1 to define more specifically the Christian faith—such as in the expression "gospel of the glory of Christ" (εὐαγγέλιον τῆς δόξης τοῦ Χριστοῦ) in 2 Cor 4:4, where this is preceded by the term "light" (φωτισμός)—, but rather to stress quite simply that faith in Christ is not consistent with favoritism'. (c) The KJV translates: 'the faith of our Lord Jesus Christ, the Lord of glory'. This requires that one gratuitously add τοῦ κυρίου to the final clause or assume *hyperbaton* ('the faith of Jesus Christ, our Lord of glory'). See Bowyer, *Conjectures*, 314. Alford, 290, who favors this construction, yet calls it 'somewhat harsh and unusual'. Cf. Brinktrine, 'Jak 2.1', positing an Aramaism. (d) 'Glory' is in apposition to 'Jesus Christ'. That is, Jesus Christ is here 'the Glory', the Shekinah. Bengel, 492, may have been the first to suggest this possibility, which Hort, 47-48; Mayor, 79-82; Laws, 94-95; and McKnight, 178, endorse. Yet, although one can find Jesus Christ associated with God's glory (e.g. Eph 1.17; Phil 3.21), where else in Christian literature of the same period is he called, without further ado, 'the Glory'? Further, according to J. Fossum, 'Jewish-Christian Christology and Jewish Mysticism', *VC* 37 (1983), 260-87, 'the name "the Glory" is not expressly given to Christ in Jewish Christianity'. (e) One can insert a comma after ἡμῶν: 'our Lord, Jesus Christ of glory'. This breaks up what naturally goes together, namely, 'our Lord Jesus Christ'. (f) The NRSV has, 'our glorious Lord Jesus Christ'. This makes δόξης a qualitative genitive (cf. Jas 1.25; 2.4) and a probable Semitism. This is today the most common solution; cf. Cantinat, 120-21; Martin, 60; Wachob, *Voice*, 68-69; Krüger, *Kritik*, 159. One of its recent proponents, however, can do no more than call it 'not impossible' (Chester, 'Theology', 44), hardly a recommendation. Where is the parallel to an attribute being added at the end of ὁ κύριος ἡμῶν Ἰησοῦ Χριστός? Mayor, 80, remarks: 'It is very improbable that such a genitive would be appended to a phrase which is already complete in itself; and we may safely say that no one would have thought of such a construction for this passage if the other suggested interpretations had not involved equal or even greater harshness'. (g) Parry, *Discussion*, 24, 36-39, renders the words, 'our Lord Jesus Christ, our glory'. Cf. Cantinat, 120-21. Adamson, 104, gains the same sense by moving ἡμῶν to the end of the sentence. This is to concede that the text as it stands is corrupt. (h) Bowyer, *Conjectures*, 314, translates: 'Have not the faith of our Lord Jesus Christ with regard to honourable appearances'. (i) For Lowe, 'Debate', τῆς δόξης 'is a word-clue alerting readers that a rhetorical argument has commenced, and that such an argument will be constructed around honour'. He paraphrases: 'My dear brothers and sisters, here is my proposition (to be discussed according to honour): show no partiality as you possess the faith of our Lord Jesus Christ'. Lowe concedes, however, that τῆς δόξης remains 'clumsy' (even though he takes it to be a 'word-clue', 252). Moreover, none of the parallels he cites from Graeco-Roman rhetoric display the sort of ambiguity and cryptic compression he finds in Jas 2.1. (j) Assaël-Cuvillier, 'Interprétation', propose: 'Do not find in προσωποληvψίαις reliable evidence of the glory that accords with our Lord Jesus Christ'. This not only has the disadvantage of being a reading that may not have occurred to any reader of James in the last 2,000 years—Assaël and Cuvillier call their proposal 'new' and I know of no evidence to the contrary—but it gives to πίστις a sense it does not seem to have elsewhere in James.

(iii) The grammatical difficulties vanish if one removes ἡμῶν Ἰησοῦ Χριστοῦ. (iv) We know that scribes added 'Jesus', 'Christ', and 'Jesus Christ' elsewhere to their manuscripts; cf. e.g. the textual variants for Mt 16.21; Col 1.2; Jas 5.14. There are, moreover, places in the NT where there is strong evidence of an interpolation notwithstanding the unanimity of the textual tradition; see e.g. the commentaries on 2 Cor 6.14-7.1. (v) Once ἡμῶν Ἰησοῦ Χριστοῦ is subtracted, the result is a title, 'Lord of glory', that is attested in both Jewish and Christian sources; see above. (vi) There is a long and striking series of parallels between Jas 1–2 and 1 Pet 1–2; and where, in the common sequence, one expects a Petrine parallel to Jas 2.1, the reference is to God, not Jesus Christ. The discrepancy is all the more notable if one sees 1 Peter as a source for James, because in other cases our author mutes the christological elements in 1 Peter; see above, 141. (vii) The interpolation could have been suggested to a scribe familiar with the traditional phrase, 'our Lord Jesus Christ'—which occurs over thirty-five times in the NT and is otherwise common in Christian sources—and perhaps with 1 Cor 2.8, where 'the Lord of glory' is Jesus. In sum, the words are best omitted.

Davids raises the standard objections to this conclusion: '(1) the phrase is difficult enough that one would have to posit an interpolator with an unusual lack of ability, (2) the expression κύριος τῆς δόξης does indeed have its parallels (see Spitta, 59-60), but τὴν πίστιν τοῦ κυρίου is a Christian, not a Jewish, expression, (3) this interpolation theory is normally used to support [a] Jewish origin for the work, which is too much weight for such a tentative hypothesis to bear, and (4) the piling up of titles and descriptions is well known in liturgical and homiletic usage'. The last point is true enough yet does not speak to the grammatical difficulties as long as one can cite no close liturgical or homiletical parallel to 2.1. The second and third points are irrelevant because the reasons for finding an interpolation are independent of the dubious thesis that James was originally not a Christian work. The first reason is peculiar, although others have made it. Someone must be responsible for the awkward phrase, and why should we think of James, who is otherwise a decent stylist, rather than an unknown interpolator? Why does Davids in effect think it more natural to attribute 'an unusual lack of ability' to James rather than to someone else?

More forceful are the objections of Wettlaufer, 'Variants', 218-35, among which are these: (i) title creep did not occur often; (ii) it is more frequent in later witnesses; (iii) in other NT texts title creep does not change the referent. But (i) title creep did occur, and one can see it elsewhere in James: 5.7 (1729: Χρίστου; L1440: τοῦ κυρίου ἡμῶν 'Ιησοῦ Χριστοῦ; 2674: τοῦ σωτῆρος), 8 (1367: τοῦ κυρίου ἡμῶν 'Ιησοῦ Χριστοῦ), 14 (88 915(*f) S:P^ms: τοῦ κυρίου 'Ιησοῦ; 6 Ä^ms: 'Ιησοῦ Χριστοῦ). Indeed, the additions in 5.7 L1440 and 5.8 1367 are precisely the change hypothesized for 2.1—ἡμῶν 'Ιησοῦ Χριστοῦ added immediately after κυρίου. (ii) The relevant statistic would not be the rate of title creep in the Greek Christian mss. in general or in Vaticanus or Sinaiticus in particular but the rate of title creep in second-century copies of James, about which we know nothing. Our earliest witnesses (P20 and P23) come from the third century (and are indeed deficient for 2.1). (iii) The interpolator presumably read 2.1 not as a statement about God but as a statement about Jesus, just as many commentators have read other sentences in James with unqualified κύριος as being about Jesus. So he was not in his own mind changing the referent.

It is worth noting that, if one declines to emend 2.1, our epistle can be taken to imply that many or even most Jews in the diaspora were Christian; cf. Hippolytus, *Apoc.* 7.4-8 GCS 1.2 ed. Achelis, 231; Gill, 779; Bardenhewer, 12.

* * *

Verse 2. The following situation, vividly depicted, is introduced as a hypothetical; but, as already argued, the circumstances, or something very close to them, were probably known to James and his readers.

This verse and those following assume that many or most of the readers belong neither in the top economic class nor at the bottom.[83]

---

[83] See further Popkes, *Adressaten*, 53-55.

ἐὰν γὰρ εἰσέλθῃ εἰς συναγωγὴν ὑμῶν.[84] The conditional ἐάν introduces a question, and more questions follow immediately and throughout the chapter. This stands in striking contrast to the first chapter, which has no questions, only imperatives. The rhetorical strategy has changed.

γάρ introduces an illustration that makes the preceding general imperative vivid and specific. ἐὰν γάρ + ἀνήρ is a rare construction that recurs in Herm. *Mand.* 6.2.7. In the LXX, συναγωγή most often translates עדה and so denotes, as usually in Philo, an assembled community or congregation.[85] But Philo also knew that the word could be used of a meeting place or building.[86] Here συναγωγή (Jas: 1×)—the absence of an article shows no particular synagogue is meant, which corresponds to the general audience of 1.1—can refer, on the one hand, to a Christian (i) religious gathering,[87] (ii) building,[88] or (iii) court[89] or, on the other

---

[84] 01Z 02 025 5 33 69 81 88 *et al.* **Byz** Antioch Cyr PsOec insert τὴν before συναγωγήν. This makes for conformity to usual NT usage, which almost always places the definite article before the singular 'synagogue'. One may compare the addition of ἡ in Acts 17.1 v.l.

[85] E.g. LXX Exod 12.3; 38.22; Obad 13. Cf. Pss. Sol. 10.7; 17.16, 43, 44; T. Levi 11.5; Benj. 11.2-3.

[86] Philo, *Prob.* 81. Cf. Josephus, *Bell.* 2.285, 289; 7.44; *Ant.* 19.300, 305; CIJ 1.718 = IJO 1.Ach47; CIJ 1.1936 = IJO 1.Ach58; CIJ 2.878 = IJO 3.Syr12; CIJ 2.861 = IJO 3.Syr34; CIJ 2.1404= CII/P 1.10; CIG 9894, 9904; SEG 17.823 = CJZC 72. In inscriptions, the meaning alternates between building (the dominant sense in Palestine) and community (so typically in the diaspora). Sometimes the word may mean both at the same time—the community in the synagogue; cf. IHierapMir 14. For much of the relevant data see M. Hengel, 'Proseuche und Synagoge', in *Judaica et Hellenistica. Kleine Schriften I*, Tübingen, 1996, 171-95.

[87] So most modern exegetes; cf. Trollope, 607; Ewald, 195; Meinertz, 28; Dibelius, 132-34; Vouga, 71. Cf. Ign. *Pol.* 4.2 ('Let the meetings [συναγωγαί] be more numerous'); Herm. *Mand.* 11.9 ('So when the man... comes into the assembly', ὅταν οὖν ἔλθῃ ὁ ἄνθρωπος... εἰς συναγωγήν; cf. 11.13, 14); Irenaeus, *Haer.* 4.31.1-2; Dionysius of Alexandria in Eusebius, *H.E.* 7.9.2; cf. 7.11.11 (181), 12 (182), 17 (183). See further Lampe, s.v. For συναγωγή in secular Greek as a designation for assemblies and corporations see Dibelius, 133. Smit, 'Background', and Webber, *Response*, 83-84, suggest that Christian communal meals especially may be in view.

[88] So Rost, 'Bemerkungen'; Maser, 'Synagoge', 278; McKnight, 183. Rost interprets Jas 2.2-3 in terms of Galilean synagogues that are now known to be from the third century CE or later. Maser compares more recent discoveries. R. Riesner, 'Synagogues in Jerusalem', in *The Book of Acts in Its First Century Setting, Volume 4*, ed. R. Bauckham, Grand Rapids, MI, 1995, 208, finds in James evidence of Jewish Christian synagogues in pre-70 Jerusalem or Judaea. According to Epiphanius, *Pan.* 30.18.2 GCS 25 ed. Holl, 357, the Ebionites call their ἐκκλησία a συναγωγή; and a Christian building is a 'synagogue' in Dittenberger OGIS 608 (the superscription of a Marcionite church). Is this the meaning in T. Benj. 11.2-3? Christian buildings are also synagogues in Acts Phil. 50 ed. Bonnet, 22; Commodian, *Inst.* 1.24.11 CSEL 15 ed. Dombart, 31.

[89] See especially Ward, 'Concern', 92-94; idem, 'Partiality'. Although this interpretation explains the appearance of κριταί in v. 4, it requires that the rich man of v. 2 be a Christian, which otherwise seems unlikely.

hand, to a Jewish (iv) religious gathering, (v) building,[90] or (vi) court.[91] Most recent commentators prefer (i), (ii), or (iii). This writer demurs: the reference is probably to entering a synagogue building (v) for a judicial convocation (vi).

The reasons are as follows: (i) Much more often than not in the NT and early Christian literature, 'synagogue' is a Jewish building or gathering.[92] (ii) More specifically, the construction εἰς + συναγωγήν can refer to entering a synagogue building.[93] (iii) 1.1 declares the audience to be Jews of the dispersion, not Christians. (iv) Although the rich come εἰς συναγωγήν, they hardly seem to be Christian; see above. (v) People both stood and sat in Jewish synagogues, and there were seats of honor in them.[94] (vi) Matthew 23.6; Mk 12.39; Lk 11.43; 14.7-11; and 20.46 suggest that few early Christian gatherings had comparable seats of honor.[95] (vii) Before the third century, Christians typically assembled in private domestic settings,[96] yet our text seems to presuppose a room with a raised platform, benches, and places for standing.[97] This better matches

---

[90] 'Synagogue' could refer either to a gathered community or meeting place; see above. In SEG 17.823 (= CJZC 72), the word means first one and then the other: 'In the second year of the emperor Nero Claudius Caesar Drusus Germanicus, on the 16th of Chorach. It was resolved by the synagogue of the Jews in Berenice that (the names of) those who donated to the repairs of the synagogue be inscribed on a stele of Parian marble.' Many older commentators, in dependence upon C. Vitringa, *De synagoga vetere libri tres*, Weissenfels, 1726, 448-50, argued or assumed that a Jewish synagogue building is meant. This position has been thought to confirm an early (pre-70) date for James, the idea being (wrongly) that only then did Christians still frequent Jewish synagogues; cf. Acts 6.19; 9.4; 15.21; 22.19. So e.g. W. Sanday, *Inspiration*, London, 1903, 346: 'The description of the Church as a "synagogue" in which it is assumed that all the members are not Christians' is evidence that James belongs to the apostolic age, for 'such mixed communities, in which believing and unbelieving Jews worshipped side by side, are not likely to have existed after the Fall of Jerusalem...' Given the possibility that James was composed in Rome, it is worth noting that epitaphs in the catacombs refer to at least thirteen Roman synagogues, and P. Richardson, 'Augustan-Era Synagogues in Rome', in *Judaism and Christianity in First-Century Rome*, ed. K.P. Donfried and P. Richardson, Grand Rapids, MI, 1998, 17-29, believes that five of those synagogues go back to the turn of the era.

[91] Those who have thought of a Jewish gathering or building or court include Clarke, 809; B. Weiss, *Manual*, 101-102; J. Weiss, *Christianity*, 2.668, 745-46; Maynard-Reid, *Poverty*, 55.

[92] E.g. Mt 4.23; 6.2; Mk 1.21; 6.2; Lk 4.15; 6.6; Jn 18.20; Acts 6.9; 13.5, 14; 17.17; 18.19. Exceptions in nn. 87, 88.

[93] For εἰσέρχομαι + εἰς + συναγωγή see Mk 1.21; 3.1; Lk 4.16; 6.6; Acts 13.14; 14.1; 18.19; 19.8. Cf. 1QM 3.11: בוא אל העדה.

[94] Cf. Philo, *Prob*. 81-82; Mt 6.5; 23.6; Lk 4.16-20; Acts 13.14-16; t. Meg. 2.5; 3.12, 14, 21; y. Mo'ed Qat. 82b-c (3.5). See further C.S. Spigel, *Ancient Synagogue Seating Capacities: Methodology, Analysis and Limits*, Tübingen, 2012, 38-42.

[95] The earliest evidence for seats of honor in a Christian assembly appears to be Herm. *Vis*. 3.9.7.

[96] L.M. White, *The Social Origins of Christian Architecture*, vol. 1, Valley Forge, PA, 1996, 103-10.

[97] So too A. Runesson, *The Origins of the Synagogue*, Stockholm, 2001, 253.

what we know of early synagogues.⁹⁸ (viii) James 2.1-7 largely reproduces a rabbinic tradition that had to do with Jewish courts; see above. Admittedly, that tradition is, in the Didascalia and the Apostolic Constitutions, transferred to Christian religious services. Yet James, unlike those later church orders, does not explicitly address itself to Christian believers, and there is certainly nothing distinctly Christian about what is said in Jas 2.1-4. (ix) Whereas we have evidence of law courts being conducted in synagogues,⁹⁹ it is hard to imagine a rich Christian ca. 100 entering a house church in order to engage in legal actions.

The ancient synagogue¹⁰⁰ was a place for reading and studying Torah as well as for housing visitors.¹⁰¹ It was further, to judge from the synonymous προσευχή,¹⁰² probably a place of prayer and worship, although the

⁹⁸ Cf. Deines, 'Sources', 57: James' 'very vivid description in v. 3 of standing or sitting at the feet of somebody else' is 'reminiscent of the benches in the excavated synagogues of first-century Palestine'. He adds in a note: 'Benches seem to be less common in early Christian churches', although admittedly 'the available examples are very limited'. For the scant archaeological evidence see R. Riesner, 'What Does Archaeology Teach Us about Early House Churches?', *TTKi* 78 (2007), 159-89.

⁹⁹ Mt 10.17; 23.34; Mk 13.9; Lk 12.11; 21.12; Acts 22.19; 26.11; Josephus, *Vita* 293-303; m. Mak. 3.12; b. Yeb. 65b; Epiphanius, *Pan.* 30.11.5 GCS 25 ed. Holl, 346. Cf. Num 15.32-36; Ezek 23.46-47. See further Ward, 'Partiality'; D.D. Binder, *Into the Temple Courts*, Atlanta, 2001, 445-49.

¹⁰⁰ Recent literature: L.J. Hoppe, *The Synagogues and Churches of Ancient Palestine*, Collegeville, MN, 1994; D. Urman and P.V.M. Flesher, ed., *Ancient Synagogues*, Leiden, 1995; J. Gutman, *The Ancient Synagogue*, 2 vols., New Haven, 2000; Binder, *Courts* (as in n. 99); Runesson, *Origins* (as in n. 97); P. van der Horst, *Japheth in the Tents of Shem*, Leuven, 2002, 55-82; C. Claussen, *Versammlung, Gemeinde, Synagoge*, Göttingen, 2002; B. Olsson and M. Zetterholm, eds., *The Ancient Synagogue from Its Origins until 200 C.E.*, Stockholm, 2003; Riesner, 'Synagogues' (as in n. 88); S.K. Catto, *Reconstructing the First-Century Synagogue*, London, 2007; A. Runesson, D.D. Binder, and B. Olsson, *The Ancient Synagogue from Its Origins to 200 CE*, Leiden, 2008; Spigel, 'Synagogues' (as in n. 94).

¹⁰¹ Cf. the famous Theodotus inscription, SEG 8.170 (= CIJ 2.1404; CII/P 1.10), which is probably from first-century CE Jerusalem: 'Theodotus... built this synagogue for the reading of the law and for the teaching of the commandments and the guest room and the chambers of the installations of water for a hostelry for those needing from abroad...' See J.S. Kloppenborg, 'Dating Theodotos (CIJ II 1404)', *JJS* 51 (2000), 243-80.

¹⁰² According to Davids, 'Tradition', 46, 'synagogue' was characteristic of Palestine, not the diaspora. This accords with Hengel, 'Proseuche und Synagoge' (as in n. 86), who argues that συναγωγή was used for the בית הכנסת of Palestine, προσευχή for places of worship in the diaspora. But the use συναγωγή for a meeting place had entered Diaspora discourse by the first century; cf. E. Schürer, *The History of the Jewish People in the Age of Jesus Christ*, vol. 2, rev. ed. G. Vermes et al., Edinburgh, 1979, 440. Relevant inscriptions include SEG 17.823 (= CJZC 72: Berenice in Cyrenaica); CIJ 1.88 (= JIWE 2.288: Rome), 433 (= JIWE 2.1: Rome); 2.751 (= IJO 2.53: Sardis in Lydia), 766 (= IJO 2.168: Akomenia in Phrygia), 781 (= IJO 2.219: Side in Pamphilia). See further Binder, *Courts* (as in n. 99), 92-118. In any case the two words can designate the same thing; see F.G. Hüttenmeister, '"Synagogue" und "Proseuche" bei Josephus und in anderen antiken Quellen', in *Begegnungen zwischen Christentum und Judentum in Antike und Mittelalter*, ed. D.-A. Koch and H. Lichtenberger, Göttingen, 1993, 163-81.

evidence for that is not abundant.¹⁰³ It additionally served as a place to settle community disputes; see n. 99.

Probable evidence for pre-second-century synagogues has been uncovered in several places, both in the diaspora (including Ostia, Delos, Acmonia, and Bernice)¹⁰⁴ and Palestine (including Masada, the Herodium, the NT Jericho, Magdala, Modi'in, Qiryat Sepher, and Gamla).¹⁰⁵ Few architectural generalizations can be made about them. It would appear that, before the end of the second century CE, many synagogues were not independent structures with their own history but rather modified rooms and buildings constructed originally for other purposes.¹⁰⁶

ὑμῶν is plural and so indicates general responsibility. James fails to mention or allude to anyone like the חזן הכנסת, the synagogue official who directed people to their seats.¹⁰⁷

ἀνὴρ χρυσοδακτύλιος ἐν ἐσθῆτι λαμπρᾷ. χρυσοδακτύλιος (Jas: 1×) first appears here in Greek literature.¹⁰⁸ One would expect instead δακτύλιος χρυσός.¹⁰⁹ Did James coin the word? Do we have here evidence of his desire for novelty in the midst of tradition? In our society most married people wear gold bands, but in the biblical books a ring is often a sign of wealth and status.¹¹⁰ Some think here of a Roman equestrian or senator.¹¹¹

---

¹⁰³ Note Philo, *Flacc.* 122; Mt 6.5; and see D.K. Falk, 'Jewish Prayer Literature and the Jerusalem Church in Acts', in Bauckham, *The Book of Acts* (as in n. 88), 277-85.

¹⁰⁴ But only for Ostia and Delos do we have the remains of a building.

¹⁰⁵ J.F. Strange, 'Archaeology and Ancient Synagogues up to about 200 C.E.', in *When Judaism and Christianity Began*, vol. 2, ed. A.J. Avery-Peck, D. Harrington, and J. Neusner, Leiden, 2004, 483-508; Catto, *Synagogue* (as in n. 100), 49-105; Runesson *et al.*, *Synagogue* (as in n. 100), 20-254; J.K. Zangenberg, 'Archaeological News from the Galilee', *Early Christianity* 1 (2010), 471-84.

¹⁰⁶ L.M. White, *Building God's House in the Roman World*, Baltimore, 1990.

¹⁰⁷ m. Yoma 7.1; m. Soṭah 7.8; 9.15; m. Šab. 1.3; b. Sukk. 51b; etc.

¹⁰⁸ And thereafter only in quotations of our verse and lexicons.

¹⁰⁹ Cf. LXX Exod 25.11, 25; 26.29; 30.4; 36.23-27; 38.3, 18; Plato, *Resp.* 359E; Plutarch, *Galba* 7.3; Epictetus, *Diatr.* 1.22.18; PGM 12.207; etc. The similar χρυσόχειρ, with the exception of Lucian, *Tim.* 20.14, appears only in very late sources.

¹¹⁰ Gen 38.18, 25; 41.42; Isa 3.21; Esth 3.10, 12; 8.2, 8, 10; Lk 15.22. Cf. Juvenal 7.139 ('No one would give Cicero himself a hundred pence nowadays unless a huge ring were blazing on his finger'); Lucian, *Tim.* 20 (wearing rings and being dressed in purple are signs of wealth); Cassius Dio 48.45 (Caesar decorated Sextus with gold rings [δακτυλίοις...χρυσοῖς]); ibid. (among the ancient Romans, 'no one was allowed to wear gold rings [δακτυλίοις χρυσοῖς] except the Senators and the Knights; and for this reason they are given to such freedmen as the ruler may choose, even though these are already wearing gold in other ways, as a mark of honor indicating that they are superior for the status of freedmen and are eligible to become Knights'); Epictetus, *Diatr.* 1.22.18 ('some white-haired old man with many a gold ring on his fingers', χρυσοῦς δακτυλίους ἔχων πολλούς); and see the discussion of rings and wealth in Pliny the Elder, *N.H.* 33.6. *Neuer Wettstein*, 1276-81, contains additional texts on rings and their ostentatious display.

¹¹¹ E.g. Streeter, *Church*, 203; Reicke, 27; idem, *Diakonie*, 242-43; Laws, 98-99. Criticism in Tsuji, *Glaube*, 142.

ἐσθής[112] means 'robe' or 'raiment'. Elsewhere in early Christian literature, ἐν ἐσθῆτι λαμπρᾷ refers to the shining clothes of angels.[113] But λαμπρός,[114] which means 'radiant' or 'shining' when used with clothes, can also mean 'bright' or 'clean'—in effect, 'fine' or 'luxurious'.[115] Here it is in antithesis to ῥυπαρός, 'filthy', 'shabby'. Cf. Philo, *Jos.* 105 ('bright raiment instead of filthy', ἀντὶ ῥυπώσης λαμπράν); Artemidorus, *Onir.* 2.3 (when dreaming, it is better to see oneself in 'clean and fine [λαμπρά] clothing' than in 'shabby [ῥυπαρά], dirty clothing'). Note the consonance and assonance created by λαμπρᾷ and ῥυπαρᾷ (α-πρα, παρα).

Some recent scholars have suggested that the rich man is a potential patron of the church.[116] This commentary takes the view that he instead enters the synagogue for purposes of a legal dispute: the issue is partiality in court. Nonetheless, the alternative proposal could be harmonized with the view that Jas 2 envisages a synagogue. Privileged seating is attested as a reward for patrons, including patrons of synagogues.[117] Moreover, James employs kinship language—esp. 'brother'—and otherwise advocates reciprocity among equals, which would be consistent with a concern to counter a patronage system; and the same concern can be found in 1.5 and 17, which speak of divine giving in terms that makes the deity unlike human patrons.

εἰσέλθῃ δὲ καὶ πτωχὸς ἐν ῥυπαρᾷ ἐσθῆτι. πτωχός appears four times in James, all in the present passage: vv. 2, 3, 5, 6. The word itself means 'one who is poor, dependent on others, a beggar'.[118] It occurs 100× in the

---

[112] LXX: 4×. NT: 7×; Jas: 3×. Gk. Pseudepigrapha (Denis): 4×. The word is common in Philo and Josephus.

[113] E.g. Acts 10.30; Chrysostom, *Asc. dom.* PG 50.449 (cf. Lk 24.4); *Hom. Acts* PG 60.178, 21 (cf. Acts 10.30). Note also T. Abr. RecLng. 16.6, where the angel of Death wears a 'most radiant' (λαμπροτάτην) robe.

[114] LXX: 7×. NT: 9×; Jas: 2×. Gk. Pseudepigrapha (Denis): 15×. Both Philo and Josephus use the word often.

[115] E.g. Philo, *Jos.* 105; Josephus, *Vita* 334; *Ant.* 8.72; Rev 15.6; 19.8. The Vulgate translates our text with 'candidus' = '(clothed in) shining white'.

[116] E.g. Vyhmeister, 'Rich'; Kloppenborg, 'Status', 150-54; idem, 'Avoidance'; Batten, *Friendship*, 127-34. Like Batten, Webber, *Response*, at several points interprets James as promoting a vision opposed to ancient patronage: God is the only patron; all clients are equals; there is no place for social climbing. Cf. Garleff, *Identität*, 265-69.

[117] E.g. CIJ 2.738 = IJO 2.36. For an introduction to the subject of benefactors of synagogues see L.H. Feldman, 'Diaspora Synagogues', in *Sacred Realm*, ed. S. Fine, New York, 1996, 51-55.

[118] Literature: L.E. Keck, 'The Poor among the Saints in the New Testament', *ZNW* 56 (1965), 100-137; idem, 'The Poor among the Saints in Jewish Christianity and Qumran', *ZNW* 57 (1966), 54-78; S. Légasse, 'Pauvreté et salut dans le Nouveau Testament', *RThL* 4 (1973), 162-72; F. Hauck and E. Bammel, 'πτωχός κτλ.', *TDNT* 6.885-915; C. Osiek, *Rich and Poor in the Shepherd of Hermas*, Washington, DC, 1983; E. Bammel, 'The Poor and the Zealots', in *Jesus and the Politics of his Day*, ed. E. Bammel and C.F.D. Moule, Cambridge, UK, 1984, 109-28; P. Coulange, *Dieu, ami des pauvres*, Göttingen, 2007; W.R. Domeris, *Touching the Heart of God: The Social Construction of Poverty among Biblical Peasants*, New York, 2007.

LXX, 39× for עָנִי (= 'poor', 'afflicted', 'humble'), 22× times for דַּל (= 'low', 'weak', 'poor', 'thin'), 11× times for אֶבְיוֹן (= 'needy', 'poor'). The primary reference is to economic poverty,[119] which is the exclusive meaning in Greek literature outside of Jewish and Christian texts.[120] But already in the Hebrew Bible, especially in the Psalms, the Greek and its Hebrew equivalents refer to those who are in special need of God's help[121] and so receive special protection;[122] and in time 'poor' became a self-designation for the meek, humiliated, and oppressed people of God.[123] As the poor person is in shabby clothes, the economic meaning is obviously to the fore here.[124] Verse 5, however, implies that the poor love God, so the religious associations of the word are also present; cf. 1.9. Indeed, given the links between James and traditions about the Ebionites, whose name derived from אֶבְיוֹן, πτωχός likely stands in part for Christians within the synagogue.[125]

Galatians 2.10 attributes to James, along with Peter and John, a special interest in the poor saints of Jerusalem, and James was remembered in Christian circles not only as being himself poor but also as being no respecter of persons.[126] So our book is here in character: Jas 2.1-7 coheres well with traditions about its purported author.

Verse 3. James accuses his readers, or rather some of them, of honoring the rich and shaming the poor. Comparable is Ecclus 11.2: 'Do not praise individuals for their good looks, or loathe anyone because of appearance alone'. James does not, however, go so far as Apost. Const. 1.3.9 ed. Funk, 11, which insists that the faithful foreswear gold rings and fine clothes.

---

[119] Cf. Prov 13.8; Mk 12.42; 14.7; Lk 21.3; Jn 12.5; Josephus, *Bell.* 5.570; T. Job 10.6-7; 12.1.

[120] Cf. LSJ, s.v.

[121] E.g. Ps 12.5; 14.6; 22.24; 37.14; 69.29; 70.5; 86.1; 88.15; Isa 61.1. Cf. Pss. Sol. 5.11: 'Who is the hope of the poor and needy, if not you, Lord?' In LXX Pss 35.10; 37.14; 40.17; 70.5; 86.1; and 109.22, πτωχὸς καὶ πένης is a fixed expression used of one's attitude in prayer.

[122] Cf. Exod 21–23; 2 Sam 22.28; Ezek 22.29; Pss 72.2, 4,12, 13; 132.15.

[123] Cf. Isa 10.2; 26.6; Pss. Sol. 5.2, 11; 10.6; 15.1; 18.2; 5 Apoc. Syr. Ps. 2.18; 1QpHab. 12.3; 1QM 14.7; 1QH 13(5).13-14.

[124] Cf. LXX Zech 3.4 (clothed in 'filthy [ῥυπαρά] garments'); Josephus, *Ant.* 7.267 ('a soiled garment', ῥυπαράν ἐσθῆτα); Sib. Or. 5.188 ('a white shirt over a dirty one', λευκὸν ἐπὶ ῥυπαρῷ); BGU 1564.10 (a garment 'without any filth', ῥύπου).

[125] Kloppenborg, 'Poverty', 225-32, rather emphasizes that the contrast between rich and poor was a standard trope in Graeco-Roman moral literature.

[126] Hegesippus *apud* Eusebius, *H.E.* 2.23.10: 'We (the Jewish leaders) and all the people bear testimony that you [James] are just and are no respecter of persons (πρόσωπον οὐ λαμβάνεις)'.

ἐπιβλέψητε δὲ ἐπὶ τὸν φοροῦντα τὴν ἐσθῆτα τὴν λαμπρὰν καὶ εἴπητε.[127] ἐπιβλέπω (Jas: 1×) literally means 'look at' but can connote care or favor.[128] φορέω (Jas: 1×) here means 'wear', as in Mt 11.8 (οἱ τὰ μαλακὰ φοροῦντες ἐν τοῖς οἴκοις τῶν βασιλέων). τὴν ἐσθῆτα τὴν λαμπρὰν rewrites the ἐν ἐσθῆτι λαμπρᾷ of the previous sentence.

σὺ κάθου ὧδε καλῶς. Cf. LXX Ruth 4.2 (καθίσατε ὧδε); Mk 14.32 (καθίσατε ὧδε). κάθημαι occurs twice in this verse and nowhere else in James[129] while ὧδε is a Jamesian *hapax*. καλῶς (cf. 2.8, 19) has been variously assessed. The NRSV translates it as 'please', the solution also of Ropes, 190: 'Some polite idiom in the sense of "please", "pray", is to be suspected. In various Greek liturgies the minster's direction to the worshipping congregation, στῶμεν καλῶς, presents the same difficulty and suggests the same explanation.'[130] The KJV, however, renders καλῶς 'in a good place', and BAGD, s.v., affirming that this is the meaning, cites Lucian, *Paras.* 50: 'reclining well (καλῶς κατακειμένῳ) as at an elegant banquet'. This is probably correct.[131] One is reminded of texts from the Jesus tradition that refer disparagingly to distinguished places in the synagogue[132] and of Herm. *Vis.* 3.9.7,[133] which presupposes seats of honor in Christian churches.[134]

καὶ τῷ πτωχῷ εἴπητε. The reference to the clothing of the poor (v. 2) is dropped.

σὺ στῆθι.[135] Cf. 1 Βασ 9.27: σὺ στῆθι (= MT: אתה עמד). For the rabbinic parallels see above, 378. ἵστημι recurs in 5.9.

---

[127] P74V 01 02 5 33 69 81 88 *et al.* Byz Antioch PsOec L:V K:SB A Sl:ChDMSi open with καὶ ἐπιβλέψητε instead of ἐπιβλέψητε δέ. This avoids two consecutive uses of δέ; cf. v. 2. Byz also adds καί at the beginning of v. 4. 025 5 69 88 322 *et al.* Byz Antioch PsOec L:T K:SB S:P Sl:ChDMSi naturally add αὐτῷ after εἴπητε. Is this original?

[128] E.g. LXX 1 Βασ 1.11; 9.16; Pss 25.16; 69.16; Tob 3.3; Jdt 13.4; Lk 1.48; 9.38; Josephus, *Ant.* 1.20; Aristotle, *Eth. nic.* 1122A-23A2.

[129] On the Attic form of the imperative (cf. LXX Ps 109.1) see BDF 100.

[130] Ropes cites Brightman-Hammond, *Liturgies*, 43, 49 (the Liturgy of St. James), 383 (the Liturgy of St. John Chrysostom), 471 (the Liturgy of Antioch). Cf. Dibelius, 131.

[131] Mayor, 84, supplies additional parallels.

[132] Mt 23.6; Mk 12.39; Lk 11.43; 20.46; cf. CIJ 2.738 = IJO 2.36: a synagogue bestowed upon a female benefactor a 'seat of honor' (προεδρίᾳ). Although the texts from the gospels join the wearing of conspicuous clothes with the desire to have good seats, James does not appear to draw upon the Jesus tradition here.

[133] 'I speak...to the leaders of the church and to those who take the chief seats (τοῖς πρωτοκαθεδρίταις)'.

[134] Seats of honor were a usual part of communal gatherings, Jewish, Greek, and Roman alike; cf. Lk 14.7-11 (when at a wedding banquet do not take the place of honor but sit at the lowest place); Plutarch, *Mor.* 58C (on giving up good seats to flatter the rich); 148E (Alexidemos has his honor insulted by the seating arrangements).

[135] Many witnesses, including 01 02 025 044 33 81 206 *et al.* Byz Cyr PsOec L:V K:BS^ms S:HP Ä G:G-D Sl:ChDMSi, have ἐκεῖ at the end of this clause (so NA²⁷) rather than after the next verb, as in 03 945 1175 *et al.* L:F K:S^mss (so the *Editio Critica Maior*). One can hardly decide the original. See J.K. Elliott, 'Changes to the Exegesis of the

ἢ κάθου ἐκεῖ ὑπὸ τὸ ὑποπόδιόν μου.[136] This may well be James' addition to his tradition. It has no counterpart in the similar instructions in rabbinic texts or church orders. Whereas the rich sit in a good place, the poor have a choice between standing[137] anywhere or, even worse, sitting in a humble place, that is, on the floor at the feet of the speaker, who thereby displays superiority. Note the contrast between ὧδε and ἐκεῖ: the rich individual is near the speaker, the poor rather removed. Although ὑποπόδιον[138] means 'footstool', a literal interpretation seems out of place here.[139] We have rather a figure of speech meaning 'at my feet'.[140] 'Footstool' appears otherwise never to be used literally in the Greek Bible.[141] One is reminded of the idiom, τιθέναι τινὰ ὑποπόδιον τῶν ποδῶν τινος—'make someone a footstool for someone'.[142]

The oldest buildings widely recognized as synagogues have stone benches on their walls. Masada has four tiers of stone benches on three walls.[143] Three such tiers line the Herodium synagogue[144] and that at Gamla.[145] Less elaborately, the building at Delos so often identified as a synagogue has one tier of benches on two walls.[146] There is, further, some benching on the eastern wall of the earliest synagogue at en-Nabratein.[147]

Catholic Epistles in the Light of the Text in the *Editio Critica Maior*', in *History and Exegesis*, ed. S.-W. Son, New York, 2006, 325; Metzger, *Commentary*, 680-81.

[136] On the variants for the first three words see the previous note. ἐπί replaces ὑπό in 03Z 025 044 33 206 218 *et al.* L593 L596 L:V^ms K:S^mss Sl:Ch—a natural improvement. ὑποπόδιον μου becomes ὑποπόδιον ποδῶν μου in 02f 33 L:V, presumably under the influence of LXX Ps 109:1; Isa 66.1.

[137] The attempt of T.H. Gaster, *The Dead Sea Scriptures in English Translation*, Garden City, NY, 1956, 16, to connect 'stand' with the Hebrew idiom for 'be excluded from society' has not been taken up.

[138] Nowhere else does biblical Greek use ὑπό before ὑποπόδιον, and everywhere else it follows ὑποπόδιον by τῶν ποδῶν: LXX Pss 98.5; 109.1; Isa 66.1; Lam 2.1; Mt 5.35; Mk 12.36; Lk 20.43; Acts 2.35; 7.49; Heb 1.13; 10.13.

[139] Some texts do, however, speak of a raised podium (בימה; cf. ἄμβων) for reading Torah; cf. t. Soṭah 7.8; b. Sukk. 51b; and already 1 Esd 9.42 ('Ezra the priest and reader of the law stood on the wooden platform [βήματος] that had been prepared').

[140] Cf. Ward, 'Concern', 95: James, 'in exaggerating the shabby treatment of the poor man in this example, has drawn on a biblical phrase (God's footstool) which connotes at least the place of the humble (Ψ 98:5) and at most the place of the enemies in judgment (Ψ 109:1)'.

[141] Cf. LXX Ps 98.5; 109.1; Isa 66.1; Lam 2.1, always for הדם.

[142] LXX Ps 109.1; Lk 20.43; Acts 2.35; Heb 1.13; etc. If one were to find an allusion to the oft-cited Ps 110.1, then one might think of the speaker as sufficiently pompous to speak ironically like God. But this seems far-fetched.

[143] See the photographs in H. Shanks, *Judaism in Stone*, New York, 1979, 22, 25.

[144] Shanks, *Stone* (as in n. 143), 28.

[145] S. Gutman, 'The Synagogue at Gamla', in L.I. Levine, *Ancient Synagogues Revealed*, Jerusalem, 1981, 30-34.

[146] L.M. White, 'The Delos Synagogue Revisited', *HTR* 80 (1987), 133-60.

[147] E.M. Meyers, J.F. Strange, and C.L. Meyers, 'Second Preliminary Report on the 1981 Excavations at en-Nabratein, Israel', *BASOR* 246 (1982), 40. Note also the benching at the Hasmonean synagogue at Jericho: E. Netzer, 'A Synagogue from the

So it seems that, notwithstanding all the architectural variety, the earliest synagogues were 'assembly halls with banked stone seating around the walls'.[148] Later synagogues also frequently featured benches along the walls.[149] Thus one wonders whether James envisions a synagogue in which the seats around the sides are reserved for the well-to-do while others are expected to occupy the floor[150] or stand in the middle. We may in any case surmise from Mt 23.6 and its parallels that some seats were considered more honorable than others,[151] and b. Sukk. 51b informs us that, at least at a later time, congregants could be sorted by social status: 'They moreover did not occupy their seats promiscuously but goldsmiths sat separately, silversmiths separately, blacksmiths separately, metalworkers separately and weavers separately, so that when a poor man entered the place he recognized the members of his craft'.

Verse 4. οὐ διεκρίθητε ἐν ἑαυτοῖς.[152] The introductory οὐ anticipates that the question asked will receive an affirmative response. διακρίνω can mean 'doubt, waver',[153] as in 1.6.[154] But ἀδιάκριτος seems to mean 'partiality' in 3.17, and the present context is all about drawing distinctions between rich and poor. So one inclines to give the verb middle sense: 'have you not made distinctions?'[155] ἐν ἑαυτοῖς then means 'among

---

Hasmonean Period Recently Exposed in the Western Plain of Jericho', *IEJ* 49 (1999), 203-21.

[148] So D.E. Groh, 'The Stratigraphic Chronology of the Galilean Synagogue from the Early Roman Period through the Early Byzantine Period (CA. 420 C.E.)', in Urman and Flesher, *Ancient Synagogues* (as in n. 100), 1.69. Groh also believes that the small assembly hall in Migdal, with benches along one wall, was a first-century synagogue.

[149] M.J.S. Chiat, *Handbook of Synagogue Architecture*, Chico, CA, 1982, passim. Note the summarizing chart on 336. Cf. the legend about the golden thrones for elders in the synagogue in Alexandria: t. Suk. 4.6; y. Suk. 55b (5.1).

[150] Cf. the situation in b. B. Bat. 8b ('At first the Master would not sit on the mats in the synagogue'); Ambrosiaster, *In Ep. 1 ad Cor.* 12.1-2 PL 17.258 ('in all religious assemblies the people should be sitting, the nobler ones on stools, those who are after them on benches, the rest on mats, which are spread out on the floor').

[151] See n. 94. The fourth-century synagogue at Sardis features prominent apse seating, presumably for the elders; see Shanks, *Stone* (as in n. 143), 170-71. Cf. t. Meg. 3.21 'How did the elders sit in session? It was facing the people with their back toward the sanctuary.'

[152] καί is added to the beginning of v. 4 in 025 5 69 88 218 *et al.* **Byz** PsOec **G**:G-D **Sl**:Ch. 322 323 629 have καί but omit οὐ, which turns a question into a statement. The same result is gained by the omission of οὐ—due to *homoioteleuton*? cf. the μοῦ at the end of v. 3—in 03T 1852 L:F.

[153] So Ropes, 192; Moo, 104; *et al.*

[154] See the discussion above, 179-91.

[155] So also Dibelius, 136-37; Mussner, 119; Ward, 'Concern', 94-96; Davids, 110; cf. NRSV and Acts 11.12; 15.9. Mayor, 85, translates, 'Are you not divided in yourselves?' For the various options in translating διεκρίθητε and their earlier proponents see Beyschlag, 103-104. The verb surely does not, against Ps.-Oecumenius *ad loc.* PG 119.473B, and Theophylact *ad loc.* PG 125.1152D, mean 'you use your critical abilities'.

yourselves', not 'inside yourselves',[156] and v. 4 is the antithesis of v. 1: whereas James denounces partiality (μὴ ἐν προσωπολημψίαις ἔχετε), his readers make distinctions among themselves based upon financial considerations.

James' opposition to class distinctions makes him, as Oesterley, 437, observes, sound like many moderns. It also makes him resemble Paul, who could oppose distinctions based upon worldly status.[157]

καὶ ἐγένεσθε κριταὶ διαλογισμῶν πονηρῶν; Cf. the two-way tradition behind Did. 5.2 and Barn. 20.2, which condemns 'advocates of the rich and lawless judges of the poor', πενήτων ἄνομοι κριταί. καὶ ἐγένεσθε κτλ. stands under the preceding οὐ. κριταί[158] creates a wordplay with διεκρίθητε. διαλογισμῶν πονηρῶν (= 'with evil thoughts')[159] is a traditional expression deriving from the Hebrew מחשבה + רע or רשע.[160] The genitive with adjectival sense is probably also a Semitism.[161] Perhaps it should be linked with the יצר הרע; see on 1.14. One may compare the μὴ κρίνετε of the Jesus tradition,[162] but the chief background is Lev 19.15.[163]

Verse 5. James now reminds readers of how God treats the poor: they are in truth honored. The *imitatio dei* is presupposed.

ἀκούσατε. The imperative is often said to reflect Hellenistic diatribe, especially as the rhetorical questions of this section of James are also characteristic of diatribe. But there are parallels in the Pentateuch,[164] the prophets,[165] wisdom texts,[166] the Qumran literature,[167] the Jesus

---

[156] Contrast Mussner, 119: 'in eurem Innern'.

[157] E.g. Gal 3.28. Interestingly enough, the *Catena ad loc.* ed. Cramer, 9, links our text with Paul by using the apostle's language about Christians being one body with one head: all are members of one another. Cf. Calvin, 276.

[158] κριτής: Jas: 4×; cf. 4.11, 12; 5.9.

[159] διαλογισμός: LXX: 27×. NT: 14×; Jas: 1×. Gk. Pseudepigrapha (Denis): 7×. Philo: 0×. Josephus: 1×. πονηρός: Jas 2×; cf. 4.16. Laws, 102, translates, 'who give corrupt decisions'; cf. MHT 3.213: 'by false standards'. Contrast MHT 4.118, which reckons with a Semitism (the Hebrew genitive of quality): 'judges of evil thoughts' = 'evil-thinking judges'.

[160] Cf. Ps 56.6 (LXX: διαλογισμοί...εἰς κακόν); Ezek 38.10 (LXX: λογισμοὺς πονηρούς); 1QpHab 3.5 (מחשבתם להרע); 1QH 14(6).22 (מחשבת רשעה); 4Q286 7 2.3 (במחשבת רשעמה); 4Q398 14-17 2.5 (מחשבות רעה); 4Q399 2.2 (מחשבת רע); Mt 15.19 (διαλογισμοὶ πονηροί); Mk 7.21 (οἱ διαλογισμοὶ οἱ κακοί); T. Levi 2.3 v.l. (διαλογισμῶν τῶν πονηρῶν); Mart. Apollonius 4 ed. Musurillo, 90 (διαλογισμῶν πονηρῶν).

[161] Cf. Lk 18.6 (ὁ κριτὴς τῆς ἀδικίας); Jas 1.25 (ἀκροατὴς ἐπιλησομονῆς). See J.A. Fitzmyer, *The Gospel according to Luke (I–IX)*, Garden City, NY, 1981, 123-24.

[162] Mt 7.1; Lk 6.37; cf. Rom 2.1; 1 Clem. 13.2; Pol. *Phil.* 2.3. The additional parallels that Stulac, 91-93, draws between Mt 7 and Jas 2 are insubstantial.

[163] See above. So also Laws, 102; Johnson, 223; Moo, 105. Note that Hesychius of Jerusalem, *Lev. ad* 19.16 PG 93.1028C, cites Jas 2.2-4 when commenting on this part of Lev 19. The verse also lies behind Ecclus 35.16 and Acts 23.3.

[164] Num 12.6; 16.8; Deut 5.1; 6.3, 4 (the Shema'); 9.1; 20.3.

[165] Isa 1.10; 7.13; 33.13; 42.18; Jer 2.4; 5.21; 7.2; 13.15; Ezek 18.25; Hos 5.1; etc.

[166] E.g. Prov 4.1, 10; 8.6; 23.19; Ecclus 3.1; 6.23; 16.24; 23.7; 31.22; 39.13; Wis 6.1.

tradition,[168] Acts,[169] and elsewhere.[170] Moreover, 'listen' + 'brother(s)' is common in Jewish and Christian sources.[171]

ἀδελφοί μου ἀγαπητοί. See the comments on 1.2, 16; 2.1. Here, as in 3.12, 'brothers' is inserted for emphasis; it does not mark a change in theme.

οὐχ ὁ θεὸς ἐξελέξατο τοὺς πτωχοὺς τῷ κόσμῳ πλουσίους ἐν πίστει.[172] Whether or to what extent ἐκλέγομαι[173] expresses a considered doctrine of election such as we find in the Dead Sea Scrolls and parts of Romans— cf. perhaps the βουληθείς of 1.18—cannot be answered.[174] Yet the main point is clear: God shows a predilection for 'the poor' as opposed to the rich. One might protest that this makes God partial; but 'partiality on God's part ceases to be so once "impartiality" is understood as an explicit effort to challenge and negate prevailing arrangements of power and status'.[175]

The qualification of τοὺς πτωχοὺς (see on v. 2) by τῷ κόσμῳ (see on 1.27) probably means 'the poor in [the eyes or judgment of] the world'.[176] But the meaning could also be 'the poor in worldly goods' or 'the poor because of the world',[177] or, on the analogy of the עֲנִוֵּי־אָרֶץ of Amos 8.4[178] and the rabbinic בָּעוֹלָם הַזֶּה (= 'in this world'), 'the poor in this present

---

[167] CD 1.1; 2.1; 4Q185 1-2 1.13; 4Q270 2.2.19; 4Q298 3-4 2.4; 4Q299 3 2.9; 4Q525 13.6.

[168] Mt 11.15; 13.43; 25.29 v.l.; Mk 4.9, 23; 7.16 v.l.; Lk 8.8; 12.21 v.l.; 14.35; Gos. Thom. 8, 21, 24, 64, 65, 96.

[169] Acts 2.22; 7.2; 15.13; 22.1.

[170] E.g. Rev 2.7, 11, 17, 29; 3.6, 13, 22; 13.9. See further Ward, 'Concern', 36-37.

[171] Tob 6.16 (ἄκουσόν μου ἄδελφε); Jdt 14.1 (ἀκούσατε...ἀδελφοί); T. Reub. 1.5 (ἀκούσατε ἀδελφοί μου); T. Jos. 1.2 (ἀδελφοὶ ἀκούσατε); Acts 7.2 (ἀδελφοί...ἀκούσατε); 15.13 (ἀδελφοὶ ἀκούσατε); 22.1 (ἀδελφοί...ἀκούσατε).

[172] ἐν is inserted before κόσμῳ in 322 323 808 L:V?. Perhaps influenced by 1 Cor 1.27-28, 02C2 04C2 025 044 5 43 61 69 81 88 et al. Byz PsOec A G:A1G-D Sl:ChMSi change to τοῦ κόσμου.

[173] Most often for בחר in the LXX. Jas: 1×. NT: 22× (11× in Luke-Acts). Gk. Pseudepigrapha (Denis): 21×. Philo: 17×. Josephus: 13×.

[174] Augustine, Praed. sanct. 17(34) PL 44.986, uses the text this way. See further R. Wall, 119-20. Cf. the use of ἐξελέξατο for God's choice of Israel in LXX Deut 14.1-2. But For Davids, 111, 'that the aorist ἐξελέξατο is used might refer to some eternal election of God (Eph 1:4) but probably refers to the declarations of Jesus and reflects the constituency of the church'. In any case ἐξελέξατο has led commentators to recall 1 Cor 1.26-29—e.g. Poole, 885; Knowling, 45; Johnson, 224; et al.—and other Christians to juxtapose that text with Jas 2.5—e.g. J. Murton, Persecution for Religion Judged and Condemned, London, 1615, 65.

[175] Kloppenborg, 'Avoidance', 765.

[176] So Ropes, 193; Schlatter, 168; Dibelius, 138; Davids, 112. Cf. Acts 7.20: 'beautiful before God' (ἀστεῖος τῷ θεῷ).

[177] So Frick, 'Note', who discusses in detail multiple possible meanings for the dative.

[178] LXX: πτωχοὺς ἀπὸ τῆς γῆς.

life'.[179] But the rabbinic parallel in b. Giṭ. 30a (עניי עולם) seems rather to mean 'the world's poor'; and in b. B. Bat. 8b, עניי דעלמא appears to signify 'the poor in the world outside (that town)'. James' paradoxical formulation in any event resembles the contrasts in Rev 2.9 ('know your tribulation and poverty, but you are rich') and T. Gad 7.6 ('The man who is poor but free from envy, who is grateful to the Lord for everything, is richer than all...').[180]

ἐν πίστει[181] after πλούσιος (see on 1.10) appears to be unparalleled, although πλούσιος (see on 1.10) + ἐν + dative is attested.[182] As for the sense, 'rich in faith' could mean 'rich in the sphere of faith' in so far as they are believers who will inherit the kingdom.[183] Calvin, 278, construes ἐν as instrumental ('rich by means of faith'): James 'calls them rich in faith, not because they had a great surplus of faith, but as men whom God had made rich, with the various gifts of His Spirit, which we receive by faith'. Yet, despite Calvin, 'rich in faith' could equally mean that the poor whom James has in mind are full of faith.[184] Jewish sources as well as the Jesus tradition are familiar with the notion that people can have little faith or great faith.[185]

καὶ κληρονόμους τῆς βασιλείας. Both κληρονόμος and βασιλεία are Jamesian *hapax legomena*. κληρονομεῖν + τὴν βασιλείαν or closely related expressions appear in Mt 25.34, a few Pauline texts, and some other early Christian sources.[186] In the background is the biblical phrase,

---

[179] Cf. b. Sanh. 100a: עני בעולם הזה. Cf. the textual variant in 61 180Z 326* 398 1837 2523 2544Z 2674 L2087 PsOec—τοῦ κόσμου τούτου—and 1 Tim 6.17: τοῖς πλουσίοις ἐν τῷ νῦν αἰῶνι; also דלת הארץ = οἱ πτωχοὶ τῆς γῆς, as in 2 Kgs 24.14; 25.12; Jer 40.7 and the עשיר בעלמא (= 'the rich in the world') in b. B. Bat. 4a.

[180] Additional wordplays between 'rich' and 'poor' include: 2 Cor 6.10 ('as poor, yet making many rich'); T. Jud. 25.4 ('those who died in poverty for the Lord's sake shall be made rich'); Herm. *Sim*. 2.5 ('the rich man has much wealth, but is poor as touching the Lord...the poor is rich in intercession and confession'). Hoppe, *Hintergrund*, 80-81, also finds Mt 11.25-26 = Lk 10.21-22 comparable: God's revelation comes not to the wise but to 'babes'.

[181] Cf. the common Hebrew באמונה. For πίστις see on 1.3.

[182] Cf. Eph 2.4 ('rich in mercy'); 1 Tim 6.18 ('rich in good deeds'). One may further compare Lk 12.21: εἰς θεὸν πλουτῶν. Billerbeck 3.754, cites related rabbinic expressions with עשיר—'rich in business', 'rich in good will', 'rich in Torah'.

[183] Cf. Huther, 79-80; Dibelius, 136. Ropes, 194, paraphrases: rich 'in the domain where faith is the chief good', that is, 'rich when judged by God's standards'. In Eph 2.4, πλούσιος ὢν ἐν ἐλέει means 'being rich in (the sphere) of mercy'.

[184] So Bengel, 493; Mayor, 86. Cf. CIG 4.9668: πλούσιος γεγώς = 'rich in children'.

[185] Mt 6.30; 8.26; 14.31; 15.28; 16.8; Lk 12.28; 17.5, 20; Josephus, *Ant*. 15.87 (μεγάλης πίστεως); Mek. on Exod 14.31 (גדולה האמנה); 16.4, 19-20; Tanḥ. Yel. Beshallah 20; b. Soṭah 48a.

[186] 1 Cor 6.9-10; 15.50; Gal 5.19-21; Eph 5.5; Ign. *Eph*. 16.1 (βασιλείαν θεοῦ οὐ κληρονομήσουσιν); Acts Thom. 136 ed. Bonnet, 243. Cf. 'inherit (eternal) life', as in Pss. Sol. 14.10; 1 En. 40.9; Mt 19.29; Mk 10.17; Lk 10.25; 18.18; Sib. Or. frag. 3 47; m. B. Meṣ. 2.11; t. Sanh. 12.11; etc.

'to inherit the land'.[187] Inheriting the kingdom is like taking possession of the land. The import is close to the rabbinic idiom, נחל or ירש + חיי/העולם הבא.[188]

ἧς ἐπηγγείλατο τοῖς ἀγαπῶσιν αὐτόν;[189] See on 1.12, where the same phrase occurs. 'Has promised'[190] need not refer to any particular occasion. Ropes, 195, surmises that 'the "promise" was implicit in the very conception of the kingdom'. But those who find an allusion to the Jesus tradition (see below) can think of the beatitudes. 'To those who love him' implicitly affirms that it is not the rich but 'the poor' in particular who love God. James assumes the sort of piety found in the Jesus tradition and in many Jewish writings, such as the Psalms of Solomon, where we read not only that 'if one is exceedingly rich, he sins' (5.16), but also that God is 'the hope and refuge of the poor' (15.1).

Many have found here the likely influence of a makarism attributed to Jesus:[191]

Mt 5.3	Lk 6.20
μακάριοι οἱ πτωχοὶ τῷ πνεύματι	μακάριοι οἱ πτωχοὶ
ὅτι αὐτῶν ἐστιν ἡ βασιλεία	ὅτι ὑμετέρα ἐστὶν ἡ βασιλεία
τῶν οὐρανῶν	τοῦ θεοῦ[192]

This seems a safe inference. The paradoxical content of the two lines is similar; πτωχός is nowhere associated with βασιλεία before Matthew and Luke; and James uses βασιλεία only here, which is consistent with

---

[187] Num 33.54; Deut 1.8; 6.18; 16.20; Josh 1.6; Ps 37.11; Tob 4.12; etc. See Allison, *Jesus*, 179-81.

[188] Cf. Mek. on Exod 14.31; m. 'Abot 5.19; Tanḥ. Buber Shelah 28; ARN 40; ARN B 10, 29, 45; y. Ned. 38a (3.8); y. Ber. 11d (7.3); y. Pesaḥ. 33a (6.1); b. Qidd. 40b; b. Ber. 51a; b. Soṭah 7b; etc.

[189] ἐπαγγείλας replaces βασιλείας in 01* 02. Is this assimilation to Heb 6.17?

[190] Cf. Ep. ad Diog. 10.2: 'to whom he promised (ἐπηγγείλατο) the kingdom in heaven, and he will give it to those who loved him'. Might this reflect James?

[191] See e.g. Schlatter, 168; Mussner, 120; Laws, 103-104; Vouga, 74; Michl, 37; Deppe, *Sayings*, 89-91; Hoppe, *Hintergrund*, 82, 120-21; Johnson, 225; Wachob-Johnson, 'Sayings', 442-46; Wachob, *Voice*, 135-51; Burchard, 100; Tiller, 'Rich', 170-72; Kloppenborg, 'Reception', 95-100; S. Johnson, *Treasure*, 90-91 (arguing that 'my beloved brothers' might reflect the mention of 'disciples' in Q 6.20). Contrast Tsuji, *Glaube*, 125-26. The two texts are associated in earlier literature too; cf. Rather of Verona, *Prael*. 1.38 CCCM 46A ed. Reid, 39; Bonaventure, *Lk* 6.20; 7.21 Opera Omnia 10 ed. Peltier, 368, 401; Erasmus, *Paraphrase*, 147; Manton, 195. But even more common are citations of Mt 11.5 = Lk 7.22 (the poor have good news preached to them)—so e.g. Poole, 885; Trapp, 696; Henry, *ad loc.*; Clarke, 1838—and Lk 12.32 ('Do not worry, little flock, it is the Father's good pleasure to give you the kingdom'); so e.g. Bede *ad loc.* CCSL 121 ed. Hurst, 194; Glossa Ordinaria *ad loc.* PL 114.673C; Martin of Legio *ad loc.* PL 209.193A.

[192] Cf. also Gos. Thom. 54: 'Jesus said, "Blessed are the poor, for yours is the kingdom of heaven"'.

its coming from his tradition.[193] On the question of James' relationship to the Synoptics see the Introduction, 56-62.[194]

Verse 6. The contrast with how God treats the poor is intended to shame readers.

ὑμεῖς δὲ ἠτιμάσατε τὸν πτωχόν. This rebuke summarizes vv. 2-4. ἀτιμάζω[195] stands in absolute contradiction to the divine choice (ἐξελέξατο) and promise (ἐπηγγείλατο). The condemnation is all the stronger if one hears an echo of certain passages in the LXX: Prov 14.21 ('The one who dishonors [ἀτιμάζων] the needy [πένητας] sins, but the one who has mercy on the poor [πτωχούς] is most blessed'); 22.22 ('Do no violence to the needy, for he is poor [πτωχός], and do not dishonor [ἀτιμάσῃς] the weak in the gates'); Ecclus 10.23 ('It is not right to dishonor [ἀτιμάσαι] one who is intelligent but poor [πτωχόν]').

οὐχ οἱ πλούσιοι καταδυναστεύουσιν ὑμῶν.[196] καταδυναστεύω[197] (= 'oppress', 'dominate') was conventionally associated with exploitation of the poor and condemnation of the rich.[198] The following reference to courts helps specify the content here, although one might also think of 5.4, where fair wages are not repaid.

καὶ αὐτοὶ ἕλκουσιν ὑμᾶς εἰς κριτήρια; Is the redundant αὐτοί Semitic?[199] Although ἕλκω[200] + κριτήριον[201] appears also in PTurin 1.1.6.11 (ἑλκυσθέντων ἁπάντων εἰς τὸ κριτήριον), it is otherwise unattested except in later, mostly ecclesiastical sources. There are, however, similar constructions: LXX Exod 21.6 (προσάξει αὐτόν... πρὸς τὸ κριτήριον τοῦ θεοῦ); Herodas 5.58-59 (ἕλκεις ἐς τὰς ἀνάγκας); Acts 16.19 ('dragged them into [εἵλκυσαν εἰς] the marketplace before the authorities'); Justin,

---

[193] One might also observe that vv. 6-7 have conceptual parallels with Mt 5.10-12 = Lk 6.22-23; cf. Bonaventure, *Lk* 6.22 Opera Omnia 11 ed. Peltier, 369. Both have to do with saints being mistreated and employ ὄνομα.

[194] For the possibility that James knew not Matthew but a form of the Q^{mt} beatitudes see Hartin, *Q*, 149-51; Wachob, *Voice*, 152.

[195] NT: 7×; Jas: 1×. In the LXX (40×), the word occurs most often in Proverbs (9×) and Sirach (8×). Gk. Pseudepigrapha (Denis): 2×. Philo: 10×. Josephus: 3×.

[196] P74 01* 02 218 1359 1563 1718 2344V have ὑμᾶς. Is this original? καταδυναστεύω occurs with both the genitive (e.g. 1 Βασ 12.3; Acts Andr. 38 ed. Prieur, 491) and the accusative (e.g. Amos 8.4; Wis 2.10).

[197] NT: 2×; cf. Acts 10.38. LXX: most often for עשׁק. Gk. Pseudepigrapha (Denis): 6× (5× in Aristeas). Philo: 2×. Josephus: 1×.

[198] LXX Ezek 18.12 (πτωχὸν καὶ πένητα κατεδυνάστευσε); 22.29 (πτωχὸν καὶ πένητα καταδυναστεύοντες); Amos 4.1 (καταδυναστεύουσαι πτωχούς); 8.4 (καταδυναστεύοντες πτωχούς); Wis 2.10 (καταδυναστεύσωμεν πένητα); cf. 1 En. 94.8-9 ('Woe unto you, O rich people! ...you committed oppression'); Sent. Syr. Men. 2:101 ('Do not despise the poor'); Apost. Const. 2.5.1 ed. Funk, 37 (a bishop must not flatter the rich or despise the poor: μήτε πένητα... καταδυναστεύων).

[199] Cf. Moule, *Idiom*, 176, citing the similar Lk 19.2.

[200] NT: 2×; cf. Acts 21.39.

[201] NT: 23×; cf. 1 Cor 6.2 and 4, where it seems to mean not 'law court' but 'lawsuit'.

2 Apol. 12.4 (εἰς βασάνους εἵλκυσαν). Expositors have taken the expression in James in two different ways. Some, appealing to v. 7, have thought of religious intolerance: the court is set to judge religious matters. For this there are parallels in the Jesus tradition and Acts.[202] Others, however, think rather of more secular issues, as in 5.4 and 1 Cor 6.1-6. In this case, one could think not of Jewish tribunals but of Gentile courts.[203]

Verse 7. οὐκ αὐτοὶ βλασφημοῦσιν τὸ καλὸν ὄνομα τὸ ἐπικληθὲν ἐφ' ὑμᾶς; What matters is not a 'good (καλῶς) seat' (v. 3) but 'the good[204] name'. Whether or not αὐτοί adds emphasis, it is a likely Semitism because the rest of the clause is Semitic. βλασφημέω (Jas: 1×) owes its presence here to the old Hebrew formulas, נקב + שם and נאץ + שם.[205] ὄνομα recurs in 5.10 and 14, both times followed by the genitive κυρίου (= God).[206] The qualification by καλός is unusual, although one may compare MT Ps 52.11 (שמך כי־טוב); 54.8 (שמך יהוה כי־טוב; LXX: τῷ ὀνόματί σου, κύριε, ὅτι ἀγαθόν); LXX Ps 134.3 (ψάλατε τῷ ὀνόματι αὐτοῦ ὅτι καλόν[207]); LXX Prov 22.1 (ὄνομα καλόν); Eccl 7.1 (MT: שם טוב; LXX: ἀγαθὸν ὄνομα); Ecclus 41.13 (שם טובת; ἀγαθὸν ὄνομα); also Plato, *Leg.* 937E (καλὸν ὄνομα); Ps.-Plato, *Theag.* 122D (καλὸν ὄνομα).[208] The current texts of the Eighteen Benedictions have, in the eighteenth benediction, הטוב שמך = 'your name is good'; cf. Midr. Ps. 29.2. More common is the antithesis, 'evil name'.[209] For ἐπικαλέω (Jas: 1×) with ὄνομα see below. τὸ καλὸν ὄνομα τὸ ἐπικληθὲν ἐφ' ὑμᾶς is the precise equivalent of השם הטוב הנקרא עילכם; cf. Deut 28.10 (שם יהוה נקרא עליך); 11Q14 1 2.15 (שם קודשו נקרא עליכם).[210]

---

[202] Mt 10.17-18; Mk 13.11; Lk 21.12-15; Acts 4.3; 6.12; 12.3; 16.20; 18.12.

[203] The *Catenae ad loc.* ed. Cramer, 11, however, refers to both. Dibelius, 139-40, discusses the sorts of legal actions and their motivations that Jews and Gentiles took against early Christians. Given the larger thesis of the present commentary, that the audience envisaged is not exclusively Christian, the relevance of his data for James is unclear.

[204] καλός: Jas 3×; cf. 3.13; 4.17.

[205] Lev 24.16; Ps 74.10, 18; Isa 52.5; 2 Macc 8.4; 4 Ezra 1.22; Rom 2.24; Rev 13.6; b. Sanh. 56a; etc.

[206] Some, however, think that the Lord of 5.14 is Jesus; see the discussion there.

[207] According to R. Wall, 118, James 'echoes' this line.

[208] For the plural see Thucydides 5.89.1; Plutarch, *Thesei et Rom.* 4; Arrian, *Anab.* 1.7.2; Epictetus, *Diatr.* 3.23.35. Huther, 79, observes: 'By the addition of the attribute καλόν the shamefulness of βλασφημεῖν is still more strongly marked'.

[209] שם רע = ὄνομα πονηρόν; cf. Deut 22.14, 19; Neh 6.13; 4Q159 2-4 8; 4Q269 9 6; 4Q270 5 20.

[210] Cf. also 2 Chr 7.14; Isa 4.1; 43.7; 63.19; Jer 14.9; Dan 9.19; Amos 9.12; Bar 2.15; 2 Macc 8.15; 4Q380 1 1.5 (שם היוה נקרא עליה); Ecclus 36.17 (עם בשמך) = LXX: λαόν...κεκλημένον ἐπ' ὀνόματί σου); 4Q504 1-2 2.12 (נקרא שמכה עלינו); LAB 49.7 (*veniet nomen meum ut invocetur in vos*); Acts 15.17; 4 Ezra 4.25 (*nomini suo quod inuocatum est super nos*); 10.22; Lev. Rab. 2.8 (שמי הגדול שנקרא עליכם).

Most commentators—for whom ἐπικληθέν has almost invariably called to mind Christian prayer, baptism and/or eucharist (cf. 'epiclesis')[211]— have thought of non-Christians who oppose or speak against Jesus Christ.[212] One can cite parallels for this interpretation.[213] But because there is no naming of 'Jesus' or 'Jesus Christ', because there was a tradition of God's name being 'good' (see above), because there was (by the time of James) no comparable tradition about Jesus, because the κύριος in the parallel in Herm. *Sim.* 8.6.4 seems to be God,[214] and because nowhere else in early Christianity do we read of anyone blaspheming the name of Jesus or Christ, Spitta was almost certainly right to interpret βλασφημοῦσιν τὸ καλὸν ὄνομα as bringing God's 'good name' into disrepute.[215] That is, 'blaspheme', as so often in the LXX and elsewhere, is an arrogant insulting of God or God's people.[216] One may compare Rom 2.23-24:

---

[211] A baptismal interpretation is especially common; cf. Poole, 885; Alford, 294; Mayor, 89; Dale, 57; Oesterley, 44; Plummer, 587; Windisch-Preisker, 15; Dibelius, 141; Dimont, 633; Tasker, 60; Mussner, 122-23; Paulsen, 'Jakobusbrief', 491; Konradt, *Existenz*, 61-62, 113-14; Popkes, 170; C.A. Gieschen, 'The Divine Name in Ante-Nicene Christology', *VC* 57 (2003), 145; Assaël-Cuvillier, 'Éléments'. Cf. Acts 22.16: 'Be baptized, and have your sins washed away, calling on his name'. The phrase later become liturgical; see the Liturgy of St. James in Brightman-Hammond, *Liturgies*, 60. Against a baptismal interpretation are Spitta, 65 (the name is Yahweh); Ludwig, *Wort*, 180-83; L. Hartman, *'Into the Name of the Lord Jesus'*, Edinburgh, 1997, 49 n. 52.

[212] So e.g. Calvin, 278 ('the name of God and of Christ'); Henry *ad loc.* ('the name of Christ'); Cellérier, 67; Adamson, 112-13 (the name is 'Christian'); Davids, 113 (the name is 'Jesus', not 'Christ' or 'Christian'); Townsend, 'Christ', 117. Eichhorn, *Einleitung*, 574-75, thinking the blasphemed name to be 'Christian', and observing that this name was not bestowed until the early 40s in Antioch, takes this as a reason to deny authorship to James the Son of Zebedee, who was martyred in the early 40s. Credner, *Einleitung*, 596, seems alone in equating the good name with πτωχοί.

[213] Cf. Acts 13.45 ('When the Jews saw the crowds, they were filled with jealousy; and blaspheming, they contradicted what was spoken by Paul'); 18.6 (the Jews in Corinth 'blasphemed' Paul); 1 Tim 1.13 (Paul used to be a blasphemer, a persecutor, and a man of violence); etc.

[214] See Kloppenborg, 'Discourse', 249.

[215] Spitta, 65. So too Burchard, 102 ('very likely'); cf. idem, 'Stellen', 363-64; Kloppenborg, 'Discourse', 248-49. Frankemölle, 396-98, leans in this direction; cf. Hutchinson Edgar, *Poor*, 123-24; Fabris, 153; Ruck-Schröder, *Name*, 233-35. Why this interpretation, in the words of Laws, 106, 'strain[s] the active form of the verb', is unclear.

[216] Cf. Schnider, 62-63 (although he takes the rich to be Christians). Martin, 66, says that 'blaspheme' may here 'be tantamount simply to acts of ridicule or scoffing'. Cf. 1 En. 91.7, 11; 94.9; Mt 9.3 = Mk 2.7 = Lk 5.17 (scribes accuse Jesus of blaspheming because of his action); 1 Tim 6.1 ('Let all who are under the yoke of slavery regard their masters as worthy of all honor, so that the name of God and the teaching may not be blasphemed'); 2 Pet 2.2 ('because of these teachers the way of truth will be blasphemed'); 1 Clem. 1.1 (a few have caused such trouble that the Corinthians' name 'has been much blasphemed'); 2 Clem. 13.1, 4 ('when they see that we not only do not love those that hate us, but not even those who love us, they laugh us to scorn, and the name is blasphemed'); Herm. *Sim.* 8.6.4 (apostates are 'blasphemers of the Lord in their sins'

'You that boast in the law, do you dishonor God by breaking the law? For, as it is written, "The name of God is blasphemed among the Gentiles because of you".' As in this text and the Lord's Prayer;[217] Acts 15.17 (a quotation from Amos 9.11 attributed to James); 1 Tim 6.1; Rev 13.6; and Did. 10.2, so too in James: τὸ ὄνομα is God's name.[218]

Verse 8. One doubts that this verse shows knowledge of or anticipates readers who justify preference for the rich by appeal to Lev 19.18.[219] The point rather is to make explicit that showing partiality to the rich is not an issue of etiquette but a matter of Torah.

εἰ μέντοι νόμον τελεῖτε βασιλικόν. μέντοι[220] after εἰ,[221] although well-attested in Classical Greek, is not otherwise found in the Greek Bible. In Greek Jewish sources, the expression appears to be confined to Philo (8×) and Josephus (6×).[222] Here it seems to have intensive force ('if indeed', 'if really') although everywhere elsewhere in the NT μέντοι seems adversative.[223] Our author implies that his audience wants to heed Lev 19; his job, then, is to remind them that favoritism contradicts love of neighbor. τελέω[224] here means 'fulfill' in the sense of 'do'.[225] In the background is the Jewish notion of 'doing the law'; see on 4.11 and cf.

---

who are ashamed 'of the name of the Lord which was called over them', τὸ ὄνομα κυρίου τὸ ἐπικληθὲν ἐπ' αὐτούς); Eusebius, *H.E.* 5.1.48 ('Blasphemed the way through their apostasy'). See further R.E. Brown, *The Death of the Messiah*, vol. 1, New York, 1994, 521-23.

[217] Cf. esp. Lk 11.2 D: 'Hallowed be your name over us' (ἐφ' ἡμᾶς).

[218] For God's name being called over people, with the result that they belong to God and have divine protection, see the texts cited in n. 210; also Pss. Sol. 9.9(18): ἔθεου τὸ ὄνομα σου ἐφ' ἡμᾶς κύριε.

[219] Contrast Calvin, 279; Poole, 885; Manton, 205; Theile, 109-10; Huther, 82 (citing in agreement Lapide, Laurentius, Hornejus, Hottinger, Wiesinger); Spitta, 66-69; Plummer, 587; Ropes, 197 ('the law of love is no excuse for respect of persons'); Easton, 39; Mitton, 89; Kugelman, 26; Maynard-Reid, *Poverty*, 66.

[220] LXX: 7×. NT: 8×; Jas: 1×.

[221] Konradt, *Existenz*, 185, stresses that v. 8 is purely hypothetical; only v. 9 names the real concrete issue. This is the view of most commentators, who see partiality as contradicting love of neighbor. Contrast Spitta, 66-69 (the addressees do indeed love neighbor but nonetheless show partiality), followed by Kühl, *Stellung*, 6-7. Jackson-McCabe, *Logos*, 169-72, holds the same view, arguing from the parallels in vv. 10-11 that 2.8-9 assumes simultaneous obedience and disobedience.

[222] In Christian sources it is common from Origen on.

[223] Jn 4.27; 7.13; 12.42; 20.5; 21.4; 2 Tim 2.19; Jude 8. Cf. Beyschlag, 110-11; Hort, 53; Dibelius, 141-42; Cantinat, 131; Blackman, 83-84; Frankemölle, 399; Moo, 110-11. But Gundry, 924, construes μέντοι as 'however'. So too Mayor, 87; Mussner, 123; Davids, 114. Felder, 'Partiality', 60, thinks it 'heightens the irony'. Cf. Plumptre, 67.

[224] Jas: 1×. LXX: most often for כלה.

[225] Cf. Ecclus 7.25; Lk 2.39 (ἐτέλεσαν πάντα τὰ κατὰ τὸν νόμον κυρίου); Josephus, *Ant.* 4.243 (τὰς δεκάτας κατὰ τοὺς Μωυσέος τελέσειε); Herm. *Sim.* 5.2.4 (τὴν ἐντολήν... τετέλεκα); Heliodorus, *Aeth.* 7.11.5 (κατὰ τὸν πάτριον νόμον τελοῖεν).

Rom 2.27: τὸν νόμον τελοῦσα.[226] Perhaps James has chosen the verb because of his interest elsewhere in τέλειος.[227]

The notion of (a) 'royal law(s)' is at home in Graeco-Roman sources.[228] 'The meaning wavers between that of "a law given by or worthy of a king" (i.e. a true king as distinct from a tyrant) and "law which is itself the king"'.[229] The LXX, by contrast, does not link βασιλικός[230] with νόμος (see on 1.25); however, LXX Esth 3.8 refers to τῶν νόμων τοῦ βασιλέως, LXX 2 Esd 7.26 to the νόμον τοῦ βασιλέως.[231]

According to many, the royal law is Lev 19.18 or the commandment to love.[232] According to others, it is the whole Torah, or the whole Torah as interpreted by Jesus.[233] The antithesis is dubious.[234] Given the conventional status of Lev 19.18 as the most important principle in the Torah,[235] that verse is a part that stands for the whole, and James seems to

---

[226] On the absence of the article in James see Mayor, 90-91.

[227] Cf. 1.4, 17, 25; 3.2; so Frankemölle, 403, Klein, *Werk*, 69.

[228] Cf. Ps.-Plato, *Minos* 317C (νόμος εστὶ βασιλικός); *Ep.* 8 354C (νόμοις βασιλικοῖς); Xenophon, *Oec.* 14.7 (τῶν βασιλικῶν νόμων); Isocrates, *Nic.* 56 (τοὺς νόμους τοὺς βασιλικούς); Xenocrates frag. 49 (βασιλικοὺς νόμους); OGI 483.1 (τὸν βασιλικὸν νόμον); also Wettstein, 665, and below n. 247. Related is the notion, ultimately Persian, of the king as a living law; cf. Ps.-Archytas of Tarentum in Stobaeus 4.1.132; Musonius in Stobaeus 4.7.67; Pindar frag. 169a; Aristotle, *Polit.* 1284A; Ps.-Aristotle, *Ep. ad Alex.*; Xenophon, *Cyr.* 8.1.22; Plutarch, *Mor.* 780C; Philo, *Mos.* 2.4; etc.

[229] C.H. Dodd, *Bible*, 39.

[230] NT: 5×; Jas: 1×. LXX: most often for a form of מלך.

[231] One might also cf. מצות המלך = 'the command of the king', as in 2 Kgs 18.36; Neh 11.23; Esth 3.3; Isa 36.21, which the LXX translates in several different ways.

[232] Cf. Ps.-Andrew of Crete, *Éloge* 6 ed. Nordet, 52; Erasmus, *Paraphrase*, 149; Servetus, *Righteousness of Christ's Kingdom* 4.1 trans. Wilbur, 255; Huther, 82; Barnes, 45; Beyschlag, 111, Knowling, 49; Moffatt, 35; Barclay, 80; Mussner, 124; Laws, 107-109 (Laws separates v. 9 from v. 10: the latter 'marks a new stage in the thought of the epistle'); Ludwig, *Wort*, 171; Hutchinson Edgar, *Poor*, 126; Sawicki, 'Person', 397; Harvey, 725; Doriani, 70.

[233] Cf. Ropes, 198; Dibelius, 142-43; Meyer, *Rätsel*, 149; Seitz, 'Law'; Furnish, *Love*, 179-80; Davids, 114; Burchard, 'Nächstenliebegebot', 524-29; Johnson, 230; Wachob, *Voice*, 92; Jackson-McCabe, *Logos*, 153; Popkes, 171-72; Hartin, 121. Proponents of this view often observe that vv. 9-10 have to do with the whole law and urge that τελέω and νόμος are a bit unusual with reference to a single commandment, for which one might expect τηρέω and ἐντολή. Elsewhere in James νόμος is more than an individual commandment: 1.25; 2.9-12; 4.11. Davids, 114, and Blomberg-Kamell, 116-17, are among the many who hold that James refers to the Torah as interpreted by Jesus.

[234] Cf. Ward, 'Concern', 141-42. Also unhelpful is the distinction, introduced by some commentators here, between moral law and ritual law. This is a later Christian idea, wrongly read back into James.

[235] כלל גדול בתורה; so Akiba according to Sifra 200 on Lev 19.18; t. Soṭah 9.11; y. Ned. 41c (9:4); Gen. Rab. 24.7; cf. Mk 12.31, 33; Lk 10.27; Rom 13.8-10; Gal 5.14. The agreement of Jesus, Paul, and traditions about Akiba on this matter must mirror Jewish tradition. Further, Hillel's evaluation of the golden rule (quoted above) is also relevant, because that rule is a variant of Lev 19.18; cf. G.B. King, 'The "Negative"

be writing about both part and whole simultaneously.[236] Cf. the famous formulation attributed to Hillel: the golden rule—a variant of Lev 19.18—*is* the whole Torah.[237] The parallel with Hillel, moreover, serves to remind that James need not be read as reducing Torah: even though Lev 19.18 may be of supreme importance, observing the weightier matters does not exclude observing other matters.[238]

'Royal' stresses importance, which hardly surprises given the centrality of Torah in general and the prominence of Lev 19.18 for both Jews and Christians. Nonetheless, the precise connotations are unclear.[239] Commentators offer several glosses. (i) 'Royal' is a roundabout way of stressing significance; so the NJB: 'the supreme law of scripture'.[240]

Golden Rule', *JR* 8 (1928), 274-75, following W. Bacher, *Die Agada der Tannaiten*, 2 vols., Berlin, 1965–66, 1.4. According to the latter, Hillel's negative golden rule 'is nothing other than a negative expression of the biblical "love your neighbor as yourself"'. Cf. Maimonides, *Sefer Ha-Mitzvoh* 206; Isaac Abravanel, *Mikraot Ketanot 613 Mitsvot Ha-Torah*, Cincinnati, 1892, 19; G. Friedlander, *The Jewish Sources of the Sermon on the Mount*, New York, 1969, 230-31. Jub. 36.4 appears to conflate the golden rule with Lev 19.18. The Hebrew of Ecclus 31.15 seems to offer a rewording of Lev 19.18 whereas the Greek version recalls the golden rule; see M. Hengel, 'Zur matthäischen Bergpredigt und ihrem jüdischen Hintergrund', *TRu* 52 (1987), 392. Matthew's Gospel designates the golden rule as the sum of the law and the prophets (7.12) and says the same of Lev 19.18 (Mt 22.39). In like manner, if Akiba reportedly christened Lev 19.18 as 'the great general principle in the Torah' (see above), ARN B 26, where the subject is love of neighbor, has him bestow this honor upon the golden rule. Tg. Ps.-J. on Lev 19.18 combines the rule of reciprocity with the command to love one's neighbor. Did. 1.2 puts the two side by side, and this same combination of the golden rule and Lev 19.18 also shows up in Ps.-Clem. Hom. 12.32 GCS 42 ed. Rehm, 190-91, and other early Christian writings. All of this means that the status of Lev 19.18 in Judaism cannot be considered apart from the status of the golden rule in Judaism. Note that the *Catena ad loc.* ed. Cramer, 11, cites Mt 7.12 to illustrate Jas 2.5.

[236] Related comments appear in Mitton, 89; Sidebottom, 42; Songer, 115; Konradt, *Existenz*, 184-87; Kloppenborg, 'Didache', 210 (Lev 19.18 is an epitome of the law).

[237] b. Šabb. 31a: זו היא כל התורה. Konradt, 'Love', 279, is probably right: 'the love command formulates the basic intention or nature of the law, which is then explicated by other regulations'. Konradt sees the same understanding in Matthew, which also like James relates love to treatment of the poor.

[238] Cf. Mt 23.23; Lk 11.42. See further Jackson-McCabe, *Logos*, 176-85, who concludes: 'While it is clear that James's law is the Torah, the question of his interpretation of those aspects of it which legislate matters such as purity, diet, circumcision and the calendar must remain open'.

[239] Cf. Burchard, 104: 'one can only guess'. Note already the extended discussion of Wolf, 32-34.

[240] Cf. Vatabulus *apud* J. Pearson, *Critici sacri*, 30; Diodati *ad loc.*; Wells, 13; Pott, 194; Rosenmüller, 347; Theile, 110-11; Alford, 294; Huther, 82; Barnes, 45 (Lev 19.18 is royal 'because it has some such prominence and importance among other laws as a king has among other men'); de Wette, 227; Winkler, 36; Mayor, 90; Plummer, 587; Ropes, 198; Dibelius, 142-43 (citing 4 Macc 14.2; Philo, *Congr.* 50; *Leg.* 4.147; Justin, *1 Apol.* 12.7); Mussner, 124 (Lev 19.18 has 'royal rank'); Blackman, 84; Ward, 'Concern', 136; Michl, 38; Kugelman, 27; Popkes, 173; Maier, 116.

Perhaps the importance of Lev 19.18 (if that is the royal law) lies in this, that it should rule people's conduct with supreme authority, or should rule over all the other laws.[241] (ii) In this connection some commentators think specifically of the Torah as interpreted by and through Jesus, who emphasized Lev 19.18.[242] This may be combined with (iii): in view of the eschatological orientation of James and the mention of the kingdom in v. 5, one may suppose that James writes of the law of the kingdom of God.[243] (iv) Many modern exegetes call attention to Philo, *Post.* 101-102, which contends that 'the word of God' (= the law) is 'the royal road'[244] of LXX Num 20.17: the law is from the divine king and leads to the divine king.[245] Perhaps then we have a bit of Philo in James, or perhaps the characterization of the Torah as royal was traditional.[246] (v) Even without appeal to Philo, one can hold that the law—or Lev 19.18—is royal in so far as its giver—God or Christ—is king.[247] (vi) To obey Torah or Lev 19.18 is to behave in regal fashion.[248]

To these suggestions, four observations may be added. (i) Whatever 'royal' might precisely mean, it clearly underlines the importance of the νόμος and so implies obligation to observe it. (ii) Although there seems to

[241] So e.g. Johnstone, 158; Stier, 327; Hort, 53. Cf. Aelius Aristides, *Or.* 2.226-27, which speaks of law as the βασιλεύς of all.

[242] Cf. Davids, 114; Frankemölle, 400-402; Moo, 112.

[243] So e.g. Gibson, 29; Carr, 33; L.M. Smith, 'James ii.8'; Hobhouse, 'Law'; K. Weiss, 'Motiv', 110; Blondel, 'Fondement', 149; Laws, 110; Deppe, *Sayings*, 92-93; Hogan, 'Law', 88; Moo, 112; Hartin, 121 ('the Mosaic law that has been ratified by Jesus'); McCartney, 147; Gundry, 924.

[244] βασιλικὴν ὁδόν, βασιλικῇ ὁδῷ, βασιλικῆς ὁδοῦ.

[245] Note GenevaB., 115 ('the Law is said to be royal and like the king's high way, for that it is plain and without turnings'); Klein, *Werk*, 149. Cf. *Gig.* 64; Clement of Alexandria, *Strom.* 7.73.5 GCS 17 ed. Stählin, 53: 'So whenever one is righteous not out of compulsion or fear or hope but from free choice, this is the road called the royal (βασιλική) road, which the royal race travel'. Calvin, 280, speaks of 'a state highway, level, straight, and open'.

[246] Cf. 4 Macc 14.2, where reason, which is so closely associated with the Law (see esp. chap. 2), is royal.

[247] God as king: Pareus, 553; Calmet, 675; Bassett, 35; Schneider, 17; Martin, 67; Frankemölle, 400-402; Döpp, 'Sozialtradition', 73; Wachob, *Voice*, 92; Sleeper, 73; cf. Deissmann, *Light*, 362 n. 5, appealing to a stone inscription at Pergamum: τὸν βασιλικὸν νόμον ἐκ τῶν ἰδίων ἀνέθηκεν: 'he set up the royal law from his own means'. Cf. also 2 Macc 3.13 (βασιλικὰς ἐντολάς); Philochorus frag. 73 (ἐν τῷ τοῦ βασιλέως νόμῳ); Athenaeus, *Deipn.* 6.27; Julius Pollax, *On.* 3.39. Fabris, 154, compares the νομοθέτης of 4.12. Grotius, 1079, thinks of Christ as king; so too T. Scott, 573; Lange, 76; Plumptre, 67; Reicke, 29; Adamson, 114; Davids, 114; Johnson, 230; Moo, 109; Cheung, *Genre*, 98. Some think of both God and Christ; cf. Schnider, 63.

[248] So Jackson-McCabe, *Logos*, 153-54. Cf. T. Levi 13.9 ('those who teach and do good will be enthroned with kings'); Clement of Alexandria, *Strom.* 6.164.2 GCS 52 ed. Stählin and Früchtel, 516 (you will not be βασιλικοί unless your righteousness exceeds that of the scribes and Pharisees and you love your neighbor and do good). Ropes, 198, suggests 'an allusion to the Stoic conception of the wise as "kings", parallel to the lurking allusion in 1.25 to the conception of the wise as alone "free"'.

be no precise Jewish parallel to νόμον βασιλικόν, tradition did associate the Torah with royal motifs. The phrase, 'crown of Torah' (כתר תורה) makes an occasional appearance in rabbinic literature, and legend gave the Israelites crowns when they received the law.[249] (iii) Commentators regularly associate our verse with Jesus because he quotes Lev 19.18 in the Synoptics.[250] Given, then, that this commentary raises the possibility of Matthew's influence upon James, it becomes intriguing that, in Mt 19.16-26, Jesus quotes Lev 19.18 as a means of 'entering into life' (v. 17), which is then equated with 'entering into the kingdom' (v. 23). One might infer that the loving of one's neighbor is 'the royal (βασιλικός) law' because it gains entry into the kingdom (βασιλεία).[251]

(iv) Critical commentators regularly list exegetical options as though they are mutually exclusive. But one is uneasy about this.[252] Writers can formulate things ambiguously because they wish to evoke as well as to explain.[253] Why imagine that it was otherwise with James? Exegetes furthermore often supply multiple interpretations simultaneously. In the present passage, for example, Bengel, 494, finds the law to be royal because it is the sum of the commandments, because it is from God the king, and because it leads to the kingdom; and according to Gill, 787, Lev 19.18 is royal because God is king and because Christ is king and because it is the greatest commandment in the law and because it is obeyed by 'kings and priests to God...in a royal manner, with a princely spirit'.[254] Such fullness of exposition may not be unjustified. If νόμον βασιλικόν 'raises different conceptions',[255] if 'a world of allusiveness and manifold overtones hover around' the expression,[256] why insist upon a single sense?

---

[249] For the former see e.g. m. 'Abot 4.13; Exod. Rab. 34.2; Tg Ps.-J. Deut 34.5; for the latter see e.g. b. Šabb. 88a; Tanḥ. Yel. We'attah Tetsawweh 11; Exod. Rab. 16.24.

[250] Mt 5.43; 19.19; 22.39; Mk 12.31, 33; cf. Lk 10.27; Gos. Thom. 25.

[251] Cf. Hartin, Q, 92, appealing not to Matthew but to Wis 6.17-20: the royal law leads to inheritance of a kingdom.

[252] Important here is F.G. Downing, 'Ambiguity, Ancient Semantics, and Faith', NTS 56 (2010), 139-62.

[253] According to Dibelius, 143, since James 'neither explains this predicate nor reveals a motivation for its formulation, we may assume that he has not created this expression'. Does this follow?

[254] Ruckstuhl, 17, does something very similar, as do additional—especially older—commentators; cf. e.g. Wolzogen, 195; Kypke, 421; Clarke, 809-10; Burkitt, 1021; Stier 327. Manton, 205-206, is content to string together alternatives with 'or' while refraining from selecting any one in particular. Cf. Estius, 403; Grünzweig, 76-77; Belser, 110.

[255] Bardenhewer, 69. Cf. Ludwig, Wort, 171; Theissen, 'Nächstenliebe', 187-88 ('religious texts often consciously work with the semantic openness of many ideas'); Jackson-McCabe, Logos, 154 ('the adjective may have been attractive to the author precisely because it works on more than one level').

[256] So Cabaniss, 'Epistle', 28.

κατὰ τὴν γραφήν.[257] This secular formula[258] seems to function as a citation formula introducing Lev 19.18.[259] It appears in the LXX with reference to religious instruction.[260] James—with the singular instead of the plural accusative (cf. 1 Cor 15.3)—may supply the first and only Christian occurrence before Clement of Alexandria.[261] Elsewhere James prefers γραφή (Jas: 3×) + a form of λέγω for formal citations: 2.23; 4.5. Whether γραφή means for him 'scripture as a whole' or 'a portion of scripture' is unclear.

ἀγαπήσεις τὸν πλησίον σου ὡς σεαυτόν. So LXX Lev 19.18 (for אהבת לרעך כמוך); also Mt 19.19; 22.39; Rom 13.9; Gal 5.14. πλησίον (Jas: 2×) recurs in 4.12, where judging is again the subject (cf. 2.4) and Lev 19 is influential. Bengel, 494, glosses τὸν πλησίον σου with 'even though poor'.[262] Jewish sources often cite or allude to Lev 19.18[263] and Akiba, according to tradition, called it the great principle in the Torah; see n. 235. The NT cites it more than any other line from the Pentateuch.[264]

James probably shows knowledge of one of the exegetical traditions associated with Lev 19.18, namely, that it summarizes much of Torah in general or the second half of the decalogue in particular.[265] Philo, *Decal.* 108-11, characterized those who adhere to the first five commandments as φιλόθεοι, those who adhere to the second five as φιλάνθρωποι; and according to Rom 13.9, 'The commandments, "You shall not commit

---

[257] 322 323 L:V K:S^mssB SI:ChMSi: κατὰ τὰς γραφάς.

[258] Cf. Plato, *Apol.* 26B; Polybius 29.21; Plutarch, *Per.* 24.12; and see further Deissmann, *Studies*, 250.

[259] Contrast Johnson, 230-32: 'it is not really a formulation of introduction' but means rather, 'in accordance with Scripture'. Contrast Cheung, *Genre*, 99-100: 'according to the scripture' modifies τελεῖτε: 'so although the royal law is not equivalent to scripture, it is supported by scripture'.

[260] Deut 10.4 (the ten commandments; MT: במכתב); 1 Chr 15.15 ('as Moses commanded with a divine word κατὰ τὴν γραφήν'); 2 Chr 30.5 (MT: ככתוב); 35.4 ('according to the writing of David... though the hand of his son Solomon'; MT: במכתב); 1 Esd 1.4 ('according to the writing of David'); 2 Esd 6.18 (κατὰ τὴν γραφὴν βιβλίου Μωυσῆ).

[261] Clement of Alexandria, *Paed.* 3.11.58.3 ed. Marcovich, 182; cf. Ps.-Justin, *Qu. et resp.* 130 ed. Otto, 206; Apost. Const. 6.11.5 ed. Funk, 325. Despite 1 Cor 15.3-4, κατὰ τὰς γραφάς (see n. 257) was scarcely more popular; cf. Justin, *Dial.* 82.42; Ps.-Clem. Hom. 3.41.3 GCS 42 ed. Rehm, 72.

[262] The inner-Jewish debate over how expansively to understand 'neighbor' seems irrelevant for understanding James if all the parties concerned belong to the same synagogue (vv. 1-7). But for the argument that James equated 'neighbor' with the community see Ward, 'Concern', 142-46.

[263] E.g. Ecclus 13.15; Jub. 7.20; 20.2; 36.4, 8; 1QS 5.25; T. Reub. 6.9; T. Iss. 5.2; T. Gad 4.2; T. Benj. 3.3-4.

[264] Note also Gos. Thom. 25; Did. 1.2; Gos. Naz. frag. 16; Sib. Or. 8.481; Apost. Const. 2.25.3; 6.23.1 ed. Funk, 95, 359.

[265] Cf. Jackson-McCabe, *Logos*, 169-76, calling attention among other things to the ὅλον τὸν νόμον of v. 10.

adultery, You shall not kill, You shall not steal, You shall not covet", and any other commandment, are summed up in this sentence, "You shall love your neighbor as yourself"'. Similarly, Mt 19.18-19 cites the same commandments as does Paul, adds the imperative to love father and mother, and then cites Lev 19.18 as the general rule that contains the preceding particulars.[266] The Didache opens by citing Deut 5.6 (love God, 1.2a) and Lev 19.18 (love neighbor, 1.2b) and then instances, in illustration of the latter, commandments from the second half of the ten words (2.1-2).[267] The same exegetical tradition, that is, the use of Lev 19.18 to characterize the final four or five commandments, appears also in Aristides, Irenaeus, Tertullian, the Apostolic Constitutions, Gregory of Nyssa, and Benedict of Nursia, among others.[268] James is in harmony with all these sources when he follows his citation of Lev 19.18 with the prohibitions of adultery and murder as instances of that law.[269]

Given early Christian usage, one expects νόμος to refer not to a single commandment but to a corpus of imperatives. Yet the exegetical tradition just noted clarifies matters. Since Lev 19.18 was widely thought of as summarizing half of the decalogue, and since furthermore the decalogue was in turn thought of as a sort of summary or précis of the Torah,[270] Lev 19.18 was not an isolated commandment but an imperative that stood for a large portion of the law. In line with this, Mt 22.39 designates Lev 19.18 as the sum of the law and the prophets and, as noted, rabbinic tradition has Akiba christen that verse as 'the great general principle in the Torah'.[271]

Some commentators show surprise that James cites Lev 19.18 instead of 19.15 ('You will do no injustice in judgment; you will not be partial to the poor or defer to the great, but in righteousness will you judge your

---

[266] Hoppe, *Hintergrund*, 89, is not alone in surmising that James knew Lev 19.18 as interpreted in the Jesus tradition; cf. Weidner, 43; Hutchinson Edgar, 'Love'. Although this is quite possible, much suggests that here the gospels may follow Jewish tradition.

[267] Did. 1.3-6 is an interpolation; the link between Lev 19.18 and the decalogue was even closer in an earlier form of the tradition; see K. Niederwimmer, *The Didache*, Minneapolis, 1998, 30-52.

[268] Aristides, *Ep.* 15 TS 1 ed. J.A. Robinson, 13; Irenaeus, *Haer.* 4.16.3; Tertullian, *Adv. Jud.* 2.3-4 ed. Tränkle, 5-6; Apost. Const. 2.36 ed. Funk, 121, 123; Gregory of Nyssa, *Vit. Mos.* 1.48 SC 1 ed. J. Daniélou, 84; Benedict, *Reg.* 4.2-7 CSEL 75 ed. Hanslik, 29.

[269] Also relevant is the rabbinic tradition that all of the ten commandments can be found in Lev 19; cf. Tanḥ. Buber Qedoshim 3; Lev. Rab. 24.5.

[270] Philo called the ten words 'heads summarizing the particular laws' (*Decal.* 19–20), and he claimed that the ten commandments 'are summaries of the laws which are recorded in the sacred books and run through the whole of the legislation' (*Decal.* 154; cf. *Spec.* 1.1). Tg. Ps.-J. Exod 24.12 has God declare: 'I will give to you [Moses] the tablets of stone upon which are hinted the rest of the law and the six hundred and thirteen commandments'. Cf. Cant. Rab. 14.2: the decalogue implies the 613 commandments.

[271] כלל גדול בתורה; Sifra 200 on Lev 19.18; t. Soṭah 9.11; y. Ned. 41c (9.4); Gen. Rab. 24.7.

neighbor'). James, however, has already clearly alluded to the latter (see above), and the former is the more powerful statement given its importance in early Judaism and Christianity.[272]

καλῶς ποιεῖτε. καλῶς (cf. 2.3, 19) + a form of ποιέω, which recurs in 2.19, was a common expression, often meaning 'to do well'.[273] Those who sense irony here (cf. Mk 7.9; Jn 4.17) tend to suppose that the readers do not in fact love their neighbor. There is, however, no irony if one instead thinks that they do indeed love their neighbor and to that extent do well.[274]

Kloppenborg observes that, if καλῶς ποιεῖτε here follows a citation of Lev 19.18, which was often thought of as a heading of or summary for the second table of the decalogue, in 2.19 it follows a citation of Deut 6.4, which was similarly understood as a heading for the first table. In both instances, moreover, violation of additional commandments is discussed, so 'the structure of James's argument...suggests that James treats Deut. 6.5 and Lev. 19.18 as summaries of the Torah'.[275] To this one may add three notes. (i) According to Hutchinson Edgar, 4.12 seems to join a likely echo of the Shemaʿ (εἷς ἐστιν ὁ νομοθέτης) with a likely echo of Lev 19.18 (σὺ δὲ τίς εἶ, ὁ κρίνων τὸν πλησίον;).[276] (ii) The citation of Lev 19.18 in 2.8 closely follows 2.5, which speaks of those who love God, so yet again love of God and love of neighbor are closely associated.[277] (iii) Given the pertinent Jewish and Christian texts, it is not unexpected that James would associate the imperative to love God with the imperative to love neighbor.[278]

Verse 9. εἰ δὲ προσωπολημπτεῖτε. This is the first occurrence in James of εἰ δέ + the second person, which recurs in 2.11; 3.14; 4.11. προσωπολημπτέω echoes Lev 19.15 (LXX: οὐ λήμψῃ πρόσωπον) and harks back to the μὴ ἐν προσωπολημψίαις of v. 1, thus reiterating the subject of the whole section. Clearly 2.9-13 belongs to the argument begun in v. 1.

---

[272] Cf. Laws, 107: Lev 19.18 'carries a special authority'.

[273] See 1 Macc 12.18, 22; 2 Macc 2.16; Mk 7.37; 1 Cor 7.37-38; 2 Pet 1.19; Herm. Vis. 2.4.2; cf. Gk. LAE 17.4; Plutarch, Pyrrh. 13.8; Diogenes Laertius 2.103. Cf. the εὖ πράξετε of Acts 15.29, which some commentators try to connect with the author of our letter; cf. Benson, 57; Mayor, 91; Witherington, 459-60. Schlatter, 174, calls attention to ויפה עשה (= καὶ καλῶς ἐποίησεν) in t. Sanh. 4.5.

[274] For this interpretation see especially Ludwig, Wort, 172-74, urging parallelism between vv. 8-9 ('if you really fulfil the royal law... If, however, you show partiality, you commit sin, being convicted by the law as transgressors') and 11 ('If you do not commit adultery but nonetheless commit murder, you have become a transgressor of the law').

[275] Kloppenborg, 'Didache', 210-11.

[276] Hutchinson Edgar, 'Love', 16-17.

[277] So Johnson, 235. For related arguments see Frankemölle, 404-405; Jackson-McCabe, Logos, 174-76; Cheung, Genre, 99-121; M. Taylor, Structure, 112-13.

[278] Cf. T. Iss. 5.1-2; T. Dan 5.3; T. Jos. 11.1; Philo, Decal. 108-11; Mk 12.29-34; Lk 10.27; Did. 1.2; Sib. Or. 8.48-82.

PARTIALITY CONDEMNED (2.1-13) 409

The verb is rare[279] and indeed wholly unattested in secular Greek; but it does occur in Apost. Const. 2.58.4, which is otherwise closely related to our passage; see above. It probably comes from James' tradition. It intrigues that the verbal parallel occurs not only in a passage from the Apostolic Constitutions with very similar content but also in one featuring sentences beginning with εἰ δέ.

ἁμαρτίαν ἐργάζεσθε. ἐργάζομαι (cf. 1.20) + ἁμαρτία (see on 1.15), which seems particularly forceful,[280] occurs in T. Gad 6.5 (μεγάλην ἁμαρτίαν ἐργάσηται) and several times in Hermas.[281] Related expressions are common.[282]

ἐλεγχόμενοι ὑπὸ τοῦ νόμου ὡς παραβάται. While ἐλέγχω (Jas: 1×)—which here means 'convict';[283] cf. the ἔνοχος of v. 10—is frequent with ὑπό,[284] and while the latter is regularly joined with νόμου (cf. v. 8),[285] James is the first to link all three.[286] One is tempted to see an ironic reversal of Lev 19.17. James has just quoted 19.18 and alluded to 19.15 while v. 17 has the famous imperative, ἐλεγμῷ ἐλέγξεις. In Leviticus, judging a neighbor through rebuke is a good thing. In James, those who judge are themselves rebuked. However that may be, the specific law that here rebukes is presumably either the just-cited Lev 19.18—loving neighbor excludes favoritism—or, more likely, Lev 19.15, which belongs to the same section as Lev 19.18 (LXX: οὐδὲ θαυμάσεις πρόσωπον δυνάστου).[287] Leviticus 19.15 was the exegetical ground for the tradition

---

[279] NT: 1×. LXX: 0×. Gk. Pseudepigrapha (Denis): 0×. Philo: 0×. Josephus: 0×.

[280] Cf. Oesterley, 440: 'the strength of the expression is intended to remind hearers that it is willful, conscious sin of which they will be guilty, if they have this respect for persons on account of their wealth'.

[281] Herm. Mand. 4.1.1 (μεγάλην ἁμαρτίαν ἐργάζῃ), 2 (ἁμαρτίαν ἐργάζῃ); 8.2 (ἁμαρτίαν μεγάλην ἐργάζῃ); Sim. 7.2 (ἁμαρτίας καὶ ἀνομίας εἰργάσατο).

[282] Note e.g. Pss 6.9 (פעלי און); LXX: οἱ ἐργαζόμενοι τὴν ἀνομίαν; cf. 1 Macc 3.6; Lk 13.27); 28.3 (פעלי און); LXX: ἐργαζομένων ἀδικίαν); 141.4 (פעלי און); LXX: ἐργαζομένοις ἀνομίαν; cf. MT 28.3; 4Q88 10.12); Job 31.3 (פעלי און); LXX: τοῖς ποιοῦσιν ἀνομίαν); Ecclus 27.10 (ἁμαρτία ἐργαζομένοις ἄδικα); 1QH 6(14).14 (פועלי רשע); 6Q16 2.2 (פועלי רשע); Mt 7.23 (οἱ ἐργαζόμενοι τὴν ἀνομίαν; Hort, 54: Jas 2.9 is 'probably a reminiscence' of this); Rom 13.10 (ἡ ἀγάπη τῷ πλησίον κακὸν οὐκ ἐργάζεται· πλήρωμα οὖν νόμου ἡ ἀγάπη); Phil 3.2 (τοὺς κακοὺς ἐργάτας); 4 Ezra 6.19.

[283] Cf. Jn 8.46; 16.8; 1 Cor 14.24; Tit 1.9, 13; Josephus, Ant. 2.419.

[284] Cf. Plato, Resp. 539B; Lk 3.19; 1 Cor 14.24; Eph 5.13; Josephus, Ant. 2.160; Liv. Proph. Ezek 2; Acts Thom. 51 ed. Bonnet, 167; Apost. Const. 2.47.3 ed. Funk, 143; Sib. Or. 8.419.

[285] E.g. Herodotus 9.111; Plato, Symp. 183B; Plutarch, Mor. 274B; 4 Macc 2.9; Philo, Post. 185; Leg. 1.332 (of the Torah); Rom 3.21 (of the Torah); Justin, Dial. 1112 (of the Torah); Melito, Pascha 39(260) ed. Hall, 20 (of the Torah). The Pauline ὑπὸ νόμον = 'under the law' (Gal 3.23; 4.4-5, 21; 5.18) is a different expression altogether.

[286] But cf. Themistius, Phil. Theod. 227C: ἐλεγχθέντας ὑπὸ τοῦ νόμου.

[287] For an allusion or implicit reference to Lev 19.15 see Nicholas of Gorran, 73; Hus, 201; Wolzogen, 195; Grotius, 1079; Pott, 195; Henry, ad loc.; Baumgarten, 102; Guyse, 575; Rosenmüller, 347; Gibson, 29; Spitta, 67; Mayor, 91; Kühl, Stellung, 6-7; Ropes, 199; Hauck, 17; Windisch-Preisker, 15-16; Moffatt, 35; Tasker, 61; Mussner, 124;

James here borrows and comments on; see above, 381, and the discussion of Jas 4.11-12, which alludes to Lev 19.15 and 18 at the same time.[288]

παραβάτης[289] occurs twice in James, both times in close connection with νόμος (2.9, 11). The word occurs nowhere else in the NT save Paul, and again in each instance the topic is transgression of 'the law': Rom 2.25 (παραβάτης νόμου), 27 (παραβάτην νόμου); Gal 2.18-19 (παραβάτην...νόμου νόμῳ). One must wonder about Pauline influence here: παραβάτης + (τοῦ) νόμου[290] is unattested in pagan or Jewish texts and—depending upon the date of the textual variant in Lk 6.4 D[291]—in no other Christian sources before Hippolytus.[292]

Although ὡς (see on 1.10) before παραβάται is unattested before James,[293] the relative adverb is present because of ἐλέγχω, which it often follows.[294]

Verse 10. James might be arguing, on a general level, that to break any one commandment—whatever it might be—is to break the whole law.[295] The application to partiality is then up to the reader. But one might also take him to be asserting quite specifically that to exhibit partiality (the implicit content of πταίσῃ ἐν ἑνί) is to go against Lev 19.18 (love of

---

Sidebottom, 42; Mitton, 93; Ruckstuhl, 17-18; Townsend, 40; Frankemölle, 'Gesetz', 208; Johnson, 231; Ludwig, *Wort*, 172; Konradt, *Existenz*, 185-86; Theissen, 'Nächstenliebe', 184, 186; Moo, 112-13; Wachob, *Voice*, 122-25 (observing that 'there are sixteen different words in LXX Lev 19.15 and ten of them appears in our unit', that is, Jas 2.1-13); Hartin, 121; Fabris, 157-59; Keith, 'Citation', 241-43; Maier, 17; Basser, 431; *et al.* Burchard, 104: the text is either directly or indirectly influenced by Lev 19.15. Manton, 210, leaves the question open.

[288] M. Taylor, *Structure*, 64-65, notes several links between our section and 4.11-12, but they do not justify his use of the word 'inclusio'.

[289] LXX: 0×. Symmachus uses it in Pss 16.4 (for פריץ, 'violent'), 138.19 (for רשע, 'wicked'); Jer 6.28 (for סוררים, 'rebellious'). N1: 5×. Gk. Pseudepigrapha (Denis): 0×. Philo: 0×. Josephus: 0×. See further Mayor, 91-92. The sense, 'violator', occurs in secular literature from at least Aeschylus: BAGD, s.v.

[290] Presumably modeled upon παραβαίνω + τὸν νόμον (cf. עבר + תורה): LXX 1 Esd 8.24, 27; Isa 24.5; 2 Macc 7.2; 3 Macc 7.12; Ecclus 10.19; Theod. Dan 9.11; Sib. Or. 3.600; Josephus, *Bell.* 2.174; etc.

[291] 'On the next day, upon seeing someone working on the sabbath, he [Jesus] said to him: O man, if you know what you do, you are blessed; but if you do not know, you are cursed and a transgressor of the law (παραβάτης εἶ τοῦ νόμου).'

[292] Hippolytus, *Dan.* 1.1.3 GCS N.F. 7 ed. Bonwetsch and Richard, 4: ἐλέγχειν ἐν ναῷ πρεσβυτέρους παραβάτας τοῦ νόμου γεγενημένους. See further Popkes, 172-73, for additional links between 2.8-13 and Paul. But Rendall, *Christianity*, 85-86, turns this around: our epistle was 'fresh in his mind' when Paul penned Romans.

[293] Cf. Irenaeus frag. 42 ed. Harvey, 509: ὡς παραβάτης γενόμενος ὁ λαός.

[294] Cf. Plato, *Leg.* 727D; Plutarch, *Mor.* 61B (ἐλεγχόμενος ὡς ἀδικῶν); Justin, *1 Apol.* 7.4 (ἐλεγχθεὶς ὡς ἄδικος); etc.

[295] Cf. Opus Imperfectum Mt *ad* 20.22 PL 827 (drawing an analogy with armor: if only one part is exposed, an arrow can penetrate); Gregory the Great, *Mor.* 19.32 CCSL 143A ed. Adriaen, 982 (making a similar point with clothing); Trapp, 697 ('the whole law is but one copulative'); Huther, 83; Punchard, 364; Gundry, 924.

neighbor), and that to break the latter is to break all of Torah because that text encompasses so much of the meaning of Torah.[296] Both interpretations require that one read into the text what is not spelled out.[297]

ὅστις γὰρ ὅλον τὸν νόμον τηρήσῃ.[298] Although ὅστις γάρ (LXX: 0×) is well-attested in Classical Greek,[299] in Christian texts before Origen it appears only here and in Mt 12.50; 13.12. ὅλος + ὁ νόμος[300]—likewise uncommon in early Christian literature—also occurs in Matthew (22.40), but Paul too has it in Gal 5.3: ὅλον τὸν νόμον ποιῆσαι.[301] It is the Greek equivalent of the biblical כל התורה (for which the LXX prefers πάντα τὸν νόμον).[302] Its being the object of τηρέω (cf. 1.27) reflects the Hebrew idiom, התורה + שמר,[303] which also lies behind the synonymous and well-attested φυλάσσω τὸν νόμον.[304]

πταίσῃ δὲ ἐν ἑνί. 'Point' or 'commandment (in the law)' is understood.[305] For the verb—the aorist connotes a single or occasional sin— see on 3.2 and cf. Ecclus 37.12: ἐὰν πταίσῃς (with reference to the commandments, ἐντολάς). In Mt 5.18-20, neglecting 'one of the least of these commandments' is set over against doing and teaching the entirety

---

[296] See above. Cf. Ceasarius of Arles, *Serm.* 23.4; 37.5; 100a CCSL 103 ed. Morin, 106, 166, 415; Theophylact *ad loc.* PG 125.1153C; the *Catenae* ed. Cramer, 11; Erasmus, *Paraphrase*, 149; Bowyer, *Conjectures*, 315 ('The whole duty of man, in the second table of the law, being comprehended under that of loving his neighbour, whoever transgresses any branch of that law violates what is called the royal law, and is guilty of all'); Easton, 38; Deppe, *Sayings*, 94-95; Cheung, *Genre*, 121. Doriani, 72-73, makes the case that partiality breaks each one of the ten commandments.

[297] Commentators are sometimes anxious, for theological reasons, to point out that the open clause is purely hypothetical: no one can keep the whole law; so Neander, 75; Zodhiates, *Faith*, 182-83. Cf. the polemical barb of Manton, 205, on v. 8: 'The Papists... bring this for one to show that a just man may fulfil the law of God'.

[298] Perhaps under the influence of Mt 5.17, some witnesses have πληρώσει. On the omission of ἄν see Mayor, 92. On the several links between Mt 5.17-20 and Jas 2.10 see especially Bottini, *Introduzione*, 118-20.

[299] Cf. also Josephus, *Ant.* 4.17.

[300] ὅλος: Jas: 4×. νόμος: see on 1.25.

[301] For Lüdemann, *Opposition*, 141-43, it is a 'possibility' that James here reflects either Gal 3.10 or 5.3. For Nienhuis, *Paul*, 187-97, James is here trying to prevent a heterodox interpretation of Paul.

[302] Cf. MT Num 5.30 (את כל־התורה...עשה); Josh 1.7 (לעשות בכל־התורה); 2 Kgs 17.13; 21.8 (לעשות...לכל־התורה); 23.25; 2 Chr 33.8 (לעשות...לכל־התורה); cf. 1QS 5.16; 8.1-2; 4Q174 1-3 2.2 (עשו את כל התורה); 4Q216 2.16; 4Q256 9.10; 4Q470 1.4 לעשות את כל־התורה); m. Qidd. 4.14 (התורה כולה); t. Dem. 2.4; b. Šabb. 31a; b. Qidd. 39b.

[303] As in Exod 16.28; 1 Chr 22.12; 14.3; Ps 119.34; Prov 28.4; 29.18 (the LXX in each case using a verb other than τηρέω). For the Greek expression see Tob 14.9; T. Dan 5.1; Acts 15.5; Josephus, *C. Ap.* 2.273; *Bell.* 6.334; Herm. *Sim.* 8.3.5. Secular sources also know the idiom: Plutarch, *Mor.* 221B; Achilles Tatius 8.13.4; Libanius, *Ep.* 357.4.

[304] Cf. LXX Exod 13.10; Ps 118.34, 44, 55; Prov 28.7; 29.18; Wis 6.4; Ecclus 21.11; T. Iss. 5.1; T. Jud. 26.1 (φυλάξατε... πάντα νόμον κυρίου); T. Ash. 6.3; Acts 7.53; 21.24; Rom 2.26; Gal 6.13; etc. Against Mussner, 124, an allusion to Deut 27.26 seems remote.

[305] Cf. Mk 10.21: ἕν σε ὑστερεῖ.

of 'the law and the prophets',[306] and in m. Qidd. 1.10, the one who fails to perform one (אחת) commandment in the law will not have life in the world to come.[307] Similarly, 4 Ezra 3.7 emphasizes that God laid upon Adam but a single (*unam*) commandment, which he transgressed, whereupon death entered the world. Moreover, in b. Qidd. 39b, the discussion of doing or not doing a single commandment leads to a statement about fulfilling the whole law, כל התורה. In a different way, Gal 5.14 stresses the importance of a single commandment or word (ἑνὶ λέγω)—Lev 19.18—as the fulfillment of πᾶς νόμος; and Gal 5.2-3—which, as already noted, uses the expression, ὅλος ὁ νόμος—affirms that those who are circumcised are bound to keep the whole law. The latter has its close parallel in t. Demai 2.5 = Sifra Lev 205: 'A proselyte who accepted responsibility for all the words of the Torah (כל דברי תורה) except for one (אחד) thing, they do not accept him'; cf. Sifre Num 112. Clearly Jas 2.10 reflects not only the rhetorical habit of contrasting a single commandment with the law in its entirety but also the conventional notion—presumably rooted in Deut 4.2; 17.20; Josh 23.6—that one must keep all of Torah, not just part of it.[308]

---

[306] Christians have often associated Jas 2.10 with Mt 5.17-20: Basil the Great, *Bapt.* 1.2 SC 357 ed. Ducatillon, 110 (asserting that James formulated Jas 5.10 because he had heard what followed the beatitudes); Theodore the Studite, *Ep.* 34 ed. Fatouros, 97; Albertus Magnus, *Super Mt cap. I–XIV ad* Mt 5.18 Opera Omnia 21/1 ed. Schmidt, 128; Manton, 214. Some have also cited Mt 28.20 ('observe all that I have commanded you'): Gregory Palamas, *Hom. xxi–xlii* 38.7 ed. Chrestou and Zeses, 476; *et al.*

[307] Cf. t. Qidd. 1.12; b. 'Erub. 69a ('a person who is suspected of disregarding one matter is held suspect with regard to all'); b. Bek. 30b ('a proselyte, who accepted the teaching of the Torah, though he is suspected of ignoring only one religious law, is suspected of disregarding the whole Torah'; cf. t. Dem. 2.4-7); Exod. Rab. 25.12 ('If you virtuously observe the Sabbath, I will regard you as observing all the commandments of the law; but if you profane it, I will regard it as though you had profaned all the commandments'); 31.14 (if one lends money without interest, it is 'as if he had fulfilled all the commandments'); Midr. Ps. 15.7 ('a man who does any one of the good things of which it is written, He that does these things will never be moved, yes, does any one at all of them, it is as though he had done all of them'); Midr. Prov 1.10 ('if you do this [refrain from theft], you will find that you have fulfilled all of the commandments of the Torah, whereas if you do not, you will find that you have transgressed all of the commandments of the Torah').

[308] Cf. also Ps.-Clem. Hom. 13.14 GCS 42 ed. Rehm, 200 ('even if someone were to do all that is right, yet on a single occasion commit adultery, she must be punished'); b. Menaḥ. 43b ('as soon as a person is bound to observe this precept he is bound to observe all the precepts'). Some assume that James has in mind not just any sin but failure to observe the commandment to love neighbor; see n. 296. The context makes this understandable. But others have, according to their rhetorical needs, equated the single failure with another sin—e.g. pride (so John Climacus, *Sc.* 26 Trevisan, ed. 193) or false doctrine (so Nicephorus of Constantinople, *Ref.* 202 CCSG 33 ed. Featherstone, 324; John of Kronstadt, *My Life in Christ*, Jordanville, NY, 2000, 551: 'He who teaches all the truths soundly, but transgresses against any one of them, he shall be found guilty of all, or against the one Truth, indivisible in Its being'). Grotius, 1079, strangely suggests that the reference is to sins that merit the death penalty.

James speaks of one commandment. No qualification is added. Evidently the rabbinic distinction between light and heavy commandments is irrelevant here:[309] James is speaking of all laws and so falls in line with 1QS 8.16-17 (discipline for one shunning any command— מכול המצוה דבר); 4 Macc 5.20-21 ('to transgress the law in matters either small or great is of equal seriousness, for in either case the law is equally despised'); T. Ash. 2.5-10; Philo, *Legat.* 117 ('if a single piece [of ancestral tradition] is taken from the base, the parts that up to then seemed firm are loosened and slip away and collapse'); Mt 23.23; m. 'Abot 2.1 ('Run after a minor commandment just as after a major one').[310]

γέγονεν πάντων ἔνοχος. ἔνοχος, a Matthean favorite (5×), occurs only here in James. It is more forensic language. For the genitive construction (without LXX precedent) see 1 Cor 11.27. πάντων = 'of all of the law'. James' sentiment is again conventional; cf. Sifre Num 111 ('if one violates a single religious duty, he thereby breaks off the yoke and... so treats the Torah impudently'—the one duty being the rule against idolatry); Sifre Deut 54 ('Anyone who acknowledges idolatry denies the entire Torah'); b. Hor. 8b (adulterers break all ten commandments). Violating a single law is not excused by keeping the rest.[311] The law is 'an indivisible whole'.[312]

In this section James cites Lev 19.18, alludes to 19.15, and draws upon an exegetical tradition associated with the latter. Leviticus 19 has, moreover, influenced other passages in our book.[313] One may wonder, then, whether the train of thought in vv. 10-12 has something to do with how that famous chapter ends: 'And you will keep all my law (LXX: πάντα τὸν νόμον) and all (πάντα) my commandments and you will do (ποιήσετε) them'.[314]

The Stoic idea of the unity of virtues, which Augustine discussed in connection with our passage, and which was summed up in the watchword, 'To possess one virtue [or: vice] is to possess all',[315] has sometimes been thought by interpreters to lie behind James.[316] Philo,

---

[309] Contrast Sigal, *Emergence*, 426. Commentators, however, are sometimes anxious to introduce something like that distinction; cf. Neander, 75-76; Punchard, 364-65; Smith, 123; Robertson, 123; Plummer, 588; Blomberg-Kamell, 119 (a white lie is a lesser sin than a nuclear holocaust).

[310] Cf. 4.2. Gibson, 30, conjectures that this teaching—which he attributes to James of Jerusalem—encouraged the opponents of Paul: one had to obey all the law, including circumcision. So too Plumptre, 68.

[311] Later Christian tradition turned this into 'all virtue suffers detriment from one vice'; cf. Ps.-Augustine, *Vera et false poen.* 14.29 PL 40.1124-25.

[312] Mussner, 125.

[313] See esp. Johnson, *Brother*, 123-35; also above, 51, 381.

[314] Gibson, 29, notes the parallel demand. So too Giere, 'Midrash', 97.

[315] See Plato, *Prot.* 329E; Cicero, *Off.* 2.10.35; Seneca, *Ben.* 5.15.1; Plutarch, *Mor.* 1046F; Diogenes Laertius 7.125; Stobaeus, *Ecl.* 2.7.5.

[316] So e.g. Boyle, 'Paradox', urging the direct influence of Seneca's *De beneficiis*—which deals with benefaction without regard to social status—upon James. Contrast Ropes, 200; Ludwig, *Wort*, 173; Burchard, 106.

Mos. 2.7 ('the possession of one is the possession of all') is the proof that the idea entered Judaism and was in some circles combined with the notion of the unity of Torah. Elsewhere James appears indebted to Stoicism.[317]

Verse 11. Clarification through illustration of v. 10. Manton, 217, remarks: 'All commands are equally commanded'.

ὁ γὰρ εἰπών. ὁ γάρ + nominative participle—common in Paul but not the LXX[318]—appears also in 1.6.[319] In 2.23; 4.5, 6, James cites Scripture with the present tense of λέγω; only in 2.11 does he employ εἶπον (cf. 2.3, 16) to do so. The personal form—'the one saying'[320]—encourages the thought that it is the will of the author of the law that matters above all: to break a commandment is to sin against its divine source.[321] The idea is close to t. Šeb. 3.6: 'A person does not deny a matter of detail before he already has denied the main principle, and a person does not turn to a matter of transgression unless he already has denied the one who gave a commandment concerning it'. Cadoux remarks: 'To disobey a law of God is to injure a personal relationship, not like an examination, where nine right answers will secure a pass, despite one wrong one, but like a friendship, where a hundred faithfulnesses cannot be set against one treachery'.[322]

Given that two of the ten commandments follow, it is natural to think of the story of the giving of Torah on Sinai, especially as, according to Exod 20.1, 'God spoke all these words', that is, the ten commandments.[323]

---

[317] See on 1.21 and especially the work of Jackson-McCabe, *Logos*.

[318] Bar 4.18, 29; Rom 6.7; 13.8; 1 Cor 11.29; 14.2; Gal 2.8; Col 3.25.

[319] For later parallels note Ps.-Ign. *Eph* 14 ed. Zahn, 284 (ὁ γὰρ εἰπών, Ἀγαπήσεις κύριον τὸν θεόν σου, εἶπεν, Καὶ τὸν πλησίον σου ὡς σεαυτόν); Apophthegmata Patrum sys. 9.15 SC 387 ed. Guy, 438 (ὁ γὰρ εἰπών, Μὴ πορνεύσῃς, εἶπε καί, Μὴ κρίνῃς).

[320] Cf. 2 Cor 4.6: ὁ θεὸς ὁ εἰπών.

[321] Cf. Ps.-Sulpicius Severus, *Ep. virg.* 2.7 CSEL 1 ed. Halm, 232-33; Aquinas, *Summa* 2/1 q. 73 ('James is speaking of *sin*, not as regards the thing to which it turns and which *causes* the distinction of *sins*... but as regards that from which *sin* turns away, in as much as *man*, by *sinning*, departs from a commandment of the *law*. Now all the commandments of the *law* are from one and the same, as he also says in the same passage, so that the same *God* is despised in every *sin*; and in this sense he says that whoever "offends in one point, is become guilty of all", for as much as, by committing one *sin*, he incurs the debt of punishment through his contempt of *God*, which is the origin of all *sins*'); John Locke, *The Reasonableness of Christianity* § 2 ed. Higgins-Biddle, 13; Bengel, 494; Beyschlag, 114; Mayor, 92; Moo, 115; Johnson, 232; Carson, 'James', 1001-1002; *et al.* Parry, *Discussion*, 32, wrongly thinks Jesus the speaker and the sermon on the mount to be in the background ('we have...in this passage of St James all the elements of the discussion of the law in the Sermon on the Mount'); cf. Kittel, 'Ort', 87-88; Scaer, 83.

[322] Cadoux, *Thought*, 72.

[323] Cf. Deut 5.4, 22; 18.16.

Later tradition sometimes emphasized this.³²⁴ So ὁ εἰπών might reflect the belief that God literally uttered the decalogue.

μὴ μοιχεύσῃς, εἶπεν καί· μὴ φονεύσῃς.³²⁵ James refers to two commandments from the second half of the decalogue, Exod 20.13, 15 = Deut 5.17, 18. LXX Deuteronomy has the order: no adultery, no murder, no theft. LXX Exodus has: no adultery, no theft, no murder. The MT for both has: no murder, no adultery, no theft; so too the Samaritan Pentateuch. Both LXX texts have the future tense—οὐ μοιχεύσεις and οὐ φονεύσεις for לא תנאף and לא תרצח respectively. James' aorist subjunctives are paralleled in Mk 10.19 and Lk 18.20, and some mss. of the former have μὴ μοιχεύσῃς immediately before μὴ φονεύσῃς. This last order also appears in the Nash Papyrus and elsewhere.³²⁶ Perhaps, then, James follows an alternative Greek text or liturgical tradition. He may also, however, just be paraphrasing, so that the order means little or nothing.³²⁷

One might suppose that any two commandments would suit the logic: to break one commandment is to break Torah, even if one keeps other commandments. But James is probably indebted to exegetical tradition here. First, there was the conventional, close relationship between Lev 19.18 and the second half of the decalogue, which would entail that breaking any one of the commandments in Exod 20.13-17 = Deut 5.17-21 would mean breaking Lev 19.18; and the latter was widely considered to be a general summary of the second half of the decalogue and so of the whole Torah.³²⁸ Second, James' argument closely resembles a midrash in Mek. R. Šimon bar Yoḥai on Exod 20.14: 'One might think he is not culpable unless he has transgressed all of them [the commandments in Exod 20.13-14]. Scripture [Exodus] states, "You will not murder. You will not commit adultery. You will not steal. You will not bear false witness. You will not covet", [so that each one] is culpable for each and every one in and of itself. If so, why does Scripture [Deut 5.17] state later on, "You will not murder and you will not commit adultery and you will not steal and you will not bear false witness and you will not covet"?'³²⁹

---

³²⁴ E.g. Philo, *Decal.* 175 ('God himself gave'; cf. 32-35); LAB 11.6; Josephus, *Ant.* 3.89-93; Mek. on Exod 20.18-19; Apost. Const. 7.36.4 ed. Funk, 434 ('you gave them the law of the ten words spoken by your voice').

³²⁵ The witnesses vary considerably here, but they can all be explained by scribes assimilating James to known versions of the decalogue—whence οὐ for μή, futures for aorist subjunctives, and 'murder' before 'adultery'.

³²⁶ LXX B; Philo, *Decal.* 36, 51, 121, 168; LAB 11.10-13; Mk 10.19 v.l.; Lk 18.19-20; Rom 13.9; Barn. 20.1.

³²⁷ Cf. Jer 7.8-9; Hos 4.1-2.

³²⁸ See above. Even without citing this tradition, Erasmus, *Paraphrase*, 149, urges that adultery and murder break the law of love. Cf. Ps.-Oecumenius *ad loc.* PG 119.B; Theophylact *ad loc.* PG 125.1153C; Theissen, 'Nächstenliebe', 186; Doriani, 72.

³²⁹ See D. Flusser, 'The Decalogue in the New Testament', in *The Ten Commandments in History and Tradition*, ed. B.-Z. Segal and G. Levi, Jerusalem, 1985, 224-26. Flusser raises the possibility that Jas 2.11 means: 'For the one saying, "Do not commit

This version [which joins the commandments with]] indicates that all of them effect each other. If someone transgresses one of them, he will ultimately transgress all of them.' Although the origin of this exposition is unknown, and although it goes on (unlike James) to insist that one who murders will commit adultery and that one who commits adultery will steal and that one who steals will swear falsely, the common idea—to break one part of the decalogue is to break all of it—is presumably ancient.[330]

It is probably coincidence that 4.4 accuses certain readers of being adulterers (μοιχαλίδες) whereas 5.6 condemns others of having committed murder (ἐφονεύσατε).[331] It seems best to explain the choice of 'Do not commit adultery' and 'Do not murder' as due either to exegetical tradition (see above) or to regard them as fitting simply because they are two of the more prominent commandments.[332]

εἰ δὲ οὐ μοιχεύεις, φονεύεις δέ, γέγονας παραβάτης νόμου.[333] A statement of the obvious. If one has committed adultery, one cannot plead 'not guilty' by counting the sins one has not done. For παραβάτης νόμος see on v. 9.

adultery" said, "And do not commit murder"'. In this case, καί goes with μὴ φονεύσῃς, not εἶπεν.

[330] Cf. n. 307. There is a parallel of sorts in Ad Herennium 4.23: 'When our ancestors condemned a woman for one crime, they considered that by this single judgement she was convicted of many transgressions. How so? Judged unchaste, she was also deemed guilty of poisoning', etc. For Davids, 117, the prohibition of murder is apt because that sin was closely associated with oppression of the poor and failure to love neighbor. He cites Jer 7.6; 22.3; Amos 8.4; Ecclus 34.26; T. Gad 4.6-7; 1 Jn 3.15.

[331] R. Wall, 126-27, forges these links. Occasional attempts to relate the sins of adultery and murder to James' *Sitz im Leben*—Martin, 70, tries to link the latter to the situation of the Jewish revolt; cf. Cargal, 116—are futile given the nature of our book. Also, and against Reicke, 29, there is no justification for reading James in terms of the spiritualization of murder and adultery in Mt 5. Contrast Ward, 'Concern', 149-52, appealing to figurative meanings for adultery and murder in Jewish texts: '"You do not commit adultery"—that is, you are not faithless, you believe in one God (cf. Ep Jas 2:19). "But you do commit murder"—that is, by showing partiality.' This is also the view of Wick, 'Murder': James, much like Mt 5, interprets the prohibitions of murder and adultery in a radical way—to humiliate is to murder, to befriend the world is to commit adultery.

[332] For Hilary of Arles *ad loc*. PLSup. 3.71, murder and adultery are notorious examples of not loving one's neighbor; cf. Oecumenius *ad loc*. PG 119. 476B. For Knowling, 51, 'the best reason for the introduction here of these two commandments may be found in the fact that they are placed first amongst those which relate generally to our duty toward our neighbour, and that they are the most weighty of such'. Cf. Huther, 84; Alford, 295; Burchard, 107. For Doriani, 72, they are simply 'the central moral commands'. For Maynard-Reid, *Poverty*, 66, the selection of murder and adultery 'indicate how heinous the crime of discrimination is to James'.

[333] As with v. 11a, so here too: many authorities reverse the order of 'adultery' and 'murder'; see n. 325. P74 02 substitute ἀποστάτης for παραβάτης, and Kilpatrick, 'Übertreter', thinks this original, urging that παραβάτης may come from Rom 2.17-29.

According to Moo, 115-16, and the vast majority of commentators, James does not assume adherence to the entirety of the Mosaic law: 'Nothing in his letter would suggest that he held so strict a view'. Yet nothing in his letter suggests that he did not hold so strict a view, or that he embraced only the ethical portion of Torah as reinterpreted by Jesus.[334] James is readily understood to hold the same view as Mt 5.17-20— another text that Christian tradition has regularly misconstrued—and so to be like those Christian Jews, known from Justin, who kept the whole Torah.[335] As to what James thought regarding Gentile obligation is less clear. Justin speaks of two sorts of Christian Jews, those who compel Gentiles to live like Jews and those who do not. Exegetes who take our letter to be anti-Pauline might surmise our author to be among the former. Those who see rather a favorable reception of Pauline tradition will be strongly inclined to opt for the other view.

If James views the Torah as still in force in its entirety, so that he cannot reduce it to love, this makes for conflict with Paul, for Gal 5.13-14 seems to go beyond the idea that Lev 19.18 is the most important command in the Torah. The apostle instead appears to promote the extreme view that loving one's neighbor is the equivalent of fulfilling all of the Torah and so to imply that other commands are not obligatory.[336]

Verse 12. The law governs both words and deeds and will judge both.

οὕτως λαλεῖτε καὶ οὕτως ποιεῖτε. Although οὕτως...καὶ οὕτως occurs across Greek literature, it is especially characteristic of the LXX, where it translates וכן...כן.[337] Here the dual adverbs may look back over the preceding argument (cf. 2.17), although it is also possible that they introduce the next clause: because you will be judged by the law of freedom, speak and act accordingly.[338] In either case, the verbs—present tense for continuous action—show that, although he has referred to adultery and murder, James is concerned with far more.[339] λαλέω[340] + ποιέω (Jas: 11×) underlines the comprehensive scope of his statement.[341]

---

[334] Contrast Krüger, *Kritik*, 179-83. Mayor, 89, even speaks of 'the Christian law' (89) as opposed to the Jewish law.

[335] Cf. Justin Martyr, *Dial.* 46-47 PTS 47 ed. Marcovich, 144-48. See further the Introduction, 27.

[336] Cf. Rom 13.8-10. See further Ludwig, *Wort*, 174-75, 184-87, on the tension between Rom 13.8-10 and Jas 2.8-13. Cf. Popkes, 'Mission', 91: Jas 2.11 corrects a 'misconception' that had grown up in 'Pauline soil'.

[337] E.g. LXX Num 2.34; Deut 22.3; Ps 34.14; Hag 2.15; Ezek 42.5; cf. 1 Cor 15.11. Oesterley, 394, suggests that James' Greek is the equivalent of כן דברו וכן עשו.

[338] Cf. Mayor, 94 (comparing 1 Cor 3.15; 9.26); Konradt, *Existenz*, 97-98.

[339] For Burchard, 107, the οὕτως might encompass not just 2.8-11 but 2.1-11 or even 1.25–2.11; he also wonders whether 1.26-27 might be above all in view. Cf. Ropes, 201.

[340] Cf. 1.19; 5.10. The emphasis upon speech is characteristic; cf. 1.19, 26; 3.1-12.

[341] Cf. Ecclus 3.8; 4 Macc 5.38; T. Gad 6.1; Philo, *Mos.* 1.151; Lk 24.19; Acts 1.1; 7.22; Rom 15.18; Col 3.17; 1 Jn 3.18; Plato, *Meno* 86C; Xenophon, *Mem.* 2.3.6; Diogenes Laertius 1.50, 65; etc. Dibelius, 147, suggests that James may here reflect a 'catechetical' imperative: So act in word and deed!

In the present context, the expression counters the showing of partiality, which consists of both word and deed. The combination moreover foreshadows the emphasis of the next section, vv. 14-26, where words without deeds are empty.

ὡς διὰ νόμου ἐλευθερίας μέλλοντες κρίνεσθαι. For 'the law of freedom' see on 1.25. The expression refers to the Torah in its entirety.[342] The law is two-sided: if it can free (cf. 1.21), it can also condemn. For the expression compare Ecclus 46.14 (ἐν νόμῳ κυρίου ἔκρινεν); Jn 7.51 (ὁ νόμος...κρινεῖ); 18.31 (κατὰ τὸν νόμον...κρίνατε); Acts 23.3 (κρίνων...κατὰ τὸν νόμον); Demosthenes, *Arist.* 2 (κατὰ τοὺς νόμους...κρῖναι). Although διὰ τοῦ νόμου appears in the LXX,[343] διὰ νόμου (without the article) occurs first in extant Greek literature in Paul. In addition, given that he uses it six times, given that he once follows it with κριθήσονται,[344] and given that the remainder of Jas 2 reflects Pauline teaching, it is natural to see Pauline influence here.

διά is likely to be instrumental: judged through the agency of the law.[345] The last judgment is in view.[346] Cf. LAB 11.2: 'I have given an everlasting law into your hands and with this I will judge the whole world (*in hac...iudicabo*). For this will serve as witness.'

In view of 5.8-9, μέλλω (Jas: 1×) connotes not just future inevitability but imminence: the judgment is near.[347] κρίνω (Jas: 6×) plays off of v. 4 (διεκρίθητε...κριταί): those who judge others (cf. 4.11-12) will themselves be judged. It does not surprise that some move from this verse (and the next) to Mt 7.1-2 = Lk 6.37.[348]

---

[342] Cf. Bassett, 36: 'The whole discourse is upon the law of Moses, and the transgression of its commandments by these members of the synagogue'. See further McCabe, *Logos*. It has, however, been common to think of 'Christ's law' or the gospel or love or the OT as reinterpreted or revised by Jesus or some such; cf. Gregory Palamas, *Hom. xxi–xlii* 38.7 ed. Chrestou and Zeses, 476; Oslander, 723; Grotius, 1080 ('the law of the gospel'); M. Goguel, *The Primitive Church*, New York, 1964, 492-93; Moo, 116; Wischmeyer, 'Gebot', 169; *et al.* Calvin, 281, reading Paul into James, equates 'the law of liberty' with 'God's clemency, which frees us from the curse of the Law'.

[343] 2 Macc 2.18; Ecclus prol. 1; cf. Let. Aris. 122.

[344] Rom 2.12. Cf. Apocry. Apoc. Jn 22 ed. Tischendorf, 89: διὰ νόμου κριθήσονται.

[345] Contrast Hort, 55-56; Ropes, 201; Laws, 116: the law of freedom is 'the context within which they speak and act, and the future judgment will take account of that fact' (Laws). This interpretation derives from a Protestant doctrine of grace. Moo, 116-17, circumvents the problem by equating the law with 'the will of God expressed in Christ's teaching'.

[346] This is the near consensus of the commentaries; cf. Anastasius of Sinai, *Cap. vi. adv. monothel.* 10.5 CCSG 12 ed. Uthemann, 154. But Ward, 'Concern', 154-55, suggests instead: 'this judgment refers to that which is to be effected by the law in the community'.

[347] Cf. Acts 17.31 (μέλλει κρίνειν); 24.25 (τοῦ κρίματος τοῦ μέλλοντος); 2 Tim 4.1 (μέλλοντος κρίνειν); Barn. 7.2 (μέλλων κρίνειν); Apocry. Apoc. Jn 22 ed. Tischendorf, 89 (μέλλεις κρίνειν).

[348] E.g. Quodvultdeus, *Prom.* 37.39 SC 102 ed. Braun, 564; Rosenmüller, 347; Hort, 56; Ropes, 201; Robertson, 126; Knowling, 52; Tasker, 2; Sidebottom, 43; Townsend,

Verse 13. Against Laws, 117, one naturally relates this verse to 2.1-7: showing mercy is the antithesis of the sort of partiality James condemns.[349]

Both vv. 13a and b sound proverbial,[350] and the sentiments, as we shall see, were common. Nonetheless, the precise formulations could be James' work. He in any case likes to end sections with aphoristic formulations; cf. 2.26; 3.18; and 4.17.

ἡ γὰρ κρίσις ἀνέλεος τῷ μὴ ποιήσαντι ἔλεος.[351] James switches from the theme of love to the theme of mercy (and from the second person to the third person). Given his concerns, there is no practical difference between the two virtues: loving one's neighbor means showing mercy to the poor, and showing mercy to the poor means loving one's neighbor.[352] Commentators do indeed sometimes wonder why love here gives way to mercy; but the answer is evident. Biblical tradition associates the two divine and human virtues, love and mercy, which in the Psalms often appear in synonymous parallelism.[353] One recalls that the parable of the good Samaritan opens by asking, with reference to the commandment to love in Lev 19.18, 'And who is my neighbor?', and that it comes to its climax by asserting that 'the one who showed mercy' fulfilled the commandment.

κρίσις[354] occurs in James only in this verse and in 5.12. ἡ is definite—'the (last) judgment'—and the future tense is implied: 'will be without mercy'.[355] ἀνέλεος might be James' coinage, because with the possible exception of T. Abr. RecLng. 16.1, it is otherwise unattested before the fourth century. It is, however, similar to ἀνηλεής[356] and ἀνίλεως.[357] ποιέω (Jas: 11×) + ἔλεος appears repeatedly in the LXX, often for חסד + עשה.[358]

43; Leahy, 912; Frankemölle, 414; Bauckham, *Brother*, 87-88. For Chandler, 'Injustice', 225-28, Jas 2.1-13 is a 'creative re-expression' of the teaching in Mt 7.1-5.

[349] Contrast Dibelius, 147, who asserts that v. 13 is 'an isolated saying'. Against Dyrness, 'Mercy', 14, v. 13 does not introduce vv. 14-26.

[350] For v. 13b so already Nicholas of Gorran, 74.

[351] ἀνέλεος: P74 01 02 03 04 018 1* 6 38 69 81 88 197 *et al*. L623 L938 L1141 L1281 Apoll Dam Isid PsCaes PsOec **K**:SB. ἀνίλεως: 020 044 049 056 0142 1C 5 18 33 35 43 61 93 94 104 *et al*. L427 L590 *et al*. Chrys Cyr Dam NilAnc PsOec.

[352] Theodosius, *Enconium on Michael* ed. Budge fol. 44b, actually substitutes 'love' for 'mercy': 'love will make a man triumph over judgment'.

[353] E.g. Pss 25.6; 51.1; 103.4; cf. Pss 40.11; 69.16; Isa 63.7; Jer 16.5; Eph 2.4.

[354] Most often for משפט in the LXX.

[355] So almost all exegetes; cf. also Peter Chrysologus, *Hom*. 41.3 CCSL 24 ed. Olivar, 235; Theodosius, *Enconium on Michael* ed. Budge fol. 23b-24a; Ceasarius of Arles, *Serm*. 31.4; 142.8 CCSL 103 ed. Morin, 138, 587; Fulgentius, *Rem*. 2.6.2 CCSL 91A ed. Fraipont, 684; John of Damascus, *Sabbat*. 35 PTS 29 ed. Kotter, 144; Bernard of Clairvaux, *Serm. in Ps. 'Quit habitat'* 11.8 Bernardi Opera 4 ed. Leclercq and Rochais, 453. But Simon, 141, thinks judgment takes place now as well as in the future.

[356] Cf. 3 Macc 5.10; T. Gad 5.11; T. Abr. RecLng. 12.1; etc.

[357] Cf. Jas 2.13 v.l.; T. Abr. RecLng. 17.8; Gk Apoc. Ezra 4.9; etc.

[358] LXX Gen 24.12, 14, 44; Exod 20.6; 34.7; Deut 5.10; Judg 8.35; 21.22; 1 Βασ 15.6; 20.14; 2 Βασ 3.8; 10.2; 22.51; 3 Βασ 2.7; Tob 14.7; Pss 17.51; 108.16; Ecclus 29.1; 46.7; Jer 9.23; 39.18; Ezek 18.19; cf. Pss. Sol. 6.6; Jos. Asen. 23.3; T. Job 11.3; Lk 1.72;

Most notably, it occurs in the prologue to the ten commandments: God does mercy to thousands who love him and keep his commandments (Exod 20.6 = Deut 5.10). Showing mercy is, then, to act like God, and not to show mercy is to abandon the *imitatio Dei*.[359]

Verse 13a is the obverse of the eschatological *lex talionis* in Mt 5.7,[360] and exegetes and Christian tradition incessantly associate the two texts.[361] Perhaps James here depends upon that beatitude.[362] Yet there are good parallels in other parts of the First Gospel (e.g. 18.21-35; 25.31-46;[363] cf. Mk 11.25) as well as elsewhere: 1 En. 27.3-4 ('the merciful...will bless him [God] for the mercy which he had bestowed upon them'); Ecclus 28.1 ('The vengeful will face the Lord's vengeance'), 4 ('If one has no mercy toward another like himself, can he seek pardon for his own sins?'); T. Zeb. 5.3 ('Have mercy in your inner being...because whatever anyone does to his neighbor, the Lord will do to him'); 8.1 ('Have compassion toward every person with mercy, in order that the Lord may

---

10.37; Josephus, *Bell*. 3.133; T. Zeb. 5.1, 4; T. Naph. 4.5; 2 Clem 3.1. The idiom occurs only occasionally in non-Jewish or non-Christian sources. Oesterley, 396, suggests that James' Greek is the equivalent of the Hebrew לאשר לא־עשה חסד ('the phrase sounds more natural in Hebrew').

[359] For divine mercy see further Exod 33.19; Deut 13.17; 1 Chr 21.13; Pss 25.6; 51.1; 69.16; 119.77; Isa 30.18; 31.30; 60.10; Ezek 39.25; Dan 9.9. For mercy as a human virtue see 1 Sam 23.21; Dan 4.27; Mic 6.8; Zech 7.9; T. Zeb. 5.1, 3; 7.1–8.6; Mt 10.19; 12.7; Lk 10.37; Rom 12.8; Jude 23; Billerbeck 1.204-205. For the latter as imitation of the former see Lk 6.36; Mek. on Exod 15.2; y. Ber. 9c (5.3); y. Pe'ah 15b (1.1); y. Meg. 75c (4.10); b. Šabb. 133b; Tg. Ps.-J. on Lev 22.28. The Stoics, identifying ἔλεος with an emotion that entailed partiality, did not regard it as a virtue. See R. Bultmann, 'ἔλεος κτλ.', *TDNT* 2.477-78.

[360] Cf. 1 Clem. 13.2; Pol. *Phil.* 2.3.

[361] Cf. Ps.-Chrysostom, *Nol. thesaur.* ed. Monachus, 633; Ceasarius of Arles, *Serm.* 26.1 CCSL 103 ed. Morin, 115; Theodosius, *Enconium on Michael* ed. Budge fol. 42b; Fulgentius, *Rem*. 2.6.3 CCSL 91A ed. Fraipont, 685; Bede *ad loc.* CCSL 121 ed. Hurst, 196; Photius, *Hom*. 6.5 ed. Aristarches, 188; Albertus Magnus, *Super Mt cap. I–XIV Opera Omnia* 21/1 ed. Schmidt, 111; Nicholas of Gorran, 74; Hus, 203; Wolzogen, 197; Zegerus *apud* J. Pearson, *Critici sacri*, 34; Beza, 552; Grotius, 1080; Lapide, 101; Henry, *ad loc.*; and most commentators on James.

[362] So Brückner, *Reihenfolge*, 290. Cf. the rewrites in Benedict, *Reg.* 64.10 CSEL 75 ed. Hanslik, 150 (the abbot should always 'superexaltet misericordia iudicio, ut idem ipse consequatur'); Ps.-Ephraem, *Compunct.* ed. Phrantzoles, 101 (μακάριοι οἱ ἐλεήσαντες ὅτι ἐκεῖ ἐλεηθήσονται· καὶ οὐαὶ τοῖς μὴ ἐλεήσασιν); and the attribution of 2.13 to 'the Lord' in John Xiphilinus, *Or. Dom. 5 Lk* PG120.1228B. Townsend, 43, affirms that the saying in Mt 5.7 'surely lies behind what James says'. Cf. Davids, 119. Deppe, *Sayings*, 96-99, is just as emphatic for the opposite view: Mt 5.7 'is certainly not consciously alluded to'. Wachob-Johnson, 'Sayings', 448-49, leave the question open.

[363] Ps.-Hippolytus, *Consumm*. 47 GCS 1.2 ed. Bonwetsch and Achelis, 308; Ceasarius of Arles, *Serm*. 157.3 CCSL 104 ed. Morin, 643; Photius, *Hom*. 2.4 ed. Aristarches, 153; Calmet, 677; Brochmand, 115; Gill, 788; Jacobi, 100; de Wette, 216; Pott, 201; Baumgarten, 107; Wordsworth, 23; Cellérier, 79; Punchard, 365; B. Weiss, 100; Windisch-Preisker, 16; Chaine, 54; Michl, 39; Cantinat, 138; Martin, 72; Frankemölle, 417; McKnight, 220; *et al.* link 2.13 with one or both of these two Matthean texts.

be compassionate and merciful to you'); T. Gad 5.11 ('By whatever human capacity anyone transgresses, by that he is also chastised. Since my anger was merciless [ἀνηλεῶς] in opposition to Joseph, through this anger of mine I suffered mercilessly [ἀνηλεῶς], and was brought under judgment [ἐκρινόμην] for twelve months'); Lk 16.19-31;[364] Sifre Deut 96 ('Whenever you show mercy to others, mercy is shown to you by heaven; when you show no mercy to others, no mercy will be shown to you from heaven'; cf. b. Šabb. 151b); t. B. Qam. 9.30 ('As long as you are merciful, the merciful one is merciful to you'); y. B. Qam. 6c (8.7: 'When you are not merciful, the Omnipresent will not have mercy on you'); Gen. Rab. 33.5 ('They forgot to be merciful to their fellow men, so the Holy One...made his mercy forget them'). So James adopts a traditional Jewish sentiment, one consistent with the eschatological rule that 'everyone will be punished so that, in whatever sin he will have sinned, by that will he be judged' (LAB 44.10).

Perhaps the closest parallel is T. Abr. RecLng. 17.8: ἀνίλεως ἀπέρχομαι τοῖς ἁμαρτωλοῖς τοῖς μὴ πράξασιν ἔλεον. This belongs to a book that was probably composed by a Jew and in circulation before James wrote. The Testament, however, was copied by Christian scribes, who freely rewrote much of it, so it is possible that 17.8 supplies not proof of the proverbial nature of James' line but rather reflects the influence of our epistle.[365]

Although ἔλεος means 'mercy' in this context, some of the church fathers applied our verse to almsgiving; cf. the ἐλεημοσύνη of Mt 6.2-4. Indeed, 2.13 became 'a standard proof-text for the efficacy of almsgiving'.[366]

κατακαυχᾶται ἔλεος κρίσεως.[367] Note the repetition of sounds: κ...κ... εος κ...εως. The lack of a conjunction makes the conclusion abrupt and

[364] There is a long tradition of associating this parable with Jas 2.13; cf. Ps.-Chrysostom, *Laz.* 2 PG 59.595; Ps.-Nilus of Ancyra, *Perist.* 4.15 PG 79.845B; John Xiphilinus, *Or. Dom. 5 Lk* PG120.1228B; Albertus Magnus, *Lk ad* 16.24 Opera Omnia 23 ed. Borgnet, 448; Bonaventure, *Lk* 16.27 Opera Omnia 11 ed. Peltier, 48; Manton, 230; *et al.*

[365] See further D.C. Allison, Jr., *The Testament of Abraham*, Berlin, 2003, 16-31. Cf. also T. Abr. 10.4-5 RecShrt: 'Have mercy upon me, Lord. The judge (God) says to him: "How can I show mercy to you when did not show such to (your) daughter?"' Oddly enough, Ps.-Ephraem, *Prec. e sacr. scrip. coll.* ed. Phrantzoles, 346, is in some ways closer to T. Abr. RecLng. 17.8 than to James: ἡ γὰρ κρίσις ἀνίλεως ἔσται ἐκεῖ τοῖς μὴ πράξασιν ὧδε τὸν ἔλεον.

[366] So Johnson, 234, citing Athanasius, *Tit. Ps* 40.2 PG 27.810; Caesarius of Cappadocia, *Dial.* 3.140 PG 38.1061; Cyril of Alexandria, *Ador.* 7 PG 68.528B. Cf. Chrysostom, *Frag. in Jac. ad loc.* PG 64.1044D. It also became a standard proof-text that the wicked will have no relief from punishment; see n. 38.

[367] Some scribes felt the need for a connecting particle—δέ (01Z 02 33 81 88 *et al.* L593 L884 PsOec **L**:FV **K**:S^mss B^mss **S**:H) or καί (38 180Z 330 *et al.* L427 L590 L1441 L2087[*f] Cyr). If the latter were original, its omission could be explained by homoioteleuton (κα → κα). ἔλεον—which makes no sense unless understood as the neuter nominative τὸ ἔλεον—appears in 04 044 5 33 69 81 88 *et al.* **Byz** GregAgr PsOec.

perhaps adds solemnity (BDF 462). For the verb, which here means 'triumph over', see on 3.14.

Manton, 225, remarks: the 'clause hath been tortured and vexed with diversity of expositions'. Many commentators urge that 'the mercy shown by the merciful, as in contrast to him who shows no mercy, enables him to stand in the judgment which otherwise would overwhelm him; so mercy is full of glad confidence and knows no fear in view of the hour of judgment'.[368] In other words, human mercy allows one to triumph over divine judgment; cf. Sib. Or. 2.81: ῥύεται ἐκ θανάτου ἔλεος, κρίσις ὁππόταν ἔλθῃ.[369] This, however, creates an inconcinnity, because it does not comport with the argument that one must keep the whole law (v. 10). If showing mercy allows one to pass the judgment, then full obedience is not required.[370]

At first glance, it does not make more sense to think instead in terms of divine mercy,[371] because then again the closing aphorism—a 'memorabile axioma'[372]—seems to reduce the force of James' argument. Why end a paragraph of warning by stressing mercy? Perhaps, given the numerous parallels to ἡ γὰρ κρίσις κτλ. (see above) and the conventional nature of κατακαυχᾶται ἔλεος κρίσεως (see below), we should surmise that the habit of abutting sayings by catchword—in this case sayings about 'mercy' and 'judgment'—has here worked to James' disadvantage. Or

---

[368] Knowling, 52; cf. Benedict, *Reg.* 64.182 ed. Vogüé and Neufville, 650; Hilary of Arles *ad loc.* PLSup 3.71; Hesychius *apud* the *Catenae* ed. Cramer, 13; Dionysius bar Salībī *ad loc.* CSCO 53, 60 Scriptores Syri 101 ed. Sedlacek, 123; Erasmus, *Paraphrase*, 150; Calvin, 282; Diodati, *ad loc.*; Wells, 15; Burkitt, 1022; Gill, 788; Huther, 86; Beyschlag, 117; Pyle, 314; Johnstone, 177; Weidner, 46; de Wette, 228; Spitta, 71; Ropes, 202; Moffatt, 37; Tasker, 63; Easton, 38; Ross, 49; Michl, 39; Laws, 117-18; Cantinat, 138; Ruckstuhl, 18; Scaer, 86; Schnider, 67; Moo, 118; Burchard, 108; Hartin, 124; Maier, 120; Blomberg-Kamell, 120. Fulgentius, *Rem.* 2.6.2-3 CCSL 91A ed. Fraipont, 684-85, offers a novel variant of this by applying the line to self-care: one should have mercy upon oneself. Hus, 204, raises the possibility that the text could be construed as having to do with human mercy and human judgment.

[369] Cf. Tob 4.10; Dan 4.27.

[370] Cf. T. Ash. 2.5-10, where one who shows mercy and fasts but nonetheless steals, robs, cheats, kills, and commits adultery is 'unclean' and 'evil as a whole'. But Moffatt, 37, urges: 'mercy constitutes the essence of the Law; in fulfilling it, James implies, all other offences such as immorality and murder are avoided'.

[371] So Chrysostom *apud* the *Catenae* ed. Cramer, 13; Leo the Great, *Tract.* 11.1 CCSL 138 ed. Chavasse, 44; Braulius of Zaragoza, *Ep.* 15 PL 80.663A; *Ancrene Wisse* 5.24 ed. Millett, 126; Calvin, 313-14; Calmet, 677; Baumgarten, 107; Wesley, 861; Barnes, 48-49; Plumptre, 69; Robertson, 126; Schlatter, 183; Blackman, 86; Martin, 72-73; R. Wall, 128; *et al.* Note Jas 5.11: God is 'compassionate and merciful'. McCartney, 150-52, denies both interpretations: our line 'simply considers mercy abstractly as being of great power and glory than judgment'. So too Alford, 296. But Poole, 886; Trapp, 697; and Stier, 335-36, to the contrary, endorse both; cf. the different readings in Peter Damian, *Ep.* 106.8; 114.18 ed. Reindel, 173, 305-306.

[372] So Bengel, 494. Gibson, 30, calls it 'a cry of triumph'.

maybe Doriani, 76, is right: 'Though James has not been thinking of mercy...he simply cannot end by declaring judgment "without mercy"'. Whatever the truth, the following texts establish that James reproduces a traditional sentiment:[373]

- Philo, *Det.* 76: God 'tempers his judgment with the mercy which he shows in doing kindness even to the unworthy. And not only does this mercy follow his judgment but it also precedes it. For mercy with him is older than justice'
- Sifre Num 8.8: 'Which attribute is greater, the attribute of doing good or the attribute of punishing? One must say it is the attribute of doing good'
- Sifre Num 134: 'You (God) suppress the quality of justice with compassion'
- Mek. on Exod 15.2: 'With me, he (God) dealt according to the rule of mercy, while with my fathers he dealt according to the rule of justice'
- t. Soṭah 4.1: 'The measure of goodness is five hundred times greater than the measure of retribution'
- Tanḥ. Buber Tazria' 4.11: 'Before the holy one stand only angels of peace and angels of mercy, but the angels of wrath are far from him'
- y. Ta'an. 65b (2.1): '"Behold, the Lord is coming forth out of his place". He comes forth from measure to measure, from the measure of justice to the measure of mercy'
- b. Ber. 7a: 'May it be my will that my mercy suppress my anger, and that my mercy prevail over my other attributes, so that I may deal with my children in the attribute of mercy and, on their behalf, stop short of the limit of strict justice'[374]
- Gen. Rab. 73.3: 'Happy are the righteous who turn the attribute of judgment into the attribute of mercy'
- Lev. Rab. 29.3: 'When Israel takes their horns and blows them...he (God) rises from the throne of judgment and sits upon the throne of mercy...and he is filled with compassion for them, taking pity upon them and changing for them the attribute of justice to one of mercy'[375]

---

[373] One doubts the generalization of Hutchinson Edgar, *Poor*, 132, that James here reinterprets 'the usual balance [in Judaism] between forgiveness and condemnation in God's judgment'.

[374] The passage continues: 'R. Ishmael b. Elisha says: I once entered into the innermost part [of the temple] to offer incense and saw...the Lord of hosts... He said to me: Ishmael, my son, bless me! I replied: May it be your will that your mercy may suppress your anger and your mercy may prevail over your other attributes, so that you may deal with your children according to the attribute of mercy and may, on their behalf, stop short of the limit of strict justice. And he nodded to me with his head.'

[375] Cf. Lev. Rab. 29.6; also 3 En. 31.2; Midr. Ps 15.7 ('What measure is greater? The measure of goodness or the measure of punishment? Clearly, the measure of goodness is five hundred times greater than the measure of punishment'); Diogenes Laertius 2.14 ('he owed his acquittal to mercy [ἐλέῳ] rather than justice [κρίσει]'); Koran Al-A'raf (7) 157 ('I will inflict my punishment on whom I will; but my mercy encompasses all things').

One suspects (i) that James adopts the traditional sentiment, that divine mercy trumps divine justice, in order to convey that mercy is what matters most and (ii) that the *imitatio dei* is implicit:[376] if mercy carries the day with God, it should carry the day with human beings.[377]

---

[376] Cf. Lk 6.36 (often cited in connection with Jas 2.13; note e.g. Cyril of Alexandria, *Fest. ep.* 11.4 SC 392 ed. Burns, 270); Chrysostom in the *Catenae* ed. Cramer, 13 (citing Lk 6.36); Ps.-Andrew of Crete, *Éloge* 6 ed. Nordet, 52; Aretius, 478; Church, 359.

[377] Cf. Manton, 225-27; Hort, 57; Hutchinson Edgar, *Poor*, 132; Popkes, 182. One wonders whether such a reading of 2.13 lies behind the famous passage in Shakespeare's *Merchant of Venice* (4.1), where 'the quality of mercy is not strained', for these words are followed by this: 'mercy... is an attribute of God himself, and earthly power doth then show likest God's, when mercy seasons justice'.

XI

FAITH WITHOUT WORKS (2.14-26)[1]

(14) What good is it, my brothers, if someone claims to have faith but does not have deeds? Is such faith able to save him? (15) If a brother or sister is ill-clothed or lacks daily food, (16) and one of you says to them, 'Go in peace, be warmed and eat your fill', but does not give them what is necessary for the body, what good is that? (17) So also faith by itself, if it has no deeds, is dead. (18) Yet someone will say, 'You have faith, and I have deeds'. Show me your faith without deeds, and I by my deeds will show you my faith. (19) You believe that God is one. You do well. The demons also believe and shudder.

---

[1] Recent literature: Allison, 'Polemic'; Avemarie, 'Werke'; Bacon, 'Faith'; Batten, *Friendship*, 134-43; Bauckham, *Wisdom*, 112-40; Baur, *Paul*, 297-313; Bindemann, 'Weisheit'; Böhmer, 'Glaube'; Bottini, *Introduzione*, 49-60; Buchhold, 'Justification'; Burchard, 'Jakobus 2.14-26'; Burge, 'Form'; Cargal, 'Prostitute'; Carson, 'James', 1003-1006; Chester, 'Theology', 20-28, 46-53; Coker, 'Nativism'; Compton, 'Justification'; D. Cooper, 'Analogy'; Cranfield, 'Message', 338-42; Dassmann, *Stachel*, 108-18; de Wette, 'Bemerkungen'; Donker, 'Verfasser'; Dowd, 'Faith'; Dyrness, 'Mercy'; Eckart, 'Terminologie'; Eichholz, *Glaube*; idem, *Paulus*; Fung, 'Justification'; Garleff, *Identität*, 289-302; George, 'Perspectives'; Haacker, 'Justification'; Harman, 'Faith'; Heide, 'Soteriology'; Heiligenthal, *Werke*, 26-53; Hengel, 'Polemik'; Hincks, 'Error'; Hodges, 'Light'; Hoppe, *Hintergrund*, 100-18; Hutchinson Edgar, *Poor*, 168-76; Jackson-McCabe, *Logos*, 243-53; Jacobs, 'Background'; Jeremias, 'Paul'; Johnston, 'Controversy'; Kamell, 'Soteriology', 171-87; Karo, 'Versuch'; Keith, 'Foi'; Klein, *Werk*, 69-78, 197-204; Klöpper, 'Erörterung'; Konradt, 'Kontext'; idem, *Existenz*, 207-48; Krüger, *Kritik*, 187-99; Kühl, *Stellung*; Laato, 'Justification'; Lackmann, *Fide*; Lautenschlager, 'Gegenstand'; Limberis, 'Provenance'; Lindemann, *Paulus*, 241-52; Lodge, 'Paul'; Lohse, 'Glaube'; Longenecker, 'Faith'; Lorenzen, 'Faith'; Luck, 'Theologie des Paulus'; Ludwig, *Wort*, 187-91; Lührmann, *Glaube*, 78-84; Manns, 'Jacques 2,24-26'; Marxsen, *Frühkatholizismus*, 22-38; McKnight, 'Interlocutor'; Mehlhorn, 'Erklärungsversuch'; Ménégoz, *Étude*; Meyer, *Rätsel*, 86-108; J. Miller, *Romans*, 387-92; Mitchell, 'Document'; Mozley, 'Faith'; Neitzel, '*Crux interpretum*'; Neudorfer, 'Sachkritik'; Nicol, 'Faith'; Nienhuis, *Paul*, 113-18, 212-24; Oeming, 'Glaube'; Parry, *Discussion*, 43-67; Patry, *Prédication*, 64-76; Penna, 'Giustificazione'; Penner, *Eschatology*, 47-74; Polhill, 'Prejudice'; Popkes, 'Justification'; Preisker, 'Verständnis'; Proctor, 'Faith'; Rakestraw, 'Soteriology'; Renouard, 'Foi'; Rusche, 'Glaube'; O. Robertson, 'Covenant'; Ropes, 'Faith'; Sanders, *Ethics*, 115-28; Scannerini, 'Giustificazione'; Schanz, 'Jakobus'; Schmidt, *Lehrgehalt*, 157-83; Schnackenburg, *Teaching*, 353-58; Soards, 'Abraham'; Stein, 'Faith'; Stewart, 'Soteriology'; Theobald, 'Kanon'; Tielemann, 'Versuch'; Tobac, 'Justification'; Tsuji, *Glaube*, 187-98; Travis, 'Paul'; van der Westhuizen, 'Techniques'; Usteri, 'Glaube'; Verseput, 'Prayers'; idem, 'Puzzle'; Via, 'Epistle'; R. Walker, 'Werken'; R. Wall, 'Rahab'; Ward, 'Concern', 158-67; idem, 'Paul'; idem, 'Works'; Watson, 'Schemes'; Webber, *Response*, 25-30; Wieser, *Abrahamvorstellungen*, 86-92; Young, 'Relation'; Zimmer, 'Verhältnis'.

(20) But do you want to know, you senseless person, that faith without deeds is useless? (21) Was not Abraham our father justified by deeds in that he offered his son Isaac on the altar? (22) You see that faith co-operated with his deeds and that, through deeds, faith was perfected, (23) and the scripture was fulfilled that says: 'Abraham believed God, and it was reckoned to him as righteousness'; and he was called the friend of God. (24) You see that a person is justified by deeds and not by faith alone. (25) Similarly, was not Rahab the prostitute also justified by deeds when she welcomed the messengers and sent them out by another way? (26) For just as the body without the spirit is dead, so also faith without deeds is dead.

History of Interpretation and Reception

James appeals to Abraham to teach that justification is by works and not by faith alone. Romans and Galatians, by contrast, appeal to Abraham to teach that justification is not by works but by faith.[2] Readers of the NT have often wondered what to make of this apparent contradiction. Augustine wrote much on the issue,[3] and whether justification is by faith alone, as Paul argues, or must be accompanied by works, as James clearly says, became a standard theological question for the medieval schools.[4] The Reformation greatly enlarged the debate, which has continued ever since. The upshot is that the relevant books, chapters, and articles are as the sands of the sea. Indeed, the secondary literature on Jas 2.14-26 seemingly exceeds that dedicated to the rest of James put together. The exegete here confronts an overgrown, entangled mess beyond sorting.[5] John Newton remarked already in the eighteenth century: 'It would tire you if I should relate a tenth part of the conjectures of learned men upon this very subject'.[6]

For convenience, however, one can fairly observe that there are at least six different ways of accounting for the apparent contradiction:[7] (i) James and Paul wrote independently of each other, so neither was concerned with the other; and if one did know what the other taught, he was not consciously being oppositional.[8] (ii) Paul responded to James or

---

[2] Rom 3.20, 24, 26, 28; 5.1; Gal 2.16; 3.11.

[3] See e.g. Augustine, *En. Ps* 31.2.2-3 CCSL 38 ed. Dekkers and Fraipont, 225-27; *Fide et op.* 14.21-23 CSEL 41 ed. Zycha, 61-64; Bergauer, *Jakobusbrief*, 45-81.

[4] Note e.g. Abelard, *Sic et Non* 142 ed. Boyer and McKeon, 489-92 ('Quod opera factorum non iustificent hominem et contra').

[5] The *Wirkungsgeschichte* of the passage accordingly escapes the mastery of anyone, and the present commentator feels his inadequacy here more than anywhere else.

[6] J. Newton, 'Of a Living and Dead Faith', in *The Works of the Rev. John Newton*, vol. 2, London 1824, 551. Cf. Böhmer, 'Glaube', 252: 'unzähligen Beiträge'.

[7] For helpful surveys that take one up to the twentieth century see Schmidt, *Lehrgehalt*, 157-83; Bartmann, *Paulus*, 1-17; Scannerini, 'Giustificazione'.

[8] E.g. J. Michaelis, *Introduction*, 305-306; Huther, 106; Simpson, 31; Alford, 101-103; Clarke, 811; G.V. Lechler, *The Apostolic and Post-Apostolic Times*, vol. 2,

to followers of James in order to correct or rebut him or them.[9] (iii) Paul agreed with James but sought 'to prevent a mischievous use' of his words, which the apostle 'thought likely to be perverted by the Judaisers who were corrupting the Gospel of Christ'.[10] (iv) James responded to Paul in a polemical fashion.[11] (v) James responded to Paul but sought to clarify his teaching, not counter it.[12] A recent variant of this last position is the thesis that James is a second-century, canonically conscious pseudepigraphon composed in part to stave off heterodox interpretations of

---

Edinburgh, 1886, 241; J.B. Lightfoot, *St. Paul's Epistle to the Galatians*, rev. ed., London, 1890, 164, 370; Plumptre, 69-70; Weidner, 21-22; Plummer, 590-91; Parry, *Discussion*, 52, 67-68; Knowling, xli-xlvi; Tobac, 'Justification', 804-805; Meyer, *Rätsel*, 86-108 (James and Paul independently reflect traditions of Hellenistic Judaism); Cadoux, *Thought*, 27-29; Windisch-Preisker, 20-21; Meinertz, *Theologie*, 242 (admitting also the possibility that James was responding to an isolated, distorted Pauline slogan); Reicke, 35; R. Walker, 'Werken'; Schnackenburg, *Teaching*, 353-58; Baasland, 'Weisheitsschrift', 133; Heiligenthal, *Werke*, 49-52; Davids, 121, 130-32; Rakestraw, 'Soteriology'; Fung, 'Justification', 160; Frankemölle, 473; Johnson, 249-50; Bindemann, 'Weisheit', 210-11; Penner, *Eschatology*, 47-74; Verseput, 'Puzzle'; Konradt, *Existenz*, 241-48; idem, 'Kontext'; Proctor, 'Faith'; Haacker, 'Justification'; Bauckham, *Wisdom*, 113-40; Cheung, *Genre*, 195-96.

[9] Cf. Spitta, 202-24; Mayor, xci-xcviii; J.A.T. Robinson, *Redating*, 126-28.

[10] So Dale, 75, 77. Related opinions in Hug, *Introduction*, 556-59, 582-84; Farrar, *Days*, 310-11, 355; Zahn, *Introduction*, 124-28; Maclaren, 419-21; Smith, 152-58; Rendall, *Christianity*, 78-87 ('when Paul was writing to the Romans, the words of our Epistle were fresh in his mind'); Harman, 'Faith'; Robinson, *Redating*, 126-28; Scaer, 91; Rolland, 'Dialogue'. Cf. D. Guthrie, *Introduction*: 752: 'Paul is acquainted with a perversion of the kind of teaching proposed by James'.

[11] E.g. de Wette, 237-40; A. Hilgenfeld, *Historisch-kritische Einleitung in das Neue Testament*, Leipzig, 1875, 532-34; Kühl, *Stellung*, 46-68; Kittel, 'Ort', 98-102 (James the brother of Jesus wrote against Paul before meeting him); Schneider, 23 (stressing that James did not understand Paul); Via, 'Epistle'; Sanders, *Ethics*, 115-28; Sigal, *Emergence*, 424; Hengel, 'Polemik' (contending that most of James blasts Paul); Lindemann, *Paulus*, 250-52; Lautenschlager, 'Gegenstand'; Tsuji, *Glaube*, 189-93; Ludwig, *Wort*, 187-91; Jackson-McCabe, *Logos*, 243-53; Limberis, 'Provenance' (James of Jerusalem was directly responding to reports about the letter to the Galatians and attempting to give diaspora Christians the correct understanding of Abraham and the law); Avemarie, 'Werke'; Coker, 'Nativism'.

[12] So Bede *ad loc*. CCSL 121 ed. Hurst, 198-99; M. Chemnitz, *Loci theologici*, Wittenberg, 1616, 259; C. Ness, *A Compleat History and Mystery of the Old and New Testament*, vol. 4, London, 1696, 501; Wells, 14; Wesley, 861; Bleek, *Introduction*, 147; Bartmann, *Paulus*, 151-62; the Navarre Bible, 31; Rainbow, *Way*, 213-23. This seems to be the position of McKnight, 261-63, who argues that Paul and James are 'more complementary than... contradictory': 'James is responding either to Paul in the flesh or, which is slightly more likely, to the early Paul or to early followers of Paul who had embraced his message and driven it to some distortion'. Dunn, *Beginning*, 1142-44, offers a similar take. Contrast Grimm, 'Einleitung', 380: if James were concerned to interpret Paul aright, it makes no sense that he fails to differentiate between Paul's true teaching and its distortion.

Paul.¹³ (vi) James reacted negatively not to Paul but to some form of (distorted) Pauline antinomianism, a view Augustine already held.¹⁴

Regarding the theological questions surrounding the perceived tension—questions that have often have asked more of the text than it can supply, questions that the author himself perhaps could not always answer¹⁵—those who suppose James to attack Paul can see the dissent as on target or—the dominant opinion—misplaced.¹⁶ Those who deny such

---

¹³ Mitchell, 'Document'; Nienhuis, *Paul*, 215-24. According to the latter, our author 'wanted to create a canonical collection of letters that would position James and Paul as equal authorities in creative, canonical tension with one another. He does not want to banish Paul, but he also knows what sort of distortions can result when believers rely on Paul alone.' But why then is James' discussion not more nuanced, and why does he favor formulations that are literally antithetical to Paul? Cf. Jas 2.21 ('Was not Abraham our father justified by works?') with Rom 4.2 (Paul rejects the possibility that 'Abraham was justified by works') and Jas 2.24 ('a man is justified by works and not by faith alone') with Gal 2.16 ('a man is not justified by works of the law but through faith in Jesus Christ, even we have believed in Christ Jesus, in order to be justified by faith in Christ, and not by works of the law, because by works of the law shall no one be justified').

¹⁴ So Augustine, as in n. 3; G. Bull, *Harmonia apostolica*, Oxford, 1842; Bengel, 494; Hug, *Introduction*, 582-84; Kern, 70-73; Lange, 88; Fausset, 587; Barnes, 59; Bleek, *Introduction*, 145-46; Hort, xxv, 66-67; Ropes, 35; von Soden, 176; Moffatt, 43; Dibelius, 179-80; Schammberger, *Kampf*, 40; Easton, 41; Eichholz, *Paulus*; Blackman, 101; Mussner, 18-22, 130; Marxsen, *Frühkatholizismus*, 22-38 (James seeks to interpret Paulinism rightly); Trocmé, 'Églises'; Schulz, *Mitte*, 286-87 (James counters a radical, 'Gnostic-enthusiastic' version of Paulinism); Schrage, 37; Rowston, 'Book', 556-57; Vielhauer, *Geschichte*, 575; Hoppe, 67-70; Dassmann, 'Stachel', 117; Pratscher, *Herrenbruder*, 214; Vouga, 85; Polhill, 'Prejudice', 399-400; Lorenzen, 'Faith', 234; Ruckstuhl, 9; Schrage, 35; Popkes, *Adressaten*, 63-91; G. Sellin, 'Die Häretiker des Judasbriefes', *ZNW* 77 (1986), 211-12; Schnider, 77-78; J. Roloff, 'Abraham im Neuen Testament', in *Exegetische Verantwortung in der Kirche*, ed. M. Karrer, Göttingen, 1990, 248; Ruegg, 'Recherche', 256; Kugelman, 31-32; Leahy, 913; Martin, 95-96; Perkins, 113; Moo, 121; Popkes, 188-89, 192; T.R. Schreiner, *New Testament Theology*, Grand Rapids, MI, 2008, 600. According to Pfleiderer, *Influence*, 136, although James was responding to Paulinists who misconstrued Paul, James did not know that their interpretation was incorrect, so he thought his remarks aimed at Paul. Cuvillier, 'Paul', offers a similar argument: James responds to a form of Paulinism akin to that in Ephesians and the Pastorals.

¹⁵ Among older theologians, one of the few to recognize the limitations of James' rhetoric was J.H. Newman, *Lectures on the Doctrine of Justification*, 6th ed., London, 1897, 277-82, although his remarks are driven by the conviction that Paul and James must be harmonious. See further n. 18.

¹⁶ So most famously Luther; cf. 'Licentiate Examination' 19, in *Luther's Works*, vol. 34, ed. L.W. Spitz, Philadelphia, 1960, 317: the 'epistle of James gives us much trouble, for the papists embrace it alone and leave out all the rest... If they will not admit my interpretations, then I shall make rubble also of it. I almost feel like throwing Jimmy into the stove.' Cf. W. Musculus, *In epistolas apostoli Pauli*, Basel, 1600, 70. Modern scholars who perceive an ineradicable contradiction between James and Paul include Kern, 44-54; Baur, *Paul*, 296-98; G. Bornkamm, *Paul*, New York, 1971, 153-54; Lohse, 'Glaube', 305; Souček, 'Problemen', 467; Kümmel, *Introduction*, 414; Schrage, 5; Hengel, 'Polemik'; Stuhlmacher, *Theologie*, 60-68; Lautenschlager, 'Gegenstand'; Avemarie, 'Werke'. Modern theologians of the same mind include: P. Althaus, *Die*

an attack typically seek (sometimes with appeal to the agreement between James and Paul in Acts 15) theological harmony.[17] Among the many strategies for establishing concord—often felt to be a theological necessity[18]—the following, which are not mutually exclusive but often forwarded by a single author, may be mentioned:[19]

(i) Many have urged that James and Paul use the same words—'faith', 'works', and/or 'justify'—in different ways.[20] Pelagius, after observing

lutherische Rechtfertigungslehre und ihre heutigen Kritiker, Berlin, 1951, 33-35; W. Joest, *Gesetz und Freiheit*, Göttingen, 1968, 161-65; P. Ramsey, *Basic Christian Ethics*, Louisville, 1993, 136.

[17] Nicholas of Cusa, *De pace fidei* 58 ed. Biechler and Bond, 55, even has Paul, in a fictional dialogue, quote Jas 2.26 with approval! But some who deny real inconsistency can yet denigrate James vis-à-vis Paul; so e.g. Ropes, 205 (James shows 'nothing either of Paul's subtlety or of his mystical insight into the act of faith'); Blackman, 101 ('James speaks for...the average man who craves no strong theological meat, with the sauce of controversy, but is content with a diet of straw'). Cf. Plumptre, 75 (James is 'practical', Paul 'deeper and more mystical'); Buchhold, 'Justification', 56 (Paul should be privileged as the fuller revelation).

[18] Cf. Calvin, *Inst*. 3.17.11 ('the Spirit cannot be at variance with himself'); Manton, 264-65; F. Turretin, *Institutio theologiæ elencticæ* 16.8.22 (part 2), Edinburgh, 1847, 599 ('since Paul and James were inspired by the same Spirit, they cannot be said to oppose each other on the doctrine of justification'); Newman, *Justification* (as in n. 15), 275 ('Is our Gospel like the pretended revelation of the Arabian imposter, a variable rule, the latter portion contradicting the former?'); J.C. Hare, *The Victory of Faith*, 2nd ed., London, 1847, 32 ('Grievous would it be to believe that Christ was thus divided, and that His Apostles themselves should have set the example of rending His vesture in sunder'); A.W. Pink, *The Doctrines of Election and Justification*, Grand Rapids, MI, 1974, 240 ('This is one of the "contradictions in the Bible" to which infidels appeal in support of their unbelief. But the Christian, however difficult he finds it to harmonize passages apparently opposite, knows there cannot be any contradiction in the Word of God'); Songer, 117 ('the authority of the entire New Testament' is at stake); Rakestraw, 'Soteriology', 32 (it is a question of the 'authority' of Scripture). Contrast Luther, who thought James very poorly informed about Christian matters and so criticized him in the light of Paul.

[19] In addition to what follows see especially Theile, 145-69; Huther, 103-104.

[20] Cf. Oecumenius *ad* Jas 2.14-19 PG 119.477D-81C; Theophylact *ad* Jas 2.17-19 PG 125.1157A-60A; Beza, 553-54; Cajetan, 367; Calvin, *Inst*. 3.17.11-12; W. Pemble, *Vindiciae Fidei*, 194-225; Haak *ad* 2.21; J. Owen, *The Doctrine of Justification by Faith through the Imputation of the Righteousness of Christ*, London, 1677, 557-82; Gill, 790; Bengel, 495; Henry, *ad* Jas 2.14-26; Doddridge, 824; J. Edwards, 'Justification by Faith Alone', in *Works of Jonathan Edwards*, vol. 19, New Haven, 2001, 230-37; J. Michaelis, *Introduction*, 302-306; Newman, *Justification*, 288-91; Rosenmüller, 351, 356; Pott, 305-17; Simpson, 30; Farrar, *Days*, 356-57; Ménégoz, *Étude*, 122-35; Jeremias, 'Paul'; Ward, 'Paul', 162-63; Mitton, 105-108; Harman, 'Faith'; Travis, 'Paul'; Zodhiates, *Labor*, 37-38; Cantinat, 155-56; Ruckstuhl, 20-22; Davids, 50-51; Martin, 80; Stein, 'Faith'; Maier, 127; Brosend, 71, 78-79; *et al*. Dowd, 'Faith', 202, wrote: 'the Baptist consensus' is that 'James is using Paul's vocabulary, but not his dictionary'. For a critique of this strategy for reconciling Paul and James see Compton, 'Justification'. As a parallel, some of the traditional conflicts between Roman Catholics and Protestants regarding 'justification' have to do with different understandings of the same terms; cf. Frankemölle, 462-63.

that faith, even for Paul, is not enough (cf. 1 Cor 13.2), urged that James does not contradict Rom 3.28 because Paul refers to 'the works of circumcision, the sabbath, etc., and not...the works of righteousness, concerning which St. James says: "Faith without works is dead"'. Paul's words have to do with one 'who comes to Christ and is saved when first believing by faith alone', and 'by adding "the works of the law"', he 'indicates that there are also works of grace that believers should perform'.[21] Augustine, despite his many disagreements with Pelagius, partly concurred on this point: when Paul denies justification by works, he is referring to works antecedent to faith, and when James affirms justification by works, he is referring to works that follow upon faith.[22] This strategy, which has often stressed a distinction between justification (Paul's topic) and sanctification (James' topic),[23] remains popular. According to O. Robertson, Paul is concerned with a divine declaration about guilt at conversion, James with subsequent public proof of someone being faithful and just.[24] One can likewise argue that James and Paul use

---

[21] Pelagius, *Rom. ad* 3.28 TS 9 ed. Souter, 34. Cf. Pelagius (?), *Vita christ.* 13 PL 50.398B-C.

[22] Augustine, *Div. quaest. oct. trib.* CCSL 44A ed. Mutzenbecher, 218-21. Cf. Bede *ad loc.* CCSL 121 ed. Hurst, 198-99; the *Catenae* ed. Cramer, 16; Isidore of Pelusium, *Ep.* 4.65 PG 78.1121C; Isidore of Seville, *Diff.* 233-34 CCSL 111A ed. Andrès Sanz, 89-90; Julian of Toledo, *Antikeim.* 2.77 PL 96.701-702; Dionysius bar Salībī *ad loc.* CSCO 53, 60 Scriptores Syri 101 ed. Sedlacek, 124; Atto of Vercelli, *Rom. ad.* 3.28 PL 134.163B-C; Calvin, 285; Johann Gropper, *Antididagma* 8, Venice, 1547, 33-35; J. Donne, 'Sermons Preached on Whitsunday', in *The Works of John Donne*, vol. 2, London, 1829, 117-18; Piscator, 733; Gill, 789; Bengel, 496-97; R. Rawlin, *Christ the Righteousness of his People*, Edinburgh, 1797, 244-49; Wesley, 862; A. Fuller, *The Complete Works*, vol. 1, Philadelphia, 1845, 673; Barnes, 49-50, 60; Bardenhewer, 88-89; Reicke, 34-35; Penna, 'Giustificazione'; Lorenzen, 'Faith', 234; Martin, 81; Maier, 143; Brosend, 82 (the difference being that between 'a missionary and a pastor'); Gench, 106; Rainbow, *Way*, 216-18. For Augustine's view of James and its relationship to Paul see Bergauer, *Jakobusbrief.*

[23] So e.g. Bucer, 'Wormser Buch', in *Martin Bucers Deutsche Schriften 9.1A: Religionsgespräche (1539–1541)*, Gütersloh, 1995, 354-55; R. Hooker, 'A Learned Discourse of Justification, Works, and how the Foundation of Faith is Overthrown', in *Faith and Works*, ed. P.E. Hughes, Wilton, CN, 1982, 66; J. Eaton, *The Discovery of the Most Dangerous Dead Faith*, London, 1747, 53-55. Bucer speaks of a 'primary justification' having to do with forgiveness and the imputation of righteousness—the justification of the ungodly (so Paul)—and a 'secondary justification' having to do with becoming righteous—the justification of the godly (so James).

[24] O. Robertson, 'Covenant'. Cf. Servetus, *Righteousness of Christ's Kingdom* 4.3 trans. Wilbur, 258: 'The grace of God does not detract from works, inasmuch as it has been given without works; nor would Christ have our works be of none effect on account of the gifts that he has freely given us, for in the sight of God account is to be taken of them either for good or for evil, else were God an unjust judge, punishing for evil deeds and giving no reward for good ones'. Servetus adds that James cannot be about deeds making for righteousness before God because Rahab saved the spies by lying, that is, by sinning.

'faith' in different ways.²⁵ Jeremias offered that, for James, faith is intellectual assent to theological propositions while for Paul faith is larger than belief and encompasses deeds.²⁶

(ii) One can focus upon the different audiences and so the writers' different goals. Gregory the Great contended that Rom 4 was aimed at those who prided themselves on their works over against their faith, Jas 2 at those who boasted in faith over against their works.²⁷ Here concord is obtained through positing dissimilar rhetorical ends.²⁸ Bede argued similarly: James perceived that his audience needed to hear more about works, Paul that his readers needed to hear more about faith.²⁹ For W.G.T. Shedd, Paul was arguing against 'sincere legalists', James against 'hypocritical believers', and this 'explains and harmonizes the difference between them'.³⁰ Bassett, 39-40, contended instead that, whereas Paul

---

²⁵ Or James and other early Christian texts. E.g. Bede *ad* 2.15-17 CCSL 121 ed. Hurst, 197, harmonized James with Ps.-Mark 16.16 ('he who believes and is baptized will be saved') by insisting that true belief involves acting on what is believed. Note also William Tyndale, 'The Wicked Mammon', in *Doctrinal Treatises*, Cambridge, UK, 1848, 120-25.

²⁶ Jeremias, 'Paul', followed by Longenecker, 'Faith'. Cf. also T. Söding, *Einheit der Heiligen Schrift?*, Freiburg, 2005, 375-76, and already Hemminge, 23; Bengel, 495; Knowling, xlii, 65. It intrigues that some of these harmonizations of Paul and James are not dissimilar from some modern attempts to harmonize Paul with himself, that is, to harmonize what Paul has to say about justification by faith and about justification by works; see e.g. Jeremias, 'Paul', 370; K.P. Donfried, 'Justification and Last Judgment in Paul', *ZNW* 67 (1976), 90-110; Watson, as in n. 28.

²⁷ Gregory the Great, *Mor*. 29.72 SC 476 ed. the Monks of Wisqes, 306. Cf. Plumptre, 76 ('St. Paul reproves the deadness of mere morality, St. James the deadness of mere orthodoxy'); Cadoux, *Thought*, 81.

²⁸ The approach has much to commend it. Certainly Paul's statements vary with the situation—see N.M. Watson, 'Justified by Faith, Judged by Works', *NTS* 29 (1983), 209-21—and presumably the same was true for James. 4.6 speaks of divine 'grace', and perhaps a different situation would have prodded our author to emphasize grace rather than deeds. Cf. Origen, *Rom*. 4.11 FC 2.2 Heither, 288-90, where the church father says, in turn, that salvation is through faith, through the blood of Jesus, and through deeds. Isidore of Seville, *Diff*. 3.32 CCSL 111A ed. Andrés Sanz, 89-90, says that Paul focuses on Abraham's initial experience of faith, James on his later sacrifice of his son.

²⁹ Bede *ad loc*. CCSL 121 ed. Hurst, 199; cf. Bengel, 495.

³⁰ W.G.T. Shedd, 'Connection between Faith and Works', in *Sermons to the Spiritual Man*, New York, 1884, 286-301. So too, with variations, Hus, 207; Turretin, *Institutio*, 599 (16.8.22) (Paul opposed Pharisees, James libertines); Surenhuys, 670-71; Burkitt, 1024; Bonsirven, 'Jacques', 788; Jeremias, 'Paul' (Paul attacked 'Jewish confidence in meritorious works', James a form of Christian 'Quietism'); Mitton, 104 (Paul countered 'legalism' or 'Judaizers', James antinomians); Fung, 'Justification', 161; Buchhold, 'Justification' (unlike James, Paul's context is the entrance of Gentiles into the people of God). For T. Scott, 576, 'St. Paul opposed those who objected to the doctrine of justification by faith, and St. James wrote against such as perverted it'. Doriani, 99-102, offers yet one more variation of this strategy: Paul ministered to pagans who needed to convert and learn about God, James to people who knew 'biblical religion' but 'insufficiently practiced it'.

addressed Christians and their concerns, James addressed non-Christian Jews (cf. 1.1): 'The law not the Gospel is the subject under discussion. There is no mention of sacrifice, atonement, or any other standpoints of the Christian dogma. The confession of faith or creed with which this discussion on faith and works is connected, is the Jewish creed that "God is one"... The parallel is not to be found in the writings of St. Paul to Christian churches, but in the preaching of John the Baptist...' Richard Baxter, however, saw things the other way: whereas Paul has in mind 'unbelieving Jews' who found justification in Moses, James is concerned for 'false Christians' who thought it sufficient 'barely to believe in Christ'.[31]

(iii) Many seek concordance between Paul and James by stressing that deeds were important for the former, who wrote that faith works through love (Gal 5.6) and who scarcely commended a faith devoid of good works.[32] For Paul, there is no 'hearing of faith' (Gal 3.2, 5) without 'the obedience of faith'.[33] Genuine faith inevitably produces good works, and immoral behavior prevents one from entering the kingdom of God. John Locke accordingly contended that Paul (and Jesus) as well as James require a faith that issues in obedience: 'that which availeth is Faith; But Faith working by Love. And that Faith without Works, i.e. the Works of sincere Obedience to the Law and Will of Christ, is not sufficient for our Justification, St. James shews at large, Chap. II'.[34] J.B. Lightfoot agreed: Gal 5.6 ('faith working through love') bridges 'the gap which seems to separate the language of St Paul and St James. Both assert a principle of practical energy, as opposed to a barren, inactive theory.'[35]

---

[31] R. Baxter, *Of Justification*, London, 1658, 153-54. Cf. Haak *ad* 2.21: Paul opposes false apostles, James 'verbal Christians'.

[32] See e.g. Ps.-Oecumenius *ad* PG 119.481A; J. Rotheram, *An Essay on Faith and Its Connection with Good Works*, London, 1766, 197-228; Huther, 105-106; G.C. Knapp, *Lectures on Christian Theology*, New York, 1868, 434-35; L.H. Christian, *Faith and Works*, Philadelphia, 1856, 124-38; Farrar, *Days*, 358-59; G.C. Berkouwer, *Faith and Justification*, Grand Rapids, MI, 1954, 133; Nicol, 'Faith', 21-22; Neudorfer, 'Sachkritik', 294-98; R.A. Sungenis, *'Not by Faith Alone'*, Santa Barbara, CA, 1997, 1-175. Vouga, 84, emphasizes especially the parallels between Jas 2 and Paul's insistence on proper behavior in 1 Corinthians. On the importance of 'works' for Paul see K.R. Snodgrass, 'Justification by Grace—To the Doers', *NTS* 32 (1986), 72-93; K.L. Yinger, *Paul, Judaism and Judgement according to Deeds*, Cambridge, UK, 1999.

[33] Rom 1.5; cf. 3.31; 8.4; 13.8-10; 16.26; 1 Cor 7.19; etc.

[34] J. Locke, *The Reasonableness of Christianity* 11 ed. Higgins-Biddle, 118. Locke adopted his view of James from Anglican Latitudinarians and Baxterian Presbyterians; see D.D. Wallace, Jr., 'Socinianism, Justification by Faith, and the Sources of John Locke's The Reasonableness of Christianity', *Journal of the History of Ideas* 45 (1984), 49-66.

[35] J.B. Lightfoot, *St. Paul's Epistle to the Galatians*, London, 1890, 205. Many have cited Gal 5.6—a verse Augustine made prominent in the West—when harmonizing Paul and James: Jerome, *Gal ad* 5.6 CCSL 77A ed. Raspanti, 155; Augustine, *Div. quaest. oct. trib.* 2 CCSL 44A ed. Mutzenbecher, 220; *De gratia et lib. arb. lib. 1* 7.18 PL 44.892; *Trin.* 15.18 CCSL 50A ed. Mountain, 507-508; *Epist. Ioan. ad Parthos* 10.1 PL 35.2054;

(iv) It is also possible to focus upon the biographies of the two figures. According to T.G. Selby, because Paul was a 'persecuting fanatic' who was 'arrested and brought into a full experience of the grace of the Gospels without any preparatory effort of his own', the apostle was 'transported with thoughts of the freeness of God's mercy, and…completely possessed by the truth that release from condemnation is received through faith alone'. James, by contrast, was 'a Nazarite of scrupulously regulated life' who found 'in his personal history that the exercise of faith went on side by side with the cultivation of righteousness. For him at least faith could not be separated for a moment from the complete round of moral precepts.'[36] In Selby's view, although Paul and James saw the same truths, they said different and even seemingly contradictory things because they were looking from different angles.[37]

(v) Neander, 81, suggested distinguishing between the divine and human points of view. God can see from the beginning whether one's faith is justifying faith because God knows the ultimate issue. This explains Paul. But human beings can only see the nature of faith in the light of its subsequent works, and in that sense one can say that works justify. This explains James.[38]

(vi) J. Miller, 387-92, denied any tension at all between Paul and James on the ground that Jas 2.21 and 25 are not questions but statements. He

---

Fide et op. 14.21 CSEL 41 ed. Zycha, 62; Bede *ad* 2.15-17 CCSL 121 ed. Hurst, 197; Severus of Antioch *apud* Zacharias Scholasticus, *H.E.* 19 PG 85.1178B; Julian of Vezelay, *Serm.* 24 SC 193 ed. Vorreux, 552; Robert Grosseteste, *Gal. ad* 3.11 CCCM 130 ed. McEvoy and Rizzerio, 86; Erasmus, *Paraphrase*, 150; Osiander, 723; Pareus, 554; Andreas de Vega, *De Justificatione doctrina universa*, Cologne, 1572, 131; Grotius, 1080; Bull, *Examin Censurae*, in *The Works of George Bull*, vol. 4, London, 1827, 187; Barlow, *Letters*, 88; J.J. Taylor, 'Fides Formata', in *The Sermons of the Right Rev. Jeremy Taylor*, New York, 1852, 422; J. Edwards, 1173; Trenkle, 47; Schmidt, *Lehrgehalt*, 183; Sadler, 37; J.R. Smith, 'Gospel', 147; Grosheide, 40; Mussner, 132; Mitton, 99 (Gal 5.6 'could almost be taken as the text which James is here expounding'); *et al.* Note further the conflation of Jas 2.26 and Gal 5.6 in the Westminster Confession of Faith 13.2 (on justification): Faith 'is ever accompanied with all other saving graces, and is no dead faith, but worketh through love'. Also commonly quoted in the commentaries are Rom 2.13; 8.13; 1 Cor 6.9-10; Gal 5.19-21. Less often cited (surprisingly) is 1 Cor 13.2, which denigrates faith without love; but note Augustine, *Fide et op.* 14.21 CSEL 41 ed. Zycha, 62; Grotius, 1080; J. Taylor, 'Fides Formata', 421; J. Edwards, 1173; Lodge, 'Paul', 213.

[36] T.G. Selby, 'Types of Unavailing Faith', in *The Alienated Crown*, Manchester, 1904, 119-20.

[37] A.B. Crabtree, *The Restored Relationship*, Chicago, 1963, 74-83, takes a similar approach. Cf. Pfleiderer, *Influence*, 137 ('the mystical inwardness and idealistic speculative bent of Paul's genius was met in the person of James by the sober realism of the practical understanding, which attaches exclusive importance to the uprightness of moral conduct, but is indifferent, or indeed suspicious, with regard to the emotions and intuitions of the religious nature'); Bartmann, *Paulus*, 142-45; Johnston, 'Controversy'; Nicol, 'Faith', 20-21.

[38] Cf. Heide, 'Sanctification', 91: Pauline justification is about 'objective' justification from God's viewpoint; James' practical view is by contrast 'very subjective'.

translated: 'Abraham...was not made righteous by works in that he offered Isaac his son, upon the altar'; 'Rahab...was not made righteous by works when she received the messengers'. In this way Miller could claim that, for James, salvation is by faith alone.

Although all but the last of the harmonizing strategies just catalogued are common to both Roman Catholics and Protestants, the two groups have nonetheless found much to disagree about regarding Jas 2.14-26, which has indeed become 'a battle-field strewn with the bones and weapons of countless adversaries'.[39] Many Protestants, tending to associate 'justification' with God's initial acceptance of penitent sinners, have again and again construed James so that the letter is consistent with a Protestant understanding of *sola fide*. They have emphasized that faith is the opposite of human striving, they have been leery about or dismissive of any notion of grace infused, and they have most often dismissed any notion of 'merit of condignity', that is, merit won after grace. Roman Catholics and Eastern Orthodox have, to the contrary, appealed to James to combat common Protestant construals of faith and works, understood as threatening the separation of religion and morality.[40] Surely, they have argued, justification is more than just imputed grace or imputed righteousness: it must, despite persisting concupiscence, involve a real transformation that will win a favorable verdict at the last judgment. Gasparo Contarini, however, tried, in 1541, to find a formulation about justification acceptable to both Catholics and Lutherans.[41] Ultimately he failed.

---

[39] So Punchard, 365.

[40] Cf. the 'Decree on Justification' from session 6 (January 13, 1547) of the Council of Trent in *Decrees of the Ecumenical Councils*, vol. 2, ed. N.P. Tanner, London, 1990, 671-81; Patriarch Jeremiah II, 'The Reply to the Augsburg Confession' § 4, in *Creeds and Confessions of Faith in the Christian Tradition*, vol. 2, ed. J. Pelikan and V. Hotchkiss, New Haven, 2003, 401; Peter Mogolia, 'The Orthodox Confession of the Catholic and Apostolic Eastern Church', in Pelikan and Hotchkiss, *Creeds*, 562; John Eck, *Enchiridion locorum communium* 5 Corpus Catholicorum 34 ed. Fraenkel, 94, 99; W. Fulke, *The Text of the New Testament of Iesus Christ*, London, 1601, 788; Sungenis, *Faith*; et al. Sometimes James is cited to support the proposition that faith itself is a work (e.g. Eck). Calvin, *Inst.* 3.17.11, observed: the Catholics 'constantly' hold up Jas 2 'as if it were the shield of Achilles'.

[41] Gasparo Contarini, *Epistola de justificatione* in *Gegenreformatorische Schriften (1530 c.–1542)* Corpus Catholicorum 7 ed. Hünermann, 23-34. This includes the assertion that 'those who say that we are justified by works speak the truth, and those who say that we are justified not by works but through faith also speak the truth' (34). On the 1541 Diet at Regensburg, which Contarini attended and which issued in a joint statement on justification from leading Catholics (Eck, Gropper, Pflug) and Protestants (Melanchthon, Bucer, Pistorius) see A.N.S. Lane, 'Twofold Righteousness', in *Justification*, ed. M. Husbands and D.J. Treier, Downers Grove, IL, 2004, 205-24. Girolamo Seripando, a Cardinal at the Council of Trent and General of the Augustinian Order, also attempted to harmonize Luther with Catholic teaching; see *De iustitia et libertate Christiana* Corpus Catholicorum 30 ed. Forster. Seripando distinguished between initial and progressive justification.

Protestants and Anglicans have also had intramural debates over Jas 2 and the status of good works for salvation.[42] The Anabaptists and English Nonconformists turned James into a rhetorical club with which to assail what they perceived as the easy, cheap belief of many Lutherans and Anglicans;[43] and very shortly after the Reformation began, Georg Major (1502–1574), who had been ordained by Martin Luther and taught at the University of Wittenberg, insisted on the necessity of good works for salvation, bolstering his view by appeal to James. Countering him were the so-called Gnesio-Lutherans, such as Flacius Illyricus and N. von Amsdorf. The debate raged until reaching its resolution—against Major and like-minded others—in the Formula of Concord (1577; this, incidentally, fails to cite James in its section on 'Good Works').[44]

Similarly, in seventeenth-century England, George Bull, eventually Bishop of St. Davids, published his *Harmonia Apostolica* (1669).[45] This attempt to demonstrate concord between James and Paul argued that the more obscure Paul should be interpreted in the light of the less obscure James[46]—whom, Bull thought, was responding to misinterpretation of

---

[42] Cf. Bengel, 497 (James rebukes 'the degenerate disciples of Luther'); Trapp, 697 (James rejects 'the faith of the Solifidians'). For the debate between Socinians and orthodox Protestants see especially F. Socinius, *Justificationis nostrae per Christum* in *Fausti Socini Senensis Opera omnia*, vol. 1, Amsterdam, 1656, 601-27 (620-22 on James); S. Maresius, *Hydra socinianismi expugnata*, vol. 2, Gronigen, 1654, 429-27; and for England generally in the sixteenth and seventeenth centuries see C.F. Allison, *The Rise of Moralism*, New York, 1966.

[43] Note e.g. Menno Simons, 'The True Christian Faith', in *The Complete Writings of Menno Simons*, Scottdale, PA, 1956, 333 (Lutherans 'make it appear that works were not even necessary; yes, that faith is of such a nature that it cannot tolerate any work alongside of it. And therefore the important and earnest epistle of James [because he reproves such a frivolous, vain doctrine and faith] is esteemed and treated as a "strawy epistle". What bold folly!'; in reckoning 'the important and earnest epistle of James' to be a 'strawy epistle', Lutherans have led astray 'the reckless and ignorant people, great and small, city dweller and cottager alike, into... a fruitless, unregenerate life'); W. Penn, 'The Sandy Foundation Shaken', in *The Select Works of William Penn*, vol. 1, 4th ed., London, 1825, 145-53.

[44] See G. Major, *Ein Sermon von S. Pauli und aller Gottfürchtigen Menschen bekerung zu Gott*, Leipzig, 1553; Flacius Illyricus, *De voce & re fidei*, n.p., 1563; N. von Amsdorf, *Ein kurtzer unterricht auff D. Georgen Maiors Antwort*, n.p., 1552. For the Majoristic controversy see M. Richter, *Gesetz und Heil*, Göttingen, 1996.

[45] G. Bull, *Harmonia apostolica, seu, Binae dissertationes, quarum in priore, doctrina D. Jacobi de justificatione ex operibus explanatur ac defenditur*, London, 1670; cf. idem, *Examin Censurae: sive Responsio ad quasdam animadversiones*, London, 1676; idem, *Apologia pro Harmonia*, London, 1703. The former is reprinted in *The Works of George Bull*, vol. 3, ed. E. Burton, Oxford, 1827.

[46] This is a rare move, although note Rainbow, *Way*, 220-21. Contrast J. Owen, *The Doctrine of Justification by Faith*, Philadelphia, 1841, 432, who here represents the vast Christian majority: 'it is from the writings of the Apostle Paul that we are principally to learn the truth in this matter, and to what is by him plainly declared is the interpretation of other places to be accommodated'. The dominant shape of the western canon,

Paul.⁴⁷ The book took to task the perceived extremism of certain followers of Luther and Calvin and insisted on the necessity of good works for salvation (although holding that such works are not the cause of salvation, only its condition). Bull generated a heated response, some maintaining that he had contradicted the eleventh article of the Articles of Religion, as well as the 'Homily of Justification' to which those Articles refer.⁴⁸

The past continues to be replayed. In the 1980s and 1990s, American evangelical circles witnessed an acrimonious debate over 'Lordship salvation'. Adherents of such, in contrast to proponents of the 'free grace' movement, were resolute that salvation necessarily involves repentance and discipleship.⁴⁹ Their opponents, sharply distinguishing between justification and sanctification, were equally adamant that such a view amounts to 'work-righteousness', and that justification by faith and eternal life (although not heavenly rewards) are independent of good works.⁵⁰ Those promoting 'Lordship salvation' naturally found Jas 2.14-26 congenial. Those on the other side argued to the contrary that the passage does not contradict their position. This involved affirming, among other things, that the σῶσαι of Jas 2.14 concerns not eternal salvation—the readers, it is assumed, are 'believers' and so 'saved'—but with rescue from the consequences of sinful behavior in this life or with failing to win rewards at the last judgment.⁵¹

---

in which the letters of Paul come before James, and in which Paul is represented by thirteen letters, James by one, has surely encouraged most to read James through Pauline eyes.

⁴⁷ His chief strategy was to argue that James has a 'simple' understanding of faith, Paul a more 'complex' understanding that includes works of love. Such a distinction, while expressed in varied terminology, appears again and again in the commentaries on James.

⁴⁸ Note e.g. Barlow, *Letters*; T. Gataker, *An Antidote against Errour [sic] concerning Justification*, London, 1679; J. Truman, *An Endeavour to rectifie some Prevailing Opinions contrary to the Doctrine of the Church of England*, London, 1671. For a helpful account of the controversy see the sympathetic 'Life of Bishop Bull' by R. Nelson, one of Bull's students, in *The Works of George Bull*, vol. 1, Oxford, 1828, esp. 79-153. During the same period—the mid-seventeenth century—a similar debate surrounded the writings of Richard Baxter and his understanding of what James has to say about works; see J. Boersma, *A Hot Pepper Corn*, Zoetermeer, 1993.

⁴⁹ See especially J. MacArthur, Jr., *The Gospel according to Jesus*, Grand Rapids, MI, 1988. For a succinct overview of the debate see K.L. Gentry, 'Lordship Controversy', in *The Westminster Handbook to Evangelical Theology*, ed. R.E. Olson, Louisville, 2004, 317-19. For additional debates within evangelical circles on this issue see Rainbow, *Way*, 20-22.

⁵⁰ See e.g. Z.C. Hodges, *The Gospel Under Siege*, 2nd ed., Dallas, 1992 (21-38 on James); idem, *Absolutely Free!*, Dallas/Grand Rapids, MI, 1989. This movement generated 'The Grace Evangelical Society', which has its own journal, *The Journal of the Grace Evangelical Society*.

⁵¹ See e.g. C.C. Bing, *Lordship Salvation*, Dallas, 1991, 30-36; Hodges, 60-61; idem, '*Dead Faith': What Is It? A Study on James 2:14-26*, Dallas, 1987. Cf. Witness Lee, in his *Life-Study of James, First Peter, Second Peter*, Anaheim, CA, 1985, 54, 60. For

One of the lesser known theological debates surrounding Jas 2.14-26 involved the so-called Glasites or Sandemanian Calvinists of eighteenth- and nineteenth-century Scotland. In an attempt to eliminate the human will and affections from the act of salvation, followers of Scottish ministers John Glas (1695–1773) and Robert Sandeman (1718–1771) emphasized that faith need be no more than 'bare belief of the bare truth'.[52] They contended, with reference to Jas 2.19, that 'whosoever among men believes what devils do, about the Son of God, is born of God, and shall be saved'.[53] The most prominent critic of Sandemanianism was the polemicist, A. Fuller of Kettering (1754–1815), the leading Baptist theologian of the day. His response insisted that 'nominal' Christians and genuine Christians do not share the same sort of faith, and that 'bare belief of the bare truth' cannot suffice. Fuller argued at length that to believe what demons believe will not of itself win salvation: that hardly accords with James' intention.[54]

Although, as noted, most Christian readers have sought harmony between James and Paul, some more recent theologians have conceded ineradicable differences. According to G. Eichholz, although Paul and James share a common theology of obedience to the word, and although Christian theology needs both writers, because James can prevent misapplying Paul, the two men promote different conceptions of faith.[55] From a Roman Catholic perspective, Hans von Balthasar has written that, although there is a 'unity' between Paul and James, this being a 'common looking upwards to the one personal centre of all theologies, to Jesus the Christ of God, the appearing and exposition of the love of the Father', there remain nonetheless 'tensions', 'opposite accents', and 'contradictory emphases'.[56]

Although Contarini failed in his attempt to unify Protestants and Catholics on the issue of justification, recent ecumenical discussions have

---

critical analysis see Heide, 'Soteriology'. Hodges is in part anticipated by Tielemann, 'Versuch'. That being 'justified by works' in James refers not to passing the final judgment but to being rewarded at the end appears also occasionally in the earlier commentary tradition; note e.g. Weidner, 51-53.

[52] See esp. R. Sandeman, *Letters on Theron and Aspasio*, 2nd ed., Edinburgh, 1759.

[53] S. Ecking, *Essays on Grace, Faith, and Experience*, Liverpool, 1806, 107.

[54] A. Fuller, *Strictures on Sandemanianism*, New York, 1812. This is a collection of letters on the subject. Letter 4 (61-76) discusses Jas 2.19 and is reprinted in *The Complete Works of Andrew Fuller*, 3rd ed., vol. 3, Philadelphia, 1852, 583-89. J. Wesley also attacked Sandeman; see his 'A Sufficient Answer to "Letters to the Author of 'Theron and Aspasio'"', in *The Works of John Wesley*, vol. 10, London, 1872, 298-306.

[55] Eichholz, *Glaube*. He appeals for support to Kierkegaard. Cf. Kümmel, *Introduction*, 415-16 (while James cannot be a basis for Christian theology, it can be a corrective); Nicol, 'Faith', 21 ('Paul is constantly in danger of being misunderstood in such a way that ethics are emasculated. James combats this tendency in an inspired way, which is enough to warrant his proper place in the canon'); Childs, *Canon*, 443 (one stresses Paul or James depending on the situation).

[56] H.U. von Balthasar, *The Glory of Lord*, vol. 7, San Francisco, 1991, 111-12.

more successfully wrestled with overcoming long-standing differences.[57] Indeed, it was already possible in the nineteenth century to suggest that 'the disputes on the subject of justification all lie in the region of speculative theology, but about practical duties all are now agreed'.[58] Although overly optimistic as a generalization about that time as well as subsequent decades, it is nonetheless true that, since the modern ecumenical movement, commentaries on Jas 2.14-26 generally exhibit a goodwill that has displaced the passion and vitriol of their predecessors. Most modern Protestant and Catholic exegetes tend to be generous in spirit when writing on 2.14-26 or to pass over past disagreements in silence. Carping about the mistakes of others, once a staple, has receded.

Despite the far-reaching theological debates over Jas 2.14-26, one should not forget that the passage has, more than anything else, served practical Christian exhortation. Again and again theologians and preachers have appealed to James to warn their audiences that just being more or less 'good' does not suffice,[59] that one cannot maintain a safe distance from those who suffer (cf. 2.15-17),[60] and that baptism and profession of Christian faith are not enough.[61]

While James' emphasis upon deeds has supplied ammunition for those wanting to motivate the seemingly contented or apathetic, his contention that right belief is insufficient has not always sat well with Christian leaders wanting to insist on the supreme importance of an orthodox

---

[57] Symptomatic of recent developments are K. Lehmann and W. Pannenberg, *The Condemnations of the Reformation Era*, Minneapolis, 1990, and *The Joint Declaration on the Doctrine of Justification* by The Lutheran World Federation and The Roman Catholic Church, Grand Rapids, MI/Cambridge, UK, 2000. (While the latter cites Paul often, James plays no role.) For a helpful review of modern Catholic discussions of justification and Luther see J. Heinz, *Justification and Merit*, Berrien Springs, MI, 1981.

[58] Salmon, *Introduction*, 577. Salmon was an Irish Anglican.

[59] E.g. Leo the Great, *Tract.* 10.2 CCSL 138 ed. Chavasse, 43; Dale, 81-83; MacDougall, *Conflict*, 59; Baker-Ellsworth, 78.

[60] Cf. F.J. van Beeck, *God Encountered, Vol. Two: The Revelation of the Glory, Part III*, Collegeville, MN, 1995, 101, arguing against 'widespread residual Jansenism and other forms of "dolorism"' that irresponsibly idealize suffering.

[61] E.g. Fulgentius of Ruspa, *Ep.* 3.27 SC 487 ed. Bachelet, 188-90; idem, *Rem.* 2.19.2 CCSL 91 ed. Fraipont, 703; Gregory the Great, *Ev. hom.* 19.5 FC 28.1 ed. Fiedrowicz, 330; Opus Imperfectum 52 PG 56.931; Severus of Antioch, *Hom. cath.* 1.27 PO 38.2.175 ed. Brière *et al.*, 266; Caesarius of Arles, *Serm.* 186.1; 209.2 CCSL 104 ed. Morin, 757-58, 835; Maximus the Confessor, *Ascet.* 34 CCSG 40 ed. Van Deun and Gysens, 72-74; Symeon the New Theologian, *Eth.* 10.188-210 SC 129 ed. Darrouzès, 272-74; Nersēs Šnorhali, *Gen. Ep.* trans. Aljalian, 22-23 (interpreting the single talent of Mt 25.18 as faith, the profit of the talent as works); T. Cranmer, 'A Short Declaration of the True, Lively, and Christian Faith', in *The Remains of Thomas Cranmer*, ed. H. Jenkyns, Oxford, 1833, 160-63; H. White, *Profession and Practice*, Philadelphia, 1849, 72-76; *et al.* By contrast, Lee, 81-85, regrettably turns Jas 2.14-26 into uninformed polemic against non-Christians: only the church—unlike 'non-Christian lands', 'mothers in India', 'Oriental religions', 'Mohammedanism', and 'Mormonism'—has filled the world with good works.

dogma. Cyril of Alexandria wrote: 'Excellency in actions...without the evidence of sound doctrines and irreproachable faith can, I believe, in no way benefit a man's soul. "Faith without works is dead", and by the same token we assert the truth of the converse, namely, works without right doctrine is dead.'[62] As several church fathers shared this sentiment, 'Deeds without faith are dead' became a stock phrase with several functions.[63]

Much closer to the spirit of James is John Howe (1630–1705) who wrote, with reference to v. 19: 'I doubt not but that there is entire orthodoxy in hell, there is very little error in hell, very little of untrue notions, the truth of things is very clearly apprehended there...false doctrine doth not obtain there...and therefore, let no man value himself too much upon this, that he understands aright, that he thinks right thoughts, doth believe that there is one God, one, and but one. He may do no more in this, than the devils do, they may be as orthodox as he.'[64]

Probably the most famous use of v. 19 is in John Wesley's sermon, 'Salvation by Faith' (preached in 1738). In this, 'the faith of a devil' is a sort of refrain.[65] But the most brilliant homiletical treatment of 'the demons believe' known to this writer is an imaginative sermon of T.G. Selby, entitled, 'Types of Unavailing Faith'. This urges that 'the faith of devils is grounded in compulsion rather than in free moral choice. They believe in spite of themselves', the reason being that they 'belong to spheres of being in which the fact of God's existence is forced upon them, just as faith in the objects of the external universe is forced upon us by the five senses'. For this reason their faith 'cannot influence character, or work towards moral ends'. The upshot is that 'faith is entirely worthless if it rest entirely upon the testimony of involuntary senses and perceptions', for 'the choice of the will and the mighty play of sovereign affections' must enter into faith. The devils 'are not one whit the less malignant for their apprehension of' theological truths; they are 'not one shade holier in disposition, nor one step nearer the ascent out of hell'. The lesson is this: 'when irrefragable events force a truth upon us, it is a sign that the desires, the sentiments, and all the deeper sympathies have been running in a counter direction'.[66]

---

[62] Cyril of Alexandria, *Ep.* 55.2 ed. Wickham, 94. Cf. the related problem that 2.19 creates for idem, *Jn.* 11.5 ed. Pusey, 668-69: if eternal life is 'knowledge' (as in John's Gospel), how does this comport with James? Cyril solves the problem by insisting on the difference between 'barren speculation' and 'the true knowledge of God' that is 'life'.

[63] Note Origen, *Rom.* 2.13; 8.1 FC 2.1, 4 ed. Heither, 194, 282; Gregory of Nazianzus, *Or.* 40.45 SC 358 ed. Moreschini and Gallay, 306; Chrysostom, *Hom. 1–67 in Gen.* 2.5 PG 53.31; Maximus the Confessor, *Lib. ascet.* 33.643 CCSL 40 ed. van Deun and Gysens, 75; John of Damascus, *F.O.* 82 (4.9) PTS 12 ed. Kotter, 184; Hist. Bar. et Ios. 19 PTS 60 ed. Volk, 188; Peter Martyr Vermigli, *In Epistolam S. Pauli Apostoli ad Romanos*, Basel, 1558, 543.

[64] J. Howe, 'Principles of the Oracles of God', in *The Posthumous Works of the Late Rev. John Howe*, vol. 2, London, 1822, 515.

[65] J. Wesley, *Sermons on Several Occasions*, vol. 1, New York, 1845, 13-19.

[66] T.G. Selby, *The Alienated Crown*, Manchester, 1904, 119-37.

In v. 20, James addresses his hapless opponent with the words, ὦ ἄνθρωπε κενέ. Earlier commentators often wondered how James can use what seems to be the Greek equivalent of רֵיקָא, a word Jesus prohibited: 'Whoever says "Raca!" to a brother will be liable to the council, and whoever says, "You fool!" will be liable to the hell of fire' (Mt 6.22). Exegetes typically suggested that Jesus' imperative must be hyperbolic or, for some other reason, not applicable to James' purpose.[67] Manton, 243, wrote: 'Christ does not forbid the word, but the word used in anger', and 'there is a difference between necessary corrections and contemptuous speeches or reproofs'. Benson, 65, generalized: 'Some of the same words, or actions, may be right, or wrong, according to the temper of mind, or the principles, or views, from which they proceed'. Those who discussed this problem regularly noted that Matthew's Jesus seemingly ignores his own command later in the Gospel when he addresses the scribes and Pharisees as 'You blind fools!' (23.17).

The remark in v. 23, that Abraham became the 'friend of God', has often moved exegetes momentarily to lay aside their theological concerns and to inform readers that they too can become friends of God. Like many, Burkitt, 1023, spoke in this connection of communion, conformity of wills, and mutual affection. Manton, 260, became emotional: 'Here is comfort to the righteous, to those that have found any-friend like affection in themselves towards God, any care to please him. God is your friend... God delighteth in your persons, in your prayers, in your graces, your outward welfare. It is a great honour to be the king's friend; you are favourites of heaven! Oh! this is your comfort that delight in his presence.'[68]

Readers of v. 24 have sometimes wondered how James could commend a woman whose livelihood was prostitution and whose heroic act involved telling a lie.[69] Some have implausibly urged that πόρνη, or at least the Hebrew behind it in Joshua, need not mean 'harlot',[70] Barnes, 57, gave a more common rationalization: 'When we commend the faith of a man who has been a profane swearer, or an adulterer, or a robber, or a drunkard, we do not commend his former life, or give a sanction to it. We commend that which has induced him to abandon his evil course.'[71]

---

[67] E.g. Grotius, 1081; Wolzogen, 200; Henry, *ad loc.*; Rosenmüller, 354-55; Baumgarten, 120; Carr, 37; Knowling, 59; Plummer, 593.

[68] The British Puritan Noncomformist, John Howe, managed to preach, over a period of six months, nine sermons on Jas 2.23, with the focus upon friendship with God; see *The Whole Works of the Rev. John Howe*, ed. J. Hunt, vol. 8, London, 1827, 376-484.

[69] Indeed, the deist M. Tindal, *Christianity as Old as the Creation*, London, 1731, 238-39, wrote: 'When Men find the Harlot Rahab celebrated, even in the New Testament, for lying to the Government, and betraying her Country to its most cruel Enemies... are they not in danger, if they find their advantage in it, & 'tis for the Service of those they judge to be true Israelites, to do the same?' The subject received some discussion; note J. Brenz, *Brevis et pia explicatio in librum Josuae*, Frankfurt, 1553, 10-14.

[70] See below n. 432. Blomberg and Kamell, 140-41, still ask, 'What were the Israelite spies doing in the house of a prostitute?'

[71] Cf. Trollope, 609: 'her sins were committed in heathen ignorance, and were, doubtless, pardoned after her faithful adherence to the religion of the true God'.

This takes care of the issue of sex for hire. But what about commending Rahab precisely for an act of deception? Matthew Henry, conceding that Rahab's lie must have been 'a good deed' because 'it is canonized' by Jas 2.25, made several observations: (i) telling the truth or keeping silence would have betrayed the spies, which also would have been a sin;[72] (ii) 'none are bound to accuse themselves, or their friends, of that which, though enquired after as a crime, they know to be a virtue'; (iii) the case was extraordinary and so cannot serve as an example for others; (iv) although Christians should never lie, Rahab was a Canaanite and had not been taught the evil of dishonesty,[73] so God judged her by her good intentions.[74] Burkitt, however, had a more edifying take: 'Rahab's faith was mixed with great infirmity, she told a lie; but that is overlooked by God, and her faith only recorded, not her failing divulged; Rahab's lie, Sarah's laughter, Job's impatience, are not mentioned: We discover our corruption in the very exercise of our graces; but oh! how good a Master do we serve, that pardons our infirmities, and accepts our sincerity.'[75]

Exegesis

2.14-26, which some regard as the theological center of our epistle,[76] is a protracted argument that can be outlined in various ways.[77] The following analysis suggests six main parts:

---

[72] Such a thought may well have occurred to an ancient reader; cf. Lev. Rab. 35.15: 'When you see your neighbor fleeing violent men, then if he goes in one direction tell them that he went in the other direction, and if he did not go in this direction say that he did'.

[73] So too J. Gill, *An Exposition of the Old Testament Volume I*, London, 1852, 843; Benson, 68 (she was 'educated among a loose and idolatrous people'); Macknight, 593; R. Jamieson, *The Pentateuch and the Book of Joshua*, Philadelphia, 1860, 160; *et al.*

[74] M. Henry, *Commentary on the Whole Bible*, vol. 1, New York, *ad* Josh 2.1-7. Henry also felt a need to defend Rahab, who betrayed her own country, against the charge of being unpatriotic. Cf. Calvin, *Commentaries on the Book of Joshua*, Grand Rapids, MI, 1979, 46; Macknight, 593 (Rahab 'hath been represented by the enemies of revelation as a traitor to her country').

[75] Burkitt, 1024. Cf. Manton, 267: 'Many times God may choose the worst of sinners. Faith in a harlot is acceptable: "The last shall be first"'. Manton, 268, added that Abraham likewise lied when he 'equivocated with his servants: "I and the lad will return"' and that 'God hideth his eyes from the evil that is in our good actions'.

[76] So Schulz, 285; R. Walker, 'Werken', 163; Preisker, *Herrenbruder*, 213 (citing others in agreement); Martin, 77. Cf. Baur, *Paul*, 296 (2.24 is 'the main doctrinal position of the Epistle of James'); L. Goppelt, *Theology of the New Testament*, vol. 2, Grand Rapids, MI, 1982, 208 (the letter reaches its 'theological peak' in 2.14-16). Contrast Popkes, *Adressaten*, 42-43; Frankemölle, 421; Bindemann, 'Weisheit', 209. For the present commentator, there is no such center.

[77] R. Wall, 130, suggests three main parts: vv. 14-17, 18-20, 21-26. Close to this is Nicol, 'Faith', 7-11: vv. 14-17 offer an illustration, vv. 18-19 an argument, vv. 20-26 two scriptural proofs. Many commentators see a major divide between vv. 17 and 18; so e.g. Fabris, 175. For an analysis in terms of Graeco-Roman rhetoric see Watson, 'Schemes',

I. Introduction of subject via two questions (14)[78]
   A. Question 1: What good is faith without deeds? (14a)
   B. Question 2: Can faith alone save? (14b)
II. Introductory illustration (Question 3, 15-16)
   A. Depiction of unfortunates: 'If a brother or sister...' (15)
   B. Response to unfortunates: 'and you say...' (16a)
   C. 'What good is it?' (16b)
III. Inference to statement of thesis: Faith without deeds is dead (17)
IV. Objection to thesis: one can have faith, another deeds (18a)[79]
V. Response to objection: one cannot have faith without deeds (18b-25)
   A. Retort I: deeds demonstrate faith (18b)
   B. Retort II: the inadequacy of simple belief (19)
   C. Retort III through two illustrations (20-25)[80]
      1. Introductory question: 'Do you want to know...?' (20)
      2. The example of Abraham (21-24)
         a. Question about Gen 22: 'Was not Abraham...?' (21)
         b. The working together of faith and deeds (22)
         c. Scriptural support and clarification (23)
         d. Conclusion about Abraham: 'You see that...' (24)
      3. The example of Rahab (25)
VI. Conclusion: restatement of thesis (26)
   A. Similitude (26a)
   B. Assertion (26b)

James begins by addressing readers directly, continues by addressing his opponent directly, and ends by again addressing readers directly:

- James addresses readers (plural), indirectly quoting 'someone' (singular, 14)
- James continues to address readers (plural) (15-17)
- Statement of 'someone' (singular) addressing James (18a? 18a-b?)
- James answers 'someone' (singular, 18b or 19-23)
- James addresses readers (plural, 24-26)

As with other portions of the letter, parallelism and repetition are prominent:

---

who views v. 14 as the *propositio*, vv. 15-16 as the *ratio*, vv. 17-19 as the *confirmatio*, vv. 20-25 as the *exornatio*, v. 26 as the *complexio*. Cf. Hartin, 157-62; Batten, *Friendship*, 134-36. Contrast Van der Westhuizen, 'Techniques', 95: v. 14 is the *proem*, vv. 14 and 17 the proposition; vv. 15-16 a narration; vv. 18-25 are the proof that includes a refutation; v. 26 is the epilogue. Iovino, 'Struttura', divines a chiastic arrangement: 2.14 (A), 15-19 (B), 20-25 (B'), 26 (A'). Ruegg, 'Recherche', 248-49, sees 2.1-13 and 14-26 as structurally parallel, as indeed forming a diptych.

[78] Bengel, 495, proposes that v. 14 outlines the whole section. 'What is the profit' anticipates vv. 15-17; 'If some says, etc.' anticipates vv. 18-19; 'Is faith able to save him?' anticipates vv. 20-26. So too Wesley, 861.

[79] The proper analysis of v. 18 is more than unclear; see below.

[80] Lodge, 'James', 201, finds a chiasmus in vv. 20-24.

FAITH WITHOUT WORKS (2.14-26)

14	τί τὸ ὄφελος
16	τί τὸ ὄφελος

14	ἐάν...λέγῃ τις
15-16	ἐάν...εἴπῃ δέ τις

14	ἔργα δὲ μὴ ἔχῃ
17	μὴ ἔχῃ ἔργα

17	οὕτως καὶ	ἡ πίστις ἐὰν μὴ ἔχῃ	ἔργα νεκρά	ἐστιν
20		ἡ πίστις χωρὶς	τῶν ἔργων ἀργή	ἐστιν
26	οὕτως καὶ	ἡ πίστις χωρὶς	ἔργων νεκρά	ἐστιν

18	σὺ πίστιν ἔχεις
18	κἀγὼ ἔργα ἔχω

18	δεῖξόν μοι τὴν πίστιν σου χωρὶς τῶν ἔργων
18	κἀγώ σοι δείξω ἐκ τῶν ἔργων μου τὴν πίστιν.

21	Ἀβραὰμ ὁ πατὴρ ἡμῶν οὐκ ἐξ ἔργων ἐδικαιώθη + participle + object
	(question)
25	Ῥαὰβ ἡ πόρνη οὐκ ἐξ ἔργων ἐδικαιώθη + participle + object
	(question)

22	βλέπεις ὅτι... ἐκ τῶν ἔργων
24	ὁρᾶτε ὅτι ἐξ ἔργων

26	ὥσπερ γὰρ τὸ σῶμα χωρὶς πνεύματος	νεκρόν ἐστιν
26	οὕτως καὶ ἡ πίστις χωρὶς ἔργων	νεκρά ἐστιν

The argument is complete in itself.[81] It sets up a contrast between two sorts of faith. The first is no more than theological belief (v. 19). It has no deeds (vv. 14-17) and so is dead (vv. 17, 26) and barren (v. 20). It cannot make one righteous (vv. 21-25). But there is also a second and superior sort of faith. This is the saving faith that co-operates with deeds and is perfected by them (vv. 21-26). It is the faith of Abraham and Rahab, who were justified by their works.

The burden of the section is not to establish that genuine faith will produce works, although James certainly believes that. Nor is the main point that salvation requires both faith and works, although that too is his belief. The argument is not positive but negative. We have here not affirmation but denial. James is rejecting a view which allegedly claims that faith does not need works, a view associated with a scriptural argument that he seeks to overturn.

The literary setting for James' reflections on ineffectual and effectual belief is the demand that readers be not just hearers but doers who act

---

[81] Davids, 119, entertains the hypothesis that vv. 14-26 were 'separately composed as a self-contained unit'.

(1.22-25; 2.12), the contention that true religion is service to others, especially the unfortunate (1.26-29; 2.1-7), and the demand to love one's neighbor (2.8).[82] For James, religion is walking, not talking; it is halakah, a way of life, not dogma.

This commentator, however, must also conjecture a particular historical setting beyond the literary context. As interpreters have always recognized, the language of Jas 2.14-26 at many points echoes Paul. 'At first glance', moreover, 'nothing can be spoken more contrary to St. Paul's doctrine in Romans'; here we seem to have 'harsh discord',[83] and it is hard to avoid surmising that Jas 2.14-26 contains some sort of reaction to Paul or Paulinists.[84]

Johnson, 247, declines to interpret 2.14-16 as a response to Paul and protests that commentators on our epistle too often fail to approach it on its own terms: 'These verses...have been seen in relationship to Paul's teaching on righteousness by faith and have, in fact, been primarily read with a view to that point of reference. The verses have therefore...been distorted, for their meaning must be determined not with reference to another author, but from their place in the composition's argument. But by having been taken out of James' context and read over against Paul, James' argument has been lost and these verses distorted.'[85] Maybe, however, this begs the question. Why is it that all the commentators have, seemingly from the beginning, interpreted James with Paul in mind? The undeniable answer is that our book moves anyone acquainted with Romans or Galatians to think of passages in those epistles. Indeed, one

---

[82] Such connections are obvious; cf. Wesley, 861 ('From Jas i ?? the apostle has been enforcing Christian practice. He now applies to those who neglect this, under the pretense of faith'); Mussner, 127-28; Martin, 78-79; Frankemölle, 421-25, 436-37; Johnson, 245-46; Moo, 120; M. Taylor, Structure, 91-92. Burchard, 110, even calls 2.14-16 an 'excursus' on 2.12-13, and Keith, 'Foi', argues that the formal structure of 2.14-26 mirrors that of 2.1-13: introduction of theme (vv. 1, 14), illustration through a concrete case (vv. 2-3, 15-16), lesson from that case (vv. 4, 17), refutation of an objection (vv. 5-6, 18-20), demonstration through scripture (vv. 8-11, 21-25), concluding aphorism (vv. 12-13, 26). When Dibelius, 149, asserts that one cannot establish a connection with the previous pericope, form-critical presuppositions are obstructing the obvious. (Augustine, *Ep.* 167.20 CSEL 44 ed. Goldbacher, 608, implausibly affirms that 2.14-26 aims to comfort those disturbed by the high standards of 2.8-12: one gains consolation by knowing that works—giving and forgiving—atone. Cf. Bede *ad loc.* CCSL 121 ed. Hurst, 197.)

[83] Pemble, *Vindiciae Fidei*, 187-88.

[84] According to Hartin, 22, 'those scholars who see' Jas 2.14-26 'as an attack on Paul's understanding of "justification through faith alone" are influenced by an ideological perception that wishes to see everything in the New Testament as related to Paul and his thought'. Whether this fairly targets others I cannot say. I can only speak for myself: I have no theological investment at all in this issue, and I do not see everything in the NT in relationship to Paul.

[85] Cf. already the objection of Usteri, 'Glaube', 214.

wonders whether any informed readers of the NT have ever read 2.14-26 wholly on its own terms, without thinking about Paul.[86]

This matters because it is a sensible principle that the history of interpretation can be a fairly reliable guide to discerning deliberate intertextuality. The more that text A has reminded readers of text B, the more likely it is that text A was in fact designed to do just that.[87] The point to emphasize with regard to James and Paul is simply this: the constant reading of the former in terms of the latter is exactly what one would expect if the author of James intended auditors of his work to think about Pauline theology. To complain that readers too often and too readily turn to Paul may be akin to objecting that Heb 13.2—'Do not neglect to show hospitality to strangers, for thereby some have entertained angels unawares'—has regularly moved readers to recall Gen 18, where Abraham hosts three mysterious visitors. Hebrews 13.2 is supposed to prod an intertextual exchange, to move informed readers to go back to Genesis. Maybe, in like fashion, Jas 2.14-24 is also a deliberately allusive text: it wants us to recall Paul.

If the history of interpretation tends strongly in a certain direction, the main reason is obvious: 2.14-26 and the relevant Pauline texts share a number of words and phrases. Moreover, those words and phrases are, prior to Paul, either rare or wholly unattested:

- Paul is the first Greek writer known to us to use δικαιόω in the passive + instrumental ἐκ, and it appears seven times in Romans and Galatians.[88] So even though the construction also occurs in Mt 12.37, it is definitely characteristic of the apostle. It shows up in James three times: 2.21, 24, 25.[89]
- ἐξ ἔργων is only meagerly attested before Paul, appearing (with quite different sense) once in Homer, once in Hesiod, once in the LXX, and never in the Pseudepigrapha, Philo, or Josephus.[90] But Paul likes it: he uses it not once or twice but repeatedly.[91] Prior to later church fathers

---

[86] It should also be noted that commentators on Romans and Galatians have regularly been reminded of Jas 2.14-26; note from early times Origen, *Rom* 4.1 FC 2.2 ed. Heither, 164; Pelagius, *Rom. ad* 3.28 TS 9.2 ed. Souter 34; Cyril of Alexandria, *Frag. Rom ad* 4.2 ed. Pusey, 180.

[87] Cf. R.B. Hays, *The Faith of Jesus Christ*, 2nd ed., Grand Rapids, MI, 2002, xlvii-lii.

[88] Rom 3.20; 4.1; 5.1; Gal 2.16 (three times); 3.24.

[89] One should add, following Laws, 132, that 'the use of justification as a term for salvation is in the Christian tradition peculiarly associated with Paul... The likelihood is, therefore, that when James heard the slogan "justification by faith alone" used (or misused) it was carrying the authority of Paul'.

[90] Homer, *Od.* 24.388; Hesiod, *Op.* 308; LXX B Judg 19.16 (ἀνὴρ πρεσβύτης ἤρχετο ἐξ ἔργων αὐτοῦ ἐξ ἀγροῦ). Note also Hippocrates, *De morbis pop.* 4.1.27; Appian, *Mith.* 433.4; Galen, *In Hipp. de vic. acut. comm. iv.* ed. Kühn, 15.584. The closest parallel in the Pseudepigrapha is Gk. frag. Jub. 2.17, a paraphrase of LXX Gen 2.2: ἀνεπαύσατο ὁ θεὸς ἐκ πάντων τῶν ἔργων; but here ἐκ has a different sense.

[91] Rom 3.20; 4.2; 9.11, 32; 11.6; Gal 2.16 (thrice); 3.2, 5, 10. Cf. its use in the Deutero-Paulines: Eph 2.9; Tit 3.5.

such as Origen and John Chrysostom, the only comparable density is in James, where ἐξ ἔργων appears three times: 2.21 (ἐξ ἔργων ἐδικαιώθη), 24 (ἐξ ἔργων δικαιοῦται), 25 (ἐξ ἔργων ἐδικαιώθη).
- James employs δικαιόω only three times, all in connection with ἐξ ἔργων; and with the exception of our letter, ἐξ ἔργων is linked to δικαιόω only in Pauline literature or texts influenced by Paul and/or James.[92] Indeed, Jas 2.21 ('Αβραάμ...οὐκ ἐξ ἔργων ἐδικαιώθη) sounds like a direct response to Rom 4.2 (εἰ γὰρ 'Αβραὰμ ἐξ ἔργων ἐδικαιώθη).
- The situation is similar regarding the δικαιοῦται ἄνθρωπος of Jas 2.24, which has its exact parallel in Gal 2.16 (δικαιοῦται ἄνθρωπος) and also reminds one of Rom 3.28 (δικαιοῦσθαι πίστει ἄνθρωπον).[93] While ἄνθρωπος is ubiquitous as the subject of a sentence, ἄνθρωπος/ν + a passive form of δικαιόω is confined to Paul, James, and later Christian literature familiar with the NT writings.
- Aside from Jas 2.24 and before the latter half of the second century, ἐκ πίστεως occurs once in the LXX (Hab 2.4), once in Hebrews (10.38, quoting Hab 2.4), and once in Justin Martyr (*Dial.* 135.6), and, by contrast, 21 times in Paul (all in Romans and Galatians).[94] So, the rarely attested expression is, just like ἐξ ἔργων, characteristic of the apostle.
- χωρὶς (τῶν) ἔργων is another Pauline expression. Although χωρὶς ἔργου appears in Philo, *Mos.* 1.318, the noun is there in the singular; and if we look instead for the plural, χωρὶς (τῶν) ἔργων, this is confined, in Jewish and Christian literature, to Paul (Rom 3.28; 4.6), to James (2.18, 20, 26), and to Christian theologians from Origen on.

This is a rather remarkable series of correlations. One would be hard pressed to find a similar concatenation of rare expressions in two texts that are not directly related.

The point is reinforced when one takes into account the relationship of James to the Jesus tradition, which is considerable: James draws directly upon several logia that circulated under the name of Jesus.[95] Now the verbal overlap between our letter and the Jesus tradition is typically minimal. James does not quote Jesus word for word but prefers to rewrite the tradition. The point for us is that, leaving aside the saying about oaths in 5.12, none of the relevant lines in James shares with its Synoptic counterpart the number of distinctive and extensive parallels that the section of faith and works shares with Romans and Galatians. So would it not be odd to urge that James freely employed the Jesus tradition on multiple occasions and yet contend that he did not know Paul? On verbal and thematic grounds, the parallels with Paul are much more impressive.

---

[92] Rom 3.20; 4.2; Gal 2.16 (thrice); Clement of Alexandria, *Strom.* 1.7.38; Ps.-Justin, *Qu. et resp.* 103; etc. The parallel in Mt 11.9 diff. Lk 7.35 (ἐδικαιώθη ἡ σοφία ἀπὸ τῶν ἔργων αὐτῆς) uses ἀπό.

[93] Some have thought Jas 2.14-26 intentionally turns Rom 3.28 upside-down; so e.g. Sanders, *Ethics*, 120-21.

[94] Rom 1.17 (*bis*); 3.26, 30; 4.16 (*bis*); 5.1; 9.30, 32; 10.6; Rom 14.23 (*bis*); Gal 3.7, 8, 9, 11, 12, 22, 24; 5.5.

[95] See further the Introduction, 56-62.

FAITH WITHOUT WORKS (2.14-26)

One might take another lesson from James' use of the Jesus tradition. None of the reworked sayings of Jesus is attributed to him. That is, despite the clear dependence, not once does James say anything like 'remembering the words of the Lord Jesus' (Acts 20.35) or 'I give this command—not I but the Lord' (1 Cor 7.20) or 'the Lord commanded' (1 Cor 9.14). We have in this circumstance proof that James could rework materials without naming their source. This diminishes the protest that our author must be explicit about what exactly he is doing.[96]

The points made so far do not stand alone. Several additional observations strongly bolster the conclusion to which they naturally lead:

(i) The linguistic parallels catalogued in the previous section all appear, in both Paul and James, within or near discussions of Abraham and whether he was justified by faith or by works. They also occur near citations of Gen 15.6 (which does not have δικαιόω).[97]

(ii) James 2.14-26 is not unrelated to its literary context; see n. 82. Nothing before or after 2.14-26, however, poses the issue of integrity, love, or action in terms of 'faith' and 'deeds'. Why, for a few verses, does this way of speaking become dominant? πίστις and ἔργα occur repeatedly in this section, and the two nouns are consistently set over against each other, as though one could claim to have faith without works or works without faith:

- v. 14:   πίστιν ἔχειν // ἔργα δὲ μὴ ἔχῃ
- v. 17:   ἡ πίστις // μὴ ἔχῃ ἔργα
- v. 18:   σὺ πίστιν ἔχεις // κἀγὼ ἔργα
- v. 18:   πίστιν // χωρὶς τῶν ἔργων
- v. 20:   ἡ πίστις // χωρὶς τῶν ἔργων
- v. 24:   ἐξ ἔργων // οὐκ ἐκ πίστεως μόνον
- v. 26:   ἡ πίστις // χωρὶς ἔργων

The manner of argument is unexpected. James distinguishes faith from works precisely in order to contend that they cannot be separated. What explains this? He is not likely to have come across their severance in Judaism. We know of no Jewish teacher who promoted the notion that

---

[96] One should also keep in mind that there are many examples of writers not naming opponents. Paul, for instance, does not name any of the so-called superlative apostles in 2 Cor 11.5; 12.11 nor any of 'those from James' in Gal 2.12. Furthermore, several ancient texts that attack Paul do not do so by name. In the Epistula Petri, Peter calls him 'the man who is my enemy' (2.3). The Ascents of James refers to him as 'a certain hostile man'. Other portions of the Pseudo-Clementines identify him with 'Simon Magnus'. And if D.C. Sim, *The Gospel of Matthew and Christian Judaism*, Edinburgh, 1998, is justified in finding anti-Pauline polemic in the First Gospel, then it goes without saying that he is not named therein also.

[97] Rom 4.3 (cf. 4.9, 22); Gal 3.6; Jas 2.23. As Jas 2.23 and Rom 4.3 agree at two points against the LXX (δέ for καί and an added α in 'Αβράμ), some have suggested a literary link here; so e.g. Lüdemann, *Paul*, 143; Ludwig, *Wort*, 190-91. But here we could equally have a non-LXX reading; see on v. 23.

faith and works might somehow be divorced.⁹⁸ Beyond that, although the rabbis often discussed the relationship of deeds to study or learning,⁹⁹ they did not much reflect on the relationship between faith and works. Nor is there much evidence that others did before them.

Admittedly, commentators on Jas 2.14-26 regularly call attention to a few Jewish texts that seem pertinent in this connection, among them Sib. Or. 3.584-86, which implies that those with faith do not do deceitful deeds, and 4.152-55, which correlates a lack of faith with a deficiency of good deeds.¹⁰⁰ They are further wont to cite 4 Ezra 9.7, which speaks of those who will be saved on account either of their deeds or faith, as well as 13.23, which has God, in the latter days, protecting those who have deeds and faith.¹⁰¹ Texts such as these, however, are very few in number, and their assertions remain undeveloped. Certainly none of them dwells upon the subject of faith or the subject of works or undertakes to discuss the relationship of those two things. Nor do these Jewish sources raise the possibility that someone might have faith but not works.

To the extent of our knowledge, it was Paul, in response to issues arising from the Gentile mission, who first turned the relationship of faith to works into a topic for discussion and who further first declared that people are justified by the former without the latter. Is it not then natural to see Pauline ideas or slogans as somehow informing James—or rather unnatural not to see such?¹⁰² This is all the more so as Jas 2.14-26 is more denial than affirmation, less commandment than clarification. Not only does James here directly address someone with an opposing point of view, but the section, although preceded by an imperative (2.12: λαλεῖτε, ποιεῖτε) and followed by an imperative (3.1: μὴ γίνεσθε), is itself bereft of moral exhortations.¹⁰³ This differentiates it from every other portion of our letter. It appears that, in 2.14-26, James is not trying to change bad behavior but to refute a defective opinion.

---

⁹⁸ The command to 'do' or 'perform' Torah is all over the Pentateuch: Lev 19.37; 20.8; Num 15.35; Deut 5.1; etc.

⁹⁹ Sifre Deut 41, 48; m. 'Abot 3.10; ARN A 24; b. 'Abod. Zar. 17b; etc.

¹⁰⁰ Sib. Or. 3.584-86: 'For to them alone did the great God give wise counsel and faith and excellent understanding in their breasts. They do not honor with empty deceits works of men'; 4.152-55: 'But when faith in piety perishes from among men, and justice is hidden in the world, untrustworthy men, living for unholy deeds, will commit outrage, wicked and evil deeds'.

¹⁰¹ 4 Ezra 9.7-8: 'It will be that all who will be saved and will be able to escape on account of their works, or on account of the faith by which they have believed, will survive the dangers that have been predicted'; 13:23: 'The one who brings the peril at that time will protect those who fall into peril, who have works and faith toward the Almighty'. According to M.E. Stone, *Fourth Ezra*, Minneapolis, 1990, 296, 'works' and 'faith' are, in 4 Ezra, 'not very clearly differentiated and are used interchangeably'.

¹⁰² Cf. Syreeni, 'Legacy', 406: 'Had not Paul contrasted faith and works, it would hardly have occurred to the author of Jas to do that so vehemently; for obviously the whole thrust of the letter is that these two *cannot* be separated from each other'.

¹⁰³ Wischmeyer, 'Beobachtungen', 323-24, has a helpful chart of imperatives in James.

(iii) Those who suppose that James is not responding to Paul but to some other individual or movement have not been without alternative scenarios, among them these: (a) James counters lax or antinomian Christian Jews.[104] (b) He attacks the book of Hebrews and its famous adulation of faith.[105] (c) He opposes an arrangement whereby Christian missionaries allowed Gentile converts into the faith 'on particularly favorable terms. The newcomer need only profess a certain minimum faith. The representatives of the church assume responsibility for the requisite deeds.'[106] (d) He battles some variety of libertine Gnosticism.[107] (e) He counters followers of Peter or Peter himself, who was associated with the tradition that faith saves (Mk 5.34; 10.52; *et al.*) and who could have been thought of as a man who confessed faith (Mk 8.29) but did not follow through (Mk 14.66-72).[108] The truth, however, is that we have not a crumb of evidence that any of these imagined opponents ever put forward the thesis, which James opposes, that justification is by faith and not by works. We do, however, know of someone who undeniably did speak in those terms: Paul.

(iv) Burchard proposes that 2.14-26 is designed not to address any of the scenarios just noted but rather to focus on the problem, common to all religions for which conversion is central, that a change in convictions is not always accompanied by an authentic change of behavior.[109] Yet James

---

[104] Cf. Benson, 61; J.C. Hare, *The Victory of Faith*, 2nd ed., London, 1847, 33; Neander, 80-82 (Jewish Christians who imagined that they were saved in virtue of believing in one God); Macknight, 590 (Jewish Christians negligent of good works); Smith, 142-43 (some Jews thought that faith without works sufficed); Robertson, 128; Schlatter, 184-88. Several of those just named along with other older exegetes (e.g. Mayor, 96) quote, at second hand, Maimonides, *Comm. Mish.* on Sanh. 11.1—'As soon as a man has mastered the thirteen heads of the faith, firmly believing therein...though he may have sinned in every possible way...still he inherits eternal life'; 'practice depends upon doctrine and not doctrine on practice; and so we find God punishes more severely for doctrine than for practice'—as though these words, torn from their context, fairly represent a first-century strain of Jewish thought. For Simeon, 65, James is denouncing specifically those who show partiality; cf. vv. 1-13.

[105] So Bacon, 'Faith'. See further above, 70.

[106] So Reicke, 33. Cf. Davids, 21: 'a Jewish Christian attempt to minimize the demands of the gospel'. Where is the evidence for such a teaching in the early churches?

[107] This thesis is associated especially with Schammberger, *Kampf*. Cf. earlier Pfleiderer, *Christianity*, 301-305 ('doctrinaire Gnostic Paulinists'), and later Schoeps, *Theologie*, 343-45 (endorsing Schammberger). Blackman, 90, envisages a sort of Gnostic spirituality, akin to 'some forms of mysticism and pietism which have adopted a distinction between "spiritual" exercises and practical Christian living'. Against a Gnostic reading see Hoppe, *Hintergrund*, 106-107.

[108] This is the idiosyncratic thesis of Haacker, 'Justification'—which he forwards very tentatively. He also proposes that James has in view Christians who put too much stock in their miracle-working faith as opposed to acts of charity; cf. 1 Cor 13.

[109] Burchard, 113, observing that a 'weak Christian' might find the rigoristic ethic of James too difficult and noting how often early Christian texts warn against not living one's faith (Mt 7.21, 26; 21.30; 1 Jn 1.6; 2.4, 9; 4.20; Rev 3.15-16; etc.). Parry,

could readily have insisted upon right action without bringing in the topic of 'justification' (he ignores it outside of 2.21-24) and without naming Abraham.[110] Burchard's thesis fails to explain precisely why James links his discussion of faith and works with the patriarch and with justification, just as it fails to elucidate why James discusses in particular Gen 15.6, a text the NT quotes only in Romans, Galatians, and James. If, however, Paul is in the background, a straightforward explanation offers itself.

In line with this, although James wishes to stress the importance of works, not the value of faith, he quotes a text, Gen 15.6, that mentions only belief: 'Abraham believed and it was reckoned to him as righteousness'. Nothing is here said of works. Near to hand is the inference that James turns his attention to Gen 15.6 because someone before him had drawn from that Scripture a conclusion—Abraham was justified by faith, not works—with which he disagrees. It very much looks as though James is saying: No, contrary to what someone else teaches, Gen 15.6 does not demonstrate justification by faith apart from works, because Abraham's faith did not exist without deeds: 'faith co-operated with his deeds and... through deeds, faith was perfected' (2.22). As others have observed, 'one gets the impression that James refers to Gn 15[6] only because he anticipates this text as an objection to his argument'.[111] And, once more, we have sufficient explanation for this in Paul, who uses Gen 15.6 to support his belief in justification by faith rather than works.

(v) Those who see things otherwise regularly emphasize that Judaism was much interested in Gen 15.6, and they further stress that Jewish tradition tied that verse to Abraham's deeds.[112] Yet James and Paul set themselves apart from the comparable Jewish texts insofar as not one of the latter intimates that faith and works might be differentiated or implies that one of those two things might exist without the other.[113] James and Paul further distinguish themselves because they alone share the verbal expressions catalogued above. The Jewish parallels do not explain James nearly as effectively as the Pauline parallels do.

Discussion, 67, seems to have a similar view, and maybe already Calvin, *Inst.* 3.17.11. See also Bauckham, *Wisdom*, 126-27. Ropes, 204, observes: 'The contrast of faith and works will appear wherever faith is held to be the fundamental characteristic of the true members of the religious community, while at the same time a body of laws regulating conduct is set forth as binding', and 'this will always call out protests like that of James'. Maier, 126, calls the issue 'zeitunabhängig'. Cf. Tertullian, *Paenit.* 5.10 CSEL 76 ed. Borleffs, 152 ('some say that the Lord is satisfied if he is looked up to with the heart and mind even if one does not act'); Jerome, *Mic.* 1.3.5/8 CCSL 76 ed. Adriaen, 460 (some say: 'if you have faith it is not necessary to be always holy').

[110] Cf. Popkes, 'Justification'.

[111] Lorenzen, 'Faith', 232.

[112] See below, on v. 23, and Penner, *Eschatology*, 63-65.

[113] Note also Lüdemann, *Paul*, 143: 'Prior to Paul no one had ever advocated that Abraham was not justified by works'.

(vi) That Jas 2.14-26 is a negative response to Paul coheres with what we learn from Paul's own epistles: the apostle had opponents, and his teaching about justification by faith in particular was controversial. We also know, from Paul's self-defense in Galatians and from his more balanced presentation in Romans, that Abraham and Gen 15.6 were for him keys to the debate in which he found himself. So when we find another early Christian writer citing Gen 15.6 and then arguing for a position that, at least on the surface, seems to be the exact opposite of Paul's position—'You see that a man is justified by works and not by faith alone' (Jas 2.24)—one's thoughts naturally tend in a certain direction.

(vii) Our letter is attributed to 'James'—presumably, as argued in the Introduction, James of Jerusalem, the brother of Jesus. Now Paul, in Gal 2.12, declares with some bitterness that, 'before certain men came from James', Peter 'ate with the Gentiles; but when they came he drew back and separated himself, fearing the circumcision party'. This is evidence that, whatever James of Jerusalem thought of Paul, some who professed association with James opposed what they understood, rightly or wrongly, to be Paul's teaching about faith.

The fact looms large when one recalls that, in later times, some still thought of James and Paul as opponents. In the Epistula Petri, a short pseudepigraphon written in the third or fourth century, Peter addresses James, defending himself with these words: 'Some from among the Gentiles have rejected my lawful preaching and have preferred a lawless (ἄνομον) and absurd doctrine of the man who is my enemy'.[114] This is a clear allusion to Paul and his purported antinomianism, and the author assumes that James will concur with Peter's negative assessment. Similar is the so-called Ascents of James, which traces authentic Christianity not to the twelve disciples but to James of Jerusalem. In this book, most likely written in the second century, James comes into fierce conflict with 'a certain hostile man', a thinly veiled reference to Paul.[115] The latter even tries to kill James, and while in this he fails, his law-free mission prevents the wholesale conversion of the Jewish people.

Given that some Christians in the first and later centuries thought of James and Paul as theological rivals, and given that Jas 2.14-26 appears to contradict Paul, can it be nothing save coincidence that our passage belongs to a pseudepigraphon ascribed to James? Should we not rather find in Jas 1.1 a signal that our epistle's discussion of faith and works may represent a community that took itself to be at odds with Paul?

---

[114] 2.3 GCS 42 ed. Rehm, 2. For introductory issues see J. Irmscher and G. Strecker, "The Pseudo-Clementines," in *New Testament Apocrypha II: Writings Related to the Apostles, Apocalypses, and Related Subjects*, rev. ed., Cambridge, UK, 2003, 483-94; also G. Strecker, *Das Judenchristentum in den Pseudoklementinen*, rev. ed., Berlin, 1981, 58-62.

[115] See especially R.E. Van Voorst, *The Ascents of James*, Atlanta, 1989.

To sum up the argument so far: the evidence that Jas 2.14-16 is a negative response to Paul is considerable. Indeed, that James 'addresses a position which claims its roots in Paul's teaching' is a view that is not just probable but, as Popkes puts it, 'obvious'.[116]

This result inevitably raises the question of whether James responds to Romans and/or Galatians in particular or instead to oral reports or rumors about Pauline theology. Unfortunately, we cannot confidently settle the issue of whether James had read or heard one or more Pauline letters, although this commentary tends toward that opinion.[117] We can, however, make a good guess as to how James might have thought of Paul's teaching, no matter how he learned of it.

Paul several times insists that he is not, in effect, an antinomian.[118] Particularly instructive is Rom 3.8: some, Paul tells us, accuse him of teaching that one can do evil that good may come. This is all the evidence we need to establish that, whatever Paul himself believed or taught, some perceived him—for reasons one can understand[119]—as teaching a dangerous lawlessness.[120]

Romans 3.8 is further of note because it belongs to Paul's discussion of justification by faith; and the same is true of Rom 6.1-2,[121] from which it seems to follow that some who accused Paul of antinomianism

---

[116] Popkes, 'Justification', 135. Cf. Pfleiderer, *Influence*, 136; Schoeps, *Theologie*, 346.

[117] For the view that James knew some of Paul's letters see above, 62-67.

[118] Rom 3.8 ('And why not do evil that good may come?—as some people slanderously charge us with saying'); 6.1-2 ('What shall we say then? Are we to continue in sin that grace may abound? By no means!'); 6.15 ('What then? Are we to sin because we are not under law but under grace? By no means!'); 1 Cor 6.12 ('"All things are lawful for me", but not all things are beneficial. "All things are lawful for me", but I will not be dominated by anything'); 10.23 ('"All things are lawful", but not all things are helpful. "All things are lawful", but not all things build up'); Gal 5.13 ('you were called to freedom, brothers; only do not use your freedom as an opportunity for the flesh, but through love be servants of one another'). I leave aside here the possibility that James addresses hyper-Paulinists, not Paul himself. Although a very common thesis, it is otiose. Cf. Lüdemann, *Paul*, 145: 'No text known to us illustrating the gnostic use of Paul corresponds to the position presupposed in James 2. Further, in deutero-Pauline literature, which theoretically must also be considered when enumerating Paul's opponents, the term "works" is adopted in a positive sense, so that a supposed attack of James against Paul's followers would be even less likely than against Paul himself. (In this case, James would be laboring under an even greater misunderstanding than if he were attacking Paul himself.)'

[119] See K. Haacker, 'Der "Antinomismus" des Paulus im Kontext antiker Gesetzestheorie', in *Geschichte—Tradition—Reflexion, vol. 3*, ed. H. Cancik, H. Lichtenberger, and P. Schäfer, Tübingen, 1996, 387-404.

[120] One recalls that Luther coined the word 'antinomian' for people he opposed, some of whom—e.g. Johann Agricola—thought of themselves as only carrying forward Luther's own ideas.

[121] One might even urge that Rom 6–8 in its entirety is largely driven by the specter of antinomianism.

did so precisely in connection with his claims about justification by faith.[122]

Discussions of James and Paul sometimes go awry here. Many Christian theologians and commentators have insisted, rightly, that Paul was not a libertine, from which they have inferred, wrongly, that James can hardly be attacking him for such. The implicit premise is that James must have understood Paul aright. But what reason, apart from theological reverence for a canonical author, do we have for supposing that James had plumbed the depths of Pauline theology and accurately understood it?[123] Paul is a very difficult author, his thoughts sometimes dense, his arguments not always pellucid. Some understandably still wonder whether his teaching about faith and works is really coherent.[124] Whatever the resolution of that matter, Paul had the habit of formulating stark and provocative antinomies, such as 'justified by faith in Christ, and not by works of the law' (Gal 2.16). It would not be at all remarkable if the author of James, as a representative of some sort of Christian Judaism, and as one who was so keen on the integrity of word and deed, was troubled by Paul's apparent denigration of 'works'—whether he understood Paul to be disparaging 'works of the law' or 'good works' in general.

The correct understanding of Paul is here beside the point, because we know that the apostle's self-understanding did not correlate with the perceptions of everyone else; and if some of his contemporaries found his teaching about justification by faith to be implicitly antinomian, why not also the author of our epistle?[125] The recurrent observation that, if James is answering Paul, he misunderstands him and so does not hit the target, may be theologically pertinent, even consoling; but it is beside the historical point, which is that polemic is by its nature typically less than fair.[126] Matthew 23 does not accurately portray the scribes and Pharisees. Irenaeus and Epiphanius are scarcely spot on when they depict this or that heretic. Roman Catholic theologians sometimes caricatured the Protestants' *sola fide*.[127] And John Henry Newman incorrectly related

---

[122] Lüdemann, *Paul*, 147-48, observes that 1 Clem. 32–33 shows the same transition—from teaching justification by faith to repudiating antinomianism.

[123] Even intelligent people of goodwill often misunderstand what they read, as any author who has published enough books knows all too well.

[124] See especially H. Räisänen, *Paul and the Law*, 2nd ed., Tübingen, 1983.

[125] And all the more if Syreeni, 'Legacy', 406, is near the truth in his conjecture that 'the Pauline slogan of faith without works was repeated in a situation where not all community members received the care and protection they needed'.

[126] Note Farrar, *Days*, 353: 'the teaching of St. Paul was intensely original. It was not easy for anyone to grasp its full meaning; and it was quite impossible for any hostile and prejudiced person to understand it at all.'

[127] Note W.H. van de Pol, *The Christian Dilemma*, New York, 1953, 33, regarding Catholic and Protestant relations: 'The greatest grievance either party has is exactly this: that the other side persists in attacking points of view that are merely imaginary, and in imputing motives that have been distorted out of all recognition'.

what Luther and Calvin had to say about justification. 'It is the nature of disagreements that *opponents do not understand each other*'.[128] More than that, opponents often caricature[129] or misrepresent each other deliberately.[130]

All we require for a plausible reading of James is the knowledge that some Christian Jews in the ancient world found Paul's formulations about faith and works problematic. And that knowledge we have, in Paul's own writings.

Additionally pertinent in this connection is James' knowledge of the Jesus tradition, for it recurrently emphasizes the eschatological consequences of one's behavior. In Mt 7.24-27 = Lk 6.47-49 (Q), the one who does what Jesus demands weathers the eschatological storm whereas the one who behaves otherwise comes to ruin. In Mt 10.32-33 = Lk 12.8-9 (Q), those who confess Jesus win salvation while those who deny him lose salvation. In Mt 12.37, the right words will justify their speakers at the end just as the wrong words will condemn those who uttered them.[131] And in Mt 25.31-46, entering into life is contingent upon showing kindness to the unfortunate whereas the sentence of darkness falls upon those who do not show such kindness. In sum, to do evil is to receive condemnation at the end; to do good is to receive reward at the end.[132]

What do such texts have to do with Paul and James? Commentators since Origen have knit their brows over the presence in Paul's letters of justification by faith and judgment by works. Many have indeed detected here a 'contradiction', others a 'paradox'.[133] They have done so because

---

[128] Limberis, 'Provenance', 410. Cf. E.L. Allen, 'Controversy in the New Testament', *NTS* 1 (1954–55), 144: 'One would have thought that the history of theological discussion shows clearly that no limits whatsoever can be set *a priori* to the possibilities of misunderstanding'. According to K. Lehmann and W. Pannenberg, *The Condemnations of the Reformation Era*, Minneapolis, 1990, 56, 'in the sixteenth century, mutual condemnations could be pronounced in a number of cases only because the two sides did not listen carefully enough to each other'.

[129] Cf. Jackson-McCabe, 'Politics', 617 n. 65: 'Those Paul refers to in Rom 3:8... clearly had both some knowledge of his teaching and some intention to make a mockery of it. This is obvious regardless of whether their own position on ethics...represented an actual, logical contradiction' of what Paul himself taught.

[130] Cf. U. Schnelle, *Theology of the New Testament*, Grand Rapids, MI, 2009, 625: 'James could have intentionally misrepresented the Pauline position or simply misunderstood it'.

[131] ἐκ γὰρ τῶν λόγων σου δικαιωθήσῃ; cf. Jas 2.21, 24, 25.

[132] See further A.P. Stanley, *Did Jesus Teach Salvation by Works?*, Eugene, OR, 2006. Although a strong theological agenda drives this book, it rightly sees the fundamental soteriological significance of works in the Jesus tradition.

[133] Cf. Bultmann, *Theology*, 1.75 ('It is noteworthy and indicative of the extent to which Paul keeps within the framework of general Christian preaching, that he does not hesitate, in at least seeming contradiction to his doctrine of justification by faith alone, to speak of judgment according to one's works'); H.A.A. Kennedy, *St. Paul's Conceptions of the Last Things*, London, 1904, 201 (Paul's invocation of the last judgment is part of a 'profound paradox').

they understand Paul's teaching about justification to sit uneasily beside a soteriological role for works.[134] Now whether or not this is a fair take on Paul does not matter. The point is rather this. If, because of one's immersion in the Jesus tradition, one believed that salvation is not independent of how one behaves, and if one further failed to see how Paul's ideas about justification harmonize with the prospect of an eschatological judgment according to works, would one not almost inevitably find Paul problematic?

According to Rom 10.9-10, 'If you confess with your lips that Jesus is Lord and believe in your heart that God raised him from the dead, you will be saved. For a person believes with his heart and so is justified, and he confesses with his lips and so is saved'. It takes little imagination to envision a non-Pauline Christian wondering about these words.[135] How do they comport with the texts from the Jesus tradition cited above? Paul seemingly avows that confession and belief suffice for salvation. But was not Jesus remembered as having said just the opposite, that confession is not enough? Calling Jesus 'Lord, Lord' without doing what he asks will not, according to Mt 7.21-23, save.[136] Maybe it is only because Jesus and Paul now appear side by side in the NT canon, and because Christians have such a long history of reading the one in the light of the other harmoniously, that they fail to see how easy it must have been for some to find what Paul taught to be at odds with what Jesus taught.[137]

The view of this commentary is that James was just such a Christian. How then does Jas 2.14-26 function in his epistle? The audience ostensibly addressed—Jews of the diaspora—contains Christian Jews and non-Christian Jews; see on 1.1. It follows that we should consider 2.14-26 from two points of view and ask not only what a Christian Jew might have made of the section but also what a non-Christian Jew might have made of it. The function of the passage depends upon the knowledge and religious location of the readers.

Christian Jews reading James and more or less familiar with rumors regarding Paul's teaching on justification by faith would have understood the passage to be polemical. James denies what Paul was taken to affirm, and he does so in a tone far from congenial. The intention of the author and the implications for informed readers are obvious.

---

[134] Cf. the famous assertion of A. Schweitzer, *The Mysticism of Paul the Apostle*, New York, 1968, 225, that there is no pathway from Paul's theory of justification by faith to ethics.

[135] Note T. Rees, *The Racovian Catechism*, London, 1818, 322-23 (an attempt to resolve the tension between Jas 2.26 and Rom 10.9), and see the discussion of Nienhuis, *Paul*, 222-23.

[136] Cf. Lk 6.46. On the parallels between Jas 2.14-26 and Mt 7.21-23 note Theobald, 'Kanon', 185-86; also below n. 293.

[137] There is another relevant consideration. If, as this commentator holds, James, like the evangelist Matthew (cf. 5.17-20), reckoned the entire Torah to be yet in force, it goes without saying that such a conviction would have required opposition to Pauline theology, which regards the law as being, in fundamental respects, passé.

What might non-Christian Jews have thought? My suggestion is that our author was likely trying to correct a misinterpretation of Christianity that he knew to be current among some outsiders. If, as we know happened, some Christians accused other Christians of antinomian tendencies, surely some Jews must have accused Christians in general of such tendencies.[138] The sorts of rumors that gathered around Paul (cf. Acts 21.20-21) almost certainly became rumors about Christians in general. Do not the followers of Jesus, some must have asserted, exalt belief at the expense of doing? But James argues to the contrary. Whatever readers may have heard, our author's religious group does not disparage works.

2.14-26, when read by non-Christian Jews, would have functioned neither as exhortation nor as polemic, but rather as apologetics.[139] For Torah-observant outsiders, the passage would be a strong statement that Christians, or at least those James speaks for, do not, despite the rumors, put belief above works. The upshot would not be direct refutation of Paul—about whom non-Christian Jews may have known or cared little or nothing—but proper perception of and sympathetic appreciation for the Christian Judaism of James.

The manner of James' argument is more than consistent with this proposal. It is quite telling that whereas Paul, when he reasons about Abraham, faith, and works, appeals to specifically Christian themes—the role of Jesus, for instance, and the faith of the uncircumcised[140]—James, in reacting to Paul, somehow manages to avoid such themes altogether. Unlike the man he implicitly criticizes, he says nothing at all about the crucifixion or Jesus' resurrection or the coming of Gentiles to faith.[141] He instead conducts his argument in purely Jewish terms, not making use of a single distinctively Christian idea.[142] He cites Genesis and refers to Abraham (vv. 21-23). He refers to Rahab and summarizes her story in Joshua (v. 25). And he writes of demons trembling not in response to a Christian *theologoumenon* but in response to the substance of the Shema', the closest thing to an ancient Jewish creed (εἶς ἐστιν ὁ θεός, v. 19).

This last fact is particularly striking. James uses πιστεύω + ὅτι in v. 19. Now the idiom in other sources can introduce properly Christian confessions,[143] and it would have been easy enough for our author, like some later exegetes,[144] to allude to or quote a Christian statement of faith,

---

[138] Cf. Bonsirven, 'Jacques', 788: Jews who understood the Christian doctrine of salvation by faith as something not entailing good works would have been scandalized.

[139] Although Theissen, 'Intention', 70-77, has also urged that Jas 2.14-26 is best characterized not as polemic but as an apology, his reading is very different from the one proposed here. For him, James corrects Pauline distortions of Jewish Christianity.

[140] Rom 3.21-26; 4.9-12, 24-25; Gal 3.1, 8-9, 13-14, 16.

[141] He also, unlike Paul, 'does not use Abraham in any way to issue a specifically Christian critique of Judaism'; so J. Siker, *Disinheriting the Jews*, Louisville, 1991, 101.

[142] Although lines within 2.14-26 have reminded commentators of this or that saying of Jesus, clear dependence is not once indicated.

[143] E.g. Jn 11.42; 8.24; 20.31; 1 Thess 4.14; 1 Jn 5.1, 5; Gk. Apoc. Ezra 4.35.

[144] Theophylact *ad loc.* PG 125.1157B; Leigh, 370-71; Manton, 241; *et al.*

such as that Jesus is Lord or that God raised Jesus from the dead.[145] Certainly the argument would work just as well. Why then does our Christian writer not refer here to a distinctively Christian belief? Or why does he not appeal to Jesus as the great exemplar of faith and works (cf. Heb 12.1-3)? We have an answer if we take Jas 1.1 seriously. Even when countering the thoroughly Christian argument of Paul, James makes his case without adverting to Christian beliefs because he hopes his letter will fall into the hands of people who do not share such beliefs, and he wants his argument to work for them.

Verse 14. The section opens (asyndetically) with two rhetorical queries; cf. 4.1. Additional questions follow in vv. 15-16, 20, 21, and 25, so that the whole unit is largely interrogatory. The questions go unanswered, on the assumption that an appeal to common sense, to the consciences of readers, and to shared religious convictions will summon the obvious responses. Everyone should know that 'charity is neither mere speech nor simple salutation but support and showing forth works';[146] and all readers of the Tanak will be familiar with its recurrent demand to 'keep my decrees and laws' (Lev 18.5); and anyone acquainted with the Jesus tradition will know that its central figure was remembered as demanding people do difficult things in order to inherit eternal life.[147] Who then in James' mind could deny that faith without works is dead, or that 'orthodoxy must prove itself in orthopraxis'?[148]

τί τὸ ὄφελος.[149] Johnson, 237, suggests a contemporary paraphrase: 'What difference does it make?' The Greek, which literally means, 'What is the profit?',[150] appears again in v. 16, where the connotations might be different. In the present context, where it is followed by μὴ δύναται κτλ., the sense is: What will it profit him at the last judgment? Cf. the Vulgate's future: *quid proderit*.

The phrase occurs repeatedly in Epictetus and can be reckoned a feature of diatribe.[151] Yet Philo, Paul, and other early Christian writers

---

[145] The lack of a Christian confession puzzles some commentators. Oesterley, 446, citing 1 Cor 8.6 ('there is one God, the Father...and one Lord, Jesus Christ'), writes: a christological addition 'might well have been expected in the verse before us; its omission must perhaps be accounted for owing to the very pronounced Judaistic character of the writer'.

[146] Chrysostom, *Hom. Rom* 7.5 PG 60 447.

[147] See above, 454. Cf. also Mk 9.43-48.

[148] So Fay, 'Weisheit', 409.

[149] 03 04* 1175 1243 omit τό. This reading, which Mayor, 96, accepts, assimilates James to common usage. 03 04* 631 1175 L593 Dam also have τὶ ὄφελος in v. 16.

[150] ὄφελος: NT: 3×. LXX: Job 15.3. Gk. Pseudepigrapha (Denis): 0×. Philo: 48×. Josephus: 10×.

[151] Epictetus, *Diatr.* 1.4.16; 1.6.4; 1.25.29; 2.17.20, 34; 3.1.30; 3.7.31; 3.10.7; 3.24.51, 75; 4.1.94; 4.4.4; 4.8.7; *Ench.* 24.5. Cf. Aristotle, *Eth. nic.* 1155A; Polybius 3.7.5; Dio Chrysostom 38.29; 48.9; Lucian, *Ind.* 2.3; Iamblichus, *Protr.* 25.29; etc. It is not typically a transitional phrase.

also use the expression,[152] which likewise has a precise Hebrew equivalent, מה־בצע.[153] Moreover, the closely related interrogatory τίς/τί + ὠφέλεια or a form of ὠφελέω appears over half a dozen times in the LXX, including LXX wisdom literature, as well as in the Jesus tradition and elsewhere.[154]

ἀδελφοί μου. See on 1.2. The expression will be used next in 3.1, where it again opens a new section.

ἐὰν πίστιν λέγῃ τις ἔχειν ἔργα δὲ μὴ ἔχῃ; Cf. v. 18 (ἀλλ' ἐρεῖ τις) and 5.19 (ἐάν τις...πλανηθῇ) and note the ἐάν in the next verse. The hypothetical sunders two things James wishes to hold together, things which evidently someone else has been thought to divide. πίστις (see on 1.3) occurs eleven times in this section. The anarthrous noun signals a new subject beyond 2.1-13.

πίστις has various shades of meaning in James, so one must judge its connotations from the immediate context.[155] It has a robust and positive sense in 1.3, 6; 2.5; 5.15, being in these places (and 2.1?) perhaps something like whole-hearted allegiance and commitment to and unconditional trust in God. In 2.14, 17, 18, 20, 22, and 24, however, it can be understood to mean something close to intellectual consent, like *credo* + accusative, or perhaps a purely professed or confessed faith (and so, from the point of view of other verses, a diminished or inadequate faith).[156] The latter sort of faith ('belief'), which resides in the head but not the heart,

---

[152] Philo, *Leg.* 1.79; 3.41, 121; *Post.* 86, 87; *Deus* 152; *Agr.* 134; *Migr.* 55; *Abr.* 73; *Mos.* 1.235; *Spec.* 3.203; *Flacc.* 186; *Legat.* 337, 357; 1 Cor 15.32; Justin Martyr, *Dial.* 4.5; 14.1 PTS 47 ed. Marcovich, 78. 92; Acts Jn 20.8 ed. Bonnet, 162.

[153] Gen 37.26; Ps 30.10; Mal 3.13. Cf. also the Aramaic ממון מה in Tg. Ps.-J. Gen 37.26 and the מה תועלת of b. Pesaḥ. 108b.

[154] LXX Ps 29.9; Job 21.15; Hab 2.18; Wis 5.8; Ecclus 20.30; 34.23-25; 41.14; Let Aris. 241; Mt 16.26; Mk 8.36; Lk 9.25; Rom 3.1; 1 Cor 14.6; Ign. *Smyr.* 5.2; Gk. Apoc. Ezra 6.23; Apoc. Sed. 7.8. Cf. also the comparable τί χρήσιμον, as in LXX Gen 37.26; T. Job 34.2; Plutarch, *Mor.* 865C; Epictetus, *Diatr.* 1.6.34 (τίς χρῆσις); etc., as well as the οὐδὲν ὠφελοῦμαι of 1 Cor 13.3, where Paul declares that faith without love counts for nothing, and Ps.-Clem. Hom. 8.7.4-5 GCS 42 ed. Rehm, 124 (explicating Mt 7.21): οὐ γὰρ ὠφελήσει τινὰ τὸ λέγειν, ἀλλὰ τὸ ποιεῖν. ἐκ παντὸς οὖν τρόπου καλῶν ἔργων χρεία. Frankemölle, 430-31, observes that elements of diatribe were not confined to philosophers and their writings, and James may have picked up such elements from other sources, including Ecclesiasticus.

[155] For Davids, 'Traditions', 42, different meanings for the same word are a sign that James consists of 'originally independent sayings and sermons'.

[156] Cf. the two definitions of 'faith'—believing doctrine on the one hand, trust and hoping in God on the other—in John of Damascus, *F.O.* 83 (4.10) PTS 12 ed. Kotter, 186. Exegetes often apply such distinctions to our verse; cf. Bede and Hus, as in n. 281. Verseput, 'Puzzle', offers a novel interpretation of 'faith' in our passage: it is not an internal quality but piety or religious practice. Thus 'faith without works' is religion without obedience, εὐσέβεια or θεοσεβής without δικαιοσύνη or φιλανθρωπία. Against this, Verseput has to deny, implausibly, a Pauline background; and it is not clear that his reading makes good sense of v. 19. Does demonic faith stand for Christian religious rites?

can exist without deeds. The former (cf. *credo* + dative) cannot lack such: for such faith to come without deeds would be a contradiction in terms.[157]

Interpreters sometimes discuss whether the faith of v. 14 is false (Osiander, 723: 'pseudoChristian') or genuine,[158] and whether λέγῃ expresses pretense.[159] Calvin, 283, argues that James here employs a 'shorn sense of faith' as a concession to rhetoric.[160] Böhmer contends that James here approximates the sense that his opponent gives to πίστις.[161] Yet it matters little whether the speaker truthfully professes to possess a purely intellectual faith (cf. v. 19) or (incorrectly) claims such.[162] Nor is the degree of the speaker's conscious hypocrisy relevant (there need not be any). All that matters is that the claim to faith is unaccompanied by corresponding deeds.[163]

The Christian character of πίστις goes unremarked and, in view of the recipients named in 1.1, cannot be assumed.[164] Certainly the faith of v. 19 (εἷς ἐστιν ὁ θεός) is not distinctively Christian.[165] It rather characterizes Judaism.

---

[157] Cf. Calvin, 283: 'it is not in fact faith at all'. Indeed, for Calvin, 284, 'our whole discussion is not on the subject of faith but on a certain uninformed opinion of God'. The intriguing proposal of R. Walker, 'Werken', that 'faith' stands for 'Gesetzesfrömmigkeit', and that James opposes a love of the law unaccompanied by action, does not seem to have won a following. Although the thesis fits well with 1.19-27 and 4.17, 'faith' involves much more than 'Gesetzesfrömmigkeit' in 2.5 and most of chap. 1. For effective criticism see Nicol, 'Faith', 11-15.

[158] Medieval Catholic exegetes tended to read our passage in terms of 'unformed faith' (*fides informis*)—this being assent to Christian truths without infused grace—and 'formed faith' (*fides formata*)—this being faith active through love; cf. P. Lombard, *Sent.* 3.23.4-5 PL 192.805-806; Aquinas, *Summa* 2/2 q. 4. a. 3-4; q. 5 a. 2, and see Beumer, 'Daemones'. The Reformers stridently rejected finding such a distinction here; cf. Calvin, 282-83.

[159] Review of discussion in Huther, 86-87. According to Cranfield, 'Message', 398, λέγῃ 'should be allowed to control our interpretation of the whole paragraph': James 'does not regard the faith which is without works as really faith at all'.

[160] Jeremias, 'Paul', 370, *et al.* say much the same thing.

[161] Böhmer, 'Glaube'. He judges James to hold that 'πίστις without ἔργα is not πίστις' (255).

[162] In either case, the remark of Maclaren, 416, seems appropriate: 'The people who least live their creeds are not seldom the people who shout loudest about them'.

[163] Cf. Nicol, 'Faith', 16 ('James' point is not that faith without works is not faith; as faith he does not criticize it, but merely stresses that faith does not fulfil its purpose when it is not accompanied by works'); Fabris, 180 (the issue is not the content of faith but its quality or character).

[164] Although commentators regularly read such in; cf. Manton, 232; Guyse, 577 ('boast of his belief in Christ, and expecting salvation from him'); Musser, 130; Adamson, 121 ('to "have faith" in our Lord Jesus Christ'); Frankemölle, 430 ('faith in Jesus as the exalted Lord'); Proctor, 'Faith', 313-14 ('faith' = 'the Christian religion'); Fabris, 179; *et al.* Contrast Bartlet, *Age*, 242-43.

[165] Contrast Ropes, 203-204, who even speaks of 'adherence to Christianity' and 'church-membership'. This is to read the rest of the NT into James.

ἔργον—the word is invariably positive in our letter—is the other key word of 2.14-26. It is employed twelve times in the section and means '(good) deeds'.[166] It is perhaps the functional equivalent of the rabbinic גמילות חסדים, usually translated 'deeds of loving kindness'.[167] m. 'Abot 1.2 makes such deeds one of the three pillars upon which the world stands, and גמילות חסדים are often acts that would fall under Lev 19.18 (quoted in Jas 2.8) and its close relative, the golden rule.[168] See further below. On λέγῃ, Knowling, 53, remarks: 'an inoperative faith can only testify to itself by saying, not by doing'. This may in fact explain why the verb has been inserted: the profession of faith is its only evidence.

ἔχω + πίστιν (cf. also v. 18) appears in Rom 14.22; 1 Cor 13.2; and Phlm 5, and as James is otherwise interacting with Paul, one might wonder about influence here. The idiom, however, is also attested in Jas 2.1, the Jesus tradition (including a saying that James likely knew; see on 1.6), other Christian sources, 4 Macc 16.22, and Josephus, not to mention secular sources, above all Plutarch.[169] ἔχω + ἔργα/ον (cf. also vv. 17, 18) is also a traditional idiom.[170]

Despite the correlation with 1.22, James is not here exhorting his audience to be more than hearers. He is instead addressing a theological issue. The closest parallels to 2.14-26 are not Mt 7.24-27 = Lk 6.47-49 and other scriptures that seek to stir individuals to action.[171] They are

---

[166] For this use of ἔργον (cf. καλῆς ἀναστροφῆς τὰ ἔργα in 3.13) note LXX Isa 32.17; Prov 10.16; T. Naph. 2.10; T. Ash. 4.2; T. Benj. 5.3; Let. Aris. 272; Sib. Or. 3.220, 233; Mt 5.16; Acts 9.36; 2 Cor 9.8; Heb 10.24; etc.; cf. the rabbinic מעשה, as in m. 'Abot 3.17. See further Spitta, 72-76. As James supplies only a couple of concrete illustrations, Christian tradition has often sought to clarify and enlarge. E.g. John of the Cross, *Subida del Monte Carmelo* 3.16.1 ed. Rodríguez and Salvador, 414, thinks of 'works of love'. So too Augustine, *De gratia et lib. arb. lib. 1* 7.18 PL 44.892; Bernard of Clairvaux, *Ad Henricum arch.* 4.14 Bernardi Opera 7 ed. Leclercq and Rochais, 111, Nicholas of Gorran, 74; P. Lombard, *Sent.* 3.23.4 PL 192.805; Gasparo Contarini, *Epistola de justificatione* Corpus Catholicorum 7 ed. Hünermann, 33-34; Gilpin, 594. Gal 5.6 has played a role here; see n. 35; also 1 Jn 3.16-18; see n. 219. Contrast the complaint of Manton, 232: 'It is folly of the Papists to restrain it to acts of charity'. Seraphim of Sarov explicates James with this: 'the works of faith are: love, peace, patience, mercy, humility, tranquility, acceptance of the cross, life in union with the Holy Spirit'; quoted in V. Zander, *St. Seraphim of Sarov*, Crestwood, NY, 1975, 104.

[167] Cf. Mayor, 96: ἔργα = the ἔλεος of v. 13. For an attempt to relate James to the rabbinic concept of גמילות חסדים see Döpp, 'Sozialtradition'.

[168] Cf. P.H. Peli, 'The Havurot That Were in Jerusalem', *HUCA* 55 (1984), 68.

[169] The saying of Jesus appears in Mt 17.20; 21.21; Mk 11.22; Lk 17.6. Cf. also Mk 4.40; 1 Tim 1.19; Herm. *Vis.* 3.6.5; *Mand.* 5.2.3; 11.9; Justin, *1 Apol.* 52.1; Sib. Or. 5.285; Josephus, *Ant.* 15.134; 4 Ezra 13.23; Plutarch, *Mor.* 365F, 503D, 507C, 809F, 812F, 833F; etc.

[170] Cf. Jas 1.4; LXX Isa 62.11 (ἔχων... τὸ ἔργον); Philo, *Decl.* 6 (ἔργον ἔχει τίμιον); 4 Ezra 8.32 (*habentibus opera iusticiae*); 13.23 (*habent operas et fidem*); 2 Clem. 6.9 (ἔργα ἔχοντες ὅσια καὶ δίκαια); Acts Phil. 143 ed. Bonnet, 83 (ἐχέτω τὰ ἔργα ἴσα τοῖς λόγοις); Cassius Dio 52.4.1 (τὸ ἔργον δικαιότατον ἔχει); etc. The comparable rabbinic idiom is יש בו מעשים, as in ARN A 24.

[171] Those texts, however, are often cited; see n. 293.

rather those texts where Paul discusses faith and works in a theoretical fashion.[172]

The first issue for Paul was not faith as opposed to good deeds in general but faith as opposed to 'works of the law' in particular, and some scholars suppose these works to be boundary markers of the covenant with Israel.[173] Many have urged that James, by contrast, is interested in good deeds or 'works' in general (cf. 1.26–2.7); this then becomes an objection to interpreting James as a retort to Paul,[174] or at least for urging that, despite the apparent overlap of theme, James, if engaged with Paul, argues past him. But (i) the meaning of 'works' in Paul is controversial.[175] (ii) Paul uses the unqualified 'works' more often than 'works of the law'. (iii) Writings in the Pauline school or tradition often speak simply of 'works' instead of 'works of the law'.[176] (iv) For a Jew such as James, 'works of the law' and 'good works' would scarcely be distinguished. This is all the more apparent since Torah is central to the argument of the passage just before this one and since 1.25 clearly associates the law with ποιητὴς ἔργου.[177]

μὴ δύναται ἡ πίστις σῶσαι αὐτόν; For the traditional link between faith and being saved see on 5.15 (where the sense is admittedly different). Interrogatory μή occurs again in 3.12. The issue here is manifestly eschatological salvation; cf. 1.21; 2.12-13. Those who, because they are

---

[172] See above, 445-57. Contrast B. Weiss, 101 (James is concerned with a 'perverse practice'); Parry, *Discussion*, 48; Plummer, 588; Dibelius, 178; R. Walker, 'Werken'; Eckart, 'Terminologie'; Burchard, 114 (James is related to ancient discussions of the relationship of piety and righteousness); *et al.*

[173] So J.D.G. Dunn, *The Theology of Paul the Apostle*, Grand Rapids, MI, 1998, 554-66. Cf. Origen, *Rom.* 8.7 FC 2.4 ed. Heither, 248. For further discussion see C.E.B. Cranfield, '"The Works of the Law" in the Epistle to the Romans', *JSNT* 43 (1991), 89-101. One wonders whether some modern translations prefer rendering ἔργα in Jas 2 as 'deeds' or 'action(s)' (e.g. NIV, ISV, REB, TEV, Weymouth) instead of 'works' in order to discourage readers from surmising conflict with Paul. But Moo, 123, suggests a different reason: there is concern that the negative use of 'works' in Paul might detract from the positive use in James. Some of the older translations in any case also used 'deeds': Tyndale (1543), Cranmer (1539), Geneva (1557).

[174] See Pelagius, *Rom. ad* 3.28 TS 9.2 ed. Souter, 34; Beza, 563-64; Cajetan, 367; Calmet, 678; Wolzogen, 197-98; W. Wall, 346-47; F. Taylor, 55-56; Knowling, xli, xliv; Chaine, 56; Childs, *Canon*, 440; Johnson, 62-63; *et al*. This well-attested tradition goes back to Origen's commentary on Romans and appears in the early Luther, *Lectures on Romans*, Philadelphia, 1961, 102: in agreement with James, Paul 'does not say that faith justifies without its own works (for then it would not be faith...), but what he does say is that faith justifies without the works of the law'.

[175] Cf. Syreeni, 'Legacy', 402 n. 19: this is a matter for 'quite sophisticated exegesis'. See now J.C.R. de Roo, *Works of the Law at Qumran and in Paul*, Sheffield, 2007.

[176] E.g. Eph 2.9-10; 2 Tim 1.9; Pol. *Phil.* 1.3.

[177] See further Klein, *Werke*, 200; Avemarie, 'Werke', 302-303 ('works' in James and 'works of the law' in Paul are functionally equivalent); McCabe, *Logos*, 244-46; McKnight, 227-28. It is also possible that James deliberately modified Paul's expression; see Tsuji, *Glaube*, 194-95.

without works, are not saved will find themselves in Gehenna.[178] As Walker has it, from the first line of 2.14-26, 'all is seen *sub specie aeternitatis*'.[179] James is fond of δύναμαι (6×) and follows convention in linking it three times to σώζω.[180] ἡ is probably resumptive or has demonstrative sense: 'such/that faith'.[181]

It is an early Christian refrain that faith saves, one the Synoptic tradition notably uses several times.[182] Our writer might be thought implicitly to deny this theologoumenon. He does not, however, oppose faith as such (cf. 1.3; 2.1; 5.15) but 'faith alone' (v. 24), which means faith 'without works' (vv. 20, 26). Further, one must do justice to αὐτόν, as Huther, 87, observes: 'James does not affirm generally that faith cannot save, but that it cannot save him whose faith, on which he trusts, is destitute of works; for αὐτόν refers back to the subject τις'. So it would be over-subtle to imagine that 2.14 really counters a far-flung way of speaking.[183] James does not deny the importance of faith but rather a misapprehension or misuse of faith.

Verse 15. This verse, which illustrates the μὴ ποιήσαντι ἔλεος of v. 13, assumes that most readers are not naked and hungry but rather have enough of life's necessities to share with the needy.[184] That one can infer anything beyond this about the concrete situation of James or his envisaged audience is dubious.[185] We may have here little more than rhetorical caricature.

---

[178] Cf. Jas 3.6. See further Moo, 123-24. Some interpreters assure readers that infants or new converts who die soon after baptism and so never have the opportunity to do good works will not for that cause be damned; cf. John Mayer, *Ecclesiastica interpretatio*, London, 1627, 28; Wordsworth, 24. But this has nothing to do with James.

[179] R. Walker, 'Werken', 165. Cf. Lautenschlager, 'Gegenstand', 174: the question of what wins eschatological salvation is the theme of the whole section.

[180] 1.21; 2.14; 4.12. The idiom, which has Hebrew counterparts—יכל + ל + Hiphil of נצל as in 2 Kgs 18.29; Isa 36.14 and יכל + ל + Hiphil of ישׁע as in Jer 14.9; b. Soṭah 39b—occurs in LXX Isa 20.6; 46.2; Ezek 33.12; Mk 10.26; 15.31; Acts 15.1; Heb 5.7; 7.25; Josephus, *Ant.* 14.95; Herm. *Mand.* 12.6.3; Barn. 12.3; etc. It is also known to secular writers: Xenophon, *Mem.* 4.2.33; Epictetus, *Diatr.* 1.27.14; Dio Chrysostom 11.91; Atticus *apud* Eusebius, *P.E.* 15.9.3 ed. GCS 43.2 ed. Mras, 369; etc. Cf. Rom 1.16: δύναμις…εἰς σωτηρίαν.

[181] So Bengel, 495; Moo, 123; *et al.*

[182] E.g. Mk 5.34; 10.52; 16.16; Lk 17.19; 18.42; Acts 14.9; Rom 10.9; Eph 2.8; 1 Clem. 12.1; Ign. *Phil.* 5.2; Did. 16.5; Barn. 12.7; Herm. *Vis.* 3.8.3.

[183] Burchard, 112: 'James speaks against the *Sprache* of the tradition but not against its spirit'.

[184] Hilary of Arles *ad loc.* PLSup 3.71, even infers that James here addresses esp. 'the rich' (*divitibus*).

[185] Ropes, 206; Dibelius, 152-53; Mussner, 131; Davids, 121; and Frankemölle, 432, find stylized rhetoric. Others, including Plumptre, 70-71 (who sees the famine of Acts 11.28-30 in the background; so too Punchard, 366); Reicke, 32; Martin, 84-85; Burchard, 116; Popkes, 192, think of a situation known to the writer. Sanders, *Ethics*, 122-23, proposes that the main point of 2.14-26 is to prod the rich in the congregation to assist

Verses 15-16, which stand at the beginning of a small discourse, are much like 2.2-4, which also stand at the beginning of a small discourse: both are long rhetorical questions that feature ἐάν + description of unethical situation + εἴπητε/εἴπῃ + quoted words.[186] The verses do not exactly offer an example of faith without works. We rather have an illustration by way of analogy: James compares faith without works to expressions of good will without works. The worthlessness of the latter suggests the worthlessness of the former.[187] As Pemble puts it: 'If Charity towards the poore professed in words, but without workes be counterfeit, then faith in God professed in like manner without Obedience is also counterfeit not true'.[188]

ἐὰν ἀδελφὸς ἦ ἀδελφή.[189] This is the only occurrence of ἀδελφή in James, whereas ἀδελφός appears throughout; see on 1.2. The combination is less common than one might guess.[190] The reason 'brother' and 'sister' are joined here is that the words characterize not the recipients of the letter—who seem to be rhetorically envisioned as male—but rather describe human objects of compassion, who naturally belong to both sexes. Indeed, given the circumstances of James' world, women may have been more prominent among the needy; cf. the 'widow' of 1.27. They are in any case members of his community, part of the 'spiritual fraternity' (Hus, 205) to which he and his readers belong,[191] and they must

---

the poor; cf. 2.1-13. According to Coker, 'Nativism', 42, 2.15-16 may reflect James' opinion that Paul had failed to 'remember the poor' (Gal 2.10). For Moo, 122, the situation is 'hypothetical' yet 'typical'. Watson, 'Schemes', 120, offers that, while vv. 15-16 need not 'correspond exactly to an actual situation... we are on firm ground in inferring that partiality is exhibited by the audience'. Perhaps; but might this not be true of any human group of significant size? Some sins we always have with us. Bishop, *Apostles*, 185, commenting on James, observes of twentieth-century Jerusalem: '"go in peace"—*rūh ma'-as-salāmi*—[is] said to beggars in various stages of poverty outside places of worship or without the verb "go" to travelers being "seen off"'. Even if this corresponds to life two thousand years ago, a text can be true to life without addressing a concrete situation.

[186] Burge, 'Form', urges that vv. 15-17 are displaced, that vv. 18-20 originally followed v. 14. The argument is based upon a formal analysis of the structure of the section, not textual witnesses.

[187] So too Belser, 120; Dibelius, 152; Mussner, 131; Mozley, 'Faith', 484; Burchard, 116. Contrast Mayor, 96.

[188] Pemble, *Vindiciae Fidei*, 199.

[189] 02 04 044 206 **Byz** PsOec **L**:V **K**:B^mss insert δέ in second place. 621 1735 1842 Cyr K:S insert γάρ.

[190] But note Plato, *Leg.* 838A, 868E, 877B; LXX Num 6.7; 1 Cor 7.15; Mk 10.29 (plural); Apost. Const. 2.58.1 ed. Funk, 167. This last introduces a section that is closely related Jas 2.1-4; see above, 378. Against Cantinat, 141-42, one does not here think of husband and wife. And against Oesterley, 444, the mention of a 'sister' is not 'distinctively Christian'.

[191] Although most commentators assume and assert that this is the Christian community—e.g. Piscator, 732; Popkes, 192, even declares: 'doubtless a designation for "Mit-Christen"'—1.1 rather suggests that it is the Jewish community of the diaspora.

be included within the love command of v. 8. Some understandably draw a connection with the poor in the previous section.¹⁹²

γυμνοὶ ὑπάρχωσιν. γυμνός (Jas: 1×) can signify 'naked' (cf. Mk 14.51-52) or, as here, 'scantily clad'.¹⁹³ It means, in effect, 'in need of clothing', just as the subsequent λειπόμενοι κτλ. means, in effect, 'in need of food'. The subsequent θερμαίνεσθε shows that the individuals envisaged cannot get warm. The description is designed to evoke sympathy. Verse 2 ('a poor person with filthy clothes') is perhaps comparable. ὑπάρχω (Jas: 1×) + γυμνός was not a traditional idiom;¹⁹⁴ but clothing the naked or ill-clad—in imitation of the deity (Gen 3.21)¹⁹⁵—was standard in Jewish and Christian lists of good deeds, just as not doing the same appears in numerous accounts of vices.¹⁹⁶

Care for the hungry was conventionally associated with care for the naked.¹⁹⁷ That these ministries appear together memorably in Mt 25.31-46 has led many exegetes of James to cite the latter or even suggest that our author may have had that Synoptic text in mind.¹⁹⁸ One cannot, however, make the case for an intentional allusion or for conscious borrowing.¹⁹⁹

καὶ λειπόμενοι τῆς ἐφημέρου τροφῆς. Although λείπω²⁰⁰ occurs also in 1.4-5, ἐφήμερος²⁰¹ and τροφή²⁰² are Jamesian *hapax*. As ἐφήμερος + τροφή was a traditional Greek expression for 'daily food' or 'the day's supply of

---

¹⁹² So e.g. Hutchinson Edgar, *Poor*, 169-70: the brother or sister must be 'poor' (2.2, 5). He less plausibly thinks of itinerant radicals in both instances.

¹⁹³ Cf. Mayor, 97. Examples in LSJ., s.v. 5; BAGD, s.v. 2. REB: 'in rags'. Huther, 88: the word can be used of 'clothing that can hardly be considered as clothing'. Gundry, 924: 'lots of skin exposed to the cold'. Cf. ערום in 1 Sam 19.24; Job 22.6. According to BDF 135.4, the singular 'γυμνός or γυμνή [to match ἀδελφός or ἀδελφή] would have been harsh',

¹⁹⁴ Thus the reason for the use of ὑπάρχω instead of the synonymous ἔχω remains unclear. Adamson, 122-23; Popkes, 193; *et al.* suggest that it hints at a protracted condition, not a one-time affair.

¹⁹⁵ Cf. Tg. Ps.-J. Deut 34.6 (God 'taught us to clothe the naked because of his having clothed Adam and Eve'); Midr. Ps 118.17.

¹⁹⁶ Job 22.6-7; Isa 58.6-7; Ezek 18.7, 16; Tob 1.17; 4.16; T. Zeb. 7.1-4; Mt 25.36-44; 2 En. 9.1; 10.5; 42.8; 63.1; T. Jacob 7.25; Mek. on Exod 14.19; Midr. Ps 118.17; etc. Manton, 234, citing several biblical passages that pair food and clothing, comments: 'Till the world drew to a height of luxury, this was enough'.

¹⁹⁷ See all of the texts cited in n. 196.

¹⁹⁸ See esp. Chase, *Prayer*, 48; cf. Hus, 204; Grotius, 1080; Wolzogen, 198; Benson, 63; Plumptre, 70; Farrar, *Days*, 335 n. 11; Carr, 35; F. Taylor, 51-52; Knowling, 54; Cranfield, 'Message', 340; Mitton, 100-101; Adamson, 124; Laws, 119; Townsend, 44; Moo, 125-26; Bottini, *Introduzione*, 121-22; Brosend, 73.

¹⁹⁹ See further Deppe, *Sayings*, 247, who argues against an allusion.

²⁰⁰ Mayor, 97: the plural is a 'very natural irregularity'.

²⁰¹ NT: 1×. LXX: 0×. The word is rare in Jewish sources, although it does occur over ten times in Philo as well as in Apoc. Ezek frag. 5 (P. Chester Beatty 185 ed. Bonner, 185). Josephus: 0×.

²⁰² NT: 16×. LXX: 34×, several times for לחם.

FAITH WITHOUT WORKS (2.14-26)

food',[203] one need not discern an allusion to the story of the manna in Exod (see 16.4) or the Lord's prayer, although some commentators cite the latter.[204]

Verse 16. This verse and the next correlate with v. 14:[205]

Empty declaration	v. 14: 'someone says that he has faith'
	v. 16: 'one of you says to them, "Go in peace..."'
Absence of deeds	v. 14: 'but has not deeds'
	v. 16: 'fail to give them what is necessary'
Inadequacy of faith alone	v. 14: 'Is faith able to save him?'
	v. 17: 'faith of itself, if it has no deeds, is dead'

The words quoted are not in themselves shocking. Indeed, they would be wholly appropriate, even comforting, if accompanied by the proper action. What makes them 'cheap alms' (Manton, 235) is that they exist by themselves. Cf. m. 'Abot 1.17 ('not the expounding [of the law] is the chief thing but the doing [of it]; and he that multiples words occasions sin'); Ps.-Justin, *Coh.Gr.* 110 ed. Otto, 110: 'the matters of our religion have to do not with words but with deeds'. Not to do good is to do wrong, and faith is no excuse.

εἴπῃ δέ τις αὐτοῖς ἐξ ὑμῶν. For τις...ὑμῶν see on 1.5.

ὑπάγετε ἐν εἰρήνῃ. Cf. Plautus, *Trin.* 439: '"Good wishes"! That's a useless phrase without good actions'. The plural corresponds to γυμνοί and λειπόμενοι in v. 15. 'Go in peace'[206] was an old Jewish expression (שלום + ילך) that came into Greek most often as an imperatival form of ὑπάγω or πορεύομαι or βαδίζω + εἰς εἰρήνην or ἐν εἰρήνῃ.[207] Not only

---

[203] E.g. Tryphon I, Περὶ τρόπων ed. Spengel, 194; Diodorus Siculus 3.32; Dionysius of Halicarnassus, *Ant.* 8.4.51; 12.1.2; Plutarch, *Mor.* 499C; Aelius Aristides, Περὶ τοῦ παραφθέγματος ed. Jebb, 398; Heliodorus, *Aeth.* 6.10.2; Iamblichus, *Pyth.* 5.24. Cf. F. Field, *Notes on Select Passages of the Greek New Testament*, Oxford, 1881, 148. Additional examples in H. Fränkel, 'Man's "Ephemeros" Nature according to Pindar and Others', *TAPA* 57 (1946), 143.

[204] Mt 6.11 = Lk 11.3: τὸν ἄρτον ἡμῶν τὸν ἐπιούσιον. Note e.g. Poole, 886; Chase, *Lord's Prayer*, 47-49 (observing that some Latin texts of Lk 11.3 and Jas 2.15 use *quotidianus* and that Chrysostom, *Mt ad loc.* PG 57.280; idem, *Gen ad* 29.22 PG 54.478, uses both ἐφήμερος and τροφή in explicating Jesus' line about bread); Blomberg-Kamell, 130.

[205] Cf. Burge, 'Form'—although the present commentator finds the parallelism less expansive than he does.

[206] ὑπάγω: Jas: 1×. εἰρήνη: Jas: 2×; cf. 3.18.

[207] Cf. Exod 4.18 (MT: לך לשלום; LXX: βάδιζε ὑγιαίνων); Judg 18.6 (MT: לכו לשלום; LXX B: πορεύεσθε ἐν εἰρήνῃ); 1 Sam 1.17 (MT: לכי לשלום; LXX: πορεύου εἰς εἰρήνην); 20.42 (MT: לך לשלום; LXX: πορεύου εἰς εἰρήνην); 2 Sam 15.9 (MT: לך בשלום; LXX: βάδιζε εἰς εἰρήνην); 2 Kgs 5.19 (MT: לך לשלום; LXX: δεῦρο εἰς εἰρήνην); Jdt 8.35 (πορεύου εἰς εἰρήνην); Tob 10.12 S (βάδιζε εἰς εἰρήνην); Jub. 12.29; 4 Bar. 7.9, 30 (ἄπελθε ἐν εἰρήνῃ); Mk 5.34 (ὕπαγε εἰς εἰρήνην); Lk 7.50 (πορεύου εἰς εἰρήνην); Acts 16.36 (πορεύεσθε ἐν εἰρήνῃ); Acts Phil. 93 ed. Bonnet, 36 (πορεύεσθε ἐν εἰρήνῃ); Ps.-Clem. Hom. 3.73.3 GCS 42 ed. Rehm, 83 (πορεύεσθε μετὰ εἰρήνης); Ep. Apost. 51.

does speech alone—'mouth-mercy' (Trapp, 697)—not feed the hungry or clothe the naked, but there is likely both irony and cruelty:[208] perhaps the naked and hungry can depart, but certainly not 'in peace'. שלם, one should remember, can designate welfare, health, safety, soundness in body (BDB, s.v.), and the same is true of its Greek equivalent. 'Peace of mind' and 'physical well-being' are well-attested meanings in the LXX.[209] According to BDAG, s.v., 2a, in James, ὑπάγετε ἐν εἰρήνῃ is 'approx. equiv. to "keep well"'. Bengel, 495, paraphrases: 'God help you; I will not'. If one understands 'Go in peace' as a religious blessing, then irresponsibility here hides behind a sham religious piety.[210]

θερμαίνεσθε καὶ χορτάζεσθε. James may have been the first to bring θερμαίνομαι[211] into close connection with χορτάζω.[212] The verbs may bear either passive ('be warmed', 'be fed') or middle sense ('warm and feed yourselves').[213] In either case, and as with 'Go in peace', one senses mockery, even cruelty.[214] Without deeds, the unaccompanied words are callous, the antithesis of Lev 19.18 (just quoted in v. 8). One cannot eat or wear words. The stomach can starve while the ears are full. Pelagius remarks: 'If one sees that one's neighbor is in danger of starvation, does one not kill him if, while one has an abundance, one does not give him food, though one has not used up one's own provision?'[215]

μὴ δῶτε δὲ αὐτοῖς τὰ ἐπιτήδεια τοῦ σώματος. The plural imperative, δῶτε, perhaps picks upon the earlier ὑμῶν, but 'the plural is often used after an indefinite singular' (Mayor, 98). For δέ in third place see BDF 475.2. Although a favorite of both Philo (72×) and Josephus (115×),

---

[208] Erasmus, *Paraphrase*, 151: 'People think they are being mocked when you say to them, "Keep warm and well fed", and give them neither food nor clothing'. Cf. Mayor, 97: 'mere mockery'.

[209] Muraoka, *Lexicon*, s.v., εἰρήνη.

[210] Cf. Popkes, 193: pious speech is useless. Reicke, 32, asserts that James directs his admonitions especially to deacons because they, at the close of communion services, pronounced the blessing, 'Depart in peace'. Cf. Trocmé, 'Églises', 663; Scaer, 89. It is true that ἐν εἰρήνῃ προέλθωμεν became standard in the liturgies, but that seems beside the point. One is also inclined to dismiss Laws, 121, who urges that the speaker is not 'simply callous. He is the man who says that he has faith, and his words should be read as expressing a pious hope, if not actually a prayer.'

[211] NT: 6×. LXX: 13×, mostly for חמם. Gk. Pseudepigrapha (Denis): 0×. Philo: 1×. Josephus: 1×.

[212] NT: 16×. LXX: 14×, for שׂבע. Gk. Pseudepigrapha (Denis): 4×. Philo: 0×. Josephus: 0×. For clothing and warmth see 1 Kgs 1.1; Job 31.20.

[213] Cf. Mk 14.67. The passive: Grotius, 1080; Mayor, 97-98 (with copious parallels); Ropes, 207; Laws 121. The middle: Huther, 88; Beyschlag, 121; Martin, 85; Popkes, 194; Witherington, 474. For Laws, 121; Cargal, 120; and Popkes, 194, the passive is the so-called divine passive. Oesterley, 444, imagines that the well-wisher has in mind Mt 6.25-34. Davids, 66, and Maier, 129, also implausibly see a connection with that text. Plumptre, 71, suggests a mocking indicative: 'ye are warming and filling yourselves'.

[214] Cf. Diodati, *ad loc.*; Knowling, 55: 'James was a master of irony'.

[215] Pelagius, *Rom. ad* 13.10 TS 9 ed. Robinson, 104.

FAITH WITHOUT WORKS (2.14-26)

ἐπιτήδιος[216] is a NT *hapax legomenon*. Its use as a qualifier of σῶμα (Jas: 5×)—'bodily needs'—is otherwise attested.[217]

τί τὸ ὄφελος; The expected answer is: Nothing. The repetition (see on v. 14) adds emphasis. One could supply either 'for you' ('profit for you' regarding salvation) or 'for them' ('profit for them' in their need). Both make sense, although the parallelism with v. 14 argues for the former.[218] Commentators regularly cite 1 Jn 3.17: 'How does God's love abide in anyone who has the world's goods and sees a brother or sister in need and yet refuses to help'.[219] One could equally cite Prov 3.27-28[220] or those prophetic texts that reject cultic worship if it is not accompanied by obedience (e.g. Hos 6.6) or Hellenistic texts which insist that reason or speech without action counts for nothing.[221] Any serious moral tradition rejects 'quiescent charity' (Oesterley, 445).

Verse 17. This statement of James' thesis answers v. 14. What is the profit of faith without deeds? Nothing: it is the same as being dead. 'The invisibility of faith speaks against its reality.'[222] The contrast throughout this chapter is not between faith and works but between faith without works and faith with works.

οὕτως καὶ ἡ πίστις, ἐὰν μὴ ἔχῃ ἔργα, νεκρά ἐστιν καθ' ἑαυτήν.[223] Cf. 1.11 (οὕτως καί + subject); 2.20 (ἡ πίστις χωρὶς τῶν ἔργων ἀργή ἐστιν), 26 (οὕτως καὶ ἡ πίστις χωρὶς ἔργων νεκρά ἐστιν); 3.5 (οὕτως καί); also 1 Cor 14.9 (οὕτως καὶ ὑμεῖς...ἐὰν μή); 15.14 (κενὴ καὶ ἡ πίστις), 17 (ματαία ἡ πίστις); Heb 6.1 (νεκρῶν ἔργων καὶ πίστεως); Herm. *Sim.* 9.21.2 (τὰ ῥήματα αὐτῶν μόνα ζῶσι, τὰ δὲ ἔργα αὐτῶν

---

[216] LXX: 10×, mostly in 1–3 Maccabees. Gk. Pseudepigrapha (Denis): 0×.

[217] E.g. Dionysius of Halicarnassus, *Ant.* 6.53.2; Philo, *Mut.* 89; Epictetus, *Diatr.* 2.22.5; Galen, *Plac. Hipp. et Plat.* 5.2.3. For τὰ ἐπιτήδεια of life's 'necessities' in general see Wettstein, 667; Kypke, 422-23; Dibelius, 153 n. 24.

[218] Manton, 235; Bardenhewer, 77; and Mussner, 131 n. 5, however, opt for the latter. Moo, 125, finds both readings true at once.

[219] Cf. Bede *ad loc.* 2.15-17 CCSL 121 ed. Hurst, 197; Moffatt, 40; Ross, 51; Mitton, 102; Laws, 119; Royster, 55; *et al.* For Maier, 129, the similarities with James indicate a common early Christian Palestinian teaching tradition. Nienhuis, *Paul*, 214-15, sets out a series of parallels between Jas 2.14-17 and 1 Jn 3.16-18 and rather urges that the former depends upon the latter.

[220] 'Do not withhold good from those to whom it is due, when it is in your power to do it. Do not say to your neighbor, "Go, and come again, tomorrow I will give it"—when you have it with you'.

[221] E.g. Philo, *Mos.* 2.130 ('reason...is of no value, however admirable and excellent are its lofty pronouncements, unless followed by deeds in accordance with it'); see further on Jas 1.22 and note the discussion of the relationship between theory and practice in Musonius Rufus, *Diss.* 5.

[222] Lorenzen, 'Faith', 232.

[223] 2374 2464* 2805 L:FU.IS have χωρὶς τῶν ἔργων instead of ἐὰν μὴ ἔχῃ ἔργα. This is assimilation to vv. 20, 26.

νεκρά ἐστιν); Sent. Sext. 7b (ἄπιστος ἐν πίστει νεκρὸς ἄνθρωπος ἐν σώματι ζῶντι); Epictetus, *Diatr.* 3.23.28 ('if the philosopher's discourse does not produce this effect, it is dead [νεκρός] and so is the speaker himself').

ἔργα comes from v. 14. νεκρός (Jas: 3×) will occur twice in the climax of the discourse (v. 26), so here the ending is anticipated.[224] One is reminded of the use of the word in Mt 8.22; Lk 9.60; and Eph 5.14: the living can be (spiritually) dead.[225] καθ' ἑαυτήν probably qualifies ἡ πίστις and means 'by itself', 'alone'; cf. the μόνον of v. 24.[226] The phrase 'underscores the solitariness of faith already expressed in the conditional clause, ἐὰν μὴ ἔχῃ ἔργα';[227] cf. Simplicius, *Comm. in Epic. Enchr.* ed. Dübner, 3.43: τὸ μὲν σῶμα καθ' αὑτὸ ἀκίνητον καὶ νεκρόν ἐστιν.[228]

Verse 18. It is clear that an interlocutor is responding to v. 17, and further that our writer's point is that, although faith and deeds can be conceptually distinguished, they cannot be separated in real life. Beyond that, however, the verse is a stumbling block. To whom do the pronouns refer? Is the speaker friend, foe, or another? Is the speaker in v. 18 the same as the person of faith without works in v. 14? How far does the quoted material extend?[229] How can the interlocutor claim to have works if James has said he does not have works? Is the text corrupt? Does the speaker forward a real position or a sophism? The exegetical explanations are manifold:[230]

---

[224] One guesses that our verse and its parallel in 26 led to the expression, 'living faith', which one finds in both Greek and Latin sources (*fides viva*); cf. Gregory Palamas, *Hom. xliii–lxiii* 59.8 ed. Chrestou and Zeses, 492: 'He is the living and true God, and seeks from us true promises, and living faith, not dead faith (πίστιν ζῶσαν ἀλλ' οὐ νεκράν), for "faith without works is dead"'.

[225] Cf. also Epictetus, *Diatr.* 1.9.19 ('you are νεκροί'); 3.16.7 ('your fine talk comes merely from your lips; that is why what you say is languid and νεκρά'); 3.23.28 (see text above).

[226] So most, including KJV, RSV, NRSV. Cf. LXX Gen 30.40; 43.32; 2 Macc 13.13; Acts 28.16; Rom 14.22 and see further Fung, 'Justification', 147-48. Mussner, 132: καθ' ἑαυτήν = κατὰ μόνας; cf. Mk 10.1. But Ropes, 208, argues for 'in itself' (cf. the Vulgate: *in semet ipsam*): 'defective in its own power to act'. Cf. Huther, 89; Alford, 298; Wordsworth, 23 ('A tree in winter may not have signs of life, but is not dead in itself; it will put forth shoots and leaves in the spring. But faith has no winter: if it has not works, it has no life in it'); Beyschlag, 122; Mayor, 99; Vouga, 87; Moo, 126.

[227] So Verseput, 'Puzzle', 106.

[228] Cited by BAGD, s.v., κατά, B.1.c., for comparison.

[229] It seemingly has to stop somewhere before v. 20, where James responds with 'O foolish man'.

[230] Theile, 128-31, and Huther, 89-92, supply helpful surveys of the older commentaries.

(i) The speaker—whose words appear in v. 18 or vv. 18-19—is an ally of James, introduced out of modesty or to add vividness. Addressing the person attacked in vv. 15-17, the ally urges that one cannot claim faith[231] without having anything to show for it, that authentic faith will always have deeds.[232] This solution avoids the awkwardness of an opponent claiming to have deeds, the very thing James denies to him; and it makes the 'you' consistent throughout. But it comes up against the difficulty that ἀλλ' ἐρεῖ τις (cf. 1 Cor 15.35) at the beginning of our sentence is unlikely to introduce a friendly voice (even if ἀλλά can otherwise mean 'indeed').[233] Where is the parallel to this?[234] And why does James speak in so roundabout a way?[235] And why does he go on in v. 20 to use the impolite, ὦ ἄνθρωπε κενέ? It is much more natural to correlate vv. 14 and 18: either ἐάν...λέγῃ τις and ἀλλ' ἐρεῖ τις introduce two closely related dissenters, or the same dissenter speaks twice.[236]

(ii) Böhmer seems to urge a slightly different position. The τις of v. 18 is not an ally but James himself, who is addressing the τις of v. 14. James says: 'you have "faith" (according to your sense of the word) and I have works. Come, let's put the thing to the test. You show me your works apart from works (which is impossible), and I will show you my faith by my works (which can be done).' The unexpected and indirect τις is to be explained by our author's 'excitable disposition'. The objections to (i) apply here as well.[237]

(iii) Perhaps an opponent asks a question, 'Do you really have faith?' (v. 18a), to which James retorts: '(Yes), and I have deeds'; that is, an objector accuses our author, because of his stress on deeds, of not having faith at all. James in turn affirms that he does indeed have faith, as his deeds prove.[238] Against this, however, the proposed question (σὺ πίστιν ἔχεις) does not begin with μή; cf. v. 14. More importantly, κἀγώ does not plausibly introduce a new speaker. It seems rather to mark continuation. One would expect, if this interpretation were correct, something like λέγω δὲ ὅτι ἔργα ἔχω or even λέγω δὲ ὅτι πίστιν ἔχω. Further, one wonders why James has an opponent interrupt just to ask, 'Do you really have faith'.[239]

---

[231] This interpretation takes σὺ πίστον ἔχεις to mean, 'you (claim to) have faith'.

[232] Cf. Gill, 789; Neander, 79; Dale, 70; Johnstone, 188-89; Schegg, 111-12; Beyschlag, 122-27; Mayor, 99-100; Belser, 122-25; Maclaren, 417-18; Bardenhewer, 78-79; Easton, 43; Mussner, 136-38; Adamson, 124-25; Gundry, 925. Cantinat, 146, seems to think this plausible.

[233] As in Jn 16.2; 1 Cor 3.2. For this argument see especially Karo, 'Versuch'.

[234] Mayor, in his appended 'Further Studies', 32, concedes that he has not found 'an exact parallel' for his interpretation of ἀλλ' ἐρεῖ τις. He seems to have missed Sextus Empiricus, *Adv. math.* 3.53, where ἀλλὰ μὴν ἐδείξαμεν, ἐρεῖ τις does introduce the statement of an ally. Still, this is not an exact parallel, and Mayor's reading does not easily follow the strong denial in v. 17.

[235] Hincks, 'Error', 200: 'Mayor's suggestion that he [James] adopts this form because he is too modest to say "I have works" is trivial'.

[236] But on the latter view, the one who says, in v. 18, πίστιν ἔχεις, claims in v. 14 to himself have faith, which is a bit clumsy.

[237] Böhmer, 'Glaube'.

[238] So Neitzel, 'Crux interpretum'; cf. Hort, 60-61 (equating 'works' with 'works of the law'); von Soden, 173-74; Moffatt, 41 (although he takes σὺ πίστιν ἔχεις to mean: 'And you claim to have faith!'); Schnider, 70-71; Fung, 'Justification', 148-50; Frankemölle, 171; Klein, *Werk*, 70-72; Edgar, *Poor*, 170-71; Cargal, 125-26.

[239] Ropes, 212, adds: 'this interpretation gives the passage too much the character of a personal debate...to suit the style proper to general hortatory moral writing'.

(iv) Burkitt, 1023, offers a variant of (iii): v. 18a is the objection of an opponent—'a false-hearted hypocrite'—vv. 18b-19 the response not of James but of a 'sincere believer that has true faith'.

(v) The claim of the opponent, whose words extend through v. 19, is that one can have good deeds without faith; that is, one can choose either faith or deeds.[240] But surely v. 18b supports James and so is odd coming from an opponent; and, as we have seen, the issue being discussed stems from Pauline theology, which raises the problem of faith without deeds, not deeds without faith. The former, not the latter, is the topic in vv. 21-26. Furthermore, the example of the demons in v. 19 supports the direction of James' argument and is not likely to come from an opponent.

(vi) Although v. 18a represents an opponent, the speech is indirect and James is writing from his own perspective. Thus 'you' is the opponent, 'I' the letter writer.[241] In line with this, indirect discourse does not demand ὅτι. Still, equating σύ with the opponent right after ἀλλ' ἐρεῖ τις remains exceedingly awkward.

(vii) τις introduces an opponent who doubts that faith and deeds are necessarily connected. σὺ πίστιν ἔχεις κἀγὼ ἔργα ἔχω means, in effect, one has faith, another deeds.[242] Cf. 1 Cor 12.9-10: one person has the gift of faith, another person has some other gift (tongues, miracles, etc.).[243] δεῖξόν μοι κτλ. then becomes James' retort. But this divests 'you' and 'I' of their normal signification.[244] This is especially problematic given that, in the immediately following v. 19, 'you' is indeed the opponent. And why use σύ...κἀγώ when the meaning is εἷς...ἕτερος?[245]

(viii) For Nienhuis, the τις is a new speaker who seeks a mediating position between James and the speaker in v. 14: 'But what if I do not have the gift of service, aid-giving or mercy? My gift is prophecy; my faith is exercised by what I say on God's behalf. Others are gifted to do works of mercy' (cf. 1 Cor 12.7-11). Verses 18bff. are James' riposte.[246]

(ix) τις introduces an outsider, a non-Christian Jew. He says in effect: You Christians claim to have something you call faith, but I have deeds. You cannot really show me without works the value of what you believe, but I have works which demonstrate that

---

[240] So Donker, 'Verfasser'; Laato, 'Justification', 81.

[241] So Weiss, 101-102; Martin, 86-89 (extending the opponent's words through v. 19); Blomberg-Kamell, 134.

[242] Cf. Erasmus, *Paraphrase*, 151; Pott, 206-209; Barnes, 52; Bouman, 136-42; Ropes, 'Faith', 208-14 (proposing as a parallel Teles, Περὶ αὐταρκείας ed. Hense, 5); Tasker, 65-66; Dibelius, 150, 154-58 (the point 'is not the distribution of faith and works to "you" and "me", but rather the total separation of faith and works in general'); Lorenzen, 'Faith', 232; Laws, 123-24; Hoppe, *Hintergund*, 101-104; Davids, 123-24; McKnight, 'Interlocutor' (stressing against Ropes that σὺ πίστιν κτλ. sets forth not two different ways to salvation but underlines that faith need not have deeds); Johnson, 240; Proctor, 'Faith', 316-17; Townsend, 46-47; Hartin, 151; Moo, 129-30; McKnight, 236-39.

[243] According to Ropes, 'Faith', 553, 555, James has heard of Paul's ideas about diversity in the church.

[244] Cf. McKnight, 'Interlocutor', 364: 'It must be admitted that this proposal requires that the personal pronouns be undervalued'.

[245] Adamson, 137, quotes from a personal letter of C.F.D. Moule, 137: 'To tell the truth, I cannot think of a less likely way to express what J.H. Ropes wants the James passage to mean than what there stands written'.

[246] Nienhuis, *Paul*, 219.

my faith is good enough.[247] One problem with this conjecture is that it implausibly has the outsider claim πίστιν. It also ill suits the likelihood that the passage is in part a response to Paul.

(x) R. Wall, 138-42, urging that the original had δεῖξόν μοι τὴν πίστιν σου ἐκ τῶν ἔργων (see n. 257), proposes that the objector's words extend through v. 19a: 'Someone will say: "You have faith and I have works. Show me your faith by your works and I will show you by my works my faith. You believe that God is one; you do right".' What follows is then James' retort. This rests upon what is generally thought to be a secondary text.

(xi) According to Bindemann, James sets forth two different positions. Verse 14 represents one conversation partner, someone who claims faith and represents an intellectualized faith without social obligations. A second individual, responding to the first, speaks in vv. 18-19: you have faith; I have works; you pride yourself in your monotheism. This second speaker represents a Jewish-Christian 'Gesetzesfrömmigkeit'. James then sets forth his own view in vv. 20-26.[248]

(xii) One can posit textual corruption. Perhaps the words of the opponent have inadvertently dropped out, οὐ πίστιν ἔχεις κτλ. being James' response to a protest no longer extant.[249] Or maybe the reading of L:F ('you have deeds and I have faith') represents the original.[250] Or ἀλλ' ἐρεῖ τις could be a marginal gloss that worked itself into the text.[251]

Not one of these explanations satisfies,[252] and as this commentator is unable to offer anything better in their place, he reluctantly concludes either that the text is corrupt, the original beyond recovery,[253] or that James expressed himself so poorly that we cannot offer any clear exposition of his words. If every interpretation seems dubious, it is best to defend none.

Despite its enigmatic character, v. 18 seems artfully constructed: πίστιν...ἔργα is followed by πίστιν...ἔργων, after which the verse ends by reversing the order: ἔργων...πίστιν. Further, κἀγώ occurs twice, and σοι δείξω balances δεῖξόν μοι.

ἀλλ' ἐρεῖ τις. Cf. v. 14: ἐάν...λέγῃ τις. Apparently a hypothetical objector asserts what James rejects. The Greek expression, which occurs in 1 Cor 15.35 and was a favorite of Origen and the Pseudo-Clementine Homilist, also has secular parallels.[254] Diatribe features closely related

---

[247] See Zahn, *Introduction*, 97-98. Criticism in Ropes, 214.
[248] Bindemann, 'Weisheit', 211-15.
[249] So Spitta, 77-79; Windisch-Preisker, 17.
[250] So Hincks, 'Error', following O. Pfleiderer, *Das Urchristenthum*, Berlin, 1887, 874. Cf. Baljon, 42.
[251] Beyschlag, 123, raises this possibility only to reject it.
[252] Cf. Hincks, 'Error', 201 ('a self-consistent and intelligible interpretation...cannot be performed'); Burchard, 121; Brosend, 74 ('Frankly, there is no acceptable solution').
[253] If one judges James to oppose Paul, then it is possible that our text originally named the apostle and that later theological sensibility removed his name.
[254] Xenophon, *Cyr.* 4.3.10; Cassius Dio 50.28; Dio Chrysostom 31.47; cf. Josephus, *Bell.* 2.365; 3.367; Ps.-Clem. Hom. 9.16; 11.12, 16, 31; 13.10, 14; 17.8 GCS 42 ed. Rehm, 138, 159, 162, 169, 198, 200, 233; Origen, *Jn* 2.37.223 SC 120bis ed. Blanc, 364;

expressions. Those who see an attack on Paul may identify him as the implicit opponent.[255]

σὺ πίστιν ἔχεις κἀγὼ ἔργα ἔχω. 'You have faith' presumably means 'you have faith (without works)'. κἀγώ occurs twice in James, both times in this verse. Some have thought that the assertion, which features consonance (χ, γ, γ, χ) and assonance (ε, ω, ε, ε, ω), would, if aimed at Paul, work better were it reversed: 'you have deeds and I have faith' (the reading of L:F). Others, as already noted, construe 'you' and 'I' as, in effect, 'one' and 'another' and then advert to 1 Cor 12.7-11, where different individuals have different gifts, one such gift being faith, another a gift featuring the εργ- root (ἑτέρῳ πίστις...ἄλλῳ δὲ ἐνεργήματα δυνάμεων). Even if this gives σύ and κἀγώ unlikely sense, it is indeed tempting to see an implicit if distorted criticism of the teaching in 1 Cor 12.[256]

δεῖξόν μοι τὴν πίστιν σου χωρὶς τῶν ἔργων.[257] James uses δείκνυμι thrice, each time in close connection with ἔργα—twice in this verse and then again in 3.13 (δειξάτο...τὰ ἔργα αὐτοῦ). On χωρὶς τῶν ἔργων see above, 446: it is Pauline. Whether we pass here from quotation to response is debated; so too the sense. In any case, James would have judged a claim to faith without works impossible.

κἀγώ σοι δείξω ἐκ τῶν ἔργον μου τὴν πίστιν.[258] Cf. 3.13; Jn 5.20 (δείξει...ἔργα); 10.32 (ἔργα καλὰ ἔδειξα ὑμῖν); also Theophilus of Antioch, *Autol.* 1.2.1 PTS 44 ed. Marcovich, 16: δεῖξον μοι τὸν ἄνθρωπόν

13.49.328 SC 222 ed. Blanc, 214; *Or.* 25.2 GCS 3 ed. Koetschau, 357; etc. Note also 4 Macc 2.24 (πῶς οὖν, εἴποι τις ἄν); 7.17 (ἴσως δ' ἂν εἴποιέν τινες); Rom 9.19; 11.19; 1 Cor 10.28 (ἐὰν δέ τις ὑμῖν εἴπῃ); Barn. 9.6 (ἀλλ' ἐρεῖς).

[255] Limberis, 'Provenance', 414; James 'gives a flimsy disguise as to the possible identity of this tricky interlocutor—a guy who talks a great deal about works and faith'. Limberis prefers to translate the indefinite τις as 'some guy' because 'it fits the derogatory tone of the passage'.

[256] For Dibelius, 156, however, the interlocutor represents no 'known historical viewpoint'. We have here instead 'simply a *sophistic separation of faith and works*. Nor does the author combat this [opinion] because it is being advocated as a doctrine in his community, but *because he wants to develop his own opinion in contrast to this*. It is for this reason that the objection in v. 18a is delivered in such a brief, subtle, and as a result, enigmatic manner'.

[257] P54V 442 L596 **L**:F **Ä**^mss omit σου and (with the exception of P54V L:F) add it after ἔργων. 5 04 61A 69 104 197 218 *et al.* **Byz L**:CAr **A**^mss **Ä**^mss **G**:A1BG-D **Sl**:ChDMSi have it both places. The addition at the end increases the parallelism with the remainder of the clause (ἐκ τῶν ἔργων μου) as do the substitution of ἐκ for χωρίς in P54V 5 218 252 322 *et al.* **Byz L**:CAr **G**:G-D **Sl**:ChDMSi (cf. Gregory Palamas, *Hom. i–xx* 8.4; 17.17 ed. Chrestou and Zeses, 216, 506) and the reversal, in the next clause, of σοι δείξω in P74 02 04 044 5 33 81 88 *et al.* **Byz** PsOec **L**:V **S**:PH **A G**:A1B **Sl**:ChDMSiS (cf. the earlier δεῖξόν μοι). Hodges, 'Light', defends the originality of ἐκ. So too R. Wall, 139. See further Martin, 76-77.

[258] P74 02 025V 5 69 *et al.* **Byz** PsOec **L**:GV **S**:PH **K**:S^ms **A**^mss **G**:G-D **Sl**:ChDMSi **Ä** add μου at the end.

FAITH WITHOUT WORKS (2.14-26) 473

σου, κἀγώ σοι δείξω τὸν θεόν μου.[259] James here reverses the previous clause. Exegetes often latch upon this line to insist that, for James, faith is 'the root and principle, and works only the fruit and evidence, of justification... Good works are secondary to faith, as being its effect and evidence.'[260] But one can just as readily take the line to show the superiority of works, because whereas the latter entail faith, faith (at least of the sort James speaks of here) does not entail works.

Some find in this phrase a definitive contrast with Paul. According to one modern Christian ethicist, James commends a faith that displays itself by means of works: 'Faith working through love is concerned only to show what love is and to discover the neighbor's needs, not to demonstrate that it itself is faithful. While Christian faith is related to deeds and cannot exist without being related to deeds, it is not self-centeredly related to them... Christian faith does not *claim* good works; it *gives* them.'[261] Whether or not these words are fair to James—the obscurities of the verse prevent a verdict—it is undeniable that 2.18 has been employed, like Mt 5.13-16, to exhort believers to display their good works before others.[262]

Verse 19. In this verse 'faith' equals 'belief', for the 'faith' of demons can be nothing more than the conviction that Israel's God exists. To use later theological terminology, the demons have *notitia*, not *assensus* or *fiducia*.

σὺ πιστεύεις ὅτι εἶς ἐστιν ὁ θεός.[263] Cf. Herm. *Mand.* 1.1 (πίστευσον ὅτι εἶς ἐστιν ὁ θεός);[264] Ps.-Clem. Hom. 3.59.2; 16.7.9 GCS 42 ed. Rehm, 78, 221-22 (ὅτι εἶς ἐστιν ὁ θεός). The words, which can be punctuated as a question,[265] allude to Deut 6.4, the Shema', the monotheistic—originally henotheistic—confession of Judaism: 'The Lord is our God, the Lord

---

[259] Is Dibelius, 154 n. 29, correct to doubt that Theophilus knew James? The oft-cited parallel in Epictetus, *Diatr.* 1.6.43 is not so close (ἐγὼ σοὶ δείξω...ἐμοὶ δείκνυε).

[260] So W.G.T. Shedd, 'Connection between Faith and Works', in *Sermons to the Spiritual Man*, New York, 1884, 296. The thought is ancient; cf. Philo, *Abr.* 268 (faith is 'fertile in good' [ἀγαθῶν], that is, it produces good works); Origen, *Rom* 4.1 FC 2.2 ed. Heither, 176; Augustine, *En. Ps* 31.2.3 CCSL 38 ed. Dekkers and Fraipont, 226.

[261] P. Ramsey, *Basic Christian Ethics*, Louisville, 1993, 136.

[262] E.g. Chrysostom, *Jn* 72.4 PG 59.395.

[263] There are many variants to the order of εἶς ἐστιν ὁ θεός (so P74 01 02 442 621 1735 1842 2464 L596 AnastS Cyr): ὁ θεὸς εἶς ἐστιν (5 88 218 322 *et al*. **Byz** Cyr Did PsOec); θεὸς εἶς ἐστιν (38T 43 69 93 319 *et al*. L427 L1441 AnastS); ἐστιν θεὸς (044 Ath), θεὸς ἐστιν (365 Phot); ὁ θεὸς ἐστιν (018* 2197* 2544T L2087); εἶς ἐστιν θεὸς (945 1241 1739 2298); εἶς ὁ θεός (Cyr **L**:FT); εἶς ὁ θεός ἐστιν (04 33V 81 1175 1243 2344 2492 2805); εἶς θεὸς ἐστιν (03 206 *et al*. L1440). Three of these readings omit εἶς and so miss the allusion to the Shema'. Discussion in Metzger, *Commentary*, 681.

[264] Irenaeus, *Haer.* 4.20.2, cites Hermas' opening line as 'scriptura'; so too Origen, *Jn* 32.16.187 GCS 10 ed. Preuschen, 451; Eusebius, *H.E.* 5.8.7; and other church fathers.

[265] So von Soden, 173-74; Chaine, 62. Contrast Mayor, 101: 'it seems to me more impressive to regard it as stating a simple matter of fact'.

alone' or 'The Lord our God, the Lord is one'.[266] This was a liturgical text for ancient as for modern Jews, and probably already by the first century, Deut 6.4-9 + 11.13-21 + Num 15.37-41 was recited at sunrise and sunset.[267] Deuteronomy 6.4-9 was also affixed to doorposts and inserted into phylacteries (in accord with the command in 6.9), and 6.4-5 was often linked to both Lev 19.18 (cf. Jas 2.8) and the decalogue (cf. Jas 2.11).[268] As the opening line of the Nicene Creed ('We believe in one God') indicates, Christians made the confession their own.[269] Whether or not εἷς (ἐστιν ὁ) θεός was, by the time of James, a standard exorcistic formula (this would explain why the devils tremble),[270] and whether or not our writer knew εἷς θεός as a formula on synagogue walls,[271] certainly *mezuzot* containing Deut 6.4 were by then reckoned to be apotropaic.[272] See 63 for the possibility that James' thought turned to Deut 6.4 because Paul associated his discussion of Abraham, faith, deeds, and justification with God's oneness or unity (Rom 3.30; Gal 3.20).

On πιστεύω + ὅτι[273] see above, 456. The construction does not introduce a Christian belief but rather Judaism's closest thing to a confession.

[266] MT: יהוה אלהינו יהוה אחד; LXX: κύριος ὁ θεὸς ἡμῶν κύριος εἷς ἐστιν. Cf. Zech 14.9; Sib. Or. 3.11 (εἷς θεός ἐστι μόναρχος); Ps.-Hecataeus frag. 3 *apud* Clement of Alexandria, *Strom.* 5.14.113.1 ed. Holladay, 318 (εἷς ἐστιν θεός); Philo, *Opif.* 171 (θεὸς εἷς ἐστι); *Plant.* 138 (εἷς ἐστιν ὁ θεός); *Spec.* 1.30 (θεὸς εἷς ἐστι), 68 (εἷς ἐστιν ὁ θεός); Ps.-Phoc. 54 (εἷς θεός ἐστι σοφός); Josephus, *Ant.* 3.91 (θεός ἐστιν εἷς); 4.201; 5.112. Fulgentius, *Ep.* 8.4 CCSL ed. Fraipont, 259, naturally moves from Deut 6.4 to Jas 2.19.

[267] Cf. m. Ber. 1-4; m. Tamid 5.1; b. Ber. 21b, 47b; also perhaps Philo, *Spec.* 4.141; Josephus, *Ant.* 4.212. Discussion in Verseput, 'Prayers'.

[268] See on v. 8. The Nash papyrus (first–second century BCE, from Egypt, in Hebrew) combines, on one sheet (perhaps used for lectionary purposes), the ten commandments and the Shema'; see W.F. Albright, 'A Biblical Fragment from the Maccabean Age', *JBL* 56 (1937), 145-76. Cf. 4QPhyl[b], which contained in part Deut 5.1–6.9, that is, both the decalogue and the Shema'. Rabbinic sources inform us that, in the second temple period, recitation of the Shema' followed recitation of the decalogue; so e.g. m. Tamid 5.1; b. Ber. 12a. See further Y. Yadin, *Tefillin from Qumran (XQ Phyl 1-4)*, Jerusalem, 1969, 32-35. Christian literature reflects the traditional association of the Shema' with the decalogue; see e.g. Methodius of Olympus, *Symp.* 8.13 SC 95 ed. H. Musurillo, 236.

[269] Cf. Mk 12.29, 32; Rom 3.30; 1 Cor 8.4, 6; Gal 3.20; Eph 4.6; 1 Tim 2.5; Theophilus of Antioch, *Autol.* 2.34.4 PTS 44 ed. Marcovich, 86; Apoc. Elijah 2.10, 49; CII/P 2.1184; etc. Fulgentius, *Ep.* 10.19 CCSL 91 ed. Fraipont, 329, uses our verse to argue for the unity of the Trinity.

[270] For later usage see E. Peterson, *ΕΙΣ ΘΕΟΣ*, Göttingen, 1926, 276-95. He interprets Jas 2.19 in terms of apotropaic traditions (295-99). Cf. Mussner, 139; Laws, 127; Schrage, 32. L. Di Segni, 'Εἷς θεός in Palestinian Inscriptions', *Scripta classica Israelica* 13 (1994), 94-115, stresses that most of the relevant texts are Samaritan, Gnostic, or Christian, and one cannot just assume that the acclamation, εἷς θεός, first became popular in Jewish circles.

[271] For this phenomenon see L. Di Segni, 'A Jewish Greek Inscription from the Vicinity of Caesarea Maritima', *'Atiqot* 22 (1993), 133-36.

[272] Cf. 4QMez B-D and see E. Eshel, H. Eshel, and A. Lange, '"Hear, O Israel" in Gold: An Ancient Amulet from Halbturn in Austria', *JAJ* 1 (2010), 43-64.

[273] This combination renders כי + אמן in LXX Exod 4.5 and Job 9.16.

Once more, then, the text lines up with a literal, not metaphorical, reading of 1.1.[274]

Given that the subject is eschatological salvation (v. 14), and that James speaks only of faith in God and good deeds, perhaps he supposed that faith in the Jewish God and good deeds are enough for salvation in this world and the world to come. He is close to Matthew in many ways, and in Mt 25.31-46—a text commentators on Jas 2.14-26 recall incessantly—religious affiliation plays no role: deeds of loving-kindness trump everything else. This early Christian text seemingly does not limit salvation to those in the church.[275] Implicit is a rejection of *extra ecclesiam nulla salus*; cf. Apoc. Sedr. 14.5, which declares that people outside the church can have God's Spirit and, upon death, can enter 'the bosom of Abraham'; also parts of the Ps.-Clementines, where one can be saved either by believing in Jesus or by keeping the law.[276] Did James think along similar lines?

Laws observes that the theme of God's oneness or unity appears elsewhere in James (e.g. 1.5; 4.12), where it stands over against the duplicity of human beings.[277] For James, the divine integrity should find its correlate in human integrity—an ideal already anticipated in the Shema', where the unity of God prefaces a call to whole-hearted commitment: 'you shall love the Lord your God with all your heart, and with all your soul, and with all your might'.

καλῶς ποιεῖς. See on 2.8. Perhaps there is an implicit contrast with pagans who do not believe in the one God,[278] in which case James might be saying: although you best them in the matter of belief, that is not enough.[279] The words in any event 'cannot be purely ironical, because the article is truth', and 'they cannot be purely laudatory, because the true article is falsely held' (Lange, 84). Perhaps καλῶς ποιεῖς is, if one may so put it, half-ironical.[280]

---

[274] Lange, 84, anachronistically affirms that James criticized the traditional confession of monotheism because in some circles it prevented belief in the incarnation. Robertson, 135, makes v. 19 the opportunity to denigrate Islam: it is monotheistic, but that 'is not enough'.

[275] See A.J. Hultgren, *The Parables of Jesus*, Grand Rapids, MI, 2000, 309-27.

[276] Ps.-Clem. Rec. 4.5 GCS 51 ed. Rehm, 148-49; Hom. 8.5-7 CGS 42 ed. Rehm, 123-24.

[277] Laws, 'Basis'. Cf. 1.6-8; 4.1, 8.

[278] Yet monotheism was not confined to Jewish and Christian circles, although the issues here are very complex; see S. Mitchell and P. van Nuffelen, *One God*, Cambridge, UK, 2010.

[279] Cf. the gratuitous accusation of Justin Martyr, *Dial.* 141.2 PTS 47 ed. Marcovich, 313: some Jews imagine that, even though they are sinners, their sins will not be reckoned to them, because they 'know God' (θεὸν γινώσκωσιν).

[280] Cf. Mayor, 101 (the expression is 'ironical from its context'); Ropes, 216 ('a slight touch of irony'); Davids, 125 ('semi-ironic'); Popkes, 200. Contrast Frankemölle, 444: there is no ironic undertone. McKnight, 241-42, observes: James 'is not kind to his opponent'.

καὶ τὰ δαιμόνια πιστεύουσιν καὶ φρίσσουσιν. Maximus the Confessor speaks in this connection of 'mere faith', Schleiermacher of 'that shadow of faith which even devils may have'.[281] The logic is clear. Demons are not atheists but rather have religious 'doctrines' (1 Tim 4.10), among which is monotheism, and shuddering proves their sincerity.[282] But to no avail: τί τὸ ὄφελος; Caesarius of Arles puts it this way: 'The demons believe that God exists, but they do not perform what he commands'.[283]

καί = 'even'.[284] Both δαιμόνιον[285] and φρίσσω[286] appear only here in James. The latter refers to something like fearful amazement, the traditional English rendering being 'shudder'.[287] Here fear must be connoted. Certainly it is fitting that demons, who instill fear in human beings, become the victims of fear before God.

[281] Maximus the Confessor, *Cent.* 1.39 PG 90.968C; Schleiermacher, *Christliche Glaube* 167.2. According to Bede *ad* 2.19 CCSL 121 ed. Hurst, 198, one can believe what God says (even the wicked can do this) or believe that God exists (as do demons) or believe 'in' God. Only the latter involves love. Hus, 206, too, when discussing demonic faith, distinguishes between *credere Deo*, *credere Deum*, and *credere in Deum*. Both Hus and Bede are following Augustine; cf. e.g. *Tract. Jn* 29.6 CCSL 36 ed. Willems, 286-87.

[282] Cf. Hort, 62. For Laws, 128, and Cargal, 127, the point is that even with demons faith evokes a response. This was also the view of Calvin, 284, who argued that James puts those attacked below demons.

[283] Caesarius of Arles, *Serm.* 12.5 CCSL 103 ed. Morin, 62. He continues: human beings are shown not to believe when they are 'unwilling to fulfill in deed' what they 'seem to promise in word'. Cf. the Ethiopic Epistle of Pelagia ed. Goodspeed *AJSL* 20 (1903), 102. J. Locke, *The Reasonableness of Christianity* 11 ed. Higgins-Biddle, 109-11, argues that the faith of the devils is not salvific because it does not exist within a 'covenant of grace'. More common is the assertion that they lack love; cf. Bernard of Clairvaux, *Ad Henricum arch.* 4.15 Bernardi Opera 7 ed. Leclercq and Rochais, 113; Thierry of Chartres, *Trin.* 1.3 ed. Häring, 133; Peter Lombard, *Sent.* 3.77 (Dist. 23.4) ed. Brady, 144; J. Newton, 'Of a Living and Dead Faith', in *The Works of the Rev. John Newton*, vol. 2, London, 1824, 561; Wordsworth, 23; Popkes, 201 (the latter appealing to Deut 6.4-5).

[284] See BDAG, s.v., 2b.

[285] LXX: 19×. It is qualified by πονηρός in Tob 3.8, 17 (cf. T. Sol. 5.1; PGM 1.115), and 6.8 BA uses the phrase, δαιμόνιον ἢ πνεῦμα πονηρόν. NT: 63×. Philo: 2×. Josephus: 34×.

[286] = φρίττω. NT: 1×. LXX: 6×. Gk. Pseudepigrapha (Denis): 7×. Philo: 5×. Josephus: 6×.

[287] Cf. LXX Job 4.15; Jer 2.12; Theod. Dan 7.15; Ezekiel the Tragedian frag. 12 *apud* Eusebius, *Praep. ev.* 9.29.11 ed. Holladay, 374; Pr Man 4 (πάντα φρίττει καὶ τρέμει ἀπὸ προσώπου δυνάμεώς σου; cf. Gk. Apoc. Ezra 7.7); Sib. Or. 3.679 (the eschatological shuddering of animals and people); Philo, *Det.* 140; Josephus, *Bell.* 5.378; T. Abr. RecLng 9.5; Herm. *Vis.* 1.2.1. Reicke, 33, finds an allusion here to the so-called God-fearers, which accords with his dubious thesis that James is opposing missionaries who, in order to win large numbers, are lax in making requirements of their converts. Adamson, 126, suggests: φρίσσω originally 'means "to bristle up", with an allusion perhaps to particular OT demons, "hairy ones" or *śe'irim* (Isa. 13:21; 34:14)'. Although he is correct about the verb (LSJ, s.v.), it is unclear that he is correct about Isaiah's *śe'irim*, which most scholars now take to refer to 'goat-demons'. To this writer's knowledge, moreover, there is no tradition of forging the link he proposes.

James was not the first to link φρίσσω, which is sometimes paired with τρέμω, to the demonic. Indeed, we have here a far-flung *topos*; cf. 4Q510 1 (a prayer that the ravaging angels may be frightened and terrified); T. Abr. RecLng 16.3 (personified Death shudders and trembles before God, ἔφριξεν καὶ ἐτρομάξεν); T. Sol. 2.1 (τὸν δαίμονα φρίσσοντα καὶ τρέμοντα); Ps.-Ign. *Phil.* 3.5 (the ruler of this world 'shudders' [φρίττει] at the cross); Justin, *Dial.* 49.8 ('before whom [that is, before Christ] the demons and all the principalities and authorities of the earth shudder [φρίσσει]'); Clement of Alexandria, *Strom.* 5.24.125.1 GCS 32 ed. Stählin and Früchtel, 411 (an Orphic fragment: 'Ruler of Ether...before whom demons shudder [φρίσσουσιν], and before whom the throng of gods fear'); Acts Phil. 132 ed. Bonnet, 63 ('God, before whom all the aeons shudder [φρίττουσιν]...principalities and powers of the heavenly places tremble [τρέμουσιν] before you'); Lactantius, *Ira* 23 SC 289 ed. Ingremeau, 208 ('the Milesian Apollo, consulted about the Jewish religion, introduced this verse into his response: "God, the king and begetter of all, before whom the earth trembles [τρομέει]...whom the depths of Tartarus and demons dread" [δαίμονες ἐρίγγασιν]'); PGM 3.226-27 ('god's seal, at whom all deathless gods of Olympus and demons... shudder', φρίσσουσι...δαίμονες); 4.2541-42 ('demons throughout the world shudder at you', δαίμονες...φρίσσουσι), 2829-30 (δαίμονες ἣν φρίσσουσιν καὶ ἀθάνατοι τρομέουσιν); 12.118 (πᾶς δαίμων φρίσσει); 3 En. 14.2 (Schäfer, *Synopse* 17 = 898: Sammael fears and trembles before God); Ps.-Bartholomew, *Book of the Resurrection of Jesus Christ* ed. Budge, fol. 2a (Death personified is greatly afraid and trembles and shakes before the triumphant Jesus).[288] James was, however, evidently the first to associate this motif with the 'faith' of demons, an effective and memorable rhetorical move.

Although originally used of both good and bad deities, δαιμόνιον came, in post-exilic Judaism, to refer to malevolent spirits closely associated with Satan.[289] James' audience was presumably familiar with a large body of lore surrounding them. They were often identified with pagan gods (LXX Deut 32.17; 1 Cor 10.20); held to inflict disease (Sib. Or. 3.331; Mt 12.22); understood as sources of temptation and vice (T. Jud. 23.1); reported to indwell or possess unfortunate human beings (Mk 5.9; 9.26); and said to have issued from the mating of the sons of God with human women (Gen 6.1-4; 1 En. 6-21).[290] But all that matters

---

[288] Given the many parallels, Mayor, 102, is unjustified in asserting that the texts in Ps.-Ignatius, Justin, the Acts of Philip, and Clement are 'reminiscences' of James.
[289] Cf. LXX Pss 90.6; 105.37; Bar 4.35; Lk 11.16 ('Beelzebul, the ruler of demons')
[290] See esp. O. Böcher, *Christus Exorcista*, Stuttgart, 1972. Their equation with (fallen) angels cannot be taken for granted for the earliest Christian sources; see D.B. Martin, 'When Did Angels Become Demons?', *JBL* 129 (2010), 657-77. Contrast Kern, 171: the demons are the sinful angels.

here is the notion that they, although corrupt, nonetheless recognize the ultimate power in the universe.[291]

Why the demons are afraid of the one God goes unsaid. Commentators often assume that they know God will destroy or punish them in the latter days.[292] But that may read too much into the text. Perhaps we have something here like the magic of powerful names: evil cannot tolerate the presence or name or even thought of the divinity; cf. Josephus, *Bell.* 5.438 (τὸ φρικτόν...ὄνομα τοῦ θεοῦ); PGM 36.261 (τῶν μεγάλων καὶ φικτρῶν ὀνομάτων ὧν οἱ ἄνεμοι φρίζουσιν); Apost.Const. 2.22.12 ed. Funk, 87 (ὀνόματί σου, ὃν πάντα φρίσσει καί τρέμει); PLond. 46.80-81 (τὸ μέγα ὄνομα...ὄν...πᾶς δαίμων φρίσσει).

Ecclesiastical interpreters have often expounded our verse and those surrounding it by associating it or them with the empty confession of Mt 7.21 = Lk 6.46.[293] Bare brain belief comes to naught.

Verse 20. This verse, so close to vv. 17 and 26 (the summarizing conclusion), is, unlike them, interrogatory. The line both reinforces an earlier assertion and introduces two famous illustrations from Scripture (Abraham, vv. 21-24; Ruth, v. 25), illustrations designed to buttress the argument in vv. 14-19.[294] Cargal, 128, speaks in this connection of

---

[291] Cf. Mk 1.24; 3.11; 5.7. Augustine, *Ep.* 194.11 CSEL 57 ed. Goldbacher, 185, already cites these gospel texts: 'For the devils also believe and shudder, but do they love? If they had not believed, they would have said neither "You are the holy one of God" nor "You are the Son of God". And if they had loved, they would not have said, "What have you to do with us?"' Cf. idem, *Trin.* 15.18 CCSL 50A ed. Mountain, 508; *Fide et op.* 14.23 CSEL 41 ed. Zycha, 64; Bede *ad* 2.19 CCSL 121 ed Hurst, 197-98, the *Catenae* ed. Cramer, 15; Wolzogen, 199, *et al.* Knowling, 58, even hazards that James may here advert to the stories about demons encountering Jesus. Jerome, *Mt* SC 242 ed. Bonnard, 164, seemingly alludes to our text in a discussion of what demons and the devil know about the Son of God, and interpreters can expand upon our text to list a slew of demonic beliefs. E.g. Thomas Cranmer, 'A Homily on the Salvation of Mankind', in *Faith and Works*, ed. P.E. Hughes, Wilton, CN, 1982, 57, recounts their belief in the virgin birth, Jesus' resurrection and ascension, and indeed 'all things written in the New and Testament'. According to Leigh, 370-71, devils believe in God, Christ, the judgment, and eternal punishment. Cf. Manton, 241: 'the devils assent to the articles of the Christian religion'.

[292] Cf. Mk 5.7 and see Anastasius of Sinai, *Quaest.* 91 CCSG 59 ed. Richard and Munitiz, 145; Gill 789; Bengel, 496; Wesley, 862; Weidner, 49. This would bring eschatological terror into the present; cf. Lk 21.11; Rev 18.10; 4 Ezra 5.23-24; etc.

[293] E.g. Origen, *Rom.* 2.13 FC 2.1 ed. Heither, 282; Cyril of Alexandria, *Jn.* 10.2 ed. Pusey, 563; Augustine, *Div. quaest. oct. trib.* 2 CCSL 44A ed. Mutzenbecher, 221; Caesarius of Arles, *Serm.* 157.6 CCSL 104 ed. Morin, 644; Fulgentius, *Ep.* 3.27 SC 487 ed. Bachelet, 188; Gregory Palamas, *Hom. xliii–lxiii* 59.8 ed. Chrestou and Zeses, 490-92; Manton, 265; Ewald, 199; Beyschlag, 119; Hort, 57; Knowling, 53; Plummer, 589; Smith, 146-47; Chaine, 57; Tasker, 64; Davids, 12; Royster, 54; *et al.* Yet there is no clear allusion or dependence here; see Deppe, *Sayings*, 247.

[294] According to Mussner, 139-40, there is no οὖν because v. 20 looks forward.

'rhetorical jujitsu', by which he means that James, in appealing to clear scriptural examples, uses his opponent's own belief system against him.

θέλεις δὲ γνῶναι. The words anticipate 'the still-furrowed brows of the imaginary interlocutor who needs more evidence' (Davids, 126). θέλω occcurs elsewhere only in the traditional formula of 4.15. All three instances of γινώσκω refer to readers knowing this or that; cf. 1.3; 5.20. Although one finds θέλεις δὲ γνῶναι introducing a question otherwise only in patristic sources,[295] related constructions appear in Jewish texts, Hermas, and Epictetus.[296]

ὦ ἄνθρωπε κενέ.[297] On the emotional content of ὦ see BDF 146. Although ὦ ἄνθρωπε[298] is an exceedingly common idiom,[299] ἄνθρωπε + qualifying vocative is not so well attested,[300] and ἄνθρωπε + κενέ[301] is otherwise attested not at all, except for quotations of James and very late Christian texts.[302] κενέ may be a Greek version of the disparaging direct address, (ה)ריקא.[303] The LXX often translates ריק or ריקם with κενός; note esp. Judg 9.4: 'worthless/vain (MT: ריקים; LXX: κενούς; cf. 11.3 A) and reckless fellows'. In any case, the rhetorical function of ὦ ἄνθρωπε κενέ is evident. κενός literally means 'empty', and applied to human beings it presumably means something like 'empty-headed'; cf. the Vulgate's *o homo inanis*.[304] Whether or not there is also a connotation of boasting[305]

---

[295] Cf. Ps-Athanasius, *Virg.* 15 TU 29 ed. von der Goltz, 50 (with ὅτι); idem, *Frag. Cant.* 1 PG 27.1352B; Ps.-Chrysostom, *Eleem.* PG 48.1062; idem, *Trin.* 2 PG 48.1090 (with ὅτι); Didymus of Alexandria, *Ps 29–34 ad* 34.15 ed. Gronewald, 350 (with ὅτι); Cyril of Jerusalem, *Catech. 1–18* 10.17; 13.12 PG 33.684A, 788C (with ὅτι *bis*); Ps.-Ephraem, *In illud: Attende tibi ipsi* 4 ed. Phrantzoles, 152 (θέλεις δὲ γνῶναι, ἀγαπητέ).

[296] E.g. Philo, *Her.* 115 (εἰ θέλεις γνῶναι); T. Job 3.3 (γνῶναι θέλεις); Epictetus, *Diatr.* 1.20.14 (εἰ θέλεις γνῶναι); Herm. *Vis.* 3.6.1 (θέλεις γνῶναι;); 3.7.3 (θέλεις γνῶναι...;).

[297] The *Editio Critica Maior* cites 38T 321 1367 as omitting ὦ. Ps.-Ephraem, *Consil. vit. spirit.* 91 ed. Phrantzoles, 247, also omits the exclamation.

[298] LXX: 0× (although LXX Mic 6.8 uses the simple ἄνθρωπε in direct address, for vocative אדם). NT: 4×.

[299] Plato, *Apol.* 28B; *Resp.* 337B; Philo, *Mos.* 2.199; *Leg.* 2.82; Rom 2.1, 3; 9.20; 1 Tim 6.11; Plutarch, *Alex.* 43.4; 69.4; Epictetus, *Diatr.* 1.21.2; 2.6.16; 2.17.33; Dio Chrysostom 7.100; Justin, *Dial.* 9.1; Lucian, *Electr.* 5.2; 3 Bar. 1.3; etc.

[300] Cf. LXX Ps 54.14 (ἄνθρωπε ἰσόψυχε); T. Abr. RecLng. 2.6 (δίκαιε ἄνθρωπε); Epictetus, *Diatr.* 3.21.14 (ἀσεβέστατε ἄνθρωπε); Herm. *Sim.* 1.3 (ἄφρον καὶ δίψυχε καὶ ταλαίπωρε ἄνθρωπε); Lucian, *Pseudol.* 1.21 (ὦ κακόδαιμον ἄνθρωπε).

[301] κενός: Jas: 1×.

[302] E.g. Cyril of Alexandria, *Frag. Rom ad* 4.2 ed. Pusey, 180; Arethas, *Scrip. min.* 14 ed. Westerink, 171.

[303] Cf. Mt 5.22; Mek. on Exod 20.2; b. Ber. 22a, 32b; b. Ned. 4b; b. B. Bat. 75a; b. Ta'an. 20b; b. Giṭ. 58a; etc. So many exegetes: Grotius, 1081; Gill, 789; Wolf, 50; Benson, 65; Davids, 126; *et al.* Contrast Oesterley, 447; Dibelius, 161 n. 62.

[304] Plutarch couples κενός with ἀνόητος: *Mor.* 35E; 541B; 599C; *Alc.* 4.3; *Phil.* 13.9. Cf. also Aristophanes, *Ran.* 530 (ἀνόητον καὶ κενόν): Philo, *Leg.* 1.311 (οἱ κενοὶ φρενῶν); Sib. Or. 5.280 (στομάτεσσι κενοῖς καὶ χείλεσι μωροῖς); Pol. *Phil.* 6.3; Justin, *Dial.* 64.2.

[305] So Dibelius, 161 n. 62. Cf. Epictetus, *Diatr.* 2.19.8; 4.4.35.

or of being 'empty' of deeds[306] or of being 'empty' of faith,[307] κενέ intimates that nobody with sense could counter the point that James is urging; cf. Gal 3.1: ὦ ἀνόητοι Γαλάται. For our author, his argument is beyond reasonable objection. He has scorn for any who might disagree.[308]

As diatribe commonly addresses an interlocutor directly as 'man' or 'fool',[309] one might, like many commentators on Rom 2.1, 3; 9.20, detect the influence of Hellenistic discourse here. Yet one should keep in mind that the same phenomenon appears in texts that do not stand under the influence of diatribe, such as Deut 32.6 ('Do you thus requite the Lord, you foolish and senseless people?'); Prov 8.5 ('O simple ones, learn prudence; O foolish men, pay attention'); Jer 5.21 ('Hear this, O foolish and senseless people'); Mic 6.8 ('He has showed you, O man [LXX: ἄνθρωπε], what is good'); Mt 23.17 ('You blind fools!'); Lk 11.40 ('You fools!'); 24.25 (ὦ ἀνόητοι); 4 Ezra 10.6 ('you most foolish of women'); 2 Clem. 11.3 (ἀνόητοι, quoting a lost apocryphon). Furthermore, Paul uses ὦ ἄνθρωπε in Rom 2.1, 3; 9.20 and ὦ ἀνόητοι Γαλάται in Gal 3.1, so once again we may have to do not with James directly borrowing from diatribe but rather—and ironically—mimicking the language of the one he is disputing; see above, 67.

ὦ ἄνθρωπε κενέ is in the singular despite the plural of v. 24. Those who see polemic aimed directly at Paul might think this appropriate: James rebukes a single figure.

ὅτι ἡ πίστις χωρὶς τῶν ἔργων ἀργή ἐστιν;[310] This rewrites v. 17, with ἀργή = 'useless'[311] replacing νεκρά, probably for the sake of variation—cf. the βλέπεις ὅτι of v. 22 with the ὁρᾶτε ὅτι of v. 24—and/or to create a wordplay: ἔργων ἀργή; cf. the wordplays in Wis 14.5 (θέλεις δὲ μὴ ἀργὰ εἶναι τὰ τῆς σοφίας σου ἔργα); Athanasius, *Inc.* 13.5 SC 199 ed. Kannengiesser, 312 (ἀργὸν αὐτοῦ τὸ ἔργον γένηται). The word—appropriately chosen for the gas Argon, an inert element—here connotes moral disgrace.[312] Easton, 44, suggests that English could reproduce the

---

[306] Cf. Did 2.5: 'Your word must not be false or empty (κενός) but confirmed by action'. Cargal, 129: 'a faith isolated from works can only be "empty words"'. For Blomberg and Kamell, 136, the expression connotes 'moral error' more than 'deficient understanding'.

[307] Cf. Oecumenius *ad loc.* PG 119.480C.

[308] Cf. Easton, 40: James shows 'impatience with a theory...he regards as so futile that its falsity ought to be obvious to everyone'. Against Martin, 90, a 'wisdom background' is not 'evident'.

[309] Epictetus employs the vocative ἄνθρωπε over sixty times.

[310] P74 **L**:F have κενή instead of ἀργή. This echoes the preceding κενέ. 01 02 04C2 025 044 5 33 69 81 88 206 *et al.* **Byz** Cyr PsOec **L**:T,CAr **K**:B **S**:PH **G**:BG-D **Sl**:D **Ä** substitute νεκρά, which is likely assimilation to vv. 17 and 26.

[311] ἀργός: LXX: 5× (2× in Wisdom, 2× in Ecclesiasticus). NT: 8×; Jas: 1×. Gk. Pseudepigrapha (Denis): 2×. Philo: 18×. Josephus: 21×. The word can also mean 'idle', as in Mt 20.3, 6; cf. BAGD, s.v., 1. Popkes, 202, finds both meanings present: a faith lacking works does nothing and is useless.

[312] Cf. Mt 12.36; 2 Pet 1.8.

wordplay with: 'faith apart from works does no work'.³¹³ Does the definite article τῶν (as in v. 18 but not 26) allude to the works of mercy in vv. 15-16?³¹⁴

Verse 21. This verse refers to Abraham's famous deed of obedience, v. 22 to his faith. Together the two lines set the stage for v. 23 and the right interpretation of Gen 15.6: that verse does not support a doctrine of faith without works because Abraham's faith was not without works.

Verses 20-24 offer two examples of faith with deeds, examples that serve as general illustrations.³¹⁵ The verses balance and stand in antithesis to the two examples in vv. 15-19—someone ignoring the needy, demons believing that God is one.³¹⁶ One should note, however, that Abraham and Rahab behave in unethical ways: the patriarch seeks to kill his son, and the harlot tells lies.³¹⁷ Should readers infer that context and intention make acts 'become good, and assume a justifying character'?³¹⁸ Or does the text, which has just endorsed the decalogue (2.10-11), here deconstruct itself?

Ἀβραὰμ ὁ πατὴρ ἡμῶν. The title implies: 'as the father, so also the children'.³¹⁹ If Abraham was not justified without works, no one will be.

Because, in Jewish and Christian texts, descent from Abraham is the basis for membership in the people of God, he is often called 'father',³²⁰

---

³¹³ R. Wall, 138, proposes an allusion to 'the birth images used earlier to chart spiritual failure as the "conception" of sin (1:14) that "brings forth" death (1:15) rather than life (1:12)'. This subtle reading is otherwise unattested in the commentary tradition. Dowd, 'Faith', 199, also offers a novel suggestion: 'James could be alluding to the Pauline use of "fruit" to denigrate the behaviors and attitudes that result from life in the Spirit...the author of James wants to makes the point that faith can be "unfruitful"'.

³¹⁴ Cf. Frankemölle, 448; Popkes, 202.

³¹⁵ Cf. Jn 8.39: 'If you were Abraham's children, you would do what Abraham did'. One should keep in mind that Abraham at least was traditionally an exemplum of various virtues—of obedience, of hospitality, and of faith.

³¹⁶ Doriani, 82, refers to the 'four case studies' of 2.15-26.

³¹⁷ Cf. Darby, *Synopsis*, 361: 'One was a father going to put his son to death, the other a bad woman betraying her country'.

³¹⁸ So Mozley, 'Faith', 483. Cf. Moffatt, 40: 'the two examples...were of actions inspired by faith which had no direct relation to the important duty of charity'. On Rahab's dissembling see above, 441-42. Christian interpreters of James almost universally avoid the question of the morality of Abraham's act. Darby, as in n. 317, is an exception. So too the deist, T. Chubb, 'Treatise XIX', in *A Collection of Tracts*, London, 1730, 245: James commends only Abraham's trust and confidence, not his judgment or reasoning that led him to attempt murder. But Theissen, 'Intention', 72, 76, finds it relevant because he takes the implicit argument to be this: if Abraham was called God's friend for the extreme act of human sacrifice, how much more should the harmless practices of Jewish Christianity be acceptable.

³¹⁹ So Pemble, *Vindiciae Fidei*, 211-12.

³²⁰ Gen 17.4-5; Exod 3.6; Josh 24.3; Isa 51.2; Tob 4.12; Ecclus 44.19; LAB 32.1; Philo, *Gig.* 64; Josephus, *Ant.* 1.158; Lk 1.55, 73; Jn 8.39, 53; Par. Jer. 4.10; 31.2; *T. Jac.* 7.22 ('father of fathers'); etc. Hence the correlative term, 'son of Abraham': 4 Macc 6.17, 22; Mt 3.9; Gal 3.7; m. B. Qam 8.6; etc.

and Ἀβραὰμ ὁ πατὴρ ἡμῶν, with its plural possessive, was a common designation.[321] It is the Greek equivalent of אברהם אבינו, the usual rabbinic title,[322] and consistent with our author being Jewish.[323] Given the content of the rest of our letter, there is no need to spiritualize the expression so that it applies to all Christians, Gentiles as well as Jews.[324] James speaks as a Jew to fellow Jews, including non-Christian Jews; see on 1.1. Thus 'our father' is for him an ecumenical expression: it reaches beyond the church.

Davids, 128-29, observing that Jewish tradition made Abraham out to be the first monotheist (see n. 449), suggests that v. 19 ('You believe that God is one') fittingly leads to reflections on the patriarch.

As it is possible that James was familiar with Romans, one should observe that the latter refers to Abraham as τὸν προπάτορα ἡμῶν (4.1) and τοῦ πατρὸς ἡμῶν respectively (4.12).

οὐκ ἐξ ἔργων ἐδικαιώθη. For the argument that this phrase shows knowledge of Paul see above, 445-46. Regarding ἐδικαιώθη,[325] harmonizers of Paul and James have sometimes insisted that the two use δικαιόω in different ways.[326] Roman Catholic exegetes have traditionally tended to think of a first justification without works (Paul's subject) and then a second justification involving meritorious works (James' subject). Protestant exegetes have more typically distinguished between being approved and such approval being declared or evidenced, so that in James, as opposed to Paul, 'justified by works' means something like 'his faith was declared/evidenced by good deeds'.

In the LXX, the chief meaning of δικαιόω is 'declare just and righteous', that is, 'vindicate' or 'acquit'.[327] This is also the first meaning

---

[321] Cf. 4 Macc 16.20; T. Levi 6.9; 8.15; Lk 1.73; Jn 8.53; Acts 7.2; Rom 4.12; 1 Clem. 31.2; Gk. Apoc. Ezra 2.6; 3.10.

[322] m. Ned. 3.11; m. Qidd. 4.14; m. 'Abot 3.12; 5.3; t. Ber. 6.12; t. Ḥag. 2.1; b. Ned. 32a; etc.

[323] The expression occurs in 1 Clem. 31.2, but Pauline influence explains this.

[324] Cf. Mayor, 102: 'Its use favours the supposition that the epistle is addressed principally to Jews'. Hort, 63, argues to the contrary; so too Mussner, 141.

[325] δικαιόω: Jas: 3×: 2.21, 24, 25.

[326] See above n. 20; also W. Tyndale, *Answer to Sir Thomas More's Dialogue*, Cambridge, UK, 1850, 202; M. Bucer, 'Bestendige Verantwortung' in *Martin Bucers Deutsche Schriften* 11.3 ed. Wilhelmi, 157; Osiander, 723; Diodati *ad loc.*; H. Knollys, *Mystical Babylon Availed*, London, 1679, 23-24 ('faith justifies our Persons, and good Works justifies our Faith'); Manton, 244-46; J. Edwards, 'Justification by Faith Alone', in *Works of Jonathan Edwards*, vol. 19, New Haven, 2001, 230-37; Guyse, 579 (justification of one's good character vs. justification of one's person before God); J. Buchanan, *The Doctrine of Justification*, Edinburgh, 1867, 358; Grosheide, 41; Pink, *Doctrines*, 241 ('Paul treats of the justification of *persons*; James, of the justification of our *profession*'); Moo, 134-35, 141-42; *et al.*

[327] So Muraoka, *Lexicon*, s.v.; cf. LXX Gen 38.26; Exod 23.7; Deut 25.1; Isa 5.23; Ecclus 10.29; 13.22; 42.2; etc. See further C. VanLandingham, *Judgment and Justification in Early Judaism and the Apostle Paul*, Peabody, MA, 2006, 254-72 (who thinks that the meaning in James is 'to make righteous').

in the Greek Pseudepigrapha as well as the earliest Christian literature.[328] One is inclined, with most modern commentators, to read James accordingly: God declared Abraham righteous because of his faithful obedience (a verdict which anticipates the eschatological verdict).[329] Some, as noted, instead think of the verb not as declarative but as demonstrative: his works showed him to be righteous in truth.[330] But the difference, although often thought highly significant for reconciling Paul and James, need not amount to much. In view of Abraham's reputation in Judaism, there can be no question of the patriarch having been, to use the theological jargon, a justified sinner. He is no example of *simul iustus et peccator*. On the contrary, God's speech-act must correspond to the truth: Abraham was indeed righteous.[331] One could say that God declared what Abraham demonstrated.[332]

James (unlike Paul) is not writing about Gentiles entering the faith community; nor is he concerned with the justification of the ungodly or with an imputation of righteousness.[333] Our author is rather concerned with a divine declaration of righteousness that is in accord with the facts; and his burden is to insist that professed faith without good deeds is insufficient, that it is a grossly deficient faith, no better than that of demons, and so without divine approval.

James' use of Abraham in this connection is altogether natural, perhaps indeed more natural than the Pauline reading (which avoids referring to the Aqedah). Because of Gen 22, Abraham was famed as an exemplar of obedience, as one who did the will of God.[334]

---

[328] E.g. 1 En. 102.10; Pss. Sol. 2.15; 3.5; 4.8; T. Sim. 6.1; T. Dan 3.3; Mt 11.19; Lk 7.29; 10.29; 16.15; T. Abr. RecLng. 13.13; Barn. 6.1; Apoc. Sed. 14.8. The generalization does not hold for Philo and Josephus.

[329] Usteri, 'Glaube', 230, puts it this way: δικαιοῦν = 'gerechtsprechen'.

[330] So e.g. Calvin, 285-86; Grotius, 1081; Dickson, 690-91; Barlow, *Letters*, 81-92 (justification in Paul is *coram deo*, in James *coram hominibus*); Davids, 127-28; Fung, 'Justification', 152-54; Johnson, 242 ('shown to be'); Hartin, 154; Compton, 'Justification', 41; Kamell, 'Soteriology', 181; also many of those named in n. 20 as well as Gregory Palamas, *Hom. i–xx* 8.3 ed. Chrestou and Zeses, 214. Criticism in Usteri, 'Glaube', 230-31; Moo, 135. R. Baxter, *Aphorismes of Justification*, 2nd ed., The Hague, 1655, 188, counters the interpretation by observing that the sacrifice of Isaac was 'a secret Action'.

[331] Cf. Aristotle, *Eth. nic.* 1103A: 'one becomes just by doing just things'.

[332] Cf. McKnight, 247: 'Even if one can distinguish God declaring that a person is righteous... from the one who is forensically declared righteous in the final courtroom... that final court's decision is undoubtedly connected to the more earthly recognition by God'.

[333] James leads more naturally to Augustine, who taught that justified humanity gains an inherent righteousness, than to Luther, who thought rather in terms of an imputed righteousness.

[334] Note LXX Gen 22.18 (ὑπήκουσας τῆς ἐμῆς φωνῆς); 26.5 (ὑπήκουσεν Ἀβραάμ ὁ πατήρ σου τῆς ἐμῆς φωνῆς); Ecclus 44.20 (Abraham kept the law even before it was given; cf. 2 Bar. 57.1-2); Jub. 21.2-3; Philo, *Her.* 8 (citation of Gen 26.5); Heb 11.8 (Ἀβραὰμ ὑπήκουσεν); Josephus, *Ant.* 1.225 (Abraham deemed 'that nothing would

Although the aorist ἐδικαιώθη refers to an event or events in the life of Abraham, the immediate setting in James has to do with eschatological salvation (vv. 13-14), and δικαιόω must be closely related to the σῶσαι in v. 14: the one who is righteous and/or wins the approving verdict of God now will be saved at the end.[335] Justification by works in the present means salvation in the future. And as with Abraham, so with everyone else.[336]

That justification is by works does not exclude a role for faith. Rather, as the context makes clear, ἐξ ἔργων ἐδικαιώθη really means 'justified by works (that are joined with faith)'. James does not counter one extreme—justification by faith alone—with another extreme—justification by works alone.[337] He instead stakes out the middle ground: faith and deeds are necessary.[338]

The modern philosophical theologian, John Hick, has written: 'Recent investigations of the nature of belief have emphasized the close connection...between believing that such-and-such is the case and acting appropriately to such-and-such being the case... "Belief" is largely a dispositional word... There are strong reasons for holding that to be in a state of believing some proposition is, primarily, to possess (or be possessed by) a set of tendencies, liabilities, or dispositions to act in ways appropriate to the truth of that proposition in situations to which the proposition is seen to be relevant. Further, in so far as such tendencies demand and find occasion for expression in overt actions, their existence is a public fact, as readily observable by others as by ourselves... [For a man to say] that he believes p, is not conclusive: for he may find out in a "moment of truth", when for the first time circumstances require him to act upon his belief, that he does not in fact believe what he supposes that he believed... Our actions alone reveal infallibly what we believe.'[339]

---

justify disobedience [παρακούειν] to God'); 1 Clem. 10.1 ('Ἀβραάμ... πιστὸς εὑρέθη ἐν τῷ αὐτὸν ὑπήκοον γενέσθαι); Tg. Ps.-J. Gen 22.18 ('you obeyed my word'). The disobedience of Abraham in The Testament of Abraham is a comedic parody of this far-flung tradition.

[335] Against Ménégoz, *Étude*, 122-25, James does nothing to associate δικαιόω directly with the forgiveness of sins.

[336] Cf. Mussner, 147. Augustine's nuanced remarks about 'justification' in *Hom.* 158 and 159 PL 38.864-68, come to mind: Christians are 'partly justified' now; justification can grow; perfect justification belongs to the eschatological future.

[337] *Pace* Luther, *Table Talk*, in Luther's Works, vol. 54, ed. T.G. Tappert, Philadelphia, 1967, 424 (no. 5443); Baur, *Paul*, 301-302 ('ἔργα and they alone are regarded as real and substantial'; 'πίστις has scarcely any real existence in itself at all'); R. Walker, 'Werken'; Klein, *Werke*, 76-77; Lautenschlager, 'Gegenstand', 181.

[338] Cf. Mussner, 144; Nicol, 'Faith'; Frankemölle, 449-50, 454; Popkes, 208; Nienhuis, *Paul*, 221; Theissen, 'Intention', 76 ('His ethical Christianity treads the correct middle way. Faith and works are in equal respects important').

[339] J. Hick, *Faith and Knowledge*, 2nd ed., Ithaca, NY, 1966, 247-48. I owe the reference to Hick to Harman, 'Faith', 37. Hick's words are taken from a chapter entitled 'Faith and Works', which opens by citing Jas 2.26.

These words may serve as an analysis of what James thinks of Abraham: the Aqedah proved the reality of his faith, and without the Aqedah, there would have been no faith.

For understanding the history of interpretation of James it is crucial to keep in mind that Augustine—like medieval theologians and the Council of Trent after him—'has an all-embracing understanding of justification, which includes both the *event* of justification (brought about by operative grace) and the *process* of justification (brought about by cooperative grace). Augustine himself does not, in fact, distinguish between these two aspects of justification: the distinction dates from the sixteenth century.'[340] This means that a clear division between sanctification and forensic justification, so important for Protestant discourse (e.g. Calvin), should not be read back into earlier texts, including James. Our author did not anticipate the Reformation's notional division between the on-going process of sanctification and a one-time forensic justification.

Under the influence of Ward—who insists on a close connection between vv. 14-26 and 12-13—more and more exegetes are inclined to stress the plural ἔργων and to infer that the sacrifice of Isaac is only one instance of a larger collection of deeds, among which must be hospitality, for which Abraham was, because of Gen 18, famed.[341] This then strengthens the association with Rahab, who took in strangers (2.25), and it well suits vv. 15-16, which concern helping the unfortunate. Beyond that, Jewish tradition celebrated Abraham's ten trials, of which the Aqedah was only one in a series.[342] But this may read too much into the text. The plural, ἐξ ἔργων, may be nothing more than a carry-over from previous lines,[343] or perhaps it is borrowed Pauline terminology. Further, whereas Rahab is also commended for only one act, the plural is nonetheless

---

[340] So A.E. McGrath, *Iustitia Dei*, vol. 1, Cambridge, UK, 1986, 31. Cf. 184: 'The significance of the Protestant distinction between *iustificatio* and *regeneratio* is that a fundamental discontinuity has been introduced into the western theological tradition *where none had existed before*'. See further D.F. Wright, 'Justification in Augustine', in *Justification in Perspective*, ed. B.L. McCormack, Grand Rapids, MI, 2006, 55-72. The Vulgate's rendering of δικαιόω helps explain Augustine's view: the Greek is represented by *iustificare*, which means 'make just'.

[341] Ward, 'Works'. Cf. Burge, 'Form', 39; Davids, 127; Johnson, 248-49; R. Wall, 142-443, 146-48; idem, 'Rahab', 224-26; Batten, *Friendship*, 140-41 ('it could be'); McKnight, 250-51. But note already Dibelius, 161. On Abraham's proverbial hospitality see A.E. Arterbury, 'Abraham's Hospitality among Jewish and Early Christian Writers', *PRS* 30 (2003), 359-76.

[342] See n. 367. Klein, *Werke*, 76, finds this tradition behind James.

[343] Verses 14, 17, 18, 20. Cf. Laws, 135 ('the use of *erga* in both examples [Abraham and Rahab] surely derives from the contrast between *faith* and *works* throughout vv. 14-26, the language being imposed on both illustrations of the theme, rather than emerging from a strictly literal consideration of their content'); Hartin, 160 (the plural 'is more stylistic than factual').

used,[344] and it remains odd that, were James thinking of Abraham's hospitality in particular, he does not clearly refer or allude to Gen 18.[345]

Although ἐξ ἔργων ἐδικαιώθη is a sign of Pauline influence, it is striking that Mt 11.19 diff. Lk 7.35 has this: ἐδικαιώθη ἡ σοφία ἀπὸ τῶν ἔργων. Moreover, Mt 12.37 (unique to Matthew) reads: ἐκ γὰρ τῶν λόγων σου δικαιωθήσῃ. Given that this commentary raises elsewhere the possibility that James knew Matthew, one might wonder whether our author thought that Jesus taught justification by works. One might also, and perhaps at the same time, wonder whether Matthew, like James, used Pauline terminology in an unPauline fashion.

ἀνενέγκας Ἰσαὰκ τὸν υἱὸν αὐτοῦ ἐπὶ τὸ θυσιαστήριον; The language comes from LXX Gen 22, which was widely alluded to and quoted.[346] ἀναφέρω[347] appears in 22.2 (ἀνένεγκον αὐτὸν ἐκεῖ) and 13 (ἀνήνεγκεν αὐτόν).[348] 22.3, 6, 9, and 13 are the source of Ἰσαὰκ τὸν υἱὸν αὐτοῦ. And ἐπὶ τὸ θυσιαστήριον[349] derives from 22.9.[350] There was much speculation about the sacrifice of Isaac in Jewish tradition. Lore gathered around several issues, including whether Isaac was a willing participant.[351] Christians for their part came to see Isaac as a prototype of Christ.[352] None of that, however, is to the point for James. What matters is Abraham's obedience, which demonstrates the authentic nature of his faith.[353]

Verse 22. Although this verse has been taken to imply the foundational importance of faith—deeds complete what faith begins[354]—or to intimate that faith and works are related as source to product, the question of

---

[344] But Frankemölle, 475, sees receiving messengers and sending them away as two acts.

[345] Dibelius, 162, raises the possibility that the formula simply means 'by his conduct'.

[346] E.g. Wis 10.5; Ecclus 44.20; 1 Macc 2.52; 4 Macc 16.20; Jub. 17.15–18.16; 4Q225 2.1; Philo the Epic Poet frag. 1 *apud* Eusebius, *Praep. ev.* 9.20.1 ed. Holladay, 234; Philo, *Deus* 4; *Abr.* 167-207; LAB 32.1-4; Josephus, *Ant.* 1.222-36; Heb 11.17-19; 1 Clem. 10.7. See further J. Swetnam, *Jesus and Isaac*, Rome, 1981, 23-80.

[347] Jas: 1×. For this as a technical term for sacrifice see BAGD, s.v., 3.

[348] Cf. Philo, Somn. 1.195: λάβε τὸν υἱόν...καὶ ἀνένεγκε...ἀνενηνοχότος. LXX Gen 22.9 has ἐπέθηκεν. Attempts to decide whether ἀνενέγκας is instrumental ('having offered up') or causal ('because he offered up') demand too much of James' text.

[349] θυσιαστήριον: Jas: 1×. Cf. Mt 5.23.

[350] The proposal of Reicke, 34, that 'the allusion to the altar may reflect the practice in the early church of placing the love offerings on the table or altar' is a reminder that sometimes commentators, in their quest to say something new, prefer the obscure and incredible over the obvious.

[351] So e.g. 4 Macc 16.20; LAB 32.2-3; Tg. Ps.-J. Gen 22.10.

[352] So already Barn. 7.3, and perhaps Rom 8.32.

[353] Manton, 251: 'Isaac is counted offered, because he was so in Abraham's purpose'.

[354] Cf. W. Ames, *Medulla theologica* 2.3.27, citing Jas 2.22 ('the internal produces the external and in it is brought to its end'); Wesley, 863; Bartmann, *Paulus*, 125; Mussner, 142; Compton, 'Justification', 39; Kamell, 'Soteriology', 182. Laato, 'Justification', argues at length for 'the priority of faith' as opposed to works for James.

whether faith or work is primary for James is likely misplaced. Our author, although he may well have believed that the religious life begins in faith,[355] addresses other matters.[356] For him, the crux is that Abraham's faith was not without deeds.[357] A later theologian might have said that there is no 'forensic justification' without 'effective justification'.

Although Abraham's faith has not yet been mentioned, v. 22 makes it sound as though it has. The explanation is that a debate over the meaning of Gen 15.6 is here anticipated. James assumes that his interlocutor will respond to his argument by appealing to the famous text about Abraham's faith and righteousness. So the subject of vv. 21-23 is the right interpretation of a biblical passage.

βλέπεις ὅτι ἡ πίστις συνήργει τοῖς ἔργοις αὐτοῦ. Cf. T. Gad 4.7 (τὸ δὲ πνεῦμα τῆς ἀγάπης…συνεργεῖ τῷ νόμῳ τοῦ θεοῦ); Musonius Rufus, *Diss*. 5 (συνεργεῖ μὲν γὰρ καὶ τῇ πράξει ὁ λόγος διδάσκων ὅπως); Herm. *Mand*. 5.1.6 v.l. (βλέπεις ὅτι ἡ μακροθυμία); *Sim*. 5.6.6 (συνεργήσασαν ἐν παντὶ πράγματι). The point is that, in the case of Abraham, faith and works together attained the goal of righteousness (v. 23).[358] The words are more forceful as an assertion rather than (as in the Vulgate) a question.[359]

βλέπω and συνεργέω[360]—the latter stands in stark contrast to the ἀργή of v. 20 and, like it, creates a wordplay: ηργει/εργοι[361]—occur only here in our epistle. For the latter used of virtues or vices working together see T. Reub. 3.6. Here συνήργει—the imperfect seemingly implies the

---

[355] In much early Christian discourse, one's pilgrimage commences with faith, that is, with believing the Christian message; cf. Ps.-Mk 16.16; Jn 3.15-16; Acts 10.43; Rom 10.9-10; Heb 4.3; etc. If this was James' view, he might have approved of the simile in Baxter, *Aphorismes* (as in n. 330), 194: 'The continuance and accomplishment of Justice is not without the joynt procurement of obedience. As a woman is made a mans wife, and instated in all that he hath, upon meer acceptance, consent, and contracts; because conjugall actions, affections, the forsaking of others, &c. are implied in the Covenant, & expressed as the necessary for future; therefore if there be no conjugall actions, affections or fidelity follow, the Covenant is not performed, nor shall the woman enjoy the benefits expected.'

[356] Cf. Rainbow, *Way*, 222: 'In vain do we search in James 2:14-26 for any statement of a causal relationship between faith and works or between righteousness and obedience'.

[357] See further Huther, 96-97. But for the argument that deeds are 'primary' see Heiligenthal, *Zeichen*, 28. For the opposite view see Lodge, 'Paul'.

[358] Precise interpretation at one time was a point of dispute between Catholics and Protestants; cf. Manton, 253: 'The Papists urge it to prove that faith needeth the concurrence of works in the matter of justification, as if works and faith were joint causes; but then the apostle would have said, that works wrought with his faith, and not faith with his works'—a dubious retort.

[359] So too Mayor, 103-104, and most interpreters.

[360] LXX: 2×. NT: 4× (3× in Paul); cf. Ps.-Mk 16.20. Gk. Pseudepigrapha (Denis): 6× (all in the Testaments of the Twelve Patriarchs; cf. T. Iss. 3.7: God working together with human integrity; T. Gad 4.7: the spirit of love working together with the law). Philo: 28×. Josephus: 32×.

[361] Cf. Aristotle, *Physiog*. 809B: συνεργεῖ καί τι ἔργον ῥώμης ἀπεργάζεται.

continual coordination of faith and works—functions as the antithesis of χωρίς in v. 20: instead of being separated, faith and deeds join together. Abraham's faith was, because of Gen 15.6 (which James quotes in the next line), proverbial.[362] In Josephus, *Ant.* 1.233, τὸ ἔργον is used of the sacrifice of Isaac. For the plural see on v. 21.

καὶ ἐκ τῶν ἔργων ἡ πίστις ἐτελειώθη.[363] Note the chiastic arrangement:

ἡ πίστις...   τοῖς ἔργοις
τῶν ἔργων   ἡ πίστις

Cf. Clement of Alexandria, *Strom.* 7.10.55.1 GCS 17 ed. Stählin, 40: τελειοῦται ἡ πίστις. Although τελειόω occurs only here in our epistle, τέλειος is used on multiple occasions: 1.4, 17, 25; 3.2. For the verb with ἐκ—nowhere else in the NT—see Philo, *Agr.* 42 ('Jacob was perfected as a result of [τελειωθέντι ἐξ] discipline'); *Conf.* 181 ('made perfect [τελειωθέντος ἐξ] through practice'); *Praem.* 49 (faith is the reward for the one ἐκ διδασκαλίας τελειωθέντι); Plutarch, *Mor.* 582F (ἐξ ἀμφοῖν τελειοῦται).

Commentators sometimes insist that ἐτελειώθη indicates not that Abraham's faith was perfected in time but that, when he offered Isaac, it was shown to have been perfect from the beginning.[364] This is to construe James in terms of Paul and later theology.[365] It is better to read our text in the light of 1.2-4: faith is not a static given (cf. 2 Thess 1.3), and it becomes fully what it should be through trial, when it exercises itself and overcomes the obstacles that face it.[366] Trials—for which Abraham was famed[367]—are a means of testing faith, and besting them results in the

---

[362] Cf. Neh 9.7; 1 Macc 2.52; 2 Macc 2.1; Ecclus 44.20; Jub. 14.6; 17.17-18; 19.8-9; 4Q226 7.1; Philo, *Deus* 4; *Abr.* 262, 273; *Virt.* 216; *Praem.* 27; Rom 4.9, 12, 16; Gal 3.7, 9; Heb 11.8; 1 Clem. 10.1, 7; 31.2; Mek. on Exod 14.15, 31; etc.

[363] αὐτοῦ is added after ἔργων to balance ἔργοις αὐτοῦ in 6 206 429 *et al.* K:S^mss S:H.

[364] Cf. the use of τελεῖται in 2 Cor 12.9 (God's strength 'perfected' in weakness) and Calvin, 286: 'Abraham's faith was formed, indeed it was burnished, before ever he was called to sacrifice his son... James only means that his integrity was made certain in that action where he revealed the remarkable fruition of his loyalty.' Similar comments in H. Bullinger, *The Decades: The Third Decade*, Cambridge, UK, 1850, 333; Barlow, *Letters*, 89; Trapp, 698; Bardenhewer, 83. Appropriate criticism in Huther, 97-98.

[365] For Oesterley, 448, if James really means that faith was 'made perfect', this is at odds with 'the purely Christian idea of faith'.

[366] Cf. Ign. *Eph.* 14.1 ('faith is the beginning and love is the end'); Manton, 254; W. Lyford, *The Instructed Christian*, Philadelphia, 1847, 342 ('Faith grows stronger and stronger, the more it is exercised; and by works faith is made perfect... it attains its end, as the tree is perfect, when it has brought forth its fruit, and until it has yield its fruit, it is not perfect'); Adamson, 130; Klein, *Werke*, 77; Soards, 'Abraham', 25. The Council of Trent may, in this particular, approximate what is implicit in James: 'faith is the first stage of human salvation, the foundation and root of all justification'; see 'Decree on Justification' from session 6 (January 13, 1547) in *Decrees of the Ecumenical Councils*, vol. 2, ed. N.P. Tanner, London, 1990, 674.

[367] For the tradition of multiple trials of Abraham see Jub. 17.17-18 (this lists seven trials); 19.2-3, 8 (this mentions ten trials); m. 'Abot 5.3 ('Abraham our father was tested

'patient endurance' that 'produces a perfected work'.³⁶⁸ One might also, despite the plural ἔργων, think not of a series of trials but of the single episode in Gen 22: that act 'perfected' Abraham's faith.³⁶⁹

τελειόω is particularly apt because of the tradition that Abraham was perfect.³⁷⁰ Its origin lies in Gen 17.1, where God says to him: 'Walk before me and be blameless'.³⁷¹ Exegetes reasoned that, if God called Abraham to be blameless, then he, who was renowned for his obedience, must have become such, esp. in view of Gen 26.5: 'Abraham obeyed my voice and kept my charge, my commandments, my statutes, and my laws'.³⁷²

Verse 23. Genesis 15.6, according to James, does not imply that Abraham was justified by faith alone: his justification involved, indeed required, deeds. The argument, which oddly appeals to a text about faith (ἐπίστευσεν) in order to substantiate a claim about works,³⁷³ seems to assume that Gen 15.6 should be connected with the sacrifice of Isaac, to which v. 21 refers; see below.³⁷⁴

---

ten times'); ARN A 33 ('with ten trials was our father Abraham tried'); b. Sanh. 89b ('I [God] have tested you with many trials'); Tg. Neof. 1 Gen 22.1 (the sacrifice of Isaac was the tenth temptation); Frag. Tg. Gen 22.1 V ('after these things, the Lord tested Abraham with the tenth test'); PRE 26-31 ('Our father Abraham was tried with ten trials', the tenth being the Aqedah).

³⁶⁸ Cf. Philo, *Conf.* 181 (Jacob was 'made perfect through practice'); *Congr.* 35 (Jacob 'was perfected as the result of discipline'); E.G. White, *Faith and Works*, Hagerstown, MD, 2003, 100 ('In order for a man to be justified by faith, faith must reach a point where it will control the affections and impulses of the heart; and it is by obedience that faith itself is made perfect'); Moo, 137.

³⁶⁹ Cyril of Jerusalem, *Catech. 1–18* 5.5 turns this completely around: πᾶν δὲ ἔργον αὐτοῦ [Abraham] κατὰ πίστιν τετέλεσται.

³⁷⁰ Cf. Jub. 23.10 ('Abraham was perfect [*feṣṣum*] with the Lord in everything he did'); Pr Man 8 ('Abraham, Isaac, and Jacob...did not sin'); Wis 10.5 (wisdom kept Abraham ἄμεμπτον); Philo, *Leg.* 3.203 (τελείου Ἀβραάμ); *Deus* 4 (Ἀβραὰμ τοῦ τελείου); *Her.* 94 (Abraham had a faith that was 'pure and unmixed'); T. Mos. 9.4 ('Never did [our] fathers nor their ancestors [the patriarchs presumably] tempt God by transgressing his commandments'); Josephus, *Ant.* 1.225 (Abraham submitted to God's will in all things); T. Abr. RecLng. 10.13 ('Abraham has not sinned'); m. Ned. 3.11 ('Abraham was not called perfect [שלם] until he was circumcised'); Gen. Rab. 46.4 ('You have no other defect but this foreskin; remove it and the defect will be gone'). Christian interpreters, however, have occasionally assured readers that Abraham could not have been perfect, because none but Jesus are; cf. Gill, 790.

³⁷¹ MT: תמים; LXX: ἄμεμπτος; cf. Jub. 15.3.

³⁷² Cf. how 1QapGen assumes that if, as Gen 13.17 has it, God ordered Abraham to walk through the entirety of the land, he must have done so, even if Genesis fails to record such a tour.

³⁷³ Popkes, 186, speaks of the verse as an 'inconvenient factor'.

³⁷⁴ Erasmus, *Paraphrase*, 153: 'If Abraham had been reluctant to sacrifice his son at God's command, he would evidently have lost the profit of his faith and the acclamation of righteousness'. Cf. Ropes, 218-19.

καὶ ἐπληρώθη ἡ γραφὴ ἡ λέγουσα. Despite 1 Kgs 2.27 (MT: למלא את־דבר יהוה אשר דבר; LXX: πληρωθῆναι τὸ ῥῆμα κυρίου ὃ ἐλάλησεν); 2 Chr 36.21 (MT: למלאות דבר־יהוה; LXX: τοῦ πληρωθῆναι λόγον κυρίου); and the theme of prophetic fulfillment in the Dead Sea Scrolls, γραφή (see on v. 3) with reference to scripture + πληρόω[375] appears to be characteristically Christian.[376] James' usage is derivative in that Christians originally and typically used the formula of prophecies coming to eschatological fulfillment. Here it rather construes an event of long ago—the Aqedah—as the fulfillment of Gen 15.6.

Exegetes wrestle with how a scripture can be fulfilled before its envisaged act. Among the proposals are these: (i) ἐπληρώθη means in effect 'brought to fruition' or 'revealed'; that is, Abraham's faith, proclaimed in chap. 15, was manifested and reached its goal and purpose in chap. 22.[377] Another way of saying this is that the event in Gen 22 confirmed the declaration in Gen 15.[378] (ii) According to Moo, 138, the sense is: Abraham's faith 'found its ultimate significance and meaning in Abraham's life of obedience'. (iii) The declaration that the Lord 'reckoned it to him as righteousness' (Gen 15.6) is soon followed (15.8) by Abraham asking, 'O Lord God, how am I to know that I shall possess it' (the land)? If this reflects an imperfect faith, then perhaps the later action in Gen 22 reflects a perfected faith.[379] (iv) The point is not that the scripture was fulfilled in the life of Abraham but that the Scripture confirms James' argument.[380] (v) James may indeed regard Gen 15.6 as a prophecy that was fulfilled in chap. 22.[381] Early Christians certainly had no trouble construing other biblical passages as prophecies against their apparent intent and original context; recall, for example, Mt 2.15, which finds a prophecy of Jesus in

---

[375] Jas; 1×. LXX: most often for מלא.

[376] Cf. Mt 26.54, 56; Mk 14.49; Lk 4.21; Jn 13.18; 17.12; 19.24 (ἡ γραφὴ πληρωθῇ ἡ λέγουσα), 36; Acts 1.16; Apost. Const. 5.19.6 ed. Funk, 293 (ἐπληρώθη ἡ γραφὴ ἡ λέγουσα). T. Sol. 23.4 (ἐπληρώθη ἡ γραφὴ ἡ λέγουσα) and Liv. Proph. Isa prologue Dor. (ἐπληρώθη ἡ γραφή) are presumably Christian, not Jewish.

[377] So e.g. Bede *ad* 2.22-23 CCSL 121 ed. Hurst, 200 (inferring from this that one can be saved although dying immediately after baptism if one's intention to make amends is truly fixed); Barlow, *Letters*, 91 (with the unique argument that Gen 15.6 was not 'scripture' until Moses wrote it down centuries later, so there was in Abraham's day no prophetic 'scripture' to be fulfilled); Benson, 67; Adam, 209 (the earlier scripture was 'verified' by the later act); Dibelius, 164 (appealing to Philo, *Abr.* 262: Gen 15.6 is not 'an item from the story of Abraham' but a 'generalization about this life'); Mitton, 113 (Gen 15.6 is a 'motto which stands, as it were, over the whole life of Abraham'); Fung, 'Justification', 155; Maier, 139-40; McKnight, 254.

[378] Bauckham, *Wisdom*, 123: 'By means of' the Aqedah, 'Abraham's faith in God stood the test'; that is, the verdict of Gen 15.6 'is confirmed when his faith is tested and proves itself in Genesis 22'.

[379] Knowling, 62, seems to be alone in suggesting this.

[380] Davids, 129; Martin, 93.

[381] Cf. Huther, 98-99; Beyschlag, 139-40; Ropes, 221; Lindemann, *Paulus*, 246; Johnson, 243; Hartin, 155.

FAITH WITHOUT WORKS (2.14-26)

the retrospective Hos 11.1. But perhaps (vi) it suffices to recall the rabbinic dictum that there is no before or after in Scripture,[382] so that a verse can be fulfilled before what it envisages takes place.

ἐπίστευσεν δὲ 'Αβραὰμ τῷ θεῷ καὶ ἐλογίσθη αὐτῷ εἰς δικαιοσύνην.[383] LXX Genesis 15.6 reads: καὶ ἐπίστευσεν 'Αβραὰμ τῷ θεῷ καὶ ἐλογίσθη αὐτῷ εἰς δικαιοσύνην;[384] cf. Ps 106.31 (Phinehas' zeal 'was reckoned to him as righteousness'); Jub. 30.17 (when Simeon and Levi slaughtered the Shechemites, 'it was reckoned to them as righteousness'); 31.23 ('he made the two sons of Jacob sleep, one on his right and one on his left, and it was counted to him as righteousness'); 4QHalakhic Letter (see below).[385] If James knew the LXX as we have it, he substituted δέ for καί and added an α to 'Αβράμ. Both changes could be stylistic, the latter assimilation to the fuller spelling in v. 21. Yet Philo, *Mut.* 177; Rom 4.3; 1 Clem. 10.6; and Justin, *Dial.* 92.3, agree exactly with James, so we plausibly have here a non-LXX reading. There is also the possibility, if James knew Romans, that here he follows Paul.[386]

For James, Abraham's faith cannot have been empty belief because it was confirmed by sacrificial obedience: his faith was faithfulness. Philo, *Abr.* 262, similarly associates Gen 15.6 with the remark that faith 'is a little thing if measured in words, but a very great thing if made good by action'. Cf. 1 Clem. 10.1: 'Abraham...was found faithful when he became obedient to the words of God'.

Jewish and Christian sources cite and allude to Gen 15.6 often.[387] Philo, *Abr.* 262, just quoted, shows us how it could be related to Abraham's deeds.[388] 1 Macc 2.52, which applies Gen 15.6 to Abraham having been found faithful in testing,[389] probably shows us that the verse was traditionally related to the Aqedah; cf. Jub. 17.15-16 (Mastema proposed the sacrifice of Isaac as a challenge to Abraham being 'faithful in

---

[382] See D. Daube, *New Testament Judaism*, vol. 2, ed. C. Carmichael, Berkeley, 2000, 412-14. This would be quite ironic because Paul's argument about Abraham in Gal 3 is grounded in the biblical sequence: the promise to Abraham is more fundamental than Torah because it was prior to and became effective before the law.

[383] δέ is omitted from the quotation in P20 020 044 5 38C 94 206 429 *et al.* L1281 L:FV **K**:SB **S**:PH **A** **G**:A1BG-D. This conforms James to the LXX.

[384] MT: והאמן ביהוה ויחשבה לו צדקה.

[385] On the idiom of 'being counted as' see R.H. Gundry, 'The Nonimputation of Christ's Righteousness', in Husbands and Treier, *Justification* (as in n. 41), 19-22.

[386] So Lüdemann, *Paul*, 143; Ludwig, *Wort*, 190-91. Gal 3.6 might attest a slightly different text.

[387] 1 Macc 2.52; Jub. 14.6; 4Q225 2 1.7-8; Philo, *Leg.* 3.228; *Migr.* 44; *Abr.* 262; *Her.* 90, 94; *Mut.* 177, 186; Rom 4.3, 22; Gal 3.6; Barn 13.7; Justin, *Dial.* 92.3; Mek. on Exod 14.15, 31; Tanḥ. Buber Metsora' 5. Allusions include Philo, *Deus* 4; *Her.* 101; *Virt.* 216; Rom 4.9; Heb 11.2; Barn. 13.7; Justin, *Dial.* 23.4. Literature: Dibelius, 168-74; Hahn, 'Genesis 15.6'; Oeming, 'Glaube'.

[388] Cf. Cyril of Alexandria, *Jn.* 10.2 ed. Pusey, 579: Abraham's faith was shown in his obedience when he left his country to go to the promised land (Gen 12.1).

[389] ἐν πειρασμῷ εὑρέθη πιστός; cf. LXX Gen 22.1: ὁ θεὸς ἐπείραζεν τὸν 'Αβραάμ.

everything');³⁹⁰ 18.16 (after the attempted sacrifice: 'I have made known to all that you are faithful to me in everything'); Ecclus 44.20 (ἐν πειρασμῷ εὑρέθη πιστός; cf. 1 Mac 2.52); Philo, *Deus* 4 (an account of Abraham offering Isaac is followed by this: 'for in this [in the unwavering steadfastness of the Existent] we are told that he had put his trust', πεπιστευκέναι); Heb 11.17 (Abraham offered Isaac 'by faith'); and 1 Clem. 10.6-7 (this quotes Gen 15.6 and passes to the Aqedah).³⁹¹ Perhaps Gen 15.6 was linked with the Aqedah in part because of the associative principle, גזרה שוה. 15.6 immediately follows God's promise to make Abraham's descendants as the stars (15.5) whereas Abraham's willingness to offer Isaac wins the promise, 'I will make your offspring as numerous as the stars of heaven' (22.17). So it might have been natural to associate the two texts, and indeed to see the faith spoken of 15.6 as demonstrated and vindicated in the Aqedah. Whether or not this is the right explanation of the conventional association, James assumes it, as well as the notion that Abraham's belief was shown in radical obedience.

Nehemiah 9.7-8 may already reflect this association: 'You are the Lord, the God who chose Abram and brought him forth out of Ur of the Chaldeans and gave him the name Abraham; and you found his heart faithful (LXX: εὗρες...πιστήν) before you and made with him the covenant to give to his descendants the land...and you fulfilled your promise, for you are righteous'. According to Oeming, these words are an overview of Abraham's story that bring together Gen 12 (the promise of the land), 15 (Abraham's faith), 17 (the renaming of the patriarch), and 22 (the sacrifice of Isaac).³⁹²

How should we construe εἰς δικαιοσύνην, which with ἐλογίσθη αὐτῷ must give us some sort of accounting metaphor?³⁹³ As in 1.20, so in 2.23: one should not assimilate James to Paul. δικαιοσύνη is naturally taken to mean moral conduct in accord with the divine will. This gives the word a sense in line with common Jewish and Christian usage, for δικαιοσύνη was 'a sort of "code word" in Judeo-Greek for faithful adherence to Torah statutes—the righteousness expressed by religious observance—it being the Septuagint translation of the biblical Hebrew word [צדק] in

---

³⁹⁰ Cf. 4Q225 2 2.8; 4Q226 7 1.

³⁹¹ Cf. later Gregory Palamas, *Hom. i–xx* 8.1 ed. Chrestou and Zeses, 212-14. Note also the link between the promise of a son and Isaac's sacrifice in Tg. Ps.-J. on Exod 12.42. On the possible connection between Gen 15 and 22 in the Apocalypse of Abraham see R. Rubinkiewicz, *L'Apocalypse d'Abraham*, Lublin, 1987, 86.

³⁹² Oeming, 'Glaube', 23-24. Note that both Ecclus 44.20 and 1 Macc 2.52 use εὑρέθη πιστός of the Aqedah.

³⁹³ Dibelius, 173, followed by Davids, 130, finds an allusion to heavenly book-keeping; cf. Spitta, 84; Jub. 19.9; 30.19-20. This reads a great deal into the passage. Contrast Burchard, 130: God 'is not here a bookkeeper because he crowns Abraham's righteousness through his friendship'. One also hesitates to follow Dibelius, 164-65, when he proposes that ἐλογίσθη itself alludes to works. For criticism see Nicol, 'Faith', 17-19.

many of the contexts in which it is found'.[394] This further harmonizes with the conventional characterization of Abraham as having been especially 'righteous' or 'just',[395] as well as with 4QHalakhic Letter, which ends with an allusion to Gen 15.6 that shows how presumably many Jews read the text: 'And it will be reckoned to you as righteousness[396] when you do what is upright and good before him (God)' (4Q398 14-17 2.7). So we should think of the divine judge reckoning Abraham to be righteous because Abraham has behaved righteously.[397]

James presumably cites the verse because of Paul's use of it to promote justification by faith. Romans 4.3 (cf. vv. 9, 22) and Gal 3.6 quote Gen 15.6. In both places, Paul's application is idiosyncratic. James, by contrast, stands in the well-attested interpretive tradition that related Gen 15.6 to the Aqedah. So, while our author may otherwise be guilty of 'over-condensation' (Mayor, cclix), at least readers familiar with that exegetical tradition would understand his argument. Further, James seemingly assumes such readership, which is why he can write in the confidence that informed and sincere readers will concur with him.[398]

καὶ φίλος θεοῦ ἐκλήθη.[399] Cf. Irenaeus, *Haer*. 4.16.2: '*Abraham* without *circumcision* and without *Sabbath observance believed God, and it was reckoned to him as righteousness, and he was called the friend of God*.'[400] This might show a knowledge of James,[401] for while Abraham is often called God's friend, James and Irenaeus appear to be the first to link that motif with a clear citation of Gen 22.12.

---

[394] So N.G. Cohen, 'The Jewish Dimension of Philo's Judaism—An Elucidation of de Spec. Leg. IV 132-150', *JJS* 38 (1987), 180. See further the whole of Cohen's article (165-86), the commentary on 1.20 above, and M.J. Fiedler, 'Δικαιοσύνη in die diasporajüdischen und intertestamentlichen Literatur', *JSJ* 1-3 (1972), 120-43.

[395] Gen 18.19; 20.5; 21.23; 24.27; Wis 10.5; Ecclus 44.19; Jub. 23.10; Josephus, *Ant.* 1.158; 2 Bar. 57.2; 58.1; T. Abr. RecLng. 1.1; Clement of Alexandria, *Strom*. 1.5.30.4 GCS 52 ed. Stählin and Früchtel, 19; b. Meg. 11a; Memar Marqah 4.12; etc. Abraham was sometimes said to have kept the law before it was given: Jub. 24.11; Ecclus 44.20; m. Qidd. 4.14; Gen. Rab. 64.4; etc.

[396] ונחשבה לך צדקה; cf. MT Gen 15.6: ויחשבה לו צדקה.

[397] But the forgiveness of sins is not implied; contrast Servetus, *Righteousness of Christ's Kingdom* 4.3 trans. Wilbur, 258: 'When love is added to faith, or some good work, sins are much more emphatically forgiven, and the reward of glory is prepared for him that loves more than for him that does not so love of his own accord; and it could even then be said, Because thou hast done this, thy sins are forgiven, as James argues from Genesis xxii'.

[398] Cf. Theissen, 'Intention', 72. Contrast Knowling, xliv: it is strange that, if James is countering Paul, his exegetical argument is not more developed.

[399] 206 429 522 *et al.* S:H^T have δοῦλος instead of φίλος. Cf. MT Exod 32.13; Deut 9.27; 1 Chr 16.13; Ps 105.6, 42; 2 Macc 1.2; b. B. Bat. 15b.

[400] 'Credidit Deo et reputatum est illi ad iustitiam et amicus Dei vocatus est.'

[401] Contrast Ropes, 223 ('probably a mere coincidence'); Nienhuis, *Paul*, 36 ('there is nothing to safeguard against the possibility that both Irenaeus and the author of James are each appealing to an earlier source'). Clement of Alexandria, *Strom*. 2.5.20.1-2 GCS 32 ed. Stählin and Früchtel, 123, might also reflect James: 'Ἀβραάμ... φίλος... κεκλημένος.

καὶ φίλος θεοῦ ἐκλήθη might be governed by ἐπληρώθη ἡ γραφή (see below); but it could also be the fourth clause in a series:

22a βλέπεις ὅτι:
22a ἡ πίστις συνήργει τοῖς ἔργοις αὐτοῦ
22b καὶ ἐκ τῶν ἔργων ἡ πίστις ἐτελειώθη
23a καὶ ἐπληρώθη ἡ γραφὴ ἡ λέγουσα...
23b καὶ φίλος θεοῦ ἐκλήθη

One can also separate v. 23 from v. 22 and then view καὶ φίλος κτλ. as an independent statement.

καλέω—the passive is divine, as in the previous clause—appears only here in James. Here it connotes public reputation and prestige.[402] It is assumed that to be called something by God is to be that something.

Abraham was widely known as God's 'beloved' and 'friend',[403] as high an honor as a human being might obtain, one that puts him on a par with Moses; see n. 403. Our text—which stands over against Gen 22.12, where the Aqedah issues in Abraham being called a fearer of God[404]— may imply that he became God's friend precisely because of his faith on a particular occasion (cf. the aorist tense) or his willingness to sacrifice

---

[402] Cf. 1 Chr 11.7. Bunyan, 410: 'God's friend reputed'.

[403] Cf. 2 Chr 20.7 (MT: אֹהַבְךָ; LXX: ἠγαπημένῳ); Isa 41.8 (MT: אֹהֲבִי; LXX: ὃν ἠγάπησα); LXX 51.2 (ἠγάπησα αὐτόν); LXX Theod. Dan 3.35 (τὸν ἠγαπημένον); Jdt 8.22 (Dei amicus); Jub. 19.9; 30.20; CD 3.2 (אוהב); 4Q176 1-2 1.10 (אהבי); 4Q252 2.8 (אהבו); Philo the Epic Poet frag. 1 apud Eusebius, Praep. ev. 9.20.1 ed. Holladay, 234 (θεοφιλῆ); Philo, Sobr. 56 ('Ἀβραὰμ τοῦ φίλου μου; cf. LXX Gen 18.17); Abr. 89 (θεοφιλοῦς), 273 (φίλος); T. Abr. RecLng. 1.4, 6; 2.3, 6; 4.7; 8.2, 4; 9.7; 15.12-14; 16.5, 9; 20.14 (φίλος throughout); RecShrt. 4.10; 8.2; 14.6 (φίλος throughout), 4 Ezra 3.14; 1 Clem. 10.1 (φίλος); 17.2 (φίλος... τοῦ θεοῦ); Apoc. Abr. 9.6; 10.6; Ps.-Clem. Hom. 18.13.6 GCS 42 ed. Rehm, 247; Rec. 1.32.2 GCS 51 ed. Rehm, 26; Mek. on Exod 13.11; Sifre Num 115; Sifre Deut 352; Tanḥ. Buber Wayyera 36, Bo 7; Tg. Neof. 1 to Gen 18.17; b. Soṭah 31a; b. Menaḥ. 53b; Koran 4.125; etc. The present name of Hebron, the traditional site of the patriarchs' tombs, is el-Khalil (er Rahman) = 'the friend (of the Merciful One)'. Gen 18.17, where God asks, 'Shall I hide from Abraham what I am about to do?', might be the origin of the notion of the patriarch as God's special friend; see above. Moreover, given that Jewish tradition sometimes drew parallels between Abraham and the law-giver, who was also known as God's 'friend' (Exod 33.11; Philo, Mos. 1.156; Sib. Or. 2.245; etc.), it would have been natural to transfer the epithet to the patriarch. Cf. Origen, Lk frag. 182 GCS 49 ed. Rauer, 302. For others as the friend of God see Wis 7.27 (Lodge, 'Paul', 210; Bindemann, 'Weisheit', 215; and Dowd, 'Faith, 201, unaccountably think this lies behind our verse); Jub. 30.20-21; Jos. Asen. 23.10; Philo, Her. 21; Fug. 58; 3 Bar. 15.2 ('our friends...who have diligently done good deeds'); m. 'Abot 6.1. 'Friend of God' or 'gods' is also widely attested outside of Jewish and Christian sources: Homer, Il. 1.381; 20.347; Epictetus, Diatr. 3.22.95-96; 3.24.60; 4.3.7-10; Dio Chrysostom, 3.51, 115; 4.43; etc. See E. Peterson, 'Der Gottesfreund', ZKG 42 (1923), 161-202; 161-202; Johnson, 243-44.

[404] Note, however, that according to b. Soṭah 31a, fearing God, with reference to Abraham, means loving God; so too Gen. Rab. 56.7. According to Jacobs, 'Background', 459-60, Philo likely knew this notion; cf. Abr. 170.

his son.⁴⁰⁵ Related ideas were certainly in James' tradition. According to Philo, *Abr.* 273, it was because of Abraham's faith that God 'no longer talked with him as God but with man as a friend with a familiar'.⁴⁰⁶ Cf. CD 3.2-3 (Abraham 'was counted as a friend for keeping God's commandments and not following the desire of his spirit'); Jub. 19.9 ('he was found faithful and he was recorded as a friend of the Lord in the heavenly tablets');⁴⁰⁷ 1 Clem. 10.1 ('Abraham, who was called the friend, was found faithful in becoming obedient to the words of God'); m. 'Abot 5.3 (Abraham stood steadfast in his ten temptations because his love was great).

Although verses in 1 Chronicles, Isaiah, and Daniel speak of Abraham as God's 'friend' (see n. 403), none of the Greek texts use φίλος.⁴⁰⁸ But according to Philo, *Sobr.* 56, God asked concerning Abraham: μὴ ἐπικαλύψω ἐγὼ ἀπὸ 'Αβραὰμ τοῦ φίλου μου; This must be a version of Gen 18.17, even though the LXX is different: μὴ κρύψω ἐγὼ ἀπὸ 'Αβραὰμ τοῦ παιδός μου ἃ ἐγὼ ποιῶ; One doubts that Philo knew only our LXX,⁴⁰⁹ because the quotation illustrates his point that wisdom is God's φίλος, not God's δοῦλος. It is doubtful that, in search of a proof for that claim, his mind moved to a text with παῖς. This is all the more likely as Tg. Neof. 1 Gen 18.17 has this: 'Am I to hide from my friend (רחמי) Abraham what I am going to do?' The same reading appears in Frag. Tg. P. The agreement between Philo and the targums means that James might have known a version of Genesis in which Abraham is called, in Gen 18.17, God's φίλος. So καὶ φίλος θεοῦ ἐκλήθη might be a 'mixed citation'—a well-attested phenomenon⁴¹⁰—of Gen 15.6 and 18.17.

Within the broader context, 2.23 may be linked with 4.4, which equates being a friend of the world with being an enemy of God. Abraham is the

---

⁴⁰⁵ Other guesses were possible. For Peter of Alexandria, *Riches* 39 ed. Pearson and Vivian, 76, Abraham was called the friend of God because of his hospitality. Christian homiletical tradition often makes Abraham's friendship with God a goal to be sought; so e.g. Didymus of Alexandria, *Ps ad* 138.17-18a PTS 16 ed. Mühlenberg, 329. See further above, 440.
⁴⁰⁶ Cf. Clement of Alexandria, *Strom.* 4.106.16.1 GCS 32 ed. Stählin and Früchtel, 294, just perhaps interpreting James.
⁴⁰⁷ Here Abraham becomes God's friend after being found faithful in the burial of Sarah, his final test. Cf. Pachomius, *Instr.* ed. Budge fol. 18b.
⁴⁰⁸ Jas: 2×; cf. 4.4.
⁴⁰⁹ In *Leg.* 3.27, he quotes the reading of our LXX.
⁴¹⁰ E.g. 11QTemple 23.13-14 combines the similar Ezek 43.20 and Lev 4.25; Mt 2.5-6 attributes to 'the prophet' a quotation from Mic 5.2 + 2 Sam 5.2 = 1 Chr 11.2; Mt 21.5 prefaces its conflation of Isa 62.11 and Zech 9.9 with 'the word through the prophet saying'; Mk 1.2 attributes Mal 3.1 + Isa 40.3 to Isaiah; Acts 3.22-3 mixes LXX Deut 18.15-20 with Lev 23.29; Rom 9.27 assigns Hos 2.1 + Isa 10.22 to Isaiah; 2 Cor 6.16 fuses Lev 26.12 with Ezek 37.27. Discussion and additional examples in J. Koenig, *L'herméneutique analogique du Judaïsme antique d'après les témoins textuelles d'Isaïe*, Leiden, 1982, 1-103, 199-291.

antithesis of this. Being a friend of God, his faith and deeds make him an enemy of the world.[411]

Jerome remarks that Abraham was God's friend even though rich.[412] The comment interests because Abraham was indeed fabled for his great wealth[413] whereas James repeatedly deprecates 'the rich'.[414] Commentators, however, typically ignore the question this might raise for an informed reader of James.

Verse 24. This sounds like a deliberate, straightforward denial of Paul's theology.

ὁρᾶτε ὅτι ἐξ ἔργων δικαιοῦται ἄνθρωπος.[415] This simply generalizes: what was true for Abraham is true for all—everyone is declared justified when one is in fact just, that is, when one has appropriate deeds. The plural hints that the discourse is moving to its conclusion: James addresses not just his opponent but everyone. Some words of Origen catch the sense: anyone 'who truly believes works the work of faith and righteousness'.[416] ὁρᾶτε ὅτι is probably indicative, not imperatival or interrogatory. The use of ἄνθρωπος reinforces the impression that Paul is here in mind; see above, 480.

καὶ οὐκ ἐκ πίστεως μόνον. 'Where faith cannot be shown it does not exist, because where it exists it is shown'.[417] For the construction cf. 1.22: καὶ μὴ ἀκροαταὶ μόνον. Note also Herm. *Mand*. 10.1.4: πιστεύσαντες μόνον. Although attested in LXX Hab 2.4, ἐκ πίστεως is yet one more sign of Paul's influence; see 446. μόνον[418] shows again that James has in view a position that emphasizes faith at the apparent expense of deeds;[419]

---

[411] Cf. Batten, *Friendship*, 142-43. As friendship is a two-way relationship, the occasional discussion as to whether 'friend of God' means that Abraham loved God or God loved Abraham posits a false antithesis. Friends love each other. Cf. Exod 20.6; Deut 5.10; Prov 8.17 (wisdom: 'I love those who love me'); m. 'Abot 6.1; y. Ber. 10d (9.5).

[412] Jerome, *Ep*. 79.1 CSEL 55 ed. Hilberg, 87.

[413] See 1QapGen 21.3; 22.29-32; Josephus, *Ant*. 1.165; T. Abr. RecLng. 1.5; 13.2; 24.1; *Sefer ha-Yashar* 3.7-9.

[414] E.g. 1.10-11; 2.6; 5.1-6.

[415] 5 69 88 322 *et al*. **Byz** PsOec **L**:PEL **G**:A1 **Sl**:ChDMSiS add τοίνυν in second place.

[416] Origen, *Rom*. 4.1 FC 2.2 ed. Heither, 164.

[417] Epistola de malis doctoribus 6.2 PLSup 1.1425.

[418] Jas: 2×; it goes with πίστεως, not οὐκ. Cf. BDAG, s.v., μόνος, 2cβ: 'not by faith viewed in isolation'. This is a rare use of the adverb, but BDAG cites Clement of Alexandria, *Strom*. 3.15.98.2 GCS 52 ed. Stählin und Früchtel, 241: 'for being a eunuch does not of itself justify' (οὐ γὰρ μόνον ἡ εὐνουχία δικαιοῖ). Contrast Compton, 'Justification', 43: μόνον goes with the verb—'a man is justified by works and not only by faith'—thereby implying an initial justification by faith and a secondary justification by works.

[419] Ironically, Jas 2.24 may have contributed to Luther's translation of Rom 3.28, 'allein durch den Glauben', and to the Protestant slogan, *sola fides justificat*. For Luther's

FAITH WITHOUT WORKS (2.14-26)

and while the word does not appear in Paul's formulations about faith, it is certainly, as Luther famously insisted, implicit in Rom 3.28 ('justified by faith apart from works of the law')[420] and Gal 2.16 ('not justified by works of the law but through faith in Jesus Christ').[421] Maier, 142, rightly comments: 'the theology of James' is 'a struggle against the μόνον'.

ἐκ πίστεως μόνον entails, as Protestant commentators have been wont to emphasize, that James is not dismissing faith,[422] only contending that it, or rather perhaps its profession (cf. v. 14), is not all-sufficient or even close to being such. Ropes, 223-24, remarks: 'It is not to be inferred that James held to a justification by works without faith. Such a misunderstanding is so abhorrent to his doctrine of the inseparability of faith and works that it does not occur to him to guard himself against it'.[423] One recalls that Augustine, who so emphasizes justification by faith, can nonetheless use *sola fide* in pejorative contexts, of professing Christians who have failed to forsake vices and pursue good works.[424]

Statements in line with James' teachings are ubiquitous in early Christian literature. Representative are 1 Clem. 11-12 (Lot and Rahab were 'saved' because of their 'faith and hospitality'; cf. 50.5); Barn. 19.1 ('if any desire to make their way to the designated place, let them be diligent with respect to their works'; cf. 4.12-13); Justin, *1 Apol.* 16.8 (those not 'living as he taught are not to be recognized as Christians, even if they speak the teachings of Christ with their tongues. For he said that not those who only speak but those who also do the works will be saved'); Origen, *Dial. Heracl.* 8 SC 67 ed. Scherer, 72-74 ('It is necessary to know that, at God's tribunal, we are not judged for faith only, as if

---

discussion and defense of his translation, which takes no notice of James, see his 'On Translating: An Open Letter', in *Works*, vol. 35, ed. E.T. Bachmann, Philadelphia, 1960, 181-202. Cf. also Calvin, *Inst.* 3.11.19.

[420] According to J. Fitzmyer, *Romans*, New York, 1993, 360-61, Luther's translation (see n. 419) has precedent in the writings of Origen, Hilary, Basil, Marius Victorinus, Ambrosiaster, Chrysostom, Pelagius, Augustine, Cyril of Alexandria, Theodoret, Bernard of Clairvaux, Theophylact, Aquinas. To this list one may add the Nuremberg Bible of 1483 and three Italian translations (Genoa 1476; Venice 1538; Venice 1546). Note U. Wilckens, *Der Brief an die Römer*, vol. 1, Zurich/Neukirchener–Vluyn, 1978, 247: 'That πίστει has exclusive sense, something which the Reformers insisted upon so emphatically, is also recognized in more recent Catholic exegesis'.

[421] At the same time, the Reformers also famously insisted: 'Sola fides justificat, sed non fides quae est sola'.

[422] Indeed, Adam, 206-208, is not alone in urging that James implies justification by faith—with the proviso that such faith is authentic, active. Popkes, 187: James could not have written of justification 'without faith'.

[423] Cf. the formulation of Melanchthon, *Apologia Confessionis* in *Philippi Melanthonis Opera*, Corpus Reformatorum 27, ed. C.G. Bretschneider and H.E. Bindseil, 491: according to James, people are 'justified by faith and works'.

[424] See A. Zumkeller, 'Der Terminus "sola fides" bei Augustinus', in *Christian Authority*, ed. G.R. Evans, Oxford, 1988, 87-100. Medieval theology followed suit: C.P. Carlson, *Justification in Earlier Medieval Theology*, The Hague, 1975, 66-68.

life were left unexamined, nor for life only, as if faith were not subject to scrutiny. We are justified by both when both [faith and life] are correct. We are not justified by both when both are incorrect'); Evagrius, *Exh.* 2.39 PG 79.1240A ('Without deeds of righteousness, faith and baptism do not save from the eternal fire'); Chrysostom, *Jn.* 31.1 PG 59.175-76 ('Even if someone believes rightly in the Father and the Son and in the Holy Spirit yet does not live rightly, his faith will avail him nothing for salvation'); idem, *Rom.* on 2.6, 7 PG 58 ('It is not right to trust in faith only. For that [eschatological] court will also inquire into deeds'); idem, *Gal* 5 PG 61.666 ('to believe is not all that is required but also to abide in love'); Augustine, *De fide et op.* 15.25 CSEL 41 ed. Zycha, 66 ('I fail to understand why the Lord said, "If you want to enter into eternal life, keep the commandments", and then mentioned the commandments relating to good behavior if one can enter eternal life without observing them'); Maximus the Confessor, *Cent.* 1.39 PG 90.968C ('Do not say: Bare faith in our Lord Jesus can save me. For this is ineffective unless you also possess charity for him through good works').[425] One should not forget that all those just quoted admired Paul, and that many others of whom the same may be said could also sound very much like James.[426] First Clement, which teaches that Christians are 'not justified' (δικαιούμεθα) through themselves but 'through faith' (διὰ τῆς πίστεως, 32.4), insists at the same time that believers are 'justified by deeds (ἔργοις δικαιούμενοι) and not by words' (30.3). One finds much the same in many other early

---

[425] Cf. also Irenaeus, *Dem.* 98 SC 406 ed. Rousseau, 218 (the Christian way of life 'must be kept in all security' and established 'through good works'); Cyprian, *Eccl. cath. unit.* 2 CCSL 3 ed. Bévenot, 250 ('How can one who does not do what Christ commanded him to do say that he believes in Christ?'); Ambrose, *Off.* 2.2.5 CCSL 15 ed. Testard, 98 ('eternal life rests upon knowledge of things divine and the fruit of good works'); Basil the Great, *Const.* 15 PG 31.1377B ('the grace from above does not come to the one who is not striving'); Cyril of Jerusalem, *Cat.* 4.2 PG 33.456 ('True religion consists of these two elements: pious doctrines and virtuous actions... God does not accept doctrines apart from good works'); Augustine, *Trin.* 15.18 CCSL 50A ed. Mountain, 507 ('*faith* itself is only rendered profitable by *love*, since *faith* without *love* can indeed exist but cannot profit'); Ambrosiaster, *Ad Tit.* 3.7 CSEL 81.3 ed. Vogels, 332 ('By his mercy God has saved us through Christ; by his grace we are born again and have received abundantly of his Holy Spirit, so that relying on good works, with him helping us in all things, we might be able to lay hold of the inheritance of the kingdom of heaven'); Mark the Monk, *De his qui putant se ex oper. just.* 5 SC 445 ed. Durand, 132 ('The one who relies on knowledge alone is not yet a faithful servant, but the one who through obedience puts his faith in the commanding Christ'); Maximus the Confessor, *Lib. ascet.* 1 CCSG 40 ed. van Deun and Gysens, 7 (the Son of God gave 'us holy commandments and promised the kingdom of heaven to those who conduct their lives by them'; cf. 34). For the argument that the nomistic soteriology of Theophilus of Antioch might be especially close to James see R. Rogers, *Theophilus of Antioch*, Lanham, MD, 2000, 173-83.

[426] Cf. (although with different conclusions from those of this author) Mitchell, 'Document', 95-98.

FAITH WITHOUT WORKS (2.14-26)

Christian texts. Part of the explanation has to do with rhetoric: if in one context it is important to stress divine grace, in another it is crucial to insist that the faithful live their lives rightly.[427] James, however, sees more in his opponent's formulations than understandable, circumstantial rhetoric.

Verse 25. As in 3.3-4 and 11-12, James employs a second illustration to reinforce his point.

The question in v. 25 has the same structure as the question in v. 21:

Introduction of biblical hero:
        v. 21: 'Abraham our father'
        v. 25: 'also Rahab the harlot'
Question about justification:
        v. 21: 'was he not...justified by deeds?'
        v. 25: 'was she not...justified by deeds?'
Summary of activity:
        v. 21: 'he offered Isaac his son on the altar'
        v. 25: 'she welcomed the messengers and sent them out'

J. Edwards, 1172, implicitly but effectively links v. 25 to vv. 15-16: 'Had Rahab the Harlot said to the spies, "I believe God is yours, and Canaan yours, but dare not show you any kindness", her faith had been dead and unactive, and would not have justified her'.

ὁμοίως δὲ καὶ 'Ραὰβ ἡ πόρνη. ὁμοίως (Jas: 1×) refers to vv. 20-23, not 24. ὁμοίως δὲ καί[428] + personal name in the nominative was conventional.[429] Does καί here mean 'even'? James' spelling of 'Ραάβ agrees with the LXX.[430] 'Ραὰβ ἡ πόρνη became, because of Josh 6.17, 25 (MT: רחב הזונה; LXX: 'Ρααβ τὴν πόρνην), a common designation.[431] The epithet is part of the formal parallelism with v. 21, where 'our father' qualifies Abraham. That James can use πόρνη—which must mean

---

[427] Cf. Clement of Alexandria, *Strom.* 6.4.44.4 GCS 52 ed. Stählin and Früchtel, 453-54: 'For to those who were righteous according to the law, *faith* was lacking. Wherefore the Lord said, when healing them, "Your *faith* has saved you". But to those righteous according to *philosophy*, not just *faith* alone (οὐχ ἡ πίστις μόνον) in the *Lord*, but also the rejection of *idolatry*, were necessary.'

[428] Cf. LXX 1 Esd 6.29; 8.20.

[429] Polybius 3.23, 24; Diodorus Siculus 4.12.8; Strabo 9.1.17; Let. Aris. 115; Lk 10.32 (cf. 5.10); Josephus, *Bell.* 2.575; 7.128; Plutarch, *Cic.* 20.3; Aelian 10.17; Acts Jn 25 ed. Bonnet, 164; Clement of Alexandria, *Strom.* 1.16.74.2 GCS 52 ed. Stählin and Früchtel, 48; Diogenes Laertius 7.87, 148; 10.136; etc. But the LXX lacks it.

[430] Cf. Heb 11.31; 1 Clem. 12.1-3. Mt 1.5 has 'Ραχάβ, Josephus 'Ραάβη.

[431] Cf. LXX Josh 6.23; Heb 11.31; 1 Clem. 12.1; Justin, *Dial.* 111.4; Clement, *Strom.* 4.17.105.4 GCS 52 ed. Stählin and Früchtel, 294; Mek. on Exod 15.2; 18.11; Sifre Deut 52; Sifre Num 78; b. Meg. 14b; b. Zebaḥ. 116a; Num. Rab. 8.9. But she can also be mentioned without the derogatory qualification: Mt 1.5; Josephus, *Ant.* 5.8; Sifre Deut 22, 306; Exod. Rab. 27.4; etc.

'prostitute'[432]—without explanation of a woman he praises implies an expectation that his audience not only knows her story but knows the tradition that she mended her ways.[433]

Rahab, who appears in Josh 2 and 6, receives a good report in both Jewish and Christian tradition.[434] The rabbis praise her as a proselyte, a prophetess, and one of the most beautiful women in the world.[435] Legends grew out of Josh 2, where she, although a pagan prostitute, not only rescues the two spies but confesses her faith in their God: 'The Lord your God is indeed God in heaven above and on earth below' (2.11). First Clement 12.1 ('Because of her faith and hospitality Rahab the harlot was saved') and Heb 11.31 ('By faith Rahab the harlot did not perish with those who were disobedient because she had received the spies in peace') suffice to show us that she was, in Christian circles, renowned for both faith—about which James says nothing[436]—and hospitality.[437]

Despite rabbinic traditions about Rahab and the attention that Christian texts pay to her, she appears in the Tanak only in Joshua and is absent from intertestamental literature.[438] Neither the Apocrypha nor the Pseudepigrapha mention her. The two spies of Josh 2 can even be introduced in LAB 20.6-7 without intimation of her role. She is also missing from the Dead Sea Scrolls[439] and Philo. Between Joshua and the Mekilta, the only extant Jewish work to comment on the woman is Josephus, who tells her story in *Ant.* 5.5-15, 26, 28-30. Here she is not a

---

[432] A few older commentators sought to avoid this meaning, proposing instead 'hostess' or 'idolater' (cf. 'playing the harlot' as in Jer 3.6; etc.); note e.g. Nicholas of Lyra *ad loc.*; Grotius, 1082; Gilpin, 595; and the discussion in Aretius, 479-80. Cf. Hug, *Introduction*, 556. J.F. Schleusner, *Novum Lexicon Graeco-Latinum in Novum Testamentum*, Leipzig, 1819, 661, gives the second meaning of πόρνη as 'hospita, xenodocha' and puts Jas 2.25 in this category.

[433] H. Windisch, 'Zur Rahabgeschichte', *ZNW* 37 (1917/18), 191, compares Mt 21.31 ('harlots go into the kingdom of God before you'), which assumes that those mentioned have since mended their way. Cf. Marty, 108.

[434] See M.D. Johnson, *The Purpose of the Biblical Genealogies*, Cambridge, UK, 1969, 162-65; A.T. Hanson, 'Rahab the Harlot in Early Christian Theology', *JSNT* 1 (1978), 53-60; B.H. Mehlman, 'Rahab as a Model of Human Redemption', in *'Open Thou Mine Eyes...'*, ed. H.J. Blumberg et al., Hoboken, NJ, 1992, 193-207.

[435] Billerbeck 1.20-23; Mehlman, 'Rahab' (as in n. 434).

[436] Contrast Royster, 62: 'It was evidently St. James' intention to show that her works were a testimony of her faith'. Many commentators remark on her faith in passing—Estius, 414; Disconi, 692; Hemminge, 26; Winkler, 44; Sadler, 45; Johnson, 206; *et al.*

[437] Note Gregory of Nazianzus, *Or.* 40.19 SC 358 ed. Moreschini, 240: 'Rahab was justified by one thing alone, hospitality'.

[438] Despite Heb 11.30-31, where Rahab is the climactic individual on a list of heroes of faith, she does not appear on any of the analogous Jewish lists: Wis 10; Ecclus 44–50; 1 Macc 2.51-60; 4 Macc 16.16-23; 18.11-19; CD 2-3; 4 Ezra 7.105-11.

[439] The only possibility seems to be 4Q517 19.1; but nothing more survives than]ב לרח[. This could be any number of words.

prostitute but an innkeeper.[440] Perhaps the seemingly scant attention paid to her before the common era was due partly to unease with her occupation.[441] Later on, however, her vocation was for many not an embarrassment but a proof that God is graceful to those who repent of their sins, it being assumed that, by becoming a proselyte, she mended her earlier ways, which could accordingly be emphasized and enlarged.[442]

Why James follows the example of Abraham with that of Rahab is unknown; the relevant OT texts mention neither her 'faith' nor 'works'. Perhaps there is something to the comment of Gundry, 926, that tradition requires two or three witnesses to establish a case.[443] James' sequence is in any case intriguing given Rahab's relative unimportance vis-à-vis other biblical worthies. The debate with Paul seems beside the point as his extant epistles do not speak of or allude to her.[444] Beyond that, the occasional claim that the two figures were associated in Hellenistic Jewish tradition is doubtful;[445] and the patriarch and the prostitute are not directly linked in Mt 1.1-5 or Heb 11.4-21 or in early rabbinic sources.[446] The closest parallel to James' juxtaposition is 1 Clem. 10-12, which offers short synopses of 'the faith and hospitality' of both Abraham (chap. 10) and Rahab (chap. 12). Even here, however, where there is also a thematic link—faith is accompanied by deeds—a précis of Lot's 'hospitality and godliness' stands between those two summaries.

---

[440] Cf. Tg. Josh 2.1: פונדקיתא = πανδοκεύτρια ('innkeeper'). The original story probably presents her as a tavern prostitute; cf. Sifre Num 78: 'Rahab the harlot, who kept an inn'.

[441] 'Ραάβ ἡ ἐπιλεγομένη πόρνη occurs in Heb 11.31 v.l.; 1 Clem. 12.1 v.l.; Ps.-Ephraem, Cap. cent.: Quomdod quis humil. 33 ed. Phrantzoles, 304. On prostitution in the biblical and Graeco-Roman worlds see the survey of materials in J.M. Ford, 'Bookshelf on Prostitution', BTB 23 (1993), 128-34.

[442] Cf. Mek. on Exod 18.11 (she practiced harlotry for forty years); b. Meg. 14a-b; b. Zebaḥ. 116b ('there was no prince or ruler who had not possessed Rahab the harlot'); Num. Rab. 8.9; Pesiq. Rab. 40.3/4; Origen, Josh 3.4 SC 71 ed. Jaubert, 138; Chrysostom, Paen. 7 PG 49.331; Adam, 211 ('Her former infamy only enhanced the sovereignty and power of that grace by which she was forgiven, sanctified, and saved'). Knoch, 189, recalls the Synoptic Jesus' 'dealings with publicans, harlots, and the outcasts'.

[443] Num 35.30; Deut 17.6; 19.15. So too Pink, Doctrines, 246.

[444] We have no evidence that Paul made use of Rahab, who was in fact a Gentile sinner. Yet one cannot, given the incomplete and occasional nature of what has survived, exclude the possibility that he nonetheless did so. Moreover, if Hebrews represents a Pauline school, as some have thought, it is worth noting that 11.31 takes notice of her.

[445] Contrast Limberis, 'Provenance', 417 ('Rahab...is connected to Abraham in much of contemporaneous Jewish literature because of her spontaneous acts of hospitality that brought about good results'); R. Wall, 'Rahab', 220. I know of no evidence for Limberis' assertion, only inferences from Christian texts; see Dibelius, 166-67.

[446] But the later Cant. Rab. 1.3.3 follows a discussion of Abraham and Sarah as proselytes with mention of Jethro and Rahab; and Gen. Rab. 56.1, in commenting on Gen 22.4 ('on the third day'), lists events associated with the number three, including Josh 2.16 ('and hide yourselves there three days').

Calvin, 286-87, comments: it is 'strange...to link such dissimilar characters. Why not select some one from the great number of the noble Patriarchs, to cite along with Abraham?' Commentators return numerous answers, explaining the juxtaposition of patriarch and prostitute—who appear here in both the order of their importance and the order of their appearance in the Bible—in the following ways: (i) Perhaps James had access to a Jewish or Christian résumé of sacred history or a catalogue of heroes or *exempla virtutis* that mentioned both Abraham and Rahab, perhaps one after the other—although, if true, we would still need to ask why James chose to mention precisely those two and no others.[447] (ii) James, perhaps responding polemically to Hebrews, borrowed the first and last names from Heb 11.8-31.[448] (iii) The two figures were both remembered as pagans who recognized the one true God (cf. v. 19), that is, they were proselytes.[449] James, however, fails to highlight their ethnic origins, which are irrelevant to his argument. (iv) They were both paragons of hospitality.[450] This motif is consistent with ὑποδεξαμένη in v. 25 (see below), but

---

[447] See Davids, 133; Hartin, 161; Burchard, 125. Cf. Neh 9.6-37 (an outline of sacred history, including Abraham); Ps 78 (sacred history from the exodus to David); Wis 10 (exemplars of wisdom, including Abraham); Ecclus 44.1–51.24 (the great leaders of Israel, including Abraham); 1 Macc 2.51-60 (biblical heroes who underwent testing, including Abraham); 4 Macc 16.16-23 (recollection of Abraham, Isaac, Daniel, Hananiah, Azariah, Mishael); 18.10-19 (heroic figures from Israel's past); CD 2.14-3.12 (a list of those who strayed and did not stray, including Abraham); Philo, *Virt.* 187-227 (ignoble and noble characters, including Abraham); Acts 7 (a polemical version of Israel's history); Heb 11.4-40 (exemplars of faith, including Abraham and Rahab); 1 Clem. 4–6 (incidents of jealousy and those who endured it); 9–12 (ancient examples of proper behavior: Abraham, Lot, Rahab; does this depend upon Hebrews?); 17–18 (examples of humility, including Abraham); 4 Ezra 7.106-10 (a list of great intercessors, including Abraham); Apost. Const. 8.12.21-27 ed. Funk 502-506 (a list of ancient heroes, including Abraham). For comparable Graeco-Roman texts see P.M. Eisenbaum, *The Jewish Heroes of Christian History*, Atlanta, 1997, 59-73. K. Haacker, 'Glaube II/3. Neues Testament', *TRE* 13, 299, posits behind James a Jewish tradition that warned proselytes, through appeal to famous proselytes of old, that monotheism should not remain theoretical.

[448] For scholars who see dependence upon Hebrews see 70. Contrast Wiesinger, 139-40; Salmon, *Introduction*, 462 ('it seems to me that one who had read Hebrews xi. would have found in that chapter other examples of faith more tempting for discussion than the case of Rahab').

[449] Cf. Bartlett, 'Document', 173 (the issue is 'what is the appropriate faith for a proselyte'; he cites relevant rabbinic texts on 176-78); Laws, 138; Perkins, 114; Tsuji, *Glaube*, 195. For Rahab recognizing the one true God see Josh 2.11. For Abraham's conversion to monotheism note Jub. 11.16-17; 12.1-8, 16-21; Philo, *Abr.* 69-71; LAB 6.4; Josephus, *Ant.* 1.154-57; Apoc. Abr. 1–9; Heb. T. Naph. 9.5. For Laato, 'Justification', 66, it is important that both Abraham and Rahab lived before or apart from the law: 'the reforming activity of James therefore is not driven by Judaizing tendencies'.

[450] See below, 505; cf. Ward, 'Works'; Patterson, *Thomas*, 183-84; Church, 364 ('may'). For Hartin, 161, James wished to promote hospitality among Christian communities and chose Rahab accordingly.

the verses on Abraham refer only to the sacrifice of Isaac. (v) According to Carson, 'perhaps James wants maximum diversity: both the ultimate ancestor of all of Israel and an obscure Gentile prostitute woman exemplify the importance of the truth that genuine faith works itself out in actions'.[451] Others too think of Abraham as representing Jews, Rahab Gentiles or Gentile proselytes.[452] (vi) In v. 15, James sensed a rhetorical need to be gender inclusive ('brother or sister'), so perhaps here too: together, Abraham and Rahab represent both sexes.[453] (vi) Maybe the inclusivity is that of social opposites—rich honored patriarch, poor marginal prostitute.[454] (vii) The key is character. Bede suggests that, if readers found Abraham too exalted a figure to imitate, they could make no such protest about Rahab, a sinful and foreign female.[455] Related is the view of Calvin, 287: James 'puts together two persons so different in character in order more clearly to show that no one...has ever been counted righteous without good works'.[456] (viii) Rahab was chosen

---

[451] Carson, 'James', 1006. Cf. Erasmus, *Paraphrase*, 153; Calvin, 287 ('he deliberately brought together two such different people, in order to exhibit more plainly that at no time was any person, of whatever condition or race or class, reckoned among the justified and believing if they did not show works'); Diodati *ad loc*. ('James doth joyn this example of Rahab with that of Abraham, to shew, that there is no degree of faith, neither high as Abraham's was, nor low and weak as Rahab's was, which may not, and ought not, produce its fruit of good work'); Fausset, 589; Wiesinger, 140; Mayor, 105-106 ('an example the furtherst removed from Abraham'); Ropes, 225; Robertson, 140 (an 'example at the further possible remove from Abraham'); Ross, 55; Moo, 143 ('James wanted variety').

[452] Cf. Turnbull, 140 ('In these two examples, all men are contained, whether Jewes or Gentiles, whether righteous or profane, and openly wicked'); Bengel, 498; Wettstein, 668 ('an example for proselytes, of which there were many in the diaspora'); Jacobi, 124; Lange, 87; Ewald, 202; Schegg, 124; Zahn, *Introduction*, 91; Hort, 65; R. Wall, 'Rahab', 231 (Rahab is not an Israelite and so illustrates 'that true religion is contretemps to any faith community where orthodoxy is valued over orthopraxy, where even orthodox demons qualify for membership'); G. and H. Hart, *Analysis*, 84. Contrast Meinertz, 35. Commentators on Mt 1.5 have often posited that her presence in Jesus' genealogy is due to her being a Gentile.

[453] Note Wesley, 863 ('in every nation and sex true faith produces works'); Knowling, 66; Burchard, 131 (adding: Rahab calls to mind a deed other than the Aqedah); Maier, 144 (a 'Vater des Glaubens' and a 'Mutter des Glaubens'). Cf. Mt 6.26-29; 13.31-33; Lk 15.4-10. Johnson, 245, wonders whether one might link Abraham and Rahab with the 'brother or sister' of v. 15. He leaves this as a question. Cf. Batten, *Friendship*, 143. Surprisingly, our verse has generated only a few gratuitous comments about women. Adam, 210, however, does speak of the 'feebler' sex.

[454] Cf. R. Wall, 'Rahab', 221; Baker-Ellsworth, 72.

[455] Bede *ad loc*. CCSL 121 ed. Hurst, 201. So too Manton, 265; Baumgarten, 130; Winkler, 44; Plummer, 595; Lackmann, *Fide*, 74; van der Westhuizen, 'Techniques', 102; Witherington, 479. Henry, *ad loc*., suggests that while Abraham had great faith, Rahab had a 'much lower degree' of faith. Cf. Guyse, 580; Diodati, as in n. 451.

[456] Cf. Scaer, 94, who makes the intriguing observation that 'Rahab is given no explicit command. She carries out God's will without command. She is in fact a better

because she, like Abraham, was famed for her 'faith', which both Heb 11.31 and 1 Clem. 12.1 speak of, and which may have its roots in MT Josh 2.12 (אות אמת = 'sign of faith').[457] Unlike almost all of his commentators, however, James fails to remark on her faith. (ix) Popkes, 186, urges exactly the opposite: Rahab is included in order to gain a scriptural example of justification that fails to mention faith. (x) Plumptre, 75, offers the wild conjecture that our author, the brother of Jesus, knew of the latter's descent from Rahab (Mt 1.5) and would have pondered her significance because Jesus ministered to harlots (Mt 21.31-32). (xi) Abraham and Rahab were similar in that they defied death. Abraham was willing to kill his only son. Rahab risked her life to protect the spies.[458] (xii) Pemble holds that Abraham and Rahab underwent 'singular triialls of a lively faith which was able in that sort to overcome what was hardest to bee conquered, viz. Naturall affection. In Abraham both fatherly affection to the life of a deere and only sonne; and in Rahab the naturall love to ones country and a mans owne life did all stoppe and give way.'[459] (xiii) Keith suggests that Abraham and Rahab were linked (by James) through word association, through the ידע תדע כי of Gen 15.13 ('know of a surety that your descendants will be sojourners in a land that is not theirs') and the ידעתי כי of Josh 2.9 ('I know that the Lord has given you the land').[460] (xiv) James turned to the story of Rahab because, according to Kamell, it illustrates the fact that bare recognition of Israel's God (Josh 2.11) does not save.[461] (xv) For Puech, Abraham demonstrates the love of God, Rahab the love of neighbor, so together they exemplify the two chief imperatives of the law.[462]

We have no means of deciding between these alternative suggestions. Is there perhaps then something to be said for those commentators who opt for several explanations at once?[463]

---

example than Abraham in demonstrating that faith must express itself in works, as she acts in response to no specific directive.'

[457] Cf. Johnson, 206 ('no persons could well be further apart in everything except their faith'); Bauckham, *Wisdom*, 124-25. The latter observes that while the LXX omits the relevant Hebrew from Josh 2.12, it does, in v. 18, speak of the scarlet cord she displays as a σημεῖον.

[458] Cf. Ruth Rab. 2.1 (Rahab 'gave up her life' and 'was ready to be burned'); Erasmus, *Paraphrase*, 153 ('she took no account of the risk to her own life'); Simeon, 67 ('at the peril of her life she concealed the Jewish spies'); Klöpper, 'Erörterung', 301.

[459] Pemble, *Vindiciae Fidei*, 219.

[460] Keith, 'Foi', 325-26.

[461] Kamell, 'Faith', 430.

[462] So Puech, 'Qumrân', 34-35.

[463] Note Gill, 790: 'This instance is produced with the other, to show, that wherever there is true faith, whether in Jew or Gentile, in man or woman, in greater or lesser believers, or in such who have been greater or lesser sinners, there will be good works'. Cf. Doriani, 97; Blomberg and Kamell, 146 (Rahab is 'at the opposite end of almost every spectrum from Abraham').

οὐκ ἐξ ἔργων ἐδικαιώθη. The words are taken from v. 21, not from Joshua's story of Rahab. No other ancient source speaks of Rahab being justified, much less justified by works.[464]

ὑποδεξαμένη τοὺς ἀγγέλους καὶ ἑτέρᾳ ὁδῷ ἐκβαλοῦσα;[465] James has ὑποδέχομαι, ἄγγελος, and ἐκβάλλω only here; ὁδός recurs in 1.8 and 5.20. Only the latter comes from the LXX account of Rahab.[466] The other words serve to summarize Josh 2.16, 21-22.

Although ὑποδέχομαι (= 'to receive hospitably'[467]) is not from LXX Josh 2 or 6, later sources recognize Rahab's hospitality (a virtue especially associated in Jewish tradition with Abraham and Job). δεξαμένη is used of her welcoming messengers in Heb 11.31, εἰσδεξαμένη of the same act in 1 Clem. 12.3, and Tanḥ. Buber Shelah 1 says that she 'received' (קיבלה) those men; cf. Num. Rab. 16.1. James' formulation appears to be informed by a tradition that stressed Rahab's hospitality. Perhaps, then, even though he does not write about Abraham's hospitality (see above), his mind—or the mind behind his source, if he had one—naturally moved from the patriarch to Rahab.

Here ἄγγελος means '(human) messenger'.[468] LXX Joshua 7.22 has Joshua send out 'messengers' (ἀγγέλους), but this has nothing to do with Rahab. The MT, however, twice refers to those Rahab guarded as המלאכים, 'the messengers'.[469] So, although a few suggest that James consciously substituted the more positive ἄγγελος for the potentially embarrassing κατάσκοπος,[470] it is no less likely that his tradition spoke of Rahab harboring 'messengers'.[471] Another possibility is that our author

---

[464] Against Manns, 'Jacques 2,24-26', rabbinic texts that speak of Rahab as 'just' or 'righteous' do not seem directly relevant.

[465] 945 1241 1739 have δεξαμένη, which is from Heb 11.31. τοὺς ἀγγέλους: so P74V 01 02 03 025 044 5 33Vf. 69 81 206 322 *et al.* **Byz** PsOec **L**:V **K**:SA **S**:H^T **SI**:S. τοὺς ἀγγέλους τοῦ 'Ισραήλ: so 61 326 1837 L1281. This clarification comes from Joshua (2.2), as does the proper name in τοὺς ἀγγέλους 'Ιησοῦ: so 996 1661; cf. Josh 2.1, 23-24. τοὺς κατασκόπους: so 04 018Z 020 88 94Z 218 252T 307Z 330 *et al.* L593 L596 *et al.* **S**:P **A G**:A1BG-D **SI**:ChDMSi; cf. Chrysostom, *Paen.* 7 PG 49.331: δεξαμένη τοὺς κατασκόπους καὶ ἑτέρᾳ ὁδῷ ἐκβαλοῦσα. κατάσκοπος occurs in the accounts of Rahab in Heb 11.31 and 1 Clem. 12, and κατασκοπεύω recurs in LXX Josh 2 and 6. 918Z (τοὺς ἀγγέλους κατασκόπους) and 918T (ἄγγελους κατασκόπους) combine the two readings. **L**:F: κατασκόπους ἐκ τῶν δώδεκα φυλῶν τῶν υἱῶν 'Ισραήλ.

[466] 2.7, 16, 22; cf. 1 Clem. 12.5.

[467] Cf. Tob 7.8; Jdt 13.13; 4 Macc 13.17; Lk 10.38; 19.6; Acts 17.7; Josephus, *Ant.* 1.259; Ign. *Smyr.* 10.1; T. Abr. RecLng. 1.2; T. Sol. 16.2.

[468] Cf. LXX Gen 32.3; 2 Chr 36.15; Isa 44.26; Hag 1.13; Mal 2.1; 1 Macc 1.44; Mt 11.10; Mk 1.2; Lk 7.27; 9.52; etc.

[469] 6.17 ('she hid the messengers that we sent'; the LXX drops this clause), 25 ('she hid the messengers'; LXX: τοὺς κατασκοπεύσαντας). LAB 20.6 identifies them as Cenaz and Naam, sons of Caleb; Tanḥ. Buber Shelah 1 identifies them as Phinehas and Caleb; so too Num. Rab. 16.1 and other sources.

[470] Some authorities have κατασκόπους in 2.25; see n. 465. Cf. LXX Josh 2.1-13; 6.21-24; Heb 11.31; 1 Clem. 12.2, 4. Note also the derogatory use of κατασκοπέω in Gal 2.4.

[471] Origen, *Hom. Josh* 3.3 SC 71 ed. Jaubert, 136, speaks of them as *angeli Dei*.

assimilated the story of Rahab to that of Abraham, who received and entertained angels.[472]

ἕτερος (Jas: 1×) + ὁδός has no precise counterpart in the biblical story of Rahab.[473] That story does not indicate that the spies went back a different way than they came.[474] The expression likely underlines the danger the spies were in while being pursued.[475]

Although ἐκβάλλω[476] can mean simply 'send forth', it perhaps here connotes haste or urgency because of danger.[477] While the LXX episode concerning Rahab does not use the verb, we find this in 2.21: καὶ ἐξαπέστειλεν αὐτούς. These words translate the MT's ותשלחם. Does James preserve an alternative rendering of the latter?[478] He in any case adverts to Josh 2.21.

Verse 26. The summarizing conclusion—which more than one theologian has ironically attributed to Paul[479]—recalls esp. vv. 17 and 20 and so lends unity to the discourse.

ὥσπερ γὰρ τὸ σῶμα χωρὶς πνεύματος νεκρόν ἐστιν.[480] Cf. Simplicius, *Comm. in Epic. Ench.* ed. Dübner, 3.43: τὸ μὲν σῶμα καθ' αὑτὸ ἀκίνητον καὶ νεκρόν ἐστιν. Although γάρ ties v. 26 to v. 25, our line concludes the entire section that v. 14 opens: this is not just a statement about Rahab but a statement about everybody. ὥσπερ (Jas: 1×) γάρ + οὕτως καί,[481] found

---

[472] Gen 19.1; Heb 13.2. R. Wall, 'Rahab', 225-26, suggests that 'angels' might encourage an astute intertextual reader to associate vv. 21-24 with Abraham entertaining three angels in Gen 18. He further offers (228) that James may have thought of the two figures in Josh 2 as angels in disguise.

[473] Josh 1 implies that Rahab sent the king's servants to the east (v 7) and directed the spies, who had come from the east, to the west, where they were to hide for three days, after which they could return as they came (v. 16).

[474] Young, 'Relation', 343, contends that the ἄγγελοι in James are the king's searchers. This would create an agreement with 1 Clem. 12.5: Rahab pointed the king's men 'in the opposite direction'. But this seems to misconstrue James.

[475] Cf. Plato, *Polit.* 268D; Appian, *Bell. civ.* 1.10.88; 5.6.50; Josephus, *Vita* 138; also the use of ἄλλος + ὁδός in 1 Βασ 14.5; 3 Βασ 13.10 (for דרך אחר); 18.6; Mt 2.12. Cargal, 'Prostitute', 118, suggests, in the light of 1.6-8 and 5.19-20, that James may present Rahab 'as an example of one who acts on her faith to save herself and others'. This suggestion to my knowledge has no support from the commentary tradition.

[476] Most often in the LXX for a form of גרש.

[477] Cf. Beyschlag, 144: 'it designates an urgent rush'. Cf. Acts 9.40.

[478] The LXX translates שלח with ἐκβάλλω in Exod 12.33; Josh 24.12; Ps 43.2.

[479] Symeon the New Theologian, *Hymn* 15.35-36 SC 156 ed. Koder, 280; Euthymius Zigabenus, *Mk* 16 PG 129.849D.

[480] γάρ drops out (due to homoioteleuton, ρ → ρ) in 03 378* 1175 1243 2492 AnastS Did S:P **A** G:A1B Sl:D **Ä**. Spitta, 88, needlessly conjectures an original κινήματος instead of πνεύματος. Isaiah of Scetis, *Ascetic Discourses* 21 ET Chryssavgis and Penkett, Kalamazoo, MI, 2002, 158, reveals how easy memory can flip meaning: 'Just as the spirit is dead when it is away from the body, faith, when it is apart from works, is dead'.

[481] οὕτως καί occurs 4× in Jas; cf. 1.11; 2.17; 3.5.

occasionally in secular Greek sources, the LXX, and Philo,[482] occurs a full seven times in the NT.[483] σῶμα (cf. v. 16) appears thrice in the next discourse (3.2, 3, 6), but nothing should be made of that.[484] χωρίς takes up the language of vv. 18 and 20. πνεῦμα is used elsewhere only in 4.5, where it probably refers to the prophetic spirit. Here, contrasted with σῶμα,[485] it likely designates the inner 'soul' or 'spirit' that can live even apart from the body. A reference to 'breath'[486] or the 'breath of life'[487]— unless James equated the latter with the 'soul'—is less likely.[488] Unlike a modern materialist, who might assert that the spirit without the body is dead, James affirms the opposite. His language presupposes an anthropological dualism popular in ancient Jewish and Christian circles.[489]

οὕτως καὶ ἡ πίστις χωρὶς ἔργων νεκρά ἐστιν.[490] This concluding statement in effect conflates vv. 17 and 20:

---

[482] Aristotle, *Mete.* 349A, 368A; Ps.-Aristotle, *Aud.* 804B; Galen, *In Hipp. de victu acut. comm.* iv 15.448; Eccl 5.14; Ecclus 23.10; Philo, *Leg.* 1.91; 2.37; *Gig.* 16; *Sobr.* 43; also Gk. Apoc. Ezra 25.7. ὥσπερ γάρ...οὕτως (without καί) is much more common.

[483] Jn 5.21, 26; Rom 5.19; 11.30; 1 Cor 11.21; 15.22; Jas 2.26.

[484] Although there is an exegetical tradition that identifies the 'body' of 3.1-12 with the church, there is no such tradition regarding our verse.

[485] Wis 2.3 supplies the only LXX instance of these two words functioning in tandem as 'soul' and 'body'. Cf. Popkes, 210: James' terminology is Graeco-Roman, not Semitic.

[486] Cf. Gen 6.17; 4 Macc 11.11; 2 Thess 2.8.

[487] Cf. Gen 1.30; 2.7; Isa 57.16; 4 Ezra 3.5; Rev 11.11.

[488] So Ropes, 225; Popkes, 210-11; against W. Perkins, *A Commentary on Galatians*, London, 1617, 338 ('as the body without breath, is dead, and it shewes it selfe to be alive by breathing: so faith that is without workes, is dead, and it shewes it selfe to be alive by works'); Hort, 66; Chaine, 72. Many commentators cite Gen 2.7 in connection with our verse. J.V. Fesko, *Justification*, Phillipsburg, NJ, 2008, 295, seems to be alone in proposing an allusion to Ezek 36–37. In several places, Didymus of Alexandria uses James to argue that the 'spirit' (πνεῦμα) is the same as the 'soul' (ψυχή); note e.g. *Ecclus ad* 2.11 PTA 25 ed. Binder and Liesenborghs, 220; cf. Cyril of Alexandria, *Ps ad* 30.6 PG 69.860B. So already Origen, *Sel. Ps* 30 PG 12.1300B

[489] So too Popkes, 211 (adding however that James implies nothing about the body being a prison for the soul); contrast Blackman, 97 (James knew nothing of the possibility of a soul apart from a body); Frankemölle, 477 (James held a 'biblical-creation theology', not a 'philosophical' understanding of πνεῦμα). Relevant texts include Wis 2.3; 15.8; Bar. 2.17; 4 Macc 14.6; Jub. 23.31; Philo, *Gig.* 15 (the body is a 'dead thing', νεκρόν); *Leg.* 3 69 ('the body' plots 'against the soul and is even a corpse [νεκρόν] and a dead thing'); Mt 10.28; Acts 7.59; 2 Cor 12.1-4; 1 Pet 3.18-19; 2 Pet 1.13; Josephus, *Bell.* 2.154; 3.362; *Ant.* 12.282 (θνητὰ τὰ σώματα ἡμῶν); 2 Bar. 30.2-5; Gk. LAE 13:6; 31:4; 32:4; T. Abr. RecLng. 20; b. Ber. 60b; b. Sanh. 91a-b. See further R.H. Gundry, *Sōma in Biblical Theology*, Cambridge, UK, 1976, and cf. Dio Chrysostom 3.68: when the soul departs from the body, the latter 'suffers immediate decay and dissolution'. Our text is one of many that contradicts those, such as O. Cullmann, *Immortality of the Soul or Resurrection of the Dead?*, London, 1958, who have argued for a profound contradiction between Hellenism dualism and the anthropology of canonical Christian sources.

[490] In accord with vv. 18, 20, 22, τῶν precedes ἔργων in 02 04 025 5 33 69 88 218 *et al*. **Byz** Eustr GregNaz PsOec **K**:SB **A**ms. Omit: P20 P74 01 03 044 81 206 *et al*.

```
17   οὕτως καὶ ἡ  πίστις ...                        νεκρά  ἐστιν
20               ἡ  πίστις χωρὶς τῶν  ἔργων ἀργή     ἐστιν
26   οὕτως καὶ ἡ  πίστις χωρὶς       ἔργων νεκρά    ἐστιν
```

Exegetes regularly remark that James' comparison is odd, because they suppose that he is comparing faith to the body, deeds to the soul, whereas faith and soul, being the primary and internal elements, should be correlated, just as the body and works, both visible things, should correspond.[491] Luther exclaimed: 'O Mary, mother of God! What a terrible comparison that is!'[492] This may press the content unduly.[493] For it may be the statements themselves—τὸ σῶμα κτλ. and ἡ πίστις κτλ.—and not their members that are being compared: just as body and spirit require each other, so too is it with faith and deeds. Faith without deeds is a corpse.[494] Even so, the comparison remains a bit awkward if one takes 2.14-25 to mean that faith and works cannot be separated, because body and soul can, in James' world, be separated.

---

[491] But some regard the unexpected simile as intentional: James wants to say that deeds are the animating, inner principle; cf. Dale, 73; Dowd, 'Faith', 202; Witherington, 480. Note Alford, 302: 'Faith is the body, the sum and substance... works (= obedience), the moving and quickening of the body; just as the spirit is the moving and quickening principle of the natural body'. Burchard, 133 (calling attention to Ign. *Trall.* 8.1, where 'faith' is 'the flesh of the Lord'), denies that either principle is, so to speak, inside the other: they are rather integrated.

[492] M. Luther, *Table Talk*, in Luther's Works, vol. 54, ed. T.G. Tappert, Philadelphia, 1967, 424 (no. 5443).

[493] But comparing x to the soul, spirit, or mind and y to the body was rhetorically common; cf. Isocrates, *Areop.* 14 ('the soul [ψυχή] of a state is nothing else than its polity, having as much power over it as does the mind over the body [σώματι]', cf. *Panath.* 138); Cicero, *Pro A. Cluen.* 146 ('the state without law would be like the human body without mind'); Philo, *Abr.* 74 ('it cannot be that while in yourself there is a mind [νοῦς] appointed as your ruler which all the community of the body [σώματος] obeys and each of the senses follows, the world... is without a king who holds it together and directs it with justice'; cf. 272); *Leg.* 1.289 ('just as the soul [ψυχή] causes bodies [σώματα] to escape corruption, so does salt, which more than anything else keeps them together and makes them in a sense immortal'); *Contempl.* 78 ('the whole law book seems to resemble a living creature with the literal ordinances for its body [σῶμα] and for its soul [ψυχήν] the invisible mind laid up in its wording'); Curtius Rufus, *Alex.* 10.6.8 ('a throng of soldiers without a leader is a body without a soul'); T. Naph. 2.2 ('just as a potter knows the pot, how much it holds, and brings clay for it accordingly, so also the Lord forms the body [σῶμα] in correspondence to the spirit [πνεύματος] and instills the spirit [πνεῦμα] corresponding to the power of the body [σώματος]'); Plutarch, *Mor.* 142E ('control ought to be exercised by the man over the woman... as the soul [ψυχήν] controls the body [σώματος]'); 2 Clem. 14.4 ('if... the flesh is the church and the Spirit [πνεῦμα] is Christ, then the one who abuses the flesh abuses the church'); Diogenes, *Ep.* 6.1 ('what the soul is the body [σώματι ψυχή], Christians are to the world'); Ps.-Philo, *Jonah* 1.3 ed. Siegert, 9 ('as the corpse is useful for nothing when it has no soul to animate it, so likewise the artisan, when he receives no understanding to inspire his handicraft').

[494] Cf. Neander, 82-83; Huther, 103; Dibelius, 167; Easton, 45; Cranfield, 'Message', 342; Frankemölle, 477; Watson, 'Schemes', 116; Cargal, 133-34; Fabris, 203-204; McKnight, 258-59.

XII

THE SINS OF SPEECH (3.1-12)[1]

(1) Not many of you should become teachers, my brothers, knowing that we will receive the greater judgment. (2) For we all make many mistakes; and if any one makes no mistakes in speech, he is a perfect man, able to bridle also the whole body. (3) If we put bits into the mouths of horses, so that they obey us, we direct their whole bodies. (4) Consider also the ships. While they are so large and are driven by hard winds, they are guided, wherever the inclination of the pilot wills, by the smallest rudder. (5) So likewise the tongue is a little member and boasts of great things. Behold, such a small fire sets ablaze such a large forest! (6) And the tongue is a fire; it is the world of unrighteousness. The tongue appoints itself among our members, staining the whole body, setting on fire the whole creation—and it will be set on fire by Gehenna. (7) For every species of quadruped and bird, of reptile and fish, can be subdued and has been subdued by the human species, (8) but no human is able to subdue the tongue. It is a restless evil, full of deadly venom. (9) With it we bless the Lord and Father, and with it we curse human beings made in the likeness of God. (10) From one and the same mouth come forth blessings and curses. This need not be, my brothers. (11) Does a spring pour forth from the same opening fresh water and brackish water? (12) Is a fig tree, my brothers, able to make olives, or a grapevine figs? No more than a salt spring can make fresh water.

History of Interpretation and Reception

Given that the tongue, the chief subject of 3.1-12, is, as James teaches, hard to govern, it does not surprise to learn that many have cited Jas 3 when counseling silence or moderation in speaking.[2] Such advice has

---

[1] Recent literature: Allison, 'Blessing'; Baker, *Speech-Ethics*, 123-34; Bauckham, 'Tongue'; idem, *Wisdom*, 88-91; Carr, 'James iii. 6'; Culpepper, 'Words'; Elliott-Binns, 'Jas. iii. 5'; Fletcher, 'Buddhism'; Giroud, 'Epitre'; Jackson-McCabe, *Logos*, 224-30; Kittel, 'Τὸν τροχόν'; Klostermann, 'Texte'; Konradt, *Existenz*, 274-85; Lockett, *Purity*, 120-26; MacGorman, 'Exposition'; Ng, 'Father'; Ong, *Strategy*, 92-99; Stiglmayr, 'Jak 3,6'; Trocmé, 'Églises'; Wandel, 'Auslegung'; Wanke, 'Lehrer'; D.F. Watson, 'Rhetoric'; Wettlaufer, 'Variants', 104-27; Wolmarans, 'Tongue'; Zimmermann, *Lehrer*, 194-208.

[2] E.g. Ps.-Clement, *1 Ep. virg.* 1.11 ed. Diekamp, 19; Cassiodorus, *Ps* 38.2 CCCL 97 ed. Adriaen, 354; Ps.-Andrew of Crete, *Éloge* 7 ed. Noret, 52; Symeon Metaphrastes 10 PG 115.208B-C; John of Salisbury, *Metalog.* 2.8 CCCM 98 ed. Hall, 68. Nicodemus of the Holy Mountain, *Handbook of Spiritual Counsel*, trans. P.A. Chamber, 113-14, follows a quotation of Jas 3.6 with this illustration: 'The elder Agathon kept a stone in

often come with pleas to recognize the central importance of the tongue for all human activity. Isaac Barrow preached: 'One half of our religion consisteth in charity toward our neighbour; and of that charity much the greater part seemeth exercised in speech; for as speaking doth take up the greatest part of our life, (our quick and active mind continually venting its thoughts, and discharging its passions thereby; all our conversation and commerce passing through it, having a large influence upon all our practice,) so speech commonly having our neighbour and his concernments for its objects, it is necessary, that either most of our charity will be employed therein, or that by it we shall most offend against that great duty, together with its associates, justice and peace.'[3]

Recent commentators universally take the meaning of διδάσκαλοι in v. 1 to be 'teachers'. A few earlier English exegetes, however, working with the AV's translation of διδάσκαλοι as 'masters', urged that James here addresses not a public instructor but 'a supercilious reprover...one that is seated in a chair of arrogance, whence he *pro imperio*, magisterially inveighs against the practice of other men'.[4] Manton, who took this view, stressed that Jas 3 prohibits neither public reproof nor private admonition, and he went on to discuss the proper way to censure others. His chief concern seems to have been to bring the text into line with his own denominational practice.

Verse 1 has played a small role in debates over whether women should teach in the churches. The use of 'brother' has been taken to imply that, when James turns to the subject of teachers, he envisages only men.[5]

'We all make many mistakes' (v. 2) naturally became a proof text for the ubiquity of sin, including post-baptismal sin.[6] This is why Oecumenius could cite it in a discussion of purgatory: as all have failed, all will need purgation in the afterlife.[7] Others, however, such as Rufinus of Aquileia, applied 3.2 to 'slips' or 'venial faults'.[8]

---

his mouth for three years in order to learn to keep silent'. D. Bonhoeffer, *Gemeinsames Leben*, Dietrich Bonhoeffer Werke 5, ed. Müller and Schönherr, Munich, 1987, 78, uses Jas 3 to urge that community members should not talk about others in secret.

[3] Cf. I. Barrow, 'Against Detraction', in *Sermons*, 415. In a sermon on v. 2 (ibid., 287), Barrow observes that 'the extent of speech must needs be vast, since it is nearly commensurate to thought itself'; it is 'the rudder that steereth human affairs'.

[4] So Manton, 271. Cf. Trapp, 698, following Manton.

[5] Note e.g. V. Poythress and W. Gruden, *The Gender-Neutral Bible Controversy*, Nashville, 2000, 266.

[6] Cf. Origen, *Adnot. in Deut ad* 23.12-14 PG 17.32C; Cyril of Alexandria, *Ador.* 11 PG 68.757D; *Isa* 4.1 PG 70.913B; Gregory the Great, *XL Hom. ev.* 39.8 FC 28.2 ed. Fiedrowicz, 824; the 418 Council of Carthage art. 7; Bede *ad loc.* CCSL 121 ed. Hurst 202-203; Acta sinc. S. Petri Alex. PG 18.466C; S. Maresius, *Hydra Socinianismi expugnata*, Groningen, 1651, 769; F. Turretin, *Institutio theologiæ elencticæ* 16.2.9, Edinburgh, 1847, 563; *et al.*

[7] Oecumenius, *Apoc.* 8.21 TEG 8 ed. de Groote, 205.

[8] Rufinus, *Apol. contra Hier.* 1.19 CCSL 20 ed. Simonetti, 53. Cf. the similar applications/explanations in Jerome, *Ep.* 57.7 CSEL 54 ed. Hilberg, 515; Rabanus Maurus,

As v. 2 also seems to imply the possibility of post-baptismal sin, it has often been quoted beside Mt 18.15-19, which offers guidelines for dealing with Christian error, as well as 1 Jn 1.8-10: 'if we say that we have no sin, we deceive ourselves'.[9] Additionally common has been the citation of 3.2 in appeals to mercy.[10] Yet Clarke, 813-14, as a Methodist who believed in Christian perfection, thought all this quite 'dangerous', and he adamantly insisted that 'were we to suppose that where he [James] appears by the use of the plural pronoun to include himself, he means to be thus understood, we must then grant that himself was one of those many teachers who were to receive a great condemnation, ver. 1; that he was a horse-breaker, because he says, "we put bits in the horses' mouths, that they may obey us," ver. 3; that his tongue was a world of iniquity, and set on fire of hell, for he says "so is the tongue among our members," ver. 6; that he cursed men, "wherewith curse we men," ver. 9. No man possessing common sense could imagine that James, or any man of even tolerable morals, could be guilty of those things.' Wesley, 864, made the same point more succinctly: 'None of which, as common sense shows, are to be interpreted either of him or of the other apostles'.

According to Martin, 103-105, 110-11, 123, 'the whole body' in v. 2 (cf. v. 3) is the church, which allows him to interpret the entire paragraph in ecclesiastical terms and to find a concern with the misuse of the tongue in worship. In this, Reicke, 37, anticipated Martin: James 'is actually thinking of the congregation whose 'tongue' is the teacher or preacher... The "body" is here, as often in the writings of Paul, a symbol of the church.' Wandel, 'Auslegung', already forwarded this interpretation in 1893. But long before any of these, Gill, 792, offered this exegesis in the eighteenth century: in v. 2, bridling the whole body might advert to governing 'the whole body, the church', to teaching 'a society of Christians' and feeding 'them with knowledge, and with understanding'. Again, in commenting on v. 3, Gill remarked that 'churches, societies, and bodies of Christians, which are large and numerous' and 'tossed to and fro with

---

Ecclus ad 14.1 PL 109.854-55; John of Ávila, *Sant. Sacr.* 51.5-8 Obras completas de San Juan de Ávila 3 ed. Balust and Hernández, 658-660; Sebastian Franck, *280 Paradoxes or Wondrous Sayings*, ET E.J. Furcha, Lewiston, 1986, 12; J. Flavel, 'Of Antinomianism', in *The Whole Works of John Flavel*, vol. 3, London, 1820, 570; T. Slater, *A Manual of Moral Theology*, vol. 1, 6th ed., London, 1928, 85. Abelard, *Ethics* ed. Luscombe, 68, takes James to imply that human beings cannot avoid behaving in unfitting fashion (but if sin is defined properly, so that it is 'contempt of God', then it is possible to live without sin, although only with much difficulty).

[9] E.g. Acta sinc. S. Petri Alex. PG 18.466C; Zwingli, *True and False Religion* 8; Peter Martyr Vermigli, *Free Will* 18; Bengel, 498; Wolfhart Pannenberg, *Systematic Theology*, vol. 3, Grand Rapids, MI/Edinburgh, 1998, 246. Bernard of Clairvaux, *Praecepto et disp.* 10 S. Bernardi Opera 3 ed. Leclercq and Rochais, 270, cites 3.2 in order to comfort those overmuch concerned with their lesser failings.

[10] E.g. Ps.-Ephraem, *De abstin. a cupid. carn.* ed. Phrantzoles 229.13; Leo the Great, *Tract.* 49.5 CCSL 138A ed. Chavasse, 289.

tempests, driven by Satan's temptations and the world's persecutions, and ready to be carried away with the wind of false doctrine' can yet be 'influenced and directed aright by those that are at the helm, the faithful ministers of the word'. Gill in turn was following others, above all Grotius, 1083.[11]

In vv. 1-2, James, adopts the first person plural. His commentators, in response, have often done the same. That is, they have moved from our author's autobiographical statements to candid statements about themselves or their teaching office.[12] In this way, the text's rhetoric has become the commentator's rhetoric.

One of the major themes of 3.1-12 is the great effect of small things such as bit, rudder, and tongue. This has become an opportunity for preachers to expound on the importance of seemingly inconsequential things.[13] Typical is the exposition of the eighteenth-century preacher, John Venn, who emphasized how evil, which grows out of the smallest trifle, must be attacked when still small: 'Watch against the beginnings'.[14] Manton, 285, focused rather on how great good can grow from the smallest seed. He instanced Luther's protest against indulgences—a quarrel about 'trifles'—that ended up dividing Europe and changing the world. Manton exhorted: 'Learn not to despise the low beginnings of providence and deliverance: there is a "day of small things", Zech. iv. 10'. Horace Bushnell had another take on this principle: when it comes to religion, human beings have no power of 'self-impulsion, but only a steering power'; so what is required of them is that they turn themselves 'into the track of another, more sufficient power'. God is that great power, and human beings can decide in what direction that power will carry them.

3.8-9 has occasionally called to mind the *Birkat ha-minim*, the rabbinic curse upon heretics. Macknight glossed the verses with this: 'Perhaps the apostle in this [verse] glanced at the unconverted Jews, who, as Justin Martyr informs us, in his dialogue with Trypho the Jew, often cursed the Christians bitterly in their synagogues'. This reading also appears, with much more confidence, in Whitby, 591, and Wells, 20.[15]

James 3.9 has played a minor role in dogmatic theology. It uses 'the image of God' without restriction, and in a context in which all human

---

[11] Cf. also Clarke, 813-14. Other proponents of this view include Vouga, 97; Reese, 'Exegete', 83; Hartin, 184, 189; Ong, *Metaphorical Reading*, 93-96; Albl, 'Health', 129; McKnight, 276.

[12] E.g. Zwingli, *Von den Predigtamt*, Sämtliche Werke 4 ed. Egli *et al.*, 431; Poole, 889; Moo, 150; Brosend, 104-105; Blomberg-Kamell, 163.

[13] See e.g. F. Wagstaff, 'The Influence of Little Things', *Christian World Pulpit* 22 (1882), 170-72.

[14] John Venn, *Sermons*, vol. 1, Boston, 1822, 209-18.

[15] Benson, 1749, and Adamson, 146, reject this interpretation. See further Allison, 'Blessing'.

beings fail (v. 2). The implication is that the image of God was not erased by the fall, and that even sinful human beings retain the image of God.[16] Calvin, 292, wrote: 'If it is objected, that the image of God in human nature was removed by the sin of Adam, we must admit that it was sadly deformed, yet in such a way that certain lineaments of it still appear. Righteousness, equity, the freedom to seek after good, these things have gone; but many gifts are left to us, by which we are superior to beasts. The man who has a true respect and reverence towards God will beware of being insulting towards people'.[17]

3.1-12 has regrettably moved several Western commentators to revert to stereotypes about Mideastern peoples. Commenting on v. 5, Oesterley, 451, imagined 'an excited audience in some place of meeting; when an Eastern audience has been aroused to a high pitch, the noise of tongues, and gesticulation of the arms occasioned by the discussion following upon the oration which has been delivered, might most aptly be compared to a forest fire; the tongue of the one speaker has set ablaze all the inflammable material which controversy brings into being'. According to Moffatt, 49, the hissing tongue of the serpent (see v. 8) 'suggested a comparison with the human tongue of Orientals who were singularly gifted in abuse and malignity of utterance'. Knoch, 193, assured readers that James' 'remarks are relevant, not only for excitable Orientals who love to talk, but for us all'.[18]

Exegesis

Although there is no obvious or firm link between Jas 2 and 3, some readers have often conjured one. The most common move has been to stress that speech, the subject of Jas 3, should not contradict one's deeds, the subject of Jas 2.[19] 3.1 thus becomes a warning against hypocrisy.

---

[16] See e.g. Epiphanius, *Pan.* 70.3 GCS 37 ed. Holl, 236; J. Fuchs, *Natural Law*, New York, 1965, 62; O. Weber, *Foundations of Dogmatics*, vol. 1, Grand Rapids, MI, 1981, 564-65. Cf. Poole, 890: although people 'have lost that spiritual knowledge, righteousness, and true holiness, in which that image of God, after which man was created, principally consists; yet still have some relics of his image continuing in them'.

[17] Cf. Bengel, 500: 'We have lost God's likeness. But there remains from it an indestructible nobleness, which we should reverence both in ourselves an others'. Wesley, 864, says almost exactly the same thing.

[18] Cf. N. Lardner, 'The Difficulty of Governing the Tongue', in *The Works of Nathaniel Lardner*, vol. 9, London, 1838, 272 (James' Jewish contemporaries 'had an impetuous and turbulent zeal'; they were 'conceited of themselves and despised others'; they 'were imposing and uncharitable'); Maclaren, 431 ('Eastern peoples are looser tongued than we Westerns are'); Knowling, xl ('sins of speech were generally characteristic of the Jews').

[19] See e.g. Dionysius of Alexandria frag. 3.2 ed. Feltoe 253; Chrysostom, *Frag. in Jac.* PG 64.1048.

According to Knowles, 'Nowhere was the separation of faith and works likely to be more frequent or more offensive than in that arising from vain and empty speech on the part of men who, while claiming to be instructors of the foolish, "say and do not"'.[20] Most exegetes, however, concede that 3.1 marks a break in the argument of the letter. At the same time, the topic of speech has already been introduced, if in cursory fashion, in 1.19, 26; and 2.12. So as 4.11-12 will return yet again to that subject, it is clearly a major theme of the letter, and repeated recourse to it lends unity to the whole.[21]

The importance of controlling the tongue, the difficulty of doing so, and the great harm done by failure in this matter are common *topoi* in almost every time and place, and within the context of ancient literature, Jewish and otherwise, James' concerns and advice are thoroughly conventional.[22] Indeed, several of the sentiments and illustrations, as the verse-by-verse commentary shows, have especially close parallels in Graeco-Roman moral and religious writings. For this reason, Knox considers 3.1-12 'a purely Hellenistic commentary on the theme of bridling the tongue'.[23] In James, however, Graeco-Roman *topoi* are mingled with Jewish elements. Verse 1 adverts to the eschatological judgment. Verse 6 shows a concern for purity, contains a Semitism, and mentions Gehenna. Verse 7 alludes to Gen 1, where God instructs humankind to exercise dominion over the animal kingdom, here as there divided into four categories. Verse 9 refers to blessing 'the Lord and Father' and speaks, in the idiom of Genesis, of 'the image of God'. Windisch-Preisker, 21, appropriately characterize 3.1-12 as a 'small treatise' that combines 'Jewish wisdom and Greek diatribe'.

In addition to its intertextual links to Gen 1, just noted, the little section may also owe something to the Jesus tradition.[24] The end of v. 1 has a strong parallel in Mk 12.40 (cf. Mt 23.14 v.l.; Lk 20.47), and v. 12 could echo the tradition in Mt 7.16-18; 12.22-25 = Lk 6.43-45. Beyond that, Jas 5.12 establishes that our author paid attention to what Jesus purportedly had to say about oaths (cf. Mt 5.33-37); and with this in

---

[20] Knowles, 68, quoting Mt 23.3. Cf. Manton, 119; Alford, 302; Plummer, 595 ('it is precisely those who neglect good works that are given to talk much about the excellence of their faith, and are always ready to instruct and lecture others'); Wandel, 'Auslegung', 679-80.

[21] Ecclesiastical readers have not missed the links; cf. Ps.-Maximus the Confessor, *Loc. comm.* 15 PG 91.813A.

[22] See especially Baker, *Speech-Ethics*, who offers an abundance of helpful comparative material. From the Hebrew Bible one may note especially the texts cited above, on 1.19.

[23] Knox, 'Epistle', 15.

[24] Shepherd, 'Matthew', 46, remarks that 'the whole diatribe of James on the tongue may be considered as a homiletic illustration of the saying of Jesus in Mt 12. 36, with its commentary in Q material supplemented by M in Mt 12 33 and 7 16-20 (cf. Lk 6 43-45)'.

mind, one may observe that Jas 3, like the Jesus tradition, stresses the importance of words at the last judgment (Mt 12.26-37), affirms that the tongue reveals one's true character (Mt 12.34 = Lk 6.45; Mk 15.20-23; Gos. Thom. 45), threatens Gehenna as a punishment for speaking against others (Mt 5.22), warns against cursing others (Mt 5.44 = Lk 6.28), and condemns religious activity by those not reconciled with others (Mt 5.23-26).

James 3.1-12 also recalls Ecclus 28.12-26, an extended discussion on the evil tongue. This stresses that speech produces contradictory effects (28.12), emphasizes its destructive capacity (28.13-16), and features several similes, including that of fire (28.22-23). Frankemölle, 478-521, believes these and additional parallels suffice to establish literary dependence. The inference is plausible.

Because Jas 3.1-12 could stand on its own, some have suggested it once did: the verses preserve an independent diatribe.[25] In line with this, vv. 3-12 contain a number of words occurring nowhere else in James,[26] and much of the material has parallels elsewhere and so must be regarded as conventional.[27] Moreover, some have discerned tensions between James' illustrations and their present context. According to Dibelius, 182, for example, 'it is out of the question that Jas seriously wished to ascribe to the teachers of the community, or to those who wished to become such...all of the sins to which he alludes in what follows'. But the case falls short. We should expect most portions of a relatively short work to contain *hapax legomena*, and each topic will naturally have its own vocabulary, especially if, as here, there are one-time illustrations. Beyond that, James discusses the tongue also in 1.19, 26; 2.12; and 4.11-12, and the section contains words and idioms that appear elsewhere in his work.[28] If, then, 3.1-12 or some part of it ever circulated by itself, James

---

[25] See e.g. J. Geffcken, *Kynika und Verwandtes*, Heidelberg, 1909, 45-53; Dibelius, 182, 184, 189-90 (James adopted a source which he did not wholly conform to his own aims); Easton, 48-49.

[26] στόμα, ἵππος, χαλινός, βάλλω, πείθω, μετάγω, πλοῖον, τηλικοῦτος, ὤν, ἄνεμος, σκληρός, ἐλαύνω, ἐλάχιστος, πηδάλιον, ὁρμή, εὐθύνω, μικρός, μέγας, αὐχέω, ἡλίκος, ὕλη, ἀνάπτω, ἀδικία, σπιλόω, φλογίζω, τροχός, γέενα, φύσις, θηρίον, πετεινόν, ἑρπτετόν, ἐνάλιος, δαμάζω, ἀνθρώπινος, εὐλογέω, καταράομαι, ὁμοίωσις, μήτι, πηγή, ὀπή, βρύω, γλυκύς, συκῆ, ἐλαία, ἔλαιον, ἄμπελος, οὔτε, ἁλυκός, ὕδωρ.

[27] Cf. the citation of Jas 3.1-12 amid the collection of traditional sayings about the tongue, culled from the Bible and church authorities, in John of Damascus, *Parall.* Γ 14 PG 95.1340D-1347A.

[28] Note e.g. γίνομαι (1.12, 22, 25; 2.4, 10, 11; 3.1, 9, 10; 5.2), ἀδελφοί μου (1.2, 16, 19; 2.1, 5, 14; 3.1, 10, 12; 5.12, 19), οἶδα (1.19; 3.1; 4.4, 17), μεῖζον (3.1; 4.6); λαμβάνω (1.7, 12; 3.1; 4.3; 5.7, 10), πόλυς (3.1, 2; 5.16), γάρ (1.6, 7, 11, 13, 20, 24; 2.2, 10, 11, 13, 26; 3.2, 7, 16; 4.14), πταίω (2.10; 3.2), εἴ τις (1.5, 23, 26; 3.2), λόγος (1.18, 21, 22, 23; 3.2), οὗτος (1.23, 25; 3.2), τέλειος (1.4, 17, 25; 3.2), ἀνήρ (1.8, 12, 20, 23; 2.2; 3.2), χαλιναγωγέω (1.26; 3.2), ὅλος (2.10; 3.2, 3, 6), σῶμα (2.16, 26; 3.2, 3, 6), εἰ δέ (2.9; 3.3, 14; 4.11), ἰδού (3.4, 5; 5.4, 7, 9, 11), ὅπου (3.4, 16), βούλομαι (1.18; 3.4; 4.4), οὕτως καί (1.11; 2.17, 26; 3.5), γλῶσσα (1.26; 3.5, 6, 8), μέλος (3.5, 6; 4.1), πῦρ (3.5, 6; 5.3),

rewrote it thoroughly.[29] Yet the best guess is that James has here simply reworked sentiments and illustrations common in the ancient Mediterranean world, including Jewish and Christian circles.

The section, characterized by an abundance of metaphors, stands as a unity.[30] (i) Verse 1 introduces a new subject that v. 12 brings to conclusion. (ii) Verse 13 turns to a new topic.[31] (iii) The entirety, apart from v. 1, lacks imperatives, which James as a whole otherwise features. (iv) The vocative, 'my brothers', marks the beginning and end (3.1, 9, 12). (v) The train of thought progresses through a series of antitheses:[32]

(large) horse vs. (small) bit	3
large ship vs. small rudder	4
small tongue vs. large boasts	5
small fire vs. large forest fire	5
animals subdued vs. tongue not subdued	7-8
blessing God vs. cursing people	9-10
fresh water vs. salt water	11-12

(vi) A number of words or closely related words are repeated:

πολλοί, πολλά	1, 2
ἀδελφοί μου	1, 10, 12
πταίομεν, πταίει	2
δυνατός, δύναται	2, 8, 12
χαλιναγωγῆσαι, χαλινούς	2, 3
στόματα, στόματος	3, 10
ὅλον τὸ σῶμα	2, 3, 6
μετάγομεν, μετάγεται	3, 4
ἰδού	4, 5
τηλικαῦτα, ἡλίκον	4, 5
γλῶσσα, γλῶσσαν	5, 6, 8
πῦρ	5, 6
φλογίζουσα, φλογιζομένη	6

κόσμος (1.27; 2.5; 3.6; 4.4), καθίστημι (3.6; 4.4), γένεσις (1.23; 3.6), δύναμαι (1.21; 2.14; 3.8, 12; 4.2, 12), οὐδείς (1.13; 3.8), ἄνθρωπος (1.7, 19; 2.20, 24; 3.8, 9; 5.17), ἀκατάστατος (1.8; 3.8; cf. ἀκαταστασία in 3.16), κακός (1.13; 3.8), κύριος (1.1, 7; 2.1; 3.9; 4.10, 15; 5.4, 7, 8, 10, 11, 14, 15), πατήρ of God (1.17, 27; 3.9), κατά (2.8, 17; 3.9), θεός (1.1, 5, 13, 20, 27; 2.5, 19, 23; 3.9; 4.4, 6, 7, 8), πικρός (3.11, 14), ποιέω (2.8, 12, 13, 19; 3.12, 18; 4.13, 15, 17; 5.15). For rhetorical questions see 2.1, 4, 5, 6, 7, 14, 16, 20, 21, 25; 3.11-12, 13; 4.1, 4, 5, 12, 14; 5.13, 14. For an interest in the sea note 1.6; 3.4-5, 12. For alliteration and assonance (here in vv. 2, 5, 6, 7, 8) see the Introduction, 83.

[29] To my knowledge, no one has suggested that James himself was the author and that he incorporated his own pre-formed essay—a possibility some have suggested for Paul and 1 Cor 13.

[30] See esp. Frankemölle, 479-81; M. Taylor, *Structure*, 53-54, 66; Watson, 'Rhetoric'. Contrast Trocmé, 'Églises'; Vouga, 93-94, 102-104: v. 13 concludes vv. 1-12.

[31] There are, however, two verbal links between vv. 1-12 and 13-18: πικρόν in vv. 11 and 14, ἀκατάστατον in v. 8 and ἀκαταστασία in v. 16.

[32] Frankemölle, 481-82, highlights the antitheses in this section.

φύσις, φύσει	7
δαμάζεται, δεδάμασται, δαμάσαι	7, 8
ἀνθρωπίνῃ, ἀνθρώπων, ἀνθρώπους	7, 8, 9
καταρώμεθα, κατάρα	9, 10
γλυκύ	11, 12
ποιῆσαι	12

Homiletical and theological commentators have most often found an ethical lesson in vv. 3-4, construing them as encouragement for the possibility of controlling speech. Many modern scholars, however, demur. According to Bertram, the images of bit and rudder must be understood 'pessimistically... As the horse cannot resist the bridle or the ship the rudder, so many are helpless against the ὁρμή or caprice of the tongue... little though the member is.'[33] This reading assuredly suits the broader context: all err (v. 2), and the tongue is a destructive fire (vv. 5-6). And yet the images of bit and rudder, taken on their own, suggest the possibility of control, as does the reference to the taming of beasts in v. 7. Furthermore, vv. 3-4 immediately follow a statement about the 'perfect' individual who can 'bridle the whole body', which strongly intimates that what immediately follows is about control, not the lack of such.

It is not so clear, then, that the old homiletical approach misconstrues the text. This commentary takes the view that vv. 3-4 elaborate the end of v. 2 ('able to bridle the whole body') and so concern control of the tongue whereas with v. 5 the subject shifts to lack of control.[34] As Laws, 148-49, observes, we do not have here alternative illustrations but a 'chain of associated ideas: to control the tongue is to control the whole body (v. 2b), as a bit...in a horse's mouth controls the whole body of the horse (v. 3); in v. 4 the idea of control remains, and now it is explicitly the control of a small object over a great one; in v. 5b this small/great contrast is stressed, but the idea of control gives way to that of destructive power'. In brief, we may think of vv. 2-4 as setting forth the ideal (control of the tongue), vv. 5-8 as documenting what is actually the case (the destructive tongue cannot be tamed), vv. 9-10 as making the application to a particularly odious religious practice, and vv. 11-12 as exclaiming via a parable over the contradiction between the ideal and the sad reality (the tongue seemingly does the impossible, working good and evil).[35]

3.1-12 is more lament than help, because James offers no counsel on how to tame the tongue. But to do so would undo his own rhetoric, which emphasizes that the tongue is untamable. His chief goal is to warn, not instruct. As Culpepper puts it, 'James does not provide "A Practical

---

[33] G. Bertram, 'ὁρμή κτλ.', *TDNT* 5.471. Cf. Konradt, *Existenz*, 278.

[34] Cf. Poole, 890; Frankemölle, 490, 494-95, 499; Popkes, 225.

[35] But Watson, 'Rhetoric', outlines the argument this way: *propositio* (v. 1a), *ratio* (v. 1b), *confirmatio* (v. 2), *exornatio* (vv. 3-10a), *conplexio* (vv. 10b-12). Hartin, 181-82, offers a very similar analysis: theme (v. 1), reason (v. 2), proof (vv. 3-5a), embellishment (vv. 5b-10), conclusion (vv. 11-12).

Guide to Controlling Your Tongue" or "Ten Steps to More Christlike Speech". Instead, James paints graphic, disturbing pictures of the tongue's potential for perversity and allows each individual to decide what to do about the problem of unrestrained speech.'[36]

Regarding *Sitz im Leben*, it is clear that some teachers are doing something wrong, but what exactly? For Bede, Jas 3 rebukes those who demanded the circumcision of Gentiles.[37] Modern expositors, while they seem to agree in not taking up this scenario, are otherwise in disagreement. According to Wolmarans, 'The situation presupposed...is a community torn apart by strife and dissension (3:14, 16; 4:1) because of too many people vying for the office of teacher (3:1)... Prospective teachers, in an attempt to acquire a following, probably entered into bitter debates with one another... Opponents were cursed (3:9).'[38] Trocmé discerns behind chaps 2 and 3 a Pauline Christianity that, among other things, paid too much heed to social hierarchy, lacked active charity, was oriented to a purely intellectual faith, and had disordered assemblies with numerous insufficiently educated teachers.[39] Vouga, 94-96, also upholds continuity with the polemical diatribe in chap. 2.[40] Wanke wonders whether a 'gnosticising' heresy lies in the background.[41]

Others dismiss all such readings as having insufficient warrant. According to Dibelius, 182, 'The interpreter must guard against regarding these examples as actual events and imputing them to the readers'. Thus the chapter is not a transparent window into an early Christian community, nor does it clearly contain inner-ecclesiastical polemic.[42] This is a reasonable position to take. One can imagine the section serving well in a variety of settings. Wherever there are teachers, some think too highly of themselves, and wherever there are human beings, some speak ill of others.

This commentary, however, posits a particular *Sitz im Leben*, one that takes its bearings from the plain sense of 1.1, from the consistent absence of explicitly Christian themes,[43] from the several references to conflict among the addressees, and from the mention of blessings and cursing in

---

[36] Culpepper, 'Tongue', 410.
[37] Bede *ad loc*. CCSL 121 ed. Hurst, 202.
[38] Wolmarans, 'Tongue', 524.
[39] Trocmé, ' Églises'.
[40] So also Draper, 'Apostles', 169-70.
[41] Wanke, 'Lehrer', 492.
[42] But many have certainly put it to good use as polemic; see already Ps.-Clement, *1 Ep. virg.* 1.11 ed. Diekamp, 19; also Peter of Callinicum, *Contra Damianum* 20.69-92 CCSG 29 ed. Ebied, Van Roey, and Wickham, 295-96 (countering Trinitarian heresy); Trapp, 698 (attacking the 'pope's parasites', among others). Cf. Isho'dad of Merv *ad loc*. HSem 10 ed. Gibson, 50: the issue in James is not the number of teachers but false doctrine.
[43] Which the commentators typically ignore. E.M. Goullburn, *The Idle Word*, New York, 1866, can even interpret 3.1-12 in terms of the imitation of Christ.

3.9-10. The view taken here is that these last verses advert to the practice of cursing human beings within the context of blessing God. In other words, James sets himself against some version of a liturgical ban on Christian Jews. But as the party James represents remains within the synagogue, such a ban was, in his time and place, likely a threat on the horizon, that is, in the process of spreading, rather than a universal fait accompli.[44]

The movement of the passage accords with this reading. For the traditional *topoi* in vv. 1-8 all serve as introduction to vv. 9-10, and the latter verses are then elaborated in vv. 11-12. The central concern of the passage is not control of the tongue in general but the problem of blessing and cursing in particular.

Verse 1. 3.1-12 opens by admonishing those who aspire to teach but quickly goes on to warn about speech in general.[45] The admonition fits the present context presumably because teaching is a prominent exercise of the tongue.[46] That is, v. 1 introduces 'the general topic by reference to a particular instance'.[47] Still, the reference to 'many teachers', which is not closely linked to either what has come or with what follows, is unexpected. This explains why some have resorted to conjectural emendation; see n. 49.

Ropes, 226, contends that the whole section addresses itself not to all but to teachers.[48] This is problematic. (i) The introductory 'my brothers' (v. 1; cf. vv. 10, 12) is not elsewhere confined to teachers. (ii) As the dominant history of interpretation makes plain, the following verses are of universal relevance. (iii) 3.1 addresses itself precisely to those who are not teachers, for clearly the meaning cannot be, 'Not many of you (teachers) should become teachers'. (iv) One can compare Mt 10, the missionary discourse. Although it explicitly addresses the twelve and through them later itinerant missionaries, half way through the chapter it begins to issue imperatives applicable to all Christians, including those who stay at home and support missionaries (10.40-42). So there is no one audience in mind; or rather, as the chapter moves forward, a specialized audience becomes a generalized audience. James 3 is similar.

---

[44] J. Marcus, 'A Jewish-Christian *'Amidah?'*, *Early Christianity* 3 (2012), 215-25, on the basis of an analysis of the Eighteen Benedictions, argues that there may have been rabbinic synagogues whose members included Christian Jews, synagogues which witnessed debates over the form of the *'Amidah* and whether it should include the ban on heretics.

[45] The citation of 3.1 in Ps.-Clement, *1 Ep. virg.* 11 ed. Funk, 10-11, similarly introduces a catena of quotations about the tongue.

[46] Contrast Dibelius, 182, who regards 3.1 as 'totally isolated'.

[47] Laws, 141. Cf. Frankemölle, 487.

[48] So too Cabaniss, 'Homily'; Adamson, 140; Reese, 'Exegete', 83.

μὴ πολλοὶ διδάσκαλοι γίνεσθε, ἀδελφοί μου.[49] Cf. the Hebrew אַל־תִּהְיוּ, which the LXX translates with μὴ γίνεσθε.[50] James separates μή from the verb also in 1.7 and 2.1. The suggestion that the meaning is, 'Do not serve as teachers much or frequently', is implausible.[51] διδάσκαλος is a *hapax*, here undefined. Whatever the relationship of 'teacher' to 'elder' (cf. 5.14)—the latter overlaps with the former if 'every leader of the primitive Church was a teacher'[52]—διδάσκαλος presumably involves (depending on the audience one envisages for James) public interpretation of Torah and/or Christian instruction, a function reserved in either case for a small number of individuals.[53] 'Teachers must always be a minority.'[54]

διδάσκαλος may here be more or less the Greek equivalent of 'rabbi'.[55] One thinks not of itinerants but of community leaders.[56] The issue of how to tell true from false teachers, so important in Paul, 1 John, Jude, and other early Christian literature,[57] does not arise here, where the subject is not heresy but ethics; cf. Herm. *Sim.* 9.22.2-3.

Why many should wish to become teachers goes unsaid. Commentators—themselves teachers—sometimes think of a desire for power and

---

[49] 020 630 have πολυδιδάσκαλοι, which may be due to an error of sight. Most of the other variants have to do with word order and do not alter the sense. D. Völter, 'Zwei neue Wörter für das Lexikon des griechischen Neuen Testaments?', *ZNW* 10 (1909), 328-29, argues that the original was ἐθελοδιδάσκαλοι. Dibelius, 183 n. 9, rejects the unattributed proposal of an original πλάνοι διδάσκαλοι. Much more tempting is the conjectural emendation of Wettlaufer, 'Variants', 104-27; μὴ πολύλαλοι διδάσκαλοι γίνεσθε; cf. Mt 6.7; 12.36-37; Jas 1.19. Haplography would then explain the dominant reading: an eye skipped from the first λ in πολύλαλοι to the last λ, creating πολλοί.

[50] 2 Chr 30.7; Ps 32.9; Zech 1.4.

[51] Cf. Dibelius, 182 (remarking that here γίνεσθαι = εἶναι); Wanke, 'Lehrer', 491; Frankemölle, 487. Contrast the v.l. πολυδιδάσκαλοι and Mussner, 159, who suggests an original πολύ instead of πολλοί. Bengel, 498, supports both meanings: not many teachers, not much speaking. For a history of the English translations of this line see Goodspeed, *Problems*, 190-91.

[52] So F.V. Filson, 'The Christian Teacher in the First Century', *JBL* 60 (1941), 322.

[53] Cf. Acts 13.1; Rom 12.7; 1 Cor 12.28-29 ('are all teachers?'); Eph 4.11; 1 Tim 2.7; Did. 11.1-2; 13.2.

[54] So Plummer, 595. On teachers in the early church see A. Harnack, *The Mission and Expansion of Christianity in the First Three Centuries*, vol. 1, 2nd ed., New York, 1908, 333-68; K.H. Rengstorf, 'διδάσκω κτλ.', *TDNT* 2.135-65; Zimmermann, *Lehrer*; P. Pilhofer, 'Von Jakobus zu Justin', in *Religiöses Lernen in der biblischen, frühjüdischen und frühchristlichen Überlieferung*, ed. B. Ego and H. Merklein, Tübingen, 2005, 253-69.

[55] Cf. Mt 23.7-8; Jn 1.38; 3.2; Jesus is often addressed as διδάσκαλος = רַבִּי in the gospels: Mt 8.19; Mk 10.17; Jn 8.4; etc. Although a few (e.g. Weidner, 56; Knowles, 69) have wondered whether Jas 3.1 alludes to Mt 23.7-10, which forbids being called 'rabbi', a connection is tenuous: the former has nothing to do with honorifics.

[56] See further Laws, 142-43.

[57] Cf. 1 Tim 6.3; 2 Tim 4.3; 2 Pet 2.1; Did. 11.3-12.

privilege.[58] The text, in any case, seemingly assumes that it was possible for a person 'who believed himself competent for the work to put himself forward and take up the activities of a teacher'.[59] One recalls how often the Synoptic Jesus walks into a synagogue and is allowed to speak, and how often Acts reports the same of Paul.[60]

ἀδελφοί μου (see on 1.2) also opens major sections in 1.2; 2.1, and 14. The vocative recurs in the present section in 3.10 and 12, the latter creating an *inclusio*. It generates sympathy, for although our author is, as the first person ληυψόμεθα entails, a teacher and so in this respect different from most of his readers, 'my brothers' sets him alongside them. It also reinforces the imperative, as Barrow observes: 'that appellation doth imply a strong argument enforcing the precept: brethren, with especial tenderness of affection, should love one another, and delight in each others good; they should tender the interest and honour of each other as their own'.[61]

εἰδότες ὅτι μεῖζον κρίμα λημψόμεθα.[62] εἰδότες ὅτι is a favorite of Paul, who uses it to refer to traditional teaching.[63] μεῖζων recurs in 4.6. The implicit agent behind λημψόμεθα is God; cf. the λήμψεται of 1.7 and 12 and the λαμβάνετε of 4.3. By employing the first person plural—apart from 1.1, this is our author's only real autobiographical statement[64]—the author identifies his pseudonym, James, as a teacher, which is consistent with the traditions about him.[65]

Only here does the author use κρίμα. But 2.12 (which speaks of judgment according to words as well as deeds) and 5.9 employ the related κρίνω with eschatological sense. 3.1, with its future tense (λημψόμεθα),

---

[58] E.g. R. Wall, 162. Cf. Mt 23.6-7; Heb 13.7; m. 'Abot 4.12; m. B. Meṣi'a 2.11. Evagrius of Pontus, *Antirrhet.* 7.42 ed. Frankenberg, 537, cited Jas 4.3 as an antidote to 'the thought of vainglory' that can motivate teaching. Luther quipped in the margin beside Jas 3.1 in one his Bibles: 'Would that you yourself had observed that'; see W. Walther, 'Zu Luthers Ansicht über den Jakobusbrief', *TSK* 66 (1883), 597.

[59] So Ropes, 227. M. Skaballanovitch, *Tolkovii Tipikon*, 2nd ed., Moscow, 2008, 32, finds in Jas 3.1 evidence that preaching was not yet a special office reserved for a particular person: in James' world, teachers were self-appointed.

[60] Mk 1.21; Lk 4.16; 6.6; Acts 13.5, 14-16; etc.

[61] Barrow, 'Against Detraction', in *Sermons*, 429.

[62] Some late Greek mss., supported by some Latin and Boharic texts, have the second person plural: 'you will receive' (cf. the Vulgate: *scientes quoniam majus judicium sumitis*). This excludes the author from the threat. One finds the same anxiety in some later exegetes: Grotius *et al.*, persuaded that an apostle could never speak of his own condemnation, accordingly urged that κρίμα must here mean 'responsibility'.

[63] Rom 5.3; 6.9; 13.11; 1 Cor 15.58; 2 Cor 1.7; 4.14; 5.11; Gal 2.16; Phil 1.16; Col 3.24. Cf. Eph 6.8; 1 Pet 1.18; Pol. *Phil.* 1.3; Epicurus, *Ep. ad Men. apud* Diogenes Laertius 10.123.

[64] The first person plurals in 1.18; 2.2; 3.3, 6, 9, 11, 21; 4.5; and 5.17 are generic: they include all or most of the writer's audience.

[65] Acts 15.12-21; Hegesippus in Eusebius, *H.E.* 2.23.1-19; the Apocryphon of James; etc.

probably also has the universal judgment in view; cf. 4.11-12; 5.1-3. Also comparable are Rom 13.2—'The one who resists the authorities resists what God has appointed, and those who resist will incur judgment' (κρίμα λήμψονται)[66]—and the eschatological warnings regarding speech in Matthew: 5.21-26; 12.36. On this reading, λαμβάνω + κρίμα is akin to λαμβάνω + μίσθον in eschatological contexts.[67] Some exegetes, however, think instead of the community, which holds leaders to a higher standard.

If the eschatological reading is right, μεῖζον κρίμα λημψόμεθα means that the greater one's responsibility on earth, the greater one's responsibility on the last day. 3.1, then, implies that the faithful can suffer judgment; cf. 1 Cor 3.12-15. Does the verse assume that they may even find themselves in Gehenna?[68] Or did the author think that eschatological judgment will correct and lead to deliverance, or alternately that it will establish ranks in heaven?[69]

The general principle seems to be that of Lk 12.48: 'From everyone to whom much has been given, much will be required, and from one to whom much has been entrusted, even more will be demanded'. James does not, however, clarify exactly why teachers will be judged more harshly: he leaves us with the bare εἰδότες ὅτι. One possibility is that, as in Mt 23.13-15, the sins of teachers inevitably mislead those taught, so the ill-effects are multiplied.[70]

James 3.1 has a parallel in Mk 12.40: οὗτοι λήμψονται περισσότερον κρίμα; cf. Mt 23.14 v.l.; Lk 20.47. This too employs λαμβάνω in the future + κρίμα, and James' μεῖζον is the functional equivalent of Mark's περισσότερον. Further, the Markan lines belongs to a denunciation of 'scribes', who in the Synoptics are teachers.[71] Perhaps, then, Jas 3.1 rewrites a saying of Jesus.[72] This would be consistent with the introductory εἰδότες ὅτι.

---

[66] The shared expression, which is likely a Semitism (cf. לקח + דין, as in m. Ketub. 10.6), is not common. Additional parallels include Mk 12.40; Rom 3.8; 1 Tim 5.12; 1 Clem. 21.1; 51.3; Ign. *Eph.* 11; Hippolytus, *Ruth* 15 GCS 1.2 ed. Achelis, 120.

[67] Cf. Mt 10.41; 1 Cor 3.8, 14; Col 3.24; 4 Ezra 7.98; 8.33; etc.

[68] Cf. v. 5; Mt 7.21; 2 Clem. 4.5.

[69] Cf. Mt 5.12, 19; 10.41-42; 20.23. Oecumenius, *Apoc.* 8.21 TEG 8 ed. de Groote, 205, cites Jas 3.2 ('we all make many mistakes') in arguing that all the saints will suffer a purging judgment. Jerome, *Eph ad* 5.5 PL 26.553C, cites it when urging that heaven will have different mansions corresponding to the virtues people have practiced.

[70] Cf. Lk 11.52; Gos. Thom. 39; also Mk 9.42, where leading others astray is again the cause of eschatological loss.

[71] E.g. Mt 13.52; Mk 12.28-34. Recall that Enoch, the supposed author of numerous revelations, was remembered as 'the scribe of righteousness' (1 En. 12.4; 15.1), and that Jesus Ben Sira was both scribe and teacher.

[72] Cf. Knowles, 69; Plumptre, 78; Schlatter, 211. Mussner, 159, leaves the question open. Deppe, *Sayings*, fails to discuss the parallel.

THE SINS OF SPEECH (3.1-12)

Verse 2. James offers an additional reason for not teaching: one will inexorably err and so be subject to the greater strictness of judgment just mentioned.

πολλὰ γὰρ πταίομεν ἅπαντες. Cf. IG 14.1201, a grave stone whose inscription includes these words: 'My child, guard yourself lest you trip: the tongue itself is not troubled, indeed, whenever it speaks; but whenever it errs it contributes many evils'.[73] The first person plural in *paraenesis* is common.[74] According to MHT 4.117, adverbial πολλὰ is a 'likely Aramaism' (cf. סגי = 'much', as often in the targumim); but 'possible Aramaism' would be a more prudent judgment. πταίω[75] occurs in the LXX most often for the Niphal of נגף. Its first and literal meaning is 'lose one's footing', but it commonly means 'go astray' or 'sin'.[76] Aelius Aristides, *Or.* 34.62, uses it of speech: ῥήματι πταίσῃ.[77]

James' incontrovertible proposition, with its striking alliteration (π, π, απ), harmonizes with the far-flung theological conviction that all human beings—note the intensive ἅπαντες—sin; cf. 4Q299 1 ('although all nations loathe sin and praise truth, not one lip or tongue persists in the latter'); Ecclus 8.5; 19.6 ('Who has not sinned with his tongue?'); Philo, *Deus* 75 ('No one...has run the course of life from birth to death without stumbling' [ἄπταιστον]); *Spec.* 1.252 ('even the perfect person [τέλειος]...never escapes from sinning').[78] James, however, may have in mind less a formal *theologoumenon* than the universal human experience that everyone fails in one way or the other; cf. Seneca, *Clem.* 1.6 ('We have all erred, some in serious, some in trivial things; some from deliberate intention, some by chance impulse, or because we were led astray by the wickedness of others'); Epictetus, *Diatr.* 1.11.7 ('to err is in accord with nature, just as practically all of us, or at least most of us, do err'); etc.[79]

On the assumption that James is a pseudepigraphon, the inclusion of the author in the generalization ('we all make many mistakes') exhibits humility and adds rhetorical force (cf. 1 Jn 1.8–2.2): even the great apostle, famous for his piety, was not free of error; cf. Trapp, 698: the one 'worthily called James the Just...affirmeth here of himself and other sanctified persons, We offend or stumble all. Near to hand is an inference

---

[73] See further Horsley-Llewelyn, *Documents*, 4.42-46.

[74] See Rom 13.12-13; 14.13, 19; Heb 10.22-24; 1 Jn 3.18-24; 4.7-16; 2 Bar. 83.5; 85.3-9.

[75] Jas: 2×; NT: 4×.

[76] As in 2.10; cf. LXX Deut 7.25; Rom 11.11; T. Job 18.2; Apoc. Sed. 1.2; also the varied senses of כשל.

[77] Apoc. Sed. 1.2—'For we make many mistakes (πολλὰ γὰρ πταίομεν) every day and night and hour'—which also appears in Ps.-Ephraem, *Serm. comm. res., de paen. et de carit.* ed. Phrantzoles, 47, and idem, *Abstin. a cup. carn.* ed. Phrantzoles, 229— presumably depends upon James.

[78] Note also 1 Kgs 8.46; Pss 14.3; 51.7; Eccl 7.20; 1QH 9(1).21-22; Ecclus 8.5; Philo, *Mut. nom.* 1.585; Mt 19.17; Rom 3.9-18; 1 Jn 1.8-10; 4 Ezra 8.35; 1 Clem. 17.4; etc.

[79] *Neuer Wettstein*, 1291-1301, supplies additional material.

from the greater to the lesser: how much more the rest of us'.[80] Given, moreover, that James addresses itself to a non-Christian audience (1.1), 'we all make many mistakes' is conciliatory. The Christian writer does not pretend to be without blame. His 'indictment...includes even himself among the defendants'.[81]

εἴ τις ἐν λόγῳ οὐ πταίει, οὗτος τέλειος ἀνήρ. ἀνήρ is pleonastic, as in 1.12. Notwithstanding 1.4, where being τέλειος is the goal of faith, and despite the author's likely knowledge of the tradition that Abraham was 'perfect' (see on 2.22), the conditional may be hypothetical, an expression of the impossible.[82] This coheres with v. 8 ('no human being can tame the tongue'), with the author's inclusion of himself as one who stumbles, and with the direction of the main argument: control of the tongue is all but impossible.[83] That ἐν λόγῳ[84] means 'in doctrine' as opposed to 'in speech' is the opinion of Clarke, 814, and a few others. It finds support in patristic usage[85] and coheres with the view of those who find in Jas 3 an attack against heretical teachers. In view of the rest of the passage, however, a more general sense seems indicated.

δυνατὸς χαλιναγωγῆσαι καὶ ὅλον τὸ σῶμα. For χαλιναγωγέω, which prepares for χαλινός in the next verse, see on 1.26, where it is the tongue that is held in check; cf. also Herm. *Mand.* 12.1.1, which exhorts bridling 'evil desire'.[86] The assumption here is that the tongue is the hardest member to master, so if one can bridle it, one will be in full control of everything else; cf. Bede: 'If anyone avoids a slip of the tongue...this person by fixed habit of the same restraint also learns how to keep guard over the other members of the body, which are more easily restrained'.[87]

---

[80] Cf. Bede *ad loc.* CCSL 121 ed. Hurst 202; Acta sinc. S. Petri Alex. PG 18.466C; Oecumenius, *Apoc.* 2.7 TEG 8 ed. de Groote, 89. Contrast Wesley and Clarke, quoted on 511.

[81] Verseput, 'Plutarch', 516. One might wonder how 3.2 harmonizes with 2.10, where the one who sins in one thing is guilty of sinning against the whole law, but this is not a topic in the commentary tradition.

[82] Cf. Brosend, 88, who asks whether James suggests an 'impossible possibility' or a 'possible impossibility'. He observes that the following metaphors themselves seem at odds: while the bit and rudder suggest control, the fire implies lack of control.

[83] Bede *ad loc.* CCSL 121 ed. Hurst 203, urges that the perfect can offend and yet remain perfect, for the righteous can fail and yet remain righteous; and in *Thomas the Contender* 140.9-30, which shares several motifs with Jas 3 (see 14 above), perfection is obtainable. Cf. also Origen, *Hom. Ps 36-38 ad* 36.23-24 SC 411 ed. Prinzivalli, Crouzel, and Brésard, 190; Lactantius, *Inst.* 6.13 CSEL 19 ed. Brandt and Laubmann, 532-34.

[84] NT: 11×; Jas: 1×. The LXX often uses ἐν λόγῳ to translate בדבר: 2 Sam 16.23; 1 Kgs 13.1-2; Eccl 8.3; 2 Chr 30.12; etc.

[85] Cf. Lampe, s.v., λόγος, IA12.

[86] James appears to be the first to associate the verb to σῶμα. The link is found thereafter only in writers familiar with James, beginning with Origen.

[87] Bede *ad loc.* CCSL 121 ed. Hurst, 203. Gill, 792, however, thinks of how 'the force of language, the power of words, and strength of argument' keep individual and communal bodies in check.

In other words, the text is about the will to self-control; cf. the βούλεται of v. 4. Ancient Christians, influenced by Stoicism, naturally took James to allude to the ability of 'reason' (λόγος) to command the body.[88]

'The whole body', a common expression[89] that recurs in vv. 3 and 6, might be what we call 'the whole person'.[90] More likely, it adverts to the physical flesh and its varied impulses. Not only is this the dominant reading in exegetical history, but in the very next verse, ὅλον τὸ σῶμα αὐτῶν refers to the physical bodies of horses.[91] One may compare Mt 5.29: 'it is better for you to lose one of your members than for your whole body (ὅλον τὸ σῶμά σου) to go into hell'.

Another option in the history of interpretation finds here a reference to the ecclesiastical 'body'; cf. 1 Cor 12 and see above. But James does not make such an equation explicit. Moreover, as Brosend, 96, argues, the physical images from the human and animal worlds in Jas 3.1-12 do not 'push the reader beyond the text to find meaning'. At the same time, one should not deny the social dimension of James' concern.[92] Our author is not addressing individuals who are talking to themselves but rather a group of people (ἀδελφοί μου) who can hurt others with their words; cf. 4.1-12; 5.9. Verses 9-10, moreover, readily call to mind a communal worship setting.[93]

Verses 3. Just as a bit in the mouth of a horse directs its whole body, so does a human being in control of the tongue master the whole body. As the simile in the next verse contains more details than the simile in this one—the ship is described ('large', 'driven by strong winds') while the horse is not, and the will of the helmsman is mentioned while the will of the rider is not—it is natural to interpret the latter in the light of the former.[94]

---

[88] E.g. Gregory of Nyssa, *Beat.* 2 Opera 7/2 ed. Callahan, 96; Ps.-Oecumenius *ad loc.* PG 119.484D; *Catenae ad loc.* ed. Cramer, 20; Ps.-Andrew of Crete, *Éloge* 7 ed. Noret, 52. For Jackson-McCabe, *Logos*, 224-30, Jas 3.2 makes most sense if one assumes the close Stoic link between speech and right reason.

[89] It is frequent in medical writers, such as Galen and Oribasius. NT: 9×. Philo: 3×. Cf. also Jos. Asen. 6.1; 16.8; 23.15; 1 Clem. 37.5; 38.1; Apoc. Sedr. 11.3, 13. Although there are Hebrew equivalents (cf. כל בשר, כל גופ[ה]), ὅλον τὸ σῶμα is absent from the LXX.

[90] E.g. Bengel, 498; E. Käsemann, *Leib und Leib Christi: Eine Untersuchung zur paulinischen Begrifflichkeit*, Tübingen, 1933, 95.

[91] Cf. Poole, 889, and see further R.G. Gundry, *Sōma in Biblical Theology*, Cambridge, UK, 1976, 27.

[92] See especially Popkes, 219-20.

[93] See further Locket, *Purity*, 121-24, arguing that 'the purity language here is a figurative label for social/ideological location'.

[94] See further Wolmarans, 'Tongue', 526-27.

εἰ δὲ τῶν ἵππων τοὺς χαλινοὺς εἰς τὰ στόματα βάλλομεν εἰς τὸ πείθεσθαι αὐτοὺς ἡμῖν, καὶ ὅλον τὸ σῶμα αὐτῶν μετάγομεν.[95] Cf. Acts Phil. 104 ed. Bonnet, 40: βάλλων χαλινὸν εἰς τὸ στόμα τοῦ δράκοντος. James' observation, which contains four *hapax legomena* (ἵππος, χαλινός, βάλλω, πείθω) and two words that appear elsewhere in James only in this section (στόμα: vv. 3, 10; μετάγω: vv. 3, 4), echoes the habit of the Greek moral tradition of likening control of the passions or rule of the earth to a charioteer in control of steeds.[96] Particularly close is Plato, *Leg.* 701C: 'I must, every time, rein in my discourse like a horse, and not let it run away with me as though it had no bridle [ἀχάλινον] in its mouth'. Yet the simile is natural, and the Hebrew Bible supplies parallels; cf. Ps 32.9 ('Do not be like a horse or a mule, without understanding, whose temper must be curbed with bit and bridle'); 39.1 ('I will guard my ways, that I may not sin with my tongue; I will bridle my mouth'); Isa 37.29 ('Because...your arrogance has come up to my ears, I will put my hook in your nose and my bit in your mouth').[97]

χαλινός,[98] which picks up on χαλιναγωγέω in v. 2, means either 'bridle' or 'bit'—the latter often made of bronze or iron—or both together.[99] Here 'bit' may be preferable,[100] although texts do not always distinguish between an animal's bridle and the parts.[101] For χαλινός

---

[95] 056 0142 6 18 35 38 81 197 206 218 252 *et al.* A have ἴδε rather than εἰ δέ. Mayor, 108-10, defends the former at great length; cf. Ropes, 229; Laws, 146. But James nowhere else has ἴδε. Recent critical editions prefer εἰ δέ. It is characteristic of James (cf. 2.9; 3.14; 4.11) and is supported by 03C2 020 044 049 1 5 33 43 61 69 88 93 94 *et al.* L590 L884 L2087 Dam PsOeo L.FV K:B. Weakly attested are εἶδε γάρ (01* S:PH^ms) and ἰδού (1874 PsOec SI:DSiS; cf. the next verse). One guesses that an original εἰ δέ became εἶδε and ἴδε, and that the latter in turn became ἰδού. Cf. Metzger, *Commentary*, 681-82.

[96] Plato, *Phaedr.* 246A-47C; Plutarch, *Mor.* 33F; Philo, *Opif.* 86-88; *Leg.* 3.223-24; *Agr.* 67-85; Ps.-Phoc. 57; etc.; also Origen, *Frag. 1–71 in Jer.* 11 GCS 6 ed. Klostermann, 202: τοιοῦτοι δὲ καὶ ἐπιβεβήκασιν ἐφ᾽ ἅρμασί τε καὶ ἵπποις, χαλιναγωγοῦντες τὸ σῶμα. But Jas 3.3 has led some to think of riding a horse.

[97] For other parallels between the horse with a bit and human experience note Horace, *Ep.* 1.2.64-71 ('bridle' anger); Ovid, *Am.* 1.2.9-20 (the unwilling horse with bridle illustrates a person being unwillingly assailed by love).

[98] NT: 2×; cf. Rev 14.20. For מֶתֶג in LXX 4 Βασ 19.28; Ps 31.9; Isa 37.29.

[99] Cf. Philo, *Opif.* 86; Rev 14.20; Apoc. Sed. 7.12; and the rabbinic בלינוס, a loanword.

[100] Cf. Dibelius, 185, citing Xenophon, *Eq.* 6.7, and Plato, *Phaedr.* 254B-D, which distinguish bit from reins.

[101] Cf. 2 Kgs 19.28; Prov 26.3. For χαλινός as the object of (ἐμ)βάλλω see LXX Isa 37.29 (ἐμβαλῶ...χαλινόν); Theognis of Megara 1.551 (ἵπποισ᾽ ἔμβαλλε...χαλινούς); Xenophon, *Eq.* 3.3 (ἐμβάλλοιτο ὁ χαλινός; cf. 6.7); Cyranides 2.31.8 (βάλῃ τὸν χαλινόν). For pictures of bridles see M.C. Bishop, 'Cavalry Equipment of the Roman Army in the First Century A.D.', in *Military Equipment and the Identity of Roman Soldiers*, ed. J.C. Coulston, Oxford, 1988, 69, 70, 72-73, 75-76, 78, 82, 85, 90.

with μετάγω,[102] BDAG, s.v. μετάγω, cites a philosophical maxim in F. Mullach, *Fragmenta Philosophorum Graecorum*, vol. 1, Paris, 1860, 486.18: οἱ ἵπποι τοῖς χαλινοῖς μετάγονται.

According to Ropes, 230, 'The smallness of the member hardly comes into consideration here'. Yet commentators often remark upon the small size of the horse's bit; cf. Dibelius, 186, 'the whole body' in the apodosis 'shows that the author has in mind the contrast which exists between the smallness of the instrument and the greatness of its effect'.[103] Given that James does not always unfold with a linear logic, it is natural to read this verse in the light of what follows; cf. v. 5: μικρόν...μεγάλα.[104]

The use of the first person plural in v. 3 may imply that readers have first-hand experience with horses. The next verse returns to the third person, perhaps because first-hand acquaintance with ships at sea cannot be presumed of all.[105]

Verse 4. Another conventional illustration of the proposition that control of the tongue means control of the body (v. 2). There seems to be an analogy: large ship ≈ human body // small rudder ≈ human speech // desire of steersman ≈ human will.[106]

ἰδοὺ καὶ τὰ πλοῖα. Cf. T. Naph. 6.2: καὶ ἰδοὺ πλοῖον. Philo, *Leg.* 3.223-24, when explaining why mind should rule sense-perception, illustrates by recalling first a charioteer guiding horses, second a helmsman steering a ship: 'A ship...keeps to her straight course when the helmsman grasping the tiller steers accordingly, but capsizes when a contrary wind has sprung up over the sea, and the surge has settled in'. Even closer to James is Plutarch, *Mor.* 33F: both 'character and speech' persuade, 'or rather character by means of speech, just as a horseman uses a bridle (χαλινοῦ) or a helmsman uses a rudder (πηδαλίου), since virtue has no instrument so humane or so akin to itself as speech'. The

---

[102] The latter occurs in the NT only in Jas 3.3-4.

[103] Cf. Manton, 124; Gill, 792; Plummer, 596; Watson, 'Rhetoric', 58; Frankemölle, 493.

[104] Cf. the use of the diminutive χαλινάριον in Apoc. Sedr. 7.12: 'among the four-footed beasts the mule is a crafty animal...yet with a small bridle we can turn it where we will'.

[105] Yet some have found in v. 4 evidence that James was written near a sea port; see 95 above. The argument is weak. Among other things, ancients could see artistic representations of boats in many places. The Hellenistic mausoleum in west Jerusalem known as Jason's tomb features drawings of boats with some detail, including rudders. See L.Y. Rahmani, 'Jason's Tomb', *IEJ* 17 (1967), 69-73. The tombs at Bet Shearim also include sketches of boats (representing the ferry to the afterlife?); see B. Mazar, *Beth She'arim*, vol. 1, Jerusalem, 1973, plates 7.3; 9.3-4; 20.2; 23.1-2.

[106] Popkes, 225, objects that the rudder cannot represent the tongue as the latter has not yet been mentioned; but James often anticipates himself, and does not οὕτως καί in v. 5 imply as much in the present case? Bede *ad loc.* CCSL 121 ed. Hurst 204, construes James this way: large ship ≈ human mind // strong winds ≈ appetites of the mind // rudder ≈ intentions of the heart.

pairing of chariotcer and pilot was clearly conventional;[107] so too all of the language in 3.3-4.[108] Artemidorus, *Onir.* 1.56, supplies partial explanation for the traditional conjoining of ships and horses: 'A horse resembles a ship. For just as the poet calls ships "the horses of the sea",[109] we call Poseidon "Hippios" and a horse is to the land as the ship is to the sea.'

ἰδού (cf. Hebrew הנה), which appears also in 3.5; 5.4, 7, 9, and 11, is not common in the canonical wisdom literature.[110] It is much more characteristic of narrative traditions, visionary and apocalyptic literature, and sayings attributed to Jesus.[111] Its unusual frequency in James—it occurs nine times in all of Paul's epistles—may be a sign that our author spoke a Semitic language.[112] The demonstrative particle also introduces an illustration in 3.5 and 5.7.

Vouga, 98, who offers an ecclesiastical reading of vv. 3-4—'the whole body' = the church—observes that, in the Gospels, a boat can symbolize the church.[113]

τηλικαῦτα ὄντα καὶ ὑπὸ ἀνέμων σκληρῶν ἐλαυνόμενα. Cf. MT Isa 27.8 (ברוחו הקשה); LXX Prov 27.16 (σκληρὸς ἄνεμος); Mk 6.48 (ἐν τῷ ἐλαύνειν...ὁ ἄνεμος); Josephus, *Ant.* 5.205 (ἤλαυνε...ἄνεμος); Dio Chrysostom 3.49 (ὑπὸ ἀνέμων σκληρῶν); Origen, *Mart.* 48 CGS 7 ed. Koetschau, 44 (ἄνεμοι σκληροί). ἄνεμος, σκληρός, ἐλαύνω and τηλικοῦτος appear only here in James.[114] The latter, a strong form of τηλίκος, means in this context 'so large' or 'so great'.[115] Revelation 16.18 uses it to describe an unprecedented violent earthquake, but Lucian, *Nav.* 15, supplies a closer parallel: τηλικαῦτα πλοῖα, 'ships of such large size'. The image is of 'hard' or 'stiff' winds driving a large ship.[116] Although

---

[107] Cf. also Philo, *Det.* 53; *Agr.* 69-70; *Conf.* 115; *Flacc.* 26; Dio Chrysostom 4.25; Stobaeus, *Ecl.* 3.17.17.

[108] Full demonstration in Dibelius, 186-90. Note the interest in ships in Jewish wisdom texts: Job 9.26; Prov 30.19; 31.14; Wis 5.10; 14.1. For Egyptian parallels see S. Herrmann, 'Steuerruder, Waage, Herz und Zunge in ägyptischen Bildreden', *Zeitschrift für ägyptische Sprache und Altertumskunde* 79 (1954), 106-15. Frankemölle, 502, disputes Herrmann's claim that James is under Egyptian influence.

[109] Homer, *Od.* 4.708. Interestingly enough, v. 4 reminds both Bede *ad loc.* CCSL 121 ed. Hurst, 204, and Dante, *Inferno* 26, of Ulysses' perils at sea.

[110] Prov: 1×; Eccl: 6×; Wis: 0×; Ecclus: 3×.

[111] Mt 7.4; 10.16; 11.8, 10, 19; 12.41, 42, 49; 13.3; 20.18; 22.4; 23.34, 38; 24.23, 25, 26; 25.6; 26.45, 46; 28.7; Mk 4.3; 10.33; 13.23; 14.41, 42; Lk 6.23; 7.25, 27, 34; 10.3, 19; 11.31, 32, 41; 13.30, 32, 35; 15.29; 17.21, 23; 18.31; 22.10, 21, 31; Jn 4.35; 16.32. It is much less frequent in Paul: Rom 9.33; 1 Cor 15.51; 2 Cor 5.17; 6.2, 9; 7.11; 12.14; Gal 1.20.

[112] P. Fiedler, *Die Formel 'und siehe' im Neuen Testament*, Munich, 1969, 41-42.

[113] E.g. Mt 8.23-27; cf. Martin, 105; Reese, 'Exegete', 83.

[114] But cf. ἡλίκος in v. 5.

[115] Cf. 2 Macc 12.3; 3 Macc 3.9; 4 Macc 16.4; T. Sol. 23.4 v.l.; T. Abr. RecShrt 8.7.

[116] Popkes, 224-25, supplies data on the size of ships in antiquity. Josephus, *Vita* 15, claims to have traveled on one that carried 600 passengers.

THE SINS OF SPEECH (3.1-12)

James' analogy would work even if nothing were said about fierce winds, the latter add drama and intimate that there are great forces at loose in the human arena. One also recalls 1.6, where the doubter is like a surging wave of the sea, driven and tossed by the wind.[117]

For the traditional use of steering a ship in religious discourse see, in addition to the texts already cited, Philo, *Cher.* 36 ('divine reason' is the 'steersman of all'); Dio Chrysostom 12.34 (the gods direct the universe 'like a skillful pilot'); Lucian, *Bis ac.* 2 (Zeus is like the master of a ship with the tiller in his hands). Also comparable is *Amen-em-Opet* 18 (20.4-6): 'Steer not with thy tongue (alone). If the tongue of a man (be) the rudder of a boat, the All-Lord is its pilot.'[118]

μετάγεται ὑπὸ ἐλαχίστου πηδαλίου ὅπου ἡ ὁρμὴ τοῦ εὐθύνοντος βούλεται. As with the previous line, this contains several Jamesian *hapax legomena*: ἐλάχιστος, πηδάλιον, ὁρμή, εὐθύνω. μετάγω makes for a verbal link with v. 3. For the smallness—ἐλαχίστου may be a genuine superlative[119]—of the rudder (πηδάλιον)[120] see Lucretius, *Rer. nat.* 896-906 ('there is no need to be surprised that elements so small can sway so large a body and turn about our whole weight. For indeed the wind, which is thin and has a fine substance, drives and pushes a great galleon with mighty momentum, and one hand rules it however fast it may go, and one rudder steers it in any direction'); Ps.-Aristotle, *Quaest. mech.* 850B ('Why does the rudder, which is small and at the end of the vessel, have so great power that it is able to move the huge mass of the ship, although it is moved by a smaller tiller and by the strength of but one man, and then without violent exertion'?)[121]

ὁρμή, which means 'impulse' or 'inclination',[122] goes with τοῦ εὐθύνοντος, literally 'the one making straight'.[123] εὐθύνω often has a nautical reference.[124] As the verb carries moral sense in LXX Josh 24.23;

---

[117] Cf. Eph 4.14; 2 Pet 2.17. It is far from obvious that σκληρός intimates religious or moral content (cf. Mt 25.24 and σκληροκαρδία). Bishop, *Apostles*, 186, fantasizes that our verse might reflect the circumstance that James heard Peter recount the story of the stilling of the storm in the language of Lk 8.23.

[118] J.B. Pritchard, *Ancient Near Eastern Texts Relating to the Old Testament*, Princeton, 1950, 423-24.

[119] BDAG, s.v., ἐλάχιστος 2.

[120] Cf. Acts 27.40 (literal usage). LXX: 0×. Pseudepigrapha (Denis): 0×. Philo: 3×. Josephus: 0×. LXX 4 Macc 7.1 however has the related πηδαλιουχέω (with metaphorical sense). According to some earlier commentators, the reference in James is not to the rudder but to the tiller; see e.g. Gill, 792; Mayor, 112. Cf. Lucian, *Nav.* 5-6: a description of a high ship is followed by this: 'and all this a little old man, a wee fellow, has kept from harm by turning the huge rudders with a tiny tiller'.

[121] The stark contrast between small and large might recall several sayings attributed to Jesus: Mt 23.24 (gnat vs. camel); Mk 4.31 (mustard seed vs. large tree); 10.25 (eye of needle vs. camel).

[122] Cf. Let. Aris. 7, 222, 256; Acts 14.5.

[123] Cf. LXX Isa 40. 3; Jn 1.23; T. Job 36.4.

[124] Philo, *Leg.* 3.224; *Conf.* 115; *Abr.* 70; Porphyry, *In Arist. cat. exp.* ed. Busse 116 (πηδαλίῳ εὐθύνεται); Gregory of Nyssa, *Eun.* 2.1.188 ed. Jaeger, 279 (πηδαλίῳ...

Prov 20.24; T. Sim. 5.2; and often in Sirach,[125] one wonders whether it intimates such here; cf. the use of εὐθύς in religious contexts to mean 'proper' or 'upright'.[126]

One wonders whether, in the present context, ἡ ὁρμὴ τοῦ εὐθύνοντος βούλεται (an unusual expression) highlights the issue of the will: one's internal disposition and fortitude make controlling the tongue possible.[127] Mayor, 111-12, however, asserts that ὁρμή 'is used of the origin of motion either moral or physical' and claims that it here refers to 'the slight pressure of the hand on the tiller'.[128]

Verse 5. This verse is Janus-faced: it looks forward and backward, summarizing and adding to the gist of the previous lines while at the same time introducing the motif of destructive fire. The theme moves from hypothetical control to the dismal reality that human beings by and large fail to tame the tongue, with dire consequences.[129]

οὕτως καὶ ἡ γλῶσσα μικρὸν μέλος ἐστὶν καὶ μεγάλα αὐχεῖ.[130] Note the alliteration: μικρὸν μέλος...μεγάλα. The personification of a part of the body as though it has an individual identity recalls 1 Cor 12.14-26 (where the various members speak), while the alienation of the self from its own members calls to mind Mt 5.29-30; Mk 9.43-48. Also related are Midr. Ps 39.2, where the body parts argue about which is the greatest, with the conclusion being that the tongue rules all, and 12.3: 'Should your tongue become perverse and speak slander of your neighbor, go to, and instruct it diligently with words of Torah'.

The inferential οὕτως καί,[131] a favorite of LXX Ecclesiasticus,[132] looks back to vv. 3-4 and ahead to vv. 5b-6: just as a (small) bit guides the

---

εὐθύνειεν); cf. Dio Chrysostom 13.18 (τῷ πηδαλίῳ κατευθύνων); Strabo, *Geog.* 2.3.5 (κατευθύνειν τὸ πλοῖον); Posidonius frag. 13.216 (κατευθύνειν τὸ πλοῖον).

[125] 2.2, 6; 6.17; 37.15; 38.10; 49.9.

[126] LXX Ps 7.11; Acts 8.12; 2 Pet 1.15; etc.

[127] Such a reading might raise the question of who or what controls the will. Cf. T. Spurgeon, 'The Ship of Life', *Christian World Pulpit* 49 (1896), 346: 'Well then, what controls the will? We seem to have a ship within a ship... A steersman has orders from his owners... We are ships, and we can control both wind and wave, or at least outride them and outlive their anger, but we must be ourselves controlled by God, lest we cannot control the speech that controls our lives.'

[128] Yet against this see G. Bertram, 'ὁρμή κτλ.', *TDNT* 5.467-74. Bertram cites Sym. Ezek 1.12 (ὅπου ἦ ἡ ὁρμὴ τοῦ πνεύματος) as well as classical texts that emphasize the freedom and caprice of the steersman.

[129] Some think v. 5 begins a 'new paragraph'. So Davids, 140; cf. Frankemölle, 482, 490, 499.

[130] Although quite a few witnesses, including P20 01 04C2 044 5 69 88 *et al.* **Byz** Dam GregAgr PsOec Sl:ChDMSiS, have μεγαλαυχεῖ, modern critical editions prefer μεγάλα αὐχει, attested in P74 02 03 04* 025 33V 43 81 *et al.* L884. Either could be original.

[131] Cf. 1.11; 2.17, 26; 3.5.

[132] 2.18; 6.17; etc.; cf. בן.

(large) horse (v. 3), and just as a small rudder steers a large ship (v. 4), and just as a small fire sets ablaze a large forest (v. 5b), so too the small tongue produces far-reaching consequences in human experience (v. 6). Cf. Euripides, *Andr.* 642-43 ('From a small [σμικρᾶς] beginning the tongue contrives great [μέγα] strife'); Dio Chrysostom 12.43 ('an ignorant tongue causes no small injury to an audience'). Poole, 890, puts it this way: 'The tongue, though little, is of great force and efficacy, and it will tell you so itself; it not only boasts what its fellow members can do, but especially what itself can'.

γλῶσσα takes up a word from 1.26 that now becomes the focus (vv. 5, 6a, 6b, 8). μικρὸν harks back to the ἐλαχίστου of the previous verse; μέλος links up with v. 6 and prepares for 4.1 ('passions at war in your members').[133] μικρόν is to be taken literally—the tongue is a small body part—although Mayor, 112, supposes that 'by the smallness of the tongue is meant the insignificance, as we deem it, of speech in comparison with action'.[134]

ἡ γλῶσσα...μεγάλα αὐχεῖ recalls 3 Macc 2.17 (καυχήσωνται...ἐν ὑπερηφανίᾳ γλώσσης); 6.4 (γλώσσῃ μεγαλορρήμονι); Ps 12.3-4 ('May the Lord cut off all flattering lips, the tongue that makes great boasts [MT: שׁוֹן מדברת גדלות; LXX: γλῶσσαν μεγαλορήμονα], those who say, "With our tongues we will prevail [LXX: τὴν γλῶσσαν ἡμῶν μεγαλυνοῦμεν]; our lips are our own—who is our master?"'). The parallel with the Psalter is especially intriguing because of the thematic links between Ps 12.1-4 and Jas 3.1-12. The former indicts 'everyone' (v. 2; cf. Jas 3.2, 8); it divines a 'double heart' behind human speech (v. 2; cf. Jas 3.9-12); it depicts the tongue as speaking proudly (v. 3; cf. Jas 3.5); and it pledges that God will punish the tongue (v. 3; cf. Jas 3.6). Has Ps 12 influenced James?

According to Mayor, 112, 'There is no idea of vain boasting: the whole argument turns upon the reality of the power which the tongue possesses'. In other words, the boast is true. This, however, does not entail that the harmful nature of the tongue comes into view only in what follows ('how great a forest is set ablaze by a small fire').[135] Early

---

[133] μικρός is a *hapax*, as are μέγας and αὐχέω.

[134] With μεγάλα αὐχεῖ cf. Scholia in Lucianum 41.24 (μεγάλα καυχωμένοις); Ps.-Callisthenes, *Hist. Alex. Magn.* rec. γ 2.59 (σὲ τὸν μεγάλα καυχώμενον); Didymus of Alexandria, *Trin.* 3.29 PG 39.948C (μὴ μεγάλα αὐχεῖν); Asterius, *Comm. Ps* ed. Richard 24.14.4 (μεγάλα καυχώμενος); also μεγαλαυχέω (a v.l. for Jas 3.5) as in Sir 48.18 and Philo, *Mut.* 155, and μεγαλαυχία, as in Philo, *Conf.* 113. BDAG, s.v., αὐχέω, cites a grave inscription in G. Kaibel, *Epigrammata graeca ex lapidibus conlecta*, Berlin, 1878, 489: [ὃν μεγάλ' αὐ]χήσασα πατρὶς Θή[β]η, 'in whom his homeland Thebes took great pride'. Earlier exegetes sometimes link αὐχεῖ, which is etymologically related to αὐχήν = 'neck', to v. 3, remarking that untamed horses lift their heads in pride; cf. Trapp, 698.

[135] But this is the view of many; cf. Gill, 279; Wells, 19; Dibelius, 190; Frankemölle, 493-44; Culpepper, 'Tongue', 409. Wesley, 864, paraphrases with the neutral, 'hath great influence'. Contrast Easton, 47; Mussner, 161; Davids, 140; Popkes, 225 (remarking that μεγάλα αὐχεῖ is a very 'subjektive Aussage'); Konradt, *Existenz*, 276.

Christian writers strongly tend to follow Jewish tradition in reckoning boasting about anything other than God to be sin and the antithesis of humility.[136] Furthermore, our passage, as just noted, is reminiscent of Ps 12.3-4, which speaks against the boasting of tongue, and it leads to a paragraph that attacks boasting: 3.14.[137] So while the factual content of the boast in v. 5 cannot be disputed, the connotations appear pejorative: one can speak the truth out of vanity.[138] μεγάλα αὐχεῖ marks, then, a change of emphasis: the subject is passing from the possibility of control to the inherently contrary and destructive nature of the tongue, which 'is arrogant in pride'.[139]

ἰδοὺ ἡλίκον πῦρ ἡλίκην ὕλην ἀνάπτει. Literally: 'Behold, what a fire sets ablaze what a wood'. The exclamation features alliteration and assonance: ἡλίκον...ἡλίκην ὕλην. With ἰδοὺ ἡλίκον cf. Epictetus, *Diatr.* 4.7.25 (ἰδοὺ ἡλίκαι εἰσί, sc. τὰς μαχαίρας); Chrysostom, *Hom. 1–55 in Ac.* 42.4 PG 60.302 (ἰδοὺ ἡλίκη πόλις). James employs ὕλη and ἀνάπτω[140]—their combination was conventional[141]—only here. The former in this context probably means 'forest', as in LXX Isa 10.17, where fire devours the ὕλην like grass.[142] ὕλη can also mean '(pile of) wood' or 'undergrowth' or 'brushwood';[143] but the rhetorical contrast—very large over against very small—suggests the other meaning here.

Often in the Bible a forest fire represents calamity.[144] The closest parallel to James' wordplay, in which ἡλίκος[145] means, first, 'how

---

[136] 1 Sam 2.3; 1 Kgs 20.11; 2 Chr 15.19; Ps 5.5; Prov 25.14; 27.1; Isa 10.12; Jer 9.23-24; Wis 17.7; Ecclus 17.9; 50.20; Rom 1.30; 1 Cor 1.31; 2 Cor 10.17; Eph 2.9; 4 Ezra 7.98; T. Jud. 13.2; T. Reub. 3.5; 1 Clem. 13.2. For Graeco-Roman criticisms of boasting and discussion of when it might be appropriate see the texts in D.F. Watson, 'Paul and Boasting', in *Paul in the Greco-Roman World*, ed. J.P. Sampley, Harrisburg, PA, 2003, 77-100.

[137] Cf. 4.16 and Bede *ad loc.* CCSL 121 ed. Hurst, 204. The acceptable boasting of 1.9 comes from God's eschatological action.

[138] Clarke, 814, offers: 'he seems to refer here to the powerful and all commanding eloquence of the Greek orators'.

[139] Isho'dad of Merv *ad loc.* HSem 10 ed. Gibson, 50.

[140] NT: 2×; cf. Lk 12.49; Acts 28.2 v.l. Most often for יצת in the LXX.

[141] Cf. Heron of Alexandria, *Auto.* 12.3-4 (ὕλη...ἀνάπτεσθαι); Philo, *Aet. mund.* 127 (ἀναφθείσης ὕλης); Plutarch, *Mor.* 132A (ὕλης ἀναπτόμενον); Polyaenus, *Strat.* 4.7.9 (πῦρ ἐμβαλὼν ἀνῆψε τὴν ὕλην).

[142] Cf. ὕλη τοῦ καλάμου = 'forest/thicket of reeds' in Jos. Asen. 24.19-20; 27.8; 28.7-8, 16.

[143] As in Artapanus *apud* Eusebius, *P.E.* 9.27.21 ed. Holladay, 216. Cf. Erasmus, *Annotationes*, 741; Elliott-Binns, 'Jas. iii.5', as well as the KJV's 'matter'. Elliott-Binns prefers 'brushwood', in part because he places James in Palestine, which has few forests but did commonly witness farmers burning off thorns, briars, and grass before ploughing. See further the discussions of Hort, 70, 104-106 (favoring 'wood' or 'timber'); Mayor, 112-13, Appendix, 7-12 (favoring 'forest').

[144] Ps 83.14; Isa 9.18; Jer 21.14; Ezek 15.6; 20.47; 39.10; 4 Ezra 4.16; 15.62.

[145] LXX: 0×; cf. τηλικοῦτος in v. 4.

THE SINS OF SPEECH (3.1-12)

small',[146] and then, second, 'how large',[147] appears in Philostratus, *Apoll.* 2.11.2, where the subject is a boy riding an elephant and guiding it with a crook: 'It seems to me a superhuman feat...for someone so tiny (τηλικούτῳ) to manage so huge (τηλικόνδε) an animal'; cf. also Plato, *Apol.* 25D: 'Do you mean to say that you, who are so much younger (τηλικούτου) than I, are yet so much more (τηλικόσδε) wise than I?'[148]

James has reproduced something close to a proverb; see Pindar, *Pyth.* 3.36-38 ('Fire [πῦρ] leaps from a single spark on a mountain and destroys a great forest' [ὕλαν; cf. Homer, *Il.* 2.455-56]); Euripides frag. 411.2-4 ('With but a little torch one might set fire to Ida's rock' [quoted by Plutarch, *Mor.* 507B]); Ecclus 11.32 ('From a spark of fire coals are multiplied' [מניצוץ ירבה גחלת]; cf. Prov 26.20]); Seneca the Elder, *Contr.* 5.5 ('One does not set fire to everything, only to some one thing from which a fire can arise, a fire that will spread to the whole'); Philo, *Migr.* 123 ('A smoldering spark, even the very smallest, when it is blown up and made to blaze, lights a great pyre'); Philo, *Decl.* 173 ('Nothing escapes desire...like a flame in the forest [ἐν ὕλῃ] it spreads abroad and consumes and destroys everything'); *Spec.* 4.27 ('a single smoldering spark is often fanned into a blaze and sets fire to great cities, particularly when the flame streams along under a carrying wind'); Ps.-Phoc. 144 v.l. ('By a tiny spark a great wood [ὕλη] is set ablaze');[149] Diogenes of Oenoanda frag. 44 ('The soul experiences feelings far greater than the cause that generated them, just as a fire great enough to burn down ports and cities is kindled by an exceedingly small spark').[150]

James not only preserves a traditional sentiment but also a traditional association. In Plutarch, *Mor.* 507B, the saying from Euripides (see above) concludes a discussion about the consequences of speech that features a maritime analogy: 'Neither when you let go from your hands a winged thing is it easy to get it back again, nor when a word is let slip from the mouth is it possible to arrest and control it, but it is borne circling on swift wings, and it is scattered abroad from one to another. So when a ship has been caught by a wind, they try to check it...but if a story runs out of harbor, so to speak, there is no roadstead or anchorage for it, but, carried away with a great noise and reverberation, it dashes upon the man who uttered it and submerges him in great and terrible danger.' Even closer is Philo, *Leg.* 3.223-24: 'When the charioteer is in command and guides the horses with the reins, the chariot goes the way he wishes... A ship, again, keeps to her straight course, when the

---

[146] As in Epictetus, *Diatr.* 1.12.26. Cf. the v.l., ὀλίγον, in 02*V 04* 044 5 33 *et al.* **Byz** Dam GregAgr **L**:FV^ms **A G Sl**:ChDMSiS.

[147] As in Col 2.1; Josephus, *Bell.* 1.626.

[148] For the rhetorical use of one word with two meanings see Quintillian 9.3.68; *Rhet. ad Her.* 4.14.21.

[149] This is in illustration of the maxim: 'Nip evil in the bud and heal the wound'.

[150] καὶ σπιν[θῆρι] μεικρῷ πάνυ τη[λικό]νδε ἐπεξάπτεται [πῦρ ἡ]λίκον καταφλέ[γει λ]ιμένας καὶ πόλεις. See further R. Strömberg, *Greek Proverbs*, Gothenburg, 1954, 64.

helmsman grasping the tiller steers accordingly, but capsizes when a contrary wind has sprung up over the sea, and the surge has settled in it. Just so, when mind, the charioteer or helmsman of the soul, rules the whole living being as a governor does a city, then life holds a straight course, but when irrational sense gains the chief place, a terrible confusion overtakes it, just as when slaves have risen against masters: for then, in very deed, the mind is set on fire and is all ablaze, and that fire is kindled by the object of sense which sense-perception provides.' Although this is not about speech or the tongue,[151] the resemblance to James suggests dependence upon a common tradition.

Because the subject of v. 5 is speech, the small fire has naturally moved some commentators, such as Bede, to remark on how seemingly insignificant words can grow into large problems.[152] This, although homiletically pleasing, reads too much into James' simile. The comparison is with the small size of the tongue, not with the trivial nature of the words it produces.

Verse 6. The syntax of this pessimistic line, 'among the most controversial in the New Testament' (Dibelius, 193), is highly problematic. While καὶ ἡ γλῶσσα [ἐστίν] πῦρ does not cause difficulty, and while the closing words (καὶ φλογίζουσα κτλ.) are clear enough, ὁ κόσμος τῆς ἀδικίας... ὅλον τὸ σῶμα succumbs to no wholly satisfying analysis. It is hard to link ὁ κόσμος to what comes before. It rather seems to be a new predicate. Yet then the connection with the following ἡ γλῶσσα is difficult. For Dibelius, 194-95, the awkward ὁ κόσμος...ἡμῶν is likely a gloss, although he cannot summon support from the textual tradition. Spitta, 96-100, urges that ἡ γλῶσσα πῦρ was originally a marginal gloss characterizing vv. 6-12, ὁ κόσμος τῆς ἀδικίας a scribe's summary of 3.13ff. After those phrases worked their way into the text, a scribe inserted ἡ σπιλοῦσα ὅλον τὸ σῶμα. Ropes, 233-34, counters by quipping that 'exegesis by leaving out hard phrases is an intoxicating experience'. Ropes nonetheless deems the text corrupt, although he refrains from conjecturing the original, opining that 'no satisfactory interpretation is possible'. Chaine, 80-81, prefers to link ὁ κόσμος τῆς ἀδικίας with what precedes: 'And the tongue (is) a fire, (it is) the world of unrighteousness'.[153] The Peshitta presents yet one more option, for it adds the equivalent of ὕλη after ἀδικίας, thereby creating an allegorical equation: 'Fire is the tongue, the forest is the world of unrighteousness'.[154]

---

[151] Graeco-Roman sources tends to associate fire with the passions, not the tongue: Plutarch, *Mor.* 138F; 454E; Philo, *Mos.* 2.58; Lucian, *Amores* 2; etc.

[152] Bede *ad loc.* CCSL 121 ed. Hurst, 204. Cf. Eccl 10.13, which Manton, 126, cites.

[153] Cf. Bede *ad loc.* CCSL 121 ed. Hurst, 205; Schnider, 81; Frankemölle, 478; Fabris, 230-31. This is the punctuation of the KJV.

[154] Adamson, 158-59, accepts this as the original; so too Bauckham, 'Tongue', 118 n. 1.

THE SINS OF SPEECH (3.1-12)

Although the present commentator suspects that the text is corrupt, he has been unable to surmise a satisfying original. For want of a better solution, then, he follows Chaine. The result is extreme hyperbole: the tongue is the world of unrighteousness. This has the advantage of allowing the second ἡ γλῶσσα to mark a new beginning. Further, the variants οὕτως[155] and οὕτως καί[156] after ἀδικίας seem to be evidence of Greek scribes construing the text along these lines. Perhaps most exegetes, however, now view ὁ κόσμος as the start of a new sentence, ἡ γλῶασσα as the subject of καθίσταται, and interpret the words to mean: 'The tongue, which defiles the whole body, represents the evil world among our members';[157] or, 'The tongue is placed among our members as a world of iniquity; it stains the whole body' (NRSV); or, 'The tongue among our members turns out to be the world of iniquity; it defiles the whole body' (Grünzweig, 103); or some such.[158]

καὶ ἡ γλῶσσα πῦρ. Both πῦρ and γλῶσσα create verbal links with the previous verse. The metaphor is perfectly natural given that (i) the human tongue might be thought to look a bit like a flame (cf. Trapp, 698) and (ii) Jewish tradition associates the tongue or speech with fire; see Isa 5.24 (לשון אש);[159] Prov 16.27 ('their speech is like scorching fire'); 26.21; Ecclus 28.22 (the godly will not be burned by the tongue's flame), 23 (slander 'will burn among them and will not be put out');[160] Vulgate Ecclus 20.15 ('the opening of his mouth is the kindling of a fire');[161] Gk. Pss. Sol. 12.1-2 ('O Lord, deliver my soul from the...lawless and slandering tongue that speaks falsehood and deceit. Infinitely agile are the words of the tongue of the lawless person, like fire burning among the people'); 4 Ezra 13.10 ('from his tongue he shot often a storm of sparks'); Lev. Rab. 16.4 (saliva passes beneath the tongue, which yet causes many conflagrations). Note also Jer 5.14, where God tells Jeremiah, 'I am making my words in your mouth a fire, and this people wood, and the fire shall devour them'.[162] This last resembles Ps 52.4, where words 'devour', which is exactly what fire does. Additionally relevant is the mythological image of fire coming forth from the mouths of God and supernatural beings.[163]

---

[155] 025 5 69 88 *et al.* **Byz** PsOec S:H^A.

[156] 020 056 0142 104 252 *et al.* L427 L1440 Sl:ChDMSiS.

[157] So H. Sasse, 'κοσμέω', *TDNT* 3.884.

[158] For additional discussion see esp. Mayor, 113-14.

[159] For 'tongue(s) of fire' see 1Q29 1.3; 2.3; 4Q376 1 2.1; 4Q530 2 2.9; 1 En. 14.9, 10, 14; 71.5; Acts 2.3.

[160] Frankemölle, 500-501, believes that James is rewriting these and surrounding verses.

[161] Bede *ad loc.* CCSL 121 ed. Hurst, 205, cites this parallel, which recent commentators have missed.

[162] 4Q381 24 2 seems conceptually related: 'my tongue is like a coal...which no-one can extinguish'.

[163] 2 Sam 22.9; Job 41.19; Ps 18.8; Isa 30.27 (God's 'tongue is like a devouring flame'); 4 Ezra 13.10; Rev 9.17-18; 11.5; Apoc. Abr. 14.31 ('burned by the fire of

Although James' remarks about the tongue become at this juncture wholly pejorative, theologians and preachers have felt the need for some balance. So they have, when commenting on v. 6, often said something positive about the tongue. According to Bede, in addition to the destructive fire that consumes the foolish, there is a 'saving fire' that kindles 'holy teachers', who 'burn with loving' and 'set others on fire with fiery tongues'.[164] Erasmus notes that, just as 'fire has many different uses if it is employed correctly, but it becomes utterly destructive if allowed to wander where it wishes', so too 'there can come from the human tongue both the greatest benefit and on the other hand the ultimate ruin to human life. Do you not see that nature's fabricator signified this very thing when he willed the human tongue to have the appearance and colour of fire?'[165] Gill, 792, similarly observes that the tongue, like fire, 'is very useful in its place, to warm and comfort'.

ὁ κόσμος τῆς ἀδικίας. 'Not a city or country only, but a world' (Trapp, 698)—or rather, given the definite article, 'the world'. ὁ κόσμος[166] τῆς ἀδικίας is an unusual Greek expression, without precise parallel in the Bible. It appears to be a genitive of quality, as in 1.23, 25; and 2.12.[167] It is surely a Semitism—cf. the Hebrew construct chain—and recalls from elsewhere in the NT especially Lk 16.8 (οἰκονόμον τῆς ἀδικίας), 9 (μαμωνᾶ τῆς ἀδικίας); and 18.6 (ὁ κριτὴς τῆς ἀδικίας); see BDF 165. The Hebrew עולם של + noun as well as Aramaic עלמא ד + noun are common enough, and one thinks in particular of the rabbinic עלמא דשקר = 'world of falsehood', which is the antithesis of עלמא דקשוט = 'world of truth' in Tanḥ. Buber Emor 2, 4 and Lev. Rab. 26.7—especially as the LXX often translates שקר with ἀδικία.[168] That James indeed has the Greek equivalent of this phrase is confirmed by this, that Lk 16.9's μαμωνᾶς τῆς ἀδικίας is the Greek equivalent for the Aramaic, ממון דשקר;[169] that is, here τῆς ἀδικίας renders דשקר. So, behind James lies a conflation of עלמא דשקר with the well-known idiom, לשון שקר.[170] The tongue of unrighteousness is the world of unrighteousness.

Azazel's tongue'); *et al.* Graeco-Roman tradition of course knows of fire-breathing monsters (Pindar, *Pyth.* 4.225; Ovid, *Metam.* 7.104-105; Apollonius of Rhodes 3.1302-305; etc.) as does world-wide mythology. That the world is fire (Heraclitus, the Stoics) and that it will end in a great conflagration (cf. 2 Pet 3.7-12) are not implicit in James.

[164] Bede *ad loc.* CCSL 121 ed. Hurst, 205.
[165] Erasmus, *Paraphrase*, 155.
[166] κόσμος: Jas: 5×: 1.27; 2.5; 3.6; 4.4 (*bis*). On 'the world' in James see especially Lockett, 'God'.
[167] Cf. LXX 1 Βασ 21.31; Ezek 14.4 (τὴν κόλασιν τῆς ἀδικίας αὐτοῦ = מכשול עונו); 44.12 (κόλασιν ἀδικίας = מכשול עון); Dan 3.6.
[168] Pss 7.14 v.l.; 51.3; 118.29, 69, 104, 163; 143.8, 11.
[169] As in Tg 1 Sam 12.3; 8.3; Tg. Prov 15.27.
[170] Cf. Ps 109.2; Prov 6.17 (LXX: γλῶσσα ἄδικος; cf. Sib. Or. 3.496); 12.19 (LXX: γλῶσσαν ἔχει ἄδικον); 26.28; 1QH 13(5).27; 4Q381 45 5; 4Q501 4; Tanḥ. Buber Wayyiqra' 10; etc.

Some have understood James' Greek to mean 'the whole of unrighteousness',[171] others 'the ornament of unrighteousness',[172] that is, the deceitful tongue seeks to make unrighteousness attractive.[173] But 'world of unrighteousness' is to be preferred, as the parallels just cited indicate; cf. also 1 En. 48.7: 'age of unrighteousness' (ḥmḍ). Further, given that elsewhere in James ὁ κόσμος must mean 'the world' (see esp. 1.27: ἄσπιλον ἑαυτὸν τηρεῖν ἀπὸ τοῦ κόσμου), that is surely the sense here. So we have once more James' pessimistic worldview, which sees the present age as evil, under the sway of wicked forces. Cf. the temptation narrative in Mt 4.1-11 = Lk 4.1-13, where Satan presumes authority to give Jesus 'the kingdoms of the κόσμου'; Jn 16.11 (Satan is 'the ruler of this κόσμου'); 2 Cor 4.4 (Satan is 'the god of this world'); 1 Jn 5.19 ('ὁ κόσμος ὅλος lies in the power of the evil one'); Corp. Herm. 6.4 ed. Nock and Festugière, 1.74 ('ὁ κόσμος is full of evil').[174]

James' pessimism about the tongue has a parallel of sorts in Rom 3.13-14: 'Their throats are opened graves; they use their tongues to deceive. The venom of vipers is under their lips. Their mouths are full of cursing and bitterness.' This combination of Pss 5.9; 10.7; and 140.3 illustrates the universality of the power of sin: all are under its power. The implication is that all people sin with their speech.

ἡ γλῶσσα καθίσταται ἐν τοῖς μέλεσιν ἡμῶν. The sense of καθίσταται[175] is uncertain. Ropes, 235, renders: 'presents itself'. The NRSV appears to regard the verb as an insignificant copula: 'The tongue is an unrighteous world among our members'. Popkes, 228, prefers 'sie steht da' or 'sitz'.[176] Baker construes it as a passive, 'appointed', which for him stresses 'the divinely ordained function of the tongue within the human body';[177] cf. 4Q185 1-3 3.12-13: 'God made the tongue'. One might then compare Lev. Rab. 16.4: 'the tongue is set (by God) between (נתון בין) two cheeks'. James' context, however, concerns the rebellious nature of the sinful tongue, not its divine origin. It seems better, then, to follow Laws, 149. Appealing to 4.4, where the verb has reflexive force ('makes himself an enemy of God'), she translates: 'appoints itself'. As the verb elsewhere is used of elevation to office,[178] a connotation of self-exaltation

---

[171] So Michl, 48; cf. LXX Prov 17.6 and the Vulgate: *universitas iniquitatis*.
[172] Cf. 1 Pet 3.3, where κόσμος = 'adorning'.
[173] So Elsner, 391-92; Chaine, 81, the latter citing Isidore of Pelusium, *Ep.* 1298 (4.10) SC 422 ed. Évieux, 322. Cf. Knox, 'Epistle', 15, and see esp. Carr, 'Jas iii.6', who stresses that this interpretation coheres well with the strong biblical theme of the tongue being full of guile and deceitfulness (Ps 12.2; Mic 6.12; etc.).
[174] Also Ps.-Mk 16.14 032; Jn 12.31; 14.30. For bibliography see H. Balz, 'κόσμος', *EDNT* 2.309-10.
[175] καθίστημι: Jas: 2×; cf. 4.4.
[176] Cf. Frankemölle, 504.
[177] Baker, *Speech-Ethics*, 127.
[178] LXX Gen 39.4-5; 1 Βασ 8.5; Ps 104.21; Philo, *Jos.* 38; Mt 24.45; Jos. Asen. 20.9; Tit 1.5; Heb 2.7; 8.3; etc.

is probably present. This harmonizes with the αὐχεῖ of v. 5. The objection of Baker, that the end of v. 6 disallows that the tongue is its own agent, rests upon a misinterpretation of that clause.[179] For μέλος (Jas: 2×) see on 4.1.

ἡ σπιλοῦσα ὅλον τὸ σῶμα. The last three words, which hark back to vv. 2 and 3, underline the far-reaching consequences of the tongue's behavior.[180] σπιλόω occurs in James only here.[181] The verb occurs once in the LXX, in Wis 15.4, and in the rest of the NT only in Jude 23, where the image may be of a garment spotted by excrement.[182] The literal meaning is 'stain' or 'soil'. Most commentators give it metaphorical sense here; cf. T. Ash. 2.7 (τὴν ψυχὴν σπιλοῖ) and the use of σπίλος in Eph 5.27 and 2 Pet 2.13. Although other texts associate speaking with impurity, they do not use this verb.[183]

According to 1.27, true religion is to keep oneself unstained by the world; according to 3.6, the tongue is 'the world of unrighteousness' that stains the whole body. Putting the two together, 'James' shocking news is that that inimical world is already present in the human body in the form of the tongue, which in the words of Sent. Syr. Men. 424, "brings to misery". And the stakes run higher than one's own purity, for the tongue sets on fire "the cycle of nature" and is itself "set on fire by hell".'[184] James has 'rhetorically configured "the world", "true religion", and "the tongue" in such a way that to use the tongue abusively (in cursing) is actually to grant "the world" access to one's mouth'.[185]

---

[179] See below. James does nothing with the fact that the tongue is 'lodged in a place of obscurity and darkness' (Midr. Ps 39.2); cf. b. 'Arak. 15b: all the members of the body are outside, except the tongue, which is inside. Nor do his words imply what Trapp, 698, finds in them. the tongue was set between brain and heart 'that it might take the advice of both'.

[180] Popkes, 230, appealing to Herm. Sim. 9, urges that 'the whole body' here stands for the entire Christian community. Cf. Reicke, Diakonie, 345.

[181] Although the related ἄσπιλος is in 1.27: ἄσπιλον ἀπὸ τοῦ κόσμου.

[182] See R.J. Bauckham, Jude, 2 Peter, Waco, TX, 1983, 116. Gk. Pseudepigrapha (Denis): 1×. Philo: 0×. Josephus: 0×.

[183] Ecclus 21.28 ('a whisperer soils [μολύνει] his own soul'); CD 5.11-13 ('they defile [טמאו] their holy spirit and open their mouth with a blaspheming tongue against the laws of the covenant of God'); Philo, Dec. 93-94 (the one who takes an oath should have a body free of 'pollution' [μιασμάτων] and not swear in 'impure' [ἀκαθάρτοις] places); Mt 15.11 ('that which comes out of the mouth defiles [κοινοῖ] a person'); Jos. Asen. 11.16 ('my mouth is defiled [μεμίαται] from the sacrifices of the idols and from the blessings of the gods of the Egyptians'; cf. 11.17-18; 12.5). Frankemölle, 505-506, discusses the possibility of a background in Gnosticism, where the body is soiled or impure.

[184] J.F. Hultin, The Ethics of Obscene Speech in Early Christianity and Its Environment, Leiden, 2008, 135.

[185] Hultin, ibid., 136. He continues: James 'makes speech a cosmic issue involving hell and creation, and places the tongue at the center of religious purity. This approach stands at some remove from the wisdom in Proverbs or Sirach or the Didache, with their emphasis on the social and ethical consequences that follow from inappropriate speech'.

THE SINS OF SPEECH (3.1-12)

καὶ φλογίζουσα τὸν τροχὸν τῆς γενέσεως.[186] φλογίζω (cf. ἀνάπτει in v. 5) is a NT *hapax* meaning 'set on fire', as in LXX Exod 9.24 (πῦρ φλογίζον); Ecclus 3.10 (πῦρ φλογίζομενον); T. Job 16.1. Although commentators have long struggled with τὸν τροχὸν τῆς γενέσεως—which sounds like a fixed expression—a consensus appears to have been reached. ὁ τροχὸς τῆς γενέσεως = ὁ κύκλος τῆς γενέσεως, 'the circle of existence' or 'creation'. Used in Orphic and Pythagorean circles with reference to metempsychosis,[187] the term was also known to Jews[188] and 'seems to be used here...as a rhetorical expression suggesting the vast extent of the devastation'.[189] It was 'a very popular metaphor'[190] that had come to mean, as Dibelius, 198, puts it, something like 'the ups and downs of life', that is, life in its entirety, past, present, and future.[191] So the phrase, a nice rhetorical flourish, reinforces the implications of ὅλον τὸ σῶμα: the tongue affects everything.[192] The link to fire seems to be James' peculiar contribution.[193]

---

[186] 617 996 1661 have τῆς γεέννης; cf. the end of the verse. This calls to mind the image of Hades' wheel of torture; cf. Kypke, 423-24; Sib. Or. 2.290-96; Apoc. Pet. 12.4-6; Acts Thom. 55; etc.

[187] Cf. Simplicius, *In coel.* 7.377: ἐν τῷ τῆς εἱμαρμένης τε καὶ γενέσεως τροχῷ οὕπερ ἀδύνατον ἀπαλλαγῆναι κατὰ τὸν Ὀρφέα. Additional texts and discussion in Ropes, 235-39; Dibelius, 196-98. Earlier commentators sometimes propose that James alludes to the torture wheel (cf. the previous note; also 4 Macc 5.3, 32 ['get your torture wheels ready and fan the fire']; 8.13; 9.12-20 ['while fanning the flames they tightened the wheel further']; etc.), as if to say: life is full of torment, which the tongue increases. But Clarke, 815, refers to the circulation of the blood, which heats up with irritating language.

[188] See Sib. Or. 2.87 (βίοτος τροχός); Philo, *Somn.* 2.44 (κύκλον καὶ τροχὸν ἀνάγκης); Ps.-Phoc. 27 (ὁ βίος τροχός). In rabbinic literature, the metaphor of the wheel (גלגל) is typically associated with poverty, as in b. Šabb. 151b (poverty is 'a wheel that revolves in the world'); Exod. Rab. 31.3 ('there is an ever rotating wheel in this world, and he who is rich today may not be so tomorrow, and also he who is poor today may not be so tomorrow'); cf. Tanḥ. Buber Mishpatim 8; Lev. Rab. 34.3; Ruth Rab. 5.9. In b. B. Bat. 16b, however, it is used of mourning. See further Kittel, 'Τὸν τροχόν'. There is no connection between James and Ezekiel's 'wheel' or 2 Macc 7.23; and although some Christians before Origen certainly believed in reincarnation—note e.g. Pist. Soph. 3.113; Test. Truth 30.17; Irenaeus, *Haer.* 1.25.4; Tertullian, *De anima* 35 CSEL 20 ed. Reifferscheid and Wissowa, 360-62; Origen, *Mt* 10.20 GCS 40 ed. E. Klostermann, 26-28—one doubts that James or anyone in his audience would have entertained that prospect. Cf. Stiglmayr, 'Jak 3,6', against Keenan, 102-105.

[189] Cranfield, 'Message', 344. But a few readers have indeed found in the expression a statement of a cyclical view of nature; see e.g. Isidore of Pelusium, *Ep.* 1566 (4.1) SC 454 ed. Évieux, 260. For secondary literature see BAGD, s.v., τροχός.

[190] So Frankemölle, 508.

[191] Cf. *Chaîne Arménienne* 47 ed. Renoux, 110. For γένεσις (see on 1.23) meaning 'life' see Wis 7.5 and Jdt 12.18.

[192] Given that, in the LXX, γένεσις most often translates תולדה = 'generation' (Gen 2.4; 5.1; 10.1; etc.), Christian Jews who knew the LXX might have understood the Greek to mean something like 'wheel of the generations'. This is surely what Jewish hearers would understand were they to run across גלגל תולדת in a context similar to that of James.

[193] Frankemölle, 508-509, contrasts the fluctuation of human existence with the unchangeable nature of God, in whom there is no change (1.17).

Fletcher, 'Buddhism', suggests influence from the wheel of life or becoming (the *Bhavacakra* or *mandala*) of Tibetan Buddhism. This wheel is a pictorial representation of the cycle of *samsara*, of birth and death. Moreover, as Fletcher observes, the famous 'Fire Sermon' attributed to Buddha has him declare, 'the tongue is on fire'. One should not dismiss this proposal as impossible, especially as James is close in many respects to Matthew, and Luz, *Matthew* 2.322, has given it as his opinion that, in view of the close parallels between Mt 14.22-33 and the story of Buddha walking on water in the Jatakas, 'an indirect Buddhist influence on the New Testament is entirely possible'. Maybe then Fletcher is half right: although James did not take his phrase from Buddhist sources, the latter may have informed Orphism and so ultimately be the source of ὁ τροχὸς τῆς γενέσεως.[194]

καὶ φλογιζομένη ὑπὸ τῆς γεέννης. Cf. Ecclus 51.3-6, which associates unclean tongue and lying words with fire and Hades, and note the wordplay with the previous clause: καὶ φλογίζουσα...τῆς γενέσεως // καὶ φλογιζομένη...τῆς γεέννης. γέεννα, the Greek equivalent of the rabbinic גיהנם(י), is the antithesis of heaven, the frightful place of post-mortem or end-time punishment.[195] It was often imagined to be a place of fire.[196] In the NT, it appears only in Jas 3.6 and the Synoptics, most often Matthew.[197] Why the place of torment came to have this name, the name of the valley south of Jerusalem, now Wadi er-Rababi, is uncertain. The familiar view, found in David Kimchi's commentary on Ps 27, that the valley was where the city's garbage was incinerated and that the constantly rising smoke and smell of corruption conjured up the fiery

---

[194] For early and on-going traffic between East and West see T. McEvilley, *The Shape of Ancient Thought*, New York, 2002. Contrast F. Büschel, 'γεννάω κτλ.', *TDNT* 1 684: 'There may be connections between Buddhism and Orphism, but they cannot be shown, and it is hardly likely that they will be'. For further discussion of the Indian parallels see Kittel, 'Τὸν τροχόν', 152-58. J.D.M. Derrett, 'The Epistle of James and the Dhammapada Commentary', *STK* 82 (2006), 36-39, argues that Jas 4.13-17 influenced an important Buddhist text. For Philonenko, 'Écho', the parallels he discerns between James and Buddhist texts may have been mediated by an Essene source.

[195] See 1 En. 27.2-3; 90.24; Sib. Or. 1.104; 2.292; 4.186; 2 Bar. 59.10; 85.13; POxy. 840 recto; Asc. Isa 1.3; 4.14; Gk. Apoc. Ezra 1.9; m. Qidd. 4.14; t. Sanh. 13.3; y. Pe'ah 15c (1.1); b. 'Erub. 19a; Tg. Isa 66.24; etc. Lit.: J.A. Montgomery, 'The Holy City and Gehenna', *JBL* 27 (1908), 24-47; J. Jeremias, 'γέεννα', *TDNT* 1.657-58; W.J.P. Boyd, 'Gehenna—According to J. Jeremias', in *Studia Biblica 1978 II. Papers on The Gospels*, ed. E.A. Livingstone, Sheffield, 1980, 9-12; C. Milikowsky, 'Which Gehenna? Retribution and Eschatology in the Synoptic Gospels and Early Jewish Texts', *NTS* 34 (1988), 238-49; B.T. Viviano, 'Hakeldama, The Potter's Field, and the Suicide of Judas (Matthew 27:3-10; Acts 1:16-20)', in *Jerusalem und die Länder*, ed. G. Theissen *et al.*, Göttingen, 2009, 203-10.

[196] 1 En. 10.6; 54.1-2; 90.24-25; 100.9; Sib. Or. 3.53-54; Mt 5.22; Mk 9.47; 4 Ezra 7.36-38; 13.10-11; Apoc. Abr. 15.6; 31.2-5; 2 Clem. 5.4; Tg. Isa 30.33; 33.14; 65.5; etc. But Aquinas, *Summa* 1 q. 64 a. 4, refers to a gloss on our verse which has it that devils 'carry fire of hell with them wherever they go'.

[197] Mt 5.22, 29-30; 10.28; 18.9; 23.15, 33; Mk 9.43-47; Lk 12.5.

torments of the damned, lacks ancient support.[198] Perhaps the abode of the wicked dead gained its name because children had there been sacrificed in fire to the god Molech (2 Chr 28.3; 33.6), or because Jeremiah, recalling its defilement by Josiah (2 Kgs 23.10; cf. 21.6), thundered against the place (Jer 7.31-2; 19.2-9; 32.35), or because some believed that valley held the entrance to the underworld home of the pagan chthonian deities (cf. b. 'Erub. 19a).

Martin, 116, represents most commentators in urging that 'Gehenna' here is in effect a circumlocution for the devil (cf. 4.7), who was thought to dwell in that place and be the source of evil in the world.[199] This is an old way of understanding our text, found already in Bede: Gehenna stands for 'the devil and his angels'.[200] In support, 3.15 speaks of a wisdom that does not come from above but is demonic. Bauckham, however, rightly questions this standard exegesis.[201] No first-century text depicts Gehenna as a source of evil on earth or as home for the devil.[202] Following Schlatter, Bauckham proposes that Jas 3.6 features the eschatological *ius talionis*.[203] The tongue that sets the wheel of existence on fire will itself be set on fire (φλογιζομένη): the present participle has future sense.[204] Such a correlation appears in many texts.[205] James 2.13 itself offers another example: 'Judgment will be without mercy to the one who has shown no mercy'. Moreover, the notion that God will punish a sinning tongue was widespread; cf. esp. Pss. Sol. 12.1-4 ('Lord, save me from...the criminal and slandering tongue... The words of the wicked

---

[198] Cf. L. Bailey, 'Gehenna', in *IDBSup* (1976), 353.

[199] Cf. Trapp, 699; Gill, 890; Weidner, 57-58; Mayor, 118-19; Smith, 181-82; Dibelius, 198; Frankemölle, 507; *et al.* For Fabris, 235, James is referring not only to the infernal origin of the evil tongue but at the same time alluding to its eschatological destruction.

[200] Bede *ad loc.* CCSL 121 ed. Hurst, 205. Cf. Gill, 793, who observes that this is analogous to 'heaven' as a periphrasis for 'God'.

[201] Bauckham, 'Tongue'.

[202] Apoc. Abr. 14.5 and 31.5, although usually cited to the contrary, are about Azazel's future fate. Nor does b. 'Arak. 15b, which features the 'Prince of Gehinnom', have anything to do with evils on earth; cf. Tanḥ. Buber Metsora' 5. See Bauckham, 'Tongue', 120-22.

[203] Schlatter, 223-24; cf. McKnight, 286.

[204] So Grotius, 1084. Cf. BDF 351 and Isho'dad of Merv *ad loc.* HSem 10 ed. Gibson, 50: the tongue 'burns in punishment from God'. So too Elsner, 392; Guyse, 583. Lapide, 3, uses our line this way when he speaks of Luther's blasphemous tongue being burned forever.

[205] E.g. 1 En. 100.7-9 ('you afflict the righteous...and burn them with fire...in the heat of a blazing fire you will burn'); Ecclus 28.1 ('the one who takes vengeance will suffer vengeance'); Mt 10.32-33; Mk 8.38; Lk 12.8-9; 1 Cor 3.17 ('if anyone destroys God's temple, God will destroy that person'); Jude 6; Rev 11.18; 16.6; 22.18-19; Apoc. Abr. 31.3 ('I will give those who have poured scorn on me to the scorn of the age to come'). Cf. the application of Jas 3.6 in Dante, *Inferno* 26.89, where 'the tongue of fire' that speaks is a hellish flame of torment. On this see A. Cornish, 'The Epistle of James in Inferno 26', *Traditio* 45 (1990), 367-79.

man's tongue...are as a fire among a people which scorches its beauty... May he [God] destroy the slanderous tongue in flaming fire far from the devout'); also LAB 63.4 ('a fiery worm will go up into his tongue and make him rot away'); Apoc. Pet 7.2 ('By their tongues, with which they have blasphemed the way of righteousness, they will be hung up'); Acts Thom. 56 ('the souls hung up by the tongue are slanderers and such as have spoken false and disgraceful words and are not ashamed'); b. 'Arak. 15b (on the last day, God will condemn the slanderer from above while the prince of Gehenna will condemn him from below; cf. Midr. Ps 12.2); Tg. Ps 120.2-4 ('O Lord, deliver my soul...from the deceitful tongue. What will he give you, O slanderer? And what will he add to you, O accuser, O deceitful tongue? A warrior's sharp arrows like lightning from above, with the glowing coals of the broom tree that burn in Gehenna from below').[206] Bauckham further shows that, at some point, Jewish readers—like the targumist just quoted—found eschatological sense in Ps 120.3-4: 'And what more shall be done to you, you deceitful tongue? A warrior's sharp arrows, with glowing coals of the broom tree!'[207] The upshot is that James' wordplay is a way of saying what Midr. Ps 120.3 (not cited by Bauckham) affirms: 'Even as you (the tongue) did act towards the world from the beginning...so will I (God) act towards you'.[208] This interpretation of 3.6 means that it has a parallel in Mt 5.22 ('If you say, "You fool", you will be liable to the Gehenna of fire'; here too Gehenna is the punishment for harmful or inappropriate speech) and the Book of Thomas the Contender 143.15-21 (the fire of lust becomes the eschatological fire that 'will devour your flesh openly and rend your souls secretly').[209]

Verse 7. πᾶσα γὰρ φύσις θηρίων τε καὶ πετεινῶν ἐρπετῶν τε καὶ ἐναλίων δαμάζεται. Cf. Isocrates, *Or.* 2.12: 'Do not deem us, the human kind, so unfortunate that, although in dealing with wild beasts we have discovered arts by which we tame their spirits and decrease their worth, yet in our own case we are powerless to help ourselves in the pursuit of virtue. On the contrary, be convinced that education and diligence are in the highest degree potent to improve our nature...' The contrast or comparison between taming animals and taming oneself evidently had some currency in the Graeco-Roman world.[210]

---

[206] For a later example of this sort of logic see Bonaventure, *Lk ad* 16.24 Opera Omnia 11 ed. Peltier, 43-45: the rich man in Lk 16.22-31 begs Lazarus, 'Cool my tongue', because God has punished his tongue for its sins. Cf. also Peter Chrysologus, *Serm.* 120.5 CCSL 24a ed. Olivar, 734-35. Older commentaries on James occasionally cite the words from Lk 16: e.g. Elsner, 392; Kypke, 424.

[207] See b. 'Arak. 15b; Chron. Jerah 14.4.

[208] See further Tanh. Buber Metsora' 1, where Gehenna is the fate of those who speak wrongly.

[209] On the relationship of Nag Hammadi's Book of Thomas the Contender to Jas 3.6 see the Introduction, 14.

[210] See also Dio Chrysostom 1.14.

THE SINS OF SPEECH (3.1-12)

Although details varied, the division of the animal kingdom into three or four major groups was conventional.[211] For the latter the following may be noted:

LXX Gen 1.26	ἰχθυῶν	πετεινῶν	κτηνῶν	ἑρπετῶν
LXX Gen 1.28	ἰχθυῶν	πετεινῶν	κτηνῶν	ἑρπετῶν
LXX Gen 7.14	θηρία	κτήνη	ἑρπετόν	πετεινόν
LXX Gen 7.21	πετεινῶν	κτηνῶν	θηρίων	ἑρπετόν
LXX Gen 8.1	θηρίων	κτηνῶν	πετεινῶν	ἑρπετῶν
LXX Gen 8.19	θηρία	κτήνη	πετεινόν	ἑρπετόν
LXX Gen 9.2	θηρίοις	ὄρνεα	κινούμενα	ἰχθύας
LXX Deut 4.17-18	κτήνους	ὀρνέου	ἑρπετοῦ	ἰχθύος
3 Βασ 5.13	κτηνῶν	πετεινῶν	ἑρπετῶν	ἰχθύων
LXX Ps 148.10	θηρία	κτήνη	ἑρπετά	πετεινά
LXX Ezek 38.20	ἰχθύες	πετεινά	θηρία	ἑρπετά
LXX Hos 4.3	θηρίοις	ἑρπετοῖς	πετεινοῖς	ἰχθύες
1 En. 7.5	πετεινοῖς	θηρίοις	ἑρπετοῖς	ἰχθύσιν
Acts 10.12 v.l.	τετράποδα	θηρία	ἑρπετά	πετεινά
Acts 11.6	τετράποδα	θηρία	ἑρπετά	πετεινά

Note also Gk. LAE 29.11: θηρία...πετεινά...ἑρπετά ἐν τῇ γῇ καὶ θαλάσσῃ.

James agrees closely with none of these. His ἐνάλιος is unique,[212] and only Gk. LAE 29.1 follows θηρία with πετεινά. Despite this, and despite the absence from the lists in Genesis of φύσις[213] and ἐνάλιος,[214] an informed Jew or Christian would immediately think of the biblical creation account,[215] which v. 9 indisputably calls to mind.[216] James, it seems, can rewrite the Bible as much as the sayings of Jesus. In this case, φύσις is his substitute for the γένος = 'species' of Gen 1 (cf. Philo, *Spec.* 4.116), ἐνάλιος his alternate for ἰχθύς (LXX Gen 1.26, 28), and δαμαζέται his synonym for ἄρχω (LXX Gen 1.26, 28). He retains, however, the πετεινά and ἑρπετά of Gen 1.26 and 28.

δαμαζέται,[217] soon repeated twice,[218] is the key word: the issue is how to control the uncontrollable. Although Jewish religious texts held that

---

[211] For the former see Gen 1.30; 6.7, 20; 7.8, 23; Lev 20.25; Hos 1.12; Jub. 3.16, 28; Acts 10.12; Rom 1.23.

[212] Epiphanius, *Pan.* 3.36.14 GCS 37 ed. Holl, 374—'And so with beasts and birds; so with domestic animals, reptiles and sea creatures' (ἐναλίων)—is much later and may be influenced by James.

[213] Cf. Wis 7.20: φύσεις ζῴων.

[214] A biblical *hapax*; cf. Philo, *Dec.* 54; Sib. Or. 5.157.

[215] As have the commentators: Dionysius bar Salībī *ad loc.* CSCO 53, 60 Scriptores Syri 101 ed. Sedlacek, 126; Meyer, *Rätsel*, 116-17; Robertson, 162; Michl, 48; Knoch, 197; Burdick, 188; Townsend, 62; Motyer, 124; *et al.* But Peter Damian, *Ep.* 86 ed. Reindel, 499, and Ng, 'Father', associate James instead with Gen 9.2.

[216] Cf. also perhaps the γενέσεως of v. 6.

[217] Cf. LXX Dan 2.40; Mk 5.4; Josephus, *Ant.* 3.86; T. Abr. RecLng. 2.9.

[218] Cf. the word-play in Apoc. Abr. 7.1: 'even things that are otherwise unsubdued are subdued by it', viz., fire.

the animals were tame before the fall[219] and will be tame again at the eschaton,[220] experience taught that wild beasts can be subdued or domesticated even now.[221] James' next assertion, however, certainly seems hyperbolic: every species has already been tamed. This is why Poole, 890, paraphrases: 'some of every kind'.[222] But the exaggeration magnifies the contrast and so serves the illustration. Precision is irrelevant.

καὶ δεδάμασται τῇ φύσει τῇ ἀνθρωπίνῃ. This makes for a little chiasmus with what precedes:

φύσις
   δαμαζέται
   δεδάμασται
φύσει

For Manton, 290, the present tense followed by the perfect tense (cf. the similar constructions in Jn 10.38 and Heb 6.10) shows that James 'doth not only intend the subjection of the creatures before the fall, which was full and voluntary, or some miraculous effects...but what is usual and ordinary, and falleth out often in common experience'.[223] Although one hesitates to divine here a distinction between prelapsarian and postlapsarian existence, James is clearly trying to be comprehensive.

ἡ ἀνθρωπίνη φύσις was a set phrase,[224] and according to Diogenes Laertius 5.59, Strato of Lampsacus wrote a treatise entitled, Περὶ φύσεως

---

[219] Gen 2.18-20; Gk. LAE 16.2; 24.4; 2 En 58.2-3.

[220] Isa 11.6-9; 65.25; Hos 2.18; Philo, *Praem.* 85-90; 2 Bar. 73.6; Sib. Or. 3.788-95.

[221] Cf. Gen 9.2; Ps 8.6-8; Ecclus 17.4; Philo, *Opif.* 83-88 (here appear also the comparisons of human beings to drivers of chariots and pilots of ships), 148-49; *Decal.* 113; also Sophocles, *Ant.* 332-52; Cicero, *Nat. deo.* 2.60.151; Seneca, *Benef.* 2.29; Epictetus, *Diatr.* 4.1.24-28; Galen, *Usu part.* 3.1; Aelian 8.4.

[222] Cf. Wesley, 864 ('The expression perhaps is not to be taken strictly'); so too Calvin, 291; Trapp, 699 ('Some creatures indeed may be taken, but not tamed, as the tiger, panther... Such unruly talkers and deceivers the Church is pestered with...sons of Belial, untamable, untractable, untouchable, unteachable'). According to Gill, 793, Pliny documents the taming of elephants, lions, tigers, eagles, crocodiles, asps, serpents, and fish (cf. Quistorp, 399), but Gill adds that some take James to speak only of 'being mastered or subdued, by one means or another; or of their being despoiled of their power, or of their poison'. Cf. Bede *ad loc.* CCSL 121 ed. Hurst, 206; Glossa Ordinaria *ad loc,* the former citing cases of tamed serpents and tigers. Bede goes on to make a point similar to Trapp's: the tongues of some human beings are so depraved that they surpass the deadliness and cruelty of wild beasts.

[223] Laws, 153, may have the same thought: the two tenses 'indicate that the present was established in the past, at creation'. Smith, 184, opines that James probably had in view not the creation and the present but Noah (cf. Gen 9.2) and the present. Henry, *ad loc.*, thinks of miraculous tamings in the biblical past (Elijah, Jonah, Daniel) and of mundane tamings later.

[224] Note e.g. Plato, *Theaet.* 149C (ἡ ἀνθρωπίνη φύσις); T. Job 3.3 (ἡ ἀνθρωπίνη φύσις); Gk. LAE 11.2; Liv. Proph. Dan 8; T. Reub. 3.3; Philo, *Spec.* 2.225 (μεταξὺ θείας καὶ ἀνθρωπίνης φύσεως); Appian, *Bell. civ.* 3.9.69 (ὑπὲρ φύσιν ἀνθρωπίνην); Iamblichus,

ἀνθρωπίνης. The expression was well known among Hellenistic writers, and Eusebius, like James (3.9), associates it with the biblical 'image of God'.[225]

Here 'human nature' is set over against the animal kingdom, and exegetes regularly revert for clarification to Gen 1.28: 'Have dominion (ἄρχετε) over the fish of the sea and over the birds of the air and over every living thing that moves upon the earth'.[226] As observed, James is intentionally echoing Genesis.

Verse 8. More hyperbole.[227] Dibelius, 200, observes that the verse has 'a rich and poetic sound'.

τὴν δὲ γλῶσσαν οὐδεὶς δαμάσαι δύναται ἀνθρώπων. Cf. v. 12: μὴ δύναται. δέ here seems emphatic and οὐδεὶς—the only new word in this clause—makes for a strong contrast with the πᾶσα of v. 7. It further creates assonance and alliteration: οὐδεὶς δαμάσαι δύναται. The sense is clearly reflexive: the subject is how to control one's own tongue, not the tongues of others.[228] Does the distance between ἀνθρώπων, placed at the end (and strictly unnecessary), and οὐδείς perhaps, as Cranfield has it, suggest 'the thought that, though man cannot tame this "restless evil", God can'?[229] For Augustine, James 'does not say that no one can tame the tongue, but no one of men; so that when it is tamed we confess that this is brought about by the piety, the help, the grace of God'.[230]

Pyth. 3.15 (κατὰ τὴν ἀνθρωπίνην φύσιν); Ps.-Callisthenes, *Hist. Alex. Magn.* rec. γ 24.16 (φύσεως ἀνθρώπων).

[225] Eusebius, *P.E.* 7.10.9 GCS 43 ed. Mras, 381.

[226] Whether δεδάμασται τῇ φύσει τῇ ἀνθρωπίνῃ means 'subjected to human nature' or 'subjected by human nature' is unclear (BDF 191.5); but the general import is the same.

[227] Cf. Lardner, 'Tongue' (as in n. 18: 'he would not be at the pains to admonish and argue as he does, if there were no hopes of success'); Oesterley, 453 (the 'exaggerated character' of vv. 7-8 'reminds one of the orator carried away by his subject'); Moffatt, 49 ('a hyperbole like the opposite exclamation in ver. 2'); Laws, 153-54 (v. 8 is hyperbole, and when taken with v. 2, we have an implicit exhortation 'to do precisely what is said to be impossible'). Priestly, 510, with his interest in practical exhortation, finds the hyperbole too much: 'There is rather too much of rhetoric in this charge. For strictly speaking there is no more difficulty in restraining the tongue than any other member; language is only one manner in which passion vents itself, and sometimes actions are more prompt than words.' Cf. Cone, 286: 'This assertion can hardly be regarded as true... and is shown false by many examples. The declaration that in general the tongue is untamable... is somewhat hazardous, and is certainly too pessimistic and extravagant to be accepted without question.'

[228] Although Wesley, 864, mentions the latter alternative.

[229] So Cranfield, 'Message', 344. Cf. Manton, 293; Wesley, 864; Marty, 132; Reicke, 39; R. Wall, 172; Konradt, *Existenz*, 279. Contrast Moo, 161-62.

[230] Augustine, *Nat. et. grat.* 15 (16) CSEL 60 ed. Urba and Zycha, 243; cf. idem, *Serm.* 55.1 PL 38.375. Augustine's interpretation was in response to the optimistic Pelagian interpretation of Jas 3.8, which found not denial but a question, 'Can anyone tame the tongue?'

Although Proverbs and Ecclesiasticus have much to say about the tongue, they do not share James' exaggerated pessimism. Most of their relevant sayings assume, without further ado, that the wise and righteous, unlike the wicked, can or will control the tongue.[231] But the difficulty of self-control and taming one's tongue does appear in other sources, such as Philo, *Det.* 23 (the 'willful and rebellious course' of the tongue requires it be curbed 'with the reigns of conscience'); Iamblichus, *Pyth.* 31.195 ('mastery of the tongue is the most difficult of all instances of self-control').[232]

ἀκατάστατον κακόν.[233] The expression, which creates more assonance and consonance (α, α, α, α, α, κ, κ, κ, τ, τ, τ), is unparalleled. Dio Chrysostom 32.23, comes closest: the populace is ἄστατον κακόν.[234] ἐστίν is understood: 'No one is able to tame the tongue; (it is) a chaotic evil'.[235] For ἀκατάστατος see on 1.8 and cf. the ἀκαταστασία of 3.16.[236] The word means 'restless', 'chaotic', 'unstable' (cf. T. Job 36.4-6), and Herm. *Mand.* 2.3 has this: 'Slander is evil; it is a restless (ἀκατάστατον) demon, never at peace but always at home with dissension'.[237] Hermas might allude to LXX Prov 26.28, as may James: 'A false tongue (γλῶσσα) hates truth, and an unguarded mouth works instability' (ἀκαταστασίας). κακός occurs also in 1.13, which asserts that God is not tempted by such. Here then is a strong contrast between the human world and the divine nature.

Earlier commentators often express themselves as does Manton, 290: 'It is a metaphor taken from beasts that are kept within rails or chains. God hath, in the structure of the mouth, appointed a double rail to it, teeth and lips...and yet it breaketh out'. One likely sees here the influence of Midr. Ps 52.6 and its parallels (via Christian Hebraists) upon Christian commentaries: 'the tongue is imprisoned, with the cheeks and teeth surrounding it... Yet no man can withstand it.'

Manton associates ἀκατάστατον κακόν with what comes immediately before: the tongue is chaotic or restless because one cannot subdue it. In 1.8, however, ἀκατάστατος has to do with double-mindedness, with the self's internal division, and this too well suits 3.9-12. What connotations are to the fore in 3.8 are unclear.

---

[231] Prov 10.20; 13.3; Ecclus 14.1; 25.8; 28.22; etc.

[232] See also Ps 39.1-3 (where the Psalmist tries to keep quiet but cannot); Philo, *Somn.* 2.150-54; Plutarch, *Mor.* 509C-10B; Midr. Ps 52.6 (quoted below).

[233] The Majority text and Cyr Dam Epiph FlavC PsOec **L**:S,CAr.Hl.PEL **S**:H G **Sl**:Si have ἀκατάσχετον. This is usually explained as an emendation, as it is a more common word.

[234] Cf. Demosthenes, *Or.* 19.136: 'The populace is like θάλαττ' ἀκατάστατον'.

[235] So BDF 137.3; cf. Mayor, 121.

[236] Ps.-Phoc. 96 uses ἀκατάσχεται of fire, an element prominent in James' essay.

[237] Note also Herm. *Mand.* 12.1.1-2, where 'the evil desire' is 'savage' and 'tamed only with difficulty'. This is similar to Herm. *Mand.* 12.4.2-3, where the visionary asks, 'If humankind is lord of all God's creatures and rules over everything, cannot humankind also master these commandments?'

THE SINS OF SPEECH (3.1-12)

James remains vague at this point. What exactly is the evil that the tongue works? Should one think of slander[238] or of gossip[239] or of cursing (cf. vv. 9-10) or of lying (cf. v. 14) or of boasting (cf. vv. 5, 14), or of something else again? Although the text goes on soon enough to denigrate 'cursing', the lack of specification here allows the text to be comprehensive, and the history of interpretation does not focus on one sin of the tongue but addresses numerous verbal failings.

μεστὴ ἰοῦ θανατηφόρου. For μεστός see on 3.17. Cf. Pss 58.3-4 ('The wicked...speak lies. They have venom like the venom of a serpent'); 140.3 ('They make their tongue sharp as a snake's, and under their lips is the venom of vipers'); Job 20.16 ('the tongue of the viper will kill them'); Ecclus 28.18 ('Many have fallen by the edge of the sword, but not as many as have fallen because of the tongue'), 21 (the tongue brings 'an evil death'); 1QH 13(5).27 ('a lying tongue, like vipers' venom that spreads to the extremities...serpents' [poison]'); 4Q525 15 ('eternal curses and vipers' venom'); T. Job 43.12 ('the poison [ἰόν] of asps in his tongue'); Herm. *Sim.* 9.26.7 ('just as the beasts poison and kill a person with their poison [ἰῷ] so also the words of such people poison and kill a person'); Lucian, *Fugit.* 19 ('foam, or rather ἰοῦ, fills the mouths' of false philosophers). μεστός is a synonym of πλήρης meaning 'full'.[240] Once more there is assonance: τη ου...τη...ου.

Although ἰός means 'rust' in 5.3, the sense here must be 'poison'.[241] θανατηφόρος[242]—common with ἰός in patristic texts[243]—refers to deadly speech in Sib. Or. frag. 3 33: 'from their mouths pour deadly poison' (θανατηφόρος ἰός). More distant parallels to James include Prov 18.21 (death and life are in the power of the tongue); Ecclus 23.12 ('There is a manner of speaking comparable to death'); Did. 2.4 ('the double tongue is a snare of death'; cf. Barn. 19.8); b. 'Arak. 15b (offering commentary on Prov 18.21).

In Romanus, θανατηφόρος appears in a retrospect of Gen 2–3,[244] and one wonders whether μεστὴ ἰοῦ θανατηφόρου continues James' interaction with Genesis. Not only have commentators very often read μεστὴ ἰοῦ θανατηφόρου as an allusion to poisonous serpents,[245] but ἰός occurs

---

[238] Cf. Lev 19.16; Ps 15.3; 4Q425 2; Col 3.8; Midr. Ps 12.2.

[239] Cf. Prov 20.19; Ecclus 19.6; Rom 1.29.

[240] Cf. LXX Nah 1.10; Prov 6.34; T. Naph. 6.2; Jn 19.29; 21.11.

[241] As in LXX Ps 139.4 (ἰὸν ἀσπίδων; cf. Rom 3.13); Philo, *Legat.* 166 (most Egyptians were 'a seed bed of evil in whose souls both the ἰόν and the temper of the native crocodiles and asps were reproduced'); T. Job 43.9 (ἰὸν ἄσπιδος); Papias frag. 11.2 ed. Bihlmeyer, 139 (ἰὸν ἐχίδνης); *et al.*

[242] NT: 1×. LXX: 5×: Num 18.22; Job 33.23; 4 Macc 8.18, 26; 15.26. Philo: 0×. Josephus: 0×. Cf. T. Abr. RecLng 8.10; 17.17.

[243] Eusebius, *H.E.* 7.31.2; Theodoret, *Ps 1–150* 90.13 PG 80.1613C; Ps.-Ephraem, *Ad ever. sup.* ed. Phrantzoles, 92.13; etc.

[244] Romanus, *Cant.* 1.12, 16 SC 82 ed. de Matons, 82, 87.

[245] Bede *ad loc.* CCSL 121 ed. Hurst, 206-207; Erasmus, *Paraphrase*, 156; Gill, 890; Kypke, 425; Henry, *ad loc.*; Clarke, 816; Doddridge, 843; Meyer, *Rätsel*, 117; Ropes,

elsewhere with ὄφις, the word for 'serpent' in LXX Gen 3.1;[246] and the rabbis thought of the נחש of Gen 3.1 as poisonous.[247] Furthermore, the fruit in Eden brought death,[248] and some held that it was poisonous (Gk. LAE 19.3) while others spoke of the ἰός of the devil;[249] and the devil was regularly identified with the serpent or thought of as having spoken through him.[250] On this intertextual reading, which has support from the history of interpretation,[251] the human tongue recapitulates the work of the serpent's tongue in Eden: it brings death. Interestingly enough, Midr. Ps 58.2 moves from Ps 58.3-4 (see above) to Gen 3: God destroyed the feet and teeth of the serpent so that he 'now eats dust'.[252]

Verse 9. The theme is still the tongue and its restless evil, but the stress is now on the duplicity of the tongue. With this change of emphasis is a change in the logic. If, in the previous verses, James declares it nearly impossible to control the tongue, in vv. 9-12 he urges 'that it is impossible, or at least a contradiction of his own natural theology, for those in the community to do anything less'. Having just proceeded as though 'the "default setting" of the tongue...is to cause harm, in vv. 9-12 he argues the opposite: because the default setting is praise of the Creator, cursing the creature is a contradiction and thus impossible'.[253]

According to Diogenes Laertius 1.105, Anacharsis, when asked, 'What in people is both good and bad?', answered: 'The tongue'. James makes the same point, albeit with theological language. In doing so, he belongs to a rich tradition. Relevant texts for comparison are T. Benj. 6.5

241; Moffatt, 49; Ross, 63; Laws, 154; Songer, 123; Deiros, 176; Hartin, 186, Tidball, 105; *et al.*

[246] T. Job 43.6; Chrysippus, *Frag. log. et phys.* 1181; Eusebius, *Ad coet. sanc.* 20.3 GCS 7 ed. Heikel, 183.

[247] ARN B 43. Cf. Eusebius, *P.E.* 7.16.3 GCS 43 ed. Mras, 395, where the dragon who led the fall of the angels carries ἰοῦ θανατηφόρου.

[248] Gen 2.16-17; Wis 2.23-24; Ecclus 25.24; Rom 5.17; 2 Bar. 56.6.

[249] E.g. Gk. LAE 19.3; T. Gad 5.1 (ἰοῦ διαβολικοῦ); T. Ash. 1.9 ('the devil's storehouse is filled with the ἰόν of the evil spirit'); Acts Phil. 111 ed. Bonnet, 43.

[250] 1 En. 69.6; 4 Macc 18.7-8; Gk. LAE 16.4; 17.4; Rev 12.9; 20.2; 3 Bar 9.7; Apoc. Sed. 4.5; etc. Note also that, according to Josephus, *Ant.* 1.50, after Adam and Eve's calamity, God put poison (ἰόν) beneath the tongue (γλῶτταν) of the serpent.

[251] Note e.g. Gregory of Nyssa, *Nativ.* Gregorii Nysseni Opera 10/2 ed. Mann, 244; Bassett, 153; O. Michel, 'ἰός, κατιόομαι', *TDNT* 3.335; Hanson, 'Report', 527; Davids, 145; R. Wall, 173; Hartin, 186 ('a clear reminder of the serpent in Genesis'); Witherington, 496; Baker-Ellsworth, 88 (James' words are apt 'because of how a serpent was Satan's vehicle for cleverly deceiving Eve to sin against God').

[252] See further Deut. Rab. 5.10 (God cut off the serpent's feet and his tongue because the latter slandered the creator when he lied to Eve); Midr. Ps 120.3 ('I will tell you, O evil tongue, how I am going to act toward you. Even as you did act toward the world from the beginning—as a serpent you spoke evil to Adam—so will I act toward you').

[253] Brosend, 91. Some commentators compare 1 Jn 4.20: one cannot love God and hate one's brother.

('The good set of mind does not talk from both sides of its mouth: praises and curses, abuse and honor...but it has one disposition, uncontaminated and pure, toward all people'); Philo, *Dec.* 93 ('It would be sacrilege to employ the mouth by which one pronounces the holiest of all names, to utter any words of shame'); Test. Domini 1.28 ed. Rahmani, 64 ('a corporeal tongue through which truth and lying go out'); Lev. Rab. 33.1 ('Good comes from it [the tongue] and bad comes from it. When the tongue is good, nothing is better; and when it is bad, nothing worse').[254] Graeco-Roman parallels include Plato, *Leg.* 659A ('swearing falsely out of the same mouth with which he invoked Heaven when he first took his seat as judge'); Plutarch, *Mor.* 38B ('speech contains both injuries and benefits in the largest measure'), 506C (the tongue is 'the instrument of both the greatest good and the greatest evil'); Vit. Aesop 53-55 ('What is better or finer than the tongue? All philosophy and education depend upon the tongue. Without it, nothing could happen—no giving, no receiving, no enterprise... And what bad thing does not come via the tongue? On account of it there are enemies, plots, conflicts, battles, jealousy, strife, wars. Surely there is nothing worse than the abominable tongue').

ἐν αὐτῇ εὐλογοῦμεν τὸν κύριον καὶ πατέρα. In accord with vv. 2-4, James shows himself not to be unremittingly negative. This requires that the invective in vv. 5-8 is hyperbole for the sake of the main point.

ἐν αὐτῇ marks a transition: instead of the tongue acting as its own agent, it is now the agent of the will or self: 'by it we...' The instrumental ἐν reminds one of the Hebrew ב; cf. Lk 22.49; Rev 6.9.

εὐλογέω + τὸν κύριον (= את־יהוה + ברך) was a common liturgical idiom, known especially from the Psalms.[255] Appearing only here in the NT and rarely in Christian literature before Origen,[256] the expression often conjures up a communal setting for exegetes, even though Jews uttered blessings also at private meals and in private prayer. Whatever the precise *Sitz im Leben* (see below), for James the chief point is to create a rhetorical contrast: the highest use of the tongue—praising God—vs. the lowest use of the tongue—cursing others. The first person plural harks back to vv. 1-2, and again the author includes himself with his readers in order to stress the universality of his generalization. Martin, 119, wonders whether the plural ('we bless') might also reflect liturgical language.

---

[254] Ecclus 5.13; 28.12; 37.18; Lev. Rab. 33.1. Plummer, 599, wonders whether James has Ecclus 28.12 specifically in mind. Although some commentators mention the διγλωσσία of Did. 2.4 and Barn. 19.7 v.l., that expresses the hypocritical distance between word and feeling or belief, not contradictory speech.

[255] Cf. Deut 8.10; Judg 5.2, 9; 1 Chr 29.20; Neh 9.5; Pss 16.7; 26.12; 34.1; 103.1-2, 20-22; 104.1, 35; 115.18; 134.1-2; 135.19-20; Tob 4.19; Ecclus 39.14; Pr Azar 35-66; 1 En. 106.11; etc. Schlatter, 227, notes that James uses not the common Greek εὐχαριστεῖν but the Jewish εὐλογεῖν. For 'tongue' with εὐλογέω or ברך see 4Q215a 1 2.7-8; 4Q503 7-9 3-4; Lk 1.64.

[256] Note Mart. Pol. 19.2. More common is εὐλογητός with θεός or κύριος, as in Lk 1.68; Rom 9.5; 2 Cor 1.3; Eph 1.3; 1 Pet 1.3.

'Lord and Father' seems unattested in Jewish sources, although close are 1 Chr 29.10 (LXX: 'Blessed are you, κύριε ὁ θεὸς 'Ισραηλ, ὁ πατὴρ ἡμῶν from ages and to ages'); Isa 63.16 (LXX: σὺ κύριε πατὴρ ἡμῶν); Ecclus 23.1 (κύριε, πάτερ, καὶ δέσποτα), 4 (κύριε, πάτερ, καὶ θεέ); 51.10 (κύριον, πατέρα κυρίου μου);[257] Josephus, *Ant.* 5.93 (ὁ θεός, πατὴρ καὶ δεσπότης τοῦ 'Εβραίων). The double title is rare also in Christian texts.[258] Perfect secular parallels exist, however (e.g. Plutarch, *Alex.* 28.2), and the Corpus Hermeticum knows the phrase as a religious title.[259]

Only here in James is God 'Lord and Father'. Although 5.4 has 'Lord of hosts', our author generally prefers the unqualified κύριος in reference to God.[260] πατήρ, however, on the other two occasions that it refers to God, is qualified: 'Father of lights' in 1.17, 'God and Father' in 1.27. Is 'Father' subjoined in 3.9 to anticipate 'the image of God' and to underline the unity of humanity, which makes cursing others all the worse? Or does it emphasize divine love, which is like parental love? Or does our text allude to the Eighteen Benedictions, in which God is addressed as both 'Lord' and 'Father' (see below)? Whatever the explanation for James' rare phrase, the 'Lord' is God the Father, not Jesus Christ.

καὶ ἐν αὐτῇ καταρώμεθα τοὺς ἀνθρώπους. This makes for antithetical parallelism:

ἐν αὐτῇ + first person plural, εὐλογοῦμεν + divine object, τὸν κύριον καὶ πατέρα.
ἐν αὐτῇ + first person plural, καταρώμεθα + human object, τοὺς ἀνθρώπους.

In order to avoid the notion that James—believed to be both saint and author of our book—ever cursed anyone, exegetes have sometimes construed the Greek that follows as a question.[261]

The contrast between blessing and cursing was conventional.[262] Note especially 2 En. A 52.1-4; this concerns speaking and is in some ways reminiscent of James: 'Blessed is he who opens his heart for praise and praises the Lord... Blessed is he who opens his lips, both blessing and praising the Lord. Cursed is he who opens his lips for cursing and

---

[257] Frankemölle, 514, believes that James is influenced by these lines in Ecclesiasticus, which have to do with controlling the tongue or being delivered from slander.

[258] But note Clement of Alexandria, *Strom.* 5.14.134 GCS 52 ed. Stählin and Früchtel, 417, and perhaps Mt 11.25 = Lk 10.21: πάτερ, κύριε. Contrast the well-attested v.l., θεὸν καὶ πατέρα (69 88 206 218 *et al.* **Byz** Dam Epiph PsOec **L**:V[mss], AU.CAr.Hl K:SB[pt]A S:H A[ms] G Sl:ChDMSiS); this was a popular title: 3 Macc 5.7; Rom 15.6; Gal 1.4; *et al.*

[259] Hermes to Tat 2 ed. Nock and Festugière, 1.60 (εὔξαι πρῶτον τῷ κυρίῳ καὶ πατρὶ καὶ μόνῳ); Frag. Varia 23.8 ed. Nock and Festugière, 4.23 (πάντων... κύριος καὶ πατήρ).

[260] See 1.7; 4.10, 15; 5.4 ('Lord of hosts'), 7, 8 (?), 10, 11, 14, 15.

[261] Cf. Theophylact *ad loc.* PG 125.1169A.

[262] Gen 12.3; 27.29; Num 23.25; 24.9-10; Deut 30; Ps 62.4 (cf. 1 Clem. 15.3); Prov 3.33; Tob 13.12; Ecclus 33.12; 1QS 2.10; 4Q171 3.9; Philo, *Her.* 177; T. Levi 4.6; 2 En. 52; etc.

blasphemy, before the face of the Lord.'²⁶³ καταράομαι²⁶⁴ appears elsewhere in the NT in Mt 25.41; Mk 11.21; Lk 6.28; Rom 12.14. In the latter two verses, as here, the word is the antithesis of εὐλογέω. Although James does not specify its meaning, the context leaves open the possibility that more than disparaging words of abuse may be in view, perhaps indeed something like a formal curse, 'which in virtue of a supernatural nexus of operation' intends to bring 'harm by its very expression to the one against whom it is directed'.²⁶⁵

Given the earlier reference to Genesis (see on v. 7) as well as the next clause, which draws upon Gen 1.26, we may have here an ironic allusion to the primeval history, which declares that God 'blessed' human beings: Gen 1.28 (ηὐλόγησεν); 5.2 (εὐλόγησεν); 9.1 (ηὐλόγησεν). All three of these texts occur near statements that God made human beings in the divine image: Gen 1.26-27; 5.1; 9.6. Such an intertextual reading would imply that to curse human beings is to contradict a divine act.²⁶⁶

καταρώμεθα, like εὐλογοῦμεν, is in the present tense. Most exegetes think of the contrasting activities as alternating: on one occasion people praise God, on another they curse people.²⁶⁷ Others suppose that the two overlap: even in the midst of blessing God, human beings can curse each other.²⁶⁸

The argument of Dibelius, 202-203, that our line must be from a Jewish source because Christians did not engage in cursing—'the presupposition that "we" curse other people does not conform with the ethos of the early Christian community'—is odd.²⁶⁹ Matthew 5.44 = Lk 6.28 and Rom 12.14, which prohibit cursing, are not records of how all believers behaved, and the apostle who penned the latter also wrote Gal 1.8-9 ('if we or an angel from heaven should proclaim to you a gospel contrary to what we proclaimed to you, let that one be accursed!')

---

²⁶³ Note also Ephraem, *Hymn. fide* 81.15 CSCO 154 Scriptores Syri 73 ed. Beck, 251: 'Prayer and prying inquiry come from one and the same mouth'.

²⁶⁴ Only here in James; most often for קלל in the LXX.

²⁶⁵ F. Büschel, 'κατάρα', *TDNT* 1.449. See further below. Reicke, 39, imagines that James had in view 'prophets of doom' who thought it 'part of the Christian message to pronounce curses upon degraded mankind'.

²⁶⁶ Cf. Tanḥ. Buber Lekh-Lekh 5: if God initially blessed Adam and Eve in Gen 1.28, the responsibility for blessing later became the responsibility of human beings.

²⁶⁷ Cf. Plummer, 599: 'The singing of *Te Deum* after massacres and *dragonnades* is perhaps no longer possible; but alternations between religious services and religious prosecutions, between writing pious books and publishing exasperating articles, are by no means extinct'.

²⁶⁸ See Calvin, 291-92; Hort, 77; Mitton, 130-31. Cf. Ps 62.4: 'they bless with their mouths, but inwardly they curse'.

²⁶⁹ One should keep in mind that, while parts of the Hebrew Bible assume that God and the saints sometimes curse others (Gen 12.3; Judg 5.23; 21.18; Prov 3.33; 11.26; 24.24; Eccl 7.21-22; Jer 11.3), other passages speak against cursing other human beings: Exod 19.14; 20.9; 21.17; 22.28; Job 31.29-30.

and 1 Cor 16.22 ('Let anyone be accursed who has no love for the Lord').[270]

Although Dibelius' reasons for his view fall short, James nonetheless, given his ostensible audience (see on 1.1), likely has in view not Christians speaking against each other but activity in a Jewish synagogue.[271] Modern commentators on 3.9 have sometimes been put in mind of the Eighteen Benedictions. They have not, however, observed that the Amidah, as we have it, also contains a curse upon heretics, including the so-called Nazoraeans, that is, Christians. If the author of our epistle was familiar with Jewish services in which such cursing took place, his words would denounce it. Several considerations make this reading plausible. (i) Despite recent doubts, some version of the *Birkat Ha-Minim* almost certainly goes back to the end of the first century at least.[272] (ii) That the authors of the Gospels of Matthew and John were familiar with that curse and responded to it is quite likely;[273] and if they knew of it, and if James was a Jewish Christian who wrote shortly after them, he too would probably have been aware that the cursing of Christians occurred in some synagogues. (iii) Most ancient texts that speak of blessing and cursing in the same breath refer either to God blessing and cursing human beings or to human beings blessing and cursing others. In Jas 3.9-10, however, the subjects are people blessing God and people cursing people. We find exactly the same thing in the *Birkat Ha-Minim*, which immediately follows its curse of human beings with 'Blessed are you, O Lord, who subdues the arrogant'.[274] (iv) The object of blessing in Jas 3.9 is τὸν κύριον καὶ πατέρα. The compound title, as we have seen, is extremely rare. So it may not be coincidence that, in the Amidah, God is blessed as both 'Lord' (יי) and '(Our) Father' (אבינו). (v) James uses καταρώμεθα and κατάρα. This interests because, in apparent references to the benediction against heretics, Justin Martyr uses that very verb and that very noun.[275] (vi) James 3.9-10 has, as we have seen, put some commentators

---

[270] Note also Acts 8.20; Rom 3.8; Gal 5.18; Phil 3.2; Rev 22.18-19. Davids, 146, counters Dibelius and maintains that James has in mind cursing as part of inner-church strife. Cf. Keenan, 110-11: James, as against Paul and Jude, 'is forbidding formal church cursing, formal exclusion from the community'. The commentary tradition does not address the issue of how James can condemn cursing human beings while Paul practices it; but note Countryman, 722.

[271] Cf. 2.1-7 and see Allison, 'Blessing'.

[272] See J. Marcus, 'Birkat Ha-Minim Revisited', *NTS* 55 (2009), 523-51.

[273] See especially Davies, *Setting*; J.L. Martyn, *History and Theology in the Fourth Gospel*, 3rd ed., Louisville, 2003.

[274] *Birkat Ha-Minim*, we should note, is actually a euphemism: the curse is called a blessing.

[275] Justin, *Dial*. 16.4: καταρώμενοι ἐν ταῖς συναγωγαῖς ὑμῶν τοὺς πιστεύοντας ἐπὶ τὸν Χριστόν; 96.2: ὑμεῖς γὰρ ἐν ταῖς συναγωγαῖς ὑμῶν καταρᾶσθε πάντων τῶν ἀπ' ἐκείνου λεγομένων Χριστιανῶν, [ὡς] καὶ τὰ ἄλλα ἔθνη, ἃ καὶ ἐνεργῆ τὴν κατάραν ἐργάζονται. On the meaning of these lines see Marcus, 'Birkat Ha-Minim', 532-33. Cf. Epiphanius, *Pan*. 29.9.2 GCS 25 ed. Holl, 332: ἐπικαταράσαι ὁ θεὸς τοὺς Ναζωραίους.

in mind of Jewish liturgy, and a few have even thought of the *Birkat ha-Minim*. Whitby, 591, wrote: 'This the unbelieving Jews did toward the Christians, cursing and anathematizing them in their synagogues; as Justin Martyr often testifieth to the face of Trypho the Jew'.[276]

τοὺς καθ' ὁμοίωσιν θεοῦ γεγονότας. This continues the series of allusions to Genesis; cf. LXX Gen 1.26: καθ' ὁμοίωσιν. Genesis 1.27; 5.1; 9.6; Wis 2.23; Ecclus 17.3; and Col 3.10 also refer to 'the image of God' but use εἰκών (cf. 1 Cor 11.7). James seems to have in mind Gen 1.26, which has both εἰκών and ὁμοίωσις.[277] Unlike other parts of the NT, there is no trace of a christological interpretation of 'image';[278] and it is typical of James that he argues not from a specifically Christian conviction, such as one should not curse one 'for whom Christ died' (1 Cor 8.11), but from a conventional Jewish belief.[279] Unlike certain ecclesiastical commentators, we need not wonder whether the application is to the saints or to all.[280] Jewish tradition, upon which James is drawing, held all human beings to be created in the image of God.[281]

James does nothing to clarify the meaning of 'the image of God', which has borne so many varied meanings in Jewish and Christian history.[282] Some ancients understood it in a straightforward, physical sense: human beings look like the Supreme Being.[283] Others thought human beings were like God in having dominion (Ecclus 17.1-8), or in

---

[276] Cf. Wells, 20 ('the men thus curs'd were the Orthodox Christians curs'd by the unbelieving Jews and Judaizing Believers'); Adamson, 146 ('thrice daily the devout Jew recited "the Eighteen Benedictions", with their ending, "Blessed art Thou, O God". But the tongue of blessing can also curse—a reference perhaps to the practice of imprecation but more probably to the disputes and slanders within the community').

[277] Cf. 1 Clem. 22.5; Barn. 5.5; 6.12.

[278] Contrast Rom 8.29; 1 Cor 11.7; 15.49; Col 1.15.

[279] See further Schlatter, 230-31.

[280] Contrast Poole, 890; Wells, 20; and see further Burchard, 149.

[281] Dale, 105, appropriately comments that the verse covers even those 'whose perversities, or whose weaknesses irritate us, anger us, provoke our scorn'.

[282] Literature: P.H. Merki, *'ΟΜΟΙΩΣΙΣ ΘΕΩ*, Freiburg, CH, 1952; J. Jervell, *Imago Dei*, Göttingen, 1960; G.A. Jónsson, *The Image of God*, Stockholm, 1988; S. Vollenweider, 'Der Menschgewordene als Ebenbild Gottes: Zum frühchristlichen Verständnis der Imago Dei', in *Ebenbild Gottes—Herrscher über die Welt*, ed. H.-P. Mathys, Neukirchen, 1998, 123-46; T. Frymer-Kensky, 'The Image: Religious Anthropology in Judaism and Christianity', in *Studies in Bible and Feminist Criticism*, Philadelphia, 2006, 91-107; G.H. van Kooten, *Paul's Anthropology in Context*, Tübingen, 2008 (the latter includes a survey of the image of God in Graeco-Roman paganism). Obviously, the distinction between 'likeness' and 'image', so important for much Christian theology from Irenaeus on, has nothing to do with James, as Rufinus of Syria, *Fide* 23 ed. Miller, 84, correctly observes.

[283] Cf. Sib. Or. 1.22-24; LAE 13-15; T. Isaac 6.33–7.1; ARN B 30.

being intelligent and rational,[284] or in being immortal.[285] What James thought, we know not.[286]

Our author understands humanity's status as the image of God to come with a moral imperative: one should not curse people. Perhaps to hand is the notion that, just as to see the image of something is to see that thing, so too to curse the image of something is to curse that thing. In any event, the link between the divine image and how one should act goes back to Gen 9.6 ('Whoever sheds the blood of a human, by a human will that person's blood be shed; for in his own image God made humankind'; cf. LAB 3.11), and later texts refer to the divine image when promoting compassion or discouraging evil.[287] Particularly close to James is 2 En. 44.1-2: 'The Lord with his own two hands created mankind; in a facsimile of his own face, both small and great, the Lord created them. And whoever insults a person's face, insults the face of a king, and treats the face of the Lord with repugnance. He who treats with contempt the face of any person treats the face of the Lord with contempt...' Alexander of Aphrodisias, *Metaph.* 710, supplies a pagan parallel: the mythologists, 'wishing to prevent people from beating each other, have made the gods in the image of the human being, intimating by this that the one striking a human being strikes and wantonly insults the divine image'.

Verse 10. Although the vocabulary shifts from 'tongue' to 'mouth', everything in this verse is either repetitive or implicit in what has come before. Its sole function is to add emphasis, to reiterate how outrageous and offensive the tongue can be. It acts against God, against good sense, and against the natural order.

ἐκ τοῦ αὐτοῦ στόματος ἐξέρχεται εὐλογία καὶ κατάρα. αὐτοῦ (cf. v. 11) is emphatic: 'out of one and the same mouth'. The NT typically uses ἐκπορεύομαι with ἐκ στόματος;[288] but ἐκ στόματος + ἐξέρχομαι has parallels in the LXX.[289] Moo, 164, cites Mt 15.11-20 ('it is not what goes into the mouth that defiles a person, but it is what comes out of the mouth that defiles... What comes out of the mouth proceeds from the heart, and

---

[284] Cf. Sib. Or. 8.395-402; 2 En. 30.10; cf. 4Q504(DibHamᵃ) 8 4-7(?).

[285] Cf. Wis 2.21-23; Ps.-Phoc. 105-108.

[286] But Wolmarans, 'Tongue', 526, appeals to ἡ ὁρμή in v. 3 and infers: for James, the image of God is probably humanity's will or reason. Cf. Wells, 31: 'intellectual faculties and free will'.

[287] Cf. 4 Ezra 8.41-45; Gk. LAE 10.3; 33.5; 35.2; T. Isaac 6.33–7.1; Apoc. Sed. 13.1-3; Mek. on Exod 20.13; t. Yeb. 8.6; Gen. Rab. 24.7 ('If you do so [that is, put your neighbor to shame], know whom you put to shame, for "in the likeness of God he made him"').

[288] Mt 15.11, 18; Lk 4.22; Eph 4.29 (of evil words); Rev 11.5; 19.15; cf. LXX Prov 3.16; Ecclus 28.12.

[289] Num 30.3; Judg 11.36; 1 Βασ 2.3; Job 37.2; Isa 45.23; 55.11; Lam 3.38—in each case for פֶּה + יָצָא. Cf. Jos. Asen. 12.11; 16.11; Gk. LAE 2.3; 20.10; Rev 19.21; 4 Bar. 6.9. The idiom is not classical, but it does appear in Aristotle, *Prob.* 11.27.

THE SINS OF SPEECH (3.1-12)

this is what defiles. For out of the heart come evil intentions, murder... slander') and suggests dependence upon the Jesus tradition. But the Synoptics say nothing about blessing or cursing, and few commentators on James have recalled the saying of Jesus.[290]

εὐλογία καὶ κατάρα—both words are *hapax legomena* for James—is strongly biblical language, recalling Deut 11.26 (εὐλογίαν καὶ κατάραν = ברכה וקללה); 30.1 (ἡ εὐλογία καὶ κατάρα), 19 (τὴν εὐλογίαν καὶ τὴν κατάραν); cf. Josh 8.34 (LXX 9.2e: 'Joshua read all the words of the law, τὰς εὐλογίας καὶ τὰς κατάρας, according to all that was written in the book of the law'); also 4QMMT C 1-17 13;[291] Josephus, *Ant*. 4.307 (τὰς εὐλογίας καὶ τὰς κατάρας, in a retelling of Deuteronomy); Ps.-Justin, *Quaest et. resp*. 92 ed. Otto, 132 (εὐλογίας καὶ κατάρας, also a reference to Deuteronomy); T. Benj. 6.5 ('The good set of mind does not talk from both sides of its mouth: praises and curses [εὐλογίας καὶ κατάρας], abuse and honor').

Although other NT authors curse people,[292] James may represent a different viewpoint, one perhaps inspired by Job 31.29-30 and/or a saying of Jesus: to curse is to sin.[293]

οὐ χρή. Cf. Midr. Pss 12.3 (one 'cannot speak slander against his fellow without denying the existence of the Lord'); 52.6 (practicing 'mercy towards God' is at odds with 'slander and an evil tongue'). οὐ χρή, although occurring only here in the Greek Bible, is otherwise common enough.[294] BDF 358.2 says that the impersonal imperfect χρή[295] is 'not Hell[enistic]', and it is has been called 'strictly classical'.[296] In *koine*, δεῖ largely replaced it.

ἀδελφοί μου. See on 1.2 and cf. 3.1, 12. Here the address appropriately follows a reference to God as 'Father' and a characterization of human beings as created in the image of God.

ταῦτα οὕτως γίνεσθαι. The exact expression appears also in Philo, *Legat*. 315; Josephus, *Ant*. 12.242; Alexander of Aphrodisias, *Metaph*. 130. For the reader, the words become a moral imperative: one must, despite the seeming impossibility of the task, master the tongue.[297] In the end, and despite his pessimism, James agrees with Tanh. Buber Toledot 21: the tongue should be under a person's control; cf. Gen. Rab. 67.3.

---

[290] Deppe, *Sayings*, does not discuss the parallel.

[291] הבר[כה ו]הקללה—an allusion to the end of Deuteronomy; cf. 4QMMT C 18-24 1, 3; C 9-16 6-7.

[292] Gal 1.8-9; 1 Cor 16.22; 2 Pet 2.14.

[293] Cf. Lk 6.28; Did. 1.3; Pol. *Phil*. 2.2-3.

[294] Philo, *Somn*. 1.227; Josephus, *C. Ap*. 2.234; *Bell*. 1.215; 2.443; etc. Early Christian writers tend to use instead δεῖ or ὀφείλει.

[295] NT: 1×; cf. LXX Prov 25.27; Let. Aris. 231; 4 Macc 8.26 v.l.

[296] So A. Robertson, *Grammar*, 126.

[297] Against interpreting v. 10 as a fatalistic statement—nothing can be done—see Frankemölle, 519-20; Baker, *Speech-Ethics*, 132-33.

Verse 11. What is absurd or impossible in nature should be absurd or impossible among human beings. The choice of an image from the natural world well suits the creation motifs in the previous verses.

μήτι ἡ πηγὴ ἐκ τῆς αὐτῆς ὀπῆς βρύει τὸ γλυκὺ καὶ τὸ πικρόν; μήτι (only here in James) requires a negative answer. ἡ πηγή[298] means 'spring', 'fountain', or 'well';[299] cf. Philo, *Somn.* 2.281: 'the lips of that πικρᾶς πηγῆς, briny as the sea'. Against Wolmarans, πηγή does not stand for a teacher.[300] ἐκ τῆς αὐτῆς echoes the ἐκ τοῦ αὐτοῦ of v. 10, just as ὀπή, which means 'opening' or 'hole',[301] recalls the 'mouth' of that verse. Whether we are to think of a hole in the ground or a split in a rock face is unclear. βρύω means 'abound'[302] or, as here, 'pour forth'.[303] Its use with πηγή is otherwise attested.[304] Commentators naturally allegorize.[305]

τὸ γλυκὺ καὶ τὸ πικρόν[306]—ὕδωρ, added in some mss., is understood (cf. v. 12)—was a very common phrase,[307] probably too common for auditors to think in particular of Isa 5.20,[308] although a few exegetes cite that verse. Here the sense is 'fresh (water) and brackish (water)'.[309] Moo, 165, suggests that James preferred πικρός over ἁλυκός because Jewish literature used the former of bad speech.[310] One could equally urge that he avoided ἁλυκός because his tradition linked salt with good speech.[311]

Exegetes often find in v. 11 a hint of the Palestinian setting of our author. For Hort, 79, James was probably thinking of the hot salt springs

---

[298] Often for מעין in the LXX.
[299] As in Jn 4.6; Rev 8.10; 14.7; 16.4.
[300] Wolmarans, 'Tongue', 527.
[301] Cf. LXX Exod 33.22; Heb 11.38.
[302] Cf. Josephus, *Ant.* 13.66; Jos. Asen. 16.16. LXX: 0×. NT: 1×.
[303] Cf. Justin, *Dial.* 114.4.
[304] Sib. Or. 6.8; Ps.-Clem. Hom. 2.45.2 GCS 42 ed. Rehm, 54; Acts Thom. 37; Ps.-Callisthenes, *Hist. Alex. Magn.* rec. a 1.46a.
[305] Bengel, 500, suggests that the fountain represents the heart, the opening the mouth. Cf. Burchard, 150, appealing to Isa 58.11 ('you will be like a spring of water'); 4Q418 81 1 ('your lips he has opened, a spring to bless the holy ones'); Philo, *Det.* 40 ('mind is the fountain of words and speech is its outlet'); *Migr.* 71 ('"logos" in the understanding resembles a spring, and is called "reason", while utterance by mouth and tongue is like its outflow, and is called "speech"'). Burchard could also have cited 4Q511 63-64 3 1-2: 'you have placed on my lips a fountain of praise'. Dibelius, 203, protests that this sort of reading is 'superfluous'. He is strictly speaking correct, but the text invites it nonetheless.
[306] πικρός will recur in 3.14 and so prepares for that verse, which concerns 'bitter jealousy'.
[307] See Aristotle, *De an.* 422B; Hippocrates, *Carn.* 13.15; etc.
[308] 'Ah, you who call evil good and good evil, who put darkness for light and light for darkness, who put bitter for sweet and sweet for bitter!'
[309] Cf. Herodotus 7.35; LXX 15.23-25; Jer 23.15; Josephus, *Bell.* 3.506; 4.476; *Ant.* 3.38.
[310] Ps 64.3; Prov 5.4; Ecclus 29.25; etc.
[311] Cf. Col 4.6; Plutarch, *Mor.* 514E-F, 685A.

of Tiberias. Mayor, 124, suggests rather a reference to the bitter and fresh springs around the Dead Sea.[312] James, however, does not record a phenomenon but rather denies its existence. As Laws, 157, notes: 'James' argument would hardly be assisted by pointing to a situation where... opposites in fact co-exist'.[313] Much more instructive are the literary parallels: Isa 5.20 (see n. 308); T. Gad 5.1 ('Hatred is evil, since it continually consorts with lying, speaking against the truth; it says that the γλυκύ is πικρόν, teaches slander'); 4 Ezra 5.9 (in the latter days, salt waters will become sweet);[314] 4 Bar. 9.18 (the same expectation as 4 Ezra); Pliny the Elder, *N.H.* 2.103 (Dionysius the tyrant of Sicily 'encountered the portent that one day the sea-water in the harbor became fresh water'); Philostratus, *Apoll.* 4.8 ('nor can τὸ πικρόν be wholesomely blended γλυκεῖ'); Antigonus, *Mirab.* 133.1-3 (a report of a river that, ἐκ μιᾶς πηγῆς, produces a salty stream and a drinkable stream).

Bede, citing 1 Cor 5.6 ('a little leaven leavens the whole lump'), goes beyond James to stress that, if one mixes bitter water with sweet water, the result is bad water; likewise, bitter speech destroys the sweetness of blessing. The point is a natural one, and others make it.[315]

Verse 12. After the illustration from springs in v. 11, James speaks of figs and olives, grapes and figs and then reverts to the former illustration:

11	first question:	Does a spring pour forth from the same opening fresh water and brackish?
12a	second question:	Can a fig tree... yield olives?
13b	third question:	or a grapevine figs?
13c	concluding assertion:	No more can salt water yield fresh.

The composition has a ring structure: γλυκύ...συκῆ...σῦκα...γλυκύ.

μὴ δύναται, ἀδελφοί μου, συκῆ ἐλαίας ποιῆσαι ἢ ἄμπελος σῦκα; Cf. vv. 8 (οὐδεὶς...δύναται) and 11 (μήτι...καί); also the Semitism in Mt 3.8 = Lk 3.8: ποιήσατε καρπόν/ύς. For 'my brothers' (cf. vv. 1, 10) see on 1.2. συκῆ, ἐλαία, ἄμπελος, and σῦκον appear only here in James. The application to human nature is made the easier by the traditional figurative use of 'fruit' in ethico-religious speech (cf. also Jas 3.17-18),

---

[312] See further Knowling, xxiv; Bishop, *Apostles*, 187; Ross, 64.

[313] Cf. the application of Calvin, 292: 'God has so distinguished things that are opposites, that inanimate objects should persuade us to avoid confusions and ambiguities, of the sort that a double-dealing tongue reveals'.

[314] Cf. T. Gad 5.7; Rev 10.9-10. In the light of 4 Ezra, Knowling, 82, takes James to be illustrating his point by reference 'monstrosities in nature which could only occur in the last days...when everything was disordered and ripe for destruction'. So too Witherington, 498: 'the apocalyptic reversal scenario is in view'. This seems overdone.

[315] Bede *ad loc.* CCSL 121 ed. Hurst, 207; cf. e.g. Martin, 121; Blomberg-Kamell, 161.

including the Jesus tradition.³¹⁶ Nothing requires a Palestinian setting: figs, olives, and grapes were common throughout the Mediterranean. Reicke, 39-40, links v. 12 to v. 11 by observing that figs are sweet, olives sour.

Interpreters often cite the following parallels: Plutarch, *Mor.* 472F ('We do not expect the vine to bear figs, nor the olive grapes'); Seneca, *Ep.* 87.25 ('Good does not spring from evil any more than figs grow from olive trees'); *Ira* 2.10.6 ('Do you think a sane person would marvel because apples do not hang from the brambles of the woodland? Would he marvel because thorns and briars are not covered with some useful fruit?'); Epictetus, *Diatr.* 2.20.18 ('How can a vine be moved to act, not like a vine, but like an olive, or again an olive to act, not like an olive, but like a vine?'); Marcus Aurelius 10.8.6 ('It will greatly help you…to be as the fig tree doing the fig tree's work').³¹⁷ These texts enshrine a sort of proverbial illustration that 'must have been common over the whole Mediterranean area'.³¹⁸

3.12a also calls to mind words attributed to Jesus in Mt 7.16-18; 12.33-35 = Lk 6.43-45.³¹⁹ Does that logion inform James?³²⁰ The Synoptic mashal concerns grapes and thorns, figs and thistles.³²¹ In some respects, James is even closer to Plutarch, *Mor.* 472F, which concerns vines, figs, olives, and grapes; see above. Further, the Synoptic saying is about evil not producing good and good not producing evil whereas the illustration

---

³¹⁶ Mt 7.16-20; 12.33; Lk 13.6-9; Jn 15.2, 4, 5, 8, 16; also Ps 1.3; Prov 1.31; Isa 3.10; Hos 10.1; Ecclus 23.25; Rom 6.22; Josephus, *Ant.* 20.48; 2 Bar. 32.1; Apoc. Adam 6.1; b. *Qidd.* 40a; etc.

³¹⁷ Cf. 4.6.1; 8.15, 46; 12.16.2. For Frankemölle, 520-21, Ecclus 27.5-7 has influenced James: 'The test of a person is in his conversation. Its fruit discloses the cultivation of a tree; so a person's speech discloses the cultivation of his mind…'

³¹⁸ So Davids, 148, rightly denying a specifically Stoic provenance.

³¹⁹ Cf. also Gos. Thom. 45 ('Grapes are not harvested from thorns, nor are figs gathered from thistles, for they do not produce fruit… An evil man…says evil things'); Ep. Apost. 32 ('Do the fruitbearing trees give the same fruit? Do they not bring forth fruit according to their nature?'); Coptic Apoc. Pet. 76.4-8 ('They do not gather figs from thorns of from thorn trees, if they are wise, nor grapes from thorns').

³²⁰ So Kirk, 'Wisdom', 27; Moo, 165-66; McCartney, 193. Brosend, 92, cautiously says only 'may'; cf. Plumptre, 83; Adamson, 147-48 (James 'possibly' goes back to a tradition antecedent to what we find in Matthew and Luke); Martin, 121 ('possible'); Watson, 'Rhetoric', 63; Bottini, *Introduzione*, 117; Witherington, 498; S. Johnson, *Treasure*, 95-97. According to Bauckham, *Wisdom*, 91, 'James is not *quoting or alluding* to the saying of Jesus, but, in the manner of wisdom sage, he is *re-expressing* the insight he has learned from Jesus' teaching'. Deppe, *Sayings*, 99-102; Dibelius, 204-205; and C.-H. Hunzinger, 'συκῆ κτλ.', *TDNT* 7.755, deny dependence. Chaine, 89, wonders whether James and the Jesus tradition independently draw upon a popular figure of speech.

³²¹ Reese, 'Exegete', 83, suggests, without argument, that whereas James 'seems to allude to words attributed to Jesus in the Sermon on the Mount', he 'speaks rather of figs and grapes, perhaps because both are symbols of the community of Israel'.

THE SINS OF SPEECH (3.1-12)

in James concerns one good not producing another good. Still, the possibility that James owes something to the Jesus tradition cannot be excluded. (i) James elsewhere shows himself adept at rewriting sayings of Jesus with considerable freedom. (ii) Both Matthew and Luke apply their agricultural figures to speech (Mt 12.34; Lk 6.45). This is not true of any of the extra-biblical parallels. (iii) Some words are shared.[322] (iv) In both James and Matthew the material takes an interrogatory form.[323] (v) Although Jas 3.12a, unlike its Synoptic parallels, is not about evil coming from good or *vice versa*, James' next line (12b) does declare that evil cannot produce good. (vi) Commentators on Jas 3.11-12, all of whom have known Matthew and Luke, often recall the dominical saying.[324] Those in James' audience also familiar with that logion could equally have recalled it.

οὔτε ἁλυκὸν γλυκὺ ποιῆσαι ὕδωρ.[325] Cf. μή...ποιῆσαι in the previous clause. The aorist infinitive is awkward but explained by the parallelism. Readers naturally supply δύναται (from 12a) for the whole and πηγή (cf. v. 11) as the compliment of ἁλυκόν. As typical of our author, this conclusion looks forward, anticipating vv. 13-18, for the topic is no longer how contradictory products come from one source but rather how a bad source cannot produce good results.[326]

That this is a statement, not a question, reveals the emphasis—the bad tongue cannot produce good speech—as does the fact that the line fails to make the reciprocal point, that fresh water does not produce salt water. ἁλυκός (NT: 1×), which is used of the 'Salt Sea' (ים המלח) = Dead Sea in the LXX,[327] substitutes for the πικρός of v. 11 and means 'salty'.[328] We do not know whether James or his audience knew the legend that, among

---

[322] μήτι (Jas 3.11; Mt 7.16; both James and Matthew pose a rhetorical question that demands a negative answer), ἤ (Jas 3.12; Mt 7.16), στόμα (Jas 3.11; Mt 11.34; Lk 6.45), συκῆ (Jas 3.12; Mt 11.34; Lk 6.45).

[323] According to *CEQ*, 88, Q also had a question.

[324] See those named in n. 320.

[325] The variants are copious. 01 33f. 81 88 322 323 1739 2344 Cyr correct οὔτε (only here in James) to οὐδέ (cf. Rev 9.21); for this variation see BDF 445.1 ('Ja 3:12 is completely corrupt'); Ropes, 243. Many authorities add οὕτως (01 04C2 025 044 5 33 69 81 206 *et al.* **Byz** Cyr PsOec **L**:FV **K**:B **S**:PH^A **G Sl**:ChDMSi **Ä**), many following with οὐδεμία πηγή ἁλυκὸν καὶ γλυκὺ ποιῆσαι ὕδωρ (5 206[*f2] 218 398 400 614 **Byz** Ps Oec **Sl**:DMSi). 025 1505 1890 2138 2495 have: οὔτε μία πηγή ἁλυκὸν καὶ γλυκὺ ποιῆσαι ὕδωρ. This last makes 12b restate 12a. But the printed text reflects James' habit of anticipating his next point. For discussion see Metzger, *Commentary*, 682. Dibelius, 206-207, and Laws, 157-58, suppose the text corrupt, the former dubbing the whole clause a gloss. Klostermann, 'Texte', thinks the original was: οὕτως οὔτε.

[326] Burchard, 153, accordingly regards v. 12 as the start of a new section, vv. 12-18.

[327] Gen 14.3; Num 34.3, 12; Deut 3.17; Josh 15.2, 5. Gk. Pseudepigrapha (Denis): 0×. Philo: 1×. Josephus: 0×.

[328] Cf. Aristotle, *Hist. an.* 574A (τὸ ἁλυκὸν ὕδωρ); Theophrastus, *Hist. plant.* 4.3.5 ('the water in some places is γλυκὺ σφόδρα but in others quite close it is ἁλυκόν'); Strabo, *Geogr.* 4.1.7 ('in the middle stand ὕδατα and salt springs [ἁλυκίδες]').

the miracles God wrought at the Red Sea, was his turning of salt water into fresh.[329]

Ropes, 243, rightly comments regarding v. 12: 'No application of these illustrations is made', and 'the passage well illustrates' James' 'vividness and fertility of illustration, as well as his method of popular suggestiveness, rather than systematic development of thought'.[330]

---

[329] See Mek. on Exod 14.16 ('He brought forth sweet water [מתוקים] from the salt water [מלוחים]'); 15.8 ('there came out for them tubes with sweet water [מתוקין] from the midst of the salt water [מלוחים]'). A few have wondered whether James had in mind Exod 15.22-27, the story of waters of Marah, which Moses made sweet; so e.g. Chaine, 88; Cantinat, 183.

[330] Bede *ad loc.* CCSL 121 ed. Hurst, 207-208, turns 3.12 into an allegory: the olive represents the fig leaves of Adam and Eve and so the covering of making excuses; the olive stands for fruits of mercy; the grapevine is the warmth of love. The moral: just as the fig cannot produce olives, so those who make excuses for themselves cannot do works of mercy; and those who are inebriated with divine love blame only themselves.

XIII

WISDOM, HUMILITY, PEACE (3.13-18)[1]

(13) Who among you is wise and understanding? He must, by his good conduct, show that his deeds are done in the humility that comes from wisdom. (14) And if you have bitter envy and strife in your hearts, do not become boastful and false to the truth. (15) This is not the wisdom that comes down from above but is earth-bound, unspiritual, demonic. (16) For where there is envy and strife, there also will be turmoil and every vile deed. (17) But the wisdom from above is first pure, then peaceable, gentle, willing to yield, full of mercy and good fruits, not divisive, without deception. (18) And the fruit of righteousness is sown in peace by those who make peace.

History of Interpretation and Reception

The *Catenae* ed. Cramer, 24, introduces our section with these words: 'Concerning good conduct and being peaceable toward each other' (ἀμάχου πρὸς ἀλλήλους). This rightly emphasizes the communal dimension of vv. 13-18—their 'social-ethical engagement' (Frankemölle, 525)—and their call for humility and peace. It is fitting that most preachers and ecclesiastical exegetes have used the verses to exhort their audiences to good deeds and to discourage quarreling among Christians.[2] Manton, 318, was eloquent: the 'truly wise Christian' should be 'moderate' in 'his opinions; not urging his own beyond their weight, nor wresting

---

[1] Recent literature: Aymer, *Pure*; D. Beck, 'Composition', 171-82; A. Calmet, 'Sagesses'; Culpepper, 'Tongue'; Giroud, 'Epitre'; Hartin, *Q*, 97-113; Hoppe, *Hintergrund*, 44-71; Jobes, 'Minor Prophets'; Johnson, *Brother*, 182-201; Kirk, 'Wisdom'; Klein, *Werk*, 154-61; Konradt, *Existenz*, 250-60; Lockett, *Purity*, 126-30; MacGorman, 'Exposition'; Marconi, 'Sapienza'; Mbwilo, 'Wisdom'; Perkins, 'James 3:16–4:3'; M. Taylor, *Structure*, 54-55, 86-88; Trocmé, 'Églises'; Varner, 'Theme'; Wanke, 'Lehrer'.

[2] Edifying representatives are Pelagius, *Rom ad* 14.4 TS 9 ed. Souter, 105; Facundus of Hermiane, *Def. Tri. Cap.* 12.44 SC 499 ed. Clément and Vander Plaetse, 152; Gregory the Great, *Past. reg.* 3.22 SC 382 ed. Judic, Rommel, and Morel, 404; P.J. Spener, *The Spiritual Priesthood* 42, Philadelphia, 1917, 26-27; Gill, 793-95; Plummer, 605; Dale, 107-20; and Church, 377-81. Note also the repeated citation of Jas 3.13-18 in J. Edwards's essay, 'Peaceable and Faithful amid Division and Strife', in *Sermons and Discourses 1734–1738*, The Works of Jonathan Edwards 19, ed. M.X. Lesser, New Haven, 2001, 658-79. The verses understandably move Motyer, 133, to mourn that Christians are born into 'a divided, wretchedly denominational situation'.

those of his adversaries beyond their intention to odious consequences which they disclaim, a fault which hath much disturbed the peace of Christendom. Charity should consider not what followeth of itself upon any opinion, but what followeth in the conscience of those that hold it... A man may err in logic that doth not err in faith.'

As vv. 13-18 name vices as well as virtues, many have naturally thought not of themselves but of their opponents.[3] In this way, those vices have again and again become the stereotypical characteristics of one's real or imagined enemies—the Jews, the Greeks, Valentinians, Origenists, deniers of the Trinity, anti-Hesychists, Jesuits, Roman Catholics, and even Nietzsche.[4] Bonaventure offered the generality that the wisdom which is 'earthly, sensual, and devilish' is 'the wisdom of heretics'.[5]

Given such an attitude, one understands why our passage has often occasioned the insistence that Christians should not always be meek, peaceable, and gentle. Augustine, for example, held that James' words do not prohibit rebuking those who need rebuking.[6] Calvin, 295, made the same point: 'there is no intention here...of doing away with unruffled words of admonition'. Trapp, 700, observing that Athanasius was normally 'sweet' and 'gentle', added that he was yet 'an adamant in his wise and stout deportment toward those that were evil'. Wells, 21, paraphrased v. 14 thus: 'But if ye have bitter Envying and Strife in your hearts against the Orthodox Christians'—implying that one could rightly hold such bitter feelings against those not orthodox. These interpreters all relativized 3.13-18 by specifying its scope and so reproducing in their Christian contexts the thought of m. 'Abot 5.17: some controversies are 'for God's sake', others are not. To judge from 4.13–5.6, the author of our epistle would have concurred.

---

[3] Brosend, 103, observes: 'the inevitable human tendency is to accentuate the negative to an extent that the positive is lost'.

[4] Against Jews: Dionysius of Alexandria, *Catena Eccl ad* 12.4-5 CCSG 24 ed. Labate, 201. Against Greeks or Greek wisdom: Dionysius of Alexandria, *Catena Eccl ad* 8.16 CCSG 24 ed. Labate, 140; Peter Damian, *Ep.* 117.13 ed. Reindel, 322; Gregory Palamas, *Hesych.* 1.1.19 ed. Meyendorff, 55; also John of Damascus' polemic against natural reasoning in *F.O.* 84 PTS 12 ed. Kotter, 187. Against Valentinians: Epiphanius, *Pan.* 31.34 GCS 25 ed. Holl, 436. Against Origenists: Barsanuphius and John, *Resp.* 601 SC 451 ed. Neyt, Angelis-Noah, and Regnault, 812. Against deniers of the Trinity: Cyril of Alexandria, *Hom. Pasch.* 12.4.24-26 SC 434 ed. Burns, Boulnois, and Meunier, 62. Against anti-Hesychists: John VI Kantakouzenos, *Refut.* 1.7 CCSG 16 ed. Voordecker and Tinnefeld, 11; *Ep. Cant.* 4.4.1 ed. Voordecker and Tinnefeld, 202. Against Jesuits: Trapp, 700. Against Roman Catholics: Clarke, 817. (Clarke's vicious rant against 'the Romish Church', which follows his outrageous remark that 'the Jews were the most intolerant of all mankind', makes disturbing reading. He does, however, at least muster a modicum of criticism for his own kind—Christians 'who are in continual broils'.) Against Nietzsche: Robertson, 181.

[5] Bonaventure, *Lk* 4.15 Opera Omnia 10 ed. Peltier, 309.

[6] Augustine, *De dono persev.* 17.44 PL 45.1020. Cf. Songer, 126.

The 1549 Book of Common Prayer borrowed the language of Jas 3.15 (ἐπίγειος, ψυχική, δαιμονιώδης; Vulgate: *terrena, animalis, diabolica*) for its Litany, in the line: 'From fornicacion, and all other deadlye synne, and from al the deceytes of the worlde, the fleshe,[7] and the devil: Good lorde deliver us'. From there the triad, 'the world, the flesh, and the devil', entered popular English and American culture, becoming among other things the title of several novels and movies, as well as of a famous essay by the controversial English scientist, J.D. Bernal (1929). After becoming separated from James, the phrase has taken on a life of its own.

3.13-18 was important for the African-American abolitionist, Frederick Douglass.[8] More than once in his earlier speeches he characterized the religion of 'our blessed Saviour', in contradiction to the soul-destroying religion of slave-holders, as coming from above, as the wisdom that is pure, peaceable, gentle, easy to be entreated, full of mercy, without partiality, and without hypocrisy. Jas 3.13-18 thus became a statement of the essence of true religion. At a later time, however, Douglass stressed that this religion is 'first pure, *then* peaceable', which he took to mean that there can be no peace without purity, that the one must come before the other. In this way he defended the violence of John Brown and opposed the idea of peace at any cost.[9]

Exegesis

This carefully crafted unit, which prominently features parallelism,[10] sets up an antithetical series that reflects James' dualistic outlook. On the one side are those who understand. Their good conduct is manifest in their wisdom, which begets a host of virtues. On the other side are those driven by jealousy and strife. Their nether wisdom fosters boasting, falsehood, disorder, and vile practices. The structure is straightforward:[11]

---

[7] Cf. the translations of Jude 19's ψυχικοί in Tyndale (1534: 'fleshlie'), Cranmer (1539: 'fleshlye'), and Geneva (1557: 'fleshly'). Note also the German of Paret, 'Wort', 114: 'Fleisch, Welt und Teufel'.

[8] For what follows see Aymer, *Pure*, passim.

[9] For related thoughts see the discussions of Dale, 112; Nystrom, 212-20.

[10] Note the repeated linking καί: σοφὸς καὶ ἐπιστήμων // ζῆλον πικρὸν... καὶ ἐριθείαν // κατακαυχᾶσθε καὶ ψεύδεσθε // ζῆλος καὶ ἐριθεία // μεστὴ ἐλέους καὶ καρπῶν ἀγαθῶν.

[11] Cf. Hartin, *Q*, 98. Fabris, 248, offers another analysis:
1. Theme, vv. 13-14
    a. Positive invitation, v. 13
    b. Negative invitation, v. 14
2. Wisdom from above, vv. 15-17
    a. Negative portrayal, vv. 15-16
    b. Positive portrayal, v. 17
3. Conclusion, v. 18

Frankemölle, 525, discerns a ring structure: v. 13 corresponds to vv. 17-18, v. 14 corresponds to v. 16, and v. 15 is the center.

3.13   the proof of true wisdom: good conduct
3.14-16   the vices that accompany an absence of wisdom from above
3.17-18   the virtues that accompany the wisdom from above

The key theme is not really wisdom but peace: the former counts because it produces the latter.[12] Not only does εἰρήνη appear twice in the final clause as the climax and even the last word (v. 18), but εἰρηνικός occurs in the previous sentence. Moreover, the vices of jealousy and strife, both mentioned in vv. 14 and 16, are recipes for a lack of communal peace whereas the virtues of meekness, gentleness, reasonableness, and mercy, named in vv. 13 and 17, are the prerequisites for such peace.

Promoting peace by analyzing wisdom is a rhetorical strategy, constructed to persuade. Readers, it goes without saying, will want to be wise. James' argument is that, if they are to become such, they will have to be peacemakers. Wisdom without peace cannot be wisdom; those who do not make peace cannot be wise.

Modern scholars have read 3.13-18 against various historical settings. For Martin, 128, the passage represents an 'anti-Zealot reaction' to Judean politics in the 60s. Many have instead insisted that James was countering other Christian teachers.[13] According to Kugelman, 41, vv. 13-18 address 'self-righteous teachers who are disrupting the peace of Christian communities by their distortion of the Pauline teaching on Christian liberty'.[14] Reicke, 42, wonders whether James had in view Christians influenced by the Stoics, the Cynics, or some other school of Hellenistic philosophy; cf. Schrage, 43. Wilckens divines behind v. 15 a 'Gnostic wisdom teaching'.[15] Hoppe, 62-66, suggests parallels between James' opponents and some of Paul's opponents in Corinth.[16] For Mussner, 169, 173, unrest raised by Judaizers may be in the background.[17] Dibelius, 208-209, however, urged that James' *paraenesis* is uninterested in 'some

---

[12] Cf. Plummer, 213; Klein, *Werk*, 155; Tsuji, *Glaube*, 81. Manton, 299, succinctly characterizes 3.13-18 without even mentioning wisdom: 'an exhortation to meekness, as opposed to envy and strife'.

[13] So e.g. Wanke, 'Lehrer'. On this view, vv. 13-18 continue the topic introduced in v. 1.

[14] Similarly Schnider, 90: the opponents are the same as those addressed in 2.14-26. Cf. G. Sellin, 'Die Häretiker des Judasbriefes', *ZNW* 77 (1986), 218 n. 40.

[15] U. Wilckens, 'σοφία κτλ.', *TDNT* 7.525. He claims: 'The adversaries speak of a heavenly wisdom which comes down from above, which contrasts with everything earthly, psychic, and devilish, and which is thus heavenly, spiritual and divine by nature'. Cf. Hauck, 24; Vouga, 105; Koester, *History*, 163 ('a criticism of Gnostic circles'); and long before them Baumgarten, 154; Priestly, 511. For an extended presentation of this thesis, now out of favor, see Schammberger, *Kampf*, 33-37 (claiming that 'the clearest trace of Gnosticism' in James is found in 3.15). Criticism in Frankemölle, 540-41.

[16] Cf. Klein, *Werk*, 160-61. See esp. 1 Cor 1-3.

[17] So earlier Wells, 22; Plumptre, 84-85. Cf. Acts 15; Galatians.

actually existing historical situation' because its concern is for what is *'generally* valid'.[18]

Given the theory of James' *Sitz im Leben* adopted herein, 3.13-18 was composed in part or chiefly to promote irenic relations between Christian and non-Christian Jews in a synagogal setting.[19] Our author wished to associate traditional vices with those guilty of religious intolerance, traditional virtues with those tolerating religious diversity.

The implied author of 3.13-18 lines up well with the traditions about James in Acts 15, which present him as endorsing a compromise on an issue of great dissension. Similarly, Acts 21 has him working to diminish conflict between Paul and certain Christian Jews in Jerusalem. Acts, then, offers an image of James that harmonizes with the spirit of Jas 3—a sign perhaps that similar traditions about James of Jerusalem lie behind both books.

The virtues that 3.13-18 commends are largely conventional, as is their appearance together. One can see this by comparing 3.13-18 with 1QS 4.2-8, which reflects a moral dualism akin to that of James.[20] The latter commends righteousness (4.2: צדק; cf. Jas 3.18: δικαιοσύνης), meekness (4.3: ענוה; cf. Jas 3.13: πραΰτητι), understanding (4.3: בינה; cf. Jas 3.13: ἐπιστήμων), wisdom (4.3: הכמת; cf. Jas 3.13: σοφός, σοφίας; 3.15: σοφία), mercy (4.5: חסדים; cf. Jas 3.17: ἐλέους), truth (4.5: אמת; cf. Jas 3.14: μή...ψεύδεσθε), purity (4.5: טהרת; cf. Jas 3.17: ἀγνή), and peace (4.7: שלום; cf. Jas 3.17: εἰρηνική; 3.18: εἰρήνη, εἰρήνην). 1QS 4.2-8 also pays attention to the heart (לבב; cf. Jas 3.4: καρδία) and it is followed by a recapitulation of evil that denounces falsehood (4.9: כחש, שקר, עולה; cf. Jas 3.14: ψεύδεσθε), pride and haughtiness (4.9: רום לבב, גוה; cf. Jas 3.14: κατακαυχᾶσθε), and 'appalling acts' (4.10: זדון מעשי; cf. Jas 3.16: πᾶν φαῦλον πρᾶγμα). See further on 3.17.

3.13-18, which addresses sins at the root of communal conflict, pulls together a number of themes and motifs already introduced:[21]

---

[18] Cf. Dibelius, 213, and, from a different point of view, the skepticism of Fabris, 150.

[19] Against Davids, 149, there is insufficient cause to imagine that 3.13-18 'was originally independent, an exhortation to peace circulating in the James tradition'.

[20] D. Beck, 'Composition', discusses at length the following and additional parallels between James and 1QS, but his theory of a direct literary relationship falls short of demonstration.

[21] Cf. C.F.G. Heinrici, *Der litterarische Charakter der neutestamentliche Schriften*, Leipzig, 1908, 75 (the 'cohesive idea' of James is the inculcation of the wisdom from above as outlined in 3.13-18); Hartin, *Q*, 97-98 (3.13-18 belongs to 'the very heart and centre of the body of the epistle'); Frankemölle, 523 (the paragraph is formally the center of James, indeed a summary of the whole); M. Taylor, *Structure*, 116 ('3.13-18 gathers key concepts raised in 2.1-3.12 and anticipates the next major movement of the discourse'); Varner, 'Theme' (3.13-18 is 'a summary of the entire discourse'; cf. idem, *Perspective*, 28-38). Contrast Dibelius, 207: there is 'no connection' between 3.13-18 and 3.1-12.

- The opening question, τίς σοφός;, reminds the reader of 1.5: 'If any of you lacks σοφία...'
- The call for τὰ ἔργα (v. 13) takes up a theme prominent throughout 1.22–2.26.
- ἐν πραΰτητι (v. 13) highlights a virtue that 1.21 (with ἐν πραΰτητι; cf. 1.9: ταπεινός) has already stressed; cf. also v. 17: ἐπιεικής.
- 'If you have bitter envy and strife in your hearts' (v. 14; cf. v. 16) calls to mind the social strife already met in 2.1-7 and 3.5-12.[22]
- μὴ κατακαυχᾶσθε counters an action that 3.5 declares to be characteristic of the tongue (μεγάλα αὐχεῖ).
- The wisdom that comes from above (v. 15: ἄνωθεν κατερχομένην; cf. v. 17) must be one of the 'good gifts' of 1.17, which come down from above: ἄνωθέν ἐστιν καταβαῖνον.
- ἀκαταστασία (v. 16) harks back to the 'unstable' (ἀκατάστατος) character of 1.8 and to the 'restless' (ἀκατάστατον) tongue of 3.8.
- ἁγνή links up with 1.27, which defines religion that is 'pure' and 'undefiled', καθαρὰ καὶ ἀμίαντος.
- μεστὴ ἐλέους matches the emphasis upon mercy (ἔλεος) in 2.13.
- καρπῶν ἀγαθῶν (v. 17; cf. v. 18) follows nicely upon the simile employing figs and grapevines in 3.12.
- ἀνυπόκριτος (v. 17) names a virtue whose corresponding vice—hypocrisy—both 1.22-25 and 2.14-16 have vividly denounced.[23]
- δικαιοσύνη (v. 18) is a pivotal word in 1.20 and 2.23; cf. the δικαιόω of 2.21, 24, 25.
- 3.13-18, in its entirety, surely disallows cursing others, the chief sin of the previous section; see 3.9-10.[24]

Johnson, 268-69, and Hartin, 203-15, regard 3.13-18 as of a piece with 4.1-10: the single unit treats the *topos* of envy.[25] Hartin suggests this outline: 3.13 (theme); 3.14 (reason); 3.15-18 (proof); 4.1-6 (embellishment); 4.7-10 (conclusion). This is an intriguing proposal, and if this commentator goes another direction, it is only with hesitation.[26] Nonetheless (i) the key words σοφός, σοφία, εἰρήνη, and εἰρηνικός (vv. 13, 15, 17, 18) are absent from 4.1-10; (ii) 3.13-18 exhibits links not only with what follows but also, as we have just seen, with preceding sections;

---

[22] According to Martin, 131, 'it takes little imagination to see that the problem discussed [in 3.13-18] reflects the scene in 2:1-7'. Cf. Bassett, 56.

[23] Cf. Plummer, 601: 'this paragraph is...a continuation of the uncompromising attack upon sham religion which is the main theme throughout a large portion of the Epistle'.

[24] Cf. Poole, 891 ('The apostle having shown the disease of the tongue, comes now to remove the cause, viz. men's opinion of their own wisdom; (they censure others, because they take themselves to be wiser than others;) and to point out the remedy, godly meekness, which is the truest wisdom'); Henry *ad loc*. ('As the sins before condemned arise from an affectation of being thought more wise than others, and being endued with more knowledge than they, so the apostle in these verses shows the difference between men's pretending to be wise and their being really so').

[25] So too Batten, *Friendship*, 145-49. Cf. earlier Doddridge, 844.

[26] In addition to what follows see the critical observations of M. Taylor, *Structure*, 54-55, 86-88.

WISDOM, HUMILITY, PEACE (3.13-18)

(iii) there is no grammatical tie between 3.18 and 4.1; (iv) one may doubt that 'envy' is the dominant theme in 3.13-18;[27] (v) v. 18 communicates a sense of closure.[28]

3.13-18, which does not appear to draw upon the Jesus tradition (although see on v. 18), begins and ends with likely allusions to Scripture—v. 13 to Hos 14.9, v. 18 to Isa 32.15-20—and it is possible that v. 13 rewrites Ecclus 3.17. On the whole, however, the passage is primarily a pastiche of conventional Jewish and Christians vices, virtues, and expressions.

Verse 13. The line seems to have a ring structure:

σοφός
    ἐν ὑμῶν
    ἐν πραΰτητι
σοφίας

τίς σοφὸς καὶ ἐπιστήμων ἐν ὑμῶν; Cf. LXX Ps 106.43 (τίς σοφός;); Jer 9.11; Hos 14.9 (see below); Ecclus 6.34 (καὶ τίς σοφός;); Mt 24.45 (τίς ἄρα ἐστὶν ὁ πιστὸς δοῦλος καὶ φρόνιμος;); m. 'Abot 4.1 (איזהו חכם). σοφός (Jas: 1×) + ἐπιστήμων (NT: 1×)—the two are here practically synonymous[29]—is a variant of a traditional combination that goes back to the Hebrew חכם + בין or ידע.[30]

Against many, little save proximity suggests equating the wise individual of 3.17 primarily or exclusively with the teacher of 3.1.[31] A σοφός

---

[27] Cf. Frankemölle, 523.
[28] Cf. Hoppe, *Hintergrund*, 44; Klein, *Werk*, 154.
[29] Cf. Alford, 309 ('It is not easy to mark the difference, if any is intended'); Easton, 50 ('rhetorical pleonasm'); and note Plato, *Theaet*. 145E: 'Are not knowledge (ἐπιστήμη) and wisdom (σοφία) the same thing?' Contrast Blomberg-Kamell, 171, following Kistemaker: ἐπιστήμων is more practical and connotes experience. That such a distinction is irrelevant for James appears to follow from this, that he goes on to speak only of σοφία, not of σοφία and ἐπιστήμη.
[30] As in Deut 1.13, 15; 4.6 (Frankemölle, 529-30, thinks James may be influenced by this text; but he is inclined to see more influence from Ecclus 10.25 ['Free persons will be at the service of a wise (σοφῷ) servant, and a man of understanding (ἐπιστήμων) will not grumble'] and 21.15-16 ['A wise (σοφόν) word, if one who understands (ἐπιστήμων) hears it...']); Prov 16.21; Isa 29.14; Hos 14.10; 1QS 4.3; 1QSa 1.28; CD 6.2-3; 2 Bar. 45.6; Sifre 13 on Deut 1.13 and 304 on Deut 31.14; etc. Greek parallels include LXX Deut 4.6 (σοφὸς καὶ ἐπιστήμων; cf. 1.13, 15); Dan 2.21 (σοφοῖς σοφίαν καὶ σύνεσιν τοῖς ἐν ἐπιστήμῃ); Philo, *Migr*. 58 (ὁ σοφὸς καὶ ἐπιστήμων); Mt 11.25 = Lk 10.21 (σοφῶν καὶ συνετῶν; for Knowles, 84, James may 'echo...the phrase used by our Lord'); 1 Cor 1.19 (quoting LXX Isa 29.14: σοφίαν τῶν σοφῶν καὶ τὴν σύνεσιν τῶν συνετῶν); Josephus, *Ant*. 11.57 (σοφῷ...συνετῷ); Barn. 6.10 (σοφὸς καὶ ἐπιστήμων). In view of the Jewish texts and against Hoppe, *Hintergrund*, 45-46, a specifically Stoic background is scarcely obvious.
[31] One need not, however, dispute the point, often made, that 'teacher' and 'wise one' in certain contexts are near synonyms; see U. Wilckens, 'σοφία κτλ.', *TDNT* 7.505-506.

need not be a teacher: the word can designate any wise person; cf. Rom 1.14. As with 3.1-12, then, the audience of 3.13-18 is not narrowly defined. In line with this, 3.13 appears to draw upon Hos 14.9 and perhaps Deut 4.6 (see below), and neither text equates the wise and understanding with teachers. Moreover, as Laws, 158-59, writes: 'According to i. 5, it is open to anyone to ask for wisdom, and so here the opening question of v. 13 is addressed to the readers in general, to whoever, including no doubt the would-be teachers, might think himself wise and understanding'.[32]

τίς...ἐν ὑμῶν[33] does not appear to have been a Greek convention, although Epictetus does open a few sentences with τίς ὑμῶν.[34] James' Greek seems to be a Semitism, the equivalent of מי בכם.[35] It or its Aramaic equivalent appears to have been a favorite of Jesus; at least the tradition attributes a Greek counterpart to him often: Mt 6.27 = Lk 12.25 (τίς ἐξ ὑμῶν); Mt 7.9 = Lk 11.11 (τίς/τίνα ἐξ ὑμῶν); Mt 12.11 = Lk 14.5 (τίς ἐξ ὑμῶν/τίνος ὑμῶν); Lk 11.5 (τίς ἐξ ὑμῶν); 14.5 (τίνος ὑμῶν), 28 (τίς ἐξ ὑμῶν); 15.4 (τίς ἐξ ὑμῶν); 17.7 (τίς ἐξ ὑμῶν); Jn 8.46 (τίς ἐξ ὑμῶν).[36] Given James' familiarity with words attributed to Jesus, including Mt 7.9 = Lk 11.11 (see on 1.5), one suspects that the form of Jas 3.13 reflects the influence of the Jesus tradition.

As 3.13 directly follows the discourse on the tongue, one may infer that the wise and understanding are those who take 3.1-12 to heart. Such people will not curse (vv. 9-10) but make peace (vv. 17-18). They will not boast (vv. 5, 14) but abandon selfish ambition (vv. 14, 16). They will not succumb to restless evil (vv. 8, 16) but will pursue reason and righteousness (vv. 17-18).

---

[32] Cf. Manton, 299; Mitton, 134; Schnider, 89; Frankemölle, 528; Konradt, *Existenz*, 251; Moo, 168-69; Fabris, 251. But for 3.13-17 as addressing teachers or would-be teachers see Bede *ad loc*. CCSL 121, ed. Hurst, 208; *Chaîne Arménienne* 49 ed. Renoux, 112-14; Erasmus, *Paraphrase*, 158; Diodati, *ad loc.*; Grünzweig, 111-12; Hort, 80; Spitta, 105, 110; Ropes, 244; Smith, 190; von Soden, 178; Moffatt, 52; Cantinat, 185-86; Ross, 66; Adamson, 149; Davids, 149; Martin, 126-27, 136-37 (although 'church members at large are not totally out of the picture', 128); Scaer, 104; Kugelman, 41; Burdick, 190; R. Wall, 180-91. For Clarke, 817, the wise individual of v. 13 is the one who can bridle the tongue.

[33] Those who regard this as a rhetorical question will compare the rhetorical questions in 2.14; 4.1; 5.13.

[34] Epictetus, *Diatr*. 1.22.1; 1.27.15; 2.17.8. Note also 1 Clem. 54.1: τίς οὖν ἐν ὑμῖν γενναῖος...

[35] As in Isa 42.23 (LXX: τίς ἐν ὑμῖν); 50.10 (LXX: τίς ἐν ὑμῖν); Hag 2.3 (LXX: τίς ἐξ ὑμῶν); 4Q381 76-77 10; b. 'Abod. Zar. 2b; etc. See further Beyer, *Syntax*, 167. Contrast Ropes, 244, who suggests rather that James' short question is 'characteristic of the diatribe'.

[36] See H. Greeven, '"Wer unter euch...?"', *WD* 3 (1952), 86-101. As Mayor, 126, notes, ἐν ὑμῶν is 'almost equivalent' to ὑμῶν.

3.13 seems to echo the conclusion of LXX Hosea.[37] This includes a couplet in synonymous parallelism that recalls the style of wisdom literature: 'Who is wise (τίς σοφός) and will understand these things, or prudent and will comprehend them? For the ways of the Lord are upright, and the just (δίκαιοι) will walk in them, but the impious will be weak in them'.[38] Six observations on this possible intertextual link: (i) James might allude to Hosea again in 4.4. (ii) Hosea's last line was memorable. Philo quotes it twice, once speaking of his 'admiration' for it.[39] Theophilus of Antioch quotes it in full.[40] (iii) Philo considers Hos 14.9 alongside the end of Hos 14.8 (LXX: 'your καρπός has been found from me'), and Jas 3.13-18 ends with a reference to fruit (vv. 17-18: καρπῶν, καρπός). (iv) Theophilus cites Hosea's conclusion when discussing 'the wisdom of God' (τὴν σοφὶν τοῦ θεοῦ), 'righteousness' (δικαιοσύνης), 'good works' (ἀγαθοεργίας), and 'the truth' (τἀληθές)—all motifs prominent in Jas 3.13-18. (v) Hos 14.9 follows lines mentioning the olive tree (ἐλαία) and the vine (ἄμπελος, vv. 6-7). James 3.13 abuts an illustration that also refers to both (v. 12: ἐλαίας...ἄμπελος). Did the content of Jas 3.12 lead its author to think of Hos 14.9? (vi) Hosea's 'the ways of the Lord are upright, and the just will walk in them, but the impious will be weak in them' is Deuteronomic language,[41] and it may be that James used the precise phrase, σοφὸς καὶ ἐπιστήμων, because he was influenced by Deut 4.6 (see above) as well as Hosea.[42]

δειξάτω ἐκ τῆς καλῆς ἀναστροφῆς τὰ ἔργα αὐτοῦ ἐν πραΰτητι σοφίας. δειξάτω...σοφίας remains awkward because it tries to say two things at once[43]—right action is the proof of wisdom, humility is the proof of wisdom.

James is not chiefly interested in philosophical or even scriptural learning. His first concern is not Socratic erudition but Solomonic wisdom—practical wisdom.[44] Commentators are occasionally reminded of Mt 7.20 = Lk 6.44 ('each tree is known by its own fruit') and Mt 12.33

---

[37] See Jobes, 'Minor Prophets'. While the commentary tradition sometimes notes the formal parallel in passing (e.g. Mayor, 125; Knowling, 83; Burchard, 154), it does not develop it.

[38] Hos 14.9. The MT is different: 'Who is wise? Let him understand these things. Who is discerning? Let him know them. For the ways of the Lord are right, and the upright walk in them, but transgressors stumble in them.'

[39] Philo, *Mut.* 139; *Plant.* 137.

[40] Theophilus, *Autol.* 2.38 PTS 44 ed. Marcovich, 97.

[41] Cf. Deut 8.6; 10.12; 11.22; etc.

[42] Cf. Jobes, 'Minor Prophets', 138. Jobes observes that although τίς σοφός appears also in LXX Ps 106.43, 'there the context is a call to remember the Lord's gracious acts of deliverance. The context of Hosea's question better fits James's message.' Witherington, 498, suggests that James may instead intentionally echo Job 28.12; but the links are weak.

[43] Cf. Mayor, 126; Dibelius, 209.

[44] Cf. Schneider, 26: 'praktische Lebensweisheit'.

('The tree is known by its fruit').[45] Although there is no verbal overlap, there is a parallel in sentiment—which might be suggestive for those who find Mt 7.16-18; 12.33-35 = Lk 6.43-45 echoed in the previous verse, Jas 3.12a.

Although δειξάτω ἐκ—note the emphatic placement of the aorist imperative—is seemingly without parallel and may be James' coinage, the line offers a variant of the formulation in 2.18: δείξω ἐκ τῶν ἔργων μου; cf. also Jn 5.20 (δείξει...ἔργα); 10.32 (ἔργα καλὰ ἔδειξα); Heb 6.10 (ἔργου...ἐνεδείξασθε). By contrast, καλῆς ἀναστροφῆς takes up a traditional locution.[46] Moreover, on the theory, upheld herein, that James knew 1 Peter, literary dependence upon 1 Pet 2.12 is plausible: 'Conduct yourselves honorably (ἀναστροφήν...καλήν) among the Gentiles, so that, though they malign you as evildoers, they may see your honorable deeds (ἔργων) and glorify God when he comes to judge'.[47]

ἀναστροφή,[48] recurrent in 1 Peter[49] and used by Paul of his pre-Christian days,[50] appears only here in James. It means 'conduct' or 'way of life'.[51] Perhaps 'lifestyle' would be an appropriate contemporary translation; cf. the KJV's archaic 'conversation'. Its qualification by καλός[52] leaves the meaning vague, if positive; but the general is soon enough followed by the particular; see esp. v. 17.

ἔργον takes up a noun used in 1.4, 25 and throughout chap. 2. Here it is fitting as James is predominantly concerned with act rather than thought; cf. m. 'Abot 3.10: 'He whose works exceed his wisdom, his wisdom endures; but he whose wisdom exceeds his works, his wisdom does not endure' (cf. 4.18). Because drawing a line from 3.13 back to 2.18 is natural,[53] some have observed that, for James, wisdom is like faith insofar as it must be manifested in works.[54]

For σοφία in James see on 1.5, where its derivation from God and a firm connection with πίστις are affirmed. Some church fathers quoted our text without ἐν πραΰτητι σοφίας,[55] as though the phrase were of secondary importance. Far from being an afterthought, however, 'in humility' is close to James' main concern, which is getting along with

[45] E.g. Rendall, *Christianity*, 51 n. 2; A. Calmet, 'Sagesses', 25.
[46] Cf. 2 Macc 6.23 (καλλίστης ἀναστροφῆς); IPergamon 459.5 (καλῶς καὶ ἐνδόξως ἀναστραφῆναι); 496.5 (ἀναστρεφομένην καλῶς); Heb 13.18 (καλῶς...ἀναστρέφεσθαι).
[47] Cf. Nienhuis, *Paul*, 210, and see further the Introduction, 67-70.
[48] LXX: Tob 4.14; 2 Macc 5.8; 6.23.
[49] 1 Pet 1.15, 18; 2.12; 3.1, 2, 16.
[50] Gal 1.13; cf. Eph 4.22.
[51] Cf. Let. Aris. 130; Gal 1.13; Eph 4.22; Heb 13.7; and the apparent rewrite of Jas 3.13 in Hist. mon. Aeg. 11.1 ed. Festugière, 90: ἐπιδειξάτο ἕκαστος ἡμῶν τὴν ἑαυτοῦ πολιτείαν. See further G. Bertram, 'ἀναστρέφω', *TDNT* 7.715-17.
[52] See on 2.7; cf. 2 Macc 6.23.
[53] Cf. Gregory Palamas, *Hom. i–xx* 8.4; 18.14 ed. Chrestou and Zeses, 216, 536.
[54] Note e.g. Huther, 120; Hartin, *Q*, 100.
[55] E.g. Cyril of Alexandria, *Hom. Pasch.* PG 77.944A; Gregory Palamas, *Hom. i–xx* 8.4; 18.14 ed. Chrestou and Zeses, 216, 536.

others in the community; cf. 1QS 2.24: 'All will be in a community of truth, of proper meekness (עֲנָוָה), of compassionate love and upright purpose, towards each other, in a holy council, associates of an everlasting society'. The virtue of humility, prominent in Matthew,[56] should banish anger and haughtiness. For πραΰτης and ἐν πραΰτητι see on 1.21 and cf. Ecclus 3.17: ἐν πραΰτητι τὰ ἔργα σου διέξαγε.[57]

σοφίας is presumably a genitive of source ('the humility that comes from wisdom'),[58] not description ('the humility that is wise').[59] Ecclesiasticus 1.27 closely links wisdom and humility or meekness: 'For the fear of the Lord is wisdom (σοφία) and discipline, fidelity and humility (πραΰτης) are his delight', and it may be that James paid some heed to the recurrent emphasis Ben Sirach puts upon πραΰς and πραΰτης.[60] But the link between wisdom and humility was not confined to Ecclesiasticus; note Prov 11.2 ('wisdom is with the humble'); 1 En. 5.8-9 ('When wisdom is given to the chosen, they will all live, and will not again do wrong, either through forgetfulness or through pride. But those who possess wisdom will be humble'); Plato, Crito 120E (the Atlantians showed πραότητι μετὰ φρονήσεως); Appian, Bell. civ. 3.11.79 (ἐπὶ σοφίᾳ τε καὶ πραότητι). That James anywhere personifies wisdom is not evident; see on 1.5.

A few have mentioned Moses when commenting on 3.17.[61] One wonders whether any of James' original audience might have moved from ἐν πραΰτητι σοφίας to think of the lawgiver. Because of Num 12.3—Moses was 'very meek (LXX: πραΰς), more than all men that were on the face of the earth'—the lawgiver became, for Jews and Christians, the exemplar of meekness;[62] and his status as a wise man, a σοφός, was equally prominent: Eupolemus indeed said he was the first σοφός;[63] cf. b. Ned. 38a: Moses was חכם ועניו.

---

[56] 5.5; 11.29; 21.5. Kugelman, 41, wonders whether James is alluding to the saying in Mt 11.29. That seems quite unlikely, although commentators on Jas 3.13 are often reminded of it; so e.g. Lapide, 139; Mitton, 135; Martin, 129; McKnight, 302.

[57] For Aymer, Pure, 71, James is alluding to this text and its context. Cf. Spitta, 105; Knowling, 84; Frankemölle, 531.

[58] So Klein, Werk, 155, and most commentators.

[59] Against Grotius, 1085; Mussner, 170; Popkes, 246. Dibelius, 209, suggests that 'humility' modifies 'wisdom' and wonders about a 'Semiticizing' construction; cf. Lapide, 139.

[60] See 1.27; 3.17, 18; 4.8; 10.14, 28; 36.28; 45.4. Cf. Frankemölle, 532. Sirach likewise shows a fondness for the ταπειν- root: 2.17; 3.18; etc.

[61] E.g. Hort, 81; Knowles, 90; Davids, 150; Fabris, 252-53.

[62] Note e.g. Ecclus 45:4; Philo, Mos. 1.26; Mek. on Exod 20:21; Tanḥ. Buber Bereshit 1.1; Sifre 101 on Num 12.3; ARN 9, 23; Origen, Exod. hom. 11.6 SC 321 ed. Borret, 348; Jerome, Ep. 82.3 CSEL 55 ed. Hilberg, 110; Apophthegmata Patrum Syncletica 11 PG 65.425B.

[63] Eupolemus frag. 1 in Eusebius, P.E. 9.16.1 ed. Holladay, 112. Cf. Deut 34.9 ('Joshua son of Nun was full of the spirit of wisdom, because Moses had laid his hands on him'); Aristobulus frag. 2 apud Eusebius, P.E. 8.10.4 ed. Holladay, 136; Acts 7.22;

Verse 14. The antithesis of v. 13: instead of good works and meekness there is bitter jealousy, strife, vanity, and falsehood—a circumstance that Dale, 108, labels 'dreary and depressing'.

εἰ δὲ ζῆλον πικρὸν ἔχετε. ζῆλον πικρόν recalls 3.11 (πικρόν, of brackish water)[64] and anticipates v. 16 (ζῆλος; cf. also 4.2: ζηλοῦτε). The combination of the two words may have been conventional.[65] Here ζῆλος[66] means not 'zeal' for a cause[67] but rather, as πικρόν requires,[68] 'intense negative feelings over another's achievements or success' (BAGD, s.v., 2)—a meaning attested repeatedly in the Testaments of the Twelve Patriarchs.[69] The NT often uses ζῆλος when characterizing inter- and intra-community strife;[70] and 1QH 13.23 and 4Q258 2.5 employ קנאה when doing the same.[71] Also relevant for James is 1 Clem. 6.1-4, which attributes the persecution of saints to ζῆλος.

The apodosis—'do not be boastful and false to the truth'—should hold whether the protasis—'if you have bitter envy and strife in your hearts'— is realized or not.[72] The εἰ, however, is not purely hypothetical: the author assumes that his characterization suits some of his readers. At the same time, the conditional is rhetorically polite. Instead of accusing—that comes soon enough, in the next chapter—James at this point invites readers to reflect on themselves and others. He is embodying his own advice, trying to be as peaceable, gentle, and unifying as possible.[73]

Eusebius, *P.E.* 11.8 GCS 43 ed. Mras, 23. Closely related is the idea that Moses was a philosopher or even founded philosophy: Artapanus frag. 3 in Eusebius, *P.E.* 9.27.4 ed. Holladay, 208; Philo, *Mos.* 2.2; etc.

[64] Cf. Manton, 302, alluding to 3.1-12: 'Ye have bitter envying. He noteth the root of tongue-evils. We pretend zeal and justice, but the true cause is envy.'

[65] Cf. Anthologia Graeca 2.1.216: πικρῷ ζήλῳ.

[66] Jas: 3.14, 16. Often for קנאה in the LXX.

[67] Ropes, 245: 'the idea is of a fierce desire to promote one's own opinion to the exclusion of others... It is the virtue of the religious "zealot"...[that] becomes the vice of the fanatic.'

[68] So already Bede *ad loc.* CCSL 121, ed. Hurst, 208. Symeon the New Theologian, *Cat. 1–34* 5.776 SC 96 ed. Krivochéine and Paramelle, 444, takes the qualification to mean that only bitter jealousy is excluded: there can be a useful jealousy.

[69] Cf. T. Reub. 3.5; T. Sim. 2.7; 4.5; T. Jud. 13.3; T. Iss. 4.5; T. Dan 1.6. See further Johnson, *Brother*, 195-200. Frankemölle, 535, detects influence from Ecclus 40.5, where ζῆλος is part of the human condition.

[70] Acts 5.17; 7.9; 13.45; 17.5; 1 Cor 3.3; 2 Cor 12.20.

[71] Cf. from a later time Deut. Rab. 5.12: 'If the heavenly beings who are free from envy (קנאה) and hatred and rivalry are in need of peace, how much more are the lower beings, who are subject to hatred, rivalry, and envy (קנאה), in need of peace'.

[72] Knox, 'James', 16, remarks: 'he really means to say that if we have envy in our hearts, we shall fall into sins of boasting and lying; what he actually says is that even if we have envy in our hearts, we must not allow it to lead us into sins of speech'.

[73] Cf. Manton, 302: 'The apostle's modesty in reproving is observable. He doth not positively tax them, but speaketh by way of supposition. So also chap. i. 25 and ii. 15. In reproofs it is wiser to proceed by way of supposition than direct accusation.'

WISDOM, HUMILITY, PEACE (3.13-18)

καὶ ἐριθείαν ἐν τῇ καρδίᾳ ὑμῶν. ἐριθεία (cf. v. 16) may mean either 'strife' or 'selfish ambition' (BAGD, s.v.); cf. the rabbinic תחרות, as in y. Ber. 6b (3.2). Here the NRSV opts for the latter, although the former perhaps fits the context better.[74] The word, uncommon before the first century C.E.,[75] occurs on lists of vices along with ζῆλος in 2 Cor 12.20 and Gal 5.20;[76] but its appearance in Jas 3.14 may owe something to the traditional pairing of ζῆλος with ἔρις, whether the latter and ἐριθεία are etymologically related or not.[77] The word's import here, as several times in Paul, is that, like ζῆλος, it characterizes partisanship and a divided community.[78] Cf. Ign. Phil. 8.1-2, where the author declares his desire for unity, counters division and anger, and then pleads: 'Do nothing κατ' ἐρίθειαν'.

ἐν τῇ καρδίᾳ ὑμῶν,[79] with its singular καρδία and plural ὑμῶν, may be a Semitism.[80] In James' tradition, καρδία (5×) was the authentic self, the psyche at its deepest level, the seat of emotions,[81] will,[82] and the intellect and understanding,[83] as well as the internal sphere in which the divinity is encountered.[84] James' focus is on the heart's wayward nature: it can be deceived (1.26); it can be the source of communal strife (3.14); it can be impure and so in need of cleansing (4.8); and it can luxuriate in pleasure while others suffer (5.5).

---

[74] Spicq, 'ἐριθίζω κτλ.', *TLNT* 2.71, suggests: 'spirit of intrigue'. Dibelius takes the meaning to be: 'party spirit'. For discussion see Hort, 81-83; F. Büschel, 'ἐριθεία', *TDNT* 2.660-61. Although Büschel observes that 'an opprobrious epithet of this kind has no fixed meaning but is a complex term in everyday usage', he also affirms that 'base self-seeking' is the likely meaning in most early Christian texts, including Jas 3.14, 16.

[75] But note Aristotle, *Polit.* 1302B, 1303A. LXX: 0×. Gk. Pseudepigrapha (Denis): 0×. Philo: 0×. Josephus: 0×.

[76] Note also Phil 2.3; Ign. *Phil.* 8.2; 1 Ep. virg. 1.8 ed. Funk, 13 (another vice list).

[77] Cf. Rom 13.13 (ἔριδι καὶ ζήλῳ); 1 Cor 3.3 (ζῆλος καὶ ἔρις); Gal 5.20 (ἔρις ζῆλος); 1 Clem. 6.4 (ζῆλος καὶ ἔρις; cf. 3.2); 3 Bar. 8.5 (ἔρεις ζήλη); 13.4 (ἔρεις ζῆλος); Herodianus, *Marci* 3.2.7 (ζήλῳ καὶ ἔριδι); Sent. Syr. Men. 422 ('jealousy is the cause of strife').

[78] Cf. 2 Cor 12.20; Gal 5.20; and see further Hort, 81-83; Spicq, 'ἐριθίζω κτλ.', *TLNT* 2.71: 'The Greeks divinized Dispute or Emulation, who concludes that ἐριθ(ε)ία 'really means the vice of a leader of a party' and involves 'party rivalry'. Unlike James, some in the ancient world celebrated partisanship and rivalry; see Spicq, 'ἐριθίζω κτλ.', *TLNT* 2.71: 'The Greeks divinized Dispute or Emulation, which they considered the energizing spirit of the world and one of the primordial forces. They had a cult of rivalry.'

[79] Cf. LXX Isa 51.7; Lk 24.38.

[80] Cf. בלבבם as in Ps 4.5; Zech 7.10; 8.17; 11QTemple 54.13; y. Ber. 2d (1.1). 01 056 0142 2544 *et al.* L:V S:PH **A G**(f) **Sl**:Ch(f)D(f)M(f) prefer the plural ταῖς καρδίαις with ὑμῶν.

[81] Deut 28.47; Prov 27.11; Isa 35.4; Acts 14.17.

[82] Prov 6.18; Jer 3.17; 23.20; Dan 1.8.

[83] Gen 27.41; Judg 5.16; T. Gad 5.3; 1QH 4.21; Mk 2.6; 2 Bar. 20.3; m. Ber. 2.1; m. 'Abot 6.6.

[84] Pss 27.8; 51.10; 73.26; Rom 5.5; Eph 3.17.

μὴ κατακαυχᾶσθε. Cf. Epitome Sent. Syr. Men. 24-25: 'Lovely is wisdom when it is not puffed up'. For boasting see on 3.5. The association of vanity with supposed wisdom was undoubtedly common; cf. Wis 17.7; Plato, *Phileb.* 49A: 'Of all the virtues, is not wisdom (σοφίας) the one to which people in general lay claim, thereby filling themselves with strife (ἐρίδων) and false (ψευδοῦς) conceit of wisdom?' Aside from Rom 11.18, κατακαυχάομαι appears in the NT only in James, here and in 2.13.[85] Although the precise content of the boasting goes unexplained,[86] one guesses that it is the claim to be wise.[87] If so, what James views as a crime—dividing the community—others see as commendable, something of which to be proud.

If 3.9-10, as argued above, adverts to the Birkat Ha-Minim, then it may be significant that the latter condemns 'the kingdom of the arrogant' and characterizes God as the one who 'humbles the arrogant'. Perhaps James is turning the tables: speaking on behalf of those being abjured, he promotes humility (ἐν πραΰτητι) and suggests that it is those who curse others who are the arrogant ones (μὴ κατακαυχᾶσθε).

καὶ ψεύδεσθε κατὰ τῆς ἀληθείας. For ἀλήθεια see on 1.18. Here the precise connotation of the noun is unelaborated. Perhaps it is redundant: by definition, being false goes against the truth.[88] κατὰ τῆς ἀληθείας—which is presumably the object of ψεύδεσθε, not κατακαυχᾶσθε καὶ ψεύδεσθε[89]—is a common expression (cf. 2 Cor 13.8) of which Philo was particularly fond.[90] That it follows ψεύδομαι (Jas: 1×) is natural; cf. T. Gad 5.1 (τῷ ψεύδει λαλῶν κατὰ τῆς ἀληθείας); Philo, *Spec.* 1.28 (ψευδεῖς δόξας κατὰ τῆς ἀληθείας); *Aet.* 69 (ψευδολογίαν κατὰ τῆς ἀληθείας). In these texts, as in James, the expression seems, as just stated, to be strictly redundant. It does however add emphasis.[91]

---

[85] 1.9 and 4.16 use καυχάομαι. LXX: Jer 27.11, 38; Zech 10.12.

[86] Might μὴ κατακαυχᾶσθε καὶ ψεύδεσθε be an example of hendiadys—'do not glory in lying'? For this suggestion see J.E. Cellérier, *Biblical Hermeneutics*, New York, 1881, 91.

[87] Cf. v. 13; so Dibelius, 210; Martin, 131; *et al.*

[88] To avoid redundancy, exegetes sometimes explain that 'the truth' is the truth of the Christian gospel; cf. Plumptre, 85; von Soden, 178; Ropes, 246-47; Knowles, 86; Burchard, 158 (appealing to 1.18; 5.19); McKnight, 305. Contrast Mitton, 137.

[89] Contrast Dibelius, 210, and the reading of 01T 398: μὴ κατακαυχᾶσθε τῆς ἀληθείας καὶ ψεύδεσθε.

[90] *Aet.* 90; *Leg.* 3.36; *Post.* 52, 101; *Her.* 109; *Somn.* 1.107; 2.280. Later heresiologists—Athanasius, the Cappadocians, Epiphanius—also, for obvious reasons, were fond of the phrase; cf. the use of Jas 3.15-17 against Valentinians in Epiphanius, *Pan.* 31.34 GCS 25 ed. Holl, 436.

[91] Cf. Huther, 121; Mayor, 128. Grotius, 1085, appropriately cites Rom 9.1 as a parallel: ἀλήθειαν λέγω... οὐ ψεύδομαι. Manton, 302, appeals also to 1 Jn 1.6: ψευδόμεθα καὶ οὐ ποιοῦμεν τὴν ἀλήθειαν.

James does not specify what sort of falsehoods he has in mind, although one possibility is that they are what has led to cursing others.[92] In any case, their proponents are like those of 5.19, who have 'wandered from the truth'. This is the same as wandering from God, the source of truth.[93]

Verse 15. As in Ecclus 19.20-30, there is authentic wisdom and there is bogus wisdom.

οὐκ ἔστιν αὕτη ἡ σοφία ἄνωθεν κατερχομένη. For σοφία see on 1.5, where there is also no christological link.[94] Although κατέρχομαι appears only here in James, it recalls the καταβαίνω of 1.17, which likewise follows ἄνωθεν.[95] 'This (supposed) wisdom' must ironically refer back to v. 14, implying that those who, from James' point of view, are bitterly envious, full of strife, boastful, and opposed to the truth have a totally different self-perception: they wrongly imagine themselves to be wise.

ἄνωθεν (see on 1.17) is the equivalent of ἐξ οὐρανοῦ and means 'from God'; cf. the divine name, 'Most High', עליון = ὁ ὕψιστος, and note Origen, *John* frag. 46 GCS 10 ed. Preuschen, 521 (ἄνωθεν καὶ ἐκ πατρός ἔρχεται—this introduces a citation of Jas 3.15); Amphilochius of Iconium, *Seleuc.* 244-45 PTS 9 ed. Oberg, 36 (δίκαιον τὴν σοφίαν... ἄνωθεν οὖσαν ἐκ θεοῦ). Its association with σοφία, to convey that all true wisdom comes from God (see on 1.5), was conventional;[96] cf. the rabbinic חכמה של מעלה.[97] Augustine used the expression to combat those who

---

[92] See on 3.9-10. One could also relate ψεύδεσθε directly to μὴ κατακαυχᾶσθε: 'Do not become boastful and thereby become false to the truth'.

[93] Cf. 1.18. Richardson, 164-65, seems to be alone in finding in v. 14 an allusion to Gen 3 and the sin of Adam and Eve.

[94] And the commentaries generally refrain from forging one. Contrast the opening of 'O Word of God Incarnate' (lyrics by W.W. How, 1823–1897): this addresses that Word as 'O Wisdom from on high'.

[95] This verbal link between 3.15 and 1.17 presumably explains why Guigo de Ponte, *Traité sur la contemplation* 3.24 Analecta Cartusiana 72, ed. P. Dupont, Salzburg, 1985, 390, attributes words from Jas 3.16 to 'James (chapter) one'.

[96] Philo, *Fug.* 138 ('God drops from above [ἄνωθεν] the ethereal wisdom [σοφίαν]'), 166 (σοφίαν ἄνωθεν... ἀπ' οὐρανοῦ); *Mut.* 260 (σοφίαν ἣν ἄνωθεν ἐπιπέμπει); Horace, *Ep.* 1.3.27 (*caelestis sapientia*); Ps.-Callisthenes, *Hist. Alex. Magn.* rec. λ 59.12 (ὑπὸ τῆς ἄνωθεν σοφίας). But Aymer, *Pure*, 71, suggests an allusion to Prov 2.6 in particular, Knowles, 88, an allusion to Wis 7.25-30.

[97] As in Gen. Rab. 17.5; 44. 17; etc. Note also similar targumic expressions such as מימרא דלעיל = 'the memra from above' (Tg. Ps.-J. Lev 24.12) and דעתא דלעיל = 'the mind from above' (Tg. Ps.-J. Num 27.5). The natural antithesis, חכמה תתאה = 'nether wisdom', 'wisdom from below', seemingly does not appear until the Zohar and later literature. In view of κατερχομένη, perhaps relevant is the idea of Wisdom leaving heaven for earth; see Ecclus 24.1-17 and 1 En. 42 (the latter affirming that Wisdom, failing to find a home on earth, returned to heaven to dwell with the angels); contrast Dibelius, 213 n. 27. Windisch-Preisker, 25, cite Heliodorus 3.16: 'he...thought, as many wrongly do, that the wisdom of the Egyptians is always one and the same thing. But of our wisdom there is one kind that is common and—as I may term it—creeps on the ground, which is

maintain free will: wisdom is from God, of grace, not self-generated.[98] Closer to James perhaps is the thought that, since wisdom has its source outside the human being, humility (cf. vv. 13, 17) commends itself.

ἀλλὰ ἐπίγειος, ψυχική, δαιμονιώδης. Cf. Philo, *Leg*. 1.43: οὐράνιον σοφίαν...ἐπίγειον σοφίαν. James' strong triad elaborates attributes of individuals devoid of wisdom from above, or rather filled with what one might dub 'wisdom from below'. They are first of all ἐπίγειος,[99] that is, they live wholly 'upon the earth' (cf. 5.5), so that they do not allow the divine influence of heaven to enter their earthly lives; cf. T. Abr. RecLng. 4.9, where the word is paired with φθαρτῶν, 'corruptible'; T. Jud. 21.4, which speaks of 'the earthly kingdom'; Jn 3.12, which contrasts ἐπίγειος and ἐπουράνιος; Philo, *Opif*. 117, which refers to the ἐπίγεια that receive 'the principle of the number seven' from ἄνωθεν; and idem, *Leg*. 1.31-32, where Philo discusses 'heavenly man' and 'earthly man'.[100] In the idiom of 4.4, those lacking the wisdom from above are friends of the world. The spatial conception—God is above, the earth is below—is a moral conception: above is good, below is bad.[101]

Those who are 'earthly' are for that reason ψυχική, which is usually rendered 'unspiritual'; cf. 1 Cor 2.14: ψυχικὸς δὲ ἄνθρωπος οὐ δέχεται τὰ τοῦ πνεύματος τοῦ θεοῦ; Jude 19: ψυχικοί, πνεῦμα μὴ ἔχοντες.[102] Although ψυχικός[103] later became a technical term among Gnostics,[104] this

concerned with ghosts and occupied about dead bodies, using herbs and addicted to enchantments, neither tending itself nor bringing such as use it to any good end. It often is deceived by its own practices and its success is of a vile and terrible sort; that is to say it gives visions of such things as are not, as though they were, and beguileth men of such things as they looked for, a deviser of mischief and a minister of foul and unlawful pleasures. The other, my son, which is the true wisdom, from whence the counterfeit has degenerated, we priests and holy men do practice from our youth. It is conversant with heavenly things, liveth with the gods, and partakes of the higher nature, considering the moving of the stars and gaining a knowledge of the future therefrom, far removed from these earthly evils and directing all things to the honesty and commodity of men'.

[98] Augustine, *Nat. et. grat.* 16 (17) CSEL 60 ed. Urba and Zycha, 243-44. So too Henry *ad loc.*

[99] LXX: 0×. NT: 7×; Jas: 1×. Gk. Pseudepigrapha (Denis): 4×. Philo: 33×. Josephus: 2×.

[100] Most English translations, beginning with Wycliffe (1380), have had some variant of 'earth(l)y'. Perhaps 'secular' might be a fitting contemporary equivalent.

[101] Cf. Gregory Palamas, *Hesych*. 2.1.19 ed. Meyendorff, 265, who takes James to mean that there are two kinds of wisdom, one ἄνωθεν, one κάτωθεν; cf. Philo. Clarke, 1846, understandably takes ἐπίγειος to mean, 'having this life only in view'.

[102] Discussion of ψυχική has often led to discussion of 'the flesh'; see above, 563; cf. Sebastian Franck, *280 Paradoxes or Wondrous Sayings*, ET E.J. Furcha, Lewiston, 1986, 114-15, 275; W. Bates, *The Whole Works of the Rev. W. Bates*, vol. 3, London, 1815, 203. But the standard English translations have used other words: 'beestli' (Wycliffe), 'natural(l)' (Tyndale, Cranmer, NASB), 'sensual' (Rheims, KJV, NEB), 'unspiritual' (RSV, NIV, NRSV).

[103] LXX: 4 Macc 1.32. NT: 6×. Gk. Pseudepigrapha (Denis): 0×. Philo: 43×. Josephus: 1×. Popkes, 241, thinks influence from Philo here possible.

has little or nothing to do with James,[105] which is not here combating false teaching.[106] Our author uses the word—in seeming tension with 1.21 and 5.20, where the ψυχή is to be saved—in a way reminiscent of Paul; see 1 Cor 2.14 (the context refers to ἀνθρωπίνης σοφίας); 15.44, 46. One might even detect Pauline influence here, especially as 1 Cor 15.40-46 passes from talk of σώματα ἐπίγεια to talk of σῶμα ψυχικόν and as Jas 2 seemingly shows an awareness of Paul.[107] But James' use of ψυχική could equally derive from a Hellenistic Jewish anthropology that regarded the νοῦς or πνεῦμα as the heavenly, immortal part of the human being, the ψυχή as the inferior, irrational, earthly, mortal part of the soul.[108]

The third term James uses is by far the strongest: δαιμονιώδης. This is a *hapax legomenon* for the Greek Bible and otherwise quite rare—although, against Frankemölle, 539, James did not coin it.[109] The contrast with ἄνωθεν and the derivation from δαιμόνιον make the general meaning evident: those in view are on the side of evil. According to Laws, 161, δαιμονιώδης suggests 'similarity rather than origin: wisdom that is "like a demon's rather than "demon-inspired"'.[110] This seems largely to be a modern reading.[111] The dominant line in the history of interpretation has preferred to think in terms of origins: demons inspire false wisdom.[112] This harmonizes with what one finds elsewhere in Jewish and Christian

[104] See Irenaeus, *Haer.* 1.5.1; Hippolytus, *Haer.* 5.6.7 8 PTS 25 ed. Marcovich, 142; Gos. Truth 34.19; Treat. Res. 46.1; Tri. Trac. 106.10; Hyp. Arc. 67.17; etc.

[105] Cf. Dibelius, 211: even though the word may have a 'gnostic' background, the book does not. Athenagoras, *Leg.* 23.4 SC 379 ed. Pouderon, 156, where Thales is reported as saying that δαίμονας are beings possessed of ψυχικάς, is likewise irrelevant for understanding James.

[106] So rightly Laws, 162-63.

[107] See further B.A. Pearson, *The Pneumatikos-Psychikos Terminology in 1 Corinthians*, Missoula, MT, 1973, 13-14.

[108] So Pearson, *Terminology* (as in n. 107), who cites, among other texts, Plutarch, *Socr.* 591D-F; Philo, *Leg.* 1.24, 72, 123; Justin, *Dial.* 30.1. But for criticism see R.A. Horsley's review of Pearson in *HTR* 69 (1976), 270-73. According to G. Theissen, *Psychological Aspects of Pauline Theology*, Philadelphia, 1987, 364, 'the Pauline opposition of *pneumatikos* and *psychikos* was prepared by the devaluation of the *psyche* in the Roman-Hellenistic period, derives primarily from reflection on pneumatic-ecstatic experience in early Christianity, and was brought secondarily into contact with Gen. 2:7'. For further discussion see Dibelius, 210-11; F.H. Horn, *Das Angeld des Geistes*, Göttingen, 1992, 188-201.

[109] See Apollodorus frag. 67C; Sym. Ps 90.6; PMich 6.33; 7.11; 8.8, 13.

[110] Cf. Hort, 84; Cantinat, 190; McCartney, 201.

[111] Although note Bunyan, 411: 'to evil tending'.

[112] Cf. Bede *ad loc.* CCSL 121, ed. Hurst, 209 ('deluded by the evil spirit'); Erasmus, *Paraphrase*, 159; Manton, 306; Gill, 794; Guyse, 585; Wesley, 865 ('such as Satan breathes into the soul'); Huther, 122 (the words are to 'be taken not in a figurative, but in a literal sense'); Alford, 310 ('devilish' denotes both origin and character); Clarke, 817; Smith, 198-99; Spitta, 107; W. Foester, 'δαίμων κτλ.', *TDNT* 2.17; Adamson, 152-53; Davids, 153; Hoppe, *Hintergrund*, 66; Van Zyl, 'Dualism', 42-43 (James presupposes 'a dualism in the cosmos'); Hartin, 210; Burchard, 160. 1 Tim 4.1 has perhaps been influential here.

literature[113] as well as with Jas 2.19, where demons are active intelligences.[114] Moreover, ἐπίγειος, one of the other words in James' triad, seems to have commonly characterized evil spirits.[115]

Many modern interpreters see a crescendo at the end of v. 16: James is combating a wisdom that is not from heaven (ἐπίγειος), that is, merely human (ψυχική), that is, indeed, demonic (δαιμονιώδης).[116] Richardson, 165, characterizes the triad as 'a descending hierarchy of values'.

Herm. Mand. 9.11 declares that faith is ἄνωθεν whereas διψυχία (cf. Jas 1.8; 4.8) is an ἐπίγειον spirit from the διαβόλου. This strongly recalls James. Also related is Mand. 11.8. This enumerates the qualities of the individual who has the divine spirit, features a list of unqualified adjectives, speaks of that wisdom as ἄνωθεν, and emphasizes peace: 'πρῶτον, the one who has the divine spirit ἄνωθεν is gentle and quiet and humble...'[117]

Verse 16. Of the sins here listed, none is a specifically Gentile failing, such as idolatry or incest. Nor has James Christianized his list in any way. Once more the text harmonizes with the declared audience of 1.1: our epistle addresses Jews.

Comparison with early Christian lists of vices shows that James is closest to Gal 5.21-22, which denounces 'enmities, strife, jealousy, anger, quarrels, dissensions, factions, and envy'. Not only does this list include ζῆλος and ἐριθεία, but it functions chiefly to further communal concord, which is James' goal, too; cf. also 1 Tim 6.4-5.

ὅπου γὰρ ζῆλος καὶ ἐριθεία. This adopts v. 14, dropping πικρός and ἐν τῇ καρδίᾳ ὑμῶν as needless repetition: we have here abbreviation. 'Where...there' sayings appear occasionally in Jewish wisdom literature,[118] and ὅπου γάρ (cf. 1 Cor 3.3) + ἐκεῖ was a common Greek idiom.[119] Yet it may be significant that the 'where...there' form was associated especially with the speech of Jesus.[120]

---

[113] Recall e.g. 1 Kgs 22.19-23 (a 'lying spirit' sent from God speaks through the prophets); Mk 8.33 (Satan speaks through Peter).

[114] Cf. 4.7. Mussner, 172, appealing to Jn 8.44, links 'demonic' to καὶ ψεύδεσθε κατὰ τῆς ἀληθείας: falsehood is the way of demons. Cf. Baumgarten, 159; Manton, 306; Poole, 891. Fulgentius, Ep. 3.27 SC 487 ed. Bachelet, 188-90, cites Jas 3.15 in urging that, while demons may have faith (2.19), they are not humble. Cf. again Manton, 306; Poole, 891.

[115] Cf. Herm. Mand. 9.11; T. Sol. 16.3; 18.3; 22.22; PGM 4.225-26, 2697; 5.166-67.

[116] So Dibelius, 210; Laws, 163; Martin, 125; Burchard, 159; et al.

[117] On the problem of the relationship between James and Hermas see the Introduction, 20-24.

[118] MT Job 39.30; Eccl 1.7. But the LXX does not use ὅπου...ἐκεῖ for these. See further Beyer, Syntax, 193-96.

[119] Plutarch, Lys. 7.4; Epictetus, Diatr. 1.11.14; 2.5.8, 23; Ps.-Aelius Aristides, Ars. rhet. 1. Arg.1.2; Sextus Empiricus, Pyrrh. hyp. 3.71; etc.

[120] Mt 6.19-21 = Lk 12.33-34 (a saying James knew; see on 5.2); Mt 18.20; 24.28 = Lk 17.37; Mk 6.10; Jn 12.26; Gos. Thom. 18.

ἐκεῖ ἀκαταστασία καὶ πᾶν φαῦλον πρᾶγμα. This statement of the self-evident is nonspecific; cf. 1.21. πᾶν φαῦλον πρᾶγμα[121] could be just about anything a reader finds repulsive. Attempts to find a specific referent are vain.

ἀκαταστασία[122] harks back to the ἀκατάστατος in 3.8 and 1.8 and so 'points to persons who are "double-minded" and double-tongued'.[123] The word refers either to a 'tumult'[124] or to 'unrest, disorder'; cf. 2 Cor 12.20, which has: ἔρις, ζῆλος...ἐριθεῖαι...ἀκαταστασίαι.[125] In Tob 4.13, the word is linked to pride. In 1 Cor 14.33, it is the antithesis of peace. In Gk. LAE 24.4, it is the condition of untamed animals after the fall of Adam and Eve. In T. Job 35.4-6, the closely related ἀκατάστατος characterizes the unstable earth as opposed to the unchanging heaven. Cf. also the use of ταραχή in T. Dan 5.2: 'Each must speak truth to his neighbor, and you will not fall into pleasure and disorder (ταραχάς), but you will be in peace, having the God of peace'.

φαῦλος (Jas: 1×) is, in the LXX, confined to 3 Macc 3.22 and wisdom literature.[126] The meaning is probably 'base' or 'vile', that is, morally inferior or objectionable.[127] Linking it with πρᾶγμα (Jas: 1×) makes for stylistic variation (contrast τὰ ἔργα in v. 13) and gives James a traditional expression;[128] cf. also the qualification of ἔργον by φαῦλος in 1 Clem. 28.1 and the latter's use with πράσσω in Jn 3.20; 5.29; Rom 9.11. For Mussner, 172, καὶ πᾶν φαῦλον πρᾶγμα means something like 'and all the other bad things'.[129]

Verse 17. 3.13-18 ends not with condemnation but an appeal for righteous behavior. Without using the word, James asks for love.[130]

3.17, which stands over against v. 15, is an asyndetic list of virtues reminiscent especially of Wis 7.22-23, even though the latter's list of 21

---

[121] Cf. כול מעשי עולה in 1QH 10.3 and the common כל דבר רע, as in Deut 17.1; 23.9; y. Pe'ah 97a (1.1); etc.

[122] NT: 6×; Jas: 1×. LXX: 2×: Tob 4.13; Prov 26.28 ('an unguarded mouth works disorder'). Gk. Pseudepigrapha (Denis): 2×. Philo: 0×. Josephus: 0×.

[123] So Martin, 132.

[124] As in Gk. LAE 24.4; 2 Cor 6.5; 1 Clem. 3.2 (here in close connection with ζῆλος); 2 Clem. 11.4.

[125] In Lk 21.9, the word is paired with 'war' and signifies an insurrection.

[126] Job 6.3, 25; 9.23; Prov 5.2; 13.6; 16.21; 22.8, 9; Ecclus 20.16.

[127] Cf. Let. Aris. 142; Sib. Or. 3.362; Ps.-Phoc. 65; T. Sol. 8.9.

[128] In Plato, φαῦλον πρᾶγμα means 'trifle matter', as in *Euthyphr.* 2C; *Phaed.* 95E; *Symp.* 213C; *Resp.* 374E.

[129] He writes: the expression 'sounds very vague and generalized and really has only the sense of et cetera in a pejorative sense (contrast the positive in v. 17: μεστή...καρπῶν ἀγαθῶν)'.

[130] Some commentators have been put in mind of 1 Cor 13; e.g. Lapide, 141; T. Scott, 580; Plumptre, 87; Weidner, 61; Plummer, 607; Reicke, 42-43; Adamson, 154; Davids, 154; Mbwilo, 'Wisdom', 115.

characteristics does not share a single word with Jas 3.17.[131] The verse is presumably James' free composition for his immediate ends.[132] As Easton, 51, writes: James' list 'is not a commonplace, or general list, more or less imperfectly adapted to the context, but is made up of terms all strictly relevant to the theme'. Comparison with other such lists in early Christian literature[133] reveals its unconventional character:

ἁγνός:	cf. 2 Cor 6.6 (ἁγνότης); Phil 4.8; 1 Tim 4.12 (ἁγνεία)
εἰρηνικός, εἰρήνη:	cf. Gal 5.22; 2 Tim 2.22
ἐπιεικής:	------; but cf. πραΰτης in Gal 5.23; Col 3.12; 2 Tim 2.25
εὐπειθής:	------
ἔλεος:	------
ἀδιάκριτος:	------
ἀνυπόκριτος:	cf. 2 Cor 6.6

The words not in the other lists—ἐπιεικής, εὐπειθής, ἔλεος, and ἀδιάκριτος—reflect James' chief concern at this point: he is calling for virtues that promote toleration.[134]

As no Jew or Christian would oppose peace, mercy, or righteousness or celebrate communal division or urge hypocrisy, James can assume that readers will applaud his list. The issue is thus not the virtues themselves but how they should be lived out in the *Sitz im Leben* the author envisages.

---

[131] Cf. Klein, *Werk*, 158 n. 223: apart from the subject, 'wisdom', and the catalogue form, Wisdom and James have nothing in common.

[132] So too Burchard, 161. Contrast Wanke, 'Lehrer': James employed a traditional catalogue into which he inserted 'full of mercy and good fruits' and then related the whole to wisdom. Originally it was a list of the desired qualities of a teacher. Perkins, 122, also supposes that 'James may have drawn on a conventional list of virtues connected with wisdom'.

[133] 2 Cor 6.6-8; Gal 5.22-23; Eph 4.32; 5.9; Phil 4.8; Col 3.12-14; 1 Tim 4.12; 6.11; 2 Tim 2.22-25; 3.10; 1 Pet 3.8; 2 Pet 1.5-7. Literature: J.D. Charles, *Virtue Amidst Vice*, Sheffield, 1997, 99-127; B.S. Easton, 'New Testament Ethical Lists', *JBL* 51 (1932), 1-12; E. Kamlah, *Die Form der katalogischen Paränese im Neuen Testament*, Tübingen, 1964; N.J. McEleney, 'The Vice Lists of the Pastoral Epistles', *CBQ* 36 (1974), 203-19; A. Vögtle, *Die Tugend- und Lasterkataloge im Neuen Testament*, Münster, 1936; S. Wibbing, *Die Tugend- und Lasterkataloge im Neuen Testament und ihre Traditionsgeschichte unter besonderer Berücksichtigung der Qumran-Texte*, Berlin, 1959. Vögtle and Wibbing leave James altogether out of account. Non-Christian virtue lists include 1QS 4.2-8; Wis 8.7; m. 'Abot 6.1; 6.6. Such lists do not occur in the Hebrew Bible, and the later Jewish and Christian lists stand under Hellenistic influence. Ecclesiastical literature has frequently associated Jas 3.17 with Gal 5.22-23 in particular; note e.g. J. Edwards, 'True Grace', in *Sermons and Discourses 1743-1758*, Works of Jonathan Edwards 25, ed. W.H. Kimnach, New Haven, 2006, 624. Moo, 175, remarks: 'Verbal resemblances between the two lists is minimal; but humility, peaceableness, and upright behavior are the focus in both lists. In a general sense, what Paul claims that the Spirit produces, James claims true wisdom produces.'

[134] Against H. Preisker, 'ἐπιείκεια, ἐπιεικής', *TDNT* 2.590 n. 4, 'wisdom from above' is not 'a christological phrase', nor do 'the attributes mentioned' in v. 17 'all refer to Christ as depicted in the Gospels'.

This, however, is left up to the reader, a deliberate if risky rhetorical strategy. James apparently trusts readers to find the same application that he does.

ἡ δὲ ἄνωθεν σοφία πρῶτον μὲν ἁγνή ἐστιν. δέ carries a strong sense of contrast, something like 'but, on the other hand'. Only here does James have μέν; its appearance without a following δέ is found often in Luke–Acts, Paul, and elsewhere.[135] ἡ...σοφία comes from v. 15. That ἁγνός[136] is 'first' (πρῶτον; Jas: 1×)—here first in importance, not first in time—might make sense given James' use of purity language elsewhere.[137] One in any case presumes that ἁγνός is, for James, a general religious word,[138] and that it here functions as a sort of heading for what follows: those who are truly 'pure' or 'holy' will in fact be peaceable, gentle, and so on.[139] Cf. Ropes, 249: the following virtues all proceed from ἁγνός.[140] This harmonizes with the view of Lockett: ἁγνός means 'free from moral pollution' and 'entails total sincerity or devotion'.[141]

ἔπειτα. The adverb recurs in 4.14. Although πρῶτον...ἔπειτα is not a Septuagintal idiom, it appears elsewhere in the NT[142] and is otherwise common enough.[143]

εἰρηνική. This adjective[144] belongs to a chain of four words marked by strong alliteration and assonance: each word begins with ε and features ει (ἔπειτα, εἰρηνική, ἐπιεικής, εὐπειθής), three contain πει or πιε (ἔπειτα, ἐπιεικής, εὐπειθής), and two end in ης (ἐπιεικής, εὐπειθής). Such alliteration and assonance are typical of virtue and vice lists.[145] That

---

[135] See further Marty, 148.

[136] NT: 8×; Jas: 1×. LXX: 11×; for טהור in LXX Pss 11.6; 18.9; Prov 15.26. Gk. Pseudepigrapha (Denis): 22×. Philo: 8×. Josephus: 5×. There was no traditional association between this word and σοφία. Note however Wis 7.24: 'For σοφία moves more freely than any other movement; because of her καθαρότητα she pervades and penetrates all things'.

[137] Although with the καθαρ- root: 1.27; 4.8. Cf. also the link between wisdom and purity in Ps 51.6-7.

[138] Cf. LXX Prov 21.8; Let. Aris. 139, 292; 4 Macc 5.37; 18.23; Phil 4.8. For Dibelius, 213, '"pure"...sounds very general'.

[139] Cf. the contrast in Phil 1.17: 'others proclaim Christ out of selfish ambition (ἐριθείας), not sincerely (ἁγνῶς) but intending to increase my suffering in my imprisonment'. On the general links between purity and holiness see S.S. Miller, 'Stepped Pools, Stone Vessels, and other Identity Markers of "Complex Common Judaism"', *JSJ* 41 (2010), 214-43; J.C. Poirier, 'Purity beyond the Temple in the Second Temple Period', *JBL* 122 (2003), 247-65.

[140] Cf. Plummer, 207; Hoppe, *Hintergrund*, 88.

[141] Lockett, *Purity*, 128. Cf. LXX Prov 20.9; 1 Clem. 21.8; 48.5. Mayor, 130, writes: 'First, the inner characteristic, purity, then the outer, peaceableness, cf. the blessing in Matt. v. 8, 9'.

[142] 1 Cor 12.28; 1 Thess 4.16; Heb 7.2.

[143] Cf. Sib. Or. 3.197; Philo, *Opif*. 95; *Plant*. 35; Josephus, *Ant*. 4.183; etc.

[144] εἰρηνικός: NT: 2×; cf. Heb 12.11. LXX: 52×. Gk. Pseudepigrapha (Denis): 3×. Philo: 33×. Josephus: 18×. Cf. 1 Clem. 14.5.

[145] Note e.g. Mt 15.19 (-οι -οι -οι, -αι -αι -αι -αι -αι); Rom 1.29-31 (-ᾳ -ᾳ -ᾳ -ᾳ, φ- φ-, α- α- α- α- α-); 2 Tim 3.2-4 (φιλα- φιλα-, α- α- α- α- α-, α- α-, προ- προ-, φιλ- φιλ-).

James' arrangement did not go altogether unnoticed until recent times is strongly suggested by Theodore the Studite's introduction of words from Jas 3.17 with his own alliterative series: ἄκακοι, ἀκατάλαλοι, ἀόργητοι, ἀπόνηροι, ἄφθονοι.[146]

Witherington, 503, makes the interesting remark that while the three words that characterize supposed or false wisdom in v. 15—ἐπίγειος, ψυχική, δαιμονιώδης—'are very different in form and do not manifest the harmony of alliteration or assonance or rhythm or rhyme, which is only appropriate since James is arguing that this antiwisdom creates chaos and disorder and a lack of harmony', the words that characterize heavenly wisdom are just the opposite: they exhibit rhyme and rhythm. James has been 'wise enough to make the sound of the discourse comport with the content of the discourse'.

For 'peace' in virtue lists see 1QS 4.7; Gal 5.22; 2 Tim 2.22; m. 'Abot 6.6. Although Prov 3.11 says that the paths of wisdom are peace (cf. 1 Kgs 5.12; b. Ber. 64a), the latter is missing from the long list of wisdom's virtues in Wis 7.[147]

If, as just urged, πρῶτον μὲν ἀγνή ἐστιν is a general heading, then the subsequent list features an *inclusio*: εἰρηνική opens it, ἐν εἰρήνῃ...εἰρήνην ends it. Everything is designed to encourage irenic behavior. One recalls Mk 9.50 ('be at peace with one another') and Rom 12.18 ('If it is possible, so far as it depends on you, live peaceably with all').

ἐπιεικής. The word (Jas: 1×), derived from εἰκός (= 'reasonable'), is a near synonym of πραΰτης, which James has just used (v. 13) and so avoids here.[148] It means 'gentle'[149] or 'kind, considerate'.[150] Gill, 794, helpfully suggests that the virtue makes people 'moderate, and humane, so as that they bear, and forbear'. In 1 Tim 3.3 and Tit 3.2, ἐπιεικής is paired with ἄμαχος, 'not quarrelsome, peaceable'; and in Wisdom, the cognate ἐπιείκεια characterizes the humble, righteous individual who endures the torment of the godless (2.6-20). James has chosen the word in part to create alliteration and assonance; see above.

εὐπειθής. This word, which appears only one other time in the Greek Bible (4 Macc 12.6), must here mean not 'obedient', its chief and first meaning in the dictionaries,[151] but 'compliant'.[152]

---

[146] Theodore the Studite, *Parva Cat.* 53 ed. Auvray, 192. James' assonance is no more a sure sign of oral composition than is the assonance in Theodore's list.

[147] The attempt of Smith, 203, to relate ἀγνός to εἰρηνικός, ἐπιεικής to εὐπειθής, ἔλεος to καρπῶν ἀγαθῶν, and ἀδιάκριτος to ἀνυπόκριτος, to see in each case an inner quality followed by its outer aspect, while homiletically promising, does not persuade.

[148] LXX: 2×. NT: 5×. Gk. Pseudepigrapha (Denis): 5×. Philo: 27×. Josephus: 30×.

[149] As in LXX Ps 85.5; Jos. Asen. 11.10; Phil 4.5; 1 Clem. 21.7.

[150] As in LXX Ezra 8.12i; Pss. Sol. 12.5; Let. Aris. 188.

[151] Cf. Epictetus, *Diatr.* 3.12.13; 4.1.159; etc.

[152] As in Philo, *Virt.* 15; Marcus Aurelius 6.1.1. Gk. Pseudepigrapha (Denis): 0×. Philo: 5×. Josephus: 3×.

WISDOM, HUMILITY, PEACE (3.13-18)

μεστὴ ἐλέους. μεστός[153] + a virtue was a traditional way of speaking; cf. Add Esth 15.14 ('full of grace'); Rom 15.24 ('full of goodness'); also πλήρης + a virtue, as in Acts 6.5, 8; 9.36 (cf. 1 Esd 1.22). מלא + virtue is the corresponding Hebrew idiom, as in 1 Kgs 7.14 ('full of wisdom').[154] None of these texts, however, speak of being filled with ἔλεος, a word which is also not featured in early Christian virtue lists. It is, however, a central demand in Matthew's Gospel,[155] which in this particular follows the Hebrew Bible, where חסד is a fundamental divine and human virtue.[156] James has already emphasized its importance in 2.13.

καὶ καρπῶν ἀγαθῶν. If this—the antithesis of v. 16's πᾶν φαῦλον πρᾶγμα—is paired with μεστὴ ἐλέους, then James' list has a nice rhythm and balanced structure:

- triad with opening ε- and η as final vowel:
  εἰρηνική ἐπιεικής εὐπειθής
- first pair with two genitives:
  μεστὴ ἐλέους καὶ καρπῶν ἀγαθῶν
- second pair with opening α- and closing -κριτος:
  ἀδιάκριτος ἀνυπόκριτος

On 'fruit'[157] in ethico-religious speech see on 3.12. Its use in virtue lists may have been traditional.[158] 'Good fruit(s)' is an idiom known from Matthew and Luke, although there the adjective is καλός.[159] Was James influenced by Ecclus 6.19, where Wisdom offers ἀγαθοὺς καρπούς?[160]

If James has the singular, καρπός, in the next verse, here he has the plural, concerning which Robertson, 187, remarks: 'there is a variety and abundance'.

ἀδιάκριτος. Mayor, 132, with reference to 1.6, urges that ἀδιάκριτος[161] here means 'single-minded'.[162] But this does not suit the present

---

[153] NT: 9×; Jas: 2×; cf. 3.8. LXX: 4×. Gk. Pseudepigrapha (Denis): 3×. Philo: 61×. Josephus: 26×.
[154] Cf. Deut 34.9; Isa 1.21; Ecclus 24.26.
[155] Mt 9.13; 12.7; 23.23.
[156] Gen 43.14; Exod 33.19; Ps 25.6; Hos 6.6; etc. Cf. the later rabbinic, גמילות חסדים, as in m. 'Abot 1.2; t. Pe'ah 4.19; b. Sukk. 49a; etc. The rabbinic term lines up with James' social concern. Maimonides, *Commentary on the Mishnah ad* Pe'ah 1.1, argues that it includes 'interpersonal relationships', and according to P. Pelik, 'The Havurot That Were in Jerusalem', *HUCA* 55 (1984), 68, 'there are many examples in talmudic literature from which it seems that the term gemilut hasadim is especially associated with certain deeds which have the common characteristic of mutual responsibility, whose essence is embodied in the maxim "do, that it should be done to you"'.
[157] καρπός; cf. 3.18; 5.7, 18.
[158] Cf. Gal 5.22; Eph 5.9. See further Kamlah, *Paränese* (as in n. 133), 181-82.
[159] Mt 3.10; 7.17-19; Lk 3.9; 6.43. Cf. also 4Q370 1.1 (פרי טוב); Col 1.10 (ἔργῳ ἀγαθῷ καρποφοροῦντες); Plutarch, *Mor.* 913A (ἀγαθοὺς καρπούς).
[160] So Frankemölle, 555, citing also Ecclus 1.16.
[161] LXX: Prov 25.11. NT: 1×. Gk. Pseudepigrapha (Denis): 1×. Philo: 3×. Josephus: 2×.
[162] Cf. Alford, 310-11: 'without doubting'.

context, which rather suggests 'undivisive' or 'nonjudgmental'; cf. the Vulgate's *non iudicans* and the situation in vv. 9-10. The NRSV has 'without a trace of partiality', which probably gains support from Jas 2.4 (οὐ διεκρίθητε ἐν ἑαυτοῖς;) and Ign. *Magn.* 15 ('Farewell in godly harmony to you who possess an ἀδιάκριτον spirit').[163] Cf. also T. Zeb. 7.2: ἀδιακρίτως πάντας σπλαγχνιζόμενοι ἐλεᾶτε. Whereas in patristic texts the meaning can be 'undiscriminating' in a bad sense,[164] in James, 'undiscriminating' holds a positive sense and seems to refer to non-discrimination against others—something like the Hebrew idiom, 'not to lift up one's face', that is, not show partiality or favoritism.[165] 3.17, in other words, anticipates 4.12, 'Who are you to judge your neighbor?'[166]

ἀνυπόκριτος. Almost everywhere else in the NT this adjective,[167] which means 'without deception' (cf. 2 Clem. 12.3) or 'generous', 'sincere', 'respectful' (cf. Iamblichus, *Pyth.* 31[188]), qualifies 'love'.[168] Hypocrisy is the enemy of peace.

The list itself has no climax. Verse 18 rather supplies this.

Verse 18. This verse possesses, according to Dibelius, 208, 'an independent wholeness and inclusiveness in form' which implies that James borrowed it from his tradition. Deppe concurs, adding that, were James the author, he would have written 'fruit of wisdom', not 'fruit of righteousness'.[169] But (i) the compressed style is typical of James. (ii) As an isolated aphorism, 3.18 would be even more enigmatic than it is in its present context.[170] (iii) 'Fruit of righteousness' is not unusual given James' interest in the δικ- root;[171] and while one might have expected instead 'fruit of wisdom', the latter does not appear to have been a common or fixed expression[172] whereas 'fruit of righteousness' was; see below. Further, 'righteousness' was conventionally associated with

---

[163] This text is obscure; most likely the meaning is 'uncertain'. Cf. F. Büchsel, 'κρίνω', *TDNT* 3.950. This may also be the meaning of ἀδιάκριτος in Ign. *Eph.* 3.2, although that too is unclear.

[164] Lampe, s.v., Cb; cf. Philo, *Spec.* 3.57.

[165] Cf. 2.1 and Wesley, 865.

[166] It also harmonizes with Hegesippus *apud* Eusebius, *H.E.* 2.23.10, who has people confessing that James the brother of Jesus is no respecter of persons (πρόσωπον οὐ λαμβάνεις).

[167] LXX: Wis 5.18; 18.16. NT: 6×; Jas: 1×. Gk. Pseudepigrapha (Denis): 0×. Philo: 1×. Josephus: 0×.

[168] Rom 12.9; 2 Cor 6.6; 1 Tim 1.5; 1 Pet 1.22. In 1 Clem. 15.1-7, 'hypocrisy' and 'peace' are set over against each other.

[169] Deppe, *Sayings*, 103. Cf. Hartin, *Q*, 99. According to Perkins, 'James 3:16–4:3', 'Verse 18 appears to be based on a proverb which related wisdom, righteousness, and peace'. Baker-Ellsworth, 101, label it a 'curious proverb'.

[170] Clarke, *ad loc.*, labels it 'confessedly obscure'.

[171] 1.20; 2.21, 23-25; 5.6, 16.

[172] Note only Let. Aris. 269 (σοφίας καρπός) and Ecclus 1.16 (σοφίας...καρπῶν αὐτῆς).

'peace'[173] and contrasted with anger (see on 1.20). (iv) The concluding emphasis upon 'peace' is the perfect ending to vv. 13-18. Indeed, v. 18 'brings the whole unit to a natural and logical conclusion'.[174] (v) 3.18 is also an appropriate transition to 4.1.

καρπὸς δὲ δικαιοσύνης. A traditional phrase[175] that early Christians came to favor.[176] It should be classified as a Septuagintalism since it does not occur in secular Greek literature. Note that δικαιοσύνη (see on 1.20) occurs in the virtue lists in 2 Cor 6.7 and 2 Tim 2.22 (cf. also Wis 8.7; m. 'Abot 6.1), and it is 'sown' in LXX Prov 11.21 (cf. 11.18); Hos 10.12; and Tanḥ. Buber Lekh-Lekha 15. Here δικαιοσύνη can have nothing to do with Pauline 'justification'. The subject is human behavior and human relations.

Does 'fruit of righteousness' mean 'righteous deeds', that is, the fruit that consists in righteousness (genitive of definition)?[177] For Ropes, 250, the expression means rather 'product of righteousness',[178] that is, 'the reward which righteous conduct brings'. Laws, 165-66, however, suggests instead that 'fruit of righteousness' = wisdom. Her argument is intertextual. James was familiar with Proverbs (note esp. 4.6 = Prov 3.34); and if Prov 11.30 refers to the 'fruit of righteousness', Prov 3.18 says that wisdom is 'a tree of life'. Putting the two together, James is saying this: the peacemakers possess wisdom, which is the fruit of righteousness. But it would be just as natural, if the genitive is possessive, to understand καρπός to refer to the virtues just enumerated (cf. Gal 5.22; Eph 5.9): taken together, they are δικαιοσύνη in action. However one resolves the issue—δικαιοσύνης is probably epexegetical because that seems so in other texts with καρπὸς δικαιοσύνης—the thought is not of individual reward to eternal life. The place of sowing is the community, and it is there James hopes that peace will be reaped. The afterlife is, despite many commentators, here beside the point.

ἐν εἰρήνῃ σπείρεται. Does this allude to MT Zech 8.12, זרע השלום, 'seed of peace'? This last belongs to a passage that foretells a time when those who have been cursed will be blessed (cf. Jas 3.9-10). Although exegetes occasionally remark that one sows seed,[179] not fruit, the idiom is

---

[173] Ps 85.10; Isa 32.17; 48.18; 1 En. 92.1; 94.4; Rom 14.17; m. 'Abot 2.7.
[174] So Sleeper, 101. See further 564.
[175] See LXX Prov 3.9; 11.30; 13.2; Amos 6.12 (MT: פרי צדקה); Let. Aris. 232.
[176] Cf. Phil 1.11; Heb 12.11; Herm. Sim. 9.19.2; Prot. Jas. 6.2; Apoc. Sed. 12.5; Acts Paul 4 ed. Lipsius, 238. Epicurus frag. 519 apud Clement of Alexandria, Strom. 6.2.24.10 GCS 15 ed. Stählin, 441, provides a secular parallel: δικαιοσύνης καρπός. Rendall, Christianity, 51 n. 1, wonders whether Heb 12.11 was 'modelled' on James. According to Pfleiderer, Christianity, 295-96, and Zimmer, 'Verhältnis', 501-502, James here depends upon Hebrews.
[177] So most modern commentators; cf. Huther, 123; Hort, 87; Mayor, 133; Knowles, 91; Dibelius, 215; Chaine, 94; Cantinat, 193; Adamson, 156; Davids, 155.
[178] Cf. LXX Isa 32.17: τὰ ἔργα τῆς δικαιοσύνης; also Mt 3.8 = Lk 3.8; Eph 5.9.
[179] Cf. Prov 11.18: זרע צדקה = σπέρμα δικαίων.

attested elsewhere.[180] ἐν εἰρήνῃ goes with the verb (cf. 2.16), not with δικαιοσύνης.[181]

τοῖς ποιοῦσιν εἰρήνην. ποιέω + εἰρήνην was a common Greek idiom;[182] cf. also εἰρηνοποιέω as in LXX Prov 10.10; Col 1.20. In addition to the verb שלם, Hebrew has several equivalents—עשה, עבד, רדף, or בוא in the Hiphil + שלום.[183]

The NRSV translates: 'for those who make peace'.[184] The RSV has instead: 'by those who make peace'.[185] The dative of agency, even if it seems to render ἐν εἰρήνῃ redundant,[186] makes better sense in context: James is concerned with sowing peace in the community at large and its effect, not with the individual obtaining rewards in this life or the life to come.[187] Again and again, however, commentators, perhaps influenced by Mt 5.9 and Gal 6.8, have read eschatological blessing and even judgment into the text.[188] This has even allowed taking σπείρεται as a divine passive: 'the reward of righteousness is sown in peace (by God) for those who make peace'.[189]

The end of v. 18 has often reminded readers of Mt 5.9: 'Blessed are the εἰρηνοποιοί'.[190] The parallel intrigues because it exists beside additional similarities:

---

[180] E.g. Antiphanies frag. 228 4; Plutarch, *Mor.* 829B; Pausanias 1.14.2; 2 Bar. 32.1. Note also LXX Prov 11.30: 'from the fruit of righteousness grows the tree of life'.

[181] Against Hort, 87, and Hodges, 88.

[182] LXX Isa 27.5; 45.7; 1 Macc 6.49; 11.51; 2 Macc 1.4; Pss. Sol. 12.5; T. Jud. 7.7; 9.1; Eph 2.15; Demosthenes, *Or.* 19.133, 298; Dio Chrysostom 17.10; Dionysius of Halicarnassus, *Ant.* 9.17.3; etc.

[183] As in MT Isa 27.5; 45.7; Mek. on Exod 20,25; m. Pe'ah 1.1; m. 'Abot 1.12, t. B. Qam. 7.6; y. Ber. 12d (9.1); etc. Oesterley, 393-94, suggests that James' Greek is the equivalent of: בשלום יזרע לעשי השלום.

[184] Cf. Dibelius, 215; Laws.

[185] Cf. Ropes, 251; Marty, 152-53; Mitton, 144.

[186] Redundancy can add emphasis; cf. Davids, 155, and recall m. 'Abot 1.12: אוהב שלום ורודף שלום. But Deppe, *Sayings*, 104-105, argues to the contrary in this case.

[187] Wesley, 865, sees the verse as promising happiness, presumably in this life. Gill, 794-95, cannot decide whether the fruit of righteousness is enjoyed in this life or the life to come. Doddridge, 844-45, thinks both true.

[188] So Origen, *Hom. Gen* 10.3 SC 7bis ed. de Lubac, 266; Bede *ad loc.* CCSL 121, ed. Hurst, 208; Erasmus, *Paraphrase*, 159; Diodati *ad* 3.18; Manton, 323; Trapp, 700; Guyse, 585; Whitby, 592; Ropes, 251.

[189] So Hoppe, *Hintergrund*, 68; Martin, 126; Schnider, 94; Frankemölle, 559-60; Klein, *Werk*, 159. Contrast Popkes, 257.

[190] E.g. Pareus, 562; Manton, 322; Baumgarten, 165; Trapp, 700; Gill, 795; Brückner, *Reihenfolge*, 290 (James here depends upon Matthew); Plumptre, 87; von Soden, 179; Hort, 87; Knowles, 91-92; Schlatter, 239; Rendall, *Christianity*, 51 n. 2; Michl, 50; Mitton, 144; Knoch, 205; Rusche, 73; Laws, 164; Vouga, 108-109; Davids, 155; Hartin, *Q*, 112; Ruckstuhl, 25; Frankemölle, 560; Johnson, 275 ('Jesus' macarism had some influence on James' language'); Moo, 178; Brosend, 101 ('in the background may be... the seventh beatitude').

- 'Blessed are the meek' (v. 5, οἱ πραεῖς); cf. James' ἐπιεικής
- 'Blessed are the merciful' (v. 7, οἱ ἐλεήμονες); cf. James' ἐλέους
- 'hunger and thirst after righteousness' (v. 6, δικαιοσύνην), 'persecuted for righteousness' (v. 10, δικαιοσύνης); cf. James' καρπὸς δικαιοσύνης
- 'pure in heart' (v. 8, οἱ καθαροὶ τῇ καρδίᾳ); cf. James' ἁγνή

These resemblances, which are confined to special Matthean material, are very far from establishing that James had heard Matthew, especially given the differences in some of the vocabulary. But if, on other grounds, one finds evidence of such indebtedness, one could here contemplate the possibility of influence from the First Gospel.[191]

Of more credence is the suggestion that Jas 3.13-18 relates itself to LXX Isa 32.15-20. This oracle foresees God pouring out a spirit ἀφ' ὑψηλοῦ, the result being abounding fruit, δικαιοσύνη, and justice. Moreover, we here read of οἱ σπείροντες, and we are told that ἔσται τὰ ἔργα τῆς δικαιοσύνης εἰρήνη. More than a few commentators note the parallel.[192] But if, as it seems, there is an intertextual relationship, James has reversed Isaiah's point: instead of righteousness bringing peace, peace brings righteousness.[193]

James 3.13-18 is also strikingly similar to the beautiful paean to peace in Num. Rab. 11.7; cf. Sifre 42 on Num 6.26. That rabbinic text, which hyperbolically affirms that peace 'outweighs everything', (i) cites Isa 32.17 (cf. Jas 3.18); (ii) associates peace with humility (cf. Jas 3.13, 17); (iii) contrasts peace with quarrelsomeness (cf. Jas 3.14, 16); (iv) declares it to be the property of the righteous (cf. Jas 3.18); and (v) has 'destroying demons' denying peace to the unrighteous (cf. Jas 3.15). Such parallels underline the extent to which Jas 3.13-18 reworks traditional Jewish materials.[194]

---

[191] See further Deppe, *Sayings*, 103-106. According to Hartin, *Q*, 154-55, James knew an expanded form of the beatitudes related to what we find in Matthew.

[192] E.g. Manton, 322; Gill, 794; Henry *ad loc*. (borrowing from Isaiah without naming the book); J. Edwards, 1173 ('a plain reference to...Is. 32:17'); Alford, 311; Mitton, 142-43; Hanson, 'Report', 527 ('a midrash on Isa. 32.15-17'); Cantinat, 193-94; Vouga, 108; Schnider, 95; Johnson, 275; R. Wall, 191; Fabris, 261; Aymer, *Pure*, 71-72; Blomberg-Kamell, 180.

[193] Cf. Cantinat, 193-94; Johnson, 275. b. B. Bat. 9a and Num. Rab. 14.10 take Isa 32.17 to mean that 'the one who causes others to do good is greater than the doer'.

[194] Num. Rab. 11.7 also contrasts peace with a divided heart (cf. Jas 1.7; 4.8).

XIV

FRIENDSHIP WITH THE WORLD VERSUS FRIENDSHIP WITH GOD (4.1-12)[1]

(1) Whence come conflicts and disputes among you? Do they not arise from your cravings for pleasures, which war within your members? (2) You desire and you do not have. You are envious and jealous and are unable to obtain. You engage in disputes and conflicts. You do not have, because you do not ask. (3) You ask and do not receive, because you ask wickedly, in order to spend in exchange for your own cravings. (4) You unfaithful people! Do you not know that love of the world is enmity with God? Therefore whoever wishes to be a lover of the world becomes an enemy of God. (5) Or do you suppose that it is for no reason that the scripture says, 'Does the spirit that he made to dwell in us set its heart on envy? (6) But he gives all the more grace'? Thus it says, 'God opposes the proud, but gives grace to the humble'. (7) Submit yourselves then to God. Resist the devil, and he will flee from you. (8) Draw near to God, and he will draw near to you. Cleanse your hands, you sinners, and purify your hearts, you double-minded. (9) Make yourselves miserable and mourn and weep. Let your laughter be turned into mourning and your joy into dejection. (10) Humble yourselves before the Lord, and he will exalt you. (11) Do not defame one another, brothers. Whoever defames a brother or judges his brother defames the law and judges the law. If, however, you judge the law, you are not a doer of the law but a judge. (12) There is one lawgiver and judge, the one able to save and to destroy. So who are you to judge your neighbor?

---

[1] Recent literature: Allison, 'Eldad'; Alonso-Schökel, 'James 5,2'; Baker, *Speech-Ethics*, 135-36, 177-86; Batten, *Friendship*, 145-77; Bauckham, 'Spirit'; Blevins, 'Repent'; Bottini, 'Legislatore'; Bruston, 'Crux interpretum'; Cargal, 'Prostitute'; C. Carpenter, 'James 4.5'; Carson, 'James', 1006-1007; Cantinat, 'Sagesse'; Coppieters, 'Signification'; Frankemölle, 'Gesetz'; Hutchinson Edgar, *Poor*, 186-209; Engelhardt, 'Bemerkungen'; Findlay, 'James iv. 5,6'; Grimm, 'Stelle'; Jackson-McCabe, *Logos*, 201-206; Jeremias, 'Jac 4 5'; Johnson, *Brother*, 182-220; Kirn, 'Noch Kirn einmal'; idem, 'Vorschlag'; Klein, *Werk*, 106-16, 125-26, 163-65; Kloppenborg, 'Emulation', 134-37; Konradt, *Existenz*, 125-35; Laws, 'Scripture'; Lockett, *Purity*, 130-40; Marcus, 'Inclination'; Michl, 'Spruch'; Penner, *Eschatology*, 149-58; Paret, 'Wort'; idem, 'Zitat'; Parry, *Discussion*, 39-42; Perkins, 'James 3:16–4:3'; Pretorius, 'Verklaringsopsies'; Prockter, 'Noah'; Schmitt, 'Adulteresses'; Schökel, 'James 5.2'; Seitz, 'Afterthoughts'; idem, 'Antecedents'; idem, 'Hermas'; Thomson, 'James iv. 5'; Townsend, 'Warning'; Tsuji, *Glaube*, 82-88, 128-29; Turner, *Insights*, 163-64; van de Sandt, 'Way'; Wenger, *Kyrios*, 178-99; Wettlaufer, 'Variants', 128-201; Wypadlo, *Gebet*, 112-59, 328-52; Zyro, 'Erklärung'; idem, 'Noch einmal'; idem, 'Reinen'.

History of Interpretation and Reception

Expositors have often been anxious to explain how 'You ask and do not receive' (v. 3) harmonizes with Mt 7.7 = Lk 11.9 ('Ask and you will receive') as well as with the parallel to the latter in Jn 14.14. According to Origen, the gospel promises cannot be unqualified: God does not give bad things, nor does God give good things if those praying desire self-glorification.[2] Didymus of Alexandria, developing Origen's thought, explained: it is like a teacher who declares that he will teach all his students, and yet in the event not all learn; in such a case, no one convicts the teacher of lying. And so it is with regard to the biblical promise regarding prayer.[3] More recently, Brosend, 116, has offered this analogy: the saying of Jesus likens God's response to prayer to that of a parent giving bread and fish; but would a parent give a child a serpent if asked? Of course not, and so likewise God does not respond when asked for the wrong things.[4]

Some Christians have been quick to stress that James' denigration of the 'world' in v. 4 does not contradict the refrain in Gen 1, that the creation is good. John of Ávila is representative: 'world' does not here 'refer to the world that God created, which is good'; it rather 'is used of those who have no other feeling and no other love than for what is visible'.[5]

Others, however, have expressed themselves differently. Gregory the Great quoted Jas 4.4 in contending that Christians should rejoice as the end of the world approaches.[6] Still others, ignoring the possible tension with Genesis, have found in the verse support for asceticism. Tradition remembered Abba Isaiah quoting 4.4 in his argument that one should hate sleep because it is the enemy of God.[7] Similarly, Symeon the New Theologian cited the first few verses from Jas 4 and commented by quoting Mt 5.28 ('everyone who looks at a woman in order to lust after her has already committed adultery with her in his heart') and Exod 20.27 ('You will not covet anything of your neighbor'). For Symeon, 'friendship

---

[2] Origen, *Lk* 183 GCS 49 ed. Rauer, 303.

[3] Didymus of Alexandria *ad loc.* ed. Zoepfl, 6-7. Cf. the *Catenae* ed. Cramer, 25-26.

[4] Cf. Cyril of Alexandria, *Comm. Jn ad* 14.15 ed. Pusey, 463; the current 'Catechism of the Catholic Church' § 2737.

[5] John of Ávila, *Aufia, filia* 2.97.6 Obras completas de San Juan de Ávila 1 ed. Balust and Hernández, 748. Cf. Kugelman, 47-48; Brosend, 114 (James 'is not positing a gnostic or dualistic ideology that disparages and disdains the physical and material').

[6] *Ev. hom.* 1.3 FC 28/1 ed. Fiedrowicz, 56. Albertus Magnus, *Para. an.* 37 Opera Omnia 37 ed. Borgnet, 503-504, also contrasts the temporal world with the eternal world.

[7] *Les Apophtegmes des Pères: Collection Systématique* 1.10, SC 387 ed. Guy, 106. Cf. Abba Isaiah of Scetis, *Ascetic Discourses* 21 ET Chryssavgis and Penkett, Kalamazoo, MI, 2002, 214.

with the world' brought first to mind sexual issues—understandable given the μοιχαλίδες of v. 4.[8]

In Protestant homilies, however, the primary use of 4.4 has been to caution against certain social contacts. One of Wesley's sermons on the verse is typical: it urges that, although Christians must love their non-Christian neighbors, they should avoid 'needless conversation' with them. Above all, Wesley takes our verse to entail that Christians should never marry non-Christians.[9]

'Love of the world is enmity with God' (v. 4) has also found some currency outside the Christian world. It well suits the Hindu idea of the world as *maya*, illusion. Paramahansa Yogananda wrote: *Samsara*, the wheel of karma, 'induces man to take the line of least resistance. "Whosoever therefore will be a friend of the world is the enemy of God". To become the friend of God, man must overcome the devils or evils of his own karma or actions that ever urge him to spineless acquiescence in the mayic delusions of the world.'[10]

Verse 6 (= Prov 3.34; 1 Pet 5.5) was of great importance to Augustine, a statement for him of an all-important, general theological principle.[11] On 'hardly a page of Scripture', he wrote, is it 'not clearly written that God resists the proud and gives grace to the humble'.[12] In the *Confessions*, moreover, he reads himself into the verse several times in order to characterize his life before conversion as prideful and to characterize his conversion as an act of humility.[13] However, in *The City of God*, which quotes Jas 4.6 in the preface, Augustine at one point reads Jesus into the verse: the Son of God is an illustration of God exalting the lowly.[14]

Verse 7, which exhorts hearers to submit themselves to God and resist the devil, and v. 8, which pledges that God will draw near to those near to God, occasioned some debate during the Reformation. Calvin, 299, thought it necessary to argue against Roman Catholics who 'infer from this passage that the initiative lies with us, and God's grace follows after'. His counter was that the Spirit fulfills 'in us the very thing He

---

[8] Symeon the New Theologian, *Cat. 1–34* 5.781-92 SC 96 ed. Krivochéine and Paramelle, 444. Elsewhere, in *Hymn* 33.13-37 SC 174 ed. Koder and Neyrand, 414, he affirms that those loving the 'visible world' are enemies of God. Cf. the application of Jas 4.8-10 in idem, *Ep.* 7.19 SC 487 ed. Bachelet, 282: James speaks against those who seek joy in this life.

[9] J. Wesley, 'On Friendship with the World', in *Sermons on Several Occasions*, New York, 1839, 196-204.

[10] Paramahansa Yogananda, *Autobiography of a Yogi*, Los Angeles, 1990, 560.

[11] See further Pfligersdorffer, 'Demut'. The line is quoted incessantly in Christian literature from every time and place, but as it occurs also in 1 Pet 5.5 and Prov 3.34, its immediate source is most often not evident.

[12] *Doctr. christ.* 3.75 CSEL 80 ed. Green, 99.

[13] *Conf.* 4.3.5; 4.15.26; 7.9.13; 10.36.59 ed. O'Donnell, 34, 43, 80, 142.

[14] Augustine, *Civ. dei* 17.4. Cf. Wolzogen, 211.

commands'.[15] The issue was an old one. Already the Pelagians had fastened upon Jas 4.7-8 as supporting their position.[16] John Cassian, seeking a middle way, found in 4.8 an affirmation of both divine grace and the freedom of the human will: 'even by his own desire an individual can sometimes be brought to a desire for virtue, but he always needs to be helped by the Lord'.[17]

Verse 9 admonishes hearers to turn laughter into joy. Many Christians have received this as a call to a sober life, and as a demand to put away all frivolity. Abba Isaiah of Scetis advised: 'Never rejoice nor smile but always turn your laughter into mourning and your joy into sorrow. Always walk with a somber attitude.'[18] Similarly, Leander of Seville, *Inst. virg.* 21.3 ed. Velazquez, 153, cited Jas 4.9 in urging nuns not to laugh. More recently, however, there is a strong tendency for exegetes to contend that James does not oppose laughter in general but only the wrong sort of laughter. Mitton, 162, is typical: 'This is not a condemnation of all laughter, but of thoughtless laughter in a situation which should rather provoke sadness and a sense of concern. Laughter can have great healing powers, to relieve inward stress and tension, and to ease strained personal relationships.'[19] But already Basil the Great had argued that laughter is of two kinds—hilarity, which is bad, and exultation, which is good.[20]

Calvin was concerned to emphasize that vv. 11-12, with their prohibition of judgment, have to do with 'the spiritual government of the soul'. That is, they have nothing to do with 'external polity', with governments and their courts, which must judge and sometimes condemn. Likewise, Doriani, 157, insisted that 'judgments are necessary at times', and that even excommunication is something incumbent.[21] A similar nervousness about tension between the *status quo* and what James might be thought to teach appears in Manton, 325-32. Supposing the condemnation of vv. 1-2

---

[15] Cf. Manton, 369-72; Gill, 797; also still Oesterley, 460: 'We have what to Christian ears sounds rather like a reversal of the order of things; we should expect the order to be that expressed in such words as, "Ye did not choose me, but I chose you" (John xv.16)'.

[16] See Augustine, *De gratia Christi* 22(23) CSEL 42 ed. Urba and Zycha, 142-43.

[17] Cassian, *Conf.* 13.9.2 SC 54 ed. Pichery, 159-60.

[18] Abba Isaiah of Scetis, *Ascetic Discourses* 21 ET Chryssavgis and Penkett, Kalamazoo, MI, 2002, 224. Cf. Nicodemus of the Holy Mountain, *Handbook of Spiritual Counsel*, trans. P.A. Chamber, 115.

[19] Cf. Martin, 154 (James was not 'a kill-joy'; he says only 'that the actions of [foolish] laughing and [senseless] rejoicing hold no place'); Moo, 196-97; and Witherington, 516 (the verse is 'not a description of how Christians must always be solemn or puritanical').

[20] Basil of Caesarea, *Reg. fus.* 17 PG 31.961-65. See further I.M. Resnick, '"Risus monasticus": Laughter and Medieval Monastic Culture', *RBén* 97 (1987), 90-100. Does Basil's opposition to merrymaking in *Ep.* 22.3 ed. Deferrari, 130, depend upon Jas 4.9?

[21] Cf. Jacobi, 164; Smith, 255-58.

to concern literal military campaigns, he took the opportunity to argue at great length that some wars are indeed justified. Pacifists, such as George Fox, have indeed to the contrary sometimes invoked Jas 4 in presenting their case.[22]

The 'Who are you?' of the closing v. 12 has occasionally moved Protestant commentators to make disparaging remarks about the general condition of humanity. Wesley, 867, appended this laconic note: 'A poor, weak, dying worm'. Huther, 138, found here 'the insignificance of man'.

One should observe that vv. 1-10 in their entirety have often reinforced the conviction of some expositors that our epistle had in view Jews outside of the church as well as within; cf. 1.1. James demands that readers submit themselves to God, resist the devil, cleanse their hands, purify their minds, mourn and weep, and humble themselves. These readers are called 'adulterers' (4.4) and 'sinners' (4.8). They are full of covetousness (4.2) and are friends of the world and enemies of God (4.4). In calling them to repent, James appeals to their knowledge of Scripture (vv. 5-6), not to specifically Christian convictions. Plummer remarked: 'There are places...in which St. James seems to...glance at the whole Jewish nation...whether Christian or not. These more comprehensive addresses are more frequent in the second half of the Epistle than the first, and one is inclined to believe that the passage before us is one of them.'[23] Sadly, this interpretation has joined itself to the anti-Judaism of certain expositors. Doddridge, 843, for instance, wrote of the 'contentious and sanguinary temper of the Jews', and it is regrettably easy to collect similar statements.[24]

Exegesis

The widespread disagreement regarding the structure of this passage shows that, if James had a clear plan in mind, he failed to communicate it. Any number of outlines are equally credible, so although a structural analysis may assist exegesis as a convenience, it may not tell us much about the author's intentions.

---

[22] Note e.g. W.M. Swartley, *Covenant of Peace*, Grand Rapids, MI, 2006, 259-62. For Fox see D.V. Steere, ed., *Quaker Spirituality*, New York, 1984, 74. Contrast C.J. Cadoux, *The Early Christian Attitude to War*, London, 1919, 49; he, although a pacifist, admits that Jas 4.1-2 probably refers 'not to military conflicts, but to strife and dissension in the more general sense'.

[23] See further, among others, Grotius, 1086; Whitby, 593-94, 689; N. Lardner, 'A History of the Apostles and Evangelists', in *The Works of Nathaniel Lardner*, vol. 6, London, 1838, 201; Clarke, 819; Gilpin, 596; Bassett, 57; Wordsworth, 27; B. Johnson, 348; Schlatter, 92-93; Beasley-Murray, 13; Adamson, *Message*, 58.

[24] Cf. Whitby, 594; Henry, *ad loc.*; Gilpin, 596.

This commentary tentatively suggests three main parts—indictment (vv. 1-3), rationale (vv. 4-6), outline of appropriate response (vv. 7-12).[25] The indictment in turn falls into two subsections. Verses 1-2a recount conflicts. Verses 2b-3, which are a bit of a digression, describe failure in prayer. Both subsections refer to 'pleasure' (ἡδονή) and 'not having' (οὐχ ἔχετε). The subsequent rationale, which takes up the theme of jealousy from v. 2, also has two parts—a reminder of the hostility between God and 'the world' (v. 4), which should counter the behavior in vv. 2b-3, and scriptural condemnation of jealousy and promotion of humility (two quotations, vv. 5-6), which should counter the behavior of vv. 1-2a. The whole concludes with a long series of imperatives, the first few having mostly to do with one's relationship to God (vv. 7-10), the rest with not slandering and judging others (vv. 11-12):

I. Indictment (vv. 1-3)
   A. Conflicts and disputes lead to envy and jealousy (vv. 1-2a)
   B. Lack is due to not asking or not asking rightly (vv. 2b-3)
II. Rationale (vv. 4-6)
   A. God and the world are antithetical (v. 4)
   B. Scriptures countering jealously and promoting humility (vv. 5-6)
      i. Quotation from lost book (vv. 5-6a)
      ii. Quotation from Proverbs (v. 6b)
III. Call to repentance (vv. 7-12)
   A. Submission, mourning, humility (vv. 7-10)
   B. Prohibition of defaming and judging others (vv. 11-12)

4.1-12 features much repetition and a high degree of parallelism:

1   πόθεν + plural nominative noun
      πόθεν πόλεμοι
      πόθεν μάχαι
    Preposition + definite article + plural noun + ὑμῶν
      ἐκ τῶν ἡδονῶν ὑμῶν
      ἐν τοῖς μέλεσιν ὑμῶν

---

[25] Cf. Davids, 155-56, who however separates vv. 11-12 from vv. 7-10 and regards the former as 'semi-independent'. So too Frankemölle, 574-78; Klein, *Werk*, 107; Burchard, 164-65, 178. Others dissociate vv. 11-12 from what goes before and instead join them with vv. 13ff.; so e.g. Nystrom, 248-66; Hutchinson Edgar, *Poor*, 197-209; Doriani, 154-56. But Easton, 58; Laws, 186; Vouga, 120; and Hartin, 220, treat vv. 11-12 as an independent unit. Brosend, 106, sees 4.1-17 as a unit with vv. 11-12 as one of the three subsections. Moo, 167-200, associates vv. 1-3 with 13.13-18 and then treats vv. 4-10 and 11-12 as separate units. Penner, *Eschatology*, 152-56, discerns a major break between vv. 5 and 6, the latter opening a new subunit. M. Taylor, *Structure*, 116-17, sees vv. 1-6 as focused on rebuke, vv. 7-10 as focused on repentance and humility, vv. 11-12 as a separate section. Popkes, 258-84, joins vv. 1-2 with 3.13-18 and then treats 4.3-12 as a unit. For Johnson, 267-89; idem, *Brother*, 182-201, 3.13–4.10 in its entirety is a coherent unit centered around the topic of envy with 3.13-4.6 functioning as the indictment, 4.7-10 as the call to change. The difficulty of making decisions on these matters is on display in Cheung, *Genre*, 77-79.

2-3 Verb ending in -ε(ι)τε + καί + οὐ(κ) + verb in ending in -τ/θε
 ἐπιθυμεῖτε   καὶ οὐκ ἔχετε
 φονεύετε καὶ ζηλοῦτε καὶ οὐ δύνασθε
 αἰτεῖτε   καὶ οὐ λαμβάνετε
 οὐ(κ) + verb ending in -ετε + διά/διότι + middle form of αἰτέω
 οὐκ   ἔχετε διὰ τὸ μὴ   αἰτεῖσθαι
 οὐ λαμβάνετε διότι κακῶς αἰτεῖσθε
4 φιλία/φίλος + τοῦ κόσμου + ἔχθρα/ἐχθρός + τοῦ θεοῦ
 φιλία   τοῦ κόσμου ἔχθρα τοῦ θεοῦ
 φίλος εἶναι   τοῦ κόσμου ἐχθρὸς τοῦ θεοῦ
7 Imperative ending in -ητε + particle/conjunction + τῷ + noun in dative ending in ῳ
 ὑποτάγητε οὖν   τῷ θεῷ
 ἀντίστητε δέ   τῷ διαβόλῳ
8 Form of ἐγγίζω + dative
 ἐγγίσατε τῷ θεῷ
 ἐγγιεῖ   ὑμῖν
 Imperative ending in -ατε + accusative plural (part of body) + vocative plural
 καθαρίσατε χεῖρας, ἁμαρτωλοί
 ἁγνίσατε καρδίας,   δίψυχοι
9 Definite article + nominative + εἰς + accusative singular
 ὁ γέλως ὑμῶν εἰς πένθος
 ἡ χαρὰ   εἰς κατήφεραν
11 Participle ending in -ων + form of ἀδελφός
 καταλαλῶν   ἀδελφοῦ
 κρίνων τὸν   ἀδελφόν
 Present active indicative ending in -ει + form of νόμος
 καταλαλεῖ νόμου
 κρίνει νόμον
12 Contrasting word pair, each noun ending in -ης
 οὐκ ποιητής
 ἀλλὰ κριτής
 Complementary word pair, each noun ending in -ης
 νομοθέτης
 καὶ κριτής
 Contrasting infinitives, each ending in -σαι
 σῶσαι καὶ
 ἀπολέσαι

Every verse displays parallelism except the short v. 10 and vv. 5-6, which preserve quotations.[26]

The passages draw forward several themes and motifs introduced earlier:

---

[26] That parallelism runs throughout speaks against the proposal that we have here largely 'a string of quotations, not very skillfully strung together—a kind of "stromateis"—taken from a variety of sources' (Oesterley, 458). The content may be largely conventional, but the form is largely editorial.

- communal conflict, 4.1-2, 11-12; cf. 2.1-13;[27] 3.9-12, 14-16
- the source of sins, 4.1-2; cf. 1.13-15
- unanswered prayer, 4.2-3; cf. 1.5
- the vice of jealousy, 4.2, 5; cf. 3.14
- rejection of 'the world', 4.4; cf. 1.27
- explicit appeal to Scripture, 4.5-6; cf. 2.8, 11, 23
- call for humility, 4.6, 9; cf. 1.9-11, 21; 3.17
- divine generosity, 4.6; cf. 1.5, 17
- demand for purity, 4.8; cf. 1.27; 3.17
- denigration of double-mindedness, 4.8; cf. 1.5-8
- proper treatment of one's neighbor, 4.11-12; cf. 2.8
- use of Lev 19, 4.11-12; cf. 2.1, 8, 9
- the ethics of speech, 4.11; cf. 1.19, 26; 3.1-12

As elsewhere, James is largely 'concerned with that behavior which threatens or sustains the existence of the community'.[28] The link with 3.13-17, with its injunctions for communal peace, is particularly close,[29] and the view of this commentary is that the same *Sitz im Leben* partly accounts for both passages.[30] James has in view above all disputes regarding Christian Jews.[31] His take, fair or not, is that their opponents, who may well wish them out of the synagogue, enter into conflicts because they are conflicted within themselves (v. 1) as well as selfishly motivated by their own desire for gratification (vv. 2, 3). Further, they side not with God but with 'the world' and so are 'jealous', failing to allow that God's grace rests upon those who see things differently than they do (vv. 4-5). James calls these double-minded individuals to repentance, and especially to abandon slandering and judging those with whom they disagree (vv. 11-12).[32]

Chapter 4 paints the situation as black and white,[33] skewering unnamed individuals. How then did our author intend his rhetoric to function? He likely had no hope of changing the minds of any here blasted. Maybe then our text is a bit like Mt 23: although the latter condemns the scribes

---

[27] Cf. Oesterley, 457: vv. 11-12 belong 'in substance to ii. 1-13'.
[28] So Paretsky, 'Two Ways', 315.
[29] See especially Wypadlo, *Gebet*, 330-40.
[30] Blomberg-Kamell, 196, are right to observe also that by returning to the subject of sins of speech in vv. 11-12, James 'is still following the train of thought he began in 3:1'. Draper, 'Apostles', 171-72, even urges that those rebuked in chap. 4 are the teachers rebuked in chap. 3, which he in turn equates with those rebuked in chap. 2 for teaching faith without works.
[31] But Mussner, 188-89, thinks of Jewish Christians judging Gentile Christians, and Simonis, *Paulus*, 111-12, thinks of Gentile Christians judging Jewish Christians.
[32] The protest of Dibelius, 216, that 4.1-12 cannot address a concrete *Sitz im Leben* (i) wrongly presupposes an exclusively Christian audience; (ii) fails to establish that different passages in James cannot have in view different groups; and (iii) mistakenly assumes that conventional *paraenesis* cannot be directed to a specific situation.
[33] van de Sandt, 'Law'; idem, 'Way', argues that 4.1-4 in particular is closely related to the two ways tradition, especially as that appears in Did. 3.1-6. Others have associated James and the two-way tradition; cf. Lockett, 'Structure'; idem, 'Spectrum', 145-47.

and Pharisees, which it addresses directly ('Woe to you, scribes, Pharisees, hypocrites'), it was never intended to be heard by them, much less to persuade them. James, however, ostensibly addresses Israelites in the diaspora, among whom would be presumably people like those rebuked in Jas 4. So dubbing the chapter an apostrophe seems problematic.

The suggestion in this commentary is that James seeks, among other things, a sympathetic Jewish audience. That is, our book hopes to reduce hostility among Jews not yet adamantly set against the participation of Jewish Christians in the synagogue. From this perspective, the censures in Jas 4 aim to elicit agreement, to move readers to concur with the author that those he criticizes merit being censored.

The passage is intertextually rich. Verse 5 quotes an unknown scripture. Verse 6 cites Prov 3.34. Verses 11-12 interact with Lev 19.15-18. Moreover, Num 11 and traditions surrounding that chapter are probably in the background throughout. That pentateuchal chapter famously deals with the vice of ἐπιθυμία (cf. Jas 4.2), features a much-discussed remark about jealousy (cf. Jas 4.2, 5), has God giving his 'spirit' (cf. Jas 4.5), and records unkind words against others (cf. Jas 4.11-12). Moreover, the lore concerning that chapter took up the themes of the humble being exalted (cf. Jas 4.6, 10), God bestowing grace (cf. Jas 4.6), God drawing near to the saints (cf. Jas 4.8), and διψυχία (cf. Jas 4.8). See further the discussion on v. 5, which argues that the apocryphon there cited is the defunct Eldad and Modad, named after two characters from Num 11.

4.1-12 also shows the influence of the Jesus tradition. Verse 3 reflects Mt 7.7-8 = Lk 11.9-10 (Q). Verses 11-12 interpret Lev 19.15-18 through the lens of Mt 7.1-5 = Lk 6.37, 41-42. And 4.9 is probably inspired by Lk 6.25. In addition, there is strong thematic congruence between 4.4 and Mt 6.24 = Lk 16.13 and between 4.10 and Lk 14.11; cf. Mt 23.12; Lk 18.14.

Verse 1. Having just finished an exhortation to peace (3.13-17), James now rails against its opposite, war. The critical tone, dominant since 1.19, continues.

πόθεν πόλεμοι. James has πόθεν and πόλεμος (cf. πολεμέω in v. 2) only in this verse. πόλεμος means first of all 'war', as throughout the LXX (almost always for מלחמה). This could be the meaning in James, if the author wrote during a time of armed conflict, such as the Jewish revolt of CE 115–117 or the bar Kokhba rebellion, CE 132–135.[34] Such

---

[34] Interpreters who have thought of literal wars or physical violence, and sometimes of the Zealots, include Grotius, 1086; Manton, 325; Bengel, 502; Whitby, 593-94; Burkitt, 1027; Knowling, 95; Smith, 211-13 (James addresses 'Christian Jews very much as a Quaker in war-time might address Englishmen of his own persuasion'); Schlatter, 240-41; Easton, 52-53 (urging that vv. 1-2b are from a Stoic source); Reicke, 45 ('riots, sabotage, and the like'); Townsend, 'Warning'; Martin, 144. Doddridge, 845, thinks of both 'private quarrels and public wars'. Cf. Henry, *ad loc*. Despite all these names, this is the minority view.

FRIENDSHIP WITH THE WORLD VERSUS FRIENDSHIP WITH GOD (4.1-12) 597

an interpretation would be consistent with the φονεύετε of 4.2, if one supposes that to be the original reading. But (i) no other pericope in James refers to literal war; (ii) 4.1-2 is flanked by passages—3.1-18 and 4.11-12—whose focus is communal strife, or what Trapp, 700, aptly called 'word-wars';[35] (iii) πόλεμος parallels μάχη, and according to BAGD, s.v., the latter occurs in early Christian literature 'only of battles fought without actual weapons'; (iv) ἐν ὑμῖν (in the next clause) would be odd with reference to literal war; and (v) πόλεμος often designates social conflict or private quarrels.[36] Comparable then is the rabbinic מלחמה של תורה (= 'war of the Torah', that is, rabbinic debates about the law), as in b. Meg. 15b.

καὶ πόθεν μάχαι ἐν ὑμῖν;[37] The clause is strictly irrelevant—πόθεν πόλεμοι; would suffice—but James loves such parallelism, with which we may compare LXX Josh 9.8 (πόθεν ἐστὲ καὶ πόθεν παραγεγόνατε;); Isa 41.24 (πόθεν ἐστὲ ὑμεῖς καὶ πόθεν ἡ ἐργασία ὑμῶν;); and he is further keen on the sources of things; cf. 1.13-15. In the LXX, μάχη[38] most often refers not to military battle but to personal disputes.[39] The word (cf. ריב and מריבה) is naturally paired with πόλεμος;[40] cf. Jas 4.2: μάχεσθε καὶ πολεμεῖτε.

Even though the language is not intended literally, it does introduce imagery from the battlefield, as do the following lines: στρατευομένων (v. 1), μάχεσθε καὶ πολεμεῖτε (v. 2), ἐχθρός (v. 4), ἀντιτάσσεται (v. 6), ἀντίστητε...φεύξεται (v. 7). Comparable are Philo, *Migr.* 60 ('disorderly companies...commanded by pleasures or desires'), and 1 Pet 2.1 ('abstain from the desires of the flesh that wage war against the soul').

---

[35] Cf. Baker, *Speech-Ethics*, 135: 'Falling in the shadow of 3:1-18 it [4.1-2] can refer to nothing else'. See further Konradt, *Existenz*, 125-26; Moo, 181.

[36] See Pss. Sol. 12.4; Philo, *Gig.* 51; T. Gad 5.1; T. Sim. 4.8; T. Dan 5.2 (here the cessation of πόλεμος or conflict correlates with speaking the truth [ἀλήθειαν; cf. Jas 3.14], with not falling into pleasure [ἡδονήν; cf. Jas 4.1], and with keeping peace [εἰρήνη; cf. Jas 3.17-18]); T. Jud. 22.1; 1 Clem. 3.2 (this links πόλεμος to both ζῆλος [cf. Jas 3.14] and φθόνος [cf. Jas 4.2, 5]); 46.5 (the form of this sentence is close to James: 'Why is there strife and angry outbursts and dissension and schisms and πόλεμός ἐν ὑμῖν?'; some have thought this a sign of dependence upon James; cf. Johnson, 73); Epictetus, *Diatr.* 3.20.18; etc. T. Job 4.4 uses the word of battle with Satan (cf. 18.5; T. Reub. 6.12), Gk. LAE 28.3 of personal conflict within. Johnson, 276, emphasizes that war was, in both the Jewish and Graeco-Roman moral traditions, associated with envy; cf. v. 2.

[37] The order of the words varies in the Greek mss., some of which omit the pleonastic πόθεν; see the *Editio Critica Maior*, 64-65. The meaning is unaffected.

[38] Jas: 1×; cf. μάχομαι in v. 2.

[39] LXX Gen 13.7, 8; Prov 17.14; 25.10; Ecclus 8.16; 28.11; Isa 58.4. For the same sense see Plato, *Tim.* 88a; T. Reub. 3.4 (the πνεῦμα μάχης resides in the liver and gall); T. Jud. 16.3; T. Gad 6.5; T. Benj. 6.4; 2 Cor 7.5; 2 Tim 2.23; Tit 3.9.

[40] See LXX Josh 4.13; Judg 11.25 A; Job 38.23; Plato, *Tim.* 19E; Dio Chrysostom 12.78; Aelius Aristides, *Or.* 45.18; etc.

Ending a question with ἐν ὑμῖν—otherwise rare in the Greek Bible[41]—is characteristic of James.[42] Here the words underline the distance between the author and some of his readers on the particular at hand: they are 'you', not 'us'.

οὐκ ἐντεῦθεν. There is a formal parallel in Libanaius, *Or.* 24.12-13: πόθεν χρὴ νομίσαι γεγενῆσθαι; ἐγὼ μὲν γὰρ ἐντεῦθεν ἡγοῦμαι. The adverb (often in the LXX for מזה) is a Jamesian *hapax*.

ἐκ τῶν ἡδονῶν ὑμῶν τῶν στρατευομένων ἐν τοῖς μέλεσιν ὑμῶν; This line features repetition, parallelism, and a pleasant, three-step rhythm:

ἐκ τῶν ἡδονῶν   ὑμῶν
   τῶν στρατευομένων
ἐν τοῖς μέλεσιν   ὑμῶν

ἐκ immediately after ἐντεῦθεν, although foreign to Greek Jewish writings, including the LXX, is otherwise well attested.[43]

Division within the community is the product of division within individuals. Whether such is due to conflicting pleasures or strife between desires and conscience (cf. the rabbinic יצר הרע and יצר הטוב) or both goes unsaid.[44]

ἡδονή here means 'desire for pleasure'. It appears infrequently in biblical Greek aside from repeated occurrence in 4 Maccabees (10×).[45] The background for its use in James is Greek philosophy mediated via Judaism. In this connection, 4 Maccabees, whose negative view of ἡδονή matches what we find among Cynics and Stoics, is highly instructive. It defines σοφία (cf. Jas 3.13-18) as 'the knowledge of divine and human matters and the causes of these', one manifestation of such wisdom being 'rational judgment', which rules over the two most comprehensive emotions, pain and pleasure (ἡδονή).[46] 'Desire' (ἐπιθυμία; cf. Jas 4.2) precedes 'pleasure' just as 'delight' follows it; and 'in pleasure there exists...a malevolent tendency' that includes 'boastfulness (ἀλαζονεία; cf. Jas 4.16), covetousness (φιλαργυρία; cf. Jas 5.3), thirst for honor, rivalry

---

[41] LXX Judg 20.12; 1 Cor 3.16; 2 Cor 13.5.

[42] 3.13; 4.1; 5.13, 14.

[43] Aristophanes, *Thesmoph.* 219; Xenophon, *Anab.* 7.6.42; Cassius Dio 50.19.5; Epictetus, *Diatr.* 2.16.45; etc.

[44] Aquinas, *Summa* 2/2 q. 116 a. 1, expands the scope of this sin: it is 'a general evil whence all vices arise'.

[45] Jas: 2×; cf. 4.3. LXX: 14×. NT: 5×; cf. Lk 8.14; Tit 3.3; 2 Pet 2.13 (all pejorative). Given the interaction of this section of James with Num 11 (see below), perhaps it is not coincidence that the only occurrence of ἡδονή in the law and the prophets is Num 11.8, part of the setting for the story of Eldad and Modad. There, however, the word (for טעם) means 'taste'.

[46] See 1.13-35; also 5.23; 6.35. Another manifestation of σοφία is δικαιοσύνη; cf. Jas 3.18.

(cf. Jas 3.13-18), and malice...' Even though James lacks any corresponding emphasis upon 'reason', the direct relevance of 4 Maccabees is self-evident.[47]

James does not explicitly associate ἡδονή with sexual pleasure,[48] although some of the English translations might encourage some to imagine otherwise.[49] He also fails to differentiate bodily pleasure from spiritual pleasure or good pleasure from bad[50] or (despite v. 7) to attribute pleasure to diabolical instigation.[51] Nor does he promote ἀπάθεια or make it plain that some pleasures are inevitable and so legitimate if indulged with moderation.[52] At the same time, James does not leave his generalization wholly unelaborated.[53] First, he associates pleasure with social conflict, much like Philo, *Decal.* 151-52, who says that the passion for pleasure causes relatives to become estranged and to hate each other, countries to be riven by internal factions, and wars to cover sea and land.[54] Second, vv. 2-3 make it clear that covetousness is primarily to the fore, which drives the desire for money, which in turn can be spent on the pleasures one favors;[55] and Philo again offers a strong parallel: pleasure moves people to break the commandment not to covet (*Decal.* 142-43).

Many commentators recognize that τῶν ἡδονῶν, in the words of Poole, 892, stands for 'those lusts whereof pleasure is the end, which is therefore put for the lusts themselves: he means the over-eager desire of

---

[47] Cf. also T. Dan 5.2; T. Benj. 6.3; Josephus, *Bell.* 2.120 (the Essenes 'shun pleasure as a vice').

[48] Contrast Wis 7.2; T. Reub. 13.6; 14.2; T. Iss. 3.5.

[49] Tyndale (1534): 'volupteousnes'; so too Geneva (1557). Cranmer (1539): 'lustes'; so too KJV (1611). RSV (1946): 'passions'. NRSV (1989): 'cravings'. Cf. the application in Alphonsus Ligouri, *Char.* 11.22 Opere Asceteche vol. 1, Rome, 1933, 139-40.

[50] Cf. 4 Macc 1.13-35; Philo, *Opif.* 152; Herm. *Sim.* 6.5.7. Contrast Smith, 214: 'He does not condemn all pleasure by implication, for pleasure has its rightful place in life, and therefore is quite rightly one of the motives for action. We may give others pleasure or do ourselves what is pleasurable, offering our thanks to the God who wishes us to be happy.'

[51] Cf. Clement of Alexandria, *Strom.* 2.20.111.3 GCS 52 ed. Stählin and Früchtel, 173; b. B. Bat. 16a; also perhaps 11Q5 19.15-16; 4Q436 1. When Evagrius of Pontus, *Antirrhet.* 2.62 ed. Frankenberg, 493, cites Jas 4.1, he remarks that 'desires' arise from the temptations of demons.

[52] Contrast Aristotle, *Eth. nic.* 1153B.

[53] Contrast Let. Aris. 245; Herm. *Sim.* 8.8.5; and ARN A 28: 'All who take for themselves the pleasures of this world (תענוגי העולם הזה; cf. Lk 8.14 [ἡδονῶν τοῦ βίου] and Ign. *Rom* 7.3 [ἡδοναῖς τοῦ βίου τούτου]) will have the pleasures of the world to come taken from them'.

[54] Cf. T. Dan 5.2; Plato, *Phaed.* 66c; Cicero, *Fin.* 1.43-44; Lucian, *Cyn.* 15; Dio Chrysostom 17.10. Note also Ps.-Macarius, *Hom. 1-50* 37.1 PTS 4 ed. Dörries, Klostermann, Kroeger, 265, which quotes Jas 4.4 and then cautions against the ἡδονή that leads to slaying a brother.

[55] For James' interest here in economic issues see Konradt, *Existenz*, 131-35.

riches, worldly greatness, carnal delights'.[56] But as to why James here chose ἡδονή over ἐπιθυμία, one can only guess. Davids, 156-57, suggests influence from a source. Tsuji suggests a desire to counter worldly joy; cf. v. 9.[57]

στρατευομένων adds more military language; see above and cf. Paul's extended use of combat imagery in 2 Cor 10.3-6.[58] Particularly close to James in both language and thought are Rom 7.23 ('I see ἐν τοῖς μέλεσίν μου another law ἀντιστρατευόμενον with the law of my mind, making me captive to the law of sin that dwells ἐν τοῖς μέλεσίν μου');[59] 1 Pet 2.11 ('I urge you as aliens and exiles to abstain from the desires of the flesh that στρατεύονται against the soul'); Pol. *Phil.* 5.2 ('every sinful desire στρατεύεται against the spirit'); Diogentus, *Ep.* 6.5 ('the flesh hates the soul and πολεμεῖ against it...because it is hindered from indulging in its ἡδοναῖς'). The application of στρατεύομαι[60] to internal conflict well suits our author's convictions about the divided self (cf. 1.7-8; 4.8), with which one may compare 1QS 3.18-19; 4.23-24.

Hellenistic dualism is present in James' ἐν τοῖς μέλεσιν ὑμῶν (cf. 3.6), which does not refer to the members of a church or social body.[61] The phrase, which is absent from the LXX but prominent in Rom 7 (vv. 5, 23 *bis*), rather assumes that the drive for pleasure, or at least wrongful pleasure, is rooted in the human body—standard fare in antiquity; cf. Plato, *Resp.* 328D (αἱ κατὰ τὸ σῶμα ἡδοναί); Aristotle, *Eth. nic.* 1149B (ἡδονὰς σωματικάς); Diogenes Laertius 2.90; Cicero, *Tusc* 1.75 ('we separate the soul from pleasure, that is from the body'); Philo, *Leg.* 3.116 (ἡδονή is in 'the breast and the belly'); *Congr.* 59 ('the body is the region of ἡδονῶν'); 2 Bar. 49.3; Diogenes, *Ep.* 6.5; *et al.*[62] Similarly, the rabbis could locate the יצר הרע (see on 1.14) in the body.[63]

---

[56] Cf. Calvin, 296 ('*Pleasures* are taken as all illicit and lustful desires') and Plummer, 607-608 (James 'puts the pleasures which excite and gratify the lusts instead of the lusts themselves, in much the same way as we use "drink" for intemperance and "gold" for avarice').

[57] Tsuji, *Glaube*, 83.

[58] Also 1 Tim 1.18; 1 Clem. 37.1; Ign. *Pol.* 6.2.

[59] Does James here, directly or indirectly, depend upon Paul? So Brückner, *Reihenfolge*, 289; Dibelius, 216; Nienhuis, *Paul*, 211; contrast Ropes, 254. See further the Introduction, 000.

[60] LXX: 8×. NT: 7×; Jas: 1×. Gk. Pseudepigrapha (Denis): 5×. Philo: 12×. Josephus: 177×.

[61] Although this is the view of Martin, 140; Cargal, 155; R. Wall, 195; *et al*. See the criticism in Davids, 157, with the response of Martin, 140.

[62] Cf. the interpretation of Cyril of Alexandria, *Rom ad* 7.16 ed. Pusey, 206, and note the association of יצר with בשר in 1QH 18(10).23; 24(18).2; 4Q416 1.16; 4Q 418 2 8 and of ἐπιθυμία with σάρξ in Gal 5.16, 24; Eph 2.3; 1 Pet 2.11; 2 Pet 2.10, 18; 1 Jn 2.16; Barn. 10.9; Plutarch, *Mor.* 1096C; etc. According to ARN A 16, 'the evil impulse within man is monarch over his two hundred and forty-eight limbs, while the good impulse is like a captive in prison'.

[63] b. Ber. 61a; Num. Rab. 22.9; etc.; cf. 1QS 4.20-21.

Verse 2. Bonhoeffer construed 4.1-2 this way: 'Those who allow their own desire to become their god, must inevitably hate other human beings who stand in their way and impede their designs'.[64]

ἐπιθυμεῖτε καὶ οὐκ ἔχετε. Cf. MT Prov 13.4: 'The soul of the sluggard desires and (has) nothing'. Although James uses ἐπιθυμέω only here, ἐπιθυμία appears in 1.14-15; see the discussion there, which links the latter to the rabbinic יצר הרע. Both verb and noun were understandably associated with ἡδονή, and in some texts ἐπιθυμία and ἡδονή are practically synonyms, or one is the cause of the other; cf. Plato, *Phaedr.* 238A ('ἐπιθυμίας irrationally drags to ἡδονάς'; cf. 66C); Philo, *Prob.* 159 ('If the soul is driven by ἐπιθυμίας or enticed by ἡδονῆς'); Josephus, *Ant.* 18.340 ('at the bidding of ἐπιθυμιῶν καὶ ἡδονῆς'); Plutarch, *Mor.* 750E ('the end of ἐπιθυμίας is ἡδονή'); Athenagoras, *Res.* 22.3 ed. Marcovich, 47 ('when there is no ἐπιθυμίας drawing it to food or intercourse or the other ἡδονάς').[65] One wonders whether James' assertion assumes that 'the desires are incapable of satisfaction' (Cicero, *Fin.* 1.43); cf. Prov 27.20 ('Sheol and Abaddon are never satisfied, and human eyes are never satisfied'); Philo, *Leg.* 3.149 ('ἐπιθυμία is never filled up'); Sextus, *Sent.* 274b ('Having possessions will not prevent the desire for possessions'); Calvin, 297 ('man's spirit is inexhaustible, once it indulges in wicked desires... Even if he were given the earth, he would long to have a new world made for him').[66]

Because James was a Jew with a knowledge of the Bible, and because he was a Christian who paid attention to the decalogue (see 2.11), his words are naturally read in the light of the tenth commandment, LXX Exod 20.17 = Deut 5.21: οὐκ ἐπιθυμήσεις (= לא תחמד).[67] Moreover, Gen. Rab. 9.12 and Pesiq. R. 21.17 record the notion that the one 'who violates the command, "You will not covet", is as one transgressing all ten commandments'. Lactantius says the same thing.[68] That this idea, which resembles Jas 2.10, was old appears likely from Philo, *Decal.* 148-50, where ἐπιθυμία (equated with πάθος) 'works universal destruction'; from idem, *Leg.* 4.84, where ἐπιθυμία is 'the fountain of all evils';[69] and from Gk. LAE 19.3, where 'ἐπιθυμία is the source of every sin'. The sin of

---

[64] D. Bonhoeffer, *Nachfolge*, Dietrich Bonhoeffer Werke 4, Munich, 1989, 282.

[65] The words are often paired, most commonly in Plato and Philo: Plato, *Phaedr.* 81B, 83B; *Symp.* 196C; Aristotle, *Eth. nic.* 1148A; Philo, *Congr.* 57, 59, 172; *Spec.* 2.30, 46; *Praem.* 17; cf. also Plutarch, *Mor.* 445B; Tit 3.3; Dio Chrysostom 1.13; 49.9; etc.

[66] Cf. Manton, 333 ('carnal desire is a gulf that is never filled up'); Trapp, 700 ('an endless piece of work').

[67] Cf. LAB 11.13; 4 Macc 2.5; Mt 5.28; Rom 7.7; 13.9; Did. 2.2; Barn. 19.6. Few commentators, however, here think of the decalogue; exceptions include Sleeper, 105-106; Blomberg-Kamell, 198.

[68] Lactantius, *Inst.* 5.6 SC 204 ed. Monat, 156. Cf. Jacob of Serug, *Hom. Elijah* 3 (Naboth) 1-2 ed. Kaufman, 177-81.

[69] The entire context—a long discussion of desire—is instructive and shows several contacts with James.

coveting is also central in Paul's analysis of sin in Rom 7 (see vv. 7-12), a chapter with other links to Jas 4. Given all this, it is not unexpected that James roots social conflict in failure to keep the tenth commandment.

Four more observations. First, οὐκ ἔχετε prepares for φθονεῖτε καὶ ζηλοῦτε: envying others arises from not having what they have. Second, James has already, in 2.8, quoted Lev 19.18, which Philo and others held to summarize the second half of the decalogue. So the rebuke in 4.2 goes hand in hand with the imperative in 2.8: to love neighbor means not to covet. Third, although a reader of the Bible might call to mind the desire of David for Bathsheba (2 Sam 11) or of Ahab for Naboth's vineyard (1 Kgs 21), James at this point is content to generalize: he offers no concrete illustration. Fourth, if one accepts the argument offered below, that the quotation in 4.5 comes from Eldad and Modad, then it becomes relevant that, in Num 11, the story of those two is closely associated with the sin of desire or craving; see 620 below.

φθονεῖτε καὶ ζηλοῦτε καὶ οὐ δύνασθε ἐπιτυχεῖν.[70] Although φθονέω occurs only twice in the LXX (Tob 4.7, 16) and one other time in the NT

---

[70] The textual tradition is nearly unanimous in reading φονεύετε instead of φθονεῖτε. Erasmus, *Annotationes*, 742, conjectured the latter to be original, and it occurs solely in 918Z, from the sixteenth century. Favoring emendation are Tyndale; Calvin, 296 ('the word "kill" has no relevance to the context'); Benson, 85; Spitta, 114; Windisch-Preisker, 27; Dibelius, 217-18; Chaine, 98; Moffatt, 58; Hauck, 25; Adamson, 168; Deppe, *Sayings*, 70; Klein, *Werk*, 108-11; Wettlaufer, 'Variants', 128-56. Against emendation are Manton, 332-33; Alford, 312; Beyschlag, 189; Hort, 89; Oesterley, 458; Knowling, 95-96; Plummer, 609; Ropes, 256; Mitton, 149-50; Mussner, 178-79; Laws, 170; Martin, 140-41; Kugelman, 46-47; Hartin, 197; Johnson, 276-77; Frankemölle, 586-87; Sleeper, 105-106; R. Wall, 196-97; Popkes, 259; Burchard, 169; Blomberg-Kamell, 188. Mayor, 136-37, seems uncertain, offering interpretation of both readings. Another possible emendation is φονᾶτε = 'you are blood-thirsty'; but this is less naturally paired with ζηλοῦτε. The arguments against Erasmus are these: (i) as just indicated, φθονεῖτε has insignificant textual support. (ii) If φονεύετε seems unexpected or extreme, one can appeal to texts in which φονεύω has figurative sense; cf. Beyschlag, 183; Cantinat, 198-99; Konradt, *Existenz*, 129; Andria, 1514 (James is 'exaggerating'); Wesley, 866; Blomberg-Kamell, 188; Gundry, 940 ('words can kill, so to speak'). See BAGD, s.v.; cf. Mt 5.21-26 and 1 Jn 3.15, which broaden, if hyperbolically, the definition of 'murder'; also Ecclus 34.24-25; 2 En. 10.5; b. B. Meṣi'a 58b. Ps.-Oecumenius *ad loc*. PG 119.492C, thought of people 'murdering their own souls'. (iii) But, as the history of interpretation shows, one can also, in the light of 2.11 and 5.6, understand the word literally. See Plummer, 609; Rendall, *Christianity*, 30-31, 113; Farley, 45 (the latter thinking of 5.4-6: withholding fitting wages leads to malnourishment, disease, and then death). (iv) ἐπιθυμεῖτε alludes, as we have seen, to the second half of the decalogue, which also features the prohibition of murder (οὐ φονεύσεις, Exod 20.15); and would it not have been natural to move from one commandment to another?

Despite these points, this writer, albeit with great hesitation, endorses Erasmus. (i) φθονέω and ζηλόω are a natural pair, often attested; cf. 1 Macc 8.16; T. Sim. 4.5; T. Benj. 4.4; 9.4; 3 Bar. 13.4; 1 Clem. 3.2; 4.7; 5.2; Vettius Valens, *Anthol. ix* 1.20.223; Cassius Dio 38.39.2; Plotinus, *Enn.* 3.6.1. This last reads: 'the soul accepts things as its own or rejects them as alien when it feels pleasure and pain, anger, envy, jealousy, lust'

(Gal 5.26), it is prominent in the Testaments of the Twelve Patriarchs.[71] Indeed, T. Sim. 3.1-6 offers a short discourse on envy which includes the proposition that 'ὁ φθόνος dominates the whole of a man's mind and does not allow him to eat or drink or do anything good. On the contrary, it lays the foundation for him to destroy the one he envies' (φθονούμενον).[72]

ζηλόω[73] is here a synonym of φθονέω, meaning 'be filled with envy'.[74] Note that m. 'Abot 4.21 associates 'envy' and 'desire' and regards them as primary sins: 'Envy (הקנאה) and desire (התאוה) and ambition take a man out of the world'.

καὶ οὐ δύνασθε ἐπιτυχεῖν[75] is another way of saying καὶ οὐκ ἔχετε. For δύναμαι, a word James likes, see on 1.21. ἐπιτυγχάνω (Jas: 1×) can signify getting what one is after,[76] so καὶ οὐ δύνασθε ἐπιτυχεῖν signals unsatisfied desire.

μάχεσθε καὶ πολεμεῖτε. These two *hapax legomena* recall v. 1 (πόλεμοι...μάχαι), forming a small chiasmus. See the discussion there. They mark the conclusion of a sequence: 'desire' leads to envy and jealousy, which in turn lead to 'disputes and conflicts'.

(φθονούσης, ζηλούσης, ἐπιθυμούσης). (ii) More or less synonymous pairs are otherwise prominent in Jas 4.1-3: πόλεμοι...μάχαι // καὶ οὐκ ἔχετε...καὶ οὐ δύνασθε ἐπιτυχεῖν // μάχεσθε...πολεμεῖτε. (iii) A scribal error could easily have turned φθονεῖτε into φονεύετε. (iv) Modern critical editions of the NT generally print φθόνοι for Gal 5.21; but most Greek mss., with support from some versions, have φόνοι. Assuming that the new editions are correct, φθόνοι became φόνοι, supplying a parallel for the hypothesized change in James. Similarly, 1 Pet 2.1 03 has φόνους, but the correct reading is φθόνους. (v) James has the related φθόνος in 4.5. Furthermore, 181 1243 2492 for that verse have φόνον, showing once again scribes changing φθο- to φο-. (vi) If nothing hints that φονεύετε has figurative sense, and if the literal sense remains jarring, φθονεῖτε commends itself as more suitable: the subject, after all, is desiring what one does not have. (E.F.F. Bishop, *Apostles*, 181-82, offers an interesting solution that, unfortunately, seems to depend upon a Semitic original: 'Another suggestion would be that some increased form of the Semitic *q-t-l* lies behind the Greek, which might have the meaning of "quarrel", as is the case with modern Arabic, where one form means "to pick a quarrel". An Arabic MS. in the University Library at Cambridge does have this very reading as a translation of φονεύτε (kill)... It might well be that φονεύτε was employed to render an Aramaic word having the same connotation as the Arabic Increased Form. In fact in ordinary speech people use *qatala* where they should use *qātala*, which means "try to kill" with the consequent extension of "quarrel"'.)

[71] Cf. T. Gad 3.3; 7.2; T. Benj. 9.4.
[72] On the relevance of this passage for Jas 4 see Johnson, *Brother*, 198-99, and for a discussion of ancient conceptions of envy and jealousy see J.J. Pilch and B.J. Malina, *Handbook of Biblical Social Values*, Peabody, MA, 1998, 59-63, 209-12.
[73] Jas: 1×; cf. ζῆλος in 3.14, 16.
[74] Cf. LXX Gen 37.1; Num 5.14, 30—all for the Piel of אשק; Acts 7.9; 17.5; 1 Cor 13.4; 2 Clem. 4.3.
[75] Cf. Ign. *Eph.* 1.2 (ἐπιτυχεῖν δυνηθῶ); Heliodorus, *Aeth.* 4.5.1 (δυνηθείην ἐπιτυχεῖν); Iamblichus, *Comm. math.* 9.21 (ἐπιτυχεῖν δυνηθείη).
[76] As in LXX Prov 12.27; Rom 7.11; T. Job 11.9; Gk. Apoc. Ezra 6.22.

οὐκ ἔχετε διὰ τὸ μὴ αἰτεῖσθαι ὑμᾶς.[77] οὐκ ἔχετε διά seemingly appears only in James and later quotations of our lines. For αἰτέω (cf. v. 3) see on 1.5.

The statement is surprising, for surely those heretofore characterized as envious or jealous want what they should not want, as the very next verse makes evident: 'in order to spend what you get on your pleasures'. James, however, sets forth two options—the first perhaps being hypothetical—in order to be comprehensive: either the envious do not ask, presumably because they know better than to ask for what they desire, or, not knowing better, they shamelessly ask for the wrong things. In either case, they receive nothing.

The line amounts to a digression of sorts. 4.1-12 is above all concerned with communal conflict and affiliated issues, not unanswered prayer. But the οὐκ ἔχετε of v. 2a apparently moved our author to think of unanswered prayer, a topic of special interest to him, as 1.7-8 reveals. The text nonetheless retains coherence, in part because James can associate the sins of both 4.1-2a and 2b-3 with ἡδονή.[78]

Verse 3. The verse seems designed to move readers—who, whatever their faults, nonetheless pray—to ponder why they ask God for this or that.

Some have fretted about the intratextual tension between 'You ask and do not receive' in v. 3 and 'You do not ask' in v. 2. Huther, 128, found harmony this way: for James, asking badly or wickedly 'does not constitute an actual prayer, so that the foregoing declaration is nevertheless true'.[79] Does this seek more consistency than the text warrants?

αἰτεῖτε καὶ οὐ λαμβάνετε. We have already seen, in the discussion on 1.5, that James was acquainted with the saying in Mt 7.7 = Lk 11.9. Our line shows that he also knew what immediately followed that saying in Q: πᾶς γὰρ ὁ αἰτῶν λαμβάνει (Mt 7.8 = Lk 11.10).[80] For although αἰτέω

---

[77] 01 025 044 5 38 61 88 94 *et al.* L427 L590 *et al.* PsOec **L**:SFV[mss] **K**:B **S**:PH **A** G:A1BG-D **SI**:ChMSi **Ä** have καί at the beginning. Dibelius, 218, accepted this as it results in a consistent formal pattern:

ἐπιθυμεῖτε—	καὶ οὐκ ἔχετε
φθονεῖτε καὶ ζηλοῦτε—	καὶ οὐ δύνασθε
μάχεσθε καὶ πολεμεῖτε—	καὶ οὐκ ἔχετε
αἰτεῖτε—	καὶ οὐ λαμβάνετε.

But connecting μάχεσθε καὶ πολεμεῖτε with καὶ οὐκ ἔχετε remains awkward: the clauses are not readily related; cf. McKnight, 328.

[78] Townsend, 'Warning', 213, for whom James addresses Christian zealots, thinks the issue is forcing the coming of the kingdom through violence rather than prayer; cf. Lk 11.2.

[79] Earlier, Manton, 333, said much the same thing.

[80] Ecclesiastical exegetes of the gospels often cite James when commenting on Mt 7.7-8 or Lk 11.9-10; so e.g. Origen, *Lk* frag. 184 GCS 49 ed. Rauer, 303; Albertus Magnus, *Super Mt cap. I–XIV* Opera Omnia 21/1 ed. Schmidt, 252; Bonaventure, *Lk*

(cf. v. 2 and see on 1.5) + λαμβάνω (see on 1.7) was a common expression,[81] and while both words were used in connection with prayer (see on 1.5 and 7), their combination with reference to that subject appears to be unattested before the Jesus tradition. The Synoptic saying, beyond that, was manifestly popular. Not only does Q attest to it, but so does John's Gospel,[82] and there are additional variants in Mt 18.19 and Mk 11.24. Moreover, 1 Jn 3.22, like James, also alludes to it (ὃ ἐὰν αἰτῶμεν λαμβάνομεν).

Modern commentators have sometimes pondered why James uses the middle, then the active, then the middle: αἰτεῖσθε, αἰτεῖτε, αἰτεῖσθαι. Alford, 312, deems this interchange 'unaccountable'. Hartin, 198, explains it as 'a stylistic variation'. Mayor, 137-38, urges that the middle 'has a slight additional shade of meaning', and that only the active can imply 'using the words, without the spirit of prayer'. Moulton agrees.[83] Turner objects that 'it is hard to find much solid grammatical evidence for this distinction'. He suggests instead that perhaps James 'had before him a letter from his readers complaining, "We ask, and receive not". They had used the active voice, as it happened, and he therefore retained it in quoting their words. He himself preferred to use the middle voice.'[84] While the evidence for James responding to a letter is nil, Turner may nonetheless not be far off. In v. 3a, James redeploys a saying of Jesus, which has the active; that is, James' αἰτεῖτε corresponds to Jesus' αἰτῶν, just as his λαμβάνετε matches Jesus' λαμβάνει. The switch from the middle to the active back to the middle may, then, be a sign of James' indebtedness to tradition,[85] and perhaps evidence that he wished at least Christian readers to note his indebtedness.

In Matthew and Luke, the promise about prayer is unqualified: 'everyone who asks receives'. Christian reflection inevitably tamed and tempered this hyperbolic utterance. In Jn 16.24, those who ask do so in Jesus' name. This grounds the assurance not in God's universal goodness

---

11.10 Opera Omnia 10 ed. Peltier, 523. John of Damascus, *C. Jacob*. PTS 22 ed. Kotter, 112, conflates (unconsciously?) James and Matthew: αἰτεῖτε καὶ οὐ δοθήσεται ὑμῖν διότι κακῶς αἰτεῖτε. Modern scholars who believe that Jas 4.3 may depend upon the Jesus tradition include Schlatter, 243; Shepherd, 'Matthew', 46; Adamson, 169; Davidson, 159; Deppe, *Sayings*, 71-74; Hartin, *Q*, 176-79; Johnson, *Brother*, 143-46; Popkes, 260; Kloppenborg, 'Emulation', 134-37; Blomberg-Kamell, 188-89, 198.
[81] Cf. Plutarch, *Nicias* 4.3; Appianus, *Frag. hist. Rom.* 23.1; Cassius Dio 47.17.5; etc.
[82] 16.24: αἰτεῖτε καὶ λήμψεσθε; cf. 14.13; 15.7, 16; 16.26.
[83] MHT 1.160-61.
[84] Turner, *Insights*, 163-64.
[85] Cf. Kittel, 'Ort', 89; Davids, 160; Hartin, *Q*, 177-78; Popkes, 265. Although Deppe, *Sayings*, 71-74, contends that James here cites Jesus, he claims that the active and middle voices of αἰτέω were interchangeable and that therefore one cannot make any inference from the switch from one to the other. But the issue is not whether the two voices had the same meaning but whether readers would observe the alternation.

(a possibly reading of Q) but allegiance to Jesus. First John 3.22 makes a similar move: 'we receive from him whatever we ask, because we obey his commandments and do what pleases him'. The formulation in Herm. *Vis.* 3.10.6 is: 'every request requires humility'. In James, the qualification is a bit different: prayers go unanswered because the supplicants pray for their own selfish pleasures. But earlier, in 1.6-8, the blame is laid on doubt, on being double-minded. Clearly our author has pondered unanswered prayer,[86] and he has more than one explanation for it.[87]

Readers familiar with Jesus' extravagant logion about prayer can appreciate James' ironic use of it here. Our author has turned it into its opposite: a statement about prayer certainly being answered has become a statement about prayer certainly not being answered.

διότι κακῶς αἰτεῖσθαι. Both διότι and κακῶς are *hapax legomena* for our book. κακῶς + αἰτέω seems unattested before James. Perhaps it was modeled upon κακῶς + λέγω.[88] In any case, the God who gives 'good gifts' (1.17) does not answer wicked requests.[89]

ἵνα ἐν ταῖς ἡδοναῖς ὑμῶν δαπανήσητε. This elaborates the generalization just made. James uses ἵνα also in 1.4. Most translations and commentators seem to assume that ἐν here means 'on' or 'upon'. But 'in return for', as in LXX Gen 31.41; Hos 12.12; Ecclus 7.18, is equally plausible. The recurrence of ἡδονή (see on v. 1) means that those who pray in order to satisfy their own pleasures are, in effect, praying for social conflict, because such pleasures cause such conflict. God, however, does not go along: their prayers return empty.[90]

δαπανάω occurs in the LXX exclusively in so-called apocryphal books[91] where it refers to cultic offerings being expended or consumed or to something losing strength.[92] In the NT, where the word is uncommon,[93]

---

[86] As have of course many outside the Christian tradition. According to Pesiq. R. 22.7, not reverencing God's ineffable name explains unanswered prayers.

[87] Christians have found his words useful in explaining why God seemingly leaves many or most prayers unanswered; cf. H.S. Bainbridge, *Talks to Candidates for Divine Healing*, London, 1922, 72. See further 589.

[88] As in LXX Exod 22.27; Lev 20.9; Isa 8.11; etc.

[89] Aquinas, *Academic Sermons* 10.3.1 ET Hoogland, 134, cites as illustration Mt 20.20-21, where the mother of the sons of Zebedee asks for her two sons to sit on the right and left of Jesus.

[90] The history of interpretation naturally expands James' comment to cover a host of issues. Clement of Alexandria, *Strom.* 7.7.44.2 GCS 17 ed. Stählin, 33, clarifies that the wicked ask for things that seem to be good but are not. Ps.-Dionysius, *E.H.* 7 θεωρία 7 PTS 36 ed. Heil and Ritter, 128, teaches that a hierarch should not pray for any who died in a state of unholiness. Maximus the Confessor, *Quaest. ad Thal.* 59.50-54 CCSG 22 ed. Laga and Steel, 47, says that prayers uttered with *apatheia* will be answered, those without it unanswered.

[91] Tob 1.7; Jdt 11.12; 12.4; Bel 5, 17, 20; 1 Macc 14.32; 2 Macc 1.23, 32; 2.10.

[92] Cf. also Barn. 14.5; Herm. *Mand.* 12.1.2.

[93] See otherwise only Mk 5.26; Lk 15.14; Acts 21.24.

the meaning is always 'spend' or 'spend freely' (BAGD, s.v.). Its connection with ἡδονή was not James' invention.[94] Given what James has to say about the rich elsewhere, the reader may think of the well-to-do spending money on themselves.

Verse 4. Those James is countering are not only at war within themselves (v. 1) but at war with God.

μοιχαλίδες.[95] The word 'anticipates and summarises the thought expressed in the verse itself' (Ropes, 261). In Mt 12.39; 16.4; and Mk 8.38, μοιχαλίς (Jas: 1x) indicts Jesus' contemporaries as an unfaithful generation. Although there is no evidence that this usage has influenced James,[96] James uses the same insult to implicate members of his audience as unfaithful to the God of Israel (cf. 1.1). His choice of the feminine[97] is striking: everywhere else he addresses his readers with masculine forms. 'Adulteresses' does not pick out women among the readers;[98] it instead recalls especially the book of Hosea—likely just alluded to in 3.13—in which the prophet takes a woman prone to adultery for a wife in order to demonstrate the people's waywardness.[99] But the motif of God as a husband to whom some are unfaithful also appears elsewhere in the Jewish Bible,[100] and the LXX associates μοιχαλίς with sinful Israel or Jerusalem.[101] In James the term designates forsaking God to take the world as a paramour; cf. Augustine's rewrite of our verse: friendship with this world is adultery against God.[102]

---

[94] Cf. Josephus, *Ant.* 19.207 (δαπανῶντα εἰς ἡδονάς); Philostratus, *Soph.* 2.570 (δαπανώμενος ἐς ἡδονάς).

[95] The scribe responsible for the textual variant, μοιχοὶ καὶ μοιχαλίδες (01C2 025 044 5 69 88 206 218 *et al.* **Byz** Phot PsOec **S**:H^mss H^msA **G**:G-D **Sl**:ChMSi), understood the accusation literally (so Metzger, *Commentary*, 682-83), as have some commentators since; see n. 98. But see D.N. Freedman, 'Bible Critic at Work', *BR* 15 (February 1999), 42-43, for the argument that haplography explains the omission.

[96] See Schmitt, 'Adulteresses'.

[97] Cf. LXX Prov 18.22; 30.20; Ezek 16.38; 23.45; Hos 3.1; Mal 3.5.

[98] But Spitta, 114, favors a literal interpretation. Cf. Hort, 91, and Oesterley, 458: 'the depraved state of morals to which the whole section bears witness must in part at least have been due to the wickedness and co-operation of the women'. For Cabaniss, 'Homily', the entirety of 4.1-10 addresses widows in the church.

[99] Jobes, 'Minor Prophets', 139-40, argues that James alludes to Hosea as well as Mal 3.5. R. Wall, 200-201, thinks Ezek 23.45 specifically in mind. Schmitt, 'Adulteresses', finds an allusion to Prov 30.20. Criticism in Cargal, 159-60.

[100] E.g. Isa 1.21; 57.3; Jer 3.9, 20; 9.2; Ezek 16; 23; cf. also 2 Cor 11.2.

[101] Ezek 23.45; Hos 3.1; Mal 3.5. Apoc. Sed. 6.3, 4 uses it of Adam: he became a μοιχαλίς. According to Mek. on Exod 20.16, the one who worships idols is 'as though he committed adultery, breaking his covenant with God'.

[102] *Conf.* 1.13.21 ed. O'Donnell, 11. Occasionally a commentator has wondered whether addressing the readers as though they were women would add a touch of scorn in a patriarchal society; so Knowling, 98, citing Homer., *Il.* 2.225: 'women, not men, of Achaia'. Cf. Plumptre, 90, and the interesting note of Carr, 52.

οὐκ οἴδατε ὅτι. Paul uses this expression to introduce questions.[103] James 4.4 supplies the only other Christian example before Irenaeus.[104] Commentators on Paul often reckon οὐκ οἴδατε ὅτι characteristic of diatribe, as do a few commentators on James.[105] One should note, however, that all the relevant parallels[106] are inexact, lacking ὅτι or having the second person singular or else varying in some other way. The only two pre-Christian examples of the precise expression, οὐκ οἴδατε ὅτι, are from the LXX—Gen 44.15 (for הלוא ידעתם כי) and 2 Sam 3.38 (for הלוא כי תדעו)—and have nothing to do with diatribe. Cf. also the use of οὐκ οἶδας ὅτι in Judg 15.11; 2 Βασ 2.26; Jn 19.10; T. Abr. RecLng. 8.9, 12; Apoc. Sed. 10.2; 14.4; 15.3, which also have nothing to do with diatribe; so too οὐκ ᾔδειτε ὅτι in Lk 2.49 and אין אתה יודע ש in b. 'Erub. 21b; Ruth Rab. 3.3; et al.

As Johnson observes, it is unclear why the readers should know what follows, for there is 'no such proverb in all the Hellenistic literature, nor is it found in Old Testament wisdom texts or in the Hellenistic Jewish literature'.[107] Johnson highlights the close parallel in 1 Jn 2.15-17 and suggests a common Christian tradition.[108] Others would suggest, more specifically, that Mt 6.24 = Lk 16.13 stands in the background; see n. 109.

ἡ φιλία τοῦ κόσμου ἔχθρα τοῦ θεοῦ ἐστιν; Cf. Rom 8.7 (ἔχθρα εἰς θεόν) and the absolute antitheses in Mt 6.24 = Lk 16.13;[109] 2 Tim 3.4 (φιλήδονοι μᾶλλον ἢ φιλόθεοι); Poimandres 4.6 ed. Nock and Festugiére, 1.51 ('It is not possible...to attach yourself both to things mortal and to things divine... It is not possible to have both'); and especially Philo frag. 2.649: 'It is impossible for love of the world to coexist with the love of God'. James' nicely balanced, memorable aphorism is evidently his invention.[110]

---

[103] Rom 6.16; 1 Cor 3.16; 5.6; 6.2, 3, 9, 15, 16, 19; 9.13, 24.
[104] *Haer.* 1.20.2 FC 8.1 ed. Brox, 272, a variant reading for Lk 2.49.
[105] E.g. Johnson, 278.
[106] Such as Epictetus, *Diatr.* 1.4.16: οὐκ οἶδας ὅτι.
[107] Johnson, *Brother*, 209-10.
[108] Nienhuis, *Paul*, 208-11, rather suggests James' use of 1 John.
[109] Commentators are often put in mind of this: Didymus of Alexandria, *Ep. can. ad loc.* ed. Zoepfl, 8; Bede *ad loc.* CCSL 121 ed. Hurst, 212; *Chaîne Arménienne* 58 ed. Renoux, 120; Manton, 342; Gill, 796; Henry, *ad loc.*; Neander, 96; Winkler, 55 ('the text is an allusion to Christ's declaration in Matt. 6:24'); Carr, 52; Weidner, 64; Knowling, 98-99; Shepherd, 'Matthew', 46; Knoch, 213; Tamez, *Message*, 47; Hartin, 198; Konradt, *Existenz*, 131-34 (drawing a parallel between the concern for money in Mt 6.19-34 and Jas 4); Sleeper, 107; Church, 386; *et al.* Kloppenborg, 'Emulation', 134-36, thinks that James has indeed paraphrased the Synoptic saying. Deppe, *Sayings*, 106-108, however, argues against finding a deliberate allusion or conscious dependence here. This commentator leaves the question open, noting only that if James did rewrite the saying of Jesus, omission of the Aramaic mammon is expected. Oddly enough, for Benson, 88, the quotation in v. 5 is a loose paraphrase of Mt 6.24. Trudinger, 'Otherworldly', 62, seems alone in imagining 4.4 to be an 'echo' of Jn 15.18.
[110] But for Spitta, 116-17, James here quotes; ὃς ἐὰν οὖν κτλ. is then his comment.

Both φιλία (Jas: 1×) meaning 'love' or 'friendship' and ἔχθρα (NT: 6×) meaning 'enmity' are common in LXX wisdom literature; they appear together, moreover, in Prov 15.17 and 25.10; and Wis 7.14 uses φιλία of friendship with God (πρὸς θεὸν ἐστείλεντο φιλίαν); cf. 7.27; 8.18. Even beyond the LXX, however, the word pair, φιλία—ἔχθρα, lent itself to pithy formulations: Thycidides 5.95 ('your ἔχθρα does not injure us as much as your φιλία'); Isocrates, *Ad Dem.* 33 ('praise is the foundation of φιλίας, blame that of ἔχθρας'); Diodorus Siculus 27.16.1 ('The intelligent man should see to it that his φιλίας are immortal, his ἔχθρας mortal'); Philo, *Virt.* 152 ('It is a very admirable saying of the ancients that in joining φιλίας we should not ignore the possibility of ἔχθραν'); Cassius Dio 45.10.6 ('influenced by his φιλίαν for Lepidus and by his ἔχθραν for Caesar').

That Abraham was God's 'friend', φίλος (2.23), has probably encouraged translators to render the φιλία in 4.4 as 'friendship'.[111] Yet given that μοιχαλίδες precedes ἡ φιλία κτλ. and that φιλία can refer to sexual love,[112] 'love', with its potential for sexual connotation, may be the better choice: James is declaring some of his readers to be adulteresses because they are passionate about 'the world' as opposed to God.

For the concept of the hostile κόσμος in James cf. the ἐπίγειος of 3.15.[113] One may compare 2 Tim 4.10 ('Demas, in love with this present world'); 1 Jn 2.15 ('Do not love the world or the things in the world. If anyone loves the world, love for the Father is not in him'); 5.19 ('the whole world is in the hands of the evil one'); and the discussion in 2 Clem. 5.[114] We have here again James' pessimism, akin to what we meet in 4 Ezra and parts of 1 Enoch: the world—not just human society—is no longer God's world, which is why the righteous have 'hated and despised this world of oppression together with all its ways of life and its habits' (1 En. 48.7), and why God must right its wrongs (cf. Jas 5.3) and even perhaps replace it (cf. Jas 5.7?). Implicit is the transience of the present 'world of corruption' (2 Bar. 40.3) and the permanence of the superior world to come.[115]

---

[111] Which then makes ancient discussions of friendship pertinent; see Johnson, *Brother*, 213-16.

[112] E.g. Prov 7.18; Ecclus 9.8; 4 Macc 2.11.

[113] See further on 1.27; also Johnson, *Brother*, 211-13; Frankemölle, 599-601.

[114] Also 1 Cor 2.12; 7.31; 11.32; Gal 4.3-4; 6.16; Col 2.8. Christians have incessantly cited 1 Jn 2.15 in connection with Jas 4.4. Note e.g. Origen, *Rom.* 4.8.2; Didymus of Alexandria, *Ep. can. ad* 1 Jn 2.15-17 ed. Zoepfl, 47; Cyril of Alexandria, *Hom. pasch.* 25.1 PG 77.904C; Sixtus III (?), *Ep. de castitate* 13.3 PLSup 1.1493; Abba Isaiah of Scetis, *Ascetic Discourses* 21 ET Chryssavgis and Penkett, Kalamazoo, MI, 2002, 214; John of Damascus, *Parall.* B 6 PG 95.1281B; Symeon the New Theologian, *Cat. 1-34* 2.306-12; 5.781-802 SC 96 ed. Krivochéine and Paramelle, 266, 444-46; John Eugenicus, *Mem. adhort. ad Theod. Porphyr.* ed. Lampros, 91; John of Ávila, *Lecc.* 12 Obras completas de San Juan de Ávila 2 ed. Balust and Hernández, 203; Poole, 892; John of Kronstadt, *My Life in Christ*, Jordanville, NY, 2000, 298; *et al.*

[115] Cf. T. Job 33-34; 1 Cor 7.31; 1 Jn 2.17; 2 Bar 48.50.

ὃς ἐὰν οὖν βουληθῇ φίλος εἶναι τοῦ κόσμου, ἐχθρὸς θεοῦ καθίσταται. This restates the thought of the previous clause, with ἐχθρός (more battlefield language; see on v. 1) and φίλος (see on 2.23) replacing ἔχθρα and φιλία. The variation adds emphasis and also calls to mind the large number of texts that speak of God's enemies, who in the Bible are requited, defeated, crushed.[116] Nothing could be more foolish than setting oneself up as an opponent of God.

οὖν occurs for the first time here but appears four more times: 4.7, 17; 5.7, 16.[117] For βούλομαι see on 1.18. ὃς ἐάν for ὃς ἄν, although a vulgarism, is common enough in the canonical gospels (e.g. Mt 5.19, 32) and the papyri.

Verse 5. James buttresses his argument by quoting 'the scripture'.

ἢ δοκεῖτε ὅτι κενῶς ἡ γραφὴ λέγει. Cf. 2.23: ἡ γραφὴ ἡ λέγουσα. For ἤ see on 1.17, and for γραφή—the singular for the plural collection is common in Paul and already attested in Let. Aris. 155—see on 2.8. δοκέω occurs also in 1.26. Introducing a question with δοκεῖτε ὅτι might, in view of Epictetus, *Diatr.* 1.4.25 and 4.1.33, be one more sign of James' debt to Hellenistic diatribe; cf. 2 Cor 12.19. Yet δοκεῖτε ὅτι also introduces questions in Lk 12.51; 13.2 and 4, and in those places it may be pre-Lukan.[118] So one might, given what we otherwise know of James, just as well see influence from the Jesus tradition.

κενῶς[119] occurs only once in the LXX, in Isa 49.4 (for לריק). Some have found here a general statement about the Bible; cf. Isa 55.11. The Lutheran Bengel wrote: 'whatever the Scripture says is in earnest. We should revere every word.'[120]

With ἡ γραφὴ λέγει one may compare Jn 7.38, 42; 19.37 (γραφὴ λέγει); Rom 4.3 (ἡ γραφὴ λέγει); 9.17; 10.11; 11.2; Gal 4.30; 1 Tim 5.18; 1 Clem. 34.6; 35.7; 42.5; 2 Clem. 2.4; 6.8; 14.1, 2. Several of these parallels involve questions,[121] so James is employing a common rhetorical strategy. Its function is akin to the 'Have you not read?' in the Synoptics.[122] The speaker assumes the audience does in fact know scripture: he indicts not their ignorance but their failure to live by what they know.

---

[116] Num 32.21; Job 13.24; Pss 68.1, 21; 92.10 (Bede *ad loc.* CCSL 121 ed. Hurst, 212, cites this: 'O Lord...your enemies will perish'); Isa 59.18; Nah 1.2; Wis 5.17; Ecclus 49.9; 2 Macc 12.28; etc.

[117] Thurén, 'Rhetoric', 268, suggests: 'This could be interpreted so that the last sections constitute a conclusion' to the whole epistle.

[118] So at least J. Jeremias, *Die Sprache des Lukasevangeliums*, Göttingen, 1980, 223, 226.

[119] NT: 1. Gk. Pseudepigrapha (Denis): 0×. Philo: 0×. Josephus: 0×. Cf. Herm. *Mand.* 11.13.

[120] Bengel, 503; cf. Wolzogen, 210.

[121] Jn 7.42; Rom 4.3; 11.2; Gal 4.30.

[122] Mt 12.3, 5; 19.4; 22.3; Mk 12.10, 26; Lk 6.3.

πρὸς φθόνον ἐπιποθεῖ τὸ πνεῦμα ὃ κατῴκισεν ἐν ἡμῖν; This is one of the most challenging lines in early Christian literature. It is of uncertain sense and uncertain source. It is no surprise that Greek patristic tradition, aside from commentaries and anthologies, appears not to quote it even once.[123] Readers evidently did not know what to make of it.[124]

Everywhere else in the Greek Bible, φθόνος (Jas: 1×; but cf. 4.2) means '(malevolent) envy': the connotation is negative.[125] It is likewise negative in the only non-Christian example of πρὸς φθόνον, that being Demosthenes, Or. 20.165: φιλανθρωπία πρὸς φθόνον, 'philanthropy against envy'.[126] The sense in James is often thought to be 'jealously' or 'enviously', that is, πρὸς φθόνον = φθονερῶς,[127] the subject being either God or God's Spirit. The NRSV has: 'God yearns jealously for the spirit that he has made to dwell in us'.[128] πρὸς φθόνον, however, can equally indicate a goal—'longs for envy'. Moreover, the NRSV's translation ill suits the context—James has railed against envy (v. 2; cf. 3.14, 16)—and it does not harmonize with the other biblical uses of φθόνος or with the negative use of φθόνος in the Graeco-Roman world.[129] Had James (or his source) wanted to refer to the positive quality of divine zeal, he almost certainly would have used ζῆλος.[130]

ἐπιποθέω (Jas: 1×), which occurs with πρός in LXX Ps 41.2 (ἐπιποθεῖ...πρὸς σέ), means 'strongly desire', 'long for', 'feel tender affection

---

[123] There is also not a single entry for Jas 4.5 in the multi-volume *Biblica Patristica*, and my researches have failed to add anything to the deficiency.

[124] So too some modern commentators. Cf. Könnecke, *Emendationen*, 15 (it 'makes no sense'); Windisch-Preisker, 27 ('The citation is for us hardly understandable'). Clarke, 820, comments: 'There is not a critic in Europe who has considered the passage who has not been puzzled with it'.

[125] 1 Macc 8.16; 3 Macc 6.7; Wis 2.24; 6.23; Mt 27.18; Mk 15.10; Rom 1.29; Gal 5.21; Phil 1.15; 1 Tim 6.4; Tit 3.3 (following ἐπιθυμίαις καὶ ἡδοναῖς); 1 Pet 2.1. Cf. Gk. frag. Jub. 10.1; Let. Aris. 224; T. Sim. 2.13; 3.1, 2, 4, 6; 4.5, 7; 6.2; T. Dan 2.5; T. Gad 4.5; T. Jos. 1.3, 7; 10.3; T. Benj. 7.2, 5; 8.1; Sib. Or. 3.377, 662; Philo, *Fug.* 154; *Mos.* 1.2; Josephus, *Ant.* 2.10; 3 Bar. 13.4; 1 Clem. 3.2; 5.2; etc. For its common association with 'the evil eye', a term used to describe the ungenerous, see J.H. Elliott, 'The Fear of the Leer', *Forum* 4/4 (1988), 56-57, 64.

[126] Cf. T. Dan 2.5: 'a disposition to envy (εἰς φθόνον) his brother'.

[127] Cf. BAGD, s.v. πρός 3f.

[128] Cf. Jeremias, 'Jac 4 5', calling attention to the tradition that the soul is a loan from God which must be returned: Eccl 12.7; Wis 15.8; Josephus, *Bell.* 3.372; Sifre 357 on Deut 34.5; etc.

[129] See Johnson, *Brother*, 182-201, and Plutarch's essay, *De Invidia et Odio*. Cf. Clement of Alexandria, *Strom.* 7.2 GCS 17 ed. Stählin, 7: 'φθόνος does not touch the Lord...nor with the Lord is there any envy of the things of human beings'.

[130] Cf. LXX 4 Βασ 19.31; Isa 9.7; 26.11; 37.32; 63.15; Zech 1.14; 2 Cor 11.2; etc. See further Bauckham, 'Spirit', 273-74; Michl, 'Spruch', 170. According to Trench, *Synonyms*, 87, φθόνος signifies 'incapable of good' and 'is used always and only' of something evil.

for'.[131] In LXX Deut 32.11 (under the figure of an eagle, for רחף) and Jer 13.14 (for חמל), God is the subject of this verb. The same is true of Theod. Job 14.15, where ἐπιποθέω does duty for כסב (as also in LXX Ps 83.2): 'you would long for the work of your hands'.[132] But in LXX Ps 61.11, the connotations are negative: ἐπὶ ἅρπαγμα μὴ ἐπιποθεῖτε (MT: בגזל אל־תהבלו: 'set no reliance on robbery'); so too in LXX Ecclus 25.21; Aq. Ezek 23.5, 7, 9; and Philo, *Mos*. 1.184 ('the in-born short-sightedness of mortality, which ἐπιποθοῦντος that assistance should be rendered quickly and at the moment').

As for τὸ πνεῦμα ὃ κατῴκισεν ἐν ἡμῖν, all three elements raise questions. (i) τὸ πνεῦμα could be the human spirit (cf. 2.26) or God's Holy Spirit or the 'spirit of contention' among James' readers.[133]

(ii) NA[27] and the *Editio Critica Maior* read κατῴκισεν ('he made to dwell'), following P[74] 01 03 044 049 *et al*. But 025 5 33 69 88 **Byz** NilAnc PsOec attest κατῴκησεν, 'he dwelt'. If James wrote the latter and the rest of the clause is not corrupt, then 'the spirit/Spirit that dwelt in us' must be the subject. In line with this are parallels in Hermas.[134] If James instead used the causative κατοικίζω, then he could have intended to say either 'the spirit/Spirit that (God) has caused to dwell in us yearns jealously' or '(God) yearns jealously over the spirit that he has put in us'. With these possibilities one can compare Herm. *Mand*. 3.1 (τὸ πνεῦμα ὃ ὁ θεὸς κατῴκισεν ἐν τῇ σαρκὶ ταύτῃ); *Sim*. 5.6.5 (τὸ πνεῦμα τὸ ἅγιον... κατῴκισεν ὁ θεὸς εἰς σάρκα).[135] A decision is difficult. Confusing κατῴ-κισεν for κατῴκησεν or *vice versa* would have been almost inevitable: because of itacism, the two would have sounded the same. It will not do to settle the issue by urging that 'since κατοικίζειν occurs nowhere else in the New Testament, copyists were more likely to replace it with the much more common κατοικεῖν, than *vice versa*'.[136] κατοικίζειν appears over fifty times in the LXX and was hardly an exotic word. Also weak is the argument, which R. Wall, 203, forwards, that a scribe wished to avoid the possibility of taking Jas 4.5 to implicate God as the source of the spirit of envy. One might just as well contend that a scribe, understanding πρὸς φθόνον in a positive sense, wanted to clarify by making God the clear subject. Nonetheless, κατῴκισεν is the better reading. It has stronger

---

[131] Cf. LXX Deut 13.8; Ps 83.2; Wis 15.19; Rom 1.11; Phil 1.8; 1 Pet 2.2. Literature: Jeremias, 'Jac 4 5'; Spicq, 'ἐπιποθέω', *TLNT* 2.58-60; idem, ''Επιποθεῖν, Désirer ou chérir?', *RB* 64 (1959), 184-95.

[132] Jeremias, 'Jac 4 5', also observes that Frag. Tg. Gen 2.2 has: 'the memra of the Lord cherished (חמיד) on the seventh day his work that he had done'.

[133] Recent commentators do not note the possibility of identifying the πνεῦμα with Satan, a view Manton, 346, 348, attributes to 'some'. Cf. Diodati, *ad loc*.

[134] *Mand*. 5.1.2 (τὸ πνεῦμα τὸ ἅγιον τὸ κατοικοῦν ἐν σοί); 5.2.5 (οὗ καὶ τὸ πνεῦμα τὸ ἅγιον κατοικεῖ); 10.2.5 (τὸ πνεῦμα τὸ ἅγιον τὸ ἐν σοὶ κατοικοῦν).

[135] Leaving aside James, these two texts from Hermas supply the earliest Christian instances of κατοικίζω.

[136] So Metzger, *Commentary*, 683.

external attestation, and the aorist makes sense for κατώκισεν—the reference is to something God did in the past—but not for κατώκησεν: the human or divine spirit dwells in people now, not just in the past.[137]

(iii) NA[27] (without apparatus) and the *Editio Critica Maior* prefer ἡμῖν at the end, which is far better attested than ὑμῖν. Either could be attributed to itacism. One might prefer ὑμῖν for internal reasons: ἐν ὑμῖν appears in 3.13; 4.1; 5.13, 14, 19, ἐν ἡμῖν nowhere else in James. Yet the former is confined to late minuscules (e.g. 1, 5, 6, 252, 365, 378 *et al.*), three lectionaries (590, 884, 2087), and L:SF. It seems best then to follow the standard critical editions.

Given the awkward and cryptic nature of πρός...ἡμῖν as well as the text-critical issues, exegetes confront a confusing plethora of possibilities regarding the interpretation of the whole, among them the following: (i) Maybe an οὐ inadvertently dropped out immediately before or after πρὸς φθόνον, so that the original was 'The Spirit/spirit that God made to dwell in us does not yearn for envy'. (ii) Perhaps an entire line has been lost, so that several words between φθόνον and ἐπιποθει are missing, in which case we can hardly recover them. (iii) Alternatively, all or some part of πρὸς φθόνον κτλ. could be an early marginal note that worked its way into the text. (iv) A few have guessed that James wrote πρὸς τὸν θεόν κτλ., which through scribal error became πρὸς φθόνον κτλ.[138] (v) One might take πρός to mean 'with regard to'[139] and then tie πρὸς φθόνον to λέγει: 'The Scripture says regarding envy...'[140] This was the view of Ps.-Oecumenius *ad loc.* PG 119.496B-97A, who regarded ἐπιποθεῖ...χάριν as part of James' comment on the citation from Proverbs. (vi) One could also construe πρὸς φθόνον...χάριν in its entirety as editorial interpretation of the quotation that follows: vv. 5b-6a are 'an introductory gloss to the proverb designed to advance James' paraenetic aims'.[141]

(vii) The subject is God, who yearns jealously over the Holy Spirit that he has placed in Christians.[142] (viii) For McCartney, 214-15, God yearns jealously over the divinely bestowed spirit of wisdom. (ix) The subject is

---

[137] Cf. Michl, 'Spruch', 168, who observes that the Old Latin and Vulgate, which make *spiritus* the subject, have the present tense: *(in)habitat*.

[138] So Kirn, 'Noch einmal'; idem, 'Vorschlag'; Könnecke, *Emendationen*, 15-16; Wettlaufer, 'Variants', 193-201. Note also perhaps Severian of Gabala *apud* the *Catenae* ed. Cramer, 29: 'the Spirit that is in us desires fellowship πρὸς θεόν'. Although the conjecture appears to go back to J.J. Wettstein, *Prolegomena ad Novi Testamenti Graeci editionem accuratissimam*, Amsterdam, 1730, 172 (where it is listed but not discussed), I find no trace of it in Wettstein's notes *ad loc.* in the 1751 edition of his *Novum Testamentum graecum*.

[139] Cf. BAGD, s.v., 3eβ.

[140] Cf. Paret, 'Zitat', 217-18. So too Morrell, *Conjectures*, 594. Morrell then construes what follows as an imperative: 'Covet that spirit, or wisdom, which dwelleth in us', which he takes to be an allusion to Wis 1.4-6; 6.11; 7.22-23. But λέγει directly introduces the scriptural citation in v. 6, as does ἡ γραφὴ ἡ λέγουσα in 2.23; cf. Jn 19.37; Rom 4.3.

[141] So C. Carpenter, 'James 4.5'; cf. Winkler, 55.

[142] So Alford, 313-14, appealing to the story of Pentecost in Acts.

God, who yearns jealously over the human spirit entrusted to human beings; cf. Gen 2.7 (although the LXX here has πνοή, not πνεῦμα). This seems to be the most popular view among modern exegetes.[143] It is enshrined in the NRSV. (x) The subject is not God but the divine Spirit, who—reading κατῴκησεν—dwells within and yearns jealously for its own. (xi) The subject is the divine Spirit, which—reading κατῴκισεν— God has caused to dwell 'within us': that Spirit longs jealously for its own.[144] (xii) Martin, 140-41, paraphrases: 'The Spirit God made to dwell in us opposes envy'—even though he cites no other instance of ἐπιποθεῖ + πρός meaning 'oppose'.[145] (xiii) Related is the suggestion of Bauckham, 'Spirit': the subject is the divine Spirit 'who abhors envy'. He postulates quotation from an apocryphon that may have had תעב = 'abhor'. James or his sources understood this as though it were תאב = 'long for'. (xiv) The subject is 'the spirit (of strife)' that dwells (κατῴκησεν) in those James is rebuking: they, so far from shunning envy, are full of envious longing; so Manton, 346-47. (xv) The subject is the human spirit,[146] which God has made to dwell within human beings: it tragically longs for envy (πρὸς φθόνον being telic).[147] The NEB reads: 'The spirit he made to dwell in us longs for envy'. (xvi) This is the same as the KJV, except that it read κατῴκησεν instead of κατῴκισεν and rendered: 'The spirit that dwelleth in us lusteth to envy'.[148] (xvii) The subject is the divinely implanted spirit, which longs enviously (πρὸς φθόνον being adverbial), with 'earthly goods' or some such being supplied.[149] So the NIV: 'The spirit he caused to live in us envies intensely'. (xviii) The subject is the divinely implanted spirit, which ardently longs for fellowship with God.[150] (xix) Adding to

---

[143] Cf. Huther, 132; Hort, 93-94; Parry, *Discussion*, 40; Ropes, 261-65; Bardenhewer, 17-20; Windisch-Preisker, 26-27; Schlatter, 248-52; Marty, 159-60; Dibelius, 223-24; Ketter, 168-69; Jeremias, 'Jac 4 5'; Mussner, 181-82; Mitton, 154-56; Schneider, 27; Davids, 163-64; Blevins, 'Repent', 422; Frankemölle, 602-605; Klein, *Werk*, 112-15; Moo, 188-91; Blomberg-Kamell, 191-92; Gundry, 940.

[144] So Farrar, *Days*, 341; Oesterley, 459.

[145] But cf. the old translations of Tyndale and Cranmer: both have 'contrary to' envy.

[146] Marcus, 'Inclination', 609 n. 8, has disposed of the objection that, if God is the subject in 4.6, then God should also be the subject in 4.5: in 1.12, 'the (unstated) subject is God, although there was no mention of him in the previous verse', and 'it is characteristic of James's style to change suddenly the subject of his verbs without alerting the reader, and this may be what is happening in 4.5-6'.

[147] So Bruston, 'Crux interpretum'; Smith, 228-29; Coppieters, 'Signification'; Adamson, 171-73; Marcus, 'Inclination', 608-609 n. 7, 621; Prockter, 'Noah'; Tsuji, *Glaube*, 85-86; R. Wall, 202-203; Burchard, 171-74; Fabris, 280-81; W. Wilson, 'Sin', 162. For Marcus, the 'spirit' should be identified with the יצר of Gen 6.5 and 8.17 and so related to the tradition of the evil impulse; see 247, n. 196. Criticism in Bauckham, 'Spirit', 275.

[148] Cf. Isho'dad of Merv *ad loc.* HSem 10 ed. Gibson, 50: the subject is the human spirit, which lusts to envy others.

[149] E.g. Chaine, 101-103; Meyer, *Rätsel*, 258; Michl, 'Spurch'; Sidebottom, 52-53.

[150] Severus of Antioch, *Hom. cath.* 47 PO 35.3.165 ed. Brière and Graffin, 306.

the confusion, most of these readings can be turned into questions—
'Does the spirit he caused to live in us really envy intensely?', 'Does the
spirit that dwelleth in us really lusteth to envy?', etc.[151] One sympathizes
with Popkes, 269-71, who outlines various possibilities without endorsing
any.

4.5 has puzzled interpreters not just because the sense is hard to divine
but also because the quoted words are, despite the introductory ἡ γραφὴ
λέγει, not close to anything in the Jewish Bible.[152] The commentaries and
secondary literature are full of suggestions, among them the following:
(i) Despite the singular ἡ γραφή, our author may be, in his mind,
summarizing the meaning of several texts or even the message of the
entire Bible.[153] One could compare the vague, generalizing reference in
Mt 26.54 ('But how then would the scriptures be fulfilled, which say it
must happen in this way?'; cf. v. 56). That God has caused a spirit or the
Holy Spirit to dwell within human beings or the saints is a biblical idea;[154]
and that God can yearn for people appears from LXX Deut 32.11 ('Like
an eagle to protect his brood, he too yearned [ἐπεπόθησεν] for his young')
and Jer 13.14 ('"I will not yearn after [ἐπιποθήσω]", says the Lord').
Against this, however, πρὸς φθόνον κτλ. seems too awkward not to be a
quotation; and in the other cases where James introduces a formal
quotation, we have no difficulty determining the source: 2.8, 11, 23; 4.6.

(ii) We could have here a misapprehension or failure of memory:
James may have heard someone say, πρὸς φθόνον κτλ., and later
erroneously recalled it as coming from the Bible.[155] (iii) Wettstein and
others have conjectured that πρὸς φθόνον κτλ. is a corruption of πρὸς τὸν
θεόν κτλ.,[156] in which case James was paraphrasing LXX Ps 41.2: ἐπιποθεῖ
ἡ ψυχή μου πρὸς σέ, ὁ θεός. Yet μείζονα δὲ δίδωσιν χάριν (in v. 6)

---

[151] Immer, *Hermeneutics*, 179, reads our line as a question which means: 'does the Spirit, that has taken up his abode in you desire enviously, i.e. has the Spirit of God envious (worldly) lust?'

[152] Cf. W. Wall, 348: 'From what scripture or writing this is cited, interpreters cannot find'.

[153] So Turnbull, 205 (the apostles had the 'liberty' to generalize about scripture and to cite a generalization as though it were a text); Manton, 347; Gill, 796; Guyse, 588; Wesley, 866; Wells, 25; Fausset, 592; Wiesinger, 175; Alford, 314; Bassett, 60; Belser, 165; Adam, 302; Dale, 134-35; Weidner, 64; Mayor, 140-41; Knowling, 99-100; Plumptre, 91; Ross, 77; Mitton, 154; Baasland, 129; Moo, 190-91; Nystrom, 227 ('perhaps'); Farley, 46. Cf. Carson, 'James', 1007: the text refers to a scriptural 'theme'—God's jealousy—not 'a specific quotation'. Frankemölle, 603, and Brosend, 114, seem inclined to the same opinion.

[154] See especially Gen 6.3; LXX: οὐ μὴ καταμείνῃ τὸ πνεῦμά μου ἐν τοῖς ἀνθρώποις τούτοις εἰς τὸν αἰῶνα. Cf. also Gen 2.7; Rom 8.9 ('if indeed God's Spirit οἰκεῖ in you'); 1 Cor 3.16 ('Do you not know that...God's Spirit dwells [οἰκεῖ] in you?'); Eph 2.22; 2 Tim 1.14.

[155] Cf. Beyschlag, 189. Grimm, 'Stelle', 956, suggests that James misremembered a midrash or targum on some verse as though it were from the Bible itself.

[156] See above, 613.

appears to offer contrast, not confirmation. (iv) Findlay, 'James iv. 5,6', suggests that James wrote πρὸς φόνον, not πρὸς φθόνον (cf. the textual problem in v. 2): 'The spirit that took up its abode in you (when your contentions began) is yearning for murder, but he gives greater grace'. Findlay thinks this a free reference to Gen 4.7, which addresses Cain the murderer: 'If you do well, will you not be accepted? And if you do not do well, sin is lurking at the door; its desire is for you, but you must master it.'[157]

(v) Maybe James wanted to refer to the setting for the story of the flood.[158] Here we read of 'the spirit' that resides in human beings (see n. 154) and of the great 'wickedness of humankind', of how 'every inclination of the thoughts of their hearts was only evil continually'.[159] James would then be likening some of his readers to the terrible generation of the flood: the spirit that dwells in them, manifested in their conflicts and disputes, longs not for God (cf. Ps 42.1) but instead pants for envy. The polemical comparison of contemporaries to the miserable generation of Noah is a *topos* known from the Jesus tradition.[160]

(vi) πρός...χάριν is parenthetical, διὸ λέγει resumptive. So the only Scripture is Proverbs. (vii) According to Laws, our text does not cite but alludes to LXX Ps 41.2 or (more likely) 83.3, where the human spirit (ψυχή) longs (ἐπιποθεῖ) for God. James is asking rhetorical questions: 'Is scripture meaningless? (v. 5a). Is this (according to the scripture) the proper manner of the soul's desire? (v. 5b).' The questions anticipate the scripturally informed response: Surely not![161] (viii) Oesterley, 459, finds a quotation not from the OT but the NT. He takes the line to be a summary of Pauline teaching, above all Gal 5.7, and so sees in Jas 4.5 'one of the many indications which point to the late date of our Epistle, or parts of it'.[162] (ix) Alford, 314, sees a loose quotation of Deut 32.10-11, 19, where God 'yearns' (ἐπεπόθησεν) and is 'jealous' (ἐζήλωσεν) for Israel. (x) For C. Carpenter, vv. 5b-6a are an inexact citation of Prov 3.34, soon to be quoted in v. 6b.[163] (xi) Meyer perceives a 'midrashic paraphrase' of Gen 49.19.[164] (xii) According to Cajetan, 369, James borrows from Exod 20.5,

[157] Cf. Paret, 'Zitat'; Zyro, 'Jakobus 4,5', 717. For criticism of Findlay see Wettlaufer, 'Variants', 190-93.
[158] For Grotius, 1087, James is quoting Gen 6.3, 5. Cf. Le Clerc, 516. Isho'dad of Merv *ad loc*. HSem 10 ed. Gibson, 50, already notes this as the view of some (as also the view that Isa 66.2 is being quoted). Prockter, 'Noah', regards Jas 4.4-6 as a midrash on Gen 6–9. R. Wall, 203-204, seems inclined to agree.
[159] Cf. also Gen 8.21, which Beza, 559; Aretius, 483; Raphel, 1087; Calmet, 686; and Maier, 184, cite.
[160] See D.C. Allison, Jr., *The Intertextual Jesus*, Harrisburg, 2000, 58-59, 93-95.
[161] Laws, 'Scripture'. Johnson, 280-82, likewise sees two rhetorical questions here.
[162] Cf. already M. Flacius Illyricus, *Ecclesiastic historia*, vol. 2, *Secunda Centuria*, Basel, CH, 1559, 71; Bengel, 503 (James is referring either to Gal 5.17 or 1 Pet 2.1-2, 5). Storr, 48, thinks this possible.
[163] C. Carpenter, 'James 4.5'. Cf. R. Scott, 137; McCartney, 216-17.
[164] Meyer, *Rätsel*, 259.

where God is 'a jealous God'.¹⁶⁵ (xiii) For Coppieters, Jas 4.5 rewrites LXX Eccl 4.4: 'I saw all toil and all manliness of work, that it is a man's envy (ζῆλος) of his companion. Indeed, this is vanity and preference of spirit (πνεύματος).'¹⁶⁶ (xiv) Several exegetes suppose that James quotes from a lost source that he and others regarded as Scripture.¹⁶⁷ Spitta conjectures use of the lost apocryphon, Eldad and Modad, named after the two characters in Num 11.24-29.¹⁶⁸ After they prophesy, a jealous Joshua complains and Moses in turn defends them. Bauckham makes the same suggestion.¹⁶⁹

This writer shares the view of Spitta and Bauckham.¹⁷⁰ The relevant considerations are these: (i) Herm. *Vis.* 2.3.4 reads: '"The Lord is near to those who return", as it is written in the book of Eldad and Modad, who prophesied to the people in the wilderness'. This is the only citation of Eldad and Modad by name. The book has perished. It is, however, also known from the so-called Chronographia brevis (ed. Boor, 135), attributed (perhaps wrongly) to Nicephorus I of Constantinople (758–829) as well as from several other book lists.¹⁷¹

---

¹⁶⁵ Cf. Stevartius, 277-79; Burdick, 194 (James gives 'the gist of such passages as Exod 20:5 and 34:14').

¹⁶⁶ Coppieters, 'Signification'.

¹⁶⁷ So Hort, 94 (suggesting a lost targum); Dibelius, 222-23; Michl, 'Spruch', 173-74; Mussner, 184; Schrage, 44-45; Davids, 162; Kugelman, 49; Hoppe, 91; Tsuji, *Glaube*, 84-85. For other instances of books or lost books that ceased to be canonical being cited as γραφή see 1 Clem. 23.3; 46.2; Barn. 16.5; Methodius of Olympus, *Symp.* 2.6 GCS 27 ed. Bonwetsch, 23; Clement of Alexandria, *Ecl.* 41; cf. also 1 Cor 2.9; Eph 5.14; b. Ber. 58a, 62b; b. Sanh. 72a. Some have analyzed 4.5 as a hexameter and taken this as evidence that James is citing a Hellenistic Jewish didactic poem (e.g. Windisch-Preisker, 27; Schneider, 28). But BDF 487 regards the proposed hexameter as 'poor'.

¹⁶⁸ Spitta, 121-23. So too Sidebottom, 52-53; Deppe, *Sayings*, 38-42.

¹⁶⁹ Bauckham, 'Spirit'—without referring to Spitta.

¹⁷⁰ In addition to what follows see Allison, 'Eldad'. Cf. also Knoch, *Eigenart*, 115-16 ('perhaps'). Knoch's argument is largely derivative, coming from Seitz, 'Afterthoughts' and 'Relationship'. The latter, nowhere citing Spitta, argues, on the basis of linguistic agreements, that James, 1 Clement, 2 Clement, and Hermas must draw upon a lost pseudepigraphon, and further (with reference to J.B. Lightfoot on 1 Clem. 23.3-4 = 2 Clem. 11.2-4; see below) that it might be Eldad and Modad. Note also Moffatt, 60 ('possibly it was the Book of Eldad and Modat'); Deppe, *Sayings*, 38-42; Hagner, *Clement*, 74, 252-53. Hagner, who thinks 'it may well be' that Jas 4.5 comes from the same apocryphal writing quoted in 1 Clem. 23.3 and 2 Clem. 11.2, is open to Lightfoot's suggestion that 1 Clem. 23.3 and 2 Clem. 11.2 quote Eldad and Modad. Hagner (who does not in this connection mention Spitta) also asks whether Jas 1.5ff. (with its use of δίψυχος); 4.14 (cf. 1 Clem. 23.1-2; 17.6); and 5.11 (cf. 1 Clem. 23.1-2) are related to that lost book.

¹⁷¹ These are: the list of Pseudo-Athanasius (which may come from the sixth century), the 'Addition to the List of Sixty Books' (perhaps from the seventh century), and the Armenian list of Mechitar of Ayrivank (thirteenth century). See T. Zahn, *Geschichte des Neutestamentlichen Kanons, Zweiter Band*, Erlangen, 1890, 292, 300, 317; idem, *Forschungen zur Geschichte des neutestamentlichen Kanonas und der altkirchlichen*

(ii) James and Hermas share numerous close conceptual and verbal parallels. These suggest a common pool of tradition—and Hermas knew Eldad and Modad.

(iii) First Clement 23.3-4 and 2 Clem. 11.2-4 quote an unknown text that J.B. Lightfoot, with very good reason, assigned to Eldad and Modad.[172] The citation opens with ταλαίπωροί εἰσιν οἱ δίψυχοι οἱ διστάζοντες τῇ καρδίᾳ, which is striking given that the δίψυχοι of Jas 4.8 immediately precedes the imperative, ταλαιπωρήσατε (v. 9), and all the more as δίψυχος is altogether absent from pre-Christian literature. Its first appearance is in James, the quotation common to 1 Clement and 2 Clement, and Hermas.[173] So the inference that James—like Hermas[174]—knew the source behind 1 Clem. 23.3-4 = 2 Clem. 11.2-4 lies near to hand.[175]

(iv) The theme of jealousy is prominent in the short story of Eldad and Modad: 'Are you (Joshua) really jealous of me (Moses)?' (Num 11.29). Any haggadic expansion of Num 11.26-29 would surely have paid some attention to the exchange between Moses and Joshua, an exchange which Mk 9.38-40 = Lk 9.49-50 hints was sufficiently well known in some circles to be called to mind by a fleeting allusion.[176] Even the succinct summary in LAB 20.5 includes the theme of jealousy; cf. Num. Rab. 15.19. Further, although the LXX here has ζηλόω, there are ancient writers who use φθόνος when referring to Num 11.26.[177]

Literature, V. Teil, Erlangen, 1893, 115-48; W. Lüdtke, 'Beiträge zu slavischen Apokryphen', ZAW 31 (1911), 230-35; M. Stone, 'Armenian Canon Lists III', HTR 69 (1976), 289-300; idem, 'Armenian Canon Lists VI', HTR 94 (2001), 477-91.

[172] J. B. Lightfoot, The Apostolic Fathers Clement, Ignatius, and Polycarp, Part One: Clement, volume 2, 2nd ed., London, 1889, 80-81. For extended defense of this position see Allison, 'Eldad'.

[173] Spitta also notes that the quotation in 2 Clem. 11.4 includes the word ἀκαταστασία, which James has in 3.16; and further that James uses the closely related ἀκατάστατος in 1.8 and 3.8, the former in connection with δίψυχος.

[174] Hermas not only uses the rare δίψυχος but links it to ταλαίπωρος (Vis. 3.7.1; Sim. 1.2-3), to διστάζω (Mand. 9.2, 4-6), and to καρδία (Mand. 9.2, 4-5; 10.2-3; Vis. 3.10.9; 4.2.5-6).

[175] So also Seitz, 'Hermas'; Knoch, Eigenart, 111-16.

[176] Cf. Mk 9.38-39 ('John said to him, "Teacher, we saw someone casting out demons in your name, and we tried to stop [ἐκωλύομεν] him, because he was not following us". But Jesus said, "Do not stop [κωλύετε] him; for no one who does a deed of power in my name will be able soon afterwards to speak evil of me"') with Num 11.28-29 ('And Joshua son of Nun, the assistant of Moses, one of his chosen men, said, "My lord Moses, stop [LXX: κώλυσον] them!" But Moses said to him, "Are you jealous for my sake? Would that all the Lord's people were prophets, and that the Lord would put his spirit on them!"'). Cyril of Alexandria, Lk 55 TU 34 ed. Sickenberger, 90-91; Albertus Magnus, En. prim. part. Luc. (I–IX) ad Lk 9.50 Opera Omnia 22 ed. A. Borgnet, 688; Poole, 168; J. Marcus, Mark 8–16, New Haven, 2009, 684; et al. link the two texts.

[177] Cyril of Jerusalem, Myst. cat. 16.26 PG 33.956A-B; Cyril of Alexandria, Lk 55 TU 34 ed. Sickenberger, 91-92; Theodoret of Cyrus, Quaest. Oct. Num 21 ed. Petruccione, 122.

(v) Even aside from any hypothesis about Eldad and Modad, Jas 4.5 has, because it concerns jealousy and 'the spirit', sent some commentators to Num 11. Poole, 893, for example, remarks that 'Joshua's envying Eldad and Modad's prophesying, for Moses's sake, seems to be an instance' of lusting for envy whereas 'Moses' not envying them' is an illustration to the contrary. Indeed, according to Gill, 796, in the eighteenth century: 'the generality of interpreters, who suppose a particular text of scripture is referred to, fetch it from Numb. ix. 29'.[178]

(vi) If James' quotation refers to τὸ πνεῦμα, Joshua's jealousy arises from God bestowing 'the spirit' (LXX: τὸ πνεῦμα) upon Eldad and Modad.

(vii) James goes on, after his quotation, to add a second quotation, which is about grace for the humble (v. 6), and he further returns to the theme in v. 10. This matters because rabbinic tradition held that God rewarded Eldad and Modad precisely for their humility.[179] That this haggadic expansion was extant around the turn of the era follows from the fact that it is already tradition for the author of Sifre.[180] So we have here yet another parallel between Jas 4 and the lore about Eldad and Modad.

(viii) If the words from Eldad and Modad in Hermas are 'The Lord is near to those who return' (ἐγγὺς κύριος τοῖς ἐπιστρεφομένοις), Jas 4.8 has this: 'Draw near to God and he will draw near to you' (ἐγγίσατε τῷ θεῷ καὶ ἐγγιεῖ ὑμῖν). The thematic coherence is undeniable, which raises the possibility that, after quoting Eldad and Modad in v. 5, James continued to be influenced by that source as he moved forward.[181]

(ix) James 4.5 is followed by μείζονα δὲ δίδωσιν χάριν. Not only can this be related to the rabbinic tradition that God gave greater gifts to Eldad and Modad because of their humility (see above), but several patristic texts, in their brief summaries of Num 11.26-29, refer to 'grace' (χάρις), saying that it has been 'given' (δίδωμι, δωρεά) by God.[182] Now

---

[178] Cf. W. Dodd ad 4.6; Cappel, 130-32; Surenhuys, Sefer, 674-75; Elsner, Observationes, 394; Schöttgen, Horae Hebraicae, 1028. Theile, 222, lists additional commentators who take this position.

[179] Sifre 95 on Num 11.24-26; Tanḥ. Buber Beha'alotekha 3.22; b. Sanh. 17a; Num. Rab. 15.19. Cf. also Tg. Ps.-J. on Num 11.26: 'they hid themselves in order to escape honor'. On this tradition see further F. Böhl, 'Demut und Prophetie: Eldad und Medad nach der frühen rabbinischen Überlieferung', in Ich bewirke das Heil und erschaffe das Unheil (Jesaja 45,7), Würzburg, 1998, 15-29.

[180] See the previous note. He attributes the thought to 'R. Simeon', failing to indicate which Simeon this might be.

[181] Tg. Ps.-J. on Num 11.26 attributes a similar and presumably traditional line to Eldad and Modad: קירוס איטימוס להון בשעת אניקין ('The Lord is near them at the hour of distress')—a prophecy which in very short space includes three Greek loan words: קירוס = κύριος, איטימוס = ἕτοιμος, אניקין = ἀνάγκη.

[182] Cyril of Jerusalem, Myst. cat. 16.26 PG 33.956A-B; Cyril of Alexandria, John 1100A ed. Pusey, 3:139; Theodoret of Cyrus, Rom.-Phil. proem PG 82.36B; idem, Quaest. in Oct. Num 21 ed. Marcos and Sáenz-Badillos, 206.

δίδωμι belongs to the LXX story of Num 11.26-29: 'And who might grant (δῴη) that all the Lord's people be prophets, when the Lord grants (δῷ) his spirit upon them?' But χάρις plays no role there. Despite this, the word established itself as part of the Greek ecclesiastical tradition regarding Num 11.26-29.[183] First Clement 23.1, moreover, when introducing its quotation from what Lightfoot argued is an excerpt from Eldad and Modad, has this: 'The Father, who is merciful in all things, and ready to do good, has compassion on those who fear him, and gently and lovingly gives grace (τὰς χάριτας...ἀποδιδοῖ) on those who draw near to him with singleness of mind'. Here again we meet χάρις and δίδωμι.

(x) The quotation in Jas 4.5 comes after the remark, in v. 2, ἐπιθυμεῖτε καὶ οὐκ ἔχετε, and vv. 1 and 3 speak against those who pursue ἡδονή. So Jas 4 opens by addressing the subject of desire. Numbers 11.34 has this to say about the setting for the story of Eldad and Modad: 'That place was called קברות התאוה, because there they buried the people who had the craving'. The Hebrew, קברות התאוה,[184] means 'graves of craving'. The LXX renders the sentence as: ἐκλήθη τὸ ὄνομα τοῦ τόπου ἐκείνου Μνήματα τῆς ἐπιθυμίας, ὅτι ἐκεῖ ἔθαψαν τὸν λαὸν τὸν ἐπιθυμητήν.[185] This harks back to the beginning of the story—LXX 11.4: 'the rabble among them ἐπεθύμησαν ἐπιθυμίαν'. Philo, *Leg.* 4.129-31, naturally used the story—to which Ps 78.29-31 (LXX: ἐπιθυμίαν...ἐπιθυμίας); 106.14 (LXX: ἐπεθύμησαν ἐπιθυμίαν); and 1 Cor 10.6 (ἐπιθυμητὰς κακῶν... ἐπεθύμησαν) clearly allude—as a general admonition against ἐπιθυμία; cf. *Migr.* 155. So too Origen and Gregory of Nyssa, the latter remarking on the people's lack of moderation regarding ἡδονή; cf. Jas 4.1, 3.[186] So the story of Eldad and Modad is set in the middle of a famous tale about desire run amok, and James' quotation in v. 5 trails a rebuke of people for following their own desires and pleasures.

(xi) As we have seen above, the last part of Jas 4.5 (τὸ πνεῦμα ὃ κατῴκισεν ἐν ἡμῖν) resembles several lines in Hermas.[187] Clearly, τὸ

---

[183] Note also Basil of Caesarea, *Spir.* 61 FC 12 ed. Sieben, 260-62: 'the grace (χάρις) of the Spirit in the recipient is ever present... He does not abide with those who, on account of the instability of their will, easily reject the grace (χάριν) which they have received. An instance of this is seen in Saul (1 Sam 16:14) and in the seventy elders of the children of Israel, except Eldad and Modad, with whom alone the Spirit appears to have remained'.

[184] Cf. v. 35; also Num 33.16-17; Deut 9.22.

[185] Cf. Josephus, *Ant.* 3.299: 'that spot still bears the surname of Kabrothaba, that is to say, ἐπιθυμίας μνημεῖα'.

[186] Origen, *Frag. in Ps ad* 78.31 PG 17.140A-B; Gregory of Nyssa, *Vit. Mos.* 63-64 SC 1 3rd ed. Daniélou, 94-96. Cf. also the concern with pleasure in Cyril of Alexandria's exposition of Num 11 in *Jn ad* 6.33 ed. Pusey, 1.461: the people sought σωματικὰς ἡδονάς. Given my conclusion, perhaps it is not coincidence that the only occurrence of ἡδονή in the law and the prophets is Num 11.8, part of the setting for the story of Eldad and Modad.

[187] *Mand.* 3.1; 5.1.2, 5; 5.7.1; *Sim.* 5.6.5; 5.7.1.

πνεῦμα + κατοικίζω or κατοικέω + ἐν was close to a fixed expression for the author of Hermas. Moreover, Herm. *Mand.* 3.1 and *Sim.* 5.6.5 along with Jas 4.5 preserve the only Christian uses before Justin of κατοικίζω. Since, then, Jas 4.5 comes from an unknown 'scripture' (γραφή), and since Hermas was influenced by Eldad and Modad, which he could quote with the formula, 'as it is written' (γέγραπται), one can at least ask whether τὸ πνεῦμα + κατοικίζω or κατοικέω + ἐν appeared in Eldad and Modad.

To sum up: the first half of Jas 4 displays a large number of overlaps with Num 11.26-29 and with traditions which grew out of that biblical passage. James concerns himself with desire, jealousy, 'the spirit', speaking against others, the humble being exalted, the giving of grace, and God drawing near to the saints, all of which are part and parcel of the lore surrounding Eldad and Modad. The circumstantial case that Eldad and Modad was the source of Jas 4.5 is about as strong as it can be given that the pseudepigraphon is no longer extant.

If this is the right conclusion, we can make some progress regarding the meaning of Jas 4.5. In Eldad and Modad, the quoted bit must have belonged to Moses' response to Joshua, after the latter raised his objection about Eldad and Modad prophesying; and τὸ πνεῦμα must have been the spirit that God told Moses he would give to the elders: 'I will take some of the spirit that is on you and put it on them' (Num 11.17; cf. v. 25). This is the same spirit that is explicitly said, in Num 11.26, to have rested upon Eldad and Modad. Numbers 11.29 calls it 'his spirit', that is, the Lord's spirit. It is referred to in Tg. Onq. and Tg. Ps.-J. on Num 11.26 as 'the spirit of prophecy'. It is 'the holy spirit' in Tg. Neof. 1. The varied expressions amount to the same thing.[188]

As for the meaning of πρὸς φθόνον ἐπιποθεῖ, the phrase must be part of a rebuke, just as the allusion to Num 11.26-29 in Mk 9.38-40 = Lk 9.49-50 serves as a rebuke. This is consistent with the recurrently negative connotations of φθόνος in Jewish and Christian texts. This in turn implies that the line from Eldad and Modad is a question,[189] which accords with its being a new edition of Num 11.29, for that too is a question: 'Are you (Joshua) really jealous of me (Moses)?' James' Greek admittedly remains difficult, but (as Bauckham has urged) a Semitic original is likely. My own guess is that the Hebrew might have been close

---

[188] The objection that the πνεῦμα of 4.5 must be the human spirit because that is its meaning in 2.26, the only other verse to use the word in James, does not persuade. Not only can one not generalize from a single occurrence, but James is here purportedly quoting a source.

[189] Exegetes have often recognized this possibility; cf. Calvin, 298; Poole, 893; Gill, 798; Zyro, 'Noch einmal', 768; Bruston, 'Crux interpretum'; Pretorius, 'Verklaringsopsies'; Hartin, 199. The objection that James otherwise uses μή with questions expecting a negative answer (2.14; 3.11, 12) is irrelevant: we have here a quotation, not a sample of James' writing.

to this: לְ/בְקִנְאָה הָאָב הָרוּחַ אֲשֶׁר יִשְׁבְּחוּ בְקִרְבֵּנוּ: '(Do you suppose that) the spirit that he (God) caused to dwell within us really pants with jealousy (or: has an appetite for envy)?'[190] Both בְקִנְאָה and לְקִנְאָה are well attested, and LXX Ps 118.174 translates הָאָב with ἐπιποθεῖν.

James writes as though his audience will have no trouble with πρὸς φθόνον κτλ.: he quotes and then moves on without explanation. Presumably, then, he assumes knowledge of Eldad and Modad, which was perhaps popular in his time and place.[191] In any event, we can see how the quotation functions within his larger argument. Just as Moses rebuked the jealous Joshua, who protested the grace unexpectedly given to Eldad and Modad, so James rebukes those in the synagogue who, out of envy and selfish desire, are cursing, disputing, slandering, and judging others.[192]

Verse 6. The emphasis is not on condemnation but on the possibility of repentance. At least rhetorically, James has not given up on those here addressed.

μείζονα δὲ δίδωσιν χάριν. The subject is probably God, as suggested by the sense and the following citation.[193] But πνεῦμα = God's Spirit could also be the subject.[194] The general meaning may be that, even if one's spirit is inclined to envy (v. 5), divine grace can incline it in another direction. But μείζονα is difficult—a greater favor than what? So although composition by James is possible, especially as δίδωσιν χάριν nicely anticipates the following quotation from Proverbs, μείζονα κτλ. could equally belong to the quotation introduced by 'scripture says'. That is, the comparative may have made sense in the context from which the quotation was extracted. For 'grace' in the traditions about Eldad and Modad see above.[195] For μείζονα see on 3.1. μείζονα + χάρις was a conventional idiom meaning 'greater favor' or 'more grateful'.[196]

---

[190] For the argument that Eldad and Modad was composed in Hebrew but translated into Greek before the end of the first century see Allison, 'Eldad'.

[191] Cf. Carr, 53: a quotation 'would suggest to St James' readers more than it states' and would be 'intended to recall teaching, and therefore would not appear so abrupt as it does to modern readers'.

[192] Cf. 3.9-10, 14-16; 4.1-2, 11-12.

[193] Although Trapp, 701, makes Scripture the subject.

[194] So Calvin, 298: James 'is arguing from opposites. Jealousy is a symptom of ill-will, but the Spirit of God displays a generous nature, by the gifts which He lavishes'. So too Knowling, 101.

[195] In the rabbinic tradition about Eldad and Modad, those two are given greater gifts than the seventy elders; see above, 619-20.

[196] Diodorus Siculus 21.21.13; Plutarch, *Cat. Min.* 69.2; Herm. *Sim* 5.2.10; etc. χάρις: Jas: 2×; cf. חֵן. For Batten, 'Emulation', 270-71, given that 'the provision of χάρις was regularly associated with benefactors in inscriptions', and given James' critique of patronage, the word may support 'the view that James envisions God as a divine benefactor'.

FRIENDSHIP WITH THE WORLD VERSUS FRIENDSHIP WITH GOD (4.1-12)   623

διὸ λέγει.[197] The same expression appears in Eph 4.8; 5.14; cf. Heb 3.7. διό (cf. 1.21) + λέγει (cf. v. 5: γραφὴ λέγει) is a variant of the conventional καθὼς λέγει/εἶπεν,[198] modified to mark an inference. The implicit subject is God[199] or 'the scripture' (cf. v. 5), there being, in this case, no appreciable difference between the two.[200]

ὁ θεὸς ὑπερηφάνοις ἀντιτάσσεται, ταπεινοῖς δὲ δίδωσιν χάριν.[201] The transition from jealousy (vv. 2, 5) to pride (vv. 6, 10) is natural: the two vices regularly go hand in hand. The citation is of LXX Prov 3.34, except that the subject in the latter is anarthrous κύριος.[202] As the Hebrew is very different—אִם־לַלֵּצִים הוּא־יָלִיץ וְלַעֲנָוִים יִתֶּן־חֵן[203]—James clearly uses the Greek text. First Peter 5.5 quotes the same words, also with θεός or ὁ θεός as the subject (the text is uncertain). Given that the LXX does not seem to have any variants here, one can, if so inclined, see in this additional evidence that James knew 1 Peter or *vice versa*. It is true that 1 Clem. 30.2 likewise quotes Prov 3.34 with θεός as the subject, Ign. *Eph.* 5.3 with ὁ θεός as the subject. But (ὁ) θεός is only one of several parallels between Jas 4 and 1 Pet 5:

- Quotation of Prov 3.34, with (ὁ) θεός   Jas 4.6   1 Pet 5.5
- Call for submission, with ὑποτάγητε   Jas 4.7, to God   1 Pet 5.5, to elders
- Call to resist ὁ διάβολος, with ἀντίστητε   Jas 4.7   1 Pet 5.8-9
- Call to humility, with ταπεινώθητε   Jas 4.10   1 Pet 5.6
- Promise of exaltation, with ὑψώσει/ῃ   Jas 4.10   1 Pet 5.6

Given the many other links between James and 1 Peter, some of which suggest a literary relationship, James could here borrow from Peter.[204] Dibelius, 225-26, however, discounting literary dependence, thinks in terms of 'an underlying paraenetic schema of loosely connected admonitions' that employed Prov 3.34.[205]

---

[197] Grotius, 1087, following Erasmus, suggests that διό...χάριν could be a gloss.
[198] = באשר אמר, as often in the Dead Sea Scrolls; cf. Heb 3.7; 4.3.
[199] Cf. CD 6.13; 8.9; 2 Cor 6.16.
[200] But Alford, 315, supposes 'the Spirit' to be the subject.
[201] Some later Greek witnesses have κύριος, which is assimilation to Prov 3.34.
[202] Oesterley, 459, arguing that the subject of δίδωσιν χάριν in v. 6a is the Spirit, the subject in v. 6b God, finds here evidence for 'the divinity of the Holy Spirit'.
[203] 'As for the scornful, he scorns them, but to the humble he gives favor'.
[204] Nienhuis, *Paul*, 204-11, argues for this. See further above, 67-70.
[205] He further deems it likely that 1 Clem. 30.2, which also quotes Prov 3.34, shows knowledge of the scheme, because it, like James, speaks against καταλαλιά (30.1, 3; cf. Jas 4.11) and demands ταπείνωσις (vv. 3, 8; cf. Jas 4.10). Cf. D.G. Horrell, 'The Product of a Petrine Circle? A Reassessment of the Origin and Character of 1 Peter', *JSNT* 86 (2002), 40-41 (James and 1 Peter share a non-Pauline tradition); Metzner, *Rezeption*, 95-99 (the two adopt 'an early Christian paraenetical tradition'). According to M.-E. Boismard, 'Une liturgie baptismale dans la Prima Petri', *RB* 64 (1957), 77-78, 1 Peter and James draw upon a liturgical hymn.

A scripturally informed reader might perceive links between the context of Prov 3.34 and the context of Jas 4.6. Both counter jealousy (Jas 4.2, 5; Prov 3.31), speak against quarrelling (Jas 4.1; Prov 3.30), and promote wisdom (Jas 3.13-18; Prov 3.35).

Although ὑπερήφανος (NT: 5×) appears only here in James, ἀντιτάσσω (NT: 5×)—more language from the battlefield[206]—recurs in 5.6, where the righteous do not resist their enemies.[207] Neither word appears in the Synoptic saying about the exalted being humbled and the humbled being exalted;[208] but James' ταπεινός[209] does recall that logion, which uses ταπεινόω; cf. ταπεινώθητε in v. 10.

Although James divides his audience into two groups, the proud and the humble, he does not regard the division as necessarily permanent. He rather calls for change, for the proud to become humble. The dualism here is ethical, not metaphysical, and so it can be undone.

In context, the proud are such because they despise others (cf. vv. 2, 5, 11-12). By lowering others, they raise themselves to 'the perilous pinnacle of self-exaltation'.[210]

Verse 7. If 4.1-6 offers a series of questions and assertions, 4.7-12 offers a series of imperatives. The first injunction not only looks back but also stands as a sort of heading for what follows. That is, subjection to God (v. 7a) involves opposing the devil (v. 7b), striving for moral purity (v. 8), mourning for sins (v. 9), becoming humble (v. 10), and not judging others (vv. 11-12).

Verses 7-10 constitute a call to repentance. Often such a call contains, in the Tanak, an admonition, an accusation, and a promise.[211] The same is true here. James seems to be informed by a traditional speech form.[212]

ὑποτάγητε οὖν τῷ θεῷ. The expression was conventional.[213] In context, the general admonition must include what James has just insisted

---

[206] LSJ, s.v., gives the main meaning as 'range in battle against'. Cf. the colorful comment of Trapp, 701: God '"setteth himself in battle-array against such", above all other sorts of sinners, as invaders of his territories, and foragers or plunderers of his chief treasures'.

[207] Alonso-Schökel, 'James 5,2', sees the link as important: 5.6 completes James' commentary on the quotation in 4.6.

[208] Mt 23.12; Lk 14.11; 18.14.

[209] NT: 8×; Jas: 2×; see on 1.9.

[210] Trapp, 701. Typically, Trapp goes on to cite the Pope as an illustration.

[211] See T. Raitt, 'The Prophetic Summons to Repentance', ZAW 83 (1971), 30-49. Examples include 2 Chr 30.6-9; Jer 3.12-13; 22.3-5; Ezek 18.30-32; Joel 2.12-13; Zeph 2.1-3.

[212] See further Wilson, 'Turning'.

[213] Cf. LXX Ps 61.2 (τῷ θεῷ ὑποταγήσεται); Dan 7.27; 2 Macc 9.12 (ὑποτάσσεσθαι τῷ θεῷ); Ign. *Eph.* 5.3; Ps.-Ign. *Mag.* 6 ed. Zahn, 200 (ὑποτασσόμενοι τῷ θεῷ); Epictetus, Diatr. 3.24.65 (τῷ θεῷ ὑποτεταγμένος); Theophilus of Antioch, *Autol.* 1.14.1 PTS 44 ed. Marcovich, 34 (ὑποτάγηθι... αὐτῷ, sc. θεῷ); PGM 12.261 (ὑποτέτακται τῷ ἐν οὐρανῷ θεῷ).

upon, namely, avoiding conflict, controlling ἐπιθυμία, and abandoning φθόνος. For the imperative coupled with οὖν see also 5.7, 16. ὑποτάσσω (1 Peter: 6×) is a *hapax* for James.[214]

ἀντίστητε δὲ τῷ διαβόλῳ καὶ φεύξεται ἀφ' ὑμῶν. This became a much quoted line.[215] Within Jas 3–4, which has in view people opposing people, it serves to reallocate effort and energy: one should resist not one's brothers but the devil.[216]

The notion of resisting the devil and of the devil fleeing were traditional; cf. Tob ℵ 6.17 (τὸ δαιμόνιον...φύξεται); BA 8.3 (τὸ δαιμόνιον... ἔφυγεν); T. Iss. 7.7 (πᾶν πνεῦμα τοῦ Βελιὰρ φεύξεται ἀφ' ὑμῶν); T. Dan 5.1 (φύγῃ ἀφ' ὑμῶν ὁ Βελιάρ); T. Naph. 8.4 (ὁ διάβολος φεύξεται ἀφ' ὑμῶν); 1 Pet 5.8-9 (ὁ...διάβολος...ᾧ ἀντίστητε); Herm. *Mand.* 12.5.2 (ὁ διάβολος...ἐὰν οὖν ἀντισταθῆτε αὐτῷ...φεύξεται ἀφ' ὑμῶν; similarly 12.2.4, with 'evil desire' as the subject); T. Sol. 13.6; 18.40; y. Pe'ah 21b (8.9: 'the lord of the spirits became angry and fled').[217] Moreover, ἀνθίστημι (Jas: 1×) and φεύγω (Jas: 1×) were a conventional pair known from accounts of battle.[218] So here James reverts to the martial imagery of vv. 1, 2, and 4. One recalls Eph 6.11, where one does combat with the devil, and Rev 12.7-8 and 20.8-9, where Satan is a warrior. Resisting the devil amounts to the same thing as submitting oneself to God (v. 7a), which is the same as drawing near to God (v. 8).[219] Although the image of the devil fleeing does not recall any traditional Jewish narrative, Christian expositors have sometimes thought of the temptation stories in the Synoptics.[220]

---

[214] Johnson, 283, makes the interesting observation that James, unlike other NT authors, displays no interest in the submission of individuals to ruling authorities or to ecclesiastical authorities or of slaves to masters or of women to their husbands.

[215] Cf. Didymus of Alexandria, *Ps.* 1.1 PTS 15 ed. Mühlenberg, 121; Cyril of Alexandria, *Isa.* PG 70.304B; Ps.-Ephraem, *Serm. paraen. ad mon. Aegyp.* 50.37 ed. Phrantzoles, 294; John of Damascus, *Parall.* Δ 25 PG 95.1408B; *et al.* Before recent times, the existence of the devil was taken for granted. In more recent commentaries, however, one sometimes runs across discussions of whether such a being exists. See e.g. the apologetical discussion of Plummer, 613-14.

[216] Cf. Maximus the Confessor, *Ascet.* 17 CCSG 40 ed. Gysens, 37.

[217] This tradition sometimes created tension with Mt 5.39 (μὴ ἀντιστῆναι τῷ πονηρῷ), which some took to refer to the devil. See e.g. Theophylact, *Mt ad loc.* PG 123.200B-C: 'Should we not then resist the devil? Yes, we should, but not by striking back at our neighbour, but through patient endurance'.

[218] 1 Macc 6.4 (ἀντέστησαν αὐτῷ...καὶ ἔφυγεν); Diodorus Siculus 11.7.4 (ἀντιστάντες...ἔφυγον); Josephus, *Ant.* 15.115 (ἀντιστάντες...ἔφυγον); etc.

[219] N. Beck, *Cryptograms*, 162, conjectures that the devil is 'not simply the demigod, but also the Roman State and the zealous advocates of the Roman Imperial Cult who, in the eyes of the early Christians, were in league with the devil'.

[220] E.g. Bonaventure, *Lk* 4.24 Opera Omnia 10 ed. Peltier, 308; T. Scott, 583; Mayor, 146; Hartin, 201; Doriani, 148. So too I. Watts, 'A Defense against the Temptation to Self-Murder', in *The Works of the Rev. Isaac Watts*, vol. 8, Leeds, 1813, 563—adding that using memorized scriptures, like Jesus, will defeat the devil.

Whereas Mark and Paul, without exception, use the Semitic form, Σατανᾶς, Matthew and Luke (and Q) also have διάβολος.[221] The two terms appear interchangeable in early Christian texts, which are generally optimistic about the limitations of Satan's power.[222] In James, too, he is not up for the fight: being no match for the faithful, he turns tail and runs.[223]

Except for 3 Βασ 11, where σατάν appears, the LXX uses διαβόλος to translate the שטן of the MT, where Satan is an accuser in the heavenly court, one of the sons of heaven, who incites the deity to test people.[224] By NT times, Satan, known by a variety of names, had become demonic, a wholly evil figure, sometimes imagined as a fallen angel, bent on the destruction of every good thing.[225] James shows scant interest in him. His sole function in our book is to stand as the antithesis to divine values. The nature, for instance, of the devil's relationship to the demons of 2.19 goes unexplored.

Readers of James, aware that διάβολος could mean 'slanderer' or 'enemy' and also that the word is a synonym for שטן = 'accuser' or 'adversary', might find mention of 'the devil' particularly fitting here. James is countering people who engage in disputes, make themselves enemies of God, and speak evil of others (4.1-4, 11-12), all attributes of 'the accuser'.

Pride and envy are also traditional attributes of the devil, and perhaps this was already true by the time of James.[226] If so, a reader might imagine that to oppose the devil is to oppose envy and pride. Commentators do think along these lines. Bengel, 503, remarks: the devil 'who is pride' tempts people 'especially by pride'.[227]

---

[221] Jas: 1×. See Mt 4.1, 5, 8, 11; 13.19; 25.41; Lk 4.2, 3, 6, 13; 8.12; cf. Jn 6.70; 8.44; 13.2.

[222] Cf. Mt 4.1-11 = Lk 4.1-13; Mk 3.26-27; Lk 10.17; Jn 12.31; Rom 16.20; etc.

[223] Calvin, 299, finds this odd: 'daily experience seems to contradict' James' promise, for 'the more bravely we resist, the sharper we feel his pressure... And fighting never wearies him.'

[224] See 1 Chr 21.1; Ps 109.6; Job 1–2; Zech 3.1-10.

[225] 1 En. 54; Jub. 10.1-14; 11.5; Wis 2.24; LAE 12–17; T. Ash. 1.8-9; T. Job 6–8; 16–27; 4 Macc 18.8; 4Q'Amram[b] 2; CD 4.12-13; 1QS 3.13–4.26; 2 En. 12.7-12; etc. Literature: Billerbeck 1.136-49; W. Foerster and G. von Rad, 'διαβάλλω, διάβολος', *TDNT* 2.71-81; K. Schäferdiek, 'Σατανᾶς', *TDNT* 7.151-65; J. Ernst, *Die eschatologischen Gegenspieler in den Schriften des Neuen Testaments*, Regensburg, 1967, 269-80; P. J. Kobelski, *Melchizedek and Melchiresa'*, Washington, DC, 1981, 75-98; G.J. Riley, 'Devil', *DDD*, 244-49; C. Breytenbach and P.L. Day, 'Satan', *DDD*, 726-32.

[226] Note Lat. LAE 12-15; 2 En. 28–30; Gk. Apoc. Ezra 4.32; Origen, *De prin.* 1.5.5 GCS 22 ed. P. Koetschau, 77.

[227] Cf. Wesley, 866: the devil is 'the father of pride and envy'.

Verse 8. This verse, taken in conjunction with vv. 9 and 11-12, 'invokes activity in all three zones of human personality: purposeful interaction, symbolized by the hands, emotion-fused thought, symbolized by the heart, and self-expressive speech, symbolized by the mouth'.[228]

ἐγγίσατε τῷ θεῷ καὶ ἐγγιεῖ ὑμῖν. If, in v. 7, Satan departs, in v. 8 God draws near:[229] the presence of the two is inversely proportional. The idea of 'drawing near' (cf. נגשׁ אל) God was a commonplace.[230] The *topos* was particularly associated with Moses, and a few have related our verse to him.[231] Perhaps more relevant, given the purity language that follows, are texts in which priests 'draw near' to God.[232] Also attested, although less common, is the idea of God coming near to human beings, sometimes for consolation and support, sometimes for judgment.[233] James' contribution is the combination of the two ideas in pithy, memorable fashion, on the model of similar reciprocal statements such as 'Return to me and I will return to you'.[234] The result is an instance of what E. Käsemann called a 'sentence of holy law', in which human action in the protasis correlates with divine action in the apodosis.[235]

To this point, James has used θεός repeatedly (16×). This, however, is its last occurrence. Whatever the explanation, from here on out, κύριος becomes the exclusive divine title (10× in chaps. 4–5).

καθαρίσατε χεῖρας, ἁμαρτωλοί, καὶ ἁγνίσατε καρδίας, δίψυχοι. Cf. LXX Isa 1.16: καθαροὶ γένεσθε. 'As one approaches God greater purification is necessary while the further away from God (near the world/devil) defilement is assumed'.[236] For καρδία see on 1.26, and for δίψυχος

---

[228] Hutchinson Edgar, *Poor*, 195. Cf. E. Sandys, 'The Seventh Sermon', in *The Sermons of Edwin Sandys*, Cambridge, 1841, 134: by speaking of hands and heart, James calls for removing both 'outward and inward sins'.

[229] ἐγγίζω: Jas: 3×; cf. 5.8, where the content is not spatial nearness but the temporal nearness of end.

[230] Exod 16.9; 19.22 (οἱ ἐγγίζοντες κυρίῳ τῷ θεῷ); 24.2 (ἐγγιεῖ... πρὸς τὸν θεόν); 34.30; 1 Sam 14.36; Isa 29.13; 48.16; 58.2 (LXX: ἐγγίζειν θεῷ); Jer 30.21; Ezek 40.46; LXX Hos 12.7 (ἔγγιζε πρὸς τὸν θεόν); Zeph 3.2 (πρὸς τὸν θεὸν... οὐκ ἤγγισεν); Jdt 8.27 (τοὺς ἐγγίζοντας αὐτῷ); Wis 6.19; 1QH 6(14).14; T. Dan 6.2 (ἐγγίζετε κυρίῳ τῷ θεῷ); Heb 7.19 (ἐγγίζομεν τῷ θεῷ); 11.6; etc.

[231] Note, however, Didymus of Alexandria, *Ps*. 148.14 PTS 16 ed. Mühlenberg, 361; Chaine, 105; Cantinat, 208-209; Martin, 153; Johnson, 284.

[232] E.g. Lev 9.7; Num 16.40; Ezek 43.19.

[233] Ps 69.18; Mal 3.5; 4 Ezra 6.18; Herm. *Vis*. 2.3.4; Tg. Ps.-J. on Num 11.26; etc.

[234] Zech 1.3; Mal 3.7. Ropes, 269, believes James 'very likely dependent' upon the former. Cf. Cantinat, 20. Didymus of Alexandria, *Zech ad* 1.12-14 SC 83 ed. Doutreleau, 196, links the two sentences.

[235] E. Käsemann, 'Sentences of Holy Law in the New Testament', in *New Testament Questions of Today*, London, 1969, 66-81. See also K. Berger, 'Zu den sogenannten Sätzen des heiligen Rechts', *NTS* 17 (1970), 10-40; D. Schmidt, 'The LXX *Gattung* "Prophetic Correlative"', *JBL* 96 (1977), 517-22.

[236] So Lockett, *Purity*, 135.

see on 1.8, where the emphasis is upon the antithesis, faith vs. belief. Here the focus is the chasm between God and world.[237]

As δίψυχος (see on 1.8) occurs in 1 Clem. 23.3-4 = 2 Clem. 11.2-4, in what appears to be a quotation from Eldad and Modad, and as it there appears in immediate proximity to both καρδία and ταλαίπωροί (cf. Jas 4.9: ταλαιπωρήσατε),[238] and as Hermas, which explicitly quotes Eldad and Modad (*Vis.* 2.3.4), links δίψυχος not only to ταλαίπωρος (*Vis.* 3.7.1; *Sim.* 1.2-3) but also to the imperative to purify one's heart (see below), and as Jas 4.5 plausibly comes from Eldad and Modad (see above), it follows that James is here still writing under the influence of that apocryphon. For the vocative case (twice in this line) see on 1.2.[239] ἁμαρτωλός—infrequent in secular sources—recurs in 5.20. The word usually does duty for רשע in the LXX. Here it designates not Gentiles but Jews who have departed from standards that they themselves, to James' mind, uphold or should uphold. καθαρίζω, χείρ and ἁγνίζω are *hapax legomena* for James, which is consistent with the possibility that our line is in part borrowed material.

'Clean hands' is a biblical idiom.[240] It is more precisely cultic language[241] that has been transferred to the personal religious sphere and so signifies moral integrity.[242] James has turned it into an imperative—seemingly unparalleled except in later Christian texts under Jamesian influence.[243] By metonymy, the hands stand for the whole person and that person's actions.[244] The expression is not common in early Christian texts, perhaps because of association with Jewish ritual.[245] Is this yet one more hint of James' Jewish outlook?

---

[237] Batten, 'Patron', 266, suggests that James may be 'deliberately contrasting the "single soul" tradition of friendship, in which friends share one soul together, with someone who is so divided that it is not possible to share a "soul" with another'.

[238] On the originality of 2 Clement's καρδία, which is not in 1 Clement, see Seitz, 'Hermas', 134-36.

[239] Cf. the vocative ἁμαρτωλοί in Tob 13.8; Gk. 1 En. 102.3.

[240] Cf. 2 Sam 22.21 (LXX: τὴν καθαριότητα τῶν χειρῶν); Job 17.9 (LXX: καθαρὸς χείρας); 22.30 (LXX: ἐν καθαραῖς χερσίν); Pss 18.20, 24 (LXX: τὴν καθαριότητα τῶν χειρῶν); 24.4.

[241] Cf. Exod 30.17-21; Lev 15.11; Mt 15.2; Mk 7.2-5; m. Ḥag. 2.5.

[242] Cf. Job 22.30; Isa 1.16; Jer 4.14; Josephus, *Bell.* 5.403.

[243] I have found no other examples before Didymus of Alexandria, in the fourth century.

[244] Cf. 2 Sam 4.11; Ezek 33.8; also Mt 27.24, where Pilate washes his hands, and Demosthenes, *Or.* 19.66, where 'clean hands' means 'free of responsibility'. Note Gregory the Great, *Mor.* 32.3 CCSL 143B ed. Adriaen, 1626: 'in the language of the sacred text, the hand signifies action'.

[245] Before Clement of Alexandria, its only other occurrence seems to be in a quotation of Exod 20.8 = Deut 5.12 in Barn. 15.1, 6. 1 Clem. 29.1 (ἁγνὰς καὶ ἀμιάντους χεῖρας) uses a slightly different idiom.

'Clean' or 'pure heart' is also a biblical figure of speech.[246] Unlike 'clean hands', early Christians were fond of this expression.[247] The idiom is typically formed with the καθαρ- root. James, however, uses ἁγνίζω, presumably because he has just used καθαρίζω and wants verbal variation with the parallelism (as in v. 9b and often). Perhaps he also wishes to forge a link with 3.17, where ἁγνή characterizes the wisdom that comes from above. However that may be, the meaning of his imperative—which presupposes as its counterpart external, ceremonial purity—has to do with moral and religious integrity, something like single-minded, unwavering intention. It is precisely what the δίψυχοί lack.

Psalms 24.4 ('clean hands a pure heart') and/or 73.13 ('I have kept my heart clean and washed my hands in innocence') might lie behind Jas 4.8.[248] Matthew 5.8 probably alludes to the former while 1 Cor 10.26 quotes Ps 24.1; and the LXX version of the latter is preceded by a line with ἁμαρτωλοί (72.12). One hesitates, however, to make much of the correlations. LXX Psalm 72.13 uses neither the καθαρ- root nor the ἁγν- root; and LXX Ps 23.4 (ἀθῷμος χερσὶν καὶ καθαρὸς τῇ καρδίᾳ) is less close to James in Greek than in English. Our text does not seem to allude to these verses any more than it does to Gen 20.5 (LXX: ἐν καθαρᾷ καρδίᾳ καὶ ἐν δικαιοσύνῃ χειρῶν).

'Purity of heart' is set over against δίψυχος not only in Jas 4.8 (ἁγνίσατε καρδίας) but also in 2 Clem. 11.1-2 (καθαρᾷ καρδίᾳ) and Herm. Mand. 9.5-7 (καθάρισον...τὴν καρδίαν σου). This agreement may be one more sign of dependence upon a common, lost apocryphon, especially as 2 Clem. 11.1-2 introduces a quotation from Eldad and Modad, as argued above.[249]

Verse 9. ταλαιπωρήσατε καὶ πενθήσατε καὶ κλαύσατε. Cf. 5.1 (κλαύσατε...ταλαιπωρίαις) and LXX Joel 1.9-10: 'Lament... Mourn (πενθεῖτε) O priests...the plains have suffered misery (τεταλαιπώρηκεν). Let the land mourn (πενθείτω), for the grain has suffered misery (τεταλαιπώρηκεν).' James' triad is awkward. The rest of the chapter is full of dyadic structures, not threes. Further, πενθέω (Jas: 1×) and κλαίω (Jas: 2×; cf. 5.1: κλαύσατε) characteristically appear in pairs.[250] Indeed, they are often

---

[246] Gen. 20.5-6; Pss 24.3-4; 51.10; 73.1; Ecclus 38.10 (ἀπόστησον πλημμέλειαν καὶ εὔθυνον χεῖρας καὶ ἀπὸ πάσης ἁμαρτίας καθάρισον καρδίαν); cf. 4Q436 1.10; 4Q525 2 2+3.1; T. Naph. 3.1; T. Jos. 4.6; Apocr. Ezek frag. 5 (PChBeatty, 187).

[247] Mt 5.8; 1 Tim 1.5; 2 Tim 2.22; Heb 10.22; Herm. Mand. 9.5.7; Sim. 6.5.2. On the relationship of James to Mt 5.8 in particular see Hartin, Q, 156-57.

[248] Cf. Oesterley, 450: 'the thought... is an adaptation of Ps. lxxii. (lxxiii.) 13'.

[249] Cf. Moffatt, 63: v. 9 'looks like another reminiscence of the Book of Eldad and Modat'.

[250] Isa 19.8 ('mourn and lament'); Gk. LAE 29.3 ('weeping and praying'); T. Abr. RecLng. 11.6 ('weeping and wailing'; cf. 11.8, 11); Josephus, Ant. 6.358 ('wailing and lamenting'); 13.28 ('weep and gnash your teeth'); Jn 16.20 ('weep and lament'); 3 Bar. 13.1 ('crying and lamenting'); 4 Bar. 9.8 ('weeping and crying'); Apoc. Sedr. 11.1 ('crying and lamenting'); etc.

paired with each other.[251] So ταλαιπωρέω[252]—which anticipates the ταλαιπωρίαις of 5.1—is a bit odd here, and even odder perhaps because there appear to be no pre-Christian instances of the imperatival form, ταλαιπωρήσατε. Perhaps then it is not unexpected that ms. 330 omits ταλαιπωρήσατε, that some church fathers quote our line using only two of James' three imperatives,[253] that some textual witnesses create a dyad by dropping καὶ πενθήσατε, and that others fashion a pair by striking καὶ κλαύσατε.[254]

One suspects that ταλαιπωρήσατε is yet another element from Eldad and Modad. For if the citation in 1 Clem. 23.3-4 = 2 Clem. 11.2-3, which Lightfoot assigned to Eldad and Modad (see above), opens with ταλαίπωροί εἰσιν οἱ δίψυχοι, the ταλαιπωρήσατε of our verse immediately follows δίψυχοι (v. 7). Moreover, Hermas, who quotes from Eldad and Modad in *Vis.* 2.3.4, also links the rare δίψυχος to ταλαίπωρος.[255]

In context, ταλαιπωρήσατε stands in contrast to 4.1-2: those ruled by ἐπιθυμεία and ἡδονή should become miserable,[256] that is, act as at a funeral, mourning a death (πενθήσατε καὶ κλαύσατε) and withdrawing from normal worldly activities; cf. Isa 32.11-12. Some readers have thought of corporal austerities.[257]

Although the second person imperatives ταλαιπωρήσατε and πενθήσατε are unattested in pre-Christian sources, it is otherwise with the command to weep, κλαύσατε,[258] which sounds like a prophetic warning, a call to repent in the face of judgment.

As our book purports to come from James the brother of Jesus, it is worth recalling those early Christian traditions that remember him as an ascetic of sorts.[259]

---

[251] LXX 2 Βασ 19.2; 2 Esd 11.4; 18.9; Sib. Or. 1.190; T. Zeb. 4.8; Ps.-Mk 16.10; Lk 6.25; Rev 16.10; 18.11, 15, 19; Josephus, *Ant.* 7.40; Acts Andr. 55; etc.; cf. בכה + אבל as in 2 Sam 19.1; Neh 8.9; y. Mo'ed. Qat. 82c (3.5).

[252] NT: 1. LXX: 17×, all but once for שדד, usually in the pual. Gk. Pseudepigrapha (Denis): 1×. Philo: 3×. Josephus: 24×. See further Spicq, 'ταλαιπωρέω κτλ.', *TLNT* 3.366-68.

[253] E.g. Chrysostom, *Frag. Jas ad loc.* PG 64.1048D (ταλαιπωρήσατε καὶ πενθήσατε); Ps.-Ephraem, *Quod lud. reb. abst.* ed. Phrantzoles, 239 (πενθήσατε καὶ κλαύσατε); Antiochus the Monk, *Pand. script. sacr.* Hom. 95 PG 89.1725A (ταλαιπωρήσατε γὰρ φησὶν καὶ κλαύσατε).

[254] καὶ πενθήσατε is not in 049 43 93 378T 665T Antioch G:A1; καὶ κλαύσατε is absent from 307 453 468 629 *et al.* L:V^ms,AU K:B^ms S:P.

[255] Hermas, *Vis.* 3.7.1; *Sim.* 1.2-3.

[256] For the intransitive use of ταλαιπωρέω see LXX Ps 37.7; Sib. Or. 5.75; Josephus, *Ant.* 2.334; 2 Clem. 19.4; Herm. *Vis.* 3.7.1; Epictetus, *Diatr.* 1.26.11.

[257] Cf. Maximus the Confessor, *Ascet.* 41 CCSG 40 ed. Gysens, 109; Grotius, 1087-88; Mayor, 147 ('voluntary abstinence from comforts and luxuries'); Smith, 244; John of Kronstadt, *My Life in Christ*, Jordanville, NY, 2000, 23-24. But Dimont, 635-36, is anxious to oppose a 'Puritan attitude', which would, to his mind, regard all joy as sinful.

[258] See LXX 2 Βασ 1.24; Jer 22.10; Joel 1.5; cf. Gk. Apoc. Ezra 6.25, 26.

[259] Eusebius, *H.E.* 2.23.4-18; Jerome, *Vir. ill.* 2 TU 14.1a ed. Richardson, 7-8.

FRIENDSHIP WITH THE WORLD VERSUS FRIENDSHIP WITH GOD (4.1-12)

ὁ γέλως ὑμῶν εἰς πένθος μετατραπήτω καὶ ἡ χαρὰ εἰς κατήφειαν. Trapp, 701, colorfully comments: 'Turn all the streams into this one channel, that may drive the mill, that may grind the heart. Meal was offered of old, and not whole corn.' James' double imperative, which assumes that some of his readers are characterized by inappropriate gaiety,[260] has a strong biblical feel; cf. 2 Sam 19.2-3 ('victory...turned into mourning' [LXX: εἰς πένθος]; this immediately follows κλαίει καὶ πενθεῖ); Job 30.31 ('My lyre is turned to mourning [LXX: εἰς πένθος], and my pipe to [εἰς] the voice of those who weep'); Lam 5.15 ('The joy of our hearts has ceased; our dancing has been turned to mourning' [LXX: εἰς πένθος]); Amos 8.10 ('I will turn your feasts into mourning [LXX: εἰς πένθος], and all your songs into lamentation'); Tob 2.6 ('Your feasts will be turned εἰς πένθος'); 1 Macc 1.39-40 ('her feasts were turned εἰς πένθος...her exaltation was turned εἰς πένθος'); 9.41 ('wedding was turned εἰς πένθος'). Note also 4Q166 2.17 ('[joy] will be turned into mourning for them'); 4 Bar. 6.6 (τὸ πένθος σου γὰρ μετεστράφη εἰς χαράν); Acts Phil. 27 ed. Bonnet, 14 (στραφῆναι εἰς πένθος). Most of these texts use (μετα)στρέφω when rendering the Hebrew idiom, הפך + ל‏אבל. None employs μετατρέπω.[261] This explains the textual variant, μεταστραφήτω:[262] it is the word we would expect. James, however, wants to use a traditional idiom and yet desires novelty at the same time.

Many have found in 4.9 the influence of Lk 6.25, which has no Matthean counterpart: 'Woe to you who are laughing (γελῶντες) now, for you will mourn and weep (πενθήσετε καὶ κλαύσετε)'.[263] The parallels just cited might discourage one from thinking this. And yet (i) none of them save Lk 6.25 has either γελάω or γέλως.[264] So (ii) as James and Luke also share the second person plural address; (iii) as both polemicize against worldly individuals; and (iv) as the nearby Jas 5.1 is also close to Lk 6.24-25, the saying attributed to Jesus probably does lie behind our text. But whatever one thinks of that matter, 'your laughter' sends one back to vv. 1-3: the reader imagines the double-minded laughing as they pursue and obtain ἡδονή.

---

[260] For other pejorative texts about laughter see K.H. Rengstorf, 'γελάω κτλ.', *TDNT* 1.658-62; Frankemölle, 613-16.
[261] NT: 1×. LXX: only in 4 Maccabees, never with εἰς. Gk. Pseudepigrapha (Denis): Let. Aris. 99. Philo: 8×, never with εἰς. Josephus: 0×. I have been unable to find any other example of μετατρέπω + εἰς πένθος before John of Thessalonica (ob. ca. 630), *Mir. Dem.* 14 ed. Lemerle, 153.
[262] In 01 02 044 5 33 69 81 88 218 *et al.* **Byz** AmEp Antioch PsOec.
[263] Cf. Calvin, 300; Knowling, 105 ('may have had in mind'); Knoch, 223; Davids, 167 ('perhaps'); Deppe, *Sayings*, 108-10; Hartin, *Q*, 151-53; Church, 389; Bottini, *Introduzione*, 134-35.
[264] γέλως: NT: 1×. LXX: 20×, usually for שחק. Gk. Pseudepigrapha (Denis): 7×. Philo: 63×. Josephus: 13×.

With ἡ χαρὰ εἰς κατήφειαν compare Lam 5.15; 4Q166 2.17; and 4 Bar. 6.6, all cited above. χαρά (cf. 1.2) might supply one more link to Lk 6: χάρητε appears in Luke's final makarism (v. 23). κατήφεια[265] means 'gloominess', and 'it is frequently used of dejection due to shame, and this association may have governed the choice of it here' (Ropes, 272). It is the antithesis of χαρά elsewhere.[266]

Verse 10. This call to humility helps unify chaps. 3–4. The humble should act peaceably (3.13-18), not curse others (3.8-12), be content with what they have (4.2), not enter into conflicts (4.1), submit themselves to God (4.6), not succumb to jealousy (4.5),[267] set aside boasting (4.13-16), not judge others (4.11-12).

The verse has the same two-fold structure as vv. 7b and 8a:

	present imperative	*future promise*
7a	resist the devil	and he will flee from you
8a	draw near to God	and he will draw near to you
10	be humble before the Lord	and he will exalt you

ταπεινώθητε ἐνώπιον κυρίου καὶ ὑψώσει ὑμᾶς. This statement of religious cause and effect, which takes the reader back to v. 6, is very similar to Lk 14.11: ὁ ταπεινῶν ἑαυτὸν ὑψωθήσεται.[268] Is this then another allusion to the Jesus tradition?[269] One is uncertain. Not only is the theme of God exalting the humble part of the tradition about Eldad and Modad,[270] which seemingly has otherwise influenced this part of James, but there are, beyond that, additional close parallels: Ps 75.7 (LXX: τοῦτον ταπεινοῖ καὶ τοῦτον ὑψοῖ, with God as the subject); Prov 29.23 ('A person's pride will bring humiliation, but one who is lowly in spirit will obtain honor'); Ezek 17.24 (LXX: ὑψῶν ξύλον ταπεινόν); Let. Aris. 263 (θεός...ταπεινοὺς ὑψοῖ); Diogenes Laertius 1.69 (τὰ μὲν ὑψηλὰ ταπεινῶν, τὰ δὲ ταπεινὰ ὑψῶν: Zeus is the subject); b. 'Erub. 13b ('He who humbles himself the Holy One, blessed be he, raises up, and whoever exalts himself the Holy One, blessed be he, humbles'); Lev. Rab. 1.5 ('my self-abnegation is my exaltation', purportedly a by-word of

---

[265] LXX: 0×. NT: 1×. Pseudepigrapha (Denis): 0×. Philo: 15×. Josephus: 12×.

[266] E.g. Philo, *Plant.* 167; *Abr.* 151; *Legat.* 15 ('every household and city was filled with anxiety and κατηφείας, their recent χαρᾶς being counter-balanced by a grief no less intense'); Libanius, *Or.* 35.6.17.

[267] Cf. Calvin, 300: 'We are jealous and envious, because we long to be high and mighty'.

[268] Cf. also Mt 23.12; Lk 18.14.

[269] So Winkler, 58; Plumptre, 91; Schlatter, 257; Deppe, *Sayings*, 113-17; Hartin, 219; idem, *Q*, 185-86; S. Johnson, *Treasure*, 94; McKnight, 357. Contrast Tsuji, *Glaube*, 128.

[270] Sifre 95 on Num 11.24-26; Tanḥ. Buber Beha'alotekha 22; b. Sanh. 17a; Num. Rab. 15.19.

Hillel); *Ahiqar* 60 ed. Lindenberger, 150 ('If [y]ou wis[h] to be [exalted], my son, [humble yourself before Šamaš], who humbles the [exalted] and [exalts the humble]').[271]

ταπείνω (Jas: 1×) + ἐνώπιον (Jas: 1×)—an idiom that occurs only in the LXX, James, and later Christian sources—is a Semitism, the Greek equivalent of לפני + נפל[272] or of לפני + ענה.[273] ἐνώπιον κυρίου (NT: 30×) is another Semitism, regularly representing לפני יהוה in the LXX.[274] ὑψόω (Jas: 1×), often paired with ταπείνω, recalls those biblical passages in which God exalts selected individuals.[275] In James, the exaltation is eschatological: it correlates with the σῶσαι of v. 12.[276]

Verse 11. The call not to speak against others or to judge them takes readers back to the condemnation of social conflict in vv. 1-2 and forms an *inclusio*.[277] Slander and judging manifest and foster personal 'conflicts and disputes' (v. 1), just as shunning the role of judge undoes enmity.

This verse and the next, which feature extensive repetition—καταλαλέω (3×), ἀδελφός (3×), κρίνω (4×), νόμος (4×; cf. νομοθέτης), κριτής (2×)—advert to LXX Lev 19.15-18, the classical Jewish locus on the topic of judgment: 'You will not render an unjust judgment (κρίσει)... with justice you will judge your neighbor (κρινεῖς τὸν πλησίον σου). You will not go around in deceit among your people... You will not hate your brother (τὸν ἀδελφόν σου) in your mind; you will reprove with reproof your neighbor (τὸν πλησίον σου) and so not incur sin on account of him. Your hand will not take vengeance, and you will not hate the sons of your people, and you will love your neighbor (τὸν πλησίον σου) as yourself.' James 2.8 has already quoted part of this famous passage, and James' use of τὸν πλησίον at the end of v. 12 confirms it is in mind again here; so too

---

[271] Note also 1 Sam 2.7; Job 22.29; Ps 18.27; Prov 3.34 (quoted in v. 6); Ezek 21.26; LXX Dan 5.19; 1 Cor 11.7; 1 Pet 5.6; 1 Clem. 59.3. Additional materials in L. Zunz, 'Alte Sentenzen über Hochmuth und Demuth', in *Gesammelte Schriften*, vol. 3, Berlin, 1876, 214-21.

[272] As in Deut 9.18, 25; Esth 6.13 (where the LXX has: ταπεινοῦσθαι ἐνώπιον θεοῦ); 2Q21 1.4; etc. Oesterley, 394, observes that James' Greek could be translated into Hebrew as: השפלו לפני יהוה.

[273] As in Dan 10.12 (LXX: ταπεινωθῆναι ἐναντίον κυρίου); Ezra 8.21 (LXX: ταπεινωθῆναι ἐνώπιον θεοῦ); y. Ta'an. 66b (3.1); etc. Note also Ecclus 2.17: ἐνώπιον αὐτοῦ ταπεινώσουσιν (the Hebrew is not extant).

[274] Lev 4.4, 18; Judg 11.11; 20.23; 2 Chr 1.6; etc. One might also regard the linking καί as a Semitism; see Beyer, *Syntax*, 253.

[275] In addition to the texts already cited see Josh 3.7 (LXX: ὑψῶσαί σε); 4.14; 2 Sam 22.49 (LXX: ὑψώσεις με); 1 Kgs 14.7 (LXX: ὑψωσά σε); 16.2 (LXX: ὕψωσά σε); etc.; cf. T. Jos. 18.1 (ὑψώσει ὑμᾶς).

[276] So Bede *ad loc.* CCSL 121 ed. Hurst, 214; Chaine, 107; Hauck, 27; Mitton, 163; R. Wall, 210; Popkes, 279; *et al.* Contrast McKnight, 357: 'The exalted place into which God will elevate them is nothing more than living before God properly'.

[277] Cf. Stier, 418; Carr, 55 ('the argument reverts to the main subject').

the reference to 'the law' and 'the law-giver' and the repetition of ἀδελφός, which is another key word from Lev 19.[278]

This creates a problem, for whereas Leviticus requires judging,[279] James asserts that judging others contradicts the law. Four observations: (i) The holiness code opposes vindictiveness, demands love over against hate (vv. 17-18), and calls for justice in dealing with others (v. 15). All of this is in harmony with the spirit of James. (ii) James may have taken the levitical imperative to concern formal communal discipline,[280] which is not his topic. He is condemning slander, which Lev 19 also condemns. (iii) Much Jewish tradition went out of its way to soften 'you will reprove your neighbor', to make sure that attempts to correct a neighbor were undertaken in meekness and compassion.[281] The Jesus tradition does the same thing.[282] (iv) The Synoptic Jesus speaks against judging: μὴ κρίνετε.[283] James has probably been influenced by this provocative imperative, itself a response to Lev 19.15-17.[284]

Brosend, 120, helpfully outlines the structure of the argument in 4.11-12 this way:

- Prohibition: Do not speak against one another
- Reason: To speak against or judge a brother is to speak against and judge the law
- Result: If you judge the law, you are not a doer of the law but a judge

---

[278] 19.17; cf. Barn. 19.4. Those who see Lev 19 in the background include Lapide, 163; Manton, 380; Plummer, 616; Ropes, 274; Hauck, 27; Dibelius, 228 (specifically Lev 19.18); Easton, 58 ('the most likely passage'); Mussner, 185; Knoch, 217; Mitton, 166; Burdick, 196; Ruckstuhl, 26; Laws, 187; Davids, 169-70; Vouga, 120-21; Schnider, 106; Frankemölle, 620-25; Baker, *Speech-Ethics*, 178-79; Moo, 197-98; Hartin, 218; Keenan, 136-37; Fabris, 289-90; Brosend, 118, 120; McCartney, 221; Witherington, 517; Blomberg-Kamell, 196, 198; McKnight, 363, 366. Note also that Cyril of Alexandria, *Amos ad* 2.6-7 ed. Pusey, 401-402, passes from discussing Lev 19.15 to Jas 4.12 and that Aquinas, *Summa* 2/2 q. 74 a. 2, in expounding Jas 4.11, says that the backbiter detracts from the law by despising the precept to love one's neighbor. Popkes, 282-83, highlighting the tension between James and Lev 19.16, ineffectively disputes the levitical background.

[279] LXX 19.15: κρινεῖς τὸν πλησίον σου; cf. v. 17: ἐλεγμῷ ἐλέγξεις.

[280] Cf. CD 9.2-8; Mt 18.15-20.

[281] E.g. 1QS 5.24–6.2; 4QBerakoth; T. Gad 6.1-5; Ps.-Phoc. 10.

[282] Mt 18.15-20; Lk 17.3-4.

[283] Mt 7.1-5 = Lk 6.37, 41-42 (Q); cf. Pol. *Phil.* 2.2-3.

[284] So e.g. Bouman, 207; Carr, 56; Hartin, 'Sermon', 453-54; Klein, *Werk*, 125-26; Johnson, *Brother*, 128-29; Popkes, 283 ('possibly'). Kloppenborg, 'Reception', 111, regards Jas 4.11 as among the 'likely contacts' between James and Q. Cf. Dionysius bar Salībī *ad loc.* CSCO 53, 60 Scriptores Syri 101 ed. Sedlacek, 129; Andrew of Caesarea, *Rev ad* 7.8 ed. Schmid, 81; Lapide, 163. But Deppe, *Sayings*, 117-19, denies James here uses a particular saying of Jesus. Commentators often also refer to Mt 5.21-22, which condemns the use of denigrating epithets. But despite the congruity in thought, there is no significant overlap in vocabulary.

- Affirmation: There is one lawgiver and judge, who is able to save and destroy
- Indictment: Who are you to judge your neighbor?

μὴ καταλαλεῖτε ἀλλήλων, ἀδελφοί. Cf. 5.9: μὴ στενάζετε, ἀδελφοί, κατ' ἀλλήλων. This subsection opens with καταλαλέω, which occurs three times in this verse but nowhere else in James.[285] The verb means 'speak ill of', 'defame', 'slander',[286] as in T. Iss. 3.4 (οὐ κατελάλησά τινος); T. Gad 3.3; 5.4 (οὐ καταλαλεῖ ἀνδρός); 2 Clem. 4.3 (μηδὲ καταλαλεῖν ἀλλήλων); Herm. Mand. 2.2-3 (μηδενὸς καταλάλει).[287] As the texts just cited have a negative particle + καταλαλέω + genitive object, the construction was clearly conventional. At the same time, given that James here interacts with Lev 19.15-18, our imperative might reflect MT Lev 19.16: 'You will not go around as a slanderer (רכיל) among your people'.[288] For the vocative 'brothers'—which makes the envisaged behavior all the worse—see above and on 1.2. Not too much should be made of the switch from ἁμαρτωλοί to ἀδελφοί because the latter belongs to the intertext, Lev 19.

ὁ καταλαλῶν ἀδελφοῦ ἢ κρίνων τὸν ἀδελφὸν αὐτοῦ καταλαλεῖ νόμου καὶ κρίνει νόμον. This is the rationale for the preceding imperative: to slander or judge a neighbor is to slander or judge the law, to forsake Torah.[289] The idea may be related to 2.10, where those who fail to keep the whole law are guilty of the whole law. Here similarly those criticized choose not to obey a commandment of Torah, so they in effect set themselves above the law.[290] κρίνων τὸν ἀδελφὸν αὐτοῦ supplies synonymous parallelism. Its function is two-fold: to help forge the link with Lev 19.15-18 (where κρίνω and ἀδελφός occur) and to add to the series of paired words and phrases in this passage; see above, 593-94. It might

---

[285] NT: 5×; cf. 1 Pet 2.1; 3.16. LXX: 13×. Gk. Pseudepigrapha (Denis): 6×. Philo: 5×. Josephus: 0×.

[286] The old English translations—Wycliffe, Tyndale, Cranmer—translated with 'backbyte'.

[287] Cf. also LXX Num 12.8; Pss 49.20 (κατὰ τοῦ ἀδελφοῦ σου καταλάλεις); 100.5 (τὸν καταλαλοῦντα λάθρᾳ τοῦ πλησίον αὐτοῦ); Prov 12.13; Wis 1.11; Gk. 1 En. 5.4; 1 Clem. 30.1, 3; 35.8 (κατὰ τοῦ ἀδελφοῦ σου κατελάλεις); Herm. Sim. 8.7.2 (with δίψυχοι); T. Abr. RecShrt. 12.6.

[288] Those who cite this verse include: Bede ad loc. CCSL 121 ed. Hurst, 215; Estius, 438; Pareus, 565; Gill, 797; Guyse, 590; Henry ad loc.; T. Scott, 584; Winkler, 58; Windisch-Preisker, 28; Schneider, 30; Mitton, 166; Cantinat, 213; Schrage, 47; Davids, 169; Vouga, 1984; Martin, 163; Blevins, 'Repent', 423; Frankemölle, 621; Giere, 'Midrash', 98; Ong, Strategy, 137; Sleeper, 115; Perkins, 128; Moo, 197-98; Fabris, 289; Witherington, 517; Blomberg-Kamell, 201; Gundry, 941. But the LXX has: οὐ πορεύσῃ δόλῳ.

[289] Not 'the law of Christ' (Gal 6.2, against Hammond, 93) nor 'the law of Christian life which... is none other than the law of love' (Huther, 136; cf. Gundry, 941) nor 'the gospel message, the new covenant as the (qualitatively) royal law, as in 2:18-23' (so Blomberg-Kamell, 197; cf. Mitton, 166, et al.).

[290] Cf. Mayor, 149; Ludwig, Wort, 177.

also, for Christian readers, serve to recall Jesus' reinterpretation of Lev 19.15-18 as Mt 7.1-5 and Lk 6.37, 41-42 likewise have κρίνω and ἀδελφός. For νόμος see on 1.25. καταλαλεῖ νόμου is an odd expression; but it is the product of a desire for parallelism: it is modeled upon ὁ καταλαλῶν ἀδελφοῦ.

That κρίνων is parallel to καταλαλῶν shows that simple ethical judgments cannot be in view: James is not countering critical thinking. Nor is he dismissing the practice of communal expulsion.[291] Interpreters have regularly understood this; see 591. His text rather blasts those who fail to exercise mercy, humility, and tolerance. κρίνω here approaches κατακρίνω.[292]

εἰ δὲ νόμον κρίνεις, οὐκ εἶ ποιητὴς νόμου ἀλλὰ κριτής. Cf. Apost. Const. 2.36 ed. Funk, 123: ἐὰν γὰρ κρίνῃς τὸν ἀδελφόν, κριτὴς ἐγένου μηδενός σε προχειρισαμένου.[293] ποιητὴς νόμου (cf. 1.22 v.l.; Rom 2.13) picks up on both 1.22-25 (with ποιηταὶ λόγου, οὐ ποιηταί, ποιητὴς ἔργου) and 2.12-16 and so draws earlier lines to bear on this verse. Readers persuaded there are prepared to be persuaded here. For ποιητής see on 1.22. Although one finds ποιητὴς νόμων in both Ps.-Plato, *Def.* 415, and Ps.-Plutarch, *Musica* 1133A, the singular, νόμου, refers to the Torah, and ποιητὴς νόμου has its immediate background in the traditional Hebrew combination, תורה + עשה.[294] κριτής (see on 4.2) is the equivalent of שפט, a 'judge'. Perhaps we should supply νόμου—'judge of the law'.[295] In any event, the word designates standing not under the law but over it. That would be to usurp the place of God; cf. v. 12.[296]

Does James invite deconstruction here? The text criticizes others for criticizing others. The ecclesiastical commentaries do not typically notice the irony. One is in any case reminded of Matthew's Jesus, who can demand love of enemies (5.44) and enjoin hearers not to insult others (5.22) yet then turn around and insult and attack opponents in the terms he has prohibited, as in chap. 23.[297]

---

[291] Cf. Mt 7.1-5 with 18.15-17.

[292] Cf. Ps.-Oecumenius *ad loc.* PG119.497C.

[293] This is followed closely by a citation of Mt 7.1 = Lk 6.37.

[294] As in 2 Chr 14.3 (LXX: ποιῆσαι τὸν νόμον); Neh 9.34; 1QpHab 7.11 (עושי התורה = 'doers of the Torah'); 8.1 (עושי התורה); 12.4-5 (עושה התורה); 4Q171 2.15 (עושי התורה), 23 (עושה התורה); Sifre Deut 306 on 32.2; y. B. Meṣi'a 10d (5.8); etc.

[295] But for the case against this see Huther, 137.

[296] Pfleiderer, *Christianity*, 303, hears a criticism of Marcion or the like. Carr, 55-56, thinks of Jewish Christians who viewed the law as transitory. Martin, 164, supposes that James is attacking antinomian followers of Paul.

[297] Interestingly enough, H.U. von Balthasar, *The Glory of the Lord: A Theological Aesthetics, vol. VII*, Edinburgh, 1989, 119, recognizes that one might find a contradiction between Jas 4.11-12 and the behavior of Jesus in the gospels. His solution is this: one cannot 'apply to him what is said in the Letter of James' because Jesus not only keeps the law but is the 'one lawgiver and judge'.

Verse 12. The argument now finds its theological grounding.

εἷς ἐστιν ὁ νομοθέτης καὶ κριτής.[298] Cf. m. 'Abot 4.8: 'Judge not alone, for none may judge alone save One'. Jewish hearers of James would likely recall Deut 6.4: 'The Lord our God is one Lord', especially as James has already referred to the Shema' in 2.19, which also uses the εἷς of LXX Deut 6.4.[299]

Philo and Josephus often speak of Moses as the νομοθέτης;[300] so too the church fathers after them.[301] James does not reject that tradition here: it is just not in view.

Although many ecclesiastical commentators and some modern exegetes identify the lawgiver and judge with Jesus Christ,[302] this must be a mistake. It is true that Jesus is often, in early Christian writings, the eschatological judge,[303] and also that patristic sources occasionally refer to him as νομοθέτης.[304] But, if we put the present text aside, no one before Justin bestows the latter title upon Jesus; and of the three times Justin does so, it is twice qualified by καινός so that Jesus is distinguished from Moses. The other time it follows a reference to the 'new covenant', which gains the same result.[305] Beyond that, the νόμος must be the Jewish Scripture (cf. 2.8-12) and must include specifically the holiness code, with its teaching on judging others (Lev 19.15-18). Nothing hints at νόμος being the teaching of Jesus.

νομοθέτης and κριτής are not typically paired in Graeco-Roman or Jewish literature. Their combination seems to be James' novelty, prompted by the previous phrase.

As in 5.9, James moves from people judging others to God judging them. This reflects the logic of the tradition in Mt 7.1-5 = Lk 6.37, 41-42, where those who judge others will be judged (by God).[306] One may compare further several Pauline texts that may also be indebted to the

---

[298] It is impossible to judge whether ὁ is original. 01 02 044 5 33 69 81 *et al.* **Byz** Antioch Dam Did PsOec have it. P74 P100 03 025 88 L1281 *et al.* omit.

[299] Cf. Mk 12.29, 32; 1 Cor 8.4. Commentators put in mind of the Shema' include Hartin, 218; Popkes, 282; Blomberg-Kamell, 202; McKnight, 366; Gundry, 941. See further Hutchinson Edgar, 'Love', 9-10.

[300] NT: 1×. LXX: only Ps 9.21. Cf. Let. Aris. 131, 139, 148; Aristobulus frag. 2 *apud* Eusebius, *P.E.* 8.10.3, 6, 9 ed. Holladay, 136, 138.

[301] Lampe, s.v., νομοθέτης, 3.

[302] So Grotius, 1088; Hammond, 94; T. Scott, 584; Macknight, 599; H.P. Liddon, *The Divinity of Our Lord and Saviour Jesus Christ*, London, 1868, 289-90; Smith, 260; Davids, 185; Martin, 162; Baker, 'Christology', 54-55. Cf. Apost. Const. 5.20.12 ed. Funk, 297: χριστόν...κριτήν, νομοθέτην. Contrast Ropes, 275; Laws, 213. Gill, 798, identifies both God and Christ as the lawgiver.

[303] Mt 25.31-46; 2 Cor 5.10; 2 Tim 4.1; *et al.*

[304] Lampe, s.v., νομοθέτης, 2.

[305] Justin, *Dial.* 12.2; 14.3; 18.3.

[306] Cf. also 1 Clem. 13.2; Pol. *Phil.* 2.3.

Jesus tradition.³⁰⁷ We seem to have here an early Christian *topos* inspired by Jesus' word against judging: human judgment in the present should abdicate in favor of divine judgment in the future.³⁰⁸

ὁ δυνάμενος σῶσαι καὶ ἀπολέσαι. The words, which specify the actions of the divine judge,³⁰⁹ recall Herm. *Mand.* 12.6.3 (φοβήθητε τὸν πάντα δυνάμενον, σῶσαι καὶ ἀπολέσαι); *Sim.* 9.23.4 (δυνάμενος ἀπολέσαι ἢ σῶσαι).³¹⁰ One could posit a common lost source or Hermas' knowledge of James. But the issue is complicated by the fact that Hermas equally resembles Mt 10.28 diff. Lk 12.5—φοβεῖσθε...τὸν δυνάμενον... ἀπολέσαι.³¹¹ Do James and Hermas reflect a variant of the Synoptic saying? Or do both depend upon Matthew?³¹²

For δύναμαι + σῴζω see on 2.14, and for the latter paired with ἀπόλλυμι (see on 1.11) see Lk 9.55 v.l. (οὐκ...ἀπολέσαι ἀλλὰ σῶσαι); Cassius Dio 44.26.4 (σῶσαι καὶ ἀπολέσαι).³¹³ In the LXX, God is the subject of both σῴζω³¹⁴ and ἀπόλλυμι,³¹⁵ although never in the same sentence.³¹⁶ Here their content must be eschatological, as in Mt 10.28. This follows from God's role as 'judge' and the strong eschatological content of verses soon to follow, 5.1-9. For ὁ δυνάμενος of God see Rom 16.25; Eph 3.20; Heb 5.7 (τὸν δυνάμενον σῴζειν); Jude 24; Herm. *Mand.* 4.1.11.³¹⁷

James offers no details about the eschatological scenario, but it is possible that ἀπολέσαι assumes that the wicked will not suffer forever but will cease to exist.³¹⁸

---

³⁰⁷ Rom 2.1; 14.4, 10-13; 1 Cor 4.4; 5.12-13. These Pauline verses have often been linked to Jas 4.11-12; note e.g. Pelagius, *Rom* 14.4 TS 9 ed. Souter, 106-107; Calvin, 301 (James uses 'the same reasoning as Paul'); Lapide, 164.

³⁰⁸ James' argument also has a formal parallel in Mt 23.8-12, where none should be called 'rabbi' because there is only one true teacher (the Messiah), nor should any be called 'father', because there is only one father, God.

³⁰⁹ Burkitt, 1030, draws a contrast with the devil of v. 7: like God, the latter can destroy; unlike God, the latter cannot save.

³¹⁰ Cf. also 2 Clem. 5.4: 'Do not fear those who, though they kill you, are not able (δυναμένους) to do anything else to you, but fear the one who, after you are dead, has the authority to cast soul and body into the flames of hell'.

³¹¹ Brückner, *Reihenfolge*, 291, thinks James here depends upon Matthew.

³¹² For the possibility that James knew Matthew see the Introduction, 56-62. For the strong possibility that Hermas knew Matthew see J. Verheyden, 'The Shepherd of Hermas and the Writings that Later Formed the New Testament', in Gregory-Tuckett, *Reception*, 293-329.

³¹³ Note also Mk 8.35; Lk 6.9; Homer, *Il.* 17.227-28; Demosthenes, *Or.* 57.60.

³¹⁴ = ישע; e.g. Deut 33.29; Hos 13.4; Zeph 3.17.

³¹⁵ E.g. Gen 19.13; Lev 20.3; Zeph 2.5.

³¹⁶ Although LXX Deut 32.39 (ἐγὼ ἀποκτενῶ καὶ ζῆν ποιήσω) and 1 Βασ 2.6 (κύριος θανατοῖ καὶ ζωογονεῖ) are conceptually similar.

³¹⁷ With insufficient cause, Braumann, 'Hintergrund', 407, associates 'able to save and destroy' with baptism.

³¹⁸ Cf 1 En. 98.9-10; Pss. Sol. 3.10-12; 13.11; 4 Ezra 12.33; 13.38; t. Sanh. 13.4-5 (some sinners will be annihilated after twelve months); m. Sanh. 10.3; Gen. Rab. 6.6.

σὺ δὲ τίς εἶ ὁ κρίνων τὸν πλησίον;[319] Cf. Rom 14.10: σὺ δὲ τί κρίνεις τὸν ἀδελφόν σου; Has Romans influenced the formulation here?[320] σὺ (δὲ) τίς εἶ (like the corresponding plural: τίνες ἐστὲ ὑμεῖς) was a fixed idiom.[321] Here it stands for: 'Who do you think you are that you can do this?' The introduction of πλησίον reinforces the allusion to Lev 19.18; see on 2.8. The neighbor is to be loved, not judged.

Judaism much pondered the identity of the 'neighbor' in Lev 19.18, there left unspecified. Like Let. Aris. 207 and T. Iss. 207 but unlike Sifra 200 *ad loc.*; Sifre 89 on Deut 13.9; ARN B 26, the Jesus tradition shows a universalizing tendency; cf. Lk 10.29. But James may here have in mind Christian Jews desirous of remaining within the synagogue: they are being defamed.

The Jesus tradition speaks of both destruction and 'everlasting' fire or punishment: Mt 3.12; 7.13; 10.28; 25.41, 46; Mk 9.48.

[319] 88 400 629 *et al.* **Byz** PsOec have ὃς κρίνεις. ἕτερον replaces πλησίον in 69 88 398 *et al.* **Byz** PsOec; cf. perhaps Rom 14.4: ὁ κρίνων ἀλλότριον. At the end, 018 94 180 307 321 453 720 918 1678 2197 2818 add ὅτι οὐκ ἐν ἀνθρώπῳ ἀλλ' ἐν θεῷ τὰ διαβήματα ἀνθρώπου (2818: ἀνθρώπων) κατευθύνεται. This is presumably a marginal gloss (inspired by LXX Ps 36.23) that worked its way into the text.

[320] For the possibility that James knew Romans see the Introduction, 62-67.

[321] Cf. Aristophanes, *Lys.* 851; Epictetus, *Diatr.* 3.1.23; Lucian, *Cat.* 14.4; Jdt 8.12; Rom 9.20 (σὺ τίς εἶ ὁ ἀνταποκρινόμενος τῷ θεῷ); 14.4; T. Sol. 21.7.

XV

DENUNCIATIONS OF THE PROSPEROUS (4.13–5.6)[1]

(13) Come now, you who say, 'Today or tomorrow we will go to this city and spend a year there, carrying on business and making money'. (14) Yet you do not know what will happen tomorrow, what your life will be like. For you are a mist that appears for a while, after which it disappears. (15) Instead you ought to say, 'If the Lord wishes, we will both live and do this or that'. (16) But as it is, you boast in your arrogant pretensions. All such boasting is evil. (17) So it is sin to know the good and yet not do it.
(1) Come now, you rich people, lament and wail for the miseries that are coming to you. (2) Your riches have rotted, and your clothes are moth-eaten. (3) Your gold and silver have rusted, and their rust will be a witness against you, and it will eat your flesh like fire. You have laid up treasure in the latter days. (4) Behold! The pay of the workers who harvested your fields—which you have unjustly withheld—screams out. And the cries of the harvesters have reached the ears of the Lord of hosts. (5) You have lived on the earth in luxury and in wanton pleasure. You have fattened your hearts on a day of slaughter. (6) You have condemned, you have murdered the righteous one, who does not resist you.

History of Interpretation and Reception

Christians have both broadened and narrowed this passage's condemnation of the rich. On the one hand, some have enlarged the scope of James' harsh words to include everyone. Mark the Hermit wrote: 'A person can, even without wealth, be a rich person, whether in speech or understanding or any sort of attachment, if he greedily hangs on to those things that are freely granted in common to everyone else. One receives in order to share with someone else who has nothing.'[2] On the other hand, and

---

[1] Recent literature: Ahrens, *Arm*; Alana, 'Rich'; Alonso-Schökel, 'James 5,2'; Backhaus, 'Condicio'; Blevins, 'Repent'; Böttrich, 'Gold'; J. Byron, 'Cain'; Deppe, *Sayings*, 111-13, 120-31; Hutchinson Edgar, *Poor*, 197-215; Feuillet, 'Parousie'; Hainthaler, *Ausdauer*, 301-305; Jebb, *Literature*, 258-68; S. Johnson, *Treasure*, 80-109; Klein, *Werk*, 127-28, 180-84; Konradt, *Existenz*, 148-65; Krüger, *Kritik*, 201-42; Maier, *Reich*, 25-45; Maynard-Reid, *Poverty*; Mayordomo-Marin, 'Gericht'; Noack, 'Reichen'; Omanson, 'Judgment'; Peck, 'James 5:1-6'; Penner, *Eschatology*, 172-77; Pretorius, 'Verklaringsopsies'; Prieto, 'Malédiction'; Rusche, 'Glaube'; Tiller, 'Rich'; Tsuji, *Glaube*, 89-92, 135-48; Weiser, 'Edelmetall'; Wheeler, *Wealth*, 91-106; R.L. Williams, 'Piety'; Wypadlo, *Gebet*, 352-66.
[2] So Mark the Hermit, *Paen.* 5 SC 445 ed. Durand, 228-30, quoting Lk 6.24 and Jas 5.1-2. Calvin, 306, enlarges the scope of 5.1-6 in a different way: 'The vices condemned

more characteristically, many have constricted James' words, anxiously insisting that the prophetic threats cannot extend to all who are well off. Surely God disapproves only those who obtain their wealth unjustly.[3] Surely only those who are avaricious or fail to show mercy or do not adhere to 'plain living' (Calvin) fall under James' condemnation.[4]

All interpreters concur that, in James, 'one's relationship to money is a litmus test for one's relationship with God'.[5] But what exactly this implies varies from exegete to exegete. Many avow that our text does not implicate modern capitalism or Christians who run businesses for profit.[6] For Gill, 798, the apostle does not 'condemn merchandise, and the lawful practice of buying and selling, and getting gain; but that men should not resolve upon those things without consulting God, and attending to his will, and subjecting themselves to it'. Nor does James, according to Gill, speak in 5.1 of 'all rich men', for 'there are some rich who are good men, and make a good use of their riches, and do not abuse them'.[7] In like fashion, some have been keen to stress that the denunciation in 4.13-16 is no condemnation of prudent planning. Smith, 277-79, endeavored to show that hoarding in James' day—a bad thing—is not the same as saving in modern times—generally a good thing. Mitton, 169, affirmed: 'James' rebuke is not a condemnation of wise planning in advance.

here do not apply to each and every one. Some employ their wealth in a life of luxury, some lay a great deal out on display and ostentation, some cheat the social virtues and live like misers in squalor. So note that various faults are blamed on various sorts, but there is a general condemnation passed on all who either accumulate unjust riches for themselves or make a wrongful abuse of riches.'

[3] Cf. Isho'dad of Merv *ad loc.* HSem 10 ed. Gibson, 51.

[4] Cf. Caesarius of Arles, *Serm.* 35.4 CCSL 103 ed. Morin, 154; Calvin, 307; Hemminge, 43-83 (almost half of Hemminge's commentary is an excursus on wealth and business); Poole, 894 ('He doth not condemn merchants traveling into other countries, nor trading there, nor designing gain by their trade, nor forecasting their business; but their promising themselves the continuance of their life, the accomplishing [of] their designs, and the success of their labours, without respect to God's providence and direction, as if their times and their works were in their own hands, not in his'); Felder, 1799.

[5] Kamell, 'Economics', 157.

[6] Cf. Keenan, 145: 'The ferocity of James' denunciation of the rich has long been an embarrassment to prudent and balanced Christian scholars'. He illustrates with quotations from Dibelius. Writing in Australia in 1980, H.P. Hamann, *James, Jude*, Adelaide, 1980, 73, contends that, since everyone has access to 'social welfare programs', direct application of James is problematic.

[7] Cf. Burkitt, 1030; Smith, 265-67 (who goes on at length about how much 'the world owes to its Merchant Princes'); Easton, 60; Moo, 202-203; Doriani, 173; Baker-Ellsworth, 123; *et al.* One can indeed plausibly urge that, in chap. 4, James fails to 'place in question the economic structures'; so Hoppe, 106, who asserts that a more critical stance is needed today. In line with this, Wheeler, *Wealth*, 101, observes that, in 2.1-12, James does not oppose the wealthy entering the assembly, only their being treated differently from others. Contrast, however, Hutchinson Edgar, *Poor*, 199 n. 52: 'as far as the author is concerned, they are unwelcome outsiders'. See further on v. 13.

Efficient community life requires such planning, as Joseph as "prime minister" in Egypt proved'.[8]

The tendency of such comments is to uphold an author's status quo. Some, however, have been less blasé. Catholicos Nerses IV of Armenia drew upon Jas 5.4 when imploring princes not to cut the wages of workers.[9] In 1826, Edward Irving used 5.1-7 to denounce the sins and infidelities that accompanied the gathering of multitudes in large British manufacturing towns.[10] More recently, some Christian exegetes have been adamant that James is not just commending an attitude, and that his words should raise questions for the capitalistic culture of consumerism. According to L. Evans, 'there is such a thing as a just and living wage; to pay anything less than that, James suggests, is unjust and sinful'.[11] For Townsend, 95, James implies Christian sponsorship of 'fair world trade and political liberty', even if that involves Christians 'paying high prices for some of the goods they consume, as well as higher taxes': 'charity is not enough'. Church, 395, insists that Christians not read James as though the only problem is greedy individuals; they rather need to 'think in terms of a culture of corruption... When we focus on the greedy individual, the solution is conversion—CEOs with better hearts. When we focus on the systemic problem...then the solution is social reform. In theological terms, the problem is the sinful nature of the corporate structure, one of the powers and principalities of this age... We need forces that counter-balance the power of corporations.'[12] Reyes, 'Grito', turns James into a critique of the modern global economy, which puts profits ahead of exploited workers. He calls the church to agitate for the 'redignification' of the industrial workforce in the global south. Even more forceful are Tamez and Maynard-Reid. The former reads James so that the rich 'must cease being rich'; the latter holds that 'there is no hope for any rich persons as long as they are members of that class'.[13]

The critical characterizations of merchants and the rich in 4.13–5.6 have regrettably become an opportunity for some Christians to indulge in

---

[8] Cf. Stier, 429; Simeon, 94 ('nor, if prospective plans were unlawful, would any one branch of agriculture or commerce, or even of liberal education, be carried forward'); Smith, 269 ('Men are to exercise forethought—it is a God-given faculty; they are to plan and to labour—God demands industry in the use of their talents'); W. Carpenter, 226 ('It is not the making of plans which He rebukes, it is the forgetfulness of God'); Moo, 295 ('James is not rebuking these merchants for their plans or even their desire to make a profit'). This group of expositors could appeal to 5.7, for this holds no criticism of farmers, whose patience requires planning.

[9] Nerses Šnorhali, *General Epistle*, trans. A. Aljalian, 1966, 70.

[10] E. Irving, 'God's Controversy with the Land', in *Sermons, Lectures and Occasional Discourses*, vol. 3, London, 1828, 893-963.

[11] L. Evans, *Faith*, 116.

[12] Cf. G. Byron, 469: 'This passage is a warning and a summons to all who participate in the personal and systematic economic crisis that is plaguing the world today'.

[13] Tamez, *Message*, 48; Maynard-Reid, *Poverty*, 82. Cf. Alana, 'Rich': James speaks against capitalism and for 'the redistribution of wealth'.

ethnic stereotyping. Carr, 56-57, spoke of 'the Semite's born instinct for trading' and added that the instinct 'is still eminently characteristic of the [Jewish] race'. According to Smith, 'the Jew was ever an optimist when business was to be done' (263), he 'had ever been inclined to overestimate the importance of wealth', and he was 'unscrupulous as to how he acquired it' (275). Schlatter, 263, wrote of the 'oriental psychology', and Easton, 63, asserted that 'Orientals spend large sums on expensive garments'. Equally offensive is the outrageous assertion of Macknight, 599: 'The unbelieving Jews being exceedingly addicted to sensual pleasures, and very covetous, were of course grievous oppressors of the poor'. And then there is the sweeping generalization of W. Carpenter, 73: 'the faults St. James censures in his letter are many of them faults to which the Jews as a race are specially liable'.

The conditional in v. 15, ἐὰν ὁ κύριος θελήσῃ (= Vulgate: *si Dominus voluerit*), 'if God wills', has an interesting history. Taken over from the pagan world, it (or a variant) has been a recurrent refrain in the speech of many Christians. In the West it is traditionally known as the *Conditio Jacobaea*. Calvin, 303, with qualification, recommended using it: 'There may well be times when godly folk, with a modest opinion of themselves, recognizing their steps to be led by the will of God, may say unconditionally that they will do this or that. Let us, however, say it is right and useful, when we make any promise for future time, to make a habit of these expressions: "God willing", or "God permitting". Naturally I do not want to make a fetish of this, as though the omission should be an offence.' He went on to observe that, although 'we frequently read in Scripture how the holy servants of God spoke of future events without qualification', nonetheless it is 'a careful practice for all men of religion' to say 'If God will' or 'If God grant'.[14] Theologians have sometimes warned against such phrases becoming formal banalities, uttered by rote and habit instead of from heartfelt sincerity.[15] Some, going further, have held that James' 'you ought to say' need not be taken literally: James is instilling an attitude, not demanding use of a formula.[16]

The corresponding Arabic is *'in sha'Allah*. According to Ropes, 279, it is 'not unlikely' that Muslims adopted the expression 'from the Syrians, and that these had it from the Greeks'. Ropes fails to note that Muslims regard recitation of *'in sha'Allah* as a scriptural commandment because the Koran says: 'Do not say of anything, "I will do such and such tomorrow", without adding, "If Allah wills"'.[17] This is strikingly close to

---

[14] Cf. Manton, 392 (giving several reasons for using the formula); Henry, *ad loc.*; Plummer, 620-21; Martin, 167.

[15] E.g. Tasker, 104, who complains among other things of abbreviating *deo volente* to 'd.v.'; cf. Neander, 103; Martin, 167.

[16] E.g. Smith, 270-71 (with extended critical remarks on 'd.v.'); Mitton, 171.

[17] Koran Al-Kahf (18).23-24.

James, so much so that one wonders whether what James wrote became a proverb that eventually entered Muhammad's world. Or does Jas 4.16 preserve what was already proverbial?

4.17 has played a role in theological reflections on the nature of sin. Origen, anticipating later discussions of 'the age of reason', thought that the idea of knowing what is right yet doing what is wrong implies, in what seems like a reversal of Plato, that one does not sin until one knows.[18] In *On First Principles*, Origen quotes Jn 15.22 and remarks that it is only after 'the reason implanted within' has begun to reveal the difference between good and evil that an individual no longer has an excuse for sin. He then cites Jas 4.17 as substantiation.[19]

Augustine, as one might anticipate, had a different take on our verse. In *De coniugiis adulterinis* he asks, after quoting James, whether one can sin even though one does not know how to do good. He responds in the affirmative.[20] He then adds, however, that those who know the good and do not do it sin more grievously. Here then we find gradations of sin and responsibility.[21] Naturally, our verse has sometimes served to validate the category of 'sins of omission'.[22]

The ἐθρέψατε of 5.5 and its translations have lent themselves to being used in exhortations against gluttony. John of Kronstadt cited the verse to authorize his advice: 'Food and drink must only be used for strengthening our powers, and not as dainties, and we must not eat when nature does not require it'.[23]

Christian pacifists have welcomed the phrase in v. 6, 'the righteous one, who does not resist you'. But exegetes who believe that, on occasion, the oppressed may be forced to join in violent revolution, have found a different way of appropriating the text. Maynard-Reid, prefers, for obvious reason, to punctuate the end of v. 6 as a question: 'Should he not resist you?'[24]

---

[18] Cf. how ignorance reduces responsibility in Acts 3.17; 17.30; 1 Tim 1.13; Tanḥ. Yel. Bereshit 7; also the generalization of b. Roš. Haš. 28b: 'For committing a sin, intention is required'.

[19] Origen, *Prin.* 1.3.6 GCS 22 ed. Koetschau, 57.

[20] Augustine, *Con. adult.* 1.9 CSEL 41 ed. Zycha, 355-56. See further the discussion of Manton, 396-98. Cf. earlier Pss. Sol. 3.7-8; 13.7.

[21] Cf. Peter Damian, *Ep.* 31.14 ed. Reindel, 291, citing 4.17: 'The more knowledge an individual has, the more blameworthy the offense, because anyone who, had he wanted, was able prudently to avoid sin, will inevitably deserve punishment'. J. Plumptre, in his *Four Discourses on Subjects Relating to the Amusement of the Stage*, Cambridge, UK, 1809, 69-98, makes 4.17 his point of departure for warning playwrights, actors, censors, and others involved with the stage to beware of unedifying comedy, and especially ridicule.

[22] Cf. W. Ames, *Medulla theologica* 1.14.9.

[23] John of Kronstadt, *My Life in Christ*, Jordanville, NY, 2000, 293. Cf. Nicodemus of the Holy Mountain, *Handbook of Spiritual Counsel*, trans. P.A. Chamber, 111.

[24] Maynard-Reid, *Poverty*, 74.

Exegesis

James has already, in this chapter, rebuked enemies of God who covet, crave pleasure, and love the world (vv. 1-4). He has further reprimanded them for defaming others and judging their neighbors (vv. 11-12). In this new section, the sins of such continue to pile up: we learn of their avarice, their arrogance, their oppression of employees, and even their murder of the righteous. Adopting the role of prophet, James upbraids such, foretelling their eschatological misery.

4.13–5.6, despite the high number of *hapax legomena*,[25] expands on a number of themes already introduced. 1.10-11 has mentioned the brevity of life in connection with the rich and their approaching ruin; cf. 4.14. 4.7-10 has demanded submission to God's will; cf. 4.15. 3.5 and 14 have countered boasting; cf. 4.16. 2.14-26 has discussed at length the importance of doing and not just knowing; cf. 4.17. 2.6-7 has referred to the oppressive behavior of the rich; cf. 5.1-6. And 4.1-3 has condemned the pursuit of pleasure as the source of much conflict; cf. 5.5.[26]

5.4 borrows from the woe-oracle in Isa 5.7-9, and Jas 4.13–5.6 in its entirety is 'delivered with all the impassioned energy of an Amos or a Joel'.[27] As often observed, the section—especially 5.1-6—is full of prophetic elements, including some elements characteristic of 'woe oracles' or הוֹי-pericopae.[28] Among the parallels are these:

- 4.13-16 rebukes merchants: 'Come now, you who say, "Today or tomorrow we will go to this city and spend a year there, carrying on business and making money". Yet...'; cf. Isa 23.2-3, 8; Ezek 27.3; Nah 3.16
- 4.13 quotes those rebuked: 'Come now, you who say, "Today or tomorrow..."'; cf. Isa 5.19; 22.13; 30.10; 42.17; 65.5; Jer 14.15; Ezek 13.5-6; Amos 6.13; 8.5-6, 14; 9.10; Mic 4.11; Zeph 1.12; etc.
- 5.1 issues a call to weep: 'lament and wail for the miseries that are coming to you'; cf. Isa 13.6; 15.3; 16.7; 23.1; Jer 9.10; 25.34; 49.3; Ezek 30.3; Joel 1.5; 5.8; Zeph 1.11; etc.

---

[25] Verse 13: σήμερον, πορεύομαι, ὅδε, πόλις, ἐμπορεύομαι, κερδαίνω; v. 14: ἐπίσταμαι, ποῖος, ἀτμίς, ὀλίγος, φαίνω, ἀφανίζω; v. 15: ἀντί, ζάω; v. 16: ἀλαζονία, καύχησις, τοιτοῦτος; 5.1: ὀλολύζω, ἐπέρχομαι; 5.2: σήπω, ἱμάτιον, σητόβρωτος; 5.3: χρυσός, ἄργυρος, κατιόομαι, μαρτύριον, ἐσθίω, σάρξ, θησαυρίζω, ἔσχατος; 5.4: μισθός, ἐργάτης, ἀμάω, ἀποστερέω, κράζω, βοή, θερίζω, οὖς, σαβαώθ 5.5: τρυφάω, σπαταλάω, τρέφω, σφαγή; 5.6: καταδικάζω. Words that appear more than once but are confined to 4.13–5.6: ἄγε (4.13; 5.1), νῦν (4.13, 16; 5.1), αὔριον (vv. 13-14).

[26] For links between 4.13–5.6 and the rest of James see further Frankemölle, 634-36.

[27] Stanley, *Sermons*, 315. Cf. Jebb, *Literature*, 258 ('It is almost as though one of the old prophets had risen from the dead'); Wordsworth, 30 (James is here 'a Christian Jeremiah')

[28] W. Janzen, *Mourning Cry and Woe Oracle*, Berlin, 1972. Cf. Isa 1.4; 5.8, 11, 18, 20, 21, 22-23; 10.1; 29.15; 30.1; 31.1; 45.9-10; Jer 22.13; 23.1; Ezek 34.2; Amos 5.18; 6.1; Mic 2.1; Nah 3.1; Hab 2.6, 9, 12, 15, 19; Zeph 3.1.

- 5.2-3 employs the so-called prophetic perfect: 'Your riches have rotted...'; cf. Isa 5.13; 9.1; 10.28-32; Jer 23.2; Amos 5.2; Joel 2.21-24; etc.
- 5.3 threatens fire: 'will eat your flesh like fire'; cf. Isa 10.16-17; 27.11; Jer 5.14; Ezek 15.7; Amos 1.12-14; 5.6; 7.4; etc.
- 5.4 uses ἰδού; cf. Isa 13.9; 19.1; Jer 6.19; 7.20; Ezek 5.8; Amos 4.2; Mic 2.3; etc.
- 5.5 refers to a coming 'day' of judgment, 'a day of slaughter'; cf. Isa 13.6, 9; Jer 46.10; Ezek 30.3; Joel 1.15; 2.1, 11, 31; 3.14; Amos 5.18, 20; Zeph 1.7, 8, 14; Zech 14.1; Mal 4.5; etc.
- 5.5-6 envisages punishment that fits the crime: those who 'have condemned and murdered the righteous one' will themselves be 'slaughtered'; cf. Isa 5.8-9; 10.5-15; 29.1-3; Hos 4.4-6; Hab 2.6-8, 15-16; etc.

Characteristically, Dibelius, 230, discerns 'no connection' between 4.13–5.6 and 4.1-12. He qualifies this, however: 'it is understandable how the author could continue the general warning of people with a worldly mind with a polemic against a specific instance of this worldly disposition. It is more a question here of a similar mood in two adjacent sections.'[29] This underestimates the connections. Not only does 4.13–5.6, like 4.1-12, address a 'worldly disposition', but the sinners rebuked in 4.13–5.6 are a subset of the group addressed in 4.1-12. Common above all is their arrogance.[30]

Jonathan Edwards, like Bede, Grotius, and so many others, thought that 5.1-6 and perhaps 4.13-17, two paragraphs that noticeably lack the address, ἀδελφοί, speak to non-Christian Jews.[31] Mayor, cxliii, asked, 'Is

---

[29] Cf. perhaps Mayor, 149, drawing a connection with the 'Who are you' of v. 12: 'The thought of his own weakness and ignorance should deter man from judging his fellows and finding fault with the law; it should also prevent him from making confident assertions as to the future'.

[30] See further Johnson, 291-92, who entitles 4.11-5.6, 'Examples of arrogance'. Martin, 159-60, suggests a continuation of the theme of the abuse of the tongue. More helpful is Schnider, 108: those who fail to live according to the *Conditio Jacobaea* will fall victim to desire (cf. 4.1-3) and pride (4.6) and will love the world (4.4) whereas those who live with that *Conditio* will have an attitude of prayer (cf. 4.3), be humble (4.6), submit to God (4.7), and be near God (v. 8). For additional links between 4.13–5.6 and 4.1-12 see M. Taylor, *Structure*, 117-18.

[31] J. Edwards, *An Humble Inquiry* Part II.8, The Works of Jonathan Edwards 12, ed. Stout, New Haven, 1994, 238; Bede *ad loc*. CCSL 121 ed. Hurst, 183; Grotius, 1089. Cf. Calmet, 689; W. Wall, 348; Guyse, 562, 593; Macknight, 596 (who includes 4.1-12 as addressed to non-Christians); Theile, 239-40; T. Scott, 586; de Wette, 257; R. Scott, 140; Wordsworth, 29-30; Carr, 58; Beyschlag, 206-207; B. Johnson, 350; Plummer, 622; Ropes, 282; Bardenhewer, 132; McNeile, *Teaching*, 90; Dibelius, 231; Ross, 85; Feuillet, 'Parousie'; Beasley-Murray, 13; Schneider, 31; Mitton, 175; Mussner, 189; Laws, 189-90; Burdick, 199; Adamson, 183; Ruckstuhl, 29; Maynard-Reid, *Poverty*, 70-75; Davids, 171-72, 174; Tamez, *Message*, 31; Stulac, 162-63; Townsend, 94; Hoppe, 97; Klein, *Werk*, 183; Hutchinson Edgar, *Poor*, 198-99; Moo, 210-11; N. Beck, *Cryptograms*, 161-62 ('superpatriotic supporters of the Romans and the Roman state itself'); Hartin, 223, 26; Fabris, 297-99; Witherington, 519, 527; Blomberg and Kamell, 215; Gundry, 942. Most of these see non-Christians only in 5.1-6. A few think James

it possible to suppose that the rich oppressors described in v. 1-6 can belong to the Church?' One understands the question. If the rich have murdered 'the righteous one' (v. 6) and are without eschatological hope, it is not so easy to think of them as belonging to the author's immediate religious circle.

The standard view is that the section is an apostrophe. In the words of Benson, it is 'a figurative address to persons that he did not expect would read his epistle'.[32] This is a possible reading. A feigned turning from one's audience to address an absent person or group is a common rhetorical move. The Hebrew Bible prophets, whom James here imitates, supply numerous examples.

Yet James contains other exhortations seemingly aimed at outsiders, and sometimes these are seamlessly woven into exhortations clearly directed to faithful readers (e.g. 1.9-11, 21). Beyond that, it is the opening verse, 1.1, that should settle the issue. Our letter is addressed, without qualification, to the twelve tribes in the diaspora. Given this, the positing of recurrent apostrophes begs the question. Our letter fictively addresses the Jewish diaspora, to which just and unjust, rich and poor belong. So 4.13–5.6 should be read not as an apostrophe but as a rebuke of a portion of the audience named in 1.1.[33] The epistle assumes that James of Jerusalem had the authority to rebuke non-Christian Jews.[34]

Although he rejected the theory that James presents itself as addressed partly to non-Christian Jews, J. Michaelis expressed unease with the view that 5.1-6 is an apostrophe.[35] He rightly noted that 'this figure is not very suitable to the epistolary style'. He nonetheless asserted that postulating a non-Christian audience 'rests entirely on the supposition, that none of the primitive Christians could have deserved this censure, and that they were all in a state of perfect regeneration, a supposition, which is absolutely inconsistent with the description, which St. Paul has given of the

---

may have pagans in view. See further B. Weiss, *Kritik*, 4-13. Exceptions include Gill, 799; Zahn, *Introduction*, 83-91; von Soden, 181; Chaine, 112-13; Frankemölle, 630-32; Tsuji, *Glaube*, 90, 138-41. One argument for their position, that James assumes the merchants and the rich know better, falls away if one assumes that his audience is the twelve tribes (1.1). Cf. Witherington, 528: 'James can call rich non-Christian Jews to account with some force, since Leviticus 19 has moral authority over them and they know that they must obey it'. A better argument, although far from decisive, is the observation that 4.13-17 and 5.1-6 belong together, and if the former addresses Christians (as often held), then so too the latter. For Garleff, *Identität*, 261-65, 5.1-6 has in view rich individuals both within and without the community.

[32] Benson, 14. Cf. Pareus, 568; Henry, *ad loc.*; W. Dodd *ad loc.*; Meinertz, 45, 47; Dibelius, 231, 235; Vouga, 127; Konradt, *Existenz*, 159-65; Fabris, 'Tradizione', 250; et al.

[33] Cf. Manton, 398: 'I may argue from the inscription of the whole epistle "to the twelve tribes" promiscuously, without any express mention of their holy calling or faith'.

[34] See further 30 of the Introduction.

[35] J. Michaelis, *Introduction*, 292-95.

Corinthians in his two Epistles to them'. This, however, is little more than a groundless caricature of the position Michaelis opposes. Equally without force was his conjecture that 'You have condemned and murdered the righteous one' (5.6) refers to nothing more than theft. He went on to confess that 1.1, which does not restrict the audience to Christians, is against his position, as is the use of 'synagogue' in 2.2.[36] The present commentator concurs and so interprets 4.13–5.6 as ostensibly directed not to Christians but rather to the group signaled by 1.1, among which were, it goes without saying, wealthy, non-Christian Jews who attended synagogue. Who actually read 4.13–5.6 and how the author hoped his words might function are different questions. See further on 5.1.

Even though 4.12-5.6 must be related to what James saw in his world, it is difficult to infer much concretely.[37] Surely our author was acquainted with merchants who, to his mind, were insufficiently pious, and surely he knew some rich individuals whose passion for wealth led them to mistreat others, which sometimes perhaps resulted in death, maybe from hunger or imprisonment. We can, moreover, safely presume that the wealthy were a minority, which is why James could anticipate that his condemnation of them would resonate with most of his readers. But his poetical fervor and unforgiving, hyperbolic rhetoric do not allow us to go much further. We can say little more than has S. Friesen, in his overview of wealth in James: the book 'provides a relatively simple explanation for economic inequality... [It] blames local elites for economic injustice but also criticizes the general population for complicity [see 2.1-6]. In this sense it is reminiscent of the Israelite prophets who denounced the ruling class for their exploitation of the poor and called the people to repentance. I call the model "relatively simple" because it reflects primarily on local conditions. It does not address larger issues of empire or social discourse, locating the problems instead in personal desire and temptation.'[38]

Whatever one's take on the problem of audience, it is clear that, notwithstanding the identical introductions ("Αγε νῦν), the related subject matter—both address prosperous people who are on the side of 'the

---

[36] After his rebuttal, Michaelis lamely added: 'At the same time I believe that as St. James was highly respected by the Jews in general, that it was his wish and intention, that unbelieving Jews also should read it, and be converted, and that this wish and intention had some influence on the choice of his materials'. This gives back much of what Michaelis tried to take away and shows that, despite himself, he could not altogether avoid supposing that the implicit audience of James included non-Christians.

[37] Hengel, 'Jakobusbrief', 255-56, sees the merchants in chap. 4 as representatives of the Pauline mission. This seems far-fetched. By contrast, although Pearson, *Sense*, 251-76, finds polemic against Paul in Jas 1-4, he does not find such in the latter part of 4 or in 5.

[38] S.J. Friesen, 'Injustice or God's Will? Explanations of Poverty in Proto-Christian Communities', in *A People's History of Christianity, Volume 1*, ed. R.A. Horsley, Minneapolis, 2005, 244.

world'—and the similar length of the two sections, 4.13-18 and 5.1-6 are in certain respects very different.³⁹ The rhetoric in 5.1-6 is stronger than the rhetoric in 4.13-18, and the variation in tone exists beside additional dissimilarities:

- 4.13-18 issues a mild rebuke that counsels a change of course; 5.1-6 offers severe condemnation without any call for repentance.⁴⁰
- 4.13-18 quotes those it addresses; 5.1-6 does not.
- 4.13-18 is about people who first of all harm themselves; 5.1-6 attacks individuals who harm others.
- 4.13-18 makes no use of eschatological expectations; 5.1-6 is full of eschatological judgment.
- 4.13-18 indicates that its addressees know what they should do; 5.1-6 says nothing similar.
- 4.13-18 is silent as to what merchants do with their money; 5.1-6 declares that the rich have used their resources to live in luxury and pleasure.⁴¹

It is understandable that whereas some regard 4.13–5.6 as a unity,⁴² others treat 4.13-17 and 5.1-6 as separate units.⁴³ A compromise seems best: although this is a single section focused on sins associated with business,

---

³⁹ Cf. M. Taylor, *Structure*, 56-57; also Laws, 195-96; Burchard, 182. But for stress on the similarities see Frankemölle, 630-32; Konrad, *Existenz*, 154-55. A few, including Huther, 144, and Hutchinson, *Poor*, 198-99, deny that 5.1 introduces a change in addressees.

⁴⁰ Isaacs, 235, labels those in 5.1-6 'irredeemably wicked'. This is the consensus of the commentators. Yet there are exceptions, such as Frankemölle, 630-66, and Maier, 201-202.

⁴¹ Burchard, 189, contrasts the 'weisheitlich' character of 4.13-17 with the 'prophetisch-apokalyptische' polemic of 5.1-6. But the latter contains wisdom elements just as the former contains prophetic elements. Moreover, scriptural 'woe-oracles' exhibit both prophetic and wisdom elements; see E. Gerstenberger, 'The Woe-Oracles of the Prophets', *JBL* 81 (1962), 249-63.

⁴² E.g. Johnson, 291 (including 4.11-12); Tsuji, *Glaube*, 89-90; Hartin, 231-32; Taylor, *Structure*, 94-95, 117-18; McKnight, 367-68.

⁴³ Cf. Felder, 1799, and see n. 39. Krüger, *Kritik*, 205, see a chiasmus of contrasts in 4.13-17:

    A   v. 13: bragging
        B   v. 14: displacing the impermanent
            C   v. 15: what one should do
        B   v. 16: evil boasting
    A   v. 17: doing good

Krüger also finds a chiasmus in 5.1-6 (219). No more convincing is Reyes, 'Grito', who associates 5.1-6 with 7-11 and offers this analysis:

    A   v. 1: coming miseries of the rich
        B   vv. 2-3: corruption of their treasures
            C   v. 4: cries of the oppressed
        B   vv. 5-6: sins of the wealthy
    A   vv. 7-11: consolation of the suffering

it consists of two subsections that address two different sorts of sins, or rather sinners, the second being the more guilty.[44]

The Jesus tradition has influenced 4.13–5.6. Not only does it show a knowledge of Mt 6.19-21 = Lk 12.33-34 (see on 5.2) and the woes in Lk 6.24-25 (see on 5.1), but warnings about wealth, sins of omission, and eschatological judgment are prominent in sayings attributed to Jesus. In other words, we have here, as throughout James, strong thematic similarities.

Jewish scripture has also shaped James' materials. In addition to reproducing themes and motifs from prophetic oracles of judgment (see above), 5.4 incorporates a phrase from LXX Isa 5.9, and 5.5 seems to rewrite LXX Jer 12.3. There may also be indebtedness to the Book of Wisdom. Quite a few readers of Jas 4.13–5.6 have recalled Wis 2, some inferring James' use of it.[45] The parallels are intriguing:

Jas 4.13–5.6	Wis 2
4.14: 'For you are a mist that appears for a while, after which it disappears'	vv. 2-4: the impious think of life as 'smoke', as 'mist', as a 'shadow'
5.4: 'The pay of the workers who harvested your fields, which you have unjustly withheld, screams out, and the cries of the harvesters have reached the ears of the Lord of hosts'	v. 10, oppression of poor by the rich: 'Let us oppress the righteous poor man'
5.5: 'You have lived on the earth in luxury and in wanton pleasure'	vv. 6-9: self-indulgence of the rich: 'Let us enjoy the good things...let us take our fill of costly wine and perfumes... Let none of us be without share in our revelry; everywhere let us leave signs of enjoyment'
5.6: 'You have condemned (κατεδικάσατε), you have murdered the righteous one (τὸν δίκαιον), who does not resist you'	vv. 12-20: oppression and murder of the righteous: 'Let us lie in wait for the righteous man (τὸν δίκαιον)... Let us condemn (καταδικάσωμεν) him to shameful death'

These similarities do not, in and of themselves, suffice to demonstrate literary dependence; but as additional parallels of this sort appear elsewhere in James, it seems likely that our author was familiar with Wisdom.

---

[44] Webber, *Response*, 88, proposes this distinction: James first attacks merchants, the 'nouveau riche', who might boast of 'their status as self-made men'; he then attacks the landowners, those with inherited wealth.

[45] E.g. Spitta, 135; Belser, 183; Plummer, 620; Moffatt, 70-71; Tasker, 115; Keenan 151-53 ('perhaps'); Johnson, 304. Cf. Dibelius, 27: dependence is 'likely', and 'Wis 2 contains an important piece of evidence for the religious antithesis between rich and poor which is so significant for Jas'. For Plumptre, 95, James might be using Wis 5.9-14.

DENUNCIATIONS OF THE PROSPEROUS (4.13–5.6)

Verse 13. As in 2.3 and 16, James now quotes those against whom he inveighs. Their words show them to embody vices already condemned. They boast (cf. 3.5; 4.14). They heed selfish ambition (3.16). They covet (cf. 4.2). And they love the world (cf. 4.4). This is some reason for doubting that James has in view here a completely new audience.

Brosend, 126, remarks that 4.13 'looks very much like a model business plan':[46]

Time frame	Today or tomorrow
Travel plan	we will go to
Destination	such and such a city
Duration	spend a year there
Activity	doing business
Goal	making money[47]

ἄγε νῦν οἱ λέγοντες. ἄγε by itself can, in Graeco-Roman sources, serve to call attention to an imperative,[48] or it can introduce a line of reasoning.[49] In Epictetus it appears in addresses to imaginary opponents who are quoted.[50] In its present context, it at least 'indicates a shift of focus'.[51]

The imperatival interjection, ἄγε, although confined in the NT to James, does show up as a call to attention in other Christian sources as well as in a few Jewish texts.[52] By contrast, ἄγε νῦν—here seemingly 'an insistent...brusque address' (Ropes, 276) with scoffing tone[53]—is foreign to Jewish texts as well as to Christian texts uninfluenced by James. It is instead an old Greek expression known from Homer and especially Greek

---

[46] Several commentators, including Mayor, 150, suggest that James' words call to mind someone looking at a map.

[47] Perhaps James' words invite the response of Plummer, 620: 'The frequent conjunctions separate the different items of the plan, which are rehearsed thus one by one with manifest satisfaction. The speakers gloat over the different steps of the program...' Johnson, 307, discerns something different: the speech 'betrays a perception of the world as a closed system of limited resources, available to...control and manipulation, yielding to...market analysis and sales campaign'.

[48] E.g. Aristophanes, *Pax* 358; Diogenes Laertius 6.36, 79; Corpus Herm. frag, 23.27 ed. Festugière, 8.

[49] E.g. Plato, *Phileb.* 39E; *Resp.* 474C; *Leg.* 893B. See further Mayor, 149. Cf. the use of δεῦτε = הבה in LXX Gen 11.3, 4, 7; Exod 1.10; Isa 1.18; 2.2; Mic 4.2; also 1 En. 6.2; Josephus, *Ant.* 6.111; 4 Bar. 9.22.

[50] Epictetus, *Diatr.* 1.6.37; 1.17.24; 1.19.3-4, 28; 3.14.13-14. Cf. φέρε νῦν in Plato, *Polit.* 294D; Josephus, *Ant.* 6.88; Epictetus, *Diatr.* 1.6.37; Diogenes Laertius 2.85; etc.; also ἴδε νῦν as in Philo, *Leg.* 2.87; Mt 26.65; Jn 16.29.

[51] M. Taylor, *Structure*, 56. He observes additional ways in which 4.13 marks a shift from the preceding material: lack of grammatical connection, change in topic, use of future tense.

[52] E.g. LXX Judg B 19.6; 4 Βασ 4.14; Isa 43.6; Sib. Or. 3.562; 5.1 = 12.1; Diognetus, *Ep.* 2.1. On the singular—a 'frozen imperative'—with the plural see BDF 144 364.2.

[53] Gundry, 941, reads it as an 'ironic, almost sarcastic command that a traveling businessman had better get going—at once'.

drama.⁵⁴ It may then be a sign of James' Hellenistic education.⁵⁵ One should perhaps not overlook, however, that there is a Hebrew equivalent: לְכוּ־נָא; cf. Isa 1.18 ('Come now, let us argue it out, says the Lord'⁵⁶); 1 Sam 23.22 (a literal usage); Jer 7.12 (a literal usage).

νῦν adds emphasis and ties together the two sections as it occurs in 4.13, 16; 5.1 and nowhere else in James. The addition of οἱ + participle after ἄγε νῦν, which may be James' linguistic novelty, also helps unite 4.13-17 and 5.1-6 (the latter opens with ἄγε νῦν οἱ πλούσιοι). λέγοντες presumably means: 'saying (to themselves)'. 'As so often in James, it is speech as revealing the orientation of the heart that is the special target' (Johnson, 295). Here λέγοντες is indebted to LXX oracles of judgment: often a prophet quotes the condemned with the formula, οἱ λέγοντες.⁵⁷ Note further that quoting the rich or well-to-do in particular in order to expose their folly may have been convention, occurring as it does also in 1 En. 97.8-9⁵⁸ and Lk 12.19.⁵⁹ In both of the latter cases, moreover, the rich are fools because they fail to understand that their current prosperity will not endure.

Whereas 5.1 attacks 'the rich' without qualification, 4.13 attacks merchants 'who say' such and such. Perhaps, then, might James not disapprove of merchants who do not say such and such?⁶⁰ Would our author rebuff the Christian merchants we learn of from Acts, such as Lydia and

---

⁵⁴ E.g. Homer, *Il.* 19.108; *Od.* 12.298; 18.55; Theocritus, *Id.* 25.177; Arg. Orphica 255; Sophocles, *Trach.* 1259; Aristophanes, *Ach.* 485; *Eq.* 1011; *Pax* 469; etc. Note M.E. Thrall, *Greek Particles in the New Testament*, Leiden, 1962, 30-31: James' non-temporal use of νῦν is 'classical in origin'.

⁵⁵ See further the Introduction, 56. In the Homeric texts cited in n. 54, ἄγε νῦν introduces an imperative, as in Jas 5.1. In 4.13, no imperative immediately follows. There is, however, an implicit imperative—a call to reflect on the circumstances James recounts. Dibelius, 231, offers a different take: ἄγε should introduce the rhetorical question he finds in v. 14, 'What is your life, really?' James interrupted the construction by adding a long, subordinate clause, generating anacoluthon.

⁵⁶ The LXX here has καὶ δεῦτε.

⁵⁷ See above, 645; cf. also 4Q185 1-2 2.9: 'The wicked people should not brag, saying...'

⁵⁸ 'Woe unto you who gain silver and gold by unjust means. You will then say, "We have grown rich and accumulated goods... for we have gathered silver, we have filled our treasuries like water. And many are the laborers in our houses..." Your wealth will not endure but it will take off from you quickly.' Spitta, 130, suggests this as the source of Jas 5.2-3.

⁵⁹ Readers have often associated Lk 12.13-21 with the latter part of Jas 4; see e.g. Bonaventure, *Lk* 8.18 Opera Omnia 10 ed. Peltier, 558; Wolf, 72; Baumgarten, 193, 205; Rosenmüller, 384; Plummer, 619 (supposing it 'remarkable', since Jas 4.13-17 immediately follows the prohibition of judging others, 'that it was just after our Lord had refused to be made a judge over two contending brothers that He spoke the parable of the Rich Fool'); Bardenhewer, 127; Mitton, 169; Schnider, 108; Johnson, 300-301; Hartin, 234; Witherington, 519 (Lk 12.16-21 'may well be in the background here'); Ringe, 373.

⁶⁰ Cf. Ahrens, *Arm*, 117. According to Popkes, 289, James does not teach that business enterprises are *eo ipso* sinful or dangerous. See further above, 640-43.

Aquila and Priscilla?[61] Or would he, on the contrary, agree with Gos. Thom. 64: 'buyers and merchants will not enter the places of my father'? σήμερον ἢ αὔριον πορευσόμεθα εἰς τήνδε τὴν πόλιν.[62] This is close to Lk 13.33: σήμερον καὶ αὔριον...πορεύεσθαι. Perhaps the coincidence preserves a common idiom.[63] σήμερον, πορεύομαι, ὅδε,[64] and πόλις occur only here in James, αὔριον only here and the next verse. πορεύομαι + εἰς (τὴν) πόλιν, although attested in secular Greek[65] is much more common in Jewish Greek literature, where it represents (ה)עיר + אל + בוא/הלך.[66]

'Today or tomorrow' (not a common Hebrew or Greek expression) perhaps underlines the confident, self-centered orientation of the speakers: they and no one else will decide when they will go, and they have not yet decided—maybe they will resolve to go today, or maybe they will resolve to go tomorrow.

'Going into this city' might initially move readers to think of local traders who live outside a city and pass through its gates in order to conduct business at its markets. Hellenized readers could then think of the agora. The following words, however, modify that scenario: 'spend a year there' indicates that we are dealing with traveling traders, the mercantile class.[67] So the image that comes to mind is of people of means using the numerous roads and shipping lanes of the Roman world.[68] That we should think of seafaring merchants[69] in particular is not evident.[70] But

---

[61] Acts 16.14, 40; 18.1-3, 18-21; cf. Rom 16.3; 1 Cor 16.19.

[62] 02 025 69 88 206 *et al.* **Byz** Cyr GregAgr PsOec **K**:B^ms **S**:H **A** have καί, which creates a common expression, σήμερον καὶ αὔριον (= היום ומחר); cf. LXX Exod 19.10; 2 Βασ 11.12; Ecclus 10.10; Lk 12.28; 13.32, 33. Dibelius, 232 n. 9, raises the possibility that a scribe desired 'to place into the mouth of the planners as confident a declaration as possible'. On the issue of whether to read πορευσόμεθα (P100V 01 03 018 025 38 43 61 88 104 *et al.* L590 L596T L921 L1141 L2087 Cyr GregAgr **L**:FV **K**:SB) or πορευσώμεθα (02 044 5 33 69 81 206 *et al.* **Byz** PsOec **L**:S) and the future or subjunctive for the next three verbs see Dibelius, 232 n. 10. One guesses that o was misheard as ω or *vice versa* and that scribes then assimilated the tenses of the other verbs.

[63] Does Evagrius, *Ad mon.* 80 TU 39.4 ed. Gressmann, 160—μὴ εἴπῃς· σήμερον μενῶ καὶ αὔριον ἐξελεύσομαι—depend upon James?

[64] Dibelius, 232 n. 12, urges that ὅδε = 'such and such' is 'vernacular'. BAGD, s.v., denies this, and Wifstrand, 'Problems', 175, regards τήνδε not as a 'vulgarism' but rather as a common feature of *koine*. See further L. Rydbeck, *Fachprosa, Vermeintliche Volkssprache und Neues Testament*, Uppsala, 1967, 88-97.

[65] E.g. Xenophon, *Hell.* 4.8.36; *Cyr.* 8.5.21.

[66] See LXX Gen 23.10, 18; 1 Βασ 9.10; Ps 106.7; Ezek 26.10; 3 Macc 4.11; Ecclus 10.15; Theodotus *apud* Eusebius, *P.E.* 9.22.8 ed. Holladay, 120.

[67] Cf. Mt 13.45; 25.14; Rev 18.3, 11, 15, 23.

[68] For a general introduction see L. Casson, *Travel in the Ancient World*, Toronto, 1974. Against Maynard-Reid, *Poverty*, 77-78, it is not evident that merchants from Syro-Palestine in particular are in view.

[69] Cf. Prov 31.14; Isa 23.2-3; Ezek 37.

[70] Nor is it evident that Davids, 171-72, is correct to suggest that 'the merchants were not wealthy yet, for in Palestine trade was seen as a way to obtain the fortune needed to

perhaps we have evidence that our author lived in a sizeable city: large land owners (cf. 5.1-6) and long-distance traders (cf. 4.13-17) typically spent their time in cities.[71]

According to Dibelius, 231, the words James puts into the mouths of merchants 'are intended to ring as animated and as true to everyday life as possible'. He then suggests the textual variants that are more in 'the vernacular style'—σήμερον ἢ αὔριον instead of σήμερον καὶ αὔριον, ἐνιαυτόν without ἕνα, τήνδε meaning 'such and such'—might for that reason alone be original. Whether or not he is right, this section contains a stylistic feature that is undeniable: it favors paired words and expressions:[72]

vv. 13, 15	οἱ λέγοντες... ἀντὶ τοῦ λέγειν ὑμᾶς
v. 13	σήμερον ἢ αὔριον
v. 13	πορευσόμεθα... καὶ ποιήσομεν
v. 13	ἐμπορευσόμεθα καὶ κερδήσομεν
v. 14	φαινομένη... ἀφανιζομένη
v. 15	ζήσομεν καὶ ποιήσομεν
v. 15	τοῦτο ἢ ἐκεῖνο
v. 16	καυχᾶσθε... καύχησις
v. 17	ποιεῖν καὶ μὴ ποιοῦντι

Note also the extensive repetition of sound in v. 13:

v. 13	ρον... ριον
v. 13	ην... ην... ιν... εν
vv. 13, 15	σομε... σομε... σομε... σομε... σομε... σομε
vv. 13-14	πορ... πο... πο... πορ... πο... προ

καὶ ποιήσομεν ἐκεῖ ἐνιαυτόν.[73] ποιέω commonly means 'spend time'.[74] ἐνιαυτός appears again in 5.17, where it means 'year', as also often in the LXX.[75] That must be the meaning here, too.[76] Calvin, 303, aptly catches James' intent: some people 'take charge of the whole course of a year' and yet 'have no power over one single minute'. Contrast the attitude in Ps 31.15: 'my times are in your hand'.

---

purchase the estates on which the "good life" might be lived'. On the ambiguity of James' description as well as of the identity of so-called merchants in many ancient texts see Ahrens, *Arm*, 122-24.

[71] Cf. Ahrens, *Arm*, 131.

[72] For the same proclivity in 5.1-6 see below, 670.

[73] ἕνα qualifies ἐνιαυτόν in 02 044 5 33 69 81 *et al.* **Byz** Cyr GregAgr PsOec **L**:Hl S:PH **A G**:G-D **Sl**:ChMSi. It is missing from 01 03 025 94 307 *et al.* **L**:SFV **K**:SB. One cannot determine whether the adjective was inadvertently dropped or added to enhance specificity.

[74] See LXX Prov 13.23; Eccl 6.12; Acts 15.33; 18.23; 20.3; T. Job 21.1; Gk. LAE 31.2; etc.

[75] E.g. Gen 47.17, 28; Deut 14.21. NT: 14×.

[76] Cf. T. Jud. 10.4 (ποιήσας σὺν αὐτῇ ἐνιαυτόν); Demosthenes, *Or.* 24.197 (ἐποίεις ἐνιαυτόν).

DENUNCIATIONS OF THE PROSPEROUS (4.13–5.6) 655

καὶ ἐμπορευσόμεθα καὶ κερδήσομεν. The goal is to carry on business and make a profit. In the LXX, ἐμπορεύομαι (NT: 2×) means either 'trade' (e.g. Prov 3.14, for סחר) or 'import' (Hos 12.2). The word need carry no negative connotations; indeed, in T. Job 11.3, 8-9, engaging in business (ἐμπορεύομαι) has a noble end: it makes charity possible. In 2 Pet 2.3, however, the word comes close to meaning 'exploit' (BAGD, s.v.); and, in James, it must likewise carry negative connotations, as the context suggests. Note Ecclus 26.29: 'It is difficult for a merchant (ἔμπορος) to keep from wrongdoing'; also 27.2: 'sin is wedged in between selling and buying'. Several OT oracles of judgment threaten merchants.[77]

κερδαίνω[78] in connection with ἐμπορεύομαι seems unattested before our book; so too the future form, κερδήσομεν.[79] Here the verb means 'procure profit', as in Mt 25.16-17, 20, 22; cf. also Let. Aris. 270, which addresses personal gain without thought of others.

Verse 14. James sets the uncertainty of every person's future over against the current self-assurance of the short-sighted rich, who think themselves masters of their fate. Presumably their financial success has bred confidence in their own powers. James counters with common sense. In the words of Erasmus, 'Life is in itself very, very short, and so many accidents, so many diseases make it thoroughly uncertain as well. And here you are, as if you had a treaty with death, speeding over land and sea to prepare some provision for your old age, which you will perhaps never reach since no one can guarantee even his own tomorrow.'[80]

οἵτινες οὐκ ἐπίστασθε τὸ τῆς αὔριον.[81] αὔριον comes from v. 13, so here James turns the words of the merchants against themselves: they do not know what they think they know. The negation of ἐπίσταμαι (Jas: 1×) undoes the four, self-confident future tenses in the previous verse: maybe the rich will not go to the city and spend a year there and carry on business and make money. The future is uncertain and so unknown—a commonplace of all wisdom literature;[82] cf. The Eloquent Peasant 183 ('Do not prepare for tomorrow before it is come. One knows not what evil may be in it'); Instruction of Amen-em-Opet 19.11-13 ('Do not spend the night in fear of tomorrow. At dawn what is the morrow like? One knows not what tomorrow is like'); LXX Prov 3.28 ('you do not know what the next day will bring'); 27.1 ('Do not boast about tomorrow,

---

[77] See above, 645; note also Rev 18.3.
[78] LXX: 0×; Symmachus: Job 22.3. NT: 17×; Jas: 1×. Gk. Pseudepigrapha (Denis): 3×. Philo: 5×. Josephus: 29×.
[79] See further Mayor, 150.
[80] Erasmus, *Paraphrase*, 164-65.
[81] 03 L:S omit τό. Metzger, *Commentary*, 683, notes that 03 exhibits 'a certain tendency...to omit the article'. 01 044 5 69 88 *et al.* **Byz** GregAgr PsOec have it. Other witnesses have τά, which may mark assimilation to LXX Prov 27.1 (τὰ εἰς αὔριον); cf. also the plural in Lk 20.25; Rom 14.19; 2 Cor 11.30.
[82] Cf. Popkes, 290: James here operates with a 'cultural commonplace'.

for you do not know what a day may bring forth');[83] Ps.-Phoc. 116-20 ('Nobody knows what will be after tomorrow or after an hour...the future is uncertain'); b. Sanh. 100b = b. Yeb. 63b ('Do not fret over tomorrow's troubles, for you know not what a day may bring forth. Tomorrow may come and you will be no more and so you will have grieved over a world that is not yours'); Philodemus, *Mort.* 37.26-27 ('not only is tomorrow unclear but also indeed the immediate future, for in relation to death we all live in an unprotected city'); Seneca, *Ep.* 101.4-5 ('He who was venturing investments by land and sea...and left no type of business untried, during the very realization of financial success and during the very onrush of the money that flowed into his coffers, was snatched from the world... How foolish it is to set out one's life, when one is not even owner of the morrow'); Stobaeus, *Ecl.* 4.41 (an anthology of texts on the subject).[84]

The saying in Mt 6.34 uses αὔριον twice, and an occasional commentator has recalled that verse.[85] The thought there, however, is different. Matthew's Jesus encourages those have little not to fret over the morrow. James warns those who have much to do just the opposite, to think about what the future will sooner or later bring them.[86]

ποία ἡ ζωὴ ὑμῶν. Instead of continuing the previous clause, this could be an independent question: Of what character is your life?[87] Moulton raised the possibility that ποία here means 'grass' or 'herb': 'For your life is a green herb, for you are a vapour'.[88] Seemingly no one has taken up this proposal. It is instead exegetical custom to construe ποία as the feminine form of ποῖος (Jas: 1×), meaning, 'what sort of?' or 'of what character?'[89]

---

[83] Basser, 433, labels 4.13-16 'an extended paraphrase of Prov 27.1'. For McKnight, 312, 'James's saying is rooted in Proverbs 27:1'.

[84] Cf. also Eccl 8.7; Ecclus 11.19; Philo, *Leg.* 3.226-27; Theognis 159-60; Plutarch, *Cons. ad Apoll.* 11.

[85] Cf. e.g. Pareus, 566; Plummer, 631. Contrast Deppe, *Sayings*, 242. For Shepherd, 'Matthew', 46, 'the woe in James is in fact an exposition of the gospel teaching on anxiety, where in the Q tradition Matthew specifically stresses the thought of being without anxiety'.

[86] Cf. Sidebottom, 55: Jas 4.13-16 is 'the opposite' of Mt 6.34 as the latter 'counsels not caution but unconcern for the morrow because it is unknown'.

[87] So e.g. Ropes, 278; Dibelius, 230, 233; Moo, 203; NRSV. ζωή: Jas: 2×; cf. 1.12.

[88] J.H. Moulton, 'Lexical Notes on the Papyri', *Expositor* ser. 7.10 (1910), 566: 'Two metaphors succeed each other naturally, each introduced with γάρ: we can imagine James watching the sun burst out after heavy rain—the green herb which would so soon fade (ch. 1. ii), and the steam that rises for a few minutes from the drenched soil'. This, however, presumes a text with γάρ after ποία, found in P74 P100 01Z 02 025 044 5 33 69 81 88 *et al.* **Byz** GregAgr PsOec **K**:B **S**:P **G**:G-D **Sl**:ChMSi. NA[27] and the *Editio Critica Maior* omit, following 01T 03 614 *et al.* Dam **L**:S **K**:SB[mss] **S**:H. See further Metzger, *Commentary*, 684.

[89] Cf. Jn 12.33; 1 Pet 1.11; etc. and the emphasis on this point in Henry's Drummond's charming sermon on our verse in *The Ideal Life and Addresses Hitherto Unpublished*, New York, 1898, 190-211.

ἀτμὶς γάρ ἐστε ἡ πρὸς ὀλίγον φαινομένη.[90] ἀτμίς (NT: 2×) refers to an insubstantial rising column, as of fumes or smoke[91] or, less frequently, 'mist' or 'steam'.[92] It is a fitting symbol of human temporality and frailty: such a column never lasts for long. Here then is the same thought as in 1.10-11, just with a different metaphor.[93]

The ephemeral nature of human existence or of evildoers was a commonplace in the Jewish and Graeco-Roman worlds;[94] it is indeed world-wide wisdom. In addition to the texts discussed in connection with 1.10-11, see Pss 37.20 ('like smoke they vanish away'); 39.11 ('everyone is a mere breath'); 90.10; 102.3 ('my days pass away like smoke'); 1 Chr 19.15 ('we are...transients before you...our days on the earth are like a shadow'); Hos 13.3 ('they will be like the morning mist'); 1 En. 108.9 ('a passing breath'); Wis 2.2-5 ('our allotted time is a passing shadow'; cf. 5.9-14); 4 Ezra 7.61 ('the great number of those who perish; for it is they who are now like a mist, and are similar to a flame and smoke'); 2 Bar. 82.6 ('as smoke they will pass away'); Plutarch, *Mor.* 360C (quoting Empedocles: 'Swift in their fate, like smoke in the air'); Marcus Aurelius 10.31 (human beings are like 'smoke'); Apost. Const. 7.33.3 ed. Funk, 424 (God has showed that 'the possession of wealth is not eternal...that outer beauty is not everlasting, that physical power is easily dissolved, and that all these things are nothing but ἀτμός and vanity').[95] Commentators usually cite at least a few of these texts as well as, sometimes, the refrain from Ecclesiastes: 'All is vanity'.[96] πρὸς ὀλίγον[97] is an abbreviation for

---

[90] The text is uncertain. 02 33 61 1735 2344 **L**:V **K**:B omit γάρ. 03 81 104 197 218 *et al.* L422 L427 **L**:Hl **S**:H have ἔστε. 018 025 044 049 1 6 38 69 88 93 94 180 *et al.* L590 L593 *et al.* PsOec **L**:S have ἔσται. But ἔστιν appears in 020 056 0142 5 18 33 35 43 61 206 *et al.* L596 L921 *et al.* Dam GregAgr **L**:V **K**:SB **Sl**:ChMSi. For discussion see Metzger, *Commentary*, 684, where the text earns a D rating, indicating 'a very high degree of doubt concerning the reading'.

[91] Cf. LXX Gen 19.28; 2 Macc 7.5; Philo, *Her.* 251; *Leg.* 1.72; Acts 2.19; Gk. LAE 33.4.

[92] Cf. 1 Clem. 17.6; Phrynichus, *Praep. soph.* epitome 8.11. Most English translations have preferred either (following the Vulgate's *vapor*) 'vapo(u)r' (e.g. Tyndale, Cranmer, Geneva, Rheims, KJV, RV, NASB) or 'mist' (e.g. RSV, NRSV, NIV, REB).

[93] Homiletical treatments typically seek to awaken hearers to the reality of their own death; see e.g. Spurgeon, 325-30, and H.C. McCook, 'Mist, or Vapor of Water', in *The Gospel in Nature*, Philadelphia, 1887, 27-40.

[94] Apart from LXX Job 11.2 and 14.1, a quotation of the former in 1 Clem. 30.5, and Pap. Eg. 5 recto, ancient Jewish and early Christian sources avoid ὀλιγόβιος to express this idea.

[95] This may be a reminiscence of James; see P.W. van der Horst and J.H. Newman, *Early Jewish Prayers in Greek*, Berlin, 2008, 44. Additional parallels: Job 7.6-9; Pss 39.6; 103.15; 144.4; 1QM 15.10; 1Q27 1 1.6; 4Q171 3.7; 4Q185 1-2 1.9-13.

[96] Note e.g. Philoxenus, *Diss.* 7.40 PO 39.4.181 ed. Brière and Graffin, 625; Bernard of Clairvaux, *Conv.* 16 SC 457 ed. Callerot, Miethke, Jaquinod, 362; Mayor, 151; R. Wall, 215-16, 220-21. Blomberg-Kamell, 208 n. 16, cite J.-L. Marion, *God Without Being*, Chicago, 1991, 222 n. 20: '*Atmis* usually translates *hebhel*, only the LXX makes the exception in preferring *mataiotēs*... James 4:14 therefore is closest to the Qoheleth in

πρὸς ὀλίγον χρόνον.⁹⁸ ὀλίγος and φαίνω are *hapax* for James. Their combination was conventional.⁹⁹

First Corinthians 15.32 offers a hypothetical and cynical application of Isa 22.13: 'Let us eat and drink, for tomorrow we die'. The apostle imagines people inferring, from life's uncertainty and brevity, that they should selfishly indulge themselves without thought of tomorrow; cf. Wis 2.5-6. James, for whom life's brevity and uncertainty are calls to repent,¹⁰⁰ sees things differently, in part because of his eschatology. He knows what tomorrow will bring—'the coming of the Lord' (5.7), the judgment (4.12; 5.9), punishment (3.6; 5.1-3), reward (1.12).¹⁰¹

First Clement 17.6 attributes to Moses these words: ἐγὼ δέ εἰμι ἀτμὶς ἀπὸ κύθρας.¹⁰² Although the source of the quotation is unknown, given that it is on the lips of Moses, given that Clement appears to have known Eldad and Modad, and given that James is otherwise, in chap. 4, influenced by that pseudepigraphon, which must have contained words of Moses (see on 4.5), it is possible that Jas 4.14 preserves another tidbit from that book.¹⁰³ However that may be, the closest parallel to 1 Clem. 17.6 appears in the Peshitta, in its version of 1 Chr 29.15, where David says, 'We are comparable to the smoke of a pot, and we sojourn with you (God) and are of little account in the world'.¹⁰⁴

ἔπειτα καὶ ἀφανιζομένη. The point is implicit in the preceding clause, but stating it adds emphasis and creates a wordplay, φαινομένη...ἀφα-

---

saying: *atmis...pros oligon phainomenē epeita kai aphanizomenē*; which the Vulgate retranscribes—Jerome very logically using the same Latin term to render *atmis* and to rendel *hebhel*—as *vapor...ad modicum parens et deinceps exterminabitur*.' Both Aquila and Theodotion have ἀτμίς in their translations of Eccl 1.2.

⁹⁷ Cf. Wis 16.6; T. Benj. 5.4; 1 Tim 4.8.

⁹⁸ Cf. Chrysippus, *Frag. mor.* 636; 4 Macc 15.27; Philo, *Gig.* 53; *Abr.* 71.

⁹⁹ See Aristotle, *Hist. an.* 563B (φαίνεται ἐπ' ὀλίγον χρόνον); Ps.-Callisthenes, *Hist. Alex. Magn.* rec. E 127.3 (εἰς ὀλίγους χρόνους φαίνεσαι). R. Wall, 221, wonders whether 'the "appearing/disappearing" idiom echoes the "coming Son of Man" tradition found in the Gospels (cf. Matt. 24:27-30)'.

¹⁰⁰ Cf. the saying attributed to R. Eliezer in m. 'Abot 2.10: 'Repent one day before your death'.

¹⁰¹ Human life is short only from one point of view: from another it continues after death. This is why an occasional sermon on our verse insists that the analogy with mist is limited or must be extended; cf. e.g. W.J.K. Little, 'Life is a Serious Matter', in *The Perfect Life: Sermons*, London, 1898, 93: 'though a vapour disappears—seeing that no particle of matter is ever destroyed—it reappears in another form'.

¹⁰² Cf. Clement of Alexandria, *Strom.* 4.17.106.4 GCS 52 ed. Stählin and Früchtel, 295, quoting Clement and with χύτρας at the end.

¹⁰³ So e.g. J.B. Lightfoot, *The Apostolic Fathers Clement, Ignatius, and Polycarp, Part One: Clement, volume 2*, 2nd ed., London, 1889, 65. Cf. Moffatt, 65: 'there is a possibility that James had read and recollected this'.

¹⁰⁴ See further J.R. Harris, 'On an Obscure Quotation in the First Epistle of Clement', *JBL* 29 (1910), 190-95. Against Frankemölle, 638, one doubts that James was the first to use ἀτμίς in the way that he does.

DENUNCIATIONS OF THE PROSPEROUS (4.13–5.6)   659

νιζομένη.[105] For ἔπειτα see on 3.17. Juxtaposing ἀφανίζω[106] and φαίνω is natural.[107] Here the former may begin to rework the saying in Mt 6.19-21 = Lk 12.33-34, for Mt 6.19-20, probably preserving Q, has ἀφανίζει twice; see further on 5.2.

Verse 15. This verse answers to v. 13 and to the 'practical atheism' (Gibson, 179) of those who there speak.

ἀντὶ τοῦ λέγειν ὑμᾶς. Cf. LXX Ps 108.4 (ἀντὶ τοῦ ἀγαπᾶν με); Ezek 29.9 (ἀντὶ τοῦ λέγειν σε); Thucydides 1.69.5 (ἀντὶ τοῦ ἐπελθεῖν αὐτοί); Dio Chrysostom 47.14 (ἀντὶ τοῦ λυπεῖν ὑμᾶς). ἀντί is a *hapax legomenon* for our book. As opposed to v. 13, where James puts into the mouths of merchants words that he imagines to be in character, here he places in their mouths his own words, which are for them out of character. Most commentators construe ἀντί κτλ. as an imperative. One can also, however, regard v. 14 as an interruption and see v. 15 as the continuation of v. 13: 'Come now, you who say, "Today or tomorrow we will go to this city and spend a year there, carrying on business and making money"...instead of saying, "If the Lord wishes, we will both live and do this or that"'.[108]

ἐὰν ὁ κύριος θελήσῃ. A conventional cliché of piety which Backhaus labels 'the foundational law' of James' anthropology;[109] cf. Ecclus 39.6 (ἐὰν κύριος ὁ μέγας θελήσῃ); 1 Cor 4.19 (ἐὰν ὁ κύριος θελήσῃ); Plato, *Alcib.* 135D (ἐὰν θεὸς ἐθέλῃ—in answer to the question, 'What should I say?');[110] Demosthenes, *Or.* 25.2 (ἐὰν θεὸς θέλῃ); Epictetus, *Diatr.* 4.6.21 (ἂν ὁ θεὸς θέλῃ); Corp. Herm. frag. 2A 2 (ἐὰν ὁ θεὸς θέλῃ); Plautus, *Cap.* 455 (*si dis placet*); Sallust, *Jug.* 14.19 (*dis volentibus*); Minicius Felix, *Oct.* 18.11 CSEL 2 ed. Halm, 25 (*si deus dederit* is 'the natural discourse of the common people'); etc.[111] Note also T. Iss. 4.3: 'the single-hearted person does not make plans to live a long life but awaits only the will of God'. There are no close rabbinic parallels.[112] Ropes, 280, speaks for

---

[105] The same wordplay occurs in Mt 6.16: ἀφανίζουσιν...φανῶσιν.

[106] Jas: 1×; cf. Mt 6.16, 19-20; Acts 13.41.

[107] Cf. Aristotle, *Hist. an.* 563B; Ps.-Aristotle, *Mund.* 399A; Libanius, *Orat.* 42.37; Ps.-Callisthenes, *Hist. Alex. Magn.* rec. γ. 35C.45; etc.

[108] Cf. Benson, 96; Moule, *Idiom*, 128.

[109] Backhaus, 'Condicio', 145.

[110] The phrase is quite common in Plato: *Theaet.* 151D; *Lach.* 201C (the closing words of the book: 'I will not fail...to come to you tomorrow, God willing'); *Ion* 530B; *Leg.* 688E, 739E, 778B; etc.

[111] Also 1 Chr 13.2; Acts 18.21; 1 Cor 16.7; Heb 6.3; Josephus, *Ant.* 2.333, 347; 7.373; Aristophanes, *Pax* 939; Xenophon, *Hell.* 2.4.17; 5.1.14; *Cyr.* 5.4.21; Epictetus, *Diatr.* 1.1.17; Apoc. Paul L¹ 49 ed. Silverstein and Hilhorst, 167. For parallels from the papyri see Deissmann, *Studies*, 252. Additional texts in Mayor, 151-52.

[112] The custom in the commentaries is to assert that 'If God wills' (אם יגזור/גוזר השם) appears only in the parodic Alphabet of Ben Sira; cf. Grotius, 1089; Schöttgen, *Horae Hebraicae*, 1030-31; Hammond-Le Clerc, 517; Whitby, 691; Oesterley, 464; Ropes, 280;

many when he avows: 'James is here recommending to Christians a Hellenistic pious formula of strictly heathen origin';[113] and according to Dimont, 636, 'James is saying that even pagans have more piety than those who glory in their vauntings'. Yet given the appearance of the formula in Ben Sirach, Acts, Paul, Hebrews, and Josephus, the use of κύριος instead of θεός, and the frequency of the related θέλημα θεοῦ in early Jewish and Christian writings,[114] it is far from clear that our author or readers would recognize the foreign origin of the formula.[115]

James does not accuse the merchants of deliberately flouting God's will.[116] He rather accuses them of a lesser sin: neglecting that will, not taking it into account. This is not, one should note, a specifically Christian critique, and the formula he appeals to has no distinctive Christian content.[117] As throughout the letter, James appeals to ethical teaching common to Jews and Christians. Our letter is theocentric, not christocentric.

The ἐάν presumes that God's will is, in some sense, unknown. This allowed Poole, 894, to distinguish between God's 'directive will', that is,

---

Billerbeck 3.758. The problem with this is threefold: (i) אם גזור הקב"ה occurs in the earlier Tanḥ. Buber Noah 28. (ii) גזר means not 'will' but 'enact a prohibition' or 'decree' (Jastrow, s.v.; Clines, s.v.). (iii) The closer parallel to ἐὰν ὁ κύριος θελήσῃ is אם ירצה השם, which appears not only in Alphabet of Ben Sira but in other late texts as well, such as מדרש לעולם in Ozar Midrashim ed. Eisenstein, 1.273. Nonetheless, the parallel in the Alphabet (see Eisenstein, 1.39) is worth quoting: 'A bride went up to her chamber, not knowing what would happen to her there. Always a man should say, not that a thing is set, but rather, If God has decreed. There was a man who said, Tomorrow I will be with my bride in her chamber, and I will be intimate with her. They said to him, If God so decrees. He said to them, Whether he decrees or does not decree, tomorrow I will be with my bride in her chamber. And thus he did: he went with his bride to her chamber and stayed with her all day; and in the night the two of them went in to lie down together; but before he could join with his bride, they both died.'

[113] Laws, 192, entertaining the possibility that the merchants are pagans, suggests that, by using a pagan formula, 'James is imaginatively thinking himself into their position: even in their own terms, they can give expression to a proper attitude towards their plans for the future'.

[114] T. Iss. 4.3; T. Naph. 3.1; Philo, *Leg.* 3.197; Mk 3.35; Rom 12.2; 1 Cor 1.1; 2 Cor 8.5; Eph 1.1; 6.6; Col 1.1; 4.12; 1 Thess 4.3; 5.18; 2 Tim 1.1; Heb 10.36; 1 Pet 4.2; 1 Jn 2.17; 1 Clem. 42.2; 49.6; Ign. *Trall.* 1.1; Pol. *Phil.* 1.3; Acts Phil. 7.5; etc.

[115] Cf. Johnson, 297: 'James' language... is thoroughly at home in the early Christian usage'. It is no surprise that some readers have recalled the Lord's Prayer ('your will be done') and Jesus' prayer in Gethsemane; see e.g. W.G.T. Shedd, 'The Duty of Reference to the Divine Will', in *Sermons on the Spiritual Man*, New York, 1884, 127-28; Marty, 172; Cantinat, 218; Doriani, 160.

[116] 'The Lord' is God, not Jesus. So most commentators, despite Mt 8.2; Lk 5.12. Contrast L. Hurtado, 'Christology', in R.P. Martin and P.H. Davids, eds., *The Dictionary of the Later New Testament and Its Development*, Downers Grove, IL, 1997, 173.

[117] Contrast Ign. *Eph.* 20.1 (where 'if it is his will' refers to 'Jesus Christ') and the formula in Mart. Pionii 7.5 ed. Gebhart, 102: ἐὰν ὁ θεὸς θέλῃ, ναί· Χριστιανοὶ γάρ ἐσμεν.

the imperatives known through Scripture, and God's 'providential will', which is not known.

καὶ ζήσομεν καὶ ποιήσομεν τοῦτο ἢ ἐκεῖνο. The Vulgate, like a few later interpreters, including Calvin, 304, connects ζήσομεν with ἐὰν ὁ κύριος θελήσῃ: *si Dominus voluerit et vixerimus faciemus hoc aut illud*.[118] But, as the texts cited above show, ἐὰν ὁ κύριος θελήσῃ was a fixed and complete formula, and 'the mention of a second proviso along with the will of God would be strange from a religious perspective' (Dibelius, 234). The first verb[119] makes human life contingent upon God's will.[120] The second verb harks back to v. 13. There, however, ποιήσομεν comes before the definite ἐμπορευσόμεθα καὶ κερδήσομεν whereas here it precedes the undefined τοῦτο ἢ ἐκεῖνο, a traditional expression;[121] cf. the Hebrew אז ואז.[122] The indefinite expression stands for a different way of being in the world: deciding for oneself where to go and what to do gives way to acknowledging that God's will, which is not always manifest, is determinative.[123] Peter Martyr Vermigli commented: 'So the will of God is not only about the law and the commandments, but everyday human affairs as well'.[124]

Verse 15 implies that God is actively involved in the world, and perhaps even that God determines when people die. Unlike the author of Wis 14.3; 17.2, however, James nowhere uses πρόνοια. Yet he would have been familiar with some idea of providence from the Pentateuch, where God directs the stories of the patriarchs and Moses (cf. Gen 50.20), as well as from the Jesus tradition.[125] James might even have believed *nihil sine deo fiat*,[126] or at least as the Psalter has: 'God does whatever he pleases'. He does not, however, pursue or develop such a thought, and 1.13-14 reflects a desire to absolve God from responsibility for evil.

---

[118] Cf. the translations of Wycliffe ('if the lord wole, and if we lyuen: we schuln do this thing ether that thing') and Bunyan ('If God permit us life and health, we will accomplish it').

[119] ζάω: Jas: 1×; cf. ζωή in v. 14.

[120] Cf. Johnson, 297: 'James has "life" precede "doing". This is the first gift that comes "from the will of God".'

[121] Galen, *Dign. pulsib.* 4.8.937; Simplicius, *Cael.* 7.533; Olympiodorus the Younger, *Arist. cat. comm.* 96.25; etc.

[122] As in Eccl 11.6; Gen. Rab. 61.3. Note also the indefinite כך וכך ('thus and so', 'this and that') in Deut. Rab. 9.1, where the angel of death shows up 'on account of the talk of human beings who say, "This and that we will do", and yet not one of them knows when he will be summoned to die'.

[123] Pelagius, *Rom. ad* 1.11 TS 9.2 ed. Souter, 11, aptly joins our verse to Acts 16.6-8, where 'the Spirit of Jesus' prevents Paul from carrying out his plan to go into Bithynia.

[124] Peter Martyr Vermigli, *An Deus Sit Author Peccati* 26.

[125] Mt 6.26 = Lk 12.24 and Mt 10.29 (cf. Lk 12.6); cf. Gen. Rab. 79.6.

[126] So the Latin of Origen, *Prin.* 3.2.7 GCS 22 ed. Koetschau, 255. Cf. the application of our passage in Jerome, *Ep.* 133.7 PL 22.1155.

Verse 16. James again describes those he attacks.

νῦν δὲ καυχᾶσθε ἐν ταῖς ἀλαζονείαις ὑμῶν. Particularly close are Prov 27.1 ('Do not boast about tomorrow [LXX: μὴ καυχῶ τὰ εἰς αὔριον], for you do not know what a day may bring') and Jer 9.23 ('Do not let the wealthy boast in their wealth');[127] but the association between wealth and pride or boasting is found in many texts.[128]

νῦν links v. 16 to v. 13 and 5.1, for the word occurs in all three.[129] Mayor, 152, paraphrases νῦν δέ: 'But as the case really stands'. For καυχάομαι see on 1.9, where again the theme is the fleeting nature of wealth—there however the lowly boast—and the discussion on 3.5.

ἀλαζονεία appears only one other time in the NT, in 1 Jn 2.16, where the KJV famously translated: 'the pride of life'. The word (LXX: 7×)— of which the author of 1 Clement was fond[130]—refers to an arrogant, pretentious, or inflated self-estimation, or to taking undue pride in one's possessions.[131] It is linked to boasting in 1 Clem. 13.3 and 21.5. In its present context, ἀλαζονεία harks back to 4.6-10: the self-confident traders do not humble themselves but rather, in their braggadocio, embody lack of submission to God.

For some commentators, ἐν ταῖς ἀλαζονείαις ὑμῶν is the object of καυχᾶσθε: these people boast about their arrogance; they are proud to be independent.[132] Others construe ἐν κτλ. as adverbial: in their arrogance, these people boast (cf. v. 13).[133] Although a decision is difficult, perhaps one should incline to the first option, on the ground that everywhere else in the NT, καυχάομαι + ἐν[134] introduces the object of one's boast. But the

---

[127] Dionysius of Alexandria, Zech. 4.226-27 SC 83 ed. Doutreleau, 918, associates the latter with Jas 4.16.

[128] Ps 49.6; Prov 16.18-19; Isa 2.7, 11; 13.11, 17; Ezek 28.5; Wis 5.8; Ecclus 13.20; 1 En. 46.7; 94.8; 97.8-9; 1QH 18(10).25; 1QpHab 8.3, 9-12; 1 Tim 6.17; Josephus, Ant. 1.194; 4.223-24; Tg. 1 Sam 2.5; etc.

[129] Cf. the recurrence of νῦν in quick succession in LXX Gen 29.32-25; Isa 33.10-11; Jn 16.22-30; 17.5-13; Acts 20.22-32.

[130] See 13.1; 14.1; 16.2; 21.5, the latter with ἐν ἀλαζονείᾳ. Gk. Pseudepigrapha (Denis): 4×. Philo: 33×. Josephus: 5×.

[131] Cf. 2 Macc 9.8; 4 Macc 2.15; Wis 5.8; T. Job 21.3; T. Dan 1.6; T. Jos. 17.8 (ἐν ἀλαζονείᾳ); Jos. Asen. 4.12. Aristotle, Eth. nic. 1127A, defines ὁ ἀλαζών as one who 'pretends to creditable qualities that he does not possess, or possesses in a lesser degree than he makes out'. Cf. Xenophon, Cyr. 2.2.12: ὁ ἀλαζών is the name for 'those who pretend that they are richer than they are or braver than they are...who promise to do what they cannot do, and that, too, when it is evident that they do this only for the sake of getting something or making some gain'. See further Trench, *Synonyms*, 98-101; Popkes, 293-94; and on the braggart as a stock character in the Greek philosophical tradition note Johnson, 297.

[132] Cf. Ropes, 280-81, who understands καυχᾶσθε to signify 'an aggravation' of the attitude of v. 13, that is, it refers to 'the pride' the traders 'take in their own overweening self-confidence and presumption. ἐν indicates that ταῖς ἀλαζονείαις are the ground of the glorying'.

[133] This is the view of Mayor, 152, and Dibelius, 234.

[134] Cf. הלל + ב, as in Jer 9.23; 2Q23 1.8.

issue is not of great importance: arrogance is involved one way or the other, and most commentators do not even notice the issue.

πᾶσα καύχησις τοιαύτη πονηρά ἐστιν. Again James states the obvious by making explicit what has been implicit; he thereby adds emphasis. For πονηρός see on 2.4. James uses τοιτοῦτος and καύχησις[135] only here, but the latter recalls καυχᾶσθε in the previous clause.

Verse 17. According to Mussner, 192, this verse was 'certainly not first created ad hoc by James'.[136] Many have thought this, for at least three reasons. (i) How the saying functions in its current context remains far from obvious. (ii) The second person (vv. 14-16) gives way to the third person (v. 17). (iii) The line—which 'operates at the level of a universal human conscience'[137]—could stand on its own. If the inference is correct, one presumes a Jewish source in view of both language and content; see below. There is, however, no close verbal parallel: Job 31.16-23 and Ezek 3.16-21 are only distant relatives.[138]

As just noted, how v. 17 functions within 4.13–5.6 is unclear, despite the οὖν. It seems 'to come out of the blue'.[139] For Mayor, it is a sort of 'summing up' of all that 'has been said before, going as far back as i. 22, ii. 14, iii. 1, 13, iv. 11'.[140] Even if true, the placement between 4.13-16 and 5.1-6 remains puzzling. According to Mitton, 172-73, v. 17 should be printed as an independent paragraph. So too Dibelius, 231, for whom 'one cannot observe even an artificial link with the context', so 'it is difficult to say what the author's reason was for inserting the saying here'. Easton, 61, like Spitta, 129, offers that James took the saying, οὖν and all, from 'some well-known source' and 'inserted it here more or less at random'. Laws, 194, proposes that LXX Prov 3, quoted in 4.6, has made itself felt again: James, because of what he wrote about 'today or tomorrow' (vv. 13-14), recalled here Prov 3.28: 'Do not say, "Go, come back, and tomorrow I will give"', when you are able to do good, for you do not know what the next day will bring'. For Schlatter, 265, and Davids, 174, καλὸν ποιεῖν might include the giving of alms (cf. 1.27), in which case the topic is what to do with money. Tsuji thinks v. 17 refers

---

[135] LXX: 10×, usually for תפארת. NT: 11× (10× in Paul). Gk. Pseudepigrapha (Denis): 0×. Philo: 1×. Josephus: 0×.

[136] Cf. Reicke, 49; Vouga, 125 ('possible'); Schrage, 49; Davids, 174 ('a proverb'); Martin, 168; Hoppe, 97, 101-102; Hartin, 226. Contrast Frankemölle, 644.

[137] So McKnight, 378. As elsewhere in James, specifically Christian convictions are conspicuous by their absence.

[138] Laws, 193, observes that, in Origen, *Prin.* 1.3.6 GCS 22 ed. Koetschau, 57, *scienti bonum et non facienti peccatum est illi* is unattributed, so perhaps this is not from James. But is this likely given how close the words are to James and that Origen otherwise quotes James? The Vulgate has: *scienti igitur bonum facere et non facienti peccatum est illi.*

[139] So Baker-Ellsworth, 122.

[140] Mayor, 152. Cf. Weidner, 69.

back to v. 15: to do the right thing is to acknowledge the priority of God's will.[141] Moffatt, 45, without ms. authority, deems the line displaced and puts it after 2.26, where the fit is better.[142]

It seems more prudent to leave this closing aphorism, with its third-person form, where it is and to compare 5.12, which has no organic connection to its immediate surroundings, and further to observe that 4.17 is not so isolated as that. At least it is about sin, which well suits the context; and it is not without rhetorical effect. Perhaps it expands culpability: those ostensibly addressed really do know that they should behave differently than they do.[143] Or maybe the verse teaches that, although the merchants have 'heretofore erred through thoughtlessness...now that things have been made quite plain to them, they are in a position to know how to act; if, therefore, in spite of knowing now how to act aright, the proper course is neglected, then it is sinful'.[144] The line becomes even more relevant if one takes εἰδότι to mean 'able' (see below): the merchants are able to help others, so if they fail so to do, they are culpable. Beyond that, Frankemölle, 644—who dubs the topic of 4.17 'Christian schizophrenia'—observes that the verse appropriately comes right before 5.1-6, where the subject is people who leave the good undone.[145] Popkes, 312, and Fabris, 305, moreover, note the verbal ties between v. 17 and vv. 13-16: εἰδότι recalls the ἐπίστασθε of v. 14, καλόν balances the πονηρά of v. 16, and ποιεῖν...ποιοῦντι takes up the ποιήσομεν of vv. 13, 15.

However exactly one relates v. 17 to its present setting, the sentiment accords with a major theme of the Jesus tradition. Again and again people are criticized for leaving undone what they should have done: Mt 25.14-20 (a man buries a talent instead of investing it); 25.31-46 (people fail to feed the hungry, cloth the naked, etc.); Mk 7.9-13 (the institution of 'corban' takes from father and mother); Lk 10.29-37 (a priest and Levite pass by a half-dead victim); 12.47-48 ('That slave who knew what his master wanted, but did not prepare himself or do what was wanted, will receive a severe beating. But one who did not know and did what deserved a beating will receive a light beating');[146] 16.19-31 (the rich man ignores poor Lazarus).

---

[141] Tsuji, *Glaube*, 91. For support he appeals to Baker, *Speech-Ethics*, 235; Klein, *Werk*, 127-28.

[142] Könnecke, *Emendationen*, 16, thinks placement after 1.25 more likely.

[143] Cf. Bede *ad loc*. CCSL 121 ed. Hurst, 216.

[144] Oesterley, 464. Cf. Clarke, 823; Ropes, 281 (the verse means, in effect, 'you have now been fully warned').

[145] Cf. Johnson, 298: 4.17 provides 'a hinge between the example provided in 4:13-16 and that in 5:1-6'.

[146] Albertus Magnus, *En. sec. part. Luc. (X–XXIV) ad* Lk 12.47 Opera Omnia 23 ed. A. Borgnet, 271; Bonaventure, *Lk* 8.18 Opera Omnia 10 ed. Peltier, 570; and many other exegetes on Lk 12.45-47 have been reminded of Jas 4.17, just as readers of James have been reminded of Lk 12.45-47; cf. Bede *ad loc*. CCSL 121 ed. Hurst, 216; Erdmann,

εἰδότι οὖν καλὸν ποιεῖν καὶ μὴ ποιοῦντι, ἁμαρτία αὐτῷ ἐστιν. For οὖν see on 4.4. The anarthrous participle instead of a nominal subject is 'foreign to secular Greek' but characteristic of the LXX.[147]

Does the line look back over vv. 13-16 or all of James thus far? Or might οὖν be intensive rather than inferential?[148] Whatever the answer, 1.15 traces sin to desire, and 2.9 labels favoritism of rich over poor a sin whereas 4.17, by contrast, regards failure to act in certain circumstances as sinful.

One can understand our line as offering an expansive definition of ἁμαρτία (see on 1.15): it is knowing (cf. 1.19) the right thing to do—καλὸν ποιεῖν[149]—and not doing it. That is, sin is failing to live by one's conscience. Understood thus, James may be insisting, in effect, that he is not informing his readers and/or opponents of anything but rather reminding them of what they must already realize at some level, presumably through the Torah; cf. Rom 2.17-22. They know better than to act as they do.[150] Their sin stems not from ignorance but from a decision.[151]

An even closer connection between 4.17 and its immediate context results if one takes εἰδότι to mean 'be able':[152] if one is able to help and does not, it is a sin. On this reading, James exhorts merchants to put their resources to good use, as in T. Job 11.3, where some seek money from Job so that they can engage in trade (ἐμπορευσάμενοι) and thereby do 'the poor' a service; cf. LXX Prov 3.27-28 ('Do not withhold to do good to the needy, when your hand can help. Do not say, "God, come back, and tomorrow I will give", for you do not know what the next day will bring'); 1 Jn 3.17 ('How does God's love abide in anyone who has the world's goods and sees a brother or sister in need and yet refuses to help?').[153]

316; Meecham, 'Epistle', 182; Fabris, 306; *et al.* Note also Isidore of Seville, *Sent.* 2.1.9 CCSL 111 ed. Cazier, 92; Bernard of Clairvaux, *Consid. ad Eug. Pap.* 2.6.13 Bernardi Opera 3 ed. Leclercq and Rochais, 420. Oesterley, 464, thinks 4.17 'perhaps an echo of Luke xii. 47'. So too Blomberg-Kamell, 213. Cf. Grotius, 1089; Guyse, 592. I have been unable to verify the assertion of Meecham, 'Epistle', 183, that Ephraem quotes Jas 4.17 from Tatian's *Diatessaron* in such a way as to imply it was an agraphon.

[147] So Turner, *Grammar*, 117.

[148] So Baker, *Speech-Ethics*, 234-35. Cf. BAGD, s.v. οὖν 3; also the discussion below of the οὖν in 5.7.

[149] Cf. LXX Isa 1.17; Gal 6.9; 1 Clem. 8.4; Epictetus, *Diatr.* 3.1.24.

[150] Cf. Mt 21.28-32; Lk 12.45-47; and the use of 'hypocrite' in Mt 6.2, 5, 16.

[151] Cf. Calvin, 304: 'They know all too well, what is alleged, and need no warning: so he turns their awareness back upon themselves (the boast of it!), and declares that their sin is the more heinous for being the sin not of ignorance, but of contempt'.

[152] So BAGD, s.v., οἶδα 3 (citing Josephus, *Bell.* 2.91; 5.407; Mt 7.11; Lk 12.56; Phil 4.12; 1 Thess 4.4; 1 Tim 3.5; 2 Pet 2.9; 1 Clem. 16.3); Konradt, *Existenz*, 152-53 (citing also Epictetus, *Diatr.* 2.14.18); Burchard, 188-89 (citing also Xenophon, *Cyr.* 1.6.46).

[153] Lev. Rab. 25.1 supplies a later parallel: 'Though a man has learned Torah and has taught, observed, and performed it, yet if he was able to protest against wrongdoing and did not protest, or was able to maintain scholars and did not maintain them, he is included in the term, "cursed"'.

ἁμαρτία αὐτῷ ἐστιν is likely a Semitism, the equivalent of חטא + ל/ב + pronoun.[154] Beyer thinks the line 'most likely has a Hebrew original'.[155] This would be consistent with the verse preserving a proverb.

4.17 resembles Rom 7, where ἁμαρτία is not doing the good; see esp. 7.18-24, which includes the phrase, ποιεῖν τὸ καλόν (v. 21). Further, discussions of Rom 7 have sometimes found part of the background in the notion that one begins to sin at the age of reason, and Jas 4.17 has occasionally been thought to teach the same thing.[156] Those who find elsewhere in James a knowledge of Paul might find such here too, especially given that 4.1 also recalls Rom 7. Or, if one supposes that James took 4.17 from his tradition, this could be evidence for Paul's influence on that tradition.[157]

5.1. For Ropes, 282, the purpose of this and following verses 'is partly to dissuade the Christians from setting a high value on wealth, partly to give them a certain grim comfort in the hardships of poverty'.[158] The view of this commentary is rather that James, here as elsewhere, seeks sympathizers within the synagogue for his Christian party. He has already, in 2.1-13, distinguished such potential sympathizers from 'the rich' and encouraged them to side with 'the poor', a category which must include some Christians. So although James is, according to 1.1, addressing the entire diaspora, an epistolary fiction that allows him here to speak directly to the wealthy wicked, his goal is not to convert such but to make common cause with or to gain sympathy from non-Christian Jews who are not so wealthy. Presumably, Christians were not the only ones to resent those attacked in 5.1-6: the rich always draw blame for a variety of injustices.

ἄγε νῦν οἱ πλούσιοι. Cf. 1 En. 94.8-9: 'Woe to you, O rich people! For you have put your trust in your wealth... You have become ready for...the day of great judgment.' For ἄγε νῦν + οἱ see on 4.13, and for πλούσιος see on 1.10. Given that James is likely reworking Lk 6.24-25 (see below), ἄγε νῦν seems to be his rewrite of οὐαί = הוי.

---

[154] Cf. m. Ker. 6.1; t. Ker. 4.2, 11; Pesiq. R. 44.7. Related is the חמא היה בך = ἔσται ἐν σοὶ ἁμαρτία of Deut 15.9; 23.22; 24.15.

[155] Beyer, *Syntax*, 219. Cf. Davids, 174: there are 'indications of a Semitic origin: (1) in the paratactic construction (καί) instead of a hypotactic "if...then" clause, (2) in the pleonastic, but rhetorically emphatic, αὐτῷ (BDF, § 446), and (3) in the similarity to ἔστιν ἐν σοὶ ἁμαρτία of Deuteronomy (15:9; 23:21; 24:15 LXX)'.

[156] So e.g. Origen; see above, 644. For Rom 7 see Davies, *Paul*, 24-26.

[157] The commentaries, however, pay much more attention to Rom 14.23, where Paul says that whatever is not of faith is sin. Indeed, a few, such as Wordsworth, 29, think James here draws upon that verse.

[158] This is a common interpretation; cf. Calvin, 305: James 'is really looking to the men of faith, that they may attend to the sad ruin of the wealthy, and not be envious of their prosperity'.

Few commentators doubt that these rich are headed for damnation. Bede was an exception. For him, James hopes for their repentance—'Now is the acceptable time'—so that they will avoid future punishments.[159]

Even though James stands in the wisdom tradition, he rejects the idea that prosperity signals God's blessing[160] and that poverty is a punishment for sin or the upshot of sloth.[161] He sides rather with the Jesus tradition, where the poor are blessed and wealth is a problem, and where the near future will see eschatological justice done by reversing current economic circumstances. Yet already Prov 30.7-9 expresses caution about trusting in wealth[162] while 21.6-7 and 28.20-22 envisage judgment falling upon the unrighteous rich;[163] and the canonical prophets rail against the rich.[164] Further, some Dead Sea Scrolls teach that the faithful should loath riches, which are an obstacle to serving God.[165] Clearly many believed in 'the deceitfulness of riches' (Mt 13.22), and no doubt many would have concurred with Jesus' remark about the camel and the eye of a needle as well as with 1 Tim 6.9-10: 'love of money is a root of all kinds of evil'. See further below, on v. 6.

By 'the rich' James has in mind the landed aristocracy who employ serfs. He speaks of them as a class. Attempts to be more specific fail, although Furfey argues that the 'rich' were those able to support themselves by their own capital, and that 'bourgeoisie' might be a fitting translation.[166]

Because siding with the poor against the rich was a common Jewish *topos*, one can infer little about the author's social status or his *Sitz im Leben* from 5.1-6. Philo and Seneca, both of whom were privileged, could disparage wealth, warn of its temptations, and speak of it as an evil. And Matthew's Gospel, which quotes Jesus as saying that 'it is easier for a camel to go through the eye of a needle than for someone who is rich to enter the kingdom of God' (19.24), dubs Joseph of Arimathea both 'rich' and 'a disciple' (27.57). Moreover, while it is possible that our author, like some later Christians monks and ascetics, had rid himself of possessions, we have no firm evidence of this. Indeed, he speaks of the poor and oppressed in the third person, as though he is not among them,[167] and

---

[159] Bede *ad loc*. CCSL 121 ed. Hurst, 216.
[160] As in Prov 8.18; 10.4, 22; 13.21; 22.4; Ecclus 44.2-6.
[161] Cf. Job 36.8-9; Prov 10.4; 12.27; 13.4; 28.19.
[162] Cf. 28.11, 22; Job 22.5-6; 31.24-28; Ecclus 5.1-3, 8; 31.5.
[163] Cf. Job 20.20-29; 27.13-23.
[164] E.g. Isa 5.8-10; Jer 5.26-29; 15.13-14; Ezek 7.11; Amos 3.9-11; 5.10-13; 8.4-8.
[165] Cf. CD 4.15-18; 1QH 18(10).22-30; also Josephus, *Vita* 73; *Bell*. 2.122; b. Ber. 32a; b. Git. 70a; b. Sanh. 192a.
[166] P.H. Furfey, 'ΠΛΟΥΣΙΟΣ and Cognates in the New Testament', *CBQ* 5 (1943), 243-63. He suggests that 'the rich' implies 'something about the source of income rather than about the amount of wealth possessed' (261).
[167] Cf. Ahrens, *Arm*, 131. Ahrens concludes that we do not have enough information to offer social-scientific theories about James' background (136).

he commends Abraham and Job, both of whom were famously wealthy.[168] In the end, just as our text offers no theory of wealth nor any analysis of the means of production or the distribution of capital, so too it fails to clarify the author's situation.[169] We can say little more than that, in James, wealth can corrupt, and that it has corrupted some, and that they will be called to account.

Perhaps more helpful than attempts to divine the socio-economic circumstances of James and his readers is the high probability that our epistle is a pseudepigraphon. This matters when one recalls the tradition of Hegesippus, that James avoided wine and meat, did not bathe, and did not anoint his body with oil.[170] If the first recipients of our letter held this sort of image of James, our passage would nicely cohere with it.

κλαύσατε ὀλολύζοντες ἐπὶ ταῖς ταλαιπωρίαις ὑμῶν ταῖς ἐπερχομέναις. κλαίω occurs in 4.9 along with ταλαιπωρέω, so the present verse recalls that one, all the more as the ἁμαρτία of v. 17 has its counterpart in the vocative ἁμαρτωλοί of v. 8. James is repeating himself.[171] The reason is partly that there must be some overlap between those rebuked in 4.1-12 and those rebuked in 4.13–5.6.[172] One assumes that 'the rich' who have prospered at the expense of others are guilty of craving and of being friends of the world; see 4.1-4. The history of interpretation shows many moving back and forth between 4.1-12 and 4.13–5.6, as though the two sections are united in subject matter.[173]

ὀλολύζω occurs twenty times in the LXX, almost always for the Hiphil of ילל.[174] Both verbs are onomatopoetic (cf. ἀλαλάζω). The meaning is 'cry out', 'howl', 'shriek', either for joy or (as regularly in the LXX and later Greek) in pain.[175] ὀλολύζω is especially prominent in

---

[168] Gen 13.2; 24.1; 1QapGen 21.3; Job 1.3, 10; T. Job 9-12; etc.

[169] Peck, 'James 5:1-6', 295, is also right that 'there is no program of reform for the world here, any more than there is an expectation that the rich may be converted... The powerful are simply being told that their time is about to come, and the Christian poor are being urged to keep themselves "unspotted" by this kind of world'.

[170] See Eusebius, *H.E.* 2.23.5.

[171] Jebb, *Literature*, 259, cleverly (over)interprets the correlation: κλαύσατε ὀλολύζοντες ἐπὶ ταῖς ταλαιπωρίαις is 'an exact inversion of the descending series in the last example, ταλαιπωρήσατε καὶ πενθήσατε καὶ κλαύσατε [4.9]... with this only difference, that ὀλολύζατε is substituted for πενθήσατε, a more vociferous, for a more plaintive expression of sorrow: the one, indicative of penitence; the other, of despair. The descending scale marks, that the sorrows of the penitent are daily mitigated; the ascending series intimates, that the pangs of the impenitent are for ever on the increase.'

[172] Many, however, contrast the two verses on the ground that whereas 4.9 is a genuine call to repentance, 5.1 is a statement of condemnation; so e.g. Ropes, 283.

[173] In addition to the commentaries note Fulgentius, *Ep.* 7.19 SC 487 ed. Bachelet, 282.

[174] NT: 1×. Gk. Pseudepigrapha (Denis): 0×. Philo: 0×. Josephus: 0×.

[175] Cf. LXX Joel 1.5, 13; Jer 4.8; Sib Or. 1.163; Ps.-Clem. Hom. 12.22 GCS 42 ed. Rehm, 185; PGM 11a.31; Acts Paul Thec. 35 ed. Lipsius, 261.

DENUNCIATIONS OF THE PROSPEROUS (4.13–5.6)   669

LXX Isaiah, where it often occurs in oracles of condemnation, as here in James.[176]

κλαίω + ὀλολύζω was not a traditional Greek combination.[177] The background probably lies in LXX prophetic oracles, in which both words address those confronting divine judgment.[178] Particularly interesting is LXX Isa 15, which features this sequence: κλαίειν...ὀλολύζετε ἐπί... ὀλολύζετε...κλαίοντες...ὀλολυγμός (vv. 2, 3, 5, 8). Once more James speaks with the voice of a prophet.

It is also likely the voice of Jesus the prophet in particular. The commentary has already observed that 4.9 plausibly rewrites the woe in Lk 6.25. If, as much modern scholarship has tended to suppose, that woe was joined from the beginning to 6.24, it is noteworthy that the latter directly addresses the rich (οὐαὶ ὑμῖν τοῖς πλουσίοις), as does James. Once more the Lukan woes have seemingly influenced our text.[179]

ταλαιπωρία[180] means 'misery', 'distress', 'misfortune'.[181] As the word is modified by ἐπέρχομαι (Jas: 1×), the content is eschatological: the text adverts to the final assize (cf. vv. 2-3) and/or (although less likely) the birth-pangs that precede the new world.[182] Again there are parallels in LXX judgment oracles: Isa 47.11 (ἥξει ἐπὶ σὲ ταλαιπωρία); Jer 6.26 (ἥξει ταλαιπωρία ἐφ' ὑμᾶς); Amos 3.10 (θησαυρίζοντες...ταλαιπωρίαν; cf. Jas 5.3); 5.9; Mic 2.4 (ταλαιπωρία ἐταλαιπωρήσαμεν); Joel 1.15 (ταλαιπωρία ἐκ ταλαιπωρίας ἥξει); Hab 2.17.[183] The whole expression, ταῖς ταλαιπωρίαις ὑμῶν ταῖς ἐπερχομέναις, is presumably modeled upon traditional eschatological expressions such as 'the day that is coming' (cf. Jer 47.4: היום הבא = LXX 29.4: τῇ ἡμέρᾳ τῇ ἐρχομένῃ), 'the wrath that is coming' (cf. 1 Thess 1.10: τῆς ὀργῆς τῆς ἐρχομένης), and

---

[176] 10.10; 13.6; 14.31; 15.2-3; 16.7; 23.1, 6, 14.

[177] Later examples presumably stand under James' influence: Cyril of Alexandria, *Isa* ad 23.6 PG 70.525A; Mark the Hermit, *Paen.* 5 SC 445 ed. Durand, 230; *et al.*

[178] E.g. Amos 8.3; Joel 1.5; Zech 11.2; etc.

[179] See further Deppe, *Sayings*, 111-13; also Aretius, 484; Omanson, 'Judgment', 427; Davids, 'Jesus', 67; Bottini, *Introduzione*, 135-38; Maier, 201.

[180] NT: 2×; cf. Rom 3.16; 1 Clem. 15.6. LXX: most often for שד or שדד. Gk. Pseudepigrapha (Denis): 2×. Philo: 5×. Josephus: 30×.

[181] Cf. Let. Aris. 15; T. Job 34.4; Philo, *Opif.* 167; Josephus, *Bell.* 7.278-79.

[182] And not, against so many earlier commentators, the destruction of Jerusalem in CE 70; note Bede *ad loc.* CCSL 121 ed. Hurst, 218; Bengel, 505; Whitby, 692; Burkitt, 1010; Benson, 100, 102; Doddridge, 846; Jebb, *Literature*, 260-61; T. Scott, 586; McKnight, 600; Lange, 128; Bassett, 64, 66; Plummer, 622, 624; Knowling, 125; Gibson, 67; Smith 275-76, 285; Ross, 87, 90. Feuillet, 'Parousie', thinks of 5.1-6 in its entirety as retrospective. Some have viewed Jerusalem's fall as being an anticipation or prelude of the end and so could think of both things; e.g. Wesley, 867; Clarke, 824; R. Scott, 143; Plumptre, 96-97. See further 689-90.

[183] In the LXX, the word 'is used predominantly in connection with the miseries suffered by those who have resisted God' (Johnson, 299).

'the age that is coming' (cf. the rabbinic עלמא דאתי, העולם הבא).[184] Perhaps, in view of 5.7, 'impending' would be a better translation of ἐπέρχομαι than 'coming'.

Coming troubles are cause for lamentation in 5.1, and this stands in striking contrast to 1.2-4, where coming troubles issue in joy. In the former case, woes are divine judgment upon those with crooked characters. In the latter, difficulties build good character.

Verse 2. Beginning with this verse, James counts four sins against the rich: accumulating wealth (vv. 2-3), withholding pay (v. 4), living extravagantly (v. 5), and murdering 'the righteous one' (v. 6—unless this is a metaphorical recapitulation of v. 4).

Verses 2-6, like 4.13-16, feature paired words and expressions:

5.2 Definite article + subject + ὑμῶν + perfect verb with seven letters, duplicated consonant, -εν ending
ὁ πλοῦτος ὑμῶν σέσηπεν καὶ
τὰ ἱμάτια ὑμῶν... γέγονεν

5.3 ὁ + noun ending in ρυσος or υρος
ὁ χρυσός καὶ
ὁ ἄργυρος
ὁ + noun ending in -ος + plural possessive pronoun ending in -ων + verb ending in -ται
ὁ χρυσὸς ὑμῶν... κατίωται καὶ
ὁ ἰὸς αὐτῶν... ἔσται

5.4 Definite article + subject + τῶν + noun ending in -των + finite verb
ὁ μισθὸς τῶν ἐργατῶν... κράζει καὶ
αἱ βοαὶ τῶν θερισάντων... εἰσεληλύθασιν

5.5 Synonymous verbs in the aorist with second person plural ending in ἡσατε
ἐτρυφήσατε καὶ
ἐσπαταλήσατε

5.6 Synonymous verbs in the aorist with second person plural ending in -σατε
κατεδικάσατε
ἐφονεύσατε

Not only does the parallelism add to the prophetic feel of the text, but it has its counterpart in the extensive parallelism of Mt 6.19-21 = Lk 12.33-34, with which James is working.

That James here depends upon the Synoptic logion has seemed clear to many.[185] The verbal overlap is extensive, the common themes evident:

---

[184] As in ARN 21; Tanḥ. Buber Lekh-Lekha 12; y. Moʿed. Qat. 83b (3:7) v.l.; y. Ḥag. 77a (2.1); b. ʿAbod. Zar. 3b; etc.; cf. Eph 2.7: ἐν τοῖς αἰῶσιν τοῖς ἐπερχομένοις. Note, however, the parallel in Scholia in Lucianum 13.6.5: ἐπερχόμενα ταλαιπωρίαν. Burchard, 190, cites additional texts in which participial ἐπέρχομαι is used of coming 'Unheil'—LXX Prov 27.12; Jos. Asen. 4.7; Josephus, Ant. 2.86; 7.325; 11.326; 1 Clem. 56.10; Herm. Vis. 3.9.5.

[185] E.g. Wolzogen, 216; Shepherd, 'Matthew', 46; Adamson, 185 ('may'); Omanson, 'Judgment', 427; Davids, 'Jesus', 67 ('close allusion'); Maynard-Reid, Poverty, 83;

DENUNCIATIONS OF THE PROSPEROUS (4.13–5.6)

Jas 4.14-5.5	Mt 6.19-21; Lk 12.33-34
ἀφανιζομένη	ἀφανίζει (Matthew, bis)
σέσηπεν, σητόβρωτα	σῆς (Matthew and Luke)
σητόβρωτα	βρῶσις (Matthew)
τὰ ἱμάτια	clothing is implicit in the Synoptics
ἐθησαυρίσατε ἐν	θησαυρίζετε...ἐν, θησαυρούς (Matthew)
	θησαυρόν (Luke)
	θησαυρός (Matthew and Luke)
ἐπὶ τῆς γῆς	ἐπὶ τῆς γῆς (Matthew)
καρδίας ὑμῶν	καρδία ὑμῶν (Luke), καρδία σου (Matthew)
eschatological application	eschatological application

The appearance in Matthew alone of βρῶσις and ἐπὶ τῆς γῆς is consistent with James being under the influence of that Gospel. But those elements may be pre-Matthean. The International Q Project judges them to come from Q.[186]

ὁ πλοῦτος ὑμῶν σέσηπεν. Cf. Ecclus 29.10-11: 'Lose your silver for the sake of a brother or a friend, and do not let it rust under a stone and be lost. Lay up your treasure according to the commandments of the Most High, and it will profit you more than gold.'[187] That wealth was ephemeral was proverbial in James' world, as it has been in most times and places.[188] The combination of πλοῦτος[189] with σήπω[190] appears to be James' invention. The verb means 'waste away' or 'rot'.[191] Here it echoes σῆς in the saying attributed to Jesus in Mt 6.19-20 = Lk 12.33 = Gos. Thom. 76. James has turned Jesus' noun into a verb.

Hartin, Q, 179-81; Popkes, 306 ('could'); Maier, 203; S. Johnson, Treasure, 97-100; cf. Albertus Magnus, Super Mt cap. I–XIV Opera Omnia 21/1 ed. Schmidt, 228. Deppe, Sayings, 120-31, has an exhaustive discussion, which concludes: 'That a particular saying of the Jesus-tradition is in the mind of James is evidenced by 1) similar subject matter as well as some verbal connections; 2) the identical approach to the subject of wealth in the teachings of James and Jesus; 3) another allusion to a saying of Jesus at 5:1 within this traditional material; and 4) the support given by numerous exegetes in the last centuries where this is the fifth most frequently cited parallel between James and the Synoptic Gospels'. Such dependence suffices to undo the thesis, forwarded by Oesterley, 465-67, that Jas 5.1-6 is an extract from a Jewish writing. Contrast Easton, 64: 'the apparent relation of vss. 2-3 to Matt. 6:19 is purely superficial'.

[186] CEQ, 328. See further W. Pesch, 'Zur Exegese von Mt 6,19-21 und Lk 12,33-34', Bib 40 (1960), 356-78.

[187] This is only one of several texts in Ecclesiasticus that recall Jas 5.1-6; see Frankemölle, 649-51, 654-55, 659-60. According to B.M. Metzger, An Introduction to the Apocrypha, New York, 1957, 165-66, James here shows an awareness of Sirach.

[188] Cf. Prov 23.4-5; 27.24; 1 En. 97.10; Philo, Post. C. 112; Jos. 131-35; etc.

[189] Jas: 1×. LXX: most often for עשר.

[190] NT: 1×. LXX: 8×; cf. בלה and the Niphal of מקק.

[191] Cf. LXX Job 16.7 (of Job's flesh; so too 33.21); Ps 37.6 (of wounds); Ecclus 14.19 (of human deeds, with σηπόμενον); Ep Jer 71 (of the decaying coverings of idols); Ezek 17.9 (of fruit); T. Job 43.5 (of a throne); Philo, Aet. mund. 125 (of stones); Josephus, C. Ap. 2.143 (of gangrene); 1 Clem. 25.3 (of bird flesh); Herm. Sim. 2.3 (of fruit); Diognetus, Ep. 2.2 (of wood), 4 (of a list of manufactured products).

Some commentators, supposing our text to concern three sorts of riches—fancy foodstuffs, costly garments, precious metals—take ὁ πλοῦτος ὑμῶν σέσηπεν to refer to food.[192] This interpretation suits the verb but not the noun, which unqualified hardly suggests grain or foodstuffs. Rather, ὁ πλοῦτος ὑμῶν 'is the general term, under which garments and coin (ver. 3) are the specifications'.[193]

The perfect—also used in the next line—is probably prophetic rhetoric: events can be 'conceived so vividly and so realistically that they are regarded as having virtually taken place and are described by the perfect. This happens often in making promises or threats... This usage is very common in the elevated language of the Prophets, whose faith and imagination so vividly project before them the event or scene which they predict that it appears already realized. It is part of the purpose of God, and therefore, to the clear eyes of the prophet, already as good as accomplished.'[194] Jude 14, which uses an aorist of the *parousia*, supplies an obvious NT example: 'the Lord came (ἦλθεν) with tens of thousands of his holy ones'.[195] James has an 'apocalyptic way of understanding the present',[196] and for those addressed here, it is too late: their treasures are 'already as good as rotted'.[197]

Ps.-Oecumenius and others have rather taken σέσηπεν to indicate that the rich are so selfish that, instead of sharing or investing their goods, they hide them away until they rot.[198] For this Philo, *Praem.* 104, provides

---

[192] Cf. Guyse, 593; Clarke, 824; Theile, 248; Macknight, 600; Smith, 277; Mayor, 154 (comparing manna, which did not keep); Tasker, 111; Mitton, 176; Deppe, *Sayings*, 122; and note the parallel to this reading in 1 En. 97.9-10.

[193] Winkler, 62. Cf. Gregory of Nazianzus, *Or.* 19.11 PG 35.1056C: 'let us not... stain our wealth (πλοῦτον) with others' tears, which will devour it like rust and moths (ἰοῦ καὶ σητός)'.

[194] So A.B. Davidson and J. Maucline, *An Introductory Hebrew Grammar*, 25th ed., Edinburgh, 1962, 194-95. Cf. Erasmus, *Paraphrase*, 165-66 ('Imagine that the time has already arrived'); Bassett, 67; Mayor, 154; A. Robertson, *Grammar*, 898 (citing Jn 17.10, 22); von Soden, 182; Dibelius, 236; Mitton, 177; Mussner, 194; Reicke, 50-51; Adamson, 185; Maynard-Reid, *Poverty*, 84 ('the prosperity of the rich is still very much evident'); Cantinat, 222; Davids, 175; Peck, 'James 5:1-6', 294; Hoppe, 103; Popkes, 299; Hartin, 227; Witherington, 525; Gundry, 942; and note perhaps the application in Palladius, *H. Laus.* 40 ed. Butler, 126: τὸν πλοῦτον ὑμῶν σήπετε εἰς κατάκριμα τῶν ψυχῶν ὑμῶν. The strategy has always been well known; cf. *Old English Homilies of the Twelfth Century*, second series, ed. R. Morris, London, 1873, 146: 'he spake of what should happen as though it had come to pass, for he knew surely that it would come'. Note LXX Isa 31.2; 44.23; 53.5-10; 60.1-2; Hab 2.16-17.

[195] Recall also the concluding ἐδόξασεν of Rom 8.30: the aorist is used even though the glorification of believers has not yet been achieved.

[196] So Tiller, 'Rich', 177.

[197] Burchard, 190. Ropes, 284, insists that the perfect reflects the view that, to those who understand, wealth is of no worth compared with enduring values. But this reading need not disallow finding prophetic perfects here. Given James' eschatological outlook, the one circumstance entails the other.

[198] So too Bede *ad* 5.3 CCSL 121 ed. Hurst, 217; Calvin, 305-306; Diodati *ad loc.*; Guyse, 593; Gill, 799; Schlatter, 267; Tasker, 111; Mitton, 178; Mussner, 194; Laws,

a parallel: 'So then let not the rich man collect great store of gold and silver and hoard it at his house, but bring it out for general use that he may soften the hard lot of the needy'. But in James the preceding ταῖς ταλαιπωρίαις ὑμῶν ταῖς ἐπερχομέναις and the following φάγεται τὰς σάρκας ὑμῶν ὡς πῦρ are eschatological, and the switch in tenses does not indicate a change in point of view; see on v. 3.

καὶ τὰ ἱμάτια ὑμῶν σητόβρωτα γέγονεν.[199] Cf. LXX Isa 51.8: 'Just as a garment (ἱμάτιον) it will be devoured (βρωθήσεται) by time, and like wool it will be devoured (βρωθήσεται) by a moth' (σητός). James moves from wealth in general to clothing (ἱμάτιον: Jas: 1×) in particular, the latter being perhaps the chief public evidence of the former.[200] It is possible that the reference is not to fancy clothing in general but to the outer garment in particular, the robe or cloak,[201] what the rabbis called the שמלה; cf. the Roman *toga*.

σητόβρωτος[202] can be explained as deriving from the saying in Mt 6.19, which features both σής and βρῶσις; see below. σής is the 'moth', whose larvae eat clothing; cf. the biblical and rabbinic סס. In the Tanak, it destroys what is feeble: Prov 25.20 (σὴς ἐν ἱματίῳ); Isa 33.1 (σὴς ἐφ' ἱματίου); cf. Ecclus 42.13: 'From garments (ἱματίων) comes the moth (σής)'.

The sense of βρῶσις is less clear. Although it typically means 'eating' (Rom 14.17) or 'food' (Jn 6.27), it can also refer to 'decay' (Galen 6.422; 12.879—of teeth); and many suppose 'rust' to be the meaning in Mt 6.19-20.[203] Yet in LXX Mal 3.11 A, the word translates אכל = 'devourer' = 'locust' or 'grasshopper', and in Ep Jer 10 v.l., βρῶσις is next to ἰός, and hendiadys is doubtful. So Mt 6.19-20 probably has in view two insects (cf. LAB 40.6) that devour costly textiles. This appears to be how Gos. Thom. 76 construes the logion: 'Do you also seek for the treasure which fails not, which endures, there where no moth (ẋooλec) comes near to devour and no worm (qñт) destroys'. Given that James has ἱμάτιον (Jas: 1×), and despite his use of 'rust' in the next line, he likely presupposes the interpretation common to Matthew and Thomas.

198; Schrage, 49-51; Vouga, 128; Schnider, 112; Townsend, 91; Mayordomo-Marin, 'Gericht'; Hainthaler, *Ausdauer*, 304-305; Konradt, *Existenz*, 155; Böttrich, 'Gold', 521. Mayordomo-Marin, 'Gericht', observes that this allows for a link with 4.17: by not sharing what they have, the rich are committing a sin of omission. He also observes, in favor of the position he takes, that, in Mt 6.19-21 = Lk 12.33-34 and Ecclus 29.10, wealth fails even now.

[199] Against the proposal, forwarded by J. Wordsworth, 'Corbey', that a Latin variant here suggests an Aramaic original for James, see Dibelius, 236 n. 33.

[200] Cf. 2.3; Mt 11.8; Lk 16.19; Acts 20.33.

[201] 1 Sam 28.8, 14; Mt 5.40; 9.20-21; 26.65; Rev 19.16.

[202] NT: 1×. LXX: Job 13.28: ἱμάτιον σητόβρωτον (Hainthaler, *Ausdauer*, 300-305, thinks James depends upon Job here). Gk. Pseudepigrapha (Denis): 0× (but Sib. Or. frag. 3.26 has σητόβρωτα). Philo: 0×. Josephus: 0×.

[203] Luke's parallel is different, but Matthew here probably preserves the earlier form; see Pesch, 'Exegese' (as in n. 186).

Verse 3. James continues his eschatological interpretation of the fact that 'prosperity is unstable' (Ps.-Phoc. 27); cf. 1 En. 97 10: 'your wealth will not endure but will take off from you quickly'.

ὁ χρυσὸς ὑμῶν καὶ ὁ ἄργυρος κατίωται. κατιόω[204]—note again the perfect tense—derives from ἰός = 'rust' (cf. the next line) and means 'to become rusty', 'rust through', or 'become tarnished'.[205] Especially interesting for comparison is Ep Jer 10: 'They decorate them as people with clothing, gods of silver (ἀργυροῦς) and gold (χρυσοῦς) and wood, which cannot save themselves from ἰοῦ and corrosion (βρωμάτων)'; but it is unclear exactly what ἰός here means.[206]

One does not normally think of gold and silver as subject to rust.[207] So how do we explain our texts? (i) According to BAGD, s.v., ἰός, 'some metals in a gold object would be subject to oxidation' or to chemical pollution if they were not 'adequately refined'. (ii) Maybe James knew that gold and silver do not rust, and that is precisely his point. Stern and graphic prophetic denunciations do not always concern themselves with factual details, and such denunciations may even have God overthrowing the facts.[208] (iii) James erred because he employed a slightly inaccurate proverb, or because his focus was elsewhere, or because he used 'popular language' (Mayor, 154), or because he was thinking of treasure in general (cf. Mt 6.20) despite speaking of gold and silver in particular.[209] (iv) Perhaps unacquainted first-hand with gold and silver, our author did not know they cannot rust.[210] (v) κατιόω bears a figurative sense: it means 'are ruined' or 'are worthless'.[211] (vi) According to Weiser, 'Edelmetall', James is thinking of coins or objects only plated to look like gold or silver: the metal within will eventually rust.[212] The correct interpretation cannot be determined. But that matters little because the main point is clear: wealth does not endure.

---

[204] NT: 1×. LXX: Ecclus 12.11. Although both Philo (3×) and Josephus (5×) use the word, it is much more common in secular Greek than in Jewish Greek. Gk. Pseudepigrapha (Denis): 0×.

[205] Cf. Ecclus 12.11; Epictetus, *Diatr.* 4.6.14; and see Böttrich, 'Gold', 521-22.

[206] It could mean not 'rust' but 'tarnish'; cf. Strabo 16.2.42.

[207] Cf. Philo, *Her.* 217. For additional texts which state that gold does not rust see Böttrich, 'Gold', 528-32; Burchard, 191. Ecclus 29.10 appears to be about silver coins.

[208] Cf. Jebb, *Literature*, 260 ('James intimates something beyond the order of nature'); Lange, 128; Alford, 321; Frankemölle, 630-31, 648, 652-53; Mayordomo-Marin, 'Gericht', 133 n. 4; Gundry, 942 ('even the riches that don't rust will in fact do so under God's judgment'). This, however, disturbs the parallelism with the line about moths eating clothing: there is nothing supernatural about that.

[209] Cf. Smith, 277; Dibelius, 236; Mussner, 194; Sidebottom, 56; Martin, 177; Böttrich, 'Gold'.

[210] So Windisch-Preisker, 31: 'the editor seems not to know, that precious metal in general does not admit rust'.

[211] Cf. Wordsworth, 30; Ropes, 285; Mitton, 177; Deppe, *Sayings*, 122.

[212] Criticism in Böttrich, 'Gold', 523-24.

χρυσός (Jas: 1×) and ἄργυρος (Jas: 1×) were—like הַזָּהָב וְהַכֶּסֶף[213]—a regular pair, although their order was not fixed.[214] Their joint appearance in texts of judgment is attested.[215] That one cannot securely possess them forever was a truism.[216]

καὶ ὁ ἰὸς αὐτῶν εἰς μαρτύριον ὑμῖν ἔσται. In 3.8, ἰός means 'poison'. In 5.3, it apparently means 'rust'.[217] εἰς μαρτύριον[218] was a fixed expression and it often appears with ἔσται (cf. הָיָה לְ).[219] Here the verb is eschatological. εἰς μαρτύριον does not appear in secular Greek texts and should be reckoned a Semitism or Septuagintalism. It can mean 'as a visible sign or proof of' for either good or ill. As our passage is a sweeping condemnation, not a call to repentance, the idiom must mean 'witness against you'.

The future tense, ἔσται, has troubled some commentators, who have fretted over how it harmonizes with the perfects just used. But the LXX supplies clear instances of proleptic aorists and futures standing side by side.[220] Further, that James can use more than one tense when discussing the same event or circumstance is manifest from v. 6: κατεδικάσατε (aorist), ἐφονεύσατε (aorist), ἀντιτάσσεται (present).

To declare, in a poetic figure, that rust—a thing without use and of no value—will witness against the rich at the last judgment is to assert that the gold and silver they now have will by then be gone, having deteriorated into what is worthless. What seemingly aids them now will not help them then; cf. Ezek 7.19 ('Their silver and gold cannot save them on the day of wrath of the Lord'); 1 En. 94.6 ('Your money makes you appear like the righteous…this very matter will be a witness against you'); 100.6 ('their wealth will not be able to save them').

The rich have already appeared in court in 2.1-7, and they will reappear in 5.6, to condemn the just. Here, however, they lose their day in court, offering proof of 4.6: God opposes the proud.

καὶ φάγεται τὰς σάρκας ὑμῶν ὡς πῦρ. Cf. LXX Num 12.12 (κατεσθίει τὸ ἥμισυ τῶν σαρκῶν αὐτῆς); Mic 3.3 (κατέφαγον τὰς σάρκας τοῦ λαοῦ μου). Moffatt, 68, calls James' words 'a Dantesque touch of horror'. The rust that eats gold and silver and will fail as a witness at the

---

[213] As in Exod 35.32; 2 Kgs 14.14; 1QM 5.5, 14; 12.12; etc.

[214] Note Plato, Resp. 417A; LXX Exod 35.32; Sib. Or. 3.641; Philo, Cher. 48; Mt 10.9; Acts 17.29; Rev 18.12; Josephus, Ant. 2.167; etc.

[215] E.g. Ezek 7.19; 28.4; Hos 8.4; Sib. Or. 3.179.

[216] Cf. Bar 3.17-19; T. Levi 13.7; Jos. Asen. 12.12; and recall the tales about Croesus.

[217] As in LXX Ezek 24.6; Ep Jer 11; Diogentus, Ep. 2.2.

[218] = לְעֵד. μαρτύριον: Jas: 1×.

[219] See LXX Gen 21.30; 31.44 (ἔσται εἰς μαρτύριον); Deut 31.19, 26 (ἔσται…εἰς μαρτύριον); Josh 24.27 (ἔσται…εἰς μαρτύριον); 1 Βασ 9.24; Job 16.9; Prov 29.14; Hos 2.14; Amos 1.11; Mic 1.2 (ἔσται…εἰς μαρτύριον); 7.18; Zeph 3.8; Mt 10.18 (εἰς μαρτύριον αὐτοῖς); Mk 1.44 (εἰς μαρτύριον αὐτοῖς; cf. 13.9); Heb 3.5; Ign. Trall. 12.3; Phil. 6.3; Barn. 8.3, 4; 9.3.

[220] E.g. Isa 5.13-17; 31.1-2; Hab 2.15-17.

last judgment will feed—this is reminiscent of the worms in Isa 66.24; Jdt 16.17 (πῦρ καὶ σκώληκας εἰς σάρκας αὐτῶν); Mk 9.48; Vis. Pauli 42 ed. Silverstein and Hilhorst, 156—upon the flesh of the rich.[221] That rust 'eats' is a natural metaphor,[222] one encouraged by the reference to moths in v. 2. ἐσθίω (Jas: 1×) + σάρξ (Jas: 1×) was a normal idiom for eating meat.[223] In some biblical passages, however, the meat is human flesh, and its being devoured is a sign of divine judgment.[224] Closely related are especially Ezek 39.17-18 (φάγεσθε κρέα, part of an eschatological summons to wild animals and birds to devour the carrion of the mighty) and Rev 19.18 (φάγητε σάρκας, part of a call to birds to eat the carrion of God's eschatological opponents). The horror and disgust of those texts should be read into James.

The adverbial ὡς πῦρ[225]—the expression occurs in the LXX for כאש[226]—leaves little doubt that we should think of Gehenna, which 3.7 has already named.[227] It was traditionally conceived of as a place of fire; see on 3.7. In the background is the notion that fire 'eats' things.[228] James seems to assume the resurrection of the wicked,[229] whose bodies will be sent to Gehenna, where they will be destroyed.[230]

Fire sometimes appears in prophecies of eschatological judgment as an instrument of purification, as in 1 Cor 3.12-15, where 'the fire' will 'test what sort of work each has done', revealing whether one has built with gold, silver, precious stones.[231] In James, however, the rich seemingly will have no precious metal left to be refined, only rust.

---

[221] Cf. Gill, 799. Several witnesses repeat ὁ ἰός before ὡς· 01 C2 02 025 044 5 33 81 et al. L884f Dam K·SA S:H Ä^mss. Is this original?

[222] Cf. Diogenes Laertius 6.5: 'As iron is eaten away (κατεσθίεσθαι) by rust (ἰοῦ), so...the envious are consumed by their own passion'.

[223] Cf. LXX Exod 12.8; Acts Phil. 99 ed. Bonnet, 38; Artemidorus, Onir. 1.70.

[224] LXX Gen 40.19; Lev 26.29; 4 Βασ 9.36; Isa 49.26; Bar 2.3; cf. Sib. Or. 5.224.

[225] ὡς: Jas: 5×. πῦρ: Jas: 3×.

[226] Isa 9.17; 30.27; Jer 4.4; 21.12; Amos 5.6; Mal 3.2; Ecclus 48.1. All but the last are texts of judgment.

[227] So most commentators. Cf. Peter Damian, Ep. 24.2 ed. Reindel, 227-28; Trapp, 702; et al. Manton, 406, thinking instead of the destruction of Jerusalem (see n. 182), observes that 'many thousands perished by fire'.

[228] Homer, Il. 23.182; Ps 21.10 (LXX: καταφάγεται αὐτοὺς πῦρ); Isa 30.27 (LXX: ὡς πῦρ ἔδεται); Amos 5.6; Ezek 15.7; 1QH 11(3).29 (כאש אובלה); 16(8).30; Rev 11.5; 20.9; Sib. Or. 7.157; etc.

[229] Cf. Sib. Or. 4.179-90; T. Benj. 10.8; 4 Ezra 7.32; Jn 5.28-29; Acts 24.15.

[230] Cf. Mt 5.28-29; 10.18; Mk 9.43-48.

[231] For eschatological fire see Ezek 38.22; Mal 4.1; Jub. 9.15; 1 En. 10.6; 54.1-2, 6; 90.24-25; 91.9; 100.9; 102.1; Pss. Sol. 15.4-5; 1QS 28, 15; 1QpHab 10.5, 13; Ecclus 21.9; Sib. Or. 2.303-305; 3.53-54, 672-74; 4 Macc 9.9; Jos. Asen. 12.11; Mt 3.10, 12 = Lk 3.9, 17; 2 Pet 3.10; Rev 3.18; 20.10; Josephus, Ant. 1.20; T. Zeb. 10.3; T. Jud. 25.3; 4 Ezra 7.36-38; 2 Bar. 44.15; T. Abr. RecLng. 13.12-13; Apoc. Elijah 5.22-24, 37; b. Ḥag. 15b; etc.

Ropes, 287, takes ὡς πῦρ with what follows: 'Since you have stored up fire...'[232] In favor of this, he insists that ἐθησαυρίσατε demands an object and notes that θησαυρίζει πῦρ occurs in LXX Prov 16.27.[233] But ἐθησαυρίσατε does not need an object.[234]

ἐθησαυρίσατε ἐν ἐσχάταις ἡμέραις.[235] This is blunt irony. The treasure the rich have stored has been gathered on the earth (cf. Mt 6.19), and it will avail nothing at the end.[236] So it is not in truth treasure. θησαυρίζω (Jas: 1×) derives from the saying in Mt 6.19-20 = Lk 12.21; see above.

'In the latter days'[237] is a Semitism, the Greek equivalent of בְּאַחֲרִית הַיָּמִים, also often translated into Greek as ἐπ' ἐσχάτων (τῶν) ἡμερῶν.[238] Here the expression may be a roundabout way of speaking of the last judgment, which will occur in the end times. The NRSV translates: 'You have laid up treasure for the last days'. But might we then rather expect ἐν τῇ ἐσχάτῃ ἡμέρᾳ (cf. Jn 6.44; 12.48) or εἰς τὴν ἐσχάτην ἡμέραν (cf. LXX Jer 12.3)? ἐν + the plural can also be interpreted in the light of 5.8: as the end is near, these must be 'the latter days' (an early Christian commonplace). That is, the rich foolishly store up treasure even though they live in the end times. The REB translates: 'you have piled up wealth in an age that is near its close'. Of what use will riches be in the approaching age to come?[239]

According to Clement of Alexandria, some early Christians understood treasuring up treasure on earth to refer to procreation.[240] James'

---

[232] Cf. Ps.-Oecumenius *ad loc.* PG 119.504A (ὁ πλοῦτος ὑμῶν, ὃν ὡς πῦρ ἐθησαυρίσατε, καταφάγεται τὰς σάρκας ὑμῶν); Ephraem Chersonensis, *Mir. Clem.* 18 PG 2.645B (ὡς τὸ αἰώνιον καὶ ἀτελεύτητον πῦρ ἑαυτοῖς θησαυρίζομεν).

[233] Cf. also perhaps LXX Mic 6.10.

[234] See LXX Ps 38.7; Lk 12.21; 1 Cor 16.2; 2 Cor 12.14; Justin, *1 Apol.* 15.11.

[235] PsOec L:V^mss add ὀργήν, and 629 has: ὑμῖν ὀργήν. These readings show the influence of Rom 2.5.

[236] Cf. LXX Prov 1.18 ('store up evil for themselves'); Philo, *Leg.* 3.105-106; Rom 2.5 ('storing up wrath for yourself on the day of wrath'). Contrast the positive use of 'treasure' in Tob 4.8-9 ('a good treasure you will be storing up for yourself against the day of necessity'); Ecclus 29.10-13; 1 En. 38.2; Pss. Sol. 9.5; Philo, *Praem.* 104; Mt 6.19-20; Mk 10.21; Col 2.3; 4 Ezra 6.5; 7.77; 8.33; 2 Bar. 14.12; 24.1; 2 En. 50.5; m. Pe'ah 1.1; t. Pe'ah 4.18; b. B. Bat. 11a; etc. For Rendall, *Christianity*, 85, Rom 2.5 shows a knowledge of Jas 5.3.

[237] ἔσχατος: Jas: 1×; ἡμέρα: Jas: 2×; cf. 5.5.

[238] Cf. Isa 2.2; Dan 11.20; T. Zeb. 9.5; T. Jud. 18.1; T. Dan 5.4; T. Jos. 19.10; Acts 2.17; 2 Tim 3.1; Did. 16.3; Barn. 4.9; 4 Ezra 7.84, 95; 10.59; 12.28; 13.20; 14.22; y. Sanh. 10b (28.3).

[239] Cf. Bengel, 505: 'you have collected it too late'. A few, such as Carr, 60, have emptied the expression of eschatological content, and some earlier commentators thought it might refer to old age; so e.g. Gill, 799. Although Calvin, 306, did not go along, he noted the possibility of taking the meaning to be: 'the rich, as if they would live for ever, are never content, but always struggle to lay things up sufficient to last to the end of time'. Others have observed that James' words assume a near *parousia* and then sought to explain why that is not a theological problem; cf. Plummer, 623.

[240] Clement of Alexandria, *Strom.* 3.12.86 GCS 52 ed. Stählin and Früchtel, 235-36.

application shows his tradition to have construed the saying of Jesus in its more natural, literal sense.[241]

Moffatt, 67, is probably right to affirm that, because of James' eschatological orientation, 'there was no call to demand social justice for the victims; the whole order of things was to be swept away immediately, and the thought of any reform and redress on earth never entered the mind of James'.

Verse 4. Just like the rust that eats their treasure, so too the pay withheld from workers will witness against the rich, who have failed to love their neighbors; cf. 2.8. Calvin, 306, observes: cruelty 'is the inseparable companion of avarice'.

ἰδού. See on 3.4. The particle is common in oracles of prophetic judgment.[242] Johnson, 301, comments: 'Just as the rich were to contemplate the miseries coming on them, now they are to gaze on the cause of those miseries'.[243]

ὁ μισθὸς τῶν ἐργατῶν τῶν ἀμησάντων τὰς χώρας ὑμῶν ὁ ἀπεστερημένος ἀφ' ὑμῶν κράζει.[244] Cf. Herm. Mand. 3.9.6: 'Beware, therefore, you who exult in your wealth, lest those in need groan, and their groaning rise up to the Lord'. The combination of μισθός[245] and ἐργάτης[246] is rare in Greek literature and seems to be the equivalent of פעלה + שכיר.[247] The expression recalls the saying attributed to Jesus in Lk 10.7 (ἄξιος γὰρ ὁ ἐργάτης τοῦ μισθοῦ αὐτοῦ[248]) and the parable of the workers in Mt 20.1-16 (v. 8: τοὺς ἐργάτας…ἀπόδος αὐτοῖς τὸν μισθόν). But we do not have here an allusion to the Jesus tradition. James harks back rather to the legislation in Lev 19.13 ('You shall not defraud your neighbour; you shall not steal; and you shall not keep for yourself the wages of a laborer [LXX: ὁ μισθὸς τοῦ μισθωτοῦ] until morning') and Deut 24.14-15 ('You shall not withhold the wages [μισθόν] of poor and needy laborers, whether other Israelites or aliens who reside in your land in one of your towns. You will pay them their wages [τὸν μισθόν] daily before sunset, because they are poor and their livelihood depends on them; otherwise they might cry to the Lord against you, and you would incur guilt').[249] As in 4.11-12, those denounced break the Torah.

---

[241] Cf. Justin, *1 Apol.* 15.12.

[242] LXX Isa 10.33; 13.9; Jer 4.13; Mal 4.1; Sib. Or. frag. 1.28; Mt 23.38 = Lk 13.35; etc.

[243] Jebb, *Literature*, 262, links ἰδού to the ἄγε of v. 1: 'Come, behold'.

[244] 01 03* have ἀφυστερημένος. Metzger, *Commentary*, 685, regards this as 'an Alexandrian refinement'. Parker, 'Text', 329, thinks the rarer word original.

[245] Jas: 1×. LXX: most often for שכר.

[246] Jas: 1×. LXX: Wis 17.17; Ecclus 19.1; 40.18; 1 Macc 3.6.

[247] As in Lev 19.13; 4Q367 2a-b 12; m. B. Meṣi'a 9.11; m. 'Abot 2.14; 6.5; y. B. Meṣi'a 9a (12.1); etc.

[248] Cf. 1 Cor 9.14-18; 1 Tim 5.8; Did. 13.1-2.

[249] Cf. Jer 22.13; Mal 3.5 (Wordsworth, 30, thinks James here depends upon Mal 3); Tob 4.14 BA (μισθὸς παντὸς ἀνθρώπου, ὃς ἐὰν ἐργάσηται, παρὰ σοὶ μὴ αὐλισθήτω);

In the LXX, ἀμάω (NT: 1×) renders קָצַר, which means 'cut short' and so, in an agricultural context, 'mow', 'cut', 'reap', 'harvest'.[250] This is the meaning in James,[251] as both the use of χώρα (Jas: 1×) = 'field' and the synonymous θερίζω in the next line show.[252] But whether our text has in mind day-laborers (cf. Mt 20.1-16) or hired-hands (cf. Jn 10.12) or slaves (cf. Ecclus 7.20) is unclear.[253]

ἀποστερέω[254] means 'unjustly withhold'; cf. LXX Exod 21.10. LXX Ecclesiasticus 34.22 (ἀποστερῶν μισθὸν μισθίου) and Mal 3.5 (ἀποστεροῦντας μισθὸν μισθωτοῦ) use it of holding back the pay of laborers. The sin of deliberate fraud sometimes appears in vice lists; cf. Mk 10.19 (μὴ ἀποστερήσῃς); Herm. *Mand.* 8.5 (ἀποστέρησις); *Sim.* 6.5.5 (ὁ ἀποστερητής); Acts Jn 36 ed. Bonnet, 169 (ὁ ἀποστερητής).

That the withheld wages cry out[255] employs a standard way of speaking, in which inanimate objects cry out for truth or justice when people do not or cannot; see Gen 4.10 ('your brother's blood is crying out to me from the ground'; cf. Heb 12.24); Job 31.38 ('if my land has cried out against me'); Hab 2.11 ('the very stones will cry out'); 1 En. 47.1 (the blood of the righteous ascends to heaven with their prayers); Lk 19.40 ('if these were silent, the very stones would cry out').[256] Many commentators have thought of Gen 3.10 in particular.[257] J. Byron even urges that lore about Cain and Abel lies beneath the whole of Jas 5.1-6.[258] Abel was known as 'righteous',[259] and Jas 5.6 speaks enigmatically of τὸν δίκαιον being killed (ἐφονεύσατε), so Byron suggests that the latter refers 'to Abel as the archetype of all righteous individuals'. Congruent with this, some came to think of Cain as greedy for economic gain;[260] and (although Byron does not note the point) it intrigues that Irenaeus, in what might be the earliest allusion to our verse, wrote of those who 'had in themselves

---

Ecclus 34.25-26; Philo, *Spec.* 4.195-96; T. Job 12.4; Ps.-Phoc. 19; Josephus, *Ant.* 20.220; b. B. Meṣi'a 111a. See further K. Berger, *Die Gesetzesauslegung Jesu: Ihr historischer Hintergrund im Judentum und im Alten Testament. Teil I*, Neukirchen, 1972, 382-84.

[250] Lev 25.11; Deut 24.19; Isa 17.5; 37.30; Mic 6.15.
[251] Cf. Philo, *Somn.* 2.77; Josephus, *Ant.* 4.231.
[252] See further Mayor, 157, who shows that ἀμησάντων = θερισάντων.
[253] On small farmers vs. large land owners see Maynard-Reid, *Poverty*, 83-93.
[254] Jas: 1×; NT: 6×; cf. Mk 10.19; 1 Cor 6.7-8; 7.5; 1 Tim 6.5.
[255] κράζω: Jas: 1×.
[256] Cf. also those texts in which the oppressed cry out to God: Gen 18.20-21; 19.12; Exod 2.23; 1 Sam 9.16; 1 En. 22.5-7; 3 Macc 5.7-9; Jdt 7.29; etc.
[257] Cf. Grotius, 1090; Wolzogen, 216; Quistorp, 401; Guyse, 594; Gill, 800; Ropes, 289; Dibelius, 238; Reicke, 51; Songer, 132; Martin, 179; Wheeler, *Wealth*, 99. Cf. already Didymus of Alexandria, *Ps.* 9.12-13 PTS 15 ed. Mühlenberg, 152: ὡς τοῦ Ἄβελ τὸ αἷμα βοᾷ πρὸς τὸν θεὸν καί ὁ μισθὸς ὁ ἀποστερηθεὶς τῶν ἐργατῶν. Ἰδοὺ γὰρ φησίν ὁ μισθὸς τῶν ἀμησάντων τὰς χώρας ὑμῶν κράζει. Johnson, 302, seems to be alone in judging that James instead 'clearly' recalls Exod 3.7.
[258] Byron, 'Cain'.
[259] Mt 23.34; Heb 11.4; 1 Jn 3.12; Josephus, *Ant.* 1.53; Tg. Neof. 1 Gen 4.8; Frag. Tg. Gen 4.10.
[260] E.g. Philo, *Cherub.* 52, 65; Josephus, *Ant.* 1.60-61.

jealousy like that of Cain and so slew the just one,[261] slighting the counsel of the Word, as did also Cain'.[262] One is unsure, however. The verbal overlap with Gen 4 is minimal, and Cain himself is, in that chapter, a worker in the field, not an employer.

ἀφ' ὑμῶν is conventionally taken to mean 'by you', with reference to ὁ ἀπεστερημένος: 'unjustly withheld by you'. Blomberg-Kamell, 223, however, suggest—seemingly unaware that others have done likewise—taking it with κράζει: 'the wages that were defrauded cry out from you';[263] that is, 'if the wages were not paid, they remain in the pockets, as it were, of the landowners and can be viewed as crying out from that location; after all, they don't belong there but in the possession of the workers'.[264]

καὶ αἱ βοαὶ τῶν θερισάντων εἰς τὰ ὦτα κυρίου σαβαὼθ εἰσεληλύθασιν.[265] A second cry. This one borrows the language of LXX Isa 5.7-9, a 'woe-oracle': 'I waited for him (Judah) to produce justice, but he produced lawlessness—nor did he produce righteousness but a cry...so that they may take something from their neighbor... For these things were heard in the ears of the Lord Sabaoth (ἠκούσθη γὰρ εἰς τὰ ὦτα κυρίου σαβαώθ)'.[266] βοή[267] + θερίζω (= 'harvest'),[268] however, seems to be James' novel construction. Perhaps LXX Exod 2.23-24 suggested the noun: 'the sons of Israel groaned from their labors (ἔργων) and cried out (ἀνεβόησαν), and their cry (βοή) rose up to God from their labors (ἔργων). And God listened to their groaning.'[269]

'The ears of the Lord' occurs several times in the Tanak.[270] James seemingly had no problem with this anthropomorphism, reproducing it as it stands in Isaiah. Did he have an anthropomorphic conception of the deity? Or did he understand the phrase in a figurative fashion? Later interpreters often note that God does not have ears, that this is just a way of speaking.[271] Note, for example, the theological clarification of Benson, 102: 'God is, in reality, an infinite spirit, and has no body, nor any bodily parts; he is omnipresent, and has a power of perceiving, or of knowing, perfectly, whatever happens throughout the whole universe'.

The LXX transliterates צבאות (= 'hosts', 'armies') with σαβαώθ over sixty times—the vast majority in Isaiah—in the phrase, κύριος σαβαώθ

---

[261] The Latin is: *occiderunt iustum*; cf. the Vulgate for Jas 5.6: *occidistis iustum*.
[262] Irenaeus, *Haer.* 4.18.3.
[263] Cf. LXX Gen 4.10 and Exod 2.23.
[264] Cf. Huther, 148; Alford, 322; Carr, 61.
[265] For discussion of the variant, εἰσελήλυθαν (so 03 025 81 *et al.*), see Parker, 'Text', 327-28.
[266] The MT is very different at the end: 'The Lord of hosts has sworn in my hearing'.
[267] LXX: 18×. NT: 1×; cf. βοάω.
[268] Jas: 1×. Cf. LXX Lev 23.10, 22; Mt 6.26; Jn 4.36 (with μισθός).
[269] Cf. 1 En. 9.10 ('those who have died will bring their suit up to the gate of heaven. Their groaning has ascended, but they could not get out from before the face of the oppression that is being wrought on the earth'); Herm. *Vis.* 3.9.6 ('Beware you who exult in your wealth, lest those in need groan, and their groaning rise up to the Lord').
[270] E.g. Num 14.28; 1 Sam 8.21; 1 Chr 28.8; Pss 18.6; 34.15; Isa 37.29; cf. Pss. Sol. 18.3; 3 Bar 1.5 (εἰσῆθεν εἰς τὰ ὦτα κυρίου τοῦ θεοῦ).
[271] So e.g. Hilary of Arles *ad loc.* PLSup 3.80.

(= יהוה צבאות).²⁷² Although early Christian literature, like the Pseudepigrapha,²⁷³ generally shies away from σαβαώθ, it eventually became popular among Christians and in magical texts.²⁷⁴ Its only other early Christian occurrences are in Rom 9.29, a citation of LXX Isa 1.9, and 1 Clem. 34.6, a quotation of LXX Isa 6.3. In James, where the word adds solemnity and perhaps emphasizes God's power,²⁷⁵ no explanation is needed. The text takes for granted an audience that knows the term from Scripture.

Although Isa 5 lies behind the parable of the vineyard in Mk 12.1-11 par., the chapter as a whole, unlike Isa 6, does not seem to have been a prime source of *testimonia* in the early churches. Moreover, Isa 5.7-9 does not appear to be quoted elsewhere. Nor does it play much of a role in pre-Christian Jewish literature.²⁷⁶ James' use of it is probably a sign that he was well acquainted with LXX Isaiah.

One can construe the perfect tense, εἰσεληλύθασιν, as either prophetic—at the last judgment the withheld pay will testify—or as a statement of current circumstance, because the injustice has already been done. In a case such as this, however, both readings suggest themselves at once.

Verse 5. 'St. James' words here are of a highly tragical character, and therefore the sentences are brief, abrupt, concise, and broken; the graphic metaphor reminds us in style of the outpourings of Hosea.'²⁷⁷

ἐτρυφήσατε ἐπὶ τῆς γῆς καὶ ἐσπαταλήσατε.²⁷⁸ τρυφάω²⁷⁹ here means 'live for' or 'indulge in pleasure', 'carouse'.²⁸⁰ It thus sends one back to

---

[272] 1 Sam 1.3; Zech 13.2; etc.; cf. 1QpHab 10.7; 4Q358 2.8; 3.3. See further T.N.D. Mettinger, 'Yahweh Zebaoth', in *DDD*, 920-24, and the literature cited there.

[273] With the exception of Sib. Or. 1.304, 316. Philo and Josephus also avoid the expression.

[274] Cf. T. Sol. 1.6, 7; 5.9; PGM 2.15; 3.76; etc. For צבאות and variants on magical amulets and bowls see J. Naveh and S. Shaked, *Amulets and Magic Bowls*, Jerusalem, 1985, 40, 56, 94, 96, 102, 164, 180.

[275] Calvin, 307: 'he calls God the Lord of Sabaoth, to indicate His power and might, and make His judgment more to be dreaded'. Bede *ad loc*. CCSL 121 ed. Hurst, 218, offers: 'He calls him the Lord of sabaoth...to terrify those who think the poor have no protector'. Penner, *Eschatology*, 175, notes that, in Isaiah, 'Lord of Hosts' occurs 'almost always in the context of imminent judgment upon the wicked'.

[276] 4QBenediction does, however, rework the prophecy of Isa 5.1-7.

[277] So Bassett, 69. Cf. Gundry, 943: 'The staccato-like effect of these short, unconnected statements sharpens the charges contained in them'. Note also the repetition of sounds: ησ/ς occurs five times, five words end in ς, and σ/ψατε concludes three words.

[278] 02 044 81 *et al*. L884 L1440 K:B^pt omit καί. Jebb, *Literature*, 267, urged its secondary character on the ground that James here sought an increased effect through asyndeton, like that generated by the omission of ו in parts of the old victory song in Judg 5.

[279] NT: 1×. LXX: Neh 9.25; Ecclus 14.4; Isa 66.11. Gk. Pseudepigrapha (Denis): T. Jos. 9.2. Philo: 17×. Josephus: 3×. Hermas: 14×.

[280] Cf. Plato, *Euthy*. 12a; T. Jos. 9.2; Philo, *Migr*. 204; Josephus, *Ant*. 4.167; Herm. *Sim*. 6.1.6 (with σπαταλῶντα; Mayor, 159, thinks Hermas here 'no doubt' dependent

the ἡδονῶν of 4.1.[281] James would presumably have concurred with the author of T. Iss. 4.2: 'ὁ ἁπλοῦς (cf. Jas 1.5) does not desire (ἐπιθυμεῖ; cf. Jas 1.14-15; 4.2) gold (χρυσίον; cf. Jas 5.3), does not defraud his neighbor, does not long for fancy foods, nor want fine clothes'. Cf. also Sifre Deut 318 on 32.15: abundance of food and drink and 'ease of life' (שׁלוה) lead to rebellion against God. That ἐπὶ τῆς γῆς (cf. 5.17) is strictly unnecessary[282] is consistent with its derivation from the saying in Mt 6.19-21 = Lk 13.33-34. The phrase adds no information—where else could the activities envisaged take place?—but perhaps supplies a rhetorical foil for the forthcoming ἐν ἡμέρᾳ σφαγῆς and helps informed Christian readers catch an allusion to Jesus' logion, where 'on the earth' contrasts with 'in heaven'. Or is there an implicit contrast with 'Lord Sabaoth', which might have moved ancients to think of the night sky and its 'heavenly hosts' (= the stars)? Or does the phrase mean 'on the land (of Israel)' and so go with the allusion to the agricultural legislation from the Pentateuch?

σπαταλάω,[283] rare in pre-Christian sources, is a synonym of τρυφάω,[284] invariably with negative sense; so it means something like 'indulge in wanton or excessive comfort'.[285] Johnson, 303, speaks in this connection of 'conspicuous consumption'.

ἐθρέψατε τὰς καρδίας ὑμῶν ἐν ἡμέρᾳ σφαγῆς. Cf. 1 En. 98.3: the rich will perish in dishonor, 'in slaughter (Gk: σφαγήν) and great misery'.[286] Perhaps the words look back over the entirety of vv. 2-5: by hoarding up

upon James); Dio Chrysostom 9.9. Cf. also the use of τρυφή in Lk 7.25; 2 Pet 2.13. For Josephus, τρυφή can be part of the excesses of corrupt royalty: *Ant.* 6.34; cf. Strabo 17.1.11; Plutarch, *Comp. Dem. Ant.* 3. On royal associations see further G. Husson, 'Le paradis de délices (Genèse 3, 23-24)', *REG* 101 (1988), 64-73.

[281] τρυφή and ἡδονή were often linked: Ps.-Plato, *Ep.* 7 327A; Josephus, *Ant.* 5.32; 11.27; Libanius, *Or.* 42.40; etc.

[282] Commentators often compare the 'in your lifetime' of Lk 16.25; cf. n. 285.

[283] NT: 2×; cf. 1 Tim 5.6. LXX: Ecclus 21.15; Ezek 16.49. The latter condemns those who prosper and indulge in excess; their sins include boasting and neglecting the poor and needy. Gk. Pseudepigrapha (Denis): 0×. Philo: 0×. Josephus: 0×. Hermas: 2×.

[284] The two verbs appear in synonymous parallelism in Herm. *Sim.* 6.1.6; 6.2.6.

[285] Cf. Ps.-Diogenes, *Ep.* 28.7; 1 Tim 5.6; Herm. *Sim.* 6.2.6 (τὰ σπαταλῶντα καὶ τρυφῶντα); Barn. 10.3 (an analogy with pigs). See further Hort, 107-109. Although James shows no knowledge of the parable of the rich man and Lazarus, readers of 5.1-6 have incessantly referred to Lk 16.19-31; cf. Bede *ad loc.* CCSL 121 ed. Hurst, 217; Peter Damian, *Ep.* 24.2 ed. Reindel, 227-28; Martin of Legio *ad loc.* PL 209.206; Aretius, 484; Guyse, 594; Trapp, 703; Carr, 62; Carson, 'James', 1010; *et al.* They have also sometimes recalled Lk 6.25, some version of which James knew; cf. Ps.-Maximus the Confessor, *Loc. comm.* 27 PG 91.871C.

[286] Does Minucius Felix, *Oct.* 37 CSEL 2 ed. Halm, 52-53 (the rich 'are fattened as victims for punishment, as sacrifices they are crowned for the slaughter') depend upon James? Or do we have here a rhetorical tradition? Cf. Dio Chrysostom 8.13-14: 'Or do you think those potbellies are good for anything? Creatures whom sensible people ought to...kill, quarter, and use as food just as people do with the flesh of large fish... I think these men have less souls than hogs.'

wealth (vv. 2-3), withholding pay (v. 4), and living extravagantly (v. 5), the rich have—unconsciously, like beasts—fatted their hearts for the day of slaughter and 'divine execution'.[287]

James seemingly borrows the language of LXX Jer 12.3: ἅγνισον αὐτοὺς εἰς ἡμέραν σφαγῆς (MT: לְיוֹם הֲרֵגָה) αὐτῶν. He has substituted 'fatten your hearts' for 'purify them', probably in part because he wants to reserve the language of purity for positive statements; cf. 4.8, with ἁγνίζω. His ἐν, which might reflect the common eschatological use of ἐν (τῇ) ἡμέρᾳ,[288] could mean 'at'.[289] Perhaps it renders Jeremiah's לְ;[290] the Hebrew preposition can mean 'at' as well as 'for' or 'in'. Jeremiah 12.3 has also influenced 1 En. 16.1 (Gk: ἀπὸ ἡμέρας σφαγῆς καὶ ἀπωλείας)[291] and 1QH 7(15).20 (לְיוֹם הֲרֵגָה).[292] The verse does not seem reflected in any other early Christian texts. Yet readers might nonetheless think of Jeremiah because that book recurrently uses σφαγή[293] and because it calls the Hinnom Valley 'the Valley of Slaughter': 7.32; 19.6.

Despite the absence of the definite article before ἡμέρᾳ, the text is not about 'a day of slaughter' but 'the day of slaughter';[294] that is, James is writing about the eschatological assize.[295] Contrast the interpretation of Calvin, 307: 'it was the practice on days of ritual sacrifice to feast more freely than daily use. So he says, the rich spend all their lives as one long celebration, plunged in an unending run of revelry.'[296]

The final judgment was sometimes associated with a scene of slaughter and carnage.[297] Here the *topos* conveys irony: unwittingly, people are fattening themselves for their own slaughter.

τρέφω (Jas: 1×) means, in this context, something like 'fatten' or 'stuff', for with σφαγή (NT: 3×) the word brings to mind animals being

---

[287] The phrase is from R. Wall, 226.

[288] As in LXX Isa 30.26; 1 En. 10.6; 22.13; 100.4-5; T. Dan 6.4; 1 Cor 1.8; etc.

[289] Cf. Mt 22.28; Lk 14.14; 1 Cor 15.23.

[290] Yet if one is willing to entertain James' use of a Hebrew text, one needs to ask whether his Greek is a literal translation of MT Isa 30.25: בְּיוֹם הֶרֶג.

[291] Syncellus: ἀπὸ ἡμέρας καιροῦ σφαγῆς καὶ ἀπωλείας. Note also perhaps 1 En. 94.8-9.

[292] Cf. Symmachus' translation of Isa 30.25: ἐν ἡμέρᾳ σφαγῆς.

[293] LXX: 12.1; 15.3; 19.6; 27.27; 28.40; 31.15; 32.34. This last has: αἱ ἡμέραι ὑμῶν εἰς σφαγήν. NT: 3×; cf. Acts 8.32; Rom 8.36—both OT quotations. Gk. Pseudepigrapha (Denis): 6×. Philo: 11×. Josephus: 47×.

[294] Cf. 'the day of the Lord' and 'the day of wrath', which occur in several canonical prophecies against the rich: Prov 11.4; Isa 10.1-4; Ezek 7.10-11; Zeph 1.18; etc.

[295] Cf. v. 3 and Gk. 1 En. 100.4 (ἐν ἡμέρᾳ κρίσεως); Mt 10.15; 11.22, 24; 12.36 (ἐν ἡμέρᾳ κρίσεως); Rom 2.5 (ἐν ἡμέρᾳ ὀργῆς); 1 Pet 2.12 (ἐν ἡμέρᾳ ἐπισκοπῆς).

[296] This was once a popular reading; cf. Diodati, *ad loc.*; Manton, 414; Bengel, 506; Gill, 800; *et al.*

[297] Isa 34.2-7 (nations are like animals fattened for sacrifice and slaughter, σφάγη); 65.12; Ezek 39.17-20; Zech 9.15; 11.4; Sib. Or. 5.375-400; Rev 19.17-21. Note also 1 En. 90.1-5, although this is not about the latter days but the continued oppression of Israel. See further S. Grill, 'Der Schlachttag Jahwes', *BZ* 2 (1958), 278-83.

prepared for slaughter.[298] In James, however, it is people, or rather their hearts, that are prepared for slaughter.[299]

καρδία (see on 3.14), which is a bit odd as the object of τρέφω,[300] is another word from the saying in Mt 6.19-21 = 13.33-34. The heart delights in pleasure and so desires it.[301]

The preceding exegesis offers an eschatological reading of ἐθρέψατε... ἐν ἡμέρᾳ σφαγῆς. But some rather think of the rich, as they indulge themselves, slaughtering the poor. The meaning then becomes, in the words of Dibelius, 239, 'You can live riotously while it goes badly for the pious'. Stulac, 165, sides with Dibelius and paraphrases: 'you have fattened yourselves—even in a day when you are slaughtering others'. In this way v. 5 leads directly to v. 6.[302]

Verse 6. This is the climax of the sins enumerated in the previous verses, and indeed of those enumerated through the entire epistle.

κατεδικάσατε. The verb basically means 'condemn' or 'pass sentence against'.[303] In James, the verb probably carries its full legal sense, so that the rich are in charge of the courtroom, if not officially then at least through their influence; cf. perhaps 2.1-7.[304]

In Lk 6.37, the sin of condemning others (μὴ καταδικάζετε) is closely linked with the sin of judging others, which Jas 4.11-12 has just highlighted. But even more relevant is Wis 2.10-20, where those who revel and enjoy the good things oppress the gentle and forbearing 'just one' (τὸν δίκαιον) and condemn (καταδικάσωμεν) him to death. As already observed above, we have some reason for supposing that at this point Wisdom influenced James.

ἐφονεύσατε τὸν δίκαιον. This seems to be traditional Christian language; cf. Acts 7.52 (τοῦ δικαίου, οὗ νῦν ὑμεῖς...φονεῖς ἐγένεσθε); Justin, *Dial.* 136.2 ('the enormity of your evil is that you hate the just

---

[298] Cf. Acts 8.32 ('like a sheep he was led to the slaughter', from Isa 53.7); Rom 8.36 ('we are accounted as sheep to be slaughtered', from Ps 44.22).

[299] Cf. MT Ps 119.70 ('their hearts are fat and gross'); Jer 46.21; Ezek 21.15; Philo, *Flac.* 178 ('my food and drink are given to me as to animals to keep them for the slaughter [θρέμμασιν ἐπὶ σφαγήν]'). Rendall, *Christianity*, 30 n. 1, suggests that the point is not 'gorging your appetite' but 'nursing your souls', that is, 'taking delight in and gloating over sanguinary reprisals'.

[300] This explains the substitution of σάρκας for καρδίας in 044 181 218 436 *et al.* L590 **L**:V^mss **S**:P **G**:A1G-D; cf. Theod. Dan. 4.12.

[301] Cf. Exod 4.14; 1 Kgs 8.66; Ps 104.15; Prov 27.9; Ecclus 50.23; etc. See E. Lerle, 'Καρδία als Bezeichnung für den Mageneingang', *ZNW* 76 (1985), 292-93, for the suggestion (based primarily upon Galen) that καρδία here means 'stomach'.

[302] Cf. Frankemölle, 656-57, who links the end of v. 5 with v. 6: the day of slaughter is the day of the murder of the righteous one.

[303] Cf. Ps 108.7; Job 34.29; Wis 11.10; Mt 12.7 (κατεδικάσατε τοὺς ἀναιτίους); T. Abr. RecLng. 14.1. Jas: 1×; NT: 4×. LXX: 10× (4× in Wisdom). Gk. Pseudepigrapha (Denis): 3×. Philo: 9×. Josephus: 13×.

[304] So Henry, *ad loc.*; Mitton, 182; *et al.*

one, whom you slew': μισεῖν τὸν δίκαιον, ὃν ἐφονεύσατε—of the Jews and Jesus);[305] Hippolytus, *Ben. Is. et Jac.* 26 ed. Brière, Mariès, and Mercier, 104 (φονεύειν πάντας τοὺς δικαίους); Apost. Const. 2.21.7 ed. Funk, 81 (δίκαιος...φονευθείς—of the just in general). The crime not only breaks the decalogue (see on 2.11) but has as its object a victim who is 'just'[306] and so innocent.[307]

Commentators have variously identified this victim of murder.[308] (i) Although only a minority think this today, many before the Reformation thought of Jesus.[309] Their view explains the transition from the plural (v. 5) to the singular (v. 6) and can appeal to Jesus being 'righteous' or 'just' in several early Christian texts[310] and likewise to tradition that he did not resist arrest or fight his fate.[311] Yet nothing in the context alludes to Jesus, and the letter is addressed to people in the diaspora, not Jerusalem (1.1).[312] Moreover, the present tense, ἀντιτάσσεται, might be unexpected if Jesus is in view. (ii) Although Ps.-Oecumenius 6 PG119.504B-C, finds a reference to Jesus, he also offers that James had his own execution in mind 'prophetically' (προφητικῶς).[313] A few modern scholars, including Frankemölle, 663-65, think of a sort of *vaticinia ex eventu*: the pseudepigraphon betrays knowledge of the martyrdom of James, who was known as 'the just'.[314] This accounts for the singular and further has in its favor the regular appearance of 'the

---

[305] So PTS 47 ed. Marcovich, 305; but the original text is uncertain.
[306] δίκαιος: Jas: 2×; cf. 5.16 and recall the Hebrew צדק.
[307] Cf. Isa 57.1; 1 En. 95.7.
[308] φονεύω: Jas: 3-4×; cf. 2.11; 4.2. In the LXX the verb most often translates רצח.
[309] Cf. Bede *ad loc.* CCSL 121 ed. Hurst, 218; Ps.-Oecumenius *ad loc.* PG 119.504B; Dionysius bar Salībī *ad loc.* CSCO 53, 60 Scriptores Syri 101 ed. Sedlacek, 131; Cassiodorus, *Ep. Jac.* 9 PL 70.1380A; Martin of Legio *ad loc.* PL 209.209C; Hilary of Arles *ad loc.* PLSup 3.80. But not all; note e.g. Isho'dad of Merv *ad loc.* HSem 10 ed. Gibson, 51 ('the just' = all who possess goods justly). Post-Reformation exegetes who see a reference to Jesus include Grotius, 1090; Guyse, 594; Manton, 416-17 (observing that some 'understand it of John the Baptist', an opinion I have not otherwise come across); McKnight, 600-601; Doddridge, 847; Gilpin, 598; Bassett, 70; T. Scott, 586; Wordsworth, 30; R. Scott, 144; Johnstone, 361-62; Mayor, 153-54; Smith, 286-88; Weidner, 72; H.L. Goudge, *The Moral Perfection of Our Lord Jesus Christ*, London, 1914, 12-13; Feuillet, 'Parousie', 275-76; R.N. Longenecker, *The Christology of Early Jewish Christianity*, London, 1970, 47; Grünzweig, 154; Scaer, 122-23; Riesner, 1261; Witherington, 529-30; Ringe, 374.
[310] Mt 27.19; Lk 23.47; Acts 3.14; 7.52 (see above); 22.14; 1 Pet 3.18; 1 Jn 2.1; Barn. 6.7. Additional texts in Laws, 205-206, who observes that some early Christians understood 'the just one' of Wis 2.12 to be Jesus Christ. For 'the righteous one' as the title of an eschatological figure other than Jesus see 1 En. 38.2; 53.6.
[311] Cf. Mt 26.51-54; Mk 14.43-50; Lk 23.6-12; Jn 18.10-12 etc.
[312] Cf. Jacobi, 208. Lange, 131, responds to this objection by observing that Jesus was killed during Passover, when many from the diaspora were present.
[313] Cf. Theophylact *ad loc.* PG 125.1184B-C. So too Bengel, 506 (*divinitus praesignificetur*) and Knowling, 125 ('anticipate in prophetic spirit').
[314] Cf. Martin, 182; Fougeras, 'Sortie', 14; Felder, 1800; Nienhuis, *Paul*, 150-52.

just' in accounts of James' martyrdom.[315] Beyond that, Jas 5.6 has sometimes been thought to echo Wis 2,[316] and that text may inform the account of James' martyrdom in Hegesippus.[317]

(iii) If James was written as late as or after the Bar Kokba war, during which some Christians were reportedly killed,[318] one could think of that crisis in particular. (iv) It is possible that we have here a reference to a particular individual or event that history has otherwise forgotten.[319]

(v) The singular noun is collective, referring to a class of individuals,[320] and the verb refers to the mistreatment, not literal murder, of one or several people; that is, the rich deprive others of their livelihood.[321] Or, alternatively, if one is living at the margin, not being paid may lead to starvation.[322] Ecclesiasticus 34.25-26 has this: 'The bread of the needy is the life of the poor; whoever deprives them of it is a murderer. To take away a neighbor's living is to commit murder; to deprive an employee of wages is to shed blood'; cf. 4.1. Sifre 279 on Deut 24.15 says the same thing: 'He who withholds the laborer's wages is considered by Scripture as if he had taken his life'.

(vi) As with (v), the reference is to a class of individuals, 'the righteous', but the expression is not purely figurative: some have been literally martyred, or at least died from being thrown into prison or executed by order of a court.[323] In favor of this, there were, by James' day, Christian stories of martyrdom (e.g. Jesus, Stephen, and James), and one can compare 1 En. 99–15 ('slaying your neighbors', in a list of economic injustices) and 103.15 ('those who devour us, scatter us, murder us', in a list of sins of the wealthy).[324] Some who take this view include Jesus as part of the larger class.[325] (vii) Whichever option one selects, one might detect an allusion to Abel, who was murdered by Cain.[326]

---

[315] E.g. 1 Apoc. Jas. 32–33, 43; 2 Apoc. Jas. 61.

[316] Verse 10: καταδυναστεύσωμεν πένητα δίκαιον; v. 20: θανάτῳ ἀσχήμονι καταδικάσωμεν.

[317] Hegesippus *apud* Eusebius, *H.E.* 2.23.15. Hegesippus cites Isa 3.10, but Nienhuis, *Paul*, 135, 150-52, argues that Wis 2.12 is the more relevant text. Even if that is not so, Wis 2.12 is itself a rewrite of Isa 3.10.

[318] See Justin, *1 Apol.* 31.6.

[319] Carr, 63, regards this view as 'the preferable interpretation'.

[320] Cf. LXX Ps 36.12, 32 (κατονεῖ ὁ ἁμαρτωλὸς τὸ δίκαιον καὶ ζητεῖ τοῦ θανατῶσαι αὐτόν); Prov 1.11; Isa 3.10; 57.1; Amos 5.12; Wis 2.12; 1QH 7(15).18; Pss. Sol. 3.4; etc.

[321] Cf. Calvin, 309; von Soden, 182; R. Wall, 232; Tsuji, *Glaube*, 144.

[322] So Countryman, 719.

[323] E.g. Wesley, 868; Huther, 150; Plummer, 625; Gaugusch, 95; Gundry, 943. For the high correlation between death and ancient imprisonment see B. Rapske, *The Book of Acts and Paul in Roman Custody*, Grand Rapids, MI, 1994, 220-23.

[324] Some, however, suppose that murder in these texts is indirect, through working people too hard or failing to pay them or cutting off all employment.

[325] Cf. Schlatter, 271; Ross, 90; Maier, 208.

[326] See J. Byron, 'Cain', and above, 679.

DENUNCIATIONS OF THE PROSPEROUS (4.13–5.6)

Perhaps options (v) and (vi) make most sense because the context is about the rich robbing the poor of their livelihood. Yet commentators should be open to the possibility of a double entendre or even an open-ended expression. One can imagine a Christian and a non-Jew hearing two different things in 5.6 or a Christian mulling several possibilities. A veiled allusion to James' fate remains an enticing possibility.

Even if one adopts (v) or (vi), one is not much helped with divining the *Sitz im Leben* behind our book. Prophetic invective lends itself to hyperbole and is otherwise hardly objective, and accusing one's enemies of murder was a common *topos*.[327] Also conventional was the association of the rich with violence.[328] One understands why Schnider, 115, instead of trying to read history into 5.6, regards it rather as rhetoric.

If one decides that 'the righteous one' stands for a class,[329] one can think of that class as including some of 'the lowly' of 1.9, some of 'the poor' of 2.2-6, and perhaps some of the oppressed laborers of 5.4.[330] Certainly 'the poor' can elsewhere be the meek, humiliated, and oppressed people of God,[331] and for many in James' time and place, 'poverty and piety, wealth and wickedness, had become synonymous'.[332]

οὐκ ἀντιτάσσεται ὑμῖν.[333] ἀντιτάσσω also means 'resist' or 'oppose' in 4.6.[334] Alonso-Schökel takes James' Greek as a question: Should/will he (God) not resist you?[335] He emphasizes the link with 4.6: ὁ θεὸς

---

[327] Cf. Ps 37.32; Wis 2.12-20; 1 En. 12.5; 1QH 10(2).21-22; 1QpHab. 11.4-8; T. Levi 16.2-3; T. Mos. 6.3-4; Philo, *Legat.* 120-31; Mt 23.34-35 = Lk 11.49-51; Josephus, *Bell.* 2.254-8; etc.

[328] Mic 6.12 ('you rich are full of violence'); Prov 1.19; 11.16 ('violent men get riches'); 1QS 10.19 = 4Q260 4.7 ('my soul will not crave wealth by violence').

[329] The plural, οἱ δίκαιοι, can refer to a group within Israel, such as the Hasidim or the sectarians of the Dead Sea Scrolls; see D. Hill, 'ΔΙΚΑΙΟΙ as a Quasi-Technical Term', *NTS* 11 (1965), 296-302.

[330] Cf. Amos 2.6, 7; 5.12; Wis 2.10. This is a common inference; cf. Prieto, 'Malédiction', 78; *et al.*

[331] Isa 10.2; 26.6; Pss. Sol. 5.2, 11; 10.6; 15.1; 18.2; 5 Apoc. Syr. Ps 2.18; 1QpHab 12.3; 1QM 14.7; 1QH 13(5).13-14; Mt 5.3; etc.

[332] So Panackel, 'Poor', 151. Cf. Prov 11.16; 15.27; 18.23; 21.26; 22.7, 16; 29.13; Ps 37.7; Isa 53.9; Jer 5.26-28; 6.13; Mic 6.10-12; Ecclus 13.19.

[333] Wolf, 70; Baumgarten, 212; and Ropes, 292, mention (without documentation) a conjecture of Bentley, which would result in: 'The Lord does not resist you'. This must refer to R. Bentley, 'Remarks upon a Discourse on Free-Thinking', in *The Works of Richard Bentley*, vol. 3, ed. A. Dyce, London, n.d., 358: 'if instead of ΟΥΚ some manuscripts, by the change of one letter, should represent ΟΚΞ... some persons would not be sorry, if what has hitherto appeared to all interpreters abrupt, incoherent, and forced, should with so slight a change be made pertinent and proper: the Lord resists, opposes, sets himself against you. For so St. James speaks before, iv.6... And then the connexion is apt and just in the following verse... be patient therefore, brethren, unto the coming τοῦ K͞Y'.

[334] Cf. LXX Prov 3.34; Hos 1.6; T. Job 47.11; 1 Clem. 36.6.

[335] Alonso-Schökel, 'James 5,2'. So too Pretorius, 'Verklaringsopsies', 659-63; Johnson, 305; Penner, *Eschatology*, 155-58; Hutchinson Edgar, *Poor*, 203. Schrage, 52,

ὑπερηφάνοις ἀντιτάσσεται. On this reading, most of 4.7-5.6 is commentary on the quotation of Prov 3.34 in 4.6. 4.7-10 expounds on grace being given to the humble whereas 4.13–5.6 focuses on God resisting the proud. The repetition of ἀντιτάσσεται then creates an *inclusio*, marking the end of the commentary on Proverbs. Alonso-Schökel outlines the sequence this way: 'God gives grace to the humble, therefore humble yourselves before God; God opposes the arrogant, you behave arrogantly; should not He oppose you?'

Although this is an intriguing suggestion, 4.11-12 does not fit the scheme very well, and it is not clear to this writer that either 4.7-10 or 4.13–5.6 is really commentary on Prov 3.34.[336] Moreover, one can hardly decide whether οὐκ ἀντιτάσσεται ὑμῖν is a question.[337] If it is, then God can be the subject.[338] Yet not only does the notion that the poor do not resist because they have no power make sense, but that the righteous would not resist the wicked is at home in Christian texts.[339] Perhaps, then, it is best to stay with the more conventional interpretation.[340]

Ropes, 292, objects that reference to the non-resistance of the righteous would be strangely anti-climactic.[341] On the contrary, it magnifies the guilt of the rich. As Mitton, 182, has it: 'The rich are represented, not as bold and fearless champions, defending a cause against dangerous enemies, but as brutal bullies, picking as the victim of their outrages those who either cannot or will not strike back'.[342] Perhaps, in addition, the slaughtered, through their nonresistance, display their faith in the world to come, a faith that does not inform the actions of the rich. And maybe, beyond that, they embody the patience that the next verse enjoins.[343]

---

thinks this 'cannot be excluded'. Cf. Carr, 63; Konradt, *Existenz*, 158-59. Others, such as Ropes, 292; Feuillet, 'Parousie', 276; Davids, 190; and Klein, *Werk*, 181, also take the words to constitute a question, but with 'the just one' as the subject: the righteous resist either at present by calling upon God or in the future by testifying against the rich at the final judgment. Gill, 800, thinks that God may be the subject but does not find a question: 'God does not resist you, as yet: he will do it shortly'. Cf. Guyse, 594-95.

[336] But see Obermüller, 'Themen'.

[337] 4.12 shows that James can end a section with a question mark.

[338] One could equally, if so inclined, make Jesus the subject: 'Will he not (at the last judgment) oppose you?'

[339] Cf. Wis 2.19; Isa 53.7; Mt 5.39; Acts 8.32; Rom 12.14-21; 1 Thess 5.15; 1 Pet 2.23.

[340] So too Krüger, *Kritik*, 237-38.

[341] The subjectivity of such judgments appears from the contrasting view of Moffatt: our phrase supplies 'a vivid climax: the helplessness of the victims aggravates the guilt of their oppressors'. Cf. Tasker, 116: 5.6 conveys 'majestic pathos'.

[342] Cf. Calvin, 308: 'the audacity of the rich increases, since those they crush are without any means of resistance'. For Wesley, 868, 'he does not resist you' underlines the self-assurance of the oppressors: 'And therefore you [the rich] are secure'.

[343] For Huther, 151, the point is 'the proximity of the vengeance of God, who interests Himself in the suffering just'.

XVI

THE NEAR END AND PATIENT ENDURANCE (5.7-11)[1]

(7) Be patient, then, brothers, until the coming of the Lord. Behold, the farmer waits for the valuable fruit of the earth, being patient over it, until it receives the early rain and the late rain. (8) You also be patient, establishing your hearts, for the coming of the Lord is near. (9) Do not, brothers, grumble against one another, so that you will not be judged. Behold, the judge is standing at the doors. (10) Make your own, as an example of readiness for suffering and patience, brothers, the prophets who spoke in the name of the Lord. (11) Behold, we bless those who were steadfast. You have heard of the steadfastness of Job, and you have seen the outcome that the Lord brought about, how the Lord is compassionate and merciful.

History of Interpretation and Reception

Verse 7 assumes that James' readers will live to see the latter days, and vv. 8-9 state plainly that the *parousia* is near. This has posed a problem for Christians with a particular view of Scripture.[2] For most of exegetical history, the difficulty was typically resolved by identifying 'the coming of the Lord' with the destruction of Jerusalem in CE 70.[3] John Lightfoot, in a sermon on Jas 5.9 preached in 1671, affirmed: 'As Christ's pouring down his vengeance in the destruction of that city and people, is called his "coming in his glory", and his "coming in judgment"; and as the destruction of that city and nation is charactered in Scripture, as the destruction of the whole world;—so, there are several passages, that speak of the nearness of that destruction, that are suited according to such characters'.[4] Regrettably, this view has often included horrific

---

[1] Recent literature: Baker, *Speech-Ethics*, 180-81; Bischoff, 'Τὸ τέλος'; C. Bultmann, 'Hiob'; Carr, 'Patience'; Davids, 'Tradition'; Eisenman, 'Rain'; Feuillet, 'Parousie'; Gemünden, *Vegetationsmetaphorik*, 296-99; Gordon, 'Τέλος'; Gray, 'Job'; Hainthaler, *Ausdauer*, 311-38; Herzer, 'Hiob'; Hutchinson Edgar, *Poor*, 204-209; Maier, *Reich*, 25-45; Oliphant, 'Waiting'; Preuschen, 'Jac 5,11'; Richardson, 'Job'; C. Seitz, 'Job'; Strobel, *Untersuchungen*, 254-64; Theophilus, 'Instans'.

[2] Or supplied a reason to reject a particular view of scripture; cf. M. Arnold, *Literature and Dogma*, New York, 1876, 152-53: it is 'as clear as anything can be' that passages such as Jas 5.8-9 show the Bible to contain 'mistakes in fact'.

[3] This interpretation became a reason for dating James as close as possible to James' death in 63: his words were thought to refer to what was for him the near future; so e.g. W. Cave, *Antiquitates apostolicae*, London, 1677, 195; Benson, 6.

[4] J. Lightfoot, *An Exposition of Three Articles on the Apostles' Creed: and Sermons*, ed. J.R. Pitman, London, 1822, 380. Cf. Ps.-Oecumenius 7 PG 119.504D-505B

generalizations about the Jewish people. Other apologetical strategies have included the following: (i) to stand at a door is to know what is happening within; in like manner, the omniscient God is making a record for the last day.[5] (ii) Divine time is different than human time.[6] (iii) God being at the door means death is near.[7] (iv) The nearness of the Lord's coming means 'that as far as we know, it could happen any day'.[8] (v) Closely related to this is Gundry, 943: 'In view of James' repeated call for patience, the nearness of the Lord's coming means not that he *will* come soon but that he's *ready* to come soon'.[9] (vi) Imminence is an expression of certainty.[10] (vii) 'If the final advent was near in the first century, it is still nearer now'.[11] (viii) 'James believes that the Lord is spatially near the righteous in his audience'.[12] (ix) Prophecies are contingent, so the end can be hastened or delayed by human behavior.[13] One can of course embrace several explanations at once.[14]

(appealing to Chrysostom); Theophylact *ad loc*. PG 125.1184D; Whitby, 693; Manton, 420; Calmet, 690-91; Wolf, 75; Benson, 109; Henry, *ad loc*.; 389; Rosenmüller, 389; Wesley, 868; Pyle, 325; Clarke, 825; Macknight, 601; Lange, 135; Knowling, 130; Ross, 92-93; Feuillet, 'Parousie'; McKnight, 406-407; *et al*.—often arguing that the judgment in 70 foreshadows the consummation, so that one may think of both the destruction of Jerusalem and the end of the world; cf. also Bassett, 72; Wardlaw, 298-99. Stanley, *Sermons*, 303, credits Chevalier Bunsen with the view, which he endorses, that James was written CE 42, because our text here has in mind events long before 70, specifically, calamities that fell upon Babylonian Jews in that year. I have not found this view in other writers.

[5] Bede *ad loc*. CCSL 121 ed. D. Hurst, 219. Cf. Turnbull, 300-301; Bengel, 507.

[6] So Manton, 423; Wolzogen, 218; Gill, 800; Doriani, 179-80; Winkler, 66; Wardlaw, 300; Punchard, 375; Johnstone, 373-74; Blomberg-Kamell, 228. Ps 90.4 and 2 Pet 3.8-9 are the typical proof-texts for this popular strategy.

[7] So Gill, 800; Winkler, 66; Simeon, 109. The latter remarks: 'Of the Day of Judgment there is frequent mention in the New Testament: and so strongly was the idea of it realized in the minds of the inspired writers, that they conveyed to the Church, unintentionally on their parts, an expectation of its speedy arrival' (107).

[8] So Doriani, 180. Cf. Richardson, 221; Zodhiates, *Patience*, 82-83; Moo, 224.

[9] Gundry, 943.

[10] So Winkler, 66; Kugelman, 59; Zodhiates, *Patience*, 82-83. Lange, 135, speaks of religious 'assurance'.

[11] Gibson, 77. Cf. Turnbull, 297-98; Fausset, 595. For Jacobi, 191, 'the coming of the Lord' is 'always nigh', and 'we are always living in the last days'.

[12] So Witherington, 537, who adds that James 'also believes that Christ could return at any time and so could be also temporally near'.

[13] Cf. Weidner, 73-74: 'Those who speak of an "error" on the part of Jesus and His Apostles, in teaching the nearness of the Second Advent, altogether misconceive the nature of Biblical prophecy, which, so far as regards its fulfilment, always remains dependent on the historical development. In this development, the relation of man to the kingdom of God forms an essential factor'; cf. Jonah's unfulfilled prophecy, 'yet three more days and Nineveh will be destroyed', and Acts 3.19-21.

[14] Cf. Poole, 896: 'his coming to the general judgment... is said to be nigh, because of the certainty of its coming, and the uncertainty of the time when it will come, and because it is continually drawing on, and the whole time of the world's duration till then

In recent centuries, however, more and more Christian commentators have come to concede the obvious.[15] One of the first was Matthew Poole (1624–1679), who wrote that 'the apostles ordinarily in their epistles speak of the world as nigh to an end in their age, though it hath since continued more than sixteen hundred years; which would incline one to think, that they thought it would have been at an end before this time' (572). But the mistake, although undeniable, has for Poole no real theological consequence. Plumptre, 100, offers a variant of this view: 'The hope was not fulfilled as men expected, but we may believe that even for those who cherished it, it was not in vain. There was a judgment at hand, in which evil-doers received their just reward, and which made glad the hearts of the righteous'. This appears to be an unconscionable construal of the events of CE 70. Less offensive is Neander, 106: 'As the traveler, beholding from afar the object of all his wanderings, overlooks the windings of the intervening way, and believes himself already near his goal; so it seemed to them [the apostolic Christians], as their eye was fixed on that consummation of the whole course of events on earth'.

Many nineteenth, twentieth, and twenty-first century Christian readers have, by contrast, often acknowledged the mistaken expectation and let it stand, without excuse.[16] Plummer, 626, supplies an early instance of this and makes the interesting observation that 'by a strange but unperceived incongruity, St. James makes the unconscious impatience of primitive Christianity a basis for his exhortations to conscious patience. Early Christians, in their eagerness for the return of their Lord, impatiently believed that his return was imminent; and St. James uses the belief as an argument for patient waiting and patient endurance.' More recently, Townsend, 98, despite writing as a Christian, has confessed that we must regard as misguided the exhortation to 'the oppressed and downtrodden to wait patiently for a very short time, at the end of which there will be justice for them'.

With the advent of higher criticism and increasing doubt about the authorship of our epistle by James of Jerusalem, the references to farming and to early and late rains in v. 7 began to gain more than illustrative import: they became for many and remain for many evidence that our author knew Palestine first-hand and so could have been the brother of Jesus, who grew up in Galilee and lived in Jerusalem.[17]

---

is but short in comparison of the eternity following; and likewise because the particular judgment of every man is nigh at hand'.

[15] And yet they often hesitate to credit Jesus with the same error; cf. Poole, 45, 166; Beyschlag, 219; and especially the excursus in Smith, 306-13.

[16] So e.g. Mitton, 185, who says of early Christians who thought the *parousia* imminent: 'Why they made this mistake we cannot be sure'. Barclay, 142-46, stresses that modern people need not take eschatological language literally and that behind the NT's symbolism is 'the truth that this world is not purposeless and aimless and painless, but that it is going somewhere, that there is one divine far-off event to which the whole creation moves'.

[17] See further the Introduction, 6, 9; also below, on v. 7.

Modern Pentecostalism has generated a novel understanding of vv. 7-8. Some, reading them in the light of Joel 2.23—a text that (i) also speaks of the former and latter rains, (ii) has to do with the Spirit, and (iii) is linked in Acts 2 to Pentecost—have inferred that 'the former rain' refers to the outpouring of the Spirit at Pentecost, 'the latter rain' to the outpouring of the Spirit in modern times. The implication is that 'the coming of the Lord is near'. Pentecostalism is sometimes known as 'the latter-rain movement', although the term has also designated particular groups or movements within Pentecostalism or offshoots of it.[18]

Regarding v. 11, although the chief protagonist of the book of Job is not a very patient man, at least after chap. 2—one preacher observed: his 'patience was plainly coincident with that which the religious world often calls impatience'[19]—our verse has encouraged many Christians to think otherwise,[20] and they have often read Job accordingly, even Christianizing its main character.[21] Thus we not only have the proverbial expression, 'the patience of Job' (from Jas 5.11 KJV),[22] but ecclesiastical exegetes of Job have regularly cited Jas 5.11, allowing it to influence their exegesis. Some have even quoted it near the beginning of their commentaries so that it stands over the whole.[23]

---

[18] See D.W. Myland, *The Latter Rain Covenant and Pentecostal Power*, Chicago, 1910, esp. 134-46; A.A. Hoekema, *What about Tongue-Speaking?*, Grand Rapids, MI, 1966, 51-53.

[19] S.A. Brook, 'The Patience of Job', in *The Onward Cry and Other Sermons*, London, 1911, 211.

[20] One can see this in the artistic tradition, where Job is usually sitting and patiently waiting; cf. L. Réau, *Iconographie de l'Art Chrétien*, vol. 2.1, Paris, 1956, 312-18.

[21] Cf. N.N. Glatzer, *The Dimensions of Job*, New York, 1969, 11. Note e.g. the anonymous metrical life of Job in the fifteenth-century ms. HM 140 (ff. 93b-96b) of the Henry E. Huntington Library: this repeatedly refers to Job's 'pacience': G.N. Garmonsway, 'A Middle English Metrical Life of Job', in *Early English and Norse Studies Presented to Hugh Smith*, ed. A. Brown and P. Foote, London, 1963, 77-98. See further below, 714-17, and the overview of the history of interpretation in C.L. Seow, *Job 1–21*, Grand Rapids, Eerdmans, 2013.

[22] Following James, ἡ ὑπομονή 'Ιώβ was likewise a fixed Greek expression; note e.g. Ps.-Athanasius, *Pat.* PG 26.1301D; Chrysostom, *Job* pro. 3 SC 346 ed. Sorlin and Neyrand, 82; Barsanuphius and John, *Ep.* 31 PO 31.3.150 ed. Chitty, 488; Theodore the Studite, *Ep.* 381 ed. Fatouros, 524; *et al.* Cf. the Coptic in the Book of the Resurrection of Jesus Christ by Bartholomew the Apostle, ed. Budge, fol. 13a: 'Job the patient' (ⲓⲱⲃ ⲡϩⲁⲣϣ). The title of G.W. Rutler's *The Impatience of Job*, La Salle, Il., 1981, more accurately captures Job's character.

[23] E.g. Olympiodorus of Alexandria, *Job* prologue PTS 24 ed. Hagedorn and Hagedorn, 2; Gregory the Great, *Mor.* Ep. 3 SC 32bis ed. Gillet and Gaudemaris, 125; Calvin, 'The Character of Job', in *Sermons from Job*, Grand Rapids, MI, 1952, 3; J. Fry, *A New Translation and Explanation of the Very Ancient Book of Job*, London, 1827, v. Cf. J.R. Baskin, 'Job as Moral Exemplar in Ambrose', *VC* 35 (1981), 222: 'James 5:7-11 established for Christianity the tradition of Job's great patience in adversity. It is to this passage that most patristic writers refer when they speak of the saintly Job'.

Many have nonetheless rightly sensed tension between James' generalization and the character who laments his birth, loathes his life, complains that he is innocent, alleges that the deity mocks innocent sufferers, and insists that he be given an explanation of his misery: this Job is 'an extremely sensitive, vehement, impatient character', with 'very little of the Stoic ἀπάθει or of Christian πραΰτης' (Mayor, 164). Some have denied the dissonance, urging a significant distinction between μακροθυμία, which Job did not exhibit, and ὑπομονή, which he did embody.[24] This, however, seems to destroy the unity of Jas 5.7-11, which hardly suggests much difference between the two words; and surely no one who thought of Job as attacking God for injustice (as the canonical Job does) would commend his ὑπομονή.

Others have recognized tension but downplayed it. Poole, 896, wrote of Job: 'though some signs of impatience be showed, yet his patience and submission to God being prevalent, and most remarkable to him, that only is taken notice of, and his failings overlooked'.[25] Still others have put the tension to good use. Spurgeon, 337, preached: 'We have heard of the impatience of Job as well as of his patience. I am glad the divine biographer was so impartial, for had not Job been somewhat impatient, we might have thought his patience to be altogether inimitable, and above the reach of ordinary men. The traces of imperfection which we see in Job prove all the more powerfully that grace can make grand examples out of common constitutions, and that keen feelings of indignation under injustice need not prevent a man's becoming a model of patience.'

5.11 has played a role in the debate as to whether Job should be understood as a fictional or historical character, a debate that goes back to the rabbis and the church fathers.[26] Aquinas, for instance, quoted the verse (along with Ezek 14.14) in his commentary on Job in order to refute Maimonides's view that Job never existed.[27] We find the same argument

---

[24] So in different ways Carr, 'Patience'; Robertson, 247; Hainthaler, *Ausdauer*, 311-38.

[25] This echoes Calvin, 311: 'Why does the apostle so greatly commend the patience of Job, who in fact under the shock of the blind catastrophe showed considerable signs of impatience? The answer is, that even though on occasion he lapses through weakness of the flesh, and actually wrestles with himself, yet he always comes back to entrusting himself wholly to God... So though his patience lack a little here and there, it well deserves praise.' Cf. also Pareus, 570; Manton, 430 ('where the bent of the heart is right, the infirmities of God's people are not mentioned'); Trapp, 703; Stier, 458-59.

[26] Note y. Soṭah 20d (5.5); b. B. Bat. 15a; Theodore of Mopsuestia, *Job* PG 66.697-98.

[27] Thomas Aquinas, *The Literal Exposition of Job*, ed. Damico and Yaffe, Atlanta, 1989, 69. Cf. F. Spanheim, *Historia Iobi*, Geneva, 1670, 9-10; Whitby, 694 ('We very probably conclude, That what is written in the Book of Job, is truly an History of what happened to him; and not, as some conceive, a Parable or Fiction of a thing not truly done: For feigned things contain no serious Motives to, nor just Examples of Patience'); Manton, 430; Gill, 801; Burkitt, 1033; Macknight, 601; Clarke, 826; Wordsworth, 32; S. Lee, *The Book of the Patriarch Job*, London, 1837, 10; A. Barnes, *Notes, Critical,*

in many later writers, especially of the nineteenth century. Stier, 458, wrote: 'We learn here from St. James, that the man Job actually existed like Noah, Daniel, and all the prophets; that the narrative of his life is not an instructive poem, but a real history'. Plummer, 627-28, in turn, devoted two long columns to refuting Stier, arguing that inspired writers could appeal to fictional characters as well as to historical individuals. Plummer went on to rebuke theologians who are impatient (!) with those who hold different opinions on matters in which certainty cannot be obtained. Long before Plummer, Grotius, 1091, although he accepted the inference that Job was a real person, believed that James does not entail the historicity of the canonical book. Rather, in his view, that book is a fictionalized account: *vera haec historia, sed tractat poetice*. Thomas Hobbes thought the same.[28]

The call to patient suffering might be considered potentially deleterious. For G. Byron, 469, the demand 'has often wrought serious consequences for African Americans who have understood the words of James...as a mandate to tolerate evil in its various manifestations of injustice and oppression'. His response is to argue that patience need not be passive: it can be exercised even as one is fighting injustice.

Exegesis

Verses 7-11, with their call to patient endurance in view of the coming *parousia*, send readers back to Jas 1. In 1.2-4, patient endurance (ὑπομονή) produces a 'perfected (τέλειον) work', so that individuals will be τέλειοι, and in 1.12, the one who exhibits patient endurance (ὑπομένει) in the midst of temptation is 'blessed' (μακάριος) and gains eschatological reward. 5.7-11 likewise commends ὑπομονή,[29] envisages suffering, and anticipates eschatological reward; and it uses words formed from the μακαρ- and τελ- roots:

ὑπομονή/ὑπομένω	1.3-4:	ὑπομονήν, ὑπομονή
	1.12:	ὑπομένει
	5.11:	ὑπομείναντας
τελ-	1.4:	τέλειον, τέλειοι
	5.11:	τέλος
μακαρ-	1.12:	μακάριος
	5.11:	μακαρίζομεν
eschatological reward	1.4:	'perfected work'
	1.12:	'crown of life'
	5.7-11:	implicit throughout

Illustrative, and Practical, on the Book of Job, New York, 1845, v. Bassett, 74, even finds in James cause to date Job to ancient times, on the ground that it would be natural to cite the first instance of something.

[28] Thomas Hobbes, *Leviathan*, ed. R. Tuck, Cambridge, UK, 1991, 263-64.
[29] Cf. also the use of μακροθυμέω in vv. 7-8.

The upshot of these links is to make the end of James like the beginning: we have here a sort of *inclusio*, which might signal to a reader that the conclusion is near.

According to Frankemölle, 668-69, 5.7-20 is the 'epilogue' or *peroratio* of James. This view has become fairly popular since Francis, 'From', argued that Hellenistic letters did not invariably include a closing formula or greeting or blessing.[30] Nonetheless, 5.7-11, 12, and 13-20 are complete in themselves, and their relationship to each other seems minimal. It is their common location at the end of James, not their content, that binds them together. The view of this commentary is that, whatever one makes of the structure of James as a whole, 5.7-11 and the following passages should be discussed as separate entities and on their own terms.

The structure of vv. 7-11 seems straightforward. We have here four imperatives, the first two followed immediately by a rationale, the next two followed immediately by two rationales:

7
- 1st imperative: 'Be patient, then, brothers, until the coming of the Lord'
- Rationale (in the form of an illustration): 'Behold, the farmer waits for the valuable fruit of the earth, being patient over it, until it receives the early rain and the late rain'

8
- 2nd imperative (repetition and expansion): 'You also be patient, establishing your hearts'
- Rationale: 'for the coming of the Lord is near'

9
- 3rd imperative: 'Do not, brothers, grumble against one another'
- 1st rationale: 'so that you will not be judged'
- 2nd rationale: 'Behold, the judge is standing at the doors'

10-11
- 4th imperative: 'Make your own, as an example of suffering and patience, brothers, the prophets who spoke in the name of the Lord'
- 1st rationale: 'Behold, we bless those who were steadfast'
- 2nd rationale: 'You have heard of the steadfastness of Job, and you have seen he outcome which Lord brought about, how the Lord is compassionate and merciful'

'Brothers' in every case belongs to an imperative (vv. 7, 9, 10). 'Behold' in every case belongs to a rationale (vv. 7, 9, 11).[31]

---

[30] Cf. also Cladder, 'Aufbau'; Davids, 26-28, 181; Reese, 'Exegete'; R. Wall, 248.
[31] Contrast the scheme of Talbert, *Suffering*, 37:
Exhortations in view of the end, 5.7-9
   1. Exhortation to patience, vv. 7-8a
   2. Exhortation to established hearts, v. 8b
   3. Exhortation not to act in the realm of speech so as to be judged, v. 9
Examples of the virtues called for in the exhortations, vv. 10-12
   1. Example of patience: the prophets, v. 10
   2. Example of steadfastness: Job, v. 11
   3. Example of speech behavior that avoids condemnation, v. 12

The recurrence of those words belongs to a larger pattern: the repetition throughout is considerable:

7a	μακροθυμήσατε ἀδελφοί	ἕως		παρουσίας	τοῦ κυρίου
7b	μακροθυμῶν	ἕως λάβῃ	ἰδού		
8	μακροθυμήσατε		ὅτι	παρουσία	τοῦ κυρίου
9a	ἀδελφοί				κριθῆτε
9b			ἰδού		κριτής
10	μακροθυμίας ἀδελφοί	λάβετε		κυρίου	
11a			ἰδού		ὑπομείναντας
11b				κυρίου	ὑπομονήν
11c			ὅτι	κύριος	

Verse 7. The rich now disappear, to be heard from no more. 'The storm of indignation is past, and from this point to the end of the Epistle St. James writes in tones of tenderness and affection'.[32] James now addresses the ἀδελφοί, with whom he identifies. Thus v. 11 resumes the inclusive first person plural; cf. 1.18; 3.1-3, 9. James 5.7-11 is nevertheless not unrelated to 4.13-5.6: both are grounded in eschatological expectation. The final day that will bring judgment upon the rich will be a day of salvation for the just.[33]

μακροθυμήσατε οὖν. Having expressed his outrage, James next counsels patience. The section opens with its keyword, μακροθυμέω.[34] The related μακροθυμία appears in v. 10, so the theme of vv. 7-11, which harks back to 1.2-4 and 13, is clear: faithful endurance in trial.

In Wis 15.1, the noun, μακροθυμία, refers to God's patience, and the verb does so in Ecclus 18.11.[35] But James, instead of invoking the *imitatio dei*, illustrates by calling to mind the typical farmer (v. 7) and Job (v. 11), even though the latter seems to say of himself, in LXX Job 7.16, that he is not patient.[36]

The verb basically means, 'be patient' or 'persevere'.[37] Here it involves 'the self-restraint which enables the sufferer to refrain from hasty retaliation' and so is the opposite of 'wrath and revenge'.[38] In religious contexts, it is used of the patience or perseverance of faith and faithfulness in trying circumstances—in suffering (T. Job 26.6), for example, or in humiliation (Ecclus 2.4), or in temptation or trial (T. Jos. 2.7), or in

---

[32] Plummer, 625.

[33] Cf. Mussner, 199-200.

[34] LXX: 5×. NT: 10×. It occurs 3× in this verse and the next. Gk. Pseudepigrapha (Denis): 7× (5× in the Testament of Job). Philo: 0×. Josephus: 0×.

[35] Cf. Ecclus 35.22; 2 Macc 6.14; Rom 2.4; Gk. Apoc. Ezra 3.6.

[36] Cf. οὐ...ἵνα μακροθυμήσω; cf. MT 6.11.

[37] Cf. Ecclus 29.8; Bar 4.25; Mt 18.26; T. Job 11.10; 28.5; 35.5.

[38] So Tasker, 117. Cf. the sermon, 'The Victory of Patience', preached in the aftermath of WWI, by W.L. Watkinson, which uses Jas 5.7 to counter violence of every sort; see *The Shepherd of the Sea and Other Sermons*, London, 1920, 39-50.

combating the devil (T. Job 27.10). The reference to Job and the application of the closely related ὑπομονή in 1.2-4—there the issue is enduring trials—make James' general interest plain.[39] Attempts to be more specific fail. One hesitates for instance to identify those addressed here primarily with those oppressed by the rich in vv. 1-6 and to suggest that James is discouraging violent retaliation for economic injustice.[40] His audience is scarcely confined to the oppressed poor; cf. 2.1-7. One is also reluctant to draw a connection with vv. 13-18 and imagine that James is thinking especially of illness. One can say little more than that the faithful will face trials (cf. 1.2-4) and find themselves opposed by 'the world' (4.4); and so they will need 'patience', a virtue so many other early Christian texts promote; see on v. 10. All this harmonizes with the Jewish tradition that the life of faith is a series of struggles to be endured patiently. One recalls Jubilees 18–19; the Testament of Joseph; and Heb 10–12; cf. 12.1: 'let us run with perseverance (ὑπομονῆς) the race that is set before us'.

Those who closely link vv. 7-11 with v. 6 or to vv. 1-6, so that those oppressed there are addressed here, will take the οὖν as supporting their view.[41] But the sense and function of οὖν (see on 4.4) are not obvious. Is it here used adversatively—'But as for you'?[42] Or does οὖν just mark continuation of the narrative, being akin to the English, 'Well, then'? Or does it signal that James is drawing a conclusion from the entire discourse, which is accordingly about to end?[43] Or does οὖν suggest that readers 'follow the example of the ideal "just man" of whom the previous verse had spoken'?[44] Or does the text assume, with Ruckstuhl, 29, that the addressees are in the same situation as the oppressed workers of v. 4? For Burchard, 198, the conjunction signals resumption of the main theme, announced in 1.2-4. Bengel, 506, comments: *quicquid interim faciant improbi*, that is, whatever the wicked of vv. 1-6 do in the meantime. Perhaps a variant of Laws' view is best: the οὖν 'does not indicate that a conclusion should be drawn specifically from v. 6, but rather that a

---

[39] One wonders, in view of Job's appearance in v. 11 and the manifest continuity of theme between vv. 7 and 11, whether the generalization of Moo, 22— μακροθυμέω more often has to do with being patient with people, ὑπομένω with enduring difficulties—is helpful here.

[40] But such is the view of Beyschlag, 217 (for him the οὖν is decisive); Plummer, 625; Kistemaker, 164-65; Johnson, 323.

[41] Cf. Manton, 418; Mussner, 200-201; Moo, 221; McCartney, 240.

[42] Cf. BAGD, s.v. 4.

[43] So R. Wall, 251. Cf. Hartin, 247. Frankemölle, 672, sees in the conjunction the start of the concluding *paraenesis* and compares 1 Cor 15.58 and Phil 4.1.

[44] So Plumptre, 99. Those who refer v. 6 to the crucifixion can interpret the transition this way: 'Since our Divine Master has met with such injurious treatment, and borne it with such steady patience; be ye therefore, my brethren, long-suffering and patient, even till the coming of the Lord Jesus Christ' (Doddridge, 847). Cf. Wordsworth, 31.

deduction should be made from the passage as a whole. The threat to the rich is an indication that there will be an end to oppression, and that the readers should therefore be patient' (208).[45]

ἀδελφοί. This vocative (see on 1.2) last appeared in 4.11. Its reappearance indicates a change of tune, and its repetition in vv. 9, 10, and 12 emphasizes that change. It is as though the author overcompensates for the previous section, which lacks 'brothers' because the endearing term would be rhetorically inappropriate given the grave sins of those charged.

ἕως τῆς παρουσίας τοῦ κυρίου. μακροθυμέω + ἕως (Jas: 1×) was not a traditional Greek expression. Its only occurrences apart from James and later Christian writings[46] are Ecclus 35.19-20 (with a negative: μὴ μακροθυμήσῃ...ἕως) and T. Job 26.6 (Job says: μακροθυμήσωμεν ἐν παντὶ ἕως οὗ ὁ κύριος σπλαγχνισθείς). The latter, like James, employs μακροθυμέω + ἕως in an exhortation related to the figure of Job that looks forward to a redemptive act of ὁ κύριος. Is this just a coincidence?[47] In any case, given the lack of a Greek background, μακροθυμέω + ἕως may be a Semitism, the equivalent of אד + ער.[48]

παρουσία[49] (lit. 'presence', cf. 2 Cor 10.10) designated both the official arrival of a high-ranking person, especially a king or emperor (cf. *adventus*), as well as the manifestation of a hidden deity. In the LXX (where the word occurs only in books first written in Greek), however, it carries the purely secular sense of 'arrival' or 'presence'.[50] More interesting is Josephus, who uses the word with reference to past entries of God into salvation-history.[51] Further, T. Jud. 22.2 (ἕως παρουσίας τοῦ θεοῦ); T. Mos. 10.12 (*ad adventum*); 2 Bar. 30.1 (מאתיתה דמשיחא); and T. Abr. RecLng. 13.4 (μέχρι...αὐτοῦ παρουσίας) raise the possibility that, in pre-Christian times, some already used the noun of the eschatological coming of God or a divine intermediary.[52] This would have been a natural step from texts such as Zech 14.5 ('the Lord my God will come') and Mal 3.2 ('the day of his coming'). In early Christian literature, however, παρου-

---

[45] Bentley offers another explanation, based upon a textual conjecture, see 687 n. 333.

[46] Beginning with Origen, *Philoc.* 27.7 SC 226 ed. Junod, 290.

[47] Spitta, *Zur Geschichte und Litteratur des Urchristentums*, vol. 3, part 2, Göttingen, 1907, 170-77, contends that James borrows from the Testament of Job. For the argument that the case falls short see Gray, 'Job'. According to Davids, 'Pseudepigrapha', 231-32; idem, 'Tradition', 117-19, James knew not the Testament of Job but the oral tradition behind it, or perhaps an Aramaic precursor.

[48] As in Dan 7.12; y. Ta'an. 65b (2.1); b. Ber. 61b.

[49] Literature: Deissmann, *Light*, 368-73; O. Oepke, 'παρουσία', *TWNT* 5 (1968), 856-69; B. Rigaux, *Les épitres aux Thessaloniciens*, Paris, 1956, 196-201; P.L. Schoonheim, *Een Semasiologisch Onderzoek van Parousia*, Aalten, 1953 (Eng. summary on 257-89); Klaus Thraede, *Grundzüge griechische-römischer Brieftopik*, Munich, 1970, 95-106.

[50] Jdt 10.18; 2 Macc 8.12; 3 Macc 3.17.

[51] Josephus, *Ant.* 3.80 (τὴν παρουσίαν τοῦ θεοῦ), 203 (θεοῦ... παρουσίαν); 9.55.

[52] Note also T. Levi 8.11; Rev 20.11; 4 Ezra 7.33.

σία adverts to the eschatological coming of Jesus.[53] This explains the dominant exegesis of Jas 5.7, which has even worked its way into the textual tradition: in place of τοῦ κυρίου, 1729 has Χριστοῦ, L1440 has τοῦ κυρίου ἡμῶν 'Ιησοῦ Χριστοῦ, and 2674 has σωτῆρος.[54] Yet it is striking that James here leaves κυρίου (see on 1.1) without specification; and everywhere else in our book, with the exception of the opening verse, the 'Lord' seems to be God. So some exegetes think it does so here too.[55] In line with this, surely 'the Lord' is God, not Jesus, in the paragraphs leading up to this one (3.9; 4.10, 15; 5.4), and 'the Lord' is likely God in the rest of our paragraph; see on vv. 10-11. In short, we have here a line that Christians could have read one way, Jews another.

If there is no clarification of 'Lord', there is equally no clarification of 'parousia'. The author assumes a common religious tradition—conventional Jewish expectations about the latter days and/or common Christian ideas about the return of Jesus.[56]

The near *parousia* functions very much as does the ephemeral nature of human life, already remarked upon in 1.10-11; 4.14. Life is soon over one way or the other—with the approach of death or with the return of the Lord. Both eventualities will bring reward for some, condemnation for others.

ἰδοὺ ὁ γεωργὸς ἐκδέχεται τὸν τίμιον καρπὸν τῆς γῆς μακροθυμῶν ἐπ' αὐτῷ ἕως λάβῃ πρόϊμον καὶ ὄψιμον.[57] This contains a string of *hapax legomena* for James: γεωργός, ἐκδέχομαι, τίμιος, πρόϊμος (NT: 1×), ὄψιμος (NT: 1×). The agricultural imagery makes for a link with vv. 4-5;

---

[53] Cf. Mt 24.3, 27, 37, 39; 1 Cor 15.23; 16.17; 1 Thess 2.19; 3.13; 4.15; 5.23; 2 Thess 2.1, 8, 9; Jas 5.7-8; 2 Pet 1.16; 3.4, 12; 1 Jn 2.28; Liv. Proph. Jer. 10; Gk. Apoc. Pet. 1; etc. But in Herm. *Sim.* 5.5.3, it may refer to God's eschatological coming.

[54] Cf. the ascription of this belief to James in Hegesippus *apud* Eusebius, *H.E.* 2.23.13: Jesus is 'about to come on the clouds of heaven'.

[55] Cf. Theile, 258; Windisch-Preisker, 31; Easton, 66; Cantinat, 232; McKnight, 408. W. Marxsen, *Introduction to the New Testament*, Philadelphia, 1968, 228, who thinks it must be God's *parousia*, finds this 'very surprising' and so reason for 'assuming that there was a pre-Christian source'. W. Bousset, *Kyrios Christos*, Nashville, 1970, 291 n. 159, expresses uncertainty as to the identity of 'Lord' here. The dominant interpretation is represented by Beyschlag, 217; Marty, 192; Laws, 208-209; Davids, 182; Jackson-McCabe, 'Messiah, 727; Burchard, 198. For Popkes, 321-22, in James, Jesus and God stand for each other; the one is Lord and so is the other.

[56] Frankemölle, 675-76, speaks of 'in-group language'. The assertion of Martin, 188, that 'the congregation to which James wrote was evidently racked by confusion over the Parousia', seems without basis.

[57] 01 025 044 5 18 35 43 61 69 88 104 *et al.* L590 L623 *et al.* Antioch PsOec S:H^M insert ἄν before λάβῃ. So too 522 629 999 1661 1890 2241 L596, with λάβοι. 02 025 044 5 33 81 88 206 218 322 323 *et al.* **Byz** PsOec **L**:V^mss **S**:PH^T **G**:G-D **Sl**:ChMSi clarify by adding ὑετόν after λάβῃ; 436 1067 1409 2541 put it before the verb. P74 03 048 945 1241 1739 2298 **L**:V **K**:S omit. 01C2 398 996 1175 1661 Antioch instead have καρπόν, 01* καρπὸν τόν.

but we have moved from large estates to small farms, and from workers being mistreated to workers doing their job.

To liken waiting for the end to waiting for a harvest was conventional eschatological rhetoric. The quotation from a lost apocryphon in 1 Clem. 23.3 = 2 Clem. 11.2-4 (see above, 618) responds to doubt about the end ever coming with an agricultural parable: 'Compare yourselves to a tree, or take a vine: first it sheds its leaves, then a shoot comes, and after these a sour grape, and then a full ripe bunch. So also my people have had turmoil and tribulation, but afterward they will receive good things'. Related is the parable of the weed among the wheat in Mt 13.24-30 and other texts that compare eschatological judgment to a harvest or some aspect of it.[58] Perhaps the closest parallel, although it is not cited in the modern commentaries, is Tg. Ps.-J. on 2 Sam 23.4: 'You [the just ones] will be raised, and it will be good for you who long for the years of consolations that are coming. Behold, like a farmer who hopes during years of scarcity that rain will fall on the earth.'

Laws, 210, observes: if James had in mind readers suffering 'under attack from outside, his parable of the farmer would be a singularly inept illustration. The farmer is in no sense persecuted by the rotation of the seasons and the variation of the climate; he simply waits for these to take their necessary and familiar course.' Laws goes on to urge that James' readers were not experiencing 'an extraordinary outburst of persecution' but rather struggling with 'the perennial difficulties of ordinary, daily human life'. If so, we must differentiate between James' audience here and the oppressed of vv. 1-6.

γεωργός[59] designates a cultivator of the land, a farmer or agricultural worker, whether contracted or not.[60] Such workers were stock characters in religious illustrations.[61] γεωργός is unassociated with ἐκδέχομαι[62] before James or in later secular literature; but the verb, which means 'wait' or 'expect', works well here as a rough synonym for μακροθυμέω. Popkes, 323 n. 101, draws a contrast between those who here wait and those who, in 5.1-6, already have what they want.

---

[58] E.g. Isa 18.4; 27.12; Jer 51.53; Hos 6.11; Mt 3.12; 13.30, 39; Rev 14.14-20; 4 Ezra 4.26-37; 9.17; 2 Bar. 70.1-2; b. B. Meṣi'a 83b; Midr. Ps. on 8.1; etc. Schlatter, 273; Reicke, 54; *et al.* think of Mk 4.26-29 in particular.

[59] Cf. the biblical אִכָּר, the rabbinic אריס. LXX: 10×. NT: 19× (all but 3 in the Synoptic parable of the wicked husbandment, Mt 21.33-46 par.).

[60] LXX Gen 9.20; Jer 14.4; Let. Aris. 111; T. Iss. 3.1; Jn 15.1; Josephus, *Bell.* 4.84; etc. That many in James' audience were farmers is possible; but against Blomberg-Kamell, 227, this is not 'clearly' the case.

[61] Cf. Ecclus 6.19; Mk 12.1-9; 2 Tim 2.6; 4 Ezra 8.41-44; 9.17; Origen, *Prin.* 3.1.14 GCS 22 ed. Koetschau, 219; Billerbeck 1.871-75.

[62] NT: 6×; cf. Heb 10.13: ἐκδεχόμενος ἕως.

Philodemus, Περὶ ποιημάτων frag. 100 (ἐξεδέξατο τὸν καρπόν) and 2 Clem. 20.3 (καρπόν...ἐκδέχεται)[63] indicate that ἐκδέχομαι was naturally linked with καρπός.[64] τίμιος καρπός has only imperfect Greek parallels.[65]

τίμιος helps explain why the farmer is so patient (so Huther, 151), and perhaps Easton, 66, is right: 'figure and fact are combined: the infinite reward of the righteous is really in mind'. καρπὸν τῆς γῆς is a biblicism.[66] The phrase refers to crops in general, not to what we usually mean by 'fruits'. μακροθυμῶν...ἕως is modeled on the previous line.[67]

The comparison with the farmer has regularly moved exegetes to contrast earthly rewards with posthumous rewards. Erasmus is characteristic: 'When you consider that he endures long-lasting toils with good hope for a transitory harvest and does not demand that what he has sown appear immediately, how much more right is it for you to bear patiently the disadvantages of this life in return for the harvest of immortality'.[68]

πρόϊμος (= πρώϊμος[69]) and ὄψιμος mean, respectively, '(the) early' and '(the) late'. Their pairing is natural[70] but is particularly characteristic of the LXX (most often for ירה(ו) and מלקוש respectively).[71] A few exegetes suppose that καρπόν is the implicit object, which is a textual variant.[72] A larger number think of the so-called early (late October and November) and 'late' (March and April) rains,[73] ὑετόν being another

[63] For Mayor, 161, this text is a reminiscence of James.

[64] For the latter see on 3.17

[65] Dionysius of Halicarnassus, *Ant.* 2.25.2; Josephus, *Bell.* 4.469; Analecta Hymn Graeca canon Julii Day 5 canon 8.2 ode 3—all with τιμιώτατον. Does James perhaps preserve here a Semitism—יוי פרי + יוקר, as in b. Ta'an. 19b; b. Giṭ. 52b?

[66] It appears in LXX Num 13.26; Deut 1.25; Ps 104.35; Mal 3.11, for פרי + האדמה or הארץ; cf. 4Q422 1.9; m. Ber. 6.1; etc.

[67] For μακροθυμέω + ἐπί + dative of αὐτός see Ecclus 18.11; 35.19; Lk 18.7; Gk. Apoc. Ezra 3.6.

[68] Erasmus, *Paraphrase*, 167. There is no reason to identify the farmer as a metaphor for God (although cf. Jn 15.1).

[69] πρώϊμος is 'the standard spelling' (BAGD, s.v.), and the mss. for 5.7 vary between πρόϊμον and πρώϊμον. See the *Editio Critica Maior*, 88.

[70] Cf. Xenophon, *Oecon.* 17.4-5; Cosmas Indicopleustes, *Top.* 2.105.

[71] Deut 11.14 (against Hutchinson Edgar, *Poor*, 205, an allusion to this text and so to the Shema' in particular is not apparent); Jer 5.24; Hos 6.3; Joel 2.23; Zech 10.1.

[72] See n. 57. Cf. Spitta, 137; Belser, 293; Vouga, 134-35; Frankemölle, 680. For early and late fruits see Jer 24.2; Hos 9.10; m. Ter. 4.6; m. Bik. 3.1-2; Sifre 301 on Deut 26.5-10; also perhaps Marcus Aurelius 4.23.

[73] See Deut 11.14; Ps 84.7; Prov 16.15; Jer 3.3; 5.24; Hos 6.3 (on the intriguing links between Jas 5.13-20 and Hos 6.1-3, which in the LXX includes ἐπιστρέψωμεν, ἰάσεται, and ἀναστησόμεθα, see J.M. Darlack, 'Pray for Reign: The Eschatological Elijah in James 5:17-18', unpublished MA Thesis, Gordon-Conwell Theological Seminary, 2007, 89-90); Joel 2.23; Zech 10.1; 4Q302 2 2.4-55 ('a good tree...plump fruit...early and late rains...he watches it'); 11Q14 1 2.9-10 ('early and late rains...to give you fruit... delicious fruits'); t. Ta'an. 1.1-4; b. Ta'an. 5a, 6a; Sifre 42 on Deut 11.14; Jerome, *Amos* 2.4.7 CSEL 76 ed. Adriaen, 263. Luther mistakenly thought of the morning and evening rain.

textual variant; see n. 57. Cf. esp. Tg. Ps.-J. on Deut 11.14; 'then I will give to your land the rain in its time, the early in Marheshvan and the late in Nisan'.[74] The latter judgment seems best: (i) All five times that the LXX pairs πρώϊμος and ὄψιμος, the subject is rain. (ii) Rain is also the subject of Jas 5.17-18, where it brings forth fruit (καρπόν) from the earth (γῆς). (iii) Although LXX Jer 24.2 speaks of 'early' figs and LXX Exod 9.32 of 'late' wheat and spelt, the LXX nowhere qualifies καρπός with πρώϊμος or ὄψιμος, and secular literature offers few illustrations of such.[75]

Those who take the text to refer to the seasonal rains often discern here evidence of James' Palestinian origin.[76] But what is true of Palestine in this respect is true of other parts of the eastern Mediterranean basin,[77] so although the circumstance is consistent with a Palestinian origin, it does not require it.[78] One does well to recall that our letter addresses itself to the diaspora and so implicitly assumes that readers outside of Palestine will understand its language. Further, the language is biblical, so any Jew might have used it,[79] just as many later Christians have used such language—sometimes metaphorically—without having lived in Palestine.[80] Maybe more to the point, then, is Moffatt, 72: 'the aptness of the figure here depends on the fact that, according to the O.T. interpretation (Deuteronomy xi. 8f.), this special feature of the Palestinian climate suggested to the pious the providential intervention of God in man's affairs'.

[74] ואיתן מיטרא דארעכון בעידניה בכיר במרחשוון ולקיש בניסן.

[75] BAGD, s.v. πρώϊμος, cites Petosiris frag. 6 (πρώϊμοι καρποί), and Geopontica 1.12.32 (οἱ πρώϊμοι καρποὶ καὶ οἱ ὄψιμοι). The latter, however, is a tenth-century agricultural sourcebook hardly free from Christian influence.

[76] So Grimm, 'Einleitung', 393; Smith, 297 (who uses the word 'prove'); Kittel, 'Ort', 81; Hadidian, 'Pictures', 228; Martin, 190-91; Hartin, 249-50; McCartney, 25; Witherington, 536. Marty, 192, sees here 'local Palestinian color' but wonders whether it could come from texts rather than first-hand experience.

[77] For details see D. Baly, *The Geography of the Bible*, New York, 1974, 43-51.

[78] Ropes, 295-96, sought to undo the force of this fact with these words: 'Elsewhere, although the dry season and rainy season are quite as well marked, the critical fall and spring months are pretty certain to secure a sufficient rainfall, as in Italy, or else there is no hope of rain in them, as in northern Egypt in the spring. But in Syria these rains are usual yet by no means uniform or certain; hence only there do they take so prominent a place in the life and thought of everybody.'

[79] See further Laws, 211-12, who appropriately refers to the thanksgiving for rain in the Book of Common Prayer ('God our heavenly Father, who by thy gracious providence, dost cause the former and the latter rain to descend upon the earth, that it may bring forth fruit for the use of man').

[80] See above, n. 9; also Didymus of Alexandria, *Ps.* frag. 657a ed. Mühlenberg, 53 ('sending the spiritual rain, the early through the old covenant and the later through the new covenant'); Michael Psellus, *Ep.* 15 ed. Maltese, 121; Theodore II Laskaris, *Ep.* 23, 184 ed. Festa, 31, 234; Grigor Narekats'i, *Prayer* 68 ed. Samuelian, 490. Alternatively, one can pick up expressions from one's travels, and many diaspora Jews spent time in Israel when they visited for major festivals.

Most interpreters do not think of the early and late rains as standing for different things. The rain simply 'express more ably how the farmers are not worn out with the tedium of such a long period that they cannot bear the delay' (Calvin, 309). But Oliphant proposes reading the one as referring to present remedies, the other to eschatological remedies: 'The farmer [the believer] waits for the previous fruit of the earth [final judgment/final reward], being patient with (the harvest) until he receives the early [intervention of Christ here and now] and late [eschatological judgment/reward] rains'.[81] This is over-interpretation.[82] So too the suggestion of Reicke, 54, that 'possibly the author has in mind here a first and a second coming of the Lord, as in Rev xx 4, 11'.

ἕως λάβῃ would mean 'until he receives' if πρόϊμον καὶ ὄψιμον designates fruit: the farmer is patient until he receives rain. But if, as it seems, πρόϊμον καὶ ὄψιμον is short for 'the early and late rain', the meaning could be that the farmer is patient until the fruit receives rain or perhaps the earth. The difference does not amount to much.

Verse 8. μακροθυμήσατε καὶ ὑμεῖς. This repeats, with the emphatic καὶ ὑμεῖς,[83] the imperative of v. 7; see *ad loc*.

στηρίξατε τὰς καρδίας ὑμῶν. This presumably is a snippet of early Christian *paraenesis*, for 1 Thess 3.13 has this: 'may he strengthen your hearts (στηρίξαι ὑμῶν τὰς καρδίας) in holiness that you may be blameless before our God and Father at the coming of our Lord (τῇ παρουσίᾳ τοῦ κυρίου) Jesus with all his saints'; cf. 2 Thess 2.17. Christians inherited the expression from the LXX, where it represents לב + סעד.[84] Given that στηρίζω[85] basically means 'establish' or 'strengthen',[86] the meaning of James' imperative is obvious: resolve, in view of the near end, to focus and maintain your will and attention.[87] Waiting for the Lord

---

[81] Oliphant, 'Waiting', 82-83. Bede *ad loc*. CCSL 121 ed. D. Hurst, 219, offers a similar analysis, and Eisenman, 'Rain', and Darlack, 'Reign' (as in n. 73), construe the rain in James as an eschatological motif.

[82] Oliphant goes on to associate Job with reward in this life and the prophets with reward in the eschaton. Cf. the allegorical interpretation of Ps.-Oecumenius *ad loc*. PG 119.505B-C: the early rain is repentance with tears during youth, the late rain such tears in old age. The same line appears in Theophylact *ad loc*. PG 125.1185B.

[83] Cf. Mt 7.12; Mk 13.29; Rom 6.11; 1 Pet 4.1.

[84] Cf. Judg 19.5, 8 (preparation for a journey with food); Pss 103.15 ('breads sustains a human heart'); 111.8 ('firm is his heart; he will never be afraid'); Ecclus 6.37 (through the commandments and wisdom God makes the heart firm); 22.16 ('a heart firmly set upon a thought from counsel will not be afraid'). The few secular instances of στηρίζω + καρδία (e.g. Thucydides 2.49.3) bear a different sense. For καρδία see on 3.14.

[85] Jas: 1×; NT: 14×. In the LXX, it is most common in Ecclesiasticus (11×).

[86] Cf. Jos. Asen. 21.21; 2 Clem 2.6; also the Syriac תקן (Aphʻel) + לבא in 2 Bar. 83.8; 85.4.

[87] Cf. Pss. Sol. 16.12 (στήρισον τὴν ψυχήν μου); Acts 14.22. The REB translates: 'be...stout-hearted'. Gundry, 943, translates the imperative with 'stabilize', which he says here means 'to settle your thinking and feeling on the nearness of "the Lord's coming"'.

is like the farmer's waiting: it is not inactivity but work.[88] Beyschlag, 218, remarks: 'Not the weak but rather only the strong hearts are able to preserve μακροθυμία'.[89] Contrast the rich of v. 5: seeking luxury, they fatten their hearts.

ὅτι ἡ παρουσία τοῦ κυρίου ἤγγικεν. For 'the parousia of the Lord' see on v. 7. For the verb see on 4.8. παρουσία + ἤγγικεν appears to be James' invention, and the combination did not catch on: later Christian literature seldom joins the two.[90] One guesses, given James' knowledge of the Jesus tradition, that he minted his expression under the influence of sentences about the kingdom of God:

> ἤγγικεν γὰρ ἡ βασιλεία τῶν οὐρανῶν, Mt 3.2; 4.17
> ἤγγικεν ἡ βασιλεία τῶν οὐρανῶν, Mt 10.7
> ἤγγικεν ἡ βασιλεία τοῦ θεοῦ, Mk 1.15
> ἤγγικεν (ἐφ' ὑμᾶς) ἡ βασιλεία τοῦ θεοῦ, Lk 10.9, 11[91]

The nearness of the *parousia*, which v. 7 assumes,[92] is now explicit.[93] James inherited the conviction from the early church, which inherited it from Jesus.[94] Jesus, like other Jewish visionaries around the turn of the era,[95] was in turn imitating prophets before him. One recalls that eschatological imminence is prominent in both Isa 40–55 and Daniel.[96] That James has a *Naherwartung* says nothing about the date of his epistle.[97]

---

[88] Tamez, *Message*, 55-56, makes the most of this: the faithful should not 'wait for God to come and do away with the oppressor... Rather it is a question of doing everything possible not to despair in spite of the desperate situation... From this angle of praxis, we see that James calls the communities to have a militant, indomitable patience that awaits opportune moments.'

[89] According to Mayor, 162, 'it is the true cure for διψυχία'.

[90] With the exception of a few quotations of our line, I have discovered examples only in Eustratius (sixth–seventh century).

[91] ἤγγικεν is also used of the end in Rom 13.12 and 1 Pet 4.7, but neither has παρουσία.

[92] The appeal to waiting for crops is perhaps all the more suitable as one waited less than half a year between planting and sowing—not a very long period of time.

[93] James does not seem to reflect any real anxiety about the end being delayed; cf. K. Erlemann, *Naherwartung und Parusieverzögerung im Neuen Testament*, Tübingen, 1995, 222-24.

[94] Cf. Mt 10.23; Mk 9.1; 13.30; Acts 3.19-21; Rom 13.11-12; 1 Cor 7.29-30; 16.22; Phil 4.5; Heb 10.37; 1 Pet 4.17; Rev 1.1, 3; 22.10, 12; etc.

[95] Cf. 4 Ezra 4.26; 8.61; 2 Bar. 82.20; 85.10.

[96] Against Songer, 134, and a few others, we cannot infer that 'the Christians James addresses felt that the time for the return of Jesus was overdue'.

[97] Kittel, 'Ort', 83-84, thought James' expectation intense and so early; but there was no unilinear rise or decline in eschatological enthusiasm; see Allison, *Jesus*, 141-43, and cf. Johnson, 322.

Verse 9. How does this verse, which forbids mutual recrimination, tie in with what surrounds it? Bede thinks of believers complaining about the rich who oppress them (vv. 1-6).[98] Isho'dad of Merv, on the contrary, believes that those rich are still addressed: 'Cease from mockery and injustice to the poor'.[99] Dibelius, 244, reads the verse as an isolated imperative. Richardson, 221, offers that 'trials are better endured with the encouragement of community than in solitude... The last thing the oppressed faithful needed was attacks against each other.'[100] For Ropes, 297, the grumbling involves some wrongly blaming others for the trials brought by eschatological tribulation: 'Do not blame one another for the distress of the present soon-to-be-ended age'. Given the drift of earlier sections of our letter, one might envisage synagogue members complaining about certain followers of Jesus. But against all this, and as Plummer, 626, observes, people in all times and places are irritated and exasperated by this or that and tend to vent their vexation upon those around them who are in no way responsible. So one can imagine any number of circumstances that explain our text. Perhaps the prudent course is to take into account both the immediate context and the close parallel in 4.11: to complain is to judge, which is inconsistent with the need for patient endurance. The divine judge will set things right soon enough. In the meantime, one should refrain from complaining about community members with whom one disagrees.

μὴ στενάζετε, ἀδελφοί, κατ' ἀλλήλων. This is very close to 4.11: μὴ καταλαλεῖτε ἀλλήλων, ἀδελφοί, which borrows from Mt 7.1-2 = Lk 6.37-38, as does ἵνα μὴ κριθῆτε in the present verse; see below. An allusion to either Israel grumbling in Egypt or the wilderness—στεναγμός appears in Exod 2.24; 6.5—or to Lev 19.15-18 seems unlikely.[101] Nor, against Gray, 'Job', 423, is there any firm connection with the conversation partners of Job, who might be said to grumble.[102]

The chief meaning of στενάζω is 'sigh' or 'groan',[103] and so the word can also mean 'bemoan' or 'complain', as in Gk. 1 En. 9.3. With κατά it can mean 'groan in front of' (LXX Ezek 21.11) or 'groan in the same manner as' or 'groan at'.[104] Here, with the following genitive, the sense is

---

[98] Bede, *ad loc*. CCSL 121 ed. D. Hurst, 219. Cf. Calvin, 308; Mitton, 187; Davids, 184. This implies that the rich of vv. 1-6 belong to the community; cf. κατ' ἀλλήλων.

[99] Isho'dad of Merv *ad* 5.9 HSem 10 ed. M.D. Gibson, 51.

[100] Richardson, on v. 11, states that Job is an exemplar because, although he complained, he 'addressed his complaints properly to God and not against others' (225).

[101] Richardson, 221-22, suggests the link with Exodus. For an allusion to Leviticus see Johnson, *Brother*, 129-30—although he confesses his own case 'fragile'.

[102] στενάζω appears neither in LXX Job nor the Testament of Job. Job uses στεναγμός of himself in LXX Job 3.24 and 23.2.

[103] Cf. Philo, *Leg*. 3.211-12; Mk 7.34; Rom 8.23; Heb 13.17; Herm. *Vis*. 3.9.6. LXX: 29×. NT: 6×; Jas: 1×. Gk. Pseudepigrapha (Denis): 8×. Philo: 9×. Josephus: 9×.

[104] For the latter two senses see Corp. Herm. frag. 23.33 ed. Festugière and Nock, 10, and Chrysostom, *Phil*. 3.4 PG 62.203, respectively.

probably 'complain against'.[105] Baker affirms that the expression, like the καταλαλεῖτε of 4.11, 'encompasses a wide assortment of verbal wrongs including: gossip, slander, mockery, cursing, angry speech, perjury, and probably also speech that reflects partiality'.[106]

James' imperative recapitulates. 3.1-12 has enjoined not cursing others; 3.13-18 has demanded keeping peace with others; and 4.11-12 has commanded not judging others. Cursing, fighting, and judging go hand in hand with complaining about them, and to cut off this last would be to do away with the other sins.[107]

Several post-Reformation commentaries divined in Jas 5.7 a reference to events leading up to CE 70. Whitby, 694, urged identifying the grumblers with Jewish zealots, who wanted to war against injustice and set up an earthly kingdom. James, who called for patient endurance instead of armed resistance, rebuked them. One finds the same exegesis in Hammond, 699-700, and Marchant, 804. This reading seems to have died out in the nineteenth century. Even Martin, who so often reads James against the Zealot ideology, fails to do so here.

ἵνα μὴ κριθῆτε. This agrees exactly with Mt 7.1, which may represent Q.[108] The same phrase also appears in Pol. *Phil.* 2.3, in words attributed to Jesus. Given that James elsewhere shows knowledge of the saying passed down in Mt 7.1-2 = Lk 6.37-38, one infers that he has made use of the same saying here.[109] This is indeed close to certain, because the precise phrase, ἵνα μὴ κριθῆτε, is unattested outside of Christian Greek texts; and it occurs only in the saying of Jesus, James, and quotations of those texts.

The threat of judgment means that 5.1-6 should not instill, on the part of those not there rebuked, complacency or self-satisfaction. God may judge the wicked; but, as 1 Pet 4.17 puts it and James here implies, judgment includes 'the household of God'.

Our text offers no guidance on how to fulfill its imperative. Photius observes how difficult this can be when one is treated poorly or unjustly. Only being philosophical and safeguarding the divine commandments, he urges, make such possible.[110] James fails to offer even that much. He appeals only to the last judgment, seemingly in the conviction that fear can motivate proper behavior.[111]

---

[105] As in V. Pach. Σ 18 ed. Halkin, 185. Cf. Gregory Palamas, *Hom. xliii–lxiii* 44.7 ed. Chrestou and Zeses, 56, rewriting Heb 13.17.

[106] Baker, *Speech-Ethics*, 180. Contrast Robertson, 244: it is 'rather the inward and unexpressed feeling than the outward expression of dissatisfaction'.

[107] Antiochus the Monk, *Pand. script.* 54 PG 89.1600C-D, appropriately juxtaposes Jas 5.9 with Jesus' command to love one's enemy.

[108] So the *CEQ*, 74.

[109] See on 4.11-12. Cf. Alford, 325; Neander, 107; Bassett, 73; Mayor, 162; Knowling, 131; Plummer, 626; Robertson, 244; Smith, 300; Schlatter, 274; Mitton, 187; Kugelman, 59; Moo, 225 ('may'); Burchard, 200 ('perhaps').

[110] Photius, *Ep. Amph.* 177 PG 101.880A-B.

[111] In v. 11, James appeals to Job, who in rabbinic tradition is sometimes said to have been motivated by fear: Tanḥ. Buber Wayyiqra' 15; b. B. Bat. 15b; etc.

ἰδοὺ ὁ κριτὴς πρὸ τῶν θυρῶν ἕστηκεν. Not only will offenders be judged, but soon: the end is near.[112] Cf. Heb 10.36-28, which counsels ὑπομονή with the promise that the *parousia* will occur shortly; also Isa 3.13 (that God 'rises' and 'stands to judge' means the judgment is near); 2 Bar. 48.39 ('the judge will come and will not hesitate'). For ἰδού see on 3.4. κριτής occurs also in 4.11-12, where God is the judge, and given the close relationship between that passage and this, it is natural to make the same identification here.[113] In this case God stands at the door. Christian readers, however, could equally think of Jesus, who is often depicted as the eschatological judge,[114] especially readers familiar with Mk 13.29 = Mt 24.33, where the imminent *parousia* is indicated by remarking that 'he (Jesus) is at the gates'.[115] Once more James can be read in two different ways.

θύρα, with which the LXX frequently translates פתח, occurs only here in James. Often there is no significant difference between the plural and the singular: a single opening could have a door or gate with two halves.[116] Although πρὸ τῶν θυρῶν does not show up in the LXX, it was a very common expression.[117] Perhaps a first- or second-century audience would have thought that God or Jesus had already arisen from his throne and was now standing at the gate(s) or door(s) of heaven.[118] That heaven has entrances was an ancient and far-flung idea.[119] One recalls, moreover, that gates were traditionally places of judgment,[120] which a few have thought makes the imagery here especially appropriate.[121]

---

[112] The suggestion of A.L. Moore, *The Parousia in the New Testament*, Leiden, 1966, 150, that the nearness is spatial rather than temporal is without basis.

[113] Cf. Ropes, 297; Laws, 213; Hartin, 243. This is a minority opinion; contrast Knowling, 131; Jackson-McCabe, 'Letter', 509; idem, 'Messiah', 727; *et al.*

[114] E.g. Mt 25.31-46; Jn 5.22; Acts 17.31; 2 Cor 5.10; 2 Tim 4.1, 8; Heb 12.23; Rev 9.11; Herm. *Sim.* 6.3.6.

[115] See further below and Bottini, *Introduzione*, 123.

[116] Cf. LXX Exod 40.5-6; Lev 1.3, 5. Against Jeremias, 'θύρα', *TDNT* 3.174, James' expression is not clearly 'Hellenistic' and 'non-Semitic'.

[117] Cf. Euripides, *Cyc.* 635; Cassius Dio 73.13.3; Josephus, *Ant.* 5.13; Jos. Asen. 5.1; etc. Note also Acts 5.23 (ἑστῶτας ἐπὶ τῶν θυρῶν); 12.14 (ἑστάναι τὸν Πέτρον πρὸ τοῦ πυλῶνος); Rev 3.20 (ἕστηκα ἐπὶ τὴν θύραν).

[118] Some take this to be the meaning of Jesus standing in Acts 7.55.

[119] Cf. Gen 28:17; Ps 78.23; 4Q213a 1 2.18; 1 En. 9.2, 10; 72–82; 3 Macc 6.18; Rev 4.1; 4 Ezra 3.19; T. Levi 5.1; T. Abr. RecLng. 11.1, 3; 3 Bar. 6.13; 11.2-5; 15.1 (cf. the 'doors' of 2.2; 3.1; 14.1; 17.1); 2 En. 13–14; Apoc. Zeph. 3.6, 9; Vis. Paul 19; Acts Pilate 19, 25; etc.; recall the gnostic conception of multiple concentric heavens around the world that feature various doors or gates. Literature: J. Jeremias, 'θύρα', *TDNT* 3.176-77; E. Brovarski, 'The Doors of Heaven', *Orientalia* 46 (1977), 107-15; W. Heimpel, 'The Sun at Night and the Doors of Heaven in Babylonian Texts', *JCS* 38 (1986), 127-51. Already in the Akkadian story of *Adapa* rec. B 37-39, heaven has an entrance gate.

[120] Deut 21.19; Isa 29.31; Amos 5.15; etc.

[121] Cf. Cantinat, 237; Gundry, 944. m. 'Abot 4.16, where this world is a vestibule to the world to come, although sometimes cited by commentators, is not here relevant.

As the eschatological discourse in Mk 13 nears its end, Jesus declares, 'So also, when you see these things taking place, you know that he is near, at the very gates'.[122] Many commentators on Jas 5.9 have recalled this synoptic text.[123] That it influenced James is a possibility given his use elsewhere of the Jesus tradition and the additional minor links between Jas 5.7-11 and Mk 13.28-32 par.[124]

An occasional exegete has been put in mind of a tradition in Hegesippus: the scribes and Pharisees asked James what he meant by 'the door of Jesus' (ἡ θύρα τοῦ 'Ιησοῦ).[125] James supposedly answered by referring to Jesus' enthronement and return, whereupon he was stoned. Wordsworth, 32, fancifully suggests that James repeatedly proclaimed, 'Behold, the judge stands at the door', and that this led people to ask, 'Which is the door of Jesus? At what door is he standing? By what door will he come? Show him to us and we will go out to meet him.' While this is pure imagination, it is conceivable that James was associated with a tradition that somehow linked his eschatological expectations with the word, 'door', and that the author of our epistle knew that tradition.[126]

Verse 10. James encourages his readers that, if they must suffer as did the prophets, they can suffer with the same mind. Affliction has a history. It is nothing new.

The basic argument of vv. 10 and 11 is this: suffering will come to the saints; saints have shown that they can persevere; those who persevere will receive reward from God, who abounds in compassion and mercy. Seemingly implicit is a rejection of taking revenge for wrongs suffered.[127]

---

[122] ἐπὶ θύραις, 13.29 = Mt 24.33; cf. also Mk 13.34; Lk 12.35-38.

[123] E.g. Poole, 896; Chaine, lxviii ('without doubt' an allusion); Moo, 225; Brosend, 144. Deppe, *Sayings*, 244, doubts that James here borrows from the Jesus tradition. Mussner, 205, leaves the question open.

[124] Ecclesiastical exegetes also often relate Jas 5.9 to Rev 3.20. John Lightfoot, in the sermon already quoted, is representative: 'At whose door doth not the judge stand, hearkening and taking notice of men's behaviour? "Behold, I stand at the door, and knock". He knocks, that, if it may be, he may be admitted; but if he be not, he stands not in vain, but takes notice of what passes in the house, that he may take account of it in his due time' (388).

[125] *Apud* Eusebius, *H.E.* 2.23.12.

[126] Note also 2 Apoc. Jas. 50 ('Once when I was sitting deliberating, he [Jesus] opened the door'), 55 ('open the good door through you'). A few earlier commentators—e.g. Poole, 896; Calmet, 691—think of Gen 4.7; but this leads nowhere.

[127] Cf. GenevaB., 117: 'Because most men are woont to object, that it is good to repell injuries by what meanes soever, hee setteth against that, the examples of the Fathers, whose patience had a most happy end, because God as a most bountifull Father, never forsaketh his'.

ὑπόδειγμα λάβετε, ἀδελφοί.[128] ὑπόδειγμα (Jas: 1×) occurs only five times in the LXX: Ecclus 44.16 (Enoch as an example of repentance); Ezek 42.15 (a model for the future temple); 2 Macc 6.28, 31 (the dying Eleazor as a noble example to the young); 4 Macc 17.23 (martyrs as an example of ὑπομονή). Besides James, the word appears five times in the NT: Jn 13.15 (Jesus' washing of feet as an example); Heb 4.11; 8.5; 9.23; 2 Pet 2.6 (Sodom and Gomorrah as examples of what will happen to the ungodly). The LXX and Josephus, *Ant.* 6.103, 106 (Jechoniah as an example of voluntary surrender) show us that some Jews employed ὑπόδειγμα when appealing to scriptural characters and earlier heroes as inspiring examples. But James may have been the first to use the word of 'the prophets' in general. Both λαμβάνω (see on 1.7) and ἀδελφός (see on 1.2) link with the surrounding materials; cf. vv. 7, 9. λαμβάνω with ὑπόδειγμα is otherwise attested.[129]

The emulation of ancient worthies is implicit in 2.21-26 while 1.4 and 2.5 seemingly presuppose the *imitatio dei*. In 5.7-11, however, the demand for imitation becomes explicit; cf. also vv. 17-18. Modern commentators sometimes express surprise that the objects of imitation are not Jesus[130] and the apostles but 'the prophets' and Job.[131] It is almost as though the text goes out of its way not to be overtly Christian.[132] By contrast, although Hebrews offers a long list of Jewish worthies (11.1-39), this leads to a paragraph in which Jesus is the prime example of faith and endurance (12.1-13).[133] James has nothing comparable.

---

[128] This is the best attested reading (03 025 18 35 38 *et al.* support it), but there are numerous variants. Some witnesses, for example, have the vocative in first place (e.g. 467 1751 L156/2), others second (e.g. 02 044 33). PsOec puts it even later in the sentence while others (e.g. 400 621T Antioch) omit it; and some witnesses (including 69 81 88 **Byz** S:P) follow it with μου.

[129] 1 Clem. 5.1; Iamblichus, *Nic. arith.* ed. Klein, 107; Chrysostom, *Jn* PG 59.433.

[130] Jesus is often a model in early Christian writings; cf. Jn 13.15, 34; 15.12; 17.16; Heb 12.1-4 (with ὑπομονή); 13.12-13; 1 Pet 2.21-22; 1 Jn 2.6; Ign. *Phil.* 7.2; Irenaeus, *Haer.* 2.22.4; Apoc. Abr. 29.10; Clement of Alexandria, *Paed.* 1.2.2 SC 70 ed. Marrou and Harl, 110; Origen, *Prin.* 4.4.4 TzF 24 ed. Görgemanns and Karpp, 796-98; *Exh. mart.* 41-42 GCS ed. Koetschau, 38-40.

[131] Cf. Mayor, 163; Knowling, 132; Moffatt, 73 ('strange'); Rendtorff, 75; Laws, 217 ('James's appeal to the prophets and to Job...has struck many as extraordinary'); Keenan, 158.

[132] And some think it originally was not Christian; cf. Easton, 67: 'It seems almost incredible that this section should ever have been treated as an original Christian exhortation; how could a Christian writer seeking examples of steadfastness content himself with O.T. prophets and Job, ignoring completely the supreme model of the sufferings and steadfastness of Christ?' For Windisch-Preisker, 32, James preserves Jewish material that has not yet been Christianized. Dibelius, 247, argues not only that the Christianization of paraenetic material took time but further 'that the Christians thought about their Lord—and especially about his "outcome"—in a different way than they did about the righteous and martyrs in the Old Testament'.

[133] Cf. how 1 Clem. 4–5 moves from ancient Jewish exemplars to recent Christian exemplars.

τῆς κακοπαθείας καὶ τῆς μακροθυμίας.[134] Cf. Josephus, *Bell.* 6.37: ἡ Ἰουδαίων μακροθυμία καὶ τὸ καρτερικὸν ἐν οἷς κακοπαθοῦσιν. The LXX has κακοπαθία/πάθεια[135] only four times.[136] The word—whose pairing with ὑπομονή (see v. 11) was probably conventional[137]—refers either to misfortune or to the strenuous, persevering effort needed to withstand misfortune. According to BAGD, s.v., 'the latter mng. is apparently the preferred one in later times, and is therefore to be accepted in Js 5:10... where it has the further advantage of fitting better into the context'. But as the LXX and Aristeas seem to know both senses,[138] and as the former appears in Philo, *Jos.* 223, context alone should decide the issue here. Judging by that, the active meaning makes more sense.[139]

μακροθυμία here means 'ability to endure'.[140] See further on v. 7, which has μακροθυμέω; cf. v. 8. Presumably both noun and verb were often associated with Job, which makes the transition to v. 11 natural; cf. T. Job 26.6 ('let us be patient in everything'); 27.10 (Job says: 'You must be patient in everything that happens to you, for patience is superior to everything').

τοὺς προφήτας οἳ ἐλάλησαν ἐν τῷ ὀνόματι κυρίου.[141] This is the only mention of 'the prophets' in our book, although James borrows throughout from Isaiah, Jeremiah, Ezekiel, and other prophetic writings. Henry, *ad loc.*, comments: 'The prophets, on whom God put the greatest honour, and for whom he had the greatest favour, were most afflicted: and, when we think that the best men have had the hardest usage in this world, we should herby be reconciled to affliction'. This is a recurrent thought with commentators.[142]

The qualification, 'who spoke in the name of Lord', perhaps serves to distinguish true prophets from false prophets, even though the latter

---

[134] Although the *Editio Critica Maior* lists numerous variants, the text here printed is solid, being attested in 03C2 18 35 206 429 522 614 *et al.* **Byz** agrees, with μου after ἀδελφοί. Most of the other variants are singly attested and/or confined to late witnesses.

[135] NT: 1×; cf. κακοπαθέω in v. 13. For the variants in spelling—both appear in the mss. for James—see BDF 23. Gk. Pseudepigrapha (Denis): 4×. Philo: 7×. Josephus: 3×.

[136] Mal 1.13; 2 Macc 2.26, 27; 4 Macc 9.8 (κακοπαθείας καὶ ὑπομονῆς).

[137] Cf. Diodorus Siculus 40.3.6; 4 Macc 9.8; Sozomen, *H.E.* 8.26.3 SC 516 ed. Bidez and Hansen, 346-48.

[138] Cf. Let. Aris. 92, 208, 259.

[139] See further Deissmann, *Studies*, 263-64; cf. W. Michaelis, 'κακοπαθέω κτλ.', *TDNT* 5.937: the sense is: 'enduring affliction'.

[140] NT: 14×; Jas: 1×. LXX: 5×. BAGD, s.v., offers two main meanings: 'state of remaining tranquil while awaiting an outcome' (cf. 2 Tim 3.10) and 'state of being able to bear up under provocation' (cf. Gal 5.22). The distinction is perhaps too fine for some texts, including James.

[141] One can hardly decide between ἐν τῷ ὀνόματι κυρίου (so 03 025 18 35 38Z 180 *et al.*) and τῷ ὀνόματι κυρίου (so 02 018 020 044 049 056 0142 1 6 33 *et al.* L156/2 L170/2 *et al.* PsOec).

[142] Cf. Calvin, 310: because 'there is no advantage in perishing with the crowd', James 'picks out the prophets, whose fellowship is blessed'.

could also speak in the name of the Lord; cf. Jer 23.25. More likely, it intimates that the prophets suffered precisely because they spoke in the name of the Lord. In any case, προφήτης (Jas: 1×) + λαλέω (see on 1.19) + ἐν τῷ ὀνόματι (ὄνομα: see on 2.7) + divine genitive is a variant of a Septuagintal idiom, one associated especially with the famous oracle about a prophet like Moses: Deut 18.19 (λαλήσῃ ὁ προφήτης ἐπὶ τῷ ὀνόματί μου);[143] 18.20 (ὁ προφήτης...λαλῆσαι ἐπὶ τῷ ὀνόματί μου...καὶ ὃς ἂν λαλήσῃ ἐπ᾽ ὀνόματι θεῶν ἑτέρων...ὁ προφήτης ἐκεῖνος); Jer 23.25 (λαλοῦσιν οἱ προφῆται...ἐπὶ τῷ ὀνόματί μου); Theod. Dan 9.6 (προφητῶν, οἳ ἐλάλουν ἐν τῷ ὀνόματί σου).[144] See further on 5.14.

Although the Tanak relates very little of the lives and deaths of most of the scriptural prophets,[145] it does tell of Daniel in the lions' den, and it further contains sweeping generalizations about the murders of 'the prophets'.[146] Later Jewish lore, firmly persuaded that the prophets must have been persecuted and slain,[147] filled in the details. Thus we have the collection known as The Lives of the Prophets, which purports that Isaiah was sawn in two[148] and that Jeremiah was stoned.[149] Cf. Heb 11.32-39, where 'the prophets' are on a list of individuals who 'shut the mouths of lions, quenched raging fire, escaped the edge of the sword...were tortured...suffered mocking and flogging, even chains and imprisonment. They were stoned to death, they were sawn in two, they were killed by the sword; they went about in skins of sheep and goats, destitute, persecuted, tormented.'[150] Ancient hearers of James might well have thought in these terms. They may also have recalled the less dramatic biblical texts in which prophets face disbelief and opposition.[151] Note that Tertullian cites Isaiah in his martyrdom as an example of patience.[152]

---

[143] ἐπί is attested as a variant for James: 181 398 1875.

[144] LXX: προφητῶν, ἃ ἐλάλησαν ἐπὶ τῷ ὀνόματί σου.

[145] For Dibelius, 245, it is 'very possible that Jas also had in mind the heroes of the Maccabean period'. Cf. Knoch, 233. Commentators sometimes think of early Christian prophets; so e.g. Bede *ad loc*. CCSL 121 ed. D. Hurst, 219; Plumptre, 101; Sleeper, 134; *et al*.

[146] Cf. 1 Kgs 18.13; 19.1, 10, 14; 2 Kgs 9.7; Neh 9.26; Jer 2.30; cf. 26.20-23. According to Schlatter, 276, James has in view not the deaths of the prophets but how they fulfilled their office during life. The distinction seems artificial.

[147] Cf. Jub. 1.12; Mt 5.12 = Lk 6.23; Acts 7.52; 1 Thess 2.15; Josephus, *Ant*. 10.38; 4 Bar. 9.21-32; etc.

[148] Cf. Mart. Isa. 5.1; Justin, *Dial*. 120.5; y. Sanh. 28c (10.2); b. Yeb. 49b.

[149] Cf. 4 Bar. 9.31; Tertullian, *Scorp*. 8 CSEL 20 ed. Reifferscheid and Wissowa, 160. Ecclus 49.7 says that people 'mistreated' Jeremiah.

[150] The list in Heb 11 probably represents a traditional genre, one with which James and his readers may have been familiar; cf. Ecclus 44-50; 3 Macc 6.4-9; 1 Clem. 9-12.

[151] E.g. Isa 6.6-13; Jer 1.17-19; 20.8-10; Ezek 2.1-7; Amos 7.10-17.

[152] Tertullian, *Pat*. 14 SC 310 ed. Fredouille, 106. 1 Clem. 17.1 calls for the imitation of Elijah, Elisha, Ezekiel, and 'the prophets', who 'went about in goatskins and sheepskins, preaching the coming of Christ'. 17.3-4, moreover, goes on to mention some saintly qualities of Job, although not his patience in particular.

Ecclesiasticus 2.1-18 is a poem on testing that stresses perseverance and patience (v. 4: μακροθύμησον; v. 14: ὑπομονήν). It further emphasizes God's mercy and compassion (vv. 7, 18: ἔλεος; v. 11: οἰκτίρμων), and it invites readers to 'consider the generations of old', asking, 'has anyone trusted in the Lord and been disappointed?' As in James, the past supplies examples of faithful endurance, and patience is rewarded by divine mercy. Given James' knowledge of Sirach, influence at this point is likely.[153] In any case, James distinguishes itself over against Sirach by being more concrete—he illustrates by appeal to the farmer (v. 7) and by naming a particular exemplar, Job (v. 11). He also differs by placing his imperatives within the context of imminent eschatology (vv. 8-9).

Verse 11. James now passes from the general to the particular, from the prophets to Job. His appeal recalls 1.3-4 and 12: constancy is needed in order to win eschatological salvation. Whether or not our text, like b. B. Bat. 15b, implies that Job was a prophet,[154] James clearly assumes on the part of his audience a familiarity with the man and his story.

ἰδοὺ μακαρίζομεν τοὺς ὑπομείναντας. For ἰδοῦ (cf. v. 9) see on 3.4. μακαρίζω,[155] which means 'consider/call blessed or fortunate' and makes for consonance with the four-fold μακρο- of the previous verses, occurs over twenty times in the LXX, ten times for אשׁר. Twice in Job the main character is the object of this verb: 29.10 (οἱ δὲ ἀκούσαντες ἐμακάρισάν με), 11 (οὓς ἤκουσεν καὶ ἐμακάρισέν με). Does James depend upon LXX Job here? Many have rather been put in mind of Theod. Dan 12.12: μακάριος ὁ ὑπομένων.[156]

According to Reicke, 54, 'Behold we bless' is not the speech of James but the speech of the prophets; that is, we have here 'a summary of what the prophets might have announced for the comfort of the Christians'. Reicke then suggests the quotation is from Daniel (see above). Very few have read the text this way, no doubt because the first person plural naturally includes the author; cf. 1.18; 3.1-3, 9. And surely a quotation of the prophets would have been introduced by 'they bless(ed)'.[157]

---

[153] See further Frankemölle, 677-78, 693-96. Popkes, 'Composition', 92, deems such dependence 'obvious'.

[154] Ecclus 49.6-10 has this list: Jeremiah, Ezekiel, Job, the twelve prophets. Does this sequence assume Job's prophetic status? One can find in Job's speeches lines that are prophetic, 19.23 being the most famous example: 'I know that my redeemer lives, and that at the last he will stand upon the earth'. Later Christians regarded this and other declarations as prophetic; cf. Ambrose, *Lk* 4.39 SC 45 ed. Tissot, 167.

[155] NT: 2×; cf. Lk 1.48; Ign. *Eph.* 5.1; Herm. *Sim.* 9.28.6.

[156] LXX: μακάριος ὁ ἐμμένων. Cf. Schlatter, 275; Strobel, *Untersuchungen*, 255; Reicke, 54.

[157] A reminder of how often Protestant exegetes have sought to score points against Roman Catholicism appears in the gratuitous remark of Benson, 111: 'The papists, to countenance their practice of beatifying, or making Saints, in the Church, have translated this text, Behold, we beatifie those, who have suffered with constancy'.

THE NEAR END AND PATIENT ENDURANCE (5.7-11)

Matthew 5.10-12 = Lk 6.22-23, which exegetes often recall here,[158] offers a thematic parallel. The logion blesses (μακάριοι) those persecuted like 'the prophets', and the blessing is made within the context of near eschatological expectation. Deppe, however, urges that Jas 5.10 does not borrow from the Jesus tradition.[159] There are some notable differences: (i) the Synoptics here say nothing about patience; (ii) they do not hold up the prophets for imitation; (iii) they say nothing about Job. Beyond all that, μακαρίζομεν alludes first to Jas 1.12 (μακάριος ἀνὴρ ὃς ὑπομένει),[160] and the notion of suffering prophets was widespread when our letter was written.[161]

Heretofore in vv. 7-10, James has used μακροθυμέω and μακροθυμία. For the final thought, he employs the closely related—and, according to some, stronger—ὑπομένω and ὑπομονή. The two roots, not paired in secular literature, appear together in T. Job 26.5-6 (οὐχ ὑπεμένομεν· ἀλλὰ μακροθυμήσωμεν); T. Jos. 2.7 (ἐμακροθύμησα· ὅτι μέγα φαρμακόν ἐστιν ἡ μακροθυμία, καὶ πολλὰ ἀγαθὰ δίδωσιν ἡ ὑπομονή); and regularly in Christian texts.[162] Chrysostom, *Glor. trib.* PG 51.162, indeed cites Jas 5.10 in this form: ὑπόδειγμα λάβετε, ἀδελφοί, τῆς κακοπαθείας καὶ τῆς ὑπομονῆς.

ὑπομονή was traditionally a Greek virtue, and ὑπομένω played an important role in Stoic ethics.[163] But the immediate background for James is the use of the root in early Christian exhortations having to do with the latter days: one must patiently endure unto the end.[164] This linguistic convention presumably developed out of several influential prophetic oracles[165] as well as the Jewish application of ὑπομονή to martyrdom.[166] It is also important to note that whereas Stoic treatments of ὑπομονή tended to focus on the independence and well-being of the self, in the LXX,

---

[158] As well as when discussing the previous verse; cf. Aretius, 485; Wolzogen, 219; Calmet, 691; Poole, 896; Manton, 426; Bengel, 507; Alford, 324; Beyschlag, 220-21; Plummer, 626; Knowling, 131-32; Schlatter, 275; Davids, 186; Martin, 193; Hartin, 158-61; Kugelman, 59; Maier, 218; Witherington, 538. Moreover, commentators on Mt 5.10-12 par. regularly recall Jas 5.10-11; cf. Albertus Magnus, *Super Mt cap. I–XIV* Opera Omnia 21/1 ed. Schmidt, 117; Bonaventure, *Lk* 11.10 Opera Omnia 10 ed. Peltier, 370; *et al.*

[159] Deppe, *Sayings*, 132-34.

[160] This is why ecclesiastical sources sometimes conflate or associate 1.12 with 5.7-11; note e.g. the Encyclical Epistle of the 649 Council of Lateran ed. Riedinger, 418.

[161] An occasional exegete also cites Mt 10.22 = Mk 13.13: the one who endures (ὑπομείνας) to the end will be saved.

[162] Col 1.11; 2 Tim 3.10; 1 Clem. 6.4; Ign. *Eph.* 3.1; Barn. 2.2; etc.

[163] Cf. Seneca, *Ep. Mor.* 67.10; Epictetus, *Diatr.* 2.2.13; also Philo, *Plant.* 169; *Det.* 30, 45, 51. See further M. Spanneut, 'Geduld', *RAC* 9.247-52.

[164] Cf. Mt 10.22; 24.13; Mk 13.13; Lk 21.14; Rom 8.25; 2 Thess 1.4-5; Rev 1.9.

[165] E.g. Isa 25.9; Dan 12.12; Hab 2.3; LXX Zech 6.14.

[166] Cf. 4 Macc 1.11; 7.9; 17.12; etc.

ὑπομονή renders מִקְוֶה, תִּקְוָה, and קָוָה and so comes to be associated with hope in God.[167]

Even though the chief protagonist of canonical Job is scarcely an exemplar of patient endurance, ὑπομένω occurs over a dozen times in the LXX version of the book (for several different Hebrew verbs); and while sometimes the meaning is simply 'remain', there are instances where the word is used by or of Job in interesting and perhaps loaded ways.[168] No doubt this contributed to associating him with patience.[169]

τὴν ὑπομονὴν 'Ιὼβ ἠκούσατε.[170] For ὑπομονή—a near synonym of μακροθυμία—see on 1.3-4. It is unlikely that 'you have heard' (for ἀκούω see on 1.19) instead of 'you have read' reflects awareness that the patience of Job—the NT names him only here[171]—is less a theme in the canonical book than in extra-canonical traditions. A few exegetes, however, have found the suggestion attractive either because it lessens the tension within the canon or explains how James could hold an opinion so at odds with the book of Job. But ἠκούσατε was a natural way to refer to Scripture as most people indeed heard it read.[172]

The book of Job likely rewrites old traditions about a consistently patient Job, traditions that lived on among Jews, Christians, and Muslims.[173] For Job's patient endurance see Aristeas *apud* Eusebius, *P.E.* 9.25.1-4 ed. Holladay, 268-70;[174] Tob 2.12 (v.l.: Tobit was tried 'so that an example of his patience might be given to posterity, just as was also

---

[167] See the analysis of C. Spicq, 'ὑπομένω, ὑπομονή', *TLNT* 3.418-19.

[168] Such as Job 6.11; 7.3; 9.4; 14.14; 17.13; 22.21.

[169] Aquila's Greek translation additionally had the word in Job 4.6; 6.8; 17.15.

[170] 38T L884 read: 'Ιακώβ. One finds the same mistake in other ancient texts; cf. e.g. T. Abr. RecLng. 15.15: mss. B Q have 'Ιώβ, ms. A 'Ιακώβ.

[171] But both 1 Clem. 26.3 and 2 Clem. 6.8 mention him.

[172] Cf. Mt 5.21, 27, 31, 33, 38; Jn 12.34; Rom 2.13.

[173] For different versions of this thesis see D.B. MacDonald, 'Some External Evidence on the Original Form of the Legend of Job', *AJSL* 14 (1898), 137-64 (MacDonald holds that James refers 'to the Job of tradition' as opposed to the Job of the canon); S. Spiegel, 'Noah, Daniel, and Job: Touching on Canaanite Relics in the Legends of the Jews', in *Louis Ginzberg Jubilee Volume*, New York, 1946, 305-55; H.A. Fine, 'The Tradition of a Patient Job', *JBL* 75 (1955), 28-32 (Job 27–28 contains the same picture of its hero as chaps. 1–2 and the epilogue); H.L. Ginzberg, 'Job the Patient and Job the Impatient', *Conservative Judaism* 21 (1967), 12-28; and especially B. Zuckerman, *Job the Silent*, New York, 1991. According to Theodore of Mopsuestia, the story of Job was well known, and not just among Jews; and he regarded the canonical version as an imperfect variant. See the excerpts from writings of Theodore on Job in G.D. Mansi, *Sacrorum conciliorum nova, et amplissima collectio*, vol. 9, Paris, 1763, 223-25.

[174] On this E.S. Gruen, *Heritage and Hellenism*, Berkeley, 1998, 199, remarks: Aristeas 'includes none of Job's anguish, his bitter laments and protest, his cursing of the day of his birth, the breaking of his spirit, and the fundamental questioning of divine justice. In Aristeas' summary, there is only steadfastness, no wavering, and no doubt. Job endures his afflictions, secure in his faith... Aristeas has shifted the direction of the tale in striking fashion.' The parallel with James is obvious.

that of holy Job');¹⁷⁵ T. Job 1.3 (ἐν πάσῃ ὑπομονῇ γενόμενος); 4.6; 5.1; 26.6; 27.10.¹⁷⁶ Some patristic texts associate Job's ὑπομονή with his being an 'athlete', ἀθλητής.¹⁷⁷

One scholar has written: 'As chapter 3 begins, Job emphatically ceases to be patient. Perhaps James never read beyond chapter 2.'¹⁷⁸ One cannot prove otherwise; and indeed 'it was the simple Job of the Book's prologue and epilogue who was best known and loved by the people'.¹⁷⁹ But ancient writers, including Paul, quote from the central sections of Job, so it was not ignored.¹⁸⁰ Furthermore, the refrain in Job 1.1, 8 and 2.3 characterizes the man from Uz as blameless, upright, God-fearing, and removed from evil, and this cannot but have greatly affected how ancients understood the entire book.¹⁸¹ Already the LXX expands the

---

¹⁷⁵ So the Vulgate: *hanc autem temptationem ideo permisit d(omi)n(u)s euenire illi ut posteris daretur exemplu(m) patientiae eius sicut et s(an)c(t)i Iob*. See S. Weeks, S. Gathercole, and L. Stuckenbruck, *The Book of Tobit*, Berlin, 2004, 99.

¹⁷⁶ Also Tertullian, *Pat.* 14.5 SC 310 ed. Fredouille, 108 (Job's patience is 'an example', as in James); Cyprian, *Mort.* 10 CCSL 3A ed. Simonetti, 21; Methodius of Olympus, *Cibis* 5.5 GCS 27 ed. Bonwetsch, 432; Jerome, *Comm. Eph.* 3.5; Apoc. Paul L¹ 49 ed. Silverstein and Hilhorst, 166-67; Hesychius of Jerusalem, *Hom. Job* 15.12.5; 21.18.12 PO 42 ed. Renoux and Mercier, 377, 524-255. See further C. Haas, 'Job's Perseverance in the Testament of Job', in *Studies on the Testament of Job*, ed. M.A. Knibb and P.W. van der Horst, Cambridge, UK, 1989, 117-54. Job's patience appears also in the Koran, in Sad (38).44. James could instead have cited the example of Abraham, who was also renowned for his patient endurance; cf. Jub. 17.15–18.19; Heb 6.15. But having already named the patriarch in chap. 2, our author may have wished to enlarge the scriptural scope of his appeals.

¹⁷⁷ E.g. Origen, *Job ad* 19.1 PG 12 1032C; Eusebius, *Ps ad* 37.3 PG 23.340D; Ps.-Basil of Caesarea, *Ps 37* 2 PG 30.85D.

¹⁷⁸ E.M. Good, 'The Problem of Evil in the Book of Job', in *The Voice from the Whirlwind*, ed. L.G. Perdue and W.C. Gilpin, Nashville, 1992, 54. Contrast C. Seitz, 'Job', 380, who thinks that ὑπομονή = 'endurance' aptly characterizes the Job of the dialogues: 'James was speaking of the Job of the whole book, especially its central section, and certainly not just the Prologue of Job'. F. Taylor, 132, has a similar view.

¹⁷⁹ J.R. Baskin, *Pharaoh's Counsellors*, Chico, CA, 1983, 27. Cf. S. Schreiner, 'Der gottesfürchtige Rebell oder Wie die Rabbinen die Frömmigkeit Ijobs deuteten', *ZTK* 89 (1992), 163.

¹⁸⁰ Ecclus 23.19 rewrites Job 3.1, 3; 10.19. Bar 3.15 borrows from Job 28.12, 20. Rom 11.25 quotes Job 41.3. 1 Cor 3.19 cites Job 5.12-13. 1 Clem. 39.3-9 runs together Job 4.16-18; 15.15; 4.19-5.5. For an overview of the NT's use of Job see Hainthaler, *Ausdauer*, passim, although one doubts that Jas 5.2 depends upon Job 13.28. Plumptre, 101, opines: 'The book would naturally be studied by one whose attention had been drawn, as St. James's manifestly had been, to the sapiential Books included in the Hagiography of the Old Testament'.

¹⁸¹ These verses were very well known; note 1 Clem. 17.3; Clement of Alexandria, *Strom.* 4.17 GCS 52 ed. Stählin and Früchtel, 295; Origen, *Fr. Luc.* 222 GCS 49 ed. Klostermann, 323; Cyprian, *Mort.* 10 CCSL 3A ed. Simonetti, 21; Eusebius, *P.E.* 7.8.30 GCS 43 ed. Mras, 375; Gregory of Nyssa, *Melet.* ed. Spira, 445; Chrysostom, *Jud.* 8.6 PG 48.936; Vit. Elis. Heracl. 2 = *AnBoll.* 91 (1973), 252; m. Soṭah 5.5; ARN A 2;

words of Job's wife in 2.9 so that she says of him: 'How long will you persist and say, "Behold, I will wait (ἀναμένω) just a little longer, while I wait for (προσδεχόμενος) the hope of my salvation"?'[182] Similarly, Qumran's Job targum evidently knew a Hebrew version of Job 13.15 which read: 'Though he slay me, yet will I wait for/trust in him'.[183] Indeed, and precisely to the point, 11Q10 18.5-6 seems to rewrite Job 31.13 so that Job is not 'impatient' (אתקצרת).[184] Perhaps even more importantly, James' image of Job matches the portrait in the Testament of Job, which 'is in the first place an exhortation to patience and endurance in a troubled and unstable world'.[185] James was less responsible for the perception of Job as patient than Johnson, 319, thinks.

We should then not explain Jas 5.11 by suggesting the author's ignorance of canonical chapters but by positing his knowledge of extra-canonical traditions.[186] In line with this, Job is an exceedingly complex and difficult book that stands in tension with itself, as modern source criticism abundantly demonstrates. That an ancient author or audience might make sense of it by latching onto one of its several themes and then making that theme central is only to be expected. This is evidently what James and his tradition did.[187] Others have done the same. Gregory the Great's *Moralia* offers a reading that regularly preserves Job's piety, and the fifteenth-century 'Life of Job' focuses on the events of his life and largely neglects the dialogues.[188]

Rabbinic texts, which often compare Job unfavorably to Abraham and occasionally identify him as a one-time counselor of Pharaoh and

---

b. B. Bat. 15b; Tanḥ. Buber Wayyeshev 5; Exod. Rab. 21.7; Num. Rab. 22.1. Cf. the summaries in Ezek 14.12-20 and Ecclus Heb 49.19 ('Job, who held fast to all the ways of justice').

[182] On the LXX Job as a bit more pious than his MT counterpart see D.H. Gard, 'The Concept of Job's Character according to the Greek Translator of the Hebrew Text', *JBL* 72 (1953), 182-86.

[183] See B. Zuckerman, 'Two Examples of Editorial Modification in 11QtgJob', in *Biblical and Near Eastern Studies*, ed. G.A. Tuttle, Grand Rapids, MI, 1978, 269-75. Cf. m. Soṭah 5.5: Job served God 'only from love'.

[184] Further, 11Q10 4.3 should probably be reconstructed to read: 'my spirit does not get impatient' (תקצר); see B. Jongeling, C.J. Labuschagne, and A.S. van der Woude, *Aramaic Texts from Qumran*, Leiden, 1976, 16.

[185] G.W.E. Nickelsburg, *Jewish Literature between the Bible and the Mishnah*, rev. ed., Minneapolis, 2005, 320.

[186] Cf. Herzer, 'Hiob', 335-38. We should also not follow Tamez, *Message*, 54, who thinks that James wishes to commend the 'militant patience' of Job, which includes the Job of the dialogues and his 'verbal fury'. Contrast Easton, 66-67: James 'certainly did not mean to encourage his readers to imitate Job's passionate outbursts'.

[187] For a similar analysis see Zuckerman, *Job*, 177-79.

[188] See G.N. Garmonsway and R.M. Raymo, 'A Middle English Metrical Life of Job', in *Early English and Norse Studies Presented to Hugh Smith*, ed. A. Brown and P. Foote, London, 1963, 77-98.

opponent of Moses, are sometimes critical of him.[189] Does James' unqualified generalization intimate that he was unaware of such criticism? Or did he know it and ignore it?[190]

καὶ τὸ τέλος κυρίου εἴδετε.[191] This clause is constructed to balance its predecessor: both have definite article + accusative singular + genitive + second person plural verb ending in -τε. The parallelism explains the cryptic genitive.[192] One may compare 2 Cor 12.1: ἀποκαλύψεις κυρίου = 'revelations given by the Lord'.[193]

As to the sense, some textual authorities clarify through emendation: τέλος (Jas: 1×) becomes ἔλεος, which lines up nicely with the next clause.[194] Augustine and much of subsequent ecclesiastical tradition, identifying the κυρίου with Jesus, find a Christological assertion—either 'you have seen the (self-sacrificial) end[195] of (our) Lord (Jesus Christ)' or 'you have seen (in advance) the end (= *parousia*) of the Lord'.[196] Most

---

[189] Cf. y. Soṭah 20d (5.5); b. Soṭah 11a; b. B. Bat. 16a-b; Exod. Rab. 21.7; Deut. Rab. 2.4. See Urbach, *Sages*, 1.407-16.

[190] Patristic writers could make Job a Christ-figure; so e.g. Jerome, *Job* PL 23.1408; Zeno of Vero, *Tract.* 1(2).15 CCSL 22 ed. Löfstedt, 60-62; Gregory the Great, *Mor.* preface 14 SC 32bis ed. Gillet and Gaudemaris, 162. See G. v. d. Osten, 'Job and Christ: The Development of a Devotional Image', *Journal of the Warburg and Courtauld Institutes* 16 (1953), 153-58. But James, whose Christology is almost wholly quiescent, contains no hint of this tradition.

[191] As in Phil 1.30 and 4.9, the mss. vary between the indicative εἴδετε (01 03* 018 1 6 18 35C 43 61 94 *et al.* L938 L1441 L1442/1 Olymp Polychr PsOec **L**:FV **K**:SBA) and the imperative ἴδετε (so 02 03C2 020 025 044 049 056 0142 5 33 35*V 69 81 88 93 *et al.* L156/2 L170/2 *et al.* LeontB). If one supposes the imperative to be original (so Hauck, 228), one can follow Huther, 152, who translates: 'see (i.e., recognize from this) that the Lord is πολύσπλαγχνός and οἰκτίρμων'.

[192] Preuschen, 'Jac 5, 11', thinks the construction sufficiently odd that the text must be corrupt. Marty, 197, wonders whether κυρίου displaced an original αὐτοῦ. So too Könnecke, *Emendationen*, 17-18. Popkes, 'Scripture', 227, unaccountably infers from the difficulties of 5.11 that our author had only a 'general and secondary knowledge' of Job.

[193] Cf. also Josephus, *Bell.* 5.459 (τὸ γὰρ τέλος εἶναι τοῦ θεοῦ); T. Gad 7.4 (ὅρον γὰρ κυρίου ἐδέξασθε).

[194] So 322 323 424A 915Z 945 1175 1241 1739T L1440*.

[195] Cf. Mt 26.58; T. Abr. RecLng. 1.3; 4.8; 15.1.

[196] Cf. Mt 10.22; 24.3; 1 Cor 1.8; also 1 Pet 2.19-25 and note Augustine, *Ep.* 140.10.26 CSEL 44 ed. Goldbacher, 176; *Sermo ad cat. symb.* 1.2.10 PL 40.633-34; Bede *ad loc.* CCSL 121 ed. D. Hurst, 220 (although he also thinks of Job 42 and Job's restoration); Hermann of Runa, *Fest. serm.* 64.3 CCCM 64 ed. Mikkers, 296; Nicholas of Lyra *ad loc.*; Estius, 452-53;Wettstein, 679; Aretius, 486; Wolf, 76; Lange, 136-37; Bischoff, 'Τὸ τέλος'; Vouga, 136-37. Cf. 1 Pet 2.19-25. But this was not the view of all pre-modern exegetes; note e.g. Olympiodorus of Alexandria, *Job* 19.23-25 PTS 24 ed. U. and D. Hagedorn, 169; also those in n. 198. For decisive criticism see Dibelius, 247. Cf. Mayor, 164: 'If τέλος is supposed to refer to the Resurrection and Ascension, the main point of the comparison (suffering) is omitted: if it refers to the Crucifixion, the encouragement is wanting'.

recent exegetes now take τέλος to refer either to the divine goal for Job—what God intended to bring about all along, namely, his enlightenment[197]—or to the cessation of Job's suffering and the restoration of his life, which followed the dramatic appearance of God.[198] Dominant Greek usage inclines one to favor the former option.[199] But, as Burchard, 203, observes, the exegetical distinction—purpose vs. termination—is likely beside the point. Surely God's intention includes all that happens at the end of the story—lessons learned, suffering stopped, fortunes restored.[200] One might compare Rom 10.4, where τέλος includes cessation—the dispensation of the law is over—but at the same time involves achieving a goal.[201]

For Strobel, 5.11 has in view not only the happy ending of Job but also the *parousia* ('double-sense').[202] The possibility is intriguing. LXX Job 42.17 adds to the MT this: 'And it is written that he will rise again with those the Lord raises up'; and (whatever the intention of the translator) some understood LXX 14.14 ('If a man dies, he will live again') and 19.26 ('my skin will arise') to be prophecies of Job's resurrection.[203] So a reader of James, familiar with the LXX, might imagine Job's happy ending as including (eventually) his resurrection from the dead, or

---

[197] Cf. Job 42.5-6. So the *Catenae* ed. Cramer, 36; Clarke, 826; Mayor, 164; Ropes, 299; Oesterley, 472; Mussner, 207; Martin, 189, 194-195; Cantinat, 240. Cf. Xenophon, *Cyr.* 3.2.29: ἦν θεὸς ἀγαθὸν τέλος διδῷ αὐτῷ.

[198] Cf. John Calvin, *Sermons from Job*, Grand Rapids, MI, 1952, 4; Beza, 560; Grotius, 1091; Wolzogen, 219; Poole, 896; Diodati, *ad loc.*; Burkitt, 1032-33; Schulthess, 172; Surenhuys, 679; Manton, 431-32; Gill, 801; Bengel, 507; Neander, 108; Belser, 190; Carr, 65; Mayor, 264; G. Delling, 'τέλος', *TDNT* 8.55; Laws, 216 ('what the Lord did in the end'); Adamson, 193; Bouttier-Amphoux, 'Prédication', 16; Hartin, 245; Moo, 230. The Peshitta already has this interpretation: דעבד לה = 'that he did for him'.

[199] See R. Badenas, *Christ the End of the Law*, Sheffield, 1985, 38-80. His survey of τέλος in biblical and cognate literature concludes that the word's 'basic connotations are primarily directive, purposive, and completive, not temporal', and that with the genitive the word 'is generally used in expression indicating result, purpose, outcome, and fate, not termination'.

[200] It is only natural that some commentators speak of both purpose and outcome; cf. Henry, *ad loc.*; Mitton, 190 ('Often, indeed, the true purpose of a process only appears at the end. The end reveals the purpose'); Zuckerman, *Job* (as in n. 173), 33 ('both nuances are to be understood'); Johnson, 321.

[201] So now many commentators on Romans; see e.g. L. Kundert, 'Christus als Inkorporation der Torah, τέλος γὰρ νόμου Χριστός', *TZ* 55 (1999), 77-78. Eventuality and goal also coincide in T. Benj. 4.1 ('the τέλος of the good man') and T. Ash. 6.4 ('men's τέλη reveal their righteousness'); note also perhaps Wis 3.19; 4 Macc 12.3; Philo, *Her.* 120.

[202] Strobel, *Untersuchungen*, 254-64. So too Gordon, 'Τέλος'; Cargal, 188-89; Hutchinson Edgar, *Poor*, 207.

[203] Full documentation in H. Tremblay, *Job 19,25-27 dans la Septante et chez les pères grecs*, Paris, 2002. Cf. 1 Clem. 26.3, which cites Job 19.26 as a proof-text of the general resurrection.

perhaps even his present state among the blessed dead.[204] This is the reading of Dionysius bar Salībī: Job received back twofold in this life but also gained life in the world to come.[205] In line with this, the context of v. 11 stresses the end's nearness. Further, one understands why Klein suggests that 'the end of the Lord' in 5.11 corresponds to 'the crown of life' in 1.12.[206] James' words do indeed recall 1.12, where steadfastness under trial produces wholeness and the crown of life. Calvin plausibly affirms that Jas 5.7-11 as a whole encourages readers to persevere because of the eschatological goal set before them.[207]

The LXX and the Testament of Job follow the MT in relating that God abundantly restored Job's worldly possessions so that he became rich again. If, then, τὸ τέλος κυρίου refers to or includes that circumstance, 5.11 implicitly agrees that God gave Job his money a second time. This is striking given the preceding verses. Those who suppose that James denounces the wealthy without exception will necessarily infer that our text here deconstructs itself. Those who hold instead that James does not contain such a sweeping condemnation might find in 5.11 support for their view.

One wonders whether τὸ τέλος κυρίου is intertextually related to the book of Job. In LXX Job 23.3, the sufferer ponders how he might find God and come to 'an end' (τέλος); and in v. 7 he longs for God to bring his case 'to an end' (τέλος). One could reasonably read Job so that its conclusion brings to Job the τέλος he spoke of and desired earlier.

Is τὸ τέλος κυρίου a Semitism? Some older exegetes cite סופו של יי as a parallel.[208] This, however, seems unattested before Rashi. More pertinent is the Aramaic קיצא דיי.[209] It is attested in Frag. Tg. P Exod 13.17, Machsor Vitry, and a fragment of Toseftic Targum on Exod 13.17, in connection with the tradition that the Ephraimites left Egypt before the 'fixed time/end of the Lord', that is, the time for the end of exile that God determined.

The switch from ἠκούσατε to εἴδετε is likely insignificant, the result of James' desire for verbal variety. Yet for Poole, 896, 'Job's patience is heard of, but God's end seen: seeing being a clearer way of perception

---

[204] The subscript to ms. V of the Testament of Job turns the future tenses of LXX Job 42.17a into aorists, obviously on the basis of Mt 27.51b-53: 'And it is written that he [Job] arose with those whom the Lord raised'. But there is no reason to believe that James knew this belief.

[205] Dionysius bar Salībī *ad loc.* CSCO 60 Scriptores Syri 101 ed. Sedlacek, 132. Cf. Calmet, 691; Schnider, 129; Burchard, 'Hiob', 15-17.

[206] Klein, *Werk*, 80. Cf. Ong, *Strategy*, 145: '"What the Lord brought about" (5:11) metaphorically represents the eschatological reward of the crown of life that the author has already mentioned in the argument of the reversal of fortunes (1:12)'.

[207] Calvin, *Sermons from Job*, Grand Rapids, MI, 1952, 4. Cf. Phil. 3.12-16.

[208] E.g. Wolf, 76; Schöttgen, *Horae Hebraicae*, 1031.

[209] Gordon, 'Τέλος', calls attention to this.

than hearing, is put in this latter clause, because God's bounty and recompense was more evident than Job's patience'. Burchard, 203, suggests that Job's perseverance is disclosed only in his words whereas one can 'see' his end in the book of Job's last chapter.[210]

More often than not, Job was thought of as a Gentile. LXX Job 42 makes him an Edomite king, and the Testament of Job tells of his conversion to monotheism. The majority opinion among the rabbis, moreover, was that he was a Gentile; see b. B. Bat. 15b. Already the Tanak implies his Gentile status by (i) making him hail from 'the land of Uz', (ii) failing to give him a genealogy, and (iii) omitting any reference to Israel's history in Job. An exegete of James might make something of this: chap. 2 commends the Gentile Rahab as well as Abraham, a Gentile by birth, while Elijah, named later in this chapter, preached to Gentiles: 1 Kgs 17.1-16; Lk 4.25-26. Yet James says nothing about Job's ethnicity, and most commentators have followed suit.[211]

ὅτι πολύσπλαγχνός ἐστιν ὁ κύριος καὶ οἰκτίρμων.[212] Cf. Pss. Sol. 16.15 (ἐν τῷ ὑπομεῖναι δίκαιον ἐν τούτοις ἐλεηθήσεται ὑπὸ κυρίου); T. Job 26.6 (μακροθυμήσωμεν ἐν παντὶ ἕως οὗ ὁ κύριος σπλαγχνισθείς). For κύριος see on 1.1. Here 'the Lord' must once again be God, not Jesus.

Both οἰκτίρμων[213] and οἰκτιρμός were conventionally paired with related adjectives and nouns to characterize God as graceful, compassionate, merciful.[214] Such language, which is first attested in the divine attribute formula of Exod 34.6, was liturgical.[215] But the combination with πολύσπλαγνος is unattested, the closest parallels before Clement of Alexandria and Origen being Phil 2.1 (σπλάγχνα καὶ οἰτιρμοί); Col 3.12 (σπλάγχνα οἰτιρμοῦ); 1 Clem. 23.1 (ὁ οἰκτίρμων...ἔχει σπλάγχνα). Here then we seemingly have again James' fondness for new variations on old ways of speaking.

πολύσπλαγχνος,[216] probably modeled upon πολυέλεος,[217] is very rare and wholly absent from pre-Christian sources. It does appear in

---

[210] Cf. Knowling, 133: 'like a drama unfolds itself scene by scene'.

[211] But note Zuckerman, *Job*, 177: 'Job was a gentile and thus proof positive that one need not necessarily be a Jew to have the special merits of chosenness and endurance'.

[212] 69 88 *et al.* **Byz G**:G-D **Sl**:ChMOSiSt omit ὁ κύριος. 01 02 025 044 5 33 81 *et al.* L170/2 *et al.* Dam PsOec have it. 03 lacks the article. 621 puts ὁ κύριος at the end.

[213] NT: 2×; cf. Lk 6.36. LXX: most often for רחום.

[214] E.g. LXX Exod 34.6; 2 Chr 30.9; Neh 9.17, 31; Pss 24.6; 39.12; 50.3; 85.15; 102.8-9 (οἰκτίρμων καὶ ἐλεήμων ὁ κύριος, μακρόθυμος...οὐκ εἰς τέλος ὀργισθήσεται; Moffatt, 74, and Hutchinson Edgar, *Poor*, 208 n. 89, suppose that James adopts the language of this text in particular; contrast Deppe, *Sayings*, 47-48); Hos 2.19; Lam 3.22; 1 Macc 3.44; Jos. Asen. 11.10; T. Jud. 19.3; cf. also 1QH 19(11).29; 4Q511 52, 54-55, 57-59; LAB 19.8; 4 Ezra 7.132-33; 2 Bar. 77.7; Apoc. Abr. 17.10.

[215] J. Scharbert, 'Formgeschichte und Exegese von Ex 34,6f und seiner Parallelen', *Bib* 38 (1957), 130-50; R.C. Dentan, 'The Literary Affinities of Exodus XXXIV 6f.', *VT* 13 (1963), 34-51. Cf. the Koranic refrain, 'In the name of Allah, the compassionate, the merciful'.

[216] LXX: 0×. NT: 1×. Gk. Pseudepigrapha (Denis): 0×. Philo: 0×. Josephus: 0×.

Herm. *Mand.* 4.3.5 (πολυεύσπλαγχνος οὖν ὢν ὁ κύριος); *Sim.* 5.4.4 (ὁ κύριος πολυεύσπλαγχνος); 5.7.4 (ὁ κύριος πάντως πολύσπλαγχνος); and Acts Thom. 119 ed. Bonnet, 229, while the related πολυσπλαγχνία appears in Herm. *Vis.* 1.3.2; 2.2.8; 4.2.3; *Mand.* 9.2; *Sim.* 8.6.1; Justin, *Dial.* 55.3. Those who accept the influence of James upon Hermas can entertain the possibility that James himself coined πολύσπλαγχνος.

In the LXX, οἰκτιρμός most often translates רחם, and σπλάγχνα does so once (Prov 12.10). This interests because, although those two Greek words play no role in the conclusion of LXX Job or the Testament of Job, רחם appears in Qumran's targum on Job 42.9-12: 'and God turned to Job in mercy' (ברחמין, 11Q10 38.3). Maybe our author had heard a targum on Job with this reading, or some other source with its sentiment.

---

[217] Cf. the LXX's formula, μακρόθυμος καὶ πολυέλεος: Exod 34.6; Num 14.18; Neh 9.17; Pss 85.5, 15; 102.8; 144.8; Ecclus 2.11; Joel 2.13 (several of these have ὁ κύριος); also Pry. Man. 7 (κύριος ὕψιστος, εὔσπλαγχνος, μακρόθυμος καὶ πολυέλεος); Jos. Asen. 11.10 (οἰκτίρμων καὶ μακρόθυμος καὶ πολυέλεος); Gk. Apoc. Ezra 1.10 (εὔσπλαγχνε καὶ πολυέλεος).

XVII

PROHIBITION OF OATHS (5.12)[1]

But above all, my brothers, do not swear—not by heaven, not by earth, not by any other oath. But let your yes be yes and your no no, so that you may not fall under judgment.

History of Interpretation and Reception

Our verse has always been read in connection with Mt 5.33-34, a close relative that also forbids oaths.[2] The two texts are in harmony with each other but in seeming conflict with the rest of the Bible. The Tanak, in which not only saints such as Abraham but also God swear, generally permits oaths in everyday speech, provided they are neither false nor irreverent.[3] One understands why Theophylact inferred that, at the time of Moses, 'it was not evil to swear; but that after Christ, it is evil'.[4] Yet even

---

[1] Recent literature: Baker, *Speech-Ethics*, 278-82; idem, 'Contexts'; Bauernfeind, 'Eid'; Bauernfeind, *Frieden*; Brunner, 'Rede'; Daube, 'Reconstruction', 67-70; Dautzenberg, 'Schwurverbot'; Deppe, *Sayings*, 134-49; Duling, 'Oaths'; Hartin, *Q*, 188-91; Ito, 'Question'; Kollmann, 'Schwurverbot'; Kutsch, 'Rede'; Marconi, 'Debolezza'; Meier, 'Oaths 1'; idem, 'Oaths 2'; Minear, 'Demand'; Puech, 'Qumrân', 39-41; Stählin, 'Beteuerungsformeln'; Vahrenhorst, *Matthäus*; idem, 'Oath'; Welborn, 'Affirmation'; Wypadlo, *Gebet*, 196-209.

[2] The two texts are often unconsciously assimilated; thus Epiphanius, *Pan.* 19.6 GCS 25 ed. Holl, 223, quotes these words as being ἐν τῷ εὐαγγελίῳ: 'Swear not, neither by heaven, nor by earth, neither any other oath. But let your yes be yes and your no no; whatever is more than these comes from the evil one.' Although the last clause is from Matthew, the rest is much closer to James. Cf. also the assimilation of Matthew to James in Chrysostom, *Hom. Mt* 17.5 PG 57.261. For the history of the interpretation of Mt 5.33-37 see H. Takaaki, *The Prohibition of Oath-Taking in the Gospel of Matthew*, Ann Arbor, MI, 1991, 18-68; Luz, *Matthew* 1.266-68.

[3] See Gen 14.22; 22.16; Exod 20.7; Lev 19.12; Num 30.3-15; Deut 6.13; 10.20; 23.21-3; 1 Kgs 17.1; 22.14; Pss 50.14; 63.11; 105.9; Isa 65.16; Jer 12.16; 23.7-8; Zech 8.17; Wis 14.28; cf. 11QTemple 53-4; T. Asher 2.6; Sib. Or. 2.68; Ps.-Phoc. 16.

[4] Theophylact, *Comm. Mt ad* 5.37 PG 123.199B, echoing Chrysostom, *Hom. Mt* 17.5 PG 57.261-62. Cf. Menno Simons, 'Confession of the Distressed Christians', *The Complete Writings of Menno Simons*, ed. J.C. Wenger, Scottsdale, PA, 1956, 518-19: 'Jesus does not...point His disciples to...the dispensation of imperfectness which allowed swearing, but He points us now from the Law to yea and nay, as to the dispensation of completeness'. As proof, Simons quotes Matthew and then James.

in the NT, Paul more than once calls upon God as his witness,[5] and in Rev 10.6, an angel 'swears by him who lives forever and ever'.

Because most Christians have been uncomfortable with the idea that Scripture contradicts itself, they have tried harmonizing strategies. One way to lessen or undo the perceived tension is to suppose that the NT prohibition of oaths is not comprehensive: the situation envisaged is not swearing on solemn formal occasions such as in court but swearing in everyday speech (which, according to Philo, was common among his Jewish contemporaries).[6] On this interpretation, Matthew's Jesus and James counter only 'the evil habit of swearing incessantly and thoughtlessly about ordinary matters',[7] or they permit swearing in God's name but ban the substitute oaths with which some thought to cheat the truth.[8] Roman Catholic theologians and exegetes have traditionally taken this view.[9] So too most Protestants.[10] It is enshrined in the 39th article of religion in the Book of Common Prayer: 'As we confess that vain and rash Swearing is forbidden Christian men by our Lord Jesus Christ, and James his Apostle, so we judge, that Christian Religion doth not prohibit,

---

[5] Rom 1.9; 2 Cor 1.23; Gal 1.20; and Phil 1.8.

[6] Philo, *Decal.* 92. As a matter of fact, the historical Jesus, if he prohibited oaths, may not have had the courtroom in his purview at all but instead the daily life of his hearers; cf. Ropes, 300-301: 'a saying such as...Mt. 5.37, would at once suggest ordinary swearing, not the rare and solemn occasion about which modern readers have been so much concerned'.

[7] Philo, *Decal.* 92.

[8] Cf. the Heidelberg Catechism, quest. 102, where 'a lawful oath is calling upon God' and Jas 5.12 is cited; also the Westminster Catechism § 24.2. For a collection of historical Christian documents on the topic see H. Gollwitzer, ed., *Eid, Gewissen, Treuepflicht*, Frankfurt am Main, 1965, 153-300.

[9] E.g. Cassiodorus, *Ep. Jac. ad loc.* PL 70.1380C; Aquinas, *Summa* 2/2 q. 89 aa. 2-3; Nicholas of Lyra, *ad loc.*; Estius, 453-55; H. Noldin, *De Praeceptis Dei et Ecclesiae*, 9th ed., Regensburg, 1911, 255-56; Bardenhewer, 147; Belser, 192-93; Mussner, 212; Knoch, 239-40; Kugelman, 62. As so often, Augustine was here influential; see especially *Serm.* 180 PL 38.972-79. Cf. the current 'Catechism of the Catholic Church' § 2154: 'The tradition of the Church has understood Jesus' words [in Mt 5.33-37] as not excluding oaths made for grave and right reasons (for example, in court)'. Occasionally, the prohibition has been applied to the so-called religious only; see e.g. Leander of Seville, *Reg.* 19 PL 72.891A-B.

[10] Cf. Calvin, 312-13; Pareus, 571-72; Aretius, 486; Grotius, 1091; Poole, 896; Manton, 436-37; Gill, 801; Burkitt, 1033; Wesley, 869; Barrow, 'Against Rash and Vain Swearing', *Sermons*, 329-53; Huther, 154-56; D.X. Junkin, *The Oath a Divine Ordinance*, Philadelphia, 1851; Beyschlag, 224; Ellicott, 378; Knowling, 153-54; Maier, 222, 224; *et al.* 'The Solid Declaration of the Formula of Concord' § 12.10, deems it an error to hold that 'a Christian cannot with a good conscience take an oath before a court, nor with an oath do homage to his prince or hereditary sovereign'. See further M. Honecker, 'Der Eid heute angesichts seiner reformatorischen Beurteilung und der abendländischen Eidestradition', in *Ich Schwöre*, ed. G. Niemeier, Munich, 1968, 27-92. The early Protestant commentaries sometimes rail against swearing by the Virgin Mary.

but that a man may swear when the Magistrate requireth, in a cause of faith and charity, so it be done according to the Prophet's teaching, in justice, judgment, and truth'.

The canonical issue explains why many discussions of Jas 5.12 have been less expositions of that verse than commentary upon the scriptural texts that together seem to trump its plain meaning. Most commonly considered from the NT are Mt 26.63-64, where Jesus has been thought to swear, Paul's several uses of an oath formula (see n. 5), Heb 6.13-18; 7.20-28; and Rev 10.6.[11] The general principle has been this: 'To interpret the Scriptures...we must not consider a part independently of the rest; but refer it to the whole, and see what will be the result by comparison'.[12]

Some, however, have nonetheless taken the prohibition at face value, even if this results in a contradiction with other parts of the canon. This was the view of the Pelagians, the Cathari, and the Waldensians, and it continues to be that of many Anabaptists, as expressed for instance in the seventh article of the Schleitheim Confession (1527).[13] Mennonites and Quakers have also tended to avoid the oath, as have the followers of Wycliffe and several Russian sects.[14] William Penn wrote a whole treatise on the subject.[15] It contains a treasure of pagan, Jewish, and Christian testimonies against oaths, testimonies that consistently recognize that oaths are only necessary because people so often lie. Penn himself states that his position contradicts the law of Moses.[16] The issue evoked much controversy during and after the Reformation, the heated nature of which is on display in Calvin's vigorous treatment of the subject.[17]

---

[11] See e.g. Wolzogen, 220; Johnstone, 392-94; Stier, 462-64; Winkler, 69; Plummer, 629-30. For a historical-critical discussion of how those passages relate to James see Stählin, 'Beteuerungsformeln'.

[12] W.C. Johnson, *The Nature, Use, and Lawfulness of Oaths*, Trenton, N.J., 1824, 30.

[13] For the Pelagians and Albigensians see F.A. Göpfert, *Der Eid*, Mainz, 1883, 111-16. For the Waldensians see K.-V. Selge, *Die Ersten Waldenser*, vol. 1, Berlin, 1967, 155-57. P. Ridemann, *Account of our Religion, Doctrine and Faith*, Suffolk, n.d., 114-20, 194-205, represents the rejection of oaths in the Hutterite tradition.

[14] For the Mennonites see H. Fast, 'Die Eidesverweigerung bei den Mennoniten', in Gollwitzer, *Eid* (as in n. 8), 136-52. Commentators on James with this understanding include Chrysostom and Cyril of Alexandria in the *Catenae* ed. Cramer, 36; Bede *ad loc.* CCSL 121 ed. Hurst, 220; Ps.-Oecumenius *ad loc.* PG 119.506C-507A; Erasmus, *Paraphrase*, 168; Theile, 266; Schneider, 35; Witherington, 541.

[15] *A Treatise on Oaths* in *The Select Works of William Penn*, 3 vols., London, 1825, 3.29-127.

[16] So too G. Fox, *A Journal or Historical Account*, Philadelphia, n.d., 162.

[17] See J. Calvin, *Treatises against the Anabaptists and Against the Libertines*, Grand Rapids, MI, 1982, 92-105. The deist, M. Tindal, *Christianity as Old as the Creation*, London, 1731, 314-18, thought the prohibition of oaths an example of an imperative that must be interpreted according to the spirit, not the letter, that is, 'explained, limited, and restrained' by reason and the promotion of human happiness.

Augustine took the injunction to let one's yes be yes and one's no no to require truth-telling without exception. That is, lying is forbidden even when the outcome is evil.[18] Gregory the Great and Aquinas held the same view.[19] But Cassian, while conceding that the demand for yes and no demands honesty, refused to see it as an absolute: what matters is intention, and one may lie to avoid a greater evil.[20] This became the dominant tradition in the East.[21]

As with so many other verses in James, 5.12 has been a recurrent occasion for condescending slurs about Jews and 'Orientals'. According to Guyse, 'the infidel Jews are abominably addicted' to 'the flagrant Sin' of 'impious Cursing and Swearing'.[22] Gibson, 70, thought it instructive to quote from a nineteenth-century travelogue: 'This people are fearfully profane. Everybody curses and swears when in a passion. No people that I have ever known can compare with these Orientals for profaneness in their use of the names and attributes of God. The evil habit seems inveterate and universal.'[23] This comment is followed by the homiletical observations of a certain Rev. C. Jerdan: 'colloquial swearing was a clamant sin among the Hebrews, as it still is among the Orientals. The people generally were adepts in the use of profane expletives'.[24] Smith, 329-30, penned these offensive words: 'The Jew was…not at all afraid of being untruthful' and 'was willing to cheat any Gentile in business' because he 'did not feel obliged to keep faith with Gentiles'.[25]

---

[18] Augustine, *Men.* 16 CSEL 41 ed. Zycha, 420-21.
[19] See n. 101 for commentators who think 5.12 prohibits lying.
[20] John Cassian, *Conf.* 17.10-11 SC 54 ed. Pichery, 256.
[21] See further B. Ramsey, 'Two Traditions on Lying and Deception in the Ancient Church', *The Thomist* 49 (1985), 504-33. Farley, 52, writing from an Eastern Orthodox viewpoint, takes James to imply that one should not use the divine name in a casual way, as in so much modern speech.
[22] Guyse, 596. Cf. Doddridge, 848. Although Manton, 435, concurs, he makes a feeble stab at fairness: swearing is also 'common…among some nations to this day—as the Dutch, French, Scottish, though the English have too much written after their copy'.
[23] The words are from W.M. Thomson, *The Land and the Book*, vol. 1, New York, 1860, 284. Johnstone, 398-99, quotes from the same passage, even more fully.
[24] Gibson, 79. Note also T. Scott, 588 ('the Jews were remarkably guilty of common swearing'); Bassett, 76 (oath-taking is 'a habit still in painful prevalence among that nation').
[25] Recognizing the prejudice in such comments should not prevent us from inferring that oath-taking was indeed common among some or many ancient Jews. According to S. Lieberman, *Greek in Jewish Palestine*, New York, 1942, 115, 'The natural tendency to swear was carried to excess; the populace swore always and everywhere, not contenting themselves with the name of God…but turning to the strangest and most varied objects to serve vicariously as surety for their veracity'. Yet note that Philo, *Spec.* 2.8, said much the same thing of Gentiles he knew: 'So highly impious are they that on any chance matter the most tremendous titles are on their lips and they do not blush to use name after name, one piled upon another, thinking that the continual repetition of a string of oaths will secure them their object'.

Exegesis

Why does the prohibition of oaths appear here, sandwiched between a call to patient endurance (vv. 7-11) and sayings about prayer and confession (vv. 13-18)? James has already, especially in 1.26; 3.1-12; and 4.11-12, addressed sins of the tongue. Bede accordingly writes: since James 'wants to draw out the deadly poison of the tongue completely from his hearers', and 'having forbidden them from slandering one another, prohibited them from judging their neighbor, and restrained them from complaining against each other in adversity', he now seeks to counter all swearing.[26] The undoubted continuity of concern, however, fails to explain why 5.12, which might have been more fittingly attached to some earlier passage, is exactly where it is.

According to Oesterley, 472-73, 'there is not the remotest connection between this verse and the section that has gone before', so it 'must be regarded as the fragment of some larger piece'.[27] Huther, 154, without positing such a source, also divines no connection with the preceding, other than an intention to address the readers' situation.[28] Similarly, Minear surmises that, in Jas 5, 'we are dealing with an unorganized jumble of oral traditions which the editor felt no pressure to reorder into a smoother literary sequence'.[29] It is understandable that commentators have sometimes treated v. 12 as its own section.[30] Rendall considers it 'so jejune, so irrelevant, and so interruptive of the general sense', that he reckons it 'an intruding adscript or gloss, originally appended perhaps as comment on iii. 9-10'.[31]

Others, however, divine links between 5.12 and its literary context. Bengel, 507, deems v. 12 a fitting introduction for v. 13: when faced with adversity, one should use the tongue to pray, not swear. He likewise links v. 12 to vv. 7-11: one swears out of impatience. Numerous expositors have had the same thought.[32] Yet πρὸ πάντων δὲ ἀδελφοί μου surely

---

[26] Bede *ad loc.* CCSL 121 ed. Hurst, 220.

[27] Cf. Dibelius, 248 ('this verse has no relationship with what precedes or follows'); Davids, 188; McKnight, 424.

[28] Cf. Moffatt, 75: 'Probably James jotted it down as an after-thought, to emphasize the warning of ver. 9'.

[29] Minear, 'Demand', 7.

[30] Cf. Chaine, 125-26; Marty, 198-203; Mussner, 211-12; Mitton, 190-95; Vouga, 138-39; Schnider, 130-32; Hartin, 257-64. From an earlier time note Pareus, 570-72; Benson, 112-15 ('a distinct section').

[31] Rendall, *Christianity*, 68 n. 1.

[32] Cf. Trapp, 703; Whitby, 695; Gill, 801; W. Wall, 349; Mayor, 167; Alford, 325; Plummer, 628; Smith, 314-15; Chaine, 425; Tasker, 124; Reicke, 56; Cantinat, 241; Motyer, 183; Martin, 203; Stulac, 177; Marconi, 'Debolezza' (who sees 5.7-12 as a unit); McCartney, 247. Some have made the implausible suggestion that the text concerns the state's demand to renounce one's faith under oath.

suggests a new topic, not continuity with the previous section. For Baker, the concluding 'so that you may not fall under judgment' is the key to the location of 5.12.[33] The verse ends a series of eschatological warnings, several of which have to do with sins of speech: 4.11-12, 17; 5.7-9. Church, 409, draws a line back to 5.1-6: those who hired but did not pay lack integrity; 'their "yes" at hiring time should have been matched by a "yes" at pay time'. Ruckstuhl, 30, like many, perceives a connection with v. 9 in particular: the mention of the judgment there encouraged placing a saying about judgment here. Bennett, 179, seemingly suggests that the conflicts of 4.1-12 are in view: 'In your bitter controversies specially restrain from taking an oath that your views are correct, or that you will not associate with those who differ from you'. Keenan, 162, finds yet another way of tying v. 12 to its context: 'the immediate focus...is upon Job and his attempts to drag God into court, to subject God's truth to human norms of validation. He has just said that the judge is standing at the door, so it follows that we should not usurp the role of judging, of validating the final truth of our statements.' Keenan goes on to urge that James also here qualifies his endorsement of Job, because the latter used oaths.[34] For Wypadlo, 5.12 fitly introduces 5.13-18 because it recapitulates James ἁπλοῦς-ideal and demands dissociation from the value-structures of the world.[35] This writer prefers the candor of the uncertain Clarke, 896: 'What relation this exhortation can have to the subject in question, I confess I cannot see. It may not have been designed to stand in any connection, but to be a separate piece of advice.'

5.7-11, according to Beyschlag, 223, would have been an appropriate ending to our epistle, especially as the verses take us back to the first chapter and so create a large *inclusio*. In his judgment, then, 5.12-20 has the character of a *Nachschrift*, a postscript.[36] Plummer, 625, 628, says much the same thing: having concluded his chief topics, James thought of two more pertinent topics and so reopened 'his letter to add them by way of a farewell word of counsel'. But according to Deppe, the grouping of *paraenesis* about the last days, oaths, healing, confession, and reconciliation reflect a primitive church order, one less developed than Did. 7–16.[37] Many others, influenced by Francis, 'Form', now regard 5.12-20 as a proper epistolary conclusion. So for instance Johnson, 325-46, who treats v. 12 as the introduction to the entire section, which he thinks of as 'a discourse on positive modes of speech in the community'. This writer, who finds in v. 12 reason to sympathize with Luther's famous remark that

---

[33] Baker, *Speech-Ethics*, 278. Also emphasizing the theme of eschatological judgment are Ropes, 300; Hauck, 31; Mussner, 211; Mitton, 191; Kugelman, 61; Davids, 188; Schrage, 54.

[34] E.g. 27.2. Belser, 192-93, and Stier, 461-62, also draw a comparison with the oppressed Job.

[35] Wypadlo, *Gebet*, 209.

[36] Cf. Zodhiates, *Patience*, 109.

[37] Deppe, *Sayings*, 135.

our author 'throws things together chaotically', is content to observe that the end of James is a bit like the end of 1 Thessalonians and the end of Hebrews: these too collect an assortment of moral injunctions.

James 5.17 reproduces a saying also known from Mt 5.33-37:[38]

Mt 5.33-37

33 πάλιν ἠκούσατε ὅτι ἐρρέθη τοῖς ἀρχαίοις· οὐκ ἐπιορκήσεις, ἀποδώσεις δὲ τῷ κυρίῳ τοὺς ὅρκους σου.
34 ἐγὼ δὲ λέγω ὑμῖν μὴ ὀμόσαι ὅλως·
μήτε ἐν τῷ οὐρανῷ ὅτι θρόνος ἐστὶν τοῦ θεοῦ
35 μήτε ἐν τῇ γῇ ὅτι ὑποπόδιόν ἐστιν τῶν ποδῶν αὐτοῦ μήτε εἰς Ἱεροσόλυμα ὅτι πόλις ἐστὶν τοῦ μεγάλου βασιλέως
36 μήτε ἐν τῇ κεφαλῇ σου ὀμόσῃς ὅτι οὐ δύνασαι μίαν τρίχα λευκὴν ποιῆσαι ἢ μέλαιναν.
37 ἔστω δὲ ὁ λόγος ὑμῶν ναὶ ναί, οὒ οὔ.
τὸ δὲ περισσὸν τούτων ἐκ τοῦ πονηροῦ ἐστιν.

Jas 5.12

πρὸ πάντων δὲ ἀδελφοί μου

μὴ ὀμνύετε
μήτε τὸν οὐρανὸν
μήτε τὴν γῆν
μήτε ἄλλον τινὰ ὅρκον

ἤτω δὲ ὑμῶν τὸ ναὶ ναὶ καὶ τὸ οὒ οὔ
ἵνα μὴ ὑπὸ κρίσιν πέσητε

In addition to sharing words, phrases, and content, the two texts have the same basic structure and order:

1. Prohibition 'do not swear at all' (Mt)
   'do not swear' (Jas)
2. Elaboration via examples 'heaven...earth...Jerusalem...your head' (Mt)
   'heaven...earth...any other oath' (Jas)
3. Demand for truthfulness 'let your word be yes yes, no no' (Mt)
   'let your yes be yes, your no no' (Jas)
4. Reason for imperative 'anything more than this comes from the evil one' (Mt)
   'that you may not fall under judgment' (Jas)

Matthew's version may be composite. 'Do not swear at all' (v. 34a) makes vv. 34b-6 ('neither by heaven, etc.') otiose. In addition, v. 33, being akin to 5.21, 27, 31, 38, and 43, is often reckoned to be editorial, and the subtraction of vv. 33 and 34b-36 leaves a perfectly coherent piece. So it is inviting to infer that the original unit consisted of 5.34a + 37.[39] Verses 34b-36, moreover, may reflect more than one developmental stage. Not only do vv. 34b-35 have the plural whereas v. 36 employs the singular, but the latter has a slightly different form than the similar clauses in vv. 34b-35,[40] and v. 36 reintroduces the verb 'to swear'.

[38] For a detailed listing of the similarities and differences between James and Matthew here see Deppe, *Sayings*, 140-41; Meier, 'Oaths 1'.
[39] For related analyses see Minear, 'Demand'; Deppe, *Sayings*, 134-49; Luz, *Matthew*, 1.260-61; Tsuji, *Glaube*, 121-22; Vahrenhorst, *Matthäus*, 256-58; Meier, 'Oaths 1'. Duling, 'Oaths', supplies a review and analysis of several tradition-histories.
[40] These last feature ὅτι + noun + ἐστίν + genitive as opposed to ὅτι οὐ δύνασαι μίαν τρίχα κτλ.

Such an analysis, many have thought, gains support from Jas 5.17. It has no equivalent to v. 33 and no parallel to the secondary v. 36. It thus appears to preserve the conjectured primitive form, with only the addition of the clause about heaven and earth.[41]

But there is room for doubt. If James knew Matthew and wished not to reproduce the saying in 5.33-37 but instead to convey its gist, it would have been altogether natural for him (i) to focus on the first and final imperatives as they contain the main points of the saying; (ii) to eliminate the antithetical format, which would serve no function in his context; and (iii) to drop the elaborations in Mt 5.35b-36, which are strictly redundant. It accords with this last possibility that James' μήτε ἄλλον τινὰ ὅρκον suggests knowledge of more than the clause about heaven and earth. Just such an editorial process may explain Justin Martyr's version of our saying: μὴ ὀμόσητε ὅλως· ἔστω δὲ ὑμῶν τὸ ναὶ ναί καὶ τὸ οὒ οὒ· τὸ δὲ περισσὸν τούτων ἐκ τοῦ πονηροῦ. This is probably a revision of Matthew without any influence from James.[42]

According to Burchard, 206-207, as James leaves 5.12 unattributed, he did not know it as a word of Jesus.[43] This is, whatever the origin of the ban on oaths, a weak argument from silence.[44] Material with close synoptic parallels is scattered throughout James, and it stretches credulity to suppose that our author thought none of it to come from Jesus. Yet he attributes not one word to him. 5.12 is of a piece with the rest.

Verse 12. In a perfect world, oaths would not be needed. They presuppose that there are two types of statements, one which demands commitment (the oath), one which does not (the statement without an oath). If, however, human beings were invariably committed to every statement, oaths would be altogether superfluous. Indeed, and ironically, Philo, like Coleridge later on ('The more oath-taking, the more lying'), observed that frequent oath-taking is really a sign of untrustworthiness.[45]

---

[41] Contrast Rendall, *Christianity*, 68: Matthew's version has the 'fuller and more authentic form'.

[42] Justin Martyr, *1 Apol.* 16.5 PTS 38 ed. Marcovich, 118. For the source-critical issues see W.-D. Köhler, *Die Rezeption des Matthäusevangelium in der Zeit vor Irenäus*, Tübingen, 1987, 211-13. Deppe, *Sayings*, 213, takes the agreements with James to be consistent with a Roman origin for our epistle: they reflect a Roman form of the saying of Jesus.

[43] Cf. Dautzenberg, 'Schwurverbot', 61-63, who denies attribution of the prohibition to the historical Jesus.

[44] Cf. Stählin, 'Beteuerungsformeln', 118 n. 2: 'the failure of a citation-formula says nothing'. See further Ito, 'Question', 10-12; Meier, 'Oaths 2', 8-16.

[45] Philo, *Leg.* 2.8. Curiously, Robertson, 248-51, wrongly associates 5.12 with 'profanity' and 'violent expletives'. But the subject is oaths, not crude, offensive, or vulgar language.

πρὸ πάντων δέ. A common Greek expression, although (if one includes the δέ) it appears only here in the Greek Bible.[46] Augustine sensibly asks, 'Is swearing after all worse than stealing? Is swearing worse than committing adultery?... Is swearing worse than killing a person?' He answers: 'Perish the thought!'[47] Mitton, 191, judges that πρὸ πάντων δέ 'ought not to be pressed too literally'. James is simply calling 'attention to something he wishes his readers to take special notice of'.[48] For Laws, 220, the emphatic transitional phrase introduces not just v. 12 but, it seems, all the imperatives through v. 20.[49] For this 1 Pet 4.8 may supply a parallel.[50] Popkes, 332, suggests that the words introduce vv. 12-18. Easton, 69, rather urges that πρὸ πάντων δέ emphasizes that what follows comes from Jesus.[51] Baker takes πρὸ πάντων δέ to signal that 5.12 is the most important of the sins of speech covered in chaps. 4–5.[52] Oesterley, 472-73, rather finds in the words evidence that James v. 12 is an excerpt: πρὸ πάντων served its function in some other context. Dibelius, 248, thinks this possible. Francis, observing that many ancient epistles use 'above all' near their conclusions and that they also often employ oaths and wishes for health, sees in πρὸ πάντων δέ indication that the epistle is nearing its end.[53] Hartin, 258, agrees and translates with 'finally'. Yet our author does not take an oath but dismisses oaths, and he associates 'above all' not with good wishes but a prohibition. Guyse, 597, proposes that πρὸ πάντων = 'before all things' and 'may refer to the profane Custom of prefixing an Oath, in common Conversation, to all that is affirmed, or denied'. In other words: 'Do not swear before everything you say'.[54] Dimont, 637, takes the sense to be: 'above all other signs

---

[46] Cf. Philo, *Ebr.* 63; Josephus, *Ant.* 17.7; 20.127; *Bell.* 1.490; Did. 10.4; Epictetus, *Diatr.* 3.22.93; Lucian, *Salt.* 36, 59; *Lex.* 23; Ps.-Justin, *Ep. Zen.* 18 ed. Otto, 84; etc. See further J.A. Robinson, *St Paul's Epistle to the Ephesians*, 2nd ed., London, n.d., 278-79. πρὸ πάντων occurs in Col 1.17 and 1 Pet 4.8 but nowhere in the LXX.

[47] Augustine, *Serm.* 180.9 PL 38.977.

[48] Cf. Carr, 65; Knowling, 135; Mussner, 211; Cantinat, 241; Deppe, *Sayings*, 135-36; McKnight, 424-25. Mitton, 191, speculates: 'Perhaps some bitter, recent experience has brought home to him how urgent this counsel is'.

[49] Cf. Vouga, 139; Martin, 198-200; Johnson, 326-27.

[50] Popkes, 332, observes that, in 1 Peter, πρὸ πάντων introduces a citation of Prov 10.12, and that James quotes this OT text in 5.20; this then is one more of the many connections between James and 1 Peter. Frankemölle, 697, further observes that, if 1 Pet 4.7-8 mentions prayer and the nearness of the end, the latter two topics are also to the fore in Jas 5. Brückner, 'Kritik', 536, posits literary dependence here. See further 67-70 above.

[51] Cf. de Wette, 261; Baker-Ellsworth, 141.

[52] Baker, *Speech-Ethics*, 279. Adamson, 194-95, seems to have a similar thought.

[53] Francis, 'Form', 125. Cf. Schnider, 130; Popkes, 332. Note e.g. POxy. 292, 294, and for oaths and wishes for health see F.X.J. Exler, *A Study in Greek Epistolography*, Washington, DC, 1923, 113-14, 127-32.

[54] Nicholas of Lyra *ad loc.* reads the Vulgate ('ante omnia autem fratres mei nolite iurare') this way.

of impatience'. This looks not ahead but back, to vv. 7-11. One remains nonplussed.[55]

ἀδελφοί μου. See on 1.2 and 5.7. According to Baker, 'brothers' links this verse to 4.11; 5.7, 9, which also use the address and have to do with sins of speech.[56] He is in any case correct in noting that 'my brothers' softens 'the seeming harshness of a stringent prohibition' by putting it in the context of the author's 'solidarity with the readers'.

μὴ ὀμνύετε. Cf. Mt 5.34: μὴ ὀμόσαι ὅλως. ὀμνύω[57] means 'take an oath'. A number of early Christian texts object to oath-taking.[58] Yet, as Augustine observes, most of the NT does not show any aversion to oaths.[59]

οὐκ ὀμεῖσθε occurs in LXX Lev 19.12 ('you shall not swear by name in an unjust manner'), and James otherwise interacts with Lev 19 while Mt 5.33-37 introduces the ban on swearing by referring to OT legislation on oaths. Against Johnson, 327, however, this is probably insufficient reason to associate our prohibition with Lev 19.12.

Although Jewish texts do not clearly ban oath-taking without qualification,[60] quite a few discourage swearing or express caution regarding the practice.[61] According to Deut 23.22, 'If you refrain from vowing, it

[55] Cf. Schrage, 56: we cannot say 'why exactly this exhortation is important to the editor "above all"'. Gryglewicz, 'Matthieu', 51, wonders whether James' πρὸ πάντων is a transformation of Matthew's ὅλως. So too Mitton, 192.

[56] Baker, *Speech-Ethics*, 279.

[57] Jas: 1×. LXX: most often for שבע.

[58] E.g. Justin, *1 Apol.* 16.5; Irenaeus, *Haer.* 2.32.1; Tertullian, *Idol.* 11, 21-23 CSEL 20 ed. Reifferscheid and Wissowa, 41, 54-57; Origen, *Princ.* 4.3.4 GCS 22 ed. Koetschau, 330; Mart. Apollonius 6 ed. Musurillo, 93; Gk. Acts Phileas 5 ed. Musurillo, 335; Eusebius, *P.E.* 1.4.9-10 GCS 43 ed. Mras, 17-18; Acts of Pilate 2.5 CCSAInstr 3 ed. Gounelle, 200-201; Epiphanius, *Pan.* 19.6 GCS 25 ed. Holl, 223; Pelagius, *1 Thess* 5.27 TS 9.2 ed. Souter, 438.

[59] Augustine, *Serm. mont.* 1.17.51 PL 34, 1255. Cf. Lk 1.73; Acts 2.30; Rom 1.9; 2 Cor 1.23; Gal 1.20; Phil 1.8; Heb 6.13-20; Rev 10.6. Note also Pliny, *Ep.* 10.96 (Christians 'bound themselves with an oath'); Prot. Jas. 4.1 (cf. Judg 8.19); Ps.-Clem. Rec. 6.9 GCS 51 ed. Rehm, 192; Acts Jn 28; Morton Smith's 'Secret Gospel of Mark', folio 1, verso 1.12; and Acts Apollonius 6 ed. Klette, 96. See further Stählin, 'Beteuerungsformeln', and for later materials G. Mead, 'Oaths', in *A Dictionary of Christian Antiquities*, vol. 2, ed. W. Smith and S. Cheetam, Hartford, CT, 1880, 1415-18.

[60] There are two possible exceptions: (i) μὴ ὀμνύετε occurs in LXX Hos 4.15. In the MT, the verse appears to ban using an orthodox oath at Bethel or Gilgal and so in an idolatrous context: 'Do not swear (אל־תשבעו), "As the Lord lives"'. But a reader of the LXX might find here a blanket prohibition of swearing. (ii) A Midrash on the decalogue, מדרש עשרת הדברות, in Bet ha-Midrash ed. Jellinek 1.72 (דבור שלישי end) has this: 'One may not swear even a true oath... and if anyone desecrates the name of God and swears falsely or even when he swears in accord with the truth... his wickedness is revealed to all people. Woe to him in this world and woe to him in the world to come.' Unfortunately this is of unknown date and provenance.

[61] On oaths in Judaism see above all Vahrenhorst, *Matthäus*, 41-214. For reviews of oaths in Greek tradition see J. Pescia, *The Oath and Perjury in Ancient Greece*,

shall be no sin in you';[62] and Eccl 5.5 says that 'it is better that you should not vow than that you should vow and not fulfill it'.[63] Ecclesiastes 2.2 refers to those 'who shun an oath', presumably out of piety.[64] Strong reservation appears in Ecclus 23.9-11 ('Do not accustom your mouth to oaths');[65] Philo, *Decal.* 84-85 ('To swear not at all is the best course and most profitable to life, well suited to a rational nature which has been taught to speak the truth so well on each occasion that its words are regarded as oaths; to swear truly is only, as people say, a "second-best voyage", for the mere fact of his swearing casts suspicion on the trustworthiness of the man'; cf. *Leg.* 2.8); m. Dem. 2.3 (those who wish to fulfill the law should not be 'profuse in vows'; cf. b. Ned. 22a); t. Ḥul. 2.17 ('best of all that you should not vow at all'); Tanḥ. Buber Mattot 1 (one is 'not entitled to swear by my name' unless one fears, serves, and holds fast to the Lord);[66] and the proverb in y. Šeb. 37a (6.6) = Lev. Rab. 6.3 ('Whether one is righteous or guilty, do not get involved with an oath').[67] According to Josephus, moreover, the Essenes believe that 'any word of theirs has more force than an oath; swearing they avoid, regarding it as worse than perjury, for they say that one who is not believed without an appeal to God stands condemned already'.[68]

Oaths were also sometimes frowned upon outside Jewish tradition. Epictetus, *Ench.* 23.5, advised: 'Avoid taking oaths, if possible, altogether; at any rate, so far as you are able'. Marcus Aurelius offered that the good person has no need of them (3.5). In Sophocles' *Oedipus at Clonus*, one

---

Tallahassee, FL, 1970; W. Burkert, *Greek Religion*, Cambridge, MA, 1985, 250-54; J.T. Fitzgerald, 'The Problem of Perjury in Greek Context', in *The Social World of the First Christians*, ed. L.M. White and O.L. Yarbrough, Minneapolis, 1995, 156-77; and the old monograph of R. Hirzel, *Der Eid*, Leipzig, 1902.

[62] Cf. 11QTemple 53.12; Deut 23.21-22.

[63] Cf. 9.2. Elsewhere the Tanak frets about the misuse of oaths—e.g. Exod 20.7; Lev 6.3; 19.11-12; Deut 5.11; Jer 5.2; 7.9; Hos 4.2; Zech 5.4; Mal 3.5; cf. Mt 5.33.

[64] MT Zech 5.3 has judgment fall upon 'everyone who swears', but this is to be read in the light of 5.4, which speaks of swearing 'falsely by my name'; cf. the targum.

[65] There is a long tradition of citing this as a parallel; cf. already Maximus the Confessor, *Loci com.* 33 PG 91.892C. Frankemölle, 698-700, thinks this text, along with Ecclus 27.11-15, may have influenced Jas 5.12.

[66] Cf. Tanḥ. Buber Wayyiqra' 15; Num. Rab. 22.1.

[67] Note also Sifre Deut 330 on 32.40, which teaches that God swore only reluctantly, because of 'those without faith'. 1 En. 69.10 ('human beings were not born…to confirm their trustworthiness through pen and ink') may be analogous to our text: if in 1 Enoch 'one need not affirm one's word by writing down what one says', in James, 'one need not affirm one's word with an oath'; so G.W.E. Nickelsburg and J.C. VanderKam, *1 Enoch 2*, Minneapolis, 2011, 302.

[68] Josephus, *Bell.* 2.135; cf. *Ant.* 15.371; Philo, *Prob.* 84. The Dead Sea Scrolls (on the assumption that they represent Essene belief) qualify Josephus' statement; see 11QTemple 53-54; CD 7.8; 9.9-12; 15-16; 1QS 5.8; 6.27; 4Q416 2 4.7-9; 4Q418 10 9-10; 4Q223-24 2 2.9; 4Q504 6.18. Discussion in Vahrenhorst, *Matthäus*, 75-95. Perhaps the Essenes required only an entrance oath; cf. Josephus, *Bell.* 2.139, 142. They certainly did not, in any case, forbid all oaths.

character says, 'You can count on me; I won't let you down'. The other responds: 'I won't swear you in like someone unreliable'. To this the first character says: 'You'd just have my word to go on anyway'.[69] Quintillian 9.2.98 was of the opinion that 'an oath, unless it is absolutely necessary, is scarcely becoming to a self-respecting man'. Already Pythagoras (or at least certain Pythagoreans) discouraged or forbade oaths.[70]

Exactly how James understood the prohibition of oaths is unclear. Did he think of a ban upon every sort of oath in every context? Or do we have here hyperbole, exaggeration for the sake of exhortation?[71] Did he have in mind a more circumscribed application and yet express himself, because he employed an unqualified tradition, as though his concern were wider?[72] We cannot answer these questions nor guess what immediate circumstance, if any, called forth the prohibition.[73] James offers no elucidation.[74]

---

[69] Note also Aeschylus frag. 394; Isocrates, *Nic.* 22; Cicero, *Balb.* 5; Plutarch, *Quaest. rom.* 2.127D; *Mor.* 46A; and the precept of Delphi in Dittenberger, *Syl.* 1268 col. 1.8, 3.396: ὅρκωι μὴ χρῶ. On the theological element in the non-Jewish sources see Kollmann, 'Schwurverbot'.

[70] Cf. Diodorus Siculus 10.9.2; Diogenes Laertius 8.22 (μηδ' ὀμνύναι θεούς); Iamblichus, *Pyth.* 47, 150; Hierocles, *Aur. carm.* 2.9-11. But the second line of the so-called Golden Verses of Pythagoras enjoins reverence for one's oath, presumably one's oath to live faithfully by Pythagorean principles. See further Dibelius, 248 n. 41.

[71] Benson, 113, speaks of 'general terms' and 'general expressions' that become, in application, 'limited'. Cf. W. Wake, *A Practical Discourse concerning Swearing*, London, 1696, xxix-xxxi: 'In Matters of this nature, tho' the Expressions be general, yet they must still be moderated with such Limitations as both the Nature of the Thing itself requires, and the general Content of Mankind agrees, ought to be put upon them. But especially, when, by so doing, there is nothing allow'd of, but what is both innocent and reasonable: And the denial whereof would unavoidably run Mankind into endless Mischiefs and Inconveniences.'

[72] Tradition, for what it is worth, had no qualms about associating James the brother of Jesus with vows, which were not always clearly distinguished from oaths; cf. Mt 5.33-37. Acts 21.22-24 has him and the elders of Jerusalem advise Paul to take a vow, and Hegesippus *apud* Eusebius, *H.E.* 2.23.5, assumes that James took a Nazarite vow.

[73] Macknight, 602, speculates that James 'forbade them, when brought before the tribunals of their persecutors, to deny their faith with oaths, which some of them, it seems, thought they might do with a safe conscience, if the oath was one of those which were reckoned not binding'. For Martin, 199-200, 5.12 is 'anti-Zealot or anti-nationalistic polemic': James opposed the Sicarii, who took oaths for their cause. Perkins, 135, speculates that 'Christians who were brought before a court by outsiders may have continued to use the oaths that were part of compulsory legal form. Similarly, the merchants would have been expected to use oaths to conclude some of their dealings'. The present writer has wondered, given his interpretation of 3.9 and the fact that curses could be reckoned a type of oath (b. Soṭah 18a; b. Šeb. 35b-36a), whether James might have had in mind specifically an oath of malediction (cf. CD 9.11-12); but the evidence is too slender to pursue. There is also not enough evidence to suggest that our author had in mind Christians swearing in synagogues, a practice which Chrysostom, *Jud.* 1.3 PG 48.847 attests.

[74] Contrast also Plutarch, *Mor.* 275C-D, which discusses why the priest of Jupiter does not take an oath.

'Lest you fall into judgment' assumes a wrong without explaining it. Did James have a gripe with those who frequently took oaths because he thought this a sure sign of telling lies?[75] Or, in accord with 2.7, was he—like Matthew's Jesus—worried that swearing would desecrate the divine name?[76] Or, given the subject matter in 4.13–5.6, was he opposed to using oaths in commercial transactions?[77] Or did he worry that swearing is, against the spirit of 4.15, an act of self-determination?[78] Or did he suppose perjury to be so heinous that he thought it best to avoid swearing altogether?[79] One can also ask whether criticism of oaths was sufficiently widespread in James' world (see above) as to require no further elucidation: maybe everybody knew the institution was, for any number of reasons, problematic.[80] We have no answers.

[75] Cf. Chrysostom, *Pop. Antioch.* PG 49.144: 'the one who swears often, both willingly and unwillingly, both ignorantly and knowingly, both in earnest and in jest, and being carried away often by anger and many other things, will frequently perjure'. Philo, *Decal.* 92; *Leg.* 2.8, says the same thing.

[76] Cf. Philo, *Spec.* 4.40; *Decal.* 93. Many commentators on James refer to the sin of blasphemy and to misusing God's name; cf. Simplicius, *Comm. in Epic. enchr.* 94 *ad* 33.5 ed. Dübner, 114: 'For an oath calls God to witness, and…to induce God upon occasion of human affairs, which is to say, for small and slight matters, implies a contempt of him. So it is necessary that we should set aside swearing, except upon occasions of necessity.' Philo, *Spec.* 2.4, knows of some who, out of reverence for the divine name, say 'Yes, by—' or 'No, by—', thereby suggesting 'the clear sense of an oath without actually making it'. This was evidently a Greek practice; cf. Suidas, *Lex.* s.v. μ 292: 'It was the custom…among the ancients sometimes to avoid swearing by God; but they were in the habit, by way of euphemy, to use such oaths as to say, "By the—", but not to add the name'; cf. Aristophanes, *Ran.* 1374; Plato, *Gorg.* 466E. Greek legend had it that Rhadamanthus, son of Zeus and judge in the underworld, taught the Cretans, out of reverence, not to swear by the gods but by lesser things—the dog, ram, goose, for instance; cf. Plato, *Apol.* 21E; Zenobius, *Epit. coll. Luc. Tarrh. et Did.* 81; Aelius Dionysius, *Attic Names* Rho 1; Philostratus, *Apoll.* 6.19; Photius, *Lex.*, s.v., Ῥαδαμάνθυος ὅρκος. Discussion in Hirzel, *Eid*, 90-104. Note the awareness of this custom in Mek. on Exod 20.2.

[77] Mayor, 167, thought that 5.12 'would have come more naturally in speaking of the sins of traders in iv. 13' and cited Clement of Alexandria, *Paed.* 3.79 ed. Marcovich, 192: 'above all, let an oath on account of what is sold be far from you'. For instances of oaths in business transactions see Cowley 14, 44; PBerlin 13587; PMoscow 135; m. Ned. 3.1; and the discussion of Pescia, *Oath*, 80-82.

[78] Some interpreters of Mt 5.33-37 have taken the prohibition to be about promissory oaths only; see Luz, *Matthew*, 1.267. Popkes, 336, thinks this may be relevant to James. Cf. H. Hammond, *A Practical Catechism*, Oxford, 1847, 148: 'let your promises and performances be all one, the first yea referring to the promise, the second to performance, which he [James] there mentions as a means to make all promissory oaths unnecessary'.

[79] Cf. Lactantius, *Epit.* 59 (64) SC 335 ed. Perrin, 228 ('he will not even swear, lest…he fall into perjury'); Augustine, *Serm.* 180.3 PL 38.973-74; Benedict, *Reg.* 4.27 CSEL 75 ed. Hanslik, 30 (one should resolve 'not to swear, for fear of perjuring oneself').

[80] See further Kollmann, 'Schwurverbot', who stresses the continuity between the tradition in James and Matthew on the one hand and Jewish and pagan criticisms of oaths on the other hand.

μήτε τὸν οὐρανὸν μήτε τὴν γῆν μήτε ἄλλον τινὰ ὅρκον. Cf. Mt 5.34-35; see above. Matthew, in accord with general LXX usage, has ἐν after ὀμνύω; cf. the Hebrew שׁבע + בּ.[81] James instead has the accusative, a classical construction.[82] Does μήτε ἄλλον τινὰ ὅρκον hint that James knew a longer form of the tradition, such as that in Matthew?[83] But one could equally conjecture that something like James' text was the occasion for the elaborations in Matthew.

Deuteronomy 6.13 and 10.20 speak of oaths in God's name. By the first century, however, that name could no longer be pronounced. Hence oaths employed substitutes,[84] including swearing by heaven and earth.[85] In the Mishnah, oaths by heaven and earth are, for some rabbinic authorities, not binding.[86] This may account for their being cited here.[87] If anyone were to imagine that oaths by heaven or earth were, because not binding, not covered by a general prohibition of swearing, James (like Matthew) anticipates the strategy and disallows it. In effect, then, all non-binding oaths are outlawed. It goes without saying that all this would be clear only to a Jewish audience.

The proposal of Baker, that 'by heaven' and 'by earth' are not particular oath formulae but rather refer to everything in the universe beside God,[88] fails to explain the following 'any other oath': the latter serves no purpose if it follows a comprehensive expression.

ἤτω δὲ ὑμῶν τὸ ναὶ ναὶ καὶ τὸ οὒ οὔ.[89] Cf. Mt 5.37 (ἔστω[90] δὲ ὁ λόγος ὑμῶν ναὶ ναί, οὒ οὔ) and 2 Cor 1.17-18 ('Was I vacillating when I wanted

---

[81] As in Deut 6.13; Isa 65.16; Dan 12.7.

[82] See BDF 149 and cf. Xenophon, *Anab.* 6.1.31; Demosthenes, *Aristocr.* 5; Josephus, *Ant.* 3.91; 7.353; etc.

[83] See above, 728-29, and cf. Maier, 223. Elliott-Binns, *Christianity*, 63, wonders whether 5.12 vis-à-vis Matthew hints at 'a reluctance to increase the prestige of Jerusalem'. An occasional commentator argues that, if James omitted the reference to swearing by Jerusalem (so Matthew), this implies a date after 70; cf. Windisch-Preisker, 32.

[84] For various sorts of oaths see Gen 42.15 (by the life of Pharaoh); 1 Chr 12.19 (by one's head; cf. Mt 5.36; m. Sanh. 3.5; b. Ber. 3a); Jdt 1.12 (by Nebuchadnezzar's throne and kingdom); Philo, *Spec.* 2.2 (by parents, living or dead), 5 (by the earth, sun, stars, heaven, the universe); Mt 23.16-22 (by the sanctuary, its gold, its altar); Gk. LAE 19.2 (by God's throne, the cherubim, and the tree of life'); Hippolytus, *Haer.* 9.15(10) PTS 25 ed. Marcovich, 361 (by heaven, water, holy spirits, angels, oil, salt, the earth); m. Ker. 1.7 ('by this temple'); t. Ḥal. 1.6 (by the covenant); m. Ned. 2.5 (by 'a net of the sea').

[85] Philo, *Spec.* 2.5; m. Šebu. 4.13; b. Šebu. 35a; Disc. 8-9 6.63.15-18. From an earlier time note Deut 4.26; 30.19; 31.28.

[86] Cf. m. Šebu. 4.13; m. Ned. 1.3; m. Sanh. 3.2; Billerbeck 1.332-4.

[87] So already Augustine, *Serm. mont.* 1.17.25 PL 34.1256.

[88] Baker, *Speech-Ethics*, 280.

[89] 01* 88 104 326Z 459 *et al.* L60 L:V^mss,AU assimilate to Mt 5.37 by inserting ὁ λόγος before ὑμῶν.

[90] James has ἔστω in 1.19 but in 5.12 prefers ἤτω; cf. LXX Ps 103.31; 1 Macc 10.31; 1 Cor 16.22. According to MHT, 1.56, 'the rarer ἤτω alternates with ἔστω, in papyri and late inscriptions, as in NT'. See further Mayor, 167.

to do this? Do I make my plans like a worldly person, ἵνα ᾖ παρ' ἐμοὶ τὸ ναὶ ναὶ καὶ τὸ οὒ οὔ; As surely as God is faithful, our word to you has not been yes and no'). The δέ is a true adversative. The meaning seems to be, 'But let your yes be truly yes and let your no be truly no' (so most exegetes) or, 'Let your yes be only yes—not yes plus an oath—and let your no be no—not no plus an oath'.[91] The differences from Matthew are probably not great, and the sense is likely the same.[92] 2 Cor 1.17-18 (which may be independent of the Jesus tradition[93]); Sifre 205 on Lev 19.36 ('your yes should be a yes'); and b. B. Meṣiʿa 49a ('let your yes be just and let your no be just'; cf. Ruth Rab. 7.6) strongly suggest that the expression was traditional and known beyond the saying attributed to Jesus.[94]

James, unlike Matthew but like Paul and several patristic witnesses, has τὸ ναὶ ναὶ καὶ τὸ οὒ οὔ, with the definite article before the first 'yes' and the first 'no'.[95] The broad attestation of this formulation shows its persistence in the oral tradition.

'Yes yes' and 'no no' are oath formulas in b. Šebu. 36a and 2 En. 49.1-2 J;[96] and while some have thought this is also the case in Mt 5.33-37, in James one type of oath is not being substituted for another.[97] The text rather calls for straightforward, truthful speech: with such, oaths are

---

[91] For the latter possibility see Origen, *Hom. Jer* 5.12 GCS 33 ed. Baehrens, 41; cf. Mayor, 167. Most commentators opt for the former alternative.

[92] Easton, 69: 'Commentators note that the force is perhaps not quite the same as in Matt. 5:37, which means, "Never say more than 'Yes, yes' or 'No, no'", where the doubling of the reply is conceivably to add emphasis; but this is fine spun and the distinction is of no consequence'. Cf. Davids, 190.

[93] The issue is disputed, the commentators divided. Discussion in D. Wenham, '1 Corinthians 1:17.18: Echo of a Dominical Logion', *NovT* 28 (1986), 271-79.

[94] For confirmation from Assyrian sources see Kutsch, 'Rede'. Cf. also Mek. on Exod 20.2, where the Israelites affirm their allegiance to God with הן והן, 'yes and yes'; also Mek. on Exod 20.3; b. Meg. 32a. For the emphatic ναί ναί in Greek texts see Sophocles, *Oed. Col.* 1747; Aristophanes, *Eq.* 749; Jdt 9.12; Ps.-Callisthenes, *Hist. Alex. Magn.* rec. γ 3.83; PGM 1.90. One may compare the double 'amen' in Num 5.22; Jn 1.51; 5.19, 24, 15; b. Šeb. 36a.

[95] Justin Martyr, *1 Apol.* 16.5 PTS 38 ed. Marcovich, 56; Clement of Alexandria, *Strom.* 5.14.99 GCS 52 ed. Stählin and Früchtel, 391; 7.11.67 GCS 17 ed. Stählin, 48; Apost. Const. 5.12.6 ed. Funk, 269; Ps.-Clem. Hom. 3.55; 19.2 GCS 42 ed. Rehm, 77, 253; Eusebius, *Dem. ev.* 3.3; and Epiphanius, *Pan.* 19.6.2 GCS 25 ed. Holl, 223. Cf. 2 Jeu 43: ⲡⲉⲩⲛⲥⲉ ϣⲱⲡⲉ ⲛⲥⲉ ⲁⲩⲱ ⲡⲉⲩⲙⲙⲟⲛ ⲛⲙⲙⲟⲛ.

[96] Yet 2 En. 42.1-2 J, which includes the words, 'not to use an oath, neither by heaven nor by earth', is likely under NT influence. 2 En. 42.1-2A lacks the relevant parallel. For various Greek oath forms with ναί see P. Meinhardt, *De forma et usu juramentorum*, Jena, 1892, 11-14.

[97] See the thorough discussion of Deppe, *Sayings*, 136-40; also Meier, 'Oaths 1', 201-204. Dibelius, 249-51, agrees regarding James but not Matthew.

superfluous.⁹⁸ This interpretation makes for continuity with James' concern elsewhere for 'the truth': 1.18; 3.14; 5.19.⁹⁹

Huther, 155-56, and Beyschlag, 225, dispute that our text enjoins truth-telling: it rather calls for simple speech. But simplicity and truth go hand in hand,¹⁰⁰ and there is no antithesis here, which is why readers have again and again taken the ban on swearing to forbid lying.¹⁰¹ James calls for the 'plain truth'.¹⁰² Indeed, although exegetes—probably under Matthean influence—typically focus on the prohibition of oaths, James' chief concern may have been truth-telling. Perhaps, that is, his focus was on the positive imperative—'let your yes be yes and your no no'—rather than the negative command—'do not swear'; but the latter came with the former in his tradition and so he included both. It is suggestive that both Justin and Clement of Alexandria understand the ban on oaths to demand truth; see n. 101.

ἵνα μὴ ὑπὸ κρίσιν πέσητε.¹⁰³ While there is no parallel to the line in Mt 5.33-37,¹⁰⁴ the sentiment is close to Mt 12.37: 'by your words you will be condemned'.¹⁰⁵ Cf. also Acts Paul Thec. 17 ed. Lipsius, 247: ἵνα μηκέτι ὑπὸ κρίσιν.¹⁰⁶

Presumably the conclusion, which covers both μὴ ὀμνύετε and ἤτω κτλ., is redactional, although πίπτω is a *hapax* for our book. κρίσις occurs twice in 2.13, and the whole clause seems a stylistic variation of

---

⁹⁸ Cf. Ps.-Oecumenius *ad loc.* PG 119.505D-507A; Daube, 'Reconstruction', 67-70.

⁹⁹ See further Baker, *Speech-Ethics*, 281-82, on how these verses about 'truth' might be related to 5.12.

¹⁰⁰ Cf. Plato, *Resp.* 382E.

¹⁰¹ E.g. Justin Martyr, *1 Apol.* 16.5 PTS 38 ed. Marcovich, 56; Clement of Alexandria, *Strom.* 7.8.51 GCS 17 ed. Stählin, 38; 7.11.67, 48; Eusebius, *Praep. ev.* 1.4 GCS 43 ed. Mras, 17-18; Ps.-Andrew of Crete, *Éloge* 7 ed. Noret, 54; Erasmus, *Paraphrase*, 168; Manton, 438; Burkitt, 1033; Pyle, 326; Stier, 468; Lange, 138; Rusche, 100; Johnson, 341; Hartin, 263; Andria, 1515; *et al.*

¹⁰² Baker, *Speech-Ethics*, 280. An occasional commentator has pondered what to do when a simple yes or no might offend or hurt. See Townsend, 103.

¹⁰³ εἰς ὑπόκρισιν appears in a well-attested variant: 025 044 5 69 81 206 *et al.* **Byz** Antioch PsOec. It was adopted by Erasmus, *Novum Testamentum*, 500; Beza, 561; Grotius, 1092; Hammond, 700; and Clarke, 826, and lies behind the translation of Tyndale: 'fall into hypocrecy'; cf. Cranmer's translation and Theophylact *ad loc.* PG 125.1185C-D. One assumes that ΥΠΟ ΚΡΙΣΙΝ became ΥΠΟΚΡΙΣΙΝ, which then motivated the insertion of ΕΙΣ. Cf. Benson, 115.

¹⁰⁴ One can hardly follow Mitton, 192, who offers that 'Matthew's "anything more than this comes from evil" may represent a rough translation of the same Aramaic, which James represents by "that you may not fall under condemnation"'. According to Luz, *Matthew*, 1.261: the conclusion in James is 'completely different' than that in Matthew.

¹⁰⁵ Bauckham, *Wisdom*, 92, thinks that 'anyone familiar with this saying of Jesus would surely find an unmistakable allusion to it'. The history of interpretation offers some support; cf. Bede *ad loc.* CCSL 121 ed. Hurst, 220; Songer, 136; Maier, 223.

¹⁰⁶ If this is an echo of James, it would be one of the earliest attestations of our book, the Acts of Paul and Thecla having been penned sometime in the second century. But the Acts otherwise shows no knowledge of James.

5.9: ἵνα μὴ κριθῆτε. πίπτω + ὑπὸ κρίσιν is unparalleled, although there are analogous expressions.[107] ὑπὸ κρίσιν is unattested in pre-Christian or Jewish sources and is, after James, rare before the fourth century. But the εἰς κρίμα ἐμπέσῃ of 1 Tim 3.6 is similar, and πίπτω + ὑπό was common enough.[108]

'Under judgment' is short for 'under (God's) judgment (at the last day)'.[109] Once again, then, James reinforces his moral teaching with eschatological expectations; cf. 4.12; 5.3, 9. The punishment—Gehenna (cf. 3.6; 5.3)—may not seem commensurate with the crime, but James here follows the Jesus tradition: sanctions for moral imperatives are often hyperbolically dire. Cf. Rev 21.8: 'liars' will find themselves in the lake of fire. Perhaps pertinent is the third commandment of the decalogue, which pledges divine retribution for wrongful speech: 'You shall not make wrongful use of the name of the Lord your God, for the Lord will not acquit anyone who misuses his name'.[110] Note also Mek. on Exod 20.7: 'after you have obligated yourself to take an oath I am a judge'.

How James reconciled the prohibition of oaths with what he found in the Tanak we cannot say. We cannot even know that he was aware of a tension[111] or whether or to what extent it would have troubled him if he were.[112] The history of interpretation, as already observed, shows us some

---

[107] E.g. LXX Ps 1.5 (οὐκ ἀναστήσονται...ἐν κρίσει); Ecclus 29.19 (ἐμπεσεῖται εἰς κρίσεις); Polybius 3.23.6 (πίπτειν ὑπὸ τὴν αὐτῶν ἐξουσίαν); Josephus, *Ant.* 2.219 (πεσὼν ὑπὸ τὴν τοῦ βασιλέως ὀργήν). Note also Mt 5.21 (ἔνοχος ἔσται τῇ κρίσει); Jn 5.24 (εἰς κρίσιν...ἔρχεται). Note also נפל + על + משפט of 1QH 11.27; 4Q432 6.2; cf. 1QM 6.5 (נפל + ב + משפט). Although Gehenna was thought of as being below the earth, James' expression is figurative, not literal. 'Falling into Gehenna' was not a fixed idiom.

[108] Cf. LXX 2 Βασ 22.39; Ps 17.39 (for תחת+נפל); Homer, *Il.* 6.453; Sib. Or. 14.145; etc.

[109] Cf. the Discourse of the Archangel Gabriel 15b-16a ed. Budge, 313: 'Do you not hear the Lord crying out to everyone, "Let your words be Yes Yes and No No, so that judgment may not be passed on you"? And let us take care to guard our life against the terrible oaths which we are in the habit of swearing, especially concerning subjects of the most trivial character, lest we receive great condemnation and punishment everlasting.'

[110] Exod 20.7; cf. Ecclus 23.11 and Beza, 561; Manton, 438-39; Baumgarten, 227; Guyse, 597; Benson, 115 (James may advert to the third commandment, 'intimating that...the christian law condemned that vice [taking God's name in vain], as well as the jewish law'). The title at the head of Book 2 of Philo's *Special Laws* holds that the third commandment has to do with 'the duty of keeping oaths'; and multiple texts reveal that 'You will not take the name of the Lord your God in vain' was understood to pertain to false oaths: Mek. on Exod 20.7; Tg. Onq. Exod 20.7; Frag. Tg. P Exod 20.7. Josephus, *Ant.* 3.91 interprets the command as banning unnecessary or frivolous oaths.

[111] Or whether he was conscious that his general prohibition of cursing those made in the image of God (3.9) seemingly sets itself against any number of biblical texts, such as Deut 27.11-26. Meier, 'Oaths 1' and 'Oaths 2' argues at length that the prohibition of oaths in James and Matthew is indeed an abrogation of Moses. But J. Klawans, 'The Prohibition of Oaths and Contra-scriptural Halakhot', *JSHJ* 6 (2008), 33-48, persuasively contends otherwise.

[112] The same issue arises in 1.13, which seems to contradict the plain sense of several biblical texts.

interpreters maintaining that the new dispensation did indeed set aside laws of the old dispensation,[113] other interpreters holding that our book has in view only everyday oaths, not oaths required in legal contexts. But these two alternatives do no exhaust the possibilities. Others have argued (i) that although God swears in scripture, 'God has the power to do what He forbids you, for everything is possible to Him';[114] or (ii) that 'do not swear' really means 'do not swear in vain' or assumes some other unspoken qualification;[115] or (iii) that while the OT enjoins swearing by God's name (Deut 6.13; 10.20), James prohibits only swearing by heaven or earth or some other substitute formula.[116]

---

[113] Cf. Theodoret, *Haer.* 16 PG 83.505; Ps.-Oecumenius *ad loc.* PG 119.505D, and see further above, on the history of interpretation, 722-24.

[114] So the 7th article of the Schleitheim Confession.

[115] Shem-Tov's Hebrew Matthew inserts 'in vain' into Mt 5.34.

[116] This has been a very popular strategy; cf. Calvin, 312-13; Gill, 801; Huther, 154-56; Stier, 465. Some have interpreted Mt 5.33-37 this way; see Luz, *Matthew*, 1.266.

XVIII

PRAYER, HEALING, RESTORATION (5.13-20)[1]

(13) Is anyone among you suffering? He should pray. Is anyone cheerful? He should sing praises. (14) Is anyone among you ill? He should call for the elders of the assembly and have them pray over him, anointing him with oil in the name of the Lord. (15) And the prayer of faith will save the sick, and the Lord will raise him up; and anyone who has committed sins will be forgiven. (16) So confess your sins to one another, and pray for one another, that you may be healed. The effectual prayer of the righteous individual works powerfully. (17) Elijah was a human being like us, and he prayed fervently that it might not rain, and for three years and six months it did not rain on the earth. (18) Then he prayed again, and heaven gave rain, and the earth yielded its fruit.

(19) My brothers, if anyone among you wanders from the way of truth and someone turns him back, (20) let him know that the one turning a sinner back from the error of his way will save his soul from death and cover a multitude of sins.

History of Interpretation and Reception

With the exception of the latter half of Jas 2, the end of chap. 5 has generated more discussion and controversy than any other portion of our letter. It has indeed played a significant role in several major ecclesiastical controversies, the most intense having to do with extreme unction.

---

[1] Recent literature: Albl, 'Health'; Allison, 'Ending'; Althaus, 'Bekenne'; Armerding, 'Afflicted'; Baker, *Speech-Ethics*, 235-41; Béraudy, 'Sacrament'; Bishop, 'Three'; Bord, *Onction*; Bottini, 'Confessione'; idem, 'Correzione'; idem, *Preghiera*; Collins, 'Anointing'; Condon, 'Healing'; Coppens, 'L'onction'; Cothenet, 'Healing'; Davids, 'Tradition', 119-21; Feiner, 'Krankensalbung', 502-508; Friesenhahn, 'Geschichte'; Hagenbach, 'Aechtheit'; Hamman, 'Prière'; Hayden, 'Elders'; Heckel, *Segen*, 342-46; L. Hogan, *Healing*, 291-97; Howard, *Disease*, 258-66; John, 'Anointing'; Kaiser, *Krankenheilung*; Karris, 'Angles'; Kilmartin, 'Catena'; Kollmann, *Jesus*, 344-47; Konradt, *Existenz*, 56-58, 191-92, 299-301; B. Kramer and J.C. Shelton, *Das Archiv des Nepheros und Verwandte Texte Teil I: Das Archiv des Nepheros*, Mainz am Rhein, 1987, 21-24; McNeile, *Teaching*, 111-16; Manns, 'Péchés'; Marconi, 'Malattia'; B. Mayer, 'Bittgebet'; Meinertz, 'Krankensalburg'; Moulton, 'Supplication'; Nielsen, *Heilung*, 210-15; Öhler, *Elia*, 257-60; Omanson, 'Judgment'; Pickar, 'Sick'; Rauch, 'Versuch'; Reicke, 'L'onction'; Rico, 'Prière'; Ruck-Schröder, *Name*, 235-37; Schenk-Ziegler, *Correctio*, 413-20; Shogren, 'Heal'; Strange, *World*; J.C. Thomas, *Devil*, 17-37; idem, 'Devil'; Verheul, 'Sacrement'; Warrington, 'Elijah'; idem, 'Healing'; L. Wells, *Healing*; Wenger, *Kyrios*, 199-210; Wilkinson, 'Healing'; idem, *Health*, 143-58; E. Wilson, 'Anointing'; Wypadlo, *Gebet*, 185-237.

For centuries, anointing with oil for healing (cf. v. 14) was in many places—before the Carolingian reform and above all in the West—not reserved for clergy or hierarchs.[2] Typically, 'the blessed oil would...be taken home, kept in the "medicine cabinet", and used as needed'.[3] By the ninth century, however, anointing for sickness had become a priestly prerogative and a ritual preparing for death; hence it became enmeshed with the rites of penance and final communion.[4] The Council of Trent affirmed extreme unction as a sacrament promulgated by James,[5] and the conventional—but not universal[6]—Roman Catholic view has been that, 'in its external details, the rite described by the Apostle James (5:14-16) is basically the same as that administered' by Roman Catholic priests throughout history.[7] This has entailed interpreting James' pledge that

[2] F.W. Puller, *The Anointing of the Sick in Scripture and Tradition*, London, 1904, and Feiner, 'Krankheit', are standard histories of the subject. For a convenient short summary see C.W. Gusmer, *And You Visited Me*, New York, 1984, 3-47. Evidence regarding anointing is scarce for the first several centuries, presumably in part because it was a private matter conducted in homes, not a public matter conducted in churches. Relevant texts include Did. 10.7 v.l. (although this might refer to anointing for baptism); Hippolytus (?), *Apost. Trad.* 5.1-2 TU 75 ed. Tidner, 127; Apost. Const. 7.27 ed. Funk, 414; Origen, *Hom. Lev.* 2.4 SC 286 ed. Borret, 110; PLond. 6.1928; Chrysostom, *Hom. Mt* 32.9 PG 57.384; POxy. 11.1384.15-22; Acts of Mār Mārī 8, 27-28 ed. Harrak, 18, 62, 64; Innocent 1, *Ep.* 25.8 PL 20.559B-561A; Caesarius of Arles, *Mart. vel phyl.* 5 PL 39.2273; Bede *ad loc.* CCSL 121 ed. Hurst, 221-22. See also the discussion of liturgical texts in E. Segelbert, 'The Benedictio Olei in the Apostolic Tradition of Hippolytus', *OC* 48 (1964), 268-81. The term, 'extreme unction'—never current in the East—came into use only during the early scholastic period, after which forgiveness of sins rather than healing of the body became generally the chief or even sole consideration; cf. Peter Lombard, *Sent.* 4.130 (Dist. 23.4) ed. Brady, 392.

[3] So P. Meyendorff, *The Anointing of the Sick*, Crestwood, NY, 2009, 36, adding: 'the anointing of the sick seems to have originated as a domestic rite'.

[4] The first full service for unction appears in the Gregorian Sacramentary; see H.B. Porter, 'The Origin of the Medieval Rite for Anointing the Sick or Dying', *JTS* 7 (1956), 211-25. Already by the fifth century, Isaac of Antioch opposed lay anointing; see G. Bickell, *Conspectus rei Syrorum litterarius*, Munich, 1871, 77-78. For a history of extreme unction see J. Kern, *De Sacramento Extremae Unctionis*, Rome, 1907.

[5] But according to Peter Lombard, *Sent.* 4.129 (Dist. 23.3) ed. Brady, 391, James indicates that 'the apostles' instituted (*institutum*) the sacrament.

[6] Cajetan, 370, does not find extreme unction in James; cf. Iacobus-M. Vosté, *Thomas de Vio, O.P. Cardinalis Caietanus*, Rome, 1935, 56-57. Erasmus, 1038, also expresses doubt.

[7] So P.F. Palmer, ed., *Sacraments and Forgiveness*, London, 1961, 274. This is the burden of Bord, *Onction*, *passim*. Cf. Stevartius, 402; the Navarre Bible, 30, 68-70. For Trent see *Creeds and Confessions of Faith in the Christian Tradition, vol. II, Part Four*, ed. J. Pelikan and V. Hotchkiss, New Haven, 2003, 856-58; and for an early response to Protestant criticisms Maldonatus, 'De extrema unctione', in *Opera Varia Theologica* 1, Paris, 1677, 381-91. Catharinus, 540, opposes Cajetan's doubt. Trent affirms that 'Christ our Lord' instituted the sacrament, which Mk 6.13 'suggested' whereas James 'recommended' and 'announced' it. Trent further states: 'There is no reason to listen to those who teach, against the open and clear meaning of the apostle James, that this anointing is either a human fabrication or a rite received from the fathers which includes neither a

'anyone who has committed sins will be forgiven' (v. 15) within the context of imminent death.[8] Vatican II, however, moderated Trent's position, preferring the phrase 'anointing of the sick' over 'extreme unction' and emphasizing that 'it is not a sacrament for those only who are at the point of death'.[9]

The Reformers and subsequent Protestants rejected extreme unction, arguing that neither Mk 6.13 nor Jas 5.14 is the mandate for a sacrament.[10] The result was that most Protestant communions ceased to practice anointing for healing, which explains its absence from editions of the Book of Common Prayer between 1552 and 1892[11]—although the

command from God nor a promise of grace; nor to those who assert that it has now ceased, as though it belonged only to the grace of healings in the primitive church; nor to those who say that the rite and usage observed by the Holy Roman Church in the administration of this sacrament are at odds with the statement of the apostle James, and so should be changed to something else; nor, finally, to those who declare that this final anointing can, without sin, be treated as negligible by the faithful'. Cf. error 48 of *Lamentabili Sane* or the *Syllabus Condemning the Errors of the Modernists* (from Pius the 10th, 1907): among propositions to be 'condemned and proscribed' is this one: 'In his Epistle (Ch. 5:14-15) James did not intend to promulgate a Sacrament of Christ but only commend a pious custom. If in this custom he happens to distinguish a means of grace, it is not in that rigorous manner in which it was taken by the theologians who laid down the notion and number of the Sacraments'. Cf. further P. Dens, *Theologia Moralis et Dogmatica*, vol. 7, Dublin, 1832, 1-2; Pickar, 'Sick'.

[8] According to Egbert of York, *Poen.* 1 *Pars altera* 15 PL 89.416A-B, true penitents who are anointed immediately before death become as pure as the 'infant who dies immediately after baptism'. Cf. Bonaventure, *Sent.* 4 dist. 23 a. 1 q. 1 Opera Omnia 6 ed. Peltier, 133-34; Aquinas, *Summa* suppl. q. 30. On this recondite subject see S.J. Brzana, *Remains of Sin and Extreme Unction according to Theologians after Trent*, Rome, 1953.

[9] 'Constitution on the Sacred Liturgy' § 73. Cf. the remarks of Frankemölle, 706.

[10] See Luther, *On the Babylonian Captivity*, in *Luther's Works*, vol. 36, ed. A.R. Wentz, Philadelphia, 1959, 118-19 ('Why do they make an extreme and a special kind of unction out of that which the apostle wished to be general? For the apostle did not desire it to be an extreme unction or administered only to the dying, but he says expressly, "Is any one sick?" He does not say: "Is any one dying?"'; Luther goes on to urge that while James fails to prescribe a divinely-instituted sacrament, the humanly instituted ritual can bring forgiveness and peace, if faith is present, 122); J. Brenz, 'Underrichtung der zwispaltigen Artickel cristenlichs Glaubens', in *Frühschriften*, 2 vols., ed. M. Brecht, G. Schäfer, and F. Wolf, Tübingen, 1970, 1974, 1.67-68; idem, 'Contiones aliquot de Sacramentis', in ibid. 2.63-66; Servetus, *Supernatural Regenration* 4 ET Hoffman and Miller, 281-82; Manton, 450 ('mere hypocritical pageantry'); Cartwright, *Confutation*, 664-66; Trapp, 704 (with his usual mean-spirited polemic); Alford, 327 (uncharacteristically harsh on this topic). Farrar, *Days*, 348, distinguishes in this connection between 'the letter and the spirit, the accident adjunct [administering oil] and the eternal principle [praying for others]'. The deist, J. Toland, 'The Original Plan of Christianity', in *The Theological and Philological Works*, London, 1732, 55, dismissed the practice as confined to Jewish Christians—the 'Nazarens'—and never intended for Gentiles.

[11] Cf. the indifference of C. Gore, *The Creed of the Christian*, London, 1905, 69-70: 'when grave illness is upon the Christian, the Church, as in the Apostolic days, is present with the remedial anointing of the Holy Oil, or, at least, where this rite has been abandoned, with other holy ministries'.

Non-jurors in the eighteenth century and the Tractarians in the nineteenth century urged a return to the practice, in large measure because of the passage in James. In recent times, with the older controversies mostly past, many Protestant groups have reintroduced anointing for the sick, for which Jas 5.14 is always the main proof text.[12]

Verse 16 has likewise found its way into polemical discourse. Roman Catholic theologians traditionally viewed the verse as a proof text for the confessional. One nineteenth-century Catholic edition of the Bible, in its footnote to Jas 5.16, has this: '*to one another*—that is, to the priests of the church, whom, v. 14, he had ordered to be called for, and brought in to the sick; moreover, to confess to persons who had no power to forgive sins would be useless. Hence the precept here means, that we must confess to men whom God hath appointed, and who, by their ordination and jurisdiction, have received the power of remitting sins in his name.'[13] Protestants, however, have been quick to latch onto the fact that James refers not to priests in this context but to 'elders' (v. 14),[14] and further that

---

[12] Cf. e.g. W.J.K. Little, *The Perfect Life*, London, 1898, 332-45; W. Pannenberg, *Systematic Theology*, vol. 3, Grand Rapids, MI/Edinburgh, 1998, 270-71, 367. Especially noteworthy and influential was the 1930 Anglican report on healing at Lambeth, which affirmed 'spiritual healing'; see *The Lambeth Conference 1930: Encyclical Letter*, London, 1930, 182-83. Symbolic of the change are today's world-wide Taizé services, which typically feature an anointing station.

[13] *The New Testament of Our Lord and Saviour Jesus Christ, translated from the Latin Vulgate*, with annotations by R. Challoner, New York, 1872, 197. Cf. Ps.-Bernard, *Medit.* 9 PL 184.500; Abelard, *Ethica* 24 PL 178.668B-C; Albertus Magnus, *Par. an.* 40 Opera Omnia 37 ed. Borgnet, 308; Aquinas, *Summa* suppl. q. 6 a. 6; Nicholas of Lyra *ad loc.*; Nicholas of Gorran, 88. Contrast Augustine, *Serm.* 253 PL 39.2212; Duns Scotus, *Sent.* 4.17 Opera Omnia 18, 518; and the gloss in Rheims, 386. Chrysostom, *Sacr.* 3.6 PG 48.644, already sees James teaching that priests can forgive sins. Since Vatican II, Catholic opinion has read less into 5.16. The 1985 edition of the New Jerusalem Bible *ad loc.* remarks: 'nothing special...may be deduced about sacramental confession'. See further Bottini, 'Confessione'.

[14] Cf. Luther, *Babylonian Captivity*, 120 ('I have my doubts...whether he would have us understand "priests" when he says "presbyters"'); Cartwright, *Confutation*, 662-63; and see esp. F. Taylor, 147-53. Contrast Ps.-Andrew of Crete, *Éloge* 4.5-10 ed. Noret, 54, and the statement of Trent (which was partly aimed at Erasmus, who translated πρεσβύτεροι by *seniores*): James' 'presbyters' are 'not the elders or leading figures among the people, but either bishops or priests duly ordained by them by the laying on of hands' (Pelikan and Hotchkiss, *Creeds* [as in n. 7], 858). Cf. the translations of Wycliffe ('preestis of the chirche') and the original Douay ('the priests of the church'). The Vulgate nonetheless has *presbuteros*, not *sacerdotes*, and it was common in the Middle Ages for Catholics to confess to someone other than a priest; cf. the 1211 Franciscan *Regula non bullata* § 20 and see D. Isabell, *The Practice and Meaning of Confession in the Primitive Franciscan Community according to the Writings of Saint Francis of Assisi and Thomas of Celano*, Assisi, 1973. Despite their other disagreements, many Protestants have concurred with Catholics in using James to argue against unordained faith-healers; cf. R. A. Torrey, *Divine Healing: Does God Perform Miracles Today?*, New York, 1924, 12-13; B. Poschmann, *Penance and the Anointing of the Sick*, New York, 1964, 234-35.

he speaks of confessing sins to 'each other'.[15] Zwingli concluded that James speaks of 'the confession which every man makes to his neighbour when he discloses to him some internal and hitherto hidden wound. Hence, nothing more can be wrung from this passage than that every man should go to his neighbour and ask him to pray with him for his shortcomings.'[16] Comments to similar effect, often snide and condescending, show up in many of the earlier Protestant commentaries.

Our passage has also been prominent in inner-Protestant debates regarding the cessation of miracles. Charismatics and faith-healers have always found in James encouragement for their view that miraculous healings continue in the Christian dispensation.[17] In the words of one advocate of miracles, 5.14-16 entails that 'prayer for physical healing and God's healing power is normal and to be expected in the life of the church'.[18] By contrast, the so-called cessationists, who believe that all miracles of the sort that appear in the NT ceased in the fourth, third, or second century or with the end of the apostolic age, so that all subsequent reports of such should be disbelieved, have had to ask why, if miracles no longer happen, one should bother to heed James' admonition to pray for the sick or anoint them with oil.[19] One common response has been to

---

[15] Cf. Calvin, 316; Benson, 121; Alford, 328; Shogren, 'Heal', 108; *et al.* Zodhiates, *Patience*, 145-85, goes on for scolding page after scolding page here, and Robertson, 260-62, becomes atypically rancorous: 'The Roman Catholic Confessional is one of the most dangerous of ecclesiastical institutions... It is difficult to conceive how a husband or father could be willing for wife or daughter to make confession to a priest. The abuses of the confessional make a horrible chapter in human history'. Others have stressed the absence of office-holders from vv. 19-20; note e.g. J. Burroughs, *The Popish Doctrine of Auricular Confession*, London, 1735, 22-23.

[16] Zwingli, *On True and False Religion* 19 trans. and ed. S.M. Jackson and C.N. Heller, Durham, NC, 1981, 255. Cf. J. Berg, *The Confessional, or an Exposition of the Doctrine of Auricular Confession*, Philadelphia, 1841, 32-33; J.H. Hopkins, *The History of the Confessional*, New York, 1850, 74-77; L.F. Bungener, *History of the Council of Trent*, New York, 1855, 259-62.

[17] See e.g. A.J. Gordon, *The Ministry of Healing*, New York, 1882, 29-34; J.B. Shelton, '"Not like it used to be?" Jesus, Miracles, and Today', *Journal of Pentecostal Theology* 14 (2006), 219-27. Note the use of Jas 5 in the contemporary miracle stories retold by C. Keener, *Miracles*, 2 vols., Grand Rapids, MI, 2011, 1.472-73, 517. C.H. Kraft, *Christianity with Power*, Eugene, OR, 1989, 161-63, argues more particularly from James that material objects can contain divine power.

[18] D.A. Oss, 'A Pentecostal/Charismatic View', in *Are Miraculous Gifts for Today?*, ed. W.A. Gruden, Grand Rapids, MI, 1996, 276.

[19] See e.g. Hemminge, 89 ('oyle was an outward signe of the gift of healing, which gift continued for a time to confirme the doctrine in the primitive Church, and nowe the Church hath not that gift: It were...foolish to keepe still the signe without the thing signified by the signe'); Hammond, 700; Benson, 119; Gilpin, 599 ('I know no greater source of fanaticism, than the application of apostolic powers to modern times'); W.E. Biederwolf, *Whipping-Post Theology*, Grand Rapids, MI, 1934, 97-108; B. Johnson, 351. Biederwolf employs our passage to attack not only 'present day Divine Healers' but also Roman Catholics, Christian Scientists, and proponents of 'auto-suggestive therapeutical

distinguish between providential blessings and extraordinary miracles: while the latter no longer occur, one can still hope that 'the ordinary operations of God's general providence in nature' may bring a special blessing.[20] Other options have been to regard miracles of healing, which God still works, as fundamentally different than other miracles, such as prophesying and speaking in tongues, which God no longer bestows; or to hold that, while God may still (in an unpredictable fashion) respond to prayer, no individual has the gift of healing.[21] B.B. Warfield, in attacking faith-healers, insisted that (i) Jas 5 does not exclude ordinary medicinal procedures; (ii) the text does not promise miraculous intervention and answers to prayer; and (iii) anointing is not a religious act; the oil is medicinal and perhaps symbolic (of the power of the Spirit), not imbued with supernatural power. In sum, then, 'what James requires of us is merely that we shall be Christians in our sickness as in our health, and that our dependence then, too, shall be on the Lord'.[22]

Two additional uses of our passage merit mention. First, v. 16 has sometimes been appealed to by those urging that one may pray to the saints in heaven. If the prayers of the righteous are powerful, then how much more the prayers of the blessed departed?[23] Second, G. Byron, 471-72, has recently posed the problem of what 5.19-20 means in a world of religious diversity. The verses assume that doctrinal or moral failure will

---

influence'. Cf. the attitude of Fausset, 595: 'Now that miraculous healing is withdrawn, to use the sign [of anointing] where the reality is wanting, would be unmeaning superstition'. A.R. Gaebelein, *The Healing Question*, New York, 1923, 78-85, argues against female faith-healers, such as Amy Semple McPherson, because James refers to 'elders', who must be men.

[20] So E.J. Carnell, *An Introduction to Christian Apologetics*, 1948, 273-74.

[21] So R.B. Gaffin, Jr., *Perspectives on Pentecost*, Phillipsburg, N.J., 1979, 112-16. Cf. R.B. Gaffin, Jr., 'A Cessationist View', in Gruden, *Miraculous Gifts* (as in n. 18), 42: the healing in James 'is not dependent on or effected by an individual empowered to do so but takes place through prayer, not only that of the elders (and then without distinction among them) but of all believers as well'. Calvin, *Inst.* 4.18, wrote: 'the gift of healing disappeared with the other miraculous powers which the Lord was pleased to give for a time, that it might render the new preaching of the gospel forever wonderful. Therefore, even were we to grant that anointing was a sacrament of those powers which were then administered by the hands of the apostles, it pertains not to us, to whom no such powers have been committed.' Cf. Manton, 449-50.

[22] B.B. Warfield, *Counterfeit Miracles*, New York, 1918, 169-73. Warfield's wife, it is worth remarking, contracted a chronic illness at a relatively young age and remained a semi-invalid. L.S. Chafer, *Systematic Theology, volume VII*, Dallas, 1948, 184, arrives at a conclusion like Warfield's by a different argument: anointing is not necessary for healing because Jesus did it only once, not consistently, and because Jas 5.14 stands alone over against the rest of the NT. Some dispensationalists have urged that this latter point has especial value because James addresses Jews, not Gentile Christians, to whom anointing does not directly apply. Cf. earlier Whitby, 695: anointing with oil was for Jews, laying on of hands for Gentiles.

[23] Note R.W. Jenson, *Systematic Theology*, vol. 2, Oxford, 1999, 268.

be evident. For Byron, however, Christianity has taken multiple legitimate forms. It follows that it may not be so easy to recognize 'the way of truth'. Moving beyond the churches, he likewise urges that the proper response to religious pluralism may not be rescuing others from the error of their ways but 'ongoing interfaith dialogue'.

Exegesis

There is no clear connection between our passage and v. 12 or preceding verses. As Manton, 439, puts it: James here 'diverteth to another matter'. A few exegetes have, nonetheless, suggested a link. According to Tasker, 127, 'instead of resorting to mutual recrimination under the trials of their earthly life, or impetuously breaking out into oaths, Christians are here bidden to turn constantly to prayer, whatever the circumstances of their life may be'.[24] Johnson, 325-26, by contrast, reckons 5.12-20 to be a 'unified discourse' whose topic is 'speech: how can the tongue be used not for the destruction of humans, but for the building up of a community of solidarity?' He is right about the concern for solidarity; but his admission that, in v. 14, 'proper speech will be performative and expressed in action', counts against his analysis. This commentary prefers to view v. 12 as isolated and to regard vv. 13-20 as dealing chiefly with two closely related subjects—healing and restoring the wayward.[25]

Although the section contains admonitions about praying,[26] singing, anointing, and confessing, its unity appears not only from the close interrelationship of all these topics but from the repetition of a number of key expressions:

```
13   κακοπαθεῖ    τις ἐν ὑμῖν   προσευχέσθω
                  τις
14                τις ἐν ὑμῖν   προσευξάσθωσαν   τοῦ κυρίου
15                              εὐχή             ὁ κύριος σώσει ἁμαρτίας
16                              εὔχεσθε
17   ὁμοιοπαθής                 προσευχῇ
                                προσηύξατο
18                              προσηύξατο
19                τις ἐν ὑμῖν
                  τις
20                                               σώσει ἁμαρτωλόν
                                                 ἁμαρτιῶν
```

[24] Cf. Bengel, 507; Weidner, 76; Mayor, 168; Smith, 333; Frankemölle, 705.
[25] Others take the chief theme of at least vv. 13-18 to be petitionary prayer; so e.g. B. Mayer, 'Bittgebet'. McKnight, 431, sees in 5.13-20 only 'random themes'.
[26] Moo, 234, citing Rom 15.30-32; Eph 6.18-20; Phil 4.6; Col 4.2-4; 1 Thess 4.17, 25; 2 Thess 3.1-2; Heb 13.18-19, observes that several NT letters end with exhortations to prayer.

PRAYER, HEALING, RESTORATION (5.13-20)   747

The section, which reminded Harnack of the Didache,[27] has parallels in ancient liturgical traditions.[28] (i) First Clement 59.4 reads: 'Save (σῶσον; cf. Jas 5.15: σώσει) those among us who are in distress... Raise up (ἔγειρον; cf. Jas 5.15: ἐγερεῖ) the fallen... Heal the weak (ἀσθενεῖς ἴασαι; cf. Jas 5.14: ἀσθενεῖ; 5.16: ἰαθῆτε). Turn back those of your people who wander (τοὺς πλανωμένους τοῦ λαοῦ σου ἐπίστρεψον; cf. Jas 5.19-20: πλανηθῇ...ἐπιστρέψῃ...ὁ ἐπιστρέψας...ἐκ πλάνης)... Raise up the weak (ἐξανάστησον τοὺς ἀσθενοῦντας; cf. Jas 5.14: ἀσθενεῖ; 5.15: ἐγερεῖ)'. This, if independent of James, is enough to establish that the concluding section of our epistle reworks liturgical tradition.[29]

(ii) One draws the same inference from the *Sacramentary* of Serapion of Thmuis. For although this document is from the fourth century, it contains many traditional prayers, and its prayer for the sick (εὐχὴ περὶ νοσούντων; cf. Jas 5.15: εὐχή), to be uttered by the bishop (cf. Jas 5.14: πρεσβυτέρους), contains the following: 'We beseech you...maker of the soul (ψυχῆς; cf. Jas 5.20: ψυχήν)...savior (σωτῆρα; cf. Jas 5.15, 20: σώσει) of all...come to the aid and heal (ἴασαι; cf. Jas 5.16: ἰαθῆτε)... raise up those who are lying sick (ἀνάστησον τοὺς κατακειμένους; cf. Jas 5.15: τὸν κάμνοντα...ἐγερεῖ). Give glory to your name (τῷ ὀνόματι; cf. Jas 5.14: τῷ ὀνόματι).'[30]

Additional parallels bolster the hypothesis of a liturgical background for Jas 5.13-20. (iii) The Testament of Our Lord, extant in Syriac and one Greek fragment and probably compiled in the fifth century, incorporates large portions of the Apostolic Tradition as well as two other sources of unknown provenance. Its priestly prayer for consecrating the oil of

---

[27] Harnack, *Geschichte*, 487.

[28] See further Allison, 'Ending'. Koester, *History*, 163, labels 5.13-20 'a short church order'. Cf. Deppe, *Sayings*, 135: 'We prefer to conceive the organizational arrangement of Jas. 5:7-20 as the presentation of a primitive church order less developed than Did. 7–16. Just as The Teaching of the Twelve Apostles combines instruction on baptism (Did. 7), fasting (8), prayers of thanksgiving at the eucharist (9–10), the receiving of prophets (11–13), confession of sins and reconciliation (14), the character qualities of church leaders (15), and the last things (16) into a primitive church order, so James groups together paraenetic exhortations about the last days (5:7-11), the forbidding of oaths (5:12), the healing ministry of the church (5:13-15), the confession of sins and prayer (5:16-18), and the reconciliation of the erring (5:19-20). Thus in piecing together a primitive church order, James moves from speaking about eschatology to various activities within the church.'

[29] On the relationship between 1 Clement and James see the Introduction, 17. 1 Clem. 59.4 belongs to a section of 1 Clement—chaps. 59–61—that, in the judgment of many, preserves in whole or in part pre-formed traditions, perhaps even Jewish prayers, just as the Apostolic Constitutions incorporate Hellenistic synagogal prayers. See H. Löhr, *Studien zum frühchristlichen und frühjüdischen Gebet*, Tübingen, 2003, 5-28. Although the proof of such a thesis falls short, there is no doubt, as Löhr has shown, that 1 Clem. 59–61 is a concatenation of traditional liturgical phrases and conventional prayer concerns. One surmises that liturgy, not James, is the source of what we find in 1 Clem. 59.4.

[30] See Serapion, *Sacr.* 7(22) ed. Funk, 164-66.

healing includes at the end a passing reference to 'those who return'. So, as in 1 Clement, the theme of return from apostasy is associated with physical healing.[31] (iv) This is also the case in Pol. *Phil.* 6.1: the duties of οἱ πρεσβύτεροι include 'turning back those who have gone astray and visiting all the sick': ἐπιστρέφοντες τὰ ἀποπεπλανημένα, ἐπισκεπτόμενοι πάντας ἀσθενεῖς.[32] (v) The Apostolic Constitutions contain a long exhortation to receive those who 'return' (ἐπιστρέφει, ἐπιστράφητε) to the faith. In the middle of it is this: 'It is necessary for us to help the νοσοῦσιν' and to 'save from death' (ῥύεσθαι ἐκ θανάτου; cf. Jas 5.20: σώσει…ἐκ θανάτου) those at risk of going astray.[33] This material also appears in the parallel in the Didascalia.[34] (vi) A short prayer for the laying on of hands for healing in Serapion twice mentions 'the name', once using the expression, ἐν τῷ ὀνόματι; cf. Jas 5.14: ἐν τῷ ὀνόματι.[35] 'The name' is also consistently invoked in later liturgies that bless the oil of healing.[36] (vii) Serapion's *Sacramentary* also contains a 'Prayer (εὐχή) for the Oil for the sick or for the Bread or for the Water', and it uses ἀσθένεια twice (cf. Jas 5.14: ἀσθενεῖ), refers to the forgiveness of sins (ἄφεσιν ἁμαρτημάτων; cf. Jas 5.15: ἁμαρτίας…ἀφεθήσεται), and appeals to the 'holy name' (τὸ ὄνομα) of God and to the name of 'the only Son' (τὸ ὄνομα; cf. Jas 5.14: ἐν τῷ ὀνόματι).[37]

Given the negligible effect of James upon the early churches in general, it is reasonable to attribute these parallels not to the impact of our book but rather to the influence of wider liturgical traditions.[38] Moreover, the same association appears in the Shemoneh Esreh, in benedictions 5-8:[39] '5. Let us return (השיבנו), our Father, to your Torah. Bring us near, our King, to your service, and bring us back in perfect repentance (בתשובה) into your presence. Blessed are you, Lord, who delights in repentance (בתשובה). 6. Forgive us, our Father, for we have sinned. Pardon us, our king, for we have transgressed. For you forgive and you pardon. Blessed are you, Lord, gracious one, who forgives abundantly. 7. Look on our affliction and plead our cause, and redeem us

---

[31] Testament of Our Lord 1.24 ed. Rahmani, 48. Apart from the parallel noted, the only evidence for the influence of James upon the Testament is the latter's use of the phrase, 'Father of lights' (1.23, 26). It is unclear, however, whether James coined the phrase; see on 1.17.

[32] There is no evidence that Polycarp knew James. See the Introduction, 17.

[33] Apost. Const. 2.14-15 ed. Funk, 51-61.

[34] Didascalia 6 ed. Vööbus, 63-72.

[35] Serapion, *Sacr.* 8(30) ed. Funk, 166.

[36] E.g. Apost. Const. 8.29 ed. Funk, 532.

[37] Serapion, *Sacr.* 19(17) ed. Funk, 190-92.

[38] It is striking that, although the Ps.-Clementine First Epistle concerning Virginity shows a knowledge of James, it makes no obvious use of the letter in its instructions for healing the sick.

[39] I quote according to what has traditionally been known as the Babylonian recension. The textual variants of this recension as well as its differences from the Cairo Geniza texts published by S. Schechter in 1898 are of little significant for our purposes.

speedily for the sake of your Name. For you are a mighty redeemer. Blessed are you, Lord, redeemer of Israel. 8. Heal us, O Lord, and we will be healed. Save us and we will be saved. For you are our praise. And bring perfect healing to all our wounds. For you, God and King, heal, being faithful and merciful. Blessed are you, Lord, who heals the sick of your people Israel.' In this standard prayer, the theme of turning back to God leads to a prayer for healing. That blessing 6 is a prayer for forgiveness is of additional significance because Jas. 5.13-20, as well as its parallels in 1 Clem. 59.4 and Pol. *Phil.* 6.1, are also associated with the theme of forgiveness.[40] We have here a traditional concatenation of themes.[41]

One may outline 5.13-20 in this manner:

1. Two contrasting situations and two exhortations (v. 13)
    a. The suffering should pray
    b. The cheerful should praise
2. Elaboration of an instance of suffering and praying (vv. 14-15)
    a. Situation: someone is sick
    b. Recommended response
        i. Call the elders
        ii. Have the elders pray
        iii. Have them anoint with oil
    c. Promised result
        i. The prayer of faith will save
        ii. The Lord will raise up the sick
        iii. Sins will be forgiven
3. General exhortation to all (v. 16)
    a. Imperatives
        i. Confess sins to one another
        ii. Pray for one another
    b. Justification: prayer is effective
4. Illustration of effective prayer (vv. 17-18)
    a. Action 1: Elijah prayed that it might not rain
    b. Outcome: it did not rain
    c. Action 2: Elijah prayed that it might rain
    d. Outcome: it rained
5. Concluding admonition to restore the wayward (vv. 19-20)
    a. Situation: one turns back someone who has wandered from the truth
    b. Outcome:
        i. A soul will be saved
        ii. Sins will be covered

---

[40] See 1 Clem. 59.4-60.2; Pol. *Phil.* 6.1-2.

[41] This conclusion is to be distinguished from the old hypothesis of Rauch, 'Versuch', according to which 5.12-20 comes from a different hand than the rest of James. Rauch argued this on the basis of several considerations, including the use of competing words and expressions (e.g. 'synagogue' in 2.2, 'church' in 5.14), the lack of NT *hapax legomena* in 5.13-20 as opposed to the rest of James, and the claim that although 1.1–5.11 is independent of the NT, 5.12-20 is not (e.g. 5.12 shows a knowledge of Mt 5.33-37 and 5.17 borrows from Lk 4.25). For criticism see Hagenbach, 'Aechtheit'.

The whole section contains a series of very optimistic promises:

'the Lord will raise him up' (v. 15)
'will be forgiven' (v. 15)
'that you may be healed' (v. 16)
'prayer...works powerfully' (v. 16)
'will save himself from death' (v. 20)
'cover a multitude of sins' (v. 20)

Our letter ends without personal details, and arguments that chap. 5 nonetheless enshrines epistolary conventions fail to persuade. The conclusion remains abrupt.[42] One does not gain a sense of closure.[43] But then quite a few endings in ancient books seem odd to us. It suffices to recall 2 Kings, Wisdom, Sirach, Pseudo-Philo, Acts, and 1 John. More important for interpretation is the stress on healing and reconciliation: we have here the ideal of a united community. One would have a wholly different impression of James were 4.12–5.6, with its threats of judgment, the conclusion.

The latter half of the passage is densely intertextual. Verses 17-18 summarize an episode from 1 Kgs 17–18. Verse 18b borrows from LXX Gen 1.11. Verses 19-20 draw upon traditions associated with Ezek 33–34. And the whole ends with a version of Prov 10.12.

Verse 13. Both the suffering and the cheerfulness to which this verse refers are left unaccounted for; but that is consistent with the imperatives being general: they hold in various circumstances. Note the parallelism, which extends into the next verse:

```
κακοπαθεῖ τις ἐν ὑμῖν;    προσ ευχέσθω
εὐθυμεῖ τις;                ψαλλέτω
ἀσθενεῖ τις ἐν ὑμῖν;      προσκαλεσάσθω⁴⁴
```

---

[42] For Plumptre, 107, the abrupt ending adds emphasis. For Felder, 1800, it feels 'as if the actual ending has been lost or the sermon-epistle was suddenly halted as the author was closing'. For E. Palmer, 83, 'it is almost as if he is interrupted before he can say everything that is on his mind'.

[43] A few exegetes believe that 5.13-20, as an epilogue, creates an *inclusio* with the prologue: chap. 1 also encourages prayer, contemplates hardship, and mentions faith. Cf. Frankemölle, 'Netz', 175-84 (adding other parallels), followed by Kaiser, *Krankenheilung*, 7-8.

[44] Burchard, 208, cites several formal parallels, including Demosthenes, *Cor.* 274; *Or.* 22.26; Marcus Aurelius 8.50.1; 1 Cor 7.18, 21, 27; 1 Pet 4.11. According to Johnson, 329, 'such rapid-fire questions' are 'common in the diatribe'. So too Dibelius, 252 (citing Teles, Περὶ αὐταρκείας 6.10-11; Philo, *Jos.* 144; Marcus Aurelius 8.50.1); Popkes, 339. But there are also old Jewish parallels. Note e.g. Deut 20.5-8; Isa 50.8 and see further Beyer, *Syntax*, 233-37.

PRAYER, HEALING, RESTORATION (5.13-20)   751

κακοπαθεῖ τις ἐν ὑμῖν; προσευχέσθω.⁴⁵ κακοπαθέω⁴⁶ is a Jamesian *hapax*, although 5.10 uses the related κακοπάθεια. The meaning here is, 'suffer misfortune', mental and/or physical, as often in Josephus.⁴⁷ The source of the suffering is not indicated, and a connection with vv. 4-6 is not obvious.⁴⁸ One cannot safely infer from this line that James wrote to a persecuted community. Given the following εὐθυμεῖ, he may be thinking chiefly of emotions.⁴⁹ Indefinite τις + ἐν ὑμῖν occurs three times in this section (see above) and nowhere else in James. It is a rare idiom.⁵⁰ For the asyndeton see BDF 494.

James also raises the subject of petitionary prayer in 1.5-8 (on praying in faith) and 4.2-3 (on praying for the wrong thing). In both of those cases the verb is αἰτέω. Here instead it is προσεύχομαι, which occurs in our book four times, all in the present section: vv. 13, 14, 17, 18. The word, which the LXX uses over a hundred times, most often for התפלל, helps unify 5.13-18, a section designed to do at least four things: to commend petitionary prayer as a response to suffering in general (v. 13); to commend petitionary prayer as a response to illness in particular (vv. 14-15); to link petitionary prayer with confession of sins (v. 16); and, by way of a famed example from olden times, to extol appropriate petitionary prayer as powerful and effective (vv. 17-18).⁵¹ As to what exactly, however, one prays for in v. 13 goes unsaid. Johnson, 329, offers: 'it would make sense to suppose that it was either for relief from suffering or for the *hypomonē* to survive it (see 5:10)'. If so, perhaps it is worth noting that, at least here, James offers no promise that the source of suffering will be removed.

---

⁴⁵ Am Antioch Cyr have ἀθυμεῖ ('disheartened'). Oddly enough, other witnesses read ἀθυμεῖ for the second verb in the sentence; see n. 54. One guesses that the εὐθυμεῖ of v. 13b became ἀθυμεῖ through an error of sight or sound, and that the corruption then migrated to v. 13a. Mayor, 168 ('the interrogative is more in accordance with the vivacity which characterizes St. James'); Ropes, 303; Mitton, 195; Davids, 191-92; and Hartin, 265, punctuate the first four words as a question. Huther, 156; Dibelius, 252; Mussner, 217; Schrage, 54; Popkes, 314, do not. Wycliffe, Tyndale, and Cranmer do not read the words as interrogatory. GenevaB., KJV, and most later English versions, including RSV and NRSV, have a question here and in the next clause.
⁴⁶ LXX: Jon 4.10. NT: 3×; cf. 2 Tim 2.9; 4.5. Gk. Pseudepigrapha (Denis): Let. Aris. 241. Philo: 8×. Josephus: 29×.
⁴⁷ *Bell.* 1.148, 159; 4.127, 135; 6.37; *Ant.* 1.185; 2.74, 103, 149, 211, 274, 314, 323; etc. Cf. LXX Jon 4.10; Let. Aris. 241. See further Kaiser, *Krankenheilung*, 26-29, and cf. Moo, 235: the word here has 'broad application, covering trials of all kinds'.
⁴⁸ Gundry, 933, thinks the suffering due to persecution. He then understands the enjoined praise as a response to deliverance from persecution. Cf. Benson, 116; Hamman, 'Prière', 40.
⁴⁹ Cf. the Vulgate: *tristatur aliquis vestrum*. Contrast Huther, 156.
⁵⁰ But note Ign. *Magn.* 10.2; Ps.-Clem. Hom. 3.30.3 GCS 42 ed. Rehm, 67 (ἐὰν ᾖ τις ἐν ὑμῖν; cf. Jas 5.19).
⁵¹ Karris, 'Angles', 207-208, seems alone in understanding the call to pray in response to suffering as encouragement to pray the Psalms of complaint.

A reader might set 5.13 within the context of earlier admonitions not to curse (3.9-12), not to judge (3.13-18), and not to grumble against others (5.9). Bede remarks: 'Because in the earlier parts of this letter our tongue is restrained from evil or useless speaking, it is appropriately made clear at the end what particularly we ought to be speaking. So we are commanded to pray and sing psalms to the Lord as often as we are struck by any adversities, also to confess our sins to one another and to pray for each other.'[52]

The imperatival form, προσευχέσθω, is unattested in non-Christian sources. It appears first in 1 Cor 14.13 and Jas 5.13, and thereafter and before the fourth century solely in texts dependent upon 1 Corinthians. Is it perhaps an echo of the liturgical injunction, προσευξώμεθα?[53]

εὐθυμεῖ τις; ψαλλέτω.[54] The intransitive εὐθυμέω[55] means 'be cheerful'.[56] ψάλλω occurs throughout the LXX Psalms for זמר, where it means either 'perform music'[57] or, less often, 'praise with music/song'.[58] In James, as elsewhere in the NT, the latter meaning is seemingly to the fore.[59] Because it closely follows προσευχέσθω, an exhortation to

---

[52] Bede, *Ep. cath.* ad loc. CCSL 121 ed. Hurst, 223. Cf. ibid., 220-21: 'The one who above restrained brothers from grumbling against one another in difficulties now shows to the contrary what should be done. If anyone among you, he says, suffers from oppressive sorrow...you should by no means...murmur against one another and lay blame on God's judgments but rather come together at the church and on bended knee to pray to the Lord.'

[53] Cf. Tob 8.4; *Mart. Perp. et Felicit.* 12 TS 1.2 ed. Robinson, 81 (σταθῶμεν καὶ προσευξώμεθα).

[54] ἀθυμεῖ appears in 044 614 945 2412 L884. See n. 45. 2805 L422 Ath Chrys Or Thdrt add ἐν ὑμῖν and so enhance the parallelism with both vv. 13a and 14a.

[55] NT: 3×; Jas: 1×. LXX: 0×; cf. Symm. Ps 31.11; Prov 15.15. Gk. Pseudepigrapha (Denis): 1×. Philo: 0×. Josephus: 4×.

[56] Cf. Plato, *Leg.* 797B; Acts 27.22, 25; Josephus, *Bell.* 6.393; *Ant.* 19.136; T. Job 40.6 v.l.; Epictetus, *Diss.* 1.1.22; *Sent. Sext.* 385. Johnson, 329, translates: 'Is anyone feeling good?' Rico, 'Prière', prefers: 'Is anyone serene?' He appeals to the Vulgate's rendering of our verse ('aequo animo est') and Acts 24.10.

[57] E.g. 1 Βασ 16.16; Pss 26.6; 56.8; Ecclus 9.4; cf. T. Job 14.2.

[58] E.g. Pss 70.22; 97.5; cf. Pss. Sol. 3.2; T. Abr. RecLng. 20.12. James supplies the earliest instance of the form, ψαλλέτω, the next being Clement of Alexandria, *Strom.* 1.1.8.3 GCS 52 ed. Stählin and Früchtel, 7.

[59] Rom 15.9; 1 Cor 14.15; Eph 5.19. NT: 5×. LXX: 53× (the vast majority in Psalms). Gk. Pseudepigrapha (Denis): 5×. Philo: 0×. Josephus: 8×. This word has been at the heart of debates regarding the use of instruments in churches, many insisting—wrongly in view of T. Job 14.2—that, by NT times, ψάλλω referred to vocal music alone; see e.g. D.F. Bonner, *Instrumental Music in the Worship of God*, Rochester, NY, 1881, 26-34, 42-47; E. Ferguson, *A Cappella Music*, Abilene, TX, 1972, 1-27. According to J. Glasgow, *Heart and Voice*, Belfast, n.d., 184, James writes about 'an individual act... and cannot therefore mean any accompaniment, unless it can be shown that the man is expected both to sing and play. This is often done; but to express it would require two verbs, or what is equivalent, a compound verb.' For a sense of how rancorous this issue has been in some quarters see *Proceedings of the Convention of United Presbyterians Opposed to Instrumental Music*, Pittsburgh, 1883.

petitionary prayer, ψαλλέτω implies sung prayers of thanksgiving.⁶⁰ Despite mention of 'the assembly' in the next verse, our author may have had in view not collective singing in a formal setting but an individual giving thanks; cf. Apost. Const. 8.34.10 ed. Funk, 542: 'if you are unable to gather together in a home or in a church, let each individual sing praises (ψαλλέτω) by himself'.⁶¹ Popkes, 340, however—who takes εὐθυμεῖ τις ψαλλέτω to mean that, if one feels good, one should express it—construes the singing as a public witness.⁶²

κακοπαθεῖ and εὐθυμεῖ represent extremes of human experience. Cothenet speaks in this connection of 'the literary genre of totality', in which a pair of expressions 'is used to represent all the situations occurring between the two extremes'.⁶³ Given that both προσευχέσθω and ψαλλέτω have to do with addressing the deity, the upshot seems to be that, whatever the situation, good or bad, orientation to God is in order.⁶⁴ One recalls 1.2, which calls for rejoicing in suffering.

Verse 14. Although v. 13 refers both to petitionary prayers and to prayers of thanksgiving, vv. 14-16 reveal James' chief interest to be the former.

The words that follow are too brief and cryptic for us to understand them as introducing a custom foreign to the readers. James must rather refer to a 'standing practice' (Popkes, 338), probably one known in both

---

⁶⁰ Cf. Pss. Sol. 15.5 (ψαλμὸν καινὸν μετὰ ᾠδῆς ἐν εὐφροσύνῃ καρδίας); Acts 16.25 (προσευχόμενοι ὕμνουν τὸν θεόν). Against the impression of the KJV ('let him sing psalms'; cf. Tyndale, Cranmer) and the remark of E. Stauffer, *New Testament Theology*, London, 1955, 200, 310 n. 656, James need not imply use of the psalter. Cf. Tasker, 128; Popkes, 340. Still, ψάλλω does refer to singing or chanting Psalms in some patristic texts; cf. Lampe, s.v., B. Marty, 207, wonders whether James knew 'Christian canticles'. Manton, 442-43, turns our text into the opportunity to criticize those who, in his time and place, discouraged public singing of the biblical Psalms. He also counters those who oppose all singing, those who oppose meter and rhyme, those who believe congregations should never sing but only respond with 'amen' to the singing of appointed psalmists, and a slew of others with views unlike his. James' imperative served a similar function in the church fathers; cf. Origen, *Sel. in Ps.* 12 PG 12.1205B; Athanasius, *Ep. Marcell.* 28 PG 27.40C; *Exp. Ps.* 46 PG 27.217C; Chrysostom, *Sanct. Bern. et Pros.* 3 PG 50.634.

⁶¹ So too Plummer, 633. Benson, 117, favors a reference to 'private devotion' for this reason: 'If one person was afflicted, and another quite easie, what would suite one, would, according to this rule of the apostle, have been unfit for the other. Accordingly; it runs in the singular number; "Is any man afflicted? let him pray".'

⁶² Cf. Bede *ad loc.* CCSL 121 ed. Hurst, 221; Bengel, 507. Plummer, 633, makes v. 13 the opportunity to rebuke people who, although they have bad voices, insist on singing publicly, with the result that others are annoyed.

⁶³ Cothenet, 'Healing', 40.

⁶⁴ Cf. the formulations of Calvin, 313 ('there is no time at which God does not call us to himself'); Bengel, 507 (one can also pray prosperity and sing in adversity); Trapp, 704 ('A Christian's whole life is divided into praying and praising, as David's Psalms are'); Burchard, 209; also J.H. Newman, *Parochial and Plain Sermons*, London, 1916, 336: 'Prayer and praise seem in his [James'] view to be an universal remedy, a panacea… which ought to be used at once, whatever it be that affects us'.

church and synagogue. The parallels to which this commentary calls attention confirm the inference.

ἀσθενεῖ τις ἐν ὑμῖν; This question and its following answer are modeled on the sentences in v. 13 and match the first in form perfectly. Although a *hapax* for James, ἀσθενέω occurs often in early Christian literature, including the gospels, with the sense, 'to be ill'.[65] That is clearly the sense here, despite occasional attempts to argue otherwise.[66] (i) James was a student of the Jesus tradition which, as we know it, uses ἀσθενέω exclusively of bodily illness.[67] (ii) Anointing with oil has to do with physical healing in Mk 6.13. (iii) Every key act and every key word in vv. 14-15 is otherwise associated with illness and physical recovery in ancient sources. (iv) The illustration in vv. 17-18 summarizes an astounding public miracle, which better suits a dramatic recovery from illness rather than a spiritual restoration. (v) The parallel in Pol. *Phil.* 6.1 (see 748 above) clearly refers to the physically ill. (vi) As already observed, 5.13-20 is influenced by liturgical traditions related to physical healing.

In what follows, James nowhere mentions physicians. Karris accordingly suggests that 'the sick person is implicitly admonished not to call the physicians to his/her bedside', that Jas 5.14 is 'anti-physician'. In support, he directs attention to ancient texts that disparage doctors.[68] Erasmus has the same take: 'If someone is suffering from bad health, he should not take refuge in magical remedies or spend huge sums of money on doctors, whose cures are often such that it is better to depart cheerfully from life'.[69] This may read too much into the text, which is mute on the topic. Only some Jews were suspicious of physicians.[70] Beyond that,

---

[65] See the texts in n. 67 and cf. T. Zeb. 5.2, 4; T. Jos. 3.5; 9.4; 1 Clem. 59.4.

[66] See further below, on v. 15; also Kaiser, *Krankenheilung*, 29-41. Howard, *Disease*, 261-63, thinks rather of mental depression, *acedia*; cf. F.J. Wright, 'Healing', *Journal of the Christian Medical Fellowship* 37 (1991), 20-21. Bede *ad loc.* CCSL 121 ed. Hurst, 221, thinks of both spiritual and bodily illness. So too Karris, 'Angles', 216-17. Strange, *World*, 31-33, takes the language to be 'multifaceted'. The verb does refer to moral weakness in LXX Hos 5.5; 14.10; Rom 4.19; 1 Cor 8.7, 11-12; 2 Clem. 17.2; etc. Hengel, 'Polemik', 540-43, forwards the fanciful thesis that Paul is the sick one who needs to be healed, turned back, and saved.

[67] Mt 10.8; 25.36, 39; Mk 6.56 (ἐτίθεσαν τοὺς ἀσθενοῦντας...ἐσῴζοντο); Lk 4.40; Jn 4.46; 5.3, 7, 13; 6.2; 11.1-3, 6. Cf. Acts 9.37; 19.12; 2 Tim 4.20.

[68] Karris, 'Angles', 211; cf. Wis 16.12; LXX Ecclus 38.15; Philo, *Sacr.* 69-71; Pliny, *N.H.* 6.15.2. To these add: 2 Chr 16.12; Job 13.4; Tob 2.10; Ecclus 10.10; m. 'Abod. Zar. 2.2; b. Pesaḥ. 113a.

[69] Erasmus, *Paraphrase*, 169. For patristic texts that employ James in order to discourage pagan cures see Ropes, 306.

[70] Note Ecclus 38.1-8 and Josephus, *Vita* 404, and see further F. Kudlien, 'Jüdische Ärzte im Römischen Reich', *Medizinhistorisches Journal* 20 (1985), 36-75. Josephus, *Bell.* 2.136, recounts that the Essenes 'make investigations into medicinal roots and the properties of stones', and Jub. 10.14-14 seems to know of healing books the use 'herbs of the earth'. For positive statements about physicians from Christians see H.C. Brennecke,

perhaps Wilson is right to wonder how many in James' audience would have had the means to employ professional healers.[71]

προσκαλεσάσθω τοὺς πρεσβυτέρους τῆς ἐκκλησίας.[72] προσκαλέομαι— note the alliteration with πρεσβυτέρους and προσευξάσθωσαν—occurs only here in our book. The verb apparently implies that the sick individual needs the presbyters to come to him because he cannot go to them; cf. Pol. *Phil.* 6.1: 'the presbyters (οἱ πρεσβύτεροι)...should visit all the sick' (ἀσθενεῖς).[73] So we have here visitation of the sick, an act praised in many Jewish and Christian texts.[74]

Although the use of προσκαλέομαι with πρεσβύτερος is unattested before James, the language echoes a biblical idiom:

- MT Exod 12.21: יקרא משה לכל־זקני ישראל ('Moses called all the elders of Israel')
- MT Exod 19.7: משה ויקרא לזקני העם ('Moses, and he called the elders of the people')
- LXX Exod 19.7: Μωυσῆς καὶ ἐκάλεσεν τοὺς πρεσβυτέρους τοῦ λαοῦ
- MT Lev 9.1: קרא משה...לזקני ישראל ('Moses called...the elders of Israel')
- MT 1 Kgs 20.7: יקרא מלך־ישראל לכל־זקני הארץ ('the king of Israel called all the elders of the land')
- 3 Βασ 21.7: ἐκάλεσεν ὁ βασιλεὺς 'Ισραηλ πάντας τοὺς πρεσβυτέρους
- Jdt 6.16: συνεκάλεσαν πάντας τοὺς πρεσβυτέρους τῆς πόλεως
- Jdt 13.12: συνεκάλεσαν τοὺς πρεσβυτέρους τῆς πόλεως

Note also LXX Joel 1.14 (συναγάγετε πρεσβυτέρους; MT: אספו זקנים); Acts 20.17 (μετεκαλέσατο τοὺς πρεσβυτέρους τῆς ἐκκλησίας); 1 Ep. Pet. ad Jas. 1.1 GCS 42 ed. Rehm, 2, where James of Jerusalem sends for the elders (μετεκαλέσατο τοὺς πρεσβυτέρους).

'Heilen und Heilung in der Alten Kirche', in *Eschatologie und Schöpfung*, ed. M. Evang, H. Merklein, and M. Wolter, Berlin, 1997, 24-45.

[71] E. Wilson, 'Anointing', 92. The church fathers could invoke James against seeking what they took to be superstitious remedies; cf. e.g. Cyril of Alexandria, *Ador.* 6 PG 68.472A; Caesarius of Arles, *Serm.* 13.3 CCSL 103.1 ed. Morin, 66-67; 184.4-5 CCSL 104.1 ed. Morin, 750-51.

[72] It is just possible that τῆς ἐκκλησίας is a secondary addition. Although τῆς ἐκκλησίας appears in the vast majority of witnesses, it is absent from 321 L:SF K:S^ms, and one can readily imagine a scribe adding it to gain a common phrase. Given the weight of the testimony, however, one guesses that an eye moved from the concluding Σ of ΠΡΕΣΒΥΤΕΡΟΥΣ to the concluding Σ of ΕΚΚΛΗΣΙΑΣ.

[73] For Christian priests or deacons or hierarchs visiting the sick see also Hippolytus (?), *Apost. Trad.* 34 TU 75 ed. Tidner, 142; Ps.-Clement, *Ep. Jas.* 12 GCS 42 ed. Rehm, 15; the Testament of Our Lord 2.21 ed. Rahmani, 142; Canons of Hippolytus 24 PO 149 ed. Coquin, 390-92. Celsus *apud* Origen, *Cels.* 6.40, claimed to know of Christian 'elders' who possessed books with the names of demons. This assertion may reflect knowledge of Christian 'elders' who were exorcists.

[74] Ecclus 7.35; Mt 25.36; Ps.-Clement, *1 Ep. virg.* 12.4 ed. Funk, 12; T. Jacob 2.23; Mek. on 18.20; Tg. Ps.-J. Deut 34.6; b. Ned. 39b-40a (there is no limit to the reward for visiting the sick); b. Soṭah 14a; etc.

'The presbyters of the church' became a common ecclesiastical phrase.[75] But it is attested in Christian sources only once before James (Acts 20.17; cf. 14.23), and whether it had become a standard expression by his time is unknown. πρεσβύτερος regularly stands for זקן in the LXX while ἐκκλησία is the equivalent of קהל (which the LXX can also translate, although much less often, with συναγωγή). Moreover, the LXX sometimes employs πρεσβύτερος to refer not just to an older person but to an older person with authority,[76] sometimes paralleling it with ἄρχων;[77] and beyond that, πρεσβύτερος and ἐκκλησία occur close together in several places.[78] It follows that 'the elders of the assembly' need not, any more than זקני העדה[79] or οἱ πρεσβύτεροι τῆς συναγωγῆς[80] or οἱ ἡγούμενοι ἐκκλησίας (Ecclus 33.19), be a distinctively Christian phrase. As Dibelius, 253, remarks: '"elders of the assembly" could indeed be understandable within a Jewish context'.[81] Cf. 2 Esd 10.8 ('Anyone who does not come within three days as the council of the rulers and the elders [τῶν ἀρχόντων καὶ τῶν πρεσβυτέρων] demands...he will be banned from the assembly [ἐκκλησίας] of the exile'), 14 (στήτωσαν δὴ οἱ ἄρχοντες ἡμῶν τῇ πάσῃ ἐκκλησίᾳ); LXX Ps 106.32 (ἐν ἐκκλησίᾳ λαοῦ καὶ ἐν καθέδρᾳ

---

[75] Cf. Ep. Clem. ad Jac. 7.5; 10.4 GCS 42 ed. Rehm, 11, 13; Epiphanius, *Pan*. 57.1.4 GCS 31 ed. Holl, 344; etc. For discussion see J. Ysebaert, *Die Amtsterminologie im Neuen Testament und in der Alten Kirche*, Breda, The Netherlands, 1994, 60-123. Roman Catholic theologians have sometimes fretted over the plural, given that a single priest typically conducts extreme unction. Cf. P.J. Toner, 'Extreme Unction', in *The Catholic Encyclopedia*, vol. 5, ed. C.G. Herbermann *et al.*, New York, 1909, 725: the plural 'does not imply that several priests are required for valid administration of the sacrament. Writing, as we may suppose, to Christian communities in each of which there was a number of priests, and where several, if it seemed well, could easily be summoned, it was natural for the Apostle to use the plural without intending to lay down as a matter of necessity that several should actually be called in... Just as one might say, "Let him call in the doctors", meaning, "Let him procure medical aid".'

[76] Gen 50.7; Deut 31.28; Judg 11.8-11; Ruth 4.2; Jdt 8.10; 10.6; Isa 24.23; 1 Macc 7.33; 11.23; 2 Macc 13.13; 14.37; Sus 5, 29, 34; cf. CIJ 1.378; 2.735, 739, 800, 801, 803, 829, 931, 1404; Lk 7.3. In the Synoptics, 'the elders' are often members of the Sanhedrin: Mt 12.23; 26.3; Mk 8.31; 11. 27; 14.43; etc. Cf. Acts 4.5, 8, 23; 6.12; 23.14; 24.1; 25.15.

[77] Gen 24.2; Exod 34.30-31; Judg 8.16; Jdt 7.23; 1 Macc 1.26; 14.28; Ps 104.22; Job 12.20-21; Isa 3.14; Lam 5.12; cf. IJO 2.5 (οἱ ἄρχοντες καὶ οἱ πρεσβύτεροι), 30 (ἀρχισυναγώγων καὶ τῶν πρεσβυτέρων); 3.Syr53 (ἀρχισυναγώγων... πρεσβυτέρων).

[78] E.g. Deut 31.28-30; Josh 9.2; 2 Chr 10.3-6; Jdt 6.16; 1 Macc 14.19-20.

[79] Cf. Lev 4.15; Judg 21.16; 4Q365 7 1.4; 11QTemple 42.12-13.

[80] Cf. LXX Lev 4.15; Judg 21.16; Sus 41.

[81] Cf. Spitta, 144. Dibelius goes on, however, to assert that there is no evidence for a Jewish office with 'ecstatic-pneumatic powers'. Meyer, *Rätsel*, 166-67, regards the phrase as a Christian interpolation into an originally Jewish text. So too Easton, 171, who also excises the reference to oil. For Christian 'presbyters' see Acts 11.30; 14.23; 15.4, 6; 1 Tim 4.14 (here the elders perform the rite of the laying on of hands); 5.17, 19; Tit 1.5; 1 Pet 5.1, 5; 2 Jn 1; 3 Jn 1.

πρεσβυτέρων); LXX Joel 2.16 (άγιάσατε εκκλησίαν, εκλέξασθε πρεσβυτέρους); LAB 11.8 (*laudes Dominum in ecclesia presbiterorum*). One should also keep in mind that πρεσβύτερος was a common title for various sorts of honored individuals in Hellenistic cities, villages, and guilds,[82] that rabbinic texts know of religious authorities, including 'elders', visiting the sick,[83] and that the NT itself uses πρεσβύτερος for lay members of the Sanhedrin (see n. 76), for Pharisaic scribes (Mk 7.3, 5), for prominent members of a Jewish synagogue (Lk 7.3), and for Jewish saints of previous generations (Heb 11.2).[84]

εκκλησία occurs in early Christian literature with two chief meanings—either the church universal or a local assembly.[85] Both senses appear in Matthew (16.18; 18.18), Acts, and Paul. In the LXX, from Deuteronomy on, εκκλησία is the equivalent of קהל, which means according to BDB, s.v., 'assembly, convocation, congregation'.[86] It never stands for עדה, which is usually rendered by συναγωγή—although, in LXX Prov 5.14, συναγωγή and εκκλησία are synonymous.[87] Whether or not the LXX supplies the immediate background to early Christian usage of εκκλησία,[88] most scholars would likely concur with Bultmann that

---

[82] See G. Bornkamm, 'πρέσβυς κτλ.', *TDNT* 6.653-54.

[83] Cf. ARN 41 ('Once, as R. Simeon ben Yohai went about visiting the sick...'); b. Sanh. 101a ('When R. Eliezer fell sick, his disciples entered to visit him'; 'When R. Eliezer fell sick, four elders [זקנים] went to visit him').

[84] R.A. Campbell, *The Elders*, Edinburgh, 1994, surveys all the relevant texts from Jewish, Graeco-Roman, and Christian sources regarding 'elders'. Although he has little to say about James, his major conclusion is relevant: 'the elders are those who bear a title of honour, not of office, a title that is imprecise, collective and representative, and rooted in the ancient family or household'. Cf. C. Claussen, 'Meeting, Community, Synagogue—Different Frameworks in Ancient Jewish Congregations in the Diaspora', in *The Ancient Synagogue from Its Origins until 200 C.E.*, ed. B. Olsson and M. Zetterholm, Stockholm, 2003, 160: 'Jewish elders must... be viewed as people who were held in high esteem. Sometimes they held more specific offices. However, most times their influence was not due to an office but rather to the honor they enjoyed as members of traditionally powerful families of high social rank.'

[85] Literature: J.Y. Campbell, 'The Origin and Meaning of the Christian Use of the Word *Ekklesia*', *JTS* 49 (1948), 130-42; J. Barr, *The Semantics of Biblical Language*, Oxford, 1961, 119-29; A. Dahl, *Das Volk Gottes*, 2nd ed., Darmstadt, 1963; W. Schrage, '"*Ekklesia*" und "Synagogue"', *ZTK* 60 (1963), 178-202; I.H. Marshall, 'New Wine in Old Wineskins: V. The Biblical Use of the Word "Εκκλησία"', *ExpTim* 84 (1973), 359-64; K. Berger, 'Volksversammlung und Gemeinde Gottes', *ZTK* 73 (1976), 167-207; N.O. Linton, *RAC* 4.905-21.

[86] Muraoka, *Lexicon*, s.v., discerns three main meanings in the LXX: act of congregating for a public meeting; large group of gathered people; social organization or body.

[87] So also apparently LXX Ps 39.10-11. Note too the linking of εκκλησία and συνάγω in 2 Chr 30.13; 2 Esd 10.1; Joel 2.16.

[88] See P. Treblico, 'Why Did the Early Christians Call Themselves ή εκκλησία?', *NTS* 57 (2011), 440-60.

'ἐκκλησία (τοῦ θεοῦ) corresponds...with (קהל יהוה)', and that 'in understanding themselves as Congregation or Church the disciples appropriate to themselves the title of the Old Testament Congregation of God'.[89] In James, however, the meaning of ἐκκλησία may be different. Read in the light of 1.1 and the implied audience throughout, it need not signify a Christian congregation or assembly but could refer to or include a Jewish congregation or assembly.[90] Comparable then would be the use of קהל in the Dead Sea Scrolls.[91]

Many modern commentators contrast what we find in Jas 5.13-15 with 1 Cor 12.9, 30. The latter speaks of the 'gifts' of healing. So whereas Paul still knows of charismatics, James, it is said, does not. He rather reflects a secondary stage of development, in which the charisma of healing had become institutionalized.[92] Perhaps this is the correct analysis. It is certainly true that, in James, healing is the concern of the community.[93] One should note, however, that some later forms of institutionalized Christianity had room for charismatic healers; cf. e.g. Irenaeus, *Haer.* 2.32.4 (some in the church still heal the sick through the laying on of hands); Hippolytus (?), *Apost. Trad.* Sahidic 38 TU 58 ed. Till and Leipoldt, 58 (if someone claims to have received gifts of healing by revelation, time will tell the truth of the matter); Apost. Const. 8.16 ed. Funk, 522 (some elders have 'the gifts of healing'; cf. 8.26, 528); Canons of Hippolytus 8 PO 149 ed. Coquin, 360 ('if someone asks for his ordination, saying, "I have received the gift of healing..."'). It is also relevant that, in Num 11, the 'elders' around Moses are charismatics, receiving the spirit and prophesying.[94]

καὶ προσευξάσθωσαν ἐπ' αὐτόν. For προσεύχομαι see on v. 13. The aorist seemingly implies a single action or a single occasion. The preposition is neither περί[95] nor ὑπέρ[96] but ἐπί, which follows προσεύχομαι nowhere else in biblical Greek. The meaning is not 'pray for' but 'pray over'. The reader envisages elders standing beside and perhaps leaning over someone prostrate with illness.[97] This reinforces the inference from

---

[89] Bultmann, *Theology*, 1.38. See further Berger and Linton, as in n. 85.

[90] Cf. LXX Deut 23.1; 31.30; Job 30.28; Ps 88.6; Pss. Sol. 10.7; Philo, *Decal.* 32; note also T. Job 32.9; 3 Bar. 13.4. Treblico, 'Christians' (as in n. 88), 449, observes: ἐκκλησία and συναγωγή 'were more or less synonymous'.

[91] 1QM 4.10; 1QSa 2.4; CD 7.17; 11.22; 12.6; etc.

[92] So e.g. Kollmann, *Jesus*, 345-56, who thinks James is related to the Matthean community, which was suspicious of wandering charismatics; cf. 7.21-23.

[93] Cf. Nielsen, *Heilung*, 213. Many regard the presbyters as representatives of the community.

[94] Cf. Windisch-Preisker, 33, and note Philo, *Fug.* 186.

[95] Cf. LXX Gen 20.7; Lk 6.28; Jn 17.20; Col 1.3; etc.

[96] Cf. 1 Βασ 12.19; Mt 5.44; Acts 8.24; 2 Cor 9.14; etc.

[97] Cf. 11Q5 27.8-9 (David performed songs 'על the possessed'); Lk 4.39 ('standing ἐπάνω her he rebuked the fever'); Acts 20.10; Ps.-Clement, *1 Ep. virg.* 12.3 ed. Funk, 11 ('over [*super*] whom they make their adjurations'); Canons of Hippolytus 24 PO 149 ed. Coquin, 390 ('when he [the deacon] prays over him').

προσκαλεσάσθω τοὺς πρεσβυτέρους, that the patient is bedridden. Cf. the situation in b. B. Bat. 116a: 'Whosoever has a sick person in his house should go to a sage who will invoke mercy for him'. Here someone must ask on behalf of an individual who cannot be up and about.

Although probably unrelated to James, it is nonetheless worth noting that the Greeks had an old proverbial phrase that underlined the value of prayers spoken by older men: 'the works of the young, the counsels of the middle-aged, and the εὐχαί γερόντων'.[98]

ἀλείψαντες αὐτὸν ἐλαίῳ. Whether or not James here refers to 'an older, pre-Christian ritual'[99] is unknown. The expression was in any case traditional.[100] It is the equivalent of סוך or משׁח + (ב)שׁמן.[101] Both ἀλείφω[102] and ἔλαιον (= specifically 'olive oil')[103] are *hapax legomena* for James. The aorist need not suggest that the anointing precedes prayer.[104]

According to Ropes, 305, James 'would hardly have been able to distinguish the parts played in the recovery' by anointing and prayer, 'or perhaps even to give any theory of the function of the oil'.[105] Yet it makes sense to see the oil as mediating divine power:[106] (i) olive oil was sometimes used in magical rituals;[107] (ii) we otherwise know of texts in which

---

[98] Hesiod frag. 321; Hyperides frag. 57; Aristophanes the Grammarian, *Paroem.* frag. 4; Harpocration the Grammarian, *Lex.*, s.v. Ἔργα νέων, ed. Dindorf, 134. Although a few of the older commentators, such as Gill, 802, cite this saying, it has fallen out of the modern commentaries.

[99] So B. Lang, *Sacred Games*, New Haven, 1997, 103.

[100] Cf. LXX Esth 2.12; Philo, *Somn.* 1.250; Mk 6.13; Lk 7.46; T. Levi 8.4; also Homer, *Il.* 10.577; 18.250; *Od.* 19.505; Aristotle, *Hist. an.* 583a; Hippocrates, *Nat. mul.* 81.

[101] As in Ps 23.5; Ezek 16.9; Mic 6.15; 4Q458 2 2.6; 11Q5 28.11; etc.

[102] Apart from James, only in the four gospels in the NT.

[103] So BDAG, s.v.

[104] Contrast Johnson, 331: 'after anointing him with oil'.

[105] Cf. Brosend, 160: 'Asking if the anointing with oil was intended medicinally, pastorally, symbolically, or sacramentally is to begin in the wrong place, assuming distinctions simply not present in the ancient Mediterranean world'.

[106] Cf. Gregory of Nyssa, *Bapt. Chr.* ed. Gebhardt, 225-27; *Chaîne Arménienne* 82 ed. Renoux, 146.

[107] See PGM 4.3004, 3209, 3248; 7.200, 212; 62.39; Artemidorus, *Onir.* 82; y. Šabb. 14c (14.3); b. Sanh. 101a; Eccl. Rab. 1.8.4. In Eccl. Rab. 1.8.4, anointing with oil breaks the spell cast by heretics. Cf. the spells against demons in T. Sol. 18.33-34: 'I am called Rhyx Anoster. I send hysteria and cause pains in the bladder. If anyone puts into pure olive oil three mashed up laurel leaves and massages himself saying, "I adjure you by Marmaraoth", immediately I withdraw... I am called Rhyx Phyikoreth. I cause drawn-out illnesses. If anyone puts salt into olive oil and massages his ill self saying, "Cherubim, seraphim, help", immediately I withdraw.' For additional texts and discussion see Kaiser, *Krankenheilung*, 151-56. On the alleged mention of the 'oil of faith' and its healing properties in a silver lamella discovered in Israel in 1967 see E. Testa, *L'Huile de la Foi*, Jerusalem, 1967; idem, 'Ancora sulla laminella guideo-cristiana', *Bib* 49 (1968), 249-53; J.T. Milik, 'Une amulette judéo-araméenne', *Bib* 48 (1967), 450-51; J. Starcky, review of Testa's *L'Onction des malades sur une lamelle du Ier siècle*, in

material substances carry extraordinary healing properties;[108] (iii) 'in the name of the Lord' likely presupposes the supernatural power of the divine name;[109] (iv) Jewish legend knew about Eden's 'oil of life' that had curative powers;[110] (v) it is the elders of the church, not physicians, who anoint with oil; and (vi) the rite 'is accompanied by prayer, not by manipulations and medications'.[111] At the same time, one must concede that oil was widely thought of as having medicinal properties in antiquity[112] and that James offers no elaboration or explanation. So 5.14 is much like Mk 6.13, where the evangelist reports, without explanation, that the disciples 'anointed with oil (ἤλειφον ἐλαίῳ) many who were sick and cured them': the extent to which either author thought of oil as having an intrinsic power or magical properties is unclear, even though a purely medicinal use seems highly improbable.[113]

RevB 75 (1968), 278-80. The magical use of oil goes back to very ancient sources; see S. Daiches, *Babylonian Oil Magic in the Talmud and in Later Jewish Literature*, London, 1913.

[108] E.g. Mk 8.22-26; Jn 9.6-7; Acts 19.11-12; Tacitus, *Hist.* 4.81.

[109] See below. Note the connection between oil and 'the name' in Clement of Alexandria, *Exc.* 82 ed. Casey, 88-90: 'the bread and the oil are sanctified by the power of the name (ὀνόματος), and they are not the same as they appeared to be when they were received, but have been transformed by power into spiritual (πνευματικήν) power'.

[110] LAE 36.2; 40.1-42.1; Gos. Nic. 19. For this tradition, which can identify Eden's tree of life with the olive-tree (cf. Ps.-Clem. Rec. 1.45 GCS 51 ed. Rehm, 34; Origen, *Cels.* 6.27 ed. Marcovich, 404), see E.C. Quinn, *The Quest of Seth*, Chicago, 1962, 25-32. Reicke, 'L'onction', sees this as the primary background for James. LAE 42.1 declares that no one can have the oil 'except in the last days'. Is this a Christian idea, or do we have here a properly Jewish expectation? Cf. 2 En. 22.8-10; also the 'unction of incorruptibility' in Jos. Asen. 8.5; 15.5; 16.16. For additional relevant sources and discussion see A. Kulik, *3 Baruch*, Berlin, 2010, 365-71.

[111] So Gordon, *Ministry of Healing*, 29-34. According to Dibelius, 252, 'the healing is not effected by the oil as a medicine'; rather, the oil is 'a medium of divine power'.

[112] Cf. Isa 1.6; Plato, *Menex.* 238A; Theophrastus, *Hist. plant.* 9.11.1-2; Menander, *Georg.* 60; Hippocrates, *Mul. affect. i–iii* 145; Philo, *Aet.* 63; *Somn.* 2.58; Lk 10.34; Josephus, *Bell.* 1.657; *Ant.* 17.172; Dioscorides Pedanius, *Mat. med.* 2.205; Pliny, *N.H.* 23.34-49; Cassius Dio 53.29.5; Celsus, *Med.* 4.26; Tertullian, *Scap.* 4.6 CSEL 76 ed. Bulhart, 14; m. Šabb. 14.4; 19.2; t. Ter. 9.13-14; t. Šabb 3.5-6; 12.11-12; y. Ma'aś Š. 70b (2.1); b. Hor. 13a-b. Robertson, 255, is hardly justified in asserting that olive oil was 'the best medicine known to the ancient world', and Karris, 'Angles', 211-14, rightly notes that anointing was invariably only one part of any treatment. It was scarcely thought of as a cure-all.

[113] This is the majority view of contemporary exegetes. Cf. Shogren, 'Heal', 103: 'Hellenistic and Jewish sources indicate that a first-century author could easily have said "use the best available medicine, then let the elders pray" if that is what he meant'. Contrast Huther, 157; Clarke, 827; Robertson, 256 (observing: 'one will decide this question according to his predilections'); Ross, 99; Zodhiates, *Patience*, 122-23; Wilkinson, 'Healing', 338-40; L. Wells, *Healing*, 128-29. Should one entertain the possibility that James thought of anointing less as an act of healing and more as an act of consecration? Cf. Gen 31.13; Exod 30.26-29; Lev 8.10-12; 1 Kgs 19.16; etc. But then might we not have expected χρίω? See Martin, 208-209; Moo, 240-41.

As James speaks simply of 'oil', not 'holy oil',[114] as he fails to mention consecration[115] or the work of the Spirit,[116] and as he emphasizes the prayer of faith,[117] prayer seems to be central, the oil less important.[118] Still, for reasons already given, one doubts that our author thought as did Hugh of St. Victor, when he asserted that it is only prayer that brings healing, that oil is only a 'symbol' (σύμβολον).[119]

---

[114] Contrast Exod 30.23-26; Num 35.25; Ps 89.20; Ecclus 45.15; Acts Thom. 67 ed. Bonnet, 184 (ἀλείψας αὐτὴν ἐλαίῳ ἁγίῳ); Palladius, *H. Laus.* 18 ed. Butler, 55 (ἀλείψας ἐλαίῳ ἁγίῳ); Vita Prima Pach. 44 ed. Halkin, 29 (ἀλείψας ἐλαίῳ ἁγίῳ); and Moses bar Kepha, *Myron-Weihe* 2.3 ed. Strothmann, 38 (James refers to consecrated oil, over which priests pray). In the Western churches, anointing has been done with undiluted olive oil. In the Eastern churches, other elements, such as water and wine (cf. Lk 10.34), have been added.

[115] Formal consecration of the anointing oil became very important in later Christian circles; see Bede *ad loc.* CCSL 121 ed. Hurst, 221; Ps.-Dionysius, *E.H.* 4.2 PTS 36 ed. Heil and Ritter, 95; Dionysius bar Salībī, *Myron* 5-6 ed. Varghese, 15-20 (citing Jas 5.13-15 as proof that 'the apostles did consecrate the myron'). James also fails to describe the anointing ritual; later readers filled in the blanks; cf. e.g. Theodulf of Orléans, *Capit. ad Eosdem* PL 105.221C: 'the Greeks trace the sign of the cross with oil on the sick person three times, pouring it cross-wise from a glass vessel on the head, the clothing, and the whole body...beginning the cross from the head and going down to the feet, then from the right hand to the shoulder and across the chest to the left hand'.

[116] For the association of anointing oil with the Spirit see the Gelasian Sacramentary 1.40 ed. Wilson, 70; Dionysius bar Salībī, *Myron* 7 ed. Varghese, 21; etc.

[117] Cf. Theognostus, *Thes.* 20.42.3 CCSG 5 ed. Munitiz, 223-24, citing Mt 8.13 ('Let it be done according to your faith'); Luther, *Babylonian Captivity*, 121-23 (also citing Mt 8.13). ἀλείψαντες is an attendant participle, not the main verb. Cf. Friesenhahn, 'Geschichte', 185: 'The rhetorical emphasis lies...on προσευξάσθωσαν'.

[118] In Christian tradition, by contrast, the anointing became increasingly important; moreover, consecrated oil often came to be thought of as having intrinsic power; cf. Serapion, *Euch.* 19(17) ed. Funk, 190-92 (this calls the oil an ἀλεξιφάρμακον and emphasizes its power against demons); Barsanuphius and John, *Ep.* 211 SC 427 ed. Neyt, Angelis-Noah, and Regnault, 171 (this rewrites James without mentioning prayer); Dionysius bar Salībī, *Myron* 52 ed. Varghese, 65 (the proximity of holy oil endangers unbelievers); Andria, 1516 ('Some in Africa believe it is actually the oil itself that has miraculous power to heal. Others think that healing depends on the quality of the oil used'). Cassian, *Conf.* 7.26 SC 42 ed. Pichery, 269, reports that, when the sick were anointed with oil that had touched Abba Paul, healing was instantaneous. For similar tales see W.E. Scudamore, 'Unction', in *A Dictionary of Christian Antiquities*, ed. W. Smith and S. Chetham, Hartford, 1880, 2004. Interestingly enough, some early Protestant commentators, in their polemic against extreme unction, argued that the apostolic oil was indeed miraculous—unlike the oil of the Catholics, which does not heal; see e.g. John Weemse, *The Christian Synagogue*, London, 1636, 265.

[119] J.A. Cramer, ed., *Catenae in Evangelia S. Matthaei et S. Marci*, Oxford, 1840, 324. Moo, 242, speaks similarly of 'symbolic connotations'. Cf. Manton, 447 ('oil was not used as an instrument, but as a symbol of the cure'); Shogren, 'Heal'; and see further Thomas, *Devil*, 26-28. Dibelius, 252-53, calls the elders 'miracle workers'. This seems imprudent.

To grant the efficacy of anointing is not to deny that, over and above such efficacy, oil would also serve a symbolic function. The substance is associated with life and gladness in a number of scriptural passages,[120] and anointing with oil is part of a healed leper's return to society in Lev 14.15-18. In line with this, mourning typically excluded anointing.[121] So anointing an ill individual might well be a hopeful sign, an implied promise of recovery.

Mark 6.13 is the only other reference to anointing as an act of healing in the earliest Christian sources. The practice is absent from Matthew, Luke, and John, and the accounts of healings in Acts also take no notice of the custom. Perhaps it was not widely practiced.

Although James says nothing about the laying on of hands, anointing inevitably involves touching, and it is natural that anointing came to be associated with the laying on of hands as a transmission of blessing and healing power;[122] cf. Origen, *Hom. Lev.* 2.4 SC 286 ed. Borret, 110 ('if anyone is ill, let him call the presbyters of the church, and let them lay hands on him, anointing him with oil');[123] Acts Thom. 67 ed. Bonnet, 184-85; Palladius, *H. Laus.* 12 ed. Butler, 35 (Benjamin healed all he laid hands upon or anointed with oil); 18, 51 (ἐλαίῳ ἁγίῳ ἀλείφων ταῖς ἑαυτοῦ χερσί καὶ προσευχόμενος).[124]

ἐν τῷ ὀνόματι τοῦ κυρίου.[125] בשם יהוה, a common OT expression,[126] came into Greek as τῷ ὀνόματι κυρίου (e.g. Pss. Sol. 6.4; 10.5), ἐν ὀνόματι κυρίου (e.g. LXX Josh 9.9; 1 Chr 16.2; Ps 118.26; Did. 12.1), ἐν τῷ ὀνόματι κυρίου (e.g. Jas 5.10), and (as here) ἐν τῷ ὀνόματι τοῦ κυρίου (cf. Acts 9.28). 'While calling upon/invoking the name of the Lord' is presumably the sense,[127] although some have thought it instead to be:

---

[120] E.g. Pss 23.5; 45.7; 104.15; Eccl 9.8; Isa 61.3; Jer 31.12.

[121] Note 2 Sam 12.16-20; 14.2; Mt 6.16-18.

[122] For hands as means of blessing see Gen 48.14; Deut 34.9; Mt 19.13; Acts 8.17; etc. For hands as means of healing see 1QapGen 20.28-29; Ps.-Mk 16.18.

[123] Very close to this is the later 'The Penitential of Cummean', in *Medieval Handbooks of Penance*, ed. J.T. McNeill and H.M. Gamer, New York, 1938, 100: 'If any be sick, let him bring the priests of the church and let them pray for him, lay their hands upon him, and anoint him with oil in the name of the Lord, and the prayer of faith shall save the sick man'.

[124] 1 Tim 4.14 was likely influential here, as it speaks of elders laying on hands.

[125] 02 044 81 104 321 *et al*. L921S AnastS Dam omit τοῦ. 03 has only ἐν τῷ ὀνόματι. Ropes, 307, citing texts with the unqualified 'the name' (e.g. Acts 5.41; 2 Clem. 13.4; m. 'Abot 4.4), seems to entertain the possibility that this could be original.

[126] Deut 18.5, 7, 22; 21.5; 1 Sam 17.45; 1 Kgs 18.32; Ps 124.8; Isa 50.10; Zech 13.3; cf. 11Q11 5.4; 11Q19 61.3.

[127] So BAGD, s.v., ὄνομα, 1.d.γ.ב. See W. Heitmüller, *'Im Namen Jesu'*, Göttingen, 1903, 86-87. He cites as parallels Jn 14.13-14; 15.16; 16.24-25; Eph 5.20; Col 3.17. Interpreters differ as to whether 'calling upon the name of the Lord' modifies the anointing or the praying or both. Grammatically, it is most natural to take it with the anointing.

'by the power and authority of the Lord'.[128] Christian readers have often—but not always—understood 'the Lord' to be Jesus.[129] Yet as elsewhere in James, the text itself does nothing to prod a christological reading,[130] and it would have been easy enough, were this the intended meaning, to have added ἡμῶν 'Ἰησοῦ Χριστοῦ.[131] Beyond that, 'the name' is certainly God's name in v. 10, and nothing in v. 14 intimates that the expression has here gained new meaning.[132] Indeed, one presumes that the prayer of the elders is directed to God, and that the κύριος of v. 15 ('the Lord will raise them up'), the κύριος who answers the prayer, must likewise be God. Certainly God was, as the eighth benediction of Amidah has it, the one 'who heals the sick of his people Israel'.[133] Is it not awkward to find a second κύριος here?

Any number of texts, including the magical papyri, reveal that special words and names were widely thought to have power.[134] Some Jews, moreover, cast out demons by the name of God.[135] On 'the name' in prayers for healing and in prayers over holy oil see above, 759-60.

---

[128] Cf. Rosenmüller, 394; K. Seybold and U.B. Mueller, *Sickness and Healing*, Nashville, 1981, 187; Thomas, *Devil*, 28-29.

[129] Note e.g. W. Rebell, *Alles ist möglich dem, der glaubt*, Munich, 1989, 99-100; Wypadlo, *Gebet*, 258-70; McKnight, 440; and cf. the textual variants in 88 915(*f) S:P^ms (τοῦ κυρίου 'Ἰησοῦ) and 6 Ä^ms ('Ἰησοῦ Χριστοῦ). The texts in which people heal in Jesus' name (Mk 9.38-39; 16.17; Lk 10.17; Acts 3.6, 16; 4.10; 16.18; 19.13) have encouraged this reading. Christian rites of anointing, however, have typically invoked 'Father, Son, and Holy Spirit'. Frankemölle, 711-13, thinks we have here a false alternative: the christological and theological ideas belong together.

[130] Cf. G. Twelftree, *In the Name of Jesus*, Grand Rapids, MI, 2007, 181: 'it is quite likely that κύριος was intended to refer to God rather than to Jesus'.

[131] Cf. 1 Cor 1.10; Acts Jn 83 ed. Bonnet, 192; Acts Phil. 9 ed. Bonnet, 5; etc. See further on 5.10.

[132] Ruck-Schröder, *Name*, 236, observes how awkward it is when commentators on Jas 5 identify 'the Lord' alternately with God and Jesus.

[133] Cf. Num 12.13; Pss 6.2; 41.4; Jer 17.14; Ecclus 38.9; Pss. Sol. 16.10; T. Job 38.12-13; PEgerton 5 recto; b. Šabb. 12a; etc.

[134] Recall the retention of the Aramaic commands in Mk 5.41; 7.34; also the talmudic tale of a certain Jacob healing 'in the name of Jesus Pandera': t. Ḥul. 2.2-3; y. 'Abod. Zar. 40d (2.2); y. Šabb. 14d-15a (14.4); b. 'Abod. Zar. 27b; Midr. Eccl. 1.8.3. See further m. Yoma 3.8 and H. Bietenhard, 'ὄνομα', *TDNT* 5.250-52. Martin, 202, insists that James does not imply 'a magical or mechanical talisman' here, and the history of interpretation shows that Christian exegetes, influenced by biblical polemic against 'magic' and 'magicians', have been allergic to associating the Bible with either; cf. Filip Stanislavov, *Abagar* FC 45 ed. Illert, 331. But everything depends upon one's point of view: a miracle to insiders usually looks like magic to outsiders.

[135] See Justin, *Dial*. 85.3; Irenaeus, *Haer*. 2.6.2; T. Sol. 4.12; 11.6; PGM 12.270-306; and perhaps 4Q511 35; 8Q5 1. On the Qumran texts see J.M. Baumgarten, 'On the Nature of the Seductress in 4Q418', *RevQ* 15 (1991), 136. See further the discussion in Origen, *Cels*. 1.24 ed. Marcovich, 24-25.

Verse 15. Although alive to the problem of unanswered prayer elsewhere, James overlooks that issue here.[136] He affirms without qualification that 'the prayer of faith' will heal.[137] Cf. Ecclus 38.9: 'When you are ill, do not delay, but pray (εὖξαι) to the Lord, and he will heal (ἰάσεται) you'.[138]

καὶ ἡ εὐχὴ τῆς πίστεως σώσει τὸν κάμνοντα.[139] εὐχή (Jas: 1×) often means 'vow' in the LXX and elsewhere.[140] Here, however, as frequently in Philo, it is a synonym of προσευχή and means 'prayer'.[141] Its association with πίστις (see on 1.3) may be James' doing as 'prayer of faith' seems to be unparalleled.[142] Whether or not we should detect influence from the Jesus tradition, which links prayer and faith,[143] the immediate background is Jas 1.5-8, which calls for asking ἐν πίστει, without doubt.[144]

---

[136] Or should we rather suppose that, by referring to 'faith', our author implies that unanswered prayers are deficient in that quality? Cf. Shogren, 'Heal', 108. Dibelius, 254-55, solves the problem by postulating an earlier formulation in which the healing was ascribed to pneumatics, not elders.

[137] The history of interpretation supplies the necessary qualifications; cf. Hugh of St. Victor, *Sacr.* 2.15.3 PL 176.577D-78B (even if health of the body does not return, the soul will be healed); Gregory Palamas, *Hom. xxi–xlii* 31.17 ed. Chrestou and Zeses, 300 (healing will occur if it is beneficial); Peter of Mogila, *Conf.* 1.10 q. 119 ed. Malvy and Viller, 70 ('health of the body does not always result'); Luther, *Babylonian Captivity*, 120 ('scarcely one in a thousand is restored to health'); Poole, 897 ('if God see it fit, and the health of body be good for the soul'); Huther, 159 ('even when the result corresponds not to the expectation in reference to the bodily sickness, yet the prayer of faith does not remain unanswered in the higher sense'); Warrington, 'Healing' (God's will, which is known imperfectly, trumps requests; cf. Moo, 244-45). Often exegetes cite Paul's thorn in the flesh (2 Cor 12.7), less often 2 Tim 4.20 ('Trophimus I left ill in Miletus'); note e.g. Plummer, 635. R.A. Torrey, *Healing* (as in n. 14), 18-26, contends that, since God gives faith, when someone is not healed, it need not be due to sin: God may, for this or that end, not give enough faith to effect a healing. Quite in contrast to this is the claim of some that, if the prayer of faith has been sincerely uttered, then physical healing has taken place, even if appearances are to the contrary; cf. E.E. Byrum, *Divine Healing of Soul and Body*, Anderson, IN, 1892, 111.

[138] Cf. 38.14. For similar confident assertions about prayer see Ps 34.17; Prov 15.29; Mk 11.24; Jn 14.14; 16.23; T. Adam 2.10 ('the priest of God mixes them [waters] with consecrated oil and anoints those who are afflicted and they are restored and healed').

[139] 025 81 322 323 945 1739 read: προσευχή. Cf. vv. 13-14. A similar textual variation between εὔχεσθε and προσεύχεσθε appears in v. 16.

[140] E.g. LXX Nah 1.15; Mal 1.14; Acts 18.18; 21.23.

[141] As in LXX Job 16.17; 2 Macc 15.26; T. Abr. RecLng. 5.2; 14.5; Pol. *Phil.* 7.2; etc. See further C. Spicq, 'εὔχομαι, εὐχή', *TLNT* 2.152-54. Horsley-Llewelyn, *Documents*, 4.249, calls attention to a fourth-century papyrus—PLond. 1926—whose wording, which includes εὐχή, may reflect a knowledge of James.

[142] L. Hogan, *Healing*, 295, asserts that תפילת האמונה probably underlies James' Greek. But he cites no examples of this phrase, and I do not know of any, although the use of an abstract genitive noun for an adjective is Semitic.

[143] Cf. Mt 21.21; Mk 11.24 and note the association of this synoptic line with James in Augustine, *Rect. cath. conv.* 5 PL 40.1173; Luther, *On the Babylonian Captivity*, 121; and many commentaries. On the links with Mk 5.34, 41 see Marconi, 'Malattia', 67.

[144] But some readers of James have found here a more specialized meaning for 'faith'—a 'miraculous faith, alluded to in the Scriptures as "the gift of faith," and the

See the discussion there.¹⁴⁵ Here, however, the issue is intercessory prayer, elders praying for a sick person.¹⁴⁶ One recalls Mk 2.1-12, where Jesus, in response to the faith of those bringing a paralytic, heals him; Mt 8.5-13 = Lk 7.1-10, where the faith of a centurion gains healing for his son or servant; and Mt 15.21-28 = Mk 7.24-30, where the possessed daughter of a Canaanite woman is freed because of her mother's faith.¹⁴⁷

James has already, in 2.14, linked σώζω (see on 1.21) with πίστις. Early Christian texts know both about faith that heals the body¹⁴⁸ and about faith that saves individuals at the last judgment.¹⁴⁹ Meinertz suggests that here the verb, like ἐγερεῖ in the next clause, is eschatological, that our text is less about the body than the 'spiritual, supernatural realm'.¹⁵⁰ This is not the natural reading, as the history of interpretation demonstrates.¹⁵¹ Most interpreters think, at least primarily, of the salvation of the body, that is, its recovery of health.¹⁵² This must be correct,

---

"gift of healing,"—a faith which we believe to be not wanting in this age, though comparatively rare'; so A.J. Gordon, *Ministry of Healing*, Boston, 1883, 33. Pickar, 'Sick', sees rather 'the faith of the Church'. Cf. Bonaventure, *Lk* 4.38 Opera Omnia 10 ed. Peltier, 322. According to Warrington, 'Healing', 358, 'the prayer of faith is... knowledge of God's will for a particular situation when no scriptural guidance is available'.

¹⁴⁵ It is not until the nineteenth and twentieth centuries that some Christians begin to move from the faith in our text to asking questions about the psycho-somatic effects of positive belief or expectation. Cf. McNeile, *Teaching*, 113, and note already M.B. Eddy, *Science and Health with Key to the Scriptures*, Boston, 1875, 12.

¹⁴⁶ On the assumption that the ritual James refers to was already fixed, Pickar, 'Sick', 169, offers that 'the prayer is not specifically mentioned... since St. James was instructing the faithful and not priests about this salutary rite'.

¹⁴⁷ Cf. also 1QapGen 20.23-29; T. Reub. 1.7-8; T. Gad 9.5; b. Ḥag. 3a; b. Ber. 34b; b. B. Bat. 116a.

¹⁴⁸ E.g. Mk 5.34; 10.52; and Lk 7.50, all with ἡ πίστις σου σέσωκέν σε. Cf. further IGUR 1240; Mt 9.22; Lk 8.48; Acts 4.9; 14.9; Justin, *Dial*. 112.1. Discussion in Kaiser, *Krankenheilung*, 201-24.

¹⁴⁹ E.g. Rom 10.9-10; Eph 2.8; 1 Tim 2.15; 1 Clem. 12.1; cf. 4 Ezra 9.7. Verheul, 'Sacrement', 370, wonders whether Joel 2.32 ('everyone who calls upon the name of the Lord will be saved'; cf. Rom 10.13) might lie in the background here.

¹⁵⁰ Meinertz, 'Krankensalbung'. Related analyses in von Soden, 184; Armerding, 'Afflicted'; H.J. Blair, 'Spiritual Healing', *EvQ* 30 (1958), 147-51; Trenkle, 389; Pickar, 'Sick', 172-73 ('primarily it will aid the sick man to overcome his spiritual evils... but its effects also will be realized against physical evils when such is necessary for the spiritual welfare of the soul'); Hayden, 'Elders'; Collins, 'Anointing'. Cf. already Hilary of Arles *ad loc*. PLSup 3.81. For more nuanced versions of this thesis see Vouga, 142; Johns, 'Anointing', 58-59.

¹⁵¹ Even more idiosyncratic is Hilary of Arles *ad loc*. PLSup 3.81: the prayer of faith is the agreement of the community (*totius Aecclaesiae consensus*).

¹⁵² Bardenhewer, 151-52; Ropes, 308; Puller, *Anointing*, 289-90; Chaine, 127; Hauck, 32-33; Dibelius, 254; Martin, 209-10 (with hesitation); Frankemölle, 715-16; Popkes, 338 (the physical interpretation is 'in the foreground'); Kaiser, *Krankenheilung*, 41-48, 77-84; *et al*. Cf. Irenaeus, *Haer*. 2.32.4: ἄλλοι δὲ τοὺς κάμνοντας διὰ τῆς χειρῶν ἐπιθέσεως ἰῶνται καὶ ὑγιεῖς ἀποκαθιστᾶσιν. R.J.S. Barrett-Lennard, *Christian Healing*

because σώζω + accusative participle of κάμνω was a standard expression for doctors saving the sick.[153] At the same time, given that bodily and spiritual health were scarcely distinct categories for early Christians, an exclusive emphasis upon the physical may assume a false dichotomy.[154]

κάμνω[155] signifies being ill; see above. BDAG, s.v., recognizes other meanings—'be hopelessly sick, waste away'[156] or even 'die'[157]—but these do not suit the context. Further, τόν refers back to the ἀσθενεῖ τις of v. 14. Also implausible is the possibility that κάμνω means 'labor (in prayer)', although note Gk. LAE 13.2: κάμῃς εὐχόμενος.

καὶ ἐγερεῖ αὐτὸν ὁ κύριος.[158] The verb is a Jamesian *hapax*. Being 'raised up' from sickness is a proof of healing in several biblical texts.[159] The image is of someone being literally raised up out of a bed.[160] As throughout James, Christian readers may identify 'the Lord' (see on 1.1) with Jesus; but the text scarcely encourages such an interpretation. Indeed, one most naturally assumes that, as prayer is offered to God (cf. 1.5), God is the one who does the healing.[161] It appears, moreover, that everywhere in the Greek Bible, when κύριος is the subject of ἐγείρω, that subject is God.[162]

---

after the New Testament, Lanham, MD, 1994, 127, thinks Irenaeus may here evidence a knowledge of James. More likely the language is traditional.

[153] Diodorus Siculus 1.82 (σῶσαι τὸν κάμνοντα); Philo, *Sacr*. 123 (τοῖς κάμνουσι τὸ σῴζεσθαι); *Decal.* 12 (σῴζουσι τοὺς κάμνοντας); Aelius Aristides 2.258 (σῴζῃ τοὺς κάμνοντας); Galen, *In Hipp. aphr. comm. vii* ed. Kühn, 523 (σωθήσεσθαι τὸν κάμνοντα); Alexander of Aphrodisias, *In Arist. top. libr. octo* ed. Wallies, 33 (σωθῆναι τὸν κάμνοντα). Cf. also the use of ῥύομαι in the prayers for healing in Apost. Const. 8.10.14; 8.11.16 ed. Funk, 490, 492; and see further Kaiser, *Krankenheilung*, 68-74.

[154] Cf. Mitton, 200. Verheul, 'Sacrement', 369-72, speaks of a 'double sense'. Cf. Caesarius of Arles, *Serm*. 19.5 CCSL 103 ed. Morin, 91; H. Vorgrimler, *Zwischenzeit und Vollendung der Heilsgeschichte*, Zurich, 1976, 506-508. Relevant here is the survey of L. Wells, *Healing*, 181-91, of σώζω in NT healing contexts. Note that the eighth benediction of the Amidah, *Rephu'a*, concerns spiritual healing in the so-called Palestinian version whereas the so-called Babylonian version clearly has to do with the physically ill.

[155] LXX: 6×. NT: 2×; cf. Heb 12.3. Gk. Pseudepigrapha (Denis): 14×. Philo: 36×. Josephus: 54×.

[156] Cf. Sib. Or. 3.3. Evagrius, *Rer. mon.* 11 PG 40.1264B, in a seeming allusion to Jas 5.15, uses ἀθυμέω, 'be disheartened'.

[157] Cf. Wis 4.16; 15.9; Sib. Or. 5.44.

[158] The Vulgate has *alleviabit*, which encouraged seeing comfort as the goal of anointing.

[159] E.g. 4 Βασ 4.31; Mk 1.31; 2.9, 11-12; 5.41; Acts 3.7. For Hartin, 268-69, the text can refer to both physical healing in the present and eschatological resurrection in the future. So too Johnson, 333. Contrast Moo, 243; Kaiser, *Krankenheilung*, 77-84.

[160] Cf. POxy. 8.1161: a sick man says that he is unable ἀναστῆναι ἐκ τῆς κοίτης μου.

[161] Note Oesterley, 474: although James 'probably' refers to Christ, 'the O.T. reference in the context would justify the contention that Jahwe is meant'.

[162] LXX Deut 18.15; Judg 2.16; 1 Βασ 2.6; 12.11; Ps 40.10; Isa 9.11; etc.

κἂν ἁμαρτίας ᾖ πεποιηκώς. For ἁμαρτία (cf. vv. 16, 20) see on 1.15. The noun with ποιέω (cf. עשׂה + חטא) occurs elsewhere.[163] The assumption here, as in the next verse, is that sickness often—not always—results from sin.[164] Recognition that sin and sickness are not inevitably correlated seems fitting from one who has just mentioned the innocent Job (v. 12). κἂν seems here to mean 'and if', not 'even though',[165] so the meaning is: 'if he has committed sins which have given rise to this sickness'.[166] Healing of the body can be proof of spiritual healing, and spiritual healing can bring physical healing.[167] Cf. b. Ned. 41a: 'A sick man does not recover from his illness until all his sins are forgiven him, as it is written: "Who forgives all your iniquities, who heals all your diseases"' (Ps 103.3).

Appealing to 1.13-17, which affirms that God gives only good gifts and is not the source of πειρασμός, Albl rejects the view that God directly sends illness or that it is divine punishment for sin. Its cause is rather ἐπιθυμία, which the devil and/or demons can employ to bring about sickness.[168] Against this, one can hardly insist that James must have been a consistent thinker, and surely a God who will execute eschatological judgment in the future (4.12; 5.3, 5, 9) might punish some sins in the present.

---

[163] LXX Num 5.7; Ezek 18.14; Tob 14.7; 12.10; Sus 52; T. Jud. 14.5; Liv. Proph. Nath. 2; Jn 8.34; 1 Jn 3.4, 8; Herm. *Mand.* 4.1.1.

[164] Cf. Bede *ad loc.* CCSL 121 ed. Hurst, 221. Relevant texts include Exod 20.5; Lev 26.14-33; Num 12.9-15; Deut 28.15-68; 1 Kgs 13.4-6; 2 Chr 21.15, 18-9; Pss 38.1-5; 103.3; Ecclus 18.19-21; 38.9-15; 1QS 3.20-4 (both sin and sickness are caused by the angel of darkness); 4Q510 1; 1QapGen. ar. 20.16-29; 4Q242; Philo, *Praem.* 119, 143-6; Mk 2.1-12; Lk 13.2; Jn 5.14; 9.2; 1 Cor 11.29-30 (Bede cites this); T. Reub. 1.7-8; T. Sim. 2.11-13; T. Zeb. 5.4-5; T. Gad 5.9-11; b. Šabb. 55a; b. Ned. 41a. Bengel, 507, and most exegetes correctly understand James' language to imply that one can be sick without sin. Cf. Popkes, 340, and note b. Ber. 5a, which asserts that illness may or may not arise from neglecting Torah. Contrast Robertson, 259, who takes the meaning to be: 'the cured man, convicted of his sins and out of gratitude to God for his goodness, repents of his sins and is forgiven'.

[165] Cf. Lk 13.9 and see Mayor, 174. Contrast Weidner, 79: 'Not as if James thought that possibly this man was not guilty of any sins... but rather "even if his sickness can be traced to certain particular sins", if he repents and confesses his sin (v. 16), it shall be forgiven him'.

[166] Mayor, 174. Cf. John, 'Anointing', 56: 'If he is in the state of having committed sins, the effect of which remains, he will be forgiven'. John adds that, in the light of 3.2, only graver sins are meant.

[167] Cf. Poole, 897: 'God will take away the cause as well as the effect'. Against Dibelius, 252, nothing implies than an exorcism is in view, although he is not alone in seeing a demonic effect here; cf. Kollmann, *Jesus*, 346-47. Contrast Wilkinson, 'Healing', 332-33, 341, observing that some NT texts clearly distinguish between demonic possession and physical disease. Note that Hippolytus (?), *Apost. Trad.* 5.1-2 TU 75 ed. Tidner, 127, does not link holy oil to demons or exorcism. James does assume that sin can cause illness; but sin does not necessitate the presence of demons.

[168] Albl, 'Health', 134.

ἀφεθήσεται αὐτῷ.[169] Unattested in secular Greek, this divine passive is a Semitism, one also found in Mt 12.32 = Lk 12.10. It represents the Hebrew נסלח לו, as in the LXX.[170] Much tradition, influenced by Mt 18.18 and Jn 20.23, has thought of the elders imparting forgiveness.[171]

In the Jesus tradition and Acts, healings are construed as miracles that confirm verbal proclamation; that is, they serve the goal of mission. In James, however, there is no trace of such a function.[172] James is wholly focused on the welfare of ill individuals.

Verse 16. Luther calls this 'one of the best verses' in James.[173]

Both the initial οὖν, which suggests continuation, and the later ἰαθῆτε, which seems roughly synonymous with the σώσει and ἐγερεῖ of v. 15, argue against finding new subject matter,[174] although some interpreters think otherwise.[175] There is also, *pace* Dibelius, 242, 255, no need, despite the switch to the present tense, to detect here materials with different origins. The tension between vv. 15 and 16 and the switch from elders to 'each other' arises from the circumstance that the focus shifts from the sick person and the elders to the rest of the community.[176] Although the subject is still prayer and forgiveness, the issue is no longer the bedridden individual but everyone. In the words of Shogren, 'James is moving to the daily life of the congregation (he switches from aorist jussives to present imperatives): if all Christians were to be admitting their sins to each other and praying for each other, the ultimate remedy of summoning the elders might be averted'.[177] Perhaps likewise the scene has shifted

---

[169] The striking third person plural, ἀφεθήσονται, appears in 025 69 436 643 676 945 *et al.* Chrys S:PH A^mss. Presumably the genitive singular ἁμαρτίας was read as an accusative plural, as in v. 16.

[170] Lev 4.26, 31, 35; 5.10, 13, 16, 18, 26; 19.22; cf. 4Q398 14-17 2.2.

[171] Note e.g. C. Harris, 'Visitation of the Sick', in *Liturgy and Worship*, ed. W.K.L. Clarke and C. Harris, London, 1932, 508: 'the natural translation is: "and if he is in a state of having committed sins, forgiveness (or more technically, 'absolution') shall be imparted to him", viz. by the presbyters, to whom he has confessed them'.

[172] Cf. Nielsen, *Heilung*, 214.

[173] M. Luther, *Table Talk*, in Luther's Works, vol. 54, ed. T.G. Tappert, Philadelphia, 1967, 454 (no. 5565).

[174] Note also that Marconi, 'Malattia', 60, sees a chiastic link:
  v. 15: εὐχὴ...ἁμαρτίας
  v. 16: ἁμαρτίας...εὔχεσθε

[175] E.g. Mussner, 227; Laws, 232-33; Vouga, 140; Burchard, 212.

[176] Cf. Huther, 159 ('From the special order James infers a general injunction, in which the intervening thought is to be conceived that the sick man confessed his sins to the presbyters for the purpose of their intercession; Christians generally are to practice the same duty of confession toward each other'); Davids, 195; Martin, 211; Kaiser, *Krankenheilung*, 13.

[177] Shogren, 'Heal', 107.

from home to public gathering; cf. Did. 4.14: ἐν ἐκκλησίᾳ ἐξομολογήσῃ τὰ παραπτώματά σου.[178]

ἐξομολογεῖσθε οὖν ἀλλήλοις τὰς ἁμαρτίας.[179] ἐξαγορεύω + ἁμαρτία[180] renders ידה + חטא in the LXX,[181] but ὁμολογέω + ἁμαρτία appears in Ecclus 4.26, ἐξομολογέω + ἁμαρτία in LXX Dan 9.20.[182] Early Christians, it appears, tended to prefer ἐξομολογέω + ἁμαρτία,[183] which occurs in the Jesus tradition (Mt 3.6; Mk 1.5).

Protestants have passionately insisted that 'to each other' is unqualified: no priest is mentioned. And it is indeed manifest that Orthodox and Catholic Christians have read much into James that is not there. Yet it is also true that James clearly presupposes religious practices about which he says next to nothing, so we remain in the dark.[184] It is, accordingly, impossible to decide whether our clause envisions public confession,[185] private confession,[186] or both,[187] or what ritual might have been involved. Nor do we know whether the text moved early readers to think of all sins or only of those committed against community members.[188]

---

[178] Also Did. 14.1: 'On the Lord's day gather together and break bread and give thanks, having first confessed your sins so that your sacrifice may be pure'. One can also see Jas 5.16 as qualifying 5.14-15; cf. Poole, 897: there 'seems to be a connexion between this and the former verse: he had said, the sick man's sins should be forgiven upon the elders' praying; and here he adds, that they must be confessed'. So too Moo, 246, although he also thinks that v. 16 moves from the ill individual to the whole community.

[179] There are several variations here: τὰς ἁμαρτίας (01 02 03 025 044 048V 6 33V 81 *et al.* Eus Phot), τὰς ἁμαρτίας ὑμῶν (206 429 614 630 945 1241 *et al.* Did S:H Sl:Ch), τὰς ἁμαρτίας ἑαυτῶν (5 623 2464), τὰ παραπτώματα (69 88 322 323 398 400 621 *et al.* **Byz** AnastS Dam Iei Or PsOec), and τὰ παραπτώματα ὑμῶν (020 378 629 631 *et al.* S:P). Did Mt 6.14-15 play a role in the rise of the latter two variants? Cf. also Did. 4.14; 14.1.

[180] The nature and scope of the sins are left undefined. See Althaus, 'Bekenne', for discussion. Bede *ad loc.* CCSL 121 ed. Hurst, 222, affirms that minor sins can be confessed to peers, but that more serious sins require a priest.

[181] LXX Lev 5.5; Num 5.7; Neh 1.6; 9.2; Ps 3.5 v.l.; Theod. Dan 9.20.

[182] Cf. also Jos. Asen. 12.3 (ἐξομολογήσομαι τὰς ἁμαρτίας μου); T. Gad 2.1 (ὁμολογῶ νῦν τὴν ἁμαρτίαν μου); Josephus, *Ant.* 8.129 (ἐξομολογουμένων τὰς ἁμαρτίας αὐτῶν).

[183] Barn. 19.12; Herm. *Vis.* 1.1.3; 3.3.6; *Sim.* 9.23.4; Acts Barn. 12 ed. Bonnet, 296; etc.

[184] Perhaps e.g. it was conventional for the sick to make confession; cf. b. Šabb. 32a: 'Our rabbis taught: If one falls sick and his life is in danger, he is told, Make confession, for all who are sentenced to death make confession'.

[185] Cf. Neh 9.4; Bar 1.14; Mt 3.6; Did. 4.14.

[186] Cf. Mt 5.23-24; Lk 18.13; 1 Jn 1.9.

[187] For rabbinic texts on the importance of confession see S. Schechter, *Aspects of Rabbinic Theology*, London, 1909, 335-39. The act was regularly understood as part of repentance. For the close link between confession and forgiveness note Ps 32.5; 1 Jn 1.9; Tg. Ps.-J. Exod 33.7 ('he confessed his sins and prayed about his sins, and praying, he was forgiven'); Lev 16.16, 20, 30.

[188] Gill, 802, opts for the latter alternative. Tyndale, Cranmer, Geneva, and KJV, translating a Greek text with τὰ παραπτώματα instead of ἁμαρτία, used 'fault' instead

Collins observes that ἀλλήλων does not always signal mutuality.[189] In Mt 24.10, for instance, 'they will hand one another (ἀλλήλους) over and will hate one another (ἀλλήλους)' seemingly refers to one party only: people betray and hate followers of Jesus, who do not betray and hate in return; cf. also Acts 19.38. So for Collins, the confession in Jas 5.16 is not mutual: the sick confess to the elders, not *vice versa*. It is not clear, however, that the elders are part of v. 16, and surely we should give ἀλλήλων its usual sense unless the context demands otherwise, and it does not do so here.

καὶ εὔχεσθε ὑπὲρ ἀλλήλων.[190] This supplies a contrast with 4.11 (καταλαλεῖτε ἀλλήλων) and 5.9 (στενάζετε...κατ' ἀλλήλων). εὔχομαι (Jas: 1×) + ὑπὲρ ἀλλήλων was not a common idiom, although it does appear in Philostratus, *Apoll.* 6.38 (ὑπὲρ ἀλλήλων ηὔξαντο),[191] and the LXX has προσεύχομαι ὑπέρ for several Hebrew expressions.[192] Later Christian usage of εὔχομαι + ὑπὲρ ἀλλήλων stands under the influence of James.[193] But perhaps Apost. Const. 8.10.19 ed. Funk, 492 (ὑπὲρ ἀλλήλων δεηθῶμεν[194]) is independent, in which case that source and James might reflect a liturgical refrain.

The implication here seems to be that effective prayer requires reconciliation, an idea at home in the Jesus tradition. Matthew 6.14-15 juxtaposes the Lord's Prayer with the insistence that one will be forgiven only if one has forgiven others. Mark 11.23-25 appends to the promise that 'if you do not doubt in your heart, but believe that what you say will come to pass, it will be done for you' the admonition, 'Whenever you stand praying, forgive, if you have anything against anyone; so that your Father in heaven may also forgive you your trespasses'. Luke 17.3-6 first implores forgiving seven times a day and then goes on to promise that faith the size of a mustard seed will uproot a tree and plant it in the sea.[195]

---

of 'sin' (cf. vv. 15 and 20), thereby implying a lesser offense in our verse. Cf. R. Bingham, *Origines Ecclesiasticae*, vol. 6, London, 1834, 562, and see the discussion of Mayor, 174-75.

[189] Collins, 'Anointing', 82-83.

[190] 02 03 048V 436 1067 1409 2541 substitute the more common προσεύχεσθε. So too Ps.-Ephraem, *Repreh. sui ip. at. Conf.* ed. Phrantzoles, 74. Cf. the variation between εὐχή and προσευχή in v. 15. According to Metzger, *Commentary*, 685, προσευχή was probably 'the result of scribal conformation to the customary Christian usage'.

[191] Ps.-Heraclitus, *Ep.* 7.6, is pejorative: ἀλλήλων σφαγὰς εὔχεσθε—that is, 'pray for each others' slaughter'.

[192] Gen 20.7 (MT: פלל + ב); 1 Βασ 1.27 (MT: פלל + אל); 2.25 (MT: פלל + ל); 12.19 (MT: פלל + ב).

[193] E.g. Ps.-Didymus of Alexandria, *Trin.* 2 PG 39.764B; Antiochus the Monk, *Pand. script. sacr.* 73 PG 89.1645C; Barsanuphius and John, *Ep.* 544 SC 451 ed. Neyt, Angelis-Noah, and Regnault, 690.

[194] This exact phrase seems otherwise unattested.

[195] On this theme in the early church see K. Stendahl, 'Prayer and Forgiveness', *SEÅ* 22–23 (1957–58), 75-86 (84 on James). Abelard, *Ethics* ed. Luscombe, 98, argues that confession is not for God, who knows all, but for those who do not know all, 'that we

ὅπως ἰαθῆτε. This may be the content of what readers ask for: εὔχεσθε ὅπως ἰαθῆτε, that is, 'pray for healing'.[196] But ὅπως (Jas: 1×) may also be consequential: 'pray, and the result will be that you will be healed'. In this case the promise is large and unqualified, which recalls certain traditions attributed to Jesus. On either reading, interpreters have been quick to add qualification by observing the obvious: sometimes people are not healed. As regularly in the LXX, ἰάομαι (Jas: 1×) refers to the healing of the physical body, at least first of all,[197] although nothing prohibits spiritual healing being included here.[198] In the Greek world and the LXX, the verb is regularly used of divine healings.[199] The attempt of Mussner, 225-29, to separate vv. 16-18 from 13-15, so that 'will be healed' refers exclusively to sins seems forced.[200]

πολὺ ἰσχύει δέησις δικαίου ἐνεργουμένη.[201] 'If this means anything, it means that the more righteous a man is, the more potent is his prayer.'[202] One recalls famous intercessory prayers of Moses (e.g. Exod 32.11-14).

Although the formulation is about prayer in general, the immediate application is to physical healing.[203] The line sounds proverbial, but there is no evidence it was.[204] Although ἰσχύω,[205] δέησις (a stylistic variant of the ἡ εὐχή of v. 15),[206] and ἐνεργέω,[207] occur only here in James, and while δίκαιος—a general term that refers to anyone who upholds the norms of

might be more helped by the prayers of those to whom we confess'. In this way Anselm connects 'confess your sins to one another' directly with 'and pray for one another'.

[196] So BAGD, s.v., ὅπως.

[197] Cf. Irenaeus, Haer. 2.32.4: ἄλλοι δὲ τοὺς κάμνοντας διὰ τῆς τῶν χειρῶν ἐπιθέσεως ἰῶνται καὶ ὑγεῖς ἀποκαθιστᾶσιν. Kaiser, Krankenheilung, 84-97, argues for an exclusively physical sense.

[198] Cf. Poole, 897; Mitton, 206. See further n. 200.

[199] See esp. L. Wells, Healing, 97-98, 119; Kaiser, Krankenheilung, 84-96.

[200] Many, however, have seen spiritual, not physical healing here: Wesley, 870; Laws, 233; Burchard, 212 (citing numerous examples of ἰάομαι with metaphorical sense); Ruckstuhl, 31; Perkins, 138; et al. Apophthegmata Patrum systematic collection 12.14 SC 474 ed. Guy, 218, interprets 'you may be healed' to mean 'you both may be healed', that is, the one praying as well as the one being prayed for.

[201] 61 326Z 629 642 1840 2186 L60 L:SV K:B^pt S:PH^A A G:G-D Sl:ChMOSiSt have γάρ. This might be original as James otherwise uses γάρ over a dozen times. But the Editio Critica Maior omits, following the majority of witnesses.

[202] So McNeile, Teaching, 110. Cf. b. Ber. 34b, where the prayer of Ḥanina b. Dosa is more effective than the prayer of Johanan b. Zakkai.

[203] Cf. the apparent application of our text in PNeph. 1.11-15: 'We entreat you therefore to pray for our health... For we believe that the Lord will hear those who are righteous' (δικαίων). But R. Wall, 267, associates v. 16b with 17-18, v. 16a with 13-15.

[204] Burchard, 212, supposes that the sentence 'could be traditional'. Cf. perhaps Gal 5.6: πίστις δι' ἀγάπης ἐνεργουμένη.

[205] Most often in the LXX for חזק.

[206] Most often in the LXX for תחנה and תחנון.

[207] LXX: 7× (2× for פעל). NT: 21×. Gk. Pseudepigrapha (Denis): 6×. Philo: 45×. Josephus: 13×.

the author[208]—appears only here and 5.6, the pithy formulation, with its emphatic placement of πολὺ ἰσχύει, could be that of our author. Gundry, 934, rightly notes that the 'shift from the plural in "be praying for one another" (5:16a) to the singular of "a righteous person" prepares for the example of Elijah as one who prayed'.

δέησις δικαίου appears to have no pre-Christian Greek parallels. Surely we have here another formulation indebted to Hebrew. תפלת צדיקים appears in Prov 15.29 (LXX: εὐχαῖς δικαίων), תפלת צדקם in CD 11.21, תפלת הצדיקים in Mek. on Exod 15.25, תפלת צדיק in b. Yeb. 64a, תפלתן של צדיקים in b. Yoma 29a; b. Suk. 14a.[209]

ἐνεργουμένη has often been understood as a middle: 'effective prayer', or 'prayer in its working'.[210] This, however, seems redundant, as though James were saying that effective prayer is effective. The passive is attested in 1 Esd 2.16 (ἐπεὶ ἐνεργεῖται τὰ κατὰ τὸν ναόν), in Let. Aris. 78 (τῶν ἐνηργημένων τὴν πολυτεχνίαν), in patristic texts,[211] and perhaps in some Pauline texts.[212] So some have suggested that James' ἐνεργουμένη is a passive: 'The supplication of a righteous man availeth much if it is wrought in him'.[213] The Spirit might in this case be the implicit subject; cf. Rom 8.26. Yet the context hardly suggests this. Maybe a vaguer 'inspired' would be more appropriate. Or maybe one should follow those, such as Dibelius, 256, who interpret ἐνεργουμένη as 'almost an adjective'. It then means 'energetic' or 'forceful' or some such,[214] in which case one

---

[208] Against Spitta, 149-50, it can scarcely refer to the dead who pray for those still on earth.

[209] For additional relevant parallels see Kaiser, *Krankenheilung*, 249-51.

[210] So BAGD, s.v., ἐνεργέω, 1b. Cf. Barsanuphius and John, *Ep.* 94, 191 SC 427 ed. Neyt, Angelis-Noah, and Regnault, 398, 612; KJV ('the effectual fervent prayer of a righteous man availeth much'); Ropes, 309 ('when it is exercised'); Mussner, 177-79; Moo, 247; Hartin, 270-71; Popkes, 351.

[211] See Lampe, s.v., ἐνεργέω, B3, giving examples of: 'be possessed by demons', 'be influenced by passions', and 'be inspired by God'.

[212] E.g. 2 Cor 4.12; Gal 5.6.

[213] J. Ross, ''Ενεργεῖσθαι in the New Testament', *Expositor* ser. 7.7 (1909), 75. See further K.W. Clark, 'The Meaning of ἐνεργέω and καταργέω in the New Testament', *JBL* 54 (1935), 98-99: 'the idea expressed is, that "the prayer of an upright man" is very powerful, when it is set in operation by supernatural force... It is not human effort, sincerity, fervor nor persistency that matters, it is rather that the prayer be...supernaturally operative'. Cf. Poole, 897; Benson, 123; Whitby, 696; Mayor, 177-79 (offering a helpful history of interpretation); Schlatter, 285-86; Baker, *Speech-Ethics*, 240. Moulton, 'Supplication', thinks the passive and middle senses can be present at the same time. Burchard, 212, asserts that a decision here makes no great interpretive difference.

[214] Cf. Beyschlag, 232-33; von Soden, 184; Laws, 234; Cantinat, 256; and the list of interpreters with this view in Huther, 169. Dibelius, 256 n. 87, observes that 'the Latin versions *ff* (*frequens*) and vulg (*assidua*) must have understood the term in Jas 5:16 in a similar way'; cf. also Theognostus, *Thes.* 18.18 CCSG 5 ed. Munitiz, 195; Gregory Palamas, *Hom. xxi–xlii* 31.17 ed. Chrestou and Zeses, 300-302; Tyndale ('if it be fervent'); T. Rees, *The Racovian Catechism*, London, 1818, 241 ('Devotion requires that, having withdrawn our thoughts as much as possible from other things, we fix them

might compare 2 Bar. 84.10 ('pray diligently') and the rabbinic imperative to utter the Amidah with 'deep earnestness'.[215] This at least matches the characterization of Elijah's prayer in v. 17, and there would then be a parallel of content with 1 Clem. 59.2: ἐκτενῆ τὴν δέησιν καὶ ἱκεσίαν ποιούμενοι—'making earnest prayer and supplication'.[216]

What precisely makes prayer ἐνεργουμένη has given rise to many suggestions, beyond those already noted. As usual, James' silence has been the opportunity for readers to fill in the gaps. Some have found here a recommendation of ascetical practices such as fasting: discipline will make prayer powerful.[217] Others have imagined faith to be the crucial factor.[218] Or sincerity.[219] Or the virtues of one's whole life.[220] Or praying with others.[221]

The so-called Epistle of the Apostles has this at one point: 'I will hear the prayer of the righteous (ⲠϢⲀⲎⲀ ⲚⲚⲆⲒⲔⲀⲒⲞⲤ) that they make for them', that is, 'sinners'.[222] Given the rarity of the expression, 'prayer of the

---

on God; and excite and invigorate in ourselves our desire of the things for which we pray; —whence fervour is wont to arise. This is what James meant'). Ps.-Clement, *1 Ep. virg.* 12.3 ed. Funk, 11, says that casting out evil spirits requires *firmis et continuis atque intenta mente.*

[215] m. Ber. 5.1: אין...להתפלל אלא מתוך כובד ראש.

[216] See further Kaiser, *Krankenheilung,* 267-69. This interpretation sometimes lies behind attacks on complacent or rote prayer; note e.g. N.R. Best, *Beyond the Natural Order,* New York, 1908, 13-26.

[217] E.g. Barsanuphius and John, *Ep.* 666 SC 468 ed. Neyt, Angelis-Noah, and Regnault, 102, citing Mt 17.21 = Mk 9.29. Idem, *Ep.* 191 SC 427 ed. Neyt, Angelis-Noah, and Regnault, 612, cites Mt 11.12 and invites great effort (βιασώμεθα). But in *Ep.* 824, 296, prayer is effective when the one asking for prayer helps (βοηθουμένη) the righteous one who has been asked. *Ep.* 824 seems to lie behind Ps.-Oecumenius *ad loc.* PG 119.508D.

[218] Cf. Barsanuphius and John, *Ep.* 234 SC 450 ed. Neyt, Angelis-Noah, and Regnault, 166. A modern twist on this is the association of James' words with the so-called power of positive thinking; see N.V. Peale, 'Try Prayer—Amazing Things will Happen', in *20 Centuries of Great Preaching,* vol. 11, ed. C.E. Fant and W.M. Pinson, Jr., Waco, TX, 1971, 238-43.

[219] So H. Bett, *The Reality of the Religious Life,* New York, 1949, 157 (expounding James). Cf. b. Ta'an. 8a: 'One's prayer is answered only if he takes his heart into his hand', that is, if he feels deeply what he prays.

[220] W. Law, *A Serious Call to a Holy and Devout Life,* London, 1898, 260, construes the text so that it recommends 'all the arts of holy living' and 'of piety and righteousness', with the upshot that prayer will 'avail much with God'. According to Theophylact *ad loc.* PG 125.11388C-D, one's behavior should coincide with one's prayers. Cf. Maximus the Confessor, *Quaest. ad Thal.* 57 CCSG 22 ed. Laga and Steel, 23: the prayer is effective if one lives God's commandments. Maximus also adds this: prayer becomes effective when the one being prayed for by a just person amends (διορθούμενος) his life.

[221] So the anonymous Maronite source edited by S.P. Brock, 'An Early Maronite Text on Prayer', *ParOr* 13 (1986), 5. Cf. Martyrius, *Perf.* 4.4.21 CSCO 200 SS 86 ed. Halleux, 123.

[222] Coptic 31(= Ethiopic 40) TU 43 ed. Schmidt, 19*.

righteous', in Christian circles,[223] given that James underlines the efficacy of such prayer, given that, in this connection, he speaks of 'sin' (v. 16), and given the close parallels between Jas 5.20 and Ep. Apost. 47 (see below), we could have here an early witness to the circulation of James—if, that is, the Epistle of the Apostles was, as so often thought, composed in the third quarter of the second century.

Hegesippus (ca. 110–180) reports that, during James' martyrdom, someone called out, 'Stop what you are doing. The just one (ὁ δίκαιος) is praying (εὔχεται) for you.'[224] The parallel with our text may be coincidence. Or Hegesippus may preserve a tradition that influenced the author of James. Or—less likely—perhaps the legend was influenced by our book, in which case we would have here another second-century witness to James.[225]

Verse 17. James reinforces his exhortations with a very concrete illustration: Elijah—certainly a 'righteous man'[226]—prayed for something very definite and was very definitely answered.[227] As to why our author thought of Elijah in this connection as opposed to Abraham, Moses, Samuel, or some other famed intercessor, or why he did not call to mind the even more dramatic encounter with the prophets of Baal, we do not know.[228] It intrigues, however, that benedictions 5-9 of the Tefillah

---

[223] The phrase remained scarce after James, although note Clement of Alexandria, *Ecl.* 15.1 GCS 17 ed. Stählin, 141 (τῆς πίστεως τὴν εὐχὴν ἰσχυροτέραν); Ps.-Ephraem, *Ad imitate. prov.* ed. Phrantzoles, 265; idem, *Serm. para. ad monach.* 22 ed. Phrantzoles, 102 (ἡ εὐχὴ τῆς πίστεως δίδωσιν αὐτῷ ἰσχὺν καὶ χάριν ἐν παντὶ ἔργῳ ἀγαθῷ). The *oratio iustitiae* ('prayer of righteousness') in Tertullian, *Orat.* 29 CSEL 20 ed. Reifferscheid and Wissowa, 199, following as it does mention of prayer stopping rain, has been thought indebted to James; cf. Mayor, 176. Yet Tertullian otherwise shows no knowledge of our epistle. See above, 14-15.

[224] Hegesippus *apud* Eusebius, *H.E.* 2.23.17. James' title as 'the just' is also associated with his prayer in 2.23.6-7, 86.

[225] Cf. the probable influence of Jas 5.17-20 upon the legend in Epiphanius, *Pan.* 78.14.1 GCS 37 ed. Holl, 464.

[226] Cf. Apoc. Zeph. 8.4; Gk. Apoc. Ezra 5.22. His 'zeal' was proverbial: 1 Kgs 19.20, 14; Ecclus 48.2; 1 Macc 2.58. But Poole, 897, comments that Elijah was not 'absolutely righteous'.

[227] Cf. the devotional application in A. Smellie, *In the Hour of Silence*, London, 1908, 79: 'let me be like him (Elijah). Too often my prayers are shot like arrows into the wide and vague expanse of the air; there is no mark set before them to which they are winged; they ask for nothing practical... I see, too, that he made entreaty about temporal matters—sunshine and storm and harvest.'

[228] Despite Gen. Rab. 33.3, there is no real evidence that Elijah was famed as a healer. Martyrius, *Perf.* 8.40 CSCO 252 SS 110 ed. Halleux, 13, appropriately adds the story of Elijah raising a dead person in 1 Kgs 17.22 to his citation of Jas 5.15-18; and according to Spitta, 150-51, James first thought of the latter episode but then moved on to something more dramatic. Plumptre, 105-106, fantasizes that our author was James the son of Zebedee, whose experience of Jesus' transfiguration and the episode in Lk 9.54 kept

contain prayers for returning to God, forgiveness, healing, salvation, and rain, all of which have their parallels in Jas 5.13-20. Is this additional evidence of a liturgical background to our passage?

Ἠλίας ἄνθρωπος ἦν ὁμοιοπαθὴς ἡμῖν.[229] ὁμοιοπαθής means, according to BAGD, s.v., 'pert[aining] to experiencing similarity in feeling or circumstances, with the same nature'.[230] In the second century and thereafter it came to be used of the incarnation.[231] Both Plutarch and Justin liked the word, which is rare in Jewish texts, although it occurs in Wis 7.3; 4 Macc 12.13; Philo, *Conf.* 7. The combination with ἄνθρωπος and a personal pronoun was conventional.[232]

That Elijah is like James' readers has suggested to many the prophet's suffering: he endured hardship, as do they.[233] Burchard, 214, instead thinks that Elijah and James' readers share the quality of 'righteousness'. Still others think the point is to stress that Elijah did not have supernatural powers but instead exercised a faith that others can exercise.[234] Whatever the truth, the notice is meant as encouragement.

Elijah in the forefront of his thoughts. Plumptre further imagines that the author may have written shortly before or after the occasion (reported by Josephus, *Ant.* 18.284-86) when a heavy shower broke a year-long drought. Martin, 201, offers that James picked the episode he did in order to 'downplay the nationalist and jingoist side of Elijah's career'. It is hard to imagine how this might be. Gilpin, 599, finds Elijah a fit example because Elijah feared 'God's threatenings against idolatry, that the whole land should be destroyed; and therefore he prayed for a drought, in order to bring the people to repentance by a slighter punishment. The apostle's inference is, that the slighter punishment of sickness was intended to save the soul from death.'

[229] The placement of ἦν is uncertain. It occurs after ἄνθρωπος (so most authorities), before ἄνθρωπος (048V 918 Sl:St), and after ὁμοιοπαθής (631 [with ἡμῖν after ἄνθρωπος] L60 [with ἡμῖν at the end]). 1874 omits. 61 1067 1241 2523* PsOec replace ἡμῖν with the distancing ὑμῖν.

[230] Cf. Plutarch, *Mor.* 708D; Corpus Herm. 26.8 ed. Festugière and Nock, 83; Justin, *Dial.* 93.3. LXX: 2×. NT: 2×.

[231] Cf. Lampe, s.v.

[232] Cf. Acts 14.15 (ἡμεῖς ὁμοιοπαθεῖ ἐσμεν ὑμῖν ἄνθρωποι); Justin, *Dial.* 48.3 (γεννηθῆναι ἄνθρωπος ὁμοιοπαθής ἡμῖν); Galen, *De simpl. med. temp. ac fac. libri xi* ed. Kühn, 559 (ἄνθρωπος γὰρ ἦν ὁμοιοπαθής ἡμῖν—nearly a perfect parallel); Acts Thom. 83 ed. Bonnet, 198 (αὐτὸς ὁμοιοπαθεῖς ὑμῶν εἰσιν ἄνθρωποι). In view of these parallels, the indefinite ἄνθρωπος = τις is not here likely to be a Semitism.

[233] Cf. 1 Kgs 19. So Bede *ad loc.* CCSL 121 ed. Hurst, 222 (citing also 1 Kgs 17.8-11, where Elijah asks to be fed); Trapp, 704-705; Gill, 803; Smith, 376; Mitton, 207; Hayden, 'Elders', 265; Warrington, 'Elijah', 224; Frankemölle, 720; Karris, 'Angles', 215.

[234] Cf. Calvin, 317; E.M. Goulburn, *The Pursuit of Holiness*, London, 1869, 1-10; Mayor, 179; Ropes, 311; W. Michaelis, 'πάσχω κτλ.', *TDNT* 5.939; R. Wall, 270 ('an extraordinary corrective to the usual adoration of Elijah within messianic Judaism'). Davids, 'Tradition', 120-21, suggests that James is countering the notion of Elijah as a 'semi-divine intermediary'. Cf. Moffatt, 82; Tasker, 141.

καὶ προσευχῇ προσηύξατο τοῦ μὴ βρέξαι.[235] For προσεύχομαι see on 5.13. Secular Greek sources do not use the singular or plural dative of προσευχή (Jas: 1×). We have here a Semitism, the Greek equivalent of the Hebrew בתפלה or Aramaic בצלו.[236] It is further the case that dative nouns with cognate verbs match the similar Hebrew construct state.[237] The result is emphasis: Elijah did not just pray, he prayed with earnest force.[238] This lines up with the ἐνεργουμένη of the previous verse.

καὶ προσευχῇ κτλ. summarizes the dramatic story in 1 Kgs 17.1-7; 18.1, 41-46, read with the belief that Elijah's miracles were wrought through prayer, that circumstance being part of Jewish lore about Elijah, as 4 Ezra 7.109; Liv. Proph. Elijah 4; and b. Sanh. 113a attest.[239] Many commentators remark that Kings says nothing about Elijah praying for rain to start or stop. But Elijah's posture in 1 Kgs 18.42 ('put his face between his knees') implies supplication; cf. b. Ber. 34b: Hanina 'put his head between his knees and prayed'.[240] One suspects, in addition, that 1 Kgs 17.1, where the prophet says that he 'stands before the Lord', encouraged the tradition that he prayed.[241] For not only was standing a

---

[235] Following προσηύξατο, 218 1359 1563 1718 1842 add πρὸς κύριον; cf. v. 15. 5 252* 322 323 et al. L1126 Cyr **Sl**:M supply the object, ὑετόν, at the end, a word other witnesses add in the next clause; see n. 250. This is likely assimilation to 5.18.

[236] As in Dan 9.21; 4Q184 3.3; m. Ta'an. 2.2; Meg. Ta'an. 12; cf. LXX Jer 11.14; 1 Macc 5.33 (ἐβόησαν ἐν προσευχῇ); Ecclus 39.5-6; 50.19 (ἐδεήθη...ἐν προσευχῇ); 51.13; Dan 9.20 (δεόμενος ἐν ταῖς προσευχαῖς); Theod. Dan 9.21 v.l. (προσευχομένου ἐν τῇ προσευχῇ); Mt 21.22 (αἰτήσητε ἐν τῇ προσευχῇ); Mk 9.29; Lk 6.12; Acts 1.14; 6.4; Rom 12.12; Phil 4.6; 4 Bar. 7.23 (ἐν ταῖς προσευχαῖς σου δεόμενος); Liv. Proph. Dan. 12. צלי צלותיה ('he prayed his prayer') and צלאן בצלותין ('they prayed their prayer'), to which some of the older commentaries call attention, do not appear until the Zohar and later sources. Turner, *Grammar*, 117, also notes that τοῦ + infinitive is 'a Hebrewism when it occurs after a verb which takes the simple infinitive in secular Greek'.

[237] Dibelius, 257 n. 92, is uncertain that James here has a Semitism, because there are also similar classical constructions e.g. Plato, *Symp*. 195B: φεύγων φυγῇ τὸ γῆρας. This overlooks the absence of the dative of προσευχή in non-Christian Greek sources.

[238] Cf. Mayor, 180, and see the discussion of Kaiser, *Krankenheilung*, 269-74.

[239] Visio Pauli L¹ 51 ed. Silverstein and Hilhorst, 167 ('Elijah...prayed and...heaven did not rain for three years and six months') probably depends upon James. In b. Sanh. 113a and elsewhere, Elijah has 'the keys of rain'. Davids, 'Tradition', 119-21, also calls attention to rabbinic texts in which Elijah is famed as an effective intercessor; cf. e.g. m. Ta'an. 2.4 ('May he that answered Elijah at Carmel answer you and hearken to the voice of your crying this day'); b. Sanh. 113a; Exod. Rab. 40.4. Note further Quest. Ezra A 39-40 and Exod. Rab. 44.1. Additionally relevant are 1 Kgs 17.8-24 (prayer for the widow of Zarephath) and 18.36-38 (prayer for fire from heaven). Earlier commentators sometimes speculated that James may have obtained some of the details in his summary from personal revelation; so e.g. Poole, 897.

[240] Cf. Neh 8.6; Lev. Rab. 31.4.

[241] The commentaries often observe this; so e.g. Mayor, 180; see already Surenhuys, 680; Baumgarten, 239.

common posture for prayer,²⁴² but b. Ber. 6b says, in interpreting Gen 19.27 ('Abraham went...to the place where he had stood before the Lord'), this: '"standing" means nothing else but prayer'. The Talmud then follows by citing Ps 106.30: 'Phinehas stood up and prayed', which matters all the more because of the old tradition that Elijah and Phinehas were one and the same.²⁴³ In line with this, Tgs. Onq., Ps.-J., and Neof. 1 on Gen 18.22 and 19.27 turn 'standing' into 'praying', and the equation is already implicit in Jer 15.1: 'Even though Moses and Samuel stood before me, yet my heart would not turn toward this people'.²⁴⁴ So it is no surprise that we find this in b. Sanh. 113a: 'Elijah...said to Ahab, "As the Lord God of Israel lives, before whom I stand, there will not be dew or rain these years, but according to my word". He prayed, and the key of rain was given him.' The tradition that the prayers of Hanina b. Dosa stopped and started rain (b. Ta'an. 24b; b. Yoma 53b) are also quite relevant, because he was likened to Elijah (cf. b. Ber. 61b). Maybe the tradition about Hanina influenced the tradition about Elijah, or maybe it was the other way around.²⁴⁵

That James knew the LXX version of the tale, not just Jewish lore about it, seems likely given the common vocabulary:²⁴⁶

James	3 Βασ 17.1-7; 18.1, 41-46
ἐπὶ τῆς γῆς, ἡ γῆ	ἐπὶ τῆς γῆς, 17.7
	ἐπὶ πρόσωπον τῆς γῆς, 18.1
	ἐπὶ τὴν γῆν, 18.42
ἐνιαυτοὺς τρεῖς	ἐν τῷ ἐνιαυτῷ τῷ τρίτῳ, 18.1
ὁ οὐρανός	ὁ οὐρανός, 18.45
ὑετόν	ὑετός, 17.1, 7; 18.44, 45
	ὑετόν, 18.1
	ὑετοῦ, 18.41
ὑετὸν ἔδωκεν	δώσω ὑετόν, 18.1

Yet James has also gone his own way: βρέχω²⁴⁷ and προσεύχομαι are absent from the LXX story; and his intensive προσευχῇ προσηύξατο

---

²⁴² Cf. 1 Sam 1.26; Jer 18.20; Pr Azar 1.2; Mt 6.5; Mk 11.25; Lk 18.11; Josephus, *Ant.* 10.255; m. Ta'an. 2.2; etc.

²⁴³ See LAB 48.1; Tg. Ps.-J. Exod 6.18; and the discussion of R. Hayward, 'Phinehas—the same is Elijah: The Origins of a Rabbinic Tradition', *JJS* 29 (1978), 22-34.

²⁴⁴ Cf. Yal. Šim. on 1 Kgs 17 and recall also that עמידה = 'standing' came to be one of the names for the Tephillah, or the standard, thrice-daily prayer of Judaism.

²⁴⁵ Recall also the similar traditions about Honi the Circle-Drawer: Josephus, *Ant.* 14.22; m. Ta'an. 3.8; y. Ta'an. 67a (3.9). Honi, too, was compared with Elijah: b. Ta'an. 23a. James' words about Elijah in turn came to influence Christian miracle stories; note e.g. Paphnutius, *Histories of the Monks in the Egyptian Desert* ed. Budge, 493-94.

²⁴⁶ Contrast Popkes, 'Scripture', 228, who proposes that James 'received his information from secondary sources...not from direct access to 1 Kings 17–18'.

²⁴⁷ NT: 6×; Jas: 2×.

seems to transfer Elijah's fervency from his prayer that rain return[248] to his word that rain cease.[249]

The story of Elijah and the rain was well-known. Josephus, *Ant.* 8.319, 328, 344-36, retells it. LAB 48.1 briefly recounts the episode. So too Liv. Proph. Elijah 4, using ηὔξατο, ἔβρεξεν, τρία, and ὑετός. 4 Ezra 7.109 (in a list of saints praying for others) mentions the tale in passing as does Ecclus 48.3 while Lk 4.25 offers a summary that uses ὁ οὐρανός, τρία, καὶ μῆνας ἕξ, and ἐπὶ πᾶσαν τὴν γῆν. Revelation 11.6 borrows elements of the legend—including τὸν οὐρανόν, ὑετός, and βρέχῃ–in order to depict two eschatological prophets.

καὶ οὐκ ἔβρεξεν ἐπὶ τῆς γῆς ἐνιαυτοὺς τρεῖς καὶ μῆνας ἕξ.[250] For βρέχω see above. ἐπὶ τῆς γῆς—does James assume a world-wide drought?—and ἐνιαυτοὺς τρεῖς come from 1 Βασ 17.7 and 18.1. καὶ μῆνας ἕξ has a perfect parallel in Lk 4.25. What is the explanation?[251] Revelation foretells Elijah-like prophets[252] who will minister for 1,260 (v. 3), that is, 42 months (v. 2), which is three and a half years. Now 'three and a half years' can serve as a round number in rabbinic texts,[253] and this might fit 1 Kgs 18.1: 'in the third year of the drought'.[254] This text indicates that rain stopped for at least parts of three years. But the number, three and a half, was symbolically charged because it is half of seven, and in Dan 7.25 and 12.7 it is the length of the apocalyptic period of distress. This explains Rev 11. It may also account for the tradition common to James and Lk 4.25: someone drew an analogy between the period of drought and famine in Elijah's day and the period of tribulation at the end of days.[255] Already Hilary of Arles *ad loc.* PLSup 3.82, when commenting on our verse, notes that three years and six months *significat tempus Antichristi.*

[248] 1 Kgs 18.42: 'he bowed himself upon the earth and put his face between his knees'; see above.

[249] James shows no awareness of later rabbinic interpretation of why Elijah put his head between his knees: he was reminding God that Israel at least observed circumcision (Lev. Rab. 31.4; Cant. Rab. 7.6) and kept the sabbath (Pesiq. Rab. Kah. 28.4).

[250] So the *Editio Critica Maior*, following most authorities. 1893 2147 2495 omit the article. A second ἐπί appears after γῆς in 996 1661, and 621 S:H[msA]H[msM] A[mss] supply ὑετόν, which other witnesses add earlier in the verse (see n. 235). 1874 agrees with **K**:B[ms] in omitting καὶ οὐκ ἔβρεξεν.

[251] On the possibility of James borrowing from Luke see above, 62. Against this see Deppe, *Sayings*, 244-45.

[252] Apoc. Elijah 4.7-19 names them as Elijah and Enoch.

[253] Billerbeck 3.761. Note also perhaps Josephus, *Bell.* 5.394; *Ant.* 14.97, 270.

[254] But a literal interpretation of numbers, when combined with a certain view of Scripture, has led many exegetes to fret; cf. Poole, 897; Manton, 467; Huther, 161; Alford, 329.

[255] This is an increasingly common explanation; cf. Laws, 237. Contrast Bishop, 'Three', who turns this around: an old tradition about a drought lasting three and a half years in Elijah's day influenced the apocalyptic scenario. Billerbeck, 3.761, notes that one ms. of Seder 'Olam marks Elijah's drought as lasting three and a half years. For a different tradition see Lev. Rab. 19.5: this counts eighteen months.

PRAYER, HEALING, RESTORATION (5.13-20)   779

Verse 18. καὶ πάλιν προσηύξατο. Cf. the account of the same incident in Liv. Proph. Elijah 4: καὶ πάλιν ηὔξατο. The immediate grammatical reference is to the καὶ προσευχῇ προσηύξατο of v. 17. The scriptural antecedent is 1 Kgs 18.41-46.[256]

καὶ ὁ οὐρανὸς ὑετὸν ἔδωκεν.[257] This combines the language of 1 Βασ 18.1 (δώσω ὑετόν) and 45 (ὁ οὐρανός). δίδωμι + ὑετόν is a Semitism. It occurs often in the LXX for גשם + נתן or מטר.[258]

For modern skeptics of nature miracles, James' illustration—which the British deists criticized[259]—will seem far-fetched. But ancient Jews knew tales of rain stopping and starting in answer to prayer, to which later Christian tradition added.[260] James himself would surely have had no quarrel with Plummer, 639-40, who argued from Jas 5.16-18 that Christians should pray about the weather and hope for an answer.[261]

The legend about James in Epiphanius, *Pan.* 78.14.1, seems to have been influenced by our line: 'he raised his hands to heaven and prayed during a drought, and heaven immediately gave rain'.[262]

καὶ ἡ γῆ ἐβλάστησεν τὸν καρπὸν αὐτῆς.[263] βλαστάνω[264] is a Jamesian *hapax legomenon*. First Kings 18.46 says only that there was a 'heavy

---

[256] The common exegetical tradition, which adds that Elijah prayed only after idolatry ceased, has no foothold in James; but note Poole, 897; Bengel, 508; Wesley, 870.

[257] The mss. differ on the relative order of ὑετόν and ἔδωκεν.

[258] Lev 26.4; Deut 11.14; Job 5.10; etc.; cf. Pss. Sol. 5.9; Acts 14.17.

[259] Cf. M. Tindal, *Christianity as Old as the Creation*, London, 1731, 240-42; T. Chubb, *The True Gospel of Jesus Christ*, London, 1738, 45-46.

[260] See 1 Sam 12.17-18 (Samuel); Josephus, *Ant.* 14.22 (Ḥoni); m. Ta'an. 3.8 (Ḥoni); b. Ta'an. 8a (the so-called whisperers), 19b-20a (Nakdimon b. Gurion), 23a (Ḥoni, Ḥoni's children), 24b (Ḥanina b. Dosa); b. Yoma 53b (Ḥanina b. Dosa); b. B. Meṣi'a 85b (R. Ḥiyya); b. Mo'ed Qat. 28a (Rabbah and R. Hisda); Eusebius, *H.E.* 5.5 (the Melitene legion). For James the brother of Jesus as a rain maker see text above. For discussion of some of these traditions see R. Patai, 'The "Control of Rain" in Ancient Palestine', *HUCA* 14 (1939), 251-86. For comparable traditions outside of Judaism note H. Diels and W. Kranz, *Die Fragmente der Vorsokratiker*, 6th ed., Berlin, 1985, 31A.14 (quoting Plutarch, Clement of Alexandria, and Philostratus; Empedocles controlled the winds); Porphyry, *Pyth.* 29 (Pythagoras predicted earthquakes, suppressed winds and hail, calmed storms on rivers and seas; Empedocles, Epimenides and Abaris learned from him how to do the same). The ninth of the Eighteen Benedictions includes a prayer for rain; cf. Treat. Shem 10.17: 'People will recite petitions and prayers and (observe) a fast and (give) alms (in hope for) rain'.

[261] Often our passage has been used to counter modern skepticism about the effectiveness of prayer; note e.g. J. Thomas, 'Prayer as a Force', in *Pulpit Prayers, Sermons, and Critical Notes*, Liverpool, 1895, 110-102; Smellie, *Silence* (as in n. 227), 79; T.G. Selby, *The Unheeding God*, New York, n.d., 83-88 (insisting that 'if prayer cannot be answered the doctrine of God's Fatherhood becomes obsolete, for a father could scarcely build up a steel-prison structure of cosmic law which leaves no room for a heart of tenderness to pulsate under its framework, no inch of play for a free and gentle hand of help').

[262] GCS 37 ed. Holl, 464: προσηύξατο καὶ εὐθὺς ὁ οὐρανὸς ἔδωκεν ὑετόν.

[263] 61 326 1837 L:S S:PH^ms Sl:ChMOSt have the plural, καρπούς.

[264] LXX: 12×. NT: 4×; cf. Mt 13.26; Mk 4.27; Heb 9.4.

rain'.²⁶⁵ James has gone back to LXX Gen 1.11: βλαστησάτω ἡ γῆ... ξύλον κάρπιμον ποιοῦν καρπόν.²⁶⁶ It is as though the rain Elijah wrought restored the creation.²⁶⁷ Given the metaphorical use of καρπός (cf. v. 7) in 3.17-18 and the appearance of βλαστάνω in two parables of Jesus (Mt 13.26; Mk 4.27), it is no surprise that a few commentators find symbolic meaning here;²⁶⁸ and Johnson, 216, draws a connection with 5.7: 'there also we have the farmer awaiting the precious fruit of the earth... which is given after a first and second rain. The vivification of the earth expressed by fruit also establishes a parallel between sickness/dry land and health/fruit-bearing land.'²⁶⁹

Verse 19. On the traditional connection in Christian sources between healing the sick and turning back the wayward see above, 747-48. It probably goes back to Jewish sources and has its ultimate source in scriptural texts that speak of people turning back and being healed.²⁷⁰ A link to Ezek 34 in particular is highly likely.²⁷¹ Verse 4 of that chapter reads: 'The weak (LXX: τὸ ἠσθενηκός) you have not strengthened, the sick (LXX: τὸ κακῶς ἔχον) you have not healed, the crippled you have not bound up, the strayed you have not brought back (LXX: τὸ πλανώμενον οὐκ ἐπεστρέψατε), the lost you have not sought'. In v. 16, God, speaking the first person, rewrites this sentence: 'I will seek the lost, and I will bring back the strayed (LXX: τὸ πλανώμενον ἐπιστρέψω), and I will bind up the crippled, and I will strengthen the weak'. These two verses²⁷² played a prominent role in the Apocryphon of Ezekiel, as we know from the fragmentary PChester Beatty 185; and it intrigues that Clement of Alexandria, *Paed.* 1.9.84.2-4 ed. Marcovich, 52, quotes from the rewrite of Ezek 34.16 in that Apocryphon and observes that it is addressed to τοὺς πρεσβυτέρους.²⁷³ Furthermore, the prayer for help and

---

²⁶⁵ Cf. Liv. Proph. Elijah 4.
²⁶⁶ Most commentators miss the borrowing; but see Huther, 162.
²⁶⁷ Cf. the return to paradise in 4 Bar 9.14, where καρπόν and βλαστήσουσι appear. R. Wall, 270, uses the term 'new creation' but fails to cite Genesis.
²⁶⁸ Cf. Estius, 467. Origen, *Or.* 13.5 GCS 3 ed. Koetschau, 330, speaks of 'the rain of the soul' in connection with Elijah's miracle.
²⁶⁹ See further the extensive reflections of Simon, 185. Martin, 213, draws a connection with 3.17-18, to wit: 'Elijah is used as a counterpoint to stress once again the need for a peaceful solution gained by prayer and submission to the divine will'.
²⁷⁰ LXX Deut 30.2-3; 2 Chr 7.14; Prov 3.7-8; Isa 6.10; Jer 3.22; Ezek 34.4; Hos 6.1-2. Note also from the NT 1 Pet 2.24-25.
²⁷¹ For use of this chapter in Jewish and Christian sources see Lk 15.4; Jn 10.11, 16; Jude 12; Apoc. Elijah 5.31; Sib. Or. 8.417.
²⁷² Which may take up Isa 6.10: 'lest they... turn and be healed'; cf. 19.22; Jer 3.22; 1 Pet 2.24-25; Herm. *Vis.* 1.3.1; Origen, *Cels.* 8.64 Marcovich, 580.
²⁷³ Apost. Const. 2.6.8-10 ed. Funk, 41, applies them to the work of the bishop. Cyprian, *Test.* 1.14, relates 34.10-16 to Christian pastors. Cf. Cyprian, *Ep.* 57.4; 68.4 CSEL 3/1 ed. Hartel, 653-55, 746-48; Tertullian, *Fug.* 11 CSEL 76 ed. Bulhart, 35.

healing in 1 Clem. 59.4, which exhibits several parallels with Jas 5.13-20, clearly depends upon Ezek 34.[274]

That turning back the wayward was traditionally linked with Ezek 34 also appears from Apost. Const. 2.18 ed. Funk, 67-71, which states: 'turn back (ἐπίστρεφε), support, exhort, heal...knowing how great a reward you will have for doing these things, and likewise how much you risk if you neglect these things' (2.18.7). This parallel to Jas 5.19-20 is then followed by line after line of supporting sentences taken from Ezek 34 (including the verse quoted at the end of 1 Clem. 59.4). Again, in Apost. Const. 2.20 ed. Funk, 71-77, the call to turn back (ἐπιστρέφω: 4, 6, 9) those who have gone astray (πλάνω: 4, 8, 9, 10) is mingled with the language of Ezek 33.10-11; 34.4, 16.[275]

Although abrupt from a formal point of view, James' final two verses are, in terms of content, most apt, because he has repeatedly promoted communal unity. Here he does so again, responding to the perceived failures of others without cursing them (cf. 3.9-12) or speaking evil of them (4.11-12); he rather seeks to return to the community those who have left or are in danger of leaving it.[276] Knowling, 149, comments: 'No words reveal more fully the tenderness of St. James than this closing exhortation'; he 'does not speak of the conversion of the many, but of one; with all his social teaching he thus never forgets to recognize...the infinite value of the individual soul.'[277]

It is noteworthy that, at the end, James speaks of correcting the errant from 'the human side, as if it were a service, a favor or accommodation which one could grant another, to convert him'.[278] Even though the subject is eschatological salvation, all the verbs have human beings as

---

[274] The closing words of Ezek 34 adopt LXX Pss 78.13 and 99.3, which matters because, in 1 Clem. 59.4, the prayer that God will 'heal the sick' and 'turn back' those of the people 'who wander', incorporates LXX Ps 78.13. So 1 Clem. 59.4, just like Ezek 34, associates turning and healing with the line from the Psalms. As if that were not enough to establish a traditional connection, the dominant theme of Ezek 34 is the failure of the shepherds to feed the sheep, a task that God then has to fill; and 1 Clem. 59.4 asks God to 'feed the hungry'.

[275] Note also Apost. Const. 2.14 ed. Funk, 51-59: this too has parallels with Jas 5.13-18 (see 748 above) and repeatedly quotes and alludes to Ezekiel.

[276] Cf. Ropes, 313: 'This seems to be a general appeal, equally related to all the preceding discussions of specific tendencies and dangers. As such, it forms a fitting conclusion and gives the motive of the whole tract'. Although the immediate background for vv. 19-20 is Jewish tradition, one should not forget the traditional praise of frank speech and friendly criticism in the Graeco-Roman world; note e.g. Philodemus' Περὶ παρρησίας and the adoption of this tradition in Philo, Her. 21: 'Frankness of speech is akin to friendship. For to whom should a man speak with frankness but to his friend?'; cf. Migr. 116-17.

[277] Cf. Reicke, 62: James' 'ultimate intention...is not to reject and condemn, but to reprove and set right. This purpose appears very plainly in the last verses of the epistle.'

[278] J.S. Jones, Seeing Darkly, Philadelphia, 1904, 122. Protestant exegetes often offer similar remarks, sometimes anxiously stressing that God alone saves.

their subjects. God is not named, and there is not even a divine passive here. So James concludes characteristically by emphasizing the importance of human beings doing what is right. Deeds are to the fore.[279]

ἀδελφοί μου. See on 1.2. The expression is particularly appropriate here. It not only adds to the correlations between beginning and end but emphasizes the author's conciliatory tone, which dominates the letter: he and his readers belong to the same community.[280]

ἐάν τις ἐν ὑμῖν. See on v. 13.

πλανηθῇ ἀπὸ τῆς ὁδοῦ τῆς ἀληθείας.[281] πλανάω (see on 1.16), ὁδός (see on 1.8), and ἀλήθεια (see on 1.18) all appear in chap. 1 and so might help an attentive reader to appreciate the unity of the whole.[282] The language is traditional.[283] Given that ἡ ὁδὸς τῆς ἀληθείας = דרך האמת and that the construct state can mean 'true way',[284] this might be the meaning of James' Greek; cf. Herm. Vis. 3.7.1: τὴν ὁδὸν αὐτῶν τὴν ἀληθινήν. But that is far from obvious, especially as the Hebrew can also mean 'the way of truth'.[285]

James alludes neither to Wis 5.6 nor Deut 11.28, nor does he define 'the way of truth'. Nonetheless, in Deuteronomy, wandering from 'the way' is the same as not doing the commandments (cf. 9.12, 16; 31.29),

---

[279] Thurén, 'Rhetoric', 274, makes the novel suggestion that vv. 19-20 are 'a slightly veiled ἔγραψα-formula': James has exhorted his audience not to be led astray (1.16), so ὁ ἐπιστρέψας 'probably does not refer to any addressee but to the author himself'.

[280] One can hardly follow Bede ad loc. CCSL 121 ed. Hurst, 223, and Adamson, 203, in imagining that James here addresses teachers in particular.

[281] The *Editio Critica Maior* has: πλανηθῇ ἀπὸ τῆς ἀληθείας, following 02 03 025 048V 5 69 88 206 322 *et al.* **Byz** Did PsOec **L**:SFV **K**:S^mss B **S**:H Ä. Perhaps this is original, a scribe having inserted ὁδοῦ under the influence of v. 20 or the common expression therein used; see n. 283. But it seems no less likely that a careless or tired eye skipped from the first τῆς to the second τῆς. P74 has: ἀπὸ τῆς ὁδοῦ. 181Z L422 have: ἀπὸ ὁδοῦ τῆς ἀληθείας. 01 33 81 218 307 *et al.* L60 L427 *et al.* AndrCr **A**^mss **G**:A have the text printed above.

[282] G. Byron, 471, forges a link with 1.1 in particular: in 1.1 James refers to 'those who are physically separated from their place of origin' whereas in 5.19-20 he speaks of 'those who are scattered or dispersed doctrinally'.

[283] Cf. LXX Gen 24.48 (ἐν ὁδῷ ἀληθείας); Deut 11.28 (πλανηθῆτε ἀπὸ τῆς ὁδοῦ; MT: סרתם מן־הדרך); Tob 1.3 (ὁδοῖς ἀληθείας); Ps 118.30 (ὁδὸν ἀληθείας); Wis 5.6 (ἐπλανήθημεν ἀπὸ ὁδοῦ ἀληθείας); Isa 53.6 (ἐπλανήθημεν, ἄνθρωπος τῇ ὁδῷ αὐτοῦ ἐπλανήθη); CD 2.13-17; 3.15; 1QS 4.17; 1QSb 1.2; 4Q259 3.4; 4Q418 9 + 9a-c 15; Gk. 1 En. 104.13 (τὰς ὁδοὺς τῆς ἀληθείας); T. Levi 2.3 v.l. (ὁδοὺς ἀληθείας); T. Ash. 5.4 (ἐπλανήθην ἀπὸ τῆς ἀληθείας); 4 Ezra 5.1; 2 Pet 2.2 (ἡ ὁδὸς τῆς ἀληθείας), 15; 1 Jn 1.8 (ἑαυτοὺς πλανῶμεν καὶ ἡ ἀλήθεια οὐκ ἔστιν ἐν ἡμῖν); 1 Clem. 35.5 (τῇ ὁδῷ τῆς ἀληθείας); Did. 6.1 (πλανήσῃ ἀπὸ ταύτης τῆς ὁδοῦ τῆς διδαχῆς).

[284] Cf. Gen 24.48; CD 3.15.

[285] Cf. CD 4.17; 1QSb 1.2; Mk 12.14. Sidebottom, 63, rightly notes that it is 'misleading to quote Greek philosophical texts over against the factual Hebrew notion of truth; the ordinary meaning in the two languages coincides: truth = what is true as opposed to false, insincere, superficial'.

and this idea seems to be present in most of the other texts cited above.[286] One guesses, then, that the same is true for our book.[287] In other words, 'the way of truth' is the way of the commandments, of the Mosaic law, which James calls in 1.25 'the perfect law, the law of freedom'.[288] Those who wander from this way[289] are apostates, in danger of flunking the eschatological judgment. As elsewhere in our book, the emphasis is upon doing.

καὶ ἐπιστρέψῃ τις αὐτόν.[290] That is, 'and someone turns him back (to the way of truth)'. Mayor, 182, comments: indefinite τις 'shows that this duty was not confined to the elders. As it belongs to the brethren in common to pray for each other and to hear each other's confessions, so here they are in common exhorted to bring back wanderers to the faith.' In the LXX, ἐπιστρέφω (Jas: 2×) most often translates שׁוב, and the Greek, like the Hebrew, can carry strong moral overtones. Here it comes close to meaning, 'turn back to repentance'.[291] For a link with Ezekiel see below.

How one is supposed to turn another back to the right way goes unsaid. One might think of something like the ecclesiastical procedure in Mt 18.15-20; see below. But Bede construes the line in the broadest fashion: one can redirect others not just by right speech but also by proper behavior, including almsgiving and hospitality.[292] Gill, 803, to the contrary, thinks chiefly of prayer for others.[293]

Verse 20. James concludes with a sentence that can be read in four different ways: the one who redirects another from the path of error will (i) save himself from death and cover his own sins[294] or (ii) save himself

---

[286] In n. 283; cf. also Gos. Truth 18.19-20.

[287] Most commentators, however, identify the way of truth with the Christian gospel, or with all that gospel entails.

[288] Contrast Erasmus, *Paraphrase*, 169: James' words include 'excessive devotion to the law of Moses'.

[289] Mayor, 182: 'It makes no difference... whether the wanderer goes astray of his own will, or is led astray by others'.

[290] 1505 1611 1890 2138 2495 **S**:H have: καὶ ἐπιστρέψητε αὐτόν.

[291] Cf. T. Jud. 23.5; T. Zeb. 9.7-8 (μετανοήσετε καὶ ἐπιστρέψει ὑμᾶς... πλάνης... πλάνης...ἐπιστρέψει); T. Dan 5.9, 11; T. Benj. 4.5 v.l.; 5.1; Acts 3.19; 9.35; 11.21; 2 Cor 3.16; 1 Thess 1.9; 1 Pet 2.25; 1 Clem. 59.4 (τοὺς πλανωμένους τοῦ λαοῦ σου ἐπίστρεψον); Herm. *Sim*. 9.26.3; Pol. *Phil*. 6.1 (οἱ πρεσβύτεροι...ἐπιστρέφοντες τὰ ἀποπεπλανημένα).

[292] Bede *ad loc*. CCSL 121 ed. Hurst, 223-24. Cf. T. Benj. 5.1: 'If you have a good mind, children, evil people will be at peace with you, and the profligate will reverence you and turn to (ἐπιστρέψουσιν) the good'.

[293] Cf. 1 Jn 5.16; Caesarius of Arles, *Serm*. 192.4 CCSL 104.1 ed. Morin, 782-83 (God can work through prayer and fasting).

[294] Bede *ad loc*. CCSL 121 ed. Hurst, 223, says the text can be interpreted this way (*ex ambiguo Graeco ita etiam recte interpretari potest*). Cf. Origen, *Hom. Lev*. 2.4 SC 286 ed. Borret, 108; Ambrosiaster, *Gal ad*. 5.10 CSEL 81.3 ed. Vogels, 57; Hilary of Arles *ad loc*. PLSup 3.83; Windisch-Preisker, 34; Bardenhewer, 159-60; Moffatt, 83;

from death and cover the sins of another[295] or (iii) save another from death and cover his own sins[296] or (iv) save another from death and cover the sins of another.[297] The history of interpretation shows that option (i) has some support, option (ii) next to no support. Most exegetes opt for (iii) or (iv).[298]

γινωσκέτω ὅτι ὁ ἐπιστρέψας ἁμαρτωλὸν ἐκ πλάνης ὁδοῦ αὐτοῦ.[299] Contrast the the formula in Sifra Lev 209.11: 'a human being who moves his fellow to stray from the way of life to the way of death...the Omnipresent should remove such a person from the world'. With the exception of γινώσκω,[300] the vocabulary reprises the previous verse, with πλανή[301] replacing its cognate verb. The line has a traditional ring; cf. LXX Ezek 34.4 (τὸ πλανώμενον οὐκ ἐπεστρέψατε), 16 (τὸ πλανώμενον ἐπιστρέψω); Wis 12.24 (τῶν πλάνης ὁδῶν); Bar 4.28 (τὸ πλανηθῆναι ἀπὸ τοῦ θεοῦ... ἐπιστραφέντες); Justin, *Dial.* 39.2 (τὴν ὁδὸν τῆς πλάνης); Acts Phil. 144 ed. Bonnet, 85 (τοῦ ἐπιστρέψαι ἐπὶ σὲ τοὺς πλανωμένους); Hippolytus, *Antichr.* 3 GCS 1.2 ed. Achelis (τοὺς δὲ πλανωμένους ἐπιστρέφειν εἰς τὴν ἑαυτοῦ ἀληθινὴν ὁδόν).[302]

We have already seen that Ezek 34 supplies part of the background to James' conclusion. So too does Ezekiel's famous refrain, according to which God does not wish the death of sinners but rather waits so that they might 'turn and live'.[303] Rabbinic and patristic authorities often cite this

---

Cantinat, 262. This seems also to be the interpretation of Cassiodorus, *Ep. Jac. ad loc.* PL 70.1380D.

[295] So Ward, 'Concern', 170-76, who argues the point at length.

[296] E.g. Jerome, *Mt ad* 18.15-17 SC 259 ed. Bonnard, 56-58; John Cassian, *Conf.* 20.8 SC 64 ed. Pichery, 65-66; 'The Bigotian Penitential', in *Medieval Handbooks of Penance*, ed. J.T. McNeill and H.M. Gamer, New York, 1938, 152; Theodore the Studite, *Ep.* 482 ed. Fatouros, 706; Erasmus, *Paraphrase*, 170; Wolzogen, 224; Wolf, 88; Hammond, 702; E. Wells, 33; Whitby, 696; Hauck, 33; Ropes, 315-16; Dibelius, 258-59; Blackman, 157; Mussner, 233; Knoch, 246; Laws, 239; Adamson, 203; Schrage, 59; Kugelman, 70; Popkes, 255-56; Witherington, 549; A.S. Kidder, *Making Confession, Hearing Confession*, Collegeville, MN, 2010, 9.

[297] E.g. Manton, 473-74; Bengel, 509; Benson, 127; Burkitt, 1035; Belser, 204; Huther, 163; Beyschlag, 237; Alford, 530 (dubbing interpretation iii 'abhorrent'); Barnes, 114-15 (observing: 'it is not easy to determine which is the true sense'); Stier, 497; Punchard, 381; Bassett, 85-86; Weidner, 82; Mayor, 237-38; Plummer, 640; Tasker, 143-44; Townsend, 111; Davids, 201; Martin, 220; Johnson, 339; Hartin, 287l; Moo, 250-51; Maier, 238-39; McKnight, 459; Gundry, 935; Varner, *Perspective*, 196.

[298] Easton, 73, however, thinks both clauses refer to both converter and converted.

[299] γινώσκετε appears in 03 69 88 1505 1890 2138 2495 S:H. For Dibelius, 258 n. 95, this is 'a revision into the style of *paraenesis* delivered to a community'. According to Metzger, *Commentary*, 686, it might conform to v. 19's ἀδελφοί μου.

[300] See on 1.3: γινώσκοντες ὅτι.

[301] Jas: 1×. LXX: 6×. For the sense, 'error', 'delusion', see Horsley-Llewelyn, *Documents*, 2.50-51.

[302] According to Mayor, 182, ὁ ἐπιστρέψας ἁμαρτωλόν, which is repetitive, might be due to James adopting a source.

[303] See Ezek 3.18; 13.22; 18.21, 23, 24, 27, 28, 32; 33.11, 19.

byword, which also plays an important role in the long recension of the Testament of Abraham[304] and the extant fragments of the Apocryphon of Ezekiel.[305] James seems to echo it and associated motifs, as one can see at a glance:[306]

Jas 5.19-20	LXX Ezekiel
ἐπιστρέψῃ, ἐπιστρέψας	ἐπιστρέψαι: 3.18 v.l.; 13.22 v.l.; 18.23 v.l.; 33.11 v.l.; ἐπιστρέψατε: 18.30 v.l., 31 v.l.; ἐπιστρέψῃ: 18.21 v.l.; ἐπίστρεψεν: 18.28 v.l.; cf. T. Abr. RecLng. 10.14
ἁμαρτωλόν	ἁμαρτωλόν: 33.19; ἁμαρτωλοῦ: 18.23 v.l., 32 v.l.; 33.11 v.l.; cf. T. Abr. RecLng. 10.14
ἐκ...ὁδοῦ αὐτοῦ	ἀπό...ὁδοῦ αὐτοῦ: 3.19; 13.22; 33.11; ἀπὸ τῶν ὁδῶν αὐτοῦ: 3.18; ἀπὸ τῆς ὁδοῦ ὑμῶν: 33.11; ἐκ τῆς ὁδοῦ: 18.23; τὴν ὁδὸν αὐτοῦ: 18.30; ταῖς ὁδοῖς αὐτοῦ: 33.20; ἡ ὁδός: 18.25 (bis), 29; 33.20
σώσει ψυχὴν αὐτοῦ	τὴν ψυχήν σου ῥύσῃ: 3.19; σὺ τὴν σεαυτοῦ ψυχὴν ῥύσῃ: 3.21; σωθῆναι: 33.12; τὴν ψυχὴν αὐτοῦ ἐφύλαξεν: 18.27
θανάτου	θάνατον: 18.23, 32; 33.11; θανάτῳ: 3.18; cf. also 18.20 (ἡ δὲ ψυχὴ ἡ ἁμαρτάνουσα ἀποθανεῖται); T. Abr. RecLng. 10.14
πλανηθῇ, πλάνης	πλανηθῇ: 33.12; πλάναι: 33.10

---

[304] See T. Abr. RecLng. 10.14. According to C.G. Montefiore and H. Loewe, *A Rabbinic Anthology* (New York, 1974), 236, 'Innumerable must be the number of times in which the Ezekiel verses are quoted'. Patristic references include 1 Clem. 8.2; Ps.-Justin, *Qu. et resp.* 78, 104 ed. Otto, 110, 160; Theophilus of Antioch, *Autol.* 3.11 PTS 44 ed. Marcovich, 111; Tertullian, *Marc.* 2.8, 13 ed. Evans, 108, 124; Clement of Alexandria, *Div.* 39.4 GCS 17 ed. Stählin, 185; Origen, *Sel. in Ps.* PG 12.1456.29; Eusebius, *H.E.* 5.1.46; Ps.-Athanasius, *Imag. Beryt.* PG 28.801A; Basil the Great, *Ep.* 44 LCL ed. Deferrari, 272; *Ascet. magn.* PG 31.1260A, 1284C; Liturgy Bas. PG 31.1649B; Liturgy Gr. Naz. PG 36.720; John Chrysostom, *Stag* 1-3 PG 47.434; *Laz.*1-7 PG 48.1027; *Poenit.* 1-9 PG 49.325; Theodoret of Cyrrhus, *Cant.* PG 81.76A; *XII Proph.* proem. PG 81.1740C; Apost. Const. 8.9.9 ed. Funk, 486 (in a prayer that some have thought was originally Jewish); Dionysius of Alexandria, *Ep. ad Fab. apud* Eusebius, *H.E.* 6.44.2-3, following his comment that God 'desires not at all the death of the sinner so much as his repentance' (Ezek 18.23; 33.11), tells the story of a certain relapsed Christian who repented and, when he became ill, called for an elder (τῶν πρεσβυτέρων μοί τινα κάλεσον).

[305] See P. Chester Beatty 185 frag. 1 *verso*; Clement of Alexandria, *Paed.* 1.84.2-4 ed. Marcovich, 52.

[306] Although most commentators overlook the links, a substantial minority notices them: B. Weiss, 117; Marty, 226; Michl, 68; Mussner, 232-33; Schnider, 137-38; Martin, 219; Omanson, 435-36; Frankemölle, 741-42; Popkes, 355; Maier, 238-39; Fabris, 348; McCartney, 263-64. Abba Isaiah of Scetis, *Ascetic Discourses* 25 ET Chryssavgis and Penkett, Kalamazoo, MI, 2002, 195-96, precedes a quotation of Jas 5.19 with a citation of Ezek 18.21-23, 30-31. Less significant are the parallels that Bottini, *Preghiera*, 168-74, notices between the final verses of James and 1 Kgs 8; Jer 14-15; and Dan 9.

Ezekiel's refrain well serves an author intent on ending with an appeal to reconciliation.

σώσει ψυχὴν αὐτοῦ ἐκ θανάτου.[307] For σῴζω + ψυχήν see on 1.21. Once more attentive readers might hear an echo of the first chapter, especially as θάνατος appears in 1.15 (q.v.) and nowhere else in James. ψυχή means something like 'the true self', that is, the self that lives beyond earthly death.[308]

σῴζω + ψυχήν + ἐκ θανάτου is yet another Semitism.[309] 'Death' is not simply physical death but the spiritual death of the individual, that is, alienation from God in the world to come; cf. 1.15, where sin is also the origin of death. The 'second death' of Revelation is analogous.[310] James 3.6 has already implied that post-mortem alienation is experienced in Gehenna, a place of fire, and 5.3 has reinforced that expectation. Note the future tense, σώσει: salvation will be won at the end.[311]

Given that the one who wanders from the right way is on the road to death, one might think of the traditional *topos* of the two ways, the way of life and the way of death. It goes back to Deut 11.26 (cf. 30.15), which Jer 21.8 rewrites as follows: 'I set before you the way of life and the way

---

[307] So 01 025 048V 5 33 307 *et al.* Cyr Did. So also 02 436 *et al.* L1126 with τήν in second place. P74V 03 614 1292 1611 2138 move αὐτοῦ to the end. 044 69 81 88 206 *et al.* **Byz** AndrCr Dam PsOec **K**:S^mss **A**^mss **G**:A1 **Sl**:ChMOSi omit the pronoun. It is impossible to be confident about the original, but it is plausible that (i) the original was the line printed above; (ii) this led, through simple transposition, or perhaps an interpretive decision, to apply the line to the converter rather than the converted, to σώσει ψυχὴν ἐκ θανάτου αὐτοῦ ('to save a soul from death itself'); and (iii) the latter reading became σώσει ψυχὴν ἐκ θανάτου when an eye skipped from the end of θανάτου to the end of αὐτοῦ. Dibelius, 258 n. 96, however, prefers an original without possessive pronoun, the latter coming into the tradition under the influence of Mt 16.25 = Mk 8.38 = Lk 9.24. See further Metzger, *Commentary*, 686.

[308] Cf. BAGD, s.v. 2d: 'the seat and center of life that transcends the earthly'.

[309] Cf. Ps 33.19 (נפשם ממות הציל); LXX: ῥύσασθαι ἐκ θανάτου τὰς ψυχὰς αὐτῶν); 56.14 (ממות נפשי הצלת; LXX: ἐρρύσω τὴν ψυχήν μου ἐκ θανάτου); 116.8 (הצלת ממות נפשי; LXX: ἐξείλατο τὴν ψυχήν μου ἐκ θανάτου); Prov 23.14 (תציל משאול נפשו; LXX: τὴν δὲ ψυχὴν αὐτοῦ ἐκ θανάτου ῥύσῃ); Job 33.30 (LXX: ἐρρύσατο τὴν ψυχήν μου ἐκ θανάτου). Although these illustrations of the idiom fail to employ σῴζω, the latter is a near synonym of ῥύομαι, it sometimes translates נצל in the LXX, and σῴζω + ἐκ θανάτου is otherwise attested; note e.g. Theod. Dan 3.88 (ἐκ χειρὸς θανάτου ἔσωσεν); Tob 14.10 (ἐσώθη ἐκ παγίδος θανάτου); Heb 5.7 (σῴζειν αὐτὸν ἐκ θανάτου); Acts Thom. 139 ed. Bonnet, 246 (τὴν ἑαυτοῦ ψυχὴν σῶσαι ἐκ...θανάτου); also Justin, *Dial.* 98.1 (σωθῆναι ἀπὸ τοῦ θανάτου).

[310] Rev 2.11; 20.6, 14; 21.8. This was not John's invention; cf. the various targumim on Deut 33.6; also Tg. Isa 22.14; 65.15; Tg. Jer 51.39, 57. Note further Jn 5.24; 8.51; Rom 6.16, 21; 2 Tim 1.10; 1 Jn 3.14; 2 Clem. 16.4; Barn. 10.5; 20.1. Diogn. 10.7 distinguishes between 'apparent death here on earth' and 'the real death' in 'eternal fire'. The LXX appears never to use θάνατος of an other-worldly fate.

[311] Many Protestant commentators are anxious to stress here that God alone is the savior; cf. the formulation of Gill, 804: one human saves another 'not efficiently, but instrumentally'.

of death'. After Jeremiah, the theme of the two ways becomes a fixed item of Jewish moral theology and is often linked with eschatological rewards and punishments.[312] The motif is equally prominent in Christian texts.[313]

Mention of death is particularly appropriate here, at the end. As James finishes his letter, he pushes readers to think of how they will finish their lives. As so often in early Jewish and Christian literature, eschatology is the last topic; cf. M 24–25 (Jesus' final discourse) and the placement of Revelation in the canon.

The identity of who is saved is less than certain, although the majority of exegetes have thought of the one who has taken the wrong path, for these reasons. (i) Surely such a one is in need of being saved. (ii) The text nowhere states, assumes, or implies that the one helping him is in danger. (iii) The nearest antecedent to αὐτοῦ is the previous αὐτοῦ, which refers to the one gone astray. (iv) In v. 15, the effort of one saves another: καὶ ἡ εὐχὴ τῆς πίστεως σώσει τὸν κάμνοντα. Nonetheless, one must concede that there is no room for confidence here. It is quite possible that James wished to say, in effect, that to help others is to help oneself. In the closely related 2 Clem. 16.4, the one who prays delivers himself from death. Second Clement 17.2 is similar: 'Let us help one another to restore to the good those who are weak so that we may all be saved (σωθῶμεν), and let us turn back (ἐπιστρέψωμεν) and admonish one another'. Furthermore, in Ezek 3.19 (τὴν ψυχήν σου ῥύσῃ) and 21 (σὺ τὴν σεαυτοῦ ψυχὴν ῥύσῃ), which are, as we have seen, relevant background for James, Ezekiel saves his own soul when he helps to turn others in the right direction. Note also Lactantius, *Inst.* 6.12.24 SC 509 ed. Ingremeau, 236-38: 'To care and support the sick, who need someone to help them...is greatly beneficial; and the one who does this will gain a living sacrifice to God, and what he has given to another for a time he will himself receive from God forever'.

---

[312] Pss 1.6; 119.29-32; 139.24; Prov 2.13; 4.18-19; Wis 5.6-7; Ecclus 2.12; 1QS 3.13–4.26; 1 En. 94.1-5; T. Ash. 1.3-5; Philo, *Sacr.* 2.20-44; 4 Ezra 7.3-9; T. Abr. RecLng. 11; 2 En. 30.15 (cf. 42.10); Mek. on Exod 14.28-29; Sifre Deut 53; m. 'Abot 2.9; ARN A 14, 18, 25; t. Sanh. 14.4; b. Ber. 28b; b. Ḥag. 3b. Additional rabbinic texts in Billerbeck 1.461-63.

[313] Mt 7.13-14; 2 Pet 2:15; Did. 1–6; Barn. 18–20; Herm. *Mand.* 6; Ps.-Clem. Hom. 7.7 GCS 42 ed. Rehm, 119; Sib. Or. 8.399-400; etc. Although the motif of the two ways is Jewish, it is also Greek. Tab. Cebes 15.2-3 describes the path to true education thus: 'Do you not also see a small gate and in front of the gate a way that is not much frequented; very few pass here; as it were through a trackless waste which seems both rough and rocky?... And there seems to be a high hill, and a very narrow ascent with a deep precipice on both sides.' Other parallels outside the Jewish and Christian traditions include Hesiod, *Op.* 287-92; Theognis, *Eleg.* 911-14; Diogenes of Sinope, *Ep.* 30; Cicero, *Tusc.* 1.30.72; Silius Italicus, *Pun.* 15.18-128; Seneca, *Lucil.* 8.3; Libanius, *Or.* 9. For Egyptian parallels see *CT* 1072, 1182, 1089.

καὶ καλύψει πλῆθος ἁμαρτιῶν.[314] This sounds very much like MT Prov 10.12: על כל־פשעים תכסה אהבה, 'love covers all trespasses'. The LXX is rather different, being further from the Hebrew: πάντας δὲ τοὺς μὴ φιλονεικοῦντας καλύπτει φιλία, 'friendship covers all those not fond of strife'. James' καλύπτω (Jas: 1×) is the natural equivalent of כסה (as often in the LXX), and ἁμαρτία is a satisfactory rendering of פשע.[315] Does James here betray a knowledge of the Hebrew? It seems more likely that we have here a witness to a lost Greek text or to a popular line based on Proverbs, also attested in 1 Pet 4.8 (ἀγάπη καλύπτει πλῆθος ἁμαρτιῶν); 1 Clem. 49.5 (ἀγάπη καλύπτει πλῆθος ἁμαρτιῶν); 2 Clem. 16.4 (ἀγάπη δὲ καλύπτει πλῆθος ἁμαρτιῶν).[316] It is true that James probably knew 1 Peter,[317] which could accordingly be his source here; and 2 Clement in turn could depend upon either 1 Peter or James; see below. First Clement, however, may be independent of both James and 1 Peter,[318] so positing an independent tradition cannot be excluded.

To 'cover' sins means to make them invisible, so the sense is the same as 'forgive'.[319] No theory of atonement is implicit. πλῆθος ἁμαρτιῶν was a conventional idiom.[320] Note further that benediction 6 of the Shemoneh Esreh has God forgiving abundantly (מרבה לסלוח).

The major exegetical question is, Whose sins are being covered,[321] the one who has gone astray[322] or the one who has turned him back?[323] Once

---

[314] 181 254 378 *et al.* S:H add ἀμήν, 43 330 2492 ὅτι αὐτῷ ἡ δόξα εἰς αἰῶνας ἀμήν. The subscripts do not hold much of interest. Almost all of them name the author with the genitive form, Ἰακώβου. Most of them use the word, ἐπιστολή. Many of them employ τέλος. A few characterize the epistle with καθολική. The only one with significant interpretive comment is 2243: τέλος τῆς Ἰακώβου καθολικῆς ἐπιστολῆς εγράφη εἰς τοὺς ἐν τῇ διασπορᾷ πιστούς. This makes the audience Christian.

[315] Cf. LXX Ps 18.13; Isa 53.6; Dan 8.12; etc.

[316] Cf. also Clement of Alexandria, *Paed.* 3.12.91.3 ed. Marcovich, 199 (Clement cites this sentiment altogether five times in his extant writings; and in *Strom.* 2.15.65 GCS 52 ed. Stählin and Früchtel, 148, it stands next to a quotation of Ezek 33.11 = 18.23, 32); Didascalia 2.2.3 ed. Funk, 34 (attributed to 'the Lord'); Apoc. Sed. 1.2.

[317] See the Introduction, 67-70.

[318] For the relationship of 1 Peter to 1 Clement see Achtemeier, *1 Peter*, 45. For James and 1 Clement see above, 000.

[319] Cf. Pss 32.1; LXX 84.2; Diogentus, *Ep.* 9.3.

[320] Cf. LXX Ezek 28.17-18; Ecclus 5.6; 4 Bar. 1.2, 8; also 1QH 12.19 (רוב פשעיהם).

[321] Smith, 382, refuses the dichotomy: 'both explanations are admissible, and both are also true'. Cf. Doddridge, 848; Knowling, 152; Nystrom, 230; Hoppe, 116; Leahy, 916; and note T. Jos. 17.2: 'love one another and in patient endurance conceal one another's shortcomings'. Others, such as Gill, 804, note the alternatives and makes no decision; cf. Vouga, 146. How intensely theological convictions can make themselves felt here appears from Clarke, 829: that hiding a multitude of sins refers to the converted is 'a dangerous doctrine'; it involves 'ignorance of God, of the nature of Divine justice, and of the sinfulness of sin'; it is 'anti-evangelical'; and it entails that 'something besides the blood of the covenant will render God propitious to man'. According to Spitta, 153, who thinks that the multitude of sins covered belong to the converter, the contrary opinion stems mostly from 'dogmatic presuppositions'.

again, we can hardly decide with confidence. That both clauses refer to the sinner who has turned back is grammatically possible and makes good sense: καλύψει πλῆθος ἁμαρτιῶν may effectively repeat σώσει ψυχὴν αὐτοῦ ἐκ θανάτου, being a sort of poetic redundancy for emphasis.[324]

But we can scarcely dismiss the other reading. That one's sins can be forgiven through good works or helping others is well attested; see LXX Dan 4.24; Tob 4.10; 12.9; Ecclus 3.30; Mt 5.7; Did. 4.6 ('if you earn something by working with your hands, you will give a ransom for your sins'); 2 Clem. 15.1 ('those who follow this advice...will save both themselves and me as their advisor'; cf. 19.1; 1 Tim 4.16); 17.2 ('let us help one another to restore those who are weak with respect to goodness, so that we may all be saved'); Pol. *Phil.* 10.2; Barn. 19.10 ('endeavoring to save a soul by the word or work with your hands for a ransom for your sins'); Pistis Sophia 104 ('He who will give life to one soul and save it, apart from the glory which he has in the kingdom of the light, he will receive further glory in return for the soul which he has saved. So that he who will save a multitude of souls, apart from the glory which he has in the kingdom of the light, he will receive much other glory in return for the souls which he has saved'); m. 'Abot 5.18 ('He that leads the many to virtue, through him will not sin befall');[325] also Dan 12.3 ('those who turn many to righteousness [will shine] like the stars for ever and ever') and the promises to the prophet Ezek in 3.19 and 21, cited above. No less importantly, there seems to have been an interpretive tradition that referred 'will cover a multitude of sins' to one's own sins, not the sins of others. While one finds the latter application in Prov 10.12; 1 Pet 4.8; and 1 Clem. 49.5, the words have to do with atonement for one's own sins in 2 Clem. 16.4; Clement of Alexandria, *Quis div.* 38 GCS 17 ed. Stählin, 184;[326] Tertullian, *Scorp.* 6 CSEL 20 ed. Reifferscheid and Wissowa, 158; and Origen, *Hom. Lev.* 2.4 SC 286 ed. Borret, 110.

Probably the most important text for comparison is Ep. Apost. Coptic 39 (= Ethiopic 47) TU 43 ed. Schmidt, 24*. The Coptic, which is here

---

[322] In which case one could implausibly hold that another person—not God—forgets the failings of one who has gone astray.

[323] Reicke, 63, and Johnson, 339, because of the future tenses, think in terms of future sins; contrast Huther, 163. It is in any case a question of divine forgiveness, not human forgiveness.

[324] Some have protested the possibility of such redundancy, but it can make for emphasis. See further Konradt, *Existenz*, 57-58, who interprets the futures as logical, not eschatological: those turned around have already gone from death to life and been forgiven.

[325] R.T. Herford, *Pirke Aboth*, New York, 1962, 140, interprets this to mean: 'the righteousness of the many which they have learned from the one acts as a defence to him so that his sin if he have any may not be reckoned against him'. Cf. the interpretation in b. Yoma 87a: 'Why? Lest he be in Gehinnom and his disciples in Gan Eden' or 'lest he be in Gan Eden and his disciples in Gehinnom'.

[326] And also perhaps in *Strom.* 1.27.6 GCS 52 ed. Stählin and Früchtel, 107, but not *Strom.* 2.15, 148.

close to the Ethiopic, reads: 'But if [someone] should fall [under the] load because of the sins he has [committed, then let] his neighbor admonish him... Now if his neighbor [has admonished] him and he returns he will be saved; (and) he who admonished him will receive a reward and life forever.' This could be an independent witness to the tradition behind James or, as Ep. Apost. 40 also contains a close parallel to James,[327] literary dependence is a possibility. In the latter case, the earliest extant interpretation of Jas 5.20 finds in that verse the salvation of two individuals.

Commentators on 5.19-20 have often called recalled Mt 18.15-20, a set of instructions on reconciliation within the church, some even suggesting the latter could have influenced James here.[328] The verbal overlap is, however, inconsequential,[329] and the Matthean text represents a Christian development of Jewish adaptations of Lev 19.17-18, to which Jas 5.19-20 does not clearly allude.[330] Nonetheless, the earliest use of Jas 5.19-20 or the tradition behind it in Ep. Apost. 47 (see above) does indeed refer to Lev 19.17-18 ('his neighbor should admonish him'). Moreover, patristic sources regularly associate Mt 18.10-20 with Ezek 33–34, chapters also, as we have seen, related to Jas 5.13-20. One guesses, then, that the tradition behind Jas 5.19-20 probably was related to Lev 19.17-18 but that James had his focus elsewhere.[331]

Second Clement 16.4 reads: 'Love covers a multitude of sin (ἀγάπη δὲ καλύπτει πλῆθος ἁμαρτιῶν) and prayer from a good conscience rescues from death (ἐκ θανάτου ῥύεται)'. The presence of ἀγάπη makes for agreement with 1 Pet 4.8 and 1 Clem. 49.5 over against James; but ἐκ θανάτου ῥύεται makes the resemblance to James strong. If additional texts suggested that 2 Clement knew James, we might infer influence here. Such evidence is lacking, however, so we should probably posit use of a common (oral?) tradition.[332]

---

[327] See the Introduction, 16.

[328] Cf. Johnson, 338 ('clearly similar'); Maier, 238; contrast Bottini, *Introduzione*, 118. Dibelius, 260, supposes that Matthew's community rule 'can be regarded as a development of the paraenesis' in Jas 5.19-20. Cf. Hartin, *Q*, 181-82. The two traditions merge in Pistis Sophia 104 and Jerome, *Mt ad* 18.15-17 SC 259 ed. Bonnard, 56-58, and are nearby in Ep. Apost. Coptic 39-40 (= Ethiopic 47-48) TU 43 ed. Schmidt, 24-25*. See text above.

[329] So too the related exhortations in Gal 6.1; 2 Thess 3.15; 1 Jn 5.16; Jude 22-23.

[330] But for the case that Lev 19.17 does lie in the background see Johnson, *Brother*, 131-32. Contrast Schenk-Ziegler, *Correctio*, 417.

[331] If so, this becomes one more reason for wondering about the scope of v. 20. According to Lev 19.17, the one who does not reprove a neighbor becomes guilty, which suggests that the one who does reprove a neighbor is not guilty; cf. 1QS 5.25–6.1.

[332] According to Cone, 295, we likely have here a 'proverbial expression'.

www.ingramcontent.com/pod-product-compliance
Lightning Source LLC
Chambersburg PA
CBHW050313240426

43673CB00042B/1391